OFFICE (

HISTORICAL DC
AND ARCHIVES,

D0782723

a division comprised of volunteers and students of Northwest history

hosted in part by the Northwest's very own

RIVER CANYON PRESS

UMPQUA, OREGON

November 26, 2010

"Preserving America's Story, One Story At A Time"

ISBN-13: 978-1456411329

ISBN-10: 1456411322

These Journals are from May 14, 1804, the day the expedition left the Mississippi River, to September 26, 1806, a day or two after they arrived back in St. Louis. It includes all possible Journal entries of Lewis and Clark. Most of the "courses and distances" and "celestial observations" have been omitted. The notes and most of the corrections of past editors have been removed. The misspellings are original. The dates with the names in the brackets are editorially provided to maintain consistency of format.

THE JOURNALS OF LEWIS AND CLARK BY MERIWETHER LEWIS AND WILLIAM CLARK, 1804-1806

[Clark, May 14, 1804] May the 14th-Monday Set out from Camp River a Dubois at 4 oClock P.M. and proceded up the Missouris under Sail to the first Island in the Missouri and Camped on the upper point opposit a Creek on the South Side below a ledge of limestone rock Called Colewater, made 41/2 miles, the Party Consisted of 2, Self one frenchman and 22 Men in the Boat of 20 ores, 1 Serjt. & 7 french in a large Perogue, a Corp and 6 Soldiers in a large Perogue. a Cloudy rainey day. wind from the N E. men in high Spirits

[Clark, May 14, 1804] Monday May 14th 1804 Rained the forepart of the day I determined to go as far as St. Charles a french Village 7 Leags. up the Missourie, and wait at that place untill Capt. Lewis Could finish the business in which he was obliged to attend to at St Louis and join me by Land from that place 24 miles; by this movement I calculated that if any alterations in the loading of the Vestles or other Changes necessary, that they might be made at St. Charles I Set out at 4 oClock P.M. in the presence of many of the Neighbouring inhabitents, and proceeded on under a jentle brease up the Missourie to the upper Point of the 1st Island 4 Miles and Camped on the Island which is Situated Close on the right (or Starboard) Side, and opposit the mouth of a Small Creek called Cold water, a heavy rain this after-noon The Course of this day nearly West wind from N. E

[Lewis, May 15, 1804] Tuesday May 15th It rained during the greater part of last night and continued untill 7 OCk. A.M. after which the Prarty proceeded, passed two Islands and incamped on the Stard. shore at Mr. Fifer's landing opposite an Island, the evening was fair. some wild gees with their young brudes were seen today. the barge run foul three several times -on logs, and in one instance it was with much difficulty they could get her off; happily no injury was sustained, tho the barge was several minutes in eminent danger; this was cased by her being too heavily laden in the stern. Persons accustomed to the navigation of the Missouri and the Mississippi also below the mouth of this river, uniformly take the precaution to load their vessels heavyest in the bow when they ascend the stream in order to avoid the danger incident to runing foul of the concealed timber which lyes in great quantities in the beds of these rivers

[Clark, May 15, 1804] Tuesday 15- rained all last night and this morning untill 7 oClock, all our fire extinguished, Some Provisions on the top of the Perogus wet, I sent two men to the Countrey to hunt, & proceed on at 9 oClock, and proceeded on 9 miles and Camped at a Mr Pip. Landing just below a Coal Bank on the South Side the prarie Comes with 1/4 of a mile of the river on the N. Side I sent to the Setlements in the Pairie & purchased fowls &. one of the Perogue are not Sufficently maned to Keep up.

Refurences from the 15th of May (2) a large Island to the Starboard; (3) passed a Small Island in the bend to the Starbord, opposit Passage De Soux and with 11/2 miles of the mississippi, observed a number of Gosselins on the edge of the river many passing down, Strong water & wind from the N E- Passed a Place Lbord Called the Plattes, a flat rock projecting from the foot of a hill, where there is a farm, (5) pass an Small Isld near the Center of the river, run on Several logs this after noon, Camped at Mr. Pipers Landing.

[Clark, May 15, 1804] May 15th Tuesday Rained the greater part of the last night, and this morning untile 7 oClock- at 9 oClock Set out and proceeded on 9 miles passed two Islands & incamped on the Starbd. Side at a Mr. Pipers Landing opposit an Island, the Boat run on Logs three times to day, owing her being too heavyly loaded a Sturn, a fair after noon, I Saw a number of Goslings to day on the Shore, the water excessively rapid, & Banks falling in-.

[Clark, May 16, 1804] Wednesday May 16th A fair morning, Set out at 5 oClock passed the Coal hill (Call by the natives Carbonear) this hill appears to Contain great quantytes of Coal, and also ore of a rich appearance haveing greatly the resemblance of Silver Arrived Opposit St Charles at 12 oClock, this Village is at the foot of a Hill from which it takes its real name Peeteite Coete or the little hill, it contains about 100 indefferent houses, and abot 450 Inhabetents principally frinch, those people appear pore and extreemly kind, the Countrey around I am told is butifull. interspursed with Praries & timber alturnetly and has a number of American Settlers

Took equal altituds with Sextion M a 68°37'30" Dined with the Comdr. & Mr. Ducetts family- (1) Passed an Island on the L Side just above the bank one just above, two Small ones oposut under the St. Shore, one on Lb. Side below St Charles, arrived at this place at 12 oClock a fine Day

[Clark, May 16, 1804] May 16th Wednesday a fair morning Set out at 5 oClk pass a remarkable Coal Hill on the Larboard Side Called by the French Carbonere, this hill appear to Contain great quantity of Coal & ore of a ____ appearance from this hill the village of St Charles may be Seen at 7 miles distance- we arrived at St. Charles at 12 oClock a number Spectators french & Indians flocked to the bank to See the party. This Village is about one mile in length, Situated on the North Side of the Missourie at the foot of a hill from which it takes its name Petiete Coete or the Little hill This village Contns. about 100 houses, the most of them Small and indefferent and about 450 inhabitants Chiefly French, those people appear pore, polite & harmonious- I was invited to Dine with a Mr. Ducett this gentleman was once a merchant from Canadia, from misfortunes aded to the loss of a Cargo Sold to the late judge Turner he has become Somewhat reduced, he has a Charming wife an eligent Situation on the hill Serounded by orchards & a excellent gardain.

[Clark, May 17, 1804] Thursday the 17th 1804 a fine Day 3 men Confined for misconduct, I had a Court martial & punishment Several Indians, who informed me that the Saukees had lately Crossed to war against the Osage Nation Som aplications, I took equal altitudes made the m a. to be 84° 39' 15" measured the Missouries at this place and made it 720 yards wide, in Banks. a Boat came up this evening, I punished Hall agreeable to his Sentence in part, a fine after noon; Suped with Mr. Ducett an agreeable man more agreeable Lady, this Gentleman has a Delightfull Situation & garden.

[Clark, May 17, 1804] May the 17th Thursday 1804 a fair day Compelled to punish for misconduct. Several Kickapoos Indians Visit me to day, George Drewyer arrive. Took equal altitudes of Suns L L made it 84° 39' 15" ap T. Measured the river found it to be 720 yards wide, a Keel Boat Came up to-day- Several of the inhabitents Came abord to day receved Several Speces of Vegatables from the inhabitents to day

[Ordway, May 17, 1804] Orders St. Charles Thursdy the 17th of May 1804- a Sergeant and four men of the Party destined for the Missourri Expidition will convene at 11 oClock to day on the quarter Deck of the Boat, and form themselves into a Court martial to hear and determine (in behalf of the Capt.) the evidences aduced against William Warner & Hugh Hall for being absent last night without leave; contrary to orders;-& John Collins 1st for being absent without leave- 2nd for behaveing in an unbecomeing manner at the Ball last night- 3rdly for Speaking in a language last night after his return tending to bring into disrespect the orders of the Commanding officer

Signd. W. Clark Comdg.
Detail for Court martial

Segt. John Ordway Prs.

members
R. Fields
R. Windsor
J. Whitehouse
Jo. Potts

The Court convened agreeable to orders on the 17th of May 1804 Sgt. John Ordway P. members Joseph Whitehouse Rueben Fields Potts Richard Windsor after being duly Sworn the Court proceded to the trial of William Warner & Hugh Hall on the following Charges Viz: for being absent without leave last night contrary to orders, to this Charge the Prisoners plead Guilty. The Court one of oppinion that the Prisoners Warner & Hall are Both Guilty of being absent from camp without leave it being a breach of the Rules and articles of war and do Sentence them Each to receive twentyfive lashes on their naked back, but the Court recommend them from their former Good conduct, to the mercy of the commanding officer.- at the Same court was tried John Collins Charged 1st for being absent without leave- 2d. for behaveing in an unbecomming manner at the ball last night idly for Speaking in a languguage after his return to camp tending to bring into disrespect the orders of the Commanding officer- The Prisoner Pleads Guilty to the first Charge but not Guilty to the two last chrges.- after mature deliberation & agreeable to the evidence aduced. The Court are of oppinion that the Prisnair is Guilty of all the charges alledged against him it being a breach of the rules & articles of War and do Sentence him to receive fifty lashes on his naked back- The Commanding officer approves of the proceedings & Desicon of the Court martial and orders that the punishment of John Collins take place this evening at Sun Set in the Presence of the Party.- The punishment ordered to be inflicted on William Warner & Hugh Hall, is remitted under the assurence arriveing from a confidence which the Commanding officer has of the Sincerity of the recommendation from the Court.- after the punishment, Warner Hall & Collins will return to their squads and Duty

The Court is Disolved.

Sign. Wm. Clark

[Clark, May 18, 1804] Friday May the 18th 1804 a fine morning took equal altitude and made it 97° 42' 37" M. A

I had the Boat & Pierogue reloded So as to Cause them to be heavyer in bow than asturn recved of Mr. Lyon 136 lb. Tobacco on act. of Mr. Choteau Gave out tin Cups & 3 Knives to the French hands, Mr. Lauriesme returned from the Kickapoo Town to day delayed a Short time & Set out for St. Louis, I Sent George Drewyer with Mr. Lauriesmus to St Louis & wrote to Cap Lewis Mr. Ducett made me a present of rivr Catts & Some Herbs our french hands bring me eggs milk &c. &. to day The wind hard from the S. W. Two Keel Boats came up to this place to day from Kentucky

[Clark, May 18, 1804] May the 18th Friday 1804 a fine morning, I had the loading in the Boat & perogue examined and changed So as the Bow of each may be heavyer laded than the Stern, Mr. Lauremus who had been Sent by Cap Lewis to the Kickapoo Town on public business return'd and after a Short delay proceeded on to St Louis, I Sent George Drewyer with a Letter to Capt Lewis Two Keel Boats arrive from Kentucky to day loaded with whiskey Hats &c. &. the wind from the SW. Took equal altitudes with Sexetn Made it 97°42' 37" MT.

[Clark, May 19, 1804] Satturday May the 19th 1804 a Violent Wind last night from the W. S W, Suckceeded by rain with lasted Som hours, a Cloudy Morning, many persons Came to the boat to day I took equal altitudes. mar time 76° 33' 7"

I heard of my Brothers illness to day which has given me much Concurn, I settle with the men and take receipts for Pay up to the 1st of Decr. next, I am invited to a ball in the Village, let Several of the men go,- R Fields Kill a Deer George Drewyear returned with a hundred Dollars, he lost

[Clark, May 19, 1804] May 19th Satturday 1804 A Violent Wind last night from the W. S. W. accompanied with rain which lasted about three hours Cleared away this morn'g at 8 oClock, I took receipt for the pay of the men up to the 1st. of Decr. next, R. Fields Kill a Deer to day, I recve an invitation to a Ball, it is not in my power to go. George Drewyer return from St Louis and brought 99 Dollars, he lost a letter from Cap Lewis to me, Seven Ladies visit me to day

[Lewis, May 20, 1804] Sunday May 20th 1804 The morning was fair, and the weather pleasent; at 10 oCk A M. agreably to an appointment of the preceeding day, I was joined by Capt. Stoddard, Lieuts. Milford & Worrell together with Messrs. A. Chouteau, C. Gratiot, and many other respectable inhabitants of St. Louis, who had engaged to accompany me to the Vilage of St. Charles; accordingly at 12 Oclk after bidding an affectionate adieu to my Hostis, that excellent woman the spouse of Mr. Peter Chouteau, and some of my fair friends of St. Louis, we set forward to that village in order to join my friend companion and fellow labourer Capt. William Clark who had previously arrived at that place with the party destined for the discovery of the interior of the continent of North America the first 5 miles of our rout laid through a beatifull high leavel and fertile prarie which incircles the town of St. Louis from N. W. to S. E. the lands through which we then passed are somewhat broken up fertile the plains and woodlands are here indiscriminately interspersed untill you arrive within three miles of the vilage when the woodland commences and continues to the Missouri the latter is extreamly fertile. At half after one P.M. our progress was interrupted the near approach of a violent thunder storm from the N. W. and concluded to take shelter in a little cabbin hard by untill the rain should be over; accordingly we alighted and remained about an hour and a half and regailed ourselves with a could collation which we had taken the precaution to bring with us from St. Louis.

The clouds continued to follow each other in rapaid succession, insomuch that there was but little prospect of it's ceasing to rain this evening; as I had determined to reach St. Charles this evening and knowing that there was now no time to be lost I set forward in the rain, most of the gentlemen continued with me, we arrived at half after six and joined Capt Clark, found the party in good health and sperits. suped this evening with Monsr. Charles Tayong a Spanish Ensign & late Commandant of St. Charles at an early hour I retired to rest on board the barge- St. Charles is situated on the North bank of the Missouri 21 Miles above it's junction with the Mississippi, and about the same distance N. W. from St. Louis; it is bisected by one principal street about a mile in length runing nearly parrallel with the river, the plain on which it stands-is narrow tho sufficiently elivated to secure it against the annual inundations of the river, which usually happen in the month of June, and in the rear it is terminated by a range of small hills, hence the appellation of petit Cote, a name by which this vilage is better known to the French inhabitants of the Illinois than that of St. Charles. The Vilage contains a

Chappel, one hundred dwelling houses, and about 450 inhabitants; their houses are generally small and but illy constructed; a great majority of the inhabitants are miserably pour, illiterate and when at home excessively lazy, tho they are polite hospitable and by no means deficient in point of natural genious, they live in a perfect state of harmony among each other; and plase as implicit confidence in the doctrines of their speritual pastor, the Roman Catholic priest, as they yeald passive obedience to the will of their temporal master the commandant. a small garden of vegetables is the usual extent of their cultivation, and this is commonly imposed on the old men and boys; the men in the vigor of life consider the cultivation of the earth a degrading occupation, and in order to gain the necessary subsistence for themselves and families, either undertake hunting voyages on their own account, or engage themselves as hirelings to such persons as possess sufficient capital to extend their traffic to the natives of the interior parts of the country; on those voyages in either case, they are frequently absent from their families or homes the term of six twelve or eighteen months and alwas subjected to severe and incessant labour, exposed to the ferosity of the lawless savages, the vicissitudes of weather and climate, and dependant on chance or accident alone for food, raiment or relief in the event of malady. These people are principally the decendants of the Canadian French, and it is not an inconsiderable proportian of them that can boast a small dash of the pure blood of the aboriginees of America. On consulting with my friend Capt. C. I found it necessary that we should pospone our departure untill 2 P M. the next day and accordingly gave orders to the party to hold themselves in readiness to depart at that hour.

Captn. Clark now informed me that having gotten all the stores on board the Barge and perogues on the evening of the 13th of May he determined to leave our winter cantainment at the mouth of River Dubois the next day, and to ascend the Missouri as far as the Vilage of St. Charles, where as it had been previously concerted between us, he was to wait my arrival; this movement while it advanced us a small distance on our rout, would also enable him to determine whether the vessels had been judiciously loaded and if not timely to make the necessary alterations; accordingly at 4 P.M. on Monday the 14th of May 1804, he embarked the party in the presence of a number of the neighbouring Citizens who had assembled to witness his departure. during the fore part of this day it rained excessively hard. In my last letter to the President dated at St. Louis I mentioned the departure of Capt. Clark from River Dubois on the 15th Inst, which was the day that had been calculated on, but having completed the arrangements a day earlyer he departed on the 14th as before mentioned. On the evening of the 14th the party halted and encamped on the upper point of the first Island which lyes near the Larbord shore, on the same side and nearly opposite the center of this Island a small Creek disimbogues called Couldwater.

The course and distance of this day was West 4 Miles the Wind from N. E.

[Clark, May 20, 1804] Sunday 20th May a Cloudy morning rained and a hard wind last night I continue to write Rolls, Send 20 men to Church to day one man Sick Capt Lewis and Several Gentlemen arrive from St Louis thro a violent Shoure of rain, the most of the party go to the Church.

[Clark, May 20, 1804] Sunday 20th May A Cloudy morning rained and hard wind from the _____ last night, The letter George lost yesterday found by a Country man, I gave the party leave to go and hear a Sermon to day delivered by Mr. _____ a romon Carthlick Priest at 3 oClock Capt. Lewis Capt. Stoddard accompanied by the Officers & Several Gentlemen of St Louis arrived in a heavy Showr of Rain Mssr. Lutenants Minford & Werness. Mr. Choteau Grattiot, Deloney, Laber Dee Ranken Dr. SoDrang rained the greater part of this evening. Suped with Mr. Charles Tayon, the late Comdt. of St Charles a Spanish Ensign.

[Clark, May 21, 1804] Monday 21st May Dine with Mr. Ducete & Set out from St. Charles at three oClock after getting every matter arranged, proceeded on under a jentle Breese, at one mile a Violent rain with Wind from the S. W. we landed at the upper point of the first Island on the Stbd Side & Camped, Soon after it commenced raining & continued the greater part of the night; 3 french men got leave to return to Town, and return early (refur to Fig. 2.)

25st refured to fig. 2 Left St. Charles May 21st 1804. Steered N. 15° W 13/4 Ms N 52°W to the upper point of the Island and Camped dureing a rain which had been falling half an hour, opposit this Isd. Corns in a Small creek on the St. Sd. and at the head one on the Ld. Side rains powerfully.

[Clark, May 21, 1804] May 21st 1804 Monday All the forepart of the Day Arranging our party and prcureing the different articles necessary for them at this place- Dined with Mr. Ducett and Set out at half passed three oClock under three Cheers from the gentlemen on the bank and proceeded on to the head of the Island (which is Situated on the Stbd Side) 3 miles Soon after we Set out to day a hard Wind from the W. S W accompanied with a hard rain, which lasted with Short intervals all night, opposit our Camp a Small creek corns in on the Lbd Side-

[Clark, May 22, 1804] Tuesday May 22nd delayed a Short time for the three french men who returned and we Set out at 6 oClock a Cloudy morning rained Violently hard last night Saw Several people on the bank to day &

passed Several Small farms. Capt. Lewis walk on Shore a little & passed a Camp of Kickapoo Indians, & incamped in the mouth of a Small Creek in a large Bend on the Stbd Side.

[Clark, May 22, 1804] May 22nd Tuesday 1804 a Cloudy morning Delay one hour for 4 french men who got liberty to return to arrange Some business they had forgotten in Town, at 6 oClock we proceeded on, passed Several Small farms on the bank, and a large creek on the Lbd. Side Called Bonom a Camp of Kickapoos on the St. Side Those Indians told me Several days ago that they would Come on & hunt and by the time I got to their Camp they would have Some Provisions for us, we Camped in a Bend at the Mo. of a Small creek, Soon after we came too the Indians arrived with 4 Deer as a Present, for which we gave them two qts. of whiskey-

This Day we passed Several Islands, and Some high lands on the
Starboard Side, Verry hard water.

[Clark, May 23, 1804] Wednesday May 23rd 8 Indians Kick. Came to Camp with meat we recved their pesents of 3 Deer & gave them Whisky.

Set out early run on a log under water and Detained one hour proceeded on the Same Course of last night, (2 miles) passed the mouth of a creek on the Sbd. Side called Woman of Osage River about 30 yds. over, abounding in fish, Stoped one hour where their was maney people assembled to See us, halted at an endented part of a Rock which juted over the water, Called by the french the tavern which is a Cave 40 yds. long with the river 4 feet Deep & about 20 feet high, this is a place the Indians & french Pay omage to, many names are wrote up on the rock Mine among others, at one mile above this rock coms in a small Creek called Tavern Creek, abov one other Small Creek, camped at 6 oClock (after expirencing great dificuselty in passing Some Drifts) on the Stb Side, examined the mens arms found all in good order except the Detachment of Solds in the Perogue-R Field Killed a Deer.

[Clark, May 23, 1804] May 23rd Course of last night S 75 W Contined 2 miles to the Said point St. Side passed the upper Point of the Island Thence S 52° W. 7 Miles to a pt. on St. Sd. passing Tavern Island two Small lsd. in a bend to the St. side the Mo. of Oge womans River at 1 m. the Cave Called the Tavern, Lbd Side at 5 m. Situated in the Clifts, opposit a Small Island on the Stbd Side (R. & Jo. Fields came in) with many people, passed the Tavern Cave, Capt Lewis assended the hill which has peninsulis projecting in raged points to the river, and was near falling from a Peninsulia hard water all Day Saved himself by the assistance of his Knife, passed a Creek 15 yds. wide at 1 mile called Creek of the Tavern on the Lbd. Side, Camped opposit the pt. which the Last Course was to. one man Sick.

[Clark, May 23, 1804] May 23rd Wednesday 1804 We Set out early ran on a Log and detained one hour, proceeded the Course of Last night 2 Miles to the mouth of a Creek on the Stbd. Side Called Osage Womans R, about 30 yds. wide, opposit a large Island and a Settlement. (on this Creek 30 or 40 famlys are Settled) Crossed to the Settlemt. and took in R & Jo. Fields who had been Sent to purchase Corn & Butter &c. many people Came to See us, we passed a large Cave on the Lbd. Side about 120 feet wide 40 feet Deep & 20 feet high many different immages are Painted on the Rock at this place. the Inds & French pay omage. many hams are wrote on the rock, Stoped about one mile above for Capt Lewis who had assended the Clifts which is at the Said Cave 300 fee high, hanging over the Water, the water excessively Swift to day, we incamped below a Small lsld. in the Meadle of the river, Sent out two hunters, one Killed a Deer

This evening we examined the arms and amunition found those mens arms in the perogue in bad order a fair evening Capt. Lewis near falling from the Pencelia of rocks 300 feet, he caught at 20 foot.

[Clark, May 24, 1804] Thursday May the 24th 1804 Set out early passed a Small lsd in the Midlle of the river, opposit the on the Lbd. Side is projecting Rock of 1/2 a mile in extent against which the Current runs, this place is called the Devils race grounds,1 above this Coms in a Small Creek called the little quiver, a Sand Island on the Stbd Side, passed Several Islands & 2 creeks, on the Stbd Side a Small Island on the Lbd Side above we wer verry near loseing our Boat in Toeing She Struck the Sands the Violence of the Current was so great that the Toe roap Broke, the Boat turned Broadside, as the Current Washed the Sand from under her She wheeled & lodged on the bank below as often as three times, before we got her in Deep water, nothing Saved her but

[Clark, May 24, 1804] May 24th Set out early, Killed a Deer last night. examined the mens arms, & Saw that all was prepared for action, passed an Island in the M. R, opposit a hard place of water called the Devill race grown, S 63° W 4 miles to a point on the Sd. Starboard Side N 68 W to a point on Lbd Side 3 ms. Passd. a Small Willow Island on the Lbd. Side to the point of a lsd. L Side- S 75° W to a point on Stbd Side 3 Miles, Passed the upper point of the Island. Crossed and in a verry bad place we got our Boat a ground & She Bocke the Toe Roap & turned the Land, the in Wheeling three times, got off returned to the head of the aforesaid Island, and Came up under a falling Bank. hard water this place being the worst I ever Saw, I call it the retregrade bend. Camped at an old house.

[Clark, May 24, 1804] May 24th Thursday 1804 Set out early passed a Verry bad part of the River Called the Deavels race ground, this is where the Current Sets against Some projecting rocks for half a mile on the Labd. Side, above this place is the mouth of a Small Creek Called queivere, passed Several Islands, two Small Creeks on the Stbd. Side, and passed between a Isld. an the Lbd. Shore a narrow pass above this Isld is a Verry bad part of the river, we attempted to pass up under the Lbd. Bank which was falling in So fast that the evident danger obliged us to Cross between the Starbd. Side and a Sand bar in the middle of the river, we hove up near the head of the Sand bar, the Sand moveing & banking caused us to run on the Sand. The Swiftness of the Current wheeled the boat, Broke our Toe rope, and was nearly over Setting the boat, all hand jumped out on the upper Side and bore on that Side untill the Sand washed from under the boat and wheeled on the next bank by the time She wheeled a 3rd Time got a rope fast to her Stern and by the means of Swimmers was Carred to Shore and when her Stern was down whilst in the act of Swinging a third time into Deep water near the Shore, we returned, to the Island where we Set out and assended under the Bank which I have just mentioned, as falling in, here George Drewyer & Willard, two of our men who left us at St. Charles to Come on by land joined us, we Camped about 1 mile above where we were So nearly being lost, on the Labd Side at a Plantation. all in Spirits. This place I call the retragrade bend as we were obliged to fall back 2 miles

[Clark, May 25, 1804]
25 May
Set out early Course West to a Point on Sbd. Side at 2 Miles passd a
Willow Isd. in a Bend to the Lbd. a creek called wood rivr Lbd. Side N
57° W. to a pt. on the Sb. Side 3 Miles passed the Mouth of a Creek St.
Side Called Le quever, this Same course continued to a Point Ld. Side
2 1/2 Miles further. opposit a Isd. on Sd Side Passed a Creek Called R.
La freeau at the pt. N 20° W 2 miles To a Small french Village called La
Charatt of five families only, in the bend to the Starbord This is the
Last Settlement of Whites, an Island opposit

[Clark, May 25, 1804] May 25th Friday 1804 rain last night river fall Several inches, Set out early psd. Several Islands passed wood River on the Lbd Side at 2 miles passed Creek on the St. Side Called La Querer at 5 miles passed a Creek at 8 mile, opsd. an Isd. on the Lbd Side, Camped at the mouth of a Creek called River a Chauritte, above a Small french Village of 7 houses and as many families, Settled at this place to be convt. to hunt, & trade with the Indians, here we met with Mr. Louisell imedeately down from the Seeeder Isld. Situated in the Countrey of the Suxex 400 Leagues up he gave us a good Deel of information Some letters he informed us that he Saw no Indians on the river below the Poncrars- Some hard rain this evening

The people at this Village is pore, houses Small, they Sent us milk & eggs to eat.

[Clark, May 26, 1804] May 26th 1804. Set out at 7 oClock after a hard rain & Wind, & proceed on verry well under Sale. Wind from the E N E

The wind favourable to day we made 18 miles a Cloud rais & wind & rain
Closed the Day

[Clark, May 26, 1804]
May the 26th Sattarday 1804.
Set out at 7 oClock after a heavy Shour of rain (George Drewyer & John
Shields, Sent by Land with the two horses with directions to proceed on
one day & hunt the next) The wind favourable from the E N E passed Beef
Island and river on Lbd Side at 3 1/2 Ms Passed a Creek on the Lbd. Side
Called Shepperds Creek, passed Several Islands to day great Deal of
Deer Sign on the Bank one man out hunting, w Camped on an Island on the
Starboard Side near the Southern extrem of Luter Island.

[Lewis, May 26, 1804] Detatchment Orders. May 26th 1804. The Commanding Officers direct, that the three Squads under the command of Sergts. Floyd Ordway and Pryor heretofore forming two messes each, shall untill further orders constitute three messes only, the same being altered and organized as follows (viz)

1 Sergt. Charles Floyd. (1)

Privates: 2 Hugh McNeal 3 Patric Gass 4 Reubin Fields (2) 5 John B Thompson + 6 John Newman 7 Richard Winsor + Francis Rivet & 8 Joseph Fields (3)

9 Sergt. John Ordway.

Privates. 10 William Bratton (4) 11 John Colter (5) X 12 Moses B. Reed 13 Alexander Willard 14 William Warner 15 Silas Goodrich 16 John Potts & 17 Hugh Hall

18 Sergt. Nathaniel Pryor. (6)

Privates. 19 George Gibson (7) 20 George Shannon (8) 21 John Shields (9) 22 John Collins 23 Joseph Whitehouse 24 Peter Wiser F 25 Peter Crusat & F 26 Francis Labuche

The commanding officers further direct that the remainder of the detatchmen shall form two messes; and that the same be constitued as follows. (viz)

Patroon, Baptist Dechamps

Engages
Etienne Mabbauf
Paul Primaut
Charles Hébert
Baptist La Jeunesse
Peter Pinaut
Peter Roi &
Joseph Collin

1 Corpl. Richard Warvington.

Privates. 2 Robert Frasier 3 John Boleye 4 John Dame 5 Ebinezer Tuttle & 6 Isaac White

The Commanding officers further direct that the messes of Sergts. Floyd, Ordway and Pryor shall untill further orders form the crew of the Batteaux; the Mess of the Patroon La Jeunesse will form the permanent crew of the red Perogue; Corpl. Warvington's mess forming that of the white perogue.

Whenever by any casualty it becomes necessary to furnish additional men to assist in navigating the Perogues, the same shall be furnished by daily detale from the Privates who form the crew of Batteaux, exempting only from such detale, Thomas P. Howard and the men who are assigned to the two bow and the two stern oars.- For the present one man will be furnished daily to assist the crew of the white perogue; this man must be an expert boatman.

The posts and duties of the Sergts. shall be as follows (viz) - when the Batteaux is under way, one Sergt. shall be stationed at the helm, one in the center on the rear of the Starboard locker, and one at the bow. The Sergt. at the helm, shall steer the boat, and see that the baggage on the quarterdeck is properly arranged and stowed away in the most advantageous manner; to see that no cooking utensels or loos lumber of any kind is left on the deck to obstruct the passage between the burths- he will also attend to the compas when necessary.

The Sergt at the center will command the guard, manage the sails, see that the men at the oars do their duty; that they come on board at a proper season in the morning, and that the boat gets under way in due time; he will keep a good lookout for the mouths of all rivers, creeks, Islands and other remarkable places and shall immediately report the same to the commanding officers; he will attend to the issues of sperituous liquors; he shall regulate the halting of the batteaux through the day to give the men refreshment, and will also regulate the time of her departure taking care that not more time than is necessary shall be expended at each halt- it shall be his duty also to post a centinel on the bank, near the boat whenever we come too and halt in the course of the day, at the same time he will (acompanied by two his guard) reconnoiter the forrest arround the place of landing to the distance of at least one hundred paces. when we come too for the purpose of encamping at night, the Sergt. of the guard shall post two centinels immediately on our landing; one of whom shal be posted near the boat, and the other at a convenient distance in rear of the encampment; at night the Sergt. must be always present with his guard, and he is positively forbidden to suffer any man of his guard to absent himself on any pretext whatever; he will at each relief through the night, accompanyed by the two men last off their posts, reconnoiter in every direction around the camp to the distance of at least one hundred and fifty paces, and also examine the situation of the boat and perogues, and see that they ly safe and free from the bank

It shall be the duty of the sergt. at the bow, to keep a good look out for all danger which may approach, either of the enimy, or obstructions which may present themselves to passage of the boat; of the first he will notify the Sergt. at the center, who will communicate the information to the commanding officers, and of the second or obstructions to the boat he will notify the Sergt. at the helm; he will also report to the commanding officers through the Sergt. at the center all perogues boats canoes or other craft which he may discover in the river, and all hunting camps or parties of Indians in view of which we may pass. he will at all times be provided with a seting pole and assist the bowsman in poling and managing the bow of the boat. it will be his duty also to give and answer all signals, which may hereafter be established for the government of the perogues and parties on shore.

The Sergts. will on each morning before our departure relieve each other in the following manner- The Sergt. at the helm will parade the new guard, relieve the Sergt. and the old guard, and occupy the middle station in the boat; the Sergt. of the old guard will occupy the station at the bow, and the Sergt. who had been stationed the preceeding day at the bow will place himself at the helm.- The sergts. in addition to those duties are directed each to keep a seperate journal from day today of all passing occurences, and such other observations on the country &c. as shall appear to them worthy of notice

The Sergts. are relieved and exempt from all labour of making fires, pitching tents or cooking, and will direct and make the men of their several messes perform an equal propotion of those duties.

The guard shall hereafter consist of one sergeant and six privates & engages.

Patroon, Dechamp, Copl. Warvington, and George Drewyer, are exempt from guad duty; the two former will attend particularly to their perogues at all times, and see that their lading is in good order, and that the same is kept perfectly free from rain or other moisture; the latter will perform certain duties on shore which will be assigned him from time to time. all other soldiers and engaged men of whatever discription must perform their regular tour of guad duty.

All detales for guard or other duty will be made in the evening when we encamp, and the duty to be performed will be entered on, by the individuals so warned, the next morning.- provision for one day will be issued to the party on each evening after we have encamped; the same will be cooked on that evening by the several messes, and a proportion of it reserved for the next day as no cooking will be allowed in the day while on the mach

Sergt. John Ordway will continue to issue the provisions and make the detales for guard or other duty.- The day after tomorrow lyed corn and grece will be issued to the party, the next day Poark and flour, and the day following indian meal and poark; and in conformity to that ratiene provisions will continue to be issued to the party untill further orders.- should any of the messes prefer indian meal to flour they may recieve it accordingly- no poark is to be issued when we have fresh meat on hand.

Labuche and Crusat will man the larboard bow oar alternately, and the one not engaged at the oar will attend as the Bows-man, and when the attention of both these persons is necessary at the bow, their oar is to be maned by any idle hand on board.

Meriwether Lewis Capt.
Wm. Clark Cpt.

[Clark, May 27, 1804] Sunday May 27th as we were Setting out this morning two Canoos loaded with Bever elk Deer Skins & Buffalow Robes, from the Mahars nation, they inform that they left that place 2 months, a gentle Breese from the S. E, we camped on an Isd in the mouth of Gasconade R, this river is 157 yards wide a butifull stream of clear water. 19 foot Deep Hills on the lower Side

[Clark, May 27, 1804] May 27th Sunday 1804 as we were pushing off this Morning two Canoos Loaded with fur &c. Came to from the Mahars nation, which place they had left two months, at about 10 oClock 4 Cajaux or rafts loaded with furs and peltres came too one from the Paunees, the other from Grand Osage, they informed nothing of Consequence, passed a Creek on the Lbd Side Called ash Creek 20 yds wide, passed the upper point of a large Island on the Stbd Side back of which Comes in three Creeks one Called Orter Creek, her the men we left hunting Came in we camped on a Willow Island in the mouth of Gasconnade River. George Shannon Killed a Deer this evening

[Clark, May 28, 1804] Monday 28th May rained hard all the last night Some wind from the S W, one Deer Killed to day, one Man fell in with Six Indians hunting, onloaded the perogue, & found Several articles Wet, Some Tobacco Spoiled. river begin to rise

[Clark, May 28, 1804] May 28th Munday 1804 Gasconnade Rained hard all last night Some thunder & lightening hard wind in the forepart of the night from the S W. Ruben Fields Killed a Deer Several hunter out to day I measured the river found the Gasconnade to be 157 yds. wide and 19 foot Deep the Course of this R. is S 29° W, one of the hunters fell in with 6 Inds. hunting, onloaded the large Perogue on board of which was 8 french hands found many things wet by their cearlenessness, put all the articles which was wet out to Dry- this day So Cloudy that no observations could be taken, the river begin to rise, examine the mens arms and equapage, all in Order

[Clark, May 29, 1804] Tuesday 29th May Sent out hunters, got a morning obsvtn and one at 12 oClock, rained last night, the river rises fast The Musquetors are verry bad, Load the pieroge

[Clark, May 29, 1804] May 29th 1804 Set out from the mouth of the gasconnade, where we took obsevn &c. left a Perogue for a man lost in the woods, Course N. 54 W 2 m to a point Lb. Side. Passed the Isd. on which we

Camped, river still rised, water verry muddey N. 78° W 2 Ms. to a pt. on Lb Side passed two willow Islands first Smaller and a Creek on Lbd. called Deer Creek one oposit the point St. Side and incamped on the Lb Side rain all night the tents together along the N; 76 W 25 Poles S 26 W, to the point above- S 19° to the pot below the River

[Clark, May 29, 1804] May 29th Tuesday rained last night, Cloudy morning 4 hunters Sent out with Orders to return at 12 oClock Took equal altitudes of Suns Lower limb found it 105° 31' 45"

Cap Lewis observed meridean altitude of sun U L-back observation with the octant & artificeal horozen- gave for altitude on the Limb 38° 44' 00" sun octant Error 2 0 0 +

had the Perogues loaded and all perpared to Set out at 4 oClock after finishing the observations & all things necessary found that one of the hunters had not returned, we deturmined to proceed on & leave one perogue to wate for him, accordingly at half past four we Set out and came on 4 miles & camped on the Lbd Side above a Small Creek Called Deer Creek, Soon after we came too we heard Several guns fire down the river, we answered them by a Discharge of a Swivile on the Bow

[Clark, May 30, 1804] May 30th, Wednesday, Set out at 7 oClock after a heavy rain, rained all last night, a little after Dark last night Several guns were herd below, I expect the French men fireing for Whitehous who was lost in the woods.

[Clark, May 30, 1804] May 30th Wednesday 1804 Rained all last night Set out at 6 oClock after a heavy Shower, and proceeded on, passed a large Island a Creek opposit on the St. Side just abov a Cave Called Monbrun Tavern & River, passed a Creek on the Lbd. Side Call Rush Creek at 4 Miles Several Showers of rain the Current Verry Swift river riseing fast Passed Big Miry River at 11 Miles on the Starboard Side, at the lower point of a Island, this River is about 50 yards Wide, Camped at the mouth of a Creek on Lbd Sd of abt 25 yds. Wide Called Grinestone Creek, opposit the head of a Isd. and the mouth of Little Miry River on the St Side, a heavy wind accompanied with rain & hail we Made 14 miles to day, the river Continue to rise, the County on each Side appear full of Water.

[Clark, May 31, 1804] May 31st Thursday 1804 rained the greater part of last night, the wind from the West raised and blew with great force untile 5 oClock p.m.which obliged us to lay by a Cajaux of Bear Skins and pelteries came down from the Grand Osarge, one french man one Indian, and a Squar, they had letters from the man Mr. Choteau Sent to that part of the Osarge Nation Settled on Arkansa River mentioning that his letter was Commited to the flaims, the Inds. not believeing that the Americans had possession of the Countrey they disregarded St Louis & their Supplies &c.- Several rats of Considerable Size was Cought in the woods to day- Capt Lewis went out to the woods & found many curious Plants & Srubs, one Deer killed this evening

[Clark, June 1, 1804] June 1st Friday 1804 Set out early, the Same Course S 48° W of Wednesday contd. 4 ms passed the Mouth of Little Miry on the Stb & high rich Land on the Lb Side, S. 45°W to an Island opposit a hill on the S. Sd. 6 Ms. this Isd is on the Lbd. passed the Mo. of Bear creek 25 yds wide at 2 ms. & three Small Isd., Some Swift water and banks falling in, Wind a head from the West, S 39° W 3 ms. to the Pt. above the mouth of Osage River Larb Side, Camped fell a number of Trees in the Point to take observation a fair after noon, Sit up untill 1 oClock to take Som observations &c.

[Clark, June 1, 1804] June 1st 1804 Friday Set out early a fair morning Passed the mouth Bear Creek 25 yds. Wide at 6 Miles, Several Small Islands in the river the wind a head from the West the Current exceedingly rapid Came to on the point of the Osarges River on the Labd Side of Missouries this osages river Verry high, felled all the Trees in the point to Make observations Sit up untill 12 oClock taken oservation this night

[Clark, June 2, 1804] June 2nd- Took the Dirts. of Son & moon &c &c. I measured the Osage & Missouris at this place made ther width as follows, the Missoure 875 yd. wide The Osage R 397 yds. wide, the distance between the 2 rivers 80 poles up is 40 Ps. Took equal altitudes & Mredian altitude also-and made them _____ I assended the hill in the point 80 ps. from the pt. found it about 100 foot high, on the top is 2 graves, or mouns, a Delightfull prospect from this hill which Comds. both rivers

Drewyer & Shields came to the opposit Side to day at SunSet we sent across & brought them over, they had been absent 7 Days Swam many creeks, much worsted. They informed us that the Countrey on both Sides of muddy river's to the hill called by the french _____ 3 ms. below this place, a Small Praries below the hill, 4 Deer Killed to day I assend a hill &. after measuring the river &c. &c. &c.

[Clark, June 2, 1804]
June 2nd Satturday Cap Lewis Took the Time & Distance of suns & moons
nearest limbs, the Sun East- and Meridean altitude of Suns U. L. with
Octant, back observation gave for altitude 37° 28'00".

Error of Octant 2° 00' 00" +. made Several other observations- I made an angle for the Wedth of the two rivers. The Missourie from the Point to the N. Side is 875 yards wide the Osage River from the point to the S. E Side is 397 yards wide, the destance between the two rivers at the pt. of high Land (ioo foot above the bottom) and 80 poles up the Missouries from the point is 40 poles, on the top of this high land under which is a limestone rock two Mouns or graves are raised- from this pt. which Comds both rivers I had a delightful) prospect of the Missouries up & down, also the Osage R. up. George Drewyer & John Shields who we had Sent with the horses by Land on the N Side joined us this evening much worsted, they being absent Seven Days depending on their gun, the greater part of the time rain, they were obliged to raft or Swim many Creeks, those men gave a flattering account of the Countrey Commencing below the first hill on the N Side and extendg Parrelal with the river for 30 or 40 Ms. The Two Muddey river passing Thro & som fine Springs & Streams our hunters kill Several Deer to day, Some Small licks on the S E of the Osage River.

[Clark, June 3, 1804] June Sunday 3rd 1804 the fore part of the day fair I attempted to take equal alltitudes, & M Altitudes, but was disapointed, the Clouds obsured the Sun, took the D. of sun & moon Capt Lewis & George Drewyer went out & Killed a Deer, We Set out at 5 oClock P M Cloudy & rain, West 5 Ms. to the mo. of Murrow Creek Lb Sd. a pt. St. Side Keeping along the Lbd Side 1 Ms., passed the mouth of a Creek on Lbd Side 3 ms., I call Cupboard, Creek, mouths behind a rock which projects into the river, Camped in the mouth of the Creek aforesaid, at the mouth of this Creek I saw much fresh Signs of Indians, haveing Crossed 2 Deer Killed to day. I have a verry Sore Throat, & am Tormented with Musquetors & Small ticks.

[Clark, June 3, 1804] June 3rd Sunday 1804 The forepart of the day fair Took meridional altitude of suns U:L with the Octant and Glass Horrison adjusted back observation. the instrument gave 38° 2' 00"- it was Cloudy and the Suns disk much obsured, and Cannot be Depended on.

We made other Observations in the evening after the return of Capt Lewis from a walk of three or four ms. round- We Set out at 5 oClock P.M. proceeded on five miles to the mouth of a Creek on the L. S. 20 yds. wide Called Murow, passed a Creek at 3 ms. which I call Cupbord Creek as it Mouths above a rock of that appearance. Several Deer Killed to dayat the mouth of the Murow Creek I Saw much Sign of war parties of Inds. haveing Crossed from the mouth of this Creek. I have a bad Cold with a Sore throat. Near West 5 Miles

[Clark, June 4, 1804] June 4th 1804 Monday, a fair Day Sent out 3 hunters, our mast broke by the boat running under a tree Passed an Islands on Stbd Side on which grow Seeder a Creek at _____ miles on the Starbd Sd. Course N. 30° W 4 ms. to pt. on St. Side below 2d Isd. passed a Creek on Lbd Side 15 yd. wide, I call Nightingale Creek. this Bird Sang all last night and is the first of the kind I ever herd, below this Creek and the last Passed a Small Isd on the Stbd. N. 25 W. 3 ms. to a pt. on St. Sd. passed a Sm. Isd. on St. Sd. and Seeder Creek on the Same Side 20 yds wide passed a Creek on Lbd Sd. 20 yd wide, I call Mast Creek, this is a Short Creek, fine land above & below the mouth. Jentle rise of about 50 foot, Delightfull Timber of Oake ash walnut hickory &c. &c. wind from N W. by W. N. 58° W. 71/2 ms. passed a Creek Called Zoncar on the Lbd Side, N 75 W 3 me. to a pt, S. Sd. called Batue a De charm, a plain on the hill opposit. I got out & walked on the L Sd. thro a Charming Bottom of rich Land about one mile then I assended a hill of about 170 foot on the top of which is a Moun and about 100 acres of Land of Dead timber on this hill one of the party says he has found Lead ore a verry extensive Cave under this hill next the river, the Land on the top is fine, This is a very bad part of the river Seven Deer Killed to day by our hunters- one of the horses is Snaged, the other lost his Shous to day the Bottom on the St. Side to day is covered with rushes, not verry good _____ the high land Comes to the bank on the Labd Side and good 2d rate land.

[Clark, June 4, 1804] June 4th Monday 1804 a fair day three men out on the right flank passed a large Island on the St. Side Called Seeder Island, this Isd. has a great Deel of Ceedar on it, passed a Small Creek at 1 ms. 15 yd. Wide which we named Nightingale Creek from a Bird of that discription which Sang for us all last night, and is the first of the Kind I ever heard. passed the mouth of Seeder Creek at 7 ms. on the S. S. abt. 20 yds. Wide above Some Small Isds. passed a Creek on the L. S. abt. 15 yds. wide. Mast Creek, here the Sergt. at the helm run under a bending Tree & broke the mast, Some delightful) Land, with a jentle assent about the Creek, well timbered, Oake, Ash, walnut &c. &c. passed, wind N W. by W. passed a Small Creek Called Zan Can C on the L. S; at this last point I got out and walked on the L. Sd. thro a rush bottom for 1 Miles & a Short Distance thro Nettles as high as my brest assended a hill of about 170 foot to a place where the french report that Lead ore has been found, I saw no mineral of that description, Capt Lewis Camped imediately under this hill, to wate which gave me Some time to examine the hill, on the top is a moun of about 6 foot high and about 100 Acres of land which the large timber is Dead in Decending about 50 foot a projecting lime Stone rock under which is a Cave at one place in this projecting rocks I went on one which Spured up and hung over the Water from the top of this rock I had a prospect of the river for 20 or 30 ms. up, from the Cave which incumposed the hill I decended by a Steep decent to the foot, a verry bad part of the river opposit this hill, the river Continu to fall Slowly, our hunters killed 7 Deer to day The land our hunters passed thro to day on the S. S. was Verry fine the latter part of to day. the high land on the S. S. is about 2d rate

[Clark, June 5, 1804] June 5th Tuesday, Jurked the Vennison Killed yesterday, after Seting over the Scouting Party or hunder of 3 men Set out at 6 oClock Course N 57° W to a pt. on S. Sd. 5 ms. passed a Creek on L. Sd. I call Lead C of 15 yds passed one on the S. Called Lit. good-womans Creek about 20 yds. wide Passed a Willow Isd. a Butifull Prarie approaching near the river above Lead C & extends to the Mine river in a westerly Derection, passed the Mouth of the Creek of the Big Rock 15 yds Wide at 4 ms. on the Lbd Sd. at 11 oClock brought a Caissie in which was 2 men, from 80 League up the Kansias River, where they wintered and caught a great qty of Beever but unfortunatey lost it by the burning of the plains, the Kansas Nation hunted on the Missourie last Winter and are now persueing the Buffalow in the Plains, passed a Projecting Rock called the Manitou a Painting from this Deavel to the Pt. on the Lbd Side N 23° W 71/2 Ms. The Same course 21/2 ms. Creek Cld. Manitou passed a on the Lbd. Side about 40 yd. wide, a Sand bar in the middle of the River passed up between the Sand & L. Shore one Mile to a Small Creek 10 yd. wide, (I call Sand C). We run on the Sand and was obliged to return to the Starbd Side, I am verry unwell with a Slight feever from a bad cold caught three days ago at the Grand so R- passed a Small Willow Isd. on S. Side, a large one in the Middle of the river, York Swam to the Isd. to pick greens, and Swam back with his greens, the Boat Drew too much water to cross the quick Sands which intervened, She draws 4 foot water, a fair wind our mast being broke by accidence provented our takeing the advantage of it passed the lower point of a large Island, opposit the Current devides between 4 Small Isds on the St Side. we found the water excessively hard for 12 Miles as we were oblged to pass up the center of the Current between two of the Isds. & round the heads of the other 2 the Current Setting imediately against the points which was choked up with Drift for a mile- Above those Isd. on the St. Side we camped altogether our Hunter or Spis discovered the sign of a war party of abt. 10 Men

[Clark, June 5, 1804] June 5th Tuesday 1804 after Jurking the meet Killed yesterday and Crossing the hunting party we Set out at 6 oClock, from the last Course & distance, N 51° W. 5 ms. to a pt. on the St. Sd. passed a Small Creek on the Ld. S. I call Lead C. passed a Creek on the S. S. of 20 yds. wide Cald. Lit. Good Womans C. on the L. S. a Prarie extends from Lead C. parrelel with the river to Mine river, at 4 ms. Passed the Creek of the big rock about 15 yds. wide on the L. Sd. at 11 oClock brought too a Small Caissee in which was two french men, from 80 Leagues up the Kansias R. where they wintered, and Cought a great quantity of Beaver, the greater part of which they lost by fire from the Praries, those men inform that the Kansas Nation are now out in the plains hunting Buffalow, they hunted last winter on this river Passed a projecting rock on which was painted a figue and a Creek at 2 ms. above Called Little Manitou Creek from the Painted rock this Creek 20 yds. wide on the L. Sd. passed a Small Creek on L. S. opposit a Verry bad Sand bar of Several ms. in extent, which we named Sand C here my Servent York Swam to the Sand bar to geather greens for our Dinner and returnd with a Sufficent quantity wild Creases or Teng grass, we passed up for 2 ms on the L. S. of this Sand and was obliged to return, the Watr. uncertain the quick Sand Moveing we had a fine wind, but could not make use of it, our Mast being broke, we passed between 2 Small Islands in the Middle of the Current, & round the head of three a rapid Current for one mile and Camped on the S. S. opsd. a large Island in the middle of the river; one Perogue did not get up for two hours, our Scout discovd. the fresh sign of about 10 Inds. I expect that those Indians are on their way to war against the Osages nation probably they are the Saukees

[Clark, June 6, 1804] Wednesday the 6th of June 1804. Mended our mast this morning and Set out at 7 oClock, under a Jentle Braise from the S, E by S N 28° W 31/2 miles to a hill on St Sd. passg the N. beige of the Island Called Split rock Island, the river rose last night a foot the Countrey about this Isd. is delightfull large rush bottom of rushes below on the St. Side N 49° W, 11/2 Ms. to the mouth of Split rock River _____ yds. wide on the Starboard Side opod. the pt. of a Isd. passed a place in the projecting rock Called the hole thro the rock, a round Cave pass thro the Pt. of rock's West 11/2 ms. to a pt. on Std. Sd. opposit a Clift of rocks abt 200 foot N 31° W. 4 ms 1/2 to a pt. on L. Side passed Saline Creek on the L. Side a large Salt Lick & Spring 9 me. up the Creek, one bushel of water will make 7 lb. of good Salt

(Information) Took Meridian altitude of sun Limb. 37° 6' 0" equat to _____ of Lattidude.

on this Creek, So great a no of Salt Springs are on it that the water is brackish N 51° W to a Belge of an Isd on the S. Sd. at 3 ms. Passed a Willow Isd. in Middle, Some wind in the after part of to day from the S E, (the Banks are falling in greatly in this part of the river) as also is one Side or the other in all the Course, we assended on the North Side of the Isd. and finding that the perogues Could not Keep up Camped 2 hs. by Sun. on the Sd Sd the land below this is good.

[Clark, June 6, 1804] June 6th Wednesday 1804 Mended our Mast this morning &, Set out at 7 oClock under a jentle breise from S. E. by S passed the large Island, and a Creek Called Split rock Creek at 5 ms. on the S. S. psd. a place to the rock from which 20 yds we. this Creek takes its name, a projecting rock with a hole thro a point of the rock, at 8 ms. passed the mouth of a Creek Called Saline or Salt R on the L. Sd. this River is about 30 yds. wide, and has So many Licks & Salt Springs on its banks that the Water of the Creek is Brackish, one Verry large Lick is 9 ms. up on the left Side the water of the Spring in this Lick is Strong as one bushel of the water is said to make 7 lb. of good Salt passed a large Isd. & Several Small ones, the water excessivly Strong,

So much So that we Camped Sooner than the usial time to waite for the pirogue, The banks are falling in Verry much to day river rose last night a foot.

Capt. Lewis took meridean altd. of Suns U. L. with the octant above
Split Rock C. &made the altitude 37° 6' 00 error of octt. as useal 2° 0' 0"
+ The Countrey for Several miles below is good, on the top of the high
land back is also tolerable land Some buffalow Sign to day

I am Still verry unwell with a Sore throat & head ake

[Clark, June 7, 1804] Thursday 7th of June 1804 Set out early passed the head of the Isd from the Isd. N. 61° W. to the mouth of a Creek Called big monitu on St. Sd. 41/2 ms. psd. a Sand bar in the river, Som Buffalow Sign Sent out George Drewyer & Newmon to hunt Capt Lewis and 6 men went to a Lick up this Creek on the right Side over 2 mes. & 2 other not far above the water runs out of the bank & not verry Strong. 3 to 500 G for a bushell.

S 88° W. 2 Miles to a pt. on Lbd. Side, high bluff on the Stbd. Side, Monitou Creek is 30 yds. Wide at the mouth, passed a painted part of a Projecting rock we found ther a Den of rattle Snakes, Killed 3 proceeded on passed, S 81°W 4 ms. to apt. on S. Side passed an Island in the Middle of the river, S. 87° W. to a pt. of high Land on the L. S. pass'g over the Middle of a willow Island, ms. 31/2 proceed on 1/2 a mile on this Course a Camped at the mouth of Good womans river on the S. S. about 35 yds wide, & navagable Som D. our hunters brought in 3 bear this evening-& infd. that the Countrey between this R. & the Monitou R is rich and well watered, Capt. Lewis went out an hour this evening

[Clark, June 7, 1804] June 7th Thursday 1804 Set out early passed the head of the Island opposit which we Camped last night, and brackfast at the Mouth of a large Creek on the S. S. Of 30 yds wide Called big Monetou, from the pt. of the Isd. or Course of last night to the mouth of this Creek is N 61° W 41/2 ms. a Short distance above the mouth of this Creek, is Several Courious Paintings and Carveing in the projecting rock of Limestone inlade with white red & blue flint, of a verry good quallity, the Indians have taken of this flint great quantities. We landed at this Inscription and found it a Den of rattle Snakes, we had not landed 3 minutes before three verry large Snakes wer observed on the Crevises of the rocks & Killed- at the mouth of the last mentioned Creek Capt. Lewis took four or five men & went to Some Licks or Springs of Salt water from two to four miles up the Creek on Rt. Side the water of those Springs are not Strong, Say from 4 to 600 Gs. of water for a Bushel of Salt passed Some Small willow Islands and Camped at the Mouth of a Small river called Good Womans River this river is about 35 yards wide and Said to be navagable for Perogues Several Leagues Capt. Lewis with 2 men went up the Creek a Short distance. our Hunters brought in three Bear this evening, and informs that the Countrey thro which they passed from the last Creek is fine rich land, & well watered.

[Clark, June 8, 1804] June 8th Friday Set out at Daylight proceeded on the Course of last night S 87° W 3 ms passed a Willow Island, from the Point of last Course S 81° W. 3 ms. to a pt. on S. S. passd a _____ Isd. in the middle of the river, passd a run on the Ld S. above a pt. of rocks 3 ms. on which thir is a number of Deer Licks, N 88° W. 3 Ms. to a pt L S. N. 83° W 2 ms. to the Mo of Mine River, psd an Isd.- This river is 90 yards wide & navagable for Perogues about 90 Ms. I went out on the L S. about 4 ms. below this R. and found the Countrey for one mile back good Land and well watered the hills not high with a gentle assent from the river, well timbered with oake, walnit Hickory ash, &c. the land Still further back becoms thin and open, with Black & rasp Berries, and Still further back the Plains Commence, The french inform that Lead ore is found on this river in Several places, it heads up between the Osagees & Kansas River the right hand folk passes in a Short distance of the Missourie at the antient Little Ozages Villages our hunter Killed, 2 Deer, after Staying one hour at the mouth of this River, Cap Lewis went out & proceeded on one Mile & came in, he fount the land in the point high and fine Course N. 64° W 1 Ms. to a pt. on S. S. N. 80° W to the Lower pot a Id. on L. S. passed a Small Isd. in the m. R. at (3 Ms.) met 3 men on a Caussee from R Dis Soux, above The Mahar Nation loaded with fur. Camped on the Lower point of an Id. L. S. called the Mills, here I found Kegs an Pummey stone, and a place that fur or Skins had been burred by the hunters our Hunters Killed 5 Deer, Some rain, the Countrey on the S. S. is Verry fine

[Clark, June 8, 1804] 8th of June, Friday 1804 Set out this morning at Daylight proceeden on the Course of last night Passed two willow Islands & a Small Creek above a Rock point on the L. S. at 6 miles on which there is a number of Deer Licks, passed the Mine River at 9 ms. this river is about 70 yards wide at its mouth and is Said to be navagable for Perogues 80 or 90 ms. the main branch passes near the place where the Little osage Village formerly Stood on the Missouries, & heads between the Osarge & Kansias Rivers, the left hand fork head with nearer Branches of the Osage River, The french inform that Lead Ore has been found in defferent parts of this river, I took Sjt. Floyd and went out 4 Ms. below this river, I found the land Verry good for a Mile or 11/2 Ms. back and Sufficiently watered with Small Streams which lost themselves in the Missouries bottom, the Land rose gradeuelly from the river to the Summit of the high Countrey which is not more that 120 foot above

High Water mark, we joined the Boat & Dined in the point above the mouth of this River, Capt. Lewis went out above the river & proceeded on one mile, finding the Countrey rich, the wedes & Vines So thick & high he came to the Boat- proceeded on passed an Island and Camped at the lower point of an Island on the L. S. Called the Island of mills about 4 ms. above Mine River at this place I found Kanteens, Axs, Pumey Stone & peltrey hid & buried (I suppose by some hunters) none of them (except the pumey Stone) was teched by one of our party, our hunters Killed 5 Deer to day, Commenced raining Soon after we Came too which prevented the party Cooking their provisions- our Spies inform that the Countrey they passed thro on S. S. is a fine high bottom, no water.

This day we met 3 men on a Cajaux from the River of the Soux above the Mahar nation those men had been hunting 12 mo. & made about 900$ in pelts. & furs they were out of Provesions and out of Powder. rained this night

[Clark, June 9, 1804] 9th of June Satterday Set out early, water verry Swift got fast on a log, detained us 1/4 hour Hard rain last night. N 39° W 31/2 Ms. to a pt. on the S. S. opposit the Commencement of the 1st Prarie, Called Prarie of the Arrows,1 the river at this place about 300 yds. Wide passed a Small Creek, Arrow Creek 8 yds. wide L. Sd. the Current exceedingly Strong

N 34° E 2 ms. to the Belg of a Small Island Situated on the L. Sd. Passed the mo. of Arrow Creek N 83°W 11/2 ms. to a pt on L. S. opposit Black bird C Small passed the head of the Isd. & a small Willow one to the L. S. (Os merdn. altd. back obsvn. 37 00' 00) N. 39° W 2 Ms. to a pt. of High Land on the L. Side opst. a pt. on St. S. River about 350 yds. wide at this pt. a Wind from the S at 4 oClock (Handson Sutn) on the High pt. a prarie & Small Lake below N 32° E 31/2 Ms. to a pt. on L. S. passed an Isld. in the mid R- in passing up on the S. S. opsd. the Isd. the Sturn of the boat Struck a log which was not proceiveable the Curt. Struck her bow and turn the boat against Some drift & Snags which below with great force; This was a disagreeable and Dangerous Situation, particularly as immense large trees were Drifting down and we lay imediately in their Course,- Some of our men being prepared for all Situations leaped into the water Swam ashore with a roap, and fixed themselves in Such Situations, that the boat was off in a fiew minits, I can Say with Confidence that our party is not inferior to any that was ever on the waters of the Missoppie we Crossed to the Island and Camped, our hunters lay on the S. S. the wind from the S. W. the river continue to rise Slowly Current excessive rapid- The Countrey on the S. S. high bottom & Delghtfull land that on the L. S. is up land or hills of from 50 to 100 foot higher than the bottom & a thinly wooded, Countrey, Lands tolerably Good; Comminced raining at 5 oClock and continued by intervales the greater part of the night. We discovered that one of our French hands had a Conpt. - We Commsd Doctering, I hope the Success in this case, usial to

[Clark, June 9, 1804] 9th of June 1804 Satturday a fair morning, the River rise a little we got fast on a Snag Soon after we Set out which detained us a Short time passed the upper Point of the Island Several Small Chanels running out of the River below a Bluff & Prarie (Called the Prariee of Arrows) where the river is confined within the width of 300 yds. Passed a Creek of 8 yds. wide Called Creek of Arrows, this Creek is Short and heads in the Praries on the L. S. passed a Small Creek Called Blackbird Creek S. S. and One Islands below & a Prarie above on the L. S. a Small Lake above the Prarie- opposit the Lower point of the 2d. Island on the S. S. we had like to have Stove our boat, in going round a Snag her Stern Struck a log under Water & She Swung round on the Snag, with her broad Side to the Current expd. to the Drifting timber, by the active exertions of our party we got her off in a fiew Mints. without engerey and Crossed to the Island where we Campd. our hunters lay on the S. S. the Perogue Crossed without Seeing them & the banks too uncertain to Send her over- Some wind from the S accompanied with rain this evening- The Lands on the S. S. is a high rich bottom the L. S. appears oven and of a good quallity runing gradually to from fifty to 100 foot.

[Clark, June 10, 1804] June 10th Sunday 1804 Some rain last night we set out early Saw a number of Goslings this morning, Continued on the Course of last night, thence N. 8 E. 21/2 ms. to a pt. on the L. S. passed a part of the River that the banks are falling in takeing with them large trees of Cotton woods which is the Common groth in the Bottoms Subject to the flud North 1 Me along the L. Side N. 40° W. 1 ms. along the L, S. opposit the two Charletons, on the N. Side, those rivers mouth together, the 1st 40 yds. wide the next 90 yds. Wide and navagable Some distance in the Countrey, the land below is high & not verry good. Came to and took Mdnl. altd. of Sons U. L. back obsvn. with the octant Made it 37° 12' 00", delayed 11/2 Hour. N. 70° W 1/2 of a me. along the L. Sd.- S 60° W 1/2 m. on L. S. the Same Course to the Pt. S. S. 11/2 Ms. We halted and Capt Lewis Killed a Buck the Current is excessively Swift about this place N. 80° W. 3 ms to a pt. on S. S. passed a Isd. Called Sheeco Islan wind from the N W Camped in a Prarie on the L. S., Capt Lewis & my Self Walked out 3 ms. found the Country roleing open & rich, with plenty of water, great qts of Deer I discovered a Plumb which grows on bushes the hight of Hasle, those plumbs are in great numbers, the bushes beare Verry full, about double the Sise of the wild plumb Called the Osage Plumb & am told they are finely flavoured.

[Clark, June 10, 1804] 10th of June 1804 A hard rain last night, we Set out this morning verry early passed Some bad placies in the river Saw a number of Goslings morning pass near a Bank which was falling in at the time we passed, passed the two River of Charletons which mouth together, above Some high land which has a great quantity of Stone Calculated for whetstons the first of those rivers is about 30 yds. Wide & the other is 70 yds wd. and heads Close to the R.

Dumoin The Aieways Nation have a Village on the head of these River they run through an even Countrey and is navagable for Perogues Cap Lewis took Medn. altd. of sun U. L with Octant, back obsvn. made it 37° 12' 00"- delayd 11/2 hours.

Capt. Lewis Killed a large Buck, passed a large Isd. called Shecco and Camped in a Prarie on the L. S. I walked out three miles, found the prarie composed of good Land and plenty of water roleing & interspursed with points of timberd land, Those Praries are not like those, or a number of those E. of the Mississippi Void of every thing except grass, they abound with Hasel Grapes & a wild plumb of a Superior quallity, called the Osages Plumb Grows on a bush the hight of a Hasel and hang in great quantities on the bushes I Saw great numbers of Deer in the Praries, the evening is Cloudy, our party in high Spirits.

[Clark, June 11, 1804] 11 June Monday- as the wind blew all this day from the N, W. which was imedeately a head we Could not Stur, but took the advantage of the Delay and Dried our wet articles examined provisons and Cleaned arms, my Cold is yet verry bad- the river begining to fall our hunters killed two Deer, G Drewry killed 2 Bear in the Prareie to day, men verry lively Danceing & Singing &c.

[Clark, June 11, 1804] 11th June 1804 Monday The N W. wind blew hard & Cold as this wind was imediately a head, we Could not proceed we took the advantage of this Delay and Dried our wet articles examin'd Provisions &c. &c. the river begining to fall the hunters killed two Deer G. Drewyer Killed two Bear in the Prarie, they were not fat. we had the meat Jurked and also the Venison, which is a Constant Practice to have all the fresh meat not used, Dried in this way.

[Clark, June 12, 1804] 12th of June, Tuesday We Set out early, passed thro a verry bad bend N. 25° W. 31/2 to apt. L. S. N. 70° W. 21/2 ms to apt. on S. S. passed a Sand bar-N 60° W 31/2 ms. to a pt. on S. S. passed Plumb. C at 1/2 a me. on L. S. and halted to Dine, and 2 Caussease Came Down from the Soux nation, we found in the party an old man who had been with the Soux 20 years & had great influence with them, we provld. on this old man Mr. Duriaur to return with us, with a view to get Some of the Soux Chiefs to go to the U. S. purchased 300 lb. of Voyagers Grece @ 5$ Hd. made Some exchanges & purchases of Mockersons & found it Late & concluded to incamp.

Those people inform that no Indians are on the river, The Countery on each Side of the river is good

[Clark, June 12, 1804] 12th of June, Tuesday 1804 Set out early passed Some bad Placies, and a Small Creek on the L. S. Called plumb Creek at abt. 1 me. at 1 oClock we brought too two Chaussies one Loaded with furs & Pelteries, the other with Greece buffalow grease & tallow We purchased 300 lb. of Greese, and finding that old Mr. Duerioun was of the party we questioned him untill it was too late to Go further and Concluded to Camp for the night, those people inform nothing of much information Colcluded to take old Durioun back as fur as the Soux nation with a view to get some of their Chiefs to Visit the Presdt.

of the United S. (This man being a verry Confidential friend of those people, he having resided with the nation 20 odd years) and to accompany them on

[Clark, June 13, 1804] 13th June Wednesday we Set out early passed a verry round bend to L. S. passed two Creeks 1 me. apt. Called Creeks of the round Bend, between those Creeks Stbd S. is a butifull Prarie, in which the antient Missourie Indians had a Village, at this place 300 of them were killed by the Saukees, a fair Day. Passed the antient Missouries villages on right Course N 40° W 21/2 pt. L S., S 29° W 3 ms. pt. S. S., this nation once the Most Noumerous is now almost extinct, about 30 of them, liveing with Otteaus on the R. Platt, the remainder all distroyed, took altd. of S. U L with qdt. which gave N 28 W. 11/2 ms to a pt. S. S. Passed some Charming land, I have not Seen any high hils above Charlton and the hits below for Several days Cannot to turmed hills but high Land, not exceeding 100 abov the high water mark N 30° W, to a pt. L. S. 2 ms. passed a verry bad Sand bar, where the boat was nearly turning & fastening in the quick Sand and came too in the mouth of Grand R. S. S. this River is about 120 yards wide and navigable for Purogues a great distance, it heads with the River Dumoine, passing the river Carlton. a Butifull open Prarie Coms to the river below its mouth, we landed and walked to the hills which is abt. 1/2 a mile. the Lower prarie over flows. the hunters Killd. a Bare & Dere, this is a butifull place the Prarie rich & extinsive, Took Some Looner Observations which Kept Cap L. & my Self up untill half past 11 oClock.

[Clark, June 13, 1804] 13th June Wednesday, 1804 We Set out early passed a round bend to the S. S. and two Creeks Called the round bend Creeks between those two Creeks and behind a Small willow Island in the bend is a Prarie in which the Missouries Indians once lived and the Spot where 300 of them fell a Sacrifise to the fury of the Saukees This nation (Missouries) once the most noumerous nation in this part of the Continent now reduced to about 80 fes. and that fiew under the protection of the Otteaus on R Platt who themselves are declineing passed Som willow lsds. and bad Sand bars, Twook Medn. altitude with Octent back observation it gave for altd. on its Low L 36° 58' 0" the E Enstrement 2° 00' 00" +. the Hills or high land for Several days past or above the 2 Charletons does not exceed 100 foot passed a Batteau or Sand roleing where the Boat was nearly turning over by her Strikeing & turning on the Sand. We came too in the Mouth of Grand River on S. S. and Camped for the night, this River is from 80 to 100 yards wide at its Mouth and navagable for Perogues a great distance This river heads with the R. Dumoine below its mouth is a butifull Plain of bbttom land the hills rise at 1/2 a mile back

The lands about this place is either Plain or over flown bottom Capt Lewis and my Self walked to the hill from the top of which we had a butifull prospect of Serounding Countrey in the open Prarie we Caught a racoon, our hunters brought in a Bear & Deer we took Some Luner observation this evening.

[Clark, June 14, 1804] 14th June, Thursday We set out at 6 oClock after a thick fog proceeded on verry well S. 33 W 2 Ms. to the lower pt of an Isld. S. S. S. 60° W. thro a narrow 1 me channel to a Small prarie S. S. opposit this lsd. on L. L. is a Butifull high Plain. from the lsd. S. 70'W. to a pt. L. S. 21/2 ms. just below a piec of High Land on the S. S. Called the place of Snakes, passed the worst place I have Seen on L. S. a Sand bar makeing out 2/3 Cross the river Sand Collecting &c forming Bars and Bars washg a way, the boat Struck and turned, She was near oversetting we saved her by Some extrodany exertions of our party (ever ready to inconture any fatigue for the premotion of the enterpris), I went out to walk on the Sand Beech, & Killed a Deer & Turky during the time I was from the boat a Caussee came too from the Pania nation loaded with furs We gave them Some whiskey and Tobacco & Settled Some desputes & parted S. 5 E. 3 ms. to pt. on S. S. passed a Creek S. S. 25 yds. wd. Called Snake Creek or (_____) passed a bad Sand bar S. S. in passing which we were obliged to run great Sesque of Loseing both Boat & men, Camped above, G. Drewyer tels of a remarkable Snake inhabiting a Small lake 5 ms. below which gobbles like a Turkey & may be herd Several miles, This Snake is of Size.

[Clark, June 14, 1804] 14th, June Thursday we Set out at 6 oClock, after a thick fog passed thro a narrow pass on the S. S. which forms a large lsd. opposit the upper point of this Island on the L. S. is one of the worst quick or moveing Sand bars which I have Seen not withstanding all our precaustons to Clear the Sands & pass between them (which was the way we were Compd. to pass from the immens Current & falling banks on the S. S.) the Boat Struck the point of one from the active exertions of the men, prevented her turning, if She had turned She must have overset. we met a Causseu from the Pania on the River Platt, we detained 2 hours with a view of engageing one of the hands to go to the Pania nation with a View to get those people to meet us on the river. I went out (Shot a Deer) we passd a highland &clay bluff on the S. S. Called the Snake bluff from the number of Snakes about this place, we passd a Creek above the Bluff about 18 yds. wide, This Creek is Called Snake Creek, a bad Sand bar Just below which we found difficuelty in passing & Campd above, our Hunters Came in. George Drewyer, gives the following act. of a Pond, & at abt. 5 miles below the S. S. Passed a Small Lake in which there was many Deer feeding he heard in this Pond a Snake makeing Goubleing Noises like a turkey. he fired his gun & the noise was increased, he has heard the indians Mention This Species of Snake one Frenchman give a Similar account

[Clark, June 15, 1804] 15 June Friday 1804, we Set out early proceeded on about 1 me. and the Boat turned on a Sawyer which was near doeing her great damage, the river is riseing fast & the water exceedingly Swift, passd. a bad Sand bar on which we Stuck for a Short time this is Said to be the worst part of the river and Camped opsd. the bend in which the Antient Villages of the little Osarge & Missouries, the lower or first of those villagies (L. Osages) is Situated in Butifull Plain at the foot of Some riseing land, in front of their Viliges next the river is a butifull bottom Plain in which they raised their Corn &c. back of the Village the high Prarie extends back to the Osarge River, about 3 Ms. above & in view the Missouries Nation resided under the protection of the Osarges, after their nation was riducd by the Saukees below, thos built their Village in the Same low Prarie and lived there many years, the war was So hot & both nations becom So reduced that the Little Osage & a fiew of the Missoures moved & built a village 5 ms near the Grand Osage, the rest of the Missoures went and took protection under the Otteaus on Platt river

[Clark, June 15, 1804] 15th, June, Friday 1804 Set out early and had not proceeded far e'er we wheeled on a Sawyer which was near injuring us Verry much, passed a plain on the L. S. a Small lsd. in the midle the river riseing, water verry Swift Passed a Creek on the L. S. passed between two Islands, a verry bad place, Moveing Sands, we were nearly being Swallowed up by the roleing Sands over which the Current was So Strong that we Could not Stem it with our Sales under a Stiff breese in addition to our ores, we were Compelled to pass under a bank which was falling in, and use the Toe rope occasionally, Continued up pass two other Small Islands and Camped on the S. S. Nearly opposit the Antient Village of the Little Osarges and below the Antt. Village of the Missoures both Situations in view an within three Ms. of each other, the Osage were Settled at the foot a hill in a butifell Plain which extends back quite to the Osage River, in front of the Vilg. Next to the river is an ellegent bottom Plain which extends Several miles in length on the river in this low Prarie the Missoures lived after They were reduced by the Saukees at Their Town Some Dists. below. The little osage finding themselves much oppressed by the Saukees & other nations, left this place & built a village 5 ms. from the Grand Osarge Town about _____ years ago. a few of the Missoures accompanied them, the remainder of that nation went to the Otteaus on the River Platt. The River at this place is about 1 ms. wide our hunters did not Come in this evening the river beginning to fall

[Clark, June 16, 1804] 16th June Satterday Set out at 7 oClock Proceed on N. 68°W. 2 1/2 ms. passed a lsd. close on the S. S. at the lower point Drewer & Willard had camped & had with them 2 bear & 2 Deer we took in the meat & proceeded on. Some rain this morning West 2 Ms. pass an lsd on S. S. & prarie, to a Belge of Snag lsd. L. S. a butifull extensive Prarie on S. S. Hills to about 9 ms. distant. Mr. Mackey has Laid down the rems. of an old fort in this Prarie, which I cannot find S 85 W. 1 me. along the lsd. L. S.- S 61° W alg L. S. 1 me. S 30° W, 3, ms. to pt. S. S. opsd. an lsd. & head of the last S 40° W 1 me. S. S. Passed a verry bad place where the Sand was moving constantly, I walked on Shore obsd. fine high Bottom land on S. S. Camped late this evening.

[Clark, June 16, 1804] 16th, June Satturday 1804 Set out at 7 oClock at about a mile 1/2 we Came to the Camp of our hunters, they had two Bear & two Deer proceeded on pass a Island on the S. S. a heavy rain came on & lasted a Short time, we came to on the S. S. in a Prarie at the place where Mr. Mackey lay down a old french fort, I could See no traces of a Settlement of any Kind, in this plain I discovered a Kind of Grass resembling Timothey which appeared well calculated for Hay, this Plain is verry extensive in the evening I walked on the S. S. to see if any timber was Convt. to make Oars, which we were much in want of, I found Som indifferent timber and Struck the river above the Boat at a bad Sand bar the worst I had Seen which the boat must pass or Drop back Several Miles & Stem a Swift Current on the opsd Side of an lsd. the Boat however assended the middle of the Streem which was diffucult Dangerious We Came to above this place at Dark and Camped in a bad place, the misquitoes and Ticks are noumerous & bad.

[Clark, June 17, 1804] June 17 1804 Rope walk Camp The Current of the River at this place is a Stick will float 48 poles 6 feet in the rapidest part in 23 Seconds, further out is 34, Still further 65 - 74 - 78 & 82 are the Trials we have made.

[Clark, June 17, 1804] June 17 Sunday 1804 Cloudy Wind, S. E. Set out early S. 65° W 1 Me. Came too to Make ores, and a Cord for a Toe Rope all this day imployed in getting out Ores, & makeing for the use of the Boat out of a large Cable rope which we have, G Drewyer Came up a Bear & 2 Deer, also a fine horse which he found in the woods, Supposed to have been left by Some war party from the osages, The Ticks are numerous and large and have been trousom all the way and the Musquetors are beginning to be verry troublesome, my Cold Continues verry bad the French higherlins Complain for the want of Provisions, Saying they are accustomed to eat 5 & 6 times a day, they are roughly rebuked for their presumption, the Country about abounds in Bear Deer & Elk and the S. S. the lands are well timbered and rich for 2 ms. to a butifull Prarie which risies into hills At 8 or 9 ms. back- on the L. S a Prarie coms. on the bank which is high and contines back rich & well watered as far

[Clark, June 17, 1804] June 17th Sunday 1804 (S. 65°W. me. S. Side-) Cloudy morning wind from the S. E. we Set out early and proceeded on one mile & came too to make oars, & repair our Cable & toe rope &c. &c. which was necessary for the Boat & Perogues, Sent out Sjt. Pryor and Some men to get ash timber for ores, and Set Some men to make a Toe Rope out of the Cords of a Cable which had been provided by Capt Lewis at Pitts burg for the Cable of the boat- George Drewyer our hunter and one man came in with 2 Deer & a Bear, also a young Horse, they had found in the Prarie, this horse has been in the Prarie a long time and is fat, I suppose he has been left by Some war party against the Osage, This is a Crossing place for the war partis against that nation from the Saukees, Aiaouez, & Souix. The party is much aflicted with Boils and Several have the Decissantary, which I contribute to the water

The Countrey about this place is butifull on the river rich & well timbered on the S. S. about two miles back a Prarie coms. which is rich and interspursud with groves of timber, the County rises at 7 or 8 miles Still further back and is roleing- on the L. S. the high lands & Prarie Corns. in the bank of the river and Continus back, well watered and abounds in Der Elk & Bear The Ticks & Musquetors are verry troublesom.

[Clark, June 18, 1804] June 18th Monday Some raind last night, Sent out 6 Hunters to day across the R. they Killed 5 Deer & Colter a Bear verry fat we continue to repare our ropes & make oars all day, heavy rain all the fore pt. of the day, the party Drying meat & greesing themselves, Several men with the Disentary, and two thirds of them with ulsers or Boils, Some with 8 or 10 of those Turners Mesquetors verry bad we finish our Cords & oars this evening Men in Spirits

[Clark, June 18, 1804] June 18th Monday Some rain last night, and Some hard Showers this morning which delay our work verry much, Send out Six hunters in the Prarie on the L S. they kill 5 Deer & Coltr a Bear, which verry large & fat, the party to wok at the oars, make rope, & jurk their meat all Day Dry our wet Sales &c. in the evening, The misquiter verry bad

[Clark, June 19, 1804] June 19th Tuesday rain last night after fixing the new Oars and makeing all necessary arrangements, we Set out under a jentle breese from the S. E. and proceeded on passed two large Islands on the S. S. leaving J. Shields and one man to go by land with the horses Some verry hard water, passed Several Islands & Sand bars to day at the head of one we were obliged to cleare away Driftwood to pass, passed a Creek on the L. Side Called Tabboe 15 yds. wide passed a large Creek at the head of an Island Called Tiger River on the S. S. The Island below this Isd. is large and Called the Isle Of Panters, formed on the S. S. by a narrow Channel, I observed on the Shore Goose & Rasp berries in abundance in passing Some hard water round a Point of rocks on the L. S. we were obliged to take out the roape & Draw up the Boat for 1/2 a mile, we Came too on the L. S. near a Lake of the Sircumfrance of Several miles Situated on the L. S. about two miles from the river this Lake is Said to abound in all kinds of fowls, great quanties of Deer frequent this Lake dureing Summer Season, and feed on the hows &c. &c. they find on the edgers the Lands on the North Side of the river is rich and Sufficiently high to afford Settlements, the Lds. on the South Side assends Gradually from the river not So rich, but of a good quallity and appear well watered

[Clark, June 20, 1804] June 20th, Wednesday Set out after a heavy Shower of rain and proceeded on the Same Course of last night passed a large butifull Prarie on the S. S. opposit a large Island, Calld Saukee Prarie, a gentle breese from the S. W. Some butiful high lands on the L. S. passed Som verry Swift water to day, I saw Pelicans to day on a Sand bar, my servant York nearly loseing an eye by a man throwing Sand into it, we came too at the lower Point of a Small Island, the party on Shore we have not Seen Since we passed Tiger R- The Land appeard verry good on each Side of the River to day and well timbered, we took Some Loner observations, which detained us untill 1 oClock a butifull night but the air exceedingly Damp, & the mosquiters verry troublesom

[Clark, June 21, 1804] 21st June Thursday 1804 river raised 3 Inches last night after our bow man Peter Crousat a half Mahar Indian examined round this Small Isd. for the best water, we Set out determined to assd. on the North Side, and Sometimes rowing Poleing & Drawing up with a Strong Rope we assended without wheeling or receving any damige more than breakeing one of my S. Windows, and looseing Some oars which were Swong under the windows

Two men Sent out to hunt this afternoon Came in with a Deer, at Sun Set The ellement had every appearance of wind, The hunters inform me that the high Countery on the S. S. is of a good quallity, and well timbd. The High lands on the L. Side is equally good The bottom land on this river is alike, 1st low and covd. with Cotton wood & willows Subject to over flow the 2nd is higher groth Cotton Walnut ash Mulberry Linn & Sycomore

[Clark, June 21, 1804] 21st June Thursday The river rose 3 Inches last night after the Bows man Peter Crousat viewed The water on each Side of the Island which presented a most unfavourable prospect of Swift water over roleing Sands which rored like an immence falls, we Concluded to assend on the right Side, and with much dificuilty, with the assistance of a long Cord or Tow rope, & the anchor we got the Boat up with out any furthr dang. than Bracking a Cabbin window & loseing Some oars which were Swong under the windows, passed four Isds to day two large & two Small, behind the first large Island two Creeks mouth Called (1) Eue-bert Creek & River & Isd. the upper of those Creeks head against the Mine River & is large, passed a verry remarkable bend in the River to the S. forming an accute angle, the high lands come to the river on the S. S. opposit the upper large Island, this Isd. is formed by a narrow chanel thro. the Pt. of the remarkable bend just mentiond below this Isd. on the L. S. is a Couenter Current of about a mile- passed between Several Small Islands Situated near the L. Side and camped above on the Same Side, Two men Sent out to hunt this evening brought in a Buck & a pore Turkey.

at Sun Set the atmespier presented every appearance of wind, Blue & white Streeks Centering at the Sun as She disappeared and the Clouds Situated to the S. W, Guilded in the most butifull manner. The Countery and Lands on each Side of the river is various as usial and may be classed as follows. viz: the low or over flown points or bottom land, of the groth of Cotton & Willow, the 2nd or high bottom of rich furtile Soils of the groth of Cotton, Walnut, Som ash, Hack berry, Mulberry, Lynn & Sycamore. the third or high Lands risees gradually from the 2nd bottom (cauht whin it Coms to the river then from the river) about 80 or 100 foot roleing back Supplied with water the Small runs of (which losees themselves in the bottom land) and are covered with a variety of timber Such as Oake of different Kinds Blue ash, walnut &c. &c. as far as the Praries, which I am informed lie back from the river at some places near & others a great Distance

[Clark, June 22, 1804] 22nd June Friday after a Violent gust of wind accompanied with rain from the West, which commenced at Day brake, and lasted about one hour, we Set out under a gentle Breeze from the N W. and proceeded on S. 14°W. 21/2 ms. to pt. on L. S. Ord Killed a goose, S 25 W 3 Ms. to a pt. on S. S. psd. Snags and Swift water on the S. S.- S. 66° W. 1/2 a me. on S pt. N 60 W 41/2 me. to pt. L. S. passed a large Isd. on the S. S.- (Ferenthiers Thermometr at 3 oClock P.M. 87 d which is 11 d above Summr heat) and one on the L. S. opposit against which there is a handsom Prarie of high Bottom & up Land, Capt Lewis went out in this Prarie & walked Several miles, Come to opposit the mouth of a large Creek on the S. S. Called River of the Fire

Prarie at the mouth of this creek the party on Shore Shields & Collins was camped waiting for our arrival & inform that they Pass'd thro Some fine Lands, and well watered G D. Killed a fine Bear to day

[Clark, June 22, 1804] 22nd June Friday river rose 4 Inchs last night. I was waken'd before day light this morning by the guard prepareing the boat to receve an apparent Storm which threttened violence from the West at day light a violent wind accompanied with rain cam from the W. and lasted about one hour, it Cleared away, and we Set out and proceeded on under a gentle breeze from the N. W. passed Some verry Swift water Crouded with Snags, pass two large Island opposit each other, and immediately opposit a large & extensive Prarie on the Labd Side, This Prarie is butifull a high bottom for 11/2 a mile back and risees to the Common leavel of the Countrey about 70 or 80 feet and extends back out of view. Capt. L walked on Shore a few miles this after noon (at 3 oClock P M. Ferents Thermometer Stood at 87°: = to 11 d above Summer heat) we came to on the L. Side opposit the mouth of a large Creek Called the River of the Fire Prarie, at the mouth of this Creek the Party on Shore were waiting our arrival, they informed that the Lands thro which they passed was fine & well watered

[Clark, June 23, 1804] 23rd June Satturday Some wind this morning from the N W. Set out at 7 oC Proceeded on N. 70 d. W 2 Ms. to an Isd. Close on the S. S. I went on Shore & walked up thro a rich bottom for about Six miles, Killed a Deer & much fatigued N. 75 E. to a point in a bend L. S. 11/2 the river fell 8 Inches last night.

[Clark, June 23, 1804] 23rd June Satturday Some wind this morning from the N. W. we Set out at 7 oClock, and proceeded on to the head of a Island on the S. S. the wind blew hard and down the river which prevented the Pty moveing from this Island the whole day, Cap. Lewis had the arms examined &c. at the lower end of this Island I got out of the boat to walk on Shore, & expected the party on Shore would overtake me at the head of the Island, they did not & I proceeded on round a round and extensive bend in the river, I Killed a Deer & made a fire expecting the boat would Come up in the evening. the wind continueing to blow prevented their moveing, as the distance by land was too great for me to return by night I concluded to Camp, Peeled Some bark to lay on, and geathered wood to make fires to Keep off the musquitor & Knats. Heard the party on Shore fire, at Dark Drewyer came to me with the horses, one fat bear & a Deer, river fell 8 Inches last night

[Lewis and Clark, June 24, 1804]
Sunday June 24th set out at 1/2 after six continuing the course on the
Lard. side N. 80 E 1/4 of a mile to point Lard. N. 551/4 of a mile to
point Lard. Due west to a point Stard 3 miles good water

(I joined the Boat theis morning with a fat Bear & two Deer, last evining I Struck the river about 6 miles (by land) abov the Boat, and finding it too late to get to the Boat, and the wind blowing So hard Down the river that She could not assend, I concluded to Camp, altho I had nothing but my hunting Dress, & the Musquitors Ticks & Knats verry troublesom, I concid to hunt on a Willow Isd. Situated close under the Shore, in Crossing from an Island, I got mired, and was obliged to Craul oat, a disegreeable Situation & a Diverting one of any one who Could have Seen me after I got out, all Covered with mud, I went my Camp & Craped off the Mud and washed my Clothes, and fired off my gun which was answered by George Drewyer who was in persute of me & came up at Dark we feasted of meet & water the latter we made great use of being much fatigued & thirsty- The meet which hung up near the water a large Snake made Several attempts to get to it and was so Detirmined that I Killed him in his attempt, the Snake appeared to make to that part of the meet which Contained the milk of a Doe, On this part of the River I observe great quantites of Bear Sign, they are after Mulbiries which are in great quantities)

N 85 d W. 41/2 ms. to a pt. on L Side, Came to above the mouth of a Creek on the L. S. abt. 20 yds. Wide Called Hay Cabbin Creek Latd. of this place is 38° 37'5" North- Capt. Lewis took Sergt. Floyd and walked on Shore, George Drewyer Killed 2 Deer R Fields Killed a Deer dureing the time we wer Jurking the meet I brought in, West 1/2 ml. along the L. S.

S 21° W. 3 ms. to a pt. on the S. S. pass 2 Creek on the S. S. just above Some rocks Some distance from Shore 1 of These Creek is Called Sharriton-Cartie, a Prarie on the L. S. near the river. Capt Lewis Killed a Deer, & Collins 3. emince number of Deer on both Sides of the river, we pass between two Sand bars at head of which we had to raise the boat 8 Inch to get her over, Camped at the Lower point of a Isd. on the L S. the Party in high Spirits.

[Clark, June 24, 1804] 24th, June Sunday Set out at half after Six. I joined the boat this morng at 8 oClock (I will only remark that dureing the time I lay on the band waiting for the boat, a large Snake Swam to the bank imediately under the Deer which was hanging over the water, and no great distance from it, I threw chunks and drove this Snake off Several times. I found that he was So determined on getting to the meet I was Compelld to Kill him, the part of the Deer which attracted this Snake I think was the milk from the bag of the Doe.) I observed great quts. of Bear Signs, where they had passed in all Directions thro the bottoms in Serch of Mulberries, which were in great numbers in all the bottoms thro which our party passed.)

Passed the mouth of a Creek 20 yds. wide name Hay Cabbin Creek from camps of Straw built on it came to about 1/2 me. above this Creek & jurked, the meet killed yesterday and this morning Lattitude of this place 38° 37' 5" N. Capt. Lewis walked on Shore & Killed a Deer, pass a bad part of the river, on the S. S. the rocks projected into the river Some distance, a Creek above Called Sharston Carta, in the evening we Passed thro betwen two Sand bars at the head we had to raise the Boat 8 Inches together over, Camped near the lower point of an Island on the L. Side, party in high Spirrits. The Countery on each Side of the river is fine interspersed with Praries, in which imence herds of Deer is Seen, on the banks of the river we observe numbers of Deer watering and feeding on the young willow, Several Killed to day

[Clark, June 25, 1804] Monday June 25th a heavy fog Detaind us about an hour Set out passed the lsd on a course from the last point S 49° W, 3 Ms to a point on the S. S. S 55° W 1/2 Me. S. S. a Coal-Bank on the opposit or L. S Side, this bank appears to Contain great quantity of excellente CoaL the wind from the N. W a Small Creek Called Coal or (Chabonea) 3 N 50° W to the Pt, L. S. 31/2 Miles Hard water & logs, Bank falling in, Passed a Small Creek L. S. Called Labeenie a Prarie is Situated on the S. S. a Short Distance from the river, which contains great quantities of wild apples of the Size of the Common apple, the French Say is well flavered when ripe, which is the time the leaves begin to fall N 70°W 1/2 me. along the right Side of a Willow lsd. Situated on the L. Side S. 80° W 1/2 me. L. S. S 55° W. 1/2 me. to Pt. of Smal lsd. L. S. S 15° W 1/2 me. L. S.- S. 2° E 2 me. pt on Lbd S. (here I will only remark that the Deer in the Morning & evening are feeding in great numbers on the banks of the River, they feed on young willow, and amuse themselves running on the open beeches or points) We have hard water this afternoon round the heads of Small lslds. on the L. Side below a Small High Prarie S. 48° W. 2 Ms. pt. S. S. passd. a small lsd. on which we Camped The party on Shore did not join us to day, or have we Seen or her of them river falling fast about 8 Inches in 24 hours, the Hills on the L. S. this evening higher than usial about 160 or 180 feet. the lands appear of a Simalier to those passed

[Clark, June 25, 1804] 25th, June Monday a thick fog detained us untile 8 oClock, passed a Island, at 3 miles passed a Coal-mine, or Bank of Stone Coal, on the South Side, this bank appears to Contain great quantity of fine Coal, the river being high prevented our Seeeing that contained in the Cliffs of the best quallity, a Small Creek mouth's below This bank Call'd after the bank Chabonea Creek the Wind from the N. W. passed a Small Creek on the L. Side at 12 oClock, Called Bennet's Creek The Praries Come within a Short distance of the river on each Side which Contains in addition to Plumbs Raspberries & vast quantities of wild apples, great numbs. of Deer are seen feeding on the young willows & earbage in the Banks and on the Sand bars in the river. our party on Shores did not join us this evening we Camped on an Island Situated on the S. Side, opposit some hills higher than Common, Say 160 or 180 feet above the Bottom. The river is Still falling last night it fell 8 Inches

[Clark, June 26, 1804] June 26th Tuesday 1804 we Set out early, the river falling a little, the wind from the S. W. Passed the mouth of a Small river on the L. Side above the upper point of a Small Island, Called Blue water river, this river heads in Praries back with the Mine River about 30 yds. wide Lattitude of a pt. 4 ms. above this river is 38° 32' 15" North, the high lands which is on the Northe Side does not exceed 80 feet high, at this Place the river appears to be Confd. in a verry narrow Channel, and the Current Still more So by Couenter Current or Whirl on one Side & high bank on the other, passed a Small lsd. in the bend to the L. Side we Killed a large rattle Snake, Sunning himself in the bank passed a bad Sand bar, where our tow rope broke twice, & with great exertions we rowed round it and Came to & Camped in the Point above the Kansas River I observed a great number of Parrot queets this evening, our Party Killed Several 7 Deer to day

[Clark, June 27, 1804] June 27th, Wednesday a fair warm morning, the river rose a little last night. we determin to delay at this Place three or four Days to make observations & recruit the party Several men out Hunting, unloaded one Perogue, and turned her up to Dry with a view of repairing her after Completeing a Strong redoubt or brest work frome one river to the other, of logs & Bushes Six feet high, The Countrey about the mouth of this river is verry fine on each Side as well as the North of the Missouries the bottom, in the Point is low, & overflown for 250 yards. it rises a little above high water mark and Continus up that hight of good quallity back to the hills _____ A high Clift, on the upper Side of the Kansis 1/2 a mile up below the Kanses the hills is about 11/2 miles from the point on the North Side of the Missouries the Hill or high lands is Several miles back, we compareed the instrmts Took equal altitudes, and the Meridian altituade of the Suns L L to day Lattitude 38° 31' 13" Longitude _____ Measured The width of the Kansas River by an angle and made it 230 yds 1/4 wide, it is wider above the mouth the Missouries at this place is about 500 yards wide, The Course from the Point down the midle. of the Missourie is S. 32° E, & turns to the North. up is N 21°W. up the right side of the Kansas is S. 54° E, & the river turns to the left, Several Deer Killed to day.

[Clark, June 28, 1804] 28 June Thursday took equal altitudes &c. &c. &c. & varaitian of the Compass repaired the Perogue Cleaned out the Boat Suned our Powder wollen articles examined every thing 8 or 10 hunts. out to day in different direction, in examineing our private Store of Provisions we found Several articles Spoiled from the wet or dampness they had received, a verry warm Day, the wind from the South, The river Missourie has raised yesterday last night & to day about 2 foot. this evening it is on a Stand, Capt. Lewis weighed the water of the Two rivers The Missouris 78° The Kansais 72° To Describe the most probable of the various accounts of this great river of the Kansas, would be too lengthy & uncertain to insert here, it heads with the river Del Norid in the black Mountain or ridge which Divides the waters of the Kansas Del Nord, & Callarado & oppsoitly from those of the Missoureis (and not well assertaind) This River recves its name from a nation which dwells at this time on its banks & 2 villages one about 20 Leagues & the other 40 Leagues up, those Indians are not verry noumerous at this time, reduced by war with their neighbours, &c. they formerly liveid on the South banks of the Missouries 24 Leagues above this river in a open & butifull plain and were verry noumerous at the time the french first Settled the Illinois, I am told they are a fierce & warlike people, being badly Supplied with fire arms, become easily conquered by the Aiauway & Saukees who are better furnished with those materials of war, This nation is now out in the plains hunting the Buffalow our hunters Killed Several Deer and Saw Buffalow, men impd Dressing Skins & makeing themselves Comfortable, the high lands Coms to the river Kanses on the upper Side at about a mile, full in view, and a butifull place for a fort, good landing place, the waters of the Kansas is verry disigreeably tasted to me.

[Clark, June 29, 1804] 29th of June 1804, Set out from the Kansas river 1/2 past 4 oClock, proceeded on passed a Small run on the L. S. at 1/2 Mile a (1) Island on the S. S. at 11/2 me. Hills above the upr. pt of lsd. L. S. a large Sand bar in the middle. Passed a verry bad place of water, the Sturn of the Boat Struck a moveing Sand & turned within 6 Inches of a large Sawyer, if the Boat had Struck the Sawyer, her Bow must have been Knocked off & in Course She must hav Sunk in the Deep water below Came to & camped on the S. S. late in the eveninge.

[Clark, June 29, 1804] 29th June Friday obsvd. the distance of (D &)) ,took Equal & maridinal altd. and after makeing Some arrangements, and inflicting a little punishment to two men we Set out at 1/2 past 4 oClock and proceeded on (i) passed a large Island on the S. Side, opposit a large Sand bar, the Boat turned and was within Six Inches of Strikeing the rapidity with which the Boat turned was so great that if her bow had Struck the Snag, She must have either turned over or the bow nocked off S W wind

[Clark, June 29, 1804] Camp mouth of the Kanseis June 29th 1804. Ordered a Court martial will Set this day at 11 oClock, to Consist of five members, for the trial of John Collins and Hugh Hall, Confined on Charges exhibited against them by Sergeant Floyd, agreeable to the articles of War.

Detail for the Court

Sergt Nat. Pryor presd.

mbs: 2 John Colter 3 John Newmon 4 Pat. Gass 1 J. B. Thompson

John Potts to act as judge advocate.

The Court Convened agreeable to order and proceeded to the trial of the Prisoners Viz John Collins Charged "with getting drunk on his post this morning out of whiskey put under his Charge as a Sentinal and for Suffering Hugh Hall to draw whiskey out of the Said Barrel intended for the party"

To this Charge the prisoner plead not guilty.

The Court after mature deliveration on the evidence abduced &c. are of oppinion that the prisoner is Guilty of the Charge exibited against him, and do therefore Sentence him to recive one hundred Lashes on his bear Back.

Hugh Hall was brought with "takeing whiskey out of a Keg this morning which whiskey was Stored on the Bank (and under the Charge of the guard) Contrary to all order, rule, or regulation"

To this Charge the prisoner "Pleades Guilty."

The Court find the prisoner guilty and Sentence him to receive fifty Lashes on his bear Back.

The Commanding Officers approve of the Sentence of the Court and orders that the Punishment take place at half past three this evening, at which time the party will Parrade for inspection-

[Clark, June 29, 1804] at the Mouth of the River Kansies June 26" 27" 28 & 29th- This river is 366 miles above the mouth of Missouri it is in Lattitude 38° 31' 13" North

it is 230 yds. wide at its mouth & wider above from the point up the Missourie for about 3 ms. N. 21° W, Down the Middle of the Missourie is S. 32° E, up the upper bank of the Kansas, is S. 54° E the river turns to the East above a pt. of high land, well Situated for a fort & in view of the Missouris one mile up & on the upper Side, the width of the Missouris at this place is about 500 yds.

Missourie Water weighs 78. The Kanseis weghs 72 river Miss raised in the time at the Kanseis 2 foot and begun to fall.

The wood land on each side of the Mouth of this river is extensive and of a good quallity as far as our hunters was back, but badly watered with Springs, only two being Seen by them

Some punishment of two men Hall & Collins for takeing whiskey out of the Barrel last night agreeable to the Sentences of a Court Mtl of the party who we have always found verry ready to punish Such Crimes

Many Deer Killed to day

Allarm post or order of Battle arms to be Situated & the Duty &c. Messes of men under a Serjiant who is to detail for every day one man of his Squad to Cook &c. who Shall have the management of the provisions dureing that day or issue, each Days rations must be divided &c. &c Order of encampment, Tents, fires & Duty

[Clark, June 30, 1804] 30th June, Set out verry early this Morng Saw a verry large wolf on the Sand bar this morning walking near a gange of Turkeys (1) at 10 miles above the Kansis passed the mouth of a Small River Call the (Petite Plate) or the little Shole river, this river is about 70 yds. Wide and has Several rapids & falls, well Calculatd for mills, the land on this river is Said to be Roaling, Killed 2 Deer Bucks Swinging the river the wind from the S. W. here we opened the Bag of Bread given us by which we found verry good, our Bacon which was given us by we examined and found Sound and good Some of that purchased in the Illinois Spoiled, a relish of this old bacon this morning was verry agreeable, Deer to be Seen in every direction and their tracks ar as plenty as Hogs about a farm, our hunts. Killed 9 Deer to day the land below the last river is good, that above, between the two rivers which is near together is Slaik'y and bad on the N. Side, the other Side is good land, Landed on the L. S. below an Isd called Dimond Island

[Clark, June 30, 1804] 30th June Satturday 1804 Set out verry early this morning, a verry large wolf Came to the bank and looked at us this morning, passd the (1) mouth of a Small river 10 ms. above the Kanseis Called by the french Petite River Platte (or Shoal river) from the number of falls in it, this river is about 60 yards wide at its mouth and runs Parrilel with the Missouries for ten or twelve miles, I am told that the lands on this Small river is good, and on its Several falls well Calculated for mills, the wind from S. W. came to at 12 oClock & rested three hours, the … being hot the men becom verry feeble, Farnsts. Thermometer at 3 oClock Stood at 96° above 0, emence numbs. of Deer on the banks, Skipping in every derection, the party Killed nine Bucks on the river & Bank to day, The Countrey on the S. S. between the Shoal River & Missouris is indifferent Subject to overflow, that below and on the L. S. is high & appers well timbered, Camped on the L. S. opsd. the Lower point of a Isd. Called diamond Island, Broke our mast

[Clark, July 1, 1804] July 1st 1804, last night one of the Sentinals Chang'd either a man or Beast, which run off, all prepared for action, Set out early passed the Dimond Isd. pass a Small Creek on the L. S. as this Creek is without name we Call it Biscuit Creek Brackfast on the upper point of a Sand beech, The river still falling a little a verry warm Day. I took Some medison last night which has worked me very much party all in helth except Boils-

passed a Sand bar in the river above the Isd. Covered for a me. with Drift Wood, Came to Capt Lewis took Medn. altitude & we delayed three hours, the day being excessively hot, Turkeys are plenty on the Shore, G. Drewyer inform that he Saw PueCanns Trees on S. S. yesterday great quantities of raspburies an Grapes, (2) pass a Creek on the L. S. called remore (Tree Frog) Creek, an Isd above in the Mid. and 2 Willow Isds on the S. S. all of the Same name; The two Willow Isds. has been made within 3 years & the Main Chant. runs now on the L S. of the large Island where there was no runing water at low water from this Island the range of Hills up the river to the N, W, pass a run on the L. S. a Butifull extensive Prarie, Two Islands just above Called (Isles des Parques) or Field Islands, those Islands are, one of our French hands tels me that the French intended to Settle here once & brought their Cows and put them on those Islands, Mr Mackey Says the first village of the Kanseis was a little above this Island & made use of as fields, no trace of anything of that Kind remains to be Seen on the Isds. fine Land on the L. Side, Hills near the river all day, Camped on the lower pot. of 1st Isd.-

[Clark, July 1, 1804] July 1st, Sunday 1804 a Small allarm last night all prepared for action, Set out early this morning passed on the North Side of Dimond Island, a Small Creek mouths opposit I call Biscuit Creek,- a large Sand bar in the middle of the river 11/2 ms. above the Isd. Covered with Drift wood. river fall a little. The wind from S. W. Came to above this Drift and delayed three hours to refresh the men who were verry much over powered with the heat, Great quantity of Grapes & raspberries, (2) passed a Small Creek on the L. S. below one large and two small Islands. This Creek and Isds. are Called Remore (or Tree Frog) a large Pond on the S. S., the main Current of Water run'g on the L. S. of the Island, I am told that Three years ago the main Current run on the S. S. of the Island and no appearance of the two Smaller Islands, Camped on the lower point of one of the two large & 2 Small Isds. Called Isles des Parques or field Islds a high butifull Prarie on the L. S. one of the french hands Says "that the french Kept their Cattle & horses on those Islands at the time they had in this quarter a fort & trading establishment."

paecaun Trees Seen on the S. S. Deer and turkeys in great quantities on the bank

[Clark, July 2, 1804] July the 2nd 1804 Set out verry early this morning passd on the Left of the Isles des parques High butiful Situation- on the L S. the land indifferent lands a Creek coms in on the S. S. Called parques, all at once the river became Crowded with drift that it was dangerous to cross this I Suppose was from the caveing in of the banks at the head of Some Island above, (3) passed a Creek on the L. S. called Turquie or Turkey Creek passed a verry bad Sand bar on the L. S. the 20 Oars & Poals could with much dificuelty Stem the Current, passed a large Island on the S. S. Called by the Inds. Wau-car-ba war-con-da or the Bear Medison Island, at 12 oClock came to on the Island and put in a mast, detained four hours, exceedingly hot, wind in forepart of the day from the S. E, George Drewyer informs that the Lands he pass through yesterday & to day on the S. S. was generally Verry fine he Saw two Springs of fresh water near the Island, Deer Sign has become So Common it is hardly necessary to mention them, we Camped after dark on the S. S. opposit the 1st old Village of the Kanzas which was Situated in a Valley between two points of high land, on the river back of their village commenced an extensive Prarie a large Island in front which appears to have made on that Side and thrown the Current of the river against the place the Village formerly Stood, and washes away the bank in that part. The french formerly had a Fort at this place, to protect the trade of this nation, the Situation appears to be a verry elligable one for a Town, the valley rich & extensive, with a Small Brook Meanding through it and one part of the bank affording yet a good Landing for Boats The High Lands above the Fere river on each Side of the Missouries appear to approach each other much nearer than below that plaice, being from 3 to 6 miles between them, to the Kansas, above that place from 3 to 5 Ms. apart and higher Some places being 160 or 180 feet the river not So wide We made a Mast of Cotton wood, to day in the Course of the evening & night it turned of a butifull red Colour

[Clark, July 2, 1804] July 2nd, 1804 Set out early and proceeed on the left of the islands, two of which are large a high bottom Situated on the L. S. passed the mouth of a Creek on the S. S. Called Turquie Creike, at this place I observed that the river was Crouded with Drift wood, and dangerous to pass as this dead timber Continued only about half an our, I concluded that Some Island of Drift had given way (3) passed a Creek on the L. S. called Turky Creek, a bad Sand bar on the L. S. we could with dificuelty Stem the Current with our 20 oars & and all the poles we had, passed a large Island on the S. S. Called by the Indians Wau-car-ba war-cand-da or the Bear Medesin Island, at 12 oClock landed on the Island & put up a mast which detained us four hours- a verry hot day winds from the S. E.- George Drewyer inform's that the Lands he passed through yesterday and to day on the S. S. was verry fine, few Springs, we Camped after dark on the S. S. above the Island & opposit the 1st old village of the Kanzes which was Situated in a valley, between two points of high Land, and imediatly on the river bank, back of the village and on a riseing ground at about one mile The French had a garrison for Some time and made use of water out of a Spring running into Turkey Creek. an extensive Prarie, as the Current of the river Sets against the banke and washes it away the landing place for Boats is indifferent- The high lands above the Fire river, approaches nearer each than below, being from 3 to 6 miles distant and above Kansas from 3 to 5 miles distant and the Hills at Some places are from 160 to 180 feet above the bottom

[Clark, July 3, 1804] July 3rd 1804 Set out verry early this morning and proceeded on under a gentle Breeze from the South passed two Islands one a Small Willow Island on the L. S. (1) The other a large Island Called Cow 1. (Isle Vache), this Island is large, opposit to the head on the S. S. is a (2) large Pond, a Bad Sand bar on the S. S. we attemptd without Success, & was oblige to Cross back, I Saw a White horse on the L. S. in view of the upper point of the Island, (3) passed a large Sand bar at the S. point, we halted to day about a mile above the Island and found a horse, which had been lost by the Indians, verry fat and jentle, Sent him on to join the others which was ahead on the L S at this place, the french had a tradeing house, for to trade with the Kanzes on a high bottom on the L. S. near the hills which is Prarie proceeded on round a large Sand bar on the L. S. & Camped (opposit a large Sand bar in the middle of the river). on the L. S. a Butifull Small Stream passes back of the trading house, before mentioned

[Clark, July 3, 1804] July 3rd, Tusday 1804 Set out verry early this morning and proceeded on under a gentle Breeze from the S. passed two Islands (1) one a Small willow Island on the L. S. the other large Called by the french Isle de Vache or Cow Island, opposit the head on the S. S. is a large Pond Containg Beever, & fowl, a bad Sandbar on the S. S. above the Island, on the L. S. we halted at an old Tradeing house, here we found a verry fat horse, which appears to have been lost a long time a butifull Small run passes back of the Tradeing house near the high land, we came to at a round bend on the L. S. and Camped

[Clark, July 4, 1804] July 4th Wednesday 1804, Set out early passed the mouth of a Beyeue leading from a Lake on the S. S. this Lake is large and was once the bend of the River, it reaches Parrelel for Several miles, Came to on the L. S. to Dine & rest a Short time, a Snake bit Jo. Fields on the Side of his foot which Swelled much, apply Barks to the wound, pass a Creek on the L. S. about 15 yards wide cuming out of an extensive

Prarie as this Creek has no name, and this day is the 4th of July, we name this Independance us. Creek above this Creek the wood land is about 200 yards, back of those wood is an extensive Prarie open and high, which may be Seen six or seven below- Saw great Nos. of Goslins to day nearly Grown, the last mentioned prarie I call Jo Fields Snake Prarie, Capt Lewis walked on Shore & Saw a large moun & 3 roads leading We Camped in the plain one of the most butifull Plains, I ever Saw, open & butifully diversified with hills & vallies all presenting themselves to the river covered with grass and a few scattering trees a handsom Creek meandering thro at this place the Kansaw Inds. formerly lived and had a verry large Town passed a Creek (4) I observed Spring braking out of the bank, a good Situation for a fort on a hill at the upper part

The Plains of this countrey are covered with a Leek Green Grass, well calculated for the sweetest and most norushing hay-interspersed with Cops of trees, Spreding ther lofty branchs over Pools Springs or Brooks of fine water. Groops of Shrubs covered with the most delicious froot is to be seen in every direction, and nature appears to have exerted herself to butify the Senery by the variety of flours Delicately and highly flavered raised above the Grass, which Strikes & profumes the Sensation, and amuses the mind throws it into Conjecterng the cause of So magnificent a Senerey in a Country thus Situated far removed from the Sivilised world to be enjoyed by nothing but the Buffalo Elk Deer & Bear in which it abounds & Savage Indians

The names of the french Ingishees, or Hirelens-

in Perogue 1 Battist de Shone Patrn 2 Joseph Le bartee 3 Lasoness 4
Paul Preemau 5 Chalo 6 E. Cann 7 Roie 8 Charlo Cougee

in the large Boat
*J. Le bartee
Rivee

bow men
Pieter Crousatt half Indian
William La Beice Mallat

3 Sergts. & 23 men for the Boat
George Drewyer. Hunter & 4 Horses
1 Corpl & 4 Privates in a Perogue to be Sent back from Plate
river
Mr. Dueron inteptr for the Sues Capt. Lewis my Self & York

in all 46 men July 4th 4 horses & a Dog

[Clark, July 4, 1804] July 4th Wednesday ussered in the day by a discharge of one shot from our Bow piece, proceeded on, passed the mouth of a (1) Bayeau lading from a large Lake on the S. S. which has the apperance of being once the bed of the river & reaches parrelel for Several Miles Came to on the L. S. to refresh ourselves &. Jos. Fields got bit by a Snake, which was quickly doctered with Bark by Cap Lewis. (2) Passed a Creek 12 yds. wide on L. S. comeing out of an extensive Prarie reching within 200 yards of the river, as, this Creek has no name, and this being the we Dine (on corn) the 4th of July the day of the independance of the U. S. call it 4th of July 1804 Creek, Capt. Lewis walked on Shore above this Creek and discovered a high moun from the top of which he had an extensive view, 3 paths Concentering at the moun Saw great numbers of Goslings to day which Were nearly grown, the before mentioned Lake is clear and Contain great quantities of fish an Gees & Goslings, The great quantity of those fowl in this Lake induce me to Call it the Gosling Lake, a Small Creek & Several Springs run in to the Lake on the East Side from the hills the land on that Side verry good- (3) We came to and camped in the lower edge of a Plain where 2d old Kanzas village formerly Stood, above the mouth of a Creek 20 yds wide this Creek we call Creek Independence as we approached this place the Praree had a most butifull appearance Hills & Valies interspsd with Coops of Timber gave a pleasing deversity to the Senery. the right fork of Creek Independence Meandering thro the middle of the Plain a point of high Land near the river givs an allivated Situation. at this place the Kanzas Indians formerley lived. this Town appears to have covd. a large Space, the nation must have been noumerous at the time they lived here, the Cause of their moveing to the Kanzas River, I have never heard, nor Can I learn; war with their neghbors must have reduced this nation and Compelled them to retire to a Situation in the plains better Calculated for their defence and one where they may make use of their horses with good effect, in persueing their enemey, we Closed the by a Discharge from our bow piece, an extra Gill of whiskey.

[Clark, July 5, 1804] July the 5th 1804 Set out verry early this morning, Swam the horse across the river, proceeded on for two miles under the bank where the old Kansas town formerly stood The Cause of those people moveing from this place I cannot learn, but naterally conclude that War has reduced their nation & compelled them to retire further into the Plains with a view of defending themselves & opposeing their enemy (more effectuall) on hors back (I neglected to mention yesterday that the Lake on the S. S. was large Say 3/4 me. wide & 7 or 8 long one creek & Several brooks running into it from the hills, it contains Great quantities of Sun fish & Gosling's from which we gave it the name,) passed Some verry bad Sand bars Situated parrelel to each other, (1) the Boat turned three times once on the _____ of a Drift wood. She recved no procieviable damage, we came to for Dinner at a Beever house, Cap Lewis's Dog Seamon went in & drove them out. the high Lands on the L. S. is open, a few trees Scattering (2) passed a Small Creek on the L. S. in the 1s bend to the left I call yellow oaker creek from a bank of that Mineral just above. we camped on the L. S. under a high bank Latd. 39° 25' 41" North

on the banks of this river I observe great quants of Grapes, berries & roses Deer is not So plenty in this three days past as they were below that. Elks are plenty about those Praries. Some Buffalow Sign.

[Clark, July 5, 1804] July 5th Thursday 1804 Set out verry early, proceeded on near the bank where the old village Stood for two miles, (Swam the hors found a few days ago) passed Some bad Sand bars, The Origan of this old village is uncertain M. de Bourgmont a French officer who Comdd. a fort near the Town of the Missouris in about the year 1724 and in July of the Same year he visited this Village at that time the nation was noumerous & well desposed towards the french Mr. Du Pratz must have been badly informed as to the Cane opposd this place we have not Seen one Stalk of reed or cane on the Missouries, he States that the "Indians that accompanied M De Bourgmont Crossed to the Canzes Village on floats of Cane"

Those people must have been verry noumerous at that time as Mr. De B. was accompanied by 300 Warriers, 500 young people & 300 Dogs of burthen out of this Village

The Cause of Those Indians moveing over to the Kanzis river I have never lernt- we passed Some bad Sand bars, Situated parrelel to each other (1) The Boat turned twice on the quick Sand & once on a raft of Drift, no procievable damage Prarie Contine on the high land on the L. S. passd a Small Creek (2) on L. S. in the first bend to the L S. I call Yellow-Oaker Creek from a quantity of that Mineral in a bank a little above

The river Continue to fall a little- I observe great quantities of Summer & fall Grapes, Berries & Wild roases on the banks- Deer is not so plenty as usual, great Deel of Elk Sign. (Wind from S E)

[Clark, July 6, 1804] 6th July Friday. We Set out early this morning & Proceeded on (the river falls Slowly) wind S. W) passed a Sand bar in 1st bend to the right (1) passed a Small Island at the S. pt. a verry warm day (worthy of remark that the water of this river or Some other Cause, I think that the most Probable throws out a greater preposn. of Swet than I could Suppose Could pass thro the humane body Those men that do not work at all will wet a Shirt in a Few minits & those who work, the Swet will run off in Streams) opposit the 3rd point passed a Prarie on the S. S. Called Reeveys Prarie (fro a man of that name being Killed in it) opposit this Prarie the river is Confined in a verry narrow Space Crowded on S. S. by Sands which were moveing and difficuelt to pass. the Hunts. Sent in 3 Deer Jurked on the 4th point of to day is a Small Island & a Sand bar 2 miles out in the river, this is Called the Grand Bend, or Grande de Tour, I walked on this Sand bar found it a light Sand intersperced with Small Pebbles of various Kinds, also pit Coal of an excellent quallity was lodged on the Sand, We camped on the L. S. at a small creek a whiper will perched on the boat for a Short time, I gave his name to the Creek

[Clark, July 6, 1804] July 6th, Friday We Set out early this morning, wind from the S. W. passed a large Sand bar in the 1st. bend to the right. (1) passed a Small Island at the S. point opposit the 3rd point we passed a Prarie on the S. S. Called Reeveys Prarie at this place the river is Confined in a verry narrow Channel Crouded by a Sand bar from the L. Point This Sand bar from the L. Point, this Sand bar is verry bad, at the 4th Point from the S. S. is a verry extensive bar, at the Point of which is a Small willow Island this is Called the Grand Detour or Great bend

I walked on this Sand bar and found the Sand was light, with Collection of Small pebble, & some Pit Coal I observe that the men Swet more than is Common from Some Cause, I think the Missouries water is the principal Cause our hunters Sent in 3 Bucks today The river Still fall a little

[Clark, July 7, 1804] 7th of July Satturday 1804 Set out early passed Some verry Swift water on the L. S. which Compelled us to Draw up by the Cord. a verry warm morning, passed a butifull Prarie on the right Side which extends back, those Praries has much the appearance from the river of farms, Divided by narrow Strips of woods those Strips of timber grows along the runs which rise on the hill & pass to the river a Cleft above, one man sick (Frasure) Struck with the Sun, Saw a large rat on the Side of the bank, Killed a wolf on the Bank passed (2) a verry narrow part of the river, all confined within 200 yards, a yellow bank above, passed a Small willow Island on the S. point, (in Low water those Small Willow Islands are joined to the Sand bars makeing out from the Points) a pond on the S. S near the prarie we passed yesterday in which G D. Saw Several young Swans we Came to and Camped on the L. S. and two men Sent out last evening with the horses did not join us this evening agreeable to orders- a hard wind with Some rain from the N, E at 7 oClock which lasted half an hour, with thunder & lightning. river fall a little

[Clark, July 7, 1804] July the 7th Satturday 1804 Set out early passed Some Swift water, which obliged us to draw up by roapes, a Sand bare at the point opposit a butifull Prarie on the S. Side Calld. (1) St. Michul, those Praries on the river has verry much the appearence of farms from the river Divided by narrow Strips of wood land, which wood land is Situatd. on the runs leading to the river. passed a Bluff of yellow Clay above the Prarie. Saw a large rat on the bank. Killed a Wolf. at 4 oClock pass a Verry narrow part of the river water Confd. in a bead not more than 200 yards wide at this place the Current runs against the L. Side. no Sand to Confine the Current on the S. S. passed a Small sand Island above the Small Islds. Situated at the points, in low water form a part of the Sand bars makeing out from those points

Incamped on the S. S. at 7 oClock a Violent Ghust of wind from the N.
E. with Some rain, which lasted half an hour (G D. informs me that he
Saw in a Pond on the S. S. which we passed yesterday; a number of young
Swans-,) one man verry Sick, Struck with the Sun, Capt. Lewis bled him
& gave Niter which has revived him much

[Clark, July 8, 1804] 8th of July Sunday Set out early this morning, the Sick man much better, Serjt. Oddeway was waiting at a Creek on the S. S. below an Island, passed (1) two Island on the S. S. and came to at the upper point, G Drewyer went out R. Fields & Guterich, five men Sick to day with a violent Head ake &c. and Several with Boils, we appoint a Cook to each mess to take Charge of the Provisions. in Serjt. Pryor's = Collens in Sjt. Ordway's Werner in Sergt. Floyd's Thompson, The french men Killed a young Deer on the Bank, (2) passed up a narrow Channel of about 80 or 100 yds wide about 5 miles to the mouth of Nadawa River which corns in to this channel from the N W. and is abt. 70 yards wide at its mouth ____ feet Deep and has a jentle Current, Perogues can navagate this river near its head, which is between the Missourie & the Grand River, passed up the gut 3/4 of a mile to the river at the head of the Island & camped opposit the head of this Island is another nearest the Middle R this Island Nadawa is the largest I have Seen, formed by a Channel washing into the Nadawa river.- "8 or 10000 acrs"

[Clark, July 8, 1804] July the 8th Sunday 1804 Set out early passed a Small Creek on the S. S. and two (1) Small Islands on the S S. five men Sick to day with a violent head ake &c. we made Some arrangements as to provisions & Messes, came to for Dinner at the lower point of a very large Island Situated near the S. S. after a delay of two hours we passed a narrow channel of 45 to 80 yds wide five miles to the mouth of (3) Nkdawa River, This river Coms in from the North and is navagable for Perogues Some distance. it is about 70 yards wide a little above the mouth, at the mouth not So wide, the mud of the Gut running out of the Missourie is thrown and Settles in the mouth half a mile higher up this Channel or gut is the upper point of the Said Island, This Island is Called Nadawa, & is the largest I have Seen in the river, containing 7 or 8000 acres of Land Seldom overflowed we Camped at the head of this Island on the S. S. opposit the head or our Camp is a Small Island near the middle of the river, river Still falling. our flank party did not join us this evening

[Lewis, July 8, 1804] Detachment Orders Nadawa Island July 8th 1804.- In order to insure a prudent and regular use of all provisions issued to the crew of the Batteaux in future, as also to provide for the equal distribution of the same among the individuals of the several messes, The Commanding Officers Do appoint the following persons to recieve, cook, and take charges of the provisions which may from time to time be issued to their respective messes, (viz) John B. Thompson to Sergt. Floyd's mess,

William Warner to Sergt. Ordway's mess, and John Collins to Sergt. Pryor's Mess.- These Superintendants of Provision, are held immediately respon sible to the commanding Officers for a judicious consumption of the provi sion which they recieve; they are to cook the same for their several messes in due time, and in such manner as is most wholesome and best calculated to afford the greatest proportion of nutriment; in their mode of cooking they are to exercise their own judgment; they shall allso point out what part, and what proportion of the mess provisions are to be consumed at each stated meal (i. e.) morning, noon and night; nor is any man at any time to take or consume any part of the mess provisions without the privity, knowledge and consent of the Superintendant. The superintendant is also held responsible for all the cooking eutensels of his mess. in considera tion of the duties imposed by this order on Thompson, Warner, and Collins, they will in future be exempt from guard duty, tho they will still be held on the royster for that duty, and their regular tour-shall be per formed by some one of their rispective messes; they are exempted also from pitching the tents of the mess, collecting firewood, and forks poles &c. for cooking and drying such fresh meat as may be furnished them; those duties are to be also performed by the other members of the mess. M. Lewis Wm. Clark

[Clark, July 9, 1804] July the 9th Monday 1804 Sent one man back to the mouth of the River to mark a tree, to let the party on Shore See that the Boat had passed the river, Set out early passed (1) the head of the Island Situated in the middle of the river a Sand bar at the head, (2) passed the mouth of a Creek or Bayou on the S. S. leading from a large Pond of about three miles in length, at 8 oClock it commenced raining, the wind changed from N E. to S. W. (3) at 6 miles passed the mouth of a Small Creek on the L. S. called Monters Creek, the river at this place is wide with a Sand bar in the Middle, passed a place on the L. S. about 2 miles above the

Creek, where Several french men camped two years to hunt- (4) passed a Island on the S S. of the river in a bend, opsd. a high Land on the L. S. wind Shifted to the N. W. in the evining, opsd. this Island, and on the L. S. Loup or Wolf River Coms in, this river is about 60 yards Wide, but little water running at the mouth, this river heads with the waters of the Kanzas, and has a perogue navigation Some distance, it abounds with Beaver, Camped opposit the head of the Island on the L. S. Saw a fire on the S. S. Supposedly the four flankers, to be theire, Sent a perogue for them, the Patroon & Bowman of the Perogue French, they returned & informed, that when they approached the fire, it was put out, which caused them to return, this report causd. us to look out Supposeing a pty. of Soux going to war, firierd the bow piec to allarm & put on their guard the men on Shore everey thing in readiness for Defence.

[Clark, July 9, 1804] July 9th Monday 1804 one man Sent back to the river we passed last night to Blase a tree with a view to notify the party on Shore of our passing Set out and passed the head of the (1) Island which was Situated opposit to our Camp last night a Sand bar at the head (2) opsd. this Island a Creek or Bayaue Corns in from a large Pond on the Starboard Side, as our flanking party Saw great numbers of Pike in this Pond, I have laid it down with that name anex'd,v at 8 oClock the wind Shifted from the N, E to S W and it commenced raining. (3) at Six miles passed the mouth of Creek on the L. S. Called Monter's Creek, about two mile above is some Cabins where our Bowman & Several frenchmen Campd. two years (4) passed an Island on the S. S. in a Bend of the river opposit Some Clifts on the L. S. the wind Shifted to the N W opposit this Island and on the L. Side (Loup) or Wolf River Coms in, this river is about 60 yards wide and heads with the waters of the Kansis, and is navagable for Perogues "Some destance up" Camped at a point on the L. S. opposit the head of the Island, our party was incamped on the Opposit Side, their not answering our Signals Caused us to Suspect the persons Camped opposit to us was a war party of Soux, we fired the Bow piece to alarm the party on Shore, ailed prepared to oppose if attacted

[Clark, July 10, 1804] July 10th Tuesday Set out this morning with a view to Land near the fire Seen last night, & recornetre, but Soon discovered that our men were at the fire, they were a Sleep early last evening, and from the Course of the Wind which blew hard, their yells were not heard by party in the perogue, a mistake altogether-. proceeded on, passed Prarie on the upper Side of Woolf River, at 4 miles passed (1) a Small Creek L. S. Called R. Pape this Creek is about 15 yds. Wide-and called after a Spanierd who killed himself at the mouth. (2) Dined on an Island Called de Selamen and delayed 3 hours, and proceeded on, opposit this Isld. on the L. S. is a (3) butifull Bottom Prarie whuch will Contain about 2000 acres of Land covered with wild rye & wild Potatoes, gread numbers of Goslings on the Banks & in the Ponds near the river, Capt Lewis Killed two this evening, we came to & Camped for the night. at a point on the S. S. opposit a yellow Clay Clift.- our men all getting well but much fatigued, the river is on a Stand nether rise nor fall, The bottom on the S. S. is verry extensive & thick. the Hills or high land is near the river on the L. S. and but thinly timbered, back of those hills is open plains.

[Clark, July 10, 1804] July 10th Tuesday 1804 Set out early this morning and Crossd the river with a view to See who the party was that Camped on the other Side, we Soon discovered them to be our men,- proceeded on passed a Prarie on the L. S. at 4 miles passed a Creek L. S Called (1) Pappie after a man who Killed himself at its mouth, this Creek is 15 yds wide- (2) Dined on an Isld. Called de Salamin Delayed 3 hours on this Island to recruit the men opposit on the L. S. is a butifull bottom Plain of about 2000 acres (3) Covered with wild rye & Potatoes, intermix't with the grass, we camped on the S. S. opposit a yellow Clay Clift, Capt. Lewis Killed two young Gees or Goslings this evening- The men of the party getting better, but much fatigued- The river on a Stand- The bottom is verry extensive on the S. S. and thickly intersperced with Vines The High Land approaches near the river on the L. S. and well timbered next to the river, back of those hills the Plains Commence.

[Clark, July 11, 1804] July 11th Wednesday, Set out early proceeded on passed a Willow (1) Island in a bend to the S. S. Sent out Dreweyer & Jo. Fields to hunt, Back of this Island a creek corns in on the S. S. called by the Indians Little Tarkio Creek I went on Shore above this Island on the S. S. found the bottom Subject for overflow wet and verry thickly interwoven with grape Vines- proceeded on at about 1/2 a miles from the river about 3 ms. and observed fresh Sign of a horse, I prosueed the track, with an expectation of finding a Camp of Indians on the river, when I got to the river, I saw a horse on the Beech, this horse as appears was left last winter by Some hunting party, probable the Othouez, I joined the Boat on the Sand Island Situated opposit the mouth of the Ne Ma har River, this river Coms in on the L. S. is about 80 yds Wide and navagable for Perogues Some Distance up the praries Commnce above the mouth and Continus on both Sides of this R Drewyer killed 6 Deer to day J. Field one Several hunters Sent out up the Nemahar R

[Clark, July 11, 1804]
July 11th, Wednesday 1804
Set out early passed a Willow Island (1) in a bend on the S. S. back of
this Island a Creek Corns in Called by the Indians Tar-ki-o

I went on Shore above this Creek and walked up parrelel with the river at ab ut half a mile distant, the bottom I found low & Subject to overflow, Still further out, the under groth & vines wer So thick that I could not get thro with ease after walking about three or 4 miles I observed a fresh horse track where he had been feeding I turned my course to the river and prosud the track and found him on a Sand beach This horse Probably had been left by Some party of Otteaus hunters who wintered or hunted in this quarter last fall or Wintr. I joined the party on a large Sand Island imediately opposit the mouth of Ne Ma haw River, at which place they had Camped, this Island is Sand about half of it Covered with Small Willows of two different Kinds, one Narrow & the other a Broad Leaf. Several hunters Sent out to day on both Sides of the river, Seven Deer Killed to day. Drewyer Killd Six of them, made Some Luner observations this evening.

[Clark, July 12, 1804] July 12th Thursday Som hunters out on the S. S. those on the L. S. did not return last night, our object in delaying here is to tak Some Observations and rest the men who are much fatigued made Sundery observations, after an early Brackfast I took five men and went up the River Ne Ma har about three miles, to an open leavel part of an emence prarie, at the Mouth of a Small Creek on the Lower Side, I went on Shore, & passed thro the plain passed Several noles to the top of a high artificial Noal from the top of this noal I had an emence, extensive & pleaseing prospect, of the Countrey around, I could See the meandering of the Little River for at least 10 miles winding thro a meadow of 15 or 20000 acres of high bottom land covered with Grass about 4 1/2 feet high, the high lands which rose irregularly, & were toped with Mounds or antent Graves which is to me a Strong evidence of this Countrey haveing been thickly Settled-.This River is about 80 yards wide with a gentle Current and heads up near the Parnee Village on River Blue a branch of Kansas, a little timbered land near the mouth for 1 mile above, only a fiew Trees, and thickets of Plumbs Cheres &c are Seen on its banks the Creeks & little reveens makeing into the river have also Some timber- I got grapes on the banks nearly ripe, observed great quantities, of Grapes, plums Crab apls and a wild Cherry, Growing like a Comn. Wild Cherry only larger & grows on a Small bush, on the side of a clift Sand Stone 1/2 me. up & on Lower Side I marked my name & day of the month near an Indian Mark or Image of animals & a boat Tried Willard for Sleeping on his post, our hunters killed some Deer, Saw Elk & Buffalow.

[Clark, July 12, 1804] July 12th, Thursday 1804 Concluded to Delay here to day with a view of takeing equal altitudes & makeing observations as well as refreshing our men who are much fatigued- after an early Brackfast I with five men in a Perogue assended the River Ne-Ma-haw about 2 miles to the mouth of a Small Creek on the Lower Side, here I got out of the Perogue, after going to Several Small Mounds in a leavel plain, I assended a hill on the Lower Side, on this hill Several Artificial Mounds were raised, from the top of the highest of those Mounds I had an extensive view of the Serounding Plains, which afforded one of the most pleasing prospects I ever beheld, under me a Butifull River of Clear water of about 80 yards wide Meandering thro a leavel and extensive Meadow, as far as I could See, the prospect Much enlivened by the fine Trees & Srubs which is bordering the bank of the river, and the Creeks & runs falling into it,-. The bottom land is covered with Grass of about 4 1/2 feet high, and appears as leavel as a Smoth Surfice, the 2 bottom is also covered with Grass and rich weeds & flours, interspersed with Copses of the Osage Plumb. on the riseing lands, Small groves of trees are Seen, with a numbers of Grapes and a Wild Cherry resembling the Common Wild Cherry, only larger and grows on a Small bush on the tops of those hills in every derection. I observed artifical mounds (or as I may more justly term Graves) which to me is a Strong indication of this Country being once Thickly Settled. (The Indians of the Missouris Still Keep up the Custom of Burrying their dead on high ground) after a ramble of about two miles about I returned to the perogue and decended down the River, gathd. Som grapes nearly ripe, on a Sandstone Bluff about 1/4 of a mile from its mouth on the Lower Side I observed Some Indian marks, went to the rock which jutted over the water and marked my name & the day of the month & year- This river heads near one of the Villages of the Pania on the River Blue, a branch of the Kansas River.- above this river about half a mile the Prarie Comes to the Missouri after my return to Camp on the Island Completed Som observations, Tred tried a man for sleeping on his Post & inspected the arms amunition &c. of the party found all complete, Took Some Luner Obsevations. three Deer killed to day. Latd. 39° 55' 56" N.

[Lewis and Clark, July 12, 1804] Camp New Island July 12th 1804. A Court matial consisting of the two commanding officers will convene this day at 1 OCk. P.M. for the trial of such prisoners as may be brought before them; one of the court will act as judge Advocate. M. Lewis Wm. Clark

The Commanding officers. Capt. M. Lewis & W. Clark constituted themselves a Court martial for the trial of Such prisoners as are Guilty of Capatol Crimes, and under the rules and articles of War punishable by Death,

Alexander Willard was brought foward Charged with "Lying down and
Sleeping on his post whilst a Sentinal, on the night of the 11th.
Instant" (by John Ordway Sergeant of the Guard)

To this Charge the prisoner pleads. Guilty of Lying Down, and not Guilty, of Going to Sleep. The Court after Duly Considering the evidence aduced, are of oppinion that the Prisoner Alexdn. Willard is guilty of every part of the Charge exhibited against him. it being a breach of the rules and articles of War (as well as tending to the probable distruction of the party) do Sentence him to receive One hundred lashes on his bear back, at four different times in equal propation.- and order that the punishment Commence this evening at Sunset, and Continue to be inflicted, (by the Guard) every evening untill Completed Wm Clark M. Lewis

[Clark, July 13, 1804] My notes of the 13th of July by a Most unfortunate accident blew over Board in a Storm in the morning of the 14th obliges me to refur to the Journals of Serjeants, and my own recollection the accurrences Courses Distance &c. of that day- last night a violent Storm from the N. N, E.- (1) passed Tar-ki-o River, at 2 miles a chant. running into this river 3 ms. abov forms St Josephs Isld. Passed an elegt Prarie in the 1st bend to the left. Containg a grass resmlg Timothy, with Seed like flax, (2) passed a Island in a bend to the S. S. at 12 ms. I walked on Shore S. S. lands, low & overflows, Killed two Goslings nearly Grown, Sailed under a Wind from the South all day, Camped on a Sand Island on the L. Pt. opposit a high & extensiv Prarie, on the S. S. the Hills about 4 or 5 me. off, this Plain appears extensive, great appearance of a Storm from the North W. this evening verry agreeable the wind Still from the South-

from the Osagies Nation with twenty odd of the Natives or chiefs of the Nation with him sailed dowen the Mississippi bound to St Louis & 3 guns fired showers of rain Showers of Rain all that night

[Clark, July 13, 1804] July 13th Friday 1804 Set out at Sun rise, and prosd. on under a gentle Breeze, at two miles passed the mouth of a Small river on the S. S. Called by the Indians Tarki-o, a Channel running out of the river three miles above (which is now filled up with Sand) runs into this Creek & and formed a Island Called St.

Josephs Several Sand bars parralel to each other above- In the first bend to the left is Situated a Butifull & extensive plain, Cover'd with Grass resembling Timothy except the Seed which resembles Flax Seed, this plain also abounds in Grapes of defferent Kinds Some nearly ripe. I Killed two Goslings nearly Grown, Several others Killed and cought on Shore, also one old Goose, with pin fethers, She Could not fly- at about 12 miles passd. a Island Situated in a bend on the S. S. above this Island is a large Sand bar Covered with willows. The wind from the South, Camped on a large Sand Bar makeing out from the L. P. opposit a high hanson Prarie, the hills about 4 or 5 miles on S. S. this plain appeard extensive, the Clouds appear to geather to the N. W. a most agreeable Breeze from the South (I walked on Shore on the S. S. the lands are low Subject to overflow)

Last night at about 10 oClock a violent Storm of wind from the N. N. E. which lasted with Great violence for about one hour, at which time a Shower of rain Succeeded.

The men on Shore did not join us this after noon- The river nearly on a Stand- the high lands on the S. S. has only been Seen at a Distance above the Nordaway River, those on the S. L. aproaching the river at every bend, on the Side next to the river well timbered, the opsd. Side open & the Commencmt. of Plains.

[Clark, July 14, 1804] July the 14th Satturday Some hard Shours of rain accompaned with Some wind detained us untill about 7 oClock, we then Set out and proceeded on about a mile and th atmispeir became Suddenly darkened by a blak & dismal looking Cloud, we wer in a Situation, near the upper point of a Sd. Isd. & the opsd Shore falling in in this Situation a Violent Storm of Wint from the N, E (passing over an Open plain, Struck the boat nearly Starboard, quatering, & blowing down the Current) the exerssions of all our Men who were out in an instant, aded to a Strong Cable and Anchor was Scrcely Sufficent to Keep the boat from being thrown up on the Sand Island, and dashed to peices the Waves dasthed over on the Side next to the wind the lockers which was covered with Tarpoling prevented them coming into the boat untill the Boat was Creaned on the Side from the Wind in this Situation we continued about 40 minits, the two perogues about a quater of a mile above, one of them in a Similer Situation with the Boat, the other under the charge of George Gibson in a much better position, with her Ster faceing the wind, this Storm Suddenly Seased, & 1 minit the river was as Smoth as glass, the wind Shifted to the S. E and we Set Sail, and proceeded on passed (1) a Small Island on the S. S. and Dined- R. Fields who has charge of the horses &c. on Shore did not join us last night-. passed a old fort where Mr. Bennet of St Louis winttered 2 years & traded with the Otteaus & Parties on the S. S. 1 me. abov the little Island, I went out on the L. S. and observed two Elk on a land in the river, in attempting to get near those elk obseved one near us I Shot one. continued on Shore & thro the bottom which was extensive, Some Small Praries, and a peponce of high rich & well timbered bottom, in the Glades I saw wild Timothy, Lams quarter Cuckle burs & rich weed, on the edges Plumbs of different kinds Grapes, and Goose berries, Camped on the L. S. Ruben Fields and Gulrich joined the Party two men unwell, one a Felin on his finger, river fall

[Clark, July 14, 1804] July 14th, Satturday 1804 Some hard Showers of rain this morning prevented our Setting out untill 7 oClock, at half past Seven, the atmispr. became Sudenly darkened by a black and dismal looking Cloud, at the time we were in a Situation (not to be bettered) near the upper point of the Sand Island, on which we lay, and the opposit Shore, the bank was falling in and lined with Snags as far as we could See down,-. in this Situation The Storm which passd over an open Plain from the N. E. Struck the our boat on the Starbd. quarter, and would have thrown her up on the Sand Island dashed to peces in an Instant, had not the party leeped out on the Leward Side and kept her off with the assistance of the ancker & Cable, untill the Storm was over, the waves Dashed over her windward Side and She must have filled with water if the Lockers which is covered with Tarpoling & Threw of the water & prevented any quantity Getting into Bilge of the Boat

In this Situation we continued about 40 Minits. when the Storm Sudenly Seased and the river become Instancetaniously as Smoth as Glass.

The two perogus dureing this Storm was in a Similar Situation with the boat about half a mile above- The wind Shifted to the S. E & We Saled up passed a Small (1) Isld. Situated on the S. S. and Dined & Continud two hours, men examine their arms- about a Mile above this Island, passed a Small Tradeing fort on the S. S. where, Mr. Bennet of St. Louis Traded with the Otteaus & Panies two years. I went on Shore to Shoot Some Elk on a Sand bar to the L. S. I fired at one but did not get him, went out into a large extensive bottom the greater part of which overflows, the part that dose not overflow, is rich and well timbered, Some Small open Praries near the hills, the Boat passed the lower part of a large Island Situated on the S. S. above the Lower point of this Island on the S. S. a (2) large Creek corns into the river Called by the Maha's Indians Neesh-nah-ba-to-na 50 yds this is a considerable Creek nearly as large as the Mine River, and runs parrelel with the Missouri, the Greater part of its Course. In those Small Praries or glades I saw wild Timothey, lambs-quarter, Cuckle burs; & rich weed. on the edges Grows Sumr. Grapes, Plum's, & Gooseberries. I Joined the boat which had Came to and Camped in a bend opposd. the large Island before mentioned on the L. S. Several men unwell with Boils, Felns, &c. The river falls a little.

[Clark, July 15, 1804] July 15th Sunday 1804. a heavy fog this morning which Detained us untill 7 oClock, put Drewyer Sgt. Floyd on Shore, at 9 I took two Men and went on Shore, with a view to Kill Some elk, passed thro open plains, and barroney lands Crossed three butifull Small Streams of water, Saw great quantity of Cherres Plums, Grapes & Berries of Difft. Kinds, the lands Generally of a good quallity, on the Streams the wood escapes the fire, at about 7 miles I Struck the river at the mouth Ne ma har Creek about 40 yds wide, near this Creek on a high part of the Prarie I had a extensive View of the river & Countrey on both Sides. on S. a contnuation of the plain as far as I could See, on the N. a bottom Prarie of about 5 ms. wide & 18 or 20 long, hills back of this Plain. I Swam across the Creek and waited for the Boat about three miles above, we camped opsd. an Island.

[Clark, July 15, 1804] July 15th, Sunday a heavy Fog this morning prevented our Setting out before 7 oClock, at nine I took two men and walked on the L. S. I crossed three butifull Streems of runnig water heading in the Praries on those Streem the lands verry fine covered with pea Vine & rich weed the high Praries are also good land Covered with Grass entirely void of timber except what grows on the water, I proceeded on thro those praries Several miles to the mouth of a large Creek on the L. S. called (2) Ne ma har this is a Small river, about 100 yds. above the mouth it is 40 yards wide, at the mouth (as all other Creeks & rivers falling into the Missourie are) much narrower than a little distance up. after continueing at the mouth of this Creek about an hour, I Swam across and proceeded on about 3 miles and halted to wate for the boat, which was Some distance below- In all this days march thro woods & Praries, I only Saw three Deer & 3 fawns- I had at one part of the Prarie a verry extensive view of all the Countrey around up and down the river a Considerable distance, on the Larbd. Sd. one Continul Plain, on the S. S. Some timber on the bank of the river, for a Short distance back of this timber is a bottom Plain of four or five miles back to the hills and under the hills between them & the river this plain appeared to extend 20 or 30 miles, those Hills have but little timber, and the Plain appears to Continu back of them- I Saw Great quantities of Grapes, Plums, or 2 Kinds wild Cherries of 2 Kinds, Hazelnuts, and Goosberries.

we Camped in a point of woods on the Larboard S. opsd. a large Island.

[Lewis, July 15, 1804] Sunday July 15th This evening I discovered that my Chronometer had stoped, nor can I assign any cause for this accedent; she had been wound up the preceding noon as usual. This is the third instance in which this instrument has stopt in a similar manner since she nas been in my possession, tho the first only since our departure from the River Dubois. in the two preceding cases when she was again set in motion, and her rate of going determined by a series of equal altitudes of the sun taken for that purpose, it was found to be the same precisely as that mentioned in the preliminary remarks to these observations, or 15 s & 5 tenths too slow in 24 h-as her rate of going after stoping, and begin again set in motion has in two instances proved to be the same, I have concluded, that whatever this impediment may procede from, it is not caused by any material injury which her works have sustained, and that when she is in motion, her error on mean time above stated, may be depended on as accurate. In consequence of the chronometer's having thus accedentally stoped, I determined to come too at the first convenient place and make such observations as were necessary to ascertain her error, establish the Latitude & Longitude, and determine the variation of the nedle, in order to fix a second point of departure.

[Clark, July 16, 1804] July 16 1804 Monday Set out verry early and proceeded on the Side of a Prarie passd the head of the Island opsd. which we Camped last night, (1) passed a Small willow Island off the L. point, hills make near the river (2) passed a large Island nearest the L. S. below the pt. a Small willow lsd. also one on the Side. this large Island is called fair Sun the wind favourable from the South. Boat run on a Sawyer, (4) pass a place on the L. S. where the hill abt. 20 acres has Sliped into the river lately just above passed under a clift of Sand Stone L. S. a number of Burds Nests in the holes & crevises of this rock which Continus 2 miles, (5) passed a willow Island in a Deep bend to the S. S. river 2 mile wide at this place, note Deed Snags across, passed the Lower point of a Island called Isle Chauvin Situated on the L. Point opposit an extensive Prarie on the S. S., This prarie I call Ball pated Prarie from the range ball hills, at from 3 to 6 miles from the river as far as my Sight will extend, we camped in a point of woods opsd. the lsd. on S. S. in a bend.

[Clark, July 16, 1804] July 16th Monday 1804 Set out this morning verry early and proceeded on under a gentle breeze from the S passed the upper point of the Island an extensive Prarie on the L. S. passed a large (1) Island Called Fair Sun lsd. a Small willow lsld. at the lower point on the L. S. the boat passd on the L. S. of those Islands Several Small Sand Islands in the Channel, the Boat run on the point of a Snag, (2) passed a place above the Island L. S. where about 20 acres of the hill has latterly Sliped into the river above a clift of Sand Stone for about two miles, the resort of burds of Different Kinds to reare their young. (5) Passed a willow Island in a Deep Bend to the S. S. opposit the river is about two miles wide, and not verry Deep as the Snag may be Seen across, Scattering, passed the Lower point of an Island called by French Chauvin's Situated off the L. Point opposit an extensive Prarie on the S. S. This Prarie I call Ball gated Prarie, from a range of Ball Hills parrelel to the river & at from 3 to 6 miles distant from it, and extends as far up & Down as I Can See, we Camped in a point of woods on the L. S. above the Lower point of the Island. river falling.

[Lewis, July 16, 1804] Monday 16th we set out at an early hour; the morning was cloudy; could find no convenient situation for observation; proceeded untill a little before noon when we came too On the Lard. Shore opposite to the center of good Island where I observed the meridian altitude of O's L. L. with Octant by the back observation, wich gave me the Latitude- 40° 20' 12" N.

I now set the Chronometer as near noon as this observation would enable me, and proceeded untill evening, when we came too on the Stard. shore opposite the lower point of the Island of the Bald prarie where we encamped.

[Clark, July 17, 1804] July 17th Tuesday, we concluded to lay by today to fix the Longitude, and get the Cronometer right, (She run down Day before yesterday), Several men out hunting to day Capt. Lewis rode out to Neesh-nahba-to na Creek which passes thro. the prarie (on which there is Some few trees) within _____ Mile of the Missoureis, wind from the S E. Several of the party have tumers of different Kinds Some of which is verry troublesom and dificuilty to cure. I took a meridian altitude (43° 27') which made the Lattitude of this place 40° 27' 6" 4/10 North.- (The Ball Hills bear N 25° W for 30 mes. The bend on L. S. passing the lsd. on the right Side is N. 28° W. 4 ms.) Took equal altitudes Tried a part of the comn pt. of the Current in 40 Seconds the water run 50 fathem 30" & 20" in places

Cap Lewers returned, Saw Some hand Som Countrey, the Creek near the high land is rapid and nearly as muddy as the river, & rising Gutrich caught two verry fat Cat fish G Drewyer Killed 3 Deer, & R Fields one, a puff of wind brought Swarms of Misquitors, which disapeared in two hours, blown off by a Continuation of the Same brees.

[Clark, July 17, 1804] Bald Pated Prarie July 17th, Tuesday 1804 We Concluded lay by at this place to day to fix the Lattitude & Longitude of this place to Correct the cromometer run down Sunday) Several men out by day light hunting Capt. Lewis Concid. to ride out to Neesh-nah-ba-to-na Creek which passes under the ball hills near this place and at one place a little above this Camp is within 300 yards of the Missouris on this Creek grows Some few trees of oake walnut & mulberry. I took Meridian altitude of sun L. L. (43° 27') which made the Lattitude 40° 27' 5" 4/10 North- wind from the South E. Several of the party much aflicted with turners of different Kinds, Som of which is verry troublesom and dificuelt to cure. Capt. Louis returned in the evening. he Saw Som hand Some Countrey & Says that the aforesaid Creek is rapid muddey and running- This Creek which is at 10 or 12 from its mouth, within 300 yds of the river is at least 16 foot Lower than the river- The high Lands from our Camp in this Bald Pated Prarie bears N 25° W. up the R.

The Common Current taken with a Log runs 50 fathen in 40"Some places much Swifter in 30" and even 20 Seconds of time- five Deer killed to day

[Clark, July 18, 1804] July 18th Wednesday a fair morning the river falling fast, Set out at Sunrise under a gentle Breeze from S. E by S. at 3 miles passed the head of the Island on L. S. called by the French Chauve or bald pate (1) opsd. the middle of this Island the Creek on L. S. is within 300 yds. of the river. back of this Island the lower point of (2) another Island in the bend to the L. S. passed large Sand bar making out from each point with many channels passing through them, "Current runs 50 fathm. in 41 Seconds" but little timber on either Side of the river, except the lsds. & points which are low wet & Covered with lofty trees, Cotton wood Mulberry Elm &c. &c. passed the head of a long Island in high water at this time no water passes thro the Channel (3) opposit the Lower point of a Island on the L. S. pass the Island and opsd. the point (4) above &

on the L. S. the hills come to the river, This Hill has Sliped into the river for about 3/4 of a mile, and leaves a Bluff of considerable hight back of it this Hill is about 200 foot high compsd. of Sand Stone inter mingled with Iron ore of an inferior quallity on a bed of Soft Slate Stone.

We passed a verry bad Sand bar (4) a little above the hill and incmpd on the L. S. opposit a Small Island in the river, Saw a Dog this evening appeared to be nearly Starved to death, he must have been left by Some party of Hunters we gave him Some meet, he would not come near, G Drewrer brought in 2 Deer this evening

[Clark, July 18, 1804] July 18th Wednesday 1804 a fair morning the river falling fast Set out this morning at Sun rise under a Gentle Breeze from the S. E. by S. passing over the Prarie, at about 3 Miles we passed the head of the Island L. S. Called by the French Chaube or Bald pate opposit the middle of (1) This Island the Creek on the S. S. is nearest the river, In high water an Island is formed in the bind above the last (2)- Measured the Current and found that in forty one Seconds it run yo fathoms but little timber is to be Seen except in the Low points on Islands & on Creeks, the Groth of timber is generally cotton Mulberry Elm Sycomore &c &c. passed a Island on the 2d point to the S. S. opposite the water (3) whin high passes out in the Plain oppsid this Island on the L. S. the hills jut to the river (4) this Hill has Sliped from the top which forms a Bluff above & 200 foot above the water, about 3/4 of a mile in length & about 200 feet in Depth has Sliped into the river it is Composed of Sand Stone intermixed with an indiffert. Iron ore near the bottom or next to the water is a Soft Slate Stone, Som pebble is also intermixt, we passed a verry bad Sand bar and incamped on the L. S. at the lower point of the oven Islands & opposit the Prarie Calld. by the french Four le Tourtue Saw a Dog nearly Starved on the bank, gave him Som meet, he would not follow, our hunters killed 2 Deer to day

[Clark, July 19, 1804] July 19th after breakfast which was on a rosted Ribs of a Deer a little and a little Coffee I walked on Shore intending only to Keep up with the Boat, Soon after I got on Shore, Saw Some fresh elk Sign, which I was induced to prosue those animals by their track to the hills after assending and passing thro a narrow Strip of wood Land, Came Suddenly into an open and bound less Prarie, I Say bound less because I could not See the extent of the plain in any Derection, the timber appeared to be confined to the River Creeks & Small branches, this Prarie was Covered with grass about 18 Inches or 2 feat high and contained little of any thing else, except as before mentioned on the River Creeks &c, This prospect was So Sudden & entertaining that I forgot the object of my prosute and turned my attention to the Variety which presented themselves to my view after continueing on this rise for Some minits, I deturmined to make my course to a line of woods to S. E. I found in this wood a butifull Streem of running water, in prosuing it down Several others Joined it and at 3 miles fell into the river between 2 clifts, I went up & under one clift of dark rich Clay for 1/2 me. above this a Clay bank which had Sliped in here I found Sand Stone Containing Iron ore, this ore appears to be inbeded under the Clay just above the water

[Clark, July 19, 1804] July 19th Thursday 1804 Set out early pass between 2 Islands one in mid. & the other L. S. opsd. wher Prarie aproaches the river S. S. This place is called the Bakers oven or in french Four le Tour tere passd. Some highlands 41/2 ms. above the lsds. on the L. S. forming a Clift to the river of yellow earth, on the top a Prarie, passd. many a bad Sand bar in this distance, & the river wide & Shallow, above this Clift 2 Small butiffull runs Come from the Plains & fall into the river, a Deer lick on the first, above those two Creeks, I found in my walk on Shore Some ore in a bank which had Sliped in to the river 3/4 me. above the Creeks, I took a cerequite around & found that those two runs mentioned contained a good proposion of wood Surrounded by a plain, with grass about 18 lnchs. high, (Capt Lewis walked on Shore after Dinner) in the first bind to the right above those Runs passed a Small Island opsd. is a Sand bar I call this Island Butter Island, as at this place we mad use of the last of our butter, as we approach this Great River Platt the Sand bars are much more noumerous than they were, and the quick & roleing Sands much more danjerous, where the Praries aproach the river it is verry wide, the banks of those Plains being much easier to undermine and fall than the wood land passed (4) a willow Island Situated near the middle of the river, a Sand bar on the S. S. and a Deep bend to the L S. camped on the right Side of the Willow Island-W. Bratten hunting on the L. S Swam to the Island. Hunters Drewyer killed 2 Deer, Saw great numbers of young gees. The river Still falling a little Sand bars thick always in view.

[Clark, July 19, 1804] July 19th, Thursday 1804 Set out early passed between two Small Islands, one in the middle of the river, the other Close on the L S. opposit a prarie S. S. Called (1) by the french Four le tourtre, The Bakers oven Islands, passed (2) Some high Clift 41/2 miles above the Islands on the L. S. of yellow earth passed Several Sand bars that were wide and at one place verry Shallow (two Small butifull runs falls into the river near each other at this Clift, a Deer Lick 200 yards up the Lowest of those runs) Those runs head at no great distance in the plains and pass thro of timber to the river. In my walk on Shore I found Some ore in the bank above those runs which I take to be Iron ore (3) at this place the Side of the hill has Sliped about half way into the river for 3/4 of a Mile forming a Clift from the top of the hill above. In the first bend to the right passed a Small Island a Sand bar opposit,- worthey of remark as we approach this great River Plate the Sand bars much more numerous and the quick or moveing Sands much worst than they were below at the places where Praries approach the river it is verry wide those places being much easier to wash & under Mine than the wood Land's. (4) passed a Willow lsd. Situated near the Middle of the river and a large Sand makeing out from the S. S. a Deep bend to the L S. we Camped at the head of this Island on the Starboard Side of it, Hunters Killed Two Deer. Saw great numbers of young Gees River falling a little.

[Clark, July 20, 1804] July 20th Friday 1804, a fog this morning and verry Cool George Drewyer Sick proceed on over a Sand bar, Bratten Swam the river to get his gun & Clothes left last night psd a large willow lsd. on the L. S. (1) passed the mouth of l'Eau que pleure the English of which is the water which Cry's this Creek is about 20 yards wide falls into the river above a Gift of brown Clay L. S. opposit a willow Island, at this Creek I went on Shore took R Fields with me and went up this Creek Several miles & crossed thro the plains to the river above with the view of finding Elk, we walked all day through those praries without Seeing any, I killed an emence large yellow Wolf-The Countrey throu which we walked after leaveing the Creek was good land covered with Grass interspersed with Groves & Scattering timber near and about the heads of Branches one of them without Suckcess, Camped above the bar on the L. S. a verry agreeable Breeze all night Serjt. Pryor & Jo. Fields brought in two Deer river Still falling. a large Spring 3/4 me. below camp

[Clark, July 20, 1804] July 20th, Friday 1804 a cool morning passed a large willow Island (1) on the S. S. and the mouth of Creek about 25 yds. wide on the L. S. Called by the french l'Eue-que pleure, or the the Water Which Cry's this Creek falls into the river above a Clift of brown Clay opposit the Willow Island, I went out above the mouth of this Creek and walked the greater part of the day thro Plains interspesed with Small Groves of Timber on the branches and Some Scattering trees about the heads of the runs, I Killed a Verry large yellow wolf, The Soil of Those Praries appears rich but much Parched with the frequent fires-" after I returned to the Boat we proceeded around a large Sand bar makeing out from the L. S. opsd. a fountain of water comeing out of a hill L. S. and affording water Suffient to turn a mill

The Praries as far as I was out appeared to be well watered, with Small Streems of running water Serjt. Pryor & Jo. Fields brought in two Deer this evening- a verry Pleasent Breeze from the N. W. all night- river falling a little, It is wothey of observation to mention that our party has been much healthier on the Voyage than parties of the Same Number is in any other Situation Turners have been troublesom to them all

From this evenings incampment a man may walk to the Pane Village on the S bank of the Platt River in two days, and to the Otteaus in one day all those Indians are Situated on the South bank of the Plate River, as those Indians are now out in the praries following & Hunting the buffalow, I fear we will not See them.

[Lewis, July 21, 1804] July 21, 1804 by a boiling motion or ebolition of it's waters occasioned no doubt by the roling and irregular motion of the sand of which its bed is entirely composed. the particles of this sand being remarkably small and light it is easily boied up and is hurried by this impetuous torrent in large masses from place to place in with irristable forse, collecting and forming sandbars in the course of a few hours which as suddenly disapated to form others and give place perhaps to the deepest channel of the river. where it enters the Missouri it's superior force changes and directs the courant of that river against it's northern bank where it is compressed within a channel less than one third of the width it had just before occupyed. it dose not furnish the missouri with it's colouring matter as has been asserted by some, but it throws into it immence quantities of sand and gives a celerity to it's courant of which it abates but little untill it's junction with the Mississippy. the water of this river is turbid at all seasons of the year but is by no means as much so as that of the Missourie. The sediment it deposits, consists of very fine particles of white sand while that of the Missoury is composed principally of a dark rich loam-in much greater quantity

21st July from the experiments and observations we were enabled to make with rispect to the comparative velocities of the courants of the rivers Mississippi Missouri and Plat it results that a vessel will float in the Mississippi below the entrance of the Missouri at the rate of four miles an hour. in the Missouri from it's junction with the Mississsippi to the entrance of the Osage river from 51/2 to 6 from thence to the mouth of the Kanzas from 61/2 to 7. from thence to the Platte 51/2 while the Plat is at least 8.- The Missouri above the junction of the river plat is equal to about 31/2 miles an hour as far as the mouth of the Chyenne where its courant still abates and becomes equal to about three miles an hour from information it dose not increase it's velocity for

[Clark, July 21, 1804] July 21st Satturday, Set out verry early and a Gentle Breeze from the S. E proceeded on very well, passed a (1) Willow Island L. S. opsd. a bad Sand bar passed Some high land covered with Timber, in this Hill is Semented rock & Limestone the water runs out and forms Several little Islands in (2) high water on the S. S. a large Sand bar on the S. S. above and opposit the wooded High Land, at about 7 oClock the wind Seased and it Commenced raining passed many Sand bars opposit or in the Mouth of the Great River Plate this river which is much more rapid than the Missourie has thrown out imence quantities of Sand forming large Sand Banks at its mouth and forced the Missourie Close under the S. S. the Sands of this river Comes roleing down with the Current which is Crowded with Sand bars and not 5 feet water at any place across its mouth, the

Rapidity of the Current of this river which is greater than that of the Missourie, its width at the Mouth across the bars is about 3/4 of a mile, higher up I am told by one of the bowmen that he was 2 winters on this river above and that it does not rise 7 feet, but Spreds over 3 miles at Some places, Capt Lewis & my Self went up Some Distance & Crossed found it Shallow. This river does not rise over 6 or 7 feet

Proceeded on passed the mouth of Papillion or Butter fly Creek 3 miles on the L. S. a large Sand bar opposit on that Side Camped above this baron L. S. a great number of wolves about us all night R. Fields killed a Deer hard wind N. W. cold

[Clark, July 21, 1804] July 21st, Satturday 1804 Set out early under a gentle breeze from the S. E. proceeded on verry well, passed (1) a willow Island on the L. S. opposit a bad Sand bar, Some high lands covered with timber L. S in this hill is limestone & Seminted rock of Shels &c. (2) in high water the opposit Side is cut thro by Several Small Channels, forming Small Islands, a large Sand bar opposit the Hill at 7 oClock the wind luled and it Commnc'd raining, arrived at the lower Mouth of the Great River Platt at 10 oClock (about 3 ms. above the Hill of wood land, the Same range of High land Continus within 3/4 of a mile of the mouth below) This Great river being much more rapid than the Missourie forces its current against the opposit Shore, The Current of This river Comes with great Velocity roleing its Sands into the Missouri, filling up its Bend & Compelling it to incroach on the S Shore- we found great dificuelty in passing around the Sand at the mouth of this River Capt Lewis and My Self with 6 men in a perogue went up this Great river Plate about 1 miles, found the Current verry rapid roleing over Sands, passing through different Channels none of them more than five or Six feet deep, about 600 yards Wide at the mouth- I am told by one of our Party who wintered two winters on This river that "it is much wider above, and does not rise more than five or Six feet" Spreds verry and from its rapidity & roleing Sands Cannot be navagated with Boats or Perogues- The Indians pass this river in Skin Boats which is flat and will not turn over. The Otteaus a Small nation reside on the South Side 10 Leagues up, the Panies on the Same Side 5 Leagus higher up- about 10 Leagus up this river on the S. Side a Small river Comes into the Platt Called Salt River, "The waters So brackish that it Can't be Drank at Some Seasons" above this river & on the North Side a Small river falls into the Platt Called Elk River This river runs Parralal withe the Missouri- at 3 miles passed a Small river on the L. S. Called Papillion or Butterfly C. 18 yds. wide a large Sand bar off the mouth, we proceeded on to get to a good place to Camp and Delay a fiew days, passed around this Sand bar and Came to for the night on the L. S. a verry hard wind from the N. W. I went on Shore S. S. and proceeded up one mile thro high Bottom land open a Great number of wolves about us this evening

[Clark, July 22, 1804] July 22nd Sunday Set out verry early with a view of getting Some timbered land & a good Situation to take equil altitudes in time proceeded on nearly a North 15° W 7 ms. to a pt. S. S. opposit Some high Lands on L. S. above the upper point of a long willow Island in the middle of the river 6 Deer killed to Day we deturmined to Stay here 4 or 5 days to take & make obsvts. & refresh our men also to Send Despatches back to govement- Wind hard N. W. Cold

[Clark, July 22, 1804] 22nd of July 1804 Completlly arranged our Camp, posted two Sentinals So as to Completely guard the Camp, formd bowers for the min $cc. &. Course from R Plate N 15° W. 10 Ms.

[Clark, July 22, 1804] July 22nd, Sunday 1804 Set out verry early with a view of Getting to Some Situation above in time to take equal altitudes and take Observations, as well as one Calculated to make our party Comfortabl in a Situation where they Could recive the benifit of a Shade- passed a large Sand bar opposit a Small river on the L. S. at 3 miles above Plate Called Papillion or Butterfly Creek a Sand bar & an Willow Island opposit a Creek 9 ms. above the Plate on the S. S. Called Mosquitos Creek Prarie on both Sides of the river. Came too and formed a Camp on the S. S. above a Small Willow Island, and opposit the first Hill which aproach the river on the L. S. and covered with timbers of Oake Walnut Elm &c. &. This being a good Situation and much nearer the Otteaus town than the Mouth of the Platt, we concluded to delay at this place a fiew days and Send for Some of the Chiefs of that nation to let them Know of the Change of Government, The wishes of our Government to Cultivate friendship with them, the Objects of our journy and to present them with a flag and Some Small presents

Some of our Provisions in the French Perogue being wet it became necessary to Dry them a fiew days- Wind hard from N W. five Deer Killed to day- The river rise a little

[Lewis, July 22, 1804] July 22nd 1804. A summary discription of the apparatus employed in the following observations; containing also some remarks on the manner in which they have been employed, and the method observed in recording the observations made with them.

1st- a brass Sextant of 10 Inches radius, graduated to 15 which by the assistance of the nonius was devisible to 15"; and half of this sum by means of the micrometer could readily be distinguished, therefore-7.5" of an angle was perceptible with this instrument; she was also furnished with three eye-pieces, consisting of a hollow tube and two telescopes one of which last reversed the images of observed objects. finding on experiment that the reversing telescope when employed as the eye-piece gave me a more full and perfect image than either of the others, I have most generally imployed it in all the observations made with this instrument; when thus prepared I found from a series of observations that the quantity of her index error was 8' 45"-; this sum is therefore considered as the standing error of the instrument unless otherwise expressly mentioned. the altitudes of all objects, observed as well with this instrument as with the Octant were by means of a reflecting surface; and those stated to have been taken with the sextant are the degrees, minutes, &c shewn by the graduated limb of the instrument at the time of observation and are of course the double altitudes of the objects observed.

2ed- A common Octant of 14 Inches radius, graduated to 20', which by means of the nonius was devisbile to 1', half of this sum, or 30" was perceptible by means of a micrometer. this instrument was prepared for both the fore and back observation; her error in the fore observation is 2°+, & and in the back observtion 2° r 1' 40.3" + at the time of our departure from the River Dubois untill the present moment, the sun's altitude at noon has been too great to be reached with my sextant, for this purpose I have therefore employed the Octant by the back observation. the degrees ' & ", recorded for the sun's altitude by the back observation express only the angle given by the graduated limb of the instrument at the time of observation, and are the complyment of the double Altitude of the sun's observed limb; if therefore the angle recorded be taken from 180° the remainder will be the double altitude of the observed object, or that which would be given by the fore observation with a reflecting surface.

3rd- An Artificial Horizon on the construction recommended and practiced by Mr. Andrw. Ellicott of Lancaster, Pensyla., in which water is used as the reflecting surface; believing this artificial Horizon liable to less error than any other in my possession, I have uniformly used it when the object observed was sufficiently bright to reflect a distinct immage; but as much light is lost by reflection from water I found it inconvenient in most cases to take the altitude of the moon with this horizon, and that of a star impracticable with any degree of accuracy.

4th- An Artificial Horizon constructed in the manner recommended by Mr. Patterson of Philadelphia; glass is here used as the reflecting surface. this horizon consists of a glass plane with a single reflecting surface, cemented to the flat side of the larger segment of a wooden ball; adjusted by means of a sperit-level and a triangular stand with a triangular mortice cut through it's center sufficiently large to admit of the wooden ball partially; the stand rests on three screws inserted near it's angles, which serve as feet for it to rest on while they assist also in the adjustment. this horizon I have employed in taking the altitude of the sun when his image he has been reather too dull for a perfect reflection from water; I have used it generally in taking the altitude of the moon, and in some cases of the stars also; it gives the moon's image very perfectly, and when carefully adjusted I consider it as liable to but little error.

5th- An Artificial Horizon formed of the index specula of a Sextant cemented to a flat board; adjusted by means of a sperit level and the triangular stand before discribed. as this glass reflects from both surfaces it gives the images of all objects much more bright than either of the other horizons; I have therefore most generally employed it in observing the altitudes of stars

6th- A Chronometer; her ballance-wheel and escapement were on the most improved construction. she rested on her back, in a small case prepared for her, suspended by an universal joint. she was carefully wound up every day at twelve oclock. Her rate of going as asscertained by a series of observations made by myself for that purpose was found to be 15 Seconds and a 5 tenths of a second too slow in twenty four howers on Mean Solar time. This is nearly the same result as that found by Mr. Andrew Ellicott who was so obliging as to examine her rate of going for the space of fourteen days, in the summer 1803. her rate of going as ascertained by that gentleman was 15.6 s too slow M. T. in 24 h. and that she went from 3 to 4 s. slower the last 12 h, than she did the first 12 h. after being wound up.

at 12 OCk. on the 14th day of may 1804 (being the day on which the detachment left the mouth of the River Dubois) the Chronometer was too fast M. T. 6 m. 32 s. & 2/10.- This time-piece was regulated on meantime, and the time entered in the following observations is that shewn by her at the place of observation. the day is recconed on Civil time, (i e) commencing at midnight.

7th- A Circumferentor, circle 6 Inches diameter, on the common construction; by means of this instrument adjusted with the sperit level, I have taken the magnetic azimuth of the sun and pole Star. It has also been employed in taking the traverse of the river:- from the courses thus obtained, together with the distances estimated from point to point, the chart of the Missouri has been formed which now accompanys these observations. the several points of observation are marked with a cross of red ink, and numbered in such manner as to correspond with the celestial observations made at those points respectively.

[Clark, July 23, 1804] Camp 10 Ms. above the river Plate Monday July the 23rd a fair morning- Sent out a party of 5 men to look to timber for Ores two other parties to hunt at 11 oClock Sent, G. Drewyer & Peter Crusett 1/2 Indn. to the Otteaus Village about 18 ms. West of our Camp, to invite the Chiefs & principal men of that nation to come & talk with us &. &., also the panic if they Should meet with any of that nation (also on the S. Side of the Plate 30 ms. higher up) (at this Season of the year all the Indians in this quater are in the Plains hunting the Buffalow from Some Signs Seen by our hunter and the Praries being on fire in the derection of the Village induce a belief that the Nation have returned to get green Corn) raised a flag Staff put out Some provisions which got wet in the french Perogue to Sun & Dry- I commenced Coppying my map of the river to Send to the Presdt. of U S. by the Return of a pty of Soldiers, from Illinois five Deer Killed- one man a bad riseing on his left breast. Wind from the N. W.

[Clark, July 23, 1804] Camp White Catfish 10 Miles above the Platt River Monday the 23rd of July 1804 A fair morning Set a party to look for timber for Ores, two parties to hunt. at 11 oClock Sent off George Drewyer & Peter Crousett with Some tobacco to invite the Otteaus if at their town and Panies if they Saw them to Come and talk with us at our Camp &c. &c. (at this Season the Indians on this river are in the Praries Hunting the Buffalow but from Some Signs of hunters near this place & the Plains being on fire near their towns induce a belief that they this nation have returned to get Some Green Corn or rosting Ears) raised a flag Staff Sund & Dryed our provisions &c. I commence Coppying a map of the river below to Send to the P. ____ U S five Deer Killed to day one man with a turner on his breast, Prepared our Camp the men put their arms in order

Wind hard this afternoon from the N. W.

Equal altitudes taken at the White Catfish Camp, 10 miles above the river Platt-

[Clark, July 24, 1804] White Catfish Camp 24th of July Tuesday. a fair morning the wind rose with the Sun & blows hard from the S. thos Southerley Breezes are dry Cool & refreshing. the Northerley Breezes which is more frequent is much Cooler, and moist, I continue my Drawing. Cap Lewis also ingaged prepareing Som paper to Send back, one of the men cought a white Catfish, the eyes Small, & Tale resembling that of a Dolfin.

[Clark, July 24, 1804] White Catfish Camp 10 Ms. above Platt 24th, of July 1804 Tuesday a fair day the wind blows hard from the South, the Breezes which are verry frequent on this part of the Missouri is cool and refreshing. Several hunters out to day; but as the game of all Kinds are Scarce only two Deer were brought in- I am much engaged drawing off a map, Capt. Lewis also much engaged in prepareing Papers to Send back by a pirogue- Which we intended to Send back from the river Plate- observations at this place makes the Lattitude 41° 3' 19" North

This evening Guthrege Cought a white Catfish, its eyes Small & tale much like that of a Dolfin

[Clark, July 25, 1804] White Catfish Camp 25th of July Wednesday. Several hunters Sent out. at 2 oClock the Two men Sent to the Otteaz Village returned and informed that no Indians were at the Town they Saw Some fresh Sign near that place which they persued, but Could not find them, they having taken precausions to Conceal the rout which they went out from the Villagethe Inds. of the Missouries being at war with one & the other or other Indians, move in large bodies and Sometimes the whole nation Continue to Camp together on their hunting pls. Those men inform that they passed thro a open Plain all the way to the Town a feiw Trees excepted on the watercourses- they Cross the papillion or the Butterfly Creek within a feiw miles of Camp and near the Village a handsm. river of 100 yards Wide Called the Corne de chearf or the Elkhorn, which mouths below the Town in the Plate N. Side. Wind from the S. E. 2 Deer & a Turkey Killed to Day Several Grous Seen in the Prarie

[Clark, July 25, 1804] White Catfish Camp 25th of July Wednesday a fair morning Several hunters out today at 2 oClock Drewyer & Peter returned from the Otteaus Village; and informs that no Indians were at their towns, They Saw Some fresh Signs of a Small party but Could not find them. in their rout to the Towns (Which is about 18 miles West) they passed thro a open Prarie Crossed papillion or Butterfly Creek and a Small butifull river which run into the Platt a little below the Town Called Corne de charf or Elk Horn river this river is about 100 yards wide with Clear water & a gravely Channel.- wind from the S. E two Deer Killed to day 1 Turkey Several Grous Seen to day.

[Clark, July 26, 1804] Whit Catfish Camp 26th of July Thursday. the wind blew Verry hard all Day from the South with Clouds of Sand which incomoded me verry much in my tent, and as I could not Draw in the Boat was obliged Combat with the Misqutr. under a Shade in the woods-. I opened the Breast of a man the discharge gave him ease &c. 5 beaver Caught near Camp-only 1 Deer Killed to day. The Countrey back from Camp on the S. S. is a bottom of about 5 ms. wide one half the Distn. timber, the other high bottom Prarie, the opsd. Side a high Hill about 170 foot rock foundatio. Timbered back & below. a Prarie

[Clark, July 26, 1804] Catfish which is White Camp 26th of July Thursday 1804 the wind blustering and hard from the South all day which blowed the Clouds of Sand in Such a manner that I could not complete my pan in the tent, the Boat roled in Such a manner that I could do nothing in that, I was Compessed to go to the woods and Combat with the Musqutors, I opened the Turner of a man on the left breast, which discharged half a point.

five Beever Cought near this Camp the flesh of which we made use of- This evening we found verry pleasent- only one Deer Killed to day. The Countrey back from Camp on the S. S. is a bottom of about five mile wide, one half the distance wood & the ball. plain high & Dry. the opposed Side a high Hill about 170 foot rock foundation, Covd. with timber, back & below is a Plain.

[Lewis, July 27, 1804] white Catfish Camp July 27th Friday, Charged the Boat and Perogue after a Small Shower of rain, Completed our ores & poles, Crossed over the two horses, with a View of their going on the S W. Side of the Missouri and Set out at Half past 1 oClock proceeded on Verry well under a gentle Breeze. passed a high Island of high wood land on the L. Side just above Camp, this Island is formed by a pond Supplied by a great number of Springs from this hill, this Pond has 2 out lets, & when the river is high the water passes thro the pond, passed a Sand Island in the 2nd bend to the right. Camped in a bend to the L. S. in Some wood, I took R. Fields & walked on Shore & Killed a Deer, and did not get to the Boat untile after night a butifull Breeze from the N W. this evening which would have been verry agreeable, had the Misquiters been tolerably Pacifick, but thy were rageing all night, Some about the Sise of house flais

[Clark, July 27, 1804] White Catfish Camp 10 ms above Platt 27th of July Friday, a Small Shower of rain this morning, at 10 oClock Commence Loading the Boat & perogue; had all the Ores Completely fixed; Swam over the two remaining horses to the L. S. with the view of the Hunters going on that Side, after Getting everry thing Complete, we Set Sale under a gentle breeze from the South and proceeded on, passed a Island (formd by a Pond fed by Springs) on the L. S. of high Land Covered with timber, in the 2nd bend to the right a large Sand Island in the river a high Prarie on the S. S.-. as we were Setting out to day one man Killed a Buck & another Cut his Knee verry bad Camped in a Bend to the L. Side in a Coops of Trees, a verry agreeable Breeze from the N W. this evening. I Killed a Deer in the Prarie and found the Misquitors So thick & troublesom that it was disagreeable and painfull to Continue a moment Still.

I took one man R. Fields and walked on Shore with a View of examoning Som mounds on the L. S. of the river- those mounds I found to be of Deffirent hight Shape & Size, Some Composed of Sand Some earth & Sand, the highest next to the river all of which covered about 200 acres of land, in a circular form on the Side from the river a low bottom & Small Pond. The Otteaus formerly lived here I did not get to the boat untile after night.

[Clark, July 28, 1804] July 28th Satturday Set out this morning early, the wind blou from the N. W. by N. a Dark Smokey Morning, Some rain at 1 me. passed a Bluff on the S. S. it being the first high land approachig the river above the Nodaway, a Island and Creek S. S. just abov this creek I call Indian Knob G. Drewyer Came with a Deer &informs he heard fireing to the S. W. I walked on Shore on the S. S. found some good Prarie out from the S. pt. The High Lands approach the river 1st bend to left The party on Shore brought in a Missouri Indian who resides with the Otteauz, this Indian & 2 others were Hunting in the Prarie their Camp is about 4 miles off. This Indian informs that his nation is in the Plains hunting the Buffalow, the party with which he is encamped is about 20 familey Hunting the Elk, we landed on S. S. below an Island

[Clark, July 28, 1804] July the 28th, Satturday 1804 Set out this morning early, the wind from the N W. by N. a Dark Smokey morning Some rain passed at 1 me. a Bluff on the S. S. the first high land above the Nodaway aproaching the river on that Side a Island and Creek 15 yds. wide on the S. S. above this Bluff, as this Creek has no name call it Indian Knob Creek our party on Shore Came to the river and informs that they heard fireing to the S W. below this High Land on the S. S. the Aiawuay Indians formerly lived, The flank came in & informed they heard two Guns to the S. W. the highland approaches in the 1st bend to the left, we camped on the S. S. below the point of an Island, G Drewyer brought in a Missourie Indian which he met with hunting in the Prarie This Indian is one of the fiew remaining of that nation, & lives with the Otteauz, his Camp about 4 miles from the river, he informs that the great gangue of the nation were hunting the Buffalow in the Plains. hs party was Small Consisting only of about 20 Lodges, _____ miles furthr a nother Camp where there was a french man, who lived in the nation, This Indian appeard spritely, and appeared to make use of the Same pronouncation of the Osarge, Calling a Chief Inca July 29th SundayWe Sent one frenchman le Liberty & the Indian to the Camp to envite the party to meet us at the next bend of High Land on the L. S. a Dark morning wind from the W. N. W. rained all last night Set out at 5 oClock &, proceeded on passed the Island, opposit this Island on the S. S. the Creek called Indian Knob Creek which mouths Several miles on a Direct line below, is within 20 feet of the Missouri & about 5 feet higher

Cought three large Cat fish to day verry fat one of them nearly white those Cat are So plenty that they may be Cought in any part of this river but fiew fish of any other Kind.

(4) at the commencement of this course passed much fallen timber apparently the ravages of a dreadful haricane which had passed obliquely across the river from N. W. to S. E. about twelve months since. many trees were broken off near the ground the trunks of which were sound and four feet in diameter.

Willard lost his gun in Bowyers R. R. Fields Dive & brought it up All the Wood Land on this part of the Missouries Appear to be Confined to the Points & Islands.

Boyers River is provably 25 yds. Wide, Willard near loseing his Gun in this river, two men Sick & Sevral with Boils, a Cold Day Wind from the N W. Som rain the fore part of the Day.

[Clark, July 29, 1804] July 29th Sunday 1804 Sent a french man la Liberty with the Indian to Otteaze Camp to invite the Indians to meet us on the river above- a Dark rainey morning wind from the W. N. W.- rained all the last night- Set out at 5 oClock opposit the (1) Island, the bend to the right or S. S. is within 20 feet of Indian Knob Creek, the water of this Creek is 5 feet higher than that of the River. passed the Isld. we Stoped to Dine under Some high Trees near the high land on the L. S. in a fiew minits Cought three verry large Catfish (3) one nearly white, Those fish are in great plenty on the Sides of the river and verry fat, a quart of Oile Came out of the Surpolous fat of one of these fish (4) above this high land & on the S. S. passed much falling timber apparently the ravages of a Dreadfull harican which had passed obliquely across the river from N. W. to S E about twelve months Since, many trees were broken off near the ground the trunks of which were Sound and four feet in Diameter, (2) about 3/4 of a Me. above the Island on the S. S. a Creek corns in Called Boyers R. this Creek is 25 yards wide, one man in attempting to Cross this Creek on a log let his gun fall in, R. Fields Dived & brought it up proceeded on to a Point on the S. S. and Camped.

[Clark, July 30, 1804] July the 30th Monday Set out early & proceeded on West 33/4 mes. passd. one pt. to the L. S and one to the S. S. to a Clear open Prarie on the L. S. which is on a rise of about 70 feet higher than the bottom which is also a prarie covered with high grass Plumbs Grape Vine & Hezel-both forming a Bluff to the River, the Lower Prarie is above high water mark at the foot of the riseing ground & below the High Bluff we came to in a grove of timber and formed a Camp raised a flag Pole, and deturmind to waite for the Ottu Indians- The white Horse which we found below Died last night, after posting out the Guards &c. &. Sent out 4 men to hunt I am ingaged in _____ and Drawing off my courses to accompany the map Drawn at White Catfish Camp, Capt. Lewis and my Self walked in the Prarie on the top of the Bluff and observed the most butifull prospects imagionable, this Prarie is Covered with grass about 10 or 12 Inch high, (Land rich) rises about 1/2 a mile back Something higher and is a Plain as fur as Can be Seen, under those high Lands next the river is butifull Bottom interspersed with Groves of timber, the River may be Seen for a great Distance both above & below meandering thro the plains between two ranges of High land which appear to be from 4 to 20 ms. apart, each bend of the river forming a point which Contains tall timber, principally Willow Cotton wood some Mulberry elm Sycamore & ash. the groves Contain walnit coffeenut & Oake in addition & Hickory & Lynn Jo. Fields Killed Brarow or as the Ponie call it Cho car tooch, this animale burrows in the ground & feeds on Bugs and flesh principally the little Dogs of the Prarie, also Something of Vegetable Kind his Shape & Size is like that of a Beever, his head Mouth &c. is like a Dog with its ears Cut off, his tale and hair like that of a Ground hog Something longer and lighter, his interals like a Hogs, his Skin thick & loose, white & hair Short under its belly, of the Species of the Bear, and it has a white Streake from its nose to its Sholders, the Toe nails of its fore feet which is large is 1 Inch and 3/4 qtr. long and those of his hind feet which is much Smaller is 3/4 long. We have this animale Skined and Stuffed. Short legs, raseing himself just above the ground when in motion Jo & R. fields Killed Som Deer at a Distance and Came in for a horse to bring them in, they have not returned this evening, a gred number of Swans in a pond above L. S. to our Camp. Serjt. Floyd verry unwell a bad Cold &c. Several men with Boils, great qts. of Catfish G. D. Cought one Small Beever alive. Som Turkey & Gees Killed to day. arms & all things in order. a fair evining, and Cool.

[Clark, July 30, 1804] July 30th Monday 1804 Set out this morning early proceeded on to a Clear open Prarie on the L. S. on a rise of about 70 feet higher than the bottom which is also a Prarie both forming Bluffs to the river of High Grass & Plumb bush Grapes &c. and Situated above high water is a Small Grove of timber at the foot of the Riseing Ground between those two priraries, and below the Bluffs of the high Prarie we Came too and formed a Camp, intending to waite the return of the french man & Indians- the white horse which we found near the Kanzeis River, Died Last night

posted out our guard and Sent out 4 men, Captn. Lewis & went up the Bank and walked a Short Distance in the high Prarie. this Prairie is covered with Grass of 10 or 12 inches in hight. Soil of good quallity &, Still further back at the Distance of about a mile the Countrey rises about 80 or 90 feet higher, and is one Continual Plain as fur as Can be Seen, from the Bluff on the 2d rise imediately above our Camp the most butifull prospect of the River up & Down and the Countrey opsd. presented it Self which I ever beheld; The River meandering the open and butifull Plains, interspursed with Groves of timber, and each point Covered with Tall timber, Such as willow Cotton Sun Mulberry, Elm, Sucamore, Lynn & ash (The Groves Contain Hickory, Walnut, Coffeenut & Oake in addition)

Two ranges of High Land parrelel to each other and from 4 to 10 miles Distant between which the river & its bottoms are Contained. (from 70 to 300 feet high)

Joseph Fields Killed and brought in an Anamale Called by the French Brarow, and by the Ponies Cho car tooch this Anamale Burrows in the Ground and feeds on Flesh, (Prarie Dogs), Bugs, & vigatables- "His Shape & Size is like that of a Beaver, his head mouth &c. is like a Dogs with Short Ears, his Tail and Hair like that of a Ground

Hog, and longer, and lighter. his Interals like the interals of a Hog," his Skin thick and loose, his Belly is White and the Hair Short- a white Streek from his nose to his Sholders.

The toe nails of his fore feet is one Inch & 3/4 long, & feet large; the nails of his hind feet 3/4 of an Inch long, the hind feet Small and toes Crooked, his legs are Short and when he Moves Just Suffcent to raise his body above the Ground He is of the Bear Species. we hav his Skin Stuffed

Jo. & R. Fields did not return this evening, Several men with Verry bad
Boils- Cat fish is Cought in any part of the river Turkeys Gees & a
Beaver Killed & Cought every thing in prime order men in high Spirits.
a fair Still evening Great no. misquitors this evening

[Lewis, July 30, 1804] July the 30th this day Joseph Fields killed a Braro as it is called by the French engages. this is a singular anamal not common to any part of the United States. it's weight is sixteen pounds.- it is a carniverous anamal. on both sides of the upper jaw is fexed one long and sharp canine tooth.- it's eye are small black and piercing.

[Clark, July 31, 1804] July 31st Tuesday a fair Day 3 hunters out this morning G. Drewyer Killed a verry fat Buck one Inch fat on the ribs Merdn. altd Latd. is 41° 18' 0" 5/10-North. R & Jo. Fields returned at 10 oClock the Killed 3 Deer, and lost the horses, Cought a Small Beever which is already taim, Several men out hunting the horses without Sukcess, The Ottees not yet arrived, I complete the Copy of the Courses &c. &c. Musqueters verry troubleson

[Clark, July 31, 1804] July 31st, Tuesday a fair Day three Hunters out, Took meridian altitude made the Lattd. 41° 18' 1" 5/10 N. R. & Jo. Fields returned to Camp They Killed 3 Deer.- The Horses Strayed off last night. Drewyer Killed a Buck one inch of fat on the ribs, R. & Jo. Fields returned without any meet haveing been in persuit of the horses- The Indians not yet arrived. Cought a young Beever alive which is already quit tame-. Cought a Buffalow fish- The evening verry Cool, The Musqutors are yet troublesom.-

[Clark, August 1, 1804] August the 1st 1804 a fair morning, Sent out two men after the horses & one back to examine if the Indians have been there, _____ Beever Cought last night, the air is Cool and pleasing

Prepared the Pipe of Peace verry flashey. wind rose at 10 oClock and blowed from the W. S. W. very pleasent all day Several men geathering grapes &c. two men after the horses which Strayed the night before last. those Praries produce the Blue Current Common in the U. S. the Goose Berry Common in the U. S, two Kind of Honeysuckle, the Bush which I have Seen in Kentucky, with a paile Pink flower, also one which grow in Clusters about 4 or 5 feet high bearing a Short flour in clusters of the like Colour. the leaves Single. 3 Deer & an Elk Killed to day. This being my birth day I order'd a Saddle of fat Vennison, an Elk fleece & a Bevertail to be cooked and a Desert of Cheries, Plumbs, Raspberries Currents and grapes of a Supr. quallity. The Indians not yet arrived. a Cool fine eveninge Musquetors verry troublesom, the Praries Contain Cheres, Apple, Grapes, Currents, Rasp burry, Gooseberris Hastlenuts and a great Variety of Plants & flours not Common to the U S. What a field for a Botents and a natirless

[Clark, August 1, 1804] August the 1st 1804 a fair morning Despatched two men after the horses lost yesterday, one man back to the place from which the messinger was Sent for the Ottoes to See if any Indians was or had been there Since our deptr. he return'd and informed that no person had been there Sence we left it. The Prarie which is Situated below our Camp is above the high water leavel and rich Covered with Grass from 5 to 8 feet high intersperced with Copse of Hazel, Plumbs, Currents (like those of the U.S.) Rasberries & Grapes of Dift. Kinds. also produceing a Variety of Plants and flowers not Common in the United States, two Kind of honey Suckle one which grows to a kind of a Srub. Common about Harrods burgh in Kentucky the other are not So large or tall and bears a flower in Clusters Short and of a light Pink Colour, the leaves differ from any of the othe Kind in as much as the Lieves are Distinkd & does not Surround the Stalk as all the other Kind does one Elk and three Deer Killed to day also two Beever Cought

The wind rose at 10 oClock from the W. S. W. and blew a Steedy and agreeable Breeze all Day.

The Musqutors verry troublesom this evening in the bottoms.

Took equal altitudes to day and the azmuth with the Commencement of the
A.M.

[Clark, August 2, 1804] August 2nd 1804 wind from the SE G. Drewery returned with the horses & one Doe Elk the countrey thro which he passed is like what we See from the Bluff above Camp three men out Hunting one Beaver caught this morning.

at Sunset 6 chiefs and their warries of the Ottos, and Missoures, with a french man by the name of Far fonge, we Shook hands and gave them Some Tobacco & Provisions, they Sent us Water Millions Three verry large & fat

Bucks Killed to day the wind Continue hard from the S. E.- the 4 qtr. of one Buck weigh'd 147 wt 1 1/2 Inch fat on the ribs

[Clark, August 2, 1804] August 2nd Thursday 1804 A verry pleasent Breeze from the S. E. The Two men Drewyer & Colter returned with the horses loaded with Elk, those horses they found about 12 miles in a Southerly Derection from Camp.

The Countrey thro which they passed is Similar to what we See from Camp. one Beaver & a foot of Beaver caught in trap Cought this morning at Sunset Mr. Fairfong and a pt. of Otteau & Missourie Nation Came to Camp, among those Indians 6 were Chiefs, the principal Chiefs Capt. Lewis & myself met those Indians & informed them we were glad to See them, and would Speak to them tomorrow, Sent them Som rosted meat Pork flour & meal, in return they Sent us Water millions. every man on his Guard & ready for any thing Three fat Bucks Killed this evening the 4 qtrs. of one weighed 147 lbs.

[Lewis, August 2, 1804] August 2ed 1804. This day one of our Hunters brought me a white Heron. this bird as an inhabitant of ponds and Marasses, and feeds upon tadpoles, frogs, small fish &c- they are common to the Mississipi and the lower part of the ohio River, (ie) as high as the falls of that river.

this bird weighed two lbs.- it's plumage is perfectly white and very thin

F I. from extremity of beak to the extremity of toe 4 71/4 from tipp to tip of wing on the back 4 11

it's beak is yellow pointed, flated crosswise and 5 Inches in length from the upper region of the bill to the eye is one inch in length, covered with a smoth yellow skin the plumage of the head projecting towards the upper bill and coming to a point a an Inch beyond the eyes on the center of the upper bill. The mouth opens to distance of the eyes- The eye is full and projecting reather, it is 7/10 of half an inch. four joints in the wing

Inches 1st joint from body in length 6 2ed Do. 81/4 3rd Do. 31/2 4th Do. 1 1st joint Number of feathers 7 Length of 3 2nd 18 6 3 6 from 10 to 12 4th 5 12

it's legs are black- the neck and beak occupy 1/2 it's length. it has four toes on a foot- the outer toe on the right foot is from the joining of the leg to extremity of toe nale 4 Inch & 1/4 has four joints exclusive of the nail joint- the next is 43/4 inches has three joints exclusive of the nale joint. the next is 33/4 and has two joints, the heel toe has one joint only and is 3 Inches in length. the nails are long sharp and black- the eye is of a deep seagreen colour, with a circle of of pale yellow around the sight forming a border to the outer part of the eye of about half the width of the whole eye. the tale has 12 feathers of six inches in length.- the wings when folded are the same length with the tale.

has 2 remarkable tufts of long feathers on each side joining the body at the upper joint of the wing. these cover the feathers of the 1st joint of the wings when they are over extended

[Clark, August 3, 1804] August 3rd Friday prepare a Small preasent for those Indians and hold a Councul Delivered a Speech & made 8 6 chief ... gave a fiew preasents and, a Smoke a Dram, Some Powder & Ball- the man we Sent not yet come up, Those people express great Satisfaction at the Speech Delivered they are no Oreters, big, open Counternances, ottoes large Missor Small

at 4 oClock Set out under a gentle Breeze from the S. E proceeded on N. 5° E 5 Ms. Passed a Pt. on the S. S. and round a large Sand bar on the L. S. and Camped above, below a great number of Snags quit across the river, The Musquitors more numerous than I ever Saw them, all in Spirrits, we had Some rough Convasation G. Dr. about boys.

The Osage & Kansies are the Same language

the Ottoes & Mahars Speek many words of the Osarge language

The Ottos, Aiaways, & Missouries Speake the Same language the Panies & Recreries Speak the Same language also the Loups & repub. the Mahar, & Poncarar the Same Language The Cheaun, Mandin & Grovanter the Same The Probility is that those defferant tribes have once formed 3 great nats. Viz: the Missouries, Osarge, Kanzes, Ottoes, Mahars, & Poncaras & Aiauaies one nation.

The Panies, Loups, Republican, Recrerees the 2nd

The Mandans Cheeons, & Grovanters the 3rd The tribes of the Soux all retain the name 4th

It is possible that the, Mahar & Poncarear may have been a Distinct nation, as they only Speek Some words of the osage which have the Same Signification 25 Days to St Ta fee S. of W. Cross the heads of Arkansies around the head of Kanzies River after Delivering a Speech informing thos Children of ours of the Change which had taken place, the wishes of our government to Cultivate friendship & good understanding, the method of have good advice & Some Directions, we made 1 Great Chief to the who was not present, to whom we adresed the Speech & Sent Some presents or Meadels & flag, we made 2 Second Chiefs one for the Missouris & another for the Ottos (those two tribes are nearly equal 1'70 each) and 4 principal men, to thos principal men to thos we gave a Small Comtn. to each man to whom we gave authority, a preasn of Br. Ch. Gart. g. Paint & a med. or Contn a Small Corns. was delivered for the whole each Chief & principal man delivered a Speech acknowledging ther approbation to what they had heard and promised to prosue the good advice and Caustion, they were happy w new fathers who gave good advice & to be Depended on all Concluded by asking a little Powder & a Drop of Milk.

I answered those Speeches gave them 50 balls one Canister of Powder & a Dram- after Cap Lewis Shot his air gun a few times which astonished the nativs, we Set Sail. recved from thos people water millions & The Cheifs & Principal men of the Ottoes & Missouris made by M L. & W C the 3rd August 1804

   Viz. Indian Names Tribe English
Signifiation

1. We-ar-ruge-nor Ottoe Little Thief

   2. Shingo-ton go Otto Big horse
      We tha a Missourie Hospatallity

   3. Wau-pe-ur Miss.
      Au-ho-ning ga M
      Ba Za con ja Ottoe
      Au-ho-ne-ga Miss.

from this place I am told by Mr. Faufong the interpeter that it will take a man 25 Days to go to St. a fee pass, the heads of Arkansas, round the Kansas head, across Some mountains from the top of which the City may be Seen the Spaniards have envited those Indians & the Panies to trade with them & Some french & a few indians are gorn from the Panias to that City this Summer-

The Situation of this place which we Call Council Bluff which is handsom ellevated a Spot well Calculated for a Tradeing establishment, the Bank high & leavel on top well Calculated for a fort to Command the Countrey and river the low bottom above high water & well Situated under the Command of the Hill for Houses to trade with the Natives a butifull Plain both abov and below at no other bend on either Side does the High land touch the river for Some distance up, as I am told.

those Bluffs afford good Clay for Brick, a great quantity on the 3 points one Opsd. one abov &one below.- the Situation I am informed is, within 1 Days march of the Ottoes, 11/2 of the Panias, 2 of the Mahars, & 21/2 of the Loups Villages, also Convenient to the roveing Bands of Soux, Those people are now at war with each other, an establishment here would bring about peace and be the means of Keeping of it.

Augt. 3d Camped on the upper point of a large Sand bar L. S. Misquters verry bad. Some place near Conncill Bluff will be the most proper place for a tradeing establishment, for maney of the nations, the distance is to the Ottoes one Days, Ponies 11/2 days, to the Mahar, 2 days, to Loups 2 Days & a half 16 or 1800 men-and convenient for Some bands of the Sues,

[Clark, August 3, 1804] August 3rd, Friday 1804 made up a Small present for those people in perpotion to their Consiqunce. also a package with a meadile to accompany a Speech for the Grand Chief after Brackfast we Collected those Indians under an orning of our Main Sail, in presence of our Party paraded & Delivered a long Speech to them expressive of our journey the wirkes of our Government, Some advice to them and Directions how They were to Conduct themselves, the princapal Chief for the nation being absente we sent him the Speech flag Meadel & Some Cloathes. after hering what they had to say Delivered a medal of Second Grade to one for the Ottos & and one for the Missourie present and 4 medals of a third Grade to the inferior Chief two for each tribe. Those two parts of nations, Ottos & Missouries now residing together is about 250 men are the Ottoes Composeing 2/3d and Missourie 1/3 part

The names of the Chiefs we acknowledged Made this day are as follows Viz

Indian name English signftn.

1st We ar ruge nor Ottoe Called Little Theif

   2 Shon go ton go " " Big Horse
      We the a Miss. " Hospatality

Shon Guss Con Ottoe " White horse
Wau pe uh M.
Ah ho ning ga M.
Baza cou ja Ottoe
Ah ho ne ga M.

Those Chiefs all Delivered a Speech acknowledgeing Their approbation to the Speech and promising to prosue the advice & Derictions given them that they wer happy to find that they had fathers which might be depended on &c.

We gave them a Cannister of Powder and a Bottle of whiskey and delivered a few presents to the whole after giveing a Br. Cth. Some Paint quartering & a Meadele to those we made Cheifs after Capt Lewis's Shooting the air gun a feiw Shots (which astonished those nativs) we Set out and proceeded on five miles on a Direct line passed a point on the S. S. & round a large Sand bar on the L. S. & Camped on the upper point. The Misquitors excessively troublesom this evening Great appearance of wind and rain to the N. W. we prepare to rec've it- The man Liberty whome we Sent for the Ottoes has not Come up he left the Ottoes Town one Day before the Indians. This man has eithered tired his horse or, lost himself in the Plains Some Indians are to hunt for him, The Situation of our last Camp Councill Bluff or Handssom Prarie appears to be a verry proper place for a Tradeing establishment & fortification The Soil of the Bluff well adapted for Brick, Great deel of timbers abov in the two Points. many other advantages of a Small nature. and I am told Senteral to Several nations Viz. one Days march from the Ottoe Town, one Day & a half from the great Pania village, 2 days from the Mahar Towns, two 1/4 Days from the Loups Village, & Convenient to the Countrey thro which Bands of the Soux hunt. perhaps no other Situation is as well Calculated for a Tradeing establishment. The air is pure and helthy So far as we can judge.-

[Clark, August 4, 1804]
August 4th at 7 oClock the heavens darkened and a violent wind from the
N W. Suckceeded which lasted about an hour, with a little rain.

Set out this morning early thro a narrow part of the, the whole Channel Confined in Some parts between the (1) Sand on one Side & the bank on the other (which is washing in) within 200 yards, this Chanl. Crouded with Snags. at 11/2 m. passed an old tradeing house L. S. where one of our Crew passed 2 years P. C tradeing with the Mahar; & Ponies-above 1 me. a (3) Creek Coms in opsd. a large bad (3) Sand bar this (3) Creek is the outlett of 3 ponds, which recved ther water from the Smaller Streams running from the hills on the L. S, Great qts. of Gees, passed in the next bend L. S. an out let to the Pond, Butifull bottom Prarie on both Sides of the river, Pumey Stone is found on the Sides of the river of various Sizes. Wind a head. Reed the man who went back to the Camp of last night for his Knife has not Come up this evening-we Camped at a pt. on the L. S. at a Beaver house. 1 Buck Killed to daye.

[Clark, August 4, 1804] August 4th Satturdaye Set out early- (at 7 oClock last night we had a Violent wind from the N W Som little rain Succeeded, the wind lasted with violence for one hour after the wind it was clear Sereen and Cool all night.) proceeded on passed thro betwen Snags which was quit across the Rivr the Channel Confined within 200 yards one Side a Sand pt. S S. the other a Bend, the Banks washing away & trees falling in constantly for 1 mile, abov this place is the remains of an old Tradeing establishment L. S. where Petr. Crusett one of our hands Stayed two years & traded with the Mahars a Short distance above is a Creek (3) the out let of Three Ponds comunicateing with each other, those Ponds or rether Lakes are fed by Springs & Small runs from the hills. (2) a large Sand Island opposit this Creek makeing out from the L. Point, from the Camp of last night to this Creek, the river has latterly Changed its bed incroaching on the L. Side, in this Sand bar I Saw great Nos. of wild gees- passed a Small Creek on the L. S about 3 miles above the last both of those Creek's are out lets from the Small Lake which reive their water from the Small Streems running from the high land- great many Pamey Stones on the Shore of various Sises the wind blew hard- Reed a man who went back to Camp for his knife has not joined us. we camped at a Beaver house on the L. S.one Buck Killed to day-

[Clark, August 5, 1804] August 5th Set out early wind from N E. Great appearance of Wind & rain, (I have remarked that I have not heard much thunder in this Countrey) a verry large Snake was Killed to day called the Bull Snake, his Colour Some thing like a rattle Snake Something lighter- the bends of the river to day is washing away the banks, haveing nothing to oppose the turbelance of the river when Confined by large hard Sand Points, forceing this Current against the bends- the Soil of the entire bottom between the high land, being the mud or Ooze of the river of Some former period mixed with Sand & Clay easely melts and Slips, or washies into the river the mud mixes with the water & the Sand collects on the points Camped on the S. S.- I went on Shore S. S. this evening Saw Some turkeys and in persueing them Struck the river 12 miles below the place by water I went out, I think the Peninsuly is about 370 yards across Subjuct to overflow; & washes into numerous Channels, Great quantities of Graps ripe & of three Defferent Kind Some large & fine. I Killed a Turkey, and made Camp in the Night, Musqutors verry troubleson- Reed the man who went back for his Knife has not yet joined us

[Clark, August 5, 1804] 5th of August Sunday 1804 Set out early great appearance of wind and rain (I have observed that Thundor & lightning is not as common in this Countrey as it is in the atlantic States) Snakes are not plenty, one was killed to day large and resembling the rattle Snake only Something lighter-. I walked on Shore this evening S. S. in Pursueing Some Turkeys I struck the river twelve miles below within 370 yards, the high water passes thro this Peninsulia; and agreeable to the Customary Changes of the river I Concld. that in two years the main Current of the river will pass through. In every bend the banks are falling in from the Current being thrown against those bends by the Sand points which inlarges and the Soil I believe from unquestionable appearns. of the entire bottom from one hill to the other being the mud or ooze of the River at Some former Period mixed with Sand and Clay easily melts and Slips into the River, and the mud mixes with the water & the Sand is washed down and lodges on the points- Great quantites of Grapes on the banks, I observe three different Kinds at this time ripe, one Of the no. is large & has the flaver of the Purple grape. camped on the S. S. the Musquitors verry troubleson. The man who went back after his Knife has not yet come up, we have Some reasons to believe he has Deserted

[Lewis, August 5, 1804]
August 5th 1804
Killed a serpent on the bank of the river adjoining a large prarie.

F Inch
Length from nose to tail 5 2
Circumpherence in largest part- 41/2
Number of scuta on belly- 221
Do. on Tale- 53

No pison teeth therefore think him perfectly inocent- eyes, center black with a border of pale brown yellow Colour of skin on head yellowish green with black specks on the extremity of the scuta which are pointed or triangular colour of back, transverse stripes of black and dark brown of an inch in width, succeeded by a yellowish brown of half that width the end of the tale hard and pointed like a cock's spur the sides are speckled with yellowish brown and black.- two roes of black spots on a lite yellow ground pass throughout his whole length on the upper points of the scuta of the belly and tale 1/2 Inch apart this snake is vulgarly called the cow or bull snake from a bellowing nois which it is said sometimes to make resembling that anamal, tho as to this fact I am unable to attest it never having heard them make that or any other noise myself.

I have frequently observed an acquatic bird in the cours of asscending this river but have never been able to procure one before today, this day I was so fortunate as to kill two of them, they are here more plenty than on the river below. they lay their eggs on the sand bars without shelter or nest, and produce their young from the 15th to the last of June, the young ones of which we caught several are covered with down of a yellowish white colour and on the back some small specks of a dark brown. they bear a great resemblance to the young quale of ten days oald, and apear like them to be able to runabout and peck their food as soon as they are hatched- this bird, lives on small fish, worms and bugs which it takes on the virge of the water it is seldom seen to light on trees an quite as seldom do they lite in the water and swim tho the foot would indicate that they did it's being webbed I believe them to be a native of this country and probly a constant resident.

the weight of the male bird is one ounce and a half, its length from beak to toe 71/2 inches from tip to tip of wing across the back one foot seven inches and a half the beak is one 1/8 inch lonong, large where it joins the head Elated on the sides and tapering to a sharp point, a little declining and curvated, a fine yellow, with a shade of black on the extremity of upper beak; the eye is prominent, black and on a angular scale of 1/2 Inc; occupyse 3 1/3 in width. the upper part of the head is black from the beak as low as the middle of the eye and a little below the joining of the neck except however some white which joins the upper part of the beak which forks and passing over the sides of the forehead terminate above each eye- the under part of the bird, that is the throat and cheeks as high as the eye, the neck brest belly and under part of the wings and tail are of a fine white, the upper part of the neck, back, and wings are of a fine, quaker colour, or bright dove colour with reather more of a bluish tint-except however the three first or larger feathers in the wing which on upper side are of a deep black. the wing has four joints

No. Joint Length of joint No. of feathers Length of do. 1 11/2 a Clump of feathers not strong but loosly connect with the flesh of the wing 11/2 2 2 16 2 3 11/2 7 from 21/2 to 41/2 4 3/4 3 51/2

the tail has eleven feathers the outer of which are an inch longer than those in the center gradually tapering inwards which gives the tale a forked appearance like that of the swally the largest or outer feather is 23/4 that of the shortest 13/4- the leg and thye are three inches long the leg occupying one half this length the thye is covered with feathers except about 1/4 of an inch above the knee the leg is of a bright yellow and nails long sharp and black the foot is webbed and has three toes forward; the heel or back toe is fixed to the leg above the palm of the foot, and is unconnected by a web to the other toes, it has no nail. the wings when foalded lap like those of the swallow and extend at least an inch and a half beyond the tale. this bird is very noysey when flying which is dose exttreemly swift the motion of the wing is much like that of kildee it has two notes one like the squaking of a small pig only on reather a high kee, and the other kit'-tee'- kit'-tee'- as near as letters can express the sound- the beak of the female is black and the black and quaker colour of the male in her is yellowish brown mixed with dove colour

[Clark, August 6, 1804] August 6th Monday 1804 at 12 oClock last night a Violent Storm of wind & rain from the N. W. one perogue (Bapteest Le joness Patroon) lost her Colours Set out early & proceeded on passed a large Island on the S. S. back of this Island Rivie de Soldiert Come in on the S. S.- the Solder's River is about the Sise of Nodaway 20 yd. wide at the mouth, passed two remarkable places, where the River had once Passed- We have every reason to belive that one man has Deserted Moses B. Reed he has been absent three Days and one french man we Sent to the Indian Camps has not joined us, we have reasons to beleve he lost himself in attempting to join us at the Council Bluff- we are deturmind to Send back 4 men to take reede Dead or alive, also hunt La Liberty and to meet us at the Mahar nation as Soon as the order is executed.

[Clark, August 6, 1804] 6th August, Monday 1804 At 12 oClock last nigh a violent Storm of wind from the N W. Some rain one pr. of Colours lost in the Storm from the bige Perogue. Set out early and proceeded on passed a large Island on the S. S. back of this Isd. Soldiers River mouths, I am told by one of the men that this river is about the Size of Nadawa river 40 yards wide at the mouth. Reed has not yet come up. neither has La Liberty the frenchman whome we Sent to the Indian Camps a fiew miles below the Council Bluffs.

[Clark, August 7, 1804]
August 7th Tuesday last night about 8 oClock a Storm of wind from the
N. W. which lasted 3/4 of an hour mosqutors more troublesom last night
than I ever Saw them, Set out late this morning wind N.

[Clark, August 7, 1804] 7th August Tuesday 1804 last night at 8 oClock a Storm from the N W. lasted 3/4 of an hour let out late this morning wind from the North- at 1 oClock dispatched George Drewyer, R. Fields, Wm. Bratten & Wm. Labieche back after the Deserter reid with order if he did not give up Peaceibly to put him to Death &c. to go to the Ottoes Village & enquire for La Liberty and bring him to the Mahars Village, also with a Speech on the occasion to the Ottoes & Missouries- and directing a few of their Chiefs to come to the Mahars, & we would make a peace between them & the Mahar and Souex, a String of wompom & a Carrot of Tobacco. proceeded on and Camped on the S. S.

I walked on Shore with one man Collies,-the bottoms Covered with very Collin Killed an elk, I fired 4 times at one & have reasons to think I Kiled him but could not find him, The Misqutors were So troublesom and Misqutors thick in the Plains that I could not Keep them out of my eyes, with a bush. in my absens Capt Lewis Killed a Pelican on Pelicans Island, at which place maney Hundreds had Collected, they left 3 fish which was. fresh and very good, we camped on the S. S. in a Streght part of the river-

[Clark, August 8, 1804] August the 8th 1804 Set out this morning at the usial time at about 2 miles (1) passed a part of the river So choked up with Snags that we found a little dificult to get thro with Safty, the wind as usial from the N W. one of the Soldiers Killed a Pilican on the Sand Isd. passed the mouth of Little (2) River de Cueoux on the S. S. this river is about 80 yards wide & navagable for Pirogus Some distance & runs parrelel to the Missourie it corns in from the River from the N E, it contains great Quantitys offish Common to the Countrey. two Miles above is (3) an Island the Channel formerly run on the right with Sand.- the Current runs to the left. many hundreds of Pelicans on this Island- we call it Pelican Isld. Cap Lewis Killed one This river Soux Called by the Sueoux Ed-Neah Wau-de-pon i'e Stone R heads in three Leagues of the river Demoin, and passes thro a Lake about 20 Legues in Sircfs. which is also within 5 Leagus of the Demoin, this lake at one place is confined by two rocks within a narrow Space- this lake of Different widths, with many Small Islands, from the Lake to the Mahars about distant 4 Days march to the Dog Plains 90 Leagues, one Principal branch of the Demoin is calld. Cat river, the Lake which this river Litt Souex heads in is Called Despree

[Clark, August 8, 1804] 8th August Wednesday 1804 Set out this morning at the usial time at two miles passed (1) a bend to L. S. Choaked up with Snags our boat run on two in turning to pass through, we got through with Safty the wind from N W. (2) passed the mouth of a River on the S. Side Called by the Soux Indians Ed-neah Wau de pon (or Stone river) the French call this river Petite Rivre de Cuouex it is about 80 yards wide and as (Mr. Durion Says whos been on the heads of it and the Country abt) is navagable for Peroques Som Distance runs Parrelel to the Missourie Some Distance, then falls down from N E thro a roleing Countrey open, the head of this river is 9 miles from the R Demon at which place the Demoin is 80 yd wide, this Little Cuouex passes thro a lake called Despree which is within 5 Leagues of the Deemoin the Said Lake is about 20 Leagues in Circumfrance and is divided into 2 by two rocks approaching Verry Near each other, this Lake is of various width, Containing many Islands- from this Lake to the Maha 4 days march, as is Said to be near the Dog Plains one princpal branch of the Demoin is Called Cat River The Demoin is Sholey

Capt. Lewis took Medn. Altitude of the Sun made it 56° 9' 00" Lat 41° 42' 34" and I took one man and went on Shore the man Killed an Elk I fired 4 times at one & did not Kill him, my ball being Small I think was the reason, the misqutors So bad in the Praries that with the assistance of a bush I could not Keep them out of my eyes, the boat turned Several tims to day on Sand bars- in my absenc the boat passed a Island 2 miles above the litte Scouex R on the upper point of the Isld Some hundreds of Pelicans were Collected, they left 3 fish on the Sand which was verry fine, Capt Lewis Killed one & took his dimentions, I joined the boat and we Camped on the S S.

worthe of remark that Snakes are not plenty in this part of the Missourie

[Lewis, August 8, 1804] August 8th 1804 we had seen but a few aquatic fouls of any kind on the river since we commenced our journey up the Missouri, a few geese accompanied by their young, the wood duck which is common to every part of this country & crains of several kinds which will be discribed in their respective places- this day after we had passed the river Souix as called by Mr. MacKay (or as is more properly called the stone river,) I saw a great number of feathers floating down the river those feathers had a very extraordinary appearance as they appeared in such quantities as to cover pretty generally sixty or seventy yards of the breadth of the river. for three miles after I saw those feathers continuing to run in that manner, we did not percieve from whence they came, at length we were surprised by the appearance of a flock of Pillican at rest on a large sand bar attatched to a small Island the number of which would if estimated appear almost in credible; they appeared to cover several acres of ground, and were no doubt engaged in procuring their ordinary food; which is fish, on our approach they flew and left behind them several small fish of about eight inches in length, none of which I had seen before- the Pellican rested again on a sand bar above the Island which we called after them from the number we saw on it. we now approached them within about three hundred yards before they flew; I then fired at random among the flock with my rifle and brought one down; the discription of this bird is as follows.

Habits

They are a bird of clime remain on the coast of Floriday and the borders of the Gulph of mexico & even the lower portion of the Mississippi during the winter and in the Spring (see for date my thermometrical observations at the river Dubois.-) visit this country and that farther north for the purpose of raising their young- this duty seems now to have been accomplished from the appearance of a young Pilacon which was killed by one of our men this morning, and they are now in large flocks on their return to their winter quarters. they lay usually two eggs only and chuise for a nest a couple of logs of drift wood near the water's edge and with out any other preperation but the thraught formed by the proximity of those two logs which form a trough they set and hatch their young which after nurture with fish their common food

Measure

F I

From beak to toe 5 8 Tip to tip of wing 9 4 Beak Length 1 3 Do.
Width from 2 to 1 1/2 Neck Length 1 11 1st joint of wing 1 1 2ed
Do. 1 41/2 3rd Do. - 7 4th do. - 23/4 Length of leg including foot
10 Do. of thy 11

Discription of Colour &c

The beak is a whiteish yellow the under part connected to a bladder like pouch, this pounch is connected to both sides of the lower beak and extends down on the under side of the neck and terminates in the stomach- this pouch is uncovered with feathers, and is formed two skins the one on the inner and the other on the center side a small quantity of flesh and strings of which the anamal has at pleasure the power of moving or drawing in such manner as to contract it at pleasure. in the present subject I measured this pouch and found it's contents 5 gallons of water

The feet are webbed large and of a yellow colour, it has four toes the hinder toe is longer than in most aquatic fouls, the nails are black, not sharp and 1/2 an inch in length

The plumage generally is white, the feathers are thin compared with the swan goose or most aquatick fouls and has but little or no down on the body. the upper part of the head is covered with black feathers short, as far as the back part of the head- the yellow skin unfeathered extends back from the upper beak and opening of the mouth and comes to a point just behind the eye

The large feathers of the wings are of a deep black colour- the 1st & 2nd joint of from the body above the same is covered with a second layer of white feathers which extend quite half the length of those large feathers of the wing- the thye is covered with feathers within a quarter of an inch of the knee. Inch 1st joint of wing has feathers No. 21 Length 9 Black 2ed Do. No. 17 Length 13 Inch 3rd Do. No. 5 Length 18 Inch 4th Do. No. 3 Length 19 Inch

it has a curious frothy substance which seems to devide its feathers from the flesh of the body and seems to be composes of globles of air and perfectly imbraces the part of the feather which extends through the skin.the wind pipe terminates in the center of the lower part of the upper and unfeathered part of the pouch and is secured by an elastic valve commanded at pleasure.

The green insect known in the U States by the name of the sawyer or chittediddle, was first heard to cry on the 27th of July, we were then in latitude 41° some minutes.

The prarie hen or grouse, was seen in the praries between the Missouri and the river platte

[Clark, August 9, 1804] 9th Augt Thursday 1804 The fog of this morning detained us untill 1/2 passed 7 oClock at which time we left our moreing and proceeded on under a gentle Breeze from the S. E, I went on Shore found the Land the Same as yesterday Killed a Turkey and Camped on the L. S. great deel of Beaver Sign to day one Beaver Cought Musquetors worse this evening than ever I have Seen them.

[Clark, August 9, 1804] 9th August Thursday 1804 The fog being thick detained us untile half pasd. 7 oClock at which time we Set out and proceeded on under Gentle Breeze from the S E I walked on Shore, Saw an Elk, crossed a Istmust of 3/4 of a mile to the river, & returned to the boat Camped on the L. S. above a Beaver Den. Musqutors verry troubleson.

[Clark, August 11, 1804] August 11th Satturday 1804 about day this morning a hard wind from the N. W. followed by rain, we landed at the foot of the hill on which Black Bird The late King of the mahar who Died 4 years ago & 400 of his nation with the Small pox was buried (1) and went up and fixed a white flag bound with Blue white & read on the Grave which was about 12 foot Base & circueller, on the top of a Penical about 300 foot above the water of the river, from the top of this hill may be Seen the bends or meanderings of the river for 60 or 70 miles round & all the County around the base of this high land is a Soft Sand Stone Bluff of about 40 or 150 foot, the Crooked, passed a Creek Called Wau-Con di peche C or Bad God Creek of bad Spirits on the L. S above the Bluff on this Creek the Mahars had the Small pox 4 years ago, Lattitude 42° 1'3" 8/10 taken on the Point above the Creek. the river is verry Crooked, we are now within 3/4 of a mile of the river at a place we Shall not get around to untill tomorrow noon- We er 3 Legues from the Mahars by land and the great deel of Beaver sign induce a belief that those people do not hunt much.

I have observed a number of places where the river has Changd its Bead at different times

[Clark, August 11, 1804] 11th August Satturday 1804. about day light this Morning a hard wind from the N W. with Some rain proceeded on arround the right of the Isld.

a hard wind accompanied with rain from the S. E. after the rain was over Capt. Lewis myself & 10 men assended the Hill on the L. S. under which there was Some fine Springs to the top of a high point where the Mahars King Black Bird was burried 4 years ago. a mound of earth about 12 Diamuter at the base & 6 feet high is raised over him turfed, and a pole 8 feet high in the Center on this pole we fixed a white flage bound with red Blue & white; this hill about 300 feet above the water forming a Bluff between that & the Water of Various hight from 40 to 150 feet in hight yellow Soft Sand Stone from the tops of this Nole the river may be Seen Meandering for 60 or 70 Miles, we Decended & Set out N. 24 to W. 1/2 me. passing over a Sand bar on the S. pt. along the Willows. to the river opposit a Small Beyeau on the L. S. which is the Conveyance of the high water from a bend which appears near in a northerly direction, haveing passed a Creek in a Deep bend to the L. S. Called by the Mahars Wau can di Peeche (Great Spirrit is bad) on this Creek & Hills near it about 400 of the Mahar Died with the Small Pox- Took Medn. Altitude & made the Latd. 42° 1' 3" 8/10 N. also the Moons Distanc from the Sun I have observed a number of places where the River has onced run and now filled or filling up & growing with willows & cottonwood

[Clark, August 12, 1804] 12th August Sunday 1804 a South wind We Set out early the river wider than usial, and Shallow, at 12 we halted in a bend to the left to take the Meridian altitude, & Dine, & Sent one man across where we took Dinner yesterday to Step off the Distance across Isthmus, he made it 974 yards, and the bend around is 183/4 miles above this bend about 4 miles, a yellow & Brown Bluff Comnuces and Continus 3 or 4 miles on the L. S. this Bluff has Some Sand Stone, Some rich Black mole mixed with yellow Clay, a fiew Red Ceeder on the tope, which is, from 20 to 150 foot high the hill Still riseing back, I think may be estemated at 200 foot on the top is timber, the wind for a few hours this evening was hard and from the S. E. In the evening about 5 oClock Cap L. & My Self wen on Shore to Shoot a Prarie wolf which was barking at us as we passed This

Prarie Wolf barked like a large fest and is not much larger, the Beaver is verry plenty, not with Standing we are almost in Sight of the Mahar Town- Cought a verry Large Catfish this morniong, prepared the Indian present which we intend given to the Mahars. P. Wiser apt. Cook to Serjt. Floyds Squad from to day

[Clark, August 12, 1804] 12th August Sunday 1804 Set out early under a gentle Breeze from the South the river wider than usial and Shallow (1) at 12 oClock we halted to take a meridian altd. of the Sun & Sent a man back or I may Say across to the Bind of the river where Capt. Lewis took the Mdn. altitude yesterday, to Step off the distance, he made it 974 yards across, the Distance arround the bend is 183/4 miles- about 4 miles above the bend on the L. S. is the Commencement of a Bluff which is about 4 miles extending on the river, of yellow and brown Clay in Some parts in it near the river a Soft Sand Stone is inbeded on the top (which is from 20 to 150 feet above the water, & rises back) is Covered with timber, a fiew red Ceider is on this Bluff, the wind Comes round to the S. E. a Prarie Wolf Come near the bank and Barked at us this evening, we made an attempt but could not git him, this Animale Barkes like a large feste Dog. Beever is verry Plenty on this part of the river. I prepare Some presents for to give the Indians of the Mahars nation. Wiser apt. Cook & Supentdt. of the Provisions of Sergt. Floyds Squad. we Camped on a Sand Island in a bend to the S. S. Musquitors verry troublesom untile the wind rose. at one or 2 oClock

[Clark, August 13, 1804] 13th of August Munday 1804. Set out this morning at Day light the usial time and proceeded on under a gentle Breeze from the S. E. passed the Island.

From this Fish Camp the River is N 55° West as far as Can be Seen, the Sand bar only changeing the Derection of the Current the Hills leave the river on the L. Side

[Clark, August 13, 1804]
August 13th Monday 1804
Set out this morning at Light the usial time and proceeded on under a
gentle Breeze from the S E

[Clark, August 14, 1804] 14th of August at 12 oClock the Party Sent yesterday to the Towns returned, and informed that they Could not find any Indians, they had not returned from hunting the Buffalow in the Praries, wind Shifted to the N W. Our party Sent after the Deserter and to the Otteau towns, have not Came up as yet

The Situation of this Village, now in ruins Siround by enunbl. hosts of grave the ravages of the Small Pox (4 years ago) they follow the Buf. and tend no Corn

[Clark, August 14, 1804] 14th August Tuesday 1804 a fine morning wind from the S E The men Sent to the Mahar Town last evening has not returned we Conclude to Send a Spye to Know the cause of Their delay at about 12 oClock the Party returned and in-formed. us that they Could not find the Indians nor any fresh Sign, those people have not returned from their Buffalow hunt, Those people haveing no houses no Corn or any thing more than the graves of their ancesters to attach them to the old Village, Continue in pursuite of the Buffalow longer than others who had greater attachments to their native Villagethe ravages of the Small Pox (which Swept off 400 men & women & Children in perpoposion) has reduced this Nation not exceeding 300 men and left them to the insults of their weaker neighbours which before was glad to be on friendly turms with them- I am told whin this fatal malady was among them they Carried ther franzey to verry extroadinary length, not only of burning their Village, but they put their wives & Children to Death with a view of their all going together to Some better Countrey- They burry their Dead on the tops of high hills and rais mounds on the top of them,- The cause or way those people took the Small Pox is uncertain, the most Probable from Some other Nation by means of a warparty

Observed Time and Distance of the Sun & Moon the Moon East the 13th of
August Monday 1804, three Miles NE of the Mahars old village at Fish
Camp-

[Clark, August 15, 1804] August 15th Wendesday I took ten men & went out to Beaver Dam across a Creek about a mile S W from Camp, and with a Brush Drag caught 308 fish, of the following kind (i'e) Pike, Samon, Bass, Pirch, Red horse, Small Cat, & a kind of Perch Called on the Ohio Silverfish I also Caught the Srimp which is Common to the Lower part of the Mississippi, in this Creek & in the Beaver Pond is emince beads of Mustles Verry large & fat- in my absence Capt Lewis Send the Souex interpr & a party to a Smoke which appeared to rise at no great distance to the north with a view to find Some Band of that nation, they returned and informed that they had been made Some time by Some Small party, and the hard wind of to day had set the Prarie on fire from Some high trees, which was left burning all well, Party from Ottoes not come up.

Camp three Miles N. E of the Mahar Village

[Clark, August 15, 1804] August 15th Wednesday 1804 I went with ten men to a Creek Damed by the Beavers about half way to the Village, with Some Small willow & Bark we mad a Drag and haulted up the Creek, and

Cought 318 fish of different kind i'e Peke, Bass, Salmon, perch, red horse, Small Cat, and a kind of perch Called Silverfish, on the Ohio.- I cought a Srimp prosisely of Shape Size & flavour of those about N. Orleans & the lower party of the Mississippi in this Creek which is only the pass or Streight from Beaver Pond to another, is Crouded with large Mustles Verry fat, Ducks, Pliver of different Kinds are on those Ponds as well as on the river in My absence Capt. Lewis Sent Mr. Durioue the Souix interpeter & three men to examine a fire which threw up an emence Smoke from the Praries on the N. E. Side of the River and at no great distance from Camp- the Object of this party was to find Some Bands of Seouex which the inptr. thought was near the Smoke and get them to Come in- in the evening this Party returned and infoermed, that the fire arrose from Some trees which had been left burning by a Small party of Seoux whom had passed Several Days- the wind Setting from that point, blew the Smoke from that pt. over our Camp. our party all in health and Sperrits the men Sent to the Ottoes & in pursute of the Deserter Reed has not yet returned or joined our party.

[Clark, August 16, 1804] Aug. 16th 1804 a Verry cool morning the winds as usial from the N W. Capt Lewis with men went out to the Creek & Pond & Caught about 800 fine fish with a Bush Drag of the following kind i.e. 79 Pike, 8 Salmon, 1 Rock, 1 flat Back, 127 Buffalow & readHorse, 4 Bass & 490 Cat, with many Small & large Silver fish,- I had a mast made & fixed to day The Party Sent to the Ottoes not yet arrived. the wind Shifted around to the S E. the night's are Cool & a Breeze rises after generally; Sometimes before night which Blows off the Musquitors cools the atmospere.

[Clark, August 16, 1804] 16th August Thursday 1804 Fishing Camp 3 ms. N. E. of the Mahars. a verry cool morning the wind as usial from the N W.

Capt Lewis took 12 men & went to the Pond & Crek between Camp and the old Village and Cought upwards of Boo fine fish, 79 Pike, 8 Salmon, 1 Rock,flat Back, 127 Buffalow & red horse 4 Bass & 490 Catt. with many Small Silver fish I had a Mast made &fixed to the Boat to day, the Party Sent to the Ottoes not yet joined us- the wind Shifted arround to the S. E. everry evening a Breeze rises which blows off the Musquitors & Cools the atmispeire.

[Clark, August 17, 1804] 17th August 1804. a fine morning Wind from the S. E. I will here annex the Latds & Distances of the Different notable placies from the River Dubois or Mouth up.

The Longitudes are not yet Calculated, We must be at this time about 99° 45' 00" West of Greenwich- I Collected a grass much resembling wheet with a grain like Rye, much fuller of grain, one like Rye & one like Barley Grass Small, a Grass like Timothey except the Seed which is on branches from the main Stalk-

Late this evening one of the party Sent after the deserters returned & joined us, he left the party 3 miles back, they cought both Deserters, one of them La liberty, got away from them, the Great Chief & 2nd Chief of the ottoes accompaned the Party with a view to bring about a Peice between themselves & the Mahar a great missfortune that the Mahars have not returned from the hunt- Sent & fiered the Prarie near Camp to bring in the Mahars & Souex if any are near. a Cool evening, 2 Beever Cought

[Clark, August 17, 1804] 17th August Friday 1804. a fine Morning the wind from the S. E. I collected a grass much resembling wheat in its grouth the grain like Rye, also Some resembling Rye & Barly. a kind of Timothey, the Seed of which branches from the main Stalk & is more like flax Seed than that of a Timothey

at 6 oClock this evening Labieche one of the Party Sent to the Ottoes joined, and informed that the Party was behind with one of the Deserters M B. Reed and the 3 principal Chiefs of the Nations- La Liberty they cought but he decived them and got away- the object of those Chiefs comeing forward is to make a peace with the Mahars thro us-. as the Mahars are not at home this great object cannot be accomplished at this time Set the Praries on fire to bring the Mahars & Soues if any were near, this being the usial Signal.

a Cool evining two Beaver Cought to day.

[Clark, August 18, 1804] 18th August 1804 a fine morning, despatched Jo. Fields for the Party from the Ottoes, whom did not Come up last night Wind from the S. E. (Panies returned from their hunt, the 12th of August) in the after Part of the Day the Party arrived, we had a Short talk after which we gave them Provisions to eate & proceeded to the trial of Reed, he confessed, & we Sentenced him only to run the Ganelet four times thro the Detachment & party, and not to be considered in the future as one of the Permonant Party, after the Punihment of about 500 Lashes, at night we had Some talk with the Chiefs about the Cause of War between them and the Mahars. posponed the further consultation untill tomorrow. had a Dance which lasted untile 11 oClock, the Close of Cap Lewis Birthday. a fine evening wind S. E

Sent to the Towns, i e Reiubin Fields Will. Brattin G. Drewyer & W Labieche.

[Clark, August 18, 1804] 18th August Satday 1804 a fine morning. Wind from the S. E. in the after part of the Day the Party with the Indians arrivd. we meet them under a Shade near the Boat and after a Short talk we gave them Provisions to eat & proceeded to the trail of Reed, he Confessed that he "Deserted & Stold a public Rifle Shot-pouch Powder & Bals" and requested we would be as favourable with him as we Could consistantly with our Oathes-which we were and only Sentenced him to run the Gantlet four times through the Party & that each man with 9 Swichies Should punish him and for him not to be considered in future as one of the Party

The three principal Chiefs petitioned for Pardin for this man After we explained the injurey Such men could doe them by false representation, & explang. the Customs of our Countrey they were all Satisfied with the propriety of the Sentence & was witness to the punishment. after which we had Some talk with the Chiefs about the orrigan of the war between them & the Mahars &c. &c.- it commenced in this way i'e' in two of the Missouries Tribe resideing with the Ottoes went to the Mahars to Steel horses, they Killed them both which was a cause of revenge on the part of the Missouris & Ottoes, they also brought war on themselves Nearly in the Same way with the Panea Loups and they are greatly in fear of a just revenge from the Panies for takeing their Corn from the Pania Towns in their absence hunting this Summer.

the evening was Closed with an extra Gill of Whiskey & a Dance untill 11 oClock.

[Clark, August 19, 1804] 19th of August Sunday 1804 a fine morning wind from the S. E I prepd. a present from the Chiefs & Warriers, the main Chief Brack fast with us naked; & beged for a Sun glass.- at 10 oClock we assembled the Cheifs & Warriers under an Orning and delivered a Speech, explanatory of the One Sent to this Nation from the Council Bluff, &c. &c.-

Children When we Sent the 4 men to your towns, we expected to See & Speake with the Mahas by the time you would arrive and to lay the foundation of a peace between you and them

The Speech of Petieit Villeu Little Thief, If you think right and Can waite untill all our Warriers Come from the Buffalows hunt, we Can then tell you who is our men of Consequnce- My fathers always lived with the father of the B together & we always live with the Big hose-all the men here are the Suns of Chief and will be glad to get Something from the hands of their fathers.- My father always directed me to be friendly with the white people, I have always done So and went often to the french, give my party pieces of Paper & we will be glad- The names

a Meddel to Car ka pa ha or Crow's head

a Comsi or Cfte. Sar na no ne or Iron Eyes a Ottoe approves & says he is Brave Nee Swor un ja Big ax a Ottoe approves Star gra hun ja Big blue Eyes a Ottoe Delivers up his comm Ne ca sa wa-Black Cat a Missouris approves the Council & he wants paper for his men at home, he after wards came & petitioned for his Paper War-sar sha co-Brave Man aproves

The Speach of the Big Horse I went to the hunt Buffalow I heard your word and I returned, I and all my men with me will attend to your wordsyou want to make peace with all, I want to make peace also, the young men when they want to go to war where is the goods you give me to Keep them at home, if you give me Some Whisky to give a Drop to my men at home.

I came here naked and must return home naked. if I have Something to give the young men I can prevent their going to war. You want to make peace with all, It is good we want Something to give my men at home. I am a pore man, and cant quiet without means, a Spoon ful of your milk will quiet all.

2nd Speech of the Little Thief I want Mr. Faufon & Mr. La bieche to make a piece with the Panies Loups. I want William to go & make a piece with the Loups, he can Speake english & will doe will to go.- refused that William LaBiech shall accompany Faufon

Those people were not well Satisfied with the Presents given them, they were much Surprised at the air gun and Several curiosities which were Shown them none more than the magnet, those people became extreemly troublesom to us begging Whisky & little articles. Sergt. Floyd was taken violently bad with the Beliose Cholick and is dangerously ill we attempt in Vain to releive him, I am much concerned for his Situation- we could get nothing to Stay on his Stomach a moment nature appear exosting fast in him every man is attentive to him york prlly

[Clark, August 19, 1804] 19th August Sunday 1804 a find morning wind from the S. E. prepared a Small Present for the Cheifs and warriers present. the main Cheif Brackfast with us, & beged for a Sun glass, those People are all naked, Covered only with Breech Clouts Blankits or Buffalow Roabes, the flesh Side Painted of Differant Colours & figures. At 10 oClock we assembled the Chiefs & warriers 9 in number under an orning, and we explained the Speech Sent to the nation from the Council Bluffs by Mr. Faufon. The 3 Chiefs and all the men or warriers made Short Speeches approveing the advice & Council their great father had Sent them, and Concluded by giveing themselves Some Credit for their acts.

We then brought out the presents and exchanged the Big horses Meadel & gave him one equal to the one Sent to the Little Thief & gave all Some Small articls & 8 Carrots of Tobacco, we gave one Small Meadel to one of the Cheifs & a Sertificate to the others of their good intentions.

Names

The Little Theif Grd. Cheif I have mentioned before
The Big horse
Crows Head (or) Kar Ka paha - Missory
Black Cat (or) Ne ma Sa wa - do
Iron Eyes (or) Sar na no no - Ottoe
Big ax (or) Nee Swar Un ja - do
Big Blue Eyes - Star gea Hun ja - do
Brave Man (or) War Sar Sha co

One of those Indians after reciving his Certificate delivd. it again to me the Big blue eyes the Chief petitioned for the Ctft. again, we would not give the Certft. but rebuked them verry roughly for haveing in object goods and not peace with their neighbours- this language they did not like at first, but at length all petitioned for us to give back the Certificate to the Big blu eyes he came forward and made a plausible excuse, I then gave the Certificate the Great Cheif to bestow it to the most Worthey, they gave it to him, we then gave them a ,Dram & broke up the Council, the Chiefs requested we would not leave them this evening. we deturned to Set out early in the morning we Showed them many Curiosities and the air gun which they were much asstonished at. those people beged much for wishey- Serjeant Floyd is taken verry bad all at one with a Beliose Chorlick we attempt to relieve him without Success as yet, he gets wordse and we are muc allarmed at his Situation, all attention to him.

[Clark, August 20, 1804] 20th August Monday after gieving faufon Some goods the Indians a Canister of whiskey, we Set out under a jentle Breeze from the S. E Shields went with the horses- I am Dull & heavy been up the greater Part of last night with Serjt. Floyd, who is as bad as he can be to live the motion of his bowels having changed &c. &c. is the Cause of his violent attack &c. &c.

we Came to make a warm bath for Sergt. Floyd hopeing it would brace him a little, before we could get him in to this bath he expired, with a great deel of composure, haveing Said to me before his death that he was going away and wished me to write a letter- we Buried him to the top of a high round hill over looking the river & Countrey for a great distance Situated just below a Small river without a name to which we name & call Floyds river, the Bluffs Sergts. Floyds Bluff-we buried him with all the honors of War, and fixed a Ceeder post at his head with his name title & Day of the month and year Capt Lewis read the funeral Service over him after paying everry respect to the Body of this desceased man (who had at All times given us proofs of his impatiality Sincurity to ourselves and good will to Serve his Countery) we returned to the Boat & proceeded to the Mouth of the little river 30 yd. wide & Camped a butifull evening

[Clark, August 20, 1804] 20th August Monday 1804 Sergeant Floyd much weaker and no better. Made Mr. Fauforn the interpter a fiew presents, and the Indians a Canister of whisky we Set out under a gentle breeze from the S. E. and proceeded on verry well- Serjeant Floyd as bad as he can be no pulse & nothing will Stay a moment on his Stomach or bowels

Passed two Islands on the S. S. and at first Bluff on the S S. Serj. Floyd Died with a great deel of Composure, before his death he Said to me, "I am going away. I want you to write me a letter"- We buried him on the top of the bluff 1/2 Miles below a Small river to which we Gave his name, he was buried with the Honors of War much lamented; a Seeder post with the (1) Name Sergt. C. Floyd died here 20th of August 1804 was fixed at the head of his grave- This Man at all times gave us proofs of his firmness and Deturmined resolution to doe Service to his Countery and honor to himself after paying all the honor to our Decesed brother we Camped in the mouth of floyds river about 30 yards wide, a butifull evening.-

[Clark, August 21, 1804] 21st August Tuesday we Set out verry early this morning under a Gentle Breeze from the S. E Course S. 82° E 3 mes to the upper pt. of a Bluff on the S. S. passed Willow Creek and Some rock below the mouth of the Seouex river on the Starboard Side those Clifts are about 170 feet high, this river heads with the St. peters and is navagable 75 Leagues (by the act. of Mr. Durien) to a fall of near 200 for, 2 large & Som Small Pitchs below the falls on the right a Creek corns in on which the red pipe Stone is percured, & in the praries about, a place of Peace with all nations.

[Clark, August 21, 1804] 21st August Tuesday 1804 We Set out verry early this morning and proceeded on under a gentle Breeze from the S. E. passed willow creek Small on the S. S. below a Bluff of about 170 feet high and one 1/2 mes. above Floyds river at 11/2 miles higher & above the Bluff passed the Soues River S. S. this River is about the Size of Grand river and as Mr. Durrien our Scones intptr. says "navagable to the falls 70 or 80 Leagues and above these falls" Still further, those falls are 200 feet or there abouts & has two princapal pitches, and heads with the St. peters passing the head of the Demoien, on the right below the falls a Creek Coms in which passes thro Clifts of red rock which the Indians make pipes of, and when the different nations Meet at those queries all is piece, passed a place in a Prarie on the L. S. where the Mahars had a Village formerly. the Countrey above the Platt R has a great Similarity. Campd. on the L. Side. Clouds appear to rise in the west & threten wind. I found a verry excellent froot resembling the read Current, the Scrub on which it grows resembles Privey & about the Common hight of a wild plumb-

The two men Sent with the horses has not joined us as yet

[Clark, August 22, 1804] 22nd of August Wendesday 1804 Set out early wind from the South. G Shannon joined the Boat last night. Course this morning is S 47° W. 11/4 on the S. point West 11/4 me. to the Commencement of a Bluff on the L. S. the High land near the river for Some distance below. This Bluff contain Pyrites alum, Copperass & a Kind Markesites also a clear Soft Substance which will mold and become pliant like wax) Capt lewis was near being Poisened by the Smell in pounding this Substance I belv to be arsenic or Cabalt. I observe great Quantity of Cops. ans and almin pure & Straters of white & brown earth of 6 Inch thick. a Creek Corns in above the Bluffs on which there is great quantities of those minerals, This Creek I call Roloje a at those Allom banks Shields joined in with two Deer

Camped on the S. S. a Great Deel of Elk Sign fresh Capt. Lewis took a Dost of Salts this evening to carry off the effects of (arsenec) or cobalt which he was trying to find out the real quallity (2) passed a Clift of Rock much impregnated with alum, Containing also a great quantity of Cabalt

ordered a Vote of the men for a Sergeant of the three highest numbers a choice to be made Gass Bratton & Gibson- Gass is worth remark, that my Ink after Standing in the pot 3 or four days Soaks up & becons thick

[Clark, August 22, 1804] 22nd August Friday 1804 Set out early wind from the South at three miles we landed at a Bluff where the two men Sent with the horses were waiting with two Deer, by examonation of this (1) Bluff Contained alum, Copperas, Cobalt, Pyrites; a alum rock Soft & Sand Stone. Capt. Lewis in proveing the quality of those minerals was near poisoning himself by the fumes & tast of the Cabalt which had the appearance of Soft Isonglass- Copperas & alum is verry pure, Above this Bluff a Small Creek Coms in from the L. S. passing under the Clifts for Several miles, this Creek I Call Roloje a name I learned last night in my Sleep. (2) Eight) Seven miles above is a Clift of Allom Stone of a Dark Brown Colr. Containing also in crusted in the Crevices & Shelves of the rock great qts. of Cabalt, Semented Shels & a red earth. from this the (3) river bends to the East and is within 3 or 4 miles of the River Soues at the place where that river Coms from the high land into the Low Prarie & passes under the foot of those Hills to its mouth.

Capt Lewis took a Dost of Salts to work off the effects of the Arsenic, we Camped on the S. S. Sailed the greater part of this day with a hard wind from the S. E. great deel of Elk Sign, and great appearance of wind from the N. W.

ordered a vote for a Serjeant to chuse one of three which may be the highest number the highest numbers are P. Gass had 19 Votes, Bratten & Gibson

[Clark, August 23, 1804] 23rd August Thursday 1804 Set out this morning verry early, the two men R. Fields & Shannon did not Come up last night, I went out and Killed a fine Buck, J. Fields Killed a Buffaloes, 2 Elk Swam by the boat whilst I was out and was not Killed, many guns fired at it R. Fields Came up with the horses & brought two Deer, Collins Killed a Small doe, Several Prarie wolves Seen Course West 4 Mls. to the mouth of a Small run between two Bluffs of yellow Clay North 31/4 miles to the upper Pt. of Some timber in the bend to S. S. near where R. fields Killed the Buffalow passed the pt. of High Land on S. S at 1/4 of a mile, Capt. Lewis went out with 8 men & brought the buffalow to the river at this bend, C. Lewis Killed a Goose, wind blew hard of the flying Sands which rasies like a Cloud of Smoke from the Bars when the wind Blows, the Sand being fine and containing a breat perpotion of earth and when it lights it Sticks to every thing it touches at this time the grass is white S 48° 3 miles to a point of willows on the S. S. haveing passed the Sand Island L. S Camped on the L S above the Island Saw an elk Standing on a Sand bar. Shields Shot it thro the neck 101/4

[Clark, August 23, 1804] 23rd August Thursday 1804 Set out this morning verry early the two men with the horses did not Come up last night I walked on Shore & Killed a fat Buck- J. Fields Sent out to hunt Came to the Boat and informed that he had Killed a Buffalow in the plain a head Cap Lewis took 12 men and had the buffalow brought to the boat in the next bend to the S S. 2 Elk Swam the river, and was fired at from the boat R. Fields came up with the Horses and brought two Deer one Deer Killed from the Boat. Several Prarie Wolves Seen to day Saw Elk Standing on the Sand bar

The Wind blew hard West and raised the Sands off the bar in Such Clouds that we Could Scercely See this Sand being fine and verry light Stuck to every thing it touched, and in the Plain for a half a mile the distance I was out every Spire of Grass was covered with the Sand or Dust We Camped on the L. S. above a Sand Island one Beaver Cought

[Clark, August 24, 1804] 24th August Friday 1804. Some rain last night & this morning, we Set out at the usial time and proceeded on the Same Course of last night Continued S. 48° W. 21/4 mes. to the Commencement of a Blue Clay Bliff on LS. about 180 or 190 feet high West under rugged Bluffs 13/4 ms. passing Several Small Dreens, falling into the river those Bluffs has been lately on fire and is yet verry Hott, Great appearance of Coal, & imence quantities of Cabalt in Side of that part oft the Bluff which Sliped in, on the Sides of the hill great quanities of a kind of Current or froot resembling the Current in appearance much richer and finer flavd. grows on a Scrub resembling a Damsen and is now fine and makes a Delightful) Tart above this Bluff I took my Servent and a french boy I have and walked on Shore I killed a Deer which york Packed on his back In the evening I Killed two Buck Elk and wounded two others which I could not pursue by the Blood as my ball was So Small to bleed them well, my boys each Shot an elk- it was late and I Crossed a Point Struck the river above and halted the boat and 12 men went out brought in the meat all the after part of the day it rained we are all wet. Capt Lewis and my Self Concluded to visit a High Hill Situated in an emence Plain three Leagues N. 20° W. from the mouth of White Stone river, this hill appear to be of a Conic form and by all the different Nations in this quater is Supposed to be a place of Deavels ors that they are in human form with remarkable large heads and about 18 inches high; that they are very watchfull and ar armed with Sharp arrows with which they can kill at a great distance; they are said to kill all persons who are so hardy as to attemp to approach the hill; they state that tradition informs them that many indians have suffered by these little people and among others that three Maha men fell a sacrefice to their murceyless fury not meany years since- so much do the Mahas Souix Ottoes and other neibbhouring nations believe this fable that no consideration is sufficient to induce them to approach this hill.

[Clark, August 24, 1804] 24th August Friday 1804 Some rain last night, a Continuation this morning; we Set out at the usial time and proceeded on the Course of last night to the (1) Commencement of a blue Clay Bluff of 180 or 190 feet high on the L. S. Those Bluffs appear to have been laterly on fire, and at this time is too hot for a man to bear his hand in the earth at any debth, gret appearance of Coal. An emence quantity of Cabalt or a Cristolised Substance which answers its discription is on the face of the Bluff- Great quantities of a kind of berry resembling a Current except double the Sise and Grows on a bush like a Privey, and the Size of a Damsen deliciously flavoured & makes delitefull Tarts, this froot is now ripe, I took my Servent and a french boy and Walked on Shore Killed Two Buck Elks and a faun, and intersepted the Boat and had all the meat butchered and in by Sun Set at which time it began to rain and rained hard, Cap Lewis & my Self walk out & got Verry wet, a Cloudey rainey night,- In my absence the Boat Passed a Small (2) River Called by the Indians White Stone River. this river is about 30 yards wide and runs thro a Plain & Prarie in its whole Course In a northerley direction from the mouth of this Creek in an imence Plain a high Hill is Situated, and appears of a Conic form and by the different nations of Indians in this quarter is Suppose to be the residence of Deavels. that they are in human form with remarkable large heads and about 18 Inches high, that they are Very watchfull, and are arm'd with Sharp arrows with which they Can Kill at a great distance; they are Said to Kill all persons who are So hardy as to attempt to approach the hill; they State that tradition informs them that many Indians have Suffered by those little people and among others three Mahar men fell a Sacrefise to their murceyless fury not many years Since- So much do the Maha, Souis, Ottoes and other neighbouring nations believe this fable that no Consideration is Suffecient to induce them to apporach the hill

[Lewis, August 24, 1804] Friday, August 24th This day the Chronometer stoped again just after being wound up; I know not the cause, but fear it procedes from some defect which it is not in my power to remedy.-

[Clark, August 24, 1804] (1) About the center of this Sand Island the river of white Stone (as Called by Mr. Evins Kenvill R.) falls in on the Stard. Side it appear to be about 25 or 30 yards Wide; at the mouth of this river 10 Indians had latterly cross Supposed be be Soues, the part of a band which are at war with the Mahars, This Soues nation are divided into bands Som 100 to 500 men in a band at peace with eath other, ther Interest & prejudices different, for instance one band the most envetterate enimy of the mahars, all the other Bands in the greatest harmony with that nation and even go with thim to War, those Soues, follow the Buffalow, & Kill them on foot, they pack their Dogs, which carry ther Bedn.

[Clark, August 25, 1804] Augt. 25th Satturday 1804 This morning Capt Lewis & my Self G D. Sjt. Ouderway Shields J. Fields colter Bratten Cane Labeeche corp Wovington Frasure & York Set out to Visit this mountain of evel Spirits, we Set out from the mouth of the White Stone Creek, at 8 oClock, at 4 miles Cross the Creek in an open plain, at 7 ms. the dog gave out & we Sent him back to the Creek at 12 oClock we rose the hill Some time before we got to the hill we obsevd. great numbers of Birds hovering about the top of this Mound when I got on the top those Birds flw off. I discovered that they wer Cetechig a kind of flying ant which were in great numbers abought the top of this hill, those insects lit on our hats & necks, Several of them bit me verry Shart on the neck, near the top of this nole I observed three holes which I Supposed to be Prarie Wolves or Braroes, which are numerous in those Plains. this hill is about 70 foot high in an emince Prarie or leavel plain from the top I could not observe any woods except in the Missourie Points and a few Scattering trees on the three Rivers in view. i e the Soues River below, the River Jacque above & the one we have crossed from the top of this Mound we observed Several large gangus of Buffalow & Elk feeding upwards of 800 in number Capt Lewis being much fatigued and verry thursty obliged us to go to the neares water which we Could See, which was the W Stone Creek at right angles from the Course we came out, and we got water in three miles in the Creek above whre the beaver had darned it up after a Delay of about one hour & a half we Set out for our boat, Cross the Creek three times wast deep, passing down an ellgent bottom of about a mile in width bordered by a ridge of about 50 feet from the top of which it was leavel to the river, we proceeded on by a Circular Derection to the place we Crossed this Creek going out where we delayed for the men to rest themselves about 40 minits in a small grove here we got Great quantities of the best largest grapes I ever tasted, Some Blue Currents still on the bushes, and two kind of Plumbs, one the Common wild Plumb the other a large Yellow Plumb growing on a Small bush, this blumb is about double the Size of the Common and Deliscously flavoured- Those plains are leavel without much water and no timber all the timber on the Stone River would not thickly timber 100 acres of land- we returned to the boat at Sunset, my Servent nearly exosted with heat thurst and fatigue, he being fat and un accustomed to walk as fast as I went was the Cause- we Set fire to the Praries in two Places to let the Sons know we were on the river and as a Signal for them to Come to the river above, our Party in the Boat & one Perogue undr. the Comd of Sergt. Pryor answered us by firing a prarie near them. we proceeded on to the place we Camped last night, and as it began to rain and verry dark, we Concluded to Stay all night, our boys prepared us a Supper of jurked meet and two Prarie Larks (which are about the Size of a Pigeon and Peculier to this country) and on a Buffalow roabe we Slept verry well in the morning we proceeded on and joined the boat at 6 miles, they had camped & were Jurking an Elk & 5 Deer which R. Fields & Shannon had brough in. from the Mound to the Hill S. S. mo. of R. Soues S 70° E. to the opsd. Hills S. 45° E. and to the woods near River au Jacque is West

[Clark, August 25, 1804] Augt. 25th Satturday wind S E The Boat under Serjt Pryor after drying some goods which got wet in the french Perogue & jurking the meet killed yesterday Set out at 12 oClock and proceeded on Six miles and Camped on the L. S. passed a Bluff of blue earth at 3 miles and a large Sand Island in a bend to the S. S. at 5 miles, R Fields brought in 5 Deer, G Shannon an Elk this eveng. rain at 3 oClock Murcky. 86 abo 0,

[Clark, August 25, 1804] 25th August Satturday 1804 a Cloudy morning Capt Lewis & my Self Concluded to go and See the Mound which was viewed with Such turrow by all the different Nation in this quarter, we Selected Shields J. Fields, W Bratten, Sergt. Ordway, J Colter, Can, and Corp Worbington & Frasure, also G. Drewyer and droped down to the mouth of White Stone River where we left the Perogue with two men and at 200 yards we assended a riseing ground of about Sixty feet, from the top of this High land the Countrey is leavel & open as far as Can be Seen, except Some few rises at a Great Distance, and the Mound which the Indians Call Mountain of little people or Spirits this mound appears of a Conic form & is N. 20° W. from the mouth of the Creek, we left the river at 8 oClock, at 4 miles we Crossed the Creek 23 yards wide in an extensive Valley and continued on at two miles further our Dog was So Heeted & fatigued we was obliged Send him back to the Creek, at 12 oClock we arrived at the hill Capt Lewis much fatigued from heat the day it being verry hot & he being in a debilitated State from the Precautions he was obliged to take to provent the affects of the Cobalt, & Mini. Substance which had like to have poisoned him two days ago, his want of water, and Several of the men complaining of Great thirst, deturmined us to make for the first water which was the Creek in a bend N. E. from the mound about 3 miles- aftr a Delay of about 1 hour & a half to recrut our party we Set out on our return down the Creek thro the bottom of about 1 mile in width, Crossed the Creek 3 times to the place we first Struck it, where we geathered Some delisious froot Such as Grapes Plumbs, & Blue Currents after a Delay of an hour we Set out on our back trail & arrived at the Perogue at Sun Set we proceedd on to the place we Campd. last night and Stayed all night.

This Mound is Situated on an elivated plain in a leavel and extensive prarie, bearing N. 20° W. from the mouth of White Stone Creek Nine Miles, the base of the Mound is a regular parallelagram the long Side of which is about 300 yards in length the Shorter 60 or 70 yards- from the longer Side of the Base it rises from the North & South with a Steep assent to the hight of 65 or 70 feet, leaveing a leavel Plain on the top of 12 feet in width & 90 in length. the North & South part of this mound is joins by two regular rises, each in Oval forms of half its hight forming three regular rises from the Plain the assent of each elivated part is as Suden as the principal mound at the narrower Sides of its Bass

The reagular form of this hill would in Some measure justify a belief that it owed its Orrigin to the hand of man; but as the earth and loos pebbles and other Substances of which it was Composed, bare an exact resemblance to the Steep Ground which border on the Creek in its neighbourhood we Concluded it was most probably the production of nature-.

The only remarkable Charactoristic of this hill admiting it to be a naturial production is that it is insulated or Seperated a considerable distance from any other, which is verry unusial in the naturul order or disposition of the hills.

The Surrounding Plains is open void of Timber and leavel to a great extent; hence the wind from whatever quarter it may blow, drives with unusial force over the naked Plains and against this hill; the insects of various kinds are thus involuntaryly driven to the mound by the force of the wind, or fly to its Leward Side for Shelter; the Small Birds whoes food they are, Consequently resort in great numbers to this place in Surch of them; Perticularly the Small brown Martin of which we saw a vast number hovering on the Leward Side of the hill, when we approached it in the act of Catching those insects; they were So gentle that they did not quit the place untill we had arrivd. within a fiew feet of them-

One evidence which the Inds Give for believeing this place to be the residence of Some unusial Spirits is that they frequently discover a large assemblage of Birds about this mound- is in my opinion a Suffient proof to produce in the Savage mind a Confident belief of all the properties which they ascribe it.

from the top of this Mound we beheld a most butifull landscape;
Numerous herds of buffalow were Seen feeding in various directions, the
Plain to North N. W & N E extends without interuption as far as Can be
Seen From the Mound to the mouth of Stone River is S. 20° E 9 miles.

to the woods near the mouth of River Jacque is West

to the High land near the mouth of Souis River is S. 70 E.

to the high land opposit Side or near the Maha Town is S. 45 E.

Some high lands to be Seen from the mound at a Great distance to the N.
E Some Nearer to the N W. no woods except on the Missouris Points

if all the timber which is on the Stone Creek was on 100 acres it would not be thickly timbered, the Soil of those Plains are delightfull Great numbers of Birds are Seen in those Plains, Such as black bird, Ren or Prarie burd a kind of larke about the Sise of a Partridge with a Short tail &c. &.

25th Augt the Boat under the Comd. of Sergt. Pryor proceeded on in our absence (after jurking the Elk I Killed yesterday) Six Miles and Camped on the Larboard Side R Fields brought in five Deer. George Shannon Killed an Elk Buck Some rain this evening.

we Set the Praries on fire as a Signal for the Soues to Come to the river.

[Lewis, August 25, 1804] August the 25th on our return from the mound of sperits saw the first bats that we had observed since we began to ascend the Missouri

also saw on our return on the Creek that passes this mound about 2 M. distant S. a bird of heron kind as large as the Cormorant short tale long leggs of a colour on the back and wings deep copper brown with a shade of red. we could not kill it therefore I can not describe it more particularly.

[Clark, August 26, 1804] 26th August Sunday 1804 arrived at the boat at 9 oClock A.M. Set out at 10 oClock after Jurking the meet & Cutting the Elk Skins for a Toe Roap and proceeded, leaveing G. Drewyer & Shannon to hunt the horses, the river verry full of Sand bars and Wide Course S. 66° W. 2 mes. to a Sand bar Makeing out from the S. S. N. 82° W. 7 mes. to a pt. of willows S S passd. a Island & large Sand bars on both sides river wide and a Clift of White earth on the L. S of 2 ms. in length to a point of Willows on the S. S opposit Arch Creek above the mouth of this Creek a Chief of the Maha nataton displeased with the Conduct of Black bird the main Chief came to this place and built a Town which was called by his name Petite Arch (or Little Bow) this Town was at the foot of a Hill in a handsom Plain fronting the river and Contained about 100 huts & 200 men, the remains of this tribe Since the Death of Petite arch has joined the remaining part of the nation This Creek is Small- we apt. Pat Gass Sergeant Vice Floyd Dicesed, Geathered great quantites of Grapes & three Kinds of Plumbs, one yellow round, & one ovel, & the Common wild Plumb. Misquetors bad to night- I have apt. you

[Clark, August 26, 1804] 26th August Sunday 1804 (Joined the Boat at 9 oClock A M) after Jurking the meat Killed yesterday and prepareing the Elk Skins for a Toe Roape we Set out Leaveing Drewyer & Shannon to hunt the horses which was lost with directions to follow us Keeping on the high lands.

proceeded on passed a Clift of White & Blue or Dark earths of 2 miles in extent on the L. S. and Camped on a Sand bar opposed the old village Called Pitite Arc a Small Creek falls into the river 15 yds wide below the Village on the Same Side L. S this village was built by a Indian Chief of the Maha nation by the name of Pitite arc (or little Bow) displeasd. with the Great Chief of that nation (Black Bird) Seperated with 200 men and built a village at this place. after his death the two villages joined. apt. Pat Gass a Sergt. Vice Floyd Deceased

Great qts. of Grape, Plumbs of three Kinds 2 yellow and large of one of which is long and a 3rd kind round & red all well flavored. perticularly the yellow Sort.

[Lewis, August 26, 1804] Orders August 26th 1804. The commanding officers have thought it proper to appoint Patric Gass, a Sergeant in the corps of volunteers for North Western Discovery, he is therefore to be obeyed and respected accordingly.

Sergt. Gass is directed to take charge of the late Sergt. Floyd's mess, and immediately to enter on the discharge of such other duties, as by their previous orders been prescribed for the government of the Sergeants of this corps.

The Commanding officers have every reason to hope from the previous faithfull services of Sergt. Gass, that this expression of their approbation will be still further confirmed, by his vigilent attention in future to his duties as a Sergeant. the Commanding officers are still further confirmed in the high opinion they had previously formed of the capacity, deligence and integrety of Sergt. Gass, from the wish expresssed by a large majority of his comrades for his appointment as Sergeant.

Meriwether Lewis
Capt. 1st U.S. Regt Infty.
Wm Clark
Cpt &.

[Clark, August 27, 1804] 27th August Monday, this morning the Morning Star was observed to be very large, G Drewyer Came up and informed that he Could neither find Shannon or the horses, he had walked all night- we Sent Shields & J. Fields back to look for Shannon & the horses and to Come up with us on the river above at the grand Callemet or River KaCure & we Set out under a Gentle Breeze from the S. E. proceeded on passed a Bluff at 7 mes. Several mile in extent of white Clay Marl or Chalk, under this bank we discovered Large Stone resembling lime incrusted with a Substanc like Glass which I take to be Cabolt, also ore, three mes above this Bluff we Set the Prarie on fire, to let the Soues Know, we wished to see them at two oClock an Indian Swam to the Perogue, we landed & two other Came they were boys, they informed us that the Souex were Camped near, on the R Jacke one Maha boy informed us his nation was gorn to make a peace with the Pania's we Send Sjt. Pryor & a frenchman with the Interptr. Mr. Durion to the Camp to See & invite their Great Chiefs to Come and Counsel with us at the Callemet Bluffs _____ Mile abov on L. S.- we proceed on 11/2 miles farther & Camped S S.

[Clark, August 27, 1804] 27th August Monday 1804 This morning the Star Calld. the morning Star much larger than Common G. Drewyer Came up and informed that he Could neither find Shannon nor horses, we Sent Shields & J Fields, back to hunt Shannon & the horses, with derections to Keep on the Hills to the Grand Calumet above on River Ka cure.

We Set Sail under a gentle Breeze from the S. E. at 7 miles passed a white Clay marl or Chalk Bluff under this Bluff is extensive I discovered large Stone much like lime incrusted with a Clear Substance which I believe to be Cabalt, also ore is imbeded in the Dark earth, resembling Slate much Softer- above this Bluff we had the Prarie Set on fire to let the Souix See that we were on the river, & as a Signal for them to Come to it.

at 2 oClock passed the mouth of River Jacque, or Yeankton one Indian at the mouth of this river Swam to the Perogue, we landed and two others came to us, those Inds. informed that a large Camp of Soues, were on R. Jacque near the mouth. we Sent Sergt. Pryor & a Frenchman with Mr. Durioin the Souls interpeter to the Camp with derections to invite the Principal Chiefs to councel with us at a Bluff above Called the Calumet- two of those Indians accompanied them and the third continued in the Boat Showing an inclination to Continue, this boy is a Mahar, and inform that his nation, were gorn to the Parnias to make a peace with that nation.

We proceeded on about one and a half miles and in Camped on a bar makeing out from the S. S. the wind blew hard from the South. a Cool & Pleasent evening, The river has fallen verry Slowly and is now low.

[Lewis, August 27, 1804]
Monday August 27th
On the Stard. shore, opposite to the lower point, or commencement of
the white Calk Bluff-

[Clark, August 28, 1804] 28th August Tuesday, 1804 The wind blew hard last night one Indian Stayed with us all night, Set out under a Stiff Breeze from S and proceedd on passe a Willow Island at two miles Several Sand bars the river here is wide & Shallow full of Sand bars- The High land appear to be getting nearer to each other passed a Bluff containing Some white earth on the L. S. below this Bluff for Some mile the Plain rises gradually to the hight of the Bluff which is 70 or 80 foot, here the Indian boy left us for his Camp- Capt Lewis & my Self much indisposed- I think from the Homney we Substitute in place of bread, (or Plumbs) we proceeded on about 3 Miles higher and Camped below the Calumet Bluff in a Plain on the L. S. to waite the return of Sergt Pryor & Mr. Durioun, who we Sent to the Soues Camp from the mouth of R. Jacque, before we landed the French rund a Snag thro their Perogue, and like to have Sunk, we had her on loaded, from an examonation found that this Perogue was unfit for Service, & Deturmined to Send her back by the Party intended to Send back and take their Perogue, accordingly Changed the loads, Some of the loading was wet wind blows hard from the South. J Shields & J. Fields joined they did not overtake Shannon with the horses who is a head of us.

[Clark, August 28, 1804] 28th August Tuesday 1804. Set out under a Stiff Breeze from the South and proceeded on passd. a willow Island at 2 miles Several Sand bars, the river wide & Shallow at 4 Miles passed a Short White Bluff of about 70 or 80 feet high, below this Bluff the Prarie rises gradually from the water back to the Hight of the Bluff which is on the Larboard Side here the Indian who was in the boat returned to the Sisouex Camp on the R Jacque, Capt. Lewis & my Self much indisposed owing to Some Cause for which we cannot account one of the Perogues run a Snag thro her and was near Sinking in the opinions of the Crew- we came too below the Calumet Bluff and formed a camp in a Butifull Plain near the foot of the high land which rises with a gradual assent near this Bluff I observe more timber in the valey & on the points than usial- The Perogue which was injurd I had unloaded and the Loading put into the other Perogue which we intended to Send back, the Perogue & changed the Crew after examoning her & finding that She was unfit for Service deturmined to Send her back by the party Some load which was in the Perogue much inju'd

The wind blew hard this after noon from the South- J. Shields & J. Fields who was Sent back to look for Shannon & the Horses joined us & informed that Shannon had the horses a head and that they Could not over take him This man not being a first rate Hunter, we deturmined to Send one man in pursute of him with Some Provisions.-

[Lewis, August 28, 1804] Orders August 28th 1804. The commanding officers direct that the two messes who form the crews of the perogues shall scelect each one man from their mess for the purpose of cooking and that these cooks as well as those previously appointed to the messes of the Barge crew, shall in future be exempted from mounting guard, or any detail for that duty; they are therefore no longer to be held on the royaster.

M. Lewis Capt. 1st US. Regt. Infty. Win Clark Cpt. &.

[Clark, August 29, 1804] 29th August Wednesday 1804- rained last night and Some this morning verry cloudy Set Some men to work to make a Toe rope of Elk Skin, and my Self to write, Sent one man to pursue Shannon a head with Some provisions, I am much engaged writeing a Speech at 4 oClock Sergt. Pryor & Mr. Durion the Soues interpeter with about 70 Soues arrived on the opposit Side of the river we Sent over for them, who came over Mr. D. & his Son who was tradeing with the Indians Came over Mr. Durion informed that three Chiefs were of the Party, we Sent over Serjt. Pryor with young Mr. Durion, Six Kettles for the Indians to Cook the meat they Killed on the way from their Camp (2 Elk & 6 Deer) a bout a bucket of Corn & 2 twists of Tobacco to Smoke intending to Speak to them tomorrow- G. Drewyer Killed a Deer-. Sergt. Pryor informs that when he approached the Indian Camp they Came to meet them Supposeing Cap Lewis or my Self to be of the party intending to take us in a roabe to their Camp-he approached the Camp which was handsum made of Buffalow Skins Painted different Colour, their Camps formed a Conic form Containing about 12 or 15 persons each and 40 in number, on the River Jacque of 100 yds wide & Deep Containing but little wood, They had a fat dog Cooked as a feest; for them, and a Snug aptmt for them to lodge on their march they passed thro plains Covd. with game &. &. &.

[Clark, August 29, 1804] 29th August Wednesday 1804 Some rain last night & this morning, Sent on Colter with Provisions in pursute of Shannon, had a Toe roap made of Elk Skin, I am much engaged rereiteing- at 4 oClock P M. Sergt. Pryor & Mr. Dorion with 5 Chiefs and about 70 men &c. arrived on the opposite Side we Sent over a Perogue & Mr. Dorrion & his Son who was tradeing with the Indians Came over with Serjt Pryer, and informed us that the Chiefs were there we Sent Serjt. Pryor & yound Mr. Dorion with Som Tobacco, Corn & a few Kitties for them to Cook in, with directions to inform the Chiefs that we would Speek to them tomorrow. Those Indians brought with them for their own use 2 Elk & 6 Deer which the young men Killed on the way from their Camp 12 miles distant.

Serjt. Pryor informs me that when Came near the Indian Camp they were met by men with a Buffalow roabe to Carry them, Mr. Dorion informed "they were not the Owners of the Boats & did not wish to be Carried"- the Sceouex Camps are handson of a Conic form Covered with Buffalow Roabs Painted different Colours and all Compact & hand Somly arranged, covered all round an orpen part in the Center for the fire, with Buffalow roabs each Lodg has a place for Cooking detached, the lodges contain 10 to 15 persons- a Fat Dog was presented as a mark of their Great respect for the party of which they partook hartily and thought it good & well flavored

The River Jacque is Deep & is navagable for Perogues a long distance up at the mouth it is Shallow & narrow but above it is 80 or 90 yards wide passing thro rich Praries with but little timber this river passes the Souex River and heads with the St Peters and a branch of Red river which which falls into Lake Winepik to the North

[Clark, August 30, 1804] 30th August Thursday 1804 A Foggeie morning I am much engagd. after Brackfast we sent Mr. Doroun in a Perogue to the other Side i'e L S. for the Chiefs and warriers of the Soues, he returned at 10 oClock with the Chiefs, at 12 oClock I finished and we delivered a Speech to the Indians expressive of the wishes of our government and explaining of what would be good for themselves, after delivering the Speech we made one grand Chief 1 2d Cheif and three third Chiefs and deliverd. to each a few articles and a Small present to the whole the grand Chief a Parole, Some wampom & a flag in addition to his present, they with Drew and we retired to dinner, Mr. Durions Sun much displeased that he could not dine with Cap Lewis and my Self- the number of Soues present is about 70 men- Dressed in Buffalow roabes a fiew fusees, Bows and arrows, and verry much deckerated with porcupine quills, a Society of which only four remains is present, this Society has made a vow never to giv back let what will happen, out of 22 only 4 remains, those are Stout likely men who Stay by them Selves, fond of mirth and assume a degree of Superiority-, the air gun astonished them verry much after night a circle was forrm around 3 fires and those Indians danced untill late, the Chiefs looked on with great dignity much pleased with what they had, we retired late and went to bead. wind hard from the South.

[Clark, August 30, 1804] 30th of August Thursday 1804 a verry thick fog this morning after Prepareing Some presents for the Chiefs which we intended make by giving Meadals, and finishing a Speech what we intend'd to give them, we Sent Mr. Dorion in a Perogue for the Chiefs & warreirs to a Council under an Oak tree near wher we had a flag flying on a high flag Staff at 12 OClock we met and Cap L. Delivered the Speach & thin made one great Chiff by giving him a meadal & Some Cloathes one 2d. Chief & three third Chiefs in the Same way, They recvd. those thing with the goods and tobacco with pleasure To the Grand Chief we gave a Flag and the parole & wampom with a hat & Chiefs Coat, we Smoked out of the pipe of peace, & the Chiefs retired to a Bourey made of bushes by their young men to Divide their presents and Smoke eate and Council Capt Lewis & my Self retired to dinner and Consult about other measures- Mr. Daurion Jr. much displeased that we did not invite him to dine with us (which he was Sorry for after wards)- The Souix is a Stout bold looking people, (the young men hand Som) & well made, the greater part of them make use of Bows & arrows, Some fiew fusees I observe among them, not with Standing they live by the Bow & arrow, they do not Shoot So well as the Northern Indians the Warriers are Verry much deckerated with Paint Porcupin quils & feathers, large leagins & mockersons, all with buffalow roabs of Different Colours. the Squars wore Peticoats & and a white Buffalow roabes with the black hair turned back over their necks & Sholders

I will here remark a Society which I had never before this day heard was in any nation of Indians- four of which is at this time present and all who remain of this Band- Those who become members of this Society must be brave active young men who take a Vow never to give back let the danger be what it may; in War Parties they always go foward without Screening themselves behind trees or any thing else to this Vow they Strictly adheer dureing their Lives- an instanc which happened not long Since, on a party in Crossing the R Missourie on the ice, a whole was in the ice imediately in their Course which might easily have been avoided by going around, the foremost man went on and was lost the others wer draged around by the party- in a battle with the Crow Indians who inhabit the Coul Noir or black mountain out of 22 of this society 18 was Killed, the remaining four was draged off by their Party Those men are likely fellows the Sit together Camp & Dance together- This Society is in imitation of the Societies of the de Curbo or Crow Indians from whome they imitate-

[Clark, August 31, 1804] 31st of August Friday rose early a fair Day- a curioes Society among this nation worthey of remark, ie, formed of their active deturmined young men, with a vow never to give back, let the danger or deficuelty be what it may, in war parties they always go forward, without Screening themselves behind trees or anything else, to this vow they Strictly adheer dureing their Lives, an Instance of it, is last winter on a march in Crossing the Missourei a hole was in the ice immediately in their Course which might easily be avoided by going around, the fore most man went on and was drowned, the others were caught by their party and draged aroundin a battle with the Crow de Curbo Indians out of 22 of this Society 18 was killed, the remaining four was draged off by their friends, and are now here- they assocate together Camp together and are merry fellows, This Custom the Souex learned of the de Carbours inhabiting the Gout Noie or Black mountain all the Chiefs Delivered a Speech agreeing to what we Said &. &. & beged which I answered from my notes. We made or gav a certificate to two Brave men the attendants of the Great Chief gave them Some tobacco and prepared a Commission for Mr. Darion to make a peace with all the nations in the neighbourhood, Mahas, Porncases, Panic, Loups, Ottoes and Missouries- & to take to the President Some of the Gt Chiefs of each nations who would accompany him allso to do certain other things, and wrot Instructions- gave him a flag and Some Cloaths- the Chiefs Sent all their young men home, and they Stayed for Mr. Dorion- in the evening late we gave the Comsn. & Instruction to Mr. Durion & he recved them with pleasa, & promised to do all which was necessary. I took a Vocabulary of the Seouex language, and a fiew answers to Some queries I put to Mr.

Pitte Dorion respecting the War No. Situation Trad &c. &. of that people which is divided into 20 tribes possessing Sepperate interest they are numerous between 2 & 3000 men, divided into 20 tribes who view their interests as defferent Some bands at War with Nations which other bands are at peace- This nation call themselves-Dar co tar. The french call them Souex Their language is not perculiar to themselves as has been Stated, a great many words is the Same with the Mahas, Ponckais, Osarge, Kanzies &c. Clearly proves to me those people had the Same Oregean - this nations inhabit the red river of Hudson bay St. Peters Missippi, Demoin R. Jacque & on the Missourie they are at War with 20 nations, and at piece with 8 only- they recved their trade from the British except a few on the Missourie they furnish Beaver Martain Loues orter, Pekon Bear and Deer and have forty Traders at least among them. The names of the Different bands of this nation are-

1st Che the ree or Bois ruley (the present band) Inhabit the Souex Jacque & Demoin Rivers

2nd Ho in de bor to or poles. They live on the head of the Suouex River

3rd Me ma car jo (or make fence on the river.) the Country near the Big bend of the Missouri.

4th Son on to ton (People of the Prarie) they rove North of the Missourie in the Praries above.

5th Wau pa Coo do (Beeds) they live near the Prarie de Chaine on the Missippi

6th Te tar ton (or Village of Prarie) on the waters of the Mississippi above Prate de Chain (Dog Prarie)

7th Ne was tar ton (Big Water Town) on the Mississippi above the mouth of the St. Peters River.

8th Wau pa to (Leaf Nation). 10 Leagues up St. Peters

9th Cass car ba (White man) 35 Lgs. up St Peters

10 Mi ac cu op si ba (Cut Bank) reside on the head of St. Peters river

11 Son on- on St. Peters in the Praries

12th Se si toons- 40 Leagues up St Peters.

The names of the other tribes I could not get In

31st August 1804 Speeches

at 8 oClock the Chiefs and warriers met us in Council all with their pipes with the Stems presented towards us, after a Silence of abt. _____ The great Chief Dressed himself in his fine Cloathes and two warriers in the uniform and armer of their Nation Stood on his left with a War Club & Speer each, & Dressed in feathurs.

The Shake hand 1st Chief Spoke

My Father. I am glad to here the word of my G. F. and all my warriers and men about me are also glad.

My Father.- now I see my two fathers the Children, of my great father, & what you have Said I believe and all my people do believ also

My Father- We are verry glad you would take pitty on them this Day, we are pore and have no powder and ball.

My Father.- We are verry Sorry our women are naked and all our children, no petiecoats or cloathes

My Father- You do not want me to Stop the boats going up if we See,

I wish a man out of your boat to bring about a peace, between all the
Indians, & he can do So.

My Father- Listen to what I say I had an English medal when I went to See them, I went to the Spanoriards they give me a meadel and Some goods, I wish you would do the Same for my people.

My Father.- I have your word I am glad of it & as Soon as the Ice is don running I will go down & take with me, Some great men of the other bands of the Soues

My Father- I will be glad to See My Grand Father but our Women has got no Cloathes and we have no Powder & Ball, take pity on us this day.

My Father- I want to listen and observe wath you Say, we want our old friend (Mr. Durion) to Stay with us and bring the Indians with my Self down this Spring.

My Father- I opend my ears and all my yound men and we wish you to let
Mr. Durion Stay, and a Perogue for to take us down in the Spring.

The speach of th White Crain Mar to ree 2d Chief

My Fathr's listen to my word, I am a young man and do not intend to talk much, but will Say a few words.

My Father- my father was a Chief, and you have made me a Chief I now think I am a chief agreeable to your word as I am a young man and inexperienced, cannot say much What the Great Chief has Said is as much as I could Say

Par nar ne Ar par be Struck by the Pana 3d Chief

My father's I cant Speek much I will Speek a litle to you

My fathers.- ther's the Chiefs you have made high, we will obey them, as also my young men, the Pipe I hold in my hand is the pipe of my father, I am pore as you See, take pity on me I believe what you have Said

My fathers- You think the great meadel you gave My great Chief pleases
me and the small one you gave me gives me the heart to go with him to
See my Great father. What the Great Chief has Said is all I could Say.
I am young and Cant Speek.

A Warrier by name Tar ro mo nee Spoke

My father- I am verry glad you have made this man our great

Chief, the British & Spaniards have acknowledged him before but never Cloathed him. you have Cloathed him, he is going to see our Great father, We do not wish to spear him but he must go and see his great father

My Fathr's, my great Chief must go and See his Gd father, give him some of your milk to Speek to his young men,

My father. our people are naked, we wish a trader to Stop among us, I would be verry glad our two fathers would give us some powder and ball and some Milk with the flag.

Speech of Ar ca we char chi the half man 3d Chief

My fathr's I do not Speak verry well, I am a pore man and

My Fathr's. I was once a Chiefs boy now I am a man and a Chief of Some note

My Fat hr's- I am glad you have made my old Chief a fine and a great man, I have been a great warrier but now I here your words, I will berry my hatchet and be at peace with all & go with my Great Chief to see my great father.

My fath-s. When I was a young man I went to the Spaniards to see ther fassion, I like you talk and will pursue you advice, Since you have given me a meadal. I will tell you the talk of the Spaniards

My Father's.- I am glad my Grand father has sent you to the read people on this river, and that he has given us a flag large and handsom the Shade of which we can Sit under

My Fathr's.- We want one thing for our nation very much we have no trader, and often in want of goods

My Fathers- I am glad as well as all around me to here your word, and we open our ears, and I think our old Frend Mr. Durion can open the ears of the other bands of Soux. but I fear those nations above will not open their ears, and you cannot I fear open them

My Fathers. You tell us that you wish us to make peace with the Ottoes & M. You have given 5 Medles I wish you to give 5 Kigz with them

My Fathers.- My horses are pore running the Buffalow give us

Some powder and ball to hunt with, and leave old Mr. Durion with us to get us a trader

My Father.- The Spaniards did not keep the Medal of the Token of our Great Chief when they gave him one You have Dressed him and I like it I am pore & take pitey on me

My fathers- I am glad you have put heart in our great Chief he can now speak with confidence, I will support him in all your Councilsafter all the chief presented the pipe to us

The Half man rose & spoke as follows viz.

My father- What you have Said is well, but you have not given any thing to the attendants of the Great Chiefs after which

In the evening late we gave Mr. Dorion a bottle of whiskey and himself with the Chiefs Crossed the river and Camped on the opposit bank Soon after a violent Wind from the N W. accompanied with rain

[Clark, August 31, 1804] 31st of August We gave a Certificate to two Men of War, attendants on the Chief gave to all the Chiefs a Carrot of Tobacco- had a talk with Mr. Dorion, who agreed to Stay and Collect the Chiefs from as many Bands of Soux as he coud this fall & bring about a peace between the Sciuex & their neighbours &. &c. &c.

after Dinner we gave Mr. Peter Darion, a Comission to act with a flag & some Cloathes & Provisions & instructions to bring about a peace with the Scioux Mahars, Panies, Ponceries, Ottoes & Missouries- and to employ any trader to take Some of the Cheifs of each or as many of those nations as he Could Perticularly the Sceiouex- I took a Vocabulary of the Scioux Language- and the Answer to a fiew quaries Such as refured to ther Situation, Trade, number War, &c. &c.- This Nation is Divided into 20 Tribes, possessing Seperate interests- Collectively they are noumerous Say from 2 to 3000 men, their interests are so unconnected that Some bands are at war with Nations which other bands are on the most friendly terms. This Great Nation who the French has given the nickname of Sciouex, Call them selves Dar co tar their language is not peculiarly their own, they Speak a great number of words, which is the Same in every respect with the Maha, Poncaser, Osarge & Kanzies. which Clearly proves that those nation at Some Period not more that a century or two past the Same nation- Those Dar ca ter's or Scioux inhabit or rove over the Countrey on the Red river of Lake Winipeck, St. Peter's & the West of the Missippie above Prarie De chain heads of River Demoin, and the Missouri and its waters on the N. Side for a great extent. They are only at peace with 8 Nations, & agreeable to their Calculation at war with twenty odd.- Their trade Corns from the British, except this Band and one on Demoin who trade with the Traders of St Louis- The furnish Beaver Martain, Loues Pikon, Bear and Deer Skins-and have about 40 Traders among them. The Dar co tar or Sceouex rove & follow the Buffalow raise no corn or any thing else the woods & praries affording a Suffcency, the eat Meat, and Substitute the Ground potato which grow in the Plains for bread The names of the Different Tribes or Canoes of the Sceoux or Dar co tar Nation

1st Che cher ree Yank ton (or bois rulay) now present inhabit the Sciouex & Demoin rivers and the Jacques.

2nd Hoin de borto (Poles) they rove on the heads of Souix & Jacqus Rivers-

3rd Me ma car jo (make fence of the river) rove on the Countrey near the big bend of the Missouries

4th Sou on, Teton (People of the Prarie) the rove in the Plains N. of the Riv Missouries above this

5th Wau pa coo tar (Leaf beds) the live near the Prare de Chain near the Missippi

6th Te tar ton (or village of Prarie) rove on the waters of the Mississippi above Prarie de Chain

7th Ne was tar ton (big water Town) rove on the Missippi above the St. Peters River

8th Wau pa tow (Leaf nation) live 10 Leagues up St Peters river

9th Cas Car ba (white man) live 35 Leagus up St Peters river

10th Mi ca cu op si ba (Cut bank) rove on the head of St. Peters

11th Sou on (-) rove on St peters river in the Prareis

12th Sou si toons (-) live 40 Legus up the St peters river

The names of the other bands neither of the Souex's interpters could inform me. in the evening late we gave Mr. Dourion a bottle of whiskey, & he with the Cheifs & his Son Crossed the river and Camped on the Opposit bank- Soon after night a violent wind from the N W. with rain the rain Continud the greater part of the night The river a riseing a little.

[Clark, August 31, 1804] August the 31st 1804 after the Indians got their Brackfast the Chiefs met and arranged themselves in a row with elligent pipes of peace all pointing to our Seets, we Came foward and took our Seets, the Great Cheif The Shake han rose and Spoke to Some length aproving what we had Said and promising to pursue the advice.

Mar to ree 2d Cheif (White Crain) rose and made a Short Speech and refured to the great Chief

Par nar ne Ar par be 3rd Cheif rose and made a Short Speech

Ar ca we char the (the half man) 3d Chief rose & spoke at Some length.
Much to the purpose.

The othe Cheif Said but little one of the warreirs Spoke after all was don & promissed to Support the Chiefs, the promisd to go and See their Great father in the Spring with Mr. Dorion, and to do all things we had advised them to do. and all Concluded by telling the distresses of ther nation by not haveing traders, & wished us to take pity on them, the wanted Powder Ball & a little milk

last night the Indians Danced untill late in their dances we gave them Som knives Tobaco & belts & tape & Binding with which they wer Satisfied

[Clark, September 1, 1804] September 1st Satturday 1804 Mr. Durion left his Kettle which we gave him, which we Sent to him and Set out under a gentle Breeze from the South (raind half the last night,) proceded on- pass Calumet Bluff of a yellowish read & a brownish white Hard clay, this Bluff is about 170 or 180 foot high here the highlands aproach the river on each Side with a jentle assent, opsd. the Bluff a large Island Covered with timber is Situated Close to the L. S. we passed the Island opposit which the high land approach the river on both Side (river ros 3 Inchs last night) passed a large Island Covered with wood on the L. S. Some rain, cloudy all day- the river wide & Hils close on each Side, Came to before night to go & See a Beaver house which is 11/2 Miles to the L. S. of the riv Cap Lewis & my self with two men went to See this house which was represented as high & situated in a Small pond. we could not find the Pon. Drewyer Killed a Buck Elk, it is not necessary to mention fish as we catch them at any place on the river, Camped at the lower point of Bonhomme Island-

[Clark, September 1, 1804] September 1st Satturday 1804 Mr. Dourion left his Kettle & Sent back for it &c. We Set out under a jentle Breeze from the S. (It rained half the last night) proceeded on pass the Bluffs Compsd. of a yellowish red, & brownish White Clay which is a hard as Chalk this Bluff is 170 or 180 feet high, here the High lands approach near the river on each Side, that on the S. S. not So high as that on the L. S. opposit the Bluffs is Situated a large Island Covered with timber close under the L. S. above the lsd the high land approach & form a Clift to the river on the S. S. this Clift is Called White Bear Clift one of those animals haveing been killed in a whole in it

[Clark, September 1, 1804] 1st of September Satturday 1804 Some hard wind and rain, Cloudy all day, the river wide & hills on each Side near the river, passd. a large (1) Island which appeared to be composed of Sand, Covered with Cotton wood close under the S. S. we landed at the Lower point of a large Island on the S. S. Called bon homme or Good man, here Capt Lewis & my Self went out a Short distance on the L. S. to See a Beave house, which was Said to be of Great hite & Situated in a Pond we could not find the house and returned after night Drewyer killed an Elk, & a Beaver. numbers of Cat fish cought, those fish is so plenty that we catch them at any time and place in the river

[Clark, September 2, 1804] 2nd of Sept. Sunday 1804- Set out early & proceeded on passed the Island & Came too above below a yellow Bluff on the S S. the Wind being hard from the N W. verry Cold Some rain all day much Thunder & lightning G Drewyer R. Fields Howard & Newmon Killed four fat Elk on the Isld. we had them Jurked &the Skins Stretched to Cover the Perogues water riseing, I observe Bear grass & Rhue in the Sides of the hills at Sunset the wind luled and cleared up cool- Aired the meet all in high Spirits- Shannon & the man Sent after him has not yet joind us

2 Sepr. description of a antient fortification

(1) From the river on the top of the antient fortification at this the 12 foot high 75 feet Base first Corse is from the river is S 76° W 96 yards. S 84° W. 53 yds. at this angle a kind of ravilene covering a Saleport, bearing East widing N 69 W 300 yds. passed a gate way at 280 yds. the bank lower & forming a right angle of 30 yards- two wings or mounds running from a high nold to the West of the way one 30 yards back of the other Covering the gate (at this place the mound is 15 feet 8 Inches higher than the plain forming a Glassee outwards & 105 feet base N. 32 W. 56 yards N. 20 W. 73 yards this part of the work is about 12 feet high, leavel & about 16 feet wide on the top) at the experation of this course a low irregular work in a Direction to the river, out Side of which is several ovel mounds of about 16 feet high and at the iner part of the Gouge a Deep whole across the Gauge N.

32 W 96 yds. to the Commencment of a wall of about 8 feet high N.81° W. 533 yards to a Deep pond 73 yds in Deamuter, and 200 yards further to a Saleport, where there is evident marks of its being Covered, the Same Course Contined 1030 yards to the river bottom.

One half of the first part of the Fortification is washed into the river, a Second line, has run from the Northrn extremity parrelel with the river (as it appears to have run at that time) N. 56 W. this of different hith from 4 to to 10 feet- The high land is about 3 me. from this fortress, and rise to Small mountains Say from 3 to 400 feet the high land on the opposit or North Side of the Missourie is 110 feet forming a yellow Clay bluff to the water and is leavel back as fur as can be Seen. I am informed by the inteperter & french, that they have Seen, numbers of those fortifications in different parts of this Cty. pirtcularly on the Platt Kansies and the North of this place on the river Jacque.

two Small fortifications is on the Arc Creek on the upper side 1st 1/4 of a mile up & the 2d 1/4 higher, nearly Square each angle 100 yards

[Clark, September 2, 1804] 2nd September Sunday 1804 Set out early and proceeded on Passed the Island and Landed on the S. S above under a yellow Clay bluff of 110 feet high, the wind blew verry hard a head from the N. W. with Some rain and verry Cold, G. Drewnyer R. Fields Newman & howard Killed four fine Elk we had the meat all jurked and the Skins Dried to Cover the Perogue, on the Side of the Bluff I observed Bear Grass & Rhue, at Sun Set the wind luled and Cleared up Cold, the high land on the L. S. is verry high, & uneaven, that on the S. S from 80 to 120 foot & is leavel back but fiew Small Streems falling into the river.

I went out and made a Survey of the antient works which is Situated in a level plain about 3 miles from the hills which are high.

A Discription of the Fortification

(1) Commenceing on the river opsid the Good Mans Island, first Course from the river is

S. 76d W. 96 yards thence

S. 84 W. 53 yards (at this angle a kind of angle or horn work)

N. 69 W. 300 yards to a high part, passing the gateway Covered by two half Circler works one back of the other lower than the main work the gate forms a right angle projecting inward

N.32 W. 56 yards

N 20 W. 73 yards This part of the work appears to have either double, or a covered way. from this Some irregular works appear to have been on mounds between this and the river with a Deep round whole in the center of a gorge formed by another angle ——— (578)

This part of the work is from 10 to 15 feet 8 Inches- the mounds of various hights- the base of the work is from 75 to 105 feet, steep inward and forming a kind of Glassee out wards

the Same Cours continued i e

N. 32°W. 96 yards to the Commencement of a wall from 8 to 10 feet high this corse not on the wall but thro to the commencment of another detached

N. 81° W 1830 yards to the river & above where this bank Strikes the river is the remains of a Circular work

in this Course at 533 yards a Deep Pond of 73 yards Diameter perfectly round is in the Course of the bank which is about 8 feet high, from this Pond the bank it lowers gradually- a bank about the Same hight runs near the river, and must have joined the main work at a part which is now washed into the river, this is also perfectly Streight and widens from the main work, as the river above has washed in its banks for A great distance I cannot form an Idear How those two long works joined- where they Strike the river above, they are about 1100 yds apart, I am informed by our freench interpeters that a great number of those antint works are in Different parts of this Countrey, on the Platt River, Kansus, Jacque, Osarge Mine river &c.

Small one is on Island opposit the one I have Discribed, and two of our Party Saw two of those antient frtresses on the Pittiet Arc Creek on the upper Side near the mouth, each angle of which were 100 yards and about 8 feet high-

[Clark, September 3, 1804] 3rd September Monday 1804. Set out at Sun rise, verry Cold morning clear and but little wind from the N W. we proceeded on, the river wide, took an obsivation below Plumb Creek which mouths on the S S. this Creek is Small & corns in between 2 white banks, Great quantities of Plumbs of a most delisious flavour, I have collected the Seed of 3 Kinds which I intend to Send to my brother, also Som grapes of a Superior quallity large & well flavoured, the river is riseing a little, Several wild Goats Seen in the Plains they are wild & fleet Elk & Buffalow is verry plenty, Scercely any timber in Countrey except a little on the river in the Points. Saw Some Signs of the 2 men who are a head, Colter has not over taken Shannon Camped on the L. S. at the edge of a Plain-

[Clark, September 3, 1804] 3rd of September Monday 1804 a verry Cold morning wind from N. W. we Set out at Sun rise, & proceeded on to a Bluff below the mouth of Plumb 12 yds. Creek on the S. S. and took an obsevation of the Suns Altitude

This Creek is Small it "abounds with blumbs of a Delicious flavour" the River is wide and Crouded with Sand bars- it is riseing a little but little timber in this Countrey all that is, is on the river in the points. we Came too on the L. Sin the edge of a Plain an Camped for the night- we Saw Some Signs of the two men Shannon & Colter, Shannon appeared to be a head of Colter- The White banks appear to Continu on both sides of the river. Grapes plenty and finely flavered-

[Clark, September 4, 1804] 4th of September Tuesday 1804. a verry Cold wind from South E. by S. we Set out early proceeded on to the mouth of a Small Creek in the bend to the L. S. Called white line at 1 1/2 miles furthr passed the mouth of a R au platte or White paint Cr about 25 yd. on Same Side Called, I walked on the top of the hill forming a Cliff Covd. with red Ceeder an extensive view from this hill, at 3 Miles from the Creek the high land jut the river forming a Bluff of Bluish Clay Continu 1 1/2 miles Came to at the mouth of Qui courre (rapid) this river Comes roleing its Sands whuch (is corse) into the Missouris from the S W by W. this river is 152 yards across the water and not exeeding 4 feet Deep it does not rise high when it Does it Spreds over a large Surface, and is not navagable it has a Great many Small Islands & Sand bars I went up this river 3 miles to the Spot the Panis once had a large Village on the upper Side in a butiful extensive Plain riseing gradialy from the river I fel into a Buffalow road joined the boat late at night at the Pania Island.

[Clark, September 4, 1804] 4th September Tuesday 1804 a verry Cold wind from the S. S. E, we Set out early and proceeded on the mouth of a Small Creek in a bend to the L. S. Called White lime, at 1 1/2 miles higher up passed a large Creek on the L. S. Called or white paint between those two Creeks (the latter of which is abt. 30 yds. wide) we passed under a Bluff of red Ceeder, at 4 mes. 1/2 passed the mouth of the River Que Courre (rapid R) on the L. S. and Came to a Short distance above, this River is 152 yards wide at the mouth & 4 feet Deep Throwing out Sands like the Platt (only Corser) forming bars in its mouth, I went up this river three miles to a butiful Plain on the upper Side where the Panias once had a Village this river widens above its mouth and is devided by Sand and Islands, the Current verry rapid, not navagable for even Canoos without Great dificulty owing to its Sands; the colour like that of the Plat is light the heads of this river is not known, it Corns into the Missourie from the S. W. by West, and I am told that is Genl. Course Some distance up is parrelel with the Missourie

[Clark, September 5, 1804] 5th September 1804 Wednesday, Set out early the wind blew hard from the South as it has for Some Days past, we Set up a jury mast & Sailed, I saw a large gangue of Turkeys, also Grous Seen Passed a large Island of about 3 miles long in the Middle of the river opposit the head of this Island the Poncarre River Coms into the Missourei on the L. S.- the S. S is a Clift under which great numbers of Springs run out of mineral water, Saw Several wild goats on the Clift & Deer with black tales,- Sent Shields & Gibson to the Poncas Towns, which is Situated on the Ponca river on the lower side about two miles from its mouth in an open butiful Plain, at this time this nation is out hunting the biffalow they raise no corn or Beens, Gibson killed a Buffalow in the Town, The two men which has been absent several Days is ahead, we came to on the upper pt. of a large Island at 3 oClock to make a mast Sent out Some hunters on the Island (which I call no preserve Island, at this place we used the last of our Preservs) They killed 3 bucks, & two Elk which welurked

[Clark, September 5, 1804] September 5th Wednesday 1804 Set out early the winds blew hard from the South, Goats turkeys Seen to day, passed a large Island (1) opsd. this Island near the head the Poncasar River Coms into the Missourie from the West this river is about 30 yards wide. dispatched two men to the Poncaries Village Situated in a handsom Plain on the lower Side of this Creek about two miles from the Missourie (the Poncasars nation is Small and at this time out in the praries hunting the Buffalow), one of the men Sent to the Village Killed a Buffalow in the town, the other, a large Buck near it, Some Sign of the two men who is a head.

above the Island on the S. S We passed under a Bluff of Blue earth, under which Seveal Mineral Springs broke out of the water of which had a taste like Salts, we Came too on the upper point of a large Island (which I call No preserves Island) here we made a Ceeder Mast, our hunters brought in three bucks, and two elks this evening which we had jurked

One of the hunter Shields, informed that he Saw Several black tailed
Deer, near the Poncaser Village

[Lewis, September 5, 1804] Sept 5th saw some wild goats or antelopes on the hill above the Glauber Salts Springs they ran off we could not discover them sufficiently distinctly to discribe even their colour their track is as large as a deer reather broader & more blont at the point

This day one of our hunters brought us a Serpent beautifully variagated with small black spotts of a romboydal form on a light yellow white ground the black pedominates most on the back the whiteis yellow on the sides, and it is nearly white on the belly with a few party couloured scuta on which the black shews but imperfectly and the colouring matter seems to be underneath the Scuta- it is not poisonous it hisses remarkably loud; it has 221 Scuta on the belly and 51 on the tale, the eyes are of a dark black colour the tale terminates in a sharp point like the substance of a cock's spur- Length 4 Ft. 6 I.

[Clark, September 6, 1804] 6th Septr Thursday 1804, a Storm this morning from the N W. at day light which lasted a fiew minits, Set out after the Storm was over and proceeded on a hard wind ahead passed the island which is Seperated from the L. Side by a narrow Channel. the morning is verry Cold.

Camped on S. Side before night no timbering in reach ahead, R. Fields killed 2 Deer Saw Buffalow, & Goats this evening, the river riseing a little

[Clark, September 6, 1804] Septr. 6th Thursday 1804 a Storm this morning from the N. W. which lasted a fiew minits, we Set out and proceeded on passed the head of the Isd. which is Seperated from the L. S by a narrow Channel, a hard wind from the N. W. a verry Cold day- we Camped on the S. S. at the upper point of Some timber, Some time before night, no timber, no timber being in reach.

I saw Several goats on the hills on the S. S. also Buffalow in great numbers

[Clark, September 7, 1804] 7th September Friday 1804. a verry Cold morning Set out at Day light

near the foot of this high Nole we discovered a Village of an annamale the french Call the Prarie Dog which burrow in the grown & with the rattle Snake and Killed one & Caught one Dog alive caught in a whole 2 frogs near the hole Killed a Dark Rattle Snake with a Prairie dog in him

The Village of those little dogs is under the ground a conisiderable distance we dig under 6 feet thro rich hard clay without getting to their Lodges Some of their wholes we put in 5 barrels of water without driveing them out, we caught one by the water forceing him out. ther mouth resemble the rabit, head longer, legs short, & toe nails

long ther tail like a ground Squirel which they Shake and make chattering noise ther eyes like a dog, their colour is Gray and Skin contains Soft fur

[Clark, September 7, 1804] 7th Septr. 1804 Septr. 7th Friday a verry Cold morning Set out at day light we landed after proceding 5 1/2 miles, near the foot of a round mounting which I saw yesterday resembling a dome.

Capt Lewis & my Self walked up, to the top which forms a Cone and is about 70 feet higher than the high lands around it, the Bass is about 300 foot in decending this Cupola, discovered a Village of Small animals that burrow in the grown (those animals are Called by the french Pitite Chien) Killed one & Cought one a live by poreing a great quantity of water in his hole we attempted to dig to the beds of one of thos animals, after diging 6 feet, found by running a pole down that we were not half way to his Lodges, we found 2 frogs in the hole, and killed a Dark rattle Snake near with a Ground rat in him, (those rats are numerous) the Village of those animals Covs. about 4 acrs of Ground on a Gradual decent of a hill and Contains great numbers of holes on the top of which those little animals Set erect make a Whistleing noise and whin allarmed Slip into their hole- we por'd into one of the holes 5 barrels of water without filling it, Those Animals are about the Size of a Small Squrel Shorter & thicker, the head much resembling a Squirel in every respect, except the ears which is Shorter, his tail like a ground Squirel which thy Shake & whistle when allarmd. the toe nails long, they have fine fur & the longer hair is gray, it is Said that a kind of Lizard also a Snake reside with those animals. Camped

[Lewis and Clark, September 8, 1804] 8th of September 1804 Satturday. Set out early and proceeded on under a Gentle breese from the S. E. at 3 mes passed the place where Trodow wintered one winter

I went out to day on the S. S with a view to find Some of the little dogs, and Coats, Traveled over a riged and mountanious Countrey without water & riseing to 5 or 600 hundred feet, Islands & Sands interveneing prevt. my getting to the boat untill after night, in my absent Capt. Lewis killed a Buffalow, I saw Greid many Buffalow & white wolves. (Sailed all day)

[Clark, September 8, 1804] 8th of September Satturday Set out early and proceeded on under a gentle Breeze from the S. E, at 3 mes. passed the house of Troodo where he wintered in 96. Called the Pania house, above is high hills on the S. S. on the S. S. much higher hills than usial appear to the North distant 8 miles recently burnt- pass 3 Small Islands at about 5 miles on this Course on the S. S. here Capt. Lewis Killed a Buffalow in the river, and this men one other Came to on the lower point of an Island in the midlle of the river Called Boat Island and incamped, jurked the meet Killed to day Consisting of 2 buffalow, one large Buck Elk one Small, 4 Deer 3 Turkeys & a Squirel, I joined the boat at this Camp, The Countrey on the S S. is pore & broken.

[Clark and Whitehouse, September 9, 1804] 9th Septembr Sunday, Set out at Sunrise and proceeded on passed the Island Several gangus of Buffalow on the Sides of the hils on the L. S. halted on L. Side took breakfast. Capt. Clark walked on Shore, we proceeded on

R. Fields came to the Boat had killed one Buffalow. passed red ceeder on the edge of the hills on bouth Sides of the river but most on the bluff on

[Clark, September 9, 1804] 9th September Sunday 1804 Set out at Sunrise and proceeded on passed the head of the Island on which we Camped, passed three Sand & willow Islands, the Sand bars So noumerous, it is not worth mentioning them, the river Shoal or Shallow wind S E Came too and Camped on a Sand bar on the L. S. Capt Lewis went out to Kill a buffalow. I walked on Shore all this evening with a view to Kill a Goat or Some Prarie Dogs in the evening after the boat landed, I Derected my Servent York with me to kill a Buffalow near the boat from a numbr. then Scattered in the plains, I saw at one view near the river at least 500 Buffalow, those animals have been in view all day feeding in the Plains on the L. S. every Copse of timber appear to have Elk or Deer. D. Killed 3 Deer, I Kiled a Buffalow Y. 2, R. Fields one.

[Lewis, September 9, 1804] Sept. 9th Capt. Clark found on the Lard shore under a high bluff issuing from a blue earth a bittuminus matter resembling molasses in consistance, colour and taste-

[Clark, September 10, 1804] 10th September Monday a Cloudy morning Set out early under a Gentle Breeze from the S E. passed two Small Islands one on the L. S. & the other on the S. S. both in the first Course at 101/2 miles passed the lower pt. of Ceder Island Situated in a bend to the L. S. this Island is about 2 miles long Covered with red Ceder, the river is verry Shallow opsd. this Island- below the Island on the top of a ridge we found a back bone with the most of the entire laying Connected for 45 feet those bones are petrified, Some teeth & ribs also Connected. at 3 mes. above ceder I passed a large Island on the S. S. to this Island Several Elk Swam above this Island on the Midle is Situated 2 Islands small one above the other, those Islands are Called mud Islands and camped on the upper Island of them 3 Buffalow 1 Elk &c. Killed to day, river falling a large Salt Spring of remarkable Salt water much frequented by Buffalow, Some Smaller Springs on the Side of the hill above less Salt, the water excesiv Salt, and is 11/2 miles from the river on the S. W. or L. S. opposit Ceder Island-

[Clark, September 10, 1804] 10th September Monday 1804. a Cloudy dark morning Set out early, a Gentle breeze from the S. E, passed two Small Islands on the L. S. and one on the S. S. all in the first Course at 101/2 miles passed the lower point of an (2) Island Covered with red Ceeder Situated in a bend on the L. S. this Island is about 2 Moles in length (1) below this on a hill on the L. S. we found the back bone of a fish, 45 feet long tapering to the tale, &c. those joints were Seperated and all petrefied, opposit this Island 11/2 miles from the river on the L. S. is a large Salt Spring of remarkable Salt water. one other high up the hill 1/2 me. not So Salt.

we proceeded on under a Stiff Breeze. three miles above Ceder Island passed a large Island on the S. S, no water on that Side (3) Several elk Swam to this Island passed a Small Island near the Center of the river, of a mile in length, and Camped on one aboav Seperated from the other by a narrow Chanel, Those Islands are Called Mud Islands- the hunters killed 3 fuffalow & one Elk to day. The river is falling a little, Great number of Buffalow & Elk on the hill Sides feeding deer Scerce

we came too at the mouth of a Creek on the L. S. at Dark in a heavy Shower of rain, it Continued to rain the greater part of the night, with a hard wind from the N W Cold

[Clark, September 11, 1804] Septr. 11th Tuesday 1804 Set out early a Cloudy morning the river verry wide from one hill to the other, with many Sand bars passed the Isd. on which we lay at a mile passed three Isds. one on the L. S. (1/4 of a mile from it on the L. S. a village of little Dogs. I Killed four, this village is 800 yards wide & 970 yds. long on a jentle Slope of a hill in a plain, those animals are noumerous) the other two Islands are on the S. S. the river is verry Shallow & wide, the boat got a ground Several times- The man G Shannon, who left us with the horses above the Mahar Village, and beleving us to be ahead pushed on as long as he Could, joined us he Shot away what fiew Bullets he had with him, and in a plentifull) Countrey like to have Starvd. he was 12 days without provision, Subsisting on Grapes at the Same the Buffalow, would Come within 30 yards of his Camp, one of his horses gave out & he left him before his last belluts were Consumed- I saw 3 large Spoted foxes today a black tailed Deer, & Killed a Buck elk & 2 Deer, one othr Elk 2 Deer & a Porkipine Killed to day at 12 oClock it became Cloudy and rained all the after noon, & night.

[Clark, September 11, 1804] Sept. 11th Tuesday 1804 a cloudy morning, Set out verry early, the river wide & Shallow the bottom narrow, & the river Crouded with Sand bars, passed the Island on which we lay at one mile-, pased three Islands one on the L. S. and 2 on the S. S. opposit the Island on the L. S. I Saw a village of Barking Squriel 970 yds. long, and 800 yds. wide Situated on a gentle Slope of a hill, those anamals are noumerous, I killed 4 with a view to have their Skins Stufed.

here the man who left us with the horses 22 days ago and has been a head ever Since joined, us nearly Starved to Death, he had been 12 days without any thing to eate but Grapes & one Rabit, which he Killed by shooting a piece of hard Stick in place of a ball-. This man Supposeing the boat to be a head pushed on as long as he Could, when he became weak and fiable deturmined to lay by and waite for a tradeing boat, which is expected Keeping one horse for the last resorse,- thus a man had like to have Starved to death in a land of Plenty for the want of Bulletes or Something to kill his meat we Camped on the L. S. above the mouth of a run a hard rain all the after noon, & most of the night, with hard wind from the N W. I walked on Shore the fore part of this day over Some broken Country which Continus about 3 miles back & then is leavel & rich all Plains, I saw Several foxes & Killed a Elk & 2 Deer. & Squirels the men with me killed an Elk, 2 Deer & a Pelican

Some rain all day to day & Cold

I walked on Shore Saw Several foxes Several Villages of Prarie dogs, and a number of Grouse

[Clark, September 12, 1804] Septr. 12th Wednesday 1804 a Dark Cloudy Day the wind hard from the N. W. we passed (1) a Island the middle of the river at the head of which we found great dificuley in passing between the Sand bars the water Swift and Shallow, it took 3/4 of the day to make one mile, we Camped on the L. S. opsd. a Village of Barking Prarie Squriels

I walked out in the morning and Saw Several Villages of those little animals, also a great number of Grous & 3 foxes, and observed Slate & Coal mixed, Some verry high hills on each Side of the river. rains a little all day.

[Clark, September 13, 1804] 13th Septr. Thursday 1804 a Dark Drizzley Day, G D Cought 4 Beaver last night the winds from the N W. Cold Set out early and proceeded on verry well passed a number of Sand bars, Capt Lewis killed a Porcupin on a Cotton treee fieeding on the leaves & bowers of the Said tree, the water is verry Shallow being Crouded with Sand bars Camped on the S. Side under a Bluff. the Bluffs on the S. S. not So much impregnated with mineral as on the L. S. muskeetors verry troublesom-.

[Lewis, September 13, 1804] September 13th Killed a bluewinged teal and a Porcupine; found it in a Cottonwood tree near the river on the Lard. Shore- the leaves of the Cottonwood were much distroyed- as were those of the Cottonwood trees in it's neighbourhood. I therefore supposed that it fed on the folage of trees at this season, the flesh of this anamal is a pleasant and whoalsome food- the quills had not yet obtained their usual length- it has four long toes, before on each foot, and the same number behind with the addition of one short one on each hind foot on the inner side. the toes of the feet are armed with long black nails particularly the fore feet- they weigh from 15 to 20 lbs- they resemble the slowth very much in the form of their hands, or fore feet. their teeth and eyes are like the bever

[Clark, September 14, 1804] Septr 14th Friday 1804 Course Dists & rifur. Set out early proceeded on passed Several Sand bars water wide & Shallow N. 68° W. 23/4 mes. to a pt. of high Land on the L. S. passed a round Island on the S S.- Caught 3 beaver last night, Some drizzeley rain Cloudy & Disagreeable and Som hard Showers, I walked on Shore with a view to find an old Volcano Said to be in this neghbourhood by Mr. McKey I was Some distance out Could not See any Signs of a Volcanoe, I killed a Goat, which is peculier to this Countrey about the hite of a Grown Deer Shorter, its horns Coms out immediately abov its eyes broad 1 Short prong the other arched & Soft the color is a light gray with black behind its ears, white round its neck, no beard, his Sides & belly white, and around its taile which is Small & white and Down its hams, actively made his brains on the back of its head, his noisterals large, his eyes like a Sheep only 2 hoofs on each foot no antelrs (more like the antelope or gazella of Africa than any other Specis of Goat). Shields Killed a Hare weighing 6 1/2 lb. verry pore, the head narrow and its ears 3 Inches wide and 6 long, from the fore to the end of the hind foot; is 2 feet 11 Inch. hite 1 foot 13/4 its tail long & thick white, clearly the mountain Hare of Europe, a rainy evening all wett The Soil of those Plains washes down into the flats, with the Smallest rain & disolves & mixes with the water we See back from the river high hills in a leavel plain, evidently the remains of mountains, what mud washed into the river within those few days has made it verry mudy, passed two Small Creeks on the L. S. & Camped below a 3rd on the L. S. rained all evening

[Clark, September 14, 1804] 14th Septr. Friday 1804. Set out early proceeded on passed Several Sand bars the river wide and Shallow 3 beaver Caught last night, Drizeley rain in the forepart of this day, cloudy and disagreeable, I walked on Shore with a view to find an old Vulcanio, Said to be in this neighbourhood by Mr. J. McKey of St. Charles. I walked on Shore the whole day without Seeing any appearance of the Villcanoe, in my walk I Killed a Buck Goat of this Countrey, about the hight. of the Grown Deer, its body Shorter, the Horns which is not very hard and forks 2/3 up one prong Short the other round & Sharp arched, and is imediately above its Eyes the Colour is a light gray with black behind its ears down its neck, and its Jaw white round its neck, its Sides and its rump round its tail which is Short & white verry actively made, has only a pair of hoofs to each foot. his brains on the back of his head, his Norstral large, his eyes like a Sheep- he is more like the Antilope or Gazella of Africa than any other Species of Goat. Shields Killed a Hare like the mountain hare of Europe, waighing 6 1/4 pounds (altho pore) his head narrow, its ears large i, e, 6 Inches long & 3 Inchs wide one half of each white, the other & out part a lead grey from the toe of the hind foot to toe of the for foot is 2 feet 11 Inches, the hith is 1 foot 1 Inche & 3/4, his tail long thick & white.

The rain Continued the Greater part of the day in My ramble I observed, that all those parts of the hills which was Clear of Grass easily disolved and washed into the river and bottoms, and those hils under which the river run, Sliped into it and disolves and mixes with the water of the river, the bottoms of the river was covered with the water and mud frome the hills about three Inches deep- those bottoms under the hils which is Covered with Grass also a great quantity of mud.

Passed 2 Small Creeks on the L. S and Camped below the third, (the place that Shannon the man who went a head lived on grapes) Some heavy Showers of rain all wet, had the Goat & rabit Stufed rained all night

[Lewis, September 14, 1804] September 14th 1804 this day Capt. Clark killed a male wild goat so called- it's weight 65 lbs.

F I length from point of nose to point of tail 4 9 hight to the top of the wethers 3 - do. behind 3 - girth of the brest 3 1 girth of the neck close to the shoulders 2 2 do. near the head 1 7

Eye deep sea green, large percing and reather prominent, & at or near the root of the horn within one 1/4 inches

[Lewis, September 14, 1804] Sept. 14th 1804. Shields killed a hare of the prarie, weight six pounds and 1/4

F. I. Length from point of hind to extremity fore feet 2 11 hight when standing erect 1 13/4 length from nose to tale 2 1 girth of body 1 23/4 length of tale - 61/2 length of the year - 51/2 width of do. do. - 3 1/8 from the extremity of the hip to the toe of the hind foot 1 31/2

the eye is large and prominent the sight is circular, deep sea green, and occupyes one third of the width of the eye the remaining two thirds is a ring of a bright yellowish silver colour. the years ar placed at the upper part of the head and very near to each other, the years are very flexable, the anamall moves them with great ease and quickness and can contrat and foald them on his back or delate them at pleasure- the front outer foald of the year is a redis brown, the inner foalds or those which ly together when the years are thrown back and wich occupy two thirds of the width of the year is of a clear white colour except one inch at the tip of the year which is black, the hinder foald is of a light grey- the head back sholders and outer part of the thighs are of a ledcoloured grey the sides as they approache the belly grow lighter becomeing gradually more white the belly and brest are white with a shad of lead colour- the furr is long and fine- the tale is white round and blounty pointed the furr on it is long and extreemly fine and soft when it runs it carry's it's tale strait behind the direction of the body- the body is much smaller and more length than the rabbit in proportion to it's height- the teeth are like those of the hair or rabbit as is it's upper lip split- it's food is grass or herbs- it resorts the open plains, is extreemly fleet and never burrows or takes shelter in the ground when pursued, I measured the leaps of one which I suprised in the plains on the 17th Inst. and found them 21 feet the ground was a little decending they apear to run with more ease and to bound with greater agility than any anamall I ever saw. this anamal is usually single seldom associating in any considerable numbers.

[Clark, September 15, 1804] September the 15th Satturday 1804 Set out early passed the Mouth of a creek on the L S. where Shannon lived on grapes waiting for Mr. Clintens boat Supposeing we had went on, Capt Lewis and my Self halted at the mouth of White River & wend up a Short Crossed &, this river is about 400 yards, the water Confined within 150 yards, the Current regularly Swift, much resembling the Missourie, Sand bars makeing out from the points, Some Islands we Sent up two men to go up this river one Day and Meet us to morrow we proceeded on passed a Small Island Covered with Ceder timber, & great number of rabits, no game except rabits, and Camped on the S. S. opposit a large Creek, on which there is more wood than usial on Creeks in this quaterr this creek raised 14 feet last rain I Killed a Buck elk & a Deer.

[Clark, September 15, 1804] 15th September Satturday 1804 Set out early passed the mo of the Creek, and the mouth of White river; (1) Capt Lewis and my Self went up this river a Short distance and Crossed, found that this differed verry much from the Plat or que Courre, threw out but little Sand, about 300 yard wide, the water confind within 150 yards, the current regular & Swift much resemblig the Missourie, with Sand bars from the points a Sand Island in the mouth, in the point is a butifull Situation for a Town 3 Gradual assents, and a much Greater quantity of timber about the mouth of this river than usial, we concluded to Send Some distance up this river detached Sjt. Gass & R. Fields. we proceeded on passed a Small (2) Island Covered with Ceeder on I Saw great numbers of Rabits & Grapes, this Island is Small & Seperated from a large Sand Isd. at its upper point by a narrow Channel, & is Situated nearest the L. Side. Camped on the S. S. opposit the mouth of a large Creek on which there is more timber than is usial on Creeks of this Size, this Creek raised 14 feet the last rains. I killed a Buck Elk & Deer, this evening is verry Cold, Great many wolves of Different Sorts howling about us. the wind is hard from the N W this evening

[Lewis, September 16, 1804] Sunday September 16th 1804. This morning set out at an early hour, and come too at 1/2 after 7 A.M. on the Lard. Shore 11/4 miles above the mouth of a small creek which we named Corvus, in consequence of having kiled a beatiful bird of that genus near it we concluded to ly by at this place the ballance of this day and the next, in order to dry our baggage which was wet by the heavy showers of rain which had fallen within the last three days, and also to lighten the boat by transfering a part of her lading to the red perogue, which we now determined to take on with us to our winter residence wherever that might be; while some of the men were imployed in this necessary labour others were dressing of skins washing and mending their cloaths &c. Capt. Clark and myself kiled each a buck immediately on landing near our encampment; the deer were very gentle and in great numbers on this bottom which had more timber on it than any part of the river we had seen for many days past, consisting of Cottonwood Elm, some indifferent ash and a considerable quanty of a small species of white oak which is loaded with acorns of an excellent flavor very little of the bitter roughness of the nuts of most species of oak, the leaf of this oak is small pale green and deeply indented, it seldom rises higher than thirty feet is much branched, the bark is rough and thick and of a light colour; the cup which contains the acorn is fringed on it's edges and imbraces the nut about one half; the acorns were now falling, and we concluded that the number of deer which we saw here had been induced thither by the acorns of which they are remarkably fond. almost every species of wild game is fond of the acorn, the Buffaloe Elk, deer, bear, turkies, ducks, pigegians and even the wolves feed on them; we sent three hunters out who soon added eight deer and two Buffaloe to our strock of provisions; the Buffaloe were so pour that we took only the tongues skins and marrow bones; the skins were particularly acceptable as we were in want of a covering for the large perogue to secure the baggage; the clouds during this day and night prevented my making any observations. Sergt. Gass and Reubin Fields whom we had sent out yesterday to explore the White river returnd at four oclock this day and reported that they had foil meanders of that stream about 12 miles r's general course West, the present or principal channel iro yards wide; the coulour of the water and rapidity and manner of runing resembled the Missouri presisely; the country broken on the border of the river about a mile, when the level planes commence and extend as far as the eye can reach on either side; as usual no timber appeared except such as from the steep declivities of hills, or their moist situations, were sheltered from the effects of the fire. these extensive planes had been lately birnt and the grass had sprung up and was about three inches high. vast herds of Buffaloe deer Elk and Antilopes were seen feeding in every direction as far as the eye of the observer could reach.

[Clark, September 16, 1804] September 16th Sunday, we proceeded on 11/4 Miles and Camped on the L. Side in a butifull Plain Surounded with timber in which we Saw Severall Der, we delayed here for the purpose of Drying the articles which were wet & the cloathes to Load the Perogue which we had intended to send back, finding the water too Shoal Deturmind to take on the Perogue also to make Some observations for Longitude &c. the two men G. & R. F. joined us and informed "that the river as far as they were up had much the Appearance of the river about the mouth, but little timber and that chiefly elm", the up land between this river & the White river is fine, Great numbers of Goat, Deer of three kinds, Buffalow, & wolves, & Barking Squrels, The fallow Deer, Cloudy, all day Cleaning out the boat examining & Drying the goods, & loading the Perogue, I killed 2 Deer Capt Lewis one & a Buffalow, one Buffalow & five other Deer Killed. I observed Pine Burs & Burch Sticks in the Drift wood up white river which Coms in on the L. S. imedeately in the point is a butifull Situation for a town 3 Gentle rises, & more timber about the mouth of this river than usial

[Clark, September 16, 1804] 16th of September Sunday 1804 We Set out verry early & proceed'd on 11/4 miles between Sand bars and Came too on the L. S. (1)- deturmined to dry our wet thig and liten the boat which we found could not proceed with the present load for this purpose we Concluded to detain the Perogue we had intended to Send back & load her out of the boat & detain the Soldiers untill Spring & Send them from our winter quarters. We put out those articles which was wet, Clean'd the boat & perogus, examined all the Locker Bails &. &c. &.

This Camp is Situated in a butifull Plain Serounded with Timber to the extent of 3/4 of a mile in which there is great quantities of fine Plumbs The two men detachd up the White river joined us here & informed that the river as far as they were up had much the appearance of the Missourie Som Islands & Sands little Timber Elm, (much Signs of Beaver, Great many buffalow) & Continud its width, they Saw & well as my Self Pine burs & Sticks of Birch in the Drift wood up this river, They Saw also Number of Goats Such as I Killed, also wolves near the Buffalow falling Deer, & the Barking Squrels Villages Capt. Lewis went to hunt & See the Countrey near the Kamp he killed a Buffalow & a Deer

Cloudy all day I partly load the empty Perogue out of the Boat. I killed 2 Deer & the party 4 Deer & a Buffalow the we kill for the Skins to Cover the Perogus, the meet too pore to eat. Capt Lewis went on an Island above our Camp, this Island is abt. one mile long, with a Great purpotion ceder timber near the middle of it

I gave out a flannel Shirt to each man, & powder to those who had expended thers

[Lewis, September 17, 1804] Monday September 17th 1804. Having for many days past confined myself to the boat, I determined to devote this day to amuse myself on shore with my gun and view the interior of the country lying between the river and the Corvus Creek- accordingly before sunrise I set out with six of my best hunters, two of whom I dispatched to the lower side of Corvus creek, two with orders to hunt the bottoms and woodland on the river, while I retained two others to acompany me in the intermediate country. one quarter of a mile in rear of our camp which was situated in a fine open grove of cotton wood passed a grove of plumb trees loaded with fruit and now ripe. observed but little difference between this fruit and that of a similar kind common to the Atlantic States. the trees are smaller and more thickly set. this forrest of plumb trees garnish a plain about 20 feet more lelivated than that on which we were encamped; this plain extends back about a mile to the foot of the hills one mile distant and to which it is gradually ascending this plane extends with the same bredth from the creek below to the distance of near three miles above parrallel with the river, and is intirely occupied by the burrows of the barking squril hertefore discribed; this anamal appears here in infinite numbers, and the shortness and virdue of grass gave the plain the appearance throughout it's whole extent of beatifull bowlinggreen in fine order. it's aspect is S. E. a great number of wolves of the small kind, balks and some pole-cats were to be seen. I presume that those anamals feed on this squirril.- found the country in every direction for about three miles intersected with deep reveries and steep irregular hills of 100 to 200 feet high; at the tops of these hills the country breakes of as usual into a fine leavel plain extending as far as the eye can reach. from this plane I had an extensive view of the river below, and the irregular hills which border the opposite sides of the river and creek. the surrounding country had been birnt about a month before and young grass had now sprung up to hight of 4 Inches presenting the live green of the spring. to the West a high range of hills, strech across the country from N. to S and appeared distant about 20 miles; they are not very extensive as I could plainly observe their rise and termination no rock appeared on them and the sides were covered with virdue similar to that of the plains this senery already rich pleasing and beatiful, was still farther hightened by immence herds of Buffaloe deer Elk and Antelopes which we saw in every direction feeding on the hills and plains. I do not think I exagerate when I estimate the number of Buffaloe which could be compreed at one view to amount to 3000. my object was if possible to kill a female Antelope having already procured a male; I pursued my rout on this plain to the west flanked by my two hunters untill eight in the morning when I made the signal for them to come to me which they did shortly after. we rested our selves about half an hour, and regailed ourselves on half a bisquit each and some jirk of Elk which we had taken the precaution to put in our pouches in the morning before we set out, and drank of the water of a small pool which had collected on this plain from the rains which had fallen some days before. We had now after various windings in pursuit of several herds of antelopes which we had seen on our way made the distance of about eight miles from our camp. we found the Antelope extreemly shye and watchfull insomuch that we had been unable to get a shot at them; when at rest they generally seelect the most elivated point in the neighbourhood, and as they are watchfull and extreemly quick of sight and their sense of smelling very accute it is almost impossible to approach them within gunshot; in short they will frequently discover and flee from you at the distance of three miles. I had this day an opportunity of witnessing the agility and superior fleetness of this anamal which was to me really astonishing. I had pursued and twice surprised a small herd of seven, in the first instance they did not discover me distinctly and therefore did not run at full speed, tho they took care before they rested to gain an elivated point where it was impossible to approach them under cover except in one direction and that happened to be in the direction from which the wind blew towards them; bad as the chance to approach them was, I made the best of my way towards them, frequently peeping over the ridge with which I took care to conceal myself from their view the male, of which there was but one, frequently incircled the summit of the hill on which the females stood in a group, as if to look out for the approach of danger. I got within about 200 paces of them when they smelt me and fled; I gained the top of the eminece on which they stood, as soon as possible from whence I had an extensive view of the country the antilopes which had disappeared in a steep revesne now appeared at the distance of about three miles on the side of a ridge which passed obliquely across me and extended about four miles. so soon had these antelopes gained the distance at which they had again appeared to my view I doubted at ferst that they were the same that I had just surprised, but my doubts soon vanished when I beheld the rapidity of their flight along the ridge before me it appeared reather the rappid flight of birds than the motion of quadrupeds. I think I can safely venture the asscertion that the speed of this anamal is equal if not superior to that of the finest blooded courser.- this morning I saws

[Clark, September 17, 1804] 17th of Septr. Monday 1804 above White river Dried all those articles which had got wet by the last rain, a fine day Capt Lewis went hunting with a vew to seethe Countrey &its productions, he was out all Day Killed a Buffalow & a remarkable bird of the Spicies of Corvus, long tail of a Greenish Purple, Varigated a Beck like a Crow white round its neck comeing to a point on its back, its belley white feet like a Hawk abt. the size of a large Pigeon Capt Lewis returned at Dark. I took the Meridian & equal altitudes to day made the Lattitude.

Colter Killed a Goat, & a Curious kind of Deer, a Darker grey than Common the hair longer & finer, the ears verry large & long a Small resepitical under its eye its tail round and white to near the end which is black & like a Cow in every other respect like a Deer, except it runs like a goat. large.

The hunters brought in 8 fallow Deer & 5 Common Deer to day, Great numbers of Buffalow in the Praries, also a light Coloured woolf Covered with hair & corse fur, also a Small wolf with a large bushey tail- Some Goats of a Different Kind Seen to day,- Great many Plumbs, rabits, Porcupines & barking Squrels, Capt Lewis Killed a rattle Snake in a village of the Squirel's and Saw a Hair to day. Wind from the S. W. we finished Drying our Provisions Some of which was wet and Spoiled,

[Clark, September 17, 1804] 17th of September Monday 1804 Dried all our wet articles this fine Day, Capt Lewis went out with a View to see the Countrey and its productions, he was out all day he killed a Buffalow and a remarkable Bird of the Corvus Species long tail the upper part of the feathers & also the wing is of a purplish variated Green, the black, a part of the wing feather are white edjed with black, white belly, white from the root of the wings to Center of the back is white, the head nake breast & other parts are black the Becke like a Crow. abt. the Size of a large Pigion. a butifull thing (See Suplement in No. 3)

I took equal altitudes and a meridian altitude. Capt. Lewis returned at Dark, Colter Killed a Goat like the one I killed and a curious kind of deer of a Dark gray Colr. more so than common, hair long & fine, the ears large & long, a Small reseptical under the eyes; like an Elk, the Taile about the length of Common Deer, round (like a Cow) a tuft of black hair about the end, this Speces of Deer jumps like a goat or Sheep

8 fallow Deer 5 Common & 3 buffalow killed to day, Capt. Lewis Saw a hare & Killed a Rattle Snake in a village of B. squerels The wind from S. W. Dryed our provisions, Some of which was much Damaged.

[Lewis, September 17, 1804] Sept. 17th one of the hunters killed a bird of the Corvus genus and order of the pica & about the size of a jack-daw with a remarkable long tale. beautifully variagated. it note is not disagreeable though loudit is twait twait twait, twait; twait, twait twait, twait.

F I from tip to tip of wing 1 10 Do. beak to extremity of tale 1 81/2 of which the tale occupys 1 1 from extremity of middle toe to hip 51/2

it's head, beak, and neck are large for a bird of it's size; the beak is black, and of a convex and cultrated figure, the chops nearly equal, and it's base large and beset with hairs- the eyes are black encircled with a narrow ring of yellowish black it's head, neck, brest & back within one inch of the tale are of a fine glossey black, as are also the short fathers of the under part of the wing, the thies and those about the root of the tale. the belly is of a beatifull white which passes above and arround the but of the wing, where the feathers being long reach to a small white spot on the rump one inch in width- the wings have nineteen feathers, of which the ten first have the longer side of their plumage white in the midde of the feather and occupying unequal lengths of the same from one to three inches, and forming when the wing is spead a kind of triangle the upper and lower part of these party coloured feathers on the under side of the wing being of dark colour but not jut or shining black. the under side of the remaining feathers of the wing are darker. the upper side of the wing, as well as the short side of the plumage of the party coloured feathers is of a dark blackis or bluish green sonetimes presenting as light orange yellow or bluish tint as it happens to be presented to different exposures of ligt- the plumage of the tale consits of 12 feathers of equal lengths by pairs, those in the center are the longest, and the others on each side deminishing about an inch each pair- the underside of the feathers is a pale black, the upper side is a dark bluefish green which like the outer part of the wings is changable as it reflects different portions of light. towards the the extremely of these feathers they become of an orrange green, then shaded pass to a redish indigo blue, and again at the extremity assume the predominant colour of changeable green- the tints of these feathers are very similar and equally as beatiful and rich as the tints of blue and green of the peacock- it is a most beatifull bird.- the legs and toes are black and imbricated. it has four long toes, three in front and one in rear, each terminated with a black sharp tallon from 3/8ths to 1/2 an inch in length.- these birds are seldom found in parties of more than three or four and most usually at this season single as the balks and other birds of prey usually are- it's usual food is flesh- this bird dose not spread it's tail when it flys and the motion of it's wings when flying is much like that of a Jay-bird-

The White turkey of the black hills from information of a french lad who wintered with the Chien Indians About the size of the common wild turkey the plumage perfectly white- this bird is booted as low as the toes-

[Clark, September 18, 1804] Septr. 18 I Killed a prarie wolf to day about the Sise of a Gray fox with a bushey tail the head and ears like a Fox wolf, and barks like a Small Dog- The annimale which we have taken for the Fox is this wolf, we have seen no Foxes.

18 Septr. Tuesday Set out early wind from the N W. Modrt. our boat being much litened goes much better than usial

[Clark, September 18, 1804] September 18th Tuesday 1804 Wind from the N W. we Set out early the boat much lightened, the wind a head proceed on verry Slowly (1) Passed an I a Island about the middle of the river at 1 Mile this Island is about a mile long, and has a great perpotion of red Cedir on it, a Small Creek comes in on the S. S. opposit the head of the Island, proceeded on passed many Sand bars and Camped on the L. S. before night the wind being verry hard & a head all Day. the hunters Killed 10 Deer to day and a Prarie wolf, had it all jurked & Skins Stretchd after Camping I walked on Shore Saw Goats, Elk, Buffalow, Black tail Deer, & the Common Deer, I Killed a Prarie Wollf, about the Size of a gray fox bushey tail head & ear like a wolf, Some fur Burrows in the ground and barks like a Small Dog.

what has been taken heretofore for the Fox was those wolves, and no Foxes has been Seen; The large wolves are verry numourous, they are of a light Colr. large & has long hair with Corrs fur.

Some Goats of a Different Kind Wer Seen yesterday Great many Porcupin rabits & Barking Squirils in this quarter. Plumbs & grapes.

[Lewis, September 18, 1804]
Sept. 18th this day saw the first brant on their return from the north-

[Clark, September 19, 1804] (1) & (2) passed a large Island Situated nearest the S. S. 1/2 a mile from the Lower pt. of this Island, the 1st of the 3 rivers mouths which is about 35 yards wide, running from the N E. one mile above the 2nd Comes in this is Small not more that 15 yards wide a Short Distance above a 3d comes in scattering its waters thro a bottom. I walked on Shore to See this great Pass of the Sioux and Calumet ground, found it a handsom Situation, and Saw the remains of their Campt on the 2d river, for many years passed- (3) passed a Creek on the L. S. 15 yds wide we (4) passed a Creek 20 yds wide (5) passed a Creek 20 yd. wide on the L. S. I call Night C. as I did not get to it untill late at night, above the mouth of this Creek we camped, the wind being favourable, for the boat I Killed a fat Buffalow Cow, and a fat Buck elk, york my Servent Killed a Buck, the Huntes Killed 4 Deer, & the boat Crew killed 2 Buffalow Swiming the river, handsom Countrey of Plains, I saw many trovs of Buffalow & a Gangue of 30 or 40 Elk and othr Scattering elk &c. a find evening I hurt my hands & feet last night

[Clark, September 19, 1804] 19th of September Wednesday 1804 Set out early, a Cool morning verry Clear the wind from the S. E a Bluff on the L. S.- here Commences a Butifull Countrey on both Sides of the Missouri, (2) passed a large Island Called Prospect Island op posit this Isd. the 3 rivers Coms in, passing thro a butifull Plain, here I walked on Shore & Killed a fat Cow & Sent her to the boat and proceeded on to the first of the 3 rivers, this river is about 35 yards wide Contains a good deel of water, I walked up this river 2 miles & Cross, the bottom is high and rich Some timber, I crossed & returned to the mouth, & proceeded up one mile to the 2d river which is Small 12 yards wide, and on it but little timber, on this Creek the Seaux has frequently Camped, as appears by the Signs- the lands betwen those two Creeks in a purpindicular bluff of about 80 feet with a butifull Plain & gentle assent back- a Short distance above the 2nd a 3rd Creek Comes into the river in 3 places Scattering its waters over the large timbered bottom, this Creek is near the Size of the middle Creek Containing a greater quantity of water, those rivers is the place that all nations who meet are at peace with each other, Called the Seaux pass of the 3 rivers.

The boat proceeded on passd. the Island (3) passed a Creek 15 yds wide on the L. Side (4) passed a Creek on the L. S. 20 yards wide which I Call Elm Creek passing thro a high Plain (5) passed a Creek on the L. S. 18 yds. wide above which the boat Came too, I joined them late at night, and Call this Creek Night Creek the winds favourable all Day, I killed a fat buck Elk late and could only get his Skin and a Small part of his flesh to Camp. My Servent Killed a Buck, the Crew in the boat Killed 2 buffalow in the river- The Hunters on Shore Killed 4 Deer with black tails one of which was a Buck with two men Prongs on each Side forked equally, which I never before Seen. I saw Several large gangs of Buffaloes 2 large Herds of Elk & goats &c. (6) pass a Small Island on the S. S. opposit to this Island on the L. S. a Creek of about 10 yards wide Coms in passing thro a plain in which great quantities of the Prickley Pear grows. I call this Creek Prickley Pear Creek, This Isld. is Called the lower Island it is Situated at the Commencement of what is Called & Known by the Grand de Tortu or Big Bend of the Missourie.

[Clark, September 20, 1804] September the 20th Thursday 1804 Detchd. 3 men across the Big bend (Called the Grand deTour) with the horse, to stay and hunt & jurk provisions untill we get around (1) passed a Island on the S. S. the river Crouded with Sand bars,

20th of September 1804 Thursday (Continued) (1) at the N W. extremity of this bend passed an Small Island on the L. S. opposit the upper Point of this Solitary Island Came too to _____ at the mouth of a Small run on the S. S. & Newmon & Tomson picked up Some Salt mixed with the Sand in the run, Such as the ottoes Indians Collect on the Sands of the Corn de Cerf R. & make use of, Camped on a Sand bar on the S. S. above the Island- I went out to examine the portage which I found quit Short 2000 yards only, the Prarie below & Sides of the hills containing great quantites of the Prickly Piar which nearly ruind my feet, I saw a hare, & I beleve he run into a hole, he run on a hill & disapeared, I Saw on this hill several holes. I Saw Several Goats Elk Ders &c. & Buffalow in every Detection feeding. R. Fields Killed a Deer & 2 Goats one a female, which differs from the male as to Size being Something Smaller, Small Straight horns without any black about the neck Camped late

[Clark, September 20, 1804] 20th of September, Thursday 1804 a fair morning wind from the S E detached 2 men to the 1st. Creek abov the big bend with the horse to hunt and wait our arrival proceeded on passed the lower Island opposit which the Sand bars are verry thick & the water Shoal. I walked on Shore with a view of examining this bend Crossed at the narost part which is a high irregular hills of about 180 or 190 feet, this place the gorge of the Bend is 1 mile & a quarter (from river to river or) across, from this high land which is only in the Gouge, the bend is a Butifull Plain thro which I walked, Saw numbrs of Buffalow & Goats, I saw a Hare & believe he run into a hole in the Side of a hill, he run up this hill which is Small & has Several holes on the Side & I could not See him after, I joined the boat in the evening- passed a Small Island on the L. S. in the N. W. extremity of the bind Called Solitary Island, and Camped late on a Sand bar near the S. S.- R. Fields killed 1 Deer & 2 Goats one of them a feemale- She Differs from the mail as to Size being Smaller, with Small Horns, Stright with a Small prong without any black about the neck None of those Goats has any Beard, they are all Keenly made, and is butifull

[Lewis, September 20, 1804] Septr. 20th on the lard. shore at the commencement of the big bend observed a clift of black porus rock which resembled Lava tho on a closer examination I believe it to be calcarious and an imperfect species of the French burr- preserved a specemine, it is a brownish white, or black or yellowish brown-

[Clark, September 21, 1804] 21st of September 1804 Friday 1804, last night or reather this morng at a half past one oClock the Sand bar on which we Camped began to give way, which allarmed the Serjt on guard & the noise waked me, I got up and by the light of the moon observed that the Sand was giving away both above & beloy and would Swallow our Perogues in a few minits, ordered all hands on board and pushed off we had not got to the opposit Shore before pt. of our Camp fel into the river. we proceeded on to the Gorge of the bend & brackfast, the Distance of this bend around is 30 miles, and 11/4 miles thro, the high lands extinds to the gauge and is about 200 feet the plain in the bend as also the two opposit Sides abov and below is delightfull plains with graduel assents from the river in which there is at this time Great number of Buffalow Elk & Goats feedg The Course from the gauge on the L. S. is S. 70 W. 41/2 Miles to the pt. of Ceder Timber on the L. S. pass Sands. worthy of remark the Cat fish not So plenty abov white river & much Smaller than usial, Great nunbers of Brant & plover, also goat and black tail Deer.

[Clark, September 21, 1804] 21st of September Friday 1804 at half past one oClock this morning the Sand bar on which we Camped began to under mind and give way which allarmed the Sergeant on Guard, the motion of the boat awakened me; I get up & by the light of the moon observed that the land had given away both above and below our Camp & was falling in fast. I ordered all hands on as quick as possible & pushed off, we had pushed off but a few minets before the bank under which the Boat & perogus lay give way, which would Certainly have Sunk both Perogues, by the time we made the opsd. Shore our Camp fell in, we made a 2d Camp for the remainder of the night & at Daylight proceeded on to the Gouge of this Great bend and Brackfast, we Sent a man to measure step off the Distance across the gouge, he made it 2000 yds. The distance arround is 30 mes. The hills extend thro the gouge and is about 200 foot above the water- in the bend as also the opposite Sides both abov and below the bend is a butifull inclined Plain in which there is great numbers of Buffalow, Elk & Goats in view feeding & Scipping on those Plains Grouse, Larks & the Prarie bird is Common in those Plains. we proceeded on passed a (1) willow Island below the mouth of a Small river called Tylors R about 35 yds. wide which corns in on the L. S. 6 miles above the Gorge of the bend, at the mouth of this river the two hunters a head left a Deer & its Skin also the Skin of a white wolfwe observe an emence number of Plover of Different kind Collecting and takeing their flight Southerly, also Brants which appear to move in the same Direction. The Cat fish is Small and not So plenty as below (2) The Shore on each Side is lined with hard rough Gulley Stones of different Sides, which has roled from the hills & out of Small brooks, Ceder is comon here, This day is worm, the wind which is not hard blows from the S. E, we Camped at the lower point of the Mock Island on the S. S. this now Connected with the main land, it has the appearance of once being an Island detached from the main land Covered with tall Cotton wood- we Saw Some Camps and tracks of the Seaux which appears to be old three or four weeks ago- one frenchman I fear has got an abscess on his they, he complains verry much we are makeing every exertion to releiv him The Praries in this quarter Contains Great qts. of Prickley Pear.

[Clark, September 22, 1804] 22nd September Saturday 1804 a thick fog this morning untill 7 oClock which detained us, Saw Some old tracks of the Indians on the S. S. proceeded on- one French man with a abscess on his thigh which pains him verry much for 10 or 12 Days a butifull Plain on both Sides low high land under which there is a number of lage Stone, we See great numbers of Buffalow feeding

[Clark, September 22, 1804] A continuation of notes taken assending the Missourie in 1804-by W. Clark Satturday the 22nd of September 1804- A Thick fog this morning detained us untill 7 oClock, The plains on both Sides of the River is butifull and assends gradually from the river; noumerous herds of Buffalow to be Seen in every derections, (1) Took the altitude of the Sun & found the Lattitude to be 44° 11' 33" N- (2) passed a Small Island on the L. S. and one on the S. S. imediately above, & about 3 m. long, on the L. S. opposit this Island a Creek of about 15 yds wide mouthes, Called the Creek of the 3 Sisters (3) passed Cedar Island 11/2 M. long & 1 M. wide Situated a little above the last and nearest the S. S.near the upper part of this Island on its S. Side a Tradeing fort is Situated built of Cedar-by a Mr. Louiselle of St Louis, for the purpose of Tradeing with the Teton Bands of Soues (or "Sieux") about this Fort I saw numbers of Indians Temporary

Lodges, & horse Stables, all of them round and to a point at top, I observed also numbers of Cotton Trees fallen for the purpose of feeding their horses on the Bark of the limbs of those trees which is Said to be excellent food for the horses- we came too on the S. S. below a Small Island called Goat island, passed a no. of large round Stones, Som distance in the river as also in the Sides of the hills,- I walked on the Shore this evening and Killed a verry large Deer- our hunters Killed 2 Deer & a Beaver, they Complain of the Mineral quallities of the high land distroying their mockersons-.

[Clark, September 22, 1804] 22nd of September Satturday 1804 a thick fog this morning detained us untill 7 oClock passed a butifull inclined Prarie on both Sides in which we See great numbers of Buffalow feeding- (1) took the Meridean altitude of the Suns upper Leimb. 92° 50' 00" the SexSecnt the Latd. produced from this Obsivation is 44° 11' 33" 3/10 North (2) passed a Small Island on the L. S. imediately above passed a Island Situated nearest the L. S. abt. 3 miles long, behind this Isd. on the L. S. a Creek Comes in about 15 yards wide, this Creek and Islands are Called the 3 Sisters a butifull Plain on both Sides of the river (3) passed a Island Situated nearest the S. S. imedeately above the last Called Ceder Island this Island is about 11/2 miles long & nearly as wide Covered with Ceder, on the South Side of this Island Mr. Louiselle a trader from St. Louis built a fort of Ceder & a good house to trate with the Seaux & wintered last winter; about this fort I observed a number of Indian Camps in a Conicel form,- they fed their horses on Cotton limbs as appears. here our hunters joined us havening killed 2 Deer & a Beaver, they Complain much of the Mineral Substances in the barren hills over which they passed distroying their mockersons.

(4) we proceeded on and Camped late on the S. Side below a Small Island in the bend S. S. Called Goat Island. The large Stones which lay on the Sides of the banks in Several places lay Some distance in the river, under the water and is dangerous &.

I walked out this evening and killed a fine Deer, the musquiters is verry troublesom in the bottoms

[Clark, September 23, 1804] 23rd Septr. Sunday 1804 (days and nights equal) Set out early under a gentle Breeze from the S E N. 46°W 33/4 Miles to the mo. of a Creek on the S. S. passd. a pt. on the L. S. (1) a Small Island opsd. in the bend to the S. S. This Island is Called goat Island, (1) this Creek is 10 yards wide. passed bad Sand bars- S. 46°W 23/4 mes. a wood at a Spring in the bend to the L. S. Saw the Prarie a fire behind us near the head of Ceder Island L. S. N. 80° W. 41/2 to the lower pt of Elk Island pass 2 Willow Islands & Sand I saw this morning 12 of those Black & white birds of the corvus Species.

Capt Lewis went out to hund on the Island a great number of Buffalow in Sight I must Seal up all those Scrips & draw from my Journal at Some other time Win Clark Cpt.

[Clark, September 23, 1804] Sunday the 23rd September 1804 Set out under a Gentle breeze from the S. E- (1) passed Goat Island Situated in a bend to the S. S- above passed a Small Creek 12 yards wide on the S. S.- we observed a great Smoke to the SW. which is an Indian Signal of their haveing discovered us, I walked on Shore and observed great numbers of Buffalows. (2) passed 2 Small Willow Islands with large Sand bars makeing from their upper points (3) passed Elk Island Situated near the L. S. about 21/2 mes. long & 3/4 wide, Covered with Cotton wood, a red berry Called by the French "grise de buff," Grapes &c. the river is wide Streight & contains a great numr of Sand bars, (4) passed a Small Creek on the S. S. 16 yds wide I call Reubens Cr.- R. Fields was the first who found it- Came too & Camped on the S. S. in a Wood. Soon after we landed three Soues boys Swam across to us, those boys informed us that a Band of Sieux called the Tetons of 80 Lodges wer Camped near the mouth of the next River, and 60 Lodges more a Short distance above them, they had that day Set the praries on fire to let those Camps Know of our approach- we gave those boys two twists of Tobacco to carry to their Chiefs & Warriors to Smoke, with derections to tell them that we wished to Speak to them tomorrow, at the mouth of the next river- Capt Lewis walked on Shore, R F. Killed a She Goat or "Cabbra."

[Clark, September 23, 1804] 23rd of September Sunday 1804 Set out under a gentle breeze from the S. E, (1) passed a Small Island Situated in a bend to the L. S. Called Goat Island, a Short distance above the upper point a Creek of 12 yards wide corns in on the S. S. we observed a great Smoke to the S W.- I walked on Shore & observed Buffalow in great Herds at a Distance (2) passed two Small willow Islands with large Sand bars makeing out from them, passed (3) Elk Island about 21/2 miles long & 3/4 mile wide Situated near the L. S. covered with Cotton wood the read Current Called by the French Gres de Butiff & grapes &c. &c. the river is nearly Streight for a great distance wide and Shoal. (4) passed a Creek on the S. S. 16 yards wide we Call Reubens Creek, as R Fields found it Camped on the S. S. below the mouth of a Creek on the L. S. three Souex boys Came to us Swam the river and informd that the Band of Soauex called the Teton of 80 Lodges were Camped at the next Creek above, & 60 Lodges more a Short distance above, we gave those boys two Carrots of Tobacco to Carry to their Chiefs, with derections to tell them that we would Speek to them tomorrow Capt Lewis walked on Shore this evening, R. F Killed a Doe Goat,-

[Clark, September 24, 1804] Monday the 24th of September 1804 a fair morning Set out early, wind from the East, passed the mouth of a Creek on the L. S. Called Creek in high water. passed a large (1) Island on the L. S.

about 21/2 Miles long on which Colter had Camped & Killed 4 Elk. the wind from the S. E.- we prepared Some Clothes a few medal for the Chiefs of the Teton band of Sioux we expected to meet at the next River- much Stone on the S. S. of the River, we Saw one hare to day- our Perogues Called at the Island for the Elk, Soon after we passed the Island Colter ran up the bank & reported that the Sioux had taken his horse, we Soon after Saw five indians on the bank; who expressed a wish to come on board, we informed them we were friends, and wished to Continue So, we were not abraid any Indians- Some of their young Men had Stolen a horse Sent by their Great Father to their great Chief, and we Should not Speak to them any more untill the horse was returned to us again- passed a Island about 11/2 m. long on which we Saw maney elk & Buffalow, we Came too off the Mouth of a Small river, The Teton of the burnt woods is Camped 2 Miles up this river, this river we Call Teton is 70 Yds wide and corns in on the S W Side-I went on Shore and Smoked with a Chief, Called Buffalow Medison, who Came to See us here. The Chief Said he Knew nothing of the horse &c &. I informed them we would call the grand Chiefs in Council tomorrow, all continued on board all night

[Clark, September 24, 1804] 24th September Monday 1804 Set out early a fair day the wind from the E, pass the mouth of Creek on the L. S. called on high water; passed (i) a large Island on the L. S. about 2 miles & 1/2 long on which Colter had Camped & Killed 4 Elk, the wind fair from the S. E. we prepared Some Clothes and a fiew meadels for the Chiefs of the Teton's hand of Seaux which we expect to See to day at the next river, observe a Great Deel of Stone on the Sides of the hills on the S. S. we Saw one Hare to day, prepared all things for action in Case of necessity, our Perogus went to the Island for the meet, Soon after the man on Shore run up the bank and reported that the Indians had Stolen the horse we Soon after met 5 Inds. and ankered out Some distance & Spoke to them informed them we were friends, & wished to Continue So but were not afraid of any Indians, Some of their young men had taken the horse Sent by their Great father for ther Chief and we would not Speek to them untill the horse was returned to us again.

passed (2) a Island on the S. S. on which we Saw Several Elk, about 11/2 miles long Called Good humered Islds. Came to about 11/2 miles above off the mouth of a Small river about 70 yards wide Called by Mr. Evins the Little Mississou River, The Tribes of the Scouix Called the Teton, is Camped about 2 miles up on the N W Side and we Shall Call the River after that nation, Teton This river is 70 yards wide at the mouth of water, and has a considerable Current we anchored off the mouth the french Perogue Come up early in the morning, the other did not get up untill in the evening Soon after we had Came too. I went & Smoked with the Chief who Came to See us here all well, we prepare to Speek with the Indians tomorrow at which time we are informed the Indians will be here, The French man who had for Some time been Sick, began to bleed which allarmed him- 2/3 of our party Camped on board The remainder with the Guard on Shore.

[Clark, September 25, 1804] 25th of September 1804 off Teton River a fair Morning the wind from the S. E. raised a Flagg Staff and formed an orning & Shade on a Sand bar in the Mouth of Teton R to Council under, the greater portion of the party to Continue on boardabout 11 oClock the 1st & 2d Chief arrived, we gave them to eat; they gave us Some meat, (we discover our interpeter do not Speak the language well) at 12 oClock the Councill Commenced & after Smokeing agreeable to the usial custom C. L. Delivered a written Speech to them, I Some explinations &c. all party Paraded, gave a Medal to the grand Chief in Indian Un-ton gar-Sar bar, or Black Buffalow- 2d Torto-hongar, Partezon (Bad fellow) the 3d Tar-ton-gar-wa-ker, Buffalow medison- we invited those Chiefs & a Soldier on board our boat, and Showed them many Curiossites, which they were much Surprised, we gave they 1/2 a wine glass of whiskey which they appeared to be exceedingly fond of they took up an empty bottle, Smelted it, and made maney Simple jestures and Soon began to be troublesom the 2d Chief effecting Drunkness as a Cloak for his vilenous intintious (as I found after wards,) realed or fell about the boat, I went in a perogue with those Chief who left the boast with great reluctians, my object was to reconsile them and leave them on Shore, as Soon as I landed 3 of their young ment Seased the Cable of the Perogue, one Soldiar Huged the mast and the 2d Chief was exceedingly insolent both in words and justures to me declareing I Should no go off, Saying he had not recived presents Suffient from us- I attempted to passify but it had a contrary effect for his insults became So personal and his intentions evident to do me injurey, I Drew my Sword at this motion Capt Louis ordered all in the boat under arms, the fiew men that was with me haveing previously taken up their guns with a full deturmination to defend me if possible- The grand Chief then took hold of the Cable & Sent all the young men off, the Soldier got out of the perogue and the 2nd Chief walked off to the Party at about 20 yards back, all of which had their bows Strung & guns Cocked- I then Spoke in verry positive terms to them all, principaly addressing myself to the 1st Chief, who let the roape go and walked to the Indian, party about, 100 I again offered my hand to the 1st Chief who refused it- (all this time the Indians were pointing their arrows blank-) I proceeded to the perogue and pushed off and had not proceeded far before the 1st & 3r Chief & 2 principal men walked into the water and requested to go on board, I took them in and we proceeded on abot a Mile, and anchored near a Small Island, I call this Island Bad humered Island

[Clark, September 25, 1804] 25th Septr a fair morning the wind from the S. E. all well, raised a Flag Staff & made a orning or Shade on a Sand bar in the mouth of Teton River for the purpose of Speeking with the Indians under, the Boat Crew on board at 70 yards Distance from the bar The 5 Indians which we met last night

Continued, about 11 oClock the 1 s & 2d Chief Came we gave them Some of our Provsions to eat, they gave us great quantites of meet Some of which was Spoiled we feel much at a loss for the want of an interpeter the one we have can Speek but little.

Met in council at 12 oClock and after Smokeing, agreeable to the usial Custom, Cap Lewis proceeded to Deliver a Speech which we oblige to Curtail for want of a good interpeter all our Party paraded. gave a medal to the Grand Chief Calld. in Indian Un ton gar Sar bar in French Beefe nure Black Buffalow Said to be a good man, 2 Chief Torto hon gar- or the Partisan-or Partizan-bad the 3rd is the Beffe De Medison his name is Tar ton gar wa ker

1. Contesabe man War zing go

2. do Second Bear = Ma to co que pan

Envited those Cheifs on board to Show them our boat and Such Curiossities as was Strange to them, we gave them 1/4 a glass of whiskey which they appeared to be verry fond of, Sucked the bottle after it was out & Soon began to be troublesom, one the 2d Cheif assumeing Drunkness, as a Cloake for his rascally intentions I went with those Cheifs (which left the boat with great reluctance) to Shore with a view of reconseleing those men to us, as Soon as I landed the Perogue three of their young men Seased the Cable of the Perogue, the Chiefs Soldr. Huged the mast, and the 2d Chief was verry insolent both in words & justures declareing I Should not go on, Stateing he had not recved presents Suffient from us, his justures were of Such a personal nature I felt my Self Compeled to Draw my Sword, at this motion Capt. Lewis ordered all under arms in the boat, those with me also Showed a Disposition to Defend themselves and me, the grand Chief then took hold of the roop & ordered the young warrers away, I felt my Self warm & Spoke in verry positive terms Most of the warriers appeared to have ther Bows Strung and took out their arrows from they quves. as I was not permited to return, I Sent all the men except 2 Inpt. to the boat, the perogu Soon returned with about 12 of our detumind men ready for any event this movement caused a no. of the Indians to withdraw at a distance,- Their treatment tome was verry rough & I think justified rough ness on my part, they all left my Perogue and Councild. with themselves the result I could not lern and nearly all went off after remaining in this Situation Some time I offered my hand to the 1 & 2 Chief who refusd to recve it. I turned off & went with my men on board the perogue, I had not progd. more the 10 paces before the 1st Cheif 3rd & 2 Brave men waded in after me. I took them in & went on board we proceeded on about 1 mile & anchored out off a willow Island placed a guard on Shore to protect the Cooks & a guard in the boat, fastened the Perogues to the boat, I call this Island bad humered Island as we were in a bad humer.

[Clark, September 26, 1804] 26th of Septr Set out early and proceeded on- the river lined with indians, came too & anchored by the particular request of the Chiefs to let their Womin & Boys See the Boat, and Suffer them to Show us some friendship- great members of men womin & Children on the bank viewing us- Those people are Spritely Small legs ille looking Set men perticularly, they grease & Black themselves when they dress, make use of Hawks feathers about thier heads, cover with a Roab each a polecat Skin to hold their Smokeables, fond of Dress, Badly armed. ther women appear verry well, fine Teeth, High Cheek Dress in Skin Peticoats, & a Roabe with the flesh Side out and harey ends turned back over their Sholdes, and look well- they doe all the Laborious work, and I may say are perfect Slaves to thier husbands who frequently have Several wives- Capt Lewis & 5 men went on Shore with the Chiefs, who appeared to wish to become friendly they requested us to remain one night & see them dance &c.- in the evening I walked on Shore, and Saw Several Mahar Womin & Boys in a lodge & was told they were Prisones lately taken in a battle in which they killed a number & took 48 prisoners- I advised the Chiefs to make peace with that nation and give up the Prisoners, if they intended to follow the words of their great father they promised that they would do So- I was in Several Lodges neetly formed, those lodges are about 15 to 20 feet Diametr Stretched on Poles like a Sugar Loaf, made of Buffalow Skins Dressed about 5 oClock I was approached by 10 well Dressed young men with a neet Buffalow Roab which they Set down before me & requested me to get in they Carried me to ther Council Tents forming 3/4 Circle & Set me down betwn 2 Chefs where about 70 men were Seated in a circle, in front of the Chief 6 feet Square was cleared & the pipe of peace raised on forks & Sticks, under which was Swans down Scattered, the Flags of Spane & the one we gave them yesterday was Displayed a large fire was made on which a Dog was Cooked, & in the center about 400 wt of Buffalow meat which they gave us,- Soon after, I took my Seat the young men went to the boat & brought Capt Lewis in the Same way & placed him by me Soon after an old man rose & Spoke approveing what we had done. requesting us to take pitty on them &C. answered- They form their Camp in a circle

The great Chief then rose in great State and Spoke to the Same purpos and with Solemnity took up the pipe of peace and pointed it to the heavens, the 4 quartrs and the earth, he made Some divistation, & presented the Sten to us to Smoke, after Smokeing & a Short Harrang to his people we were requested to take the meat, and the Flesh of the Dog gavin us to eat- We Smoked untill Dark, at which time all was cleared away & a large fire made in the Center, Several men with Tamborens highly Decorated with Der & Cabra Hoofs to make them rattle, assembled and began to Sing & Beat- The women Came forward highly decerated with the Scalps & Trofies of war of their fathes Husbands & relations, and Danced the war Dance, which they done with great chearfulness untill 12 oClock, when we informed the Chief we intended return on bord, (they offered us women, which we did not except) 4 Chiefs accompanied us to the boat and Staid all night- Those people have a Description of Men which they Call Soldiars, those men attend to the police of the Band, Correct all vices &. I Saw one to day whip 2 Squars who appeared to have fallen out, when the Soldier approached all appeared give way and flee at night they Keep 4 or 5 men at different distances walking around their Camp Singing the acursenes of the night all in Spirits this evening wind hard from the S E

I saw 25 Squars & Boys taken 13 days ago in a battle with the Mahars, in which they destroyed 40 Lodges, Killed 75 men & boys, & took 48 prisones which they promised us Should be delivered to Mr. Durion now with the Yankton _____, we gave our Mahar interpeter a few alls & &. to give those retched Prisonis, I saw Homney of ground Potatos a Spoon of the Big Horn animals which will hold 2 quarts.

[Clark, September 26, 1804] 26th Septr. 1804 bad hd lsd. 26th of September Wednesday 1804 Set out early proceeded on and Came to by the wish of the Chiefs for to let their Squars & boys See the Boat and Suffer them to treat us well great number of men women & Children on the banks viewing us, these people Shew great anxiety, they appear Spritely, generally ill looking & not well made thier legs & arms Small Generally- they Grese & Black themselves with coal when they dress, make use of a hawks feather about their heads the men a robe & each a polecats Skins, for to hold ther Bais roly for Smokeing fond of Dress & Show badly armed with fuseis &. The Squaws are Chearfull fine lookg womin not handson, High Cheeks Dressed in Skins a Peticoat and roab which foldes back over thir Sholder, with long wool. doe all ther laborious work & I may Say perfect Slaves to the men, as all Squars of nations much at war, or where the womin are more noumerous than the men- after Comeing too Capt. Lewis & 5 men went on Shore with the Chiefs, who appeared desposed to make up & be friendly, after Captain Lewis had been on Shore about 3 hours I became uneasy for fear of Some Deception & sent a Serjeant to See him and know his treatment which he reported was friendly, & thy were prepareing for a Dance this evening

The made frequent Selecitiation for us to remain one night only and let them Show their good disposition towards us, we deturmined to remain, after the return of Capt. Lewis, I went on Shore I saw Several Maha Prisoners and Spoke to the Chiefs it was necessary to give those prisoners up & become good friends with the Mahars if they wished to follow the advice of their Great father I was in Several Lodges neetly formed as before mentioned as to the Bauruly Tribe- I was met by about 10 well Dressd. yound men who took me up in a roabe Highly a decrated and Set me Down by the Side of their Chief on a Dressed robe in a large Council House this house formed a 3/4 Cercle of Skins well Dressed and Sown together under this Shelter about 70 men Set forming a Circle in front of the Chiefs a plac of 6 feet Diameter was Clear and the pipe of peace raised on Sticks under which there was Swans down Scattered, on each Side of the Circle two Pipes, The flags of Spain 2 & the Flag we gave them in front of the Grand Chief a large fire was near in which provisions were Cooking, in the Center about 400 wt. of excellent Buffalo Beif as a present for us

Soon after they set me Down, the men went for Capt Lewis brough him in the same way and placed him also by the Chief in a fiew minits an old man rose & Spoke approveing what we had done & informing us of their Situation requesting us to take pity on them &c which was answered The Great Chief then rose with great State to the Same purpote as far as we Could learn & then with Great Solemnity took up the pipe of peace whin the principal Chiefs Spoke with the pipe of Peace he took in one hand Some of the most Delicate parts of the Dog which was prepared for the feist & made a Sacrifise to the flag- & after pointing it to the heavins the 4 quarter of the Globe & the earth, , lit it and prosist presented the Stem to us to Smoke, after a Smoke had taken place, & a Short Harange to his people, we were requested to take the meal put before us the dog which they had been cooking, & Pemitigon & ground potatoe in Several platters. Pemn is buffo meat dried or baked pounded & mixed with grease raw Dog Sioux think great dishused on festivals. eat little of dog pemn & pote good we Smoked for an hour Dark & all was Cleared away a large fire made in the Center, about 10 misitions playing on tamberins. long sticks with Deer & Goats Hoofs tied So as to make a gingling noise and many others of a Similer kind, those men began to Sing, & Beet on the Tamboren, the women Came foward highly Deckerated in theire way, with the Scalps and Trofies of war of ther father Husbands Brothers or near Connection & proceeded to Dance the war Dance which they done with Great Chearfullness untill 12 oClock when we informed the Cheifs that they were fatigued &c. they then retired & we Accompd. by 4 Chiefs returned to our boat, they Stayed with us all night. Those people have Some brave men which they make use of as Soldiers those men attend to the police of the Village Correct all errors I saw one of them to day whip 2 Squars who appeared to have fallen out, when he approachd all about appeared to flee with great turrow at night thy keep two 3 4 or 5 men at deffinit Distances walking around Camp Singing the accurrunces of the night all the men on board 100 paces from Shore wind from the S. E. moderate one man verry sick on board with a Dangerass abscess on his Hip. all in Spirits this eveninge

In this Tribe I saw 25 Squars and boys taken 13 days ago in a battle with the mahars in this battle they Destroyd 40 lodges, killed 75 men, & Som boys & children, & took 48 Prisones Womin & boys which they promis both Capt. Lewis and my Self Shall be Delivered up to Mr. Durion at the Tribe, those are a retched and Dejected looking people the Squars appear low & Corse but this is an unfavourabl time to judge of them we gave our Mahar inteptr. Some fiew articles to give those Squats in his name Such as alls needle &. &c.

I Saw & eat Pemitigon the Dog, Groud potatoe made into a Kind of homney, which I thought but little inferior- I also Saw a Spoon made of a horn of an animile of the Sheep kind the spoon will hold 2 quarts.

[Clark, September 27, 1804] 27th of Septr. 1804- The Bank as usial lined with Sioux, gave the 2 principal Chiefs a blanket & a peck of Corn each, Capt Lewis accompanied the Chiefs to their Lodges, they informed us that a great part of their nation had not arrived, & would arrive to night and requested us to Delay one Day longer, that they might See us

I rote a letter to Mr. Durion, & prepared Some Commissions & a meadel & Sent to Captain Lewis- at 2 oClock Capt Lewis retuned with 4 chiefs & a Brave man named War-cha pa- after a delay of half an hour I went with them on Shore, they left the boat with reluctiance (we Suspect they are treacherous and are at all times guarded & on our guard) They again offered me a young woman and wish me to take her & not Dispise them, I wavered the Subject, at Dark the Dance began as usial and performed as last night. womin with ther Husbands & relations cloths arms Scalps on poles &c. &c. Capt Lewis joined me & we continued until about 11 oClock and 2 Chief accompaned us to the boat I with 2 Cheifs was in a Perogue going on board, by bad Stearing the parogu Struk the Cable with Such force as to brake it near the anchor (Cap Lewis) and 3 or 4 men on Shore, I had all hands up and was Compelled to Land- the Chief got allarmed & allarmed the Indians the 1s Chief & about 200 men Came down in great hast armd and for action, and found it was false, about 20 of them Camped on Shore all night- this allarm Cap Lewis & well as my Self viewed as the Signal of their intentions, one half on guard, our misfortune of loseing our anchor obliged us to lay under a falling in bank much exposed to the Accomplishment of the hostile intentions of those Tetons (who we had every reason to believe from their Conduct intended to make an attempt to Stop our progress & if possible rob us-) Peter Crusat who Spoke Mahar came in the night and informed me that the mahar Prisoners told him that the Tetons intended to Stop us- We Shew'd but little Sign of a knowledge of there intentions.

[Clark, September 27, 1804] 27th of Septr. Thursday 1804 I rose early aftr a bad nights Sleep found the Chief all up, and the bank as usial lined with Spectators we gave the 2 great Cheifs a Blanket a peace, or rethr they took off agreeable to their Custom the one they lay on and each one Peck of Corn after Brackfast Capt. Lewis & the Chiefs went on Shore, as a verry large part of their nation was Comeing in, the Disposition of whome I did not know one of us being Suffcent on Shore, I wrote a letter to Mr. P. Durion & prepared a meadel & Some Comsns. & Sent to Cap Lewis at 2 oClock Capt. Lewis returned with 4 Chiefs & a Brave man named War cha pa or on his Guard. when the friends of those people die they run arrows through their flesh above and below their elbous as a testimony of their Greaf after Staying about half an hour, I went with them on Shore, Those men left the boat with reluctience, I went first to the 2d Chiefs Lodge, where a Croud Came around after Speeking on various Subjects I went to a princpal mans lodge from there to the grand Chiefs lodge, after a fiew minits he invited me to a Lodge within the Circle in which I Stayed with all their principal men untill the Dance began, which was Similer to the one of last night performed by their womn which poles on which Scalps of their enemies were hung, Some with the Guns Spears & war empliments their husbands in their hands

Capt. Lewis came on Shore and we Continued untill we were Sleepy & returned to our boat, the 2nd Chief & one principal man accompanid us, those two Indians accompanied me on board in the Small Perogue, Capt. Lewis with a guard Still on Shore, the man who Steered not being much acustomed to Steer, passed the bow of the boat & peroge Came broad Side against the Cable & broke it which obliged me to order in a loud voice all hands all hands up & at their ores, my preempty order to the men and the bustle of their getting to their ores allarmd the Cheifs, togethr with the appearance of the men on Shore, as the boat turnd. The Cheif hollowered & allarmed the Camp or Town informing them that the Mahars was about attacting us. in about 10 minits the bank was lined with men armed the 1st Cheif at their head, about 200 men appeared and after about 1/2 hour returned all but about 60 men who Continued on the bank all night, the Cheifs Contd. all night with us- This allarm I as well as Captn. Lewis Considered as the Signal of their intentions (which was to Stop our proceeding on our journey and if Possible rob us) we were on our Guard all night, the misfortune of the loss of our Anchor obliged us to Lay under a falling bank much exposd. to the accomplishment of their hostile intentions P. C -our Bowman who Cd. Speek Mahar informed us in the night that the Maha Prisoners informed him we were to be Stoped- we Shew as little Sighns of a Knowledge of their intentions as possible all prepared on board for any thing which might hapen, we kept a Strong guard all night in the boat no Sleep

[Clark, September 28, 1804] 28th of Septr 1804 Friday I made maney attempts in defferent ways to find our anchor without Sukcess, the Sand had Covered her up, we Deturmined to proceed on to Day- and after Brackfast we with great Dificuelty got the Chiefs out of the boat, and when we were about Setting out the Class

Called the Soldiars took possession of the Cable- the 1st Cheif was Still on board and intended to go a Short distance up with us, was informed that the men Set on the Cable, he went out and told Capt Lewis who was at the Bow, they wanted tobacco The 2d Chief Demanded a flag & Tobacco which we refused to give, Stateing proper reasons to them for it, after much rangleing, we gave a Carrot of Tobacco to the 1st Cheif and he to the men &lurked the Cable from them & proceeded on under a Breeze from the S E. we took in the 3rd Cheif who was Sitting on a Sand bar 2 miles above- he told us the Rope was held by order of the 2d Chief who was a Double Spoken man- Soon after we Saw a man rideing full Speed up the bank, we brought him on board, & he proved to be the Sun of the 3d Cheif, by him we Sent a talk to the nation, explanatory of our hoisting the red flag under the white, if they were for Peace Stay at home and doe as we had Derected them and if they were for war or deturmined to attempt to Stop us, we were ready to defend our Selves (as I had before Said)- we Substituted large Stones in place of an Anchor, we came to at a Small Sand bar in the middle of the river and Stayed all night-I am verry unwell I think for the want of Sleep

[Clark, September 28, 1804] 28th of September 1804 Friday Made many attemps in different ways to find our Anchor but could not, the Sand had Covered it, from the misfortune of last night our boat was laying at Shore in a verry unfavourable Situation, after finding that the anchor Could not be found we deturmined to proceed on, with great difficuelty got the Chiefs out of our boat, and when we was about Setting out the Class Called the Soldiers took possession of the Cable the 1 s Chief which was Still on board & intended to go a Short distance up with us, I told him the men of his nation Set on the Cable, he went out & told Capt Lewis who was at the bow the men who Set on the Roap was Soldiers and wanted Tobacco Capt. L. Said would not agree to be forced into any thing, the 2d Chief Demanded a flag & Tobacco which we refusd. to Give Stateing proper reasons to them for it after much dificuelty-which had nearly reduced us to hostility I threw a Carot of Tobacco to 1 s Chief Spoke So as to touch his pride took the port fire from the gunner the Chief gives the Tobaco to his Soldiers & he jurked the rope from them and handed it to the bows man we then Set out under a Breeze from the S. E. about 2 miles up we observed the 3rd Chief on Shore beckining to us we took him on board he informed us the roap was held by the order of the 2d Chief who was a Double Spoken man, Soon after we Saw a man Comeing full Speed, thro the plains left his horse & proceeded across a Sand bar near the Shore we took him on board & observed that he was the Son of the Chief we had on board we Sent by him a talk to the nation Stateent the Cause of our hoisting the red flag undr. the white, if they were for peace Stay at home & do as we had Derected them, if the were for war ore were Deturmined to Stop us we were ready to defend our Selves, we halted one houre & 1/2 on the S. S. & made a Substitute of Stones for a ancher, refreshed our men and proceeded on about 2 miles higher up & came too a verry Small Sand bar in the middle of the river & Stayed all night, I am Verry unwelle for want of Sleep Deturmined to Sleep to night if possible, the men Cooked & we rested well.

[Clark, September 29, 1804] Capt. W. Clarks Notes Continued as first taken- 29th of September Satturday 1804- Set out early Some bad Sand bars, at 9 oClock we observed the 2d Chief with 2 men and Squars on Shore, they wished to go up with us as far as the other part of their band, which would meet us on the river above not far Distant we refused to let one more Come on board Stateing Suffient reasons, observd they would walk on Shore to the place we intended to Camp, offered us women we objected and told them we Should not Speake to another teton except the one on board with us, who might go on Shore when ever he pleased, those Indians proceeded on untill later in the evening when the Chief requested that the Perogue might put him across the river which we agreed to- Saw numbers of Elk on the Sand bars today, passed an old Ricara Village at the mouth of a Creek without timber we Stayed all night on the Side of a sand bar 1/2 a Mile from the Shore.

[Clark, September 29, 1804] 29th of Septr. Satturday 1804 Set out early Some bad Sand bars, proceeded on at 9 oClock we observed the 2d Chief & 2 principal men one man & a Squar on Shore, they wished to go up with us as far as the other part of their band, which they Said was on the river a head not far Distant we refused Stateing verry Sufhcint reasons and was plain with them on the Subject, they were not pleased observed that they would walk on Shore to the place we intended to Camp to night, we observed it was not our wish that they Should for if they did we Could not take them or any other Tetons on board except the one we had now with us who might go on Shore when ever he pleased- they proceeded on, the Chief on board askd. for a twist of Tobacco for those men we gave him 1/2 a twist, and Sent one by them for that part of their band which we did not See, & Continued on Saw great numbers of Elk at the mouth of a Small Creek Called No timber (-as no timber appeared to be on it.) above the mouth of this Creek the Parties had a Village 5 years ago,- The 2d Chief Came on the Sand bar & requested we would put him across the river, I Sent a Perogue & Crossed him & one man to the S. S. and proceeded on & Came too on a Sand bar on about 1/2 mile from the main Shore & put on it 2 Sentinals Continud all night at anchor (we Substitute large Stones for anchors in place of the one we lost) all in high Spirits &c

[Clark, September 30, 1804] 30th of September Sunday 1804 had not proceeded far before we discovered an Indian running after us, he requstd to go with us to the Ricaras, we refused to take him, I discovered at a great Distanc a great number of men women & Children decending a hill towards the river above which the Chief with us told us was the other Band, Some rain & hard wind at about 10 oClock we anchored opposit the Camps of this band and told them we took them by the hand, and Sent to each Chief a Carrot of Tobacco & Some to the principal men and farther Said that after Staying with the band below 2 days to See them we had been badly treated and Should not land again, as we had not time to Delay- refured then to Mr. Durion for a full account of us, and an explination of what had been Said, they appeard ansioes for us to eat with them and observed they were friendly we apoligised & proceeded on under a Double reafed Sale- the Chief on board threw out to those that ran up Small pieces of Tobacco & told them to go back and open thier ears, We Saw great number of white guls- refresh the party with whiskey, in the evening we Saw 2 Indians at a Distance, The boat turned by accident & was nearly filling and rocked verry much, allarmed the Indian Chief on board who ran and hid himself, we landed & the Indian express a wish to return, we gave him a Blanket Knife & Some tobacco and advised him to keep his men away, we camped on a Sand bar. verry Cold & windy-

[Clark, September 30, 1804] 30th of Septr. Sunday 1804. Set out this morning early had not proceeded on far before we discovered an Indn. running after us, he came up with us at 7 oClock & requested to come on bord and go up to the recorees we refused to take any of that band on board if he chose to proceed on Shore it was verry well Soon after I discovered on the hills at a great distance great numbers of Indians which appeared to be makeing to the river above us, we proceeded on under a Double reafed Sail, & Some rain at 9 oClock observed a large band of Indians the Same which I had before Seen on the hills incamping on the bank the L. S. we Came too on a Sand bar Brackfast & proceeded on & cast the ancher opposit their Lodgs. at about 100 yards distand, and informed the Indians which we found to be a part of the Band we had before Seen, that took them by the hand and Sent to each Chief a Carrot of tobacco, as we had been treated badly by Some of the band below, after Staying 2 days for them, we Could not delay any time, & refured them to Mr. Duron for a full account of us and to here our talk Sent by him to the Tetons, those were verry Selecitious for us to land and eate with them, that they were friendly &c. &. we appoligised & proceeded on, Sent the peroge to Shore above with the Tobacco & Delivd. it to a Soldr. of the Chief with us Several of them ran up the river, the Chf. on board threw then out a Small twist of Tobacco & told them to go back & open ther ears. they recved the Tobacco & returned to their lodges- we Saw great numbers of white guls this day is cloudy & rainey- refresh the men with a glass of whisky after Brackfast.

we Saw about 6 miles above 2 Indians who came to the bank and looked at us a about 1/2 an hour & went over the hills to the S W. we proceeded on under a verry Stiff Breeze from the S. , the Stern of the boat got fast on a log and the boat turned & was verry near filling before we got her righted, the waves being verry high, The Chief on board was So fritined at the motion of the boat which in its rocking caused Several loose articles to fall on the Deck from the lockers, he ran off and hid himself, we landed he got his gun and informed us he wished to return, that all things were Cleare for us to go on we would not See any more Tetons &c. we repeated to him what had been Said before and advised him to keep his men away, gave him a blanket a Knife & Some Tobacco, Smokd a pipe & he Set out. we also Set Sale and Came to at a Sand bar, & Camped, a verrey Cold evening, all on our guard

[Clark, October 1, 1804] 1st of October Monday 1804 The wind blew hard from the S. E. all last night, Set out early passed a large Island in the middle of the river opposit this Island the Ricaras lived in 2 Villages on the S W. Side, about 2 Miles above the upper point of the Island the Chyenne River Coms in on the L. S. and is about 400 yards wide dischargeing but little water for a R. of its Size, the Current jentle, and navagable, to the Black mountains we haule the Boat over a Sand bar, River wide & Shoal, pass'd a Creek at 5 mils we Call Sentinal Creek, a Small one above, but little timber about this river, the hills not So high as usial, the upper Creek I call lookout Creek, Camped on a Sand bar, opposit a Tradeing house, where a Mr. Valles & 2 men had Some fiew goods to trade with the Sioux, a boy came to us, This Mr. Vallie informed us he wintered last winter 300 Legus up the Chyemne River under the Black mountains, he Sais the River is rapid and bad to navagate, it forks 100 Leagus up the N. fork enters the Black mountain 40 Leagues above the forks the Countrey like that on the Missouri less timber more Cedar, the Coat Nur or Black m. is high and Some parts retain Snow all Summer, Covered with timber principally pine, Great number of goats and a kind of anamal with verry large horns about the Size of a Small Elk, White Bear no bever on the chien great numbers in the mountains, The Chyenne Nation has about 300 Lodges hunt the Buffalow, Steel horses from the Spanish Settlements, which they doe in 1 month- the Chanal of this River is Corse gravel, Those mountains is inhabited also by the white booted Turkeys worthy of remark that the Grouse or Prarie hen is Booted, the Toes of their feet So constructed as to walk on the Snow, and the Tail Short with 2 long Stiff feathers in the middle.

Sand bars are So noumerous, that it is impossible to discribe them, & think it unnecessary to mention them.

[Clark, October 1, 1804] 1st of October Monday 1804 The wind blew hard all last night from the S. E. verry Cold Set out early the wind Still hard passed a large Island in the middle of the river (1) opsd. the lower point of this Island the Ricrerees formerly lived in a large Town on the L. S. above the head of the Island about 2 miles we passed the (2) River) L. S. this river Comes in from the S W. and is about 400 yards wide, the Current appears gentle, throwing out but little Sands, and appears to throw out but little water the heads of this River is Indians live Some distance up this river, the presise distance I cant learn, above the mouth of this river the Sand bars are thick and the water Shoal the river Still verry wide and falling a little we are obliged to haul the boat over a Sand bar, after makeing Several attempts to pass. the wind So hard we Came too & Stayed 3 hours after it Slackened a little we proceeded on round a bend, the wind in the after part of the Day a head- (2) passed a Creek on the L. S. which we Call the Sentinal, this part of the river has but little timber, the hills not so high. the Sand bars now noumerous, & river more than one mile wide including the Sand bars. (2) pass a Small Creek above the latter which we Call lookout C-. Continued on with the wind imediately a head, and Came too on a large Sand bar in the middle of the river, we Saw a man opposit to our Camp on the L. S. which we discovd. to be a Frenchman, a little of the willows we observed a house, we Call to them to come over, a boy Came in a Canoo & informed that 2 french men were at the house with good to trade with the Seauex which he expected down from the rickerries everry day, Severl large parties of Seauex Set out from the rics for this place to trade with those men- This Mr. Jon Vallie informs us that he wintered last winter 300 Leagues up the Chien River under the Black mountains, he informs that this river is verry rapid and dificiult even for Canoos to assend and when riseing the Swels is verry high, one hundred Leagues up it forks one fork Comes from the S. the other at 40 Leagues above the forks enters the black Mountain. The Countrey from the Missourie to the black mountain is much like the Countrey on the Missourie, less timber & a greatr perpotion of Ceder. The black Mountains he Says is verry high, and Some parts of it has Snow on it in the Summer great quantities of Pine Grow on the mountains, a great noise is heard frequently on those mountains-, on the mountains great numbers of goat, and a kind of Anamale with large Circuler horns, This animale is nearly the Size of an Argalia Small Elk. White bear is also plenty- The Chien Inds. inhabit this river principally, and Steel horses from the Spanish Settlements This excurtion they make in one month the bottoms & Sides of R Chien is Corse gravel. This frenchman gives an account of a white booted turkey an inhabitant of the Cout Noie-

[Clark, October 1, 1804] 1st of October Monday 1804 at the Mouth of River Chien or Dog R We proceeded now from the mouth of this river 11 miles and Camped on a Sand bar in the river opposit to a Tradeing house verry windy & Cold- 11 miles above the Chien R

[Clark, October 1, 1804]
The red Berry is Called by the Rees Nar-nis-

The Ricares

Names of the nations who come to the Ricares to trafick and bring
Horses & robes

1. * Kun-na-nar-wesh Gens de vash Blue beeds 2. ° Noo-tar-wau Hill Climbers 3. * Au ner-hoo the people who pen Buffalow to Catch them 4. * To-che-wah-Coo Fox Indians 5. * To-pah-cass White hair's 6. * Cat-tar kah Paducar 7. * Kie-wah Tideing Indians 8. * Too war Sar Skin pricks 9. Shar ha (Chien) the village on the other Side 10. We hee Shaw (Chien) The villages on this Side

Those nation all live on the praries from S W. by S. to West of the
Ricaries, all Speek different languages and are numerous all follow the
Buffalow and winter in the mountains. The Mandans Call a red berry
common to the upper part of the Missouri As-say the engages call the
Same berry grease de Buff- grows in great abundance a makes a
Delightfull Tart

[Clark, October 2, 1804] 2nd of October Tuesday 1804, Mr. Vallie Came on board, Lat. 44° 19' 36 N. we observed Some Indians on a hill on the S. S. one Came to the river & fired off his gun and asked us to come he wish us to go to his Camp near at hand we refused, passed a large Island on the S. S., here we expected the Tetons would attempt to Stop us, and prepared for action, &c. opposit this Island on the L. S. a Small Creek comes in, we call this Caution Island, Camped on a Sand bar 1/2 mile from the main Shore the wind hard from the N W. Cold, the current of the river less rapid, & retains less Sediment than below.

[Clark, October 2, 1804] 2nd of Octr. 2nd of October Tuesday 1804 a Violent wind all night from the S. E. Slackened a little and we proceeded on. Mr. Jon Vallee Came on board and proceeded on 2 miles with us, a verry Cold morning Some black clouds flying took a meridian altitude & made the Lattitude 44° 19' 36" North this was taken at the upper part of the gouge of the Lookout bend, the Sentinal heard a Shot over the hills to the L. S. dureing the time we were Dineing on a large Sand bar. the after part of this day is pleasent, at 2 oClock opposit a wood on the L. S. we observed some Indians on a hill on the S. S. one Came down to the river opposit to us and fired off his gun, & beckind. to us to Come too, we payed no attention to him he followed on Some distance, we Spoke a few words to him, he wished us to go a Shore and to his Camp which was over the hill and Consisted of 20 Lodges, we excused our Selves advised him to go and here our talk of Mr. Durion he enquired for traders we informed him one was in the next bend below & parted, he returned- & we proceeded on (1) passed a large Island, the S. S. here we expected the Tetons would attempt to Stop us and under that

Hear we prepared our Selves for action which we expected every moment. opsd. this Island on the L. S. a Small Creek Comes in, This Island we call Isd. of Caution we took in Some wood on a favourable Situation where we Could defend our men on Shore & (2) Camped on a Sand bar 1/2 a mile from the main Shore. the wind changed to the N. W. & rose verry high and Cold which Continud. The Current of the Missourie is less rapid & contains much less Sediment of the Same Colour.

[Clark, October 2, 1804] 2nd of October Tuesday 1804 Proceeded on as mentioned in journal No. 2 twelve miles Camped above a large Island on a Sand bar, verry windy and Cold the after part of this day, the mid day verry worm, The Lattitude as taken to day is 44° 19' 36"- observe great Caution this day expecting the Seaux intentions Some what hostile towards our progression, The river not So rapid as below the Chien, its width nearly the Same 12 miles

[Clark, October 3, 1804] 3rd of October Wednesday 1804 The N W. wind blew verry hard all night with Some rain, we Set out early, at 12 examoned our Stores & goods, Several bags Cut by the mice and Corn Scattered, Some of our Cloth also cut by them also papers &c. &c. at 1 oClock an Indian Came to the Bank S. S, with a turkey on his back 4 other soon joined him Some rain, Saw Brant & white guts flying Southerly

[Clark, October 3, 1804] 3rd of October Wednesday 1804 wind blew hard all night from the N W. Some rain and verry Cold. we Set out at 7 oClock & proceeded on

[Clark, October 3, 1804] 3rd of October Wednesday 1804 The N. W. wind blew verry hard all night with Some rain a Cold morning, we Set out at 7 oClock and proceeded on at 12 oClock landed on a Bare L. S. examined the Perogus & factle of the boat to see if the mice had done any damage, Several bags Cut by them Corn Scattered &. Some of our Clothes also Spoiled by them, and papers &c. &. at 1 oClock an Indian Came to the bank S. S. with a turkey on his back, four others Soon joined him, we attempted Several Chanels and Could not find water to assend, landed on a Sand bar & Concluded to Stay all night, & Send out and hunt a Chanell, Some rain this after noon- Saw Brant & white gulls flying Southerly in large flocks-

[Clark, October 4, 1804] 4th of October Thursday- the Wind blew all night from the N W. Some rain we were obliged to drop down 3 miles to get a Channel Sufficient Deep to pass Several Indians on the bank, Call'd to us frequently to Land, one gave 3 yels & Sciped a Ball before us, we payed no attention to them, while at Brackfast one Swam across to us, beged for Powder, we gave him a Small piece of Tobacco & put him over on a Sand bar, passed a large Island in the middle of the river Good hope I. Passed a small Creek L. S. passed a creek L S Camped on a Sand bar at the upper point of an Island on which is the remains of an old ricara Village fortified Called La hoo It was circular, this Village appears to have been deserted about 5 or 6 years, 17 houses yet remain, the Island Contains but little timber, the evening verry Cold and wood Scerce, make use of Drift wood

[Clark, October 4, 1804] 4th of October Thursday 1804 the wind blew all night from the NW. Some rain, we were obliged to Drop down 3 miles to get the Chanel Suft. deep to pass up, Several Indians on the Shore viewing of us Called to us to land one of them gave 3 yels & Sciped a ball before us, we payed no attention to him, proceeded on and Came too on the L. S. to brackft one of those Indians Swam across to us beged for Powder, we gave him a piece of Tobacco & Set him over on a Sand bar, and Set out, the wind hard a head (1) passed a Island in the middle of the river about 3 miles in length, we call Goodhope Island, (2) at 4 miles passed a (2) Creek on the L. S. about 12 yards wide Capt. Lewis and 3 men walked on Shore & crossed over to an (3) Island Situated on the S. S. of the Current & near the Center of the river this Isld. is about 11/2 miles long & nearly 1/2 as wide, in the Center of this Island was an old Village of the rickeries Called La ho catt it was Circular and walled Containing 17 lodges and it appears to have been deserted about five years, the Island Contains but little timber. we Camped on the Sand bar makeing from this Island, the day verry Cool.

[Clark, October 5, 1804] 5th of October Friday 1804 Frost this morning, Set out early passed a Small Creek on the L. S. saw 3 Tetons on the S. S. they beged Some Tobacco, we proceed on passed a Creek on the S. S. I Saw a white brant in a gangue on the Sand bar Saw a large herd of Cabra or antelopes Swiming the River, we Killed four of them passed a Small Island on the L. S. a large Creek on the L. S. at the head of the Island White Brant Creek, I walked on the Island which is covered with wild rye, I Killed a Buck & a Small wolf this evening, Clear pleasant evening, Camped on a mud bar S. S. refreshd the men with whiskey.

[Clark, October 5, 1804] 5th of October Friday 1804 Frost this morning, we Set out early and proceeded on (1) passed a Small Creek on the L. S. at 7 oClock heard Some yels proceeded on Saw 3 Indians of the Teton band, they called to us to Come on Shore, beged Some Tobacco, we answd. them as usial and proceeded on, passed (2) a Creek on the S. S. at 3 mes. abov the mouth we Saw one white Brant in a gang of about 30, the others all as dark as usial, a Discription of this kind of Gees or Brant Shall be given here after Saw a Gang of Goats Swiming across the river out of which we killed four they were not fatt. in the evening passed a Small (3) Island Situated Close to the L. Side, at the head of this Isd. a large Creek coms in on the L. S. Saw white or Brants, we Call this Creek white Brant Creek- I walked on the Isd. found it Covered with wild rye, I Shot a Buck, Saw a large gang of Goat on the hills opposit, one Buck killed, also a Prarie wolf this evening, the high Land not So high as below, river about the Same width, the Sand bars as noumerous, the earth Black and many of the Bluffs have the appearance of being on fire, we Came too and Camped on a mud bar makeing from the L. S. The evening is Calm and pleasant, refreshed the men with a glass of whiskey-

[Clark, October 6, 1804] 6th of October Satturday 1804 Cold Wind from the N. Saw many large round Stones near the middle of the River passed an old Ricara village of 80 Lodges Picketed in those lodges in nearly an octagon form, 20 to 60 feet Diameter Specious Covered with earth and as Close as they Can Stand, a number of Skin Canoes in the huts, we found Squashes of 3 different Kinds growing in the Village Shields Killed an Elk Close by- The Magpy is common here, we Camped off the mouth of Otter Creek on the S. S. this Creek is 22 yds. wide & heads near the R. Jacque,- contains much water.

[Clark, October 6, 1804] 6th October Satturday 1804 a cool morning wind from the North Set out early passed a willow Island (1) Situated near the S. Shore at the upper point of Som timber on the S. S. many large round Stones near the middle of the river, those Stones appear to have been washed from the hills (2) passed a village of about 80 neet Lodges covered with earth and picketed around, those loges are Spicious of an Octagon form as close together as they can possibly be placed and appear to have been inhabited last Spring, from the Canoes of Skins Mats buckets & found in the lodges, we are of appinion they were the recrereis we found Squashes of 3 Different Kinds growing in the Village, one of our men killed an Elk Close by this Village, I saw 2 wolves in persute of another which appeared to be wounded and nearly tired, we proceeded on found the river Shole we made Severl. attempts to find the main Channel between the Sand bars, and was obliged at length to Drag the boat over to Save a league which we must return to get into the deepest Channel, we have been obgd to hunt a Chanl. for Some time past the river being devided in many places in a great number of Chanels, Saw Gees, Swan, Brants, & Ducks of Different kinds on the Sand bars to day, Capt Lewis walked on Shore Saw great numbers of Prarie hens, I observe but fiew Gulls or Pleaver in this part of the river, The Corvos or Magpye is verry Common in this quarter

We Camped on a large Sand bar off the mouth of Otter Creek on the S. S. this Creek is about 22 yards wide at the mouth and contains a greater perpotion of water than Common for Creeks of its Sise

[Clark, October 7, 1804] 7th of October Sunday 1804 frost last night, passed a River 90 yds. wide the Ricaras Call Sur-war-kar-ne all the water of this river runs in a chanel of 20 yards, the Current appears jentle, I walked up this River a mile, Saw the tracks of white bear, verry large, also a old Ricara village partly burnt, fortified about 60 Lodges built in the Same form of those passed yesterday, many Canoes & Baskets about the huts-about 10 oClock we Saw 2 Indians on the S. S. they asked for Something to eat & told us they were Tetons of the band we left below on ther way to the Ricaras we gave them meat & wind hard from the South, passed a large open Island covered with grass and wild rye, I walked on the Isd & 4 men they Killed a Braroe & a Black tale Doe with a black breast, the largest Deer I ever saw, the great numbers of Grous on it, we call it Grous Island, Camped opposit the Island near the S. Side.

[Clark, October 7, 1804] 7th of October Sunday 1804 a Cloudy morning, Some little rain frost last night, we Set out early proceeded on 2 miles to the mouth of a (1) river on the L. S. and brackfast this river whin full is 90 yards wide the water is at this time Confined within 20 yards, the Current appears jentle, this river throws out but little Sand at the mouth of this river we Saw the Tracks of White bear which was verry large, I walked up this river a mile- below the (2) mouth of this river, is the remains of a Rickorrie Village or Wintering Camp fortified in a circular form of a bout 60 Lodges, built in the Same form of those passed yesterday This Camp appears to have been inhabited last winter, many of their willow & Straw mats, Baskets & Buffalow Skin Canoes remain intire within the Camp, the Ricares Call this river Sur-war-kar-na or Park from this river we proceeded on under a gentle Breeze from the S. W. at 10 oClock we Saw 2 Indians, on the S. S. they asked for Something to eate, & informed us they were part of the Beiffs De Medisons Lodge on their way to the Rickerreis, passed (3) a willow Island in a bind to the S. S. (4) at 5 miles passd. a willow Island on the S. S.- wind hard from the South in the evening I walked on an (5) Island nearly the middle of the river Called Grous Island, one of the men killed a Shee Brarrow, another man killed a Black tail Deer, the largest Doe I ever Saw (Black under her breast) this Island is nearly 11/4 ms. Squar no timbr high and Covered with grass wild rye and Contains Great numbers of Grouse, we proceeded on a Short distance above the Island and Camped on the S. S. a fine evening.

[Clark, October 8, 1804] 8th of October Monday 1804 a cool Morning wind from the N. W. passed the mouth of a Small Creek on the L. S. about 21/2 Miles above the Isd. Passed the Mouth of a River on the L. S. called by the Ricaries We-tar-hoo. this river is 120 yards wide, the water Confined within 20 yards, throws out mud with little Sand, great quanties of red Berries, resembling Currents near the mouth of this river Latd. 45° 39' 5 N. this river heads in the 1s Black Mountain, 2 Miles higher up passed a Small River on the L. S. Called Maropa 25 yards wide Chocked up with mud- our hunters discovered a Ricara village on an Island a fiew miles above we passed the 1s Ricara Village about the center of the Island, in presence of Great numbers of Spectators and Camped above the Island on the L. S. at the foot of Some high land. (Mr. Gravotine a French man joined us as an intepeter) The Island on which is Ricara Village is Situated, is about 3 miles long Seperated from the Main L. Side by a Narrow Deep Channel, those Indians Cultivate on the Island Corn Beens Simmins, Tobacco &c &c. after Landing Capt. Lewis with Mr. Gravelin and 3 men went to the Village, I formd a Camp on Shore with the Perogue crew & guard, with the Boat at Anchor, Capt Lewis returned late, a french man and a Spaniard accompanied him

[Clark, October 8, 1804] 8th of October Monday 1804 a Cool morning Set out early the wind from the N. W. proceeded on passed the mouth of a Small Creek on the L. S. about 21/2 miles above Grouse Island, (3) passed a willow Island which Divides the Current equilly. (2) passed the mouth of a River called by the ricares We tar hoo on the L. S. this river is 120 yards wide, the water of which at this time is Confined within 20 yards, dischargeing but a Small quantity, throwing out mud with Small propotion of Sand, great quantities of the red Berries, ressembling Currents, are on the river in every bend- 77° 33' 0" Lattitude from the Obsevation of to day at the mouth of this river is 45° 39' 5"-North- proceeded on passed a (3) Small river of 25 yards wide Called (4) or Beaver Dam R this river is intirely Chocked up with mud, with a Streem of 1 Inch Diamiter passing through, discharging no Sand, at 1 (5) mile passed the lower pint of an Island close on the L. S. 2 of our men discovered the reckerrei village, about the Center of the Island on the L. Side on the main Shore. this Island is about 3 miles long, Seperated from the L. S. by a Channel of about 60 yards wide verry Deep, The Isld. is covered with fields, where those people raise their Corn Tobacco Beens &c. &c. Great numbers of those People came on the Island to See us pass, we passed above the head of the Island & Capt. Lewis with 2 interpeters & 2 men went to the Village I formed a Camp of the french & the guard on Shore, with one Sentinal on board of the boat at anchor, a pleasent evening all things arranged both for Peace or War, This Village (6) is Situated about the Center of a large Island near the L. Side & near the foot of Some high bald uneaven hills, Several french men Came up with Capt Lewis in a Perogue, one of which is a Mr. Gravellin a man well versed in the language of this nation and gave us Some information relitive to the Countrey naton &c

[Clark, October 8, 1804] Orders October the 8th 1804 Robert Frazer being regularly inlisted and haveing become on of the Corps of Vollenteers for North Western Discovery, he is therefore to be viewed & respected accordingly; and will be anexed to Sergeant Gass's mess.

Win Clark Cpt &.
Meriwether Lewis
River Marapa Capt. 1st U.S. Regt. Infty

[Clark, October 9, 1804] 9th of October Tuesday 1804 a windey night Some rain, and the wind Continued So high & cold We could not Speck in Council with the Indians, we gave them Some Tobacco and informed them we would Speek tomorrow, all the grand Chiefs visited us to day also Mr Taboe, a trader from St. Louis- Many Canoes of a Single Buffalow Skin made in the form of a Bowl Carrying generally 3 and Sometimes 5 & 6 men, those Canoes, ride the highest Waves- the Indians much asstonished at my Black Servent and Call him the big medison, this nation never Saw a black man before, the wind verry high, I saw at Several times to day 3 Squars in single Buffalow Skin Canoes loaded with meat Cross the River, at the time the waves were as high as I ever Saw them in the Missouri

[Clark, October 9, 1804] 9th of October 1804 Tuesday a windey rainey night, and Cold, So much So we Could not Speek with the Indians to day the three great Chiefs and many others Came to See us to day, we gave them Some tobacco and informed them we would Speek on tomorrow, the day Continued Cold & windey Some rain Sorry Canoos of Skins passed down from the 2 villages a Short distance above, and many Came to view us all day, much asstonished at my black Servent, who did not lose the oppertunity of his powers Strength &c. &. this nation never Saw a black man before.

Several hunters Came in with loads of meat, I observed Several Canoos made of a Single buffalow Skin with 2 & 3 Thre Squars Cross the river to day in Waves as high as I ever Saw them on this river, quite uncomposed I have a Slite Plurise this evening Verry Cold &c. &.

1st Chiefs name Ka kawissassa (lighting Crow.) 2d do do Pocasse (or Hay) 3d do do Piaa he to (or Eagles feather)

[Clark, October 10, 1804] 10th of October 1804 at 11 oClock the wind Shifted from S. E to N W. Mr. Taboe visited us- we hear that Some jealousy exists as to the Chiefs to be made- at 1 oclock the Cheifs all assembled under an orning near the Boat, and under the American Flag. we Delivered a Similar Speech to those delivered the Ottoes & Sioux, made three Chiefs, one for each Village and gave them Clothes & flags- 1 s Chief is name Ka-ha-wiss assa lighting ravin 2d Chief Po-casse (Hay) & the 3rd Piaheto or Eagles Feather- after the Council was over we Shot the Air gun, which astonished them, & they all left us, I observed 2 Sioux in the Council one of them I had Seen below, they Came to interceed with the Ricaras to Stop us as we were told- the Inds. much astonished at my black Servent, who made him Self more turrible in thier view than I wished him to Doe as I am told telling them that before I cought him he was wild & lived upon people, young children was verry good eating Showed them his Strength &c. &c.- Those Indians are not fond of Licquer of any Kind-

[Clark, October 10, 1804] 10th of October Wednesday 1804. a fine forming wind from the S. E at about 11 oClock the wind Shifted, to the N. W. we prepare all things ready to Speak to the Indians, Mr. Tabo & Mr. Gravolin Came to brackfast with us the Chiefs &. came from the lower Town, but none from the 2 upper Towns, which is the largest, we Continue to delay & waite for them at 12 oClock Dispatchd Gravelin to envite them to Come down, we have every reason to believe that a jellousy exists between the Villages for fear of our makeing the 1st Cheif from the lower Village, at one oClock the Cheifs all assembled & after Some little Cerrimony the Council Commenced, we informd them what we had told the others before i e Ottoes & Seaux. made 3 Cheif 1 for each Village. gave them presents.

after the Council was Over we Shot the air guns which astonished them much, they then Departed and we rested Secure all night, Those Indians wer much astonished at my Servent, They never Saw a black man before, all flocked around him & examind. him from top to toe, he Carried on the joke and made himself more turibal than we wished him to doe. (Thos Indians were not fond of Spirits Licquer. of any kind)

[Clark, October 11, 1804] 11th of October Thursday 1804 wind S. E. at 11 oClock met the 1s Chief in Council, he Thanked us for what we had given him & his people promised to attend to our advise, and Said the road was open for us and no one Dare Shut it &c. &. we took him and one Chief on board and Set out, on our way took in the 2d Chief at the mo of a Small Creek, and Came too off the 2d village which is 3 miles above the Island, we walked up with the 2 & 3 Chiefs to their villages which is Situated on each Side of a Small Creek, they gave us Something to eat in thier way, after Conversations on various Subjects & Beareing the civilities of those people who are both pore & dirtey we informed the Chiefs we would here what they had to Say tomorrow and returned on board about 10 oClock P M. Those people gave us to eat Corn & Beans, a large well flavoured Been which they rob the Mice of in the Plains and is verry nurishing-all tranquillity

[Clark, October 11, 1804] 11th October Thursday 1804 a fine morning the wind from the S. E. at 11 oClock we met the Grand Chief in Council & and he made a Short Speech thanking us for what we had Given him & his nation promisseing to attend to the Council we had given him & informed us the road was open & no one dare Shut it, & we might Departe at pleasure, at 1 oClock we Set out for the upper villages 3 miles distant, the Grand Chief & nephew on board, proceeded on at 1 mile took in the 2d Chief & Came too off the first Second village Seperated from the 3rd by a Creek after arrangeing all matters we walked up with the 2d Chief to his village, and Set talking on various Subjects untile late we also visited the upper or 3rd Village each of which gave us Something to eate in their way, and a fiew bushels of Corn Beens &. &c.

after being treated by everry civility by those people who are both pore & Durtey we returned to our boat at about 10 oClk. P M. informing them before we Departed that we would Speek to them tomorrow at there Seperate Villages. Those people gave us to eate bread made of Corn & Beens, also Corn & Beans boild. a large Been, which they rob the mice of the Prarie which is rich & verry nurrishing also

[Clark, October 11, 1804]
(Ricares)

October the 11th Thursday 1804 we met in Council to hear what the Grand
Chief Ka kaw issassa had to Say in answer to the Speech of yesterday

The Grand Chief rose and spoke as follows i, e,

My Fathers-! My heart is glader than it ever was before to See my fathers.- a repetition.

If you want the road open no one Can provent it it will always be open for you.

Can you think any one Dare put their hands on your rope of your boat.
No! not one dar

When you Get to the mandans we wish you to Speak good words with that
Nation for us. we wish to be at peace with them.

It gives us pain that we do not Know how to work the Beaver, we will make Buffalow roabs the best we Can.

when you return if I am living you will See me again the same man The Indian in the prarie know me and listen to my words, when you come they will meet to See you.

We Shall look at the river with impatient for your return. Finished

[Clark, October 12, 1804] 12th of October Friday after Brackfast we joined the Chiefs & Indians on the bank who wer waiting for us, and proceeded to the 1st village and Lodge of the Pocasse, This man Spok at Some lengths, to the Same purpote of the 1 s Chief, & Declareing his intentions of visiting his great father, Some Doubts as to his Safty in Passing the Sioux, requested us to take a Chief of their nation and make a good peace with the Mandan for them, that they Knew that they were the Cause of the war by Killing the 2 Mandan Chiefs- this Chief & people gave us about 7 bushels of Corn, Some Tobacco of their own make, and Seed Legins & a Robe We proceeded to the 3rd Chiefs Village which is the largest, after the usial Seremoney of Eating Smokg. &. he Spoke to near the Same amount of the last Chief, & more pleasently, he gave us 10 bushels of Corn, Some Beens & Simmins, after he had Spoken, and I gave Some Sketches of the Power & Magnitude of Our Countrey, we returned to our Boat, I have the rhumetism on my neck the Chiefs accompanied us on board, we gave them Some Sugar Salt and a Sun Glass each, and after eating a little they returned on Shore leaveing one to accompany us to the Mandans, and we Set out viewed by men womin & children of each village proceeded on about 91/2 miles and Camped on the S S. Clear & Cold- The Ricaras Are about 500 men Mr. Taboe say 600 able to bear arms, and the remains of ten different tribes of Panias reduced by the Small Pox & wares with the Sioux, they are tall Stout men corsily featured, their womin Small & industerous raise great quantites of corn beans &c also Tobacco for the men to Smoke, they collect all the wood and doe the Drudgery common amongst Savages- Their language is So corrupted that many lodges of the Same village with dificuelty under Stand all that each other Say- They are Dirty, Kind, pore, & extravegent; possessing natural pride, no begers, rcive what is given them with pleasure, Thier houses are close together & Towns inclosed with Pickets, thier Lodges are 30 to 40 feet in Diamuter Covered with earth on Neet Poles Set end wise resting on 4 forks Supporting Beems Set in a Square form near the Center, and lower about 5 feet high other forks all around Supt. Strong Beems, from 8 to 10 of those, with a opening at top of about 5 to 6 feet Square, on the Poles which pass to the top, Small Willow & grass is put across to Support the earth- The Sioux exchange, Some merchndze of Small value which they get from Mr. Cameron of St. Peters for Corn &c and have great influence over this people treat them roughly and keep them in contineal dread- The Ricaras are at war with the Crow Indians and Mandans-&c. &- The Ricaras, have a custom Similar to the Sioux in maney instances, they think they cannot Show a Sufficient acknowledgement without to their guest handsom Squars and think they are despised if they are not recved

The Sioux followed us with women two days we put them off. the Ricarries we put off dureing the time we were near their village- 2 were Sent by a man to follow us, and overtook us this evening, we Still procisted in a refusial-The Dress of the Ricara men is Simpally a pr. of Mockersons & Legins, a flap, and a Buffalow Robe- Their Hair is long and lais loose their arms & ears are decerated with trinkets

The womin Dress Mockersons & Legins & Skirt of the Skin of the Cabre or Antelope, long fringed & roab to the fringes & with Sleaves, verry white, and Roabes- all were Dressed to be without hare in the Summer

Those people make large Beeds of Diferrent colours, out of glass or
Beeds of Dift colours, verry ingeniously

[Clark, October 12, 1804] 12th October Friday 1804 I rose early after brackfast we joined the Indians who were waiting on the bank for us to come out and go and Council, we accordingly joined them and went to the house of the 2nd Chief Lassil where there was many Chief and warriers & about 7 bushels of Corn, a pr Leagins a twist of their Tobacco & Seeds of 2 Kind of Tobacco we Set Some time before the Councill Commenced this man Spoke at Some length declareing his dispotion to believe and prosue our Councils, his intention of going to Visit his great father acknowledged the Satisfaction in receiveing the presents &c. rais'g a Doubt as to the Safty on passing the nations below particularly the Souex. requested us to take a Chief of their nation and make a good pact with Mandins & nations above. after answering those parts of the 2d Chiefs Speech which required it, which appeared to give General Satisfaction we went to the Village of the 3rd Chief and as usial Some Serimony took place before he Could Speek to us on the Great Subject. This Chief Spoke verry much in the Stile on nearly the Same Subjects of the other Chief who Set by his Side, more Sincear & pleasently, he presented us with about 10 bushels of Corn Some beens & quashes all of which we acksepted with much pleasure, after we had ansd. his Speech & give them Some account of the Magnitude & power of our Countrey which pleased and astonished them verry much we returned to our boat, the Chiefs accompanied us on board, we gave them Some Sugar a little Salt, and a Sun Glass, & Set 2 on Shore & the third proceeded on with us to the Mandens by name, at 2 oClock we Set out the inhabitints of the two Villages Viewing us from the banks, we proceeded on about 91/2 miles and Camped on the S. S. at Some woods passed, the evening Clear & pleasent Cooler

The Nation of the Rickerries is about 600 men able to bear arms a Great perpotion of them have fusees they appear to be peacefull, their men tall and perpotiend, womin Small and industerous, raise great quantities of Corn Beens Simmins &c. also Tobacco for the men to Smoke they Collect all the wood and do the drugery as Common amongst Savages.

Thise nation is made up of 10 Different Tribes of the Pania, who had formerly been Seperate, but by Commotion and war with their neighbours have Come reduced and compelled to Come together for protection, The Curruption of the language of those different Tribes has So reduced the language that the Different Villages do not understade all the words of the others.- Those people are Durtey, Kind, pore, & extravigent pursessing national pride. not beggarley reive what is given with great pleasure, Live in worm houses large and built in an oxigon form forming a Cone at top which is left open for the Smoke to pass, those houses are generally 30 or 40 foot Diamiter. Covd. with earth on poles willows & grass to prevent the earths passing thro, Those people express an inclination to be at peace with all nations The Seaux who trade the goods which they get of the British Traders for their corn, and great influence over the Rickeres, poisen their minds and keep them in perpetial dread.

I Saw Some of the Chien or Dog Indians, also a man of a nation under the Court new-This nation is at war with the Crow Indians & have 3 Children prisoners.

a curious Cuistom with the Souix as well as the reckeres is to give handsom Squars to those whome they wish to Show Some acknowledgements to- The Seaux we got Clare of without taking their Squars, they followed us with Squars 13th two days. The Rickores we put off dureing the time we were at the Towns but 2 Handsom young Squars were Sent by a man to follow us, they Came up this evening and peresisted in their Civilities.

Dress of the men of this nation is Simply a pr. mockerson, Leagins, flap in front & a Buffalow roabe, with ther arms & ears Deckorated The women, wore Mockersons leagins fringed and a Shirt of Goat Skins, Some with Sleaves. this garment is longe & Genlry. White & fringed, tied at the waste with a roabe, in Summer without hair.

[Clark, October 12, 1804] 2nd Chief Ricaras

My Father, I am glad to See this is a fine Day to here the good Councils & talk good talk I am glad to See you & that your intentions are to open the road for all we See that our Grand father has Sent you to open the road we See it Our Grand father by Sending you means to take pity on us Our Grand father has Sent you with tobacco to make peace with all nations, we think

The first nation who has recomended the road to be clear and open. You
Come here & have Directed all nations which you have met to open &
clear the road. you come to See the water & roads to Clear them as
Clear as possible

you just now Come to See us, & we wish you to tell our Grand ftar that we wish the road to be kept Clear & open. I expect the Chief in the next Town will tell you the Same to move on & open the road

I think when you Saw the nations below they wish you to open the road- (or something to that amount) when you passd. the Souex they told you the Same I expect. we See you here to day we are pore our women have no Strouds & Knives to Cut their meat take pitty on us when you return.

you Come here & Derect us to Stay at home & not go to war, we Shall do So, we hope you will when you get to the Mandins you will tell them the Same & Cleer the road, no one Dar to Stop you, you go when you please,

The you tell us to go Down, we will go and See our grand father & here & receve his Gifts, and think fully that our nation will be covered after our return, our people will look for us with the same impatience that our Grand father looks for your return, to Give him

If I am going to See my grand father, many bad nations on the road, I am not afraid to Die for the good of my people (all Cried around him.)

The Chief By me will go to the Mandans & hear what they will Say. (we agree'd.)

The verry moment we Set out to go down we will Send out my Brother to bring all the Nation in the open prarie to See me part on this Great mission to See my Great father.

our people hunting Shall be glad to here of your being here & they will all Come to See, as you Cannot Stay they must wate for your return to See you, we are pore take pity on our wants

The road is for you all to go on, who do you think will injure a white man when they come to exchange for our Roabes & Beaver

after you Set out many nations in the open plains may Come to make war against us, we wish you to Stop their guns & provent it if possible. Finished

3d Chief of Ricares

My fathers I will see the Indians below & See if they have the hart as they tell you

The nation below is the Mahas & Ottes & but one nation, (the Souix) has not a good heart.

I always look at the 1 t Chief & the 2d whin they go & will also follow ther example & go on also

You See those 2 men they are chiefs, when I go they will take Care, they beleve your words.

Mabie we will not tell the trooth, as to the Child perhaps they will not wish to go.

My Children the old women & men whin I return I can then give them, Some a Knife Some powder & others Ball &c. What is the matter if we was to go for nothing my great Chief wish to go, I wish to go also.

when I go to See my Grand father I wish to return quicke for fear of my people being uneasy.

my Children are Small & perhaps will be uneasy whin I may be Safe

I must go, I also wish to go, perhaps I may when I return make my people glad

I will Stay at home & not go to War even if my people are Struck

we will believ your word but I fear the Indians above will not believe your word.

I will think that 1/2 of the men who will return will Stay in this
Village 1/2 below in the other villages

what did the Seaus tell you- (we informd them)

[Clark, October 13, 1804] 13th of October Satturday 1804 Newmon Confined for Mutinous expressions, proceeded on passed a Camp of Sioux on the S. S. those people did not Speak to us. passed a Creek on the S. S. 18 miles above the Ricaras I call Stone Idol Creek, this Creek heads in a Small lake at no great distance, near which there is a Stone to which the Indians asscribe great virtue &. &c. at 21 Miles passed a Creek 15 yds wide on the L. S I call Pocasse, we observed great quantites of grapes, a fine Breez from S E Camped on the L. S. Some rain thus evening, we formed a Court Martial of 7 of our party to Try Newmon, they Senteenced him 75 Lashes and banishment from the party- The river narrow current jentle & wood plenty on the Bottoms the up land is as usial Open divircified plains, generally rich & leavel.

[Clark, October 13, 1804] 13th of October Satturday 1804 one man J. Newmon Confined for mutinous expression Set out early proceeded on, passd. a Camp of Seauex on the S. S. those people only viewed us & did not Speak one word- The visiters of last evening all except one returned which is the Brother of the Chief we have on board passed (1) a Creek on the S. S. 13 yds. at 18 me. above the Town heading in Some Ponds a Short Diste. to the N. E we call Stone Idol C. (well to observe here that the Yankton or R Jacque heads at about 2 Days March of this place Easterly, the R de Seauex one Day further, the Chien a branch of R. Rouche Still beyend, and the River St. Peters 4 Days March from this place on the Same direction Informtn. of the Rickores). passed 2 large willow (2) & Sand Islands above the mouth of the last Creek- at 21 miles above the Village passed a (3) Creek about 15 yards wide on the L. S. we Call after 2d Chief Pocasse (or Hay) nearly opposit this creek a fiew miles from the river on the S. S. 2 Stones resembling humane persons & one resembling a Dog is Situated in the open Prarie, to those Stone the Rickores pay Great reverance make offerings whenever they pass (Infomtn. of the Chief & Intepeter) those people have a Curious Tredition of those Stones, one was a man in Love, one a Girl whose parents would not let marry, the Dog went to mourn with them all turned to Stone gradually, Commenceing at the feet. Those people fed on grapes untill they turned, & the woman has a bunch of grapes yet in her hand on the river near the place those are Said to be Situated, we obsd. a greater quantity of fine grapes than I ever Saw at one place.

The river about the Island on which the lower Rickores Village is
Situated is narrow and Conts. a great propotion of Timber than below,
the bottoms on both Sides is Covered with timber the up lands naked the
Current jentle and Sand bars Confined to the points Generally

We proceeded on under a fine Breeze from the S.E. and Camped late at the upper part of Some wood on the Starboard Side, Cold & Some rain this evening. we Sent out hunters Killed one Deer.

We Tried the Prisoner Newmon last night by 9 of his Peers they did
"Centence him 75 Lashes & Disbanded the party."

[Lewis and Clark, October 13, 1804] Orders 13th of October 1804 A court Martial to Consist of nine members will set to day at 12 oClock for the trial of John Newman now under Confinement Capt. Clark will attend to the forms & rules of a president without giveing his opinion

Detail for the Court Martial
Sert. John Ordaway
Sergeant Pat. Gass
Jo. Shields
H. Hall

Jo. Collins
Wm. Werner
Wm. Bratten
Jo. Shannon
Silas Goodrich
Meriwether Lewis
Capt. 1st U S. Regt. Infty.
Win Clark Capt
or E. N W D

In conformity to the above order the Court martial convened this day for the trial of John Newman, charged with "having uttered repeated expressions of a highly criminal and mutinous nature; the same having a tendency not only to distroy every principle of military discipline, but also to alienate the affections of the individuals composing this Detachment to their officers, and disaffect them to the service for which they have been so sacredly and solemnly engaged."- The Prisonar plead not guilty to the charge exhibited against him. The court after having duly considered the evidence aduced, as well as the defense of the said prisonor, are unanimously of opinion that the prisonar John Newman is guilty of every part of the charge exhibited against him, and do sentence him agreeably to the rules and articles of war, to receive seventy five lashes on his bear back, and to be henceforth discarded from the perminent party engaged for North Western discovery; two thirds of the Court concurring in the sum and nature of the punishment awarded. the commanding officers approve and confirm the sentence of the court, and direct the punishment take place tomorrow between the hours of one and two P.M.- The commanding officers further direct that John Newman in future be attatched to the mess and crew of the red Perogue as a labouring hand on board the same, and that he be deprived of his arms and accoutrements, and not be permited the honor of mounting guard untill further orders; the commanding officers further direct that in lue of the guard duty from which Newman has been exempted by virtue of this order, that he shall be exposed to such drudgeries as they may think proper to direct from time to time with a view to the general relief of the detachment.-

[Clark, October 14, 1804] 14th of October Sunday 1804 Some rain last night we Set out in the rain which continued all day passed a Creek on the L. S. Piaheto 15 yds Wide, halted on a Sand bar and had the punishmt inflicted on Newmon, which caused the indian Chieif to cry untill the thing was explained to him Camped opposit an antient fortification which is on the L. S, when I explained to the Chief the Cause of whipping N- he observed that examples were necessary & that he himself had made them by Death, but his nation never whiped even from their bearth.

[Clark, October 14, 1804] 14th of October Sunday 1804. Some rain last night all wet & Cold, we Set early the rain contind all Day at _____ miles we passed a (1) Creek in the L. S. 15 yards wide this Creek we Call after the 3rd Chief Piaheto (or Eagles feather) at 1 oClock we halted on a Sand bar & after Dinner executed the Sentence of the Court Martial So far as gieving the Corporal punishment, & proceeded on a fiew miles, the wind a head from N. E. Camped in a Cove of the bank on the S. S. imediately opposit our Camp on the L. Side I observe an antient fortification the walls of which appear to be 8 or 10 feet high, the evening wet and disagreeable, the river Something wider more timber on the banks

The punishment of this day allarmd. the Indian Chief verry much, he Cried aloud (or effected to Cry) I explained the Cause of the punishment and the necessity He thought examples were also necessary, & he himself had made them by Death, his nation never whiped even their Children, from their burth.

[Clark, October 15, 1804] 15th of October Rained all last night, passed a Ricara hunting camp on the S.S. & halted at another on the L.S, Several from the 1t Camp visited us and gave meat as also those of the Camp we halted at, we gave them fish hooks Some beeds &c. as we proceeded on we Saw a number of Indians on both Sides all day, Saw L. S some Curious Nnobs high and much the resemblance of a hiped rough house, we halted at a Camp of 10 Lodges of Ricaras on the S. S., we visited thier Lodges & were friendly recved by all- their women fond of our men- &c.

[Clark, October 15, 1804] 15th of October Monday 1804 rained all last night, we Set out early and proceeded on at 3 Miles passed an Ind. Camp on the S. S. we halted above and about 30 of the Indians came over in their Canoos of Skins, we eate with them, they give us meat, in return we gave fishhooks & Some beeds, about a mile higher we came too on the L. S. at a Camp of Ricres of about 8 Lodges, we also eate & they gave Some meat, we proceded on Saw numbers of Indians on both Sides passing a Creek, Saw many Curious hills, high and much the resemblance of a house with a hiped roof, at 12 oClock it Cleared away and the evening was pleasent, wind from the N. E.- at Sunset we arrived at a Camp of Ricares of 10 Lodges on the S. S. we Came too and Camped near them Capt Lewis & my Self went with the Chief who accompanis us, to the Huts of Several of the men all of whome Smoked & gave us Something to eate also Some meat to take away, those people were kind and appeared to be much plsd. at the attentioned paid them.

Those people are much pleased with my black Servent- Their womin verry fond of carressing our men. &.

[Clark, October 16, 1804] 16th of October Tuesday 1804 Some rain this morning 2 Squars verry anxious to accompany us we Set out with our Chief on Board by name Ar ke tar nar shar (or Chief of the Town) a little above our Camp on the L. S. passed an old Shyenne Village, which appears to have been Serounded with a wall of earth; this is the retreat & first Stand of this nation after being reduced by the Sioux and drove from their Countrey on the heads of red River of L Winipic where they Cultivated the landspassed a Creek I call So-harch or Girl Creek L. S. 2 miles higher passed Woman Crreek or Char-parts passed an Island Situated in a bend to the S. S. at the lower point of this Island a Creek comes in Called Kee-tooth

Sar-kar-nar- or the place of Beaver above the Island a Small River on the Same S. Side Called War-re-Con nee Elk shed their horns, this river is 35 yards wide & heads near the River au Jacque, Carp Island wind hard a head from the N W. Saw great numbers of goats or Antelope on Shore, Capt Lewis one man & the Ricara Chief walked on Shore, in the evening I discovered a number of Indians on each Side and goats in the river or Swiming & on Sand bars, when I came near Saw the boys in the water Swiming amongst the goats & Killing them with Sticks, and then hauling them to the Shore those on Shore Kept them in the water, I saw 58 Killed in this way and on the Shore, the hunter with Cap Lewis Shot 3 goats I came too and Camped above the Ricara Camp on the L. S. Several Indians visited us duereing the night Some with meat, Sang and were merry all night.

[Clark, October 16, 1804] 16th October Tuesday 1804 Some rain this morning, 2 young Squars verry anxious to accompany us, we Set out with our Chief on board by name Ar ke tar na Shar or Chief of the Town, a little above our Camp on the L. S. passed a Circular work, where the, Shar ha (or Chien, or Dog Indians) formerly lived, a Short distance abov passed a Creek which we Call Chien Creek, above is a willow Island Situated near (i) the L. Side a large Sand bar above & on both Sides (2) passed a Creek above the Island on the L. S. call So-harch (or Girls) Creek, at 2 miles higher up (3) passed a Creek on L. S. call Char part (or womins) Creek passed (5) an Island Situated in a bend to the S. S. this Isd. is about 11/2 miles long, Covered with timber Such as Cotton wood, opsd. the lower point a creek coms in on the S. S. called by the Indians Kee tooth Sar kar nar (or place of Beavr) above the Island a Small river about 35 yards wide corns in Called War re con ne or (Elk Shed their horns). The Island is Called Carp Island by Ivens. wind hard from the N. W. Saw great numbers of Goats on the Shore S. S. proceeded on Capt. Lewis & the Indian Chief walked on Shore, Soon after I discovered Great numbers of Goats in the river, and Indians on the Shore on each Side, as I approached or got nearer I discovered boys in the water Killing the Goats with Sticks and halling them to Shore, Those on the banks Shot them with arrows and as they approachd. the Shore would turn them back of this Gangue of Goats I counted 58 of which they had killed & on the Shore, one of our hunters out with Cap Lewis killed three Goats, we passed the Camp on the S. S. and proceeded 1/2 mile and Camped on the L. S. many Indians came to the boat to See, Some Came across late at night, as they approach they hollowed and Sung, after Staying a Short time 2 went for Some meat, and returned in a Short time with fresh & Dried Buffalow, also goat, those Indians Strayed all night, They Sung and was verry merry the greater part of the night

[Lewis, October 16, 1804] October 16th This day took a small bird alive of the order of the _____ or goat suckers. it appeared to be passing into the dormant state. on the morning of the 18th the murcury was at 30 above 0. the bird could scarcely move.- I run my penknife into it's body under the wing and completely distroyed it's lungs and heart- yet it lived upwards of two hours this fanominon I could not account for unless it proceeded from the want of circulation of the blood.- the recarees call this bird to'-na it's note is at-tah-to'-nah'; at-tah'to'-nah'; to-nah, a nocturnal bird, sings only in the night as does the whipperwill.- it's weights oz 17 Grains Troy

[Clark, October 17, 1804] 17th of October 1804 Wind S. W. I walked on Shore with the Ricara Chief and an Inteprieter, they told me maney extroadenary Stories, I Killed 3 Dear & a Elk, the Chief Killed a Deer and our hunters Killed 4 Deer, in my absenc the wind rose So high that the Boat lay too all Day; Latd 46° 23' 57" N, I caught a Small uncommon whiperwill we observe emence herds of Goats, or Antelopes flocking down from the N E Side & Swiming the River, the Chief tels me those animals winter in the Black Mountain, and in the fall return to those mounts from every quarter, and in the Spring disperse in the planes, those emence herds we See all of which is on the N E Side of the River is on their way to the mountain, and in the Spring they will be as noumeroes on their return (some ganges winter on the Missouri)- camped on the L. S.

note from the Ricares to the River Jacque near N. E. is about 40 mes. to the Chien a fork of R Rogue 20 passing the Souix River near the Chien this from information of Mr. Graveline who passed through this Countrey

[Clark, October 17, 1804] 17th October Wednesday 1804. Set out early a fine morning the wind from the N W. after brackfast I walked on Shore with the Indian Chief & Interpeters, Saw Buffalow Elk and Great numbers of Goats in large gangues (I am told by Mr. G. that those Animals winter in the Black mountains and this is about the Season they Cross from the East of the Missouris to go to that Mountain, they return in the Spring and pass the Missourie in Great numbers). This Chief tells me of a number of their Treditions about Turtles, Snakes, &.

and the power of a perticiler rock or Cave on the next river which informs of everr thing none of those I think worth while mentioning- The wind So hard a head the boats Could not move aftr 10 oClock, Capt Louis Took the altitude of the Sun Laid. 46° 23' 57" I Killed 3 Deer and the hunters with me killed 3 also the Indian Shot one but Could not get it- I Scaffeled up the Deer & returned & met the boat after night on the L. S. about 6 miles above the place we Camped last night- one of the men Saw a number of Snakes, Capt Lewis Saw a large Beaver house S. S. I Cought a Whipprwill Small & not Common-. the leaves are falling fast-. the river wide and full of Sand bars,-. Great numbers of verry large Stone on the Sides of the hills & Some rock of a brownish Colour in the Ld. Bend below this-.

Great numbers of Goats are flocking down to the S. Side of the river on their way to the Black Mountains where they winter those animals return in the Spring in the Same way & Scatter in different directions.

[Clark, October 18, 1804] 18th of October 1804. at 6 miles passed the mouth of La Bullet or Cannon Ball River on the L. Side about 140 yards Wide, and heads near the Black Mountains above the mouth of this River, in and at the foot of the Bluff, and in the water is a number of round Stones, resembling Shells and Cannon balls of Different Sises, and of excellent grit for Grindstons- the Bluff continus for about a mile, The water of this River is confined within 40 yards- we met 2 french men in a Canoe, who informed us they wer trapping near the mandans and were robed of 4 Traps, & part of their Skins and Several other articles by Indians he took to be Mandans those men return with us, Saw emence numbers of Goats all Day S. S. our hunters Kill Sevral passed a large Creek Called Che wah or fish Creek on the S. S. 28 yds. wide, passed a Small Creek at 2 m on the L. S. Camped on the L. S. Saw a no of Buffalow, & in one gangue 248 Elk our hunters Killed 6 Deer & 4 Elk this evening, The Countrey is leavel and fine Some high Short hills, and ridges at a Distance, Bottoms fine and Partially timbered with Cotton wood principally Some ash & Elm.

[Clark, October 18, 1804] 18th of October Thursday 1804 Set out early proceeded on at 6 mes. passed the mouth of (1) la Boulet (or Cannon Ball River) about 140 yards wide on the L. S. this river heads in the Court not or Black mountains) (a fine Day) above the mouth of this river Great numbers of Stone perfectly round with fine Grit are in the Bluff and on the Shore, the river takes its name from those Stones which resemble Cannon Balls.- The water of this river is Confined within 40 yards. We met 2 french men in a perogue Desending from hunting, & complained of the Mandans robing them of 4 Traps ther fur & Seeveral othr articles Those men were in the imploy of our Ricaree interpeter Mr. Gravelin they turned & followered us.

Saw Great numbers of Goats on the S. S. Comeing to the river our hunters Killed 4 of them Some run back and others crossed & prosceed on their journey to the Court Noir, at (3) passed a Small River Called Che wah or fish river on the S. S. this river is about 28 yards wide and heads to the N. E, passed a Small creek on the L. S. 1 mile abov the last, and Camped on a Sand bar on the L. S. opposit to us we Saw a Gangue of Buffalow bulls which we did not think worth while to kill- our hunters Killd. 4 Goats 6 Deer 4 Elk & a pelican & informs that they Saw in one Gang 248 Elk, (I walked on Shore, in the evining with a view to See Some of those remarkable places mentioned by evens, none of which I could find,) The Countrey in this quarter is Generally leavel & fine Some high Short hills, and some ragid ranges of Hills at a Distans

The ricara Indians inform us that they find no black tail Deer as high up as this place, those we find are of the fallow Deer Kind

The Ricareis are not fond of Spiritous liquers, nor do they apper to be fond of receiveing any or thank full for it

[Clark, October 19, 1804] 19th of October Friday 1804. Set out early under a gentle Breeze from the S. E. more timber than Common in the bottoms passed a large Pond on the S. S. I walked out on the high land L. Side and observed great numbers of Buffalows, I counted in view at one time 52 gangues of Buffalow & 3 of Elk, besides Deer & goats &c. all the Streems falling from the hills or high lands So brackish that the water Can't be Drank without effecting the person making use of it as Globesalts-, I saw in my walk Several remarkable high Conocal hills, one 90 feet, one 60 and others Smaller-the Indian Chief Say that the Callemet Bird live in the hollows of those hills, which holes are made by the water passing from the top & &. I also Saw an old Village fortified Situated on the top of a high Point, which the Ricarra Chief tels me were Mandans, we Camped on the L. S. I Killed a Deer & Saw Swans &c. our hunters Killed 4 Elk and 6 Deer to Day

[Clark, October 19, 1804] 19th October Friday 1804 a fine morning wind from the S. E. we Set out early under a gentle Breeze and proceeded on verry well, more timber than Common on the banks on this part of the river- passed a large Pond on the S. S.- I walked out on the Hills & observed Great numbers of Buffalow feedeing on both Sides of the river I counted 52 Gangues of Buffalow & 3 of Elk at one view, all the runs which come from the high hills which is Generally about one or 2 miles from the water is brackish and near the Hills (the Salts are) and the Sides of the Hills & edges of the Streems, the mineral salts appear I saw Som remarkable round hills forming a Cone at top one about 90 foot one 60 & Several others Smaller, the Indian Chief Say that the Callemet bird live in the holes of those hills, the holes form by the water washing thro Some parts in its passage Down from the top- near one of those noles, on a point of a hill 90 feet above the lower plane I observed the remains of an old village, which had been fortified, the Indian Chief with us tels me, a party of Mandins lived there, Here first saw ruins of Mandan nation we proceeded on & Camped on the L. S. opposit the upper of those Conocal hills our hunters killed 4 Elk 6 Deer & a pelican, I saw Swans in a Pond & Killed a fat Deer in my walk, Saw above 10 wolves. This day is pleasent

[Clark, October 20, 1804] 20th of October 1804 wind from the S E, I walked out to view those remarkable places pointed out by Evens, and continud all day Saw an old Village of the Mandans below the Chess chi ter R. appear to have been fortified above the village on the Same L. S. is a coal bank where we Campd. passed a Small Creek on the S. S. and an Island on the L. S Covered with willows Small Cotton the Countrey thro which I passed this day is Delightfull, Timber in the bottoms, Saw great nos. of Buffalow Elk Goats & Deer as we were in want of them I Killed 3 Deer, our hunters 10 Deer and wounded a white Bear, I Saw Several fresh tracks of that animal double the Sise of the largest track I ever Saw, great numbers of wolves, those animals follow the buffalow and devour, those that die or are Killed, and those too fat or pore to Keep up with the gangue

[Clark, October 20, 1804] 20th of October Satterday 1804 Set out early this morning and proceeded on the wind from the S. E after brackfast I walked out on the L. Side to See those remarkable places pointed out by Evins, I saw an old remains of a villige on the Side of a hill which the Chief with us Too ne tels me that nation lived in a number villages on each Side of the river and the Troubleson Seauex caused them to move about 40 miles higher up where they remained a fiew years & moved to the place they now live, (2) passed a Small Creek on the S. S. (3) and one on the L. S. passed (4) a Island Covered with willows laying in the middle of the river no current on the L. S. Camped on the L. S. above a Bluff containing Coal (5) of an inferior quallity, this bank is imedeately above the old village of the Mandans- The Countrey is fine, the high hills at a Distanc with gradual assents, I Kild 3 Deer The Timber Confined to the bottoms as usial which is much larger than below. Great numbers of Buffalow Elk & Deer, Goats. our hunters killed 10 Deer & a Goat to day and wounded a white Bear I saw Several fresh track of those animals which is 3 times as large as a mans track-, The wind hard all Day from the N. E. & East, great numbers of buffalow Swiming the river

I observe near all large gangues of buffalow wolves and when the buffalow move those Anamals follow and feed on those that are killed by accident or those that are too pore or fat to Keep up with the gangue.

[Lewis, October 20, 1804] 20th October Peter Crusat this day shot at a white bear he wounded him, but being alarmed at the formidable appearance of the bear he left his tomahalk and gun; but shortly after returned and found that the bear had taken the opposite rout.- soon after he shot a buffaloe cow broke her thy, the cow pursued him he concealed himself in a small raviene.-

[Clark, October 21, 1804] 21t of October Sunday 1804 a verry Cold night wind hard from the N. E. Some rain in the night which feesed as it fell, at Day began to Snow and Continued all the fore part of the day, at 1/4 of a mile passed the Mouth of Chess-che tar (or Heart) River L. S. 38 yards wide, this river heads near Turtle mountain with Knife River on this River is a Smothe Stone which the Indians have great fath in & Consult the Stone on all great occasions which they Say Marks or Simblems are left on the Stone of what is to take place &c. an old mandan Village above the mouth of this Little River, I saw a Single tree in the open Plains which the Mandans formerly paid great Devotion to run Cords thro their flesh & tie themselves to the tree to make them brave, passed an old Village on a Small run on the S S. one on the bank L. and Camped, I Killed a fat Buffalow this evening- Little gun all my hunting

[Clark, October 21, 1804] 21st October Sunday 1804 a verry Cold night wind hard from the N. E Some rain in the night which frosed up it fell at Day light it began to Snow and Continud all the fore part of the Day passed just above our Camp (1) a Small river on the L. S. Called by the Indians Chiss-Cho-tar this river is about 38 yards wide Containing a good Deel of water Some Distance up this River is Situated a Stone which the Indians have great fath in & Say they See painted on the Stone, "all the Calemites & good fortune to hapin the nation & partes who visit it"- a tree (an oak) which Stands alone near this place about 2 miles off in the open prarie which has with Stood the fire they pay Great respect to, make Holes and tie Strings thro the Skins of their necks and around this tree to make them brave (all this is the information of Too ne is a whipper will) the Chief of the Ricares who accompanied us to the Mandins, at 2 miles (2) passed the 2nd Villages of the Manden, which was in existance at the Same time with the 1st this village is at the foot of a hill on the S. S. on a butifull &extensive plain - at this time Covered with Buffalow- a Cloudy afternoon, I killed a fine Buffalow, we Camped on the L. S. verry Cold ground Covered with Snow. one orter KIM.

[Clark, October 22, 1804] 22nd of October 1804 last night at about 1 oClock I was violently attacked with Rhumetism in my neck, which was so violently I could not move, Cap L. applied a hot Stone raped in flannel which gave temperry ease, we passed a War party of Tetons on their way as we Supposed to the Mandons of 12 men on the L. S. we gave them nothing and refused to put them across the river, passed 2 old Villages at the mouth of a large Creek L. S and a Small Island at the head of which is a bad place, an old Village on the S. S.

and the upper of the 6 Villages the Mandans occupied about 25 years ago this village was entirely cut off by the Sioux & one of the others nearly, the Small Pox distroyed great Numbers

[Clark, October 22, 1804] 22nd October Monday 1804 last night at 1 oClock I was violently and Suddinly attacked with the Rhumitism in the neck which was So violent I could not move Capt. applied a hot Stone raped in flannel, which gave me some temporory ease,-. we Set out early, the morning Cold at 7 oClock we Came too at a Camp of Teton Seaux on the L. S. those people 12 in number were naikd and had the appearanc of war, we have every reason to believ that they are going or have been to Steel horses from the Mandins, they tell two Stories, we gave them nothing after takeing brackfast proceeded on- my Neck is yet verry painfull at times Spasms.

Camped on the L Side, passed an Island Situated on the L. Side at the head of which & Mandans village S. S. we passd a bad place- The hunters killed a buffalow bull, they Say out of about 300 buffalow which they Saw, they did not See one Cow. Great Deel of Beaver Sign. Several Cought every night.

[Clark, October 23, 1804] 23rd of October 1804 Some Snow, passed 5 Lodges fortified the place the two french men were robed Those are the hunting Camps of the mandans, who has latterly left them. we camped on the L. S.

[Clark, October 23, 1804] 23rd of October Tuesday 1804 a cloudy morning Some Snow Set out early pass five Lodges which was Diserted, the fires yet burning we Suppose those were the Indians who robed the 2 french Trappers a fiew days ago those 2 men are now with us going up with a view to get their property from the Indians thro us. cold & Cloudy camped on The L. S. of the river

[Clark, October 24, 1804] 24th of October Cloudy Some little Snow (my Rhumetism Continue, not So bad as the 2 last days,) a butufull Countrey on both Sides, bottoms covered with wood, we See no game to day, passed an old village of a Band of Me ne tarres Called Mah har ha where they lived 40 year ago on the L. S. Came too on an Island Caused by the river cutting through a narrow point 7 years ago, on this island we wer visited by the grand Chief of the mandans a 2d Chief and Some other, who wer Camped on the Island, those Chief met our Ricarra Chief with great Corduallity, & Smoked together Cap Lewis Visited the Camps 5 Lodges, and proceeded on & Camped near a 2d Camp of Mandans on the S. S. nearly opposit the old Ricara & Manden Village which the Ricarras abandaned in the year 1789

[Clark, October 24, 1804] 24th October Wednesday 1804 Set out early a Cloudy day Some little Snow in the morning I am Something better of the Rhumutim in my neck- a butiful Countrey on both Sides of the river. The bottoms Covd. with wood, we have Seen no game on the river to day a prof of the Indians hunting in the neighbourhod (1) passed a Island on the S. S. made by the river Cutting through a point, by which the river is Shortened Several miles- on this Isld. we Saw one of the Grand Chiefs of the Mandins, with five Lodges hunting, this Cheif met the Chief of the Ricares who accompanied us with great Cordiallity & Sermony Smoked the pipe & Capt. Lewis with the Interpeter went with the Chiefs to his Lodges at 1 mile distant, after his return we admited the Grand Chief & his brother for a few minits on our boat. proceeded on a Short distance and Camped on the S. S. below the old Village of the Mandins & ricares.- Soon after our landg. 4 Mandins Came from a Camp above, the Ricares Chief went with them to their Camp, 25th of October Thursday 1804. a Gentle Breeze from the S. E by E passed an (1) old Village on a high Plain where the Mandans onced lived & after they left the Village & moved higher the Ricaras took possession & live until 1799 when they abandoned it & flew from the just revenge of the Mandans, a verry extensive Bottom above the Village above the Center of which (2) the Mandans lived in the 2 villages on the L. 5., but little timber- Several parties of Indians on each Side of the River going up. in view in every directions- we are informed that the Sioux has latterly taken horses from the Big Bellies or Minitaries and on their way homerwards they fell in with the Assinniboins who killed them and took the horses & a frenchman Menard who resided with the Mandan for 20 years past was Killed a fiew days ago on his way from the Britishment astablishments on the Assineboin River, 150 miles N. of this place to the mandans by the assinniboin Indians- we were frequently Called to by parties of Indians & requested to land & talk, passed a verry bad place & Camped on a Point S S. opposit a high hill Several Indians visit us this evening the Sun of the late great Chief of the Mandans who had 2 of his fingers off and appeared to be pearced in maney places on inquiring the reason, was informed that it was a testimony to their grief for Deceased freinds, they frequently Cut off Sevral fingers & pierced themselves in Different parts, a Mark of Savage effection, wind hard from the S. W. verry Cold R Fields with a Rhumitisum in his Neck one man R. in his hips my Self much better, Those Indians appear to have Similar Customs with the Ricaras, their Dress the Same more mild in their language & justures &c. &c.

[Clark, October 25, 1804] 25th of October Thursday 1804 a Cold morning Set out early under a gentle Breeze from the S. E. by E proceeded on, passed (1) the 3rd old Village of the Mandans which has been Desd. for many years, This village was Situated on an eminance of about 40 foot above the water on the L. S. back for Several miles is a butifull plain (2) at a Short distance above this old village on a Continuation of the Same eminance was Situated the which have been avacuated only Six years, above this village a large and extensive bottom for Several miles in which the Squars raised ther Corn, but little timber near the villages, on the S. S. below is a point of excellent timber, and in the point Several miles above is fine timber, Several parties of Mandins rode to the river on the S. S. to view us indeed they are continuelly in Sight Satisying their Curiossities as to our apperance &c. we are told that the Seaux has latterly fallen in with & Stole the horses of the Big belley, on their way home they fell in with the Ossiniboin who killed them and took the horses- a frenchman has latterly been killed by the Indians on the Track to the tradeing establishment on the Ossinebine R. in the North of this place (or British fort) This frenchman has lived many years with the Mandins- we were frequently called on to land & talk to parties of the Mandins on the Shore, wind Shifted to the S. W at about 11 oClock and blew hard untill 3 OCk. clouded up river full of Sand bars & we are at a great loss to find the Channel of the river, frequently run on the Sand bars which Detain us much passed a verry bad riffle of rocks in the evining by takeing the L. S. of a Sand bar and Camped on a Sand point on the S. S. opposit a high hill on the L. S. Several Indians Come to See us this evening, amongst others the Sun of the late great Cheif of the Mandins, this man has his two little fingers off-; on inquering the Cause, was told it was Customary for this nation to Show their greaf by Some testimony of pain, and that it was not uncommon for them to take off 2 Smaller fingers of the hand and Some times more with ther marks of Savage effection

The wind blew verry hard this evening from the S. W. verry Cold

R. Fields with the rhumitim in his neck, P. Crusat with the Same Complaint in his Legs- the party other wise is well, as to my Self I feel but Slight Simptoms of that disorder at this time,

[Clark, October 26, 1804] 26th of October 1804 wind from the S. E we Set the Ricara Chief on Shore with Some Mandans, many on each Side veiwing of us, we took in 2 Chiefs (Coal and Big Man) and halted a feiw minits at their Camps, on the L. S. fortified in their way, here we Saw a trader from the Ossinniboin River Called McCracken, this man arrived 9 day ago with goods to trade for horses & Roabs one other man with him- we Camped on the L. Side a Short distanc below the r st rnandan village on the L. S. many men women & Children flocked down to See us- Capt Lewis walked to the Village with the Chief and interpeters, my Rheumitism increasing prevented me from going also, and we had Deturmined that both would not leave the boat at the Same time untill we Knew the Desposition of the Nativs, Some Chieef visited me & I Smoked with them- they appeared delighted with the Steel Mill which we were obliged to use, also with my black Servent, Capt Lewis returned late

[Clark, October 26, 1804] 26th of October Friday 1804 Set out early wind from the S W proceeded on Saw numbers of the Mandins on Shore, we Set the Ricare Chief on Shore, and we proceeded on to the Camp of two of their Grand Chiefs where we delayed a fiew minits, with the Chiefs and proceeded on takeing two of their Chiefs on board & Some of the heavy articles of his house hole, Such as earthen pots & Corn, proceeded on, at this Camp Saw a McCracken Englishmon from the N. W Company this mana Came nine Days ago to trade for horses & Buffalo robes,- one other man Came with him. the Indians Continued on the banks all day- but little wood on this part of the river, many Sand bars and bad places, water much devided between them

for the 26th. Octr. we came too and Camped on the L. S. about 1/2 a mile below the ist. Manddin Town on the L. S. Soon after our arrival many men womin & Children flocked down to See us, Capt Lewis walked to the village with the principal Chiefs and our interpters, my rhumatic Complaint increasing I could not go- if I was well only one would have left the Boat & party untill we new the Disposition of the Inds. I Smoked with the Cheifs who Came after. Those people apd much pleased with the Corn mill which we were obliged to use, & was fixed in the boat.

[Clark, October 27, 1804] 27th of October Satturday 1804 we Set out early and Came too at the village on the L. S. where we delayed a few minits, I walked to a Chiefs Logg & Smoked with them, but Could not eat, which did displease them a little, here I met with a Mr. Jessomme, who lived in this nation 13 years, I got him to interpet & he proceedd on with us we proceeded on to a Central point opposit the Knife River, & formed a Camp on the S. S. above the 2d Mandan village & opsd. the Mah-har-ha village- and raised a flag Staff- Capt Lewis & the Intepeters walked down to the 2d Village of Mandans, & returned in about an hour, we Sent 3 Carrotes of tobacco to the other villages & enviting them to come down and Council with us tomorrow,- we endeaver to precure Some Knowledge of the principal Chiefs of the Different nations &.- well to give my ideas as to the impression thais man makes on me is a Cunin artfull an insoncear - he tels me he was once empld. by my brother in the Illinois & of his description I conceve as a Spye upon the British of Michillinicknac & St Joseph,s we think he may be made use full to us & do employ him as an interpeter- no. of Indians bring their wives &c. to the campes of our party on Shore &c.

[Clark, October 27, 1804] 27th of October Satturday 1804 we Set out arly Came too at this Village on the L. S. this village is Situated on an eminance of about 50 feet above the Water in a handson Plain it Containes houses in a kind of Picket work. the houses are round and Verry large Containing Several families, as also their horses which is tied on one Side of the enterance, a Discription of those houses will be given hereafter, I walked up & Smoked a pipe with the Cheifs of this Village they were anxious that I would Stay and eat with them, my indisposition provented my eating which displeased them, untill a full explination took place, I returned to the boat and Sent 2 Carrots of Tobacco for them to Smoke, and proceeded on, passed the 2d Village and Camped opsd. the Village of the Weter Soon or ah wah bar ways which is Situated on an eminance in a plain on the L. S. this Village is Small and Contains but fiew inhabitents. above this village & also above the Knife river on the Same Side of the Missouri the Big bellies Towns are Situated a further Discription will be given here after as also of the Town of Mandans on this Side of the river i e S. Side

a fine worm Day we met with a french man by the name of jassamme which we imploy as an interpeter This man has a wife & Children in the Village- Great numbers on both Sides flocked down to the bank to view us as wee passed.

Capt. Lewis with the Interpetr. walked down to the village below our Camp After delaying one hour he returned and informed me the Indians had returned to their village &c., &c., we Sent three Carrots of Tobacco by three young men, to the three Villages above inviting them to come Down & Council with us tomorrow. many Indians Came to view us Some Stayed all night in the Camp of our party- we procured Some information of Mr. Jessomme of the Chiefs of the Different Nations

[Clark, October 28, 1804]
28th of October 1804
the wind So hard from the S. W. We could not meet the Indians in
Councils, those who visited us we Sent to the nearest village,
Consulted the Black Cat M Chief about the Chiefs of the Different
Villages, who gave his Oppinion to us.

[Clark, October 28, 1804] Sunday 28th of October 1804 a windey Day, fair and Clear many of the Grosvantres (or Big Bellies) and Watersons Came to See us and hear the Council the wind being So violently hard from the S. W. provented our going into Councel, (indeed the Chiefs of the Manodans from the lower Village Could not Cross, we made up the presents and entertained Several of the Curious Cheifs whome, wished to See the Boat which was verry Curious to them viewing it as great medison, as they also viewed my black Servent The Black Cat Grand Chief of the Mandans, Capt Lewis & my Self with an Interpeter walked up the river about 1 1/2 miles our views were to examine the Situation & Timbers for a fort, we found the Situation good but the Timber Scerce, or at least Small timbr Such as would answer us-, we Cunsulted the Grand Chief in respect to the other Chiefs of the Defferent Villages he gave the names of 12- George Drewyer Cought 2 Beaver above our Camp last night, we had Several presents from the Woman of Corn boild homney, Soft Corn &c. &c. I prosent ajar to the Chiefs wife who recved it with much pleasure our men verry Chearfull this evening- we Sent the Cheifs of the Gross Vantres to Smoke a pipe with the Grand Chef of the Mandins in his Village, & told them we would Speek tomorrow.

[Clark, October 29, 1804] 29th of October 1804 a fine morning after Brackfast we were Visited by the Old Chief of the Big Bellies or me ne tar res, this Man has Given his power to his Son who is now on a war party against the Snake Indians who inhabit the Rockey Mountains, the S W wind verry high- we met in Council under an orning and our Sales Stretched round to keep out as much wind as possible & Delivered a long Speach Similar to what had been Said to the nations below, the old Chief was restless before the Speech was half ended, observed his Camp was exposed & could wait no longer &c. at the Conclusion of the Speach we mentioned the Ricaras & requested them to make a peace & Smoke out of the Sacred Stem with their Chief which I intreduced and gave him the pipe of peace to hand around, they all Smoked with eagerness out of the pipe held by the Ricara Chief Ar-ke-tar-na-Shar we mentioned our hands that were to be discharged here, also the roberrey commited on th 2 french men below, & requested them to answere us tomorrow, gave the Chief Small preasents and a fiew presents for each village Shot the air gun which both Surprised and astonished the nativs, and Soon dispersed

our Ricara Chief Came told me he wished to return to his nation tomorrow I put him off & Said we would Send a talk by him after the Chiefs had Spoken to us- we gave a Steel mill to the mandans which was verry pleasing to them

The Chief who recved Medals to Day are as follows viz-in Council

is Mandan village Ma-too-ton kai s Chief Sha-ha-ka Big White 2nd Ka-goh-ha-me little Crows

2 do village Roop tar-hee

1 s & grand Chief Poss-cop-sa-he Black Cat

2d Chief Car-gar-no-mok-she raven man Chief

Mah har-ha village

is Chief Ta-tuck-co pin re has, white Buffalow Skin unfolded

Little Menetarre village

is Chief Omp-Se-ha-ra Black mockerson. 2d Chief Oh-hark little Fox.

The Grand village of Manetarres, The One Eye is the principal Chief and he is out on a hunting party. we Send by the Grape all the articles for this grand Chief and all the Village what goods was intended for that Village- The Prarie got on fire and went with Such Violenc & Speed as to Catch a man & woman & burn them to Death, Several escapd. among other a Small boy who was Saved by getting under a green Buffalow Skin, this boy was half white, & the Indians Say all white flesh is medisan, they Say the grass was not burnt where the boy Sat &c. &. this fire passed us at 8 oClock, and lookd truly tremendious.

[Clark, October 29, 1804] 29th October Monday 1804 a fair fine morning after Brackfast we were visited by the old Cheaf of the Big bellies or _____ this man was old and had transfered his power to his Sun, who was then out at war against the Snake Indians who inhabit the rockey mountains- at 10 oClock the S W. wind rose verry high, we Collected the Chiefs and Commened a Council ounder a Orning and our Sales Stretched around to Keep out as much wind as possible, we delivered a long Speech the Substance of which Similer to what we had Delivered to the nations below. the old Chief of the Grossanters was verry restless before the Speech was half ended observed that he Could not wait long that his Camp was exposed to the hostile Indians, &c. &. he was rebuked by one of the Chiefs for his uneasiness at Such a time as the present, we at the end of the Speech mentioned the Ricare who Accompanied us to make a firm peace, they all Smoked with him (I gave this Cheaf a Dollar of the American Coin as a Meadel with which he was much pleased) In Councel we prosented him with a Certificate of his Sincrity and good Conduct &c. we also Spoke about the fur which was taken from 2 french men by a Mandan, and informd of our intentions of Sending back the french hands- after the Council we gave the presents with much Seremoney, and put the Meadels on the Cheifs we intended to make viz. one for each Town to whome we gave Coats hats & flags, one Grand Cheif to each nation to whome we gave meadels with the presidents likeness in Councel we requested them to give us an answer tomorrow or as Soon as possible to Some points which required their Deliberation- after the Council was over we Shot the Air gun which appeared to assonish the nativs much, the greater part them retired Soon after

The Ricare Cheaf Ar-ke-tar-na-shar Came to me this evening and tells me that he wishes to return to his Village & nation, I put him off Saying tomorrow we would have an answer, to our talk to the Satisfaction & Send by him a String of wompom informing what had passed here. a Iron or Steel Corn Mill which we gave to the Mandins, was verry Thankfully recived- (rte The Prarie was Set on fire (or Cought by accident) by a young man of the Mandins, the fire went with Such velocity that it burnt to death a man and woman, who Could not Get to any place of Safty, one man a woman & Child much burnt and Several narrowly escaped the flame- a boy half white was Saved un hurt in the midst of the flaim, Those ignerent people Say this boy was Saved by the great Spirit medisin because he was white- The Cause of his being Saved was a Green buffalow Skin was thrown over him by his mother who perhaps had more fore Sight for the pertection of her Son, and less for herself than those who escaped the flame, the Fire did not burn under the Skin leaving the grass round the boy This fire passed our Camp last about 8 oClock P.M. it went with great rapitidity and looked Tremendious

The following Chiefs were made in Council to day

Mar-too-ton-ha or Lower Village of the Mandans 1st Cheif Sha-ha-ka or Big White 2 do Ka-goh-ha-mi or Little raven

Roop-tar-hee or Second Village of the Mandans 1st and Grand Cheif-Pass-cop-sa-he or black Cat 2nd Cheif Car-gar-no-mok-She raven man Cheaf

Mah-har-ha 3rd Village
Chief Ta-tuck-co-pin-re-ha (white Buffalow robe unfolded)

Me-ne-tar-re Me-te har-tar 1st Cheif-Omp-se-ha-ra. Black Mockersons 2 do. Oh-harh or Little fox

we Sent the presents intended for the Grand Chief of the Mi-ne-tar-re or Big Belley, and the presents flag and wompoms by the Old Chief and those, and those intended for the Cheif of the Lower Village by a young Cheif

The following Cheifs were recommended in addition to those Viz.

1st Village Oh-hee-nar Big Man- a Chien Sho-ta-har ro-ra

2d Village Taw nish-e-o- Bel-lar sa ra Ar-rat-ta na-mock-She- Wolf Man Chief

3rd Village
Min-nis-Sur-ra-ree (Neighing horse)
Lo-tong-gar-ti har- old woman at a distance

4th Village Mar-noh-tah the big Steeler Man-se-rus-se- tale of Callumet bird

5th Village
Ad hako ho pin nee Little Wolfs medisons
Ar-rat-toe-no mook-gu (man wolf Chief) (at war)
Cal-tar co ta- (Cherry grows on a bush) old Chief and father to the
above mentd.
Chief Maw-pah'-pir-re-cos-sa too- This chief is near this hunting and a
verry Considerable man

To the 1st Chiefs we gave a medal with the Imp. of the President of the
U S.
To the 2d Chiefs a medal of weaveing & Domestic animals.
To the 3rd Chiefs a medal with the impression of a man Sowing wheat.

4th Village 1 Ea pa no pa- Two taled Calumet bird young Chief 2 War he ras sa the red Shield young Chief of
Big belley-big town

[Clark, October 30, 1804] 30th of October Tuesday 1804 many Indian Chief visit us today I went in th Perogou
to the Island 7 miles above to look out a proper place for to winter, it being near the tim the ice begins to run
at this place, and the Countrey after a few leagues high is Said to be barron of timber, I found no place
Soutable, & we concluded to drop down to th next point below & build a fort to winter in the Party Danced
which Delited the Indians.

[Clark, October 30, 1804] 30th October Tuesday 1804 Two Chiefs came to have Some talk one the princapal of
the lower Village the other the one who thought himself the principal mane, & requested to hear Some of the
Speech that was Delivered yesterday they were gratified, and we put the medal on the neck of the Big White to
whome we had Sent Clothes yesterday & a flag, those men did not return from hunting in time to join the
Counell, they were well pleased (2d of those is a Chien) I took 8 men in a Small perogue and went up the river
as far as the 1st Island about 7 miles to See if a Situation Could be got on it for our Winter quarters, found the
wood on the Isd. as also on the pt. above So Distant from the water that, I did not think that we Could get a
good wintering ground there, and as all the white men here informed us that wood was Sceres, as well as game
above, we Deturmined to drop down a fiew miles near wood and game on my return found maney Inds. at our
Camp, gave the party a dram, they Danced as is verry Comn. in the evening which pleased the Savages much.
Wind S. E

[Clark, October 30, 1804]
Mandans

Ka gar no mogh ge the 2d Chief of the 2d Village of Mandins Came the 30t of Octr. and Spoke to us as follows.
Viz

Will you be So good as to go to the Village the Grand Chief will Speek & give Some Corn, if you will let Some
men take bags it will be well. I am going with, the Chief of the ricares to Smoke a pipe with that nation- I
concluded to go down

Mockerson Indians

The principal Chief of the Wau to Soon Came and Spoke a fiew words on Various Subjects not much to the
purpose. we Smoked and after my Shooting the air gun he departed, Those nations know nothing of reagular
Councills, and know not how to proceed in them, they are restless &c-

[Clark, October 31, 1804] 31st of October Wednesday 1804 The main Chief of the mandans Sent 2 Cheifs for to
envite us to Come to his Lodge, and here what he has to Say I with 2 interpetes walked down, and with great
Cerimony was Seated on a Robe by the Side of the Chief; he threw a Robe highly decoraterd over my Sholders,
and after Smokeing a pipe with the old men in the Circle, the Chief Spoke he belived all we had told him, and
that peace would be genl. which not only gave himself Satisfaction but all his people; they now Could hunt
without fear & their women could work in the fields without looking every moment for the ememey, as to the
Ricaras addressing himself to the Chief with me you know we do not wish war with your nation, you have
brought it on your Selves, that man Pointing to the 2d Chief and those 2 young warriers will go with you &
Smoke in the pipes of peace with the Ricaras- I will let you see my father addressing me that we wish to be at
peace with all and do not make war upon any- he continud to Speak in this Stile (refer to notes) he delivered 2

of the Traps to me which was taken from the french men, gave me 2 bushels of Corn, I answered the Speech which appeared to give general Satisfactionand returned to the boat, In the evening the Chief Visited us Dressed in his new Suit, &delayed untill late the men Dancd untill 10 oClock which was common with them wrote to the N W Copanys agent on the Ossinniboin River by a Mr. McCruckin.

[Clark, October 31, 1804] 31st of October Wednesday 1804 a fine morning, the Chief of the Mandans Sent a 2d Chief to invite us to his Lodge to recive Some Corn & here what he had to Say I walked down and with great ceremoney was Seeted on a roab by the Side of the Chief, he threw a handsom Roabe over me and after smokeing the pipe with Several old men arround, the Chief Spoke Said he believed what we had told them, and that peace would be general, which not only gave him Satisfaction but all his people, they now Could hunt without fear, & ther womin Could work in the fields without looking everry moment for the Enemey, and put off their mockersons at night, as to the Reares we will Show you that we wish peace with all, and do not make war on any without Cause, that Chief pointing to the 2d and Some brave men will accompy. the Ricare Chief now with you to his village & nation, to Smoke with that people, when you Came up the Indians in the neighbouring Villages, as well as those out hunting when they heard of you had great expectations of reciving presents they those hunting imediately on hearing returned to the Village and all was Disapointed, and Some Dessatisfied, as to himself he was not much So but his Village was- he would go and See his great father &c. &c.

he had put before me 2 of the Steel traps which was robed from the french a Short tim ago. about 12 bushels of Corn which was brought and put before me by the womin of the Village after the Chief finished & Smoked in great cerrimony, I answered the Speech which Satisfied them verry much and returned to the boat. met the princapal Chief of the 3d Village and the Little Crow both of which I invited into the Cabin and Smoked & talked with for about one hour. Soon after those Chiefs left us the Grand Chief of the Mandans Came Dressed in the Clothes we had given with his 2 Small Suns, and requested to See the men Dance which they verry readily gratified him in,- the wind blew hard all the after part of the day from the N E and Continud all night to blow hard from that point, in the mornig it Shifed N W. Capt Lewis wrote to the N W Companys agent on the Orsineboine River abt. North of this place

[Clark, October 31, 1804] black Cat or Pose-cop-sa-he 1st Chief of the Mandans & 2d Village

"I believe what you have told us in Council, & that peace will be general, which not only givs me pleasure, but Satisfaction to all the nation, they now Can hunt without fear, and our womin Can work in the fields without looking every moment for the enimey-" as to the Ricares we will Show you that we wish piace with all, and do not make war on any with out Cause, that Chief pointing to the 2d of the Village and Some young men will accompany the Ricrea Chief home to his Nation to Smoke with that people- When the Indians of the Different Villages heard of your Comeing up they all Came in from hunting to See, they expected Great presents. they were disapointed, and Some dissatisfied- as to my Self I am not much So, but my Village are- he believed the roade was open; and he would go and See his great father- he Delivered Up 2 Traps which had been taken from the french, & gave me a roabe & about 12 bushels of Corn- & smoked &c

I answered the Speech it explained, many parts which he Could not understand-of the Speech of yesterday.

[Lewis, October 31, 1804] Wednesday October 31st 1804. The river being very low and the season so far advanced that it frequently shuts up with ice in this climate we determined to spend the Winter in this neighbourhood, accordingly Capt. Clark with a party of men reconnoitred the countrey for some miles above our encampment; he returned in the evening without having succeed in finding an eligible situation for our purpose.-

[Clark, November 1, 1804] 1 November 1804 Visited by Several Chiefs of the lower Village who requested we would call on them &c. Spoke to the Same purpote with the Grand Chief. we Set out in the evening & I with the Party droped down to the place we intended to winter & Cap Lewis called at the Village 3 miles above &. &.

[Clark, November 1, 1804] 1st of November Thursday 1804 the wind hard from the N W. Mr. McCrackin a Trader Set out at 7 oClock to the fort on the Ossiniboin by him Send a letter, (incloseing a Copy of the British Ministers protection) to the principal agent of the Company- at about 10 OClock the Cheifs of the Lower Village Cam and after a Short time informed us they wished they would us to call at their village & take Some Corn, that they would make peace with the Ricares they never made war against them but after the rees Killed their Chiefs they killed them like the birds, and were tired and would Send a Chief and Some brave men to the Ricares to Smoke with that people in the evening we Set out and fell down to the lower Village where Capt. Lewis got out and continud at the Village untill after night I proceeded on & landed on the S. S. at the upper point of the 1st Timber on the Starboard Side after landing & Continuinge- all night droped down to a proper place to build Capt Lewis Came down after night, and informed me he intended to return the next morning by the perticular Request of the Chiefs.

We passed the Villages on our Decent in veiw of Great numbers of the inhabitents

[Clark, November 1, 1804] The 1st of Novr. Mandins is Village the Main Chief Big White & 2 others i e the Big Man or Sha-ha-ca and _____ Came early to talk, and Spoke as follows, after Smoking, Viz.

Is it Certain that the ricares intend to make good with us our wish is to be at peace with all, we will Send a Chief with the pania Chief and Some young men to Smoke and make good peace-? are you going to Stay abov or below this Cold.- answer by C. L We are going down a few miles to look a place we can find no place abov proper.

The panias know's we do not begin the war, they allway begin, we Sent a Chief and a pipe to the Pania to Smoke and they killed them-, we have killed enough of them we kill them like the birds, we do not wish to kill more, we will, make a good peace

We were Sorry when we heard of your going up but now you are going down, we are glad, if we eat you Shall eat, if we Starve you must Starve also, our village is too far to bring the Corn to you, but we hope you will Call on us as you pass to the place you intend to Stop

C L answered the above-

[Lewis, November 1, 1804] Thursday November 1st 1804 The wind blew so violently during the greater part of this day that we were unable to quit our encampment; in the evening it abated;- we droped down about seven miles and land on N. E. side of the river at a large point of Woodland.

[Clark, November 2, 1804] 2nd Novr. 1804 Friday- Capt Lewis returned to the Village & I fixed on a place for to build a fort and Set to work Cap Lewis returned in the eveng with 11 bushels of Corn, the Ricarre Chief Set out for his Village accompanied by Several mandans

[Clark, November 2, 1804] 2nd November Friday 1804 This morning at Day light I went down the river with 4 men to look for a proper place to winter proceeded down the river three miles & found a place well Supld. with wood, & returned, Capt. Lewis went to the village to here what they had to Say & I fell down, and formed a camp near where a Small Camp of Indian were huntig Cut down the Trees around our Camp, in the evening Capt. Lewis returned with a present of 11 bushels of Corn, our recaree Chief Set out acccompanied by one Chief and Several Brave men, he Called for Some Small article which we had given but as I could not understand him he Could not get. the wind from the S. E. a fine day- many Indians to day

[Lewis, November 2, 1804] Friday November 2nd 1804" This morning early we fixed on the site for our fortification which we immediately set about.

This place we have named Fort Mandan in honour of our Neighbours.

[Clark, November 3, 1804] 3rd of November Satturday 1804 wind hard from the west Commence building our Cabins, Dispatched 6 hunters in a perogue Down the River to hunt, Discharged the french hands, Mr. Jessomme his Squar & child moved to camp, the little Crow loaded his Squar with meat for us also a Roabe, we gave the Squar an ax & &. Cought 2 bever near Camp

[Clark, November 3, 1804] 3rd of November Satterday 1804 a fine morning wind hard from the West we commence building our Cabins, Send Down in Perogue 6 men to hunt Engaged one man, Set the french who intend to return to build a perogue, many Indians pass to hunt, Mr. Jessomme with his Squar & Children. come Down to live, as Interpter, we recive a hors for our Sirvice, in the evening the Ka goh ha mi or little ravin Came & brought us on his Squar about 60 Wt. of Dried Buffalow meat a roabe, & Pot of Meal &. they Delayed all night- we gave his Squar an ax & a fiew Small articles & himself a piece of Tobacco, the Men were indulged with a Dram, this evening two Beaver Cought This morning- and one Trap Lost

[Clark, November 4, 1804] 4th of Novr. a french man by Name Chabonah, who Speaks the Big Belley language visit us, he wished to hire & informed us his 2 Squars were Snake Indians, we engau him to go on with us and take one of his wives to interpet the Snake language The Indians Horses & Dogs live in the Same Lodge with themselves

[Clark, November 4, 1804] 4th November Sunday 1804 Fort Mandan a fine morning we Continued to Cut Down trees and raise our houses, a Mr. Chaubonee, interpeter for the Gross Vintre nation Came to See us, and informed that he came Down with Several Indians from a Hunting expedition up the river, to here what we had told the Indians in Councl this man wished to hire as an interpeter, the wind rose this evining from the East & Clouded up- Great numbers of Indians pass hunting and Some on the return-

[Clark, November 5, 1804] 5th November Monday 1804 I rose verry early and commenced raising the 2 range of Huts the timber large and heavy all to Carry on Hand Sticks, Cotton wood & Elm Som ash Small, our Situation Sandy, great numbers of Indians pass to and from hunting a Camp of Mandans, A fiew miles below us Cought within two days 100 Goat, by Driveing them in a Strong pen, derected by a Bush fence widening from the pen

&c. &. the Greater part of this day Cloudy, wind moderate from the N. W. I have the Rhumitism verry bad, Cap Lewis writeing all Day- we are told by our interpeter that 4 Ossiniboin Indians, have arrived at the Camps of the Gross Venters & 50 Lodges are Comeing

[Clark, November 6, 1804] 6th of Nov. Mr. Gravolin our Ricara Interpreter & 2 of our french hands & 2 boys Set out in a Canoe for the Ricaras Mr. ravellin is to accompany the Ricaras Chiefs to the City of Washington in the Spring, Great numbers of Geese pass to the South which is a certain approach of ice

[Clark, November 6, 1804] 6th November Tuesday 1804 Fort Mandan last night late we wer awoke by the Sergeant of the Guard to See a nothern light, which was light, not red, and appeared to Darken and Some times nearly obscered, and open, many times appeared in light Streeks, and at other times a great Space light & containing floating Collomns which appeared opposite each other & retreat leaveing the lighter Space at no time of the Same appeerence

This morning I rose a Day light the Clouds to the North appeared black at 8 oClock the wind begun to blow hard from the N W. and Cold, and Continud all Day Mr. Jo Gravilin our ricare interpeter Paul premor, Lajuness & 2 french Boys, who Came with us, Set out in a Small perogue, on their return to the ricaree nation & the Illinois, Mr. Gravilin has instructions to take on the recarees in the Spring &c.- Continue to build the huts, out of Cotton Timber, &c. this being the only timber we have.

[Clark, November 7, 1804] 7th November Wednesday 1804 a termperate day we continued to building our hut, Cloudy and fogging all day

[Clark, November 8, 1804] 8th Novr. Thursday 1804 a Cloudy morning Jussome our interpreter went to the Village, on his return he informed us that three English men had arrived from the Hudsons Bay Company, and would be here tomorrow, we Contd. to build our huts, many Indians Come to See us and bring their horses to Grass near us

[Clark, November 9, 1804] 9th Novr. Friday 1804 a verry hard frost this morning we Continue to build our Cabens, under many disadvantages, Day Cloudy wind from the N W. Several Indians pass with flying news, we got a White weasel, (Taile excepted which was black at the end) of an Indian Capt Lewis walked to the hill abt. 3/4 of a mile- we are Situated in a point of the Missouri North Side in a Cotton wood Timber, this Timber is tall and heavy Containing an imence quantity of water Brickle & Soft food for Horses to winter (as is Said by the Indians) The Mandans Graze their horses in the day on Grass, and at night give them a Stick of Cotton wood to eate, Horses Dogs & people all pass the night in the Same Lodge or round House, Covd. with earth with a fire in the middle

great number of wild gees pass to the South, flew verry high

[Clark, November 10, 1804] 10th November Satturday 1804 rose early continued to build our fort numbers of Indians Came to See us a Chief Half Partia & brought a Side of a Buffalow, in return We Gave Some fiew small things to himself & wife & Son, he Crossed the river in the Buffalow Skin Canoo & and, the Squar took the Boat and proceeded on to the Town 3 miles the Day raw and Cold wind from the N W, the Gees Continue to pass in gangues as also brant to the South, Some Ducks also pass

[Clark, November 11, 1804] 11th November Sunday 1804 Fort Mandan a Cold Day Continued at work at the Fort Two men Cut themselves with an ax, The large Ducks pass to the South an Indian gave me Several roles of parched meal two Squars of the Rock Mountain, purchased from the Indians by a frenchmen Came down The Mandans out hunting the Buffalow

[Clark, November 12, 1804] 12th November Monday 1804 a verry Cold night early this morning the Big White princapal Chief of the lower Village of the Mandans Came Down, he packd about 100 W. of fine meet on his Squar for us, we made Some Small presents to the Squar, & Child gave a Small ax which She was much pleased- 3 men Sick with the _____ Several, Wind Changeable verry cold evening, freesing all day Some ice on the edges of the river.

Swans passing to the South, the Hunters we Sent down the river to hunt has not returned

The interpeter Says that the Mandan nation as they old men Say Came out of a Small lake where they had Gardins, maney years ago they lived in Several Villages on the Missourie low down, the Smallpox destroyed the greater part of the nation and reduced them to one large Village and Some Small ones, all nations before this maladey was affrd. of them after they were reduced the Sioux and other Indians waged war, and killed a great maney, and they moved up the Missourie, those Indians Still continued to wage war, and they moved Still higher, untill they got in the Countrey of the Panias, whith this ntn. they lived in friendship maney years, inhabiting the Same neighbourhood untill that people waged war, They moved up near the watersoons &

winataree where they now live in peace with those nations, the mandans Specke a language peculial to themselves

they can rase about 350 men, the Winatarees about 80 and the Big bellies about 600 or 650 men. the mandans and Seauex have the Same word for water-The Big bellies Winitarees & ravin Indians Speake nearly the Same language and the presumption is they were origionally the Same nation The Ravin Indians have 400 Lodges & about 1200 men, & follow the Buffalow, or hunt for their Subsistance in the plains & on the Court not & Rock Mountains, & are at war with the Sioux Snake Indians

The Big bellies & Watersoons are at war with the Snake Indians & Seauex, and were at war with the Ricares untill we made peace a fiew days passd.- The Mandans are at War with all who make war on them, at present with the Seauex only, and wish to be at peace with all nations, Seldom the agressors-

[Clark, November 13, 1804] 13th The Ice begin to run we move into our hut, visited by the Grand Chief of the Mandans, and Che chark Lagru a Chief of the Assinniboins & 7 men of that Nation, I Smoke with them and gave the Chief a Cord & a Carrot of Tobacco- this Nation rove in the Plains above this and trade with the British Companes on the Ossinniboin River, they are Divided into Several bands, the decendants of the Sioux & Speak nearly their langguage a bad disposed Set & Can raies about moo men in the 3 bands near this place, they trade with the nations of this neighbourhood for horses Corn & Snow all Day Capt. L. at the village.

[Clark, November 13, 1804] 13th Novr. Tuesday 1804 The Ice began to run in the river 1/2 past 10 oClock P. M we rose early & onloaded the boat before brackfast except, the Cabin, & Stored away in a Store house- at 10 oClock A M the Black Cat the Mandin Chief and Lagru Che Chark Chief & 7 men of note visited us at Fort Mandan, I gave him a twist of Tobacco to Smoke with his people & a Gold Cord with a view to Know him again, The nation Consists of about 600 men, hunt in the Plains & winter and trade on the Ossiniboin River, they are Decendants of the Siaux and Speake their language, they Come to the nations to this quarter to trade or (make preasthts) for horses the method of this Kind of Trafick by addoption Shall be explained hereafter &, Snow'd all day, the Ice ran thick and air Cold.

[Clark, November 14, 1804] Fort Mandan 14th of November Wednesday 1804 a Cloudy morning, ice runing verry thick river rose 1/2 Inch last night Some Snow falling, only two Indians visit us to day Owing to a Dance at the Village last night in Concluding a Serimoney of adoption, and interchange of property, between the Ossinoibins, Christinoes and the nations of this neighbourhood- we Sent one man by land on hors back to know the reason of the Delay of our hunters, this evening 2 french men who were traping below Came up-with 20 beaver we are compelled to use our Pork which we doe Spearingly for fear of Some falur in precureing a Sufficiency from the Woods.

our Interpeter informs that 70 Lodges one of 3 bands of Assinniboins & Some Crestinoes, are at the Mandan Village. The Crrirstinoes are abt. 300 men Speak the Chipaway-Language, the live near Fort De peare

[Clark, November 15, 1804] 15th of November Thursday 1804 a Cloudy morning, the ice run much thicker than yesterday at 10 oClock G Drewyer & the frenchman we Dispatched yesterday came up from the Hunters, who is incamped about 30 miles below- after a about one hour we Dispatched a man with orders to the hunters to proceed on without Delay thro the floating ice, we Sent by the man Tin, to put on the parts of the Perogue exposed to the ice & a toe roape- The wind Changeable- all hands work at their huts untill 1 oClock at night Swans passing to the South- but fiew fowls water to be Seen- not one Indian Came to our fort to day

[Clark, November 16, 1804] 16th November Friday 1804 a verry white frost all the trees all Covered with ice, Cloudy, all the men move into the huts which is not finishd Several Indians Come to Camp to day, The Ossinoibins is at the Big bellie Camp, Some trouble like to take place between them from the loss of horses &c. as is Said by an old Indian who visited us with 4 buffalow robes & Corn to trade for a pistol which we did not let him have, men imployed untill late in dobing their huts, Some horses Sent down to Stay in the woods near the fort, to prevent the Ossniboins Steeling them

[Clark, November 17, 1804] 17 th November Satturday 1804 a fine morning, last night was Cold, the ice thicker than yesterday, Several Indians visit us, one Chief Stayed all day we are much engaged about our huts.

[Clark, November 18, 1804] 18th Novr. Sunday 1804 a Cold morning Some wind the Black Cat, Chief of the Mandans Came to See us, he made Great inquiries respecting our fashions. he also Stated the Situation of their nation, he mentioned that a Council had been held the day before and it was thought advisable to put up with the resent insults of the Ossinoibins & Christonoes untill they were Convinced that what had been told thim by us, Mr. Evins had deceived them & we might also, he promised to return & furnish them with guns & amunitiion, we advised them to remain at peace & that they might depend upon Getting Supplies through the Channel of the Missouri, but it requred time to put the trade in opperation. The Assiniboins &c have the trade of those nations in their power and treat them badly as the Soux does the Ricarees and they cannot resent for fear of loseing their trade &.

[Clark, November 19, 1804] 19th of November 1804 our hunters return with 32 Deerr, 12 Elk & a Buffalow Ice ran which detained the huntes much Cap lewis visit the Me ne tar rees, the 25th and returned the 27th of Nov. with 2 Chiefs &c. &c. and told me that 2 Clerks & 5 men of the N W Company & Several of the hudsons Bay Company had arrived with goods to trade with the Indians a Mr. La Roche & Mc Kinzey are the Celerks (Distant 150 Miles across)

[Clark, November 19, 1804] 19th Novr. Monday a Cold day the ice Continue to run our Perogue of Hunters arrive with 32 Deer, 12 Elk & a Buffalow, all of this meat we had hung up in a Smoke house, a timeley supply- Several Indians here all day- the wind bley hard from the N. W. by W. our men move into their huts, Several little Indian aneckdts. told me to day

[Clark, November 20, 1804] 20th November Tuesday 1804 Capt Lewis & my Self move into our huts, a verry hard wind from the W. all the after part of the day a temperate day Several Indians Came Down to Eat fresh meat, three Chiefs from the 2d Mandan Village Stay all Day, they are verry Curious in examining our works. Those Chiefs informs us that the Souix settled on the Missourie above Dog River, threten to attacked them this winter, and have treated 2 Ricares who Carried the pipe of peace to them Verry roughly. whiped & took their horses from them &c. &c. & is much displeased with Ricares for makeing a peace with the Mandans &. &. through us, &. we gave them a Sattisfactory answer. &c. &c.

[Clark, November 21, 1804] 21st Novr. Wednesday a fine Day dispatched a perogu and Collected Stone for our Chimnys, Some wind from the S. W. arrange our different articles- maney Indians visit us to day, G D hurd his hand verry bad- all the party in high Spirits- The river Clear of ice, & riseing a little

[Clark, November 22, 1804] 22nd of November Thursday 1804 a fine morning Dispatched a perogue and 5 Men under the Derection of Sergeant Pryor to the 2nd Village for 100 bushels of Corn in ears which Mr. Jessomme, let us have did not get more than 80 bushels- I was allarmed about 10 oClock by the Sentinal, who informed that an Indian was about to Kill his wife in the interpeters fire about 60 yards below the works, I went down and Spoke to the fellow about the rash act which he was like to commit and forbid any act of the kind near the fort- Some missunderstanding took place between this man & his wife about 8 days ago, and She came to this place, & Continued with the Squars of the interpeters, 2 days ago She returned to the Villg. in the evening of the Same day She came to the interpeters fire appearently much beat, & Stabed in 3 places- We Detected that no man of this party have any intercourse with this woman under the penalty of Punishment- he the Husband observed that one of our Serjeants Slept with his wife & if he wanted her he would give her to him, We derected the Serjeant Odway to give the man Some articles, at which time I told the Indian that I believed not one man of the party had touched his wife except the one he had given the use of her for a nite, in his own bed, no man of the party Should touch his Squar, or the wife of any Indian, nor did I believe they touch a woman if they knew her to be the wife of another man, and advised him to take his Squar home and live hapily together in future,- at this time the Grand Chief of the nation arrived, & lecturd him, and they both went off apparently dis

The grand Chief continued all day a warm Day fair afternoon- many Indian anickdotes one Chief & his familey Stay all night.

[Clark, November 23, 1804] 23rd , a fair warm Day, wind from the S. E. Send after Stone Several men with bad Colds, one man Sheilds with the Rhumitism the river on a Stand haveing rose 4 Inches in all

[Clark, November 24, 1804] 24th of November Satturday 1804 a warm Day Several men with bad Coalds we continue to Cover our Huts with hewed punchens, finishd. a Cord to draw our boat out on the bank, this is made 9 Straps of Elk Skin,- the wind from the S. E.

[Clark, November 25, 1804] 25th of Novr. Sunday 1804 a fine day warm & pleasent Capt. Lewis 2 Interpeters & 6 men Set out to See the Indians in the different Towns & Camps in this neighbour hood, we Continu to Cover & dob our huts, two Chiefs Came to See me to day one named Wau-ke-res-sa-ra, a Big belley and the first of that nation who has visited us Since we have been here, I gave him a Handkerchef Paint & a Saw band, and the other Some fiew articles, and paid a perticular attention which pleased them verry much, the interpeters being all with Capt. Lewis I could not talk to them. we Compleated our huts- Several men with bad Colds, river fall 1 1/2 inch

[Clark, November 26, 1804] 26th of Novr. 1804 Monday Fort Mandan a little before day light the wind shifted to the N. W. and blew hard and the air Keen & Cold all day, Cloudy and much the appearance of Snow; but little work done to day it being Cold &c.

[Clark, November 27, 1804] 27th of November Tuesday 1804 a cloudy morning after a verry Cold night, the River Crouded with floating ice wind from the N W. finished Dobing Capt. Lewis returned from the Villages with two Chiefs Mar-noh toh & Man-nes-sur ree & a Considerate man with the party who accompanied him, The Menitares, (or Big bellies) were allarmed at the tales told them by the Mandans Viz: that we intended to join the Seaux to Cut off them in the Course of the winter, many Circumstances Combind to give force to those reports i e the movements of the interpeters & their families to the Fort, the strength of our work &. &.

all those reports was contridicted by Capt Louis with a Conviction on the minds of the Indians of the falsity of those reports- the Indians in all the towns & Camps treated Capt Lewis & the party with Great respect except one of the principal Cheifs Mar par pa par ra pas a too or (Horned Weasel) who did not Chuse to be Seen by the Capt. & left word that he was not at home &.

Seven Traders arrived from the fort on the Ossinaboin from the N W Companey one of which Lafrances took upon himself to speak unfavourably of our intentions &. the princpal Mr. La Rock, (& Mr. McKensey) was informed of the Conduct of their interpeter & the Consiquinces if they did not put a Stop to unfavourable & ill founded assursions &c. &.

The two Chiefs much pleased with their treatments & the Cherefullness of the party, who Danced to amuse them &c. &c.

The river fall 2 Inches verry Cold and began to Snow at 8 oClock P M and Continued all night- Some miss understanding with Jussomm & his woman- at Day the Snow Seased

[Clark, November 28, 1804] 28th Novr. Wednesday 1804 a cold morning wind from the N. W river full of floating ice, began to Snow at 7 oClock a m and continued all day at 8 oClock the Poss-cop-so-he or Black Cat Grand Chief of the Mandans Came to See us, after Showing Those Chiefs many thing which was Curiossities to them, and Giveing a fiew presents of Curioes Handkerchiefs arm bans & paint with a twist of Tobaco they departed at 1 oClock much pleased, at parting we had Some little talk on the Subject of the British Trader Mr. Le rock Giveing Meadils & Flags, and told those Chiefs to impress it on the minds of their nations that those Simbells were not to be recved by any from them, without they wished incur the displieasure of their Great American Father- a verry disagreeable day- no work done to day river fall 1 Inch to day

[Clark, November 29, 1804] 29th November Thursday 1804 A verry Cold windey day wind from the N. W by W. Some Snow last night the Detpt of the Snow is various in the wood about 13 inches, The river Closed at the Village above and fell last night two feet Mr. La Rock and one of his men Came to visit us we informed him what we had herd of his intentions of makeing Chiefs &c. and forbid him to give meadels or flags to the Indians, he Denied haveing any Such intention, we agreed that one of our interpeters Should Speak for him on Conditions he did not Say any thing more than what tended to trade alone- he gave fair promises &.

[Clark, November 30, 1804] 30h of Nov. an Indian Chief Came and informed us that five Men of the Mandans Nation was on a hunting party to the S W, distance about Eight Leagues, they were Surprised one man Killed two wounded and nine horses taken, Severale others men wer on hunting partes & were to have returned Several days ago & had not yet returned, & that they expected to be attacked by an army of Sioux I took 23 men and went to the Village deturmined to Collect the warriers of the Different Villages and meet the Sioux- The village not expecting Such Strong aid in So Short a time was a little alarmed of the formable appearance of my party The principal Chiefs met me at 200 yards Distance from the Town, and envited me to his Lodge. I told the Nation the Cause of Comeing &. was to assist in Chastiseing the enimies of my Dutifull Children- I requested great Chief to repeat the Cercunstance of the Sioux attack as it realy happined which he did- I told them to Send runners to the other villages & assemble the warriers & we Would go and Chastize the Sioux for Spilling the Blood of my Dutifull Children- after a Conversation of a few minits amongst themselves, a Chief Said that they now Saw that what we had told them was the trooth and we were ready to protect them and Kill those who did not listen to our Councils (and after a long Speech) he concluded Said "the Sious who Spilt our Blood is gorn home- The Snow is deep and it is Cold, our horses Cannot Travel thro the plains in pursute- If you will go and conduct us in the Spring after the Snow is gorn, we will assemble all the warriers & Brave men in all the villages and go with you." I answered the Speach at Some length, explained to them their Situation declareing our intentions of Defending them at any time dureing the time we Should Stay in ther nieghbourhood, explained the Situation of the Ricaras & told them not to get angrey with them untill they were Certain of their haveing violated the treaty &c. &. I crossed the River on the Ice and returned to the fort

[Clark, November 30, 1804] 30th in the morning early a Indian Came to the river opposit & requsted to be brought over, that he had Some thing to Say from his nation we Sent for him, and after he had Smoked- he Said he thought the river was frosted across here & expected to Cross on the ice

7 or 8 Mandans out hunting in a S. W, Derection from this place about 8 Leagues, after they had made their hunt and on their return was attackted by a large Party of Seaux, one of the party a young Chief was Killed 2

wounded & 9 horses taken, the men who made their escape Say the one half of the party who attacked them was Panias-

The two Panias who Came here a fiew days ago was imediately Sent home, for fear of their being put to death by the party Defeated

Two of the attacting party was Known to be Panies. The man who was killed mentioned that after he was wounded, that he had been at war & been wounded, "this day I shall die like a man before my Enimies,! tell my father that I died bravely, and do not greive for me-"

4 of the Big bellies who were Camped near thos is missing, and Searching for him in their Camps above- no one Dare to go to the ground where the battle was for fear of the Sioux being noumerous-.

[Clark, November 30, 1804] 30th of November Friday 1804 This morning at 8 oClock an Indian Calld from the other Side and informed that he had Something of Consequence to Communicate. we Sent a perogue for him & he informed us as follows. Viz: "five men of the Mandan Nation out hunting in a S. W. derection about Eight Leagues was Suprised by a large party of Sceoux & Panies, one man was Killed and two wounded with arrows & 9 Horses taken, 4 of the We ter Soon nation was missing, & they expected to be attacked by the Souix &c. &." we thought it well to Show a Disposition to ade and assist them against their enimies, perticularly those who Came in oppersition to our Councils, and I Deturmined to go to the town with Some men, and if the Sceoux were comeing to attact the nation to Collect the worriers from each Village and meet them, thos Ideas were also those of Capt Lewis, I crossed the river in about an hour after the arrival of the Indian express with 23 men including the interpeters and flankd the Town & came up on the back part The Indians not expecting to receive Such Strong aide in So Short a time was much Supprised, and a littled allarmed at the formadable appearance of my party- The principal Chiefs met me Some Distance from the town (Say 200 yards) and invited me in to town, I ord my pty into dft. lodges & I explained to the nation the cause of my comeing in this formadable manner to their Town, was to asst and Chastise the enimies of our Dutifull Children,- I requested the Grand Cheif to repeat the Circumstancies as they hapined which he did as was mentioned by the Express in the morning- I then informed them that if they would assemble their warrers and those of the different Towns I would to meet the Army of Souix & Chastise thim for takeing the blood of our dutifull Children &c. after a conversation of a fiew minits amongst themselves, one Chief the Big Man Cien Said they now Saw that what we hade told them was the trooth, whin we expected the enimies of their Nation was Comeing to attact them, or had spilt their blood were ready to protect them, and Kill those who would not listen to our Good talk- his people had listened to what we had told them and Cearlessly went out to hunt in Small parties believing themselves to be Safe from the other Nations- and have been killed by the Panies & Seauex. "I knew Said he that the Panies were Tiers, and told the old Chief who Came with you (to Confirm a piece with us) that his people were hers and bad men and that we killed them like the Buffalow, when we pleased, we had made peace Several times and you Nation have always Commened the war, we do not want to Kill you, and will not Suffer you to Kill us or Steal our horses, we will make peace with you as our two fathers have derected, and they Shall See that we will not be the Ogressors, but we fear the Ricares will not be at peace-long- My father those are the words I Spoke to the Ricare in Your presents- you See they have not opened their ears to your good "Councils but have Spuilt our blood. two Ricarees whome we Sent home this day for fear of our peoples Killing them in their greaf-informed us when they Came here Several days ago, that two Towns of the Ricares were makeing their Mockersons, and that we had best take care of Our horses & a number of Sieuex were in their Towns, and they believed not well disposed towards us- four of the Wetersoons are now absent they were to have been back in 16 days they have been out 24 we fear they have fallen. my father the Snow is deep and it is cold our horses Cannot travel thro the the plains,- those people who have Spilt our blood have gorn back? if you will go with us in the Spring after the Snow goes off we will raise the Warriers of all the Towns & nations around about us, and go with you."

I told this nation that we Should be always willing and ready to defend them from the insults of any nation who would dare to Come to doe them injurey dureing the time we would remain in their neighbourhood, and requstd. that they would inform us of any party who may at any time be discovered by their Patroles or Scouts;

I was Sorry that the Snow in the Plains had fallen So Deep Sence the Murder of the young Chief by the Scioux as prevented, their horses from traveling I wished to meet those Scioux & all others who will not open their ears, but make war on our dutifull Children, and let you See that the Wariers of your great father will Chastise the enimies of his dutifull Children the Mandans, wetersoons & Winitarees, who have opend. their ears to his advice- you Say that the Panies or Ricares were with the Sciaux, Some bad men may have been with the Sciaux you know there is bad men in all nations, do not get mad with the racarees untill we know if those bad men are Counternoncd. by their nation, and we are Convsd. those people do not intend to follow our Councils- you know that the Sceaux have great influence over the ricarees and perhaps have led Some of them astray- you know that the Ricarees, are Dependant on the Sceaux for their guns, powder, & Ball, and it was policy in them to keep on as good terms as possible with the Siaux untill they had Some other means of getting those articles &c. &.

you know your Selves that you are Compelled to put up with little insults from the Christinoes & Ossinaboins (or Stone Inds.) because if you go to war with those people, they will provent the traders in the north from bringing you Guns Powder & Ball and by that means distress you verry much, but whin you will have Certain Suppliers from your Great American father of all those articls you will not Suffer any nation to insult you &c. after about two hours conversation on various Subjects all of which tended towards their Situation &c. I informed them I Should return to the fort, the Chief Said they all thanked me verry much for the fatherly protection which I Showed towards them, that the Village had been Crying all the night and day for the death of the brave young man, who fell but now they would wipe away their tears, and rejoice in their fathers protection- and Cry no more

I then Paraded & Crossed the river on the ice and Came down on the N. Side the Snow So deep, it was verry fatigueing arrved at the fort after night, gave a little Taffee, a Cold night the river rise to its former hite- The Chief frequently thanked me for Comeing to protect them- and the whole Village appeared thankfull for that measure

[Clark, December 1, 1804] 1s Decr. a young Chief arrived

7 Chiens Came to the Village with a pipe & the 3 Ricares who Came here a fiew days ago & Sent off yesterday have returned and Say that the Sieaux & ricares are Camped together

[Clark, December 1, 1804] 1st of December Saturday 1804 wind from the N W. all hands ingaged in pitting pickets &. at 10 oClock the half brother of the man who was killed Came and informd. us that after my departure last night Six Chiens So Called by the french Shar ha Indians had arrived with a pipe and Said that The mandans apprehended danger from the Shar has as they were at peace with the Seaux; and wished to Kill them and the Ricarees (or Parties) but the Cheifs informed the nation "it was our wish that they Should not be hurt, and forbid being Killed &c." we gave a little Tobacco &c. & this man Departed well Satisfied with our councils and advice to him in the evening a Mr. G Henderson in the imploy of the hudsons bay Company Sent to trade with the Gros ventre-or big bellies So Called by the french traders

[Clark, December 2, 1804] 2d of Decr. 1804 Visited by Several Mandan Chiefs and 4 Chyannes Inds. who Came with a pipe to the Mandans, Sent a Speech to ther Nation a flag & Some tobacco, also written a Speech to the Ricaras & Sioux, informe them what they might depend on if they would not open their ears, & &.

[Clark, December 2, 1804] 2nd of December Sunday 1804 The latter part of last night was verry warm and Continued to thaw untill _____ oClock when the wind Shifted to the North at 11 oClock the Chiefs of the Lower village of the Mandans with maney of theire young men and 4 of the Shar-ha's who had come to Smoke with the pipe of Peace with the Mandans, we explained to them our intentions our views and advised them to be at peace, Gave them a flag for theire nation, Some Tobacco with a Speech to Deliver to their nation on theire return, also Sent by them a letter to Mrs. Tabbo & Gravoline, at the Ricares Village, to interseid in proventing Hostilities, and if they Could not effect those measures to Send & informe us of what was going on, Stateing to the Indians the part we intend to take if the Rickores & Seauex did not follow our Derections and be at peace with the nations which we had addopted- We made Some fiew Small presents to those Shar ha's and also Some to the Mandans & at 3 oClock they all Departed well pleased, haveing Seen many Curisossties, which we Showed them-. river rise one inch

[Clark, December 3, 1804] 3rd December Monday 1804. a fine morning the after part of the day Cold & windey the wind from the N W. The Father of the Mandan who was killed Came and made us a present of Some Dried Simnens & a little pemicon, we made him Some Small preasents for which he was much pleased

[Clark, December 4, 1804] 4th of December Tuesday 1804 a Cloudy raw Day wind from the N. W. the Black Cat and two young Chiefs Visit us and as usial Stay all Day the river rise one inch finish the main bastion, our interpetr. we discover to be assumeing and discontent'd

[Clark, December 5, 1804] 5th December Wednesday 1804 a Cold raw morning wind from the S. E. Some Snow, two of the N W. Companey Came to See us, to let us Know they intended to Set out for the establishment on the osinniboin River in two Days-& their party would Consist of 5 men, Several Indians also visited us one brought Pumpkins or Simmins as a preasent a little Snow fell in the evening at which time the wind Shifted round to N. E.

[Clark, December 6, 1804] Fort Mandan 6th of December Thursday 1804 The wind blew violently hard from the N, N W. with Some Snow the air Keen and Cold. The Thermometer at 8 oClock A, M, Stood at 10 dgs. above o- at 9 oClock a man & his Squar Came down with Some meat for the inturpeter his dress was a par mockersons of Buffalow Skin Pr. Legins of Goat Skin & a Buffalow robe, 14 ring of Brass on his fingers, this metel the Mandans ar verry fond off- Cold after noon river rise 1 1/2 Inch to day

[Clark, December 7, 1804] at Fort mandan 7th of December 1804, we were informed by a Chief that great numbers of Buffalow were on the hills near us Cap Lewis with a party went out & Killed 11three in view of our fort, The weather so excesive Cold & wolves plenty, we only saved 5 of them, I with a party turned on the 8th out and found the Buffalow at 7 ms. distant Killed 8 & a Deer, I returned with 2 Cows leaving men with remaining meat- Several men badly frost bit- The Themormeter Stood this morning at 44 d. below Breizing.

Capt Lewis went out 9th & Stayed all night out Killed 9 buffalowmaney of the Buffalow Killed were So meager that they not fit for use Collected by the ade of Some horses the best of the meat in fact all we could Save from wolves & I went on a hunting party the 14 & 15 of Decr.- much Snow verry cold 52° below freesinge. N W. & H Bay Clerks Visit us the 16th also Mr Hainey, Cold Tem. 74° below freesing

I visit the Mandans on the 1s of January Capt Lewis the 2nd

[Clark, December 7, 1804] 7th of December Friday 1804 a verry Cold day wind from the N W. the Big White Grand Chief of the 1s Village, Came and informed us that a large Drove of Buffalow was near and his people was wating for us to join them in a Chase Capt. Lewis took 15 men & went out joined the Indians, who were at the time he got up, Killing the Buffalows on Horseback with arrows which they done with great dexterity, his party killed 14 Buffalow, five of which we got to the fort by the assistance of a horse in addition to what the men Packed on their backs- one Cow was killed on the ice after drawing her out of a vacancey in the ice in which She had fallen, and Butchered her at the fort- those we did not get in was taken by the indians under a Custon which is established amongst them i e. any person Seeing a buffalow lying without an arrow Sticking in him, or Some purticular mark takes possesion, many times (as I am told) a hunter who Kills maney Buffalow in a chase only Gets a part of one, all meat which is left out all night falls to the Wolves which are in great numbers, always in the Buffalows- the river Closed opposit the fort last night 11/2 inches thick The Thermometer Stood this morning at 1 d. below o- three men frost bit badly to day

[Clark, December 8, 1804] 8th December Satturday 1804 a verry Cold morning, the Thermometer Stood at 12 d. below 0 which is 42 d. below the freesing point, wind from the N W I with 15 men turned out Indians joined us on horseback, shot with arrows rode along side of buffaloel and killed 8 buffalow & one Deer, one Cow and Calf was brought in, two Cows which I killed at 7 miles Dst. I left 2 men to Skin & Keep off the wolves, and brought in one Cow & a calf, in the evening on my return to the fort Saw great numbers of Buffalow Comeing into the Bottoms on both Sides of the river This day being Cold Several men returned a little frost bit; one of men with his feet badly frost bit my Servents feet also frosted & his P-s a little, I feel a little fatigued haveing run after the Buffalow all day in Snow many Places 10 inches Deep, Generally 6 or 8, two men hurt their hips verry much in Slipping down- The Indians kill great numbers of Buffalow to day- 2 reflectings Suns to day

[Clark, December 9, 1804] 9th December Sunday 1804 The Thermometer Stood this morning at 7° above 0, wind from the E. Capt Lewis took 18 men & 4 horses and went out Send in the meet killed yesterday and kill more, the Sun Shown to day Clear, both interpeters went to the Villages to day at 12 oClock two Chiefs Came loaded with meat one with a dog & Slay also loaded with meat, Capt. Lewis Sent in 4 Hors's loaded with meat, he continued at the hunting Camp near which they killed 9 buffalow.

[Clark, December 10, 1804] 10th Monday Decr. 1804 Fort Mandan a verry Cold Day The Thermometer to day at 10 & 11 Degrees below 0., Capt. Lewis returned, to day at 12 oClock leaveing 6 men at the Camp to prepare the meat for to pack 4 Horse loads Came in, Capt Lewis had a Cold Disagreeable night last in the Snow on a Cold point with one Small Blankett the Buffaloe Crossed the river below in emence herds without brakeing in. only 2 buffalow killed to day one of which was too pore to Skin, The men which was frost bit is gitting better. the rise 11/2 inch wind North

[Clark, December 11, 1804] 11th December Tuesday 1804 a verry Cold morning Wind from the north The Thermomettr at (4 oClock A M at 21°) Sunrise at 21° See list. below 0 which is 53° below the freesing point and getting colder, the Sun Shows and reflects two imigies, the ice floating in the atmespear being So thick that the appearance is like a fog Despurceing

Sent out three horses for meat & with Derections for all the hunters to return to the fort as Soon as possible at 1 oClock the horses returned loaded at night all the hunters returned, Several a little frosted, The Black Cat Chief of the Mandans paid us a Visit to day continue Cold all day river at a Stand

[Clark, December 12, 1804] 12th December Wednesday 1804 a Clear Cold morning wind from the north the Thormometer at Sun rise Stood at 38° below 0, moderated untill 6 oClock at which time it began to get Colder. I line my Gloves and have a cap made of the Skin of the Louservia (Lynx) (or wild Cat of the North) the fur near 3 inches long a Indian Of the Shoe nation Came with the half of a Cabra ko ka or Antilope which he killed near the Fort, Great numbers of those animmals are near our fort but the weather is So Cold that we do not think it prudent to turn out to hunt in Such Cold weather, or at least untill our Consts. are prepared to under go this Climate. I measure the river from bank to bank on the ice and make it 500 yards

[Clark, December 13, 1804] 13th December Thursday 1804 The last night was verry Clear & the frost which fell Covered the ice old Snow & thos parts which was naked 1/6 of an inch, The Thermotr. Stands this morning at 20° below 0, a fine day. find it imposible to make an Observation with an artifical Horsison Joseph Fields kill a Cow and Calf to day one mile from the fort river falls

[Clark, December 14, 1804] 14th December Friday 1804 a fine morning. wind from the S. E. the murckerey Stood at '0' this morning I went with a party of men down the river 18 miles to hunt Buffalow, Saw two Bulls too pore to kill, the Cows and large gangues haveing left the River, we only killed two Deer & Camped all night with Some expectation of Seeing the Buffalow in the morning, a verry Cold night, Snowed.

[Clark, December 15, 1804] 15th of December 1804 Satturday a Cold Clear morning, Saw no buffalow, I concluded to return to the Fort & hunt on each Side of the river on our return which we did without Success- the Snow fell 1 1/2 inches deep last night. wind North- on my return to the fort found Several Chiefs there

[Clark, December 16, 1804] Fort Mandan 16th December, Sunday 1804 a clear Cold morning, the Thermtr. at Sun rise Stood at 22° below 0, a verry Singaler appearance of the Moon last night, as She appeared thro The frosty atmispear- Mr. Henny, from the Establishment on River Ossinnniboin, with a letter from, Mr Charles Chaboillez one of the Cos arrived in 6 Days, Mr. C in his letters expressed a great anxiety to Serve us in any thing in his power-

a root Discribed by Mr. Henry for the Cure of a Mad Dog

Mr. Le rock a Clerk, of the N W Company and Mr. George Bunch a Clerk of the Hudsons bay Compy accompanied Mr. Henny from the Village

[Clark, December 17, 1804] 17th December Monday 1804 a verry Cold morning the Thrmt. Stood a 43° below 0. We found Mr. Henny a verry intelligent man from whome we obtained Some Scetches of the Countrey between the Mississippi & Missouri, and Some Sketches from him, which he had obtained from the Indins. to the West of this place also the names and charecktors of the Sceoux &c about 8 oClock P M. the thermometer fell to 74° below the freesing pointe- the Indian Chiefs Sent word that Buffalow was in our neighbourhood, and if we would join them, in the morning they would go and kill them-

[Clark, December 18, 1804] 18th December Tuesday 1804 The Themometer the Same as last night Mr. Haney & La Rocke left us for the Grossventre Camp, Sent out 7 men to hunt for the Buffalow They found the weather too cold & returned, Several Indians Came, who had Set out with a veiw to Kill buffalow, The river rise a little I imploy my Self makeing a Small map of Connection &. Sent Jessomme to the Main Chief of the mandans to know the Cause of his detaining or takeing a horse of Chabonoe our big belly interpeter, which we found was thro the rascallity of one Lafrance a trader from the N W. Company, who told this Cheif that Chabonah owd. him a horse to go and take him he done So agreeable to an indian Custom- he gave up the horse

[Clark, December 19, 1804]
19th December Wednesday 1804
The wind from S. W. the weather moderated a little, I engage my self in
Connecting the Countrey from information. river rise a little

[Clark, December 20, 1804] 20th December Thursday 1804 The wind from the N W a moderate day, the Thermometr 37° above 0, which givs an oppertunity of putting up our pickets next the river, nothing remarkable took place to Day river fall a little

[Clark, December 21, 1804] 21st December Friday 1804 a fine Day worm and wind from the N W by W, the Indian whome I stoped from Commiting murder on his wife, thro jellousy of one of our interpeters, Came & brought his two wives and Showed great anxiety to make up with the man with whome his joulassey Sprung- a womin brought a Child with an abcess on the lower part of the back, and offered as much corn as She Could carry for Some medison, Capt Lewis administered &c.

[Clark, December 22, 1804] 22nd December Satturday 1804 a number of Squars womn & men Dressed in Squars Clothes Came with Corn to Sell to the men for little things, we precured two horns of the animale the french Call the rock mountain Sheep those horns are not of the largest kind- The mandans Indians Call this Sheep Ar-Sar-ta it is about the Size of a large Deer, or Small Elk, its Horns Come out and wind around the head like the horn of a Ram and the teckere not unlike it much larger and thicker perticelarly that part with which they but or outer part which is _____ inchs thick, the length of those horns, which we have is

[Clark, December 23, 1804] 23rd December Sunday 1804 a fine Day great numbers of indians of all discriptions Came to the fort many of them bringing Corn to trade, the little Crow, loadd. his wife & Sun with corn for us, Cap. Lewis gave him a few presents as also his wife, She made a Kettle of boild Simnins, beens, Corn & Choke Cherris with the Stones which was paletable

This Dish is Considered, as a treat among those people, The Chiefs of the Mandans are fond of Stayin & Sleeping in the fort

[Clark, December 24, 1804] 24 December Monday 1804 Several Chiefs and members of men womin and Children at the fort to day, Some for trade, the most as lookers on, we gave a fellet of Sheep Skin (which we brought for Spunging) to 3 Chiefs one to each of 2 inches wide, which they lay great value (priseing those felets equal to a fine horse), a fine Day we finished the pickingen around our works

[Clark, December 25, 1804] 25th December Christmass Tuesday I was awakened before Day by a discharge of 3 platoons from the Party and the french, the men merrily Disposed, I give them all a little Taffia and permited 3 Cannon fired, at raising Our flag, Some men went out to hunt & the Others to Danceing and Continued untill 9 oClock P, M, when the frolick ended &c.

[Clark, December 26, 1804] 26th Decr. Wednesday 1804 a temperate day no Indians to day or yesterday. A man from the N W Company Came Down from the Gross Vintres to Get one of our interpeters to assist them in trade This man informed that the Party of Gross Ventres who persued the Ossinboins that Stold their horses, has all returned in their usial way by Small parties, the last of the party bringing 8 horses which they Stole from a Camp of Asniboins which they found on Mouse river-

[Clark, December 27, 1804] 27th December 1804 Thursday a little fine Snow weather something Colder than yesterday Several Indians here to Day, much Surprised at the Bellos & method of makeing Sundery articles of Iron wind hard from the N W.

[Clark, December 28, 1804] 28th of December Friday 1804 blew verry hard last night, the frost fell like a Shower of Snow, nothing remarkable to day, the Snow Drifting from one bottom to another and from the leavel plains into the hollows &c

[Clark, December 29, 1804] 29th December Satturday 1804 The frost fell last night nearly a 1/4 of an inch Deep and Continud to fall untill the Sun was of Some bite, the Murcurey Stood this morning at 9 d below 0 which is not considered Cold, as the Changes take place gradually without long intermitions

a number of Indians here

[Clark, December 30, 1804] 30th December Sunday 1804 Cold the Termtr. at 20 d below 0 a number of Indians here to day they are much Supprised at the Bellows one Deer Killed

[Clark, December 31, 1804] Fort Mandan 31st of December Monday 1804 a fine Day Some wind last night which mixed the Snow and Sand in the bend of the river, which has the appearance of hillocks of Sand on the ice, which is also Covered with Sand & Snow, the feost which falls in the night continues on the earth & old Snow &c. &c.- a Number of indians here every Day our blckSmitth mending their axes hoes &c. &c. for which the Squars bring Corn for payment

[Clark, January 1, 1805] Fort Mandan on the N E bank of the Missouries 1600 miles up January the 1st 1805 Tuesday The Day was ushered in by the Discharge of two Cannon, we Suffered 16 men with their musick to visit the 1st Village for the purpose of Danceing, by as they Said the perticular request of the Chiefs of that village, about 11 oClock I with an inturpeter & two men walked up to the Village (my views were to alay Some little miss understanding which had taken place thro jelloucy and mortificatiion as to our treatment towards them) I found them much pleased at the Danceing of our men, I ordered my black Servent to Dance which amused the Croud verry much, and Some what astonished them, that So large a man Should be active &c. &.

I went into the lodges of all the men of note except two, whome I heard had made Some expressions not favourable towards us, in Compareing us with the trabers from the north- Those Cheifs observed what they Sayed was in just & lafture.- just as I was about to return the 2d Chief and the Black man, also a Chief returnd from a mission on which they had been Sent to meet a large party 150 of Gross Ventres who were on their way down from their Camps 10 Miles above to revenge on the Shoe tribe an injurey which they had received by a Shoe man Steeling a Gross Venters Girl, those Chiefs gave the pipe turned the party back, after Delivering up the girl, which the Shoe Chief had taken and given to them for that purpose. I returned in the evening, at night the party except 6 returned, with 3 robes, an 13 Strings of Corn which the indians had given them, The Day was worm, Themtr. 34° abov 0, Some fiew Drops of rain about Sunset, at Dark it began to Snow, and Snowed the greater part of the night, (the tempetr for Snow is about o) The Black Cat with his family visited us to day and brought a little meet

[Clark, January 2, 1805] 2nd of January Wednesdey 1805 a Snowey morning a party of men go to Dance at the 2nd Village to Dance, Capt Lewis & the interprtr visit the 2d Village, and return in the evening, Some Snow to Day verry Cold in the evining

[Clark, January 3, 1805] 3rd of January Thursday 1805 Soome Snow to day; 8 men go to hunt the buffalow, killed a hare & wolf Several Indians visit us to day & a Gross Ventre came after his wife, who had been much abused, & come here for Protection.

[Clark, January 4, 1805] Fort Mandan 4th of January Friday 1805 a worm Snowey morning, the Themtr. at 28° abov 0, Cloudy, Sent out 3 men to hunt down the river, Several Indians Came today the little Crow, who has proved friendly Came we gave him a handkerchf & 2 files, in the evening the weather became cold and windey, wind from the N W. I am verry unwell the after part of the Daye

[Clark, January 5, 1805] 5th of January Satturday 1805 a cold day Some Snow, Several Indians visit us with thier axes to get them mended, I imploy my Self drawing a Connection of the Countrey from what information I have recved- a Buffalow Dance (or Medison) for 3 nights passed in the 1st Village, a curious Custom the old men arrange themselves in a circle & after Smoke a pipe, which is handed them by a young man, Dress up for the purpose, the young men who have their wives back of the circle go to one of the old men with a whining tone and request the old man to take his wife (who presents necked except a robe) and- the Girl then takes the Old man (who verry often can Scercely walk) and leades him to a Convenient place for the business, after which they return to the lodge, if the Old man (or a white man) returns to the lodge without gratifying the man & his wife, he offers her again and again; it is often the Case that after the 2d time without Kissing the Husband throws a nice robe over the old man & and begs him not to dispise him, & his wife (we Sent a man to this Medisan last night, they gave him 4 Girls) all this is to cause the buffalow to Come near So that They may kill thim 2

[Clark, January 6, 1805] 6th of January Sunday 1805 a Cold day but fiew indians to day I am ingaged as yesterday

[Clark, January 7, 1805] 7th of January Monday 1805 Fort Mandan a verry Cold clear Day, the Themtr Stood at 22 d below 0 wind N W., the river fell 1 inch Several indians returned from hunting, one of them the Big White Chef of the Lower Mandan Village, Dined With us, and gave me a Scetch of the Countrey as far as the high mountains, & on the South Side of the River Rejone, he Says that the river rejone recves 6 Small rivers on the S. Side, & that the Countrey is verry hilley and the greater part Covered with timber, Great numbers of beaver &c.- the 3 men returned from hunting, they kill'd 4 Deer & 2 wolves, Saw Buffalow a long ways off, I continue to Draw a connected plote from the information of Traders, Indians & my own observation & idea- from the best information, the Great falls is about 800 miles nearly west,-

[Clark, January 8, 1805] 8th of January Tuesday 1805 a Cold Day but fiew indians at the fort to day wind from the N, W, one man at the Village

[Clark, January 9, 1805] 9th of January Wednesday 1805 A Cold Day Themometer at 21° below 0, Great numbers of indians go to Kill Cows, the little Crow Brackft. with us, Several Indians Call at the Fort nearly frosed, one man reported that he had Sent his Son a Small boy to the fort about 3 oClock, & was much distressed at not finding him here, the after part of this day verry Cold, and wind Keen

[Clark, January 10, 1805] 10th Of January 1805 This morning a boy of 13 years of age Came to the fort with his feet frozed, haveing Stayed out all night without fire, with no other Covering than a Small Robe goat skin leagens & a pr. Buffalow Skin mockersons- The Murcery Stood at 72° below the freesing point- Several others Stayed out all night not in the least hurt, This boy lost his Toes only-

[Clark, January 10, 1805] 10th of January Thursday 1805 last night was excessively Cold the murkery this morning Stood at 40° below 0 which is 72° below the freesing point, we had one man out last night, who returned about 8 oClock this morning The Indians of the lower Villages turned out to hunt for a man & a boy who had not returnd from the hunt of yesterday, and borrowd a Slay to bring them in expecting to find them frosed to death about 10 oclock the boy about 13 years of age Came to the fort with his feet frosed and had layen out last night without fire with only a Buffalow Robe to Cover him, the Dress which he wore was a pr of Cabra Legins, which is verry thin and mockersons- we had his feet put in Cold water and they are Comeing too- Soon after the arrival of the Boy, a man Came in who had also Stayed out without fire, and verry thinly Clothed, this man was not the least injured Customs & the habits of those people has ancered to bare more Cold than I thought it possible for man to indure

Send out 3 men to hunt Elk below about 7 miles

[Clark, January 11, 1805] 11th January Friday 1805 verry Cold, Send out 3 men to join 3 now below & hunt,

Pose-cop se ha or Black Cat came to See us and Stay all night

Sho sa har ro ra or Coal also Stayd all night, the inturpeter oldst wife Sick, Some of our men go to See a war medison made at the village on the opposit Side of the river, this is a

[Clark, January 12, 1805] Fort Manden 12th of January Satturday 1805 a verry Cold Day three of our hunters J. & R Fields withe 2 Elk on a Slay Sent one more hunter out.

[Clark, January 13, 1805] 13th of January Sunday (1805) a Cold Clear Day (great number of Indians move Down the River to hunt) those people Kill a number of Buffalow near their Villages and Save a great perpotion of the meat, their Custom of makeing this article of life General leaves them more than half of their time without meat Their Corn & Beans &c they Keep for the Summer, and as a reserve in Case of an attack from the Soues, which they are always in dread, and Sildom go far to hunt except in large parties, about 1/2 the Mandan nation passed this to day to hunt on the river below, they will Stay out Some Days, Mr. Chabonee (our inturpeter) and one man that accompanied him to Some loges of the Minatarees near the Turtle Hill returned, both frosed in their faces.

Chaboneu informs that the Clerk of the Hudsons Bay Co. with the Me ne tar res has been Speaking Some fiew expressns. unfavourable towards us, and that it is Said the N W Co. intends building a fort at the Mene tar re's- he Saw the Grand Chief of the Big bellies who Spoke Slightly of the Americans, Saying if we would give our great flag to him he would Come to See us.

[Clark, January 14, 1805] 14th of January 1805 Monday This morning early a number of indians men womin children Dogs &c & passed down on the ice to joine those that passed yesterday, we Sent Sergt Pryor and five men with those indians to hunt one of our hunters Sent out Several days arived & informs that one Man (Whitehouse) is frost bit and Can't walk home-

[Clark, January 15, 1805] Fort Mandan 15th January Tuesday 1805 between 12 & 3 oClock this morning we had a total eclips of the moon, a part of the observations necessary for our purpose in this eclips we got which is at 12h 57m 54s Total Darkness of the moon @ 1 44 00 End of total Darkness of This moon @ 2 39 10 End of the eclips-

This morning not So Cold as yesterday wind from the S. E. wind choped around to the N W. Still temperate four Considerate men of the Minetarre Came to See us we Smoked in the pipe, maney mands. present also, we Showed to those men who had been impressed with an unfavourable oppinion of us.

[Clark, January 16, 1805] 16th January Wednesday 1805 about thirty Mandans Came to the fort to day, 6 Chiefs. Those Me ne to rees told them they were liars, had told them if they came to the fort the whites men would kill them, they had been with them all night, Smoked in the pipe and have been treated well and the whites had danced for them, observing the Mandans were bad and ought to hide themselves- one of the 1st War Chiefs of the big belles nation Came to See us to day with one man and his Squar to wate on him we Shot the Air gun, and gave two Shots with the Cannon which pleased them verry much, the little Crow 2d Chf of the lower village came & brought us Corn &. 4 men of ours who had been hunting returned one frost'd

This war Chief gave us a Chart in his way of the Missourie, he informed us of his intentions of going to war in the Spring against the Snake Indians we advised him to look back at the number of nations who had been distroyed by war, and reflect upon what he was about to do, observing if he wished the hapiness of his nation, he would be at peace with all, by that by being at peace and haveing plenty of goods amongst them & a free intercourse with those defenceless nations, they would get on easy terms a great Number of horses, and that nation would increas, if he went to war against those Defenceless people, he would displease his great father, and he would not receive that pertection & Care from him as other nations who listened to his word- This Chief who is a young man 26 yr. old replied that if his going to war against the Snake indians would be displeasing to us be would not go, he had horses enough.

we observed that what we had Said was the words of his Great father, and what we had Spoken to all the nations which we Saw on our passage up, they all promis to open their ears and we do not know as yet if any of them has Shut them (we are doubtfull of the Souxs) if they do not attend to what we have told them their great father will open their ears- This Cheif Said that he would advise all his nation to Stay at home untill we Saw the Snake Indians & Knew if they would be friendly, he himself would attend to what we had told him

[Clark, January 17, 1805] 17th January Thursday 1805 a verry windey morning hard from the North Thermometer at 0, Several Indians here to day

[Clark, January 18, 1805] 18th January Friday 1805 a fine worm morning, Mr. La Rock & McKinzey Came down to See us with them Several of the Grosse Venrees.

[Clark, January 19, 1805] 19th January Satturday 1805. a find Day Messrs. Larock & McKinzey returned home, Sent three horses down to our hunting Camp for the meet they had killed, Jussoms Squar, left him and went to the Village

[Clark, January 20, 1805] 20th a Cold fair day Several Indians at the fort to day a miss understanding took place between the two inturpeters on account of their Squars, one of the Squars of Shabownes Squars being Sick, I ordered my Servent to, give her Some froot Stewed and tee at dift Tims which was the Cause of the misundstd

[Clark, January 21, 1805] Fort Mandan 21st Monday January 1805 a number of Indians hereto day a fine day nothing remarkable one ban verry bad with the pox

[Clark, January 22, 1805] 22nd January 1805 Tuesday a find warm Day attempted to Cut the Boat & the perogues out of the Ice, found water at about 8 inches under the 1st Ice, the next thickness about 3 feet

[Clark, January 23, 1805] 23rd January 1805 Wednesday a Cold Day Snow fell 4 Inches deep, the occurrences of this day is as is common

[Clark, January 24, 1805] 24th January Thursday 1805 a fine day, our inturpeters appear to understand each others better than a fiew days past Sent out Several hunters, they returned without killing any thing, Cut Coal wood

[Clark, January 25, 1805] 25th of January 1805 Friday we are informed of the arrival of a Band of Asniboins at the Villages with the Grand Cheif of those Tribes call the (Fee de petite veau) to trade, one of our interpeter & one man Set out to the Big Belley Camp opposit the Island men employ'd in Cutting the Boat out of the ice, and Collecting Coal wood.

[Clark, January 26, 1805] 26th of January Satturday 1805 a verry fine warm Day Several Indians Dine with us and are much Pleased- one man taken violently Bad with the Plurisee, Bleed & apply those remedeis Common to that disorder.

[Lewis, January 26, 1805] Saturday January 26th 1805 Observed Meridian Altitude of sun's U. L. with sextant and artificl. Horzn. of water 48° 50 Latitude deduced from this observatn. N. 47 21 47

[Clark, January 27, 1805] 27th of January Sunday 1804 a fine day, attempt to Cut our Boat and Canoos out of the Ice, a deficuelt Task I fear as we find waters between the Ice, I Bleed the man with the Plurisy to day & Swet him, Capt Lewis took of the Toes of one foot of the Boy who got frost bit Some time ago, Shabonoe our interpeter returned, & informed that the Assiniboins had returned to their Camps, & brough 3 horses of Mr. Laroches to Stay here for fear of their being Stolen by the Assiniboins who are great rogues- Cut off the boy toes

[Clark, January 28, 1805] 28th January Monday 1805 attempt to cut through the ice &c get our Boat and Canoo out without Suckcess, Several Indians here wishing to get war hatchets made this shape the man Sick yesterday is getting well Mr. Jessome our interpeter was taken verry unwell this evening warm day

[Clark, January 29, 1805] 29th January Tuesday 1805 Gave Jassome a Dost of Salts we Send & Collect Stones and put them on a large log heap to heet them with a View of warming water in the Boat and by that means, Sepperate her from the Ices, our attempt appears to be defeated by the Stones all breaking & flying to peaces in the fire, a fine warm Day, we are now burning a large Coal pit, to mend the indians hatchets, & make them war axes, the only means by which we precure Corn from them

[Clark, January 30, 1805] 30th January Wednesday 1805 a fine morning, Clouded up at 9 oClock, Mr. La Rocke paid us a Visit, & we gave him an answer respecting the request he made when last here of accompanying us on our journey &c.

[Clark, January 31, 1805] 31st January Thursday, 1805 Snowed last night, wind high from the N W. Sawed off the boys toes Sent 5 men down the river to hunt with 2 horses, our interpeter Something better, George Drewyer taken with the Ploursey last evening Bled & gave him Some Sage tea, this morning he is much better- Cold disagreeable

[Clark, February 1, 1805] 1st of February Friday 1805 a cold windey Day our hunters returnd. haveing killed only one Deer, a war Chief of the Me ne tar ras Came with Some Corn requested to have a War hatchet made, & requested to be allowed to go to war against the Souis & Ricarres who had Killed a mandan Some time past- we refused, and gave reassons, which he verry readily assented to, and promised to open his ears to all we Said this man is young and named (Seeing Snake Mar-book, She-ah-O-ke-ah) this mans woman Set out & he prosued her, in the evening

[Clark, February 2, 1805] 2nd of February Satturday 1805 a find Day one Deer Killed our interpeter Still unwell, one of the wives of the Big belley interptr taken Sick- Mr. Larocke leave us to day (this man is a Clerk to the N W Company, & verry anxious to accompany us)

[Lewis, February 3, 1805] 3rd of February Sunday 1805. a fine day; the blacksmith again commences his opperations. we were visited by but few of the natives today. the situation of our boat and perogues is now allarming, they are firmly inclosed in the Ice and almost covered with snow. The ice which incloses them lyes in several stratas of unequal thicknesses which are seperated by streams of water. this peculiarly unfortunate because so soon as we cut through the first strata of ice the water rushes up and rises as high as the upper surface of the ice and thus creates such a debth of water as renders it impracticable to cut away the lower strata which appears firmly attatched to, and confining the bottom of the vessels. the instruments we have hitherto used has been the ax only, with which, we have made several attempts that proved unsuccessful) from the cause above mentioned. we then determined to attempt freeing them from the ice by means of boiling water which we purposed heating in the vessels by means of hot stones, but this expedient proved also fruitless, as every species of stone which we could procure in the neighbourhood partook so much of the calcarious genus that they burst into small particles on being exposed to the heat of the fire. we now determined as the dernier resort to prepare a parse) of Iron spikes and attatch them to the end of small poles of convenient length and endeavour by means of them to free the vessels from the ice. we have already prepared a large rope of Elk-skin and a windless by means of which we have no doubt of being able to draw the boat on the bank provided we can free from the ice.

[Clark, February 3, 1805] 3rd of February 1805 our provisions of meat being nearly exorsted I concluded to Decend the River on the Ice & hunt, I Set out with about 16 men 3 horses & 2 Slays Descended nearly 60 miles Killed & loaded the horses back, & made 2 pens which we filed with meat, & returned on the 13th we Killed 40 Deer, 3 Bulls 19 Elk, maney So meager that they were unfit for use

[Lewis, February 4, 1805] 4th February, Monday 1805. This morning fair tho could the thermometer stood at 18° below Naught, wind from N. W. Capt Clark set out with a hunting party consisting of sixteen of our command and two frenchmen who together with two others, have established a small hut and resided this winter within the vicinity of Fort Mandane under our protection. visited by many of the natives today. our stock of meat which we had procured in the Months of November & December is now nearly exhausted; a supply of this articles is at this moment peculiarly interesting as well for our immediate consumption, as that we may have time before the approach of the warm season to prepare the meat for our voyage in the spring of the year. Capt. Clark therefore deturmined to continue his rout down the river even as far as the River bullet unless he should find a plenty of game nearer- The men transported their baggage on a couple of small wooden Slays drawn by themselves, and took with them 3 pack horses which we had agreed should be returned with a load of meat to fort mandane as soon as they could procure it. no buffaloe have made their appearance in our neighbourhood for some weeks; and I am informed that our Indian neighbours-suffer extreemly at this moment for the article of flesh. Shields killed two deer this evening, both very lean- one a large buck, he had shed his horns.

[Lewis, February 5, 1805] 5th February Tuesday 1805. Pleasent morning wind from N. W. fair; visited by many of the natives who brought a considerable quanty of corn in payment for the work which the blacksmith had done for them- they are pecuarly attatched to a battle ax formed in a very inconvenient manner in my opinion. it is fabricated of iron only, the blade is extreemly thin, from 7 to nine inches in length and from 43/4, to 6 Inches on it's edge, from whence the sides proceed nearly in a straight line to the eye where it's width is generally not more than an inch. The eye is round & about one inch in diameter. the handle seldom more than fourteen inches in length, the whole weighing about one pound- the great length of the blade of this ax, added to the small size of the handle renders a stroke uncertain and easily avoided, while the shortness of the handel must render a blow much less forceable if even well directed, and still more inconvenient as they uniformly use this instrument in action on horseback. The oalder fassion is still more inconvenient, it is somewhat in the form of the blade of an Espantoon but is attatchd to a helve of the dementions before discribed the blade is sometimes by way of ornament purforated with two three or more small circular holes- the following is the general figure it is from 12 to 15 inces in length

[Lewis, February 6, 1805] 6th February Wednesday 1805. Fair morning Wind from N. W. had a sley prepared against the return of the horses which Capt Clark had promised to send back as soon as he should be able to procure a load of meat. visited by many of the natives among others the Big white, the Coal, big-man, hairy horn and the black man, I smoked with them, after which they retired, a deportment not common, for they usually pester us with their good company the ballance of the day after once being introduced to our apartment. Shields killed three antelopes this evening. the blacksmiths take a considerable quantity of corn today in payment for their labour. the blacksmith's have proved a happy resoce to us in our present situation as I believe it would have been difficult to have devised any other method to have procured corn from the natives. the Indians are extravegantly fond of sheet iron of which they form arrow-points and manufacter into instruments for scraping and dressing their buffaloe robes- I permited the blacksmith to dispose of a part of a sheet-iron callaboos which had been nearly birnt out on our passage up the river, and for each piece about four inches square he obtained from seven to eight gallons of corn from the natives who appeared extreemly pleased with the exchange-

[Lewis, February 7, 1805] 7th February Thursday 1805. This morning was fair Thermometer at 18° above naught much warmer than it has been for some days; wind S. E. continue to be visited by the natives. The Sergt. of the guard reported that the Indian women (wives to our interpreters) were in the habit of unbaring the fort gate at any time of night and admitting their Indian visitors, I therefore directed a lock to be put to the gate and ordered that no Indian but those attatched to the garrison should be permitted to remain all night within the fort or admitted during the period which the gate had been previously ordered to be kept shut which was from sunset untill sunrise.

[Lewis, February 8, 1805] 8th February Friday 1805. This morning was fair wind S. E. the weather still warm and pleasent- visited by the black-Cat the principal chief of the Roop-tar-he, or upper mandane vilage. this man possesses more integrety, firmness, inteligence and perspicuety of mind than any indian I have met with in this quarter, and I think with a little management he may be made a usefull agent in furthering the views of our government. The black Cat presented me with a bow and apologized for not having completed the shield he had promised alledging that the weather had been too could to permit his making it, I gave him som small shot 6 fishing-hooks and 2 yards of ribbon his squaw also presented me with 2 pair of mockersons for which in return I gave a small lookingglass and a couples of nedles. the chief dined with me and left me in the evening. he informed me that his people suffered very much for the article of meat, and that he had not himself tasted any for several days.

[Lewis, February 9, 1805] 9th February Saturday 1805. The morning fair and pleasent, wind from S. E.- visted by Mr. McKinzey one the N. W. Company's clerks. this evening a man by the name of Howard whom I had given permission to go the Mandane vilage returned after the gate was shut and rether than call to the guard to have it opened scaled the works an indian who was looking on shortly after followed his example. I convinced the Indian of the impropryety of his conduct, and explained to him the riske he had run of being severely treated, the fellow appeared much allarmed, I gave him a small piece of tobacco and sent him away Howard I had comitted to the care of the guard with a determineation to have him tryed by a Courtmartial for this offence. this man is an old soldier which still hightens this offnce-

[Lewis, February 10, 1805] 10th February Sunday 1805. This Morning was Cloudy after a slight snow which fell in the course of the night the wind blue very hard from N. W. altho the thermometer stood at 18° Above naught the violence of the wind caused a degree of could that was much more unpleasant than that of yesterday when thermometer stood at 10° only above the same point. Mr. McKinzey left me this morning. Charbono returned with one of the Frenchmen and informed me that he had left the three Horses and two men with the meat which Capt. Clark had sent at some distance below on the river- he told me that the horses were heavy loaded and that not being shod it was impossible for horses to travel on the ice. I determined to send down some men with two small slays for the meat and accordingly I gave orders that they should set out early the next morning. two men were also sent to conduct the horses by way of the plain.

[Lewis, February 11, 1805] 11th February Monday 1805. The party that were ordered last evening set out early this morning. the weather was fair and could wind N. W. about five oclock this evening one of the wives of Charbono was delivered of a fine boy. it is worthy of remark that this was the first child which this woman had boarn and as is common in such cases her labour was tedious and the pain violent; Mr. Jessome informed me that he had freequently adminstered a small portion of the rattle of the rattle-snake, which he assured me had never failed to produce the desired effect, that of hastening the birth of the child; having the rattle of a snake by me I gave it to him and he administered two rings of it to the woman broken in small pieces with the fingers and added to a small quantity of water. Whether this medicine was truly the cause or not I shall not undertake to determine, but I was informed that she had not taken it more than ten minutes before she brought forth perhaps this remedy may be worthy of future experiments, but I must confess that I want faith as to it's efficacy.-

[Lewis, February 12, 1805] 12th February Tuesday 1805. The morning was fair tho could, thermometer at 14° below naught wind S. E. ordered the Blacksmith to shoe the horses and some others to prepare some gears in order to send them down with three slays to join the hunting party and transport the meat which they may have pocured to this place- the the men whom I had sent for the meat left by Charbono did not return untill 4 OClock this evening. Drewyer arrived with the horses about the same time, the horses appeared much fatieged I directed some meal brands given them moisened with a little water but to my astonishment found that they would not eat it but prefered the bark of the cotton wood which forms the principall article of food usually given them by their Indian masters in the winter season; for this purpose they cause the trees to be felled by their women and the horses feed on the boughs and bark of their tender branches. the Indians in our neighbourhood are freequently pilfered of their horses by the Recares, Souixs and Assinniboins and therefore make it an invariable rule to put their horses in their lodges at night. in this situation the only food of the horse consists of a few sticks of the cottonwood from the size of a man's finger to that of his arm. The Indians are invariably severe riders, and frequently have occasion for many days together through the whole course of the day to employ their horses in pursuing the Buffaloe or transporting meat to their vilages during which time they are seldom suffered to tast food; at night the Horse returned to his stall where his food is what seems to me a scanty allowance of wood. under these circumstances it would seem that their horses could not long exist or at least could not retain their flesh and strength, but the contrary is the fact, this valuable anamall under all those disadvantages is seldom seen meager or unfit for service.- A little after dark this evening Capt. Clark arrived with the hunting party- since they set out they have killed forty Deer, three buffaloe bulls, & sixteen Elk, most of them were so meager that they were unfit for uce, particularly the Buffaloes and male Elk- the wolves also which are here extreemly numerous heped themselves to a considerable proportion of the hunt- if an anamal is killed and lyes only one night exposed to the wolves it is almost invariably devoured by them.

[Lewis, February 13, 1805] 13th February Wednesday 1805. The morning cloudy thermometer 2° below naught wind from S. E. visited by the Black-Cat gave him a battle ax with which he appeared much gratifyed.

[Clark, February 13, 1805]
I returned last night from a hunting party much fatigued, haveing
walked 30 miles on the ice and through of wood land Points in which the
Snow was nearly Knee Deep

The 1st day I left the fort proceeded on the ice to new Mandan Island, 22 miles & Camped Killed nothing, & nothing to eat,

The 2d day the morning verry Cold & Windey, I broke thro the ice and got my feet and legs wet, Sent out 4 hunters thro a point to Kill a Deer & Cook it by the time the party Should get up, those hunters killed a Deer & 2 Buffalow Bulls the Buffalow too Meagur to eate, we eate the Deer & proceeded on to an old Indian Lodge, Sent out the hunters & they brought in three lean Deer, which we made use of for food,- walking on uneaven ice has blistered the bottom of my feat, and walking is painfull to me

3rd day Cold morning the after party of the Day worm, Camped on a Sand point near the mouth of a Creek on the S W. Side we Call hunting Creek, I turned out with the hunters, I Killed 2 Deer the hunters killed an Elk, Buffalow Bull & 5 Deer. all Meager

4th Day hunted the two bottoms near the Camp Killed 9 Elk, 18 Deer, brought to camp all the meat fit to eate & had the bones taken out. every man ingaged either in hunting or Collecting & packing the meat to Camp

5th Day Dispatched one of the party our Interpeter & 2 french men with the 3 horses loaded with the best of the meat to the fort 44 miles Distant, the remaining meat I had packed on the 2 Slays & drawn down to the next point about 3 miles below, at this place I had all the meat Collected which was killed yesterday & had escaped the wolves, Raven & Magpie, (which are verry noumerous about this Place) and put into a close pen made of logs to secure it from the wolves & birds & proceeded on to a large bottom nearly opposit the Chisscheter (heart) River, in this bottom we found but little game, Great No. of wolves, on the hills Saw Several parsels of Buffalow.- Camped. I killed a Buck

6th Day The Buffalow Seen last night provd to be Bulls. lean & unfit for to make uce of as food, the Distance from Camp being nearly 60 miles, and the packing of meat that distance attended with much difficulty determined me to return and hunt the points above, we Set out on our return and halted at an old Indian lodge 40 miles below Fort Mandan Killed 3 Elk & 2 Deer-.

7th Day a cold Day wind blew hard from the N. W. J Fields got one of his ears frosed deturmined to lay by and hunt today Killed an Elk & 6 deer,* this meat I had Boned & put onto a Close pen made of logs- *all that was fit for use

8th day air keen halted at the old Camp we Stayed in on the 2d night after we left the Fort, expecting to meat the horses at this Place, killed 3 Deer, Several men being nearly out of Mockersons & the horses not returning deturmind me to return to the Fort on tomorrow

9th day. Set out early, Saw great numbers of Grouse feeding on the young willows, on the Sand bars one mans I sent in persute of a gangue of Elk killed three near the old Ricara Village and joined at the fort, Sent him back to Secure the meat one man with him- The ice on the parts of the River which was verry rough, as I went down, was Smothe on my return, this is owing to the rise and fall of the water, which takes place every day or two, and Caused by partial thaws, and obstructions in the passage of the water thro the Ice, which frequently attaches itself to the bottom.- the water when riseing forses its way thro the cracks & air holes above the old ice, & in one night becoms a Smothe Surface of ice 4 to 6 Inchs thick,- the river falls & the ice Sink in places with the water and attaches itself to the bottom, and when it again rises to its former hite, frequently leavs a valley of Several feet to Supply with water to bring it on a leavel Surface.

The water of the Missouri at this time is Clear with little Tinges.

I saw Several old Villages near the Chisscheta River on enquirey found they were Mandan Villages destroyed by the Sous & Small Pox, they noumerous and lived in 6 Villages near that place.

[Clark, February 14, 1805] 14th Sent 4 men with the Horses Shod & 2 Slays down for the meat I had left, 22 miles below those men were rushed on by 106 Sioux who robed them of 2 of their horses- & they returned

[Clark, February 14, 1805] 14th of February Thursday 1805 The Snow fell 3 inches Deep last night, a fine morning, Dispatched George Drewyer & 3 men with two Slays drawn by 3 horses for the meat left below-

[Clark, February 15, 1805] 15th Capt. Lewis with a party of men & 4 Indians went in pursute of the Sioux, the Indians returned the next Day & informed me that the Sioux had Burnt all my meat & Born home (they Saw me but was afraid to attact me) Capt Lewis returned the 21st with 2400 I. of meat, haveing Killed 36 Deer & 14 Elk, the Sioux burnt one of my meet houses; they did not find the other

[Clark, February 15, 1805] 15th of February Friday 1805 at 10 oClock P M. last night the men that dispatched yesterday for the meat, returned and informed us that as they were on their march down at the distance of about 24 miles below the Fort about 105 Indians which they took to be Souis rushed on them and Cut their horses from the Slays, two of which they carried off in great hast, the 3rd horse was given up to the party by the intersetion of an Indian who assumd Some authority on the accasion, probably more thro fear of himself or Some of the Indians being killed by our men who were not disposed to be Robed of all they had tamely, they also forced 2 of the mens knives & a tamahawk, the man obliged them to return the tamahawk the knives they ran off with G Drewyer Frasure, S Gutterage, & Newmon with a broken Gun

we dispatched two men to inform the mandans, and if any of them chose to pursue those robers, to come down in the morning, and join Capt Lewis who intended to Set out with a party of men verry early, by 12 oClock the Chief of the 2ed Village Big white Came down, and Soon after one other Chief and Several men- The Chief observed that all the young men of the 2 Villages were out hunting, and but verry fiew guns were left,Capt. Lewis Set out at Sunrise with 24 men, to meet those Soues &c. Several Indians accompanied him Some with Bows & arrows Some withe Spears & Battle axes, a 2 with fusees - the morning fine the Thermometer Stood at 16° below 0, Nought, visited by 2 of the Big Bellies this evening,- one Chief of the Mandans returned from Capt Lewises Party nearly blind- this Complaint is as I am infomd. Common at this Season of the year and caused by the reflection of the Sun on the ice & Snow, it is cured by jentilley Swetting the part affected by throweng Snow on a hot Stone

verry Cold part of the night- one man Killed a verry large Red Fox to day

[Clark, February 16, 1805] 16th of February Satturday 1805 a fine morning, visited by but fiew Indians to day, at Dusk two of the Indians who wint down with Capt. Lewis returned, Soon after two others and one man (Howard) with his feet frosted, and informed that the Inds. who Commited the roberry of the 2 horses was So far a head that they could not be overtaken, they left a number of pars of Mockersons which, the Mandans knew to be Souix mockersons,- This war party Camped verry near the last camp I made when on my hunting party, where they left Some Corn, as a deception, with a view to induc a belief that they were Ricarras.

Capt Lewis & party proceeded on down the meat I left at my last Camp was taken.

[Clark, February 17, 1805] 17th of February Sunday 1805 this morning worm & a little Cloudy, the Coal & his Son visited me to day with about 30 w. of Drid Buffalow meat, & Some Tallow Mr. McKinsey one of the N W. Compys. Clerks visited me (one of the hoses the Sous robed a fiew Days past belonged to this man) The after part of the day fair,

[Clark, February 18, 1805] 18th of February Monday 1805 a cloudy morning Some Snow, Several Indians here today Mr. McKinsey leave me, the after part of the day fine I am much engaged makeing a discriptive List of the Rivers from Information our Store of Meat is out to day

[Clark, February 19, 1805] 19th of February Tuesday 1805 a fine Day visited by Several of the Mandans to day, our Smiths are much engaged mending and makeing Axes for the Indians for which we get Corn

[Clark, February 20, 1805] Fort Mandan 20th February Wednesday 1805 a Butifull Day, visited by the Little raven verry early this morning I am informed of the Death of an old man whome I Saw in the Mandan Village. this man, informed me that he "was 120 winters old, he requested his grand Children to Dress him after Death & Set him on a Stone on a hill with his face towards his old Village or Down the river, that he might go Streight to his brother at their old village under ground"I observed Several Mandan verry old Chiefly men

[Clark, February 21, 1805] 21st February Thursday 1805 a Delightfull Day put out our Clothes to Sun- Visited by the big white & Big man they informed me that Several men of their nation was gorn to Consult their

Medison Stone about 3 day march to the South West to know What was to be the result of the insuing year- They have great confidence in this Stone and Say that it informs them of every thing which is to happen, & visit it every Spring & Sometimes in the Summer "They haveing arrived at the Stone give it Smoke and proceed to the wood at Some distance to Sleep the next morning return to the Stone, and find marks white & raised on the Stone representing the piece or war which they are to meet with, and other changes, which they are to meet" This Stone has a leavel Surface of about 20 feet in Surcumfrance, thick and pores, and no doubt has Some mineral qualtites effected by the Sun.

The Big Bellies have a Stone to which they ascribe nearly the Same
Virtues

Capt Lewis returned with 2 Slays loaded with meat, after finding that he could not overtake the Souis war party, (who had in their way distroyd all the meat at one Deposit which I had made & Burnt the Lodges) deturmined to proceed on to the lower Deposit, which he found had not been observed by Soux he hunted two day Killed 36 Deer & 14 Elk, Several of them So meager, that they were unfit for use, the meet which he killed and that in the lower Deposit amounting to about 3000 wt was brought up on two Slays, one Drawn by 16 men had about 2400 wt on it

[Clark, February 22, 1805] Fort Mandan 22nd of February Friday 1805. a Cloudy morning, at about 12 oClock it began to rain and Continud for a fiew minits, and turned to Snow, and Continud Snowing for about one hour, and Cleared away fair The two hunters left below arrived, They killed two Elk, and hung them up out of the reach of the wolves- The Coal a Ricara who is a considerable Chief of the Mandans visited us to day, and maney others of the three nations in our neighbourhood.

[Clark, February 23, 1805] 23rd of February 1805 Satturday All hands employed in Cutting the Perogus Loose from the ice, which was nearly even with their top; we found great difficuelty in effecting this work owing to the Different devisions of Ice & water after Cutting as much as we Could with axes, we had all the Iron we Could get & Some axes put on long poles and picked throught the ice, under the first water, which was not more the 6 or 8 inches deep- we disengaged one Perogue, and nearly disingaged the 2nd in Course of this day which has been warm & pleasent vised by a no of Indians, jessomme & familey went to the Shoes Indians Villag to day

The father of the Boy whose feet were frose near this place, and nearly
Cured by us took him home in a Slay-

[Clark, February 24, 1805] 24th February Sunday 1805 The Day fine, we Commenced very early to day the Cutting loose the boat which was more difficuelt than the perogus with great exertions and with the assistance of Great prises we lousened her and turned the Second peroue upon the ice, ready to Draw out, in Lousening the boat from the ice Some of the Corking drew out which Caused her to Leake for a few minits untill we Discovered the Leake & Stoped it- Jessomme our interpeter & familey returned from the Villages Several Indians visit us today

[Clark, February 25, 1805] 25th of February Monday 1805 we fixed a Windlass and Drew up the two Perogues on the upper bank and attempted the Boat, but the Roap which we bade made of Elk Skins proved too weak & broke Several times night Comeing on obliged us to leave her in a Situation but little advanced- we were Visited by the Black mockerson Chief of the little Village of Big Bellies, the Cheef of the Shoe Inds and a number of others those Chiefs gave us Some meat which they packed on their wives, and one requested a ax to be made for hies Sun, Mr. Bunch, one of the under traders for the hudsons Bay Companey- one of the Big Bellies asked leave for himself & his two wives to Stay all night, which was granted, also two Boys Stayed all night, one the Sun of the Black Cat.

The Day has been exceedingly pleasent

[Clark, February 26, 1805] 26th of Feby 1805 Drew up the Boat & perogus, after Cutting them out of the ice with great Dificuelty-& trouble

[Clark, February 26, 1805] 26th February Tuesday 1805 a fine Day Commencd verry early in makeing preparations for drawing up the Boat on the bank, at Sunset by repeated exertions the whole day we accomplished this troublesom task, just as we were fixed for having the Boat the ice gave away near us for about 100 yds in length- a number of Indians here to day to See the Boat rise on the Bank

[Clark, February 27, 1805] 27th of February Wednesday 1805 a fine day, prepareing the Tools to make perogues all day- a feiw Indians visit us to day, one the largest Indian I ever Saw, & as large a man as ever I Saw, I commence a Map of the Countrey on the Missouries & its waters &c. &c.-

[Clark, February 28, 1805] 28th of February 1805 Thursday Mr. Gravilin 2 frenchmen and 2 Ricaras arrived from the Ricaras with letters from Mr. Tahoe &c. informing us of the Deturmination of the Ricaras to follow our councils- and the threts & intintions of the Sioux in Killing us whenever they again met us- and that a party of Several bands were formeing to attacke the Mandans &c. &c.

we informed the Mandans & others of this information & also the wish the Ricars had to live near them & fite the Sioux &c. &c. &c.

despatched 16 Men 5 Miles abov to build 6 Canoes for the voyage, being Deturmend to Send back the Barge

[Clark, February 28, 1805] 28th of February Thursday 1805 a fine morning, two men of the N W Compy arrve with letters and Sacka comah also a Root and top of a plant presented by Mr. Haney, for the Cure of mad Dogs Snakes &c, and to be found & used as follows vz: "this root is found on high lands and asent of hills, the way of useing it is to Scarify the part when bitten to chu or pound an inch or more if the root is Small, and applying it to the bitten part renewing it twice a Day. the bitten person is not to chaw nor Swallow any of the Root for it might have contrary effect."

Sent out 16 men to make four Perogus those men returned in the evening and informed that they found trees they thought would answer.

Mr. Gravelin two frenchmen & two Inds. arrive from the Ricara Nation with Letters from Mr. Anty Tabeaux, informing us of the peaceable dispositions of that nation towards the Mandans & Me ne to res & their avowed intentions of pursueing our Councils & advice, they express a wish to visit the Mandans, & Know if it will be agreeable to them to admit the Ricaras to Settle near them and join them against their common Enimey the Souis we mentioned this to the mandans, who observed they had always wished to be at peace and good neighbours with the Ricaras, and it is also the Sentiments of all the Big Bellies, & Shoe Nations

Mr. Gravilin informs that the Sisetoons and the 3 upper bands of the Tetons, with the Yanktons of the North intend to come to war in a Short time against the nations in this quarter, & will Kill everry white man they See- Mr. T. also informes that Mr. Cameron of St peters has put arms into the hands of the Souls to revenge the death of 3 of his men Killed by the Chipaways latterly- and that the Band of tetons which we Saw is desposed to doe as we have advised them- thro the influenc of their Chief the Black Buffalow

Mr. Gravilin further informs that the Party which Robed us of the 2 horses laterly were all Sieoux 100 in number, they Called at the Ricaras on their return, the Ricares being displeased at their Conduct would not give them any thing to eate, that being the greatest insult they could peaceably offer them, and upbraded them.

[Clark, March 1, 1805]
March 1st Friday 1805
a fine Day I am ingaged in Copying a map, men building perogus, makeing
Ropes, Burning Coal, Hanging up meat & makeing battle axes for Corn

[Clark, March 2, 1805] 2nd of March 1805 Satturday a fine Day the river brake up in places all engaged about Something Mr. La Rocque a Clerk of the N W Company visit us, he has latterly returned from the Establishments on the Assinniboin River with Merchindize to tarade with Indians- Mr. L informs us the N, W. & X Y Companies have joined, & the head of the N W. Co. is Dead Mr. McTavish of Monteral,- visted by the Coal & Several Indians

[Clark, March 3, 1805] 3rd of March Sunday 1805 a fine Day wind from the W, a large flock of Ducks pass up the Rivervisited by the black Cat, Chief of the Mandans 2d Cheif and a Big Belley, they Stayed but a Short time we informed those Chiefs of the news recved from the Ricaras, all hands employd

[Clark, March 4, 1805] Fort Mandan 4th March Monday 1805 a Cloudy morning wind from the N W the after part of the day Clear, visited by the Black Cat & Big White, who brought a Small present of meat, an Engage of the N W Co. Came for a horse, and requested in the name of the woman of the princapal of his Department Some Silk of three Colours, which we furnished-. The Assinniboins who visited the Mandans a fiew Days ago returned and attempted to take horses of the Minetarres & were fired on by them

[Clark, March 5, 1805]
5th March Tuesday 1805
A fine Day Themometer at 40° abo 0. Several Indians visit us to day one
frenchman cross to join a Indian the two pass through by Land to the
Ricaras with a Letter to Mr. Tabbow

[Clark, March 6, 1805] 6th of March Wednesday 1805 a Cloudy morning & Smokey all Day from the burning of the plains, which was Set on fire by the Minetarries for an early crop of Grass as an endusement for the Buffalow to feed on- the horses which was Stolen Some time ago by the Assinniboins from the minetarries were returned yesterday- visited by Oh-harh or the Little fox 2d Chief of the lower Village of the Me ne tar ries- one man Shannon Cut his foot with the ads in working at a perogue, George & Graviline go to the Village, the river rise a little to day-

[Clark, March 7, 1805] 7th of March Thursday 1805 a little Cloudy and windey N E. the Coal visited us with a Sick child, to whome I gave Some of rushes Pills- Shabounar returned this evening from the Gross Vintres & informed that all the nation had returned from the hunting- he our menetarre interpeter had received a present from Mr. Chaboilleiz of the N. W. Company of the following articles 3 Brace of Cloath 1 Brace of Scarlet a par Corduroy Overalls 1 Vests 1 Brace Blu Cloth 1 Brace red or Scarlet with 3 bars, 200 balls & Powder, 2 bracs Tobacco, 3 Knives.

[Clark, March 8, 1805] 8th of March Friday 1805 a fair morning Cold and windey, wind from the East, visited by the Greesey head & a Riarca to day, those men gave Some account of the Indians near the rockey mountains

a young Indian same nation & Differnt Village Stole the Doughter of the Black man, he went to his Village took his horse & returned & took away his doughter

[Clark, March 9, 1805]
on the 9th of March we were Visited by the Grand Chief of the Minetarres, to whome we gave a medal & Some Cloths & a flag. Sent a French Man & a Indian with a letter to Mr. Tabboe informing them the Ricarras of the desire the Mandans had to See them &. &.

[Clark, March 9, 1805] 9th of March Satturday 1805 a Cloudy Cold and windey morning wind from the North- walked up to See the Party that is makeing Perogues, about 5 miles above this, the wind hard and Cold on my way up I met The Main Chief of the Manitarres with four Indians on Thier way to See us, I requested him to proceed on to the fort where he would find Capt. Lewis I should be there my Self in corse of a fiew hours, Sent the interpeter back with him and proceeded on my Self to the Canoes found them nearly finished, the timber verry bad, after visiting all the perogues where I found a number of Indans I wind to the upper mandan Village & Smoked a pipe the greatest mark of friendship and attention with the Chief and returned on my return found the Manitarree Chief about Setting out on his return to his village, having recieved of Captain M. Lewis a medel Gorget armbans, a Flag Shirt, Scarlet &c. &c. &c. for which he was much pleased Those Things were given in place of Sundery articles Sent to him which he Sais he did not receive 2 guns were fired for this Great man

[Clark, March 10, 1805] 10th of March Sunday 1805. a Cold winday Day. we are visited by the Black mockersons, Chief of the 2d Manetarre Village and the Chief of the Shoeman Village or Mah ha ha V. those Chiefs Stayed all day and the latter all night and gave us many Strang accounts of his nation &c this Little tribe or band of Menitaraies Call themselves Ah-nah-haway or people whose village is on the hill. nation formerleyed lived about 30 miles below this but beeing oppressed by the Asinniboins & Sous were Compelled to move 5 miles the Minitaries, where, the Assinniboins Killed the most of. them those remaining built a village verry near to the Minitarries at the mouth of Knife R where they now live and Can raise about 50 men, they are intermixed with the Mandans & Minatariers- the Manclans formerly lived in 6 large villages at and above the mouth of Chischeter or Heart River five Villages on the West Side & two on the East one of those Villages on the East Side of the Missouri & the larges was intirely Cut off by the Sioux & the greater part of the others and the Small Pox reduced the others.

[Clark, March 11, 1805] Fort Mandan 11th of March Monday 1805 A Cloudy Cold windey day, Some Snow in the latter part of the day, we deturmin to have two other Perogues made for us to transport our Provisions &c.

We have every reason to believe that our Menetarre interpeter, (whome we intended to take with his wife, as an interpeter through his wife to the Snake Indians of which nation She is) has been Corupted by the _____ Companeys &c. Some explenation has taken place which Clearly proves to us the fact, we give him to night to reflect and deturmin whether or not he intends to go with us under the regulations Stated.

[Clark, March 12, 1805] 12th a fine day Some Snow last night our Interpeter Shabonah, detumins on not proceeding with us as an interpeter under the terms mentioned yesterday he will not agree to work let our Situation be what it may not Stand a guard, and if miffed with any man he wishes to return when he pleases, also have the disposial of as much provisions as he Chuses to Carrye.

in admissable and we Suffer him to be off the engagement which was only virbal wind N W

[Clark, March 13, 1805] 13th of March Wednesday 1805 a fine day visited by Mr. Mckinsey one of the Clerks of the N W Companey, the river riseing a little- maney Inds. here to day all anxiety for war axes the Smiths have not an hour of Idle time to Spear wind S W

[Clark, March 14, 1805]
14th March Thursday 1805. a fine day Set all hands to Shelling Corn &c.
Mr. McKinsey leave us to day maney Indians as usial. wind west river
Still riseing

[Clark, March 15, 1805] 15th of March Friday 1805 a fine day I put out all the goods & Parch meal Clothing &c to Sun, a number of Indians here to day They make maney remarks respecting our goods &c. Set Some men about Hulling Corn &c.

[Lewis, March 16, 1805] March 16th, 1804. Mr. Gurrow a Frenchman who has lived many years with the Ricares & Mandans shewed us the process used by those Indians to make beads. the discovery of this art these nations are said to have derived from the Snake Indians who have been taken prisoners by the Ricaras. the art is kept a secret by the Indians among themselves and is yet known to but few of them.

the Prosess is as follows,- Take glass of as many different colours as you think proper, then pound it as fine as possible puting each colour in a seperate vessel. wash the pounded glass in several waters throwing off the water at each washing. continue this opperation as long as the pounded glass stains or colours the water which is poured off and the residium is then prepared for uce. You then provide an earthen pot of convenient size say of three gallons which will stand the fire; a platter also of the same materials sufficiently small to be admitted in the mouth of the pot or jar. the pot has a nitch in it's edge through which to watch the beads when in blast. You then provide some well seasoned clay with a propertion of sand sufficient to prevent it's becoming very hard when exposed to the heat. this clay must be tempered with water untill it is about the consistency of common doe. of this clay you then prepare, a sufficient number of little sticks of the size you wish the hole through the bead, which you do by roling the clay on the palm of the hand with your finger. this done put those sticks of clay on the platter and espose them to a red heat for a few minutes when you take them off and suffer them to cool. the pot is also heated to cles it perfectly of any filth it may contain. small balls of clay are also mad of about an ounce weight which serve each as a pedestal for a bead. these while soft ar distributed over the face of the platter at such distance from each other as to prevent the beads from touching. some little wooden paddles are now provided from three to four inches in length sharpened or brought to a point at the extremity of the handle. with this paddle you place in the palm of the hand as much of the wet pounded glass as is necessary to make the bead of the size you wish it. it is then arranged with the paddle in an oblong form, laying one of those little stick of clay crosswise over it; the pounded glass by means of the paddle is then roped in cilindrical form arround the stick of clay and gently roled by motion of the hand backwards an forwards until you get it as regular and smooth as you conveniently can. if you wish to introduce any other colour you now purforate the surface of the bead with the pointed end of your little paddle and fill up the cavity with other pounded glass of the colour you wish forming the whole as regular as you can. a hole is now made in the center of the little pedestals of clay with the handle of your shovel sufficiently large to admit the end of the stick of clay arround which the bead is formed. the beads are then arranged perpindicularly on their pedestals and little distance above them supported by the little sticks of clay to which they are attatched in the manner before mentioned. Thus arranged the platter is deposited on burning coals or hot embers and the pot reversed with the apparture in it's edge turned towards coverd the whole. dry wood pretty much doated _; is then plased arron the pot in sush manner as compleatly to cover it is then set on fire and the opperator must shortly after begin to watch his beads through the apparture of the pot lest they should be distroyed by being over heated. he suffers the beads to acquire a deep red heat from which when it passes in a small degree to a pailer or whitish red, or he discovers that the beads begin to become pointed at their upper extremities he removes the fire from about the pot and suffers the whole to cool gradually. the pot is then removed and the beads taken out. the clay which fills the hollow of the beads is picked out with an awl or nedle, the bead is then fit for uce. The Indians are extreemly fond of the large beads formed by this process. they use them as pendants to their years, or hair and sometimes wear them about their necks.

[Clark, March 16, 1805] 16th of March Satturday 1805 a Cloudy day wind from the S. E one Indian much displeased with whitehouse for Strikeing his hand when eating with a Spoon for behaveing badly. Mr. Garrow Shew'd us the way the ricaras made their large Beeds

[Clark, March 17, 1805] 17th of March Sunday a windey Day attempted to air our goods &. Mr. Chabonah Sent a french man of our party that he was Sorry for the foolissh part he had acted and if we pleased he would accompany us agreeabley to the terms we had perposed and doe every thing we wished him to doe &c. &c. he had requested me Some thro our French inturpeter two days ago to excuse his Simplicity and take him into the cirvise, after he had taken his things across the River we called him in and Spoke to him on the Subject, he agreed to our terms and we agreed that he might go on with us &c &c. but fiew Indians here to day; the river riseing a little and Severall places open.

[Clark, March 18, 1805] 18th of March 1805 a cold cloudy Day wind from the N. I pack up all the merchindize into 8 packs equally devided So as to have Something of every thing in each Canoe & perogue I am informed of a Party of Christanoes & assinniboins being killed by the Sioux, 50 in Number near the Estableishments on the assinniboin R. a fiew days ago (the effect of Mr. Cammeron, revenge on the Chipaway for Killing 3 of his men) Mr. Tousent Chabono, Enlisted as an Interpreter this evening, I am not well to day.

[Clark, March 19, 1805] 19th of March 1805 Cold windey Day Cloudy Some little Snow last night Visited to Day by the big white & Little Crow, also a man & his wife with a Sick Child, I administer for the child I am told that two parties are gorn to war from the Big bellies and one other party going to war Shortly.

[Clark, March 20, 1805] I visited the Mandans on the 20th & have the canoes taken to the River, ready to Decend to the fort when the River Clears,

[Clark, March 20, 1805] Fort Mandan 20th March Wednesday 1805. I with all the men which could be Speared from the Fort went to Canoes, there I found a number of Indians the men carried 4 to the River about 1 1/2 miles thro the Bottom, I visited the Chief of the Mandans in the Course of the Day and Smoked a pipe with himself and Several old men. cloudy wind hard from N.

[Clark, March 21, 1805] I return on the 21st and on my return I passed on the points of the high hills S. S. where I saw an emence quantity of Pumice Stone, and evident marks of the hills being on fire I collected some Pumice Stone, burnt Stone & hard earth and put them into a furnace, the hard earth melted and glazed the other two a part of which i, e, the Hard Clay became a Pumice-Stone, I also collected a Plant the root of which is a Cure for the Bite of a mad dog & Snake which I shall Send- Mr. Haney (I think it grows in the Blue R Barrens) the Indians make large Beeds of Different Colours-

[Clark, March 21, 1805] 21st March Thursday 1805 a Cloudy Day Some snow, the men Carried the remaining the 2 remained Canoes to the River, all except 3 left to take care & complete the Canoes, returned to the fort with their baggage, on my return to day to the Fort I came on the points of the high hills, Saw an emence quantity of Pumice Stone on the Sides & foot of the hills and emence beds of Pumice Stone near the Tops of the hills with evident marks of the Hill haveing once been on fire, I collected Some the differnt i e Stone Pumice Stone & a hard earth and put them into a furnace the hard earth melted and glazed the others two and the hard Clay became a pumice Stone Glazed. I collected Some plants &c.

[Clark, March 22, 1805] 22nd of March 1805 Visited by the 2nd Chief of the Grand Village of the Minetarrees to whome we gave a medal & Some Clothes acknowledging him as a 2d Chief, he Delayed all night, & Saw the men Dance, which is common amusement with the men he returned the 23rd with Mr. La Rocque & McKinsey two of the N W. Companys Clerks- Some few Drops of rain this evening for the first time this Winter visited by many Indians to day

[Clark, March 22, 1805] March 22, 1805 23rd of March Friday 1805 a Cloudy Day visited by Mrs. Lack McKinsey & the 2d Chief of the Bigbellies, the white wolf and many other Menataries, we gave a Medal Some Clothes and wampoms to the 2 Chief and Delivered a Speach, which they all appeared well pleased with in The evening the men Danced Mr. Jessomme displeased

[Clark, March 24, 1805] 24th of March Satturday 1805 after Brackfast Mr. La Rocke and Mr. McKinsey and the Chiefs & men of the Minetarras leave us- Soon after we were visited by a Brother of the Burnia who gave us a Vocabulary of his Language- the Coal & many other Mandans also visit us to Day. a find Day in the fore part in the evening a little rain & the first this winter

[Clark, March 25, 1805] 25th of March Sunday 1805 a Cloudy morning wind from the N E the after part of the Day fair, Several Indians visit us today, prepareing to Set out on our journey Saw Swans & wild Gees flying N E this evening

[Clark, March 25, 1805] March 25, 1805 26h The ice broke up in Several places in the evenig broke away and was nearly takeing off our new Canoes river rise a little

[Clark, March 26, 1805] 26th of March Monday 1805 a find Day wind S. W. but fiew Inds visit us to day the Ice haveing broken up in Several places, The ice began to brake away this evening and was near distroying our Canoes as they wer decnding to the fort, river rose only 9 Inches to day prepareing to Depart

[Clark, March 27, 1805] 27th of March Tuesday 1805 The river choked up with ice opposit to us and broke away in the evening raised only 1/2 Inch all employed prepareing to Set out

[Clark, March 28, 1805] 28th had all the Canoes, the Perogus corked pitchd & lined cover the Cotton Wood, which is win Shaken (the Mandans feed their horses on the cotton wood Sticks in places of corn).

[Clark, March 28, 1805] 28th of March Friday 1805 a windey Blustering Day wind S W ice running the river Blocked up in view for the Space of 4 hours and gave way leaveing great quantity of ice on the Shallow Sand bars. had all the canoes corked pitched & tirred in and on the cracks and windshake which is universially in the Cotton wood

[Clark, March 28, 1805] March 28, 1805 25th the ice Stoped running owing to Some obstickle above all prepareing to Set out but few Indians visit us to day they are watching to catch the floating Buffalow which brake through the ice in Crossing, those people are fond of those animals tainted and Catch great numbers every Spring

[Clark, March 29, 1805] 29th of March Satturday 1805 The ice has Stoped running owing to Som obstickle above, repare the Boat & Perogues, and prepareing to Set out but few Indians visit us to day they are now attending on the river bank to Catch the floating Buffalow

[Clark, March 30, 1805] 30th of March. The Ice is passing in great quantites, river ran a little, The Plains are on fire on both Sides of the river it is common for the indians to Set those Plains on fire near their village for the advantage of early Grass for the hors & as an inducement to the Buffalow to visit them

[Clark, March 30, 1805] 30th of March Sunday 1805 The obstickle broke away above & the ice came dow in great quantites the river rose 13 inches the last 24 hours I observed extrodanary dexterity of the Indians in jumping from one Cake of ice to another, for the purpose of Catching the buffalow as they float down maney of the Cakes of ice which they pass over are not two feet Square. The Plains are on fire in view of the fort on both Sides of the River, it is Said to be common for the Indians to burn the Plains near their villages every Spring for the benifit of ther horse, and to induce the Buffalow to come near to them.

[Clark, March 31, 1805] 31 h of March Monday 1805 Cloudy Several gangus of Ducks and Gees pass up not much ice floating. All the party in high Spirits, but fiew nights pass without a Dance they are helth. except the-vn. -which is common with the Indians and have been communicated to many of our party at this place- those favores bieng easy acquired. all Tranquille

[Clark, March 31, 1805] 31t of March Monday 1805 Cloudy Day Seven Gangs of Gees and Ducks pass up the river- but a Small portion of ice floating down to-day- but fiew Inds visit us to day all the party in high Spirits they pass but fiew nights without amuseing themselves danceing possessing perfect harmony and good understanding towards each other Generally healthy except venerials complains which is verry Commion amongst the natives and the men Catch it from them

[Clark, April 1, 1805] April 1st 1805 we have Thunder lightning hail and rain to day the first rain of note Sinc the 15 of October last, I had the Boat Perogus & Canos put in the water, and expect to Set off the boat with despatches in her will go 6 Americans 3 frenchmen, and perhaps Several ricarra Chief imediately after we Shall assend in 2 perogus & 6 canoes, accompanied by 5 french who intends to assend a Short distance to trap the beavr which is in great abundance highr up our party will consist of one Interpter & Hunter, one French man as an interpreter with his two wives (this man Speaks Minetary to his wives who are L hiatars or Snake Indians of the nations through which we Shall pass, and to act as interpretress thro him)- 26 americans & french my servant and an Mandan Indian and provisions for 4 months

[Clark, April 1, 1805] Fort Mandan April the 1st Tuesday 1805 The fore part of to day haile rain with Thunder & lightning, the rain continued by intimitions all day, it is worthey of remark that this is the 1st rain which has fallen Since we have been here or Since the 15 of October last, except a fiew drops at two or three defferent times

had the Boat Perogus & Canoes all put into the water.

[Clark, April 2, 1805] April the 2nd a Cold rain day we are writeing and prepareing dispatches all day- I conclude to Send my journal to the President of the United States in its original State for his own perusial, untill I call for it or Some friend if I should not return, an this journal is from the 13th of May 1804 untill the 3rd of April 1805. wrote untill verry late at night but little time to devote to my friends, the river is falling fast.

[Clark, April 2, 1805] April the 2nd Friday 1805 a cloudy day rained all the last night we are preparing to Set out all thing nearly ready. The 2d Chief of the 2d Mandan Village took a miff at our not attending to him perticelarely after being here about ten day and moved back to his village

The mandans Killed twenty one elk yesterday 15 miles below this, they were So meager that they Scercely fit for use

[Clark, April 3, 1805] 3rd of April we Shall pack up to day and Set out tomorrow.

[Clark, April 3, 1805] April the 3rd Thursday 1805 a white frost this morning, Some ice on the edge of the water, a fine day Pack up and prepare to load

Mrs. La Roche & McKinsey Clerk to the N W. Compy. visit us. Mr. McKinzey wishes to get pay for his horse lost in our Service this winter and one of which was robed this winter by the Tetons, we Shall pay this man for his horse. we are all day ingaged packing up Sundery articles to be Sent to the President of the U. S.

bow an quiver of arrows-with some Ricara's tobacco seed

No. 11 a Martin Skin, Containing the tail of a Mule Deer, a weasel and three Squirels from the Rockey mountains.

No. 12. The bones & Skeleton of a Small burrowing wolf of the Praries the Skin being lost by accident.

No. 99 The Skeliton of the white and Grey hare.

Box No. 2, contains 4 Buffalow Robes, and a ear of Mandan Corn.

The large Trunk Contains a male & female Brarow and female's Skeliton.

a Carrote of Ricaras Tobacco

a red fox Skin Containing a Magpie.

No. 14 Minitarras Buffalow robe Containing Some articles of Indian dress.

No. 15 a Mandan robe containing two burrowing Squirels, a white weasel and the Skin of a Loucirvea.

also

13 red fox Skins.

1 white Hare Skin &.

4 horns of the mountain ram

> 1 Robe representing a battle between the Sioux & Ricaras,
> Minetarras and Mandans.

In Box No. 3.

nos. 1 & 2 The Skins of the Male & female Antelope with their Skelitons. & the Skin of a yellow Bear which I obtained from the Scions

No. 4. Box Specimens of plants numbered from 1 to 67.

Specimens of Plants numbered frome 1 to 60.

> 1 Earthen pot Such as the Mandans Manufacture and use for
> culinary purposes .

Box No 4 Continued

1 Tin box, containing insects mice &c. a Specimine of the fur of the antelope.

a Specimon of a plant, and a parcel of its roots highly prized by the natives as

an efficatious remidy in Cases of the bite of the rattle Snake or Mad Dog.

In a large Trunk

Skins of a Male and female Braro, or burrowing Dog of the Prarie, with the Skeliton of the female.

1 Skin of the red fox Containing a Magpie.

2 Cased Skins of the white hare.

1 Minitarra Buffalow robe Containing Some articles of Indian Dress

1 Mandan Buffalow robe Containing a dressed Lousirva Skin, and 2 Cased Skins of the Burrowing Squirel of the Praries.

13 red fox Skins

4 Horns of the Mountain Ram or big horn.

1 Buffalow robe painted by a mandan man representing a battle fought 8 years Since by the Sioux & Ricaras against the mandans, menitarras & Ah wah bar ways (Mandans &c. on horseback)

Cage No. 6.

Contains a liveing burrowing Squirel of the praries

Cage No. 7.

Contains 4 liveing magpies

Cage No. 9.

Containing a liveing hen of the Prarie

a large par of Elks horns containing by the frontal bone-

[Clark, April 4, 1805] April the 4th 1805 Wednesday a blustering windey Day the Clerks of the N W. Co. leave us we are arrangeing all things to Set out &c.

[Clark, April 5, 1805] April the 5th 1805 Thursday we have our 2 perogues & Six Canoes loaded with our Stores & provisions, principally provisions. the wind verry high from the N W. a number of Mandans visit us to day

[Clark, April 6, 1805] April the 6th Friday Saturday 1805 a fine day visited by a number of mandans, we are informed of the arrival of the whole of the ricarra nation on the other Side of the river near their old village. we Sent an interpreter to See with orders to return imediately and let us know if their Chiefs ment to go down to See their great father.

[Lewis, April 7, 1805] Fort Mandan April 7th 1805. Having on this day at 4 P.M. completed every arrangement necessary for our departure, we dismissed the barge and crew with orders to return without loss of time to S. Louis, a small canoe with two French hunters accompanyed the barge; these men had assended the missouri with us the last year as engages. The barge crew consisted of six soldiers and two _____ Frenchmen; two Frenchmen and a Ricara Indian also take their passage in her as far as the Ricara Vilages, at which place we expect Mr. Tiebeau to embark with his peltry who in that case will make an addition of two, perhaps four men to the crew of the barge. We gave Richard Warfington, a discharged Corpl., the charge of the Barge and crew, and confided to his care likewise our dispatches to the government, letters to our private friends, and a number of articles to the President of the United States. One of the Frenchmen by the Name of Gravline an honest discrete man and an excellent boat-man is imployed to conduct the barge as a pilot; we have therefore every hope that the barge and with her our dispatches will arrive safe at St. Louis. Mr. Gravlin who speaks the Ricara language extreemly well, has been imployed to conduct a few of the Recara Chiefs to the seat of government who have promised us to decend in the barge to St. Liwis with that view.-

At same moment that the Barge departed from Fort Mandan, Capt. Clark embaked with our party and proceeded up the river. as I had used no exercise for several weeks, I determined to walk on shore as far as our encampment of this evening; accordingly I continued my walk on the N. side of the River about six miles, to the upper Village of the Mandans, and called on the Black Cat or Pose cop'se ha, the great chief of the Mandans; he was not at home; I rested myself a minutes, and finding that the party had not arrived I returned about 2 miles and joined them at their encampment on the N. side of the river opposite the lower Mandan village. Our party now consisted of the following Individuals. Sergts. John Ordway, Nathaniel Prior, & Patric Gass; Privates, William Bratton, John Colter, Reubin, and Joseph Fields, John Shields, George Gibson, George Shannon, John Potts, John Collins, Joseph Whitehouse, Richard Windsor, Alexander Willard, Hugh Hall, Silas Goodrich, Robert Frazier, Peter Crouzatt, John Baptiest la Page, Francis Labiech, Hue McNeal, William Werner, Thomas P. Howard, Peter Wiser, and John B. Thompson.

Interpreters, George Drewyer and Tauasant Charbono also a Black man by the name of York, servant to Capt. Clark, an Indian Woman wife to Charbono with a young child, and a Mandan man who had promised us to accompany us as far as the Snake Indians with a view to bring about a good understanding and friendly intercourse between that nation and his own, the Minetares and Ahwahharways.

Our vessels consisted of six small canoes, and two large perogues. This little fleet altho not quite so rispectable as those of Columbus or Capt. Cook were still viewed by us with as much pleasure as those deservedly famed adventurers ever beheld theirs; and I dare say with quite as much anxiety for their safety and preservation. we were now about to penetrate a country at least two thousand miles in width, on which the foot of civillized man had never trodden; the good or evil it had in store for us was for experiment yet to determine, and these little vessells contained every article by which we were to expect to subsist or defend ourselves. however as this the state of mind in which we are, generally gives the colouring to events, when the immagination is suffered to wander into futurity, the picture which now presented itself to me was a most pleasing one. entertaing as I do, the most confident hope of succeading in a voyage which had formed a darling project of mine for the last ten years, I could but esteem this moment of my departure as among the most happy of my life. The party are in excellent health and sperits, zealously attatched to the enterprise, and anxious to proceed; not a whisper of murmur or discontent to be heard among them, but all act in unison, and with the most perfect harmony. I took an early supper this evening and went to bed. Capt. Clark myself the two Interpretters and the woman and child sleep in a tent of dressed skins. this tent is in the Indian stile, formed of a number of dressed Buffaloe skins sewed together with sinues. it is cut in such manner that when foalded double it forms the quarter of a circle, and is left open at one side where it may be attatched or loosened at pleasure by strings which are sewed to its sides to the purpose. to erect this tent, a parsel of ten or twelve poles are provided, fore or five of which are attatched together at one end, they are then elivated and their lower extremities are spread in a circular manner to a width proportionate to the demention of the lodge, in the same position orther poles are leant against those, and the leather is then thrown over them forming a conic figure.

[Clark, April 7, 1805] 7th of April Satturday 1805" a windey day, The Interpreter we Sent to the Villages returned with Chief of the Ricara's & 3 men of that nation this Chief informed us that he was Sent by his nation to Know the despositions of the nations in this neighbourhood in respect to the recara's Settleing near them, that he had not yet made those arrangements, he request that we would Speek to the Assinniboins, & Crow Inds. in their favour, that they wished to follow our directions and be at peace with all, he viewed all nations in this quarter well disposed except the Sioux. The wish of those recaras appears to be a junction with the Mandans & Minetarras in a Defensive war with the Sioux who rob them of every Spece of property in Such a manner that they Cannot live near them any longer. I told this Chief we were glad to See him, and we viewed his nation as the Dutifull Children of a Great father who would extend his protection to all those who would open their ears to his good advice, we had already Spoken to the Assinniboins, and Should Speeke to the Crow Indians if we Should See them &c. as to the Sioux their Great father would not let them have any more good Guns &c. would take Care to prosu Such measurs as would provent those Sioux from Murding and taking the property from his dutyfull red Children &c.- we gave him a certificate of his good Conduct & a Small Medal, a Carrot of Tobacco and a String of Wompom- he requested that one of his men who was lame might decend in the boat to their nation and returned to the Mandans well Satisfied

The name of this Chief of War is Kah-kah, we to-Raven brave.

This Cheif delivered us a letter from Mr. Taboe. informing us of the wish of the Grand Chiefs of the Ricarras to visit their Great father and requesting the privolage of put'g on board the boat 3000 w of Skins &c. & adding 4 hands and himself to the party. this preposeal we Shall agree to, as that addition will make the party in the boat 15 Strong and more able to defend themselves from the Seoux &c.

[Clark, April 7, 1805]
Fort Mandan April 7th 1805"
Sunday, at 4 oClock P M, the Boat, in which was 6 Soldiers 2 frenchmen
& an Indian, all under the command of a corporal who had the charge of
dispatches, &c.-and a Canoe with 2 french men, Set out down the river
for St. Louis. at the same time we Sout out on our voyage up the river
in 2 perogues and 6 canoes, and proceded on to the 1st villg. of
Mandans & Camped on the S. S.- our party consisting of Sergt. Nathaniel
Pryor Sgt. John Ordway Sgt. Pat. Gass, William Bratten, John Colter
Joseph & Reubin Fields, John Shields George Gibson George Shannon, John
Potts, John Collins, Jos. Whitehouse, Richard Windser, Alexander
Willard, Hugh Hall, Silas Gutrich, Robert Frazure, Peter Crouzat, John
Baptiest la page, Francis Labich, Hugh McNeal, William Werner, Thomas
P. Howard, Peter Wiser, J. B. Thompson and my Servent york, George
Drewyer who acts as a hunter & interpreter, Shabonah and his Indian
Squar to act as an Interpreter & interpretress for the snake
Indians-one Mandan & Shabonahs infant. Sah-kah-gar we a

[Lewis, April 8, 1805] April 8th Set out early this morning, the wind blew hard against us from the N. W. we therefore traveled very slowly. I walked on shore, and visited the black Cat, took leave of him after smoking a pipe as is their custom, and then proceeded on slowly by land about four miles where I wated the arrival of the party, at 12 Oclock they came up and informed me that one of the small canoes was behind in distress. Capt Clark returned foud she had filled with water and all her loading wet. we lost half a bag of hisquit, and about thirty pounds of powder by this accedent; the powder we regard as a serious loss, but we spread it to dry immediately and hope we shall be enabled to restore the greater part of it. this was the only powder we had which was not perfectly secure from geting wet. we took dinner at this place, and then proceed on to oure encampment, which was on the S. side opposite to a high bluff. the Mandan man came up after we had encamped and brought with him a woman who was extreemly solicitous to accompany one of the men of our party, this however we positively refused to permit.

From the upper point on an island (being the point to which Capt. Clark took his last course when he assended the river in surch of a place for winter quarters 1st November last) to a point of wood land Stard side, passing a high bluff on the Lard. N 40° W. 31/2

[Clark, April 8, 1805] 8th of April Monday 1805 Set out verry early wind hard a head from the N. W. proceeded on passed all the villages the inhabitents of which flocked down in great numbers to view us, I took my leave of the great Chief of the Mandans who gave me a par of excellent mockersons, one Canoe filed with water every thing in her got wet. 2/3 of a barrel of powder lost by this accedent.

Camped on the S. S. opsd. a high bluff an Indian joined us, also an Indian woman with a view to accompany us, the woman was Sent back the man being acquainted with the Countrey we allowed him to accompanie ns

[Lewis, April 9, 1805] Tuesday April 9th Set out as early as it was possible to see this morning and proceed about five miles where we halted and took beakfas- the Indian man who had promised us to accompany us as far as the Snake Indians, now informed us of his intention to relinquish the journey, and accordingly returned to his village. we saw a great number of brant passing up the river, some of them were white, except the large feathers in the first and second joint of the wing which are black. there is no other difference between them and the common gray brant but that of their colour- their note and habits are the same, and they are freequently seen to associate together. I have not yet positively determined whether they are the same, or a different species.- Capt Clark walked on shore to-day and informed me on his return, that passing through the prarie he had seen an anamal that precisely resembled the burrowing squrril, accept in point of size, it being only about one third as large as the squirrel, and that it also burrows. I have observed in many parts of the plains and praries the work of an anamal of which I could never obtain a view. their work resembles that of the salamander common to the sand hills of the States of South Carolina and Georgia; and like that anamal also it never appears above the ground. the little hillocks which are thrown up by these anamals have much the appearance of ten or twelve pounds of loose earth poared out of a vessel on the surface of the plain. in the state they leave them you can discover no whole through which they throw out this earth; but by removing the loose earth gently you may discover that the soil has been broken in a circle manner for about an inch and a half in diameter, where it appears looser than the adjacent surface, and is certainly the place through which the earth has been thrown out, tho the operation is performed without leaving any visible aperture.- the Bluffs of the river which we passed today were upwards of a hundred feet high, formed of a mixture of yellow clay and sand- many horizontal stratas of carbonated wood, having every appearance of pitcoal at a distance; were seen in the the face of these bluffs. these stratas are of unequal thicknesses from I to 5 feet, and appear at different elivations above the water some of them as much as eighty feet. the hills of the river are very broken and many of them have the apearance of having been on fire at some former period. considerable quantities of pumice stone and lava appear in many parts of these hills where they are broken and washed down by the rain and melting snow. when we halted for dinner the squaw busied herself in serching for the wild artichokes which the mice collect and deposit in large hoards. this operation she performed by penetrating the earth with a sharp stick about some small collections of drift wood. her labour soon proved successful, and she procurrd a good quantity of these roots. the flavor of this root resembles that of the Jerusalem Artichoke, and the stalk of the weed which produces it is also similar, tho both the root and stalk are much smaller than the Jarusalem Artichoke. the root is white and of an ovate form, from one to three inches in length and usually about the size of a man's finger. one stalk produces from two to four, and somitimes six of these roots.

at the distance of 6 miles passed a large wintering or hunting camp of the Minetares on the Stard. side. these lodges about thirty in number are built of earth and timber in their usual stile. 21/4 miles higher we passed the entrance of Miry Creek, which discharges itself on the Stard. side. this creek is but small, takes it's rise in some small lakes near the Mouse river and passes in it's course to the Missouri, through beatifull, level, and fertile plains, intirely destitute of timber.- Three miles above the mouth of this creek we passed a hunting camp of Minetares who had prepared a park and were wating the return of the Antelope; which usually pass the Missouri at this season of the year from the Black hills on the South side, to the open plains on the north side of the river; in like manner the Antelope repasses the Missouri from N. to South in the latter end of Autumn, and winter in the black hills, where there is considerable bodies of woodland. we proceed on 111/2 miles further and encamped on the N. side in a most beatifull high extensive open bottom

[Clark, April 9, 1805] 9th of April Tuesday 1805. Set out this morning verry early under a gentle breeze from the S. E. at Brackfast the Indian deturmined to return to his nation. I saw a Musquetor to day great numbers of Brant flying up the river, the Maple, & Elm has buded & Cotton and arrow wood beginning to bud. I saw in the prarie an animal resembling the Prarie dog or Barking Squirel & burrow in the Same way, this animal was about 1/3 as large as the barking Squirel. But fiew resident birds or water fowls which I have Seen as yet at 6 miles passed an old hunting camp of Menitarrees on the S. S. 21/2 miles higher passed the mouth of Miry Creek on the S. S. passed a hunting Camp of Minetarees on the S. S. waiting the return of the Antilope, Saw Great numbers of Gees feedin in the Praries on the young grass, I saw flowers in the praries to day, juniper grows on the Sides of the hills, & runs on the ground all the hills have more or Less indefferent Coal in Stratias at different bites from the waters edge to 80 feet. those Stratias from 1 inch to 5 feet thick. we Campd. on the S. S. above some rocks makeing out in the river in a butifull ellivated plain.

[Lewis, April 10, 1805] Wednesday April 10th 1805. Set out at an early hour this morning at the distance of three miles passed some Minetares who had assembled themselves on the Lard shore to take a view of our little fleet. Capt Clark walked on shore today, for several hours, when he returned he informed me that he had seen a gang of Antelopes in the plains but was unable to get a shoot at them he also saw some geese and swan. the geese are now feeding in considerable numbers on the young grass which has sprung up in the bottom prariesthe Musquetoes were very troublesome to us today. The country on both sides of the missouri from the tops of the river hills, is one continued level fertile plain as far as the eye can reach, in which there is not even a solitary tree or shrub to be seen except such as from their moist situations or the steep declivities of hills are sheltered from the ravages of the fire. at the distance of 12 miles from our encampment of last night we arrived at the lower point of a bluff on the Lard side; about 11/2 miles down this bluff from this point, the bluff is now on fire and throws out considerable quantities of smoke which has a strong sulphurious smell. the appearance of the coal in the blufs continues as yesterday. at 1 P.M. we overtook three french hunters who had set out a few days before us with a view of traping beaver; they had taken 12 since they left Fort Mandan. these people avail themselves of the protection which our numbers will enable us to give them against the Assinniboins who sometimes hunt on the Missouri and intend ascending with us as far as the mouth of the Yellow stone river and continue there hunt up that river. this is the first essay of a beaver hunter of any discription on this river. the beaver these people have already taken is by far the best I have ever seen. the river bottoms we have passed to-day are wider and possess more timber than usualthe courant of the Missouri is but moderate, at least not greater than that of the Ohio in high tide; it's banks are falling in but little; the navigation is therefore comparitively with it's lower portion easy and safe.- we encamped this evening on a willow point, Stard. side just above a remarkable bend in the river to the S. W. which we called the little bason.-

[Clark, April 10, 1805] 10th of April Wednesday 1805 Set out verry early. the morning cool and no wind proceeded on passed a camp of Inds. on the L. S. this day proved to be verry worm, the Misquetors troublesom. I Saw Several Antilope on the S. S. also gees & Swan, we over took 3 french men Trappers The countrey to day as usial except that the points of Timber is larger than below, the Coal Continue to day, one man Saw a hill on fire at no great distance from the river, we camped on the S. S. just above a remarkable bend in the river to the S W, which we call the little bacon.

[Lewis, April 11, 1805] Thursday April 11th Set out at an early hour; I proceeded with the party and Capt Clark with George Drewyer walked on shore in order to procure some fresh meat if possible. we proceeded on abot five miles, and halted for breakfast, when Capt Clark and Drewyer joined us; the latter had killed, and brought with him a deer which was at this moment excepable as we had had no fresh meat for several days. the country from fort Mandan to this place is so constantly hunted by the Minetaries that there is but little game we halted at two P.M. and made a comfortable dinner on a venison stake and beavers tales with the bisquit which got wet on the 8th inst. by the accidant of the canoe filling with water before mentioned. the powder which got wet by the same accedent, and which we had spread to dry on the baggage of the large perogue, was now examined and put up; it appears to be almost restored, and our loss is therefore not so great as we had at first apprehended.- the country much the same as yesterday. on the sides of the hills and even the banks of the rivers and sandbars, there is a white substance that appears in considerable quantities on the surface of the earth, which tastes like a mixture of common salt and glauber salts. many of the springs which flow from the base of the river hills are so strongly impregnated with this substance that the water is extreemly unpleasant to the taste and has a purgative effect.- saw some large white cranes pass up the river- these are the largest bird of that genus common to the country through which the Missouri and Mississippi pass. they are perfectly white except the large feathers of the two first joints of the wing which are black. we encamped this evening on the Stard. shore just above the point of woodland which formed to extremity of the last course of this day. there is a high bluff opposite to us, under which we saw some Indians, but the river is here so wide that we could not speake to them; suppose them to be a hunting party of Minetares.- we killed two gees today.

[Clark, April 11, 1805] 11th of April Thursday 1805 Set out verry early I walked on Shore, Saw fresh bear tracks, one deer & 2 beaver killed this morning in the after part of the day killed two gees; Saw great numbers of Gees Brant & Mallard Some White Cranes Swan & guls, the plains begin to have a green appearance, the hills on either side are from 5 to 7 miles asunder and in maney places have been burnt, appearing at a distance of a redish brown choler, containing Pumic Stone & lava, Some of which rolin down to the base of those hills- In maney of those hills forming bluffs to the river we procieve Several Stratums of bituminious Substance which resembles Coal; thong Some of the pieces appear to be excellent Coal it resists the fire for Some time, and consumes without emiting much flaim.

The plains are high and rich Some of them are Sandy Containing Small pebble, and on Some of the hill Sides large Stones are to be Seen- In the evening late we observed a party of Me ne tar ras on the L. S. with horses and dogs loaded going down, those are a part of the Menetarras who camped a little above this with the Ossinniboins at the mouth of the little Missouri all the latter part of the winter we Camped on the S. S. below a falling in bank. the river raise a little.

[Lewis, April 12, 1805] Friday April the 12th 1805. Set out at an early hour. our peroge and the Canoes passed over to the Lard side in order to avoid a bank which was rappidly falling in on the Stard. the red perogue contrary to my expectation or wish passed under this bank by means of her toe line where I expected to have seen her carried under every instant. I did not discover that she was about to make this attempt untill it was too late for the men to reembark, and retreating is more dangerous than proceeding in such cases; they therefore continued their passage up this bank, and much to my satisfaction arrived safe above it. this cost me some moments of uneasiness, her cargo was of much importance to us in our present advanced situation- We proceeded on six miles and came too on the lower side of the entrance of the little Missouri on the Lard shore in a fine plain where we determined to spend the day for the purpose of celestial observation. we sent out 10 hunters to procure some fresh meat. at this place made the following observations.-

The night proved so cloudy that I could make no further observations. George Drewyer shot a Beaver this morning, which we found swiming in the river a small distance below the entrance of the little Missouri. the beaver being seen in the day, is a proof that they have been but little hunted, as they always keep themselves closly concealed during the day where they are so.- found a great quantity of small onions in the plain where we encamped; had some of them collected and cooked, found them agreeable. the bulb grows single, is of an oval form, white, and about the size of a small bullet; the leaf resembles that of the shive, and the hunters returned this eying with one deer only. the country about the mouth of this river had been recently hunted by the Minetares, and the little game which they had not killed and frightened away, was so extreemly shy that the hunters could not get in shoot of them.

The little Missouri disembogues on the S. side of the Missouri 1693 miles from the confluence of the latter with the Mississippi. it is 134 yards wide at it's mouth, and sets in with a bould current but it's greatest debth is not more than 21/2 feet. it's navigation is extreemly difficult, owing to it's rapidity, shoals and sand bars. it may however be navigated with small canoes a considerable distance. this river passes through the Northern extremity of the black hills where it is very narrow and rapid and it's banks high an perpendicular. it takes it's rise in a broken country West of the Black hills with the waters of the yellow stone river, and a considerable distance S. W. of the point at which it passes the black hills. the country through which it passes is generally broken and the highlands possess but little timber. there is some timber in it's bottom lands, which consists of Cottonwood red Elm, with a small proportion of small Ash and box alder. the under brush is willow, red wood, (sometimes called red or swamp willow-) the red burry, and Choke cherry the country is extreamly broken about the mouth of this river, and as far up on both sides, as we could observe it from the tops of some elivated hills, which stand betwen these two rivers, about 3 miles from their junction. the soil appears fertile and deep, it consists generally of a dark rich loam intermixed with a small proportion of fine sand. this river in it's course passed near the N. W. side of the turtle mountain, which is said to be no more than 4 or 5 leagues distant from it's entrance in a straight direction, a little to the S. of West.- this mountain and the knife river have therefore been laid down too far S. W. the colour of the water, the bed of the river, and it's appearance in every respect, resembles the Missouri; I am therefore induced to believe that the texture of the soil of the country in which it takes it's rise, and that through which it passes, is similar to the country through which the Missouri passes after leaving the woody country, or such as we are now in.- on the side of a hill not distant from our camp I found some of the dwarf cedar of which I preserved a specimen (See No. 2). this plant spreads it's limbs alonge the surface of the earth, where they are sometimes covered, and always put forth a number of roots on the under side, while on the upper there are a great number of small shoots which with their leaves seldom rise higher than 6 or eight inches. they grow so close as perfectly to conceal the eath. it is an evergreen; the leaf is much more delicate than the common Cedar, and it's taste and smell the same. I have often thought that this plant would make very handsome edgings to the borders and walks of a garden; it is quite as handsom as box, and would be much more easily propegated.- the appearance of the glauber salts and Carbonated wood still continue.

[Clark, April 12, 1805] 12th April Friday 1805 a fine morning Set out verry early, the murcery Stood 56° above 0. proceeded on to the mouth of the Little Missouri river and formed a Camp in a butifull elivated plain on the lower Side for the purpose of takeing Some observations to fix the Latitude & Longitude of this river. this river falls in on the L. Side and is 134 yards wide and 2 feet 6 Inches deep at the mouth, it takes its rise in the N W extremity of the black mountains, and through a broken countrey in its whole course washing the N W base of the Turtle Mountain which is Situated about 6 Leagues S W of its mouth, one of our men Baptiest who came down this river in a canoe informs me that it is not navagable, he was 45 days descending.

One of our men Shot a beaver Swimming below the mouth of this river.

I walked out on the lower Side of this river and found the countrey hilley the Soil composed of black mole & a Small perportion of Sand containing great quantity of Small peable Some limestone, black flint, & Sand Stone I killed a Hare Changeing its Colour Some parts retaining its long white fur & other parts assumeing the Short grey, I Saw the Magpie in pars, flocks of Grouse, the old field lark & Crows, & observed the leaf of the wild

Chery half grown, many flowers are to be seen in the plains, remains of Minetarra & Ossinneboin hunting Camps are to be Seen on each Side of the two Missouris

The wind blew verry hard from the S. all the after part of the day, at 3 oClock P M. it became violent & flowey accompanied with thunder and a little rain. We examined our canoes &c found Several mice which had already commenced cutting our bags of corn & parched meal, the water of the little Missouri is of the Same texture Colour & quallity of that of the Big Missouri the after part of the day so Cloudy that we lost the evening observation.

[Lewis, April 13, 1805] Saturday April 13th Being disappointed in my observations of yesterday for Longitude, I was unwilling to remain at the entrance of the river another day for that purpose, and therefore determined to set out early this morning; which we did accordingly; the wind was in our favour after 9 A.M. and continued favourable untill three 3 P.M. we therefore hoisted both the sails in the White Perogue, consisting of a small squar sail, and spritsail, which carried her at a pretty good gate, untill about 2 in the afternoon when a suddon squall of wind struck us and turned the perogue so much on the side as to allarm Sharbono who was steering at the time, in this state of alarm he threw the perogue with her side to the wind, when the spritsail gibing was as near oversetting the perogue as it was possible to have missed. the wind however abating for an instant I ordered Drewyer to the helm and the sails to be taken in, which was instant executed and the perogue being steered before the wind was agin placed in a state of security. this accedent was very near costing us dearly. beleiving this vessell to be the most steady and safe, we had embarked on board of it our instruments, Papers, medicine and the most valuable part of the merchandize which we had still in reserve as presents for the Indians. we had also embarked on board ourselves, with three men who could not swim and the squaw with the young child, all of whom, had the perogue overset, would most probably have perished, as the waves were high, and the perogue upwards of 200 yards from the nearest shore; however we fortunately escaped and pursued our journey under the square sail, which shortly after the accident I directed to be again hoisted. our party caught three beaver last evening; and the French hunters 7. as there was much appearance of beaver just above the entrance of the little Missouri these hunters concluded to remain some days; we therefore left them without the expectation of seeing them again.- just above the entrance of the Little Missouri the great Missouri is upwards of a mile in width, tho immediately at the entrance of the former it is not more than 200 yards wide and so shallow that the canoes passed it with seting poles. at the distance of nine miles passed the mouth of a creek on the Stard. side which we called onion creek from the quantity of wild onions which grow in the plains on it's borders. Capt. Clark who was on shore informed me that this creek was 16 yards wide a mile & a half above it's entrance, discharges more water than creeks of it's size usually do in this open country, and that there was not a stick of timber of any discription to be seen on it's borders, or the level plain country through which it passes. at the distance of 10 miles further we passed the mouth of a large creek; discharging itself in the center of a deep bend. of this creek and the neighbouring country, Capt Clark who was on shore gave me the following discription "This creek I took to be a small river from it's size, and the quantity of water which it discharged. I ascended it 1 1/2 miles, and found it the discharge of a pond or small lake, which had the appearance of having formerly been the bed of the Missouri. several small streems discharge themselves into this lake. the country on both sides consists of beautifull level and elivated plains; asscending as they recede from the Missouri; there were a great number of Swan and gees in this lake and near it's borders I saw the remains of 43 temperary Indian lodges, which I presume were those of the Assinniboins who are now in the neighbourhood of the British establishments on the Assinniboin river-" This lake and it's discharge we call Boos Egg from the circumstance of Capt Clark shooting a goose while on her nest in the top of a lofty cotton wood tree, from which we afterwards took one egg. the wild gees frequently build their nests in this manner, at least we have already found several in trees, nor have we as yet seen any on the ground, or sand bars where I had supposed from previous information that they most commonly deposited their eggs.- saw some Bufhaloe and Elk at a distance today but killed none of them. we found a number of carcases of the Buffaloe lying along shore, which had been drowned by falling through the ice in winter and lodged on shore by the high water when the river broke up about the first of this month. we saw also many tracks of the white bear of enormous size, along the river shore and about the carcases of the Buffaloe, on which I presume they feed. we have not as yet seen one of these anamals, tho their tracks are so abundant and recent. the men as well as ourselves are anxious to meet with some of these bear. the Indians give a very formidable account of the strengh and ferocity of this anamal, which they never dare to attack but in parties of six eight or ten persons; and are even then frequently defeated with the loss of one or more of their party. the savages attack this anamal with their bows and arrows and the indifferent guns with which the traders furnish them, with these they shoot with such uncertainty and at so short a distance, that they frequently mis their aim & fall a sacrefice to the bear. two Minetaries were killed during the last winter in an attack on a white bear. this anamall is said more frequently to attack a man on meeting with him, than to flee from him. When the Indians are about to go in quest of the white bear, previous to their departure, they paint themselves and perform all those superstitious rights commonly observed when they are about to make war uppon a neighbouring nation. Oserved more bald eagles on this part of the Missouri than we have previously seen saw the small hawk, frequently called the sparrow hawk, which is common to most parts of the U States. great quantities of gees are seen feeding in the praries. saw a large flock of white brant or gees with black wings pass up the river; there were a number of gray brant with them; from their flight I presume they proceed much further still to the N. W.- we have never been enabled yet to shoot one of these birds, and cannot therefore determine whether the gray brant found with the white are their brude of the last year or whether they are the same with the grey brant common to the Mississippi and lower part of the Missouri.- we killed 2 Antelopes today which we found swiming from the S. to the N. side of the river; they were very poor.- We encamped this evening on the Stard. shore in a beautiful) plain, elivated about 30 feet above the river.

[Clark, April 13, 1805] 13th of April Satturday 1805 Set out this morning at 6 oClock, the Missouri above the mouth of Little Missouri widens to nearly a mile containing a number of Sand bars this width &c. of the River Continues Generally as high as the Rochejhone River.

Cought 3 beaver this morning, at 9 miles passd. the mouth of a Creek on the S. S. on the banks of which there is an imence quantity of wild onions or garlick, I was up this Creek 1/2 a m. and could not See one Stick of timber of any kind on its borders, this creek is 16 yds wide 1/2 a mile up it and discharges more water than is common for Creeks of its Size. at about 10 miles higher we pass a Creek about 30 yards wide in a deep bend to the N W. This creek I took to be a Small river from its Size & the quantity of water which it discharged, I ascended it 11/2 mes and found it the discharge of a pond or Small Lake which has appearance of haveing been once the bead of the river, Some Small Streams discharge themselves into this Lake. the Countery on both Side is butifull elevated plains assending in Some parts to a great distance near the aforesaid Lake (which we call Goose egg L from a Circumstance of my Shooting a goose on her neast on Some Sticks in the top of a high Cotton wood tree in which there was one egg) We Saw 8 buffalow at a distance, We also Saw Several herds of Elk at a distance which were verry wild, I Saw near the Lake the remains of 43 lodges, which has latterly been abandond I Suppose them to have been Ossinniboins and now near the british establishments on the Ossinniboin River tradeing. we camped on the S. S. in a butifull Plain. I observe more bald Eagles on this part of the Missouri than usial also a Small Hawk Killed 2 Antelopes in the river to day emence numbers of Geese to be seen pared &c. a Gange of brant pass one half of the gange white with black wings or the large feathers of the 1 s & 2d joint the remds. of the comn. color. a voice much like that of a goos & finer &c.

[Lewis, April 14, 1805] Sunday April 14th 1805. One of the hunters saw an Otter last evening and shot at it, but missed it. a dog came to us this morning, which we supposed to have been lost by the Indians who were recently encamped near the lake that we passed yesterday. the mineral appearances of salts, coal and sulpher, together with birnt hills & pumicestone still continue.- while we remained at the entrance of the little Missouri, we saw several pieces of pumice stone floating down that stream, a considerable quanty of which had lodged against a point of drift wood a little above it's entrance. Capt. Clark walked on shore this morning, and on his return informed me that he had passed through the timbered bottoms on the N. side of the river, and had extended his walk several miles back on the hills; in the bottom lands he had met with several uninhabited Indian lodges built with the boughs of the Elm, and in the plains he met with the remains of two large encampments of a recent date, which from the appearance of some hoops of small kegs, seen near them we concluded that they must have been the camps of the Assinniboins, as no other nation who visit this part of the missouri ever indulge themselves with spirituous liquor. of this article the Assinniboins are pationately fond, and we are informed that it forms their principal inducement to furnish the British establishments on the Assinniboin river with the dryed and pounded meat and grease which they do. they also supply those establishments with a small quantity of fur, consisting principally of the large and small wolves and the small fox skins. these they barter for small kegs of ruin which they generally transport to their camps at a distance from the establishments, where they revel with their friends and relations as long as they possess the means of intoxication, their women and children are equally indulged on those occations and are all seen drunk together. so far is a state of intoxication from being a cause of reproach among them, that with the men, it is a matter of exultation that their skill and industry as hunters has enabled them to get drunk frequently. in their customs, habits, and dispositions these people very much resemble the Siouxs from whom they have descended. The principal inducement with the British fur companies, for continuing their establishments on the Assinniboin river, is the Buffaloe meat and grease they procure from the Assinniboins, and Christanoes, by means of which, they are enabled to supply provision to their engages on their return from rainy Lake to the English river and the Athabaskey country where they winter; without such resource those voyagers would frequently be straitened for provision, as the country through which they pass is but scantily supplyed with game, and the rappidity with which they are compelled to travel in order to reach their winter stations, would leave therm but little leasure to surch for food while on their voyage.

The Assinniboins have so recently left this neighbourhood, that the game is scarce and very shy. the river continues wide, and not more rapid than the Ohio in an averge state of it's current. the bottoms are wide and low, the moister parts containing some timber; the upland is extreemly broken, chonsisting of high gaulded nobs as far as the eye can reach on ether side, and entirely destitute of timber. on these hills many aromatic herbs are seen; resembling in taste, smel and appearance, the sage, hysop, wormwood, southernwood and two other herbs which are strangers to me; the one resembling the camphor in taste and smell, rising to the hight of 2 or 3 feet; the other about the same size, has a long, narrow, smooth, soft leaf of an agreeable smel and flavor; of this last the Atelope is very fond; they feed on it, and perfume the hair of their foreheads and necks with it by rubing against it. the dwarf cedar and juniper is also found in great abundance on the sides of these hills. where the land is level, it is uniformly fertile consisting of a dark loam intermixed with a proportion of fine sand. it is generally covered with a short grass resembling very much the blue grass.- the miniral appearances still continue; considerable quantities of bitumenous water, about the colour of strong lye trickles down the sides of the hills; this water partakes of the taste of glauber salts and slightly of allumn.- while the party halted to take dinner today Capt Clark killed a buffaloe bull; it was meagre, and we therefore took the marrow bones and a small proportion of the meat only. near the place we dined on the Lard. side, there was a large village of burrowing squirrels. I have remarked that these anamals generally celect a South Easterly exposure for their residence, tho they are sometimes found in the level plains.- passed an Island, above which two small creeks fall in on Lard side; the upper creek largest, which we called Sharbono's Creek after our interpreter who encamped several weeks on it with a hunting party of Indians. this was the highest point to which any whiteman had ever ascended; except two Frenchmen who having lost their way had straggled a few miles further, tho to what place precisely I could not learn.- I walked on shore above this creek and killed an Elk, which was so poor that it was unfit for uce; I therefore left it, and joined the party at their encampment on the Stard shore a little after dark. on my arrival Capt Clark informed me that he had seen two white bear pass over the hills shortly after I fired, and that they appeared to run nearly from the place where I shot. the lard. shore on which I walked was very broken, and the hills in many places had the appearance of having sliped down in masses of several acres of land in surface.- we saw many gees feeding on the tender grass in the praries and several of their nests in the trees; we have not in a single instance found the nest of this bird on or near the ground. we saw a number of Magpies their nests and eggs. their nests are built in trees and composed of small sticks leaves and grass, open at top, and much in the stile of the large blackbird comm to the U States. the egg is of a bluish brown colour, freckled with redish brown spots. one of the party killed a large hooting owl. I observed no difference between this burd and those of the same family common to the U States, except that this appeared to be more booted and more thickly clad with feathers.-

[Clark, April 14, 1805] 14th of April Sunday 1805. a fine morning, a dog came to us this morning we Suppose him to be left by the Inds. who had their camps near the Lake we passd. yesterday not long Sence, I observed Several Single Lodges built of Stiks of cotten timber in different parts of the bottoms. in my walk of this day which was through the wooded bottoms and on the hills for several miles back from the river on the S. S. I Saw the remains of two Indian incampments with wide beeten tracks leading to them. those were no doubt the Camps of the Ossinnaboin Indians (a Strong evidence is hoops of Small Kegs were found in the incampments) no other nation on the river above the Sioux make use of Spiritious licquer, the Ossinniboins is said to be pasionately fond of Licquer, and is the principal inducement to their putting themselves to the trouble of Catching the fiew wolves and foxes which they furnish, and recive their liquor always in small Kegs. The Ossinniboins make use of the Same kind of Lodges which the Sioux and other Indians on this river make use of- Those lodges or tents are made of a number of dressed buffalow Skins Sowed together with Sinues & deckerated with the tales, & Porcupine quils, when open it forms a half circle with a part about 4 Inches wide projecting about 8 or 9 Inches from the center of the Streight Side for the purpose of attaching it to a pole to it the hight they wish to raise the tent, when they errect this tent four poles of equal length are tied near one end, those poles are elevated and 8 10 or 12 other poles are anexed forming a Circle at the ground and lodging in the forks of the four attached poles, the tents are then raised, by attach the projecting part to a pole and incumpassing the poles with the tent by bringing the two ends together and attached with a Cord, or laied as high as is necessary, leaveing the lower part open for about 4 feet for to pass in & out, and the top is generally left open to admit the Smoke to pass- The Borders of the river has been So much hunted by those Indians who must have left it about 8 or 10 days past and I prosume are now in the neighbourhood of British establishments on the Osinniboin; the game is Scerce and verry wild. The River Continues wide and the current jentle not more rapid than the Current of the Ohio in middle State- The bottoms are wide and low and the moist parts of them Contain Som wood such as cotton Elm & Small ash, willow rose bushes &c. &c. &. next to the hills Great quantity of wild Isoop, the hills are high broken in every direction, and the mineral appearance of Salts Continue to appear in a greater perportion, also Sulpher, Coal & bitumous water in a Smaller quantity, I have observed but five burnt hills, about the little Missouri, and I have not Seen any pumey stone above that River I Saw Buffalow on the L. S. Crossed and dureing the time of dinner killed a Bull, which was pore, we made use of the best of it, I Saw a village of Burrowing dogs on the L. S. passed a Island above which two Small Creeks falls in on the L. S. the upper of which is the largest and we call Shabonas Creek after our interpreter who incamped several weeks on this Creek and is the highest point on the Missouri to which a white man has been previous to this time. Capt. Lewis walked out above this creek and killed an Elk which he found So meager that it was not fit for use, and joined the boat at Dusk at our Camp on the S. S. opposit a high hill Several parts of which had Sliped down. on the Side of those hills we Saw two white bear running from the report of Capt. Lewis Shot, those animals assended those Steep hills with Supprising ease & verlocity. they were too far to discover their prosise Colour & Size- Saw Several gees nests on trees, also the nests & egs of the Magpies, a large grey owl killed, booted & with ears &c.

[Lewis, April 15, 1805] Monday April 15th 1805. Set out at an early hour this morning. I walked on shore, and Capt. Clark continued with the party it being an invariable rule with us not to be both absent from our vessels at the same time. I passed through the bottoms of the river on the Stard. side. they were partially covered with timber & were extensive, level and beatifull. in my walk which was about 6 miles I passed a small rivulet of clear water making down from the hills, which on tasting, I discovered to be in a small degree brackish. it possessed less of the glauber salt, or alum, than those little streams from the hills usually do.- in a little pond of water fromed by this rivulet where it entered the bottom, I heard the frogs crying for the first time this season; their note was the same with that of the small frogs which are common to the lagoons and swamps of the U States.- I saw great quantities of gees feeding in the bottoms, of which I shot one. saw some deer and Elk, but they were remarkably shy. I also met with great numbers of Grouse or prarie hens as they are called by the English traders of the N. W. these birds appeared to be mating; the note of the male is kuck, kuck, kuck, coo, coo, coo. the first part of the note both male and female use when flying. the male also dubbs something like the pheasant, but by no means as loud. after breakfast Capt. Clark walked on the Std. shore, and on his return in the evening gave me the following account of his ramble. "I ascended to the high country, about 9 miles distant from the Missouri. the country consists of beatifull, level and fertile plains, destitute of timber I saw many little dranes, which took their rise in the river hills, from whence as far as I could see they run to the N. E." these streams we suppose to be the waters of Mous river a branch of the Assinniboin which the Indians informed us approaches the Missouri very nearly, about this point. "I passed," continued he, "a Creek about 20 yards wide," which falls into the Missouri; the bottoms of this creek are wide level and extreemly fertile, but almost entirely destitute of timber. the water of this creek as well as all those creeks and rivulets which we have passed since we left Fort Mandan was so strongly impregnated with salts and other miniral substances that I was incapable of drinking it. I saw the remains of several camps of the Assinniboins; near one of which, in a small ravene, there was a park which they had formed of timber and brush, for the purpose of taking the Cabrie or Antelope. it was constructed in the following manner. a strong pound was first made of timbers, on one side of which there was a small apparture, sufficiently large to admit an Antelope; from each side of this apparture, a curtain was extended to a considerable distance, widening as they receded from the pound.- we passed a rock this evening standing in the middle of the river, and the bed of the river was formed principally of gravel. we encamped this evening on a sand point on Lard. side. a little above our encampment the river was confined to a channel of 80 yards in width.-

[Clark, April 15, 1805] 15th of April Monday 1805 Set out at an early hour, Captn Lewis walked on Shore and Killed a goose, passed a Island in a bend to the L. S. the wind hard from the S. E. after brackfast I walked on Shore and assended to the high Countrey on the S. S. and off from the Missouri about three miles the countrey is butifull open fertile plain the dreans take theer rise near the Clifts of the river and run from the river in a N E derection as far as I could See, this is the part of the River which Mouse river the waters of Lake Winnipec approaches within a fiew miles of Missouri, and I believe those dreans lead into that river. we passed a creek about 20 yds. wide on the S. S. the bottoms of this Creek is extensive & fertile, the water of this as also, all the Streams which head a fiew miles in the hills discharge water which is black & unfit for use (and can Safely Say that I have not Seen one drop of water fit for use above fort Mandan except Knife and the little Missouris Rivers and the Missouri, the other Streams being So much impregnated with mineral as to be verry disagreeble in its present State.) I saw the remains of Several Camps of ossinniboins, near one of those camps & at no great distance from the mouth of the aforesid Creek, in a hollow, I saw a large Strong pen made for the purpose of Catching the antelope, with wings projecting from it widining from the pen

Saw Several gangs of Buffalow and Some elk at a distance, a black bear Seen from the Perogues to day- passed a rock in the Middle of the river, Some Smaller rocks from that to the L. Shore, the dog that came to us yesterday morning continues to follow us, we camped on a Sand point to the L. S.

[Lewis, April 16, 1805] Tuesday April 16th 1805. Set out very early this morning. Capt. Clark walked on Shore this morning, and killed an Antelope, rejoined us at 1/2 after eight A.M.- he informed me that he had seen many Buffaloe Elk and deer in his absence, and that he had met with a great number of old hornets nests in the woody bottoms through which he had passed.- the hills of the river still continue extreemly broken for a few miles back, when it becomes a fine level country of open fertile lands immediately on the river there are many fine leavel extensive and extreemly fertile high plains and meadows. I think the quantity of timbered land on the river is increasing. the mineral appearances still continue. I met with several stones today that had the appearance of wood first carbonated and then petrefyed by the water of the river, which I have discovered has that effect on many vegitable substances when exposed to it's influence for a length of time. I believe it to be the stratas of Coal seen in those hills which causes the fire and birnt appearances frequently met with in this quarter. where those birnt appearances are to be seen in the face of the river bluffs, the coal is seldom seen, and when you meet with it in the neighbourhood of the stratas of birnt earth, the coal appears to be presisely at the same hight, and is nearly of the same thickness, togeter with the sand and a sulphurious substance which ususually accompanys it. there was a remarkable large beaver caught by one of the party last night. these anamals are now very abundant. I have met with several trees which have been felled by them 20 Inches in diameter. bark is their only food; and they appear to prefer that of the Cotton wood and willow; as we have never met with any other species of timber on the Missouri which had the appearance of being cut by them.- we passed three small creeks on the Stard. side. they take their rise in the river hills at no great distance. we saw a great number of geese today, both in the plains and on the river- I have observed but few ducks, those we have met with are the Mallard and blue winged Teal

[Clark, April 16, 1805] 16th of April Tuesday 1805 Wind hard from the S. E I walked on Shore and Killed an antilope which was verry meagre, Saw great numbers of Elk & some buffalow & Deer, a verry large Beaver Cought this morning. Some verry handsom high planes & extensive bottoms, the mineral appearances of Coal & Salt together with Some appearance of Burnt hils continue. a number of old hornets nests Seen in every bottom more perticularly in the one opposit to the place we camped this night- the wooded bottoms are more extensive to day than Common. passed three Small Creeks on the S. S. to day which take their rise in the hills at no great distance, Great numbers of Gees in the river & in the Plains feeding on the Grass.

[Lewis, April 17, 1805] Wednesday April 17th 1805. A delightfull morning, set out at an erly hour. the country though which we passed to (lay was much the same as that discribed of yesterday; there wase more appearance of birnt hills, furnishing large quanties of lava and pumice stone, of the latter some pieces were seen floating down the river. Capt. Clark walked on shore this morning on the Stard. side, and did not join us untill half after six in the evening. he informed me that he had seen the remains of the Assinniboin encampments in every point of woodland through which he had passed. we saw immence quantities of game in every direction around us as we passed up the river; consisting of herds of Buffaloe, Elk, and Antelopes with some deer and woolves. tho we continue to see many tracks of the bear we have seen but very few of them, and those are at a great distance generally runing from us; I thefore presume that they are extreemly wary and shy; the Indian account of them dose not corrispond with our experience so far. one black bear passed near the perogues on the 16th and was seen by myself and the party but he so quickly disappeared that we did not shoot at him.- at the place we halted to dine on the Lard. side we met with a herd of buffaloe of which I killed the fatest as I concieved among them, however on examining it I found it so poar that I thought it unfit for uce and only took the tongue; the party killed another which was still more lean. just before we encamped this evening we saw some tracks of Indians who had passed about 24 hours; they left four rafts of timber on the Stard. side, on which they had passed. we supposed them to have been a party of the Assinniboins who had been to war against the rocky mountain Indians, and then on their return. Capt. Clark saw a Curlou today. there were three beaver taken this morning by the party. the men prefer the flesh of this anamal, to that of any other which we have, or are able to procure at this moment. I eat very heartily of the beaver myself, and think it excellent; particularly the tale, and liver. we had a fair wind today which enabled us to sail the greater part of the distance we have travled, encamped on the Lard shore the extremity of the last course

[Clark, April 17, 1805] 17th of April Wednesday 1805 a fine morning wind from the S E. Genly to day handsom high extencive rich Plains on each Side, the mineral appearances continue with greater appearances of Coal, much greater appearance of the hills haveing been burnt, more Pumice Stone & Lava washed down to the bottoms and some Pumice Stone floating in the river, I walked on the S. S. Saw great numbs. of Buffalow feeding in the Plains at a distance Capt. Lewis killed 2 Buffalow buls which was near the water at the time of dineing, they were So pore as to be unfit for use. I Saw Several Small parties of antelopes large herds of Elk, Some white wolves, and in a pond (formed on the S. S. by the Missouries Changeing its bead) I Saw Swan Gees & different kinds of Ducks in great numbers also a Beaver house. Passed a Small Creek on the S. S. & Several runs of water on each Side, Saw the remains of Indian camps in every point of timbered land on the S. S. in the evining a thunder gust passed from the S W, without rain, about Sunset Saw Some fresh Indians track and four rafts on the shore S. S. Those I prosume were Ossinniboins who had been on a war party against the Rockey Mountain Indians- Saw a Curlow, Some verry large beaver taken this morning. those animals are made use of as food and preferred by the party to any other at this Season

[Lewis, April 18, 1805] Thursday April 18th 1805. A fine morning, set out at an early hour. one Beaver caught this morning by two traps, having a foot in each; the traps belonged to different individuals, between whom, a contest ensued, which would have terminated, most probably, in a serious rencounter had not our timely arrival at the place prevented it. after breakfast this morning, Capt. Clark walked on Stad. shore, while the party were assending by means of their toe lines, I walked with them on the bank; found a species of pea bearing a yellow flower, and now in blume; it seldom rises more than 6 inches high, the leaf & stalk resembles that of the common gardin pea, the root is pirenial. (See specimen of vegitables No. 3.) I also saw several parsels of buffaloe's hair hanging on the rose bushes, which had been bleached by exposure to the weather and became perfectly white. it every appearance of the wool of the sheep, tho much finer and more silkey and soft. I am confident that an excellent cloth may be made of the wool of the Buffaloe. the Buffaloe I killed yesterday had cast his long hare, and the poll which remained was very thick, fine, and about 2 inches in length. I think this anamal would have furnished about five pounds of wool. we were detained today from one to five P.M. in consequence of the wind which blew so violently from N. that it was with difficulty we could keep the canoes from filling with water altho they were along shore; I had them secured by placing the perogues on the out side of them in such manner as to break the waves off them. at 5 we proceed, and shortly after met with Capt. Clark, who had killed an Elk and a deer and was wating our arrival. we took the meat on board and continued our march untill nearly dark when we came too on the Stard side under a boald welltimbered bank which sheltered us from the wind which had abated but not yet ceased. here we encamped, it being the extremity of the last course of this day.-

[Clark, April 18, 1805] 18th of April Thursday 1805 Set out at an early hour one Beaver & a Musrat Cought this morning, the beaver cought in two traps, which like to have brought about a missunderstanding between two of the party &c. after brackfast I assended a hill and observed that the river made a great bend to the South, I concluded to walk thro the point about 2 miles and take Shabono, with me, he had taken a dost of Salts &c. his Squar followed on with her child, when I Struck the next bend of the river could See nothing of the Party, left this man & his wife & Child on the river bank and went out to hunt, Killed a young Buck Elk, & a Deer, the Elk was tolerable meat, the Deer verry pore, Butcherd the meat and Continued untill near Sunset before Capt Lewis and the party Came up, they were detained by the wind, which rose Soon after I left the boat from the N W. & blew verry hard untill verry late in the evening. we Camped on the S. S. in an excellent harbor, Soon after We came too, two men went up the river to Set their beaver traps they met with a Bear and being without their arms thought prodent to return &c. the wild Cheries are in bloom, Great appearance of Burnt hills Pumice Stone &c. the Coal & Salt appearance Continued, the water in the Small runs much better than below,- Saw Several old Indian Camps, the game, Such as Buffalow Elk, antelopes & Deer verry plenty

[Lewis, April 19, 1805] Friday April 19th 1805. The wind blew So hard this morning from N. W. that we dared not to venture our canoes on the river.- Observed considerable quantities of dwarf Juniper on the hillsides (see specimen No. 4) it seldom rises higher then 3 feet.- the wind detained us through the couse of this day, tho we were fortunate in having placed ourselves in a safe harbour. the party killed one Elk and a beaver today. The beaver of this part of the Missouri are larger, fatter, more abundant and better clad with fur than those of any other part of the country that I have yet seen; I have remarked also that their fur is much darker.

[Clark, April 19, 1805] 19th of April Friday 1805 a blustering windey day the wind So hard from the N, W. that we were fearfull of ventering our Canoes in the river, lay by all day on the S. Side in a good harber, the Praries appear to green, the cotton trees bigin to leave, Saw some plumb bushes in full bloom, those were the plumb bushes which I have Seen for Some time. Killed an Elk an a Beaver to day- The beaver of this river is much larger than usial, Great deal of Sign of the large Bear,

[Lewis, April 20, 1805] Saturday April 20th 1805. The wind continued to blow tolerably hard this morning but by no means as violently as it lid yesterday; we determined to set out and accordingly departed a little before seven. I walked on shore on the N. side of the river, and Capt Clark proceeded with the party. the river bottoms through which I passed about seven miles were fertil and well covered with Cottonwood some Box alder, ash and red Elm. the under brush, willow, rose bushes Honeysuccle, red willow, goosbury, currant and servicebury & in the open grounds along the foot of the river hills immence quantities of the hisop. in the course of my walk I killed two deer, wounded an Elk and a deer; saw the remains of some Indian hunting camps, near which stood a small scaffold of about 7 feet high on which were deposited two doog slays with their harnis. underneath this scaffold a human body was lying, well rolled in several dressed buffaloe skins and near it a bag of the same materials containg sundry articles belonging to the diseased; consisting of a pare of mockersons, some red and blue earth, beaver's nails, instruments for dressing the Buffalo skin, some dryed roots, several platts of the sweet grass, and a small quantity of Mandan tobacco.- I presume that the body, as well as the bag containing these articles, had formerly been placed on the scaffold as is the custom of these people, but had fallen down by accedent. near the scaffold I saw the carcase of a large dog not yet decayed, which I supposed had been killed at the time the human body was left on the scaffold; this was no doubt the reward, which the poor doog had met with for performing the _____-friendly office to his mistres of transporting her corps to the place of deposit. it is customary with the Assinniboins, Mandans, Minetares &c who scaffold their dead, to sacrefice the favorite horses and doggs of their diseased relations, with a view of their being servicable to them in the land of sperits. I have never heard of any instances of human sacrefices on those occasions among them.

The wind blew so hard that I concluded it was impossible fror the perogues and canoes to proceed and therefore returned and joined them about three in the evening. Capt. Clark informed me that soon after seting out, a part of the bank of the river fell in near one of the canoes and had very nearly filled her with water. that the wind became so hard and the waves so high that it was with infinite risk he had been able to get as far as his present station. the white perrogue and several of the canoes had shiped water several times but happily our stores were but little injured; those which were wet we put out to dry and determined to remain untill the next morning. we sent out four hunters who soon added 3 Elk 4 gees and 2 deer to our stock of provisions. the party caught six beaver today which were large and in fine order. the Buffaloe, Elk and deer are poor at this season, and of tours are not very palitable, however our good health and apetites make up every necessary deficiency, and we eat very heartily of them.- encamped on Stard side; under a high well timbered bank.

[Clark, April 20, 1805] 20th of April Satturday 1805 wind a head from the N W. we Set out at 7 oClock proceeded on, Soon after we Set out a Bank fell in near one of the Canoes which like to have filled her with water, the wind became hard and waves So rought that we proceeded with our little Canoes with much risque, our Situation was Such after Setting out that we were obliged to pass round the 1st Point or lay exposed to the blustering winds & waves, in passing round the Point Several canoes took in water as also our large Perogue but without injuring our Stores & much I proceeded on to the upper part of the 1st bend and came too at a butiful Glade on the S. S., about 1 mile below Capt Lewis who had walked thro the point, left his Coat & a Deer on the bank which we took on board,-. a Short distance below our Camp I Saw Some rafts on the S. S. near which, an Indian woman was Scaffeled in the Indian form of Deposing their dead, & fallen down She was or had been raised about 6 feet inclosed in Several robes tightly laced around her, with her dog Slays, her bag of Different coloured earths paint Small bones of animals beaver nales and Several other little trinkets, also a blue jay, her dog was killed and lay near her. Capt. Lewis joined me Soon after I landed & informed me he has walked Several miles higher, & in his walk killed 2 Deer & wounded an Elk & a Deer, our party Shot in the river four beaver & cought two, which were verry fat and much admired by the men, after we landed they killed 3 Elk 4 Gees & 2 Deer we had Some of our Provisions & which got a little wet aired, the wind Continued So hard that we were Compelled to delay all day. Saw Several buffalow lodged in the drift wood which had been drouned in the winter in passing the river; Saw the remains of 2 which had lodged on the Side of the bank & eate by the bears.

This morning was verry cold, Some Snow about 2 oClock from flying clouds, Some frost this morning & the mud at the edge of the water was frosed

[Lewis, April 21, 1805] Sunday April 21st 1805. Set out at an early hour this morning. Capt Clark walked on shore; the wind tho a head was not violent. the country through which we passed is very simelar in every rispect to that through which we have passed for several days.- We saw immence herds of buffaloe Elk deer & Antelopes. Capt Clark killed a buffaloe and 4 deer in the course of his walk today; and the party with me killed 3 deer, 2 beaver, and 4 buffaloe calves. the latter we found very delicious. I think it equal to any veal I ever tasted. the Elk now begin to shed their horns. passed one large and two small creeks on the Lard. side, tho neither of them discharge any water at present. the wind blew so hard this evening that we were obliged to halt several hours. we reached the place of incampment after dark, which was on the Lard. side a little above White earth river which discharges itself on the Stard. side. immediately at the mouth of this river it is not more than 10 yards wide being choked up by the mud of the Missouri; tho after leaving the bottom lands of this river, or even sooner, it becomes a boald stream of sixty yards wide and is deep and navigable. the course of this river as far as I could see from the top of Cut bluff, was due North. it passes through a beatifull level and fertile vally about five miles in width. I think I saw about 25 miles up this river, and did not discover one tree or bush of any discription on it's borders. the vally was covered with Elk and buffaloe. saw a great number of gees today as usual, also some swan and ducks.

[Clark, April 21, 1805] 21st of April Sunday 1805 Set out early the wind gentle & from the N. W. the river being verry Crooked, I concluded to walk through the point, the Countrey on either Side is verry Similar to that we have passed, Saw an emence number of Elk & Buffalow, also Deer Antelopes Geese Ducks & a fiew Swan, the Buffalow is about Calveing I killed a Buffalow & 4 Deer in my walk to day, the party killed 2 deer 2 beaver & 4 Buffalow Calves, which was verry good veele. I Saw old Camps of Indians on the L. Side, we passed 1 large & 2 Small Creeks on the L. Side neither of them discharge any water into the river, in the evening the wind became verry hard a head, we made Camp at a late hour which was on the L. Side a little above the mouth of White Earth River which falls in on the Stad Side and is 60 yds. wide, several Mes. up

[Lewis, April 22, 1805] Monday April 22cd 1805. Set out at an early hour this morning; proceeded pretty well untill breakfat, when the wind became so hard a head that we proceeded with difficulty even with the assistance of our toe lines. the party halted and Cpt. Clark and myself walked to the white earth river which approaches the Missouri very near at this place, being about 4 miles above it's entrance. we found that it contained more water than streams of it's size generally do at this season. the water is much clearer than that of the Missouri. the banks of the river are steep and not more than ten or twelve feet high; the bed seems to be composed of mud altogether. the salts which have been before mentioned as common on the Missouri, appears in great quantities along the banks of this river, which are in many places so thickly covered with it that they appear perfectly white. perhaps it has been from this white appearance of it's banks that the river has derived it's name. this river is said to be navigable nearly to it's source, which is at no great distance from the Saskashawan, and I think from it's size the direction which it seems to take, and the latitude of it's mouth, that there is very good ground to believe that it extends as far North as latitude 50°.- this stream passes through an open country generally.- the broken hills of the Missouri about this place exhibit large irregular and broken masses of rocks and stones; some of which tho 200 feet above the level of the water seem at some former period to have felt it's influence, fo they appear smoth as if woarn by the agetation of the water. this collection consists of white & grey gannite, a brittle black rock, flint, limestone, freestone, some small specimens of an excellent pebble and occasionally broken stratas of a stone which appears to be petrefyed wood, it is of a black colour, and makes excellent whetstones. Coal or carbonated wood pumice stone lava and other mineral apearances still continue. the coal appears to be of better quality; I exposed a specimen of it to the fire and found that it birnt tolerably well, it afforded but little flame or smoke, but produced a hot and lasting fire.- I asscended to the top of the cutt bluff this morning, from whence I had a most delightfull view of the country, the whole of which except the vally formed by the Missouri is void of timber or underbrush, exposing to the first glance of the spectator immence herds of Buffaloe, Elk, deer, & Antelopes feeding in one common and boundless pasture. we saw a number of bever feeding on the bark of the trees alonge the verge of the river, several of which we shot, found them large and fat. walking on shore this evening I met with a buffaloe calf which attatched itself to me and continued to follow close at my heels untill I embarked and left it. it appeared allarmed at my dog which was probably the cause of it's so readily attatching itself to me. Capt Clark informed me that he saw a large drove of buffaloe pursued by wolves today, that they at length caught a calf which was unable to keep up with the herd. the cows only defend their young so long as they are able to keep up with the herd, and seldom return any distance in surch of them.-

[Clark, April 22, 1805] 22nd of April Monday 1805 a verry cold morning Some frost, we Set out at an early hour and proceeded on verry well untill brackfast at which time the wind began to blow verry hard ahead, and Continued hard all day we proceeded on with much dificuelty with the assistance of the toe Ropes. Capt. Lewis & my Self walked to the _____ River which is near the Missouri four miles above its mouth, this river is 60 yards wide and contains a greater perportion of water at this time than is Common for Rivers of its Size it appears navagable as fur as any of the party was, and I am told to near its Source in morrasses in the open Plains, it passes (as far as we can See which is 6 or 7 Leagus) thro a butifull extinsive vallie, rich & fertile and at this time Covered with Buffalow, Elk & antelopes, which may be Seen also in any other direction in this quarter- this river must take its rise at no great distance Easte of the Saskashawan, and no doubt as far N. as Latd. 50°

Some of the high plains or the broken Revien of the river contains great quantity of Pebble Stones of various Sizes, The Stratum of Coal is much richer than below, the appearances of Mineral & burnt hills Still continue the river riseing a little, Saw an emence number of beaver feeding on the waters edge & Swiming Killed Several, Capt. Lewis assended a hill from the top of which he had a most inchanting prospect of the Countrey around & the meanderings of the two rivers, which is remarkable Crooked- a buffalow calf which was on the Shore alone followed Cap Lewis Some distance,- I observed a large drove of buffalow prosued by wolves the wolves cought one of their Calves in my view, those animals defend their young as long as they Can keep up with the drove

[Lewis, April 23, 1805] Tuesday April 23rd Set out at an early hour this morning. about nine A.M. the wind arose, and shortly after became so violent that we were unabled to proceed, in short it was with much difficulty and some risk that I was enabled to get the canoes and perogues into a place of tolerable safety, there being no timber on either side of the river at this place. some of the canoes shiped water, and wet several parsels of their lading, which I directed to be opened and aired we remained untill five in the evening when the wind abating in some measure, we reloaded, and proceeded. shortly after we were joined by Capt. Clark who had walked on shore this morning, and passing through the bottom lands had fallen on the river some miles above, and concluding that the wind had detained us, came down the river in surch of us. he had killed three blacktaled, or mule deer, and a buffaloe Calf, in the course of his ramble. these hard winds, being so frequently repeated, become a serious source of detention to us.- incamped on the Stard. side.-

[Clark, April 23, 1805] 23rd of April 1805 a cold morning at about 9 oClock the wind as usial rose from the N W and continued to blow verry hard untill late in the evening I walked on Shore after brackfast in my walk on the S side passed through extensive bottoms of timber intersperced with glades & low open plains, I killed 3 mule or black tail Deer, which was in tolerable order, Saw Several others, I also killed a Buffalow Calf which was verry fine, I Struck the river above the Perogus which had Come too in a bend to the L. S. to Shelter from the wind which had become violently hard, I joined Capt Lewis in the evening & after the winds falling which was late in the evening we proceeded on & encamped on the S. S. The winds of this Countrey which blow with Some violence almost every day, has become a Serious obstruction in our progression onward, as we Cant move when the wind is high without great risque, and if there was no risque the winds is generally a head and often too violent to proceed

[Lewis, April 24, 1805] Wednesday April 24th The wind blew so hard during the whole of this day, that we were unable to move. notwithstanding that we were sheltered by high timber from the effects of the wind, such was it's violence that it caused the waves to rise in such manner as to wet many articles in the small canoes before they could be unloaded. we sent out some hunters who killed 4 deer & 2 Elk, and caught some young wolves of the small kind.- Soar eyes is a common complaint among the party. I believe it origenates from the immence quantities of sand which is driven by the wind from the sandbars of the river in such clouds that you are unable to discover the opposite bank of the river in many instances. the particles of this sand are so fine and light that they are easily supported by the air, and are carried by the wind for many miles, and at a distance exhibiting every appearance of a collumn of thick smoke. so penitrating is this sand that we cannot keep any article free from it; in short we are compelled to eat, drink, and breath it very freely. my pocket watch, is out of order, she will run only a few minutes without stoping. I can discover no radical defect in her works, and must therefore attribute it to the sand, with which, she seems plentifully charged, notwithstanding her cases are double and tight.

[Clark, April 24, 1805] 24th of April Wednesday 1805 The wind rose last night and continued blowing from the N. & N W. and Sometimes with great violence, untill 7 oClock P. M, Several articles wet in the Perogues by their takeing water &c. as the wind was a head we could not move today Sent out hunters, they killed 4 Deer 2 Elk & cought Some young wolves of the Small kind, The party complain much of the Sand in their eyes, the Sand is verry fine and rises in clouds from the Points and bars of the river, I may Say that dureing those winds we eat Drink & breeth a prepotion of Sand.

[Lewis, April 25, 1805] Thursday April 25th 1805. The wind was more moderate this morning, tho still hard; we set out at an early hour. the water friezed on the oars this morning as the men rowed. about 10 oclock A.M. the wind began to blow so violently that we were obliged to lye too. my dog had been absent during the last night, and I was fearfull we had lost him altogether, however, much to my satisfaction he joined us at 8 Oclock this morning. The wind had been so unfavorable to our progress for several days past, and seeing but little prospect of a favourable chang; knowing that the river was crooked, from the report of the hunters who were out yesterday, and beleiving that we were at no very great distance from the Yellow stone River; I determined, in order as mush as possible to avoid detention, to proceed by land with a few men to the entrance of that river and make the necessary observations to determine it's position, which I hoped to effect by the time that Capt. Clark could arrive with the party; accordingly I set out at 1 t OCk. on the Lard. side, accompanyed by four men. we proceeded about four miles, when falling in with some bufaloe I killed a yearling calf, which was in good order; we soon cooked and made a hearty meal of a part of it, and renewed our march our rout lay along the foot of the river hills. when we had proceeded about four miles, I ascended the hills from whence I had a most pleasing view of the country, perticularly of the wide and fertile values formed by the missouri and the yellowstone rivers, which occasionally unmasked by the wood on their borders disclose their meanderings for many miles in their passage through these delightfull tracts of country. I could not discover the junction of the rivers immediately, they being concealed by the woods, however, sensible that it could not be distant I determined to encamp on the bank of the Yellow stone river which made it's appearance about 2 miles South of me. the whol face of the country was covered with herds of Buffaloe, Elk & Antelopes; deer are also abundant, but keep themselves more concealed in the woodland. the buffaloe Elk and Antelope are so gentle that we pass near them while feeding, without apearing to excite any alarm among them, and when we attract their attention, they frequently approach us more nearly to discover what we are, and in some instances pursue us a considerable distance apparenly with that view.- in our way to the place I had determined to encamp, we met with two large herds of buffaloe, of which we killed three cows and a calf. two of the former, wer but lean, we therefore took their tongues and a part of their marrow-bones only. I then proceeded to the place of our encampment with two of the men, taking with us the Calf and marrowbones, while the other two remained, with orders to dress the cow that was in tolerable order, and hang the meat out of the reach of the wolves, a precaution indispensible to it's safe keeping, even for a night. we encamped on the bank of the yellowstone river, 2 miles South of it's confluence with the Missouri. On rejoining Capt. Clark, the 26th in the evening, he informed me, that at 5 P.M. after I left him the wind abated in some measure and he proceeded a few miles further and encamped.

[Clark, April 25, 1805] 25th of April Thursday 1805 The wind was moderate & ahead this morning, we Set out at an early hour The morning cold, Some flying Clouds to be Seen, the wind from the N. ice collected on the ores this morning, the wind increased and became So violent about 1 oClock we were obliged to lay by our Canoes haveing taken in Some water, the Dog which was lost yesterday, joined us this morning.

finding that the winds retarded our progression for maney days past, and no apparance of an alteration, and the river being Crooked that we could never have 3 miles fair wind, Capt. Lewis concluded to go by land as far as the Rochejhone or yellow Stone river, which we expect is at no great distance by land and make Some Selestial observations to find the Situation of its mouth, and by that measure not detain the Perogues at that place any time for the purpose of makeing those necessary observations he took 4 men & proceeded on up the Missouri on the L. Side, at 5 oClock the wind luled and we proceeded on and incamped.

[Lewis, April 26, 1805] Friday April 26th 1805. This morning I dispatched Joseph Fields up the yellowstone river with orders to examine it as far as he could conveniently and return the same evening; two others were directed to bring in the meat we had killed last evening, while I proceeded down the river with one man in order to take a view of the confluence of this great river with the Missouri, which we found to be two miles distant on a direct line N. W. from our encampment. the bottom land on the lower side of the yellowstone river near it's mouth for about one mile in width appears to be subject to inundation; while that on the opposite side of the Missouri and the point formed by the junction of these rivers is of the common elivation, say from twelve to 18 feet above the level of the water, and of course not liable to be overflown except in extreem high water, which dose not appear to be very frequent there is more timber in the neighbourhood of the junction of these rivers, and on the Missouri as far below as the White earth river, than there is on any part of the Missouri above the entrance of the Chyenne river to this place. the timber consists principally of Cottonwood, with some small elm, ash and boxalder. the under growth on the sandbars and verge of the river is the small leafed willow; the low bottoms, rose bushes which rise to three or four feet high, the redburry, servicebury, and the redwood; the high bottoms are of two discriptions either timbered or open; the first lies next to the river and it's under brush is the same with that of the low timbered bottoms with the addition of the broad leafed willow, Goosebury, choke cherry, purple currant; and honeysuckle bushis; the open bottoms border on the hills, and are covered in many parts by the wild hyssop which rises to the hight of two feet. I observe that the Antelope, Buffaloe Elk and deer feed on this herb; the willow of the sandbars also furnish a favorite winter food to these anamals as well as the growse, the porcupine, hare, and rabbit. about 12 Olock I heard the discharge of several guns at the junction of the rivers, which announced to me the arrival of the paty with Capt Clark; I afterwards learnt that they had fired on some buffaloe which they met with at that place, and of which they killed a cow and several Calves; the latter are now fine veal. I dispatched one of the men to Capt Clark requesting him to send up a canoe to take down the meat we had killed and our baggage to his encampmt, which was accordingly complyed with. after I had completed my observations in the evening I walked down and joined the party at their encampment on the point of land fromed by the junction of the rivers; found them all in good health, and much pleased at having arrived at this long wished for spot, and in order to add in some measure to the general pleasure which seemed to pervade our little community, we ordered a dram to be issued to each person; this soon produced the fiddle, and they spent the evening with much hilarity, singing & dancing, and seemed as perfectly to forget their past toils, as they appeared regardless of those to come. in the evening, the man I had sent up the river this morning returned, and reported that he had ascended it about eight miles on a streight line; that he found it crooked, meandering from side to side of the valley formed by it; which is from four to five miles wide. the corrent of the river gentle, and it's bed much interrupted and broken by sandbars; at the distance of five miles he passed a large Island well covered with timber, and three miles higher a large creek falls in on the S. E. sides above a high bluff in which there are several stratas of coal. the country bordering on this river as far as he could percieve, like that of the Missouri, consisted of open plains. he saw several of the bighorned anamals in the couse of his walk; but they were so shy that he could not get a shoot at them; he found a large horn of one of these anamals which he brought with him. the bed of the yellowstone river is entirely composed of sand and mud, not a stone of any kind to be seen in it near it's entrance. Capt Clark measured these rivers just above their confluence; found the bed of the Missouri 520 yards wide, the water occupying 330. it's channel deep. the yellowstone river including it's sandbar, 858 yds. of which, the water occupied 297 yards; the depest part 12 feet; it was falling at this time & appeard to be nearly at it's summer tide.- the Indians inform that the yellowstone river is navigable for perogues and canoes nearly to it's source in the Rocky Mountains, and that in it's course near these mountains it passes within less than half a day's march of a navigable part of the Missouri. it's extreem sources are adjacent to those of the Missouri, river platte, and I think probably with some of the South branch of the Columbia river. the first part of its course lies through a mountanous rocky country tho well timbered and in many parts fertile; the middle, and much the most extensive portion of the river lies through a delightfull rich and fertile country, well covered with timber, intersperced with plains and meadows, and well watered; it is some what broken in many parts. the lower portion consists of fertile open plains and meadows almost entirely, tho it possesses a considerable proportion of timber on it's borders. the current of the upper portion is extreemly rappid, that of the middle and lower portions much more gentle than the Missouri. the water of this river is turbid, tho dose not possess as much sediment as that of the Missouri. this river in it's course recieves the waters of many large tributary strains principally from the S. E. of which the most considerable are the Tongue and bighorn rivers the former is much the largest, and heads with the river Platte and Bighorn river, as dose the latter with the Tongue river and the river Platte.- a suficient quantity of limestone may be readily procured for building near the junction of the Missouri and yellowstone rivers. I could observe no regular stratas of it, tho it lies on the sides of the river hills in large irregular masses, in considerable quantities; it is of a light colour, and appears to be of an excellent quality.-

[Clark, April 26, 1805] 26th of April Friday 1805 last night was verry Cold. the Thermometer Stood at 32 abov 0 this morning. I Set out at an early hour, as it was cold I walked on the bank, & in my walk Shot a beaver & 2 Deer, one of the Deer in tolerable order, the low bottom of the river is generaly Covered with wood willows & rose bushes, red berry, wild Cherry & red or arrow wood intersperced with glades The timber is Cottonwood principally, Elm Small ash also furnish a portion of the timber, The Clay of the bluffs appear much whiter than below, and Contain Several Stratums of Coal, on the hill Sides I observe pebbles of different Size & Colour- The river has been riseing for Several days, & raised 3 inches last night, at 12 oClock arrived at the forks of the Roche Johne & Missouri and formed a Camp on the point Soon after George Drewyer Came from Capt Lewis & informed me that he was a little way up the Roche johne and would join me this evining, I Sent a canoe up to Capt Lewis and proceeded measure the width of the rivers, and find the debth. The Missouri is 520 yards wide above the point of yellow Stone and the water covers 330 yards; the YellowStone River is 858 yards wide includeing its Sand bar, the water covers 297 yards and the deepest part is 12 feet water, it is at this time falling, the Missouri rising The Indians inform that the yellow Stone River is navagable for Perogues to near its Source in the Rocky Mountains, it has many tributary Streams, principally on the S. E. Side, and heads at no great distance from the Missouri, the largest rivers which fall into it is Tongue river which heads with the waters of River Platt, and Big horn river which also heads with Platt & Tongue R the current of this river is Said to be rapid near its mouth it is verry jentle, and its water is of a whitish colour much Clearer of Sediment than the Missouri. the Countrey on this river is Said to be broken in its whole Course & Contains a great deel of wood, the countrey about its mouth is verry fine, the bottoms on either Side is wooded with Cotton wood, ash, Elm &c. near the banks of the river back is higher bottoms and Covered with red berry, Goose berry & rose bushes &. interspersed with Small open Glades, and near the high land is Generally open rich bottoms- at our arrival at the forks I observed a Drove of Buffalow Cows & Calves on a Sand bar in the point, I directed the men to kill the fattest Cow, and 3 or 4 Calves, which they did and let the others pass, the Cows are pore, Calves fine veele.

Capt Lewis joined me in the evening after takeing equal altitudes a little way up the YellowStone river the Countrey in every direction is plains except the moist bottoms of the river, which are covered with Some indifferent timber Such as Cotton wood Elm & Small ash, with different kind of Stubs & bushes in the forks about 1 mile from the point at which place the 2 rivers are near each other a butiful low leavel plain Commences, and extends up the Missourie & back, this plain is narrow at its commencement and widens as the Missouri bends north, and is bordered by an extencive wood land for many miles up the yellow Stone river, this low plain is not Subject to over flow, appear to be a few inches above high water mark and affords a butifull commanding Situation for a fort near the commencement of the Prarie, about _____ miles from the Point & _____ yards from the Missouri a Small lake is Situated, from this lake the plain rises gradually to a high butifull Countrey, the low Plain continues for Some distance up both rivers on the Yellow Stone it is wide & butifull opsd. the point on the S. Side is Some high timbered land, about 11/2 miles below on the Same Side a little distance from the water is an elivated plain- Several of the party was up the yellow Stone R Several miles, & informed that it meandered throught a butifull Countrey Joseph Fields discovered a large Creek falling into the Yellowstone River on the S E Side 8 miles up near which he Saw a big horn animal, he found in the Prarie the horn of one of those animals which was large and appeared to have laid Several years I Saw maney buffalow dead on the banks of the river in different places Some of them eaten by the white bears & wolves all except the Skin & bones, others entire, those animals either drounded in attempting to Cross on the ice dureing the winter or Swiming across to bluff banks where they Could not get out & too weak to return we Saw several in this Situation.

emence numbers of antelopes in the forks of the river, Buffalow & Elk & Deer is also plenty beaver is in every bend. I observe that the Magpie Goose duck & Eagle all have their nests in the Same neighbourhood, and it is not uncommon for the Magpie to build in a few rods of the eagle, the nests of this bird is built verry Strong with Sticks Covered verry thickly with one or more places through which they enter or escape, the Goose I make no doubt falls a pray to those vicious eagles

[Lewis, April 27, 1805] Saturday April 27th 1805. Previous to our seting out this morning I made the following observations.

This morning I walked through the point formed by the junction of the rivers; the woodland extends about a mile, when the rivers approach each other within less than half a mile; here a beatifull level low plain commences and extends up both rivers for many miles, widening as the rivers recede from each other, and extending back half a mile to a plain about 12 feet higher than itself; the low plain appears to be a few inches higher than high water mark and of course will not be liable to be overflown; tho where it joins the high plain a part of the Missouri when at it's greatest hight, passes through a channel of 60 or 70 yards wide and falls into the yellowstone river. on the Missouri about 21/2 miles from the entrance of the yellowstone river, and between this high and low plain, a small lake is situated about 200 yards wide extending along the edge of the high plain parallel with the Missouri about one mile. on the point of the high plain at the lower extremity of this lake I think would be the most eligible site for an establishment. between this low plain and the Yellowstone river their is an extensive body of timbered land extending up the river for many miles. this site recommended is about 400 yards distant from the Missouri and about double that distance from the river yellowstone; from it the high plain, rising very gradually, extends back about three miles to the hills, and continues with the same width between these hills and the timbered land on the yellowstone river, up that stream, for seven or eight miles; and is one of the hadsomest plains I ever beheld. on the Missouri side the hills sircumscribe it's width, & at the distance of three miles up that river from this site, it is not more than 400 yards wide. Capt Clark thinks that the lower extremity of the low plane would be most eligible for this establishment; it is true that it is much nearer both rivers, and might answer very well, but I think it reather too low to venture a permanent establishment, particularly if built of brick or other durable materials, at any considerable expence; for so capricious, and versatile are these rivers, that it is difficult to say how long it will be, untill they direct the force of their currents against this narrow part of the low plain, which when they do, must shortly yeald to their influence; in such case a few years only would be necessary, for the annihilation of the plain, and with it the fortification.- I continued my walk on shore; at 11 A.M. the wind became very hard from N. W. insomuch that the perogues and canoes were unable either to proceede or pass the river to me; I was under the necessity therefore of shooting a goose and cooking it for my dinner. the wind abated about 4. P.M. and the party proceeded tho I could not conveniently join them untill night. altho game is very abundant and gentle, we only kill as much as is necessary for food. I believe that two good hunters could conveniently supply a regiment with provisions. for several days past we have observed a great number of buffaloe lying dead on the shore, some of them entire and others partly devoured by the wolves and bear. those anamals either drownded during the winter in attempting to pass the river on the ice during the winter or by swiming acrss at present to bluff banks which they are unable to ascend, and feeling themselves too weak to return remain and perish for the want of food; in this situation we met with several little parties of them.- beaver are very abundant, the party kill several of them every day. The Eagles, Magpies, and gees have their nests in trees adjacent to each other; the magpye particularly appears fond of building near the Eagle, as we scarcely see an Eagle's nest unaccompanyed with two or three Magpies nests within a short distance.- The bald Eagle are more abundant here than I ever observed them in any part of the country.

[Clark, April 27, 1805] 27th of April Satturday 1805 after take the azmuth of the Sun & brackfasting we Set out wind moderate & a head, at 11 oClock the wind rose and continued to blow verry hard a head from the N. W. untill 4 oClock P M, which blew the Sand off the Points in Such clouds as almost Covered us on the opposit bank, at 4 I Set out from my unpleasent Situation and proceeded on, Capt. Lewis walked on Shore in the Point to examine & view the Countrey and could not get to the boats untill night, Saw great numbers of Goats or antilopes, Elk, Swan Gees & Ducks, no buffalow to day I Saw Several beaver and much Sign, I Shot one in the head which imediately Sunk, altho the game of different kinds are in abundance we Kill nothing but what we can make

[Lewis, April 28, 1805] Sunday April 28th 1805. Set out this morning at an early hour; the wind was favourable and we employed our sails to advantage. Capt Clark walked on shore this morning, and I proceeded with the party. the country through which we passed today is open as usual and very broken on both sides near the river hills, the bottoms are level fertile and partially covered with timber. the hills and bluffs exhibit their usual mineral appearances, some birnt hills but no appearance of Pumicestone; coal is in great abundance and the salts still increase in quantity; the banks of the river and sandbars are incrusted with it in many places and appear perfectly white as if covered with snow or frost.- the woods are now green, tho the plains and meadows appear to abate of the verdure those below exhibited some days past. we past three small runs today. two falling in on the Stard. and one on the Lard. side, they are but small afford but little water and head a few miles back in the hills. we saw great quantities of game today; consisting of the common and mule deer, Elk, Buffaloe, and Antelopes; also four brown bear, one of which was fired on and wounded by one of the party but we did not get it; the beaver have cut great quantities of timber; saw a tree nearly 3 feet in diameter that had been felled by them. Capt. Clark in the course of his walk killed a deer and a goose; & saw three black bear; he thinks the bottoms are not so wide as they have been for some days past.

[Clark, April 28, 1805] 28th of April Sunday 1805 a fine day river falling, wind favourable from the S. E. and moderate, I walked on Shore to view the Countrey, from the top of the high hills, I beheld a broken & open Countrey on both Sides, near the river Some verry handsom low plains, I killd. a Deer & a goose, Saw three black bear great numbers of Elk antelopes & 2 Gangues of Buffalow, the hills & Bluffs Shew the Straturs of Coal, and burnt appearances in maney places, in and about them I could find no appearance of Pumice Stone, the wood land have a green appearance, the Plains do not look So green as below, The bottoms are not So wide this afternoon as below Saw four bear this evening, one of the men Shot at one of them. The Antilopes are nearly red, on that part which is Subject to change i e the Sides & 2/3 of the back from the head, the other part as white as Snow, 2 Small runs fall in on the S. Side and one this evening on the Lard Side those runs head at a fiew miles in the hills and discharge but little water, the Bluffs in this part as also below Shew different Straturs of Coal or carbonated wood, and Coloured earth, such as dark brown, yellow a lightish brown, & a dark red &c.

[Lewis, April 29, 1805] Monday April 29th 1805. Set out this morning at the usual hour; the wind was moderate; I walked on shore with one man. about 8 A.M. we fell in with two brown or yellow bear; both of which we wounded; one of them made his escape, the other after my firing on him pursued me seventy or eighty yards, but fortunately had been so badly wounded that he was unable to pursue so closely as to prevent my charging my gun; we again repeated our fir and killed him. it was a male not fully grown, we estimated his weight at 300 lbs. not having the means of ascertaining it precisely. The legs of this bear are somewhat longer than those of the black, as are it's tallons and tusks incomparably larger and longer. the testicles, which in the black bear are placed pretty well back between the thyes and contained in one pouch like those of the dog and most quadrupeds, are in the yellow or brown bear placed much further forward, and are suspended in seperate pouches from two to four inches asunder; it's colour is yellowish brown, the eyes small, black, and piercing; the front of the fore legs near the feet is usually black; the fur is finer thicker and deeper than that of the black bear. these are all the particulars in which this anamal appeared to me to differ from the black bear; it is a much more furious and formidable anamal, and will frequently pursue the hunter when wounded. it is asstonishing to see the wounds they will bear before they can be put to death. the Indians may well fear this anamal equiped as they generally are with their bows and arrows or indifferent fuzees, but in the hands of skillfull riflemen they are by no means as formidable or dangerous as they have been represented. game is still very abundant we can scarcely cast our eyes in any direction without percieving deer Elk Buffaloe or Antelopes. The quantity of wolves appear to increase in the same proportion; they generally hunt in parties of six eight or ten; they kill a great number of the Antelopes at this season; the Antelopes are yet meagre and the females are big with young; the wolves take them most generally in attempting to swim the river; in this manner my dog caught one drowned it and brought it on shore; they are but clumsey swimers, tho on land when in good order, they are extreemly fleet and dureable. we have frequently seen the wolves in pursuit of the Antelope in the plains; they appear to decoy a single one from a flock, and then pursue it, alturnately relieving each other untill they take it. on joining Capt Clark he informed me that he had seen a female and faun of the bighorned anamal; that they ran for some distance with great aparent ease along the side of the river bluff where it was almost perpendicular; two of the party fired on them while in motion without effect. we took the flesh of the bear on board and proceeded. Capt. Clark walked on shore this evening, killed a deer, and saw several of the bighorned anamals. there is more appearance of coal today than we have yet seen, the stratas are 6 feet thick in some instances; the earth has been birnt in many places, and always appears in stratas on the same level with the stratas of coal. we came too this evening in the mouth of a little river, which falls in on the Stard. side. This stream is about 50 yards wide from bank to bank; the water occupyes about 15 yards. the banks are of earth only, abrupt, tho not high- the bed, is of mud principally. Capt Clark, who was up this streeam about three miles, informed me that it continued about the same width, that it's current was gentle and it appeared navigable for perogus it meanders through an extensive, fertile, and beautifull vally as far as could bee seen about N. 30°W. there was but one solitary tree to be seen on the banks of this river after it left the bottom of the Missouri. the water of this river is clear, with a brownish yelow tint. here the highlands receede from the Missouri, leaving the vally formed by the river from seven to eight miles wide, and reather lower then usual.- This stream my friend Capt. C. named Marthas river

[Clark, April 29, 1805] 29th of April Monday 1805 Set out this morning at the usial hour. the wind is moderate & from the N E had not proceeded far eer we Saw a female & her faun of the Bighorn animal on the top of a Bluff lying, the noise we made allarmed them and they came down on the Side of the bluff which had but little Slope being nearly purpindicular, I directed two men to kill those anamals, one went on the top and the other man near the water they had two Shots at the doe while in motion without effect, Those animals run & Skiped about with great ease on this declivity & appeared to prefur it to the leavel bottom or plain. Capt Lewis & one man walkd on Shore and he killed a yellow Bear & the man with him wounded one other, after getting the flesh of the bear on bord which was not far from the place we brackfast, we proceeded on Saw 4 gangus of buffalow and great numbers of Antelopes in every direction also Saw Elk and Several wolves, I walked on Shore in the evening & killed a Deer which was So meager as to be unfit for use The hills Contain more Coal, and has a greater appearance of being burnt that below, the burnt parts appear on a parrilel with the Stratiums of Coal, we Came too in the mouth of a Little river on the S. S. which is about 50 or 60 yards from bank to bank, I was up this Stream 3 miles it continues its width and glides with a gentle Current, its water is about 15 yards wide at this time, and appears to be navagable for Canoes &c. it meanders through a butifull & extencive vallie as far as can be Seen about N 30° W. I saw only a Single tree in this fertile vallie The water of the River is clear of a yellowish Colour, we call this river Martheys river in honor to the Selebrated M. F

Here the high land widen from five to Eight miles and much lower than below, Saw Several of the big horn animals this evening. The Wolves distroy great numbers of the antelopes by decoying those animals Singularly out in the plains and prosueing them alternetly, those antelopes are Curious and will approach any thing which appears in motion near them &c.

[Lewis, April 30, 1805] Tuesday April 30th 1805. Set out at sunrise. the wind blew hard all last night, and continued to blow pretty hard all day, but not so much, as to compell us to ly by. the country as usual is bare of timber; the river bottoms are level and fertile and extensive, but possess but little timber and that of an indifferent quality even of it's kind; principally low cottonwood, either too small for building, or for plank or broken and dead at top and unsound in the center of the trunk. saw great quantities of game as usual. Capt. Clark walked on shore the greater part of the day, past some old Indian lodges built of drift wood; they appear to be of antient date and not recently inhabited. I walked on shore this evening and killed a buck Elk, in tolerable order; it appeared to me to be the largest I had seen, and was therefore induced to measure it; found it five feet three inches from the point of the hoof, to the top of the sholders; the leg and hoof being placed as nearly as possible in the same position they would have been had the anamal been standing.

[Clark, April 30, 1805] 30th of April Tuesday 1805 The wind blew hard from the N E all last night, we Set out at Sunrise the wind blew hard the greater part of the day and part of the time favourable, we did not lie by to day on account of the wind I walked on Shore to day our interpreter & his Squar followed, in my walk the Squar found & brought me a bush Something like the Current, which She Said bore a delicious froot and that great quantites grew on the Rocky Mountains, this Srub was in bloom has a yellow flower with a deep Cup, the froot when ripe is yellow and hangs in bunches like Cheries, Some of those berries yet remained on the bushes. The bottoms above the mouth of the last river is extensive level & fertile and covered with indifferent timber in the points, the up land appear to rise gradually, I saw Great numbers of Antelopes, also Scattering Buffalow, Elk, Deer, wolves, Gees, ducks & Grows- I Killed 2 Gees which we dined on to day Capt Lewis walked on Shore and killed an elk this evening, and we Came too & camped on the S. S the Countrey on both Sides have a butifull appearance.

[Lewis, May 1, 1805] Wednesday May 1st 1805. Set out this morning at an early, the wind being favourable we used our sales which carried us on at a good pace untill about 12 OCk. when the wind became so high that the small canoes were unable to proceed one of them which seperated from us just befor the wind became so violent, is now lying on the opposite side of the river, being unable to rejoin us in consequence of the waves, which during those gusts run several feet high. we came too on the Lard. shore in a handsome bottom well stocked with cottonwood timber; here the wind compelled us to spend the ballance of the day. we sent out some hunters who killed a buffaloe, an Elk, a goat and two beaver. game is now abundant. the country appears much more pleasant and fertile than that we have passed for several days; the hills are lower, the bottoms wider, and better stocked with timber, which consists principally of cottonwood, not however of large size; the under-growth willow on the verge of the river and sandbars, rose bushes, red willow and the broad leafed willow in the bottom lands; the high country on either side of the river is one vast plain, intirely destitute of timber, but is apparently fertile, consisting of a dark rich mellow looking lome. John Shields sick today with the rheumatism. Shannon killed a bird of the plover kind. weight one pound. it measured from the tip of the toe, to the extremity of the beak, 1 foot 10 Inches; from tip to tip of wings when extended 2 F. 5 I.; Beak 3 5/8 inches; tale 3 1/8 inches; leg and toe 10 Ins.- the eye black, piercing, prominent and moderately large. the legs are Hat thin, slightly imbricated and of a pale sky blue colour, being covered with feathers as far as the mustle extends down it, which is about half it's length. it has four toes on each foot, three of which, are connected by a web, the fourth is small and placed at the heel about the 1/8 of an inch up the leg. the nails are black and short, that of the middle toe is extreemly singular, consisting of two nails the one laping on or overlaying the other, the upper one somewhat the longest and sharpest. the tale contains eleven feathers of equal length, & of a bluish white colour. the boddy and underside of the wings, except the large feathers of the 1st & 2cd joints of the same, are white; as are also the feathers of the upper part of the 4th joint of the wing and part of those of the 3rd adjacent thereto, the large feathers of the 1st or pinion and the 2cd joint are black; a part of the larger feathers of the 3rd joint on the upper side and all the small feathers which cover the upper part of the wings are black, as are also the tuft of long feathers on each side of the body above the joining of the wing, leaving however a stripe of white betwen them on the back. the head and neck are shaped much like the grey plover, and are of a light brickdust brown; the beak is black and flat, largest where it joins the head, and from thence becoming thiner and tapering to a very sharp point, the upper chap being 1/8 of an inch the longest turns down at the point and forms a little hook. the nostrils, which commence near the head are long, narrow, connected, and parallel with the beak; the beak is much curved, the curvature being upwards in stead of downwards as is common with most birds; the substance of the beak precisely resembles whalebone at a little distance, and is quite as flexable as that substance their note resembles that of the grey plover, tho is reather louder and more varied, their habits appear also to be the same, with this difference; that it sometimes rests on the water and swims which I do not recollect having seen the plover do. this bird which I shall henceforth stile the Missouri plover, generally feeds about the shallow bars of the river; to collect it's food which consists of _____, it immerces it's beak in the water and throws it's head and beak from side to side at every step it takes.

[Clark, May 1, 1805] May the 1st Wednesday 1805 We Set out at Sun rise under a Stiff Breeze from the East, the morning Cool & Cloudy. one man J. Shields Sick with rhumetism- one of the men (Shannon) Shot a Gull or pleaver, which is about the Size of an Indian hen, with a Sharp pointed bill turning up & 4 Inches long, the head and neck of a light brown, the breast, the underfeathers of the 2nd and 3d joint of the wings, the Short feathers on the upper part of the 3rd joint of the wings, down the back the rump & tail white. The large feathers of the 1st joints of the wing the upper feathers of the 2d joints of the wings, on the body on the joints of the wing and the bill is black.- the legs long and of a Skie blue. The feet webed &c. This fowl may be properly Stiled the Missouri Pleaver- the wind became verry Hard and we put too on the L. Side, as the wind Continued with Some degree of violence and the waves too high for the Canoes we were obliged to Stay all day

[Lewis, May 1, 1805]
May 1st 1805.
Shannon killed a bird of the plover kind the weight one pound.- eye black percing and prominent

Measure F. Inchs from the tip of the toe to the extremity of the beak 1 10 from tip to tip of wing when extended 2 5 length of beak 3 5/8 length of tale 3 1/8 length of leg and toe 10

the legs are flat, of pale skye blue colour and but slightly imbricated. the second joint, as low as the mustle extends is covered with feathers which is about half it's length. it has three toes on a foot connected by a web. there is also a small toe on each foot placed about the eighth of an inch up the leg behind. the nails are black and short and those of the middle toes ar singular-there being two nails on each the one above the other the upper one the longest and sharpest.- the tale contains eleven feathers of the same length of a bluish white colour. the body and under side of the wings except the large feathers of the 1 & 2cd joints of the wings are white, as are also the feathers of the upper part of the 4th joint of the wing. and some of those of the 3rd adjoining.- the large feathers of the pinion or first (joint) & the second joint are black; a part of the larger feathers of the third joint on the upper side and all the smaller feathers which cover the upper part of these joints ar black; as are also the tuft of long feathers on each side of the body above the joining of the wing, leaving however a stripe of white between them on the back. the head and neck are shaped much like the grey plover, and is a light brickdust brown. the beak is black and flat, largest where it joins the head and from thence tapering every way gradually to a very sharp point the upper beak being 1/8 of an inch the longest turning down at the point. the nostrils are parrallal with the beak and are long narrow and connected. the beak is curvated and invirted; the Curvature being upwards in stead of downwards as those of most birds are- the substance of the beak is as flexable as whalebone and at a little distance precisely resembles that substance. their note is like that of the common whistling or grey plover tho reather louder, and more varied, and their habits are the same with that bird so far as I have been enabled to learn, with this difference however that this bird sometimes lights in the water and swims.- it generally feads about the shallow bars of the river; to collect it's food, it immerces it's beak in the water, and thows it's head and beak from side to side at every step it takes.

[Lewis, May 2, 1805] Thursday May 2ed 1805 The wind continued violent all night nor did it abate much of it's violence this morning, when at daylight it was attended with snow which continued to fall untill about 10 A.M. being about one inch deep, it formed a singular contrast with the vegitation which was considerably advanced. some flowers had put forth in the plains, and the leaves of the cottonwood were as large as a dollar. sent out some hunters who killed 2 deer 3 Elk and several buffaloe; on our way this evening we also shot three beaver along the shore; these anamals in consequence of not being hunted are extreemly gentle, where they are hunted they never leave their lodges in the day, the flesh of the beaver is esteemed a delecacy among us; I think the tale a most delicious morsal, when boiled it resembles in flavor the fresh tongues and sounds of the codfish, and is usually sufficiently large to afford a plentifull meal for two men. Joseph Fields one of the hunters who was out today found several yards of scarlet cloth which had been suspended on the bough of a tree near an old indian hunting camp, where it had been left as a sacrefice to the deity by the indians, probably of the Assinniboin nation, it being a custom with them as well as all the nations inhabiting the waters of the Missouri so far as they are known to us, to offer or sacrefice in this manner to the deity watever they may be possessed off which they think most acceptable to him, and very honestly making their own feelings the test of those of the deity offer him the article which they most prize themselves. this being the most usual method of weshiping the great sperit as they term the deity, is practiced on interesting occasions, or to produce the happy eventuation of the important occurrances incident to human nature, such as relief from hungar or mallady, protection from their enemies or the delivering them into their hands, and with such as cultivate, to prevent the river's overflowing and distroying their crops &c. screfices of a similar kind are also made to the deceased by their friends and relatives. the are was very piercing this evening the water friezed on the oars as they rowed. the wind dying at 5 P.M. we set out.

every thing which is incomprehensible to the indians they call big medicine, and is the opperation of the presnts and power of the great sperit. this morning one of the men shot the indian dog that had followed us for several days, he would steal their cooked provision.

[Clark, May 2, 1805] May 2nd Thursday 1805 The wind blew verry hard all the last night, this morning about Sunrise began to Snow, (The Thermomtr. at 28 abov o) and Continued untill about 10 oClock, at which time it

Seased, the wind Continued hard untill about 2 P.M. the Snow which fell to day was about 1 In deep, a verry extroadernaley Climate, to behold the trees Green & flowers Spred on the plain, & Snow an inch deep. we Set out about 3 oClock and proceeded on about five 1/2 miles and encamped on the Std Side, the evening verry cold, Ice freesing to the Ores, I Shot a large beaver & Drewyer three in walking on the bank, the flesh of those animals the party is fond of eating &c.

[Lewis, May 3, 1805] Friday May 3rd 1805. The morning being very could we did not set out as early as usual; ice formed on a kettle of water 1/4 of an inch thick. the snow has melted generally in the bottoms, but the hills still remain covered. on the lard side at the distance of 2 miles we passed a curious collection of bushes which had been tyed up in the form of a faciene and standing on end in the open bottom it appeared to be about 30 feet high and ten or twelve feet in diameter, this we supposed to have been placed there by the Indians, as a sacrefice for some purpose. The wind continued to blow hard from the West but not so strong as to compel us to ly by. Capt. Clark walked on shore and killed an Elk which he caused to be butched by the time I arrived with the party, here we halted and dined being about 12 OCk. our usual time of halting for that purpose. after dinner Capt. Clark pursued his walk, while I continued with the party, it being a rule which we had established, never to be absent at the same time from the party. the plains or high lands are much less elivated than they were, not being more than from 50 to 60 feet above the river bottom, which is also wider than usual being from 5 to 9 ms. in width; traces of the ancient beds of the river are visible in many places through the whole extent of this valley. since the hills have become lower the appearance of the stratas of coal burnt hills and pumice stone have in a great measure ceased; I saw none today. we saw vast quantities of Buffaloe, Elk, deer principally of the long tale kind, Antelope or goats, beaver, geese, ducks, brant and some swan. near the entrance of the river mentioned in the 10th course of this day, we saw an unusual number of Porcupines from which we determined to call the river after that anamal, and accordingly denominated it Porcupine river. this stream discharges itself into the Missouri on the Stard. side 2000 miles above the mouth of the latter, it is a beatifull bold runing stream, 40 yards wide at it's entrance; the water is transparent, it being the first of this discription that I have yet seen discharge itself into the Missouri; before it enters a large sand bar through which it discharges itself into the missouri it's banks and bottom are formed of a stiff blue and black clay; it appears to be navigable for canoes and perogues at this time and I have no doubt but it might be navigated with boats of a considerable size in high water. it's banks appear to be from 8 to ten feet high and seldom overflow; from the quantity of water furnished by this river, the appearance of the country, the direction it pursues, and the situation of it's entrance, I have but little doubt but it takes it's source not far from the main body of the Suskashawan river, and that it is probably navigable 150 miles; perhaps not very distant from that river. should this be the case, it would afford a very favorable communication to the Athebaskay country, from whence the British N. W. Company derive so large a portion of their valuable furs.- Capt. Clark who ascended this river several miles and passed it above where it entered the hills informed me on his return that he found the general width of the bed of the river about one hundred yards, where he passed the river the bed was 112 yards wide, the water was knee deep and 38 yard in width; the river which he could observe from the rising grounds for about 20 miles, bore a little to the East of North. there was a considerable portion of timber in the bottom lands of this river. Capt Clark also met with limestone on the surface of the earth in the course of his walk. he also saw a range of low mountains at a distance to the W of N , their direction being N. W. the country in the neighborhood of this river, and as far as the eye can reach, is level, fertile, open and beatifull beyond discription. 1/4 of a mile above the entrance of this river a large creek falls in which we called 2000 mile creek. I sent Rubin Fields to examine it, he reported it to be a bold runing stream, it's bed 30 yards wide. we proceeded about 3 miles abov this creek and encamped on the Stard. shore. I walked out a little distance and met with 2 porcupines which were feeding on the young willow which grow in great abundance on all the sandbars; this anamal is exceedingly clumsy and not very watchfull I approached so near one of them before it percieved me that I touched it with my espontoon.- found the nest of a wild goose among some driftwood in the river from which we took three eggs. this is the only nest we have met with on driftwood, the usual position is the top of a broken tree, sometimes in the forks of a large tree but almost invariably, from 15 to 20 feet or upwards high.-

[Clark, May 3, 1805] May 3rd Friday 1805 we Set out reather later this morning than usial owing to weather being verry cold, a frost last night and the Thermt. Stood this morning at 26 above 0 which is 6 Degrees blow freeseing- the ice that was on the Kittle left near the fire last night was 1/4 of an inch thick. The Snow is all or nearly all off the low bottoms, the Hills are entireley Covered. three of our party found in the back of a bottom 3 pieces of Scarlet one brace in each, which had been left as a Sacrifice near one of their Swet houses, on the L. S. we passed to day a curious collection of bushes tied up in the shape of fascene about 10 feet diamuter, which must have been left also by the natives as an offering to their medison which they Convinced protected or gave them relief near the place, the wind Continued to blow hard from the West, altho not Sufficently So to detain us, I walked on Shore and killed an Elk & had him bucchured by the time the Perogus Came up which was the usial time of dineing. The high lands are low and from 8 to 9 miles apart and there is evident marks of the bead of the river having been changed frequently but little appearance of the Coal & burnt hills to day- Great numbers of Buffalow, Elk, Deer, antilope, beaver, Porcupins, & water fowls Seen to day, Such as, Geese, ducks of dift. kinds, & a fiew Swan- I continued my walk on Shore after dinner, and arrived at the mouth of a river on the St. Side, which appeared to be large, and I concluded to go up this river a few miles to examine it accordingly I Set out North 1 mile thro wood or timbered bottom, 2 miles through a butifull leavel plain, and 1 mile over a high plain about 50 feet higher than the bottom & Came to the little river, which I found to be a butifull clear Stream of about 100 yds. from bank to bank, (I waded this river at the narrowest part and made it 112 Steps from bank to bank and at this place which was a kind of fording place the water was near Knee deep, and 38 steps wide, the bottom of a hard stiff Black Clay,) I observed a Great perportion of timber in the bottoms of this river as far as I could See which was to the East of N. 18 or 20 miles, it appears to be navigable at this time for Canoes, and from appearances must be navagable a long distance for Perogus & boats in high water. This river we call Porcupine from the great number of those anamals found about it's mouth.- a Short distance above about 1/4 mile and on the Lard Side a large Creek falls in, which R. Fields went to examine & reports that it is a bold running Stream, 30 yds wide as this Creek is 2000 miles up the Missouri we Call it the 2000 mile Creek, we proceeded on 3 miles & Camped on the S. S. here I joined Capt Lewis who had in my absens walkd. on the upper Side of Porcupine River for Some distance- This river from its Size & quantity of water must head at no great distance from the Saskashawan on this river I Saw emence herds Elk & Buffalow & many deer & Porcupine. I also Saw the top of a mountain which did not appear verry high to the West of N. & bore N W. I Saw on the high land limestone & pebble- The Countrey about the mouth of this river and as far as the eye Can reach is butifull open Countrey. The greater part of the Snow is melted.

[Lewis, May 4, 1805] Saturday May 4th 1805. We were detained this morning untill about 9 OCk. in order to repare the rudder irons of the red perogue which were broken last evening in landing; we then set out, the wind hard against us. I walked on shore this morning, the weather was more plesant, the snow has disappeared; the frost seems to have effected the vegetation much less than could have been expected the leaves of the cottonwood the grass the box alder willow and the yellow flowering pea seem to be scarcely touched; the rosebushes and honeysuckle seem to have sustaned the most considerable injury. The country on both sides of the Missouri continues to be open level fertile and beautifull as far as the eye can reach which from some of the eminences is not short of 30 miles. the river bottoms are very extensive and contain a much greater proportion of timber than usual; the fore part of this day the river was bordered with timber on both sides, a circumstance which is extreemly rare and the first which has occurred of any thing like the same extent since we left the Mandans, in the after part of the day we passed an extensive beautifull plain on the Stard. side which gradually ascended from the river. I saw immence quantities of buffaloe in every direction, also some Elk deer and goats; having an abundance of meat on hand I passed them without firing on them; they are extreemly gentle the bull buffaloe particularly will scarcely give way to you. I passed several in the open plain within fifty paces, they viewed me for a moment as something novel and then very unconcernedly continued to feed. Capt. Clark walked on shore this evening and did not rejoin us untill after dark, he struck the river several miles above our camp and came down to us. we saw many beaver some which the party shot, we also killed two deer today. much sign of the brown bear. passed several old Indian hunting camps in the course of the day one of them contained two large lodges which were fortifyed with old driftwood and fallen timber; this fortification consisted of a circular fence of timber lade horizontally laping on and over laying each other to the hight of 5 feet. these pounds are sometimes built from 20 to 30 feet in diameter and covered over with the trunks and limbs of old timber. the usual construction of the lodges we have lately passed is as follows. three or more strong sticks the thickness of a man's leg or arm and about 12 feet long are attatched together at one end by a with of small willows, these are then set on end and spread at the base, forming a circle of ten twelve or 14 feet in diameter; sticks of driftwood and fallen timber of convenient size are now placed with one end on the ground and the other resting against those which are secured together at top by the with and which support and give the form to the whole, thus the sticks are laid on untill they make it as thick as they design, usually about three ranges, each piece breaking or filling up the interstice of the two beneath it, the whole forming a connic figure about 10 feet high with a small apperture in one side which answers as a door. leaves bark and straw are sometimes thrown over the work to make it more complete, but at best it affords a very imperfect shelter particularly without straw which is the state in which we have most usually found them.

At noon the sun was so much obscured that I could not obtain his maridian Altitude which I much wished in order to fix the latitude of the entrance of Porcupine river. Joseph Fields was very sick today with the disentary had a high fever I gave him a doze of Glauber salts, which operated very well, in the evening his fever abated and I gave him 30 drops of laudnum.-

[Clark, May 4, 1805] May 4th Satturday 1805 The rudder Irons of our large Perogue broke off last night, the replaceing of which detained us this morning untill 9 oClock at which time we Set out the wind a head from the west, The Countrey on each Side of the Missouri is a rich high and butifull the bottoms are extencive with a great deal of timber on them all the fore part of this day the wood land bordered the river on both Sides, in the after part a butifull assending plain on the Std Side we Camped on the Std. Side a little above we passed a Small Creek on the L. Side near which I Saw where an Indian lodge had been fortified many year past. Saw great numbers of anamals of different kinds on the banks, I Saw the black martin to day-in the evening I walkd. on Shore on the Std Side & Struck the river Several miles above our Camp & did not get to Camp untill Some time after night- we have one man Sick, The river has been falling for Several days passed; it now begins to rise a little; the rate of rise & fall is from one to 3 inches in 24 hours.

[Lewis, May 5, 1805] Sunday May 5th 1805 A fine morning I walked on shore untill 8 A M when we halted for breakfast and in the course of my walk killed a deer which I carried about a mile and a half to the river, it was in good order. soon after seting out the rudder irons of the white perogue were broken by her runing fowl on a sawyer, she was however refitted in a few minutes with some tugs of raw hide and nales. as usual saw a great quantity of game today; Buffaloe Elk and goats or Antelopes feeding in every direction; we kill whatever we wish, the buffaloe furnish us with fine veal and fat beef, we also have venison and beaver tales when we wish them; the flesh of the Elk and goat are less esteemed, and certainly are inferior. we have not been able to take any fish for some time past. The country is as yesterday beatifull in the extreme.

saw the carcases of many Buffaloe lying dead along the shore partially devoured by the wolves and bear. saw a great number of white brant also the common brown brant, geese of the common kind and a small species of geese which differ considerably from the common canadian goose; their neck head and beak are considerably thicker shorter and larger than the other in proportion to it's size, they are also more than a third smaller, and their note more like that of the brant or a young goose which has not perfectly acquired his notes, in all other rispects they are the same in colour habits and the number of feathers in the tale, they frequently also associate with the large geese when in flocks, but never saw them pared off with the large or common goose. The white brant ascociate in very large flocks, they do not appear to be mated or pared off as if they intended to raise their young in this quarter, I therefore doubt whether they reside here during the summer for that purpose.

this bird is about the size of the common brown brant or two thirds of the common goose, it is not so long by six inches from point to point of the wings when extended as the other; the beak head and neck are also larger and stronger; their beak legs and feet are of a redish or fleshcoloured white. the eye is of moderate size, the puple of a deep sea green incircled with a ring of yellowish brown. it·has sixteen feathers of equal length in the tale; their note differs but little from the common brant, their flesh much the same, and in my opinion preferable to the goose, the flesh is dark. they are entirely of a beatifull pure white except the large feathers of the 1st and second joints of the wings which are jut black. form and habits are the same with the other brant; they sometimes ascociate and form one common flock. Capt Clark found a den of young wolves in the course of his walk today and also saw a great number of those anamals; they are very abundant in this quarter, and are of two species the small woolf or burrowing dog of the praries are the inhabitants almost invariably of the open plains; they usually ascociate in bands of ten or twelve sometimes more and burrow near some pass or place much frequented by game; not being able alone to take a deer or goat they are rarely ever found alone but hunt in bands; they frequently watch and seize their prey near their burrows; in these burrows they raise their young and to them they also resort when pursued; when a person approaches them they frequently bark, their note being precisely that of the small dog. they are of an intermediate size between that of the fox and dog, very active fleet and delicately formed; the ears large erect and pointed the head long and pointed more like that of the fox; tale long; the hair and fur also resembles the fox tho is much coarser and inferior. they are of a pale redish brown colour. the eye of a deep sea green colour small and piercing. their tallons are reather longer than those of the ordinary wolf or that common to the atlantic states, none of which are to be found in this quarter, nor I believe above the river Plat.- The large woolf found here is not as large as those of the atlantic states. they are lower and thicker made shorter leged. their colour which is not effected by the seasons, is a grey or blackish brown and every intermediate shade from that to a creen coloured white; these wolves resort the woodlands and are also found in the plains, but never take refuge in the ground or burrow so far as I have been able to inform myself. we scarcely see a gang of buffaloe without observing a parsel of those faithfull shepherds on their skirts in readiness to take care of the mamed & wounded. the large wolf never barks, but howls as those of the atlantic states do. Capt. Clark and Drewyer killed the largest brown bear this evening which we have yet seen. it was a most tremendous looking anamal, and extreemly hard to kill notwithstanding he had five balls through his lungs and five others in various parts he swam more than half the distance acoss the river to a sandbar & it was at least twenty minutes before he died; he did not attempt to attact, but fled and made the most tremendous roaring from the moment he was shot. We had no means of weighing this monster; Capt. Clark thought he would weigh 500 lbs. for my own part I think the estimate too small by 100 lbs. he measured 8 Feet 71/2 Inches from the nose to the extremity of the hind feet, 5 F. to 1/2 Inch arround the breast, 1 F. 11 I. arround the middle of the arm, & 3 F. 11 I. arround the neck; his tallons which were five in number on each foot were 4 1/8 Inches in length. he was in good order, we therefore divided him among the party and made them boil the oil and put it in a cask for future uce; the oil is as hard as hogs lard when cool, much more so than that of the black bear. this bear differs from the common black bear in several respects; it's tallons are much longer and more blont, it's tale shorter, it's hair which is of a redish or bey brown, is longer thicker and finer than that of the black bear; his liver lungs and heart are much larger even in proportion with his size; the heart particularly was as large as that of a large Ox. his maw was also ten times the size of black bear, and was filled with flesh and fish. his testicles were pendant from the belly and placed four inches assunder in seperate bags or pouches.- this animal also feeds on roots and almost every species of wild fruit.

The party killed two Elk and a Buffaloe today, and my dog caught a goat, which he overtook by superior fleetness, the goat it must be understood was with young and extreemly poor. a great number of these goats are devowered by the wolves and bear at this season when they are poor and passing the river from S. W. to N. E. they are very inactive and easily taken in the water, a man can out swim them with great ease; the Indians take them in great numbers in the river at this season and in autumn when they repass to the S. W.

[Clark, May 5, 1805] 5th of May Sunday 1805 We Set out verry early and had not proceeded far before the rudder Irons of one of the Perogus broke which detained us a Short time Capt Lewis walked on Shore this morning and killed a Deer, after brackfast I walked on Shore Saw great numbers of Buffalow & Elk Saw also a Den of young wolves, and a number of (frown wolves in every direction, the white & Grey Brant is in this part of the Missouri I shot at the white brant but at So great a distance I did not kill, The Countrey on both sides is as yesterday, handsom & fertile- The river rising & Current Strong & in the evening we Saw a Brown or Grisley beare on a Sand beech, I went out with one man Geo. Drewyer & Killed the bear, which was verry large and a turrible looking animal, which we found verry hard to kill we Shot ten Balls into him before we killed him, & 5 of those Balls through his lights This animal is the largest of the Carnivorous kind I ever Saw we had nothing that could way him, I think his weight may be Stated at 500 pounds, he measured 8 feet 71/2 In. from his nose to the extremity of the Toe, 5 feet 101/2 in. arround the breast, 1 feet 11 Ins. around the middle of the arm, 3 feet 11 Ins. arround the neck his tallents was 4 Inches &3/8 long, he was good order, and appeared verry different from the Common black bear in as much as his tallents were blunt, his tail Short, his liver & lights much larger, his maw ten times as large and Contained meat or flesh & fish only- we had him Skined and divided, the oile tried up & put in Kegs for use. we Camped on the Stard Side, our men killed three Elk and a Buffalow to day, and our Dog Cought an antilope a fair race, this animal appeared verry pore & with young.

[Lewis, May 6, 1805] Monday May 6th 1805. The morning being fair and pleasant and wind favourable we set sale at an early hour, and proceeded on very well the greater part of the day; the country still continues level fertile and beautifull, the bottoms wide and well timbered comparitively speaking with other parts of the river; no appearance of birnt hills pumice stone or coal, the salts of tartar or vegitable salts continues to appear on the river banks, sand bars and in many parts of the plains most generally in the little revines at the base of the low hills. passed three streames today which discharged themselves on the Lard. side; the first of these we call little dry creek it contained some water in standing pools but discharged none, the 2ed 50 yards wide no Water, we called it Big dry Creek, the 3rd is bed of a conspicuous river 200 yards wide which we called little dry river; the banks of these streams are low and bottoms wide with but little timber, their beds are almost entirely formed of a fine brown sand intermixed with a small proportion of little pebbles, which were either transparent, white, green, red, yellow or brown. these streams appeared to continue their width without diminution as far as we could perceive them, which with rispect to the river was many miles, they had receny discharged their waters. from the appearance of these streams, and the country through which they passed, we concluded that they had their souces in level low dry plains, which probably is the character of the country for a great distance west of this, or to the vicinity of the black hills, that the country being low on the same level nearly and in the same parallel of latitude, that the rains in the spring of the year suddonly melts the snow at the same time and causes for a few days a vast quantity of water which finds it's way to the Missouri through those channels; by reference to the diary of the weather &c it will be percieved that there is scarcely any rain during the summer Autumn and winter in this open country distant from the mountains. Fields still continues unwell. saw a brown bear swim the river above us, he disappeared before we can get in reach of him; I find that the curiossity of our party is pretty well satisfyed with rispect to this anamal, the formidable appearance of the male bear killed on the 5th added to the difficulty with which they die when even shot through the vital parts, has staggered the resolution several of them, others however seem keen for action with the bear; I expect these gentlemen will give us some amusement shotly as they soon begin now to coppolate. saw a great quantity of game of every species common here. Capt Clark walked on shore and killed two Elk, they were not in very good order, we therefore took a part of the meat only; it is now only amusement for Capt. C. and myself to kill as much meat as the party can consum; I hope it may continue thus through our whole rout, but this I do not much expect. two beaver were taken in traps this morning and one since shot by one of the party. saw numbers of these anamals peeping at us as we passed out of their wholes which they form of a cilindric shape, by burrowing in the face of the abbrupt banks of the river.

[Clark, May 6, 1805] May 6th Monday 1805 a fine morning wind from the N. E. we Set out early and proceeded on verry well under Sail the greater part of the day, passed two Creeks & a River to day on the Lard. Side, neither of them discharged any water into the Missouri, they were wide and Continued their width for Some distance, the little water of those Creeks & the little river must wash the low Country, I believe those Streams to be the Conveyance of the water of the heavy rains & melting Snows in the Countrey back &c. &c. I walked on Shore and Killed two Elk neither of which was fat, we saved the best of the meat, one beaver Shot to day. the countrey on both Sides butifull no appearances of either Coal or pumice Stone & burnt hills, The Salts of Tarter or white aprs. of Salts are yet to be Seen.

[Lewis, May 7, 1805] Tuesday May 7th 1805. A fine morning, set out at an early hour; the drift wood begins to come down in consequence of the river's rising; the water is somewhat clearer than usual, a circumstance I did not expect on it's rise. at 11 A.M. the wind became so hard that we were compelled to ly by for several hours, one of the small canoes by the bad management of the steersman filled with water and had very nearly sunk; we unloaded her and dryed the baggage; at one we proceed on the wind having in some measure abated. the country we passed today on the North side of the river is one of the most beautifull plains we have yet seen, it rises gradually from the river bottom to the hight of 50 or 60 feet, then becoming level as a bowling green. extends back as far as the eye can reach; on the S. side the river hills are more broken and much higher tho some little destance back the country becomes level and fertile. no appearance of birnt hills coal or pumicestone, that of salts still continue. vegitation appears to have advanced very little since the 28th Ulto.- we continue to see a great number of bald Eagles, I presume they must feed on the carcases of dead anamals, for I see no fishing hawks to supply them with their favorite food. the water of the river is so terbid that no bird wich feeds exclusively on fish can subsist on it; from it's mouth to this place I have neither seen the blue crested fisher nor a fishing hawk. this day we killed 3 Buffaloe 1 Elk & 8 beaver; two of the Buffaloe killed by Capt Clark near our encampment of this evening wer in good order dressed them and saved the meat, the Elk I killed this morning, thought it fat, but on examineation found it so lean that we took the tongue marrowbones and Skin only.

[Clark, May 7, 1805] May 7th Tuesday, 1805 A fine morning river rose 11/2 Inches last night, the drift wood beginning to run the water Something Clearer than usial, the wind became verry hard, and at 11 oClock one Canoe by bad Stearing filled with water, which detained us about 3 hours, had a Meridian altitude, the Laid. from which is 47°36' 11" 6/10 The Countrey on the North Side of the Missouri is one of the handsomest plains we have yet Seen on the river the plain rises from the river bottom gradually. The Hills on the South Side is high & uneavin. no appearance of Coal or burnt hills, that of Salts Still appear; vegitation appears to be Slow, I walked on the bank to day and Shot 2 beaver, in the evening Killed two Buffalow in tolerable order which we Saved and Camped on the Lard Side. 8 beaver, 3 buffalow & an Elk killed to day

[Lewis, May 8, 1805] Wednesday May 8th 1805. Set out at an early hour under a gentle brieze from the East. a black cloud which suddonly sprung up at S. E. soon over shaddowed the horizon; at 8 A.M. it gave us a slight sprinke of rain, the wind became much stronger but not so much so as to detain us. we nooned it just above the entrance of a large river which disimbogues on the Lard. side; I took the advantage of this leasure moment and examined the river about 3 miles; I found it generally 150 yards wide, and in some places 200. it is deep, gentle in it's courant and affords a large boddy of water; it's banks which are formed of a dark rich loam and blue clay are abbrupt and about 12 feet high. it's bed is principally mud. I have no doubt but it is navigable for boats perogues and canoes, for the latter probably a great distance. the bottoms of this stream ar wide, level, fertile and possess a considerable proportion of timber, principally Cottonwood. from the quantity of water furnised by this river it must water a large extent of country; perhaps this river also might furnish a practicable and advantageous communication with the Saskashiwan river; it is sufficiently large to justify a belief that it might reach to that river if it's direction be such. the water of this river possesses a peculiar whiteness, being about the colour of a cup of tea with the admixture of a tablespoonful) of milk. from the colour of it's water we called it Milk river. (we think it possible that this may be the river called by the Minitares the river which scoalds at all others or _____) Capt Clark who walked this morning on the Lard. shore ascended a very high point opposite to the mouth of this river; he informed me that he had a perfect view of this river and the country through which it passed for a great distance (probably 50 or 60 Miles,) that the country was level and beautifull on both sides of the river, with large herds of Buffaloe distributed throughout that the river from it's mouth boar N. W. for 12 or 15 Miles when it forked, the one taking a direction nearly North, and the other to the West of N. West. from the appearance of the vallies and the timber on each of these streams Capt. C. supposed that they were about the same size. great appearance of beaver on this river, and I have no doubt but what they continue abundant, there being plenty of cottonwood and willow, the timber on which they subsist. The country on the Lard. side of the river is generally high broken hills, with much broken, grey black and brown grannite scattered on the surface of the earth in a confused manner. The wild Licquorice is found on the sides of these hills, in great abundance. at a little distance from the river there is no timber to be seen on either side; the bottom lands are not more than one fifth covered with timber; the timber as below is confined to the borders of the river. in future it will be understood that there is no timber of any discription on the upland unless particularly mentioned; and also that one fifth of the bottom lands being covered with timber is considered a large proportion. The white apple is found in great abundance in this neighbourhood; it is confined to the highlands principally. The whiteapple, so called by the French Engages, is a plant which rises to the hight of 6 or 9 Inchs. rarely exceeding a foot; it puts forth from one to four and sometimes more stalks from the same root, but is most generally found with one only, which is branched but not defusely, is cylindric and villose; the leafstalks, cylindric, villose and very long compared with the hight of the plant, tho gradually diminish in length as they ascend, and are irregular in point of position; the leaf, digitate, from three to five in number, oval 1 Inch long, absolutely entire and cottony; the whole plant of a pale green, except the under disk of the leaf which is of a white colour from the cottony substance with which it is covered. the radix a tuberous bulb; generally ova formed, sometimes longer and more rarely partially divided or brancing; always attended with one or more radicles at it's lower extremity which sink from 4 to 6 inches deep. the bulb covered with a rough black, tough, thin rind which easily seperates from the bulb which is a fine white substance, somewhat porus, spungy and moist, and reather tough before it is dressed; the center of the bulb is penitrated with a small tough string or ligament, which passing from the bottom of the stem terminates in the extremity of the radicle, which last is also covered by a prolongation of the rind which invellopes the bulb. The bulb is usually found at the debth of 4 inches and frequently much deeper. This root forms a considerable article of food with the Indians of the Missouri, who for this purpose prepare them in several ways. they are esteemed good at all seasons of the year, but are best from the middle of July to the latter end of Autumn when they are sought and gathered by the provident part of the natives for their winter store. when collected they are striped of their rhind and strung on small throngs or chords and exposed to the sun or placed in the smoke of their fires to dry; when well dryed they will keep for several years, provided they are not permitted to become moist or damp; in this situation they usually pound them between two stones placed on a piece of parchment, untill they reduce it to a fine powder thus prepared they thicken their soope with it; sometimes they also boil these dryed roots with their meat without breaking them; when green they are generally boiled with their meat, sometimes mashing them or otherwise as they think proper. they also prepare an agreeable dish with them by boiling and mashing them and adding the marrow grease of the buffaloe and some buries, until the whole be of the consistency of a haisty pudding. they also eat this root roasted and frequently make hearty meals of it raw without sustaining any inconvenience or injury therefrom. The White or brown bear feed very much on this root, which their tallons assist them to procure very readily. the white apple appears to me to be a tastless insippid food of itself tho I have no doubt but it is a very healthy and moderately nutricious food. I have no doubt but our epicures would admire this root very much, it would serve them in their ragouts and gravies in stead of the truffles morella.

We saw a great number buffaloe, Elk, common and Black taled deer, goats beaver and wolves. Capt C. killed a beaver and a wolf, the party killed 3 beaver and a deer. We can send out at any time and obtain whatever species of meat the country affords in as large quantity as we wish. we saw where an Indian had recently grained, or taken the hair off of a goatskin; we do not wish to see those gentlemen just now as we presume they would most probably be the Assinniboins and might be troublesome to us. Capt C. could not be certain but thought he saw the smoke and some Indian lodges at a considrable distance up Milk river.

[Clark, May 8, 1805] May the 8th Wednesday 1805 a verry black Cloud to the S W. we Set out under a gentle breeze from the N. E. about 8 oClock began to rain, but not Sufficient to wet, we passed the mouth of a large river on the Starboard Side 150 yards wide and appears to be navagable. the Countrey thro which it passes as far as Could be seen from the top of a verry high hill on which I was, a butifull leavil plain this river forks about N W from its mouth 12 or 15 miles one fork runs from the North & the other to the West of N W. the water of this river will justify a belief that it has its Sourse at a considerable distance, and waters a great extent of Countrey- we are willing to believe that this is the River the Minitarres Call the river which Scolds at all others

the Countrey on the Lard. Side is high & broken with much Stone Scattered on the hills, In walking on Shore with the Interpreter & his wife, the Squar Geathered on the Sides of the hills wild Lickerish, & the white apple as called by the angegies and gave me to eat, the Indians of the Missouri make great use of the white apple dressed in different ways- Saw great numbers of Buffalow, Elk, antelope & Deer, also black tale deer beaver & wolves, I killed a beaver which I found on the bank, & a wolf. The party killed 3 Beaver 1 Deer I saw where an Indian had taken the hair off a goat Skin a fiew days past- Camped early on the Lard. Side. The river we passed today we call Milk river from the peculiar whiteness of it's water, which precisely resembles tea with a considerable mixture of milk.

[Lewis, May 9, 1805] Thursday May 9th 1805. Set out at an early hour; the wind being favourable we used our sails and proceeded very well; the country in appearance is much as yester, with this difference that the land appears more fertile particularly of the Lard. hills which are not so stoney and less broken; the timber has also in some measure declined in quantity. today we passed the bed of the most extraordinary river that I ever beheld. it is as wide as the Missouri is at this place or 1/2 a mile wide and not containing a single drop of runing water; some small standing pools being all the water that could be per-ceived. it falls in on the Lard. side. I walked up this river about three miles and ascended an eminence from which I could perceive it many miles; it's course about South for 10 or 12 miles, when it viered around to the E of S. E. as far as I could see. the valley of this river is wide and possesses but a scanty proportion of timber; the hills which border it are not very high nor is the country very broken; it is what may properly be designated a wavy or roling country intersperced with some handsom level plains. the bank are low and abbrupt, seldom more than 6 or eight feet above the level of the bed, yet show but little appearance of being overflown; they are of black or yellow clay or a rich sandy loam. the bed is entirely composed of a light brown sand the particles of which as well as that of the Missoury are remarkably fine. this river I presume must extend back as far as the black hills and probably is the channel through which a great extent of plain country discharge their superfluous waters in the spring season. it had the appearance of having recently discharged it's waters; and from the watermark, it did not appear that it had been more than 2 feet deep at it's greatest hight. This stream (if such it can properly be termed) we called Big dry river. about a mile below this river on the same side a large creek falls in also dry at present. The mineral salts and quarts appear in large quantities in this neighbourhood. the sand of the Missouri from it's mouth to this place has always possessed a mixture of granulated talk or I now think most probably that it is this quarts. Capt C. killed 2 bucks and 2 buffaloe, I also killed one buffaloe which proved to be the best meat, it was in tolerable order; we saved the best of the meat, and from the cow I killed we saved the necessary materials for making what our wrighthand cook Charbono calls the boudin blanc, and immediately set him about preparing them for supper; this white pudding we all esteem one of the greatest delacies of the forrest, it may not be amiss therefore to give it a place. About 6 feet of the lower extremity of the large gut of the Buffaloe is the first mosel that the cook makes love to, this he holds fast at one end with the right hand, while with the forefinger and thumb of the left he gently compresses it, and discharges what he says is not good to eat, but of which in the squel we get a moderate portion; the mustle lying underneath the shoulder blade next to the back, and fillets are next saught, these are needed up very fine with a good portion of kidney suit; to this composition is then added a just proportion of pepper and salt and a small quantity of flour; thus far advanced, our skilfull opporater C-o seizes his recepticle, which has never once touched the water, for that would intirely distroy the regular order of the whole procedure; you will not forget that the side you now see is that covered with a good coat of fat provided the anamal be in good order; the operator sceizes the recepticle I say, and tying it fast at one end turns it inwards and begins now with repeated evolutions of the hand and arm, and a brisk motion of the finger and thumb to put in what he says is bon pour manger; thus by stuffing and compressing he soon distends the recepticle to the utmost limmits of it's power of expansion, and in the course of it's longtudinal progress it drives from the other end of the recepticle a much larger portion of the _____ than was prevously discharged by the finger and thumb of the left hand in a former part of the operation; thus when the sides of the recepticle are skilfully exchanged the outer for the iner, and all is compleatly filled with something good to eat, it is tyed at the other end, but not any cut off, for that would make the pattern too scant; it is then baptised in the missouri with two dips and a flirt, and bobbed into the kettle; from whence after it be well boiled it is taken and fryed with bears oil untill it becomes brown, when it is ready to esswage the pangs of a keen appetite or such as travelers in the wilderness are seldom at a loss for.

we saw a great quantity of game today particularly of Elk and Buffaloe, the latter are now so gentle that the men frequently throw sticks and stones at them in order to drive them out of the way. we also saw this evening emence quantities of timber cut by the beaver which appeared to have been done the preceeding year, in place particularly they had cut all the timber down for three acres in front and on nearly one back from the river and had removed a considerable proportion of it, the timber grew very thick and some of it was as large as a man's body. the river for several days has been as wide as it is generally near it's mouth, tho it is much shallower or I should begin to dispair of ever reaching it's source; it has been crouded today with many sandbars; the water also appears to become clearer, it has changed it's complexin very considerably. I begin to feel extreemly anxious to get in view of the rocky mountains.

I killed four plover this evening of a different species from any I have yet seen; it resembles the grey or whistling plover more than any other of this family of birds; it is about the size of the yellow legged or large grey plover common to the lower part of this river as well as most parts of the Atlantic States where they are sometimes called the Jack curloo; the eye is moderately large, are black with a narrow ring of dark yellowish brown; the head, neck, upper part of the body and coverts of the wings are of a dove coloured brown, which when the bird is at rest is the predominant colour; the brest and belley are of a brownish white; the tail is composed of 12 feathers of 3 Ins. being of equal length, of these the two in the center are black, with traverse bars of yellowish brown; the others are a brownish white. the large feathers of the wings are white tiped with blacked. the beak is black, 21/2 inches in length, slightly tapering, streight of a cilindric form and blontly or roundly pointed; the chaps are of equal length, and nostrils narrow. longitudinal and connected; the feet and legs are smoth and of a greenish brown; has three long toes and a short one on each foot, the long toes are unconnected with a web, and the short one is placed very high up the leg behind, insomuch that it dose not touch the ground when the bird stands erect. the notes of this bird are louder and more various than any other of this family that I have seen.

[Clark, May 9, 1805] May 9th Thursday 1805 a fine Day wind from the East we proceeded on verry well the Countrey much the appearance which it had yesterday the bottom & high land rich black earth, Timber not so abondant as below, we passed the mouth of a river (or the appearance of a river) on the Lard. Side the bend of which as far as we went up it or could See from a high hill is as large as that of the Missouri at this place which is near half a mile this river did not Contain one drop of running water, about a mile below this river a large Creeke joins the river L. S. which is also Dry- Those dry Streams which are also verry wide, I think is the Conveyance of the melted Snow, & heavy rains which is Probable fall in from the high mountanious Countrey which is Said to be between this river & the Yellow Stone river- I walked on Shore the fore part of this day, & observed Great quantities of the Shining Stone which we view as quarts, I killed 2 Bucks & a Buffalow, Capt Lewis also killed one which verry good meat, I saw emuenarable herds of buffalow, & goats to day in every derection- The Missouri keeps its width which is nearly as wide as near its mouth, great number of Sand bars, the water not So muddy & Sand finer & in Smaller perpotion. Capt. Lewis killed 4 pleaver different from any I have ever before Seen, larger & have white breast & the underfeathers of the wings are white &c.

[Lewis, May 9, 1805] May 9th 1805. I killed four plover this evening of a different kind from any I have yet seen. it resembles the grey or whistling plover more than any other of this family of birds, tho it is much larger. it is about the size of the yellow leged plover common to the U States, and called the jack curlooe by some. the legs are of a greenish brown; the toes, three and one high at the heel unconnected with a webb, the breast and belly of a brownish white; the head neck upper part of the body and coverts of the wings are of a dove colured brown which when the bird is at rest is the predomanent colour. the tale has 12 feathers of the same length of which the two in the center are black with transverse bars of yellowish bron, the others are a brownish white. the large feathers of the wings are white tiped with black. the eyes are black with a small ring of dark yellowish brown- the beak is black, 21/2 inches long, cilindrical, streight, and roundly or bluntly pointed. the notes of this bird are louder and more various than of any other species which I have seen.-

[Lewis, May 10, 1805] Friday May 10th 1805. Set out at sunrise and proceeded but a short distance ere the wind became so violent that we were obliged to come too, which we did on the Lard. side in a suddon or short bend of the river where we were in a great measure sheltered from the effects of the wind. the wind continued violent all day, the clouds were thick and black, had a slight sprinkle of rain several times in the course of the day. we sent out several hunters to scower the country, to this we were induced not so much from the want of provision as to discover the Indians whome we had reasons to believe were in the neighbourhood, from the circumstance of one of their dogs comeing to us this morning shortly after we landed; we still beleive ourselves in the country usually hunted by the Assinniboins, and as they are a vicious illy disposed nation we think it best to be on our guard, accordingly we inspected the arms and accoutrements the party and found them all in good order. The hunters returned this evening having seen no tents or Indians nor any fresh sign of them; they killed two Mule deer, one common fallow or longtailed deer, 2 Buffaloe and 5 beaver, and saw several deer of the Mule kind of immence size, and also three of the Bighorned anamals. from the appearance of the Mule deer and the bighorned anamals we beleive ourselves fast approaching a hilly or mountainous country; we have rarely found the mule deer in any except a rough country; they prefer the open grounds and are seldom found in the woodlands near the river; when they are met with in the woodlands or river bottoms and are pursued, they invariably run to the hills or open country as the Elk do. the contrary happens with the common deer ther are several esscential differences between the Mule and common deer as well in form as in habits. they are fully a third larger in general, and the male is particularly large; I think there is somewhat greater disparity of size between the male and female of this speceis than there is between the male and female fallow deer; I am convinced I have seen a buck of this species twice the volume of a buck of any other species. the ears are peculiarly large; I measured those of a large buck which I found to be eleven inches long and 31/2 in width at the widest part; they are not so delicately formed, their hair in winter is thicker longer and of a much darker grey, in summer the hair is still coarser longer and of a paleer red, more like that of the Elk; in winter they also have a considerable quantity of a very fine wool intermixed with the hair and lying next to the skin as the Antelope has. the long hair which grows on the outer sides of the 1st joint of the hinder legs, and which in the common deer do not usually occupy more than 2 inches in them occupys from 6 to eight; their horns also differ, these in the common deer consist of two main beams from which one or more points project the beam graduly deminishing as the points procede from it, with the mule deer the horns consist of two beams which at the distance of 4 or 6 inches from the head divide themselves each into two equal branches which again either divide into two other equal branches or terminate in a smaller, and two equal ones; having either 2 4 or 6 points on a beam; the horn is not so rough about the base as the common deer and are invariably of a much darker colour. the most striking difference of all, is the white rump and tale. from the root of the tail as a center there is a circular spot perfectly white, of abot 3 inches radius, which occupys a part of the rump and extremitys of the buttocks and joins the white of the belley underneath; the tail which is usually from 8 to 9 inches long, for the first 4 or 5 inches from it's upper extremity is covered with short white hairs, much shorter indeed than the hairs of the body; from hence for about one inch further the hair is still white but gradually becomes longer, the tail then terminates in a tissue of black hair of about 3 Inches long. from this black hair of the tail they have obtained among the French engages the appelation of the black taled deer, but this I conceive by no means characteristic of the anamal as much the larger portion of the tail is white. the year and the tail of this anamal when compared with those of the common (leer, so well comported with those of the mule when compared with the horse, that we have by way of distinction adapted the appelation of the mule deer which I think much more appropriate. on the inner corner of each eye there is a drane or large recepicle which seems to answer as a drane to the eye which gives it the appearance of weeping, this in the common deer of the atlantic states is scarcely perceptable but becomes more conspicuous in the fallow deer, and still more so in the Elk; this recepticle in the Elk is larger than in any of the pecora order with which I am acquainted.

Boils and imposthumes have been very common with the party Bratton is now unable to work with one on his hand; soar eyes continue also to be common to all of us in a greater or less degree. for the imposthume I use emmolient poltices, and for soar eyes a solution of white vitriol and the sugar of lead in the proportion of 2 grs. of the former and one of the latter to each ounce of water.

[Clark, May 10, 1805] May the 10th Friday 1805 river fell 3/4 of an inch last night, wind from the N. W, we proceeded on but a short distance e'r'e the wind became So violent we could not proceed came to on the Lard. Side in a Short bend, the wind Continued all day Several times in the course of the day We had some fiew drops of rain from verry black Clouds, no thunder or lightning latterly, Soon after we landed a Dog came to us from the opposit Side, which induced a belief that we had not passd. the Assinniboin Indians, parties wer Sent on the hills in different derections to examine but Saw no tents or fresh Sign. examined the arms &c. of the party found all in good order. Three mule deer, two Buffalow & 5 beaver killed, 3 of the mountain ram Seen.

[Lewis, May 11, 1805] Saturday May 11th 1805. Set out this morning at an early hour, the courant strong; and river very crooked; the banks are falling in very fast; I sometimes wonder that some of our canoes or perogues are not swallowed up by means of these immence masses of earth which are eternally precipitating themselves into the river; we have had many hair breadth escapes from them but providence seems so to have ordered it that we have as yet sustained no loss in consequence of them. The wind blue very hard the forepart of last night but abated toward morning; it again arose in the after part of this day and retarded our progress very much. the high lands are broken, the hills higher and approach nearer the river, tho the soil of both hills and bottoms appear equally as furtile as below; it consists of a black looking tome with a moderate portion of sand; the hills and bluffs to the debth of 20 or thirty feet, seemed to be composed entirely of this loam; when thrown in the water it desolves as readily as loaf sugar and effervesses like marle. great appearance of quarts and mineral salts, the latter appears both on the hills and bottoms, in the bottoms of the gullies which make down from the hills it lies incrusting the earth to the debth of 2 or 3 inches, and may with a fether be swept up and collected in large quantities, I preserved several specimines of this salts. the quarts appears most commonly in the faces of the bluffs. no coal, burnt hills, or pumice stone. saw today some high hills on the Stard. whose summits were covered with pine. Capt Clark went on shore and visited them; he brought with him on his return som of the boughs of this pine it is of the pitch kind but I think the leaves somewhat longer than ours in Virginia. Capt C. also in his walk killed 2 Mule deer a beaver and two buffaloe; these last he killed about 3 miles above where we encamped this evening in the expectation that we would reach that place, but we were unable to do so from the adverse winds and other occurrences, and he came down and joined us about dark. there is a dwarf cedar growing among the pine on the hills; it rises to the hight thre sometimes 4 feet, but most generally spreads itself like a vine along the surface of the earth, which it covers very closely, puting out roots from the underside of the limbs; the leaf is finer and more delicate than the common red ceader, it's fruit and smell are the same with the red ceader. the tops of these hills which produce the pine and cedar is of a different soil from that just described; it is a light coloured poor sterile sandy soil, the base usually a yellow or white clay; it produces scarcely any grass, some scattering tuffts of sedge constitutes the greater part of it's grass. About 5 P.M. my attention was struck by one of the Party runing at a distance towards us and making signs and hollowing as if in distress, I ordered the perogues to put too, and waited untill he arrived; I now found that it was Bratton the man with the soar hand whom I had permitted to walk on shore, he arrived so much out of breath that it was several minutes before he could tell what had happened; at length he informed me that in the woody bottom on the Lard. side about 1 1/2 below us he had shot a brown bear which immediately turned on him and pursued him a considerable distance but he had wounded it so badly that it could not overtake him; I immediately turned out with seven of the party in quest of this monster, we at length found his trale and persued him about a mile by the blood through very thick brush of rosbushes and the large leafed willow; we finally found him concealed in some very thick brush and shot him through the skull with two balls; we proceeded dress him as soon as possible, we found him in good order; it was a monstrous beast, not quite so large as that we killed a few days past but in all other rispects much the same the hair is remarkably long fine and rich tho he appears parshally to have discharged his winter coat; we now found that Bratton had shot him through the center of the lungs, notwithstanding which he had pursued him near half a mile and had returned more than double that distance and with his tallons had prepared himself a bed in the earth of about 2 feet deep and five long and was perfectly alive when we found him which could not have been less than 2 hours after he received the wound; these bear being so hard to die reather intimedates us all; I must confess that I do not like the gentlemen and had reather fight two Indians than one bear; there is no other chance to conquer them by a single shot but by shooting them through the brains, and this becomes difficult in consequence of two large muscles which cover the sides of the forehead and the sharp projection of the center of the frontal bone, which is also of a pretty good thickness. the flece and skin were as much as two men could possibly carry. by the time we returned the sun had set and I determined to remain here all night, and directed the cooks to render the bear's oil and put it in the kegs which was done. there was about eight gallons of it.

the wild Hysop grows here and in all the country through which we have passed for many days past; tho from big Dry river to this place it has been more abundant than below, and a smaller variety of it grows on the hills, the leaves of which differ considerably being more deeply indented near it's extremity. the buffaloe deer and Elk feed on this herb in the winter season as they do also on the small willow of the sandbars. there is another growth that begins now to make it's appearance in the bottom lands and is becoming extreemly troublesome; it is a shrub which rises to the hight of from two to four feet, much branched, the bark of the trunk somewhat rough hard and of light grey colour; the wood is firm and stif, the branches beset with a great number of long, shap, strong, wooddy looking thorns; the leaf is about 3/4 or an inch long, and one 1/8 of an inch wide, it is obtuse, absolutely entire, veinless fleshy and gibbose; has no perceptable taste or smell, and no anamal appears to eat it. by way of designating when I mention it hereafter I shall call it the fleshey leafed thorn

[Clark, May 11, 1805] May the 11th Satturday 1805. Wind hard fore part of last night the latter part verry Cold a white frost this morning, the river riseing a little and verry Crooked the high land is rugged and approaches nearer than below, the hills and bluff exhibit more mineral quats & Salts than below, the gullies in maney places are white, and their bottoms one, two & 3 Inches deep of this mineral, no appearance of either burnt pumice Stone or Coal, the Countrey hilley on both Sides of a rich black earth, which disolves This kind of Countrey Continues of the Same quallity for maney miles on either Side, we observed Some hills which appeared to be timbered, I walked to this timber and found it to pitch pine & Dwarf Cedar, we observe in every derection Buffalow, Elk, Antelopes & Mule deer inumerable and So jintle that we Could approach near them with great ease, I killed 2 Mule Deer for the benifit of their Skins for the party, and about the place I expected the party would get to Camp I killed 2 fat Bulls for theire use, in my absence they had killed a fine fat Yellow bear below which detained them and they did not reach the place I expected, but had Camped on the Lard. Side about 2 miles below on my return to the party I killed a fat Beaver the wind blew verry hard from the S. W. all the after part of this day which retarded our progress verry much. river rose 2 In

[Lewis, May 12, 1805] Sunday May 12th 1805. Set out at an early hour, the weather clear and Calm; I walked on shore this morning for the benifit of exersize which I much wanted, and also to examine the country and it's productions, in these excurtions I most generally went alone armed with my rifle and espontoon; thus equiped I feel myself more than an equal match for a brown bear provided I get him in open woods or near the water, but feel myself a little diffident with respect to an attack in the open plains, I have therefore come to a resolution to act on the defencive only, should I meet these gentlemen in the open country. I ascended the hills and had a view of a rough and broken country on both sides of the river; on the North side the summits of the hills exhibit some scattering pine and cedar, on the South side the pine has not yet commenced tho there is some cedar on the face of the hills and in the little ravines. the choke cherry also grows here in the hollows and at the heads of the gullies; the choke Cherry has been in blume since the ninth inst. this growth has freequently made it's appearance on the Missouri from the neighbourhood of the Baldpated Prarie, to this place in the form of it's leaf colour and appearance of it's bark, and general figure of it's growth it resembles much the Morillar cherry,1 tho much smaller not generally rising to a greater hight than from 6 to 10 feet and ascociating in thick clusters or clumps in their favorit situations which is usually the heads of small ravines or along the sides of small brooks which flow from the hills. the flowers which are small and white are supported by a common footstalk as those of the common wild cherry are, the corolla consists of five oval petals, five stamen and one pistillum, and of course of the Class and order Pentandria Monogynia. it bears a fruit which much resembles the wild cherry in form and colour tho larger and better flavoured; it's fruit ripens about the begining of July and continues on the trees untill the latter end of September- The Indians of the Missouri make great uce of this cherry which they prepare for food in various ways, sometimes eating when first plucked from the trees or in that state pounding them mashing the seed boiling them with roots or meat, or with the prarie beans and white-apple; again for their winter store they geather them and lay them on skins to dry in the sun, and frequently pound them and make them up in small roles or cakes and dry them in the sun; when thus dryed they fold them in skins or put them in bags of parchment and keep them through the winter either eating them in this state or boiling them as before mentioned. the bear and many birds also feed on these burries. the wild hysop sage, fleshey leaf thorn, and some other herbs also grow in the plains and hills, particularly the arromatic herb on which the Antelope and large hare feed. The soil has now changed it's texture considerably; the base of the hills and river bottoms continue the same and are composed of a rich black loam while the summits of the hills and about half their hight downwards are of a light brown colour, poor sterile and intermixed with a coarse white sand. about 12 OClock the wind veered about to the N. W. and blew so hard that we were obliged to Ly by the ballance of the day. we saw great quantities of game as usual. the bottom lands still becomeing narrower.

About sunset it began to rain, and continued to fall a few drops at a time untill midnight; the wind blew violently all night.

[Clark, May 12, 1805] May 12th Sunday 1805. Set out at an early hour, the morning Clear and Calm, Capt. Lewis walked on Shore this morning about 12 oClock the wind becam Strong from the E. about half past one oClock the wind Shifted round to the N. W. and blew verry hard all the latter part of the day, which obliged us to Lay by- The Countrey is hilley & rugged and the earth of a lightish brown and but indifferent, Some Small Cedar is Scattered on the Sides of the hils & in the hollars, Some pine ridges is also to be Seen on the North Side, we observe great quantites of game as usual. I killed a beaver in the water, Saw Several Sitting on the bank near the waters edge about Sunset it began to rain, and rained very moderately only a fiew drops at a time for about half the night, wind Continued violent all night

[Lewis, May 13, 1805] Monday May 13th 1805. The wind continued to blow so violently this morning that we did not think it prudent to set out. sent out some hunters. At 1 P.M. the wind abated, and altho the hunters had not all returned we set out; the courant reather stronger than usual and the water continues to become reather clearer, from both which I anticipate a change of Country shortly. the country much the same as yesterday; but little timber in the bottoms and a scant proportion of pine an cedar crown the Stard. hills. Capt C. who was on shore the greater part of the day killed a mule and a Common deer, the party killed several deer and some Elk principally for the benefit of their skins which are necessary to them for cloathing, the Elk skins I now begin to reserve for making the leather boat at the falls. the hunters joined us this evening; Gibson had wounded a very large brown bear but it was too late in the evening to pursue him.

[Clark, May 13, 1805] 13th of May Monday 1805 The wind Continued to blow hard untill one oClock P M. to day at which time it fell a little and we Set out and proceeded on verry well about 9 miles and Camped on the Lard Side. the countrey much the Same appearance as yesterday but little timber in the bottoms; Some Pine in places on the Stard. Hills. I killed two deer this evening one a mule deer & the other a common Deer, the party killed Several this morning all for the use of their Skins which are now good, one man Gibson wounded a verry large brown bear, too late this evening to prosue him- We passed two Creeks in a bend to the Lard Side neither them had any water, are somewhat wider; passed some high black bluffs. saw immence herds of buffaloe today also Elk deer wolves and Antelopes. passed three large creeks one on the Stard. and two others on the Lard. side, neither of which had any runing water. Capt Clark walked on shore and killed a very fine buffaloe cow. I felt an inclination to eat some veal and walked on shore and killed a very fine buffaloe calf and a large woolf, much the whitest I had seen, it was quite as white as the wool of the common sheep. one of the party wounded a brown bear very badly, but being alone did not think proper to pursue him. In the evening the men in two of the rear canoes discovered a large brown bear lying in the open grounds about 300 paces from the river, and six of them went out to attack him, all good hunters; they took the advantage of a small eminence which concealed them and got within 40 paces of him unperceived, two of them reserved their fires as had been previously conscerted, the four others fired nearly at the same time and put each his bullet through him, two of the balls passed through the bulk of both lobes of his lungs, in an instant this monster ran at them with open mouth, the two who had reserved their fires discharged their pieces at him as he came towards them, boath of them struck him, one only slightly and the other fortunately broke his shoulder, this however only retarded his motion for a moment only, the men unable to reload their guns took to flight, the bear pursued and had very nearly overtaken them before they reached the river; two of the party betook themselves to a canoe and the others seperated an concealed themselves among the willows, reloaded their pieces, each discharged his piece at him as they had an opportunity they struck him several times again but the guns served only to direct the bear to them, in this manner he pursued two of them seperately so close that they were obliged to throw aside their guns and pouches and throw themselves into the river altho the bank was nearly twenty feet perpendicular; so enraged was this anamal that he plunged into the river only a few feet behind the second man he had compelled take refuge in the water, when one of those who still remained on shore shot him through the head and finally killed him; they then took him on shore and butched him when they found eight balls had passed through him in different directions; the bear being old the flesh was indifferent, they therefore only took the skin and fleece, the latter made us several gallons of oil; it was after the sun had set before these men come up with us, where we had been halted by an occurrence, which I have now to recappitulate, and which altho happily passed without ruinous injury, I cannot recollect but with the utmost trepidation and horror; this is the upseting and narrow escape of the white perogue It happened unfortunately for us this evening that Charbono was at the helm of this Perogue, in stead of Drewyer, who had previously steered her; Charbono cannot swim and is perhaps the most timid waterman in the world; perhaps it was equally unluckey that Capt. C. and myself were both on shore at that moment, a circumstance which rarely happened; and tho we were on the shore opposite to the perogue, were too far distant to be heard or to do more than remain spectators of her fate; in this perogue _____ were embarked, our papers, Instruments, books medicine, a great part of our merchandize and in short almost every article indispensibly necessary to further the views, or insure the success of the enterprize in which we are now launched to the distance of 2200 miles. surfice it to say, that the Perogue was under sail when a sudon squawl of wind struck her obliquely, and turned her considerably, the steersman allarmed, in stead of puting her before the wind, lufted her up into it, the wind was so violent that it drew the brace of the squarsail out of the hand of the man who was attending it, and instantly upset the perogue and would have turned her completely topsaturva, had it not have been from the resistance mad by the oarning against the water; in this situation Capt. C and myself both fired our guns to attract the attention if possible of the crew and ordered the halyards to be cut and the sail hawled in, but they did not hear us; such was their confusion and consternation at this moment, that they suffered the perogue to lye on her side for half a minute before they took the sail in, the perogue then wrighted but had filled within an inch of the gunwals; Charbono still crying to his god for mercy, had not yet recollected the rudder, nor could the repeated orders of the Bowsman, Cruzat, bring him to his recollection untill he threatend to shoot him instantly if he did not take hold of the rudder and do his duty, the waves by this time were runing very high, but the fortitude resolution and good conduct of Cruzat saved her; he ordered 2 of the men to throw out the water with some kettles that fortunately were convenient, while himself and two others rowed her ashore, where she arrived scarcely above the water; we now took every article out of her and lay them to drane as well as we could for the evening, baled out the canoe and secured her; there were two other men beside Charbono on board who could not swim, and who of course must also have perished had the perogue gone to the bottom. while the perogue lay on her side, finding I could not be heard, I for a moment forgot my own situation, and involluntarily droped my gun, threw aside my shot pouch and was in the act of unbuttoning my coat, before I recollected the folly of the attempt I was about to make, which was to throw myself into the river and indevour to swim to the perogue; the perogue was three hundred yards distant the waves so high that a perogue could scarcely live in any situation, the water excessively could, and the stream rappid; had I undertaken this project therefore, there was a hundred to one but what I should have paid the forfit of my life for the madness of my project, but this had the perogue been lost, I should have valued but little.- After having all matters arranged for the evening as well as the nature of circumstances would permit, we thought it a proper occasion to console ourselves and cheer the sperits of our men and accordingly took a drink of grog and gave each man a gill of sperits.

[Clark, May 14, 1805] 14th of May Tuesday 1805 A verry Clear Cold morning a white frost & some fog on the river the Thermomtr Stood at 32 above 0, wind from the S. W. we proceeded on verry well untill about 6 oClock a Squawl of wind Struck our Sale broad Side and turned the perogue nearly over, and in this Situation the Perogue remained untill the Sale was Cut down in which time She nearly filed with water- the articles which floated out was nearly all caught by the Squar who was in the rear. This accident had like to have cost us deerly; for in this perogue were embarked our papers, Instruments, books, medicine, a great proportion of our merchandize, and in short almost every article indispensibly necessary to further the views, or insure the success of the enterprize in which, we are now launched to the distance of 2,200 miles. it happened unfortunately that Capt. Lewis and myself were both on shore at the time of this occurrence, a circumstance which seldom took place; and tho we were on the shore opposit to the perogue were too far distant to be heard or do more than remain spectators of her fate; we discharged our guns with the hope of attracting the attention of the crew and ordered the sail to be taken in but such was their consternation and confusion at the instant that they did not hear us. when however they at length took in the sail and the perogue wrighted; the bowsman Cruzatte by repeated threats so far brought Charbono the Sternman to his recollection that he did his duty while two hands bailed the perogue and Cruzatte and two others rowed her on shore were she arrived scarcely above the water. we owe the preservation of the perogue to the resolution and fortitude of Cruzatte

The Countrey like that of yesterday, passed a Small Island and the enterence of 3 large Creeks, one on the Stard. & the other 2 on the Lard Side, neither of them had any running water at this time- Six good hunters of the party fired at a Brown or Yellow Bear Several times before they killed him, & indeed he had like to have defeated the whole party, he pursued them Seperately as they fired on him, and was near Catching Several of them one he pursued into the river, this bear was large & fat would way about 500 wt; I killed a Buffalow, & Capt. Lewis a Calf & a wolf this evening.

[Lewis, May 15, 1805] Wednesday May 15th as soon as a slight shower of rain passed over this morning, we spread the articles to dry which had got wet yesterday in the white perogue; tho the day proved so cloudy and damp that they received but little benifit from the sun or air; we were enabled to put them in such a state as to prevent their sustaining further injury. our hunters killed several deer, and saw three bear one of which they wounded.

[Clark, May 15, 1805] May 15th Wednesday 1805 Our medisons, Instruments, merchandize, Clothes, provisions &c. &c. which was nearly all wet we had put out to air and dry. the day being Cloudy & rainey those articles dried but little to-day- our hunters killed Several deer &c. and Saw three Bear one of which they wounded &c.

We see Buffalow on the banks dead, others floating down dead, and others mired every day, those buffalow either drown in Swiming the river or brake thro the ice

[Lewis, May 16, 1805] Thursday May 16th The morning was fair and the day proved favorable to our operations; by 4 oClock in the evening our Instruments, Medicine, merchandize provision &c, were perfectly dryed, repacked and put on board the perogue. the loss we sustained was not so great as we had at first apprehended; our medicine sustained the greatest injury, several articles of which were intirely spoiled, and many others considerably injured; the ballance of our losses consisted of some gardin seeds, a small quantity of gunpowder, and a few culinary articles which fell overboard and sunk, the Indian woman to whom I ascribe equal fortitude and resolution, with any person onboard at the time of the accedent, caught and preserved most of the light articles which were washed overboard all matters being now arranged for our departure we lost no time in seting out; proceeced on tolerably well about seven miles and encamped on the Stard. side. in the early part of the day two of our men fired on a panther, a little below our encampment, and wounded it; they informed us that it was very large, had just killed a deer partly devoured it, and in the act of concealing the ballance as they discovered him. we caught two Antelopes at our encampment in attempting to swim the river; these anamals are but lean as yet, and of course not very pleasant food. I walked on shore this evening and killed a buffaloe cow and calf, we found the calf most excellent veal. the country on either side of the river is broken and hills much higher than usual, the bottoms now become narrow and the timber more scant; some scattering pine and cedar on the steep declivities of the hills.- this morning a white bear toar Labuiche's coat which he had left in the plains.

[Clark, May 16, 1805] May 16th Thursday 1805 a fair morning our articles all out to Dry at 4 oClock we had every thing that was Saved dry and on bord, our loss is Some medison, Powder, Seeds, & Several articles which Sunk, and maney Spoiled had a medn. altitude which gave for Latd. °' _" N.- two of our men fired at a pant hr a little below our Camp, this animale they say was large, had Caught a Deer & eate it half & buried the ballance. a fiew antilope Swam the river near our Camp two of them were Cought by the party in the river. at half past 4 oClock we Set out and proceeded on verry well _____ miles and incamped on the Std. Side the Countrey as before hilley & broken verry Small proprotion of timber in the points, Some little pine & Ceader in the hills

Buffalow & Deer is yet plenty on the river in the small timbered bottoms Capt Lewis walked out on the Std. Side and killed a Cow & Calf the calf was verry fine their bases. it is somewhat singular that the lower part of these hills appear to be formed of a dark rich loam while the upper region about 150 feet is formed of a whiteish brown sand, so hard in many parts as to resemble stone; but little rock or stone of any kind to be seen in these hills. the river is much narrower than usual, the bed from 200 to 300 yards only and possessing a much larger proportion of gravel than usual. a few scattering cottonwood trees are the only timber near the river; the sandbars, and with them the willow points have almost entirely disappeared. greater appearance than usual of the saline incrustations of the banks and river hills. we passed two creeks the one on Stard. side, and the other just below our camp on the Lard. side; each of these creeks afford a small quantity of runing water, of a brackish tast. the great number of large beds of streams perfectly dry which we daily pass indicate a country but badly watered, which I fear is the case with the country through which we have been passing for the last fifteen or twenty days. Capt Clark walked on shore this evening and killed an Elk; buffaloe are not so abundant as they were some days past. the party with me killed a female brown bear, she was but meagre, and appeared to have suckled young very recently. Capt. Clark narrowly escaped being bitten by a rattlesnake in the course of his walk, the party killed one this evening at our encampment, which he informed me was similar to that he had seen; this snake is smaller than those common to the middle Atlantic States, being about 2 feet 6 inches long; it is of a yellowish brown colour on the back and sides, variagated with one row of oval spots of a dark brown colour lying transversely over the back from the neck to the tail, and two other rows of small circular spots of the same colour which garnis the sides along the edge of the scuta. it's bely contains 176 scuta on the belly and 17 on the tale. Capt Clark informed me that he saw some coal which had been brought down by the water of the last creek we passed; this creek also throws out considerable quantities of Driftwood, though there is no timber on it which can be perceived from the Missouri; we called this stream rattlesnake creek. Capt Clark saw an Indian fortifyed camp this evening, which appeared to have been recently occupyed, from which we concluded it was probable that it had been formed by a war party of the Menetares who left their vilage in March last with a view to attack the blackfoot Indians in consequence of their having killed some of their principal warriors the previous autumn. we were roused late at night by the Sergt. of the guard, and warned of the danger we were in from a large tree that had taken fire and which leant immediately over our lodge. we had the loge removed, and a few minutes after a large proportion of the top of the tree fell on the place the lodge had stood; had we been a few minutes later we should have been crushed to attoms. the wind blew so hard, that notwithstanding the lodge was fifty paces distant from the fire it sustained considerable injury from the burning coals which were thrown on it; the party were much harrassed also by this fire which communicated to a collection of fallen timber, and could not be extinguished.

[Clark, May 17, 1805] May 17th Friday 1805 a fine morning wind from the N W. mercury at 60° a 0. river falling a little. we Set out at an early hour and proceeded on verry well by the assistance of the Toe rope principally, the Countrey verry rugged & hills high and the river washing the base on each Side, Great appearance of the Salt Substance. a fiew Cotton trees is the only timber which is Scattered in the bottoms & the hills contain a fiew Pine & Cedar, which is Scattered. river much narrower than below from 2 to 300 yards wide, the bottoms muddey & hills rich earth except near their topes- We passed 2 large Creeks to day one on the Starbd Side and the other just below our camp on the Lard. Side each of those creeks has a little running water near their mouthes which has a brackish taste, I was nearly treading on a Small fierce rattle Snake different from any I had ever Seen &c. one man the party killed another of the Same kind. I walked on Shore after dinner & killed an Elk- the party in my absence Killed a female Brown or yellow Bear which was meagre the appearances of the Hills & Countrey is as before mentioned except a greater appearance of the white appearance of Salts or tarter and Some Coal which has been thrown out by the floods in the last Creek- Buffalow & Deer is not plenty to day, Elk is yet to be Seen in abundance we Camped in the upper part of a Small timbered bottom on the Lard. Side in which I Saw a fortified Indian Camp, which I Suppose is one of the Camps of a Mi ne tar re war party of about 15 men, that Set out from their village in March last to war against the Blackfoot Indians.

we were roused late at night and warned of the danger of fire from a tree which had Cought and leaned over our Lodge, we had the lodge moved Soon after the Dry limbs & top of the tree fell in the place the Lodge Stood, the wind blew hard and the dry wood Cought & fire flew in every direction, burnt our Lodge verry much from the Coals which fell on it altho at Some distance in the plain, the whole party was much disturbed by this fire which could not be extinguished &c

[Lewis, May 18, 1805] Saturday May 18th 1805. The wind blew hard this morning from the West. we were enabled to employ our toe line the greater part of the day and therefore proceeded on tolerably well. there are now but few sandbars, the river is narrow and current gentle. the timber consists of a few cottonwood trees along the verge of the river; the willow has in a great measure disappeared. in the latter part of the day the hills widened, the bottoms became larger, and contained more timber. we passed a creek on the Stard. side about three oclock, which afforded no water; came too and encamped on the Lard. side opposite to the lower point of a small Island, two miles short of the extremity of the last course of this day. Capt Clark in the course of his walk this evening killed four deer, two of which were the black tailed or mule deer; the skins are now good, they have not yet produced their young.- we saw a number of buffaloe, Elk, deer and Antelopes.- the saline substance frequently mentioned continues to appear as usual.-

[Clark, May 18, 1805] May 18th Satturday 1805 A windey morning wind from the West we proceeded on verry well with the assistance of the Toe Coard, river narrow but flew Sand bars, & current jentle, but a few Cotton Trees Contained in the bottoms willow is not common on the bears as usial Some little on the Sides of the river is yet to be Seen, the after part of the day was Cloudy & at about 12 oClock it began to rain and continued moderately for about 11/2 hours, not Sufficient to wet a man thro his clothes; this is the first rain Since we Set out this Spring The hills widen and the bottoms Contain more timber than for Several days past, we passed a Wisers Creek on the Std. Side about 3 oClock and Camped on the Lard Side opposit the lower point of a handsom little Island near the middle of the river. I walked on Shore and killed four Deer, 2 common & 2 mule deer, one of which had 3 fauns, 2 others had 2 each, those deer are fat, & their Skins tolerable good, which are now in demand with us for clothes Such as Legins & Mockersons, I Saw great numbers of Buffalows & Elk; Some of the party Shoot & Catch beaver every day & night

[Lewis, May 19, 1805] Sunday May 19th 1805. The last night was disagreeably could; we were unable to set out untill 8 oclock A.M. in consequence of a heavy fogg, which obscured the river in such a manner that we could not see our way; this is the first we have experienced in any thing like so great a degree; there was also a fall of due last evening, which is the second we have experienced since we have entered this extensive open country. at eight we set out and proceeded as yesterday by means of the cord principally, the hills are high and the country similar to that of yesterday. Capt Clark walked on shore with two of the hunters and killed a brown bear; notwithstanding that it was shot through the heart it ran at it's usual pace near a quarter of a mile before it fell. one of the party wounded a beaver, and my dog as usual swam in to catch it; the beaver bit him through the hind leg and cut the artery; it was with great difficulty that I could stop the blood; I fear it will yet prove fatal to him. on Capt. Clark's return he informed me that he had from the top of one of the adjacent hights discovered the entrance of a large stream which discharged itself into the Missouri on the Lard. side distant 6 or seven miles; from the same place he also saw a range of Mountains, bearing W. distant 40 or 50 miles; they appeared to proceed in a S. S. W. direction; the N. N. E. extremity of these mountains appeared abrupt.

This afternoon the river was croked, rappid and containing more sawyers than we have seen in the same space since we left the entrance of the river Platte. Capt. C. in the course of his walk killed three deer and a beaver, I also walked on shore this evening a few miles and killed an Elk, a buck, and a beaver. the party killed and caught 4 other beaver & 3 deer.

The men complain much of sore eyes and imposthumes.

[Clark, May 19, 1805] May 19th Sunday 1805 a verry cold night, the murckery Stood at 38 at 8 oClock this morning, a heavy dew which is the 2d I have Seen this Spring. The fog (which was the first) was So thick this morning that we could not Set out untill the Sun was about 2 hours up, at which time a Small breeze Sprung up from the E. which Cleared off the fog & we proceeded on by means of the Cord The hills are high & rugged the

Countrey as yesterday- I walked on Shore with two men we killed a white or grey bear; not withstanding that it was Shot through the heart it ran at it's usial pace near a quarter of a mile before it fell. Capt Lewis's dog was badly bitten by a wounded beaver and was near bleading to death-. after killing the Bear I continued my walk alone, & killed 3 Deer & a Beaver; finding that the Perogues were below I assended the highest hill I could See, from the top of which I Saw the mouth of M. Shell R & the meanderings of the Missouri for a long distance. I also Saw a high mountain in a westerley direction, bearing S. S W. about 40 or 50 miles distant, in the evening the river was verry Crooked and much more rapid & Containing more Sawyers than any which we have passed above the River Platte Capt Lewis walked on Shore this after noon & killed an Elk, Buck & a Beaver, I kiled three Deer at dinner, the hunters killed three other Deer to day Several beaver also killed. We Camped on the Stard Side in a bottom of Small Cotton wood

[Lewis, May 20, 1805] Monday May 20th 1805 Set out at an early hour as usual, the banks being favourable and water strong we employed the toe rope principally; river narrow and croked; country much as that of yesterday; immence number of the prickley pears in the plains and on the hills. At the distance of 21/4 miles passed the entrance of a large Creek, affording but little water; this stream we named Blowing Fly Creek, from the immence quantities of those insects found in this neighbourhood, they infest our meat while roasting or boiling, and we are obliged to brush them off our provision as we eat. At 11 A.M. we arrived at the entrance of a handsome bold river which discharges itself into the Missouri on the Lard. side; this stream we take to be that called by the Minnetares the _____ or Muscleshell River; if it be the same, of which I entertain but little doubt, it takes it's rise, by their information in the 1st Chain of the Rocky Mountains at no great distance from the Yellow stone river, from whence in it's course to this place it passes through a high and broken country pretty well timbered, particularly on it's borders, and intersperced with handsome fertile plains and medows. but from the circumstance of the same Indians informing us that we should find a well timbered country in the neighbourhood of it's mouth, I am induced to beleive that the timbered country of which they speak is similar to that we have passed for a day or two, or that in our view above, which consists of nothing more than a few scattering small scrubby pine and dwarf cedar on the summits of some of the highest hills nine tenths of the country being wholy destitute of timber of any kind, covered with a short grass, arromatic herbs and the prickley pear; the river bottom however, so far as we have explored it or 8 m. are well stocked with Cottonwood timber of tollerable size, & lands of excellent quality. We halted at thentrance of the river on the point formed by it's junction with the Missouri determining to spend the day, make the necessary observations and send out some hunters to explore the country. The Muscle Shell river falls into the Missouri 2270 miles above it's mouth, and is 110 yards in width, it affords much more water than streams of it's width generally do below, it's courant is by no means rappid, and from appearances it might be navigated with canoes a considerable distance; it's bed is coarse sand and gravel principally with an occasion mixture of black mud; it's banks abbrupt and about 12 feet high yet never appear to overflow; the waters of this river is of a greenish yellow cast, much more transparent than the Missouri, which last is also much more transparent than below but still retains it's whiteish hue and a proportion of it's sedement. the Missouri opposite to this point is deep, gentle in it's courant, and 222 yards in width. The hunters returned this evening and informed us that the country continued much the same in appearance as that we saw where we were or broken, and that about five miles abe the mouth of shell river a handsome river of about fifty yards in width discharged itself into the shell river on the Stard. or upper side; this stream we called Sah-ca-gar me-ah or bird woman's River, after our interpreter the Snake woman. Shields also found a bould spring or fountain issuing from the foot of the Lard. hills about 4 miles up the Missouri; a fountain in this plain country is a great novelty; I have not seen a bould fountain of pure water except one since I left the Mandans; there a number of small ones but all without exception are impregnated with the salts which abound in this country, and with which I believe the Missoury itself considerably impregnated but to us in the habit of useing it not perceptible; the exception I make is a very fine fountain under the bluffs on the Lard. side of the Missouri and at a distance from the river about five miles below the entrance of the yellowstone River. The sands of the Missouri are not so abundant as they have been for some time past, being confined to the points only; the bed of the river principally mud and still too deep to use the seting pole. Capt. Clark walked out today and killed two deer and an Elk, the hunters killed 4 deer and elk and a buffaloe. I saw two large Owls with remarkable long feathers on the sides of the head which resembled ears; I take them to be the large hooting owl tho they are somewhat larger and their colours brighter than those common to the J States.-

[Clark, May 20, 1805] May 20th Monday 1805 a fine morning wind from the N E. river falling a little We Set out at 7 oClock and proceeded on verry well as usial by the assistance of the Cord passed Some verry Swift water, river narrow and Crooked, at 11 oClock arrived at the mouth of Shell river on the Lard Side and formed a Camp for the present. haveing passed a large Creek about 4 miles below on the Ld Side which we call Blowing fly Creek from the emence quantites of those insects which geather on our meat in Such numbers that we are oblige to brush them off what we eate.

muscle Shell River falls in on Lard Side 2270 miles up Contains a greater perportion of water than Rivers of its Size below, I measured it and find it to be 110 yards wide, the water of a Greenish yellow Colour, and appers to be navagable for Small Craft, The Minetarras inform us that this river heads in the 1st of the rockey Mountains & passes through a broken Countrey. its head at no great distance from the Yellow Stone River The Countrey about this river as described yesterday we took the Meredian altitude 59° 50' 0" back observation and found the Latd. to be 47° 0' 24"

The Missouri at the mouth of Shell River is 222 yards wide with a Smoth Current the Missouri water is not So muddey as below, but retains nearly its usial Cholour, and the Sands principally Confined to the points I killed two Deer & an Elk, the hunters killed an Elk & Several deer mearly for their Skins to make Leagins,- Sent men out in every derection, the Countrey generally verry broken Some leavel plains up the Shell river The bottoms of the Shell river is well timbered as also a Small river which falls into that river on the upper Side 5 miles above its mouth. The hills on the Lard. Contain Scattering Pine & Cedar.

[Lewis, May 21, 1805] Tuesday May 21st 1805 A delightfull morning set out at an early hour and proceeded on very well, imployed the chord principally; the shores are abbrupt and bould and composed of a black and yellow clay; see no extensive collection of pure sand, the bars are composed black mud and a small poportion of fine sand; the courant still pretty strong. the Missouri in it's course downward makes a suddon and extensive bend to receive the Muscle shell river, the point of country thus formed tho high is still much lower than that surrounding it, thus forming a valley of wavey of country which extends itself for a great distance in a Northerley direction; the soil is fertile, produces a fine turf of low grass and some herbs, also immence quantities of the Prickley pear, without a stick of timber of any discription. the country on the South side is high broken and crowned with some scrubby pines and dwarf cedar; the leaf of this pine is much longer than the common pitch or red pine of Virginia, the cone is also longer and slimer, and the imbrications wider and thicker, and the whole frequently covered with rosin. Mineral appearances as usual. the growse or praire hen are now less abundant on the river than they were below; perhaps they betake themselves to the open plains at a distance from the river at this season.-

The wind which was moderate all the fore part of the day continued to encrease in the evening, and about dark veered about to N. W. and blew a storm all night, in short we found ourselves so invelloped with clouds of dust and sand that we could neither cook, eat, nor sleep; and were finally compelled to remove our lodge about eight oClock at night to the foot of an adjacent hill where we were covered in some measure from the wind by the hills. several loose articles blown over board and lost. our first station was on a bar on Stard. opposite the lower point of a small Island, which we now called windy Island. the bends of the river are short and suddon, the points covered with some cottonwood, larger willow, or broadleafed willow with an abundance of the wild rose and some small honeysuckle bushes constitute the undergrowth, the redwood is also found in small quantities. Capt. C walked on shore today and killed 2 Elk; the party killed several deer and a buffaloe Cow.-

[Clark, May 21, 1805] May 21st Tuesday 1805. a butifull morning, wind from the West, river falling a little, we Set out at an early hour and proceed on in the usial way by the assistance of the Coard principally, but little use of the Oares & less with the poles as the bottoms are muddey, we Se no great bodies of pure Sand the bars & points are rich mud mixed with fine Sand. I walked on Shore Stard. Side the river makes a great bend to the South to receve Shell River, the boint for many miles out in a Northerley direction is a rich uneaven valley Contain Some Short grass, and Prickley pears without timber The Countrey on the South Side of the Missouri is high, Soil and mineral appearance as usial, more Scattering pine & Cedar on the hills, the wind which blew moderatly all the foreparty of the day increassd and about Dark Shifted to the N W. and Stormed all night, Several loose articles were blown over board, our lodge & Camp which was on a Sand bar on the Std. Side & opposite to the lower point of an Island we were obliged to move under the hills, the dust & Sand blew in clouds. The bends of the river are Short and points Covered with Cotton wood under groth wild rose bushes I killed 2 Elk to day Several Deer Killd. & a Buffalow Cow.

[Lewis, May 22, 1805] Wednesday May 22cd 1805. The wind blew so violently this morning that we did not think it prudent to set out untill it had in some measure abated; this did not happen untill 10 A.M. when we proceeded principally by the toe lines the bottoms somewhat wider than usual, the lands fertile or apparently so tho the short grass and the scantey proportion of it on the hills would indicate no great fertility. passed Windy Island on Lard. at 1 M. 5 1/2 miles above passed a large Island in a bend on Stard. side, and three miles further on the same side passed the entrance of grows Creek 20 yds wide, affords but little water. this creek we named from seeing a number of the pointed tail praire hen near it's mouth, these are the fist we have seen in such numbers for some days. I walked on shore this morning the country is not so broken as yesterday tho still high and roling or wavy; the hills on Lard. side possess more pine than usual; some also on the Stard. hills. Salts and other mineral appearances as usual. the river continues about the same width or from 200 to 250 yds. wide, fewer sandbars and the courant more gentle and regular; game not so abundant as below the Muscle Shell river. I killed a deer in the course of my walk today. Capt. C. also walked out this evening and took a view of the country from a conspicuous point and found it the same as has been discribed. we have caught but few fish since we left the Mandans, they do not bite freely, what we took were the white cat of 2 to 5 lbs. I presume that fish are scarce in this part of the river. We encamped earlyer this evening than usual in order render the oil of a bear which we killed. I do not believe that the Black bear common to the lower part of this river and the Atlantic States, exists in this quarter; we have neither seen one of them nor their tracks which would be easily distinguished by it's shortness of tallons when compared with the brown grizly or white bear. I believe that it is the same species or family of bears which assumes all those colours at different ages and seasons of the year.

[Clark, May 22, 1805] May 22nd Wednesday 1805 The wind Continued to blow So violently hard we did not think it prudent to Set out untill it luled a little, about 10 oClock we Set out the morning Cold, passed a Small Island in the bend to the Lard Side, & proceeded on at 5 miles higher passed a Island in a bend to the Stard Side, and a Creek a Short distance above on the Stard Side 20 yds. w Capt Lewis walked out before dinner & Killed a Deer, I walked out after dinner and assended & but a few miles to view the Countrey, which I found roleing & of a verry rich Stickey Soil produceing but little vegitation of any kind except the prickley-piar, but little grass & that verry low. a great deal of Scattering Pine on the Lard Side & Some fur on the Stard. Sd. The mineral productions as described in the proceeding days, game not So abundant as below, the river Continue about the Same width, fewer Sand bars & current more regular, river falls about an inch a day We camped on the Stard. Side, earlier than we intend on account of Saveing the oil of a bear which the party killed late this afternoon.

Maney of the Creeks which appear to have no water near ther mouths have
Streams of running water higher up which rise & waste in the Sand or
gravel. the water of those Creeks are So much impregnated with the Salt
Substance that it cannot be Drank with pleasure.

[Lewis, May 23, 1805] Thursday May 23rd 1805. Set out early this morning, the frost was severe last night, the ice appeared along the edge of the water, water also freized on the oars. at the distance of one mile passed the entrance of a creek 15 yds. wide on Stard. side, this we call Teapot Creek, it affords no water at it's mouth but has runing water at some small distance above, this I beleive to be the case with many of those creekes which we have passed since we entered this hilley country, the water is absorbed by the earth near the river and of course appear dry; they afford but little water at any rate, and that is so strongly impregnated with these salts that it is unfit for uce; all the wild anamals appear fond of this water; I have tryed it by way of experiment & find it moderately pergative, but painfull to the intestens in it's opperation. this creek runs directly towards some low mountains which lye N. W. of it and appear to be about 30 mes. distant, perhaps it heads in them. This range of mountains appear to be about 70 miles long runing from E to W. having their Eastern extremity about 30 mes. distant in a northwardly direction from pot Island.- also passed two small creeks on Lard. and two others on Stard. all inconsiderable and dry at their entrances. just above the entrance of Teapot Creek on the stard. there is a large assemblage of the burrows of the Burrowing Squirrel they generally seelect a south or a south Easterly exposure for their residence, and never visit the brooks or river for water; I am astonished how this anamal exists as it dose without water, particularly in a country like this where there is scarcely any rain during Yi of the year and more rarely any due; yet we have sometimes found their villages at the distance of five or six miles from any water, and they are never found out of the limits of the ground which their burrows occupy; in the Autumn when the hard frosts commence they close their burrows and do not venture out again untill spring, indeed some of them appear to be yet in winter quarters. passed 3 Islands the two first covered with tall cottonwood timber and the last with willows only. river more rappid, & the country much the same as yesterday. some spruce pine of small size appears among the pitch pine, and reather more rock than usual on the face of the hills. The musquetoes troublesome this evening, a circumstance I did not expect from the temperature of the morning. The Gees begin to lose the feathers of their wings and are unable to fly. Capt Clark walked on shore and killed 4 deer and an Elk. We killed a large fat brown bear which took the water after being wounded and was carried under some driftwood where he sunk and we were unable to get him. Saw but few buffaloe today, but a great number of Elk, deer, some antelopes and 5 bear. The wild rose which is now in blume are very abundant, they appear to differ but little from those common to the Atlantic States, the leaves of the bushes and the bush itself appear to be of somewhat smaller size.

[Clark, May 23, 1805] May 23rd Thursday 1805 a Severe frost last night, the Thrmotr. Stood at the freesing point this morning i e 32 a 0. wind S W. the water freeses on the oars. Ice on the edge of the river we Set out at an early hour and passed the mouth a Creek at 1 mile on the Stard. Side which heads in a mountain N W of its mouth 30 or _____ miles, the Countrey on each Side is as passed yesterday passed 2 Small Creeks on the Stard & 2 on the Lard. Side to day. a mountain which appears to be 60 or 70 miles long bearing E. & W is about 25 miles distant from this river on the Stard Side Notherley of Pot Island I walked on Shore and killed 4 deer & an Elk, & a beaver in the evening we killed a large fat Bear, which we unfortunately lost in the river, after being Shot took the water & was Carried under a drift passed in course of this day three Islands, two of them Covered with tall timber & a 3rd with willows

The after part of this day was worm & the Misquitors troublesome. Saw but five Buffalow a number of Elk & Deer & 5 bear & 2 Antilopes to day. the river beginning to rise, and Current more rapid than yesterday, in maney places I saw Spruces on the hills Sides Stard. this evening.

[Lewis, May 24, 1805]
Friday May 24th 1805.

The water standing in the vessels freized during the night 1/8 of an inch thick, ice also appears along the verge of the river. the folage of some of the cottonwood trees have been entirely distroyed by the frost and are again puting forth other buds. the high country in which we are at present and have been passing for some days I take to be a continuation of what the Indians as well as the French Engages call the Black hills. This tract of country so called consists of a collection of high broken and irregular hills and short chain of mountains sometimes 120 miles in width and again becomeing much narrower, but always much higher than the country on either side; they commence about the head of the Kanzas river and to the West of that river near the Arkansas, from whence they take their course a little to the W. of N. W. approaching the rockey Mountains obliquely, passing the river platte above the forks and intercepting the Yellowstone river near the big bend and passing the Missouri at this place and probably continuing to swell the country as far North as the Saskashawan river tho they are lower here than they are discribed to the Sth. and may therefore probably terminate before they reach the Suskashawan. the black hills in their course nothwardly appear to approach more nearly to the Rocky Mountains.

We set out at an early hour this morning and proceed on principally by the chord untill about 9 A.M. when a fine breeze sprung up from the S. E. and enabled us though the ballance of the day to employ our sails to advantage; we proceed at a pretty good pace notwithstanding the courant of the river was very strong. we passed two large and four small Islands; also several streams on either side; the first of these is a large Creek or small river which disinboged on the Stard. side about 11/2 miles above our encampment of last evening, it is 30 yards wide and contains some water. the bed is gravley and intermixed with some stone, it takes its rise in the mountains which are situated in a Northwardly direction from its entrance, distant about 30 miles. the air is so pure in this open country that mountains and other elivated objects appear much nearer than they really are; these mountains do not appear to be further than 15 m. we sent a man up this creek to explore the country he returned late in the evening and informed that he had proceeded ten miles directly towards these mountains and that he did not think himself by any mean half way these mountains are rockey and covered with some scattering pine. This stream we call North Mountain creek. the next stream in order is a creek which falls in on Lard. 21/2 miles higher; this is 15 yds. wide no water; a large village of the burrowing or barking squirrels on the Stard. side opposite it's entrance, hence the name Little dog Ck. that being the name by which the French Engages call this anamal. at three miles and at 10 ms. from hence still ascending 2 Small creek fall in on the Stard. side, no water. 51/2 miles higher a small river falls in on Lard. side this we called South Mountain creek as from it's direction it appeared to take it's rise in a range of Mountains lying in a S. Westerly direction from it's entrance distant 50 or 60 m.; this creek is 40 yards wide and discharges a handsome stream of water. it's bed is rockey with gravel and sand, the banks high and country broken it's bottom narrow and no timber. The country high and broken, a considerable portion of black rock and brown sandy rock appear in the faces of the hills; the tops of the hills covered with scattering pine spruce and dwarf cedar; the soil poor and sterile, sandy near the tops of the hills, the whole producing but little grass; the narrow bottoms of the Missouri producing little else but Hysop or southern wood and the pulpy leafed thorn. Capt. Clark walked on shore this evening and killed a buffaloe cow, we left 2 Canoes and six men to dress the Cow and bring on the meat, they did not overtake us this evening. game is becoming more scarce, particularly beaver, of which we have seen but few for several days the beaver appears to keep pace with the timber as it declines in quantity they also become more scarce.

[Clark, May 24, 1805] May 24th Friday 1805 a Cold night the water in the Small vestles frosed 1/8 of an inch thick, and the thermometer Stood this morning at the freesing point. we Set out at an early hour and proceeded on, at 9 oClock we had a Breeze from the S E which Continued all day. This Breeze afforded us good Sailing, the river rising fast Current verry rapid. passed Several Small Islands, two large & two Small Creeks, the 1st of those Creeks or Small rivers 11/2 m. above our Camp is 30 yards wide and Contains water and appears to take its rise in the North Mountns. which is Situated in a northerley detection about 20 miles distant. 21/2 m. higher a Creek falls in on the Lard. Side, opposit a large village of Barking Squirels. 3 miles Still higher a Small Creek falls in on the Stard. 13 miles higher up a Small river falls in on the Lard Side which is 40 yards wide and has running water. This Stream appears to take its rise in the South Mountains which is Situated in a Southerly direction 30 or 40 miles distant. I walked on the high countrey on the Stard. Side found it broken & Dry Some pine, Spruce & Dwarf Cedar on the hill sides, I Sent one man 10 mile out he reports a Similarity of Countrey back I killed a fat buffalow a Short distance below the place we dined 2 Canoes & 6 men we left to get the meat did not join us this evening. we Camped on the Lard point. the Cotton wood in this point is beginning to put out a Second bud, the first being killed by the frost

[Lewis, May 25, 1805] Saturday May 25th 1805. The Two canoes which we left behind yesterday to bring on the meat did not arrive this morning untill 8 A M. at which time we set out; the wind being against us we did not proceed with so much ease or expedition as yesterday, we imployed the toe line principally which the banks favored the uce off; the courant strong particularly arround the points against which the courant happened to set, and at the entrances of the little gullies from the hills, those rivulets having brought down considerable quantities of stone and deposited it at their entrances forming partial barriers to the water of the river to the distance of 40 or 50 feet from the shore, arround these the water run with great violence, and compelled us in some instances to double our force in order to get a perorogue or canoe by them. as we ascended the river today I saw several gangs of the bighorned Anamals on the face of the steep bluffs and clifts on the Stard. side and sent drewyer to kill one which he accomplished; Capt. Clark and Bratton who were on shore each killed one of these anamals this evening. The head and horns of the male which Drewyer killed weighed 27 lbs. it was somewhat larger than the male of the common deer, the boddy reather thicker deeper and not so long in proportion to it's hight as the common deer; the head and horns are remakably large compared with the other part of the anamal; the whole form is much more delicate than that of the common goat, and there is a greater disparity in the size of the male and female than between those of either the deer or goat. the eye is large and prominant, the puple of a deep sea green and small, the iris of a silvery colour much like the common sheep; the bone above the eye is remarkably prominant; the head nostrils and division of the upper lip are precisely in form like the sheep. there legs resemble the sheep more than any other animal with which I am acquainted tho they are more delicately formed, like the sheep they stand forward in the knee and the lower joint of the foreleg is smallest where it joins the knee, the hoof is black & large in proportion, is divided, very open and roundly pointed at the toe, like the sheep; is much hollowed and sharp on the under edge like the Scotch goat, has two small hoofs behind each foot below the ankle as the goat sheep and deer have. the belley, inside of the legs, and the extremity of the rump and butocks for about two inches arround the but of the tale, are white, as is also the tale excet just at it's extremity on the upper side which is of a dark brown. the tail is about three inches in length covered with short hair, or at least not longer than that of the boddy; the outher parts of the anamal are of a duskey brown or reather a leadcoloured light brown; the anamal is now sheding it's winter coat which is thick not quite as long as that of the deer and appears to be intermixed with a considerable quantity of a fine fur which lyes next to the skin & conceald by the coarcer hear; the shape of the hair itself is celindric as that of the antelope is but is smaller shorter, and not compressed or flattened as that of the deer's winter coat is, I believe this anamal only sheds it's hair once a year. it has eight fore teeth in the under jaw and no canine teeth. The horns are lagest at their base, and occupy the crown of the head almost entirely. they are compressed, bent backwards and lunated; the surface swelling into wavy rings which incircleing the horn continue to succeed each other from the base to the extremity and becoming less elivated and more distant as they recede from the head. the horn for about two thirds of it's length is filled with a porus bone which is united with the frontal bone. I obtained the bones of the upper part of the head of this animal at the big bone lick. the horns of the female are small, but are also compress bent backwards and incircled with a succession of wavy rings. the horn is of a light brown colour; when dressed it is almost white extreemly transparent and very elastic. this horn is used by the natives in constructing their bows; I have no doubt but it would eligant and ucefull hair combs, and might probably answer as many valuable purposes to civilized man, as it dose to the savages, who form their watercups spoons and platters of it. the females have already brought forth their young indeed from the size of the young I suppose that they produce them early in March. they have from one to two at a birth. they feed on grass but principally on the arromatic herbs which grow on the clifts and inaccessable hights which they usually frequent. the places they gerally celect to lodg is the cranies or cevices of the rocks in the faces of inacessable precepices, where the wolf nor bear can reach them and where indeed man himself would in many instancies find a similar deficiency; yet these anamals bound from rock to rock and stand apparently in the most careless manner on the sides of precipices of many hundred feet. they are very shye and are quick of both sent and sight.

At the distance of two 3/4 miles above our encampment of last evening we passed a Creek 20 yard wide affording no runing water, we also passed 7 Islands in the course of the day. The Country on either hand is high broken and rockey; the rock is either soft brown sand stone covered with a thin strata of limestone, or a hard black rugged grannite, both usually in horizontal stratas and the Sandy rock overlaying the other.- Salts and quarts still appear, some coal and pumice stone also appear; the river bottoms are narrow and afford scarcely any timber. the bars of the river are composed principally of gravel, but little pine on the hills. We saw a Pole-cats this evening it is the first we have seen for many days. buffalow are now scarce and I begin to fear our harvest of white puddings are at an end.

[Clark, May 25, 1805] May 25th Satturday 1805" The two Canoes left for meat yesterday did not joint us untill 8 oClock this morning at which time we Set out, the morning Cool & pleasent wind a head all day from the S. W. we pass a Creek on the Lard. Side about 20 yards wide, which does not run, we also passd 7 Islands, I walked on Shore and killed a female Ibex or big horn animal in my absence Drewyer & Bratten killed two others, this animale is a species peculiar to this upper part of the Missouri, the head and horns of the male which Drewyer killed to day weighed 27 lbs it was Somewhat larger than the Mail of the Common Deer;) The body reather thicker deeper and not So long in proportion to its hight as the common Deer; the head and horns of the male are remarkably large Compared with the other parts of the animal; the whole form is much more delicate than that of the common goat, and there is a greater disparity in the Size of the mail and female than between those of either the deer or goat. the eye is large and prominant, the puple of a deep Sea green and Small, the iris of a Silvery Colour much like the common Sheep; the bone above the Eye is remarkably prominant; the head nostrils and division of the upper lip are precisely in form like the Sheep. their legs resemble the Sheep more than any other animal with which I am acquainted tho they are more delicately formed, like the Sheep they stand foward in the Knee and the lower joint of the fore leg is Smallest where it joins the Knee, the hoof is black and large in perpotion, is divided, very open and roundly pointed at the toe; like the Sheep; is much hollowed and Sharp on the under edge like the Scotch goat, has two Small Hoofs behind each foot below the ankle as the goat Sheep and Deer have. the belley, iner Side of the legs, and the extremity of the rump and buttocks for about two inches 1/2 around the but of the tail, are white, as is also the tail except just at its extremity on the upper Side which is of a dark brown. the tail is about 3 inches in length covered with Short hair, or at least not longer than that of the boddy; the outer part of the animal are of a duskey brown or reather a lead coloured light brown; the animal is now Sheding its winter coat which is thick not quite as long as that of the Deer and appears to be inter mixt with a considerable quantity of fine fur which lies next to the Skin and concealed by the Coarcer hair; the Shape of the hair itself is cylindric as that of the Antilope is, but is Smaller, Shorter and not Compressed or flattened as that of the deers winter Coat is. I believe this animal only Sheds it's hair once a year. it has Eight fore teeth in the underjaw and no canine teeth. The Horns are large at their base, and occupy the Crown of the head almost entirely, they are compressed, bent backwards and lunated; the Surface Swelling into wavey rings which incircleing the horn continue to Succeed each other from the base to the extremity and becomeing less elivated and more distant as they receed from the head. The horn for about two thirds of its length is filled with a porus bone which is united with the frontal bone (Capt. Lewis obtained the bones of the upper part of the head of this Animal at the big Bone Lick in the State of Kentucky which I Saw and find to be the Same in every respect with those of the Missouri and the Rockey Mountains) the horns of the female are Small, but are also compressed and bent backwards and incircled with a Succession of wavy rings. the horn is of a light brown Colour; when Dressed it is almost white extreamly transparent and very elastic. this horn is used by the nativs in constructing their bows; I have no doubt of it's elegance and usefullness in hair Combs, and might probably answer as maney valuable purpoces to civilized man, as it does to the native indians, who form their water Cups, Spoons and platters of it. the females have already brought forth their young indeed from the Size of the young, I Suppose that they produce them early in March. they have from one to two at a birth. they feed on grass, but principally on the arramatic herbs which grow on the Clifts and inaccessable hights which they frequent most commonly, and the places they generally collect to lodge is the Cranies or Cevices of the rocks in the face of inaccessable precepices, where the wolf nor Bear Can reach them, and where indeed man himself would in maney instances find a Similar deficiency; yet those animals bound from rock to rock and Stand apparently in the most Careless manner on the Side of precipices of maney hundred feet. they are very Shy and quick of both Sent and Sight. The flesh of this animal is dark and I think inferior to the flesh of the Common Deer, and Superior to the antilope of the Missouri and the Columbian Plains-. In my walk of this day I saw mountts. on either side of the river at no great distance, those mountains appeared to be detached, and not ranges as laid down by the Minetarrees, I also think I saw a range of high mounts. at a great distance to the S S W. but am not certain as the horozon was not clear enough to view it with Certainty. The country on either side is high broken and rockey a dark brown hard rugid Stone intermixed with a Soft white Sand Stone. the hills contain Coal or cabonated wood as below and Some Scattering pumistone. the Sides of the river is bordered with coars gravel, which in maney places have washed either together or down Small brooks and forms bars at Some distance in the water, around which the current passes with great valocity. the bottoms between hills and river are narrow and Contain Scercely any timber. The appearence of Salts, and bitumun Still Continue. we Saw a polecat to day being the first which we have Seen for Some time past. The Air of this quarter is pure and helthy. the water of the Missouri well tasted not quite So muddy as it is below, not withstanding the last rains has raised the river a little it is less muddy than it was before the rain.

[Lewis, May 26, 1805] Sunday May 26th 1805. Set out at an early hour and proceeded principally by the toe line, using the oars mearly to pass the river in order to take advantage of the shores. scarcely any bottoms to the river; the hills high and juting in on both sides, to the river in many places. the stone tumbleing from these clifts and brought down by the rivulets as mentioned yesterday became more troublesome today. the black rock has given place to a very soft sandstone which appears to be washed away fast by the river, above this and towards the summits of the hills a hard freestone of a brownish yellow colour shews itself in several stratas of unequal thicknesses frequently overlain or incrusted by a very thin strata of limestone which appears to be formed of concreted shells. Capt. Clark walked on shore this morning and ascended to the summit of the river hills he informed me on his return that he had seen mountains on both sides of the river runing nearly parrallel with it and at no great distance; also an irregular range of mountains on lard. about 50 mes. distant, the extremities of which boar W and N. W. from his station. he also saw in the course of his walk, some Elk, several herds of the Big horn, and the large hare; the latter is common to every part of this open country. scarcely any timber to be seen except the few scattering pine and spruce which crown the high hills, or in some instances grow along their sides. In the after part of the day I also walked out and ascended the river hills which I found sufficiently fortiegueing. on arriving to the summit one of the highest points in the neighbourhood I thought myself well repaid for any labour; as from this point I beheld the Rocky Mountains for the first time, I could only discover a few of the most elivated points above the horizon, the most remarkable of which by my pocket compass I found bore N. 65° W. being a little to the N. of the N. W. extremity of the range of broken mountains seen this morning by Capt. C. these points of the Rocky Mountains were covered with snow and the sun shone on it in such manner as to give me the most plain and satisfactory view. while I viewed these mountains I felt a secret pleasure in finding myself so near the head of the heretofore conceived boundless Missouri; but when I reflected on the difficulties which this snowey barrier would most probably throw in my way to the Pacific, and the sufferings and hardships of myself and party in them, it in some measure counterballanced the joy I had felt in the first moments in which I gazed on them; but as I have always held it a crime to anticipate evils I will believe it a good comfortable road untill I am compelled to beleive differently. saw a few Elk & bighorns at a distance on my return to the river I passed a creek about 20 yds. wide near it's entrance it had a handsome little stream of runing water; in this creek I saw several softshelled Turtles which were the first that have been seen this season; this I believe proceeded reather from the season than from their non existence in the portion of the river from the Mandans hither. on the Stard. shore I killed a fat buffaloe which was very acceptable to us at this moment; the party came up to me late in the evening and encamped for the night on the Lard. side. it was after dark before we finished butchering the buffaloe, and on my return to camp I trod within five inches of a rattle snake but being in motion I passed before he could probably put himself in a striking attitude and fortunately escaped his bite, I struck about at random with my espontoon being directed in some measure by his nois untill I killed him. Our hunters had killed two of the Bighorned Anamals since I had left them. we also passed another creek a few miles below Turtle Creek on the Stard. 30 yds in width which also had runing water bed rockey.- late this evening we passed a very bad rappid which reached quite across the river, the party had considerable difficulty in ascending it altho they doubled their crews and used both the rope and the pole. while they were passing this rappid a female Elk and it's fawn swam down throught the waves which ran very high, hence the name of Elk rappids which they instantly gave this place, these are the most considerable rappids which we have yet seen on the missouri and in short the only place where there has appeared to be a suddon decent. opposite to these rappids there is a high bluff and a little above on Lard. a small cottonwood bottom in which we found sufficient timber for our fires and encampment. here I rejoined the party after dark. The appearances of coal in the face of the bluffs, also of birnt hills, pumice stone salt and quarts continue as yesterday. This is truly a desert barren country and I feel myself still more convinced of it's being a continuation of the black hills. we have continued every day to pass more or less old stick lodges of the Indians in the timbered points, there are two even in this little bottom where we lye.-

[Clark, May 26, 1805] May 26th Sunday 1805 We Set out early and proceeded as yesterday wind from the S. W. the river enclosed with very high hills on either Side. I took one man and walked out this morning, and ascended the high countrey to view the mountains which I thought I Saw yesterday, from the first Sumit of the hill I could plainly See the Mountains on either Side which I Saw yesterday and at no great distance from me, those on the Stard Side is an errigular range, the two extremities of which bore West and N. West from me. those Mountains on the Lard. Side appeared to be Several detached Knobs or mountains riseing from a leven open Countrey, at different distances from me, from South West to South East, on one the most S. Westerly of those Mountains there appeared to be Snow. I crossed a Deep holler and assended a part of the plain elevated much higher than where I first viewed the above mountains; from this point I beheld the Rocky Mountains for the first time with Certainty, I could only discover a fiew of the most elivated points above the horizon. the most remarkable of which by my pocket Compas I found bore S. 60 W. those points of the rocky Mountain were Covered with Snow and the Sun Shown on it in Such a manner as to give me a most plain and Satisfactory view. whilst I viewed those mountains I felt a Secret pleasure in finding myself So near the head of the heretofore Conceived boundless Missouri; but when I reflected on the difficulties which this Snowey barrier would most probably throw in my way to the Pacific Ocean, and the Sufferings and hardships of my Self and party in them, it in Some measure Counter ballanced the joy I had felt in the first moments in which I gazed on them; but as I have always held it little Short of Criminality to anticipate evils I will allow it to be a good Comfortable road untill I am Compelled to believe otherwise The high Country in which we are at present and have been passing for Some days I take to be a continuation of what the Indians as well as the French Engages call the Black hills. This tract of Country So Called Consists of a Collection of high broken and irregular hills and Short Chains of Mountains, sometimes 100 miles in width and again becoming much narrower, but always much higher than the Country on either Side; they commence about the head of the Kanzas river and to the west of that river near the Arkansaw river, from whence they take their Cource a little to the west of N. W. approaching the Rocky Mountains obliquely passing the river Platt near the forks, and intersepting the River Rochejhone near the big bend of that river, and passing the Missouri at this place-, and probably Continueing to Swell the Country as far North as the Saskashawan river. tho they are lower here than they are discribed to the South and may therefore termonate before they reach the Saskashawan. the Black hills in their Course northerly appear to approach more nearly the Rocky Mountains. I Saw a great number of white brant, also the common brown brant, Geese of the common Size & kind and a Small Species of geese, which differs considerably from the Common or Canadian Goose; their necks, head and backs are considerably thicker, Shorter and larger than the other in propotion to its Size they are also more than a third Smaller, and their note more like that of the brant or young goose which has not perfectly acquired his note, in all other respect they are the Same in Colour habits and the number of feathers in the tail, they frequently also ascocate with the large Geese when in flocks, but never Saw them pared off with the larger or common goose. The white Brant ascocates in very large flocks, they do not appear to be mated or pared off as if they intended to raise their young in this quarter, I therefore doubt whether they reside here dureing the Summer for that purpose. this bird is larger than the Common brown brant or 2/3 of the common goose. it is not So long by Six inches from point to point of the wings when extended as the other; the back head and neck are also larger and Stronger; their beak, legs and feet are of a redish flesh coloured white. the eye of a moderate Size, the puple of a deep Sea green encircled with a ring of yellowish brown. it has 16 feathers of equal length in the tail their note differs but little from the Common brant. they are of a pure white except the large feathers of the 1st and 2d joint of the wings which are jut black.

The country which borders the river is high broken and rocky, generally imbeded with a Soft Sand Stone higher up the hill the Stone is of a brownish yellow hard and gritty those Stones wash down from the hills into the river and cause the Shore to be rocky &c. which we find troublesom to assend there is Scerce any bottom between the Hills & river and but a fiew trees to be Seen on either Side except Scattering pine on the Sides of the emence hills; we passed 2 Creeks on the Stard Side both of them had running water in one of those Creek Capt Lewis tells me he saw Soft Shell Turtle Capt Lewis in his walk killed a fat Buffalow which we were in want of our hunters killed 2 Mountain rams or bighorns in the evening late we passed a rapid which extended quite across the river we assended it by the assistance of a Cord & poles on the Lard. Side the Cliffs jut over, the opposit Side is a Small leavel bottom, we Camped a little above in a Small grove of Cotton trees on the Lard. Side in the rapid we saw a Dow Elk & her faun, which gave rise to the name of Elk & faun Riffle we had a few drops of rain at Dark.- the Salts Coal & Burnt hills & Pumicston Still Continue, game Scerce this Countrey may with propriety I think be termed the Deserts of America, as I do not Conceive any part can ever be Settled, as it is deficent in water, Timber & too Steep to be tilled. We pass old Indian lodges in the woody points every day & 2 at our camp &c

[Lewis, May 26, 1805] May 26, 1805. One of the party killed a bighorned, the head and horns of which weighed 27 lbs. a hare was also killed which weighed 8 1/2 lbs. the hare are now of a plale lead brown colour-

[Lewis, May 27, 1805] Monday May 27th 1805. The wind blew so hard this morning that we did not sent out untill 10 A.M. we employed the chord most of the day; the river becomes more rappid and is intercepted by shoals and a greater number of rocky points at the mouths of the little gulies than we experienced yesterday. the bluffs are very high steep rugged, containing considerable quantities of stone and border the river closely on both sides; once perhaps in the course of several miles there will be a few acres of tolerably level land in which two or thre impoverished cottonwood trees will be seen. great quantities of stone also lye in the river and garnish it's borders, which appears to have tumbled from the bluffs where the rains had washed away the sand and clay in which they were imbeded. the bluffs are composed of irregular tho horizontal stratas of yellow and brown or black clay, brown and yellowish white sand, of soft yellowish white sand stone and a hard dark brown free stone, also of large round kidneyformed and irregular seperate masses of a hard black Iron stone, which is imbeded in the Clay and sand. some little pine spruce and dwarf cedar on the hills. some coal or carbonated wood still makes it's appearance in these bluffs, pumicestone and birnt hills it's concommutants also are seen. the salts and quarts are seen but not in such abundance. the country more broken and barren than yesterday if possible. about midday it was very warm to this the high bluffs and narrow channel of the river no doubt contributed greatly. we passed a small untimbered Island this morning on the Lard. side of the river just above our encampment of last evening. saw a few small herds of the Bighorned anamals and two Elk only, of the last we killed one, the river is generally about 200 yds. wide, very rappid and has a perceptable fall or declination through it's whole course.

This evening we encamped, for the benefit of wood, near two dead toped cottonwood trees on the Lard. side; the dead limbs which had fallen from these trees furnished us with a scanty supply only, and more was not to be obtained in the neighbourhood.-

[Clark, May 27, 1805] May 27th Monday 1805. The wind blew hard from the S W. which detained us untill about 10 oClock, at which time we Set out and proceeded on, passed a Small nacked Island on the Lard Side imediately above the timber in which we Camped The river is verry Shoaley and the bad places are verry numerous, i e at the mouth of every Drean the rocks which is a hard dark gritey Stone is thrown out Some distance in the river which Cause a Considerable riffle on that Side, the hills approach the river verry Close on either Side, river narrow & no timber except Some Scattering pine on the hills & hill Sides, the Salts, Coal, burn hills & Pumice Stone &c. Continue, the hills are Generally Bluffs of various Coloured earth most commonly black with different quallities stone intermixed Some Stratums of Soft Sand Stone, Some hard, Some a dark brown & yellow hard grit, those Stones are loosened by the earths washing from them into the river and ultimately role down into the river, which appears to be Crowded with them. This day is verry worm- we only Saw a fiew Small herds of the big horn animals on the hills, and two Elk one of which We killed, we Camped at 2 dead top trees on the Lard Side. The river is Genly about 200 yards wide and Current very Swift to day and has a verry perceptiable fall in all its Course- it rises a little.

[Lewis, May 28, 1805] Tuesday May 28th 1805. This morning we set forward at an early hour; the weather dark and cloudy, the are smokey, had a few drops of rain; we employed the chord generally to which we also gave the assistance of the pole at the riffles and rocky points; these are as numerous and many of them much worse than those we passed yesterday; arround those points the water drives with great force, and we are obliged in many instaces to steer our vessels through the appertures formed by the points of large sharp rocks which reach a few inches above the surface of the water, here sould our chord give way the bough is instantly drivin outwards by the stream and the vessel thrown with her side on the rocks where she must inevitably overset or perhaps be dashed to peices; our ropes are but slender, all of them except one being made of Elk's skin and much woarn, frequently wet and exposed to the heat of the weather are weak and rotten; they have given way several times in the course of the day but happily at such places that the vessel had room to wheel free of the rocks and therefore escaped injury; with every precaution we can take it is with much labour and infinite risk that we are enabled to get around these points. found a new indian lodge pole today which had been brought down by the stream, it was woarn at one end as if draged by dogs or horses; a football also, and several other articles were found, which have been recently brought down by the courant; these are strong evedences of Indians being on the river above us, and probably at no great distance; the football is such as I have seen among the Minetaries and therefore think it most probable that they are a band of the Minetaries of Fort de Prarie. the river country &c continued much as yesterday untill late in the evening when we arrived at the entrance of a large Creek discharges itself on the Stard. side, is 35 Yd. wide and contains runing water; here the hills recede from the river on both sides, the bottoms extensive particularly on the Stard. side where the hills are comparitively low and open into three large vallies which extend for a considerable distance in a Northwardly direction; here also the river spreads to more than 3 times it's former width and is filled with a number of small and handsome Islands covered with cottonwood some timber also in the bottoms, the land again fertile. These appearances were quite reviving after the drairy country through which we had been passing. Capt. C. walked on shore in the early part of the day and killed a big horned anamal; he saw a great number of them as well as ourselves in the broken country. at 10 A.M. a few drops of rain again fell and were attended with distant thunder which is the first we have heated since we left the Mandans.- This evening we encamped on Stard. opposite to the entrance of a small Creek. I beleive the bighorn have their young at a very early season, say early in March for they appear now to be half grown. One of the party saw a very large bear today but being some distance from the river and no timber to conceal him he did not think proper to fire on him.

[Clark, May 28, 1805] May 28th Tuesday 1805 a Cloudy morning Some fiew drops of rain and verry Smokey wind from the S. W. we Set out at an early hour, the Shoaley places are verry numerous and Some bad to get around we have to make use of the Cord & Poles, and our tow. ropes are all except one of Elkskin, & Stretch and Sometimes brake which indanger the Perogues or Canoe, as it imedeately turns and if any rock Should chance to be below, the rapidity of the current would turn her over, She Should chance to Strike the rock we observe great Caution at those places.

I walked on Shore found the Countrey ruged and as described yesterday, I Saw great numbers of the Big horned animals, one of which I killed their fauns are nearly half grown- one of the Party Saw a verry large bear, picked up on the Shore a pole which had been made use of by the Nativs for lodge poles, & haul'd by dogs it is new and is a Certain Sign of the Indians being on the river above a foot ball and Several other articles are also found to Substantiate this oppinion-. at 1 oClock we had a few drops of rain and Some thunder whic is the first thunder we have had Sinc we Set out from Fort Mandan; at 10 miles the the hills begin to widen & the river Spreds & is crouded with Islands the bottoms Contain Some Scattering Cotton wood the Islands also Contain timber- passed a Creek of running water on the Stard Side about 35 yards wide and camped imedeately opposit to a Small Creek on the Lard. Side we call Bull Creek from the Circumstance of a Buffalow Bull swiming from the opposit Side and comeing out of the river imedeately across one of the Perogues without Sinking or injureing any thing in the Perogue, and passing with great violence thro our Camp in the night makeing 3 angles without hurting a man, altho they lay in every direction, and it was very dark The Creek below 35 yards wide I call Thompsons Creek after a valuable member of our party- this Creek contains a Greater preportion of running water than Common.

[Lewis, May 29, 1805] Wednesday May 29th 1905. Last night we were all allarmed by a large buffaloe Bull, which swam over from the opposite shore and coming along side of the white perogue, climbed over it to land, he then alarmed ran up the bank in full speed directly towards the fires, and was within 18 inches of the heads of some of the men who lay sleeping before the centinel could allarm him or make him change his course, still more alarmed, he now took his direction immediately towards our lodge, passing between 4 fires and within a few inches of the heads of one range of the men as they yet lay sleeping, when he came near the tent, my dog saved us by causing him to change his course a second time, which he did by turning a little to the right, and was quickly out of sight, leaving us by this time all in an uproar with our guns in or hands, enquiring of each other the case of the alarm, which after a few moments was explained by the centinel; we were happy to find no one hirt. The next morning we found that the buffaloe in passing the perogue had trodden on a rifle, which belonged to Capt. Clark's black man, who had negligently left her in the perogue, the rifle was much bent, he had also broken the spindle, pivit, and shattered the stock of one of the bluntderbushes on board, with this damage I felt well content, happey indeed, that we had sustaned no further injury. it appears that the white perogue, which contains our most valuable stores, is attended by some evil gennii. This morning we set out at an early hour and proceded as usual by the Chord. at the distance of 2 1/2 miles passed a handsome river which discharged itself on the Lard. side, I walked on shore and acended this river about a mile and a half in order to examine it. I found this river about 100 yds. wide from bank to bank, the water occupying about 75 yard. the bed was formed of gravel and mud with some sand; it appeared to contain much more water as the Muscle-Shell river, was more rappid but equally navigable; there were no large stone or rocks in it's bed to obstruct the navigation; the banks were low yet appeared seldom to overflow; the water of this River is Clear than any we have met with great abundance of the Argalia or Bighorned animals in the high country through which this river passes Cap. C who assended this R. much higher than I did has thought proper to call it Judieths River. The bottoms of this stream as far as I could see were wider and contained more timber than the Missouri; here I saw some box alder intermixed with the Cottonwood willow rose bushes and honeysuckle with some red willow constitute the undergrowth. on the Missouri just above the entrance of the Big Horn River I counted the remains of the fires of 126 Indian lodges which appeared to be of very recent date perhaps 12 or 15 days. Capt. Clark also saw a large encampent just above the entrance of this river on the Stard. side of reather older date, probably they were the same Indians. The Indian woman with us exmined the mockersons which we found at these encampments and informed us that they were not of her nation the Snake Indians, but she beleived they were some of the Indians who inhabit the country on this side of Rocky Mountains and North of the Missoury and I think it most probable that they were the Minetaries of Fort de Prarie. At the distance of six 1/2 ms. from our encampment of last night we passed a very bad rappid to which we gave the name of the Ash rappid from a few trees of that wood growing near them; this is the first ash I have seen for a great distance. at this place the hills again approach the river closely on both sides, and the same seen which we had on the 27th and 28th in the morning again presents itself, and the rocky points and riffles reather more numerous and worse; there was but little timber; salts coal &c still appear. today we passed on the Stard. side the remains of a vast many mangled carcases of Buffalow which had been driven over a precipice of 120 feet by the Indians and perished; the water appeared to have washed away a part of this immence pile of slaughter and still their remained the fragments of at least a hundred carcases they created a most horrid stench. in this manner the Indians of the Missouri distroy vast herds of buffaloe at a stroke; for this purpose one of the most active and fleet young men is scelected and disguised in a robe of buffaloe skin, having also the skin of the buffaloe's head with the years and horns fastened on his head in form of a cap, thus caparisoned he places himself at a convenient distance between a herd of buffaloe and a precipice proper for the purpose, which happens in many places on this river for miles together; the other indians now surround the herd on the back and flanks and at a signal agreed on all shew themselves at the same time moving forward towards the buffaloe; the disguised indian or decoy has taken care to place himself sufficiently nigh the buffaloe to be noticed by them when they take to flight and runing before them they follow him in full speede to the precepice, the cattle behind driving those in front over and seeing them go do not look or hesitate about following untill the whole are precipitated down the precepice forming one common mass of dead an mangled carcases; the decoy in the mean time has taken care to secure himself in some cranney or crivice of the clift which he had previously prepared for that purpose. the part of the decoy I am informed is extreamly dangerous, if they are not very fleet runers the buffaloe tread them under foot and crush them to death, and sometimes drive them over the precepice also, where they perish in common with the buffaloe.- we saw a great many wolves in the neighbourhood of these mangled carcases they were fat and extreemly gentle, Capt. C. who was on shore killed one of them with his espontoon. just above this place we came too for dinner opposite the entrance of a bold runing river 40 yds. wide which falls in on Lard. side. this stream we called slaughter river. it's bottoms are but narrow and contain scarcely any timber. our situation was a narrow bottom on the Stard. possessing some cottonwood. soon after we landed it began to blow & rain, and as there was no appearance of even wood enough to make our fires for some distance above we determined to remain here untill the next morning, and accordingly fixed our camp and gave each man a small dram. notwithstanding the allowance of sperits we issued did not exceed 1/2 pn. man several of them were considerably effected by it; such is the effects of abstaining for some time from the uce of sperituous liquors; they were all very merry.- The hunters killed an Elk this evening, and Capt. C. killed two beaver.

[Clark, May 29, 1805] May 29th Wednesday 1805 In the last night we were alarmed by a Buffalow which Swam from the opposit Shore landed opposit the Perogue in which Capt Lewis & my Self were in he Crossed the perogue, and went with great force up to the fire where Several men were Sleeping and was 18 inches of their heads, when one man Sitting up allarmed him and he turned his course along the range of men as they lay, passing between 4 fires and within a fiew Inches of Some of the mens heads as they lay imediately in a direction to our lodge about which Several men were lying. our Dog flew out & he changed his course & passed without doeing more damage than bend a rifle & brakeing hir Stock and injureying one of the blunder busts in the perogue as he passed through- We Set out this morning at the usial hour & proceeded on at 2 1/2 miles passed the mouth of a river ____ yards wide, discharging a great quantity of water, and Containing more wood in its bottoms than the Missouri- this river Capt Lewis walked up for a Short distance & he Saw an old encampment of Indians (I also saw large encampment on the Stard Side at the mouth of a Small Creek of about 100 Lodges which appeared to be 5 or 6 weeks past, the Indian woman examined the mockersons &c. and told us they were the Indians which resided below the rocky mountains & to the North of this river,that her nation make their mockersons differently) at 6 1/2 miles passed a considerable rapid at which place the hills approach near the river on both Sides, leaveing a narrow bottom on the Stard. Side, (ash rapid) and continue Close all day but little timber, I walked on the bank in the evening and saw the remains of a number of buffalow, which had been drove down a Clift of rocks I think from appearances that upwards of 100 of those animals must have perished here, Great numbers of wolves were about this place & verry jentle I killed one of them with my Spear. The hills above ash rapid Contains more rock and Coal, and the more rapid points. we Came too for Dinner opposit the enterence of a Small river which falls in on the Lard Side and is about ____ yards wide, has a bold running Stream, Soon after we Came too it began to rain & blow hard, and as we were in a good harbor & Small point of woods on the Stard Side, and no timber for some distance above, induced us to conclude to Stay all night. we gave the men a dram, altho verry Small it was Sufficent to effect Several men. one of our hunters killed an elk this evening- I killed 2 beaver on the Side of the bank a table Spoon full of water exposed to the air in a Saucer would avaperate in 36 hours when the mercury did not Stand higher than the temperate point in the heat of the day.

[Lewis, May 30, 1805] Thursday May 30th 1805. The rain which commenced last evening continued with little intermission untill 11 this morning when we set out; the high wind which accompanied the rain rendered it impracticable to procede earlyer. more rain has now fallen than we have experienced since the 15th of September last. many circumstances indicate our near approach to a country whos climate differs considerably from that in which we have been for many months. the air of the open country is asstonishingly dry as well as pure. I found by several experiments that a table spoon full of water exposed to the air in a saucer would avaporate in 36 hours when the murcury did not stand higher than the temperate point at the greatest heat of the day; my inkstand so frequently becoming dry put me on this experiment. I also observed the well seasoned case of my sextant shrunk considerably and the joints opened. The water of the river still continues to become clearer and notwithstanding the rain which has fallen it is still much clearer than it was a few days past. this day we proceded with more labour and difficulty than we have yet experienced; in addition to the imbarrasments of the rappid courant, riffles, & rockey point which were as bad if not worse than yesterday, the banks and sides of the bluff were more steep than usual and were now rendered so slippery by the late rain that the men could scarcely walk. the chord is our only dependance for the courant is too rappid to be resisted with the oar and the river too deep in most places for the pole. the earth and stone also falling from these immence high bluffs render it dangerous to pass under them. the wind was also hard and against us. our chords broke several times today but happily without injury to the vessels. we had slight showers of rain through the course of the day, the air was could and rendered more disagreeable by the rain. one of the party ascended the river hills and reported on his return that there was snow intermixed with the rain which fell on the hights; he also informed us that the country was level a little back from the river on both sides. there is now no timber on the hills, an only a few scattering cottonwood, ash, box Alder and willows to be seen along the river. in the course of the day we passed several old encampment of Indians, from the apparent dates of which we conceived that they were the several encampments of a band of about 100 lodges who were progressing slowly up the river; the most recent appeared to have been evacuated about 5 weeks since. these we supposed to be the Minetares or black foot Indians who inhabit the country watered by the Suskashawan and who resort to the establishment of Fort de Prarie, no part of the Missouri from the Minetaries to this place furnishes a perminent residence for any nation yet there is no part of it but what exhibits appearances of being occasionally visited by some nation on hunting excurtions. The Minnetares of the Missoury we know extend their excurtions on the S. side as high as the yellowstone river; the Assinniboins still higher on the N. side most probably as high as about Porcupine river and from thence upwards most probably as far as the mountains by the Minetares of Fort de Prarie and the Black Foot Indians who inhabit the S. fork of the Suskashawan. I say the Missouri to the Rocky mountains for I am convinced that it penetrates those mountains for a considerable distance.- Two buffaloe killed this evening a little above our encampment.

[Clark, May 30, 1805] May 30th Thursday 1805 The rain conmmenced yesterday evining, and continued moderately through the course of the night, more rain has now fallin than we have experienced Since the 15th of September last, the rain continued this morning, and the wind too high for us to proceed, untill about 11 oClock at which time we Set out, and proceeded on with great labour, we were obliged to make use of the Tow rope & the banks were So muddey & Slipery that the men could Scercely walk not with Standing we proceeded on as well as we could wind hard from the N W. in attempting to assend a rapid our toe Cord broke & we turned without injurey, those rapids or Shoaley points are noumerous and dificuelt, one being at the mouth of every drean Some little rain at times all day one man assended the high Countrey and it was raining & Snowing on those hills, the day has proved to be raw and Cold. Back from the river is tollerably leavel, no timber of any kind on the hills, and only a fiew Scattering cotton willow & ash near the river, much hard rock; & rich earth, the Small portion of rain which has fallen causes the rich earth as deep as is wet to Slip into the river or bottoms &c.

we discover in Several places old encampments of large bands of Indians, a fiew weeks past and appear to be makeing up the river- Those Indians we believe to be the Blackfoot Inds. or Menetares who inhabit the heads of the Saskashowin & north of this place and trade a little in the Fort de Prarie establishments. we Camped in a grove of Cotton trees on the Stard Side, river rise 11/2 In.

[Lewis, May 31, 1805] Friday May 31st 1805. This morning we proceeded at an early hour with the two perogues leaving the canoes and crews to bring on the meat of the two buffaloe that were killed last evening and which had not been brought in as it was late and a little off the river. soon after we got under way it began to rain and continued untill meridian when it ceased but still remained cloudy through the ballance of the day. The obstructions of rocky points and riffles still continue as yesterday; at those places the men are compelled to be in the water even to their armpits, and the water is yet very could, and so frequent are those point that they are one fourth of their time in the water, added to this the banks and bluffs along which they are obliged to pass are so slippery and the mud so tenacious that they are unable to wear their mockersons, and in that situation draging the heavy burthen of a canoe and walking ocasionally for several hundred yards over the sharp fragments of rocks which tumble from the clifts and garnish the borders of the river; in short their labour is incredibly painfull and great, yet those faithfull fellows bear it without a murmur. The toe rope of the white perogue, the only one indeed of hemp, and that on which we most depended, gave way today at a bad point, the perogue swung and but slightly touched a rock, yet was very near overseting; I fear her evil gennii will play so many pranks with her that she will go to the bottomm some of those days.- Capt. C. walked on shore this morning but found it so excessively bad that he shortly returned. at 12 OCk. we came too for refreshment and gave the men a dram which they received with much cheerfullness, and well deserved.

The hills and river Clifts which we passed today exhibit a most romantic appearance. The bluffs of the river rise to the hight of from 2 to 300 feet and in most places nearly perpendicular; they are formed of remarkable white sandstone which is sufficiently soft to give way readily to the impression of water; two or thre thin horizontal stratas of white free-stone, on which the rains or water make no impression, lie imbeded in these clifts of soft stone near the upper part of them; the earth on the top of these Clifts is a dark rich loam, which forming a graduly ascending plain extends back from 1/2 a mile to a mile where the hills commence and rise abruptly to a hight of about 300 feet more. The water in the course of time in decending from those hills and plains on either side of the river has trickled down the soft sand clifts and woarn it into a thousand grotesque figures, which with the help of a little immagination and an oblique view at a distance, are made to represent eligant ranges of lofty freestone buildings, having their parapets well stocked with statuary; collumns of various sculpture both grooved and plain, are also seen supporting long galleries in front of those buildings; in other places on a much nearer approach and with the help of less immagination we see the remains or ruins of eligant buildings; some collumns standing and almost entire with their pedestals and capitals; others retaining their pedestals but deprived by time or accident of their capitals, some lying prostrate an broken othes in the form of vast pyramids of connic structure bearing a sereis of other pyramids on their tops becoming less as they ascend and finally terminating in a sharp point. nitches and alcoves of various forms and sizes are seen at different hights as we pass. a number of the small martin which build their nests with clay in a globular form attatched to the wall within those nitches, and which were seen hovering about the tops of the collumns did not the less remind us of some of those large stone buildings in the U States. the thin stratas of hard freestone intermixed with the soft sandstone seems to have aided the water in forming this curious scenery. As we passed on it seemed as if those seens of visionary inchantment would never have and end; for here it is too that nature presents to the view of the traveler vast ranges of walls of tolerable workmanship, so perfect indeed are those walls that I should have thought that nature had attempted here to rival the human art of masonry had I not recollected that she had first began her work. These walls rise to the hight in many places of 100 feet, are perpendicular, with two regular faces and are from one to 12 feet thick, each wall retains the same thickness at top which it possesses at bottom. The stone of which these walls are formed is black, dence and dureable, and appears to be composed of a large portion of earth intermixed or cemented with a small quantity of sand and a considerable portion of talk or quarts. these stones are almost invariably regular parallelepipeds, of unequal sizes in the walls, but equal in their horizontal ranges, at least as to debth. these are laid regularly in ranges on each other like bricks, each breaking or covering the interstice of the two on which it rests. thus the purpendicular interstices are broken, and the horizontal ones extend entire throughout the whole extent of the walls. These stones seem to bear some proportion to the thickness of the walls in which they are employed, being larger in the thicker walls; the greatest length of the parallelepiped appears to form the thickness of the thiner walls, while two or more are employed to form that of the thicker walls. These walls pass the river in several places, rising from the water's edge much above the sandstone bluffs, which they seem to penetrate; thence continuing their course on a streight line on either side of the river through the gradually ascending plains, over which they tower to the hight of from ten to seventy feet until) they reach the hills, which they finally enter and conceal themselves. these walls sometimes run parallel to each other, with several ranges near each other, and at other times interscecting each other at right angles, having the appearance of the walls of ancient houses or gardens. I walked on shore this evening and examined these walls minutely and preserved a specimine of the stone. I found the face of many of the river hills formed of Clifts of very excellent free stone of a light yellowish brown colour; on these clifts I met with a species of pine which I had never seen, it differs from the pitchpine in the particular of it's leaf and cone, the first being vastly shorter, and the latter considerably longer and more pointed. I saw near those bluffs the most beautiful) fox that I ever beheld, the colours appeared to me to be a fine orrange yellow, white and black, I endevoured to kill this anamal but it discovered me at a considerable distance, and finding that I could get no nearer, I fired on him as he ran, and missed him; he concealed himself under the rocks of the clift; it appeared to me to be about the size of the common red fox of the Atlantic states, or reather smaller than the large fox common to this country; convinced I am that it is a distinct species. The appearance of coal continues but in small quantities, but little appearance of birnt hills or pumice stones the mineral salts have in some measure abated and no quarts. we saw a great number of the Bighorn some mule deer and a few buffaloe and Elk, no antelopes or common deer. Drewyer who was with me and myself killed two bighorned anamals; the sides of the Clifts where these anamals resort much to lodg, have the peculiar smell of the sheepfolds. the party killed in addition to our hunt 2 buffaloe and an Elk. the river today has been from 150 to 250 yds. wide but little timber today on the river.

[Clark, May 31, 1805] May 31st Friday 1805. A cloudy morning we dispatched all the Canoes to Collect the meat of 2 Buffalow killed last night a head and a little off the river, and proceeded on with the perogues at an early hour. I attempted to walk on Shore Soon found it verry laborious as the mud Stuck to my mockersons & was verry Slippery. I return'd on board. it continued to rain moderately untill about 12 oClock when it ceased, & Continued Cloudy. the Stone on the edge of the river continue to form verry Considerable rapids, which are troublesom & dificuelt to pass, our toe rope which we are obliged to make use of altogether broke & we were in Some danger of turning over in the perogue in which I was, we landed at 12 and refreshed the men with a dram, our men are obliged to under go great labour and fatigue in assending this part of the Missouri, as they are compelled from the rapidity of the Current in many places to walk in the water & on Slippery hill Sides or the Sides of rocks, on Gravel & thro a Stiff mud bear footed, as they Cannot keep on Mockersons from the Stiffness of the mud & decline of the Slipy. hills Sides- the Hills and river Clifts of this day exhibit a most romantick appearance on each Side of the river is a white Soft Sand Stone bluff which rises to about half the hight of the hills, on the top of this Clift is a black earth on points, in maney places this Sand Stone appears like antient ruins some like elegant buildings at a distance, Some like Towers &c. &c. in maney places of this days march we observe on either Side of the river extraodanary walls of a black Semented Stone which appear to be regularly placed one Stone on the other, Some of those walls run to the hite of 100 feet, they are from about 1 foot to 12 feet thick and are perpendicular, those walls Commence at the waters edge & in Some places meet at right angles- those walls appear to Continue their Course into the Sand Clifts, the Stones which form those walls are of different Sizes all Squar edged, Great numbers has fallen off from the walls near the river which cause the walls to be of uneaquil hite, in the evening the Countrey becomes lower and the bottoms wider, no timber on the uplands, except a few Cedar & pine on the Clifts a few Scattering Cotton trees on the points in the river bottoms, The apparance of Coal Continus Capt Lewis walked on Shore & observed a Species of Pine we had never before Seen, with a Shorter leaf than Common & the bur different, he also Collected Some of the Stone off one of the walls which appears to be a Sement of Isin glass black earth we Camped on the Stard Side in a Small timbered bottom above the mouth of a Creek on the Stard Side our hunters killed, 2 animals with big horns, 2 Buffalow & an Elk, we Saw Great numbers of those big horned animals on the Clifts, but fiew Buffalow or Elk, no antelope, a fiew mule deer, Saw a fox to day. The river rises a little it is from 150 to 250 yds. wide

[Clark, May 31, 1805] May 31st Friday 1805 Cloudy morning, we proceeded on at an early hour with the two Perogues leaving the Canoes and crews to bring on the meat of two Buffalow that were killed last evening and which had not been brought in as it was late and a little off the river. Soon after we got under way it began to rain and Continued untill 12 oClock when it Seased but Still remained cloudy through the ballance of the day. the obstructions of rocky points and riffles Still continue as yesterday; at those places the men are compelled to be in the water even to their armpits, and the water is yet very cold, and So frequent are those points that they are one fourth of their time in the water. added to this the bank and bluff along which they are obliged to pass are So Slippery and the mud So tenatious that they are unable to bare their mockersons, and in that Situation dragging the heavy burthen of a Canoe and Walking occasionally for Several hundred yards over the Sharp fragments of rocks which tumble from the Clifts; and in Short their labour is incredibly painfull and great, yet those faithfull fellows bear it without a murmer.

The toe rope of the white perogue, the only one indeed of hemp, and that on which we most depended, gave way to day at a bad point, the perogue Swong and but slightly touched a rock, yet was very near oversetting; I fear her evil Ginnie will play So many pranks with her that She will go to the bottom Some of those days.

I attempted to walk on Shore this morning but found it so excessivily bad that I Soon returned on board. at 12 oClock we came too for refreshment and gave the men a dram which they received with much Chearfulness, and well deserved all wet and disagreeable. Capt. Lewis walked on Shore, he informed one that he Saw "the most butifull fox in the world" the Colour appeared to him to be of a fine Orrange yellow, white and black, he fired at this fox running and missed him, he appeared to be about the size of the common red fox of the united States, or rather smaller.

The hills and river clifts which we pass to day exhibit a most romantic appearance. The Bluffs of the river rise to the hight of from 2 to 300 feet and in most places nearly perpendicular; they are formed of remarkable white Sandstone which is Sufficiently Soft to give way readily to the impression of water; two or three thin horizontal Stratas of white free Stone, on which the rains or water make no impression, lie imbeded in those clifts of Soft Stone near the upper part of them; the earth on the top of these clifts is a dark rich loam, which forming a gradual ascending plain extend back from 1/2 a mile to a mile where the hills commence and rise abruptly to the hight of about 300 feet more. The water in the Course of time aceending from those hills and plains on either Side of the river has trickled down the Soft Sand Clifts and woarn it into a thousand grotesque figures; which with the help of a little imagination and an oblique view at a distance are made to represent elegant ranges of lofty freestone buildings, haveing their parapets well Stocked with Statuary; Colloms of various Sculptures both Grooved and plain, are also Seen Supporting long galleries in part of those buildings; in other places on a much nearer approach and with the with the help of less immagination we See the remains of ruins of eligant buildings; Some Collumns Standing and almost entire with their pedestals and Capitals, others retaining their pedestals but deprived by time or accedint of their capitals, Some lying prostrate and broken, others in the form of vast Pyramids of connic Structure bearing a Serious of other pyramids on their tops becomeing less as they ascend and finally termonateing in a Sharp point. nitches and alcoves of various forms and Sizes are Seen at different hights as we pass. a number of the Small martin which build their nests with Clay of a globular form attached to the wall within those nitches, and which were Seen hovering about the top of the collumns did not the less remind us of Some of those large Stone buildings in the United States. The thin Stratas of hard free Stone intermixed with the Soft Sand Stone Seems to have aided the water in forming this Curious Scenery.

as we passed on it Seemed as if those Seens of Visionary enchantment would never have an end; for here it is too that nature presents to the view of the traveler vast ranges of walls of tolerable workmanship, So perfect indeed are those walls that I Should have thought that nature had attempted here to rival the human art of Masonry had I not recollected that She had first began her work. These walls rise to the hight in many places of 100 feet, are perpindicular, with two regular faces, and are from one to 12 feet thick, each wall retains the Same thickness to the top which it possesses at bottom. The Stone of which these walls are formed is black, dense and dureable, and appears to be Composed of a large portion of earth intermixed or Cemented with a Small quantity of Sand and a Considerable portion of quarts. these Stones are almost invariably regular parallelepipeds, of unequal Sizes in the wall, but equal in their horizontal ranges, at least as to debth. These are laid regularly in ranges on each other like bricks, each breaking or covering this interstice of the two on which it rests, thus the pirpendicular interstices are broken, and the horizontal ones extend entire throughout the whole extent of the walls. These Stones Seam to bear Some proportion to the thickness of the walls in which they are employd, being larger in the thicker walls; the greatest length of the parallelepiped appear to form the thickness of the thiner walls, while two or more are employed to form that of the thicker walls. Those walls pass the river in Several places rising from the waters edge much above the Sand Stone Bluffs, which they Seam to penetrate; thence Continueing their course on a Streight line on either Side of the river thorough the gradually ascending plains over which they tower to the hight of from ten to 90 feet untill they reach the hills which they finally enter and Conceal themselves. these walls Sometimes run parallel to each other, with Several ranges near each other, and at other times intersecting each other at right angles, haveing the appearance of the walls of ancient houses or gardins. both Capt Lewis and My self walked on Shore this evening and examined those walls minutely and preserved a Specimine of the Stone.- I found many clifts of very excellent free Stone of a light yellowish brown Colour. Capt. Lewis observed a Species of pine which I had never Seen, it differs from the pitch pine in the particular of its leaf and Cone, the first being partly Shorter, and the latter considerably longer and more pointed. The appearance of Coal Continues but in Smaller quantities, but little appearance of burnt hills or pumicestone. the mineral Salt in Some measure have abated and no quarts. we Saw a great number of the Big Horn, Some mule deer, and a few Buffalow and Elk, no antelopes or Common Deer-. Capt. Lewis killed a Big horn animal. the party killed 2 Buffalow one Elk and a Big horn or Ibex to day-. The river has been from 150 to 250 yards wide but little timber on the river to day. river less muddy than it was below.

[Lewis, June 1, 1805] Saturday June 1st 1805 The moring was cloudy and a few drops of rain. Set out at an early hour and proceeded as usual by the help of our chords. the river Clifts and bluffs not so high as yesterday and the country becomes more level. a mountain or a part of the N. Mountain appears to approach the river within 8 or 10 ms. bearing N. from our encampment of the last evening. Capt C. who walked on shore today informed me that the river hills were much lower than usual and that from the tops of those hills he had a delightfull view of rich level and extensive plains on both sides of the river; in those plains, which in many places reach the river clifts, he observed large banks of pure sand which appeared to have been driven by the S W. winds from the river bluffs and there deposited. the plains are more fertile at some distance from the river than near the bluffs where the surface of the earth is very generally covered with small smothe pebbles which have the appearance of having been woarn by the agitation of the waters in which they were no doubt once immerced. A range of high Mountains appear to the S. W. at a considerable distance covered with snow, they appear to run Westerly. no timber appears on the highlands; but much more than yesterday on the river and Islands. rockey points and shoals less freequent than yesterday but some of them quite as bad when they did occur. the river from 2 to 400 yards wide, courant more gentle and still becoming clearer. game is by no means as abundant as below; we killed one male bighorn and a mule deer today; saw buffalow at a distance in the plains particularly near a small Lake on Lard. side about 8 ms. distant. some few drops of rain again fell this evening. we passed six Islands and encamped on the 7th; they are all small but contain some timber. the wind has been against us all day.- I saw the choke cherry the yellow and red courant bushes; the wild rose appears now to be in full bloom as are also the prickley pear which are numerous in these plains.- We also saw some Indian Lodges of sticks today which did not appear to have been long evacuated.- some coal appear in the bluffs.

[Clark, June 1, 1805] June 1st Satterday 1805 a Cloudy morning we Set out at an early hour and proseeded on as usial with the toe rope The Countrey appears to be lower and the Clifts not So high or Common, a mountain or a part of the north Mountain about 8 or 10 miles N. of this place, I walked on Shore to day found the Plains much lower than we have Seen them and on the top we behold an extencive plain on both Sides, in this plain I observed maney noles of fine Sand which appeared to have blown from the river bluffs and collected at these points Those plains are fertile near the river a great no. of Small Stone, I observed at Some distance to the S. W. a high mountain which appears to bear westerly The Cole appear as usial, more Cotton trees Scattered on the Shores & Islands than yesterday- no timber on the high land, the river from 2 to 400 yards wide & current more jentle than yesterday but fiew bad rapid points to day- the wild animals not So plenty as below we only killed a ram & mule Deer to day, we Saw Buffalow at a distance in the plains, particularly near a Lake on the Lard. Side about 8 miles distant from the river- We passed Six Islands and encamped on the 7th all those Islands are Small but contain Some timber on them The river riseing a little Wind to day from the S. W. Som fiew drops of rain in the morning and also in the evening, flying Clouds all day

Saw Several Indian camps made of Sticks & bark Set up on end and do not appear to belong evacuated- The roses are in full bloome, I observe yellow berries, red berry bushes Great numbers of Wild or choke Cheries, prickley pares are in blossom & in great numbers

[Lewis, June 2, 1805] Sunday June 2ed 1805 The wind blew violently last night and was attended by a slight shower of rain; the morning was fair and we set out at an early hour. imployed the chord as usual the greater part of the day. the courant was strong tho regular, and the banks afforded us good toeing. the wind was hard and against us yet we proceded with infinitely more ease than the two precedeing days. The river bluffs still continue to get lower and the plains leveler and more extensive; the timber on the river increases in quantity; the country in all other rispects much as discribed yesterday. I think we are now completely above the black hills we had a small shower of rain today but it lasted only a few minutes and was very moderate. Game becomeing more abundant this morning and I thought it best now to loose no time or suffer an opportunity to escape in providing the necessary quantity of Elk's skins to cover my leather boat which I now expect I shall be obliged to use shortly. Accordingly I walked on shore most of the day with some of the hunters for that purpose and killed 6 Elk 2 buffale 2 Mule deer and a bear. these anamals were all in good order we therefore took as much of the meat as our canoes and perogues could conveniently carry. the bear was very near catching Drewyer; it also pursued Charbono who fired his gun in the air as he ran but fortunately eluded the vigilence of the bear by secreting himself very securely in the bushes untill Drewyer finally killed it by a shot in the head; the shot indeed that will conquer the farocity of those tremendious anamals.- in the course of the day we passed 9 Islands all of them small and most of them containing some timber.

we came too on the Lard. side in a handsome bottom of small cottonwood timber opposite to the entrance of a very considerable river; but it being too late to examine these rivers minutely to night we determined to remain here untill the morning, and as the evening was favourable to make some obesvations.-

[Clark, June 2, 1805] June 2nd Sunday 1805 we had a hard wind and a little rain last night, this morning fair we Set out at an early hour, wind from the S W. Some little rain to day wind hard a head, the Countrey much like that of yesterday as discribed Capt Lewis walked on Shore, himself & the hunters killed 6 Elk & a Bear and 2 mule deer, and 2 buffalow which was all in good order a beaver also killed to day, passed 9 Islands to day the Current Swift but regular, we Camped on the Lard Side at the forks of the river the Currents & Sizes of them we Could not examine this evening a fair night we took Some Luner observations of moon & Stears

[Lewis, June 3, 1805] Monday June 3rd 1805 This morning early we passed over and formed a camp on the point formed by the junction of the two large rivers. here in the course of the day I continued my observations as are above stated. An interesting question was now to be determined; which of these rivers was the Missouri, or that river which the Minnetares call Amahte Arz zha or Missouri, and which they had discribed to us as approaching very near to the Columbia river. to mistake the stream at this period of the season, two months of the traveling season having now elapsed, and to ascend such stream to the rocky Mountain or perhaps much further before we could inform ourselves whether it did approach the Columbia or not, and then be obliged to return and take the other stream would not only loose us the whole of this season but would probably so dishearten the party that it might defeat the expedition altogether. convinced we were that the utmost circumspection and caution was necessary in deciding on the stream to be taken. to this end an investigation of both streams was the first thing to be done; to learn their widths, debths, comparitive rappidity of their courants and thence the comparitive bodies of water furnished by each; accordingly we dispatched two light canoes with three men in each up those streams; we also sent out several small parties by land with instructions to penetrate the country as far as they conveniently can permiting themselves time to return this evening and indeavour if possible to discover the distant bearing of those rivers by ascending the rising grounds. between the time of my A.M. and meridian Capt. C & myself stroled out to the top of the hights in the fork of these rivers from whence we had an extensive and most inchanting view; the country in every derection around us was one vast plain in which innumerable herds of Buffalow were seen attended by their shepperds the wolves; the solatary antelope which now had their young were distributed over it's face; some herds of Elk were also seen; the verdure perfectly cloathed the ground, the weather was pleasent and fair; to the South we saw a range of lofty mountains which we supposed to be a continuation of the S. Mountains, streching themselves from S. E. to N. W. terminating abbrubtly about S. West from us; these were partially covered with snow; behind these Mountains and at a great distance, a second and more lofty range of mountains appeared to strech across the country in the same direction with the others, reaching from West, to the N of N. W., where their snowey tops lost themselves beneath the horizon. this last range was perfectly covered with snow. the direction of the rivers could be seen but little way, soon loosing the break of their channels, to our view, in the common plain. on our return to camp we boar a little to the left and discovered a handsome little river falling into the N. fork on Lard. side about 1 1/2 ms. above our camp. this little river has as much timber in it's bottoms as either of the larger streams. there are a great number of prickley pears in these plains; the Choke cherry grows here in abundance both in the river bottoms and in the steep ravenes along the river bluffs. saw the yellow and red courants, not yet ripe; also the gooseberry which begins to ripen; the wild rose which grows here in great abundance in the bottoms of all these rivers is now in full bloom, and adds not a little to the beaty of the cenery. we took the width of the two rivers, found the left hand or S. fork 372 yards and the N. fork 200. The noth fork is deeper than the other but it's courant not so swift; it's waters run in the same boiling and roling manner which has uniformly characterized the Missouri throughout it's whole course so far; it's waters are of a whitish brown colour very thick and terbid, also characteristic of the Missouri; while the South fork is perfectly transparent runds very rappid but with a smoth unruffled surface it's bottom composed of round and flat smooth stones like most rivers issuing from a mountainous country. the bed of the N. fork composed of some gravel but principally mud; in short the air & character of this river is so precisely that of the missouri below that the party with very few exceptions have already pronounced the N. fork to be the Missouri; myself and Capt. C. not quite so precipitate have not yet decided but if we were to give our opinions I believe we should be in the minority, certain it is that the North fork gives the colouring matter and character which is retained from hence to the gulph of Mexico. I am confident that this river rises in and passes a great distance through an open plain country I expect that it has some of it's souces on the Eastern side of the rocky mountain South of the Saskashawan, but that it dose not penetrate the first range of these Mountains and that much the greater part of it's sources are in a northwardly direction towards the lower and middle parts of the Saskashawan in the open plains. convinced I am that if it penetrated the Rocky Mountains to any great distance it's waters would be clearer unless it should run an immence distance indeed after leaving those mountains through these level plains in order to acquire it's turbid hue. what astonishes us a little is that the Indians who appeared to be so well acquainted with the geography of this country should not have mentioned this river on wright hand if it be not the Missouri; the river that scolds at all others, as they call it if there is in reallity such an one, ought agreeably to their account, to have fallen in a considerable distance below, and on the other hand if this righthand or N. fork be the Missouri I am equally astonished at their not mentioning the S. fork which they must have passed in order to get to those large falls which they mention on the Missouri. thus have our cogitating faculties been busily employed all day.

Those who have remained at camp today have been busily engaged in dressing skins for cloathing, notwithstanding that many of them have their feet so mangled and bruised with the stones and rough ground over which they passed barefoot, that they can scarcely walk or stand; at least it is with great pain they do either. for some days past they were unable to wear their mockersons; they have fallen off considerably, but notwithstanding the difficulties past, or those which seem now to mennace us, they still remain perfectly cheerfull. In the evening the parties whom we had sent out returned agreeably to instructions. The parties who had been sent up the rivers in canoes informed that they ascended some distance and had then left their canoes and walked up the rivers a considerable distance further barely leaving themselves time to return; the North fork was not so rappid as the other and afforded the easiest navigation of course; Six feet appeared to be the shallowest water of the S. Branch and 5 feet that of the N. Their accounts were by no means satisfactory nor did the information we acquired bring us nigher to the decision of our question or determine us which stream to take. Sergt. Pryor had ascended the N. fork and had taken the following courses and distances-viz-

Joseph and Reubin Fields reported that they had been up the South fork about 7 mes. on a streight course somewhat N of W. and that there the little river which discharges itself into the North fork just above us, was within 100 yards of the S. fork; that they came down this little river and found it a boald runing stream of about 40 yds. wide containg much timber in it's bottom, consisting of the narrow and wide leafed cottonwood with some birch and box alder undrgrowth willows rosebushes currents &c. they saw a great number of Elk on this river and some beaver. Those accounts being by no means satisfactory as to the fundamental point; Capt. C. and myself concluded to set out early the next morning with a small party each, and ascend these rivers untill we could perfectly satisfy ourselves of the one, which it would be most expedient for us to take on our main journey to the Pacific. accordingly it was agreed that I should ascend the right hand fork and he the left. I gave orders to Sergt. Pryor Drewyer, Shields, Windsor, Cruzatte and La Page to hold themselves in readiness to accompany me in the morning. Capt. Clark also selected Reubin &Joseph Fields, Sergt. Gass, Shannon and his black man York, to accompany him. we agreed to go up those rivers one day and a halfs march or further if it should appear necessary to satisfy us more fully of the point in question. the hunters killed 2 Buffaloe, 6 Elk and 4 deer today. the evening proved cloudy. we took a drink of grog this evening and gave the men a dram, and made all matters ready for an early departure in the morning. I had now my sack and blanket happerst in readiness to swing on my back, which is the first time in my life that I had ever prepared a burthen of this kind, and I am fully convinced that it will not be the last. I take my Octant with me also, this I confide La Page.

[Clark, June 3, 1805] June 3rd Monday 1805 we formed a Camp on the point in the junction of the two rivers, and dispatched a Canoe & three men up each river to examine and find if possible which is the most probable branch, the left fork which is the largest we are doubtfull of, the Indians do not mention any river falling in on the right in this part of the Missouri, The Scolding river, if there is Such a one Should have fallen in below agreeable to their accts. we also dispatched men in different dircts. by land, to a mountain Covered with Snow to the South & other up each river- Capt Lewis and my Self walked out & assended the hill in the point observed a leavel open Countrey to the foot of the mountains which lye South of this, also a River which falls into the Right hand fork about 11/2 miles above its mouth on the Lard. Side this little river discharges a great deal of water & contains as much Cotton timber in its bottoms as either of the others we saw Buffalow & antelopes &c. wild Cheries, red & yellow hurries, Goose berries &c. abound in the river bottoms, prickley pares on the high plains, we had a meridian altitude and the Lattd. produced was 47° 24' 12" N. the after part of the day proved Cloudy, we measured each river and found the one to Right hand 200 yards wide of water & the Left hand fork 372 yards wide & rapid- the right hand fork falling the other at a Stand and Clear, the right fork and the river which fall into it is Coloured & a little muddey. Several men Complain of their feet being Sore in walking in the Sand & their being Cut by the Stones They to be Sure have a bad time of it obliged to walk on Shore & haul the rope and 9/10 of their time bear footed, in the evening late the Canoes returned and the men informed us that they had assended Some miles by water & left their Canoes & walked on land the greater part of the day, their accounts by no means Satisfactory, Serjt. Pryor assended the right hand fork and took the following Courses, &c

Joseph & Rubin Fields went up the left fork 7 miles on a direct line at which place, the Small river which falls into the right hand fork approaches within 100 yards of the South fork, they Came down the Small river which is a bold Stream Covered with Elk & Some beaver, its bottoms Covered with wood, as the Information given by those parties respecting the rivers did not Satisfy us as to the main & principal branch Capt. Lewis & my Self deturmined to go up each of those rivers one Day & a half with a view to Satisfy ourselves which of the two was the principal Stream and best calculated for us to assend- The hunters Killed 2 buffalow, 6 Elk & Several deer to day we refreshed our party with a dram &c Cloudy evining.-

[Lewis, June 4, 1805] Tuesday June 4th 1805 This morning early Capt. C. departed, and at the same time I passed the wright hand fork opposite to our camp below a small Island; from hence I steered N. 30 W. 41/2 to a commanding eminence; here I took the following bearings of the mountains which were in view. The North Mountains appear to change their direction from that of being parallel with the Missouri turning to the North and terminating abruptly; their termineation bearing N. 48° E distant by estimate 30 mes. The South Mountains appear to turn to the S. also terminating abrubtly, their extremity bearing S. 8 W. distant 25 mes. The Barn Mountain, a lofty mountain so called from it's resemblance to the roof of a large Barn, is a seperate Mountain and appears reather to the wright of and retreating from the extremity of the S. mts.; this boar S. 38 W. distant 35 ms. The North fork which I am now ascending lies to my left and appears to make a considerable bend to the N. W. on it's Western border a range of hills about 10 mes. long appear to lye parallel with the river and from hence bear N. 60° W. to the N. of this range of hills an Elivated point of the river bluff on it's Lard. side boar N. 72° W. distant 12 mes. to this last object I now directed my course through a high level dry open plain. the whole country in fact appears to be one continued plain to the foot of the mountains or as far as the eye can reach; the soil appears dark rich and fertile yet the grass is by no means as high nor dose it look so luxurient as I should have expected, it is short just sufficient to conceal the ground. great abundance of prickly pears which are extreemly troublesome; as the thorns very readily perce the foot through the Mockerson; they are so numerous that it requires one half of the traveler's attention to avoid them In these plains I observed great numbers of the brown Curloos, a small species of curloo or plover of a brown colour about the size of the common snipe and not unlike it in form with a long celindric curved and pointed beak; it's wings are proportionately long and the tail short; in the act of liteing this bird lets itself down by an extention of it's wings without motion holding their points very much together above it's back, in this rispect differing ascentially from any bird I ever observed. a number of sparrows also of three distinct species I observed. also a small bird which in action resembles the lark, it is about the size of a large sparrow of a dark brown colour with some white fathers in the tail; this bird or that which I take to be the male rises into the air about 60 feet and supporting itself in the air with a brisk motion of the wings sings very sweetly, has several shrill soft notes reather of the plaintive order which it frequently repeats and varies, after remaining stationary about a minute in his aireal station he descends obliquely occasionly pausing and accomnying his decension with a note something like twit twit twit; on the ground he is silent. thirty or forty of these birds will be stationed in the air at a time in view, these larks as I shall call them add much to the gayety and cheerfullness of the scene. All those birds are now seting and laying their eggs in the plains; their little nests are to be seen in great abundance as we pass. there are meriads of small grasshoppers in these plains which no doubt furnish the principal aliment of this numerous progeny of the feathered creation. after walking about eight miles I grew thisty and there being no water in the plains I changed my direction and boar obliquely in towards the river, on my arrival at which about 3 mes. below the point of observation, we discovered two deer at feed at some distance near the river; I here halted the party and sent Drewyer to kill one of them for breakfast; this excellent hunter soon exceded his orders by killing of them both; they proved to be two Mule Bucks in fine order; we soon kindled a fire cooked and made a hearty meal. it was not yet twelve when we arrived at the river and I was anxious to take the Meridian Altd. of the sun but the clouds prevent ed my obtaining the observation. after refreshing ourselves we proceded up the river to the extremity of the first course, from whence the river boar on it's general course N. 15° W. 2 M. to a bluff point on Stard. here Drewyer killed four other deer of the common kind; we skined them and hung up a part of the meat and the skins as we did also of the first, and took as much of the meat as we thought would answer for our suppers and proceeded N. 30 W. 2 m. to the entrance of a large creek on Lard. side the part of the river we have passed is from 40 to 60 yds. wide, is deep, has falling banks, the courant strong, the water terbid and in short has every appearance of the missouri below except as to size. it's bottoms narrow but well timbered. Salts coal and other mineral appearances as usual; the bluffs principally of dark brown, yellow and some white clay; some freestone also appears in places. The river now boar N. 20° E. 12 mes. to a bluff on Lard. At the commencement of this course we ascended the hills which are about 200 feet high, and passed through the plains about 3 m. but finding the dry ravines so steep and numerous we determined to return to the river and travel through it's bottoms and along the foot and sides of the bluffs, accordingly we again reached the river about 4 miles from the commencement of the last course and encamped a small distant above on the Stard. side in a bend among the willow bushes which defended us from the wind which blew hard from the N. W. it rained this evening and wet us to the skin; the air was extremely could. just before we encamped Drewyer fired at a large brown bar across the river and wounded him badly but it was too late to pursue him. killed a braro and a beaver, also at the place of our encampment, a very fine Mule deer. we saw a great number of Buffaloe, Elk, wolves and foxes today. the river bottoms form one emence garden of roses, now in full bloe.

[Clark, June 4, 1805] June 4th Tuesday 1805 Capt. Lewis & my Self each with a Small party of men Set out earlythose who accompanied Capt Lewis were G. Drewyer Serjt. Pryor, J Shields, P. Crusat J. B. de Page, R. Winser, went up the N. side of the N. fork. those who accompanied me were Serjt. Gass Jos. & Ruben Fields G. Shannon & my black man York, and we Set out to examine the South fork, our first Course was S. 25° W. 7 miles to the S. fork at a Spring, at which place the little river which falls into the N. fork is 100 yards distant only Seperated from the South fork by a narrow ridge. our course from thence S. 20° W. 8 miles to the river at an Island where we dined below a Small river falls in on the S E Side which heads in a mountain to the S. E about 20 miles. North of this place about 4 miles the little river brakes thro a high ridge into the open Leavel plain thro which we have passd. from the point, this plain is covered with low grass & prickley pear, emence number of Prarie dogs or barking Squirel are thro this plain- after eating we proceeded on N. 45° W. Struck the river at 3 miles 5, 9 & 13 miles at which place we encamped in an old Indian lodge made of Stiks and bark at the river near our camp we Saw two white Bear, one of them was nearly catching Joseph Fields who could not fire, as his gun was wet the bear was So near that it Struck his foot, and we were not in a Situation to give him assistance, a Clift of rocks Seperated us the bear got allarmed at our Shot & yells & took the river.- Some rain all the afternoon Saw Several Gangues of Buffalow at a distance in the open plains on each Side, Saw Mule deer antilopes & wolves- The river is rapid & Closely himed on one or the other Side with high bluffs, Crouded with Islands & graveley bars Containing but a Small quantity of timber on its bottoms & none on the high land.

[Lewis, June 5, 1805] Wednesday June 5th 1805. This morning was cloudy and so could that I was obleged to have recourse to a blanket coat in order to keep myself comfortable altho walking. the rain continued during the greater part of last night. the wind hard from N. W. we set out at sunrise and proceded up the river eight miles on the course last taken yesterday evening, at the extremity of which a large creek falls in on the Stard. 25 yards. wide at it's entrance, some timber but no water, notwithstanding the rain; it's course upwards is N. E. it is astonishing what a quantity of water it takes to saturate the soil of this country, the earth of the plains are now opened in large crivices in many places and yet looks like a rich loam from the entrance of this Creek (which I called Lark C.) the river boar N. 50. W. 4 m. at the entrance of this creek the bluffs were very steep and approached the river so near on the Stard. side that we ascended the hills and passed through the plains; at the extremity of this course we returned to the river which then boar North 2 rues. from the same point, I discovered a lofty single mountain which appeard to be at a great distance, perhaps 80 or more miles it boar N. 52 W. from it's conic figure I called it tower Mountain. we now passed through the river bottoms to the extremity of the last course thence with the river S 60° W 11/2 m. S 10 W. 3 m N 50 W 11/2 at the extremity of which I again ascended the bluffs and took a course to a point of the Lard. bluffs of the river which boar West 10 m. the river making a deep bend to the south that is of at least five miles from the center of the chord line to the center of the bend. on this course we passed through the plains found the plains as yesterday extreemly leavel and beautifull, great quanties of Buffaloe, some wolves foxes and Antelopes seen. near the river the plain is cut by deep ravines in this plain and from one to nine miles from the river or any water, we saw the largest collection of the burrowing or barking squirrels that we had ever yet seen; we passed through a skirt of the territory of this community for about 7 miles. I saw a flock of the mountain cock, or a large species of heath hen with a long pointed tail which the Indians informed us were common to the Rockey Mountains, I sent Shields to kill one of them but he was obliged to fire a long distance at them and missed his aim. as we had not killed or eat anything today we each killed a burrowing squrrel as we passed them in order to make shure of our suppers. we again intersepted the river at the expiration of the last course or the lard. bluffs, from whence it now boar N 80° W. 2 mes. from this point saw some other lofty mountains to the N. W. of Tower Mtn. which boar N. 65°W. 80 or 100 mes. distant at the expiration of this course we killed five Elk and a blacktailed or mule deer and encamped on Stard. side of the river in a handsome well timbered bottom where there were several old stick lodges. in the forepart of the day there was but little timber in the river bottoms but the quantity is now greater than usual. the river is about 80 yds. wide with a strong steady courant and from 6 to 10 feet water. I had the burrowing squirrels roasted by way of experiment and found the flesh well flavored and tender; some of them were very fat.

[Clark, June 5, 1805] June 5th Wednesday 1805 Some little rain & Snow last night the mountains to our S E. covered with Snow this morning air verry Cold & raining a little, we Saw 8 buffalow opposit, they made 2 attempts to Cross, the water being So Swift they Could not, about the time we were Setting out three white bear approached our Camp we killed the three & eate part of one & Set out & proceeded on N. 20° W 11 miles. -k the river at maney places in this distance to a ridge on the N. Side t m the top of which I could plainly See a mountain to the South & W. covered with Snow at a long distance, The mountains opposit to us to the S. E. is also Covered with Snow this morning.- a high ridge from those mountains approach the river on the S E Side forming Some Clifts of hard dark Stone.- From the ridge at which place I Struck the river last, I could _____ discover that the river run west of South a long distance, and has a Strong rapid Current, as this river Continued its width debth & rapidity and the Course west of South, going up further would be useless, I determined to return, I accordingly Set out, thro the plain on a Course N. 30° E on my return & Struck the little river at 20 miles passing thro a Leavel plain, at the little river we killed 2 buck Elk & dined on their marrow, proceeded on a few miles & Camped, haveing killed 2 deer which was verry fat, Some few drops of rain to day, the evening fair wind hard from the N. E. I Saw great numbers of Elk & white tale deer, Some beaver, antelope mule deer & wolves & one bear on this little river marked my name in a tree N. Side near the ridge where the little river brakes thro

[Lewis, June 6, 1805] Thursday June 6th 1805. I now became well convinced that this branch of the Missouri had it's direction too much to the North for our rout to the Pacific, and therefore determined to return the next day after taking an observation of the sun's Meridian Altitude in order to fix the latitude of the place. The forepart of the last evening was fair but in the latter part of the night clouded up and contnued so with short intervals of sunshine untill a little before noon when the whole horizon was overcast, and I of course disappointed in making the observation which I much wished. I had sent Sergt. Pryor and Windsor early this morning with orders to procede up the river to some commanding eminence and take it's bearing as far as possible. in the mean time the four others and myself were busily engaged in making two rafts on which we purposed descending the river; we had just completed this work when Sergt. Pryor and Windsor returned, it being about noon; they reported that they had proceded from hence S 70 W. 6 m. to the summit of a commanding eminence from whence the river on their left was about 2 1/2 miles distant; that a point of it's Lard. bluff, which was visible boar S 80 W. distant about 15 ms.; that the river on their left bent gradually arround to this point, and from thence seemed to run Northwardly. we now took dinner and embarcked with our plunder and five Elk's skins on the rafts but were soon convinced that this mode of navigation was hazerdous particularly with those rafts they being too small and slender. we wet a part of our baggage and were near loosing one of our guns; I therefore determined to abandon the rafts and return as we had come, by land. I regreted much being obliged to leave my Elk's skins, which I wanted to assist in forming my leather boat; those we had prepared at Fort Mandan being injured in such manner that they would not answer. we again swung our packs and took our way through the open plains for about 12 mes. when we struck the river; the wind blew a storm from N. E. accompanyed by frequent showers of rain; we were wet and very could. continued our rout down the river only a few miles before the Abruptness of the clifts and their near approach to the river compelled us take the plains and once more face the storm; here we boar reather too much to the North and it was late in the evening before we reached the river, in our way we killed two buffaloe and took with us as much of the flesh as served us that night, and a part of the next day. we encamped a little below the entrance of the large dry Creek called Lark C. having traveled abut 25 mes. since noon. it continues to rain and we have no shelter, an uncomfortable nights rest is the natural consequence.

[Clark, June 6, 1805] June 6th Thursday 1805 a Cloudy Cold raw day wind hard from the N. E. we Set out early & traveled down the little river which was imedeately in our Course on this river we killed 7 Deer for their Skins the bottoms of this little river is in everry respect except in extent like the large bottoms of the Missouri below the forks containing a great perpotion of a kind of Cotton wood with a leaf resembling a wild Cherry-. I also observed wild Tanzey on this little river in great quantities, we halted at 12 oClock and eate a part of a fat Buck, after Dinner we assended the Plain at which time it began to rain and Continued all day, at 5 oClock we arrived at our Camp on the point, where I expected to meet Capt Lewis- he did not return this evening.- my Self and party much fatigued haveing walked Constantly as hard as we Could march over a Dry hard plain, dcending & assending the Steep river hills & gullies, in my absence the party had killed an Elk & 2 buffalow, I Sent out for the meat a part of which was brought in- nothing remarkable had transpired at camp in my absence

[Lewis, June 7, 1805] Friday June 7th 1805. It continued to rain almost without intermission last night and as I expected we had a most disagreable and wrestless night. our camp possessing no allurements, we left our watery beads at an early hour and continued our rout down the river. it still continues to rain the wind hard from N. E. and could. the grownd remarkably slipry, insomuch that we were unable to walk on the sides of the bluffs where we had passed as we ascended the river. notwithstanding the rain that has now fallen the earth of these bluffs is not wet to a greater debth than 2 inches; in it's present state it is precisely like walking over frozan grownd which is thawed to small debth and slips equally as bad. this clay not only appears to require more water to saturate it as I before observed than any earth I ever observed but when saturated it appears on the other hand to yeald it's moisture with equal difficulty. In passing along the face of one of these bluffs today I sliped at a narrow pass of about 30 yards in length and but for a quick and fortunate recovery by means of my espontoon I should been precipitated into the river down a craggy pricipice of about ninety feet. I had scarcely reached a place on which I could stand with tolerable safety even with the assistance of my espontoon before I heard a voice behind me cry out god god Capt. what shall I do on turning about I found it was Windsor who had sliped and fallen abut the center of this narrow pass and was lying prostrate on his belley, with his wright hand arm and leg over the precipice while he was holding on with the left arm and foot as well as he could which appeared to be with much difficulty. I discovered his danger and the trepedation which he was in gave me still further concern for I expected every instant to see him loose his strength and slip off; altho much allarmed at his situation I disguised my feelings and spoke very calmly to him and assured him that he was in no kind of danger, to take the knife out of his belt behind him with his wright hand and dig a hole with it in the face of the bank to receive his wright foot which he did and then raised himself to his knees; I then directed him to take off his mockersons and to come forward on his hands and knees holding the knife in one hand and the gun in the other this he happily effected and escaped. those who were some little distance bhind returned by my orders and waded the river at the foot of the bluff where the water was breast deep. it was useless we knew to attempt the plains on this part of the river in consequence of the numerous steep ravines which intersected and which were quite as had as the river bluffs. we therefore continued our rout down the river sometimes in the mud and water of the bottom lands, at others in the river to our breasts and when the water became so deep that we could not wade we cut footsteps in the face of the steep bluffs with our knives and proceded. we continued our disagreeable march through the rain mud and water untill late in the evening having traveled only about 18 miles, and encamped in an old Indian stick lodge which afforded us a dry and comfortable shelter. during the day we had killed six deer some of them in very good order altho none of them had yet entirely discarded their winter coats. we had reserved and brought with us a good supply of the best peices; we roasted and eat a hearty supper of our venison not having taisted a mosel before during the day; I now laid myself down on some willow boughs to a comfortable nights rest, and felt indeed as if I was fully repaid for the toil and pain of the day, so much will a good shelter, a dry bed, and comfortable supper revive the sperits of the waryed, wet and hungry traveler.

[Clark, June 7, 1805] June 7th Friday 1805 rained moderately all the last night and Continus this morning, the wind from the S. W, off the mountains, The Themometer Stood at 40° above 0, I allow Several men to hunt a Short time to day, the rain Continue moderately all day the bottom verry muddey 2 buffalow an Elk & Deer killed to day- Capt. Lewis not returned yet. river falling

[Lewis, June 8, 1805] Saturday June 8th 1805 It continued to rain moderately all last night this morning was cloudy untill about ten oClock when it cleared off and became a fine day. we breakfasted and set out about sunrise and continued our rout down the river bottoms through the mud and water as yesterday, tho the road was somewhat better than yesterday and we were not so often compelled to wade in the river. we passed some dangerous and difficult bluffs. The river bottoms affording all the timber which is to be seen in the country they are filled with innumerable litle birds that resort thither either for shelter or to build their nests. when sun began to shine today these birds appeared to be very gay and sung most inchantingly; I observed among them the brown thrush, Robbin, turtle dove, linnit goaldfinch, the large and small blackbird, wren and several other birds of less note. some of the inhabitants of the praries also take reffuge in these woods at night or from a storm. The whole of my party to a man except myself were fully peswaided that this river was the Missouri, but being fully of opinion that it was neither the main stream or that which it would be advisable for us to take, I determined to give it a name and in honour of Miss Maria W-d. called it Maria's River. it is true that the hue of the waters of this turbulent and troubled stream but illy comport with the pure celestial virtues and amiable qualifications of that lovely fair one; but on the other hand it is a noble river; one destined to become in my opinion an object of contention between the two great powers of America and Great Britin with rispect to the adjustment of the North westwardly boundary of the former; and that it will become one of the most interesting brances of the Missouri in a commercial point of view, I have but little doubt, as it abounds with anamals of the fur kind, and most probably furnishes a safe and direct communication to that productive country of valuable furs exclusively enjoyed at present by the subjects of his Britanic Majesty; in adition to which it passes through a rich fertile and one of the most beatifully picteresque countries that I ever beheld, through the wide expance of which, innumerable herds of living anamals are seen, it's borders garnished with one continued garden of roses, while it's lofty and open forrests, are the habitation of miriads of the feathered tribes who salute the ear of the passing traveler with their wild and simple, yet sweet and cheerfull melody.- I arrived at camp about 5 OClock in the evening much fatiegued, where I found Capt. Clark and the ballance of the party waiting our return with some anxiety for our safety having been absent near two days longer than we had engaged to return. on our way to camp we had killed 4 deer and two Antelopes; the skins of which as well as those we killed while on the rout we brought with us. Maria's river may be stated generally from sixty to a hundred yards wide, with a strong and steady current and possessing 5 feet water in the most sholly parts.

As the incidents which occurred Capt. C. during his rout will be more fully and satisfactoryley expressed by himself I here insert a copy of his journal during the days we wer seperated.-

I now gave myself this evening to rest from my labours, took a drink of grog and gave the men who had accompanyed me each a dram. Capt. Clark ploted the courses of the two rivers as far as we had ascended them. I now began more than ever to suspect the varacity of Mr. Fidler or the correctness of his instruments. for I see that Arrasmith in his late map of N. America has laid down a remarkable mountain in the chain of the Rocky mountains called the tooth nearly as far South as Latitude 45°, and this is said to be from the discoveries of Mr. Fidler? we are now within a hundred miles of the Rocky Mountains, and I find from my observation of the 3rd Inst that the latitude of this place is 47° 24' 12.8". the river must therefore turn much to the South, between this and the rocky Mountain to have permitted Mr. Fidler to have passed along the Eastern border of these mountains as far S. as nearly 45° without even seeing it. but from hence as far as Capt. C. had ascended the S. fork or Missouri being the distance of 55 miles it's course is S. 29°W. and it still appeared to bear considerably to the W. of South as far as he could see it. I think therefore that we shall find that the Missouri enters the rocky mountains to the North of 45°- we did take the liberty of placing his discoveries or at least the Southern extremity of them about a degree further N. in the sketh which we sent on to the government this spring mearly from the Indian information of the bearing from Fort Mandan of the entrance of the Missouri into the Rocky Mountains, and I reather suspect that actual observation will take him at least one other degree further North. The general Course of Maria's river from hence to the extremity of the last course taken by Sergt. pryor is N 69° W. 59 mes.

[Clark, June 8, 1805] June 8th Saturday 1805 rained moderately all the last night & Some this morning untill 10 oClock, I am Some what uneasy for Capt. Lewis & party as days has now passed the time he was to have returned, I had all the arms put in order and permited Severall men to hunt, aired and dried our Stores &c. The rivers at this point has fallen 6 Inches Sinc our arrival, at 10 oClock cleared away and became fair- the wind all the morning from the S. W. & hard- The water of the South fork is of a redish brown colour this morning the other river of a whitish colour as usual-The mountains to the South Covered with Snow. Wind Shifted to the N E in the evening, about 5 oClock Capt. Lewis arrived with the party much fatigued, and inform'd me that he had assended the river about 60 miles by Land and that the river had a bold current of about 80 or 100 yards wide the bottoms of Gravel & mud, and may be estimated at 5 feet water in Sholest parts

Some rain in the evening. the left hand fork rose a little.

[Lewis, June 9, 1805] Sunday June 9th 1805. We determined to deposite at this place the large red perogue all the heavy baggage which we could possibly do without and some provision, salt, tools powder and Lead &c with a view to lighten our vessels and at the same time to strengthen their crews by means of the seven hands who have been heretofore employd. in navigating the red perogue; accordingly we set some hands to diging a hole or cellar for the reception of our stores. these holes in the ground or deposits are called by the engages cashes; on enquiry I found that Cruzatte was well acquainted this business and therefore left the management of it intirely to him. today we examined our maps, and compared the information derived as well from them as from the Indians and fully settled in our minds the propryety of addopting the South fork for the Missouri, as that which it would be most expedient for us to take. The information of Mr. Fidler incorrect as it is strongly argued the necessity of taking the South fork, for if he has been along the Eastern side of the rocky mountains as far as even Latd. 47°, which I think fully as far south as he ever was in that direction, and saw only small rivulets making down from those mountains the presumption is very strong that those little streams do not penetrate the rocky Mountains to such distance as would afford rational grownds for a conjecture that they had their sources near any navigable branch of the Columbia, and if he has seen those rivulets as far south as 47° they are most probably the waters of some Nothern branch of the Missouri or South fork probably the river called by the Indians Medicine River; we therefore cannot hope by going Northwardly of this place being already in Latititude 47° 24" to find a stream between this place and the Saskashawan which dose penetrate the Rocky mountains, and which agreeably to the information of the Indians with rispect to the Missouri, dose possess a navigable curent some distance in those mountains. The Indian information also argued strongly in favour of the South fork. they informed us that the water of the Missouri was nearly transparent at the great falls, this is the case with the water of the South fork; that the falls lay a little to the South of sunset from them; this is also brobale as we are only a few minutes North of Fort Mandan and the South fork bears considerably South from hence to the Mountains; that the falls are below the rocky mountains and near the Nothern termineation of one range of those mountains. a range of mountains which apear behind the S. Mountains and which appear to terminate S. W. from this place and on this side of the unbroken chain of the Rocky Mountains gives us hope that this part of their information is also correct, and there is sufficient distance between this and the mountains for many and I fear for us much too many falls. another impression on my mind is that if the Indians had passed any stream as large as the South fork on their way to the Missouri that they would not have omitted mentioning it; and the South fork from it's size and complexion of it's waters must enter the Ry. Mountains and in my opinion penetrates them to a great distance, or els whence such an immence body of water as it discharges; it cannot procede from the dry plains to the N. W. of the Yellow Stone river on the East side of the Rocky Mountains for those numerous large dry channels which we witnessed on that side as we ascended the Missouri forbid such a conjecture; and that it should take it's sourses to the N. W. under those mountains the travels of Mr. Fidler fobid us to beleive. Those ideas as they occurred to me I indevoured to impress on the minds of the party all of whom except Capt. C. being still firm in the beleif that the N. Fork was the Missouri and that which we ought to take; they said very cheerfully that they were ready to follow us any wher we thought proper to direct but that they still thought that the other was the river and that they were affraid that the South fork would soon termineate in the mountains and leave us at a great distance from the Columbia. Cruzatte who had been an old Missouri navigator and who from his integrity knowledge and skill as a waterman had acquired the confidence of every individual of the party declared it as his opinion that the N. fork was the true genuine Missouri and could be no other. finding them so determined in this beleif, and wishing that if we were in an error to be able to detect it and rectify it as soon as possible it was agreed between Capt. C. and myself that one of us should set out with a small party by land up the South fork and continue our rout up it untill we found the falls or reached the snowy Mountains by which means we should be enabled to determine this question prety accurately. this expedition I prefered undertaking as Capt. C best waterman &c. and determined to set out the day after tomorrow; I wished to make some further observations at this place, and as we had determined to leave our blacksmith's bellows and tools here it was necessary to repare some of our arms, and particularly my Airgun the main spring of which was broken, before we left this place. these and some other preperations will necessarily detain us two perhaps three days. I felt myself very unwell this morning and took a portion of salts from which I feel much releif this evening. The cash being completed I walked to it and examined it's construction. it is in a high plain about 40 yards distant from a steep bluff of the South branch on it's nothern side; the situation a dry one which is always necessary. a place being fixed on for a cash, a circle abut 20 inches in diameter is first discribed, the terf or sod of this circle is carefully removed, being taken out as entire as possible in order that it may be replaced in the same situation when the chash is filled and secured. this circular hole is then sunk perpendicularly to the debth of one foot, if the ground be not firm somewhat deeper. they then begin to work it out wider as they proceed downwards untill they get it about six or seven feet deep giving it nearly the shape of the kettle or lower part of a large still. it's bottom is also somewhat sunk in the center. the dementions of the cash is in proportion to the quantity of articles intended to be deposited. as the earth is dug it is handed up in a vessel and carefully laid on a skin or cloth and then carryed to some place where it can be thrown in such manner as to conseal it usually into some runing stream wher it is washed away and leaves no traces which might lead to the discovery of the cash. before the goods are deposited they must be well dryed; a parsel of small dry sticks are then collected and with them a floor is maid of three or four inches thick which is then covered with some dry hay or a raw hide well dryed; on this the articles are deposited, taking care to keep them from touching the walls by putting other dry sticks between as you stoe away the merchandize, when nearly full the goods are covered with a skin and earth thrown in and well ramed untill with the addition of the turf furst removed the whole is on a level with the serface of the ground. in this manner dryed skins or merchandize will keep perfectly sound for several years. the traders of the Missouri, particularly those engaged in the trade with the Siouxs are obliged to have frequent recourse to this method in order to avoyd being robed. most of the men are busily engaged dressing skins for cloathing. In the evening Cruzatte gave us some music on the violin and the men passed the evening in dancing singing &c and were extreemly cheerfull.-

[Clark, June 9, 1805] June 9th Sunday a fair morning the wind hard from the S. W. the river during the night fell 1 Inch, we conclude to bury a few of our heavy articles, Some Powder & Lead provisions & a fiw Tools, in case of accident and leave one perogue at this place, and as Soon as those things are accomplished to assend the South fork, which appears to be more in our Course than the N. fork the Genl. Course of the South fork for 35 miles is S. 29° W.- that of the N. fork is N. 69° W. for 59 miles, and as we are North of Fort mandan it is probable the most Southerley fork is the best for us.- Capt. Lewis a little unwell to day & take Salts &c. Send out 7 men to make a cache or hole to burry the Stores, air out Cloathes &c. &c. finish'd the cache or Seller &c. the men all engaged dressing Skins for their clothes, in the evening the party amused themselves danceing and Singing Songes in the most Social manner. had a meridian altitude which gave 47° 24' 29" took some Luner observations which gave for Longitude _____ variation 151/2° East

[Lewis, June 10, 1805] Monday June 10th 1805. The day being fair and fine we dryed all our baggage and merchandize. Shields renewed the main Spring of my air gun we have been much indebted to the ingenuity of this man on many occasions; without having served any regular apprenticeship to any trade, he makes his own tools principally and works extreemly well in either wood or metal, and in this way has been extreenely servicable to us, as well as being a good hunter and an excellent waterman. in order to guard against accedents we thout it well to conceal some ammunicion here and accordingly buryed a tin cannester of 4 lbs. of powder and an adequate quantity of lead near our tent; a cannester of 6 lbs. lead and an ax in a thicket up the S. Fork three hundred yards distant from the point. we concluded that we still could spare more amunition for this deposit Capt. Clark was therefore to make a further deposit in the morning, in addition to one Keg of 20 lbs. and an adequate proportion of lead which had been laid by to be buried in the large Cash. we now scelected the articles to be deposited in this cash which consisted of 2 best falling axes, one auger, a set of plains, some files, blacksmiths bellowses and hammers Stake tongs &c. 1 Keg of flour, 2 Kegs of parched meal, 2 Kegs of Pork, 1 Keg of salt, some chissels, a cooper's Howel, some tin cups, 2 Musquets, 3 brown bear skins, beaver skins, horns of the bighorned anamal, a part of the men's robes clothing and all their superfluous baggage of every discription, and beaver traps.- we drew up the red perogue into the middle of a small Island at the entrance of Maria's river, and secured and made her fast to the trees to prevent the high floods from carrying her off put my brand on several trees standing near her, and covered her with brush to shelter her from the effects of the sun. At 3 P.M. we had a hard wind from the S. W. which continued about an hour attended with thunder and rain. as soon as the shower had passed over we drew out our canoes, corked, repared and loaded them. I still feel myself somewhat unwell with the disentary, but determined to set out in the morning up the South fork or Missouri leaving Capt. Clark to compleat the deposit and follow me by water with the party; accordingly gave orders to Drewyer, Joseph Fields, Gibson and Goodrich to hold themselves in readiness to accompany me in the morning. Sah-cah-gah, we a, our Indian woman is very sick this evening; Capt. C. blead her. the night was cloudy with some rain.

I saw a small bird today which I do not recollect ever having seen before. it is about the size of the blue thrush or catbird, and it's contour not unlike that bird. the beak is convex, moderately curved, black, smoth, and large in proportion to its size. the legs were black, it had four toes of the same colour on eah foot, and the nails appeared long and somewhat in form like the tallons of the haulk, the eye black and proportionably large. a bluish brown colour occupied the head, neck, and back, the belly was white; the tail was reather long in proportion and appeared to be composed of feathers of equal length of which a part of those in the center were white the others black. the wings were long and were also varigated with white and black. on each side of the head from the beak back to the neck a small black stripe extended imbrasing the eye. it appeared to be very busy in catching insects which I presume is it's usual food; I found the nest of this little bird, the female which differed but little in size or plumage from the male was seting on four eggs of a pale blue colour with small black freckles or dots.- the bee martin or Kingbird is common to this country tho there are no bees in this country, nor have we met with a honey bee since we passed the entrance of the Osage river.

[Clark, June 10, 1805] June 10th Monday 1805 a fine day dry all our articles arrange our baggage burry Some Powder & lead in the point, Some Lead a canister of Powder & an ax in a thicket in the point at Some distance, buried on this day and in the large cache or whole we buried on the up land near the S. fork 1 mile up S. S. we drew up our large Perogue into the middle of a Small Island in the North fork and covered her with bushes after makeing her fast to the trees, branded several trees to prevent the Indians injureing her, at 3 oClock we had hard wind from the S. W. thunder and rain for about an hour after which we repaired & Corked the Canoes & loadded them- Sah cah gah, we a our Indian woman verry Sick I blead her, we deturmined to assend the South fork, and one of us, Capt. Lewis or My self to go by land as far as the Snow mountains S. 20° W. and examine the river & Countrey Course & to be Certain of our assending the proper river, Capt Lewis inclines to go by land on this expedition, according Selects 4 men George Drewyer, Gibson, Jo. Fields & S. Gutrich to accompany him & deturmine to Set out in the morning- The after noon or night Cloudy Some rain, river riseing a little.

[Lewis, June 11, 1805] Tuesday June 11th 1805 This morning I felt much better, but somewhat weakened by my disorder. at 8 A.M. I swung my pack, and set forward with my little party. proceeded to the point where Rose River a branch Maria's River approaches the Missouri so nearly. from this hight we discovered a herd of Elk on the Missouri just above us to which we desended and soon killed four of them. we butchered them and hung up the meat and skins in view of the river in order that the party might get them. I determined to take dinner here, but before the meal was prepared I was taken with such violent pain in the intestens that I was unable to partake of the feast of marrowbones. my pain still increased and towards evening was attended with a high fever; finding myself unable to march, I determined to prepare a camp of some willow boughs and remain all night. having brought no medecine with me I resolved to try an experiment with some simples; and the Choke cherry which grew abundanly in the bottom first struck my attention; I directed a parsel of the small twigs to be geathered striped of their leaves, cut into pieces of about 2 Inches in length and boiled in water untill a strong black decoction of an astringent bitter tact was produced; at sunset I took a point of this decoction and abut an hour after repeated the dze by 10 in the evening I was entirely releived from pain and in fact every symptom of the disorder forsook me; my fever abated, a gentle perspiration was produced and I had a comfortable and refreshing nights rest. Goodrich who is remarkably fond of fishing caught several douzen fish of two different species- one about 9 inches long of white colour round and in form and fins resembles the white chub common to the Potomac; this fish has a smaller head than the Chubb and the mouth is beset both above and below with a rim of fine sharp teeth; the eye moderately large, the puple dark and the iris which is narrow is of a yellowish brown colour, they bite at meat or grasshoppers. this is a soft fish, not very good, tho the flesh is of a fine white colour. the other species is precisely the form and about the size of the well known fish called the Hickory Shad or old wife, with the exception of the teeth, a rim of which garnish the outer edge of both the upper and lower jaw; the tonge and pallet are also beset with long sharp teeth bending inwards, the eye of this fish is very large, and the iris of a silvery colour and wide. of the 1st species we had caught some few before our arrival at the entrance of Maria's river, but of the last we had seen none untill we reached that place and took them in Missouri above it's junction with that river. the latter kind are much the best, and do not inhabit muddy water; the white cat continue as high as the entrance of Maria's R, but those we have caught above Mandans never excede 6 lbs. I beleive that there are but few in this part of the Missouri. saw an abundance of game today even in our short march of 9 miles.

[Clark, June 11, 1805] June 11th Tuesday 1805 a fair morning wind from the S W. hard we burry 1 keg in the Cash & 2 Canisters of Powder in 2 seperate places all with Lead; & in the Cash 2 axes, auger, Plains, 1 Keg flour, 2 Kegs Pork, 2 Kegs Parchd meal 1 Keg salt, files Chisel, 2 Musquits, Some tin cups, bowel, 3 bear Skins, Beaver Skins, Horns, & parts of the mens robes & clothes.- Beaver Traps and blacksmith's tools. Capt. Lewis Set out at 8 oClock we delayed to repare Some guns out of order & complete our deposit, which took us the day the evening fair and fine wind from the N. W. after night it became cold & the wind blew hard, the Indian woman verry Sick, I blead her which appeared to be of great Service to her both rivers riseing fast

[Lewis, June 12, 1805] Wednesday June 12th 1805. This morning I felt myself quite revived, took another portion of my decoction and set out at sunrise. I now boar out from the river in order to avoid the steep ravines of the river which usually make out in the plain to the distance of one or two miles; after gaining the leavel plain my couse was a litte to the West of S. W.- having traveled about 12 miles by 9 in the morning, the sun became warm, and I boar a little to the south in order to gain the river as well to obtain water to allay my thirst as to kill something for breakfast; for the plain through which we had been passing possesses no water and is so level that we cannot approach the buffaloe within shot before they discover us and take to flight. we arrived at the river about 10 A.M. having traveled about 15 m. at this place there is a handsom open bottom with some cottonwood timber, here we met with two large bear, and killed them boath at the first fire, a circumstance which I beleive has never happend with the party in killing the brown bear before. we dressed the bear, breakfasted on a part of one of them and hung the meat and skins on the trees out of the reach of the wolves. I left a note on a stick near the river for Capt. Clark, informing him of my progress &c.- after refreshing ourselves abut 2 hours we again ascended the bluffs and gained the high plain; saw a great number of burrowing squirrels in the plains today. also wolves Antelopes mule deer and immence herds of buffaloe. we passed a ridge of land considerably higher than the adjacent plain on either side, from this hight we had a most beatifull and picturesk view of the Rocky mountains which wer perfectly covered with Snow and reaching from S. E. to the N. of N. W.- they appear to be formed of several ranges each succeeding range rising higher than the preceding one untill the most distant appear to loose their snowey tops in the clouds; this was an august spectacle and still rendered more formidable by the recollection that we had them to pass. we traveled about twelve miles when we agin struck the Missoury at a handsome little bottom of Cottonwood timber and altho the sun had not yet set I felt myself somewhat weary being weakened I presume by late disorder; and therfore determined to remain here during the ballance of the day and night, having marched about 27 miles today. on our way in the evening we had killed a buffaloe, an Antelope and three mule deer, and taken a sufficient quantity of the best of the flesh of these anamals for three meals, which we had brought with us. This evening I ate very heartily and after pening the transactions of the day amused myself catching those white fish mentioned yesterday; they are here in great abundance I caught upwards of a douzen in a few minutes; they bit most freely at the melt of a deer which goodrich had brought with him for the purpose of fishing.

The narrow leafed cottonwood grows here in common with the other species of the same tree with a broad leaf or that which has constituted the major part of the timber of the Missouri from it's junction with the Mississippi to this place. The narrow leafed cottonwood differs only from the other in the shape of it's leaf and greater thickness of it's bark. the leaf is a long oval acutely pointed, about 2 1/2 or 3 Inches long and from 3/4 to an inch in width; it is thick, sometimes slightly grooved or channeled; margin slightly serrate; the upper disk of a common green while the under disk is of a whiteish green; the leaf is smoth. the beaver appear to be extremely fond of this tree and even seem to scelect it from among the other species of Cottonwood, probably from it's affording a deeper and softer bark than the other species.- saw some sign of the Otter as well as beaver near our camp, also a great number of tracks of the brown bear; these fellows leave a formidable impression in the mud or sand I measured one this evening which was eleven inches long exclusive of the tallons and seven and 1/4 in width.

[Clark, June 12, 1805] June 12th 1805 Wednesday last night was Clear and Cold, this morning fair we Set out at 8 oClock & proceeded on verry well wind from the S. W. The interpreters wife verry Sick So much So that I move her into the back part of our Covered part of the Perogue which is Cool, her own situation being a verry hot one in the bottom of the Perogue exposed to the Sun- Saw emence No. of Swallows in the 1st bluff on the Lard. Side, water verry Swift, the bluff are blackish Clay & Coal for about 80 feet. the earth above that for 30 or 40 feet is a brownish yellow, a number of bars of corse gravil and Stones of different Shape & Size &c. Saw a number of rattle Snakes to day one of the men cought one by the head in Catch'g hold of a bush on which his head lay reclined three canoes were in great danger today one diped water, another was near turning over &c. at 2 oClock P M a fiew drops of rain I walked thro a point and killed a Buck Elk & Deer, and we camped on the Stard Side, the Interpreters woman verry Sick worse than She has been. I give her medison one man have a fellon riseing on his hand one other with the Tooth ake has taken cold in the jaw &c.

[Lewis, June 13, 1805] Thursday June 13th 1805. This morning we set out about sunrise after taking breakfast off our venison and fish. we again ascended the hills of the river and gained the level country. the country through which we passed for the first six miles tho more roling than that we had passed yesterday might still with propryety he deemed a level country; our course as yesterday was generally S W. the river from the place we left it appeared to make a considerable bend to the South. from the extremity of this roling country I overlooked a most beatifull and level plain of great extent or at least 50 or sixty miles; in this there were infinitely more buffaloe than I had ever before witnessed at a view. nearly in the direction I had been travling or S. W. two curious mountains presented themselves of square figures, the sides rising perpendicularly to the hight of 250 feet and appeared to be formed of yellow clay; their tops appeared to be level plains; these inaccessible hights appeared like the ramparts of immence fortifications; I have no doubt but with very little assistance from art they might be rendered impregnable. fearing that the river boar to the South and that I might pass the falls if they existed between this an the snowey mountains I altered my course nealy to the South leaving those insulated hills to my wright and proceeded through the plain; I sent Feels on my right and Drewyer and Gibson on my left with orders to kill some meat and join me at the river where I should halt for dinner. I had proceded on this course about two miles with Goodrich at some distance behind me whin my ears were saluted with the agreeable sound of a fall of water and advancing a little further I saw the spray arrise above the plain like a collumn of smoke which would frequently dispear again in an instant caused I presume by the wind which blew pretty hard from the S. W. I did not however loose my direction to this point which soon began to make a roaring too tremendious to be mistaken for any cause short of the great falls of the Missouri. here I arrived about 12 OClock having traveled by estimate about 15 Miles. I hurryed down the hill which was about 200 feet high and difficult of access, to gaze on this sublimely grand specticle. I took my position on the top of some rocks about 20 feet high opposite the center of the falls. this chain of rocks appear once to have formed a part of those over which the waters tumbled, but in the course of time has been seperated from it to the distance of 150 yards lying prarrallel to it and forming a butment against which the water after falling over the precipice beats with great fury; this barrier extends on the right to the perpendicular clift which forms that board of the river but to the distance of 120 yards next to the clift it is but a few feet above the level of the water, and here the water in very high tides appears to pass in a channel of 40 yds. next to the higher part of the ledg of rocks; on the left it extends within 80 or ninty yards of the lard. Clift which is also perpendicular; between this abrupt extremity of the ledge of rocks and the perpendicular bluff the whole body of water passes with incredible swiftness. immediately at the cascade the river is about 300 yds. wide; about ninty or a hundred yards of this next the Lard. bluff is a smoth even sheet of water falling over a precipice of at least eighty feet, the remaining part of about 200 yards on my right formes the grandest sight I ever beheld, the hight of the fall is the same of the other but the irregular and somewhat projecting rocks below receives the water in it's passage down and brakes it into a perfect white foam which assumes a thousand forms in a moment sometimes flying up in jets of sparkling foam to the hight of fifteen or twenty feet and are scarcely formed before large roling bodies of the same beaten and foaming water is thrown over and conceals them. in short the rocks seem to be most happily fixed to present a sheet of the whitest beaten froath for 200 yards in length and about 80 feet perpendicular. the water after decending strikes against the butment before mentioned or that on which I stand and seems to reverberate and being met by the more impetuous courant they role and swell into half formed billows of great hight which rise and again disappear in an instant. this butment of rock defends a handsom little bottom of about three acres which is deversified and agreeably shaded with some cottonwood trees; in the lower extremity of the bottom there is a very thick grove of the same kind of trees which are small, in this wood there are several Indian lodges formed of sticks. a few small cedar grow near the ledge of rocks where I rest. below the point of these rocks at a small distance the river is divided by a large rock which rises several feet above the water, and extends downwards with the stream for about 20 yards. about a mile before the water arrives at the pitch it decends very rappidly, and is confined on the Lard. side by a perpendicular clift of about 100 feet, on Stard. side it is also perpendicular for about three hundred yards above the pitch where it is then broken by the discharge of a small ravine, down which the buffaloe have a large beaten road to the water, for it is but in very few places that these anamals can obtain water near this place owing to the steep and inaccessible banks. I see several skelletons of the buffaloe lying in the edge of the water near the Stard. bluff which I presume have been swept down by the current and precipitated over this tremendious fall. about 300 yards below me there is another butment of solid rock with a perpendicular face and abot 60 feet high which projects from the Stard. side at right angles to the distance of 134 yds. and terminates the lower part nearly of the bottom before mentioned; there being a passage arround the end of this butment between it and the river of about 20 yardes; here the river again assumes it's usual width soon spreading to near 300 yards but still continues it's rappidity. from the reflection of the sun on the spray or mist which arrises from these falls there is a beatifull rainbow produced which adds not a little to the beauty of this majestically grand senery. after wrighting this imperfect discription I again viewed the falls and was so much disgusted with the imperfect idea which it conveyed of the scene that I determined to draw my pen across it and begin agin, but then reflected that I could not perhaps succeed better than pening the first impressions of the mind; I wished for the pencil of Salvator Rosa or the pen of Thompson, that I might be enabled to give to the enlightened world some just idea of this truly magnificent and sublimely grand object, which has from the commencement of time been concealed from the view of civilized man; but this was fruitless and vain. I most sincerely regreted that I had not brought a crimee obscura with me by the assistance of which even I could have hoped to have done better but alas this was also out of my reach; I therefore with the assistance of my pen only indeavoured to traces some of the stronger features of this seen by the assistance of which and my recollection aided by some able pencil I hope still to give to the world some faint idea of an object which at this moment fills me with such pleasure and astonishment, and which of it's kind I will venture to ascert is second to but one in the known world. I retired to the shade of a tree where I determined to fix my camp for the present and dispatch a man in the morning to inform Capt. C. and the party of my success in finding the falls and settle in their minds all further doubts as to the Missouri. the hunters now arrived loaded with excellent buffaloe meat and informed me that they had killed three very fat cows about 3/4 of a mile hence. I directed them after they had refreshed themselves to go back and butcher them and bring another load of meat each to our camp determining to employ those who remained with me in drying meat for the party against their arrival. in about 2 hours or at 4 OClock P.M. they set out on this duty, and I walked down the river about three miles to discover if possible some place to which the canoes might arrive or at which they might be drawn on shore in order to be taken by land above the falls; but returned without effecting either of these objects; the river was one continued sene of rappids and cascades which I readily perceived could not be encountered with our canoes, and the Clifts still retained their perpendicular structure and were from 150 to 200 feet high; in short the river appears here to have woarn a channel in the process of time through a solid rock. on my return I found the party at camp; they had butchered the buffaloe and brought in some more meat as I had directed. Goodrich had caught half a douzen very fine trout and a number of both species of the white fish. these trout are from sixteen to twenty three inches in length, precisely resemble our mountain or speckled trout in form and the position of their fins, but the specks on these are of a deep black instead of the red or goald colour of those common to the U. States. these are furnished long sharp teeth on the pallet and tongue and have generally a small dash of red on each side behind the front ventral fins; the flesh is of a pale yellowish red, or when in good order, of a rose red.

I am induced to believe that the Brown, the white and the Grizly bear of this country are the same species only differing in colour from age or more probably from the same natural cause that many other anamals of the same family differ in colour. one of those which we killed yesterday was of a creemcoloured white while the other in company with it was of the common bey or rdish brown, which seems to be the most usual colour of them. the white one appeared from it's tallons and teath to be the youngest; it was smaller than the other, and although a monstrous beast we supposed that it had not yet attained it's growth and that it was a little upwards of two years old. the young cubs which we have killed have always been of a brownish white, but none of them as white as that we killed yesterday. one other that we killed sometime since which I mentioned sunk under some driftwood and was lost, had a white stripe or list of about eleven inches wide entirely arround his body just behind the shoalders, and was much darker than these bear usually are. the grizly bear we have never yet seen. I have seen their tallons in possession of the Indians and from their form I am perswaded if there is any difference between this species and the brown or white bear it is very inconsiderable. There is no such anamal as a black bear in this open country or of that species generally denominated the black bear

my fare is really sumptuous this evening; buffaloe's humps, tongues and marrowbones, fine trout parched meal pepper and salt, and a good appetite; the last is not considered the least of the luxuries.

[Clark, June 13, 1805] June 13th Thursday 1805 a fair morning, Some dew this morning the Indian woman Verry sick I gave her a doste of Salts. We Set out early, at a mile & 1/2 passed a Small rapid Stream on the Lard Side which heads in a mountain to the S. E 12 or 15 miles, which at this time covered with Snow, we call this stream Snow river, as it is the conveyance of the melted snow from that mountain at present. numbers of gees & goslings, the gees cannot fly at this Season- goose berries are ripe and in great abundance, the yellow Current is also Common, not yet ripe Killed a buffalow & Campd on the Lard Side near an old Indian fortified campy one man Sick & 3 with Swellings, the Indian woman verry Sick. Killed a goat & fraser 2 Buffalow

The river verry rapid maney Sholes great nos of large Stones passed
Some bluffs or low cliffts of Slate to day

[Lewis, June 14, 1805] Friday June 14th 1805. This morning at sunrise I dispatched Joseph Fields with a letter to Capt. Clark and ordered him to keep sufficiently near the river to observe it's situation in order that he might be enabled to give Capt. Clark an idea of the point at which it would be best to halt to make our portage. I set one man about preparing a saffold and collecting wood to dry the meat Sent the others to bring in the ballance of the buffaloe meat, or at least the part which the wolves had left us, for those fellows are ever at hand and ready to partake with us the moment we kill a buffaloe; and there is no means of puting the meat out of their reach in those plains; the two men shortly after returned with the meat and informed me that the wolves had devoured the greater part of the meat. about ten OClock this morning while the men were engaged with the meat I took my Gun and espontoon and thought I would walk a few miles and see where the rappids termineated above, and return to dinner. accordingly I set out and proceeded up the river about S. W. after passing one continued rappid and three small cascades of abut for or five feet each at the distance of about five miles I arrived at a fall of about 19 feet; the river is hereabout 400 yds. wide. this pitch which I called the crooked falls occupys about three fourths of the width of the river, commencing on the South side, extends obliquely upwards about 150 yds. then forming an accute angle extends downwards nearly to the commencement of four small Islands lying near the N. shore; among these Islands and between them and the lower extremity of the perpendicular pitch being a distance of 100 yards or upwards, the water glides down the side of a sloping rock with a volocity almost equal to that of it's perpendicular decent. just above this rappid the river makes a suddon bend to the right or Northwardly. I should have returned from hence but hearing a tremendous roaring above me I continued my rout across the point of a hill a few hundred yards further and was again presented by one of the most beatifull objects in nature, a cascade of about fifty feet perpendicular streching at rightangles across the river from side to side to the distance of at least a quarter of a mile. here the river pitches over a shelving rock, with an edge as regular and as streight as if formed by art, without a nich or brake in it; the water decends in one even and uninterupted sheet to the bottom wher dashing against the rocky bottom rises into foaming billows of great hight and rappidly glides away, hising flashing and sparkling as it departs the sprey rises from one extremity to the other to 50 f. I now thought that if a skillfull painter had been asked to make a beautifull cascade that he would most probably have pesented the precise immage of this one; nor could I for some time determine on which of those two great cataracts to bestoe the palm, on this or that which I had discovered yesterday; at length I determined between these two great rivals for glory that this was pleasingly beautifull, while the other was sublimely grand. I had scarcely infixed my eyes from this pleasing object before I discovered another fall above at the distance of half a mile; thus invited I did not once think of returning but hurried thither to amuse myself with this newly discovered object. I found this to be a cascade of about 14 feet possessing a perpendicular pitch of about 6 feet. this was tolerably regular streching across the river from bank to bank where it was about a quarter of a mile wide; in any other neighbourhood but this, such a cascade would probably be extoled for it's beaty and magnifficence, but here I passed it by with but little attention, determining as I had proceded so far to continue my rout to the head of the rappids if it should even detain me all night. at every rappid cateract and cascade I discovered that the bluffs grew lower or that the bed of the river rose nearer to a level with the plains. still pursuing the river with it's course about S. W. passing a continued sene of rappids and small cascades, at the distance of 2 1/2 miles I arrived at another cataract of 26 feet. this is not immediately perpendicular, a rock about 1/3 of it's decent seems to protrude to a small distance and receives the water in it's passage downwards and gives a curve to the water tho it falls mostly with a regular and smoth sheet. the river is near six hundred yards wide at this place, a beatifull level plain on the S. side only a few feet above the level of the pitch; on the N. side where I am the country is More broken and immediately behind me near the river a high hill. below this fall at a little distance a beatifull little Island well timbered is situated about the middle of the river. in this Island on a Cottonwood tree an Eagle has placed her nest; a more inaccessable spot I beleive she could not have found; for neither man nor beast dare pass those gulphs which seperate her little domain from the shores. the water is also broken in such manner as it decends over this pitch that the mist or sprey rises to a considerable hight. this fall is certainly much the greatest I ever behald except those two which I have mentioned below. it is incomparably a geater cataract and a more noble interesting object than the celibrated falls of Potomac or Soolkiln &c. just above this is another cascade of about 5 feet, above which the water as far as I could see began to abate of it's valosity, and I therefore determined to ascend the hill behind me which promised a fine prospect of the adjacent country, nor was I disappointed on my arrival at it's summit. from hence I overlooked a most beatifull and extensive plain reaching from the river to the base of the Snowclad mountains to the S. and S. West; I also observed the missoury streching it's meandering course to the South through this plain to a great distance filled to it's even and grassey brim; another large river flowed in on it's Western side about four miles above me and extended itself though a level and fertile valley of 3 miles in width a great distance to the N. W. rendered more conspicuous by the timber which garnished it's borders. in these plains and more particularly in the valley just below me immence herds of buffaloe are feeding. the missouri just above this hill makes a bend to the South where it lies a smoth even and unruffled sheet of water of nearly a mile in width bearing on it's watry bosome vast flocks of geese which feed at pleasure in the delightfull pasture on either border. the young geese are now completely feathered except the wings which both in the young and old are yet deficient. after feasting my eyes on this ravishing prospect and resting myself a few minutes I determined to procede as far as the river which I saw discharge itself on the West side of the Missouri convinced that it was the river which the Indians call medicine river and which they informed us fell into the Missouri just above the falls I decended the hills and directed my course to the bend of the Missouri near which there was a herd of at least a thousand buffaloe; here I thought it would be well to kill a buffaloe and leave him untill my return from the river and if I then found that I had not time to get back to camp this evening to remain all night here there being a few sticks of drift wood lying along shore which would answer for my fire, and a few sattering cottonwood trees a few hundred yards below which would afford me at least a semblance of a shelter. under this impression I scelected a fat buffaloe and shot him very well, through the lungs; while I was gazeing attentively on the poor anamal discharging blood in streams from his mouth and nostrils, expecting him to fall every instant, and having entirely forgotton to reload my rifle, a large white, or reather brown bear, had perceived and crept on me within 20 steps before I discovered him; in the first moment I drew up my gun to shoot, but at the same instant recolected that she was not loaded and that he was too near for me to hope to perform this opperation before he reached me, as he was then briskly advancing on me; it was an open level plain, not a bush within miles nor a tree within less than three hundred yards of me; the river bank was sloping and not more than three feet above the level of the water; in short there was no place by means of which I could conceal myself from this monster untill I could charge my rifle; in this situation I thought of retreating in a brisk walk as fast as he was advancing untill I could reach a tree about 300 yards below me, but I had no sooner terned myself about but he pitched at me, open mouthed and full speed, I ran about 80 yards and found he gained on me fast, I then run into the water the idea struck me to get into the water to such debth that I could stand and he would be obliged to swim, and that I could in that situation defend myself with my espontoon; accordingly I ran haistily into the water about waist deep, and faced about and presented the point of my espontoon, at this instant he arrived at the edge of the water within about 20 feet of me; the moment I put myself in this attitude of defence he sudonly wheeled about as if frightened, declined the combat on such unequal grounds, and retreated with quite as great precipitation as he had just before pursued me. as soon as I saw him run off in that manner I returned to the shore and charged my gun, which I had still retained in my hand throughout this curious adventure. I saw him run through the level open plain about three miles, till he disappeared in the woods on medecine river; during the whole of this distance he ran at full speed, sometimes appearing to look behind him as if he expected pursuit. I now began to reflect on this novil occurrence and indeavoured to account for this sudden retreat of the bear. I at first thought that perhaps he had not smelt me before he arrived at the waters edge so near me, but I then reflected that he had pursued me for about 80 or 90 yards before I took the water and on examination saw the grownd toarn with his tallons immediately on the impression of my steps; and the cause of his allarm still remains with me misterious and unaccountable.- so it was and I feelt myself not a little gratifyed that he had declined the combat. My gun reloaded I felt confidence once more in my strength; and determined not to be thwarted in my design of visiting medicine river, but determined never again to suffer my peice to be longer empty than the time she necessarily required to charge her. I passed through the plain nearly in the direction which the bear had run to medecine river, found it a handsome stream, about 200 yds. wide with a gentle current, apparently deep, it's waters clear, and banks which were formed principally of darkbrown and blue clay were about the hight of those of the Missouri or from 3 to 5 feet; yet they had not the appearance of ever being overflown, a circumstance, which I did not expect so immediately in the neighbourhood of the mountains, from whence I should have supposed, that sudden and immence torrants would issue at certain seasons of the year; but the reverse is absolutely the case. I am therefore compelled to beleive that the snowey mountains yeald their warters slowly, being partially effected every day by the influence of the sun only, and never suddonly melted down by haisty showers of rain.

having examined Medecine river I now determined to return, having by my estimate about 12 miles to walk. I looked at my watch and found it was half after six P.M.- in returning through the level bottom of Medecine river and about 200 yards distant from the Missouri, my direction led me directly to an anamal that I at first supposed was a wolf; but on nearer approach or about sixty paces distant I discovered that it was not, it's colour was a brownish yellow; it was standing near it's burrow, and when I approached it thus nearly, it couched itself down like a cat looking immediately at me as if it designed to spring on me. I took aim at it and fired, it instantly disappeared in it's burrow; I loaded my gun and exmined the place which was dusty and saw the track from which I am still further convinced that it was of the tiger kind. whether I struck it or not I could not determine, but I am almost confident that I did; my gun is true and I had a steady rest by means of my espontoon, which I have found very serviceable to me in this way in the open plains. It now seemed to me that all the beasts of the neighbourhood had made a league to distroy me, or that some fortune was disposed to amuse herself at my expence, for I had not proceded more than three hundred yards from the burrow of this tyger cat, before three bull buffaloe, which wer feeding with a large herd about half a mile from me on my left, seperated from the herd and ran full speed towards me, I thought at least to give them some amusement and altered my direction to meet them; when they arrived within a hundred yards they mad a halt, took a good view of me and retreated with precipitation. I then continued my rout homewards passed the buffaloe which I had killed, but did not think it prudent to remain all night at this place which really from the succession of curious adventures wore the impression on my mind of inchantment; at sometimes for a moment I thought it might be a dream, but the prickley pears which pierced my feet very severely once in a while, particularly after it grew dark, convinced me that I was really awake, and that it was necessary to make the best of my way to camp. it was sometime after dark before I returned to the party; I found them extremely uneasy for my safety; they had formed a thousand conjectures, all of which equally forboding my death, which they had so far settled among them, that they had already agreed on the rout which each should take in the morning to surch for me. I felt myself much fortiegued, but eat a hearty supper and took a good night's rest.- the weather being warm I had left my leather over shirt and had woarn only a yellow flannin one.

[Clark, June 14, 1805] June 14th Friday 1805 a fine morning, the Indian woman complaining all night & excessively bad this morning- her case is Somewhat dangerous- two men with the Tooth ake 2 with Turners, & one man with a Tumor & Slight fever passed the Camp Capt. Lewis made the 1st night at which place he had left part of two bear their skins &c three men with Turners went on shore and Staycd out all night one of them killed 2 buffalow, a part of which we made use of for brackfast, the Current excesevely rapid more So as we assend we find great difficuelty in getting the Perogue & Canoes up in Safety, Canoes take in water frequently, at 4 oClock this evening Jo. Fields returned from Capt. Lewis with a letter for me, Capt Lewis dates his letter from the Great falls of the Missouri, which Fields informs me is about 20 miles in advance & about 10 miles above the place I left the river the time I was up last week Capt. L. informs that those falls; in part answer the discription given of them by the Indians, much higher the Eagles nest which they describe is there, from those Signs he is Convinced of this being the river the Indians call the Missouri, he intends examineing the river above untill my arrival at a point from which we can make a portage, which he is apprehensive will be at least 5 miles & both above & below there is Several Small pitches, & Swift troubled water we made only 10 miles to day and Camped on the Lard Side, much hard Slate in the Clifts & but a Small quantity of timber.

[Lewis, June 15, 1805] Saturday June 15th 1805. This morning the men again were sent to bring in some more meat which Drewyer had killed yesterday, and continued the opperation of drying it. I amused myself in fishing, and sleeping away the fortiegues of yesterday. I caught a number of very fine trout which I made Goodrich dry; goodrich also caught about two douzen and several small cat of a yellow colour which would weigh about 4 lbs. the tails was seperated with a deep angular nitch like that of the white cat of the missouri from which indeed they differed only in colour. when I awoke from my sleep today I found a large rattlesnake coiled on the leaning trunk of a tree under the shade of which I had been lying at the distance of about ten feet from him. I killed the snake and found that he had 176 scuta on the abdomen and i'7 half formed scuta on the tale; it was of the same kinde which I had frequently seen before; they do not differ in their colours from the rattle snake common to the middle attlantic states, but considerably in the form and figures of those colours. This evening after dark Joseph Fields returned and informed me that Capt Clark had arrived with the party at the foot of a rappid about 5 miles below which he did not think proper to ascend and would wait my arrival there. I had discovered from my journey yesterday that a portage on this side of the river will be attended by much difficulty in consequence of several deep ravines which intersect the plains nearly at right angles with the river to a considerable distance, while the South side appears to be a delighfull smoth unbroken plain; the bearings of the river also make it pobable that the portage will be shorter on that side than on this.- I directed Fields to return early in the morning to Capt. C. and request him to send up a party of men for the dryed meat which we had made. I finde a very heavy due on the grass about my camp every morning which no doubt procedes from the mist of the falls, as it takes place no where in the plains nor on the river except here.

[Clark, June 15, 1805] June the 15th Satturday 1805 a fair morning and worm, we Set out at the usial time and proceeded on with great dificuley as the river is more rapid we can hear the falls this morning verry distinctly- our Indian woman Sick &low Spirited I gave her the bark & apply it exteranaly to her region which revived her much. the curt. excessively rapid and dificuelt to assend great numbers of dangerous places, and the fatigue which we have to encounter is increatiable the men in the water from morning untill night hauling the Cord & boats walking on Sharp rocks and round Sliperery Stones which alternately cut their feet & throw them down, not with Standing all this dificuelty they go with great chearfulness, aded to those dificuelties the rattle Snakes inumerable & require great caution to prevent being bitten.- we passed a Small river on the Lard Side about 30 yards wide verry rapid which heads in the mountains to the S. E. I Sent up this river 5 miles, it has Some timber in its bottoms and a fall of 15 feet at one place, above this river the bluffs are of red earth mixed with Stratums of black Stone, below this little river, we pass a white clay which mixes with water like flour in every respect, the Indian woman much wors this evening, She will not take any medison, her husband petetions to return &c., river more rapid late in the evening we arrived at a rapid which appeared So bad that I did not think it prudent to attempt passing of it this evening as it was now late, we Saw great numbers of Gees Ducks, Crows Blackbirds &c Geese & Ducks with their young. after Landing I detached Joseph Fields to Capt. Lewis to let him know where I was &c river rises a little this evening we could not get a Sufficency of wood for our use

[Lewis, June 16, 1805] Sunday June 16th 1805 J. Fields set out early on his return to the lower camp, at noon the men arrived and shortly after I set out with them to rejoin the party. we took with us the dryed meat consisting of about 600 lbs. and several douzen of dryed trout. about 2 P.M. I reached the camp found the Indian woman extreemly ill and much reduced by her indisposition. this gave me some concern as well for the poor object herself, then with a young child in her arms, as from the consideration of her being our only dependence for a friendly negociation with the Snake Indians on whom we depend for horses to assist us in our portage from the Missouri to the columbia River. I now informed Capt. C. of my discoveries with rispect to the most proper side for our portage, and of it's great length, which I could not estimate at less than 16 miles. Capt. C. had already sent two men this morning to examine the country on the S. side of the river; he now passed over with the party to that side and fixed a camp about a mile blow the entrance of a Creek where there was a sufficient quantity of wood for fuel, an article which can be obtained but in few places in this neighbourhood. after discharging the loads four of the canoes were sent back to me, which by means of strong ropes we hawled above the rappid and passed over to the south side from whence the water not being rappid we can readily convey them into the creek by means of which we hope to get them on the high plain with more ease. one of the small canoes was left below this rappid in order to pass and repass the river for the purpose of hunting as well as to procure the water of the Sulpher spring, the virtues of which I now resolved to try on the Indian woman. this spring is situated about 200 yards from the Missouri on the N. E. side nearly opposite to the entrance of a large creek; it discharges itself into the Missouri over a precepice of rock about 25 feet, forming a pretty little _____ the water is as transparent as possible strongly impregnated with sulpher, and I suspect Iron also, as the colour of the hills and bluffs in the neighbourhood indicate the existence of that metal. the water to all appearance is precisely similar to that of Bowyer's Sulpher spring in Virginia. Capt. Clark determined to set out in the morning to examine and survey the portage, and discover the best rout. as the distance was too great to think of transporting the canoes and baggage on the men's shoulders, we scelected six men, and ordered them to look out some timber this evening, and early in the morning to set about making a parsel of truck wheels in order to convey our canoes and baggage over the portage. we determined to leave the white perogue at this place, and substitute the Iron boat, and also to make a further deposit of a part of our stores. in the evening the men who had been sent out to examine the country and made a very unfavourable report. they informed us that the creek just above us and two deep ravenes still higher up cut the plain between the river and mountain in such a manner, that in their opinions a portage for the canoes on this side was impracticable. good or bad we must make the portage. notwithstanding this report I am still convinced from the view I had of the country the day before yesterday that a good portage may be had on this side at least much better than on the other, and much nearer also. I found that two dozes of barks and opium which I had given her since my arrival had produced an alteration in her pulse for the better; they were now much fuller and more regular. I caused her to drink the mineral water altogether. wen I first came down I found that her pulse were scarcely perceptible, very quick frequently irregular and attended with strong nervous symptoms, that of the twitching of the fingers and leaders of the arm; now the pulse had become regular much fuller and a gentle perspiration had taken place; the nervous symptoms have also in a great measure abated, and she feels herself much freeer from pain. she complains principally of the lower region of the abdomen, I therefore continued the cataplasms of barks and laudnumn which had been previously used by my friend Capt Clark. I beleive her disorder originated principally from an obstruction of the mensis in consequence of taking could.- I determined to remain at this camp in order to make some celestial observations, restore the sick woman, and have all matters in a state of readiness to commence the portage immediately on the return of Capt. Clark, who now furnished me with the dayly occurrences which had taken place with himself and party since our seperation which I here enter in his own words.

[Clark, June 16, 1805] June 16th of Sunday 1805 Some rain last night a cloudy morning wind hard from the S. W. we Set out passed the rapid by double manning the Perogue & Canoes and halted at 1/4 of a mile to examine the rapids above, which I found to be an Continued Cascade for as far as could be Seen which was about 2 miles, I walked up on the Lard Side as high as a large Creek, which falls in on the Lard. Side one mile above & opposit a large Sulpher Spring which falls over the rocks on the Std. Side the wind rored from the S. W. hard & Some rain, at about 2 oClock Capt Lewis joined me from the falls 5 miles distant, & infd. that the Lard Side was the best portage I despatched 2 men this morning on the Lard. Side to examine the portage.- the Indian woman verry bad, & will take no medisin what ever, untill her husband finding her out of her Senses, easyly provailed on her to take medison, if She dies it will be the fault of her husband as I am now convinced-. we crossed the river after part of the day and formed a Camp from which we intended to make the first portage, Capt. Lewis stayed on the Std Side to direct the Canoes over the first riffle 4 of them passed this evening the others unloaded & part of the Perogue Loading taken out- I deturmined to examine & Survey the Portage find a leavel rout if possible- The 2 men despatched to examine the Portage gave an unfavourable account of the Countrey, reporting that the Creek & 2 deep reveens cut the Prarie in such a manner between the river and mountain as to render a portage in their oppinion for the Canoes impossible- we Selected 6 men to make wheels & to draw the Canoes on as the distance was probably too far for to be caried on the mens Sholders

[Lewis, June 17, 1805] Monday June 17th 1805. Capt. Clark set out early this morning with five men to examine the country and survey the river and portage as had been concerted last evening. I set six men at work to pepare four sets of truck wheels with couplings, toungs and bodies, that they might either be used without the bodies for transporting our canoes, or with them in transporting our baggage I found that the Elk skins I had prepared for my boat were insufficient to compleat her, some of them having become dammaged by the weather and being frequently wet; to make up this deficiency I sent out two hunters this morning to hunt Elk; the ballance of the party I employed first in unloading the white perogue, which we intend leaving at this place, and bring the whole of our baggage together and arranging it in proper order near our camp. this duty being compleated I employed them in taking five of the small canoes up the creek which we now call portage creek about 13/4 miles; here I had them taken out and lyed in the sun to dry. from this place ther is a gradual ascent to the top of the high plain to which we can now take them with ease; the bluffs of this creek below and those of the river above it's entrance are so steep that it would be almost impracticable to have gotten them on the plain. we found much difficulty in geting the canoes up this creek to the distance we were compelled to take them, in consequence of the rappids and rocks which obstruct the channel of the creek. one of the canoes overset and was very near injuring 2 men essencially. just above the canoes the creek has a perpendicular fall of 5 feet and the cliffts again become very steep and high. we were fortunate enough to find one cottonwood tree just below the entrance of portage creek that was large enough to make our carrage wheels about 22 Inches in diameter; fortunate I say because I do not beleive that we could find another of the same size perfectly sound within 20 miles of us. the cottonwood which we are obliged to employ in the other parts of the work is extreemly illy calculated for it being soft and brittle. we have made two axeltrees of the mast of the white peroge, which I hope will answer tolerably well tho it is reather small. The Indian woman much better today, I have still continued the same course of medecine; she is free from pain clear of fever, her pulse regular, and eats as heartily as I am willing to permit her of broiled buffaloe well seasoned with pepper and salt and rich soope of the same meat; I think therefore that there is every rational hope of her recovery. saw a vast number of buffaloe feeding in every direction arround us in the plains, others coming down in large herds to water at the river; the fragments of many carcases of these poor anamals daily pass down the river, thus mangled I pesume in decending those immence cataracts above us. as the buffaloe generally go in large herds to water and the passages to the river about the falls are narrow and steep the hinder part of the herd press those in front out of their debth and the water instally takes them over the cataracts where they are instantly crushed to death without the possibility of escaping. in this manner I have seen ten or a douzen disappear in a few minutes. their mangled carcases ly along the shores below the falls in considerable quantities and afford fine amusement for the bear wolves and birds of prey; this may be one reason and I think not a bad one either that the bear are so tenatious of their right of soil in this neighbourhood.

[Clark, June 17, 1805] June 17th Monday 1805 a fine morning wind as usial Capt. Lewis with the party unloaded the Perogue & he determined to keep the party employed in getting the loading to the Creek about 1 mile over a low hill in my absence on the Portage.

I Set out with 5 men at 8 oClock, and proceeded on up the Creek Some distance to examine that & if possable assend that Suffcently high, that a Streight Cours to the mouth of Medison river would head the 2 reveins, the Creek I found Confined rapid and Shallow generalley

Monday 17th of June passed through an open roleing Prarie, So as to head the two reveins after heading two we Stand our Course So as to Strike the river below the great pitch on our Course to the river Crossed a Deep rivein near its mouth with Steep Clifts this rivein had running water which was very fine, the river at this place is narrow & Confined in perpindicular clifts of 170 feet from the tops of those Clifts the Countrey rises with a Steep assent for about 250 feet more we proceeded up the river passing a Sucession of rapids & Cascades to the Falls, which we had herd for Several miles makeing a dedly Sound, I beheld those Cateracts with astonishment the whole of the water of this great river Confined in a Channel of 280 yards and pitching over a rock of 97 feet 3/4 of an, from the foot of the falls arrises a Continued mist which is extended for 150 yds. down & to near the top of the Clifts on L Sd. the river below is Confined a narrow Chanl. Of 93 yards having a Small bottom of timber on the Stard Side which is definded by a rock, rangeing Cross wise the river a little below the Shoot, a Short distance below this Cataract a large rock divides the Stream, I in assendending the Clifts to take the hith of the fall was near Slipping into the water, at which place I must have been Sucked under in an instant, and with deficuelty and great risque I assended again, and decended the Clift lower down (but few places Can be descended to the river) and took the hight with as much accuricy as possible with a Spirit Leavels &c. dined at a fine Spring 200 yards below the pitch near which place 4 Cotton willow trees grew. on one of them I marked my name the date, and hight of the falls,- we then proceeded up on the river passing a Continued Cascade & rapid to a fall of 19 feet at 4 Small Islands, this fall is diaguanally across the river from the Lard Side, forming an angle of 3/4 of the width from the Lard. from which Side it pitches for 2/3 of that distance. on the Stard Side is a rapid decline- below this Shoot a Deep revein falls in which we Camped for the night which was Cold (The mountains in every derection has Snow on Them) The plain to our left is leavel we Saw one Bear & inumerable numbers of Buffalow, I Saw 2 herds of those animals watering immediately above a considerable rapid, they decended by a narrow pass to the bottom Small, the rier forced those forwd into the water Some of which was taken down in an instant, and Seen no more others made Shore with difficuelty, I beheld 40 or 50 of those Swimming at the Same time those animals in this way are lost and accounts for the number of buffalow carcases below the rapids

[Lewis, June 18, 1805] Tuesday June 18th 1805. This morning I employed all hands in drawing the perogue on shore in a thick bunch of willow bushes some little distance below our camp; fastened her securely, drove out the plugs of the gage holes of her bottom and covered her with bushes and driftwood to shelter her from the sun. I now scelected a place for a cash and set tree men at work to complete it, and employed all others except those about the waggons, in overhawling airing and repacking our indian goods ammunition, provision and stores of every discription which required inspection. examined the frame of my Iron boat and found all the parts complete except one screw, which the ingenuity of Sheilds can readily replace, a resource which we have very frequent occasion for. about 12 O'Clk. the hunters returned; they had killed 10 deer but no Elk. I begin to fear that we shall have some difficulty in procuring skins for the boat. I wold prefer those of the Elk because I beleive them more durable and strong than those of the Buffaloe, and that they will not shrink so much in drying. we saw a herd of buffaloe come down to water at the sulpher spring this evening, I dispatched some hunters to kill some of them, and a man also for a cask of mineral water. the hunters soon killed two of them in fine order and returned with a good quantity of the flesh, having left the remainder in a situation that it will not spoil provided the wolves do not visit it. The waggons are completed this evening, and appear as if they would answer the purpose very well if the axetrees prove sufficiently strong. the wind blew violently this evening, as they frequently do in this open country where there is not a tree to brake or oppose their force. The Indian woman is recovering fast she set up the greater part of the day and walked out for the fist time since she arrived here; she eats hartily and is free from fever or pain. I continue same course of medecine and regimen except that I added one doze of 15 drops of the oil of vitriol today about noon.

There is a species of goosberry which grows very common about here in open situations among the rocks on the sides of the clifts. they are now ripe of a pale red colour, about the size of a common goosberry. and like it is an ovate pericarp of soft pulp invelloping a number of smal whitish coloured seeds; the pulp is a yelloish slimy muselaginous substance of a sweetish and pinelike tast, not agreeable to me. the surface of the berry is covered with a glutinous adhesive matter, and the frut altho ripe retains it's withered corollar. this shrub seldom rises more than two feet high and is much branched, the leaves resemble those of the common goosberry only not so large; it has no thorns. the berry is supported by seperate peduncles or footstalks of half an inch in length. immence quantities of small grasshoppers of a brown colour in the plains, they no doubt contribute much to keep the grass as low as we find it which is not generally more than three inches, the grass is a narrow leaf, soft, and affords a fine pasture for the Buffaloe.-

[Clark, June 18, 1805] June 18th Tuesday 1805 we Set out early and arrived at the second great Cataract at about 200 yds above the last of 19 feet pitch- this is one of the grandest views in nature and by far exceeds any thing I ever Saw, the Missouri falling over a Shelveing rock for 47 feet 8 Inches with a Cascade &c of 14 feet 7 Inches above the Shoot for a 1/4 mile I decended the Clift below this Cateract with ease measured the hight of the purpendicular fall of 47 feet 8 Inches at which place the river is 473 yards wide as also the hight of the Cascade &c. a continuel mist quite across this fall* after which we proceeded on up the river a little more than a mile to the largest fountain or Spring I ever Saw, and doubt if it is not the largest in America Known, this water boils up from under th rocks near the edge of the river and falls imediately into the river 8 feet and keeps its Colour for 1/2 a mile which is emencely Clear and of a bluish Cast, proceeded on up the river passed a Succession of rapids to the next great fall of 26 Ft. 5 I. river 580 yards wide this fall is not intirely perpdincular a Short bench gives a Curve to the water as it falls a butifull Small Island at the foot of this fall near the Center of the Channel Covered with trees, the Missouri at this fall is 36 yards wide, a Considerable mist rises at this fall ocasionally, from this pitch to the head of the rapids is one mile & has a fall of 20 feet, this is also a handsome Scenery a fall in an open leavel plain, after takeing the hight & measureing the river proceeded on, Saw a gange of Buffalow Swiming the river above the falls, Several of which was drawn in to the rapids and with dificuelty mad Shore half drowned, we killed one of those Cows & took as much meat as we wished. emence herds of those animals in every direction, passed 2 groves in the Point just above the rapids & dined in one opposit the mouth of Medison River, which fails in on the Stard. Side and is 137 yards wide at its mouth the Missouri above is 800 yards wide, as the river Missouri appears to bear S Easterley I assended about 4 miles high to a Creek which appeared to head in South mountains passed a Island of _____ and a little timber in an Easterly bend at 1 mile, passed Some timber in a point at 2 mile at or near the lower point of a large Island on which we Shot at a large white bear. passed a Small Island in the middle and one close on the Lard Shore at 3 miles behind the head of which we Camped. those 3 Islands are all opposit, Soon after we Camped two ganges of Buffalow crossed one above & the other below we killed 7 of them & a calf and Saved as much of the best of the meat as we could this evening, one man A Willard going for a load of meat at 170 yards distance on an Island was attact by a white bear and verry near being Caught, prosued within 40 yards of Camp where I was with one man I collected 3 others of the party and prosued the bear (who had prosued my track from a buffalow I had killed on the Island at about 300 yards distance and chance to meet Willard) for fear of his attacking one man Colter at the lower point of the Island, before we had got down the bear had allarmed the man and prosued him into the water, at our approach he retreated, and we relieved the man in the water, I Saw the bear but the bushes was So thick that I could not Shoot him and it was nearly dark, the wind from the S W & Cool killed a beaver & an elk for their Skins this evening

[Lewis, June 19, 1805] Wednesday June 19th 1805. This morning I sent over several men for the meat which was killed yesterday, a few hours after they returned with it, the wolves had not discovered it. I also dispatched George Drewyer Reubin Fields and George Shannon on the North side of the Missouri with orders to proceed to the entrance of Medecine river and indeavour to kill some Elk in that neigh-bourhood. as there is more timber on that river than the Missouri I expect that the Elk are more plenty. The cash completed today. The wind blew violently the greater part of the day. the Indian woman was much better this morning she walked out and gathered a considerable quantity of the white apples of which she eat so heartily in their raw state, together with a considerable quantity of dryed fish without my knowledge that she complained very much and her fever again returned. I rebuked Sharbono severely for suffering her to indulge herself with such food he being privy to it and having been previously told what she must only eat. I now gave her broken dozes of diluted nitre untill it produced perspiration and at 10 P.M. 30 drops of laudnum which gave her a tolerable nights rest. I amused myself in fishing several hours today and caught a number of both species of the white fish, but no trout nor Cat. I employed the men in making up our baggage in proper packages for transportation; and waxed the stoppers of my powder canesters anew. had the frame of my Iron boat clensed of rust and well greased. in the evening the men mended their mockersons and preparedthemselves for the portage. After dark my dog barked very much and seemed extreemly uneasy which was unusual with him; I ordered the sergt. of the guard to reconniter with two men, thinking it possible that some Indians might be about to pay us a visit, or perhaps a white bear; he returned soon after & reported that he believed the dog had been baying a buffaloe bull which had attempted to swim the river just above our camp but had been beten down by the stream landed a little below our camp on the same side & run off.

[Clark, June 19, 1805] June 19th Wednesday 1805 We went on the Island to hunt the White bear this morning but Could not find him, after plotting my Courses &c. I deturmined to dry the meat we killed and leave here, and proceed up the river as far as it bent to the S. E. and examine a Small Creek above our Camp, I Set out and found the Creek only Contained back water for 1 mile up, ascend near the Missouri 3 miles to the bend, from which place it turnd. Westerly, from this bend I with 2 men went forward towards the Camp of the party to examine the best ground for the portage, the little Creek has verry extencive bottoms which Spread out into a varriety of leavl rich bottoms quite to the mountains to the East, between those bottoms is hills low and Stoney on this declivity where it is Steep. I returned to Camp late and deturmined that the best nearest and most eassy rout would be from the lower part of the 3rd or white bear Island, the wind all this day blew violently hard from the S W. off the Snowey mountains, Cool, in my last rout I lost a part of my notes which could not be found as the wind must have blown them to a great distance. Summer duck Setting great numbers of buffalow all about our Camp

[Lewis, June 20, 1805] Thursday June 20th 1805. This morning we had but little to do; waiting the return of Capt. Clark; I am apprehensive from his stay that the portage is longer than we had calculated on. I sent out 4 hunters this morning on the opposite side of the river to kill buffaloe; the country being more broken on that side and cut with ravenes they can get within shoot of the buffaloe with more ease and certainty than on this side of the river. my object is if possible while we have now but little to do, to lay in a large stock of dryed meat at this end of the portage to subsist the party while engaged in the transportation of our baggage &c, to the end, that they may not be taken from this duty when once commenced in order to surch for the necessary subsistence. The Indian woman is qute free from pain and fever this morning and appears to be in a fair way for recovery, she has been walking about and fishing. In the evening 2 of the hunters returned and informed me that they had killed eleven buffaloe eight of which were in very fine order, I sent off all hands immediately to bring in the meat they soon returned with about half of the best meat leaving three men to remain all night in order to secure the ballance. the bufhaloe are in inimence numbers, they have been constantly coming down in large herds to water opposite to us for some hours sometimes two or three herds wartering at the same instant and scarcely disappear before others supply their places. they appear to make great use of the mineral water, whether this be owing to it's being more convenient to them than the river or that they actually prefer it I am at a loss to determine for they do not use it invaryably, but sometimes pass at no great distance from it and water at the river. brackish water or that of a dark colour impregnated with mineral salts such as I have frequently mentioned on the Missouri is found in small quantities in some of the steep ravenes on the N. side of the river opposite to us and the falls. Capt. Clark and party returned late this evening when he gave me the following relation of his rout and the occurrences which had taken place with them since their departure.

Capt. Clark now furnished me with the field notes of the survey which he had made of the Missouri and it's Cataracts cascades &c. from the entrance of portage Creek to the South Eastwardly bend of the Missouri above the White bear Islands, which are as follow.

[Clark, June 20, 1805] June 20th Thursday 1805 a Cloudy morning, a hard wind all night and this morning, I direct Stakes to be Cut to Stick up in the prarie to Show the way for the party to transport the baggage &c. &c. we Set out early on the portage, Soon after we Set out it began to rain and continued a Short time we proceeded on thro a tolerable leavel plain, and found the hollow of a Deep rivein to obstruct our rout as it Could not be passed with Canos & baggage for Some distance above the place we Struck it I examined it for Some time and finding it late deturmined to Strike the river & take its Course & distance to Camp which I accordingly did the wind hard from the S. W. a fair after noon, the river on both Sides Cut with raveins Some of which is passes thro Steep Clifts into the river, the Countrey above the falls & up the Medison river is leavel, with low banks, a chain of mountains to the west Some part of which particuler those to the N W. & S W are Covered with Snow and appear verry high- I Saw a rattle Snake in an open plain 2 miles from any Creek or wood. When I arrived at Camp found all well with great quantites of meet, the Canoes Capt. Lewis had Carried up the Creek 1 mile to a good place to assend the band & taken up. Not haveing Seen the Snake Indians or knowing in fact whither to Calculate on their friendship or hostillity, we have Conceived our party Sufficiently Small, and therefore have Concluded not to dispatch a Canoe with a part of our men to St. Louis as we have intended early in the Spring. we fear also that Such a measure might also discourage those who would in Such Case remain, and migh possibly hazard the fate of the expedition. we have never hinted to any one of the party that we had Such a Scheem in contemplation, and all appear perfectly to have made up their minds, to Succeed in the expedition or perish in the attempt. we all believe that we are about to enter on the most perilous and dificuelt part of our Voyage, yet I See no one repineing; all appear ready to meet those dificuelties which await us with resolution and becomeing fortitude.

We had a heavy dew this morning. the Clouds near those mountains rise Suddonly and discharge their Contents partially on the neighbouring Plains; the Same Cloud discharge hail alone in one part, hail and rain in another and rain only in a third all within the Space of a fiew Miles; and on the Mountains to the South & S. E. of us Sometimes Snow. at present there is no Snow on those mountains; that which covered them a fiew days ago has all disappeared. the Mountains to the N. W. and West of us are Still entirely Covered are white and glitter with the reflection of the Sun.

I do not believe that the Clouds that pervale at this Season of the year reach the Summits of those lofty mountains; and if they do the probability is that they deposit Snow only for there has been no proceptable diminution of the Snow which they Contain Since we first Saw them. I have thought it probable that these mountains might have derived their appellation of Shineing Mountains, from their glittering appearance when the Sun Shines in certain directions on the Snow which Cover them.

Dureing the time of my being on the Plains and above the falls I as also all my party repeatedly heard a nois which proceeded from a Direction a little to the N. of West, as loud and resembling precisely the discharge of a piece of ordinance of 6 pounds at the distance of 5 or six miles. I was informed of it Several times by the men J. Fields particularly before I paid any attention to it, thinking it was thunder most probably which they had mistaken. at length walking in the plains yesterday near the most extreem S. E. bend of the River above the falls I heard this nois very distinctly, it was perfectly calm clear and not a Cloud to be Seen, I halted and listened attentively about two hour dureing which time I heard two other discharges, and took the direction of the Sound with my pocket Compass which was as nearly West from me as I could estimate from the Sound. I have no doubt but if I had leasure I could find from whence it issued. I have thought it probable that it might be caused by running water in Some of the caverns of those emence mountains, on the principal of the blowing caverns; but in Such case the Sounds would be periodical and regular, which is not the Case with this, being Sometimes heard once only and at other times Several discharges in quick Succession. it is heard also at different times of the day and night. I am at a great loss to account for this Phenomenon. I well recollect hereing the Minitarees Say that those Rocky Mountains make a great noise, but they could not tell me the Cause, neither Could they inform me of any remarkable substance or situation in these mountains which would autherise a conjecture of a probable cause of this noise-. it is probable that the large river just above those Great falls which heads in the detection of the noise has taken it's name Medicine River from this unaccountable rumbling Sound, which like all unacountable thing with the Indians of the Missouri is Called Medicine.

The Ricaras inform us of the black mountains making a Simalar noise &c. &c. and maney other wonderfull tales of those Rocky mountains and those great falls.

[Lewis, June 21, 1805] Friday June 21st 1805. This morning I employed the greater part of the men in transporting a part of the bagage over portage creek to the top of the high plain about three miles in advance on the portage. I also had one canoe carryed on truck wheles to the same place and put the baggage in it, in order to make an early start in the morning, as the rout of our portage is not yet entirely settled, and it would be inconvenient to remain in the open plain all night at a distance from water, which would probably be the case if we did not set out early as the latter part of the rout is destitute of water for about 8 miles- having determined to go to the upper part of the portage tomorrow; in order to prepare my boat and receive and take care of the stores as they were transported, I caused the Iron frame of the boat and the necessary tools my private baggage and Instruments to be taken as a part of this load, also the baggage of Joseph Fields, Sergt. Gass and John sheilds, whom I had scelected to assist me in constructing the leather boat. Three men were employed today in shaving the Elk skins which had ben collected for the boat. the ballance of the party were employed in cuting the meat we had killed yesterday into thin Retches and drying it, and in bring in the ballance of what had been left over the river with three men last evening. I readily preceive several difficulties in preparing the leather boat which are the want of convenient and proper timber; bark, skins, and above all that of pitch to pay her seams, a deficiency that I really know not how to surmount unless it be by means of tallow and pounded charcoal which mixture has answered a very good purpose on our wooden canoes heretofore. I have seen for the first time on the Missouri at these falls, a species of fishing ducks with white wings, brown and white body and the head and part of the neck adjoining of a brick red, and the beak narrow; which I take to be the same common to James river, the Potomac and Susquehanna. immence numbers of buffaloe comeing to water at the river as usual. the men who remained over the river last night killed several mule deer, and Willard who was with me killed a young Elk. The wind blew violently all day. The growth of the neighbourhood what little there is consists of the broad and narrow leafed cottonwood, box alder, the large or sweet willow, the narrow and broad leafed willow. the sweet willow has not been common to the Missouri below this or the entrance of Maria's river; here attains to the same size and in appearance much the same as in the Atlantic States. the undergrowth consists of rosebushes, goosberry and current bushes, honeysuckle small, and the red wood, the inner bark of which the engages are fond of smoking mixed with tobacco.

[Clark, June 21, 1805] June 21st Friday 1805 a fine morning wind from the S W. off the mountains and hard, Capt Lewis with the men except a few take a part of the baggage & a Canoe up the Hill 3 mile in advance, Several men employed in Shaveing & Graneing Elk hides for the Iron boat as it is called- 3 men were Sent up the Medison river yesterday to kill Elk for the Skins for the boat, I fear that we Shall be put to Some dificulty in precureing Elk Skins Sufficent-, Cloudy afternoon, we dry meat for the men to eat on their return from the upper part of the portage Capt Lewis determine to proceed to the upper part of the Portage tomorrow & with 3 men proced to fix the Iron boat with Skins &c. &c.

[Lewis, June 22, 1805] Saturday June 22cd 1805. This morning early Capt Clark and myself with all the party except Sergt. Ordway Sharbono, Goodrich, york and the Indian woman, set out to pass the portage with the canoe and baggage to the Whitebear Islands, where we intend that this portage shall end. Capt. Clarke piloted us through the plains. about noon we reached a little stream about 8 miles on the portage where we halted and dined; we were obliged here to renew both axeltrees and the tongues and howns of one set of wheels which took us no more than 2 hours. these parts of our carriage had been made of cottonwood and one axetree of an old mast, all of which proved deficient and had broken down several times before we reached this place we have now renewed them with the sweet willow and hope that they will answer better. after dark we had reached within half a mile of our intended camp when the tongues gave way and we were obliged to leave the canoe, each man took as much of the baggage as he could carry on his back and proceeded to the river where we formed our encampment much fortiegued. the prickly pears were extreemly troublesome to us sticking our feet through our mockersons. Saw a great number of buffaloe in the plains, also immence quantities of little birds and the large brown curloo; the latter is now seting; it lays it's eggs, which are of a pale blue with black specks, on the ground without any preperation of a nest. there is a kind of larke here that much resembles the bird called the oldfield lark with a yellow brest and a black spot on the croop; tho this differs from ours in the form of the tail which is pointed being formed of feathers of unequal length; the beak is somewhat longer and more curved and the note differs considerably; however in size, action, and colours there is no perceptable difference; or at least none that strikes my eye. after reaching our camp we kindled our fires and examined the meat which Capt. Clark had left, but found only a small proportion of it, the wolves had taken the greater part. we eat our suppers and soon retired to rest.

[Clark, June 22, 1805] June 22nd Satturday 1805 a fine morning, Capt Lewis my Self and all the party except a Sergeant Ordway Guterich and the Interpreter and his wife Sar car gah we a (who are left at Camp to take Care of the baggage left) across the portage with one Canoe on truck wheels and loaded with a part of our Baggage I piloted thro the plains to the Camp I made at which place I intended the portage to end which is 3 miles above the Medesin River we had great dificuley in getting on as the axeltree broke Several times, and the Cuppling tongus of the wheels which was of Cotton & willow, the only wood except Boxelder & _____ that grow in this quarter, we got within half a mile of our intended Camp much fatigued at dark, our tongus broke & we took a load to the river on the mens back, where we found a number of wolves which had distroyed a great part of our meat which I had left at that place when I was up day before yesterday we Soon went to Sleep & Slept Sound wind from the _____ we deturmine to employ every man Cooks & all on the portage after to day

Canoe and baggage brought up, after which we breakfasted and nearly consumed the meat which he had left here. he now set out on his return with the party. I employed the three men with me in the forenoon clearing away the brush and forming our camp, and puting the frame of the boat together. this being done I sent Shields and Gass to look out for the necessary timber, and with J. Fields decended the river in the canoe to the mouth of Medicine river in surch of the hunters whom I had dispatched thither on the 19th inst. and from whom we had not heard a sentence. I entered the mouth of medicine river and ascended it about half a mile when we landed and walked up the Stard. side. frequently hooping as we went on in order to find the hunters; at length after ascending the river about five miles we found Shannon who had passed the Medecine river & fixed his camp on the Lard. side, where he had killed seven deer and several buffaloe and dryed about 600 lbs. of buffaloe meat; but had killed no Elk. Shannon could give me no further account of R. Fields and Drewyer than that he had left them about noon on the 19th at the great falls and had come on the mouth of Medicine river to hunt Elk as he had been directed, and never had seen them since. the evening being now far spent I thought it better to pass the Medicine river and remain all night at Shannon's camp; I passed the river on a raft which we soon constructed for the purpose. the river is here about 80 yds. wide, is deep and but a moderate current. the banks low as those of the Missouri above the falls yet never appear to overflow. as it will give a better view of the transactions of the party, I shall on each day give the occurrences of both camps during our seperation as I afterwards learnt those of the lower camp from Capt. Clark. on his return today he cut of several angles of the rout by which we came yesterday, shortened the portage considerably, measured it and set up stakes throughout as guides to marke the rout. he returned this evening to the lower camp in sufficient time to take up two of the canoes from portage creek to the top of the plain about a mile in advance. this evening the men repaired their mockersons, and put on double souls to protect their feet from the prickley pears. during the late rains the buffaloe have troden up the prairie very much, which having now become dry the sharp points of earth as hard as frozen ground stand up in such abundance that there is no avoiding them. this is particulary severe on the feet of the men who have not only their own wight to bear in treading on those hacklelike points but have also the addition of the burthen which they draw and which in fact is as much as they can possibly move with. they are obliged to halt and rest frequently for a few minutes, at every halt these poor fellows tumble down and are so much fortiegued that many of them are asleep in an instant; in short their fatiegues are incredible; some are limping from the soreness of their feet, others faint and unable to stand for a few minutes, with heat and fatiegue, yet no one complains, all go with cheerfullness. in evening Reubin Fields returned to the lower camp and informed Capt. Clark of the absence of Shannon, with rispect to whome they were extreemly uneasy. Fields and Drewyer had killed several buffaloe at the bend of the missouri above the falls and had dryed a considerable quantity of meat; they had also killed several deer but no Elk.

[Clark, June 23, 1805] June 23rd Sunday 1805 a Cloudy morning wind from the S. E, after getting the Canoe to Camp & the articles left in the plains we eate brackfast of the remaining meat found in Camp & I with the party the truck wheels & poles to Stick up in the prarie as a guide, Set out on our return, we proceeded on, & measured the Way which I Streightened considerably from that I went on yesterday, and arrived at our lower camp in Suffcent time to take up 2 Canoes on the top of the hill from the Creek, found all Safe at Camp the men mended their mockersons with double Soles to Save their feet from the prickley pear, (which abounds in the Praries,) and the hard ground which in Some & maney places So hard as to hurt the feet verry much, the emence number of Buffalow after the last rain has trod the flat places in Such a manner as to leave it uneaven, and that has tried and is wors than frozen ground, added to those obstructions, the men has to haul with all their Strength wate & art, maney times every man all catching the grass & knobes & Stones with their hands to give them more force in drawing on the Canoes & Loads, and notwithstanding the Coolness of the air in high presperation and every halt, those not employed in repairing the Couse; are asleep in a moment, maney limping from the Soreness of their feet Some become fant for a fiew moments, but no man Complains all go Chearfully on- to State the fatigues of this party would take up more of the journal than other notes which I find Scercely time to Set down. I had the best rout Staked out and measured which is 17 miles 3/4 to the river & 1/2 a mile up i.e 181/4 miles portage- from the lower rapid to the 1st Creek is 286 poles, to a Deep run of water, Called Willow Run is 6 miles thence to the river 3 miles above Medison Riv at 3 Island Called White Bear Islands is 11 miles all prarie without wood or water except at the Creek & run which afford a plenty of fine water and a little wood the plain is tolerably leavel except at the river a Small assent & passing a low hill from the Creek a rough & Steep assent for about 1/4 of a mile and Several Gullies & a gradual hill for 11/2 miles the heads of Several gullies which have Short assents & the willow run of a Steep hill on this run grows Purple & red Currents. the red is now ripe the Purple full grown, an emence number of Prarie birds now Setting of two kinds one larger than a Sparrow dark yellow the Center feathers of its tail yellow & the out Sides black Some Streeks about its neck, the other about the Same Size White tail

[Lewis, June 24, 1805] Monday June 24th 1805. Supposing that Drewyer and R. Fields might possibly be still higher up medicine river, I dispatched J. Fields up the river with orders to proceede about four miles and then return whether he found them or not and join Shannon at this camp. I set out early and walked down the South West side of the river and sent Shannon down the opposite side to bring the canoe over to me and put me across the Missouri; having landed on the Lard. side of the Missouri I sent Shannon back with the canoe to ascend the Medicine river as far as his camp to meet J. Fields and bring the dryed meat at that place to the camp at the white bear Islands which accomplished and arrived with Fields this evening. the party also arrived this evening with two canoes from the lower camp. they were wet and fatiegued, gave them a dram. R. Fields came with them and gave me an account of his & Drewyer's hunt, and informed me that Drewyer was still at their camp with the meat they had dryed. the iron frame of my boat is 36 feet long 41/2 F. in the beam and 26 Inches in the hole.

This morning early Capt. Clark had the remaining canoe drawn out of the water; and divided the remainder of our baggage into three parcels, one of which he sent today by the party with two canoes. The Indian woman is now perfectly recovered. Capt. C. came a few miles this morning to see the party under way and returned. on my arrival at the upper camp this morning, I found that Sergt. Gass and Shields had made but slow progress in collecting timber for the boat; they complained of great difficulty in geting streight or even tolerably streight sticks of 4/2 feet long. we were obliged to make use of the willow and box alder, the cottonwood being too soft and brittle. I kept one of them collecting timber while the other shaved and fitted them. I have found some pine logs among the drift wood near this place, from which, I hope to obtain as much pitch as will answer to pay the seams of the boat. I directed Fraizer to remain in order to sew the hides together, and form the covering for the boat.

[Clark, June 24, 1805] June 24th Monday 1805 a Cloudy morning I rose early had, the remaining Canoe hauled out of the water to dry and divided the baggage into 3 parcels, one of which the party took on their backs & one waggon with truk wheels to the Canoes 3 miles in advance (Those Canoes or 5 of our Canoes were Carried up the Creek 13/4 of a mile taken out on the bank and left to dry from which place they are taken up a point and intersects this rout from the mouth of the Creek at 3 miles from the foot of the rapids) after getting up their loads they divided men & load & proceeded on with 2 canoes on truck wheels as before, I accompanied them 4 miles and returned, my feet being verry Sore from the walk over ruts Stones & hills & thro the leavel plain for 6 days proceeding Carrying my pack and gun. Some few drops of rain in the fore part of the day, at 6 oClock a black Cloud arose to the N West, the wind shifted from the S to that point and in a short time the earth was entirely Covered with hail, Some rain Succeeded, which Continud for about an hour very moderately on this Side of the river, without the earths being wet 1/2 an inch, the riveins on the opposit or N W Side discharged emence torrents of water into the river, & Showed evidently that the rain was much heavyer on that Side, Some rain at different times in the night which was worm- Thunder without lightning accompanied the hail Cloud

[Lewis, June 25, 1805] Tuesday June 25th 1805. This morning early I sent the party back to the lower camp; dispatched Frazier down with the canoe for Drewyer and the meat he had collected, and Joseph Fields up the Missouri to hunt Elk. at eight OClk. sent Gass and Sheilds over to the large Island for bark and timber. about noon Fields returned and informed me that he had seen two white bear near the river a few miles above and in attempting to get a shoot them had stumbled uppon a third which immediately made at him being only a few steps distant; that in runing in order to escape from the bear he had leaped down a steep bank of the river on a stony bar where he fell cut his hand bruised his knees and bent his gun. that fortunately for him the bank hid him from the bear when he fell and that by that means he had escaped. this man has been truly unfortunate with these bear, this is the second time that he has narrowly escaped from them. about 2 P. M Shields and Gass returned with but a small quantity of both bark and timber and informed me that it was all they could find on the Island; they had killed two Elk the skins of which and a part of the flesh they brought with them. in the evening Drewyer and Frazier arrivd with about 800 lbs. of excellent dryed meat and about 100 lbs of tallow. The river is about 800 yds. wide opposite to us above these islands, and has a very gentle current the bottoms are hadsome level and extensive on both sides; the bank on this side is not more than 2 feet above the level of the water; it is a pretty little grove in which our camp is situated. there is a species of wild rye which is now heading it rises to the hight of 18 or 20 inches, the beard is remarkably fine and soft it is a very handsome grass the culm is jointed and is in every rispect the wild rye in minuture. great quantities of mint also are here it resemble the pepper mint very much in taste and appearance. the young blackbirds which are almost innumerable in these islands just begin to fly. see a number of water tarripens. I have made an unsuccessfull attempt to catch fish, and do not think there are any in this part of the river. The party that returned this evening to the lower camp reached it in time to take one canoe on the plain and prepare their baggage for an early start in the morning after which such as were able to shake a foot amused themselves in dancing on the green to the music of the violin which Cruzatte plays extreemly well.

Capt. C. somewhat unwell today. he made Charbono kook for the party against their return. it is worthy of remark that the winds are sometimes so strong in these plains that the men informed me that they hoisted a sail in the canoe and it had driven her along on the truck wheels. this is really sailing on dry land.

[Clark, June 25, 1805] June 25th Tuesday 1805 a fair worm morning, Clouded & a few drops of rain at 5 oClock A.M. fair I feel my Self a little unwell with a looseness &c. &c. put out the Stores to dry & Set Chabonah &c to Cook for the party against their return-he being the only man left on this Side with me I had a little Coffee for brackfast which was to me a riarity as I had not tasted any Since last winter. The wind from the N. W. & worm. This Countrey has a romantick appearance river inclosed between high and Steep hills Cut to pieces by revines but little timber and that Confined to the Rivers & Creek, the Missourie has but a fiew Scattering trees on its borders, and only one Solitary Cotton tree in sight of my Camp the wood which we burn is drift wood which is broken to pieces in passing the falls, not one large tree longer than about 8 or 10 feet to be found drifted below the falls the plains are inferior in point of Soil to those below, more Stone on the sides of the hill, grass but a few inches high and but few flowers in the Plains, great quantites of Choke Cheries, Goose burres, red & yellow berries, & red & Purple Currents on the edges of water Courses in bottoms & damp places, about my Camp the Cliffs or bluffs are a hard red or redish brown earth Containing Iron. we Catch great quantities of Trout, and a kind of mustel, flat backs & a Soft fish resembling a Shad and a few Cat. at 5 oClock the party returned, fatigued as usial, and proceeded to mend their mockersons &c. and G Shannon & R, Fds. to of the men who ware Sent up the medison river to hunt Elk, they killed no Elk, Several Buffalow & Deer, and reports that the river is 120 yds wide and about 8 feet deep Some timber on its borders- a powerfull rain fell on the party on their rout yesterday Wet Some fiew articles, and Caused the rout to be So bad wet & Deep thay Could with dificuelty proceed, Capt. Lewis & the men with him much employd with the Iron Boat in fitting it for the water, dispatched one man to George Drewyers Camp below medison river for meat &c. a fair after noon- great numbers of buffalow water opposit to my Camp everry day- it may be here worthy of remark that the Sales were hoised in the Canoes as the men were drawing them and the wind was great relief to them being Sufficeritly Strong to move the Canoes on the Trucks, this is Saleing on Dry land in every Sence of the word, Serjeant N Pryor Sick, the party amused themselves with danceing untill 10 oClock all Chearfullness and good humer, they all tied up their loads to make an early Start in the morning.

[Lewis, June 26, 1805] Wednesday June 26th 1805. The Musquetoes are extreemly troublesome to us. This morning early I dispatched J. Fields and Drewyer in one of the canoes up the river to hunt Elk. set Frazier at work to sew the skins together for the covering of the boat. Sheilds and Gas I sent over the river to lurch a small timbered bottom on that side opposite to the Islands for timber and bark; and to myself I assign the duty of cook as well for those present as for the party which I expect again to arrive this evening from the lower camp. I collected my wood and water, boiled a large quantity of excellent dryed buffaloe meat and made each man a large suet dumpling by way of a treat. about 4 P.M. Shields and Gass returned with a better supply of timber than they had yet collected tho not by any means enough. they brought some bark principally of the Cottonwood which I found was too brittle and soft for the purpose; for this article I find my only dependence is the sweet willow which has a tough & strong bark. Shields and Gass had killed seven buffaloe in their absence the skins of which and a part of the best of the meat they brought with them. if I cannot procure a sufficient quantity of Elk's skins I shall substitute those of the buffaloe. late in the evening the party arrived with two more canoes and another portion of the baggage. Whitehouse one of them much heated and fortiegued on his arrivall dank a very hearty draught of water and was taken almost instanly extreemly ill. his pulse were very full and I therefore bled him plentifully from which he felt great relief. I had no other instrument with which to perform this opperation but my pen knife, however it answered very well. the wind being from S. E today and favourable the men made considerable progress by means of their sails.

At the lower Camp. The party set out very early from this place, and took with them two canoes and a second alotment of baggage consisting of Parched meal, Pork, powder lead axes, tools, bisquit, portable soupe, some merchandize and cloathing. Capt. C. gave Sergt. Pryor a doze of salts this morning and employed Sharbono in rendering the buffaloe tallow which had been collected there, he obtained a sufficient quantity to fill three empty kegs. Capt. C. also scelected the articles to be deposited in the cash consisting of my desk which I had left for that purpose and in which I had left some books, my specimens of plants minerals &c. collected from fort Mandan to that place. also 2 Kegs of Pork, 1/2 a Keg of flour 2 blunderbushes, 1/2 a keg of fixed ammunition and some other small articles belonging to the party which could be dispenced with. deposited the swivel and carriage under the rocks a little above the camp near the river. great numbers of buffaloe still continue to water daily opposite the camp. The antelopes still continue scattered and seperate in the plains. the females with their young only of which they generally have two, and the males alone. Capt. Clarke measured the rout from the Camp at the Whitebear Islands to the lower camp which is as follows.-

[Clark, June 26, 1805] June 26th Wednesday 1805 Some rain last night this morning verry Cloudy the party Set out this morning verry early with their loads to the Canoe Consisting of Parched meal Pork Powder Lead axes, Tools Bisquit, P. Soup & Some Merchendize & Clothes &c. &c. I gave Serjt. Pryor a dolt of Salts, & Set Chabonah to trying up the Buffalow tallow & put into the empty Kegs &c. I assort our articles for to be left at this place buried, _____ Kegs of Pork, 1/2 a Keg of flour, 2 blunderbuts, _____ Caterrages a few Small lumbersom articles Capt Lewiss Desk and Some books & Small articles in it

The wind from the N. W. verry worm flying Clouds in the evening the wind Shifted round to the East & blew hard, which is a fair wind for the two Canoes to Sail on the Plains across the portage, I had three Kegs of Buffalow Grease tried up. Great numbers of Buffalow opposite to our Camp watering to day.

[Lewis, June 27, 1805] Thursday June 27th 1805. The party returned early this morning for the remaining canoe and baggage; Whitehouse was not quite well this morning I therefore detained him and about 10 A.M. set him at work with Frazier sewing the skins together for the boat; Shields and Gass continued the operation of shaving and fiting the horizontall bars of wood in the sections of the boat; the timber is so crooked and indifferent that they make but little progress, for myself I continued to act the part of cook in order to keep all hands employed. some Elk came near our camp and we killed 2 of them at 1 P.M. a cloud arrose to the S. W. and shortly after came on attended with violent Thunder Lightning and hail &c. (see notes on diary of the weather for June). soon after this storm was over Drewyer and J. Fields returned. they were about 4 miles above us during the storm, the hail was of no uncommon size where they were. They had killed 9 Elk and three bear during their absence; one of the bear was the largest by far that we have yet seen; the skin appear to me to be as large as a common ox. while hunting they saw a thick brushey bottom on the bank of the river where from the tracks along shore they suspected that there were bare concealed; they therefore landed without making any nois and climbed a leaning tree and placed themselves on it's branches about 20 feet above the ground, when thus securely fixed they gave a hoop and this large bear instantly rushed forward to the place from whence he had heard the human voice issue, when he arrived at the tree he made a short paus and Drewyer shot him in the head. it is worthy of remark that these bear never climb. the fore feet of this bear measured nine inches across and the hind feet eleven and - 3/4 in length & exclusive of the tallons and seven inches in width. a bear came within thirty yards of our camp last night and eat up about thirty weight of buffaloe suit which was hanging on a pole. my dog seems to be in a constant state of alarm with these bear and keeps barking all night. soon after the storm this evening the water on this side of the river became of a deep crimson colour which I pesume proceeded from some stream above and on this side. there is a kind of soft red stone in the bluffs and bottoms. of the gullies in this neighbourhood which forms this colouring matter.- At the lower camp. Capt. Clark completed a draught of the river with the couses and distances from the entrance of the Missouri to Ft. Mandan, which we intend depositing here in order to guard against accedents. Sergt. Pryor is somewhat better this morning. at 4 P.M. the party returned from the upper camp; Capt. C. gave them a drink of grog; they prepared for the labour of the next day. soon after the party returned it began to rain accompanyed by some hail and continued a short time; a second shower fell late in the evening accompanyed by a high wind from N. W.- the mangled carcases of several buffaloe pass down the river today which had no doubt perished in the falls.

[Clark, June 27, 1805] June 27th Thursday 1805 a fair warm morning wind from the S, E, and moderate. Serjt. Pryor Something better this morning, I proceed to finish a rough draugh of the river & Distances to leave at this place, the wormest day we have had this year, at 4 oClock the Party returned from the head of the portage Soon after it began to hail and rain hard and continued for a fiew minits & Ceased for an hour and began to rain again with a heavy wind from the N W. I refresh the men with a drink of grog The river beginning to rise a little the water is Coloured a redish brown, the Small Streams, discharges in great torrents, and partake of the Choler of the earth over which it passes-a great part of which is light & of a redish brown. Several Buffalow pass drowned & in passing over the falls Cloudy all night, Cold

[Lewis, June 28, 1805] Friday June 28th 1805. Set Drewyer to shaving the Elk skins, Fields to make the cross stays for the boat, Frazier and Whitehouse continue their operation with the skins, Shields and Gass finish the horizontal bars of the sections; after which I sent them in surch of willow bark, a sufficient supply of which they now obtained to bind the boat. expecting the party this evening I prepared a supper for them but they did not arrive. not having quite Elk skins enough I employed three buffaloe hides to cover one section. not being able to shave these skins I had them singed pretty closely with a blazeing torch; I think they will answer tolerable well. The White bear have become so troublesome to us that I do not think it prudent to send one man alone on an errand of any kind, particularly where he has to pass through the brush. we have seen two of them on the large Island opposite to us today but are so much engaged that we could not spare the time to hunt them but will make a frolick of it when the party return and drive them from these islands. they come close arround our camp every night but have never yet ventured to attack us and our dog gives us timely notice of their visits, he keeps constantly padroling all night. I have made the men sleep with their arms by them as usual for fear of accedents. the river is now about nine inches higher than it was on my arrival. lower Camp. early this morning Capt. C. dispatched the remaining canoe with some baggage to the top of the plain above Portage creek three miles in advance; some others he employed in carrying the articles to the cash and depositing them and others to mend the carriages which wer somewhat out of repair. this being accomplished he loaded the two carriages with the remaining baggage and set out with all the party and proceeded on with much difficulty to the canoe in the plain. portage creek had arisen considerably and the water was of crimson colour and illy tasted. on his arrival at the canoe he found there was more baggage than he could possibly take at one load on the two sets of trucks and therefore left some barrels of pork & flour and a few heavy boxes of amunition which could not well be injured, and proceeded with the canoe & one set of trucks loaded with baggage to willow run where he encamped for the night, and killed two buffaloe to subsist the party. soon after his arrival at willow run he experienced a hard shower of rain which was succeeded by a violent wind from the S. W. off the snowy mountains, accompanyed with rain; the party being cold and wet, he administered the consolation of a dram to each.

[Clark, June 28, 1805] June 28th Friday 1805 a fair morning wind from the South I dispatch the remaining Canoe with baggage in her to the top of the Hill three miles, imploy Some hands in Carrying those things we intend to deposit to the Carsh or hole, Some to repareing one of the trucks &c. &c. the water is riseing and of a redish brown Cholour after Covering the Carshe & loading the two Carrges with the remaining part of our Baggage we all Set out passed the Creek which had rose a little and the water nearly red, and bad tasted, we assended the hill to the place the Canoe lay with great labour, at the Canoe at which place we left Some boxes & Kegs of Pork & flour for another Load, and proceeded on with the Canoe & what baggage we could draw on the wheels to willow run 6 miles where we Camped, this run mearly Some water remaining in holes &c. Soon after we halted we had a Shower, and at dark we expereinced a most dredfull wind from off the Snow Mountains to the S. W. accompd. with rain which continued at intervales all night men wet. I refreshed them with a dram. Killed 2 Buffalow. Great nos. about

[Lewis, June 29, 1805] Saturday June 29th 1805. This morning we experienced a heavy shower of rain for about an hour after which it became fair. not having seen the large fountain of which Capt. Clark spoke I determined to visit it today as I could better spare this day from my attention to the boat than probably any other when the work would be further advanced; accordingly after seting the hands at their several employments I took Drewyer and seet out for the fountain and passed through a level beautiful plain for about Six miles when I reached the brake of the river hills here we were overtaken by a violent gust of wind and rain from the S. W. attended with thunder and Litning. I expected a hail storm probably from this cloud and therefore took refuge in a little gully wher there were some broad stones with which I purposed protecting my head if we should have a repetition of the seene of the 27th but fortunately we had but little hail and that not large; I sat very composedly for about an hour without sheter and took a copious drenching of rain; after the shower was over I continued my rout to the fountain which I found much as Capt. C; had discribed & think it may well be retained on the list of prodegies of this neighbourhood towards which, nature seems to have dealt with a liberal hand, for I have scarcely experienced a day since my first arrival in this quarter without experiencing some novel occurrence among the party or witnessing the appearance of some uncommon object. I think this fountain the largest I ever beheld, and the hadsome cascade which it affords over some steep and irregular rocks in it's passage to the river adds not a little to it's beauty. it is about 25 yds. from the river, situated in a pretty little level plain, and has a suddon decent of about 6 feet in one part of it's course. the water of this fountain is extreemly tranparent and cold; nor is it impregnated with lime or any other extranious matter which I can discover, but is very pure and pleasent. it's waters marke their passage as Capt. Clark observes for a considerable distance down the Missouri notwithstanding it's rapidity and force. the water of the fountain boil up with such force near it's center that it's surface in that part seems even higher than the surrounding earth which is a firm handsom terf of fine green grass. after amusing myself about 20 minutes in examining the fountain I found myself so chilled with my wet cloaths that I determined to return and accordingly set out; on our way to camp we found a buffaloe dead which we had shot as we came out and took a parsel of the meat to camp it was in very good order; the hump and tongue of a fat buffaloe I esteem great delicasies. on my arrival at camp I was astonished not to find the party yet arrived, but then concluded that probably the state of the praries had detained them, as in the wet state in which they are at present the mud sticks to the wheels is such manner that they are obliged to halt frequently and clense them. Transaction and occurrencies which took place with Capt. Clark and party today.

Shortly after the rain which fell early this morning he found it impossuble from the state of the plains for the party to reach the upper extremity of the portage with their present load, and therefore sent back almost all of the party to bring the baggage which had been left behind yesterday. he determined himself to pass by the way of the river to camp in order to supply the deficiency of some notes and remarks which he had made as he first ascended the river but which he had unfortunately lost. accordingly he left one man at Willow run to guard the baggage and took with him his black man York, Sharbono and his indian woman also accompanyed Capt. C. on his arrival at the falls he perceived a very black cloud rising in the West which threatened immediate rain; he looked about for a shelter but could find none without being in great danger of being blown into the river should the wind prove as violent as it sometimes is on those occasions in these plains; at length about a 1/4 of a mile above the falls he discovered a deep rivene where there were some shelving rocks under which he took shelter near the river with Sharbono and the Indian woman; laying their guns compass &c. under a shelving rock on the upper side of the rivene where they were perfectly secure from the rain. the first shower was moderate accompanyed by a violent rain the effects of which they did but little feel; soon after a most violent torrent of rain decended accompanyed with hail; the rain appeared to decend in a body and instantly collected in the rivene and came down in a roling torrent with irrisistable force driving rocks mud and everything before it which opposed it's passage, Capt. C. fortunately discovered it a moment before it reached them and seizing his gun and shot pouch with his left hand with the right he assisted himself up the steep bluff shoving occasionaly the Indian woman before him who had her child in her arms; Sharbono had the woman by the hand indeavouring to pull her up the hill but was so much frightened that he remained frequently motionless and but for Capt. C. both himself and his woman and child must have perished. so suddon was the rise of the water that before Capt C could reach his gun and begin to ascend the bank it was up to his waist and wet his watch; and he could scarcely ascend faster than it arrose till it had obtained the debth of 15 feet with a current tremendious to behold. one moment longer & it would have swept them into the river just above the great cataract of 87 feet where they must have inevitably perished. Sarbono lost his gun shot pouch, horn, tomahawk, and my wiping rod; Capt. Clark his Umbrella and compas or circumferenter. they fortunately arrived on the plain safe, where they found the black man, York, in surch of them; york had seperated from them a little while before the storm, in pursuit of some buffaloe and had not seen them enter the rivene; when this gust came on he returned in surch of them & not being able to find them for some time was much allarmed. the bier in which the woman carrys her child and all it's cloaths wer swept away as they lay at her feet she having time only to grasp her child; the infant was therefore very cold and the woman also who had just recovered from a severe indisposition was also wet and cold, Capt C. therefore relinquished his intended rout and returned to the camp at willow run in order also to obtain dry cloathes for himself and directed them to follow him. on Capt. Clark's arrival at camp he found that the party dispatched for the baggage had returned in great confusion and consternation leaving their loads in the plains; the men who were all nearly naked and no covering on the head were sorely mawled with the hail which was so large and driven with such force by the wind that it nocked many of them (town and one particulary as many as three times most of them were bleeding freely and complained of being much bruised. willow run raised about 6 feet with this rain and the plains were so wet they could do nothing more this evening. Capt. C. gave the party a dram to console them in some measure for their general defeat.

[Clark, June 29, 1805] Junne 29th Saltarday 1805 a little rain verry early this morning after Clear, finding that the Prarie was So wet as to render it impossible to pass on to the end of the portage, deturmined to Send hack to the top of the hill at the Creek for the remaining part of the baggage left at that place yesterday, leaveing one man to take care of the baggage at this place. I deturmined any Self to proceed on to the falls and take the river, according we all Set out., I took my Servent & one man Chabono our Interpreter & his Squar accompanied, Soon after I arrived at the falls, I perceived a Cloud which appeared black and threaten imediate rain, I looked out for a Shelter but Could See no place without being in great danger of being blown into the river if the wind Should prove as turbelant as it is at Some times about 1/4 of a mile above the falls I obsd a Deep rivein in which was Shelveing rocks under which we took Shelter near the river and placed our guns the Compass &c. &c. Under a Shelveing rock on the upper Side of the Creek, in a place which was verry Secure from rain, the first Shower was moderate accompanied with a violent wind, the effects of which we did not feel, Soon after a torrent of rain and hail fell more violent than ever I Saw before, the rain fell like one voley of water falling from the heavens and gave us time only to get out of the way of a torrent of water which was Poreing down the hill in the rivin with emence force tareing every thing before it takeing with it large rocks & mud, I took my gun & Shot pouch in my left hand, and with the right Scrambled up the hill pushing the Interpreters wife (who had her Child in her arms) before me, the Interpreter himself makeing attempts to pull up his wife by the hand much Scared and nearly without motion- we at length retched the top of the hill Safe where I found my Servent in Serch of us greatly agitated, for our wellfar-. before I got out of the bottom of the revein which was a flat dry rock when I entered it, the water was up to my waste & wet my watch, I Scrcely got out before it raised 10 feet deep with a torrent which turrouble to behold, and by the time I reached the top of the hill, at least 15 feet water, I directed the party to return to the Camp at the run as fast as possible to get to our lode where Clothes Could be got to Cover the Child whose Clothes were all lost, and the woman who was but just recovering from a Severe indispostion, and was wet and Cold, I was fearfull of a relaps I caused her as also the others of the party to take a little Spirits, which my Servent had in a Canteen, which revived verry much. on arrival at the Camp on the willow run-met the party who had returned in great Confusion to the run leaveing their loads in the Plain, the hail & wind being So large and violent in the plains, and them naked, they were much brused, and Some nearly killed one knocked down three times, and others without hats or any thing on their heads bloodey & Complained verry much; I refreshed them with a little grog- Soon after the run began to rise and rose 6 feet in a few minits-. I lost at the river in the torrent the large Compas, an eligant fusee, Tomahawk Humbrallo, Shot pouh, & horn wih powder & Ball, mockersons, & the woman lost her Childs Bear & Clothes bedding &c.- The Compass is a Serious loss; as we have no other large one. The plains are So wet that we Can do nothing this evining particilarly as two deep reveins are between ourselves & Load

[Lewis, June 30, 1805] Sunday June 30th 1805. We had a heavy dew this morning which is a remarkable event. Fraizer and Whitehouse still continue their opperation of sewing the skins together. I set Shields and gass to shaving bark and Fields continued to make the cross brases. Drewyer and myself rendered a considerable quantity of tallow and cooked. I begin to be extremely impatient to be off as the season is now waisting a pace nearly three months have now elapsed since we left Fort Mandan and not yet reached the Rocky Mountains I am therefore fully preswaded that we shall not reach Fort Mandan again this season if we even return from the ocean to the Snake Indians. wherever we find timber there is also beaver; Drewyer killed two today. There are a number of large bat or goatsucker here I killed one of them and found that there was no difference between them and those common to the U States; I have not seen the leather winged bat for some time nor is there any of the small goatsuckers in this quarter of the country. we have not the whip-poor-will either. this last is by many persons in the U States confounded with the large goat-sucker or night-hawk as it is called in the Eastern States, and are taken for the same bird. it is true that there is a great resemblance but they are distinct species of the goatsucker. here the one exists without the other. the large goat sucker lays it's eggs in these open plains without the preperation of a nest we have found their eggs in several instances they lay only two before they set nor do I beleive that they raise more than one brood in a season; they have now just hatched their young.- This evening the bark was shaved and the leather covering for the sections were also completed and I had them put into the water, in order to toughen the bark, and prepare the leather for sewing on the sections in the morning. it has taken 28 Elk skins and 4 Buffaloe skins to complete her. the crossbars are also finished this evening; we have therefore only the way strips now to obtain in order to complete the wood work, and this I fear will be a difficult task. The party have not returned from the lower camp I am therefore fearfull that some uncommon accedent has happened.

Occurrences with Capt. Clark and Party

This morning Capt. Clark dispatched two men to kill some buffaloe, two others to the falls to surch for the articles lost yesterday, one he retained to cook and sent the others for the baggage left in the plains yesterday. the hunters soon returned loaded with meat those sent for the baggage brought it up in a few hours, he then set four men at work to make axeltrees and repare the carrages; the others he employed in conveying the baggage over the run on their sholders it having now fallent to about 3 feet water. the men complained much today of the bruises and wounds which they had received yesterday from the hail. the two men sent to the falls returned with the compas which they found covered in the mud and sand near the mouth of the rivene the other articles were irrecoverably lost. they found that part of rivene in; which Capt. C. had been seting yesterday, filled with huge rocks. at 11 A.M. Capt. Clark dispatched the party with a load of the baggage as far as the 6 miles stake, with orders to deposit it there and return with the carriages which they did accordingly. they experienced a heavy gust of wind this evening from the S. W. after which it was a fair afternoon. more buffaloe than usual were seen about their camp; Capt. C assured me that he beleives he saw at least ten thousand at one view.

[Clark, June 30, 1805] June 30th Sunday 1805. a fair morning, I dispatch the party except 5 for the remaining baggage Scattered in the plains, two to hunt for meat, two to the falls, and one to Cook at 10 oClock the hunters Came in loaded with fat meat, & those were dispatched for the baggage returned with it. I Set 4 men to make new axeltrees & repare the Carrages, others to take the load across the run which had fallen & is about 3 feet water, men Complain of being Swore this day dull and lolling about, The two men dispatched in Serch of the articls lost yesterday returned and brought the Compass which they found in the mud & Stones near the mouth of the revein, no other articles found, the place I Sheltered under filled up with hugh Rocks, I Set the party out at 11 oClock to take a load to the 6 mile Stake & return this evening, and I intend to take on the ballance to the river tomorrow if the prarie will permit. at 3 oClock a Storm of wind from the S. W. after which we had a clear evening. Great numbers of Buffalow in every direction, I think 10,000 may be Seen in a view.

[Lewis, July 1, 1805] Monday July 1st 1805. This morning I set Frazier and Whitehouse to sewing the leather on the sides of the sections of the boat; Shields and J. Fields to collect and split light wood and prepare a pit to make tar. Gas I set at work to make the way strips out of some willow limbs which tho indifferent were the best which could be obtained. Drewyer and myself completed the opperation of rendering the tallow; we obtained about 100 lbs. by evening the skins were all attatched to their sections and I returned them again to the water. all matters were now in readiness to commence the opperation of puting the parts of the boat together in the morning. the way strips are not yet ready but will be done in time as I have obtained the necessary timber. the difficulty in obtaining the necessary materials has retarded my operations in forming this boat extreemly tedious and troublesome; and as it was a novel peice of machinism to all who were employed my constant attention was necessary to every part of the work; this together with the duties of cheif cook has kept me pretty well employed. at 3 P.M. Capt. Clark arrived with the party all very much fortiegued. he brought with him all the baggage except what he had deposited yesterday at the six mile stake, for which the party were too much fortiegued to return this evening. we gave them a dram and suffered them to rest from their labours this evening. I directed Bratton to assist in making the tar tomorrow, and scelected several others to assist in puting the boat together. the day has been warm and the Musquetoes troublesome of course the bear were about our camp all last night, we have therefore determined to beat up their quarters tomorrow, and kill them or drive them from their haunts about this place.

[Clark, July 1, 1805]
White Bear Islands above the Falls of the Missouri July 1st Monday 1805
I arrived at this place to day at 3 oClock P.M. with the party from the
lower part of the portage much fatigued &c.

[Clark, July 1, 1805] July 1st Monday 1805. We Set out early this morning with the remaining load, and proceeded on verry well to Capt Lewis's Camp where we arrived at 3 oClock, the Day worm and party much fatigued, found Capt. Lewis and party all buisey employd in fitting up the Iron boat, the wind hard from the S, W,- one man verry unwell, his legs & theis broke out and Swelled the hail which fell at Capt. Lewis Camp 27 Ins was 7 Inches in circumfrance & waied 3 ounces, fortunately for us it was not So large in the plains, if it had we Should most certainly fallen victims to its rage as the men were mostly naked, and but few with hats or any covering on their heads, The hunters killed 3 white bear one large, the fore feet of which measured 9 Inchs across, the hind feet 11 Inchs 3/4 long & 7 Inch's wide a bear nearly Catching Joseph Fields Chased him into the water, bear about the Camp every night & Seen on an Isld. in the day

[Lewis, July 2, 1805] Tuesday July 2cd 1805 A shower of rain fell very early this morning after which we dispatched the men for the remaining baggage at the 6 mile stake. Shields and Bratton seting their tarkiln, Sergts. Pryor and Gass at work on the waystrips and myself and all other hands engaged in puting the boat together which we accomplished in about 3 hours and I then set four men at work sewing the leather over the cross bars of Iron on the inner side of the boat, which form the ends of the sections. about 2 P.M. the party returned with the baggage, all well pleased that they had completed the laborious task of the portage. The Musquetoes uncommonly troublesome the wind hard from the S. W. all day I think it possible that these almost perpetual S. W. winds proceede from the agency of the Snowey Mountains and the wide level and untimbered plains which streach themselves along their bases for an immence distance (i e) that the air comeing in contact with the snow is suddenly chilled and condenced, thus becoming heaver than the air beneath in the plains, it glides down the sides of these mountains & decends to the plains, where by the constant action of the sun on the face of an untimbered country there is a partial vacuum formed for it's reception. I have observed that the winds from this quarter are always the coldest and most violent which we experience, yet I am far from giving full credit to my own hypothesis on this subject; if hoever I find on the opposite side of these mountains that the winds take a contrary direction I shall then have more faith. After I had completed my observation of Equal Altitudes today Capt. Clark Myself and 12 men passed over to the large Island to hunt bear. the brush in that part of it where the bear frequent is an almost impenetrable thicket of the broad leafed willow; this brush we entered in small parties of 3 or four together and surched in every part. we found one only which made at Drewyer and he shot him in the brest at the distance of about 20 feet, the ball fortunately passed through his heart, the stroke knocked the bear down and gave Drewyer time to get out of his sight; the bear changed his course we pursued him about a hundred yards by the blood and found him dead; we surched the thicket in every part but found no other, and therefore returned. this was a young male and would weigh about 400 lbs. the water of the Missouri here is in most places about 10 feet deep. after our return, in moving some of the baggage we caught a large rata it was somewhat larger than the common European rat, of lighter colour; the body and outer part of the legs and head of a light lead colour, the belly and inner side of the legs white as were also the feet and years. the toes were longer and the ears much larger than the common rat; the ears uncovered with hair. the eyes were black and prominent the whiskers very long and full. the tail was reather longer than the body and covered with fine fur or poil of the same length and colour of the back. the fur was very silkey close and short. I have frequently seen the nests of these rats in clifts of rocks and hollow trees but never before saw one of them. they feed very much on the fruit and seed of the prickly pear; or at least I have seen large quantities of the hulls of that fruit lying about their holes and in their nests.

[Clark, July 2, 1805] July 2nd Tuesday 1805 Some rain at day light this morning. dispatched the party for the remaining baggage left at the 6 mile Stake, they returned in the evening and we Crossed to a large Island nearly opposit to us to kill bear which has been Seen frequently in the Island, we killed one bear & returned at Sun Set. The Roreing of the falls for maney miles above us

[Clark, July 2, 1805] July 2nd Tuesday 1805 Some rain at day light this morn'g after which a fair morning, dispatched the men for the Kegs &c. left at the Six mile Stake, others to get timber for the boat &c. Musquetors verry troublesom to day, day worm, after the return of the men with the articles left at the 6 mile Stake Capt. Lewis my Self & 12 men Crossed to an Island on which we Saw a bear the evening before, & Several had been Seen by the party at this place, we killed one of the bear and returned. The river at this place is _____ yards wide and about 10 feet water Cought a rat in our Stores, which had done some mischief, this rat was about the Sise of a Comn. large rat, larger ears, long whiskers & toes, with a tail long & hairey like a ground Squirel, verry fine fur and lighter than the Common rat. Wind to day as usial from the S. W. and hard all the after part of the day, those winds are also Cool and generally verry hard.

[Lewis, July 3, 1805] Wednesday July 3rd 1805. This morning early we employed all hands; some were making tar or attempting to make it, others were attatching the skins on the boat, other cuting and fiting the bark for lining puting in the woodworke &c some hunters were sent out to kill buffaloe in order to make pemecon to take with us and also for their skins which we now want to cover our baggage in the boat and canoes when we depart from hence. the Indians have informed us that we should shortly leave the buffaloe country after passing the falls; this I much regret for I know when we leave the buffaloe that we shal sometimes be under the necessity of fasting occasionally. and at all events the white puddings will be irretreivably lost and Sharbono out of imployment. our tar-kiln which ought to have began to run this morning has yealded no tar as yet and I am much affraid will not yeald any, if so I fear the whole opperation of my boat will be useless. I fear I have committed another blunder also in sewing the skins with a nedle which has sharp edges these have cut the skin and as it drys I discover that the throng dose not fill the holes as I expected tho I made them sew with a large throng for that purpose. at 10 OCk A.M. we had a slight shower which scarcely wet the grass. One buffaloe only and 2 Antelopes killed today six beaver and 2 otter have been killed within the last three days. The current of the river looks so gentle and inviting that the men all seem anxious to be moving upward as well as ourselves. we have got the boat pretly well forward today and think we shall be able to complete her tomorrow except paying her, to do which will require some little time to make her first perfectly dry. she has assumed her shape and looks extreemly well. She will be very light, more so than any vessel of her size that I ever saw.

[Clark, July 3, 1805] July 3rd Wednesday 1805 all of party employd in Sowing the Skins to the boat, burning Tare, preparing timber, hunting buffalow for their meat & Skins, drying & repacking the Stores, Goods &c. &c. at 1 oClock began to rain. in the evening the hunters killed two antelopes & a Buffalow.

[Clark, July 3, 1805] July 3rd Wednesday 1805 A fine morning wind from the S. W all the party employd, Some about the boat, attaching the Skins & Sowing them to the Sections, others prepareing timber, Some, burning tar of the drift pine, Some airring and repacking the Stores & Goods, & others hunting for Meet to make pemitigon & for the use of their Skins to Cover the Canoes & boat,-. a Small Shower at 1 oClock which did Scercely wet the grass-. one buffalow and two Antelopes Killed this evening. Six beaver & 2 orters has been Killed at this camp within a fiew days we discover no fish above the falls as yet- the only timber in this part of the Countrey is willow, a fiew Cotton trees which is neither large nor tall, Boxalders and red wood. (Boil roche arrow wood)

The water tolerably clear and Soft in the river, Current jentle and bottoms riseing from the water; no appearance of the river riseing more than a few feet above the falls, as high up as we have yet explored. but few trees on the Std Side the grass is high and fine near the river. the winds has blown for Several days from the S. W. I think it possible that those almost perpetial S W. winds, proceed from the agency of the Snowey mountains and the wide leavel and untimbered plains which Streach themselves along their borders for an emence distance, that the air comeing in Contact with the Snow is Suddenly chilled and condensed, thus becomeing heavyer than the air beneath in the plains it glides down the Sides of those mountains and decends to the plains, where by the constant action of the Sun on the face of the untimbered country there is a partial vacuom formed for it's reception I have observed that the winds from this quarter is always the Coaldest and most violent which we experience, yet I am far from giveing full credit to this hypothesis on this Subject; if I find however on the opposit Side of these mountains that the winds take a contrary direction I Shall then have full faith. (The winds take a contrary direction in the morning or from the mountains on the west Side)

[Lewis, July 4, 1805] Thursday July 4th 1805. Yesterday we permitted Sergt. Gass McNeal and several others who had not yet seen the falls to visit them. no appearance of tar yet and I am now confident that we shall not be able to obtain any; a serious misfortune. I employed a number of hands on the boat today and by 4 P.M. in the evening completed her except the most difficult part of the work that of making her seams secure. I had her turned up and some small fires kindled underneath to dry her. Capt. C. completed a draught of the river from Fort Mandan to this place which we intend depositing at this place in order to guard against accedents. not having seen the Snake Indians or knowing in fact whether to calculate on their friendship or hostility or friendship we have conceived our party sufficiently small and therefore have concluded not to dispatch a canoe with a part of our men to St. Louis as we had intended early in the spring. we fear also that such a measure might possibly discourage those who would in such case remain, and might possibly hazzard the fate of the expedition. we have never once hinted to any one of the party that we had such a scheme in contemplation, and all appear perfectly to have made up their minds to suceed in the expedition or purish in the attempt. we all beleive that we are now about to enter on the most perilous and difficult part of our voyage, yet I see no one repining; all appear ready to met those difficulties which wait us with resolution and becoming fortitude. we had a heavy dew this morning. the clouds near these mountains rise suddenly and discharge their contents partially on the neighbouring plains; the same cloud will discharge hail alone in one part hail and rain in another and rain only in a third all within the space of a few miles; and on the Mountains to the S. E. of us sometimes snow. at present there is no snow on those mountains; that which covered them when we first saw them and which has fallen on them several times since has all disappeared. the Mountains to the N. W. & W. of us are still entirely covered are white and glitter with the reflection of the sun. I do not beleive that the clouds which prevail at this season of the year reach the summits of those lofty mountains; and if they do the probability is that they deposit snow only for there has been no perceptible deminution of the snow which they contain since we first saw them. I have thought it probable that these mountains might have derived their appellation of shining Mountains, from their glittering appearance when the sun shines in certain directions on the snow which covers them. since our arrival at the falls we have repeatedly witnessed a nois which proceeds from a direction a little to the N. of West as loud and resembling precisely the discharge of a piece of ordinance of 6 pounds at the distance of three miles. I was informed of it by the men several times before I paid any attention to it, thinking it was thunder most probably which they had mistaken at length walking in the plains the other day I heard this noise very distictly, it was perfectly calm clear and not a cloud to be seen, I halted and listened attentively about an hour during which time I heard two other discharges and tok the direction of the sound with my pocket compass. I have no doubt but if I had leasure I could find from whence it issued. I have thout it probable that it might be caused by runing water in some of the caverns of those immence mountains, on the principal of the blowing caverns; but in such case the sounds would be periodical & regular, which is not the case with this, being sometimes heard once only and at other times, six or seven discharges in quick succession. it is heard also at different seasons of the day and night. I am at a loss to account for this phenomenon. our work being at an end this evening, we gave the men a drink of sperits, it being the last of our stock, and some of them appeared a little sensible of it's effects the fiddle was plyed and they danced very merrily untill 9 in the evening when a heavy shower of rain put an end to that part of the amusement tho they continued their mirth with songs and festive jokes and were extreemly merry untill late at night. we had a very comfortable dinner, of bacon, beans, suit dumplings & buffaloe beaf &c. in short we had no just cause to covet the sumptuous feasts of our countrymen on this day.- one Elk and a beaver were all that was killed by the hunters today; the buffaloe seem to have withdrawn themselves from this neighbourhood; tho the men inform us that they are still abundant about the falls.

[Clark, July 4, 1805] ,July the 4th Thursday 1805 A fine morning, a heavy dew last night, all hands employed in Completeing the leather boat, gave the Party a dram which made Several verry lively, a black Cloud came up from the S. W, and rained a fiew drops I employ my Self drawing a Copy of the river to be left at this place for fear of Some accident in advance, I have left buried below the falls a Map of the Countrey below Fort Mandan with Sundery private papers the party amused themselves danceing untill late when a Shower of rain broke up the amusement, all lively and Chearfull, one Elk and a beaver kill'd to day. our Tar kill like to turn out nothing from the following cause.

The climate about the falls of Missouri appears to be Singular Cloudy every day (Since our arrival near them) which rise from defferent directions and discharge themselves partially in the plains & mountains, in Some places rain others rain & hail, hail alone, and on the mountains in Some parts Snow. a rumbling like Cannon at a great distance is heard to the west if us; the Cause we Can't account

[Lewis, July 5, 1805] Friday July 5th 1805. This morning I had the boat removed to an open situation, scaffold her off the ground, turned her keel to the sun and kindled fires under her to dry her more expeditiously. I then set a couple of men to pounding of charcoal to form a composition with some beeswax which we have and buffaloe tallow now my only hope and resource for paying my boat; I sincerely hope it may answer yet I fear it will not. the boat in every other rispect completely answers my most sanguine expectation; she is not yet dry and eight men can carry her with the greatest ease; she is strong and will carry at least 8,000 lbs. with her suit of hands; her form is as complete as I could wish it. the stitches begin to gape very much since she has began to dry; I am now convinced this would not have been the case had the skins been sewed with a sharp point only and the leather not cut by the edges of a sharp nedle. about 8 A M. a large herd of buffaloe came near our camp and Capt. Clark with a party of the hunters indeavoured to get a shoot at them but the wind proved unfavourable and they ran off; the hunters pursued and killed three of them; we had most of the meat brought in and set a party to drying it. their skins were all brought in and streached to dry for the purpose of covering the baggage. 2 Wolves and three Antelopes also killed today. we permitted three other men to visit the falls today; these were the last of the party who had not as yet indulged themselves with this grand and interesting seen. the buffaloe again appear in great numbers about our camp and seem to be moving down the river. it is somewhat remarkable that altho you may see ten or a douzen herds of buffaloe distinctly scattered and many miles distant yet if they are undisturbed by pursuit, they will all be traveling in one direction. the men who were permitted to visit the falls today returned in the evening and reported that the buffaloe were very numerous in that quarter; and as the country is more broken near the river in that quarter we conclude to dispatch a couple of canoes tomorrow with some hunters to kill as many as will answer our purposes.

The plains in this part of the country are not so fertile as below the entrance of the Cockkle or missel shell river and from thence down the Missouri there is also much more stone on the sides of the hills and on the broken lands than below.-

[Clark, July 5, 1805] July 5th Friday 1805 A fine morning and but little wind, worm and Sultrey at 8 oClock- I Saw a large gangue of Buffalow and prosued them with Several men the wind was unfavourable and we Could not get near them, the party Scattered & Killed 3 buffalow and brought in their Skins and Some meat, Killed 2 wolves & 3 Antilopes for their Skins, Capt. Lewis much engaged in Completeing the Leather boat. Three men went to See the Falls, Saw great numbers of Buffalow on both Sides of the river. great numbers of young black birds

[Lewis, July 6, 1805] Saturday July 6th 1805 In the couse of last night had several showers of hail and rain attended with thunder and lightning. about day a heavy storm came on from the S W attended with hail rain and a continued roar of thunder and some lightning. the hail was as large as musket balls and covered the ground perfectly. we hand some of it collected which kept very well through the day and served to cool our water. These showers and gusts keep my boat wet in dispite of my exertions. she is not yet ready for the grease and coal. after the hail and rain was over this morning we dispatched 4 hunters and two canoes to the head of the rappids as we had determined last evening. the red and yellow courants are now ripe and abundant, they are reather ascid as yet. There is a remarkable small fox which ascociate in large communities and burrow in the praries something like the small wolf but we have not as yet been able to obtain one of them; they are extreemly watchfull and take reffuge in their burrows which are very deep; we have seen them no where except near these falls.

[Clark, July 6, 1805] July 6th Satturday 1805 a heavy wind from the S W and Some rain about mid night last, at day light this morning a verry black Cloud from the S W, with a Contined rore of thunder & Some lightening and rained and hailed tremendiously for about 1/2 an hour, the hail was the Size of a musket ball and Covered the ground. this hail & rain was accompand. by a hard wind which lasted for a fiew minits. Cloudy all the forepart of the day, after Part Clear. dispatched 4 men in 2 Canoes to the falls, to kill Buffalow, for their Skins & Meat others emplloyd about the boat, I cought Some Small fish this evening.

[Lewis, July 7, 1805] Sunday July 7th 1805. The weather warm and cloudy therefore unfavourable for many operations; I keep small fires under the boat; the blowing flies are innumerable about it; the moisture retained by the bark prevents it from drying as fast as it otherwise would. we dispatched two other hunters to kill Elk or buffaloe for their skins to cover our baggage. we have no tents; the men are therefore obliged to have recourse to the sails for shelter from the weather and we have not more skins than are sufficient to cover our baggage when stoed away in bulk on land. many of the men are engaged in dressing leather to cloath themselves. their leather cloathes soon become rotton as they are much exposed to the water and frequently wet. Capt. Clarks black man York is very unwell today and he gave him a doze of tartar emettic which operated very well and he was much better in the evening. this is a discription of medecine that I nevr have recourse to in my practice except in cases of the intermittent fever. this evening the hunters returned with the canoes and brought thre buffaloe skins only and two Antelope 4 deer and three wolf skins; they reported that the buffaloe had gone further down the river. the two hunters whom we sent out from hence returned also without having killed anything except one Elk. I set one of the party at work to make me some sacks of the wolf skins, to transport my Instruments when occasion requirs their being carried any distance by land.- we had a light shower of rain about 4 P.M. attended with some thunder and lightning. one beaver caught this morning. the musquetoes are excessively troublesome to us. I have prepared my composition which I should have put on this evening but the rain prevented me.

[Clark, July 7, 1805] July 7th Sunday 1805 A Warm day wind from the S. W Cloudy as usial, the four men hunters did not return last night. dispatched 2 men to kill Elk for the use of their Skin for the boat. my man York Sick, I give him a dosh of Tarter. Some rain in the after part of the day in the evining the hunters returned with three buffalow Skins two goat Skins, four Deer Skins, two deer, & 3 wolve Skins, to be used in Covering the boat Canoes & to make mockersons, one Elk also killed to day

[Lewis, July 8, 1805] Monday July 8th 1805. Capt. Clark Determined to make a second effort to replace the notes which he had made with rispect to the river and falls accordingly he set out after an early breakfast and took with him the greater part of the men with a view also to kill buffaloe should there be any in that quarter. after geting some distance in the plains he divided the party and sent them in different directions and himself and two others struck the Missouri at the entrance of medicine river and continued down it to the great Cataract, from whence he returned through the plains to camp where he arrived late in the evening. the hunters also returned having killed 3 buffaloe 2 Antelopes and a deer. he informed me that the immence herds of buffaloe which we had seen for some time past in this neighbourhood have almost entirely disappeared and he beleives are gone down the river.

The day being warm and fair about 12 OCk. the boat was sufficiently dry to receive a coat of the composition which I accordingly applyed. this adds very much to her appearance whether it will be effectual or not. it gives her hull the appearance of being formed of one solid piece. after the first coat had cooled I gave her a second which I think has made it sufficiently thick. The mountains which ly before us from the South, to the N. W. still continue covered with snow. one hunter also passed the river to hunt this morning in the evening he returned having killed a Buck and a male Antelope. The party who were down with Capt. Clark also killed a small fox which they brought with them. it was a female appeared to give suck, otherwise it is so much like the comm small fox of this country commonly called the kit fox that I should have taken it for a young one of that species; however on closer examination it did apear to differ somewhat; it's colour was of a lighter brown, it's years proportionably larger, and the tale not so large or the hair not so long which formed it. they are very delicately formed, exceedingly fleet, and not as large as the common domestic cat. their tallons appear longer than any species of fox I ever saw and seem therefore prepared more amply by nature for the purpose of burrowing. there is sufficient difference for discrimination between it and the kit fox, and to satisfy me perfectly that it is a distinct species. the men also brought me a living ground squirrel which is something larger than those of the U States or those of that kind which are also common here. this is a much hadsomer anamal. like the other it's principal colour is a redish brown but is marked longitudinally with a much greater number of black or dark bron stripes; the spaces between which is marked by ranges of pure white circular spots, about the size of a brister blue shot. these colours imbrace the head neck back and sides; the tail is flat, or the long hair projecting horizontally from two sides of it only gives it that appearance. the belly and breast are of much lighter brown or nearly white. this is an inhabitant of the open plain altogether, wher it burrows and resides; nor is it like the other found among clifts of rocks or in the woodlands. their burrows sometimes like those of the mole run horizontally near the surface of the ground for a considerable distance, but those in which they reside or take refuge strike much deeper in the earth.- Slight rain this afternoon. musquetoes troublesome as usual.

[Clark, July 8, 1805] July 8th Monday 1805 A worm morning flying Clouds I deturmin take the width of the river at the falls & the Medison river and to take the greater part of the men which Can be Speared to Kill Buffalow for their Skins as well as meat, devided the party & Sent them in different directions to hunt & proceeded my Self to the mouth of Medison river measured it and found it to be 137 yards wide, in the narrowest part of the Missouri imediately above Medison river the Missouri is 300 yards wide, below and a little above the falls 1440 yards wide with the direction of the upper great fall 580 yards wide, at the great Spring 270 yards wide, at the handsom falls of 47 ft. 8 l. the river is 473 yards wide, at the lower great falls the river is confined within 280 yards, below the falls the water occupies 93 yards only- after takeing the wedth of the river at those Sundery placies I returned thro the plains in a direct line to Camp. Some rain this evening after a verry hot day.- the mountains which are in view to the South & N W. are Covered with Snow. those nearer us and forma 3/4 Circle around us is not Covered with Snow at this time. The hunters killed 3 buffalow, two antelopes, & a Deer to day- the emence herds of buffalow which was near us a fiew days ago, has proceeded on down the river, we Can See but a fiew Bulls in the plains

[Lewis, July 9, 1805] Tuesday July 9th 1805. The morning was fair and pleant. the Islands seem crouded with blackbirds; the young brude is now completely feathered and flying in common with the others. we corked the canoes and put them in the water and also launched the boat, she lay like a perfect cork on the water. five men would carry her with the greatest ease. I now directed seats to be fixed in her and oars to be fitted. the men loaded the canoes in readiness to depart. just at this moment a violent wind commenced and blew so hard that we were obliged to unload the canoes again; a part of the baggage in several of them got wet before it could be taken out. the wind continued violent untill late in the evening, by which time we discovered that a greater part of the composition had seperated from the skins and left the seams of the boat exposed to the water and she leaked in such manner that she would not answer. I need not add that this circumstance mortifyed me not a little; and to prevent her leaking without pich was impossible with us, and to obtain this article was equally impossible, therefore the evil was irraparable I now found that the section formed of the buffaloe hides on which some hair had been left, answered much the best purpose; this leaked but little and the parts which were well covered with hair about 1/8th of an inch in length retained the composition perfectly and remained sound and dry. from these circumstances I am preswaided, that had I formed her with buffaloe skins singed not quite as close as I had done those I employed, that she would have answered even with this composition. but to make any further experiments in our present situation seemed to me madness; the buffaloe had principally dserted us, and the season was now advancing fast. I therefore relinquished all further hope of my favorite boat and ordered her to be sunk in the water, that the skins might become soft in order the better to take her in peices tomorrow and deposite the iron fraim at this place as it could probably be of no further service to us. had I only singed my Elk skins in stead of shaving them I beleive the composition would have remained and the boat have answered; at least untill we could have reached the pine country which must be in advance of us from the pine which is brought down by the water and which is probably at no great distance where we might have supplyed ourselves with the necessary pich or gum. but it was now too late to introduce a remidy and I bid a dieu to my boat, and her expected services.- The next difficulty which presented itself was how we should convey the stores and baggage which we had purposed carrying in the boat. both Capt. Clark and myself recollected having heard the hunters mention that the bottoms of the river some few miles above us were much better timbered than below and that some of the trees were large. the idea therefore suggested itself of building two other canoes sufficiently large to carry the surplus baggage. on enquiry of the hunters it seemed to be the general opinion that trees sufficiently a large for this purpose might be obtained in a bottom on the opposite side about 8 miles distant by land and reather more than double that distance by water; accordingly Capt. Clark determined to set out early in the morning with ten of the best workmen and proceede by land to that place while the others would in the mean time be employed by myself in taking the Boat in peices and depositing her, together with the articles which we had previously determined to deposit at this place, and also in trasporting all the baggage up the river to that point in the six small canoes. this plan being settled between us orders were accordingly given to the party, and the ten men who were to accompany Capt. Clark had ground and prepared their axes and adds this evening in order to prepare for an early departure in the morning. we have on this as well as on many former occasions found a small grindstone which I brought with me from Harper's ferry extreemly convenient to us. if we find trees at the place mentioned sufficiently large for our purposes it will be extreemly fortunate; for we have not seen one for many miles below the entrance of musselshell River to this place, which would have answered.-

[Clark, July 9, 1805] July 9th Tuesday 1805 a clear worm morning wind from the S W. Lanced the Leather boat, and found that it leaked a little; Corked Lanced & loaded the Canoes, hurried our truk wheels, & made a Carsh for a Skin & a fiew papers I intend to leave here on trial found the leather boat would not answer without the addition of Tar which we had none of, haveing Substituted Cole & Tallow in its place to Stop the Seams &c. which would not answer as it Seperated from the Skins when exposed to the water and left the Skins naked & Seams exposed to the water this falire of our favourate boat was a great disapointment to us, we haveing more baggage than our Canoes would Carry. Concluded to build Canoes for to Carry them; no timber near our Camp. I deturmined to proceed on up the river to a bottom in which our hunters reported was large Trees &c.

[Lewis, July 10, 1805] Wednesday July 10th 1805. Capt. Clark set out with his party early this morning and passed over to the opposite side. after which I dispatched Sergt. Ordway with 4 Canoes and 8 men to take up a load of baggage as far as Capt. Clark's camp and return for the remainder of our plunder. with six others I now set to work on my boat, which had been previously drawn out of the water before the men departed, and in two hours had her fraim in readiness to be deposited. had a cash dug and deposited the Fraim of the boat, some papers and a few other trivial articles of but little importance. the wind blew very hard the greater part of the day. I also had the truck wheels buried in the pit which had been made to hold the tar. having nothing further to do I amused myself in fishing and caught a few small fish; they were of the species of white chub mentioned below the falls, tho they are small and few in number. I had thought on my first arrival here that there were no fish in this part of the river. Capt. Clark proceeded up the river 8 miles by land (distance by water 231/4) and found 2 trees of Cottonwood and cut them down; one proved to be hollow and split in falling at the upper part and was somewhat windshaken at bottom; the other proved to be much windshaken. he surched the bottom for better but could not find any he therefore determined to make canoes of those which he had fallen; and to contract their length in such manner as to clear the craks and the worst of the windsken parts making up the deficiency by allowing them to be as wide as the trees would permit. they were much at a loss for wood to make axhandles. the Chokecherry is the best we can procure for this purpose and of that wood they made and broke thir 13 handles in the course of this part of a day. had the eyes of our axes been round they would have answered this country much better. the musquetoes were very troublesome to them as well as ourselves today. Sergt. Ordway proceeded up the river about 5 miles when the wind became so violent that he was obliged to ly by untill late in the evening when he again set out with the canoes and arrived within 3 miles of Capt. Clark's Camp where he halted for the night. about five miles above whitebear camp there are two Islands in the river covered with Cottonwood box alder and some sweet willow also the undergrowth like that of the islands at this place.-

[Clark, July 10, 1805] July 10th Wednesday 1805 a fair windey day wind hard the most of the day from the S. W.rained modderately all last night (by Showers) we dispatched Serjt. Ordway with 4 Canoes loaded & 8 men by water to assend as high as I Should have found timber for Canoes & formed a Camp;-. I Set out with Sergt. Pryor four Choppers two Involids & one man to hunt, Crossed to the Std. Side and proceeded on up the river 8 miles by land (distance by water 231/4 ms.) and found two Trees which I thought would make Canoes, had them fallen, one of them proved to be hollow & Split at one End & verry much win Shaken at the other, the other much win Shaken, we Serched the bottoms for better trees and made a trial of Several which proved to be more indifferent. I deturmined to make Canoes out of the two first trees we had fallen, to Contract thir length so as to clear the hollow & winshakes, & ad to the width as much as the tree would allow. The Musquitors emencely noumerous & troublesom, Killed two deer & a goat. The Canoes did not arrive as I expected, owing to the hard wind which blew a head in maney places. we ar much at a loss for wood to make ax hilthes,13 hath been made & broken in this piece of a day by the four Choppers, no other wood but Cotton Box elder Choke Cherry and red arrow wood. we Substitute the Cherry in place of Hickory for ax hilthes ram rods, &c. &c.

[Lewis, July 11, 1805] Thursday July 11th 1805. We had now nothing to do but wait for the canoes; as they had not returned I sent out some of the small party with me to hunt; in the evening they returned with a good quantity of the flesh of a fat buffaloe which they had killed. the canoes not arrived this evening. I saw several very large grey Eagles today they are a half as large again as the common bald Eagle of this country. I do not think the bald Eagle here qute so large as those of the U States; the grey Eagle is infinitely larger and is no doubt a distinct species. this evening a little before the sun set I heared two other discharges of this unaccounable artillery of the Rocky Mountains proceeding from the same quarter that I had before heard it. I now recollected the Minnetares making mention of the nois which they had frequently heard in the Rocky Mountains like thunder; and which they said the mountains made; but I paid no attention to the information supposing it either false or the fantom of a supersticious immagination. I have also been informed by the engages that the Panis and Ricaras give the same account of the Black mountains which lye West of them. this phenomenon the philosophy of the engages readily accounts for; they state it to be the bursting of the rich mines of silver which these mountains contain.

This morning Capt. Clark dispatched Bratton to meet the canoes which were detained by the wind to get a couple of axes. he obtained the axes and returned in about two hours. this man has been unable to work for several days in consequence of a whitlow on one of his fingers; a complaint which has been very common among the men. one of the canoes arrived at Capt. Clarks camp about 10 A.M. this he had unloaded and set a few miles up the river for a buffaloe which had been killed, the party sent killed another in thir rout and brought in the flesh and skins of both they were in good order; his hunters had also killed two deer and an Antelope yesterday. the three other canoes did not arrive untill late in the evening in consequence of the wind and the fear of weting their loads which consisted of articles much more liable to be injured by moisture than those which composed the load of that which arrived in the morning. Capt. C. had the canoes unloaded and ordered them to float down in the course of the night to my camp, but the wind proved so high after night that they were obliged to put too about 8 miles above and remain untill morning. Capt. C. kept the party with him busily engaged at the canoes. his hunters killed and brought in three very fat deer this evening.

[Clark, July 11, 1805] July 11th Thursday 1805 a fair windey morning wind S. W. I dispatch W Bratten (who cannot work he haveing a turner rising on his finger) to meat the Canoes & bring from them two axes, which is necessary for the work at the perogues or Canoes, and is indespenceable he returned in about two hours & informed that one Canoe was within three miles, about 1 oClock the Canoe which Bratten left arrived haveing killed a Buffalow on the river above our Camp, at which place the bend of the river below & that above is about

1 mile apart, I dispatched Serjt. Pryor with 3 men in the Canoe to get the meat they killed another buffalow near the one killed and brought the meat of both down. at Sunset the 3 remaining Canoes arrived unloaded & returned imeadeately with orders to flote down to Camp at the portage to night for the purpose of takeing up the remaining baggage. Musquitors verry troublesom, and in addition to their torments we have a Small Knat, which is as disagreeable, our hunter killed 3 Deer to day one of them verry fat. all the men with me engaged about the Canoes hunting &c. &.

[Lewis, July 12, 1805] Friday July 12th 1805. The canoes not having arrived and the wind still high I dispatched Sergt. Gass with three men to join Capt. Clark and assist in completing the canoes retaining only a few who in addition to those in the canoes that I expect every moment, will be sufficient to man the six canoes and take up all the baggage we have here at one load. I feel excessively anxious to be moving on. the canoes were detained by the wind untill 2 P.M. when they set out and arrived at this place so late that I thought it best to detain them untill morning. Bratton came down today for a cople of axes which I sent by him; he returned immediately. Sergt. Gass and party joined Capt. Clark at 10 A.M. Capt. C. kept all the men with him busily engaged some in drying meat, others in hunting, and as many as could be employed about the canoes. Segt. Pryor got his sholder dislocated yesterday, it was replaced immediately and is likely to do him but little injury; it is painfull to him today. the hunters with Capt. C. killed three deer and two otter today. the otter are now plenty since the water has become sufficiently clear for them to take fish. the blue crested fisher, or as they are sometimes called the Kingfisher, is an inhabitant of this part of the country; this bird is very rare on the Missouri; I have not seen more than three or four of those birds during my voyage from the entrance of the Missouri to the mouth of Maria's river and those few were reather the inhabitants of streams of clerer water which discharged themselves into the Missouri than of that river, as they were seen about the entrances of such streams. Musquetoes extreemly troublesome to me today nor is a large black knat less troublesome, which dose not sting, but attacks the eye in swarms and compells us to brush them off or have our eyes filled with them. I made the men dry the ballance of the freshe meet which we had abot the camp amounting to about 200 lbs.

[Clark, July 12, 1805] July 12th Friday 1805 a fair windey morning wind from the S. W. all hands at work at Day light Some at the Canoes, & others drying meat for our voyage- Dispatched W. Brattin to the lower Camp for two axes which are necessary to carry on our work at this place &. Serjt. Pryors Sholder was put out of place yesterday Carrying Meat and is painfull to day. wind hard all day dispatched 2 hunters, they returnd in the evening with three Deer & 2 orters. four men arrived from the lower Camp by land to assist at this place in building the Canoes &c. musquitors & knats verry troublesom all day. a fiew wild pigions about our Camp.

[Lewis, July 13, 1805] Saturday July 13th 1805. This morning being calm and Clear I had the remainder of our baggage embarked in the six small canoes and maned them with two men each. I now bid a cheerfull adue to my camp and passed over to the opposite shore. Baptiest La Page one of the men whom I had reserved to man the canoes being sick I sent Charbono in his stead by water and the sick man and Indian woman accompanyed me by land. from the head of the white bear Islands I passed in a S. W. direction and struck the Missouri at 3 miles and continued up it to Capt. Clark's camp where I arrived about 9 A.M. and found them busily engaged with their canoes Meat &c. in my way I passed a very extraordinary Indian lodge, or at least the fraim of one; it was formed of sixteen large cottonwood poles each about fifty feet long and at their larger end which rested on the ground as thick as a man's body; these were arranged in a circular manner at bottom and equally distributed except the omission of one on the East side which I suppose was the entrance to the lodge; the upper part of the poles are united in a common point above and secured with large wyths of willow brush. in the center of this fabric there was the remains of a large fire; and about the place the marks of about 80 leather lodges. I know not what was the intention or design of such a lodge but certain I am that it was not designed for a dwelling of anyone family. it was 216 feet in circumpherence at the base. it was most probably designed for some great feast, or a council house on some great national concern. I never saw a similar one nor do the nations lower down the Missouri construct such. The canoes and party with Sergt. Ordway proceeded up the river about 5 miles when the wind became so violent that two of the canoes shiped a considerable quanty of water and they were compelled to put too take out the baggage to dry and clense the canoes of the water. about 5 P.M. the wind abated and they came on about 8 miles further and encamped. I saw a number of turtledoves and some pigeons today. of the latter I shot one; they are the same common to the United States, or the wild pigeon as they are called. nothing remarkable in the appearance of the country; the timber entirely confined to the river and the country back on either side as far as the eye can reach entirely destitute of trees or brush. the timber is larger and more abundant in the bottom in which we now are than I have seen it on the Missouri for many hundred miles. the current of the river is still extreemly gentle. The hunters killed three buffaloe today which were in good order. the flesh was brought in dryed the skins wer also streached for covering our baggage. we eat an emensity of meat; it requires 4 deer, an Elk and a deer, or one buffaloe, to supply us plentifully 24 hours. meat now forms our food prinsipally as we reserve our flour parched meal and corn as much as possible for the rocky mountains which we are shortly to enter, and where from the indhan account game is not very abundant. I preserved specemines of several small plants to day which I have never before seen. The Musquetoes and knats are more troublesome here if possible than they were at the White bear Islands. I sent a man to the canoes for my musquetoe bier which I had neglected to bring with me, as it is impossible to sleep a moment without being defended against the attacks of these most tormenting of all insects; the man returned with it a little after dark.

[Clark, July 13, 1805] July 13th Saturday 1805. a fair Calm Morning, verry Cool before day- we were visited by a Buffalow Bull who came within a fiew Steps of one of the Canoes the men were at work. Capt. Lewis one man &c. arrived over Land at 9 oClock, the wind rose and blew hard from the S. E. the greater part of the day both Canoes finished all to Corking & fixing ores &c. &c. The Hunters killed 3 Buffalow the most of all the meat I had dried for to make Pemitigon. The Musquetors & Knats verry troublesom all day & night

[Lewis, July 14, 1805] Sunday July 14th 1805. This morning was calm fair and warm; the Musquetoes of course troublesome. all hands that could work were employed about the canoes. which we completed and launched this evening. the one was 25 feet and the other 33 feet in length and about 3 feet wide. we have now the seats and oars to make and fit &c. I walked out today and ascended the bluffs which are high rockey and steep; I continued my rout about 3 1/2 when I gained a conspicuous eminence about 2 mes. distant from the river a little below the entrance of Fort Mountain Creek. from this place I had a commanding view of the country and took the bearings of the following places. (viz)

To the point at which the Missouri first enters the Rocky Mountains
S. 28° W.
25
To the termineation of the 1st Chain of Rocky Mountains; northwardly,
being that through which the Missouri first passes
N. 73° W
80
To the extremity or tirmineation of 2cd Chain of the Rocky Mountains
N. 65 W.
150
To the most distant point of a third and continued chain of the same
mts
N. 50°W.
200
The direction of the 2cd Do. from S 45 E. to N. 45 W.

To Fort Mountain S. 75° W. 8

The country in most parts very level and in others swelling with gentle rises and decents, or in other wirds what I have heretofore designated a wavy country destitute of timber except along the water-courses. On my return to camp found Sergt. Ordway had arrived with all the canoes about noon and had unloaded them every preperation except the entire completion of the oars poles &c is made for our departure tomorrow. the grass and weeds in this bottom are about 2 feet high; which is a much greater hight than we have seen them elsewhere this season. here I found the sand rush and nittles in small quantities. the grass in the plains is not more than 3 inches high. grasshoppers innumerable in the plains and the small birds before noticed together with the brown Curlooe still continue nomerous in every part of the plains.

had a slight shower at 4 P.M. this evening.

[Clark, July 14, 1805]
July 14th Sunday 1805
a fine morning Calm and worm musquetors & Knats verry troublesom. The
Canoes arrive at 12 oClock & unloade to Dry &c. finished & Lanced the 2
Canoes, Some rain this afternoon. all prepareing to Set out on tomorrow.

[Lewis, July 15, 1805] Monday July 15th 1805. We arrose very early this morning, assigned the canoes their loads and had it put on board. we now found our vessels eight in number all heavily laden, notwithstanding our several deposits; tho it is true we have now a considerable stock of dryed meat and grease. we find it extreemly difficult to keep the baggage of many of our men within reasonable bounds; they will be adding bulky articles of but little use or value to them. At 10 A.M. we once more saw ourselves fairly under way much to my joy and I beleive that of every individual who compose the party. I walked on shore and killed 2 Elk near one of which the party halted and dined. we took the skins marrow bones and a part of the flesh of these Elk. in order to lighten the burthen of the canoes I continued my walk all the evening and took our only invalledes Potts an LaPage with me. we passed the river near where we dined and just above the entrance of a beautifull river 80 yards wide which falls in on the Lard. side which in honour of Mr. Robert Smith the Secretary of the Navy we called Smith's River. this stream meanders through a most lovely valley to the S. E. for about 25 miles when it enters the Rocky mountains and is concealed from our view. many herds of buffaloe were feeding in this valley. we again crossed the river to the Stard. side and passed through a plain and struck the river at a Northwardly bend where there was timber here we waited untill the canoes arrived by which time it was so late that we concluded to encamp for the night. here Drewyer wouded a deer which ran into the river my dog pursued caught it drowned it and brought it to shore at our camp. we have now passed Fort Mountain on our right it appears to be about ten miles distant. this mountain has a singular appearance it is situated in a level plain, it's sides stand nearly at right angles with each other and are each about a mile in extent. these are formed of a yellow clay only without the mixture of rock or stone of any size and rise perpendicularly to the hight of 300 feet. the top appears to be a level plain and from the eminence on which I was yesterday I could see that it was covered with a similar cost of grass with the plain on which it stands. the surface appears also to possess a tolerable fertile mole of 2 feet thick. and is to all appearance inaccessible. from it's figure we gave it the name of fort mountain. those mounds before mentioned near the falls have much the same appearance but are none of them as large as this one. the prickly pear is now in full blume and forms one of the beauties as well as the greatest pests of the plains. the sunflower is also in blume and is abundant. this plant is common to every part of the Missouri from it's entrance to this place. the lambsquarter, wild coucumber, sand rush and narrow dock are also common here. Drewyer killed another deer and an Otter today. we find it inconvenient to take all the short meanders of the river which has now become cooked and much narrower than below, we therefore take it's general course and lay down the small bends by the eye on our daily traverse or chart. the river is from too to 150 yds. wide. more timber on the river than below the falls for a great distance. on the banks of the river there are many large banks of sand much elivated above the plains on which they ly and appear as if they had been collected in the course of time from the river by the almost incessant S. W. winds; they always appear on the sides of the river opposite to those winds.

The couses and distances from the White bear islands to the camp at which we made the canoes as taken by Sergt. Ordway.-

[Clark, July 15, 1805] July 15th Monday 1805 rained all the last night I was wet all night this morning wind hard from the S. W. we Set out at 10 oClock and proceeded on verry well passed a river on the Lard Side about 80 yards wide which we Call after the Secy of the Navey Smiths River the river verry Crooked bottoms extensive rich and Passes thro a butifull vally between 2 mts. Conts. high grass, our Canoes being So Small Several of the men Capt. Lewis & my Self Compelled to walked on Shore & Cross the bends to keep up with the Canoes- a round mountain on our right abt. 10 miles appears inaxcessable we Call fort mountain. The Prickley pear in bloom but fiew other flowers. Sun flowr are common, also lambs quarter & Nettles. Capt Lew Killed 2 Elk & the hunters killed 2 Deer & a Ortter, we Camped on the Stard Side at which place I Saw many beaver, the timber on the edge of the river more Common than below the falls- as I am compelled to walk on Shore find it verry dificult to take the Courses of the river, as it is verry Crooked more So than below

[Lewis, July 16, 1805] Tuesday July 16th 1805. We had a heavy dew last night sen one man back this morning for an ax that he had carelessly left last evening some miles below, and set out at an early hour. early this morning we passed about 40 little booths formed of willow bushes to shelter them from the sun; they appeared to have been deserted about 10 days; we supposed that they were snake Indians. they appeared to have a number of horses with them-. this appearance gives me much hope of meeting with these people shortly. Drewyer killed a buffaloe this morning near the river and we halted and breakfasted on it. here for the first time I ate of the small guts of the buffaloe cooked over a blazing fire in the Indian stile without any preperation of washing or other clensing and found them very good.- After breakfast I determined to leave Capt. C. and party, and go on to the point where the river enters the Rocky Mountains and make the necessary observations against their arrival; accordingly I set out with the two invalleds Potts and LaPage and Drewyer; I passed through a very handsome level plain on the Stard. side of the river, the country equally level and beautiful) on the opposite side; at the distance of 8 mes. passed a small stream on which I observed a considerable quantity of aspin. a little before 12 I halted on the river at a Stard. bend and well timbered bottom about 41/2 miles below the mountains and made the following observation.

after this observation we pursued our rout through a high roling plain to a rapid immediately at the foot of the mountain where the Missouri first enters them. the current of the missouri below these rappids is strong for several miles, tho just above there is scarcely any current, the river very narrow and deep abot 70 yds. wide only and seems to be closely hemned in by the mountains on both sides, the bottoms only a few yards in width. an Indian road enters the mountain at the same place with the river on the Stard side and continues along it's border under the steep clifts these mountains appear to be only about 800 feet above the river and are formed almost entirely of a hard black grannite. with a few dwarf pine and cedar scattered on them. at this place there is a large rock of 400 feet high wich stands immediately in the gap which the missouri makes on it's passage from the mountains; it is insulated from the neighbouring mountains by a handsome little plain which surrounds it base on 3 sides and the Missouri washes it's base on the other, leaving it on the Lard. as it decends. this rock I called the tower. it may be ascended with some difficulty nearly to it's summit, and from it there is a most pleasing view of the country we are now about to leave. from it I saw this evening immence herds of buffaloe in the plains below. near this place we killed a fat elk on which we both dined and suped. the Musquetoes are extreemly troublesome this evening and I had left my bier, of course suffered considerably, and promised in my wrath that I never will be guily of a similar peice of negligence while on this voyage.

[Clark, July 16, 1805] July 16th Tuesday 1805 a fair morning after a verry cold night, heavy dew, dispatched one man back for an ax left a fiew miles below, and Set out early Killed a Buffalow on which we Brackfast Capt Lewis & 3 men went on to the mountain to take a meridian altitude, passed about 40 Small Camps, which appeared to be abandoned about 10 or 12 days, Suppose they were Snake Indians, a fiew miles above I Saw the poles Standing in thir position of a verry large lodge of 60 feet Diamater, & the appearance of a number of Leather Lodges about, this Sign was old & appeared to have been last fall great number of buffalow the river is not So wide as below from 100 to 150 yards wide & Deep Crouded with Islands & Crooked Some Scattering timber on its edge Such as Cotton wood Cotton willow, willow and box elder, the Srubs are arrow wod, red wood, Choke Cherry, red berries, Goose beries, Sarvis burey, red & yellow Currents a Spcie of Shomake &c.

I camped on the head of a Small Island near the Stard. Shore at the Rockey Mountains this Range of mountains appears to run N W & S E and is about 800 feet higher than the Water in the river faced with a hard black rock the current of the River from the Medison river to the mountain is gentle bottoms low and extensive, and its General Course is S. 10° W. about 30 miles on a direct line

[Lewis, July 17, 1805] Wednesday July 17th 1805. The sunflower is in bloom and abundant in the river bottoms. The Indians of the Missouri particularly those who do not cultivate maze make great uce of the seed of this plant for bread, or use it in thickening their scope. they most commonly first parch the seed and then pound them between two smooth stones until) they reduce it to a fine meal. to this they sometimes mearly add a portion of water and drink it in that state, or add a sufficient quantity of marrow grease to reduce it to the consistency of common dough and eate it in that manner. the last composition I think much best and have eat it in that state heartily and think it a pallateable dish. there is but little of the broad leafed cottonwood above the falls, much the greater portion being of the narrow leafed kind. there are a great abundance of red yellow perple & black currants, and service berries now ripe and in great perfection. I find these fruits very pleasent particularly the yellow currant which I think vastly preferable to those of our gardens. the shrub which produces this fruit rises to the hight of 6 or 8 feet; the stem simple branching and erect. they grow closly accociated in cops either in the oppen or timbered lands near the watercouses. the leaf is petiolate of a pale green and resembles in it's form that of the red currant common to our gardens. the perianth of the fructification is one leaved, five cleft, abreviated and tubular, the corolla is monopetallous funnel-shaped; very long, superior, withering and of a fine orrange colour. five stamens and one pistillum; of the first, the fillaments are capillare, inserted into the corolla, equal, and converging; the anther ovate, biffid and incumbent. with rispect to the second the germ is roundish, smoth, inferior pedicelled and small; the style, long, and thicker than the stamens, simple, cylindrical, smooth, and erect, withering and remains with the corolla untill the fruit is ripe. stigma simple obtuse and withering.- the fruit is a berry about the size and much the shape of the red currant of our gardins, like them growing in clusters supported by a compound footstalk, but the peduncles which support the several berries are longer in this species and the berries are more scattered. it is quite as transparent as the red current of our gardens, not so ascid, & more agreeably flavored. the other species differ not at all in appearance from the yellow except in the colour and flavor of their berries. I am not confident as to the colour of the corolla, but all those which I observed while in blume as we came up the Missouri were yellow but they might possibly have been all of the yellow kind and that the perple red and black currants here may have corollas of different tints from that of the yellow currant.- The survice berry differs somewhat from that of the U States the bushes are small sometimes not more than 2 feet high and scarcely ever exceed 8 and are proportionably small in their stems, growing very thickly ascosiated in clumps. the fruit is the same form but for the most part larger more lucious and of so deep a perple that on first sight you would think them black.- there are two species of goosbirris here allso but neither of them yet ripe. the choke cherries also abundant and not yet ripe. there is Box alder, red willow and a species of sumac here also. there is a large pine tree situated on a small island at the head of these rappids above our camp; it being the first we have seen for a long distance near the river I called the island pine island. This range of the rocky mountains runs from S E to N. W.- at 8 A.M. this morning Capt. Clark arrived with the party. we took breakfast here, after which I had the box which contained my instruments taken by land arround tower rock to the river above the rappid; the canoes ascended with some difficulty but without loss or injury, with their loads.

After making those observations we proceed, and as the canoes were still heavy loaded all persons not employed in navigating the canoes walled on shore. the river clifts were so steep and frequently projecting into the river with their perpendicular points in such manner that we could not pass them by land, we wer therefore compelled to pass and repass the river very frequently in the couse of the evening. the bottoms are narrow the river also narrow deep and but little current. river from 70 to 100 yds. wide. but little timber on the river aspin constitutes a part of that little. see more pine than usual on the mountains tho still but thinly scattered. we saw some mountain rams or bighorned anamals this evening, and no other game whatever and indeed there is but little appearance of any. in some places both banks of the river are formed for a short distance of nearly perpendicular rocks of a dark black grannite of great hight; the river has the appearance of having cut it's passage in the course of time through this solid rock. we ascended about 6 miles this evening from the entrance of the mountain and encamped on the Stard. side where we found as much wood as made our fires. musquetoes still troublesome knats not as much so.- Capt. C. now informed me that after I left him yesterday, he saw the poles of a large lodge in praire on the Stard. side of the river which was 60 feet in diameter and appeared to have been built last fall; there were the remains of about 80 leather lodges near the place of the same apparent date. This large lodge was of the same construction of that mentioned above the white bear Islands. the party came on very well and encamped on the lower point of an island near the Stard. shore on that evening. this morning they had set out early and proceeded without obstruction untill they reached the rappid where I was encamped.

[Clark, July 17, 1805] July 17th Wednesday 1805 Set out early this morning and Crossed the rapid at the Island Cald pine rapid with Some dificuelty, at this rapid I came up with Capt Lewis & party took a Medn. altitude & we took Some Luner Observations &c. and proceeded on, the emence high Precipies oblige all the party to pass & repass the river from one point to another the river confined in maney places in a verry narrow Chanel from 70 to 120 yards wide bottoms narrow without timber and maney places the mountain approach on both Sides, we observe great deel of Scattering pine on the mountains, Some aspin, Spruce & fur trees took a meridian altd. which gave for Lattitude 46° 42' 14" 7/10 N we proceeded on verry well about 8 miles & Camped on the Stard Side The river crooked bottoms narrow, Clifts high and Steep, I assended a Spur of the Mountain which I found to be highe & dificuelt of axcess, Containig Pitch Pine & Covered with grass Scercely any game to be Seen The yellow Current now ripe also the fussey red Choke Cheries getting ripe Purple Current are also ripe. Saw Several Ibex or mountain rams to day

[Lewis, July 18, 1805] Thursday July 18th 1805. Set out early this morning. previous to our departure saw a large herd of the Bighorned anamals on the immencely high and nearly perpendicular clift opposite to us; on the fase of this clift they walked about and hounded from rock to rock with apparent unconcern where it appared to me that no quadruped could have stood, and from which had they made one false step they must have been precipitated at least 500 feet. this anamal appears to frequent such precepices and clifts where in fact they are perfectly secure from the pursuit of the wolf, bear, or even man himself.- at the distance of 21/2 miles we passed the entrance of a considerable river on the Stard. side; about 80 yds. wide being nearly as wide as the Missouri at that place. it's current is rapid and water extreamly transparent; the bed is formed of small smooth stones of flat rounded or other figures. it's bottoms are narrow but possess as much timber as the Missouri. the country is mountainous and broken through which it passes. it appears as if it might be navigated but to what extent must be conjectural. this handsome bold and clear stream we named in honour of the Secretary of war calling it Dearborn's river.- as we were anxious now to meet with the Sosonees or snake Indians as soon as possible in order to obtain information relative to the geography of the country and also if necessary, some horses we thought it better for one of us either Capt. C. or myself to take a small party & proceed on up the river, some distance before the canoes, in order to discover them, should they be on the river before the daily discharge of our guns, which was necessary in procuring subsistence for the party, should allarm and cause them to retreat to the mountains and conceal themselves, supposing us to be their enemies who visit them usually by the way of this river. accordingly Capt. Clark set out this morning after breakfast with Joseph Fields, Pots and his servant York. we proceeded on tolerably well; the current stonger than yesterday we employ the cord and oars principally tho sometimes the setting pole. in the evening we passed a large creek about 30 yds. wide which disembogues on the Stard. side; it discharges a bold current of water it's banks low and bed frormed of stones altogether; this stream we called Ordway's creek after Sergt. John Ordway. I have observed for several days a species of flax growing in the river bottoms the leaf stem and pericarp of which resembles the common flax cultivated in the U States. the stem rises to the hight of about 21/2 or 3 feet high; as many as 8 or ten of which proceede from the same root. the root appears to be perennial. the bark of the stem is thick strong and appears as if it would make excellent Hax. the seed are not yet ripe but I hope to have an opportunity of collecting some of them after they are so if it should on experiment prove to yeald good flax and at the same time admit of being cut without injuring the perennial root it will be a most valuable plant, and I think there is the greatest probability that it will do so, for notwithstanding the seed have not yet arrived at maturity it is puting up suckers or young shoots from the same root and would seem therefore that those which are fully grown and which are in the proper stage of vegitation to produce the best fax are not longer essencial to the preservation or support of the root. the river somewhat wider than yesterday and the mountains more distant from the river and not so high; the bottoms are but narrow and little or no timber near the river. some pine on the mountains which seems principally confined to their uper region. we killed one Elk this morning and found part of the flesh and the skin of a deer this evening which had been kited and left by Capt. Clark. we saw several herds of the Bighorn but they were all out of our reach on inacessable clifts.- we encamped on the Lard. side in a small grove of narrow leafed cottonwood there is not any of the broad leafed cottonwood on the river since it has entered the mountains. Capt Clark ascended the river on the Stard. side. in the early part of the day after he left me the hills were so steep that he gained but little off us; in the evening he passed over a mountain by which means he cut off many miles of the river's circuitous rout; the Indian road which he pursued over this mountain is wide and appears as if it had been cut down or dug in many places; he passed two streams of water, the branches of Ordway's creek, on which he saw a number of beaver dams succeeding each other in close order and extending as far up those streams as he could discover them in their couse towards the mountains. he also saw many bighorn anamals on the clifts of the mountains. not far beyond the mountain which he passed in the evening he encamped on a small stream of runing water. having travelled about 20 m. the water of those rivulets which make down from these mountains is extreemly cold pure and fine. the soil near the river is of a good quality and produces a luxuriant growth of grass and weeds; among the last the sunflower holds a distinguished place. the aspin is small but grows very commonly on the river and small streams which make down from the Mouts.

I also observed another species of flax today which is not so large as the first, sildome obtaining a greater hight than 9 Inches or a foot the stem and leaf resemble the other species but the stem is rarely branched, bearing a single monopetallous bellshaped blue flower which is suspended with it's limb downwards,

[Clark, July 18, 1805] July 18th Tursday 1805 a fine morning passed a Considerable river which falls in on the Stard Side and nearly as wide as the Missouri we call Dearbournes river after the Sety. of war. we thought it prudent for a partey to go a head for fear our fireing Should allarm the Indians and cause them to leave the river and take to the mountains for Safty from their enemes who visit them thro this rout. I deturmined to go a head with a Small partey a few days and find the Snake Indians if possible after brackfast I took J. Fields Potts & my Servent proceeded on. the Country So Hilley that we gained but little of the Canoes untill in the evening I passed over a mountain on an Indian rode by which rout I cut off Several miles of the Meanderings of the River, the roade which passes this mountain is wide and appears to have been dug in maney places, we Camped on a Small run of Clear Cold water, musquitors verry troublesom the forepart of the evening I Saw great maney Ibex. we Crossed two Streams of running water on those Streams I saw Several Beaver dams. ordway Creek the Countrey is Mountanious & rockey except the valey &c. which is Covered with earth of a good quallity without timber, The timber which is principally pitch pine is Confined to the mountains, the Small runs & Creeks which have water running in them Contain Cotton-Willow, Willow, & aspin. trees all Small I Saw maney fine Springs & Streams of running water which Sink & rise alternately in the Valies the water of those Streams are fine, those Streams which run off into the river are darned up by the beaver from near ther mouthes up as high as I could See up them

[Lewis, July 19, 1805] Friday July 19th 1805 The Musquetoes are very troublesome to us as usual. this morning we set out early and proceeded on very well tho the water appears to encrease in volocity as we advance. the current has been strong all day and obstructed with some rapids, tho these are but little broken by rocks and are perfectly safe. the river deep and from 100 to 150 yds. wide. I walked along shore today and killed an Antelope. whever we get a view of the lofty summits of the mountains the snow presents itself, altho we are almost suffocated in this confined vally with heat. the pine cedar and balsum fir grow on the mountains in irregular assemleages or spots mostly high up on their sides and summits. this evening we entered much the most remarkable clifts that we have yet seen. these clifts rise from the waters edge on either side perpendicularly to the hight of 1200 feet. every object here wears a dark and gloomy aspect. the towering and projecting rocks in many places seem ready to tumble on us. the river appears to have forced it's way through this immence body of solid rock for the distance of 53/4 miles and where it makes it's exit below has thown on either side vast collumns of rocks mountains high. the river appears to have woarn a passage just the width of it's channel or 150 yds. it is deep from side to side nor is ther in the 1st 3 miles of this distance a spot except one of a few yards in extent on which a man could rest the soal of his foot. several fine springs burst out at the waters edge from the interstices of the rocks. it happens fortunately that altho the current is strong it is not so much so but what it may be overcome with the oars for there is hear no possibility of using either the cord or Setting pole. it was late in the evening before I entered this place and was obliged to continue my rout until sometime after dark before I found a place sufficiently large to encamp my small party; at length such an one occurred on the lard. side where we found plenty of lightwood and pichpine. this rock is a black grannite below and appears to be of a much lighter colour above and from the fragments I take it to be flint of a yelloish brown and light creemcolourd yellow.- from the singular appearance of this place I called it the gates of the rocky mountains. the mountains higher today than yesterday, saw some Bighorns and a few Antelopes also beaver and Otter; the latter are now very plenty one of the men killed one of them today with a setting pole. musquetoes less troublesome than usual. we had a thundershower today about 1 P.M. which continued about an hour and was attended with som hail. we have seen no buffaloe since we entered the mounts. this morning early Capt. Clark pursued his rout, saw early in the day the remains of several Indians camps formed of willow brush which appeared to have been inhabited some time this spring. saw where the natives had pealed the bark off the pine trees about this same season. this the indian woman with us informs that they do to obtain the sap and soft part of the wood and bark for food. at 11 A.M. Capt. C. feell in with a gang of Elk of which he killed 2. and not being able to obtain as much wood as would make a fire substituded the dung of the buffaloe and cooked a part of their meat on which they breakfasted and again pursueed their rout, which lay along an old indian road. this evening they passed a hansome valley watered by a large creek which extends itself with it's valley into the mountain to a considerable distance. the latter part of the evening their rout lay over a hilly and mountanous country covered with the sharp fragments of flint which cut and bruised their feet excessively; nor wer the prickly pear of the leveler part of the rout much less painfull; they have now become so abundant in the open uplands that it is impossible to avoid them and their thorns are so keen and stif that they pearce a double thickness of dressed deers skin with ease. Capt. C. informed me that he extracted 17 of these bryers from his feet this evening after he encamped by the light of the fire. I have guarded or reather fortifyed my feet against them by soaling my mockersons with the hide of the buffaloe in parchment. he encamped on the river much fortiegud having passed two mountains in the course of the day and travelled about 30 miles.-

[Clark, July 19, 1805] July 19th Fryday 1805 a find morning I proceeded on in an Indian path river verry crooked passed over two mountains Saw Several Indian Camps which they have left this Spring. Saw trees Peeled & found poles &c. at 11 oC I Saw a gange of Elk as we had no provision Concluded to kill Some Killd two and dined being oblige to Substitute dry buffalow dung in place of wood, this evening passed over a Cream Coloured flint which roled down from the Clifts into the bottoms, the Clifts Contain flint a dark grey Stone & a redish brown intermixed and no one Clift is Solid rock, all the rocks of everry description is in Small pices appears to have been broken by Some Convulsion- passed a butifull Creek on the Std. Side this eveng which meanders thro a butifull Vallie of great extent, I call after Sgt Pryor the countrey on the Lard Side a high mountain Saw Several Small rapids to day the river Keep its width and appear to be deep, my feet is verry much brused & cut walking over the flint, & constantly Stuck full Prickley pear thorns, I puled out 17 by the light of the fire to night We camped on the river Same (Lard) Side Musqutors verry troublesom.

[Lewis, July 20, 1805] Saturday 20 h 1805. Set out early this morning as usual, currant strong, we therefore employ the toe rope when ever the banks permit the use of it; the water is reather deep for the seting pole in most places. at 6 A.M. the hills retreated from the river and the valley became wider than we have seen it since we entered the mountains. some scattering timber on the river and in the valley. consisting of the narrowleafed Cottonwood aspin & pine. vas numbers of the several species of currants gooseberries and service berries; of each of these I preserved some seeds. I found a black currant which I thought preferable in flavor to the yellow. this currant is really a charming fruit and I am confident would be prefered at our markets to any currant now cultivated in the U States. we killed an Elk this morning which was very acceptable to us. through the valley which we entered early in the morning a large creek flows from the mountains and discharges itself into the river behind an island on Stard. side about 15 yds. wide this we called Potts's Creek after John Potts one of our party. about 10 A.M. we saw the smoke arrose as if the country had been set on fire up the valley of this creek about 7 ms. distant we were at a loss to determine whether it had been set on fire by the natives as a signall among themselves on discovering us, as is their custom or whether it had been set on fire by Capt. C. and party accidentally. the first however proved to be the fact, they had unperceived by us discovered Capt. Clark's party or mine, and had set the plain on fire to allarm the more distant natives and fled themselves further into the interior of the mountains. this evening we found the skin of an Elk and part of the flesh of the anamal which Capt. C. had left near the river at the upper side of the valley where he assended the mountain with a note informing me of his transactions and that he should pass the mounts which lay just above us and wate our arrival at some convenient place on the river. the other elk which Capt. C. had killed we could not find. about 2 in the evening we had passed through a range of low mountains and the country bacame more open again, tho still broken and untimbered and the bottoms not very extensive. we encamped on the Lard. side near a spring on a high bank the prickly pears are so abundant that we could scarcely find room to lye. just above our camp the river is again closed in by the Mouts. on both sides. I saw a black woodpecker today about the size of the lark woodpecker as black as a crow. I indevoured to get a shoot at it but could not. it is a distinct species of woodpecker; it has a long tail and flys a good deel like the jay bird.

This morning Capt. Clark set out early and proceeded on through a valley leaving the river about six miles to his left; he fell in with an old Indian road which he pursued untill it struck the river about 18 miles from his camp of the last evening just above the entrance of a large creek which we call white paint Creek. the party were so much fortiegued with their march and their feet cut with the flint and perced with the prickly pears untill they had become so painfull that he proceeded but little further before he determined to encamp on the river and wait my arrival.- Capt. C. saw a smoke today up the valley of Pryor's creek which was no doubt caused by the natives likewise. he left signals or signs on his rout in order to inform the indians should they pursue his trale that we were not their enemies, but white men and their friends.- cloth &c

[Clark, July 20, 1805] July 20th Satturday 1805 a fine morning we proceded on thro a valley leaveing the river about 6 miles to our left and fell into an Indian roade which took us to the river above the mo. of a Creek 18 miles The Misquetors verry troublesom my man York nearly tired out, the bottoms of my feet blistered. I observe a Smoke rise to our right up the Valley of the last Creek about 12 miles distant, The Cause of this

Smoke I can't account for certainly tho think it probable that the Indians have heard the Shooting of the Partey below and Set the Praries or Valey on fire to allarm their Camps; Supposeing our party to be a war party comeing against them, I left Signs to Shew the Indians if they Should come on our trail that we were not their enemeys. Camped on the river, the feet of the men with me So Stuck with Prickley pear & cut with the Stones that they were Scerseley able to march at a Slow gate this after noon

[Lewis, July 21, 1805] Sunday July 21st 1805. Set out early this morning and passed a bad rappid where the river enters the mountain about 1 m. from our camp of last evening the Clifts high and covered with fragments of broken rocks. the current strong; we employed the toe rope principally, and also the pole as the river is not now so deep but reather wider and much more rapid our progress was therefore slow and laborious. we saw three swans this morning, which like the geese have not yet recovered the feathers of the wing and could not fly we killed two of them the third escaped by diving and passed down with the current; they had no young ones with them therefore presume they do not breed in this country these are the first we have seen on the river for a great distance. we daily see great numbers of gees with their young which are perfectly feathered except the wings which are deficient in both young and old. my dog caught several today, as he frequently dose. the young ones are very fine, but the old gees are poor and unfit for uce. saw several of the large brown or sandhill Crain today with their young. the young Crain is as large as a turkey and cannot fly they are of a bright red bey colour or that of the common deer at this season. this bird feeds on grass prinsipally and is found in the river bottoms. the grass near the river is lofty and green that of the hill sides and high open grounds is perfectly dry and appears to be scorched by the heat of the sun. the country was rough mountainous & much as that of yesterday untill towards evening when the river entered a beautifull and extensive plain country of about 10 or 12 miles wide which extended upwards further that the eye could reach this valley is bounded by two nearly parallel ranges of high mountains which have their summits partially covered with snow. below the snowey region pine succeeds and reaches down their sides in some parts to the plain but much the greater portion of their surfaces is uncovered with timber and expose either a barren sterile soil covered with dry parched grass or black and rugged rocks. the river immediately on entering this valley assumes a different aspect and character, it spreads to a mile and upwards in width crouded with Islands, some of them large, is shallow enough for the use of the seting pole in almost every part and still more rappid than before; it's bottom is smooth stones and some large rocks as it has been since we have entered the mountains. the grass in these extensive bottoms is green and fine, about 18 inches or 2 feet high. the land is a black rich loam and appears very fertile. we encamped in this beatiful valley on the Lard. side the party complain of being much fatiegued with this days travel. we killed one deer today.- This morning we passed a bold creek 28 yds. wide which falls in on Stard. side. it has a handsome and an extensive valley. this we called Pryor's Creek after Sergt. (John) Pryor one of our party. I also saw two fesants today of a dark brown colour much larger than the phesant of the U States.

this morning Capt. Clark having determined to hunt and wait my arrival somewhere about his preset station was fearfull that some indians might still be on the river above him sufficiently near to hear the report of his guns and therefore proceeded up, the river about three miles and not finding any indians nor discovering any fresh appearance of them returned about four miles below and fixed his camp near the river; after refreshing themselves with a few hours rest they set out in different directions to hunt. Capt C. killed a buck and Fields a buck and doe. he caught a young curlooe which was nearly feathered. the musquetoes were equally as troublesome to them as to ourselves this evening; tho some hours after dark the air becomes so cold that these insects disappear. the men are all fortunately supplyed with musquetoe biers otherwise it would be impossible for them to exist under the fatiegues which they daily encounter without their natural rest which they could not obtain for those tormenting insects if divested of their biers. timber still extreemly scant on the river but there is more in this valley than we have seen since we entered the mountains; the creeks which fall into the river are better supplyed with this article than the river itself.-

we saw a number of trout today since the river has become more shallow; also caught a fish of a white colour on the belly and sides and of a bluish cast on the back which had been accidentally wounded by a setting pole. it had a long pointed mouth which opened somewhat like the shad.

[Clark, July 21, 1805] July 21st Sunday 1805 a fine morning our feet So brused and Cut that I deturmined to delay for the Canoes, & if possible kill Some meat by the time they arrived, all the Creeks which fall into the Missouri on the Std. Side Since entering the Mountains have extencive Valies of open Plain. the river bottoms Contain nothing larger than a Srub untill above the last Creek the Creeks & runs have timber on them generally, the hills or mountains are in Some places thickly covered with pine & Cedar &c. &c. I proceeded on about 3 miles this morning finding no fresh Indian Sign returned down the river four miles and Camped, turned out to hunt for Some meat, which if we are Suckessfull will be a Seasonable Supply for the partey assending. emence quantities of Sarvice buries, yellow, red, Purple & black Currents ripe and Superior to any I ever tasted particularly the yellow & purple kind. Choke Cheries are Plenty; Some Goose buries- The wild rose Continue the

Willow more abundant no Cotton wood of the Common kind Small birds are plenty, Some Deer, Elk, Goats, and Ibex; no buffalow in the Mountains.

Those mountains are high and a great perportion of them rocky Vallies fertile I observe on the highest pinicals of Some of the mountains to the West Snow lying in Spots Some Still further North are covered with Snow and cant be Seen from this point The Winds in those mountains are not Settled generally with the river, to day the wind blow hard from the West at the Camp. The Missouri Continus its width the Current Strong and Crouded with little Islands and Cose graveley bars; but little fine Sand the Chanel generally a Corse gravel or Soft mud. Musquetors & Knats verry troublesom. I killed a Buck, and J. Fields killed a Buck and Doe this evening. Cought a young Curlough.

[Lewis, July 22, 1805] Monday July 22cd 1805. We set out early as usual. The river being divided into such a number of channels by both large and small Island that I found it impossible to lay it down correctly following one channel only in a canoe and therefore walked on shore took the general courses of the river and from the rising grounds took a view of the Islands and it's different channels which I laid don in conformity thereto on my chart. there being but little timber to obstruct my view I could see it's various meanders very satisfactorily. I passed though a large Island which I found a beautifull level and fertile plain about 10 feet above the surface of the water and never overflown. on this Island I met with great quantities of a smal onion about the size of a musquit ball and some even larger; they were white crisp and well flavored I geathered about half a bushel of them before the canoes arrived. I halted the party for breakfast and the men also geathered considerable quantities of those onions. it's seed had just arrived to maturity and I gathered a good quantity of it. This appears to be a valuable plant inasmuch as it produces a large quantity to the squar foot and bears with ease the rigor of this climate, and withall I think it as pleasantly flavored as any species of that root I ever tasted. I called this beatifull and fertile island after this plant Onion Island. here I passed over to the stard. shore where the country was higher and ascended the river to the entrance of a large creek which discharges itself into the Missouri on the Stard. side. it is composed of three pretty considerable creeks which unite in a beautifull and extensive vally a few miles before it discharges itself into the river. while wateing for the canoes to arrive I killed an otter which sunk to the bottom on being shot, a circumstance unusual with that anamal. the water was about 8 feet deep yet so clear that I could see it at the bottom; I swam in and obtained it by diving. I halted the party here for dinner; the canoes had taken different channels through these islands and it was sometime before they all came up. I placed my thermometer in a good shade as was my custom about 4 P.M. and after dinner set out without it and had proceeded near a mile before I recollected it I sent Sergt. Ordway back for it, he found it and brought it on. the murcury stood at 80 a. 0 this is the warmest day except one which we have experienced this summer. The Indian woman recognizes the country and assures us that this is the river on which her relations live, and that the three forks are at no great distance. this peice of information has cheered the sperits of the party who now begin to console themselves with the anticipation of shortly seeing the head of the missouri yet unknown to the civilized world. the large creek which we passed on Stard. 15 yds. we call white Earth Creek from the circumstance of the natives procuring a white paint on this crek.- Saw many gees, crams, and small birds common to the plains, also a few phesants and a species of small curlooe or plover of a brown colour which I first met with near the entrance of Smith's river but they are so shy and watchfull there is no possibility of geting a shoot at them it is a different kind from any heretofore discribed and is about the size of the yellow leged plover or jack Curlooe. both species of the willow that of the broad leaf and narrow leaf still continue, the sweet willow is very scarce. the rose bush, small honesckle, the pulpy leafed thorn, southernwood, sage Box alder narrow leafed cottonwood, red wod, a species of sumac are all found in abundance as well as the red and black goosberries, service berries, choke cherries and the currants of four distinct colours of black, yellow, red and perple. the cherries are not yet ripe. the bear appear to feed much on the currants. late this evening we arrived at Capt. Carks camp on the stard. side of the river; we took them on board with the meat they had collected and proceeded a short distance and encamped on an Island Capt. Clark's party had killed a deer and an Elk today and ourselves one deer and an Antelope only. altho Capt C. was much fatiegued his feet yet blistered and soar he insisted on pursuing his rout in the morning nor weould he consent willingly to my releiving him at that time by taking a tour of the same kind. finding him anxious I readily consented to remain with the canoes; he ordered Frazier and Jo. & Reubin Filds to hold themselves in readiness to accompany him in the morning. Sharbono was anxious to accompany him and was accordingly permitted. the musquetoes and knats more than usually troublesome to us this evening.-

[Clark, July 22, 1805] July 22d Monday 1805 a fine morning wind from the S. E. the last night verry cold, my blanket being Small I lay on the grass & Covered with it. I opened the bruses & blisters of my feet which caused them to be painfull dispatched all the men to hunt in the bottom for Deer, deturmined my Self to lay by & nurs my feet. haveing nothing to eat but venison and Currents, I find my Self much weaker than when I left the Canoes and more inclined to rest & repose to day. These men were not Suckcessfull in hunting killed only one Deer Capt Lewis & the Party arvd. at 4 oClock & we all proceeded on a Short distance and Camped on an Island the Musquitors verry troublesom this evening G Drewyer not knowing the place we Camped Continued on up the river. I deturmined to proceed on in pursute of the Snake Indians on tomorrow and directed Jo Rubin Fields

Frasure to get ready to accompany me. Shabono, our interpreter requested to go, which was granted &c. In my absence the hunters had killed Some Deer & a Elk, one fusee found &c. &c.

[Lewis, July 23, 1805] Tuesday July 23rd 1805. Set out early as usual; Capt. Clark left us with his little party of 4 men and continued his rout on the Stard. side of the river. about 10 OCk. A M. we came up with Drewyer who had seperated from us yesterday evening and lay out all night not being able to find where we had encamped. he had killed 5 deer which we took on board and continued our rout. the river is still divided by a great number of islands, it channels sometimes seperating to the distance of 3 miles; the current very rapid with a number of riffles; the bed gravel and smooth stones; the banks low and of rich loam in the bottoms; some low bluffs of yellow and red clay with a hard red slate stone intermixed. the bottoms are wide and but scantily timbered. the underbrush very thick consisting of the narrow & broad leafed willow rose and Currant bushes principally. high plains succeeds the river bottoms and extend back on either side to the base of the mountains which are from 8 to 12 miles assunder, high, rocky, some small pine and Cedar on them and ly parallel with the river. passed a large creek on Lard. side 20 yds. wide which after meandering through a beautifull and extensive bottom for several miles nearly parallel with the river discharges itself opposite to a large cluster of islands which from their number I called the 10 islands and the creek Whitehous's Creek, after Josph. Whitehouse one of the party. saw a great abundance of the common thistles; also a number of the wild onions of which we collected a further supply. there is a species of garlic also which grows on the high lands with a flat leaf now green and in bloe but is strong tough and disagreeable. found some seed of the wild flax ripe which I preserved; this plant grows in great abundance in these bottoms. I halted rearther early for dinner today than usual in order to dry some articles which had gotten wet in several of the canoes. I ordered the canoes to hoist their small flags in order that should the indians see us they might discover that we were not Indians, nor their enemies. we made great uce of our seting poles and cords the uce of both which the river and banks favored. most of our small sockets were lost, and the stones were so smooth that the points of their poles sliped in such manner that it increased the labour of navigating the canoes very considerably, I recollected a parsel of giggs which I had brought on, and made the men each atatch one of these to the lower ends of their poles with strong wire, which answered the desired purpose. we saw Antelopes Crain gees ducks beaver and Otter. we took up four deer which Capt. Clark & party had killed and left near the river. he pursued his rout untill late in the evening and encamped on the bank of the river 25 ms. above our encampment of the last evening; he followed an old indian road which lyes along the river on the stard side Capt. saw a number of Antelopes, and one herd of Elk. also much sign of the indians but all of ancient date. I saw the bull rush and Cattail flag today.

I saw a black snake today about two feet long the Belly of which was as black as any other part or as jet itself. it had 128 scuta on the belley 63 on the tail.

[Clark, July 23, 1805] July 23rd Tuesday 1805 a fair morning wind from the South. I Set out by land at 6 miles overtook G Drewyer who had killed a Deer. we killed in the Same bottom 4 deer & a antelope & left them on the river bank for the Canoes proceeded on an Indian roade through a wider Vallie which the Missouri Passes about 25 miles & Camped on the bank of the river, High mountains on either Side of the Vallie Containing Scattering Pine & Cedar Some Small Cotton willow willow &c. on the Islands & bank of the river I Saw no fresh Sign of Indians to day Great number of antelopes Some Deer & a large Gangue of Elk

[Lewis, July 24, 1805] Wednesday July 24th 1805. Set out at sunrise; the current very strong; passed a remarkable bluff of a crimson coloured earth on Stard. intermixed with Stratas of black and brick red slate. the valley through which the river passed today is much as that of yesterday nor is there any difference in the appearance of the mountains, they still continue high and seem to rise in some places like an amphatheater one rang above another as they recede from the river untill the most distant and lofty have their tops clad with snow. the adjacent mountains commonly rise so high as to conceal the more distant and lofty mountains from our view. I fear every day that we shall meet with some considerable falls or obstruction in the river notwithstanding the information of the Indian woman to the contrary who assures us that the river continues much as we see it. I can scarcely form an idea of a river runing to great extent through such a rough mountainous country without having it's stream intercepted by some difficult and gangerous rappids or falls. we daily pass a great number of small rappids or riffles which decend one to or 3 feet in 150 yards but they are rarely incommoded with fixed or standing rocks and altho strong rappid water are nevertheless quite practicable & by no means dangerous. we saw many beaver and some otter today; the former dam up the small channels of the river between the islands and compell the river in these parts to make other channels; which as soon as it has effected that which was stoped by the beaver becomes dry and is filled up with mud sand gravel and drift wood. the beaver is then compelled to seek another spot for his habitation wher he again erects his dam. thus the river in many places among the clusters of islands is constantly changing the direction of such sluices as the beaver are capable of stoping or of 20 yds. in width. this anamal in that way I beleive to be very instrumental in adding to the number of islands with which we find the river crouded. we killed one deer today and found a goat or Antelope which had been left by Capt. Clark. we saw a large bear but could not get a shoot at him. we also saw a great number of Crams & Antelopes, some gees and a few red-headed ducks the small bird of the plains and curloos still abundant. we observed a great number of snakes about the water of a brown uniform colour, some black, and others speckled on the abdomen and striped with black and brownish yellow on the back and sides. the first of these is the largest being about 4 feet long, the second is of that kind mentioned yesterday, and the last is much like the garter snake of our country and about it's size. none of these species are poisonous I examined their teeth and fund them innosent. they all appear to be fond of the water, to which they fly for shelter immediately on being pursued.- we saw much sign of Elk but met with none of them. from the appearance of bones and excrement of old date the buffaloe sometimes straggle into this valley; but there is no fresh sighn of them and I begin think that our harrvest of white puddings is at an end, at least untill our return to the buffaloe country. our trio of pests still invade and obstruct us on all occasions, these are the Musquetoes eye knats and prickley pears, equal to any three curses that ever poor Egypt laiboured under, except the Mahometant yoke. the men complain of being much fortiegued, their labour is excessively great. I occasionly encourage them by assisting in the labour of navigating the canoes, and have learned to push a tolerable good pole in their fraize. This morning Capt. Clark set out early and pursued the Indian road whih took him up a creek some miles abot 10 A.M. he discovered a horse about six miles distant on his left, he changed his rout towards the horse, on approaching him he found the horse in fine order but so wild he could not get within less than several hundred paces of him. he still saw much indian sign but none of recent date. from this horse he directed his course obliquely to the river where on his arrival he killed a deer and dined. in this wide valley where he met with the horse he passed five handsome streams, one of which only had timber another some willows and much stoped by the beaver. after dinner he continued his rout along the river upwards and encamped having traveled about 30 mes.

[Clark, July 24, 1805] July 24th Wednesday 1805 a fine day wind from the N W. I proceeded on up a Creek on the direction of the Indian road at 10 oClock discovered a horse 6 miles to my left towards the river as I approached the horse found him fat and verry wild we could not get near him, we changed our Direction to the river for water haveing previously Crossed 5 handsom Streams in one Vallie one only had any timber on it one other Willows only & a number of beaver Dams. when I Struck the river turned down to kill a Deer which we dined on & proceeded on up the river a fiew miles an Campd. on the river. the river much like it was yesterday. the mountains on either Side appear like the hills had fallen half down & turned Side upwards the bottoms narrow and no timber a fiew bushes only.

[Lewis, July 25, 1805] Thursday July 25th 1805. Set out at an early hour and proceeded on tolerably well the water still strong and some riffles as yesterday. the country continues much the same as the two preeceding days. in the forenoon we saw a large brown bear on an island but he retreated immediately to the main shore and ran off before we could get in reach of him. they appear to be more shy here than on the Missouri below the mountains. we saw some antelopes of which we killed one. these anamals appear now to have collected again is small herds several females with their young and one or two males compose the herd usually. some males are yet soletary or two perhaps together scattered over the plains which they seen invariably to prefer to the woodlands. if they happen accedentaly in the woodlands and are allarmed they run immediately to the plains, seeming to plaise a just confidence in their superior fleetness and bottom. we killed a couple of young gees which are very abundant and fine; but as they are but small game to subsist a party on of our strength I have forbid the men shooting at them as it waists a considerable quantity of amunition and delays our progress. we passed Capt. Clark's encampment of the 23rd inst. the face of the country & anamal and vegatable productions were the same as yesterday, untill late in the evening, when the valley appeared to termineate and the river was again hemned in on both sides with high caiggy and rocky clifts. soon after entering these hills or low mountains we passed a number of fine bold springs which burst out underneath the Lard. clifts near the edge of the water; they wer very cold and freestone water. we passed a large Crk. today in the plain country, 25 yds. wide, which discharges itself on the Stard. side; it is composed of five streams which unite in the plain at no great distance from the river and have their souces in the Mts. this stream we called Gass's Creek. after Sergt. Patric Gass one of our party.- two rapids near the large spring we passed this evening were the worst we have seen since that we passed on entering the rocky Mountain; they were obstructed with sharp pointed rocks, ranges of which extended quite across the river. the clifts are formed of a lighter coloured stone than those below I obseve some limestone also in the bed of the river which seem to have been brought down by the current as they are generally small and woarn smooth.- This morning Capt. Clark set out early and at the distance of a few miles arrived at the three forks of the Missouri, here he found the plains recently birnt on the stard. side, and the track of a horse which appeared to have passed only about four or five days. after taking breakfast of some meat which they had brought with them, examined the rivers, and written me a note informing me of his intended rout, he continued on up the North fork, which though not larger than the middle fork, boar more to the West, and of course more in the direction we were anxious to pursue. he ascended this stream about 25 miles on Stard. side, and encamped, much fatieued, his feet blistered and wounded with the prickley pear thorns. Charbono gave out, one of his ankles failed him and he was unable to proceede any further.- I observed that the rocks which form the clifts on this part of the river appear as if they had been undermined by the river and by their weight had seperated from the parent hill and tumbled on their sides, the stratas of rock of which they are composed lying with their edges up; others not seperated seem obliquely depressed on the side next the river as if they had sunk down to fill the cavity which had been formed by the washing and wearing of the river. I have observed a red as well as a yellow species of goosberry which grows on the rocky Clifts in open places of a swetish pine like flavor, first observed in the neighbourhood of the falls; at least the yellow species was first observed there. the red differs from it in no particular except it's colour and size being somewhat larger; it is a very indifferent fruit, but as they form a variety of the native fruits of this country I preserved some of their seeds. musquetoes and knats troublesome as usual.

[Clark, July 25, 1805] July 25th Thursday 1805 a fine morning we proceeded on a fiew miles to the three forks of the Missouri those three forks are nearly of a Size, the North fork appears to have the most water and must be Considered as the one best calculated for us to assend middle fork is quit as large about 90 yds. wide. The South fork is about 70 yds wide & falls in about 400 yards below the midle fork. those forks appear to be verry rapid & Contain Some timber in their bottoms which is verry extincive,- on the North Side the Indians have latterly Set the Praries on fire, the Cause I can't account for. I Saw one horse track going up the river about four or 5 days past. after Brackfast (which we made on the ribs of a Buck killed yesterday), I wrote a note informing Capt Lewis the rout I intended to take, and proeeded on up the main North fork thro a vallie, the day verry hot about 6 or 8 miles up the North fork a Small rapid river falls in on the Lard Side which affords a great Deel of water and appears to head in the Snow mountains to the S W. this little river falls into the Missouri by three mouthes, haveing Seperated after it arrives in the river Bottoms, and Contains as also all the water courses in this quarter emence number of Beaver & orter maney thousand enhabit the river & Creeks near the 3 forks (Pholosiphie's River)- We Campd on the Same Side we assended Starboard 20 miles on a direct line up the N. fork. Shabono our intrepreter nearly tired one of his ankles falling him- The bottoms are extencive and tolerable land Covered with tall grass & prickley pears The hills & mountains are high Steep & rockey. The river verry much divided by Islands Some Elk Bear & Deer and Some Small timber on the Islands. Great quantities of Currents, red, black, yellow, Purple, also Mountain Currents which grow on the Sides of Clifts; inferior in taste to the others haveing Sweet pineish flaver and are red & yellow, Choke Cheries, Boin roche, and the red buries also abound- musquitors verry trouble Som untill the mountain breeze Sprung up which was a little after night.

[Lewis, July 26, 1805] Friday July 26th 1805. Set out early this morning as usual current strong with frequent riffles; employ the cord and seting poles. the oars scarcely ever being used except to pass the river in order to take advantage of the shore and cur-rent. at the distance of 33/4 m. passed the entrance of a large Creek 15 yds. wide which discharges itself on Lard. near the center of a Lard. bend it is a bold runing stream this we called Howard's Creek after Thomas P. Howard one of our party. at the distance of one mile further we passed the entrance of a small run which falls in just above a rocky clift on Lard. here the hills or reather mountains again recede from the river and the valley again widens to the extent of several miles with wide and fertile bottom lands. covered with grass and in many places a fine terf of greenswoard. the high lands are thin meagre soil covered with dry low sedge and a species of grass also dry the seeds of which are armed with a long twisted hard beard at the upper extremity while the lower point is a sharp subulate firm point beset at it's base with little stiff bristles standing with their points in a contrary direction to the subulate point to which they answer as a barb and serve also to pres it forward when onece entered a small distance. these barbed seed penetrate our mockersons and leather legings and give us great pain untill they are removed. my poor dog suffers with them excessively, he is constantly hinting and scratching himself as if in a rack of pain. the prickly pear also grow here as abundantly as usual. there is another species of the prickly pear of a globular form, composed of an assemblage of little conic leaves springing from a common root to which their small points are attached as a common center and the base of the cone forms the apex of the leaf which is garnished with a circular range of sharp thorns quite as stif and more keen than the more common species with the flat leaf, like the Cockeneal plant. on entering this open valley I saw the snowclad tops of distant mountains before us. the timber and mountains much as heretofore. saw a number of beaver today and some otter, killed one of the former, also 4 deer; found a deer's skin which had been left by Capt. C. with a note informing me of his having met with a horse but had seen no fresh appearance of the Indians. the river in the valley is from 2 to 250 yds. wide and crouded with Islands, in some places it is 3/4 of a mile wide including islands. were it passed the hills it was from 150 to 200 yds. the banks are still low but never overflow. one of the men brought me an indian bow which he found, it was made of cedar and about 2 F. 9 Inh. in length. it had nothing remarkable in it's form being much such as is used by the Mandans Minetares &c. This morning Capt. Clark left Sharbono and Joseph Fields at the camp of last evening and proceeded up the river about 12 miles to the top of a mountain from whence he had an extensive view of the valley of the river upwards and of a large creek which flowed into it on Std. side. not meeting with any fresh appearance of Indians he determined to return and examine the middle fork of the missouri and meet me by the time he expected me to arrive at the forks. he returned down the mountain by the way of an old Indian road which led through a deep hollow of the mountain facing the south the day being warm and the road unshaded by timber he suffered excessively with heat and the want of water, at length he arrived at a very cold spring, at which he took the precaution of weting his feet head and hands before drank but notwithstanding this precaution he soon felt the effects of the water. he felt himself very unwell shortly after but continued his march rejoined Sharbono and Fields where the party eat of a fawn which Jo. Fields had killed in their absence Capt. C. was so unwell that he had no inclination to eat. after a short respite he resumed his march pass the North fork at a large island; here Charbono was very near being swept away by the current and cannot swim, Capt. C however risqued him and saved his life. Capt. C. continued his march to a small river which falls into the North fork some miles above the junction of the 3 forks it being the distance of about four miles from his camp of last evening here finding himself still more unwell he determined to encamp. they killed two brown or Grisley bear this evening on the island where they passed the N. fork of the Missouri. this stream is much divided by islands and it's current rapid and much as that of the missouri where we are and is navigable.-

[Clark, July 26, 1805] July 26th Friday 1805 I deturmined to leave Shabono & one man who had Sore feet to rest & proceed on with the other two to the top of a mountain 12 miles distant west and from thence view the river & vallies a head, we with great dificuelty & much fatigue reached the top at 11 oClock from the top of this mountain I could see the Course of the North fork about 10 miles meandering through a Vallie but Could discover no Indians or Sign which was fresh. I could also See Some distance up the Small River below, and also the middle fork after Satisfying my Self returned to the two men by an old Indian parth, on this parth & in the Mountain we Came to a Spring of excessive Cold water, which we drank reather freely of as we were almost famished; not with Standing the precautions of wetting my face, hands, & feet, I Soon felt the effects of the water. We Contind. thro a Deep Vallie without a Tree to Shade us Scorching with heat to the men who had killed a pore Deer, I was fatigued my feet with Several blisters & Stuck with prickley pears. I eate but verry little deturmined to Cross to the middle fork and examine that. we Crossed the Missouri which was divided by a verry large Island, the first Part was knee deep, the other waste deep & verry rapid- I felt my Self verry unwell & took up Camp on the little river 3 miles above its mouth & near the place it falls into the bottom a fiew Drops of rain this evening

we killed 2 bear which was imediately in our way. both pore emence number of Beaver and orter in this little river which forks in the bottom

[Lewis, July 27, 1805] Saturday July 27th 1805. We set out at an early hour and proceeded on but slowly the current still so rapid that the men are in a continual state of their utmost exertion to get on, and they begin to weaken fast from this continual state of violent exertion. at the distance of 13/4 miles the river was again closely hemned in by high Clifts of a solid limestone rock which appear to have tumbled or sunk in the same manner of those discribed yesterday. the limestone appears to be of an excellent quality of deep blue colour when fractured and of a light led colour where exposed to the weather. it appears to be of a very fine grain the fracture like that of marble. we saw a great number of the bighorn on those Clifts. at the distance of 33/4 ms. further we arrived at 9 A.M. at the junction of the S. E. fork of the Missouri and the country opens suddonly to extensive and beatifull plains and meadows which appear to be surrounded in every direction with distant and lofty mountains; supposing this to be the three forks of the Missouri I halted the party on the Lard. shore for breakfast and walked up the S. E. fork about 1/2 a mile and ascended the point of a high limestone clift from whence I commanded a most perfect view of the neighbouring country. From this point I could see the S. E. fork about 7 miles. it is rapid and about 70 yards wide. throughout the distance I saw it, it passes through a smoth extensive green meadow of fine grass in it's course meandering in several streams the largest of which passes near the Lard. hills, of which, the one I stand on is the extremity in this direction. a high wide and extensive plain succeeds the meadow and extends back several miles from the river on the Stard. sade and with the range of mountains up the Lard. side of the middle fork. a large spring arrises in this meadow about 1/4 of a mile from the S. E. fork into which it discharges itself on the Stard. side about 400 paces above me. from E to S. between the S. E. and middle forks a distant range of lofty mountains rose their snow-clad tops above the irregular and broken mountains which lie adjacent to this beautifull spot. the extreme point to which I could see the S. E. fork boar S. 65° E. distant 7 ms. as before observed. between the middle and S. E. forks near their junctions with the S. W. fork there is a handsom site for a fortification it consists of a limestone rock of an oblong form; it's sides perpendicular and about 25 ft high except at the extremity towards the middle fork where it ascends gradually and like the top is covered with a fine terf of greenswoard. the top is level and contains about 2 Acres. the rock rises from the level plain as if it had been designed for some such purpose. the extream point to which I can see the bottom and meandering of the Middle fork bears S. 15 E distant about 14 miles. here it turns to the right around a point of a high plain and disappears to my view. it's bottoms are several miles in width and like that of the S. E. fork form one smoth and beautifull green meadow. it is also divided into several streams. betwen this and the S. W. fork there is an extensive plain which appears to extend up both those rivers many miles and back to the mountains. the extreme point to which I can see the S. W. fork bears S. 30 W. distant about 12 miles. this stream passes through a similar country with the other two and is more divided and serpentine in it's course than either of the others; it also possesses abundanly more timber in it's bottoms. the timber here consists of the narrowleafed cottonwood almost entirely. but little box alder or sweet willow the underbrush thick and as heretofore discribed in the quarter of the missouri. a range of high mountains at a considerable distance appear to reach from South to West and are partially covered with snow the country to the right of the S. W. fork like that to the left of the S. E. fork is high broken and mountainous as is that also down the missouri behind us, through which, these three rivers after assembling their united force at this point seem to have forced a passage these bottom lands tho not more than 8 or 9 feet above the water seem never to overflow. after making a draught of the connection and meanders of these streams I decended the hill and returned to the party, took breakfast and ascended the S. W. fork 13/4 miles and encamped at a Lard. bend in a handsome level smooth plain just below a bayou, having passed the entrance of the middle fork at 1/2 a mile. here I encamped to wait the return of Capt. Clark and to give the men a little rest which seemed absolutely necessary to them. at the junction of the S. W. and Middle forks I found a note which had been left by Capt. Clark informing me of his intended rout, and that he would rejoin me at this place provided he did not fall in with any fresh sighn of Indians, in which case he intended to pursue untill he over took them calculating on my taking the S. W. fork, which I most certainly prefer as it's direction is much more promising than any other. beleiving this to be an essential point in the geography of this western part of the Continent I determined to remain at all events untill I obtained the necessary data for fixing it's latitude Longitude &c. after fixing my camp I had the canoes all unloaded and the baggage stoed away and securely covered on shore, and then permitted several men to hunt. I walked down to the middle fork and examined and compared it with the S. W. fork but could not satisfy myself which was the largest stream of the two, in fact they appeared as if they had been cast in the same mould there being no difference in character or size, therefore to call either of these streams the Missouri would be giving it a preference wich it's size dose not warrant as it is not larger then the other. they are each 90 yds. wide. in these meadows I saw a number of the duckanmallad with their young which are now nearly grown. Currants of every species as well as goosberries are found here in great abundance and perfection. a large black goosberry which grows to the hight of five or six feet is also found here. this is the growth of the bottom lands and is found also near the little rivulets which make down from the hills and mountains it puts up many stems from the same root, some of which are partialy branched and all reclining. the berry is attatched seperately by a long peduncle to the stem from which they hang pendant underneath. the berry is of an ovate form smooth as large as the common garden goosberry when arrived at maturity and is as black as jet, tho the pulp is of a cimson colour. this fruit is extreemly asced. the leaf resembles the common goosberry in form but is reather larger and somewhat proportioned to the superior size of it's stem when compared with the common goosberry. the stem is covered with very sharp thorns or bryers. below the tree forks as we passed this morning I observed many collections of the mud nests of the small martin attatched to the smooth face of the limestone rocks sheltered by projections of the same rock above. Our hunters returned this evening with 6 deer 3 Otter and a musk rat. they informed me that they had seen great numbers of Antelopes, and much sign of beaver Otter deer Elk, &c. at 3 P.M. Capt Clark arrived very sick with a high fever on him and much fatiegued and exhausted. he informed me that he was very sick all last night had a high fever and frequent chills & constant aking pains in all his mustles. this morning notwithstanding his indisposition he pursued his intended rout to the middle fork about 8 miles and finding no recent sign of Indians rested about an hour and came down the middle fork to this place. Capt. C. thought himself somewhat bilious and had not had a passage for several days; I prevailed on him to take a doze of Rushes pills, which I have always found sovereign in such cases and to bath his feet in warm water and rest himself. Capt. C's indisposition was a further inducement for my remaining here a couple of days; I therefore informed the men of my intention, and they put their deer skins in the water in order to prepare them for dressing tomorrow. we begin to feel considerable anxiety with rispect to the Snake Indians. if we do not find them or some other nation who have horses I fear the successfull issue of our voyage will be very doubtfull or at all events much more difficult in it's accomplishment. we are now several hundred miles within the bosom of this wild and mountanous country, where game may rationally be expected shortly to become scarce and subsistence precarious without any information with rispect to the country not knowing how far these mountains continue, or wher to direct our course to pass them to advantage or intersept a navigable branch of the Columbia, or even were we on such an one the probability is that we should not find any timber within these mountains large enough for canoes if we judge from the portion of them through which we have passed. however I still hope for the best, and intend taking a tramp myself in a few days to find these yellow gentlemen if possible. my two principal consolations are that from our present position it is impossible that the S. W. fork can head with the waters of any other river but the Columbia, and that if any Indians can subsist in the form of a nation in these mountains with the means they have of acquiring food we can also subsist. Capt. C. informed me that there is a part of this bottom on the West side of the Middle fork near the plain, which appears to overflow occasionally and is stony.

[Clark, July 27, 1805] July 27th Saturday 1805 I was verry unwell all last night with a high fever & akeing in all my bones. my fever &c. continus, deturmind to prosue my intended rout to the middle fork, accordingly Set out in great pain across a Prarie 8 miles to the Middle this fork is nearly as large as the North fork & appears to be more rapid, we examined and found no fresh Sign of Indians, and after resting about an hour, proceeded down to the junction thro a wide bottom which appears to be overflown every year, & maney parts Stoney this river has Several Islands and number of beaver & orter, but little timber. we could See no fresh Sign of Indians just above the Point I found Capt Lewis encamped haveing arrived about 2 oClock. Several Deer killed this evening. I continue to be verry unwell fever verry high; take 5 of rushes pills & bathe my feet & legs in hot water

[Lewis, July 28, 1805] Sunday July 28th 1805. My friend Capt. Clark was very sick all last night but feels himself somwhat better this morning since his medicine has opperated. I dispatched two men early this morning up the S. E. Fork to examine the river; and permitted sundry others to hunt in the neighbourhood of this place. Both Capt. C. and myself corrisponded in opinon with rispect to the impropriety of calling either of these streams the Missouri and accordingly agreed to name them after the President of the United States and the Secretaries of the Treasury and state having previously named one river in honour of the Secretaries of War and Navy. In pursuance of this resolution we called the S. W. fork, that which we meant to ascend, Jefferson's River in honor of Thomas Jefferson. the Middle fork we called Madison's River in honor of James Madison, and the S. E. Fork we called Gallitin's River in honor of Albert Gallitin. the two first are 90 yards wide and the last is 70 yards. all of them run with great valocity and thow out large bodies of water. Gallitin's River is reather more rapid than either of the others, is not quite as deep but from all appearances may be navigated to a considerable distance. Capt. C. who came down Madison's river yesterday and has also seen Jefferson's some distance thinks Madison's reather the most rapid, but it is not as much so by any means as Gallitin's. the beds of all these streams are formed of smooth pebble and gravel, and their waters perfectly transparent; in short they are three noble streams. there is timber enough here to support an establishment, provided it be erected with brick or stone either of which would be much cheaper than wood as all the materials for such a work are immediately at the spot. there are several small sand-bars along the shores at no great distance of very pure sand and the earth appears as if it would make good brick. I had all our baggage spread out to dry this morning; and the day proving warm, I had a small bower or booth erected for the comfort of Capt. C. our leather lodge when exposed to the sun is excessively hot. I observe large quantities of the sand rush in these bottoms which grow in many places as high as a man's breast and stand as thick as the stalks of wheat usually do. this affords one of the best winter pastures on earth for horses or cows, and of course will be much in favour of an establishment should it ever be thought necessary to fix one at this place. the grass is also luxouriant and would afford a fine swarth of hay at this time in parsels of many acres together. all those who are not hunting altho much fatiegued are busily engaged in dressing their skins, making mockersons leggings &c to make themselves comfortable. the Musquetoes are more than usually troublesome, the knats are not as much so. in the evening about 4 O'Ck the wind blew hard from South West and after some little time brought on a Cloud attended with thunder and Lightning from which we had a fine refreshing shower which cooled the air considerably; the showers continued with short intervals untill after dark. in the evening the hunters all returned they had killed 8 deer and 2 Elk. some of the deer wer in excellent order. those whome I had sent up Gallitin's river reported that after it passed the point to which I had seen it yesterday that it turned more to the East to a considerable distance or as far as they could discover the opening of the Mountains formed by it's valley which was many miles. the bottoms were tolerably wide but not as much so as at or near it's mouth. it's current is rappid and the stream much divided with islands but is sufficiently deep for canoe navigation. Our present camp is precisely on the spot that the Snake Indians were encamped at the time the Minnetares of the Knife R. first came in sight of them five years since. from hence they retreated about three miles up Jeffersons river and concealed themselves in the woods, the Minnetares pursued, attacked them, killed 4 men 4 women a number of boys, and mad prisoners of all the females and four boys, Sah-cah-gar-we-ah or Indian woman was one of the female prisoners taken at that time; tho I cannot discover that she shews any immotion of sorrow in recollecting this event, or of joy in being again restored to her native country; if she has enough to eat and a few trinkets to wear I beleive she would be perfectly content anywhere.

[Clark, July 28, 1805] July 28th Sunday 1805 I was verry unwell all night, Something better this morning, a very worm day untill 4 oClock when the wind rose & blew hard from the S W. and was Cloudy, The Thermometr. Stood at 90° above 0 in the evening a heavy thunder Shower from the S W. which continud at intervales untill after dark, Several deer killed to day men all employed dressing Skins for Clothes & Mockersons, two men went up the East fork & reports that it is nearly the Size of the N. fork, verry rapid & has maney Islands. Our present Camp is the prosise Spot the Snake Indians were Camped at the time the Minetarries came in Sight, attacked & killed 4 men 4 women & a number of boys, & made prisoners of all. the females & 4 boys.

[Lewis, July 29, 1805] Monday July 29th 1805. This morning some of the hunters turned out and returned in a few hours with four fat bucks, the venison is now very fine we have killed no mule deer since we lay here, they are all of the longtailed red deer which appear quite as large as those of the United States. the hunters brought in a living young sandhill crane it has nearly obtained it's growth but cannot fly; they had pursued it and caught it in the meadows. it's colour is precisely that of the red deer. we see a number of the old or full grown crams of this species feeding in these meadows. this young animal is very ferce and strikes a severe blow with his beak; after amusing myself with it I had it set at liberty and it moved off apparently much pleased with being releived from it's captivity. the men have been busily engaged all day in dising skins and making them into various garments all are leather dressers and taylors. we see a great abundance of fish in the stream some of which we take to be trout but they will not bite at any bate we can offer them. the King fisher is common on the river since we have left the falls of the Missouri. we have not seen the summer duck since we left that place, nor do I beleive that it is an inhabitant of the Rocky mountains. the Duckanmallard were first seen with their young on the 20th inst. and I forgot to note it; they are now abundant with their young but do not breed in the missouri below the mountains. the grasshopers and crickets are abundant in the plains as are also the small birds frequently mentioned. there is also in these plains a large ant with a redish brown body and legs, and a black head and abdomen; they construct little perimids of small gravel in a conic shape, about 10 or 12 inches high without a mixture of sticks and with but little earth. Capt. Clark is much better today, is perfectly clear of fever but still very languid and complains of a general soarness in all his limbs. I prevailed on him to take the barks which he has done and eate tolerably freely of our good venison.

[Clark, July 29, 1805] July 29 Monday 1805 A fair morning wind from the North I feel my Self something better to day, made some Celestial observations took two Merdn. altitudes which gave for Latd. 45° 22' 34" N men all dressing Skins &c.

[Lewis, July 30, 1805] Tuesday July 30th 1805. Capt. Clark being much better this morning and having completed my observations we reloaded our canoes and set out, ascending Jeffersons river. Sharbono, his woman two invalleds and myself walked through the bottom on the Lard. side of the river about 41/2 miles when we again struck it at the place the woman informed us that she was taken prisoner. here we halted untill Capt. Clark arrived which was not untill after one P.M. the water being strong and the river extreemly crooked. we dined and again proceeded on; as the river now passed through the woods the invalleds got on board together with Sharbono and the Indian woman; I passed the river and continued my walk on the Stard. side. saw a vast number of beaver in many large dams which they had maid in various bayoes of the river which are distributed to the distance of three or four miles on this side of the river over an extensive bottom of timbered and meadow lands intermixed. in order to avoid these bayoes and beaver dams which I found difficult to pass I directed my course to the high plain to the right which I gained after some time with much difficulty and waiding many beaver dams to my waist in mud and water. I would willingly have joined the canoes but the brush were so thick, the river crooked and bottoms intercepted in such manner by the beaver dams, that I found it uceless to attempt to find them, and therefore proceeded on up the river in order to intersept it where it came near the plain and woult be more collected into one channel. at length about sunset I arrived at the river only about six miles from my calculation on a direct line from the place I had left the canoes but I thought they were still below me. I found the river was divided where I reached it by an Island and was therefore fearfull that they might pass without my seeing them, and went down to the lower point of the large island; here I discovered a small Island, close under the shore on which I was; I passed the narrow channel to the small island and examined the gravly bar along the edge of the river for the tracks of the men, knowing from the appearance of the river at this place that if they had passed they would have used the cord on the side where I was. I saw no tracks and was then fully convinced that they were below me. I fired my gun and hallooed but counld hear nothing of them. by this time it was getting nearly dark and a duck lit on the shore in about 40 steps of me and I killed it; having now secured my supper I looked our for a suitable place to amuse myself in combating the musquetoes for the ballance of the evening. I found a parsel of drift wood at the head of the little Island on which I was and immediately set it on fire and collected some willow brush to lye on. I cooked my duck which I found very good and after eating it layed down and should have had a comfortable nights lodge but for the musquetoes which infested me all night. late at night I was awakened by the nois of some animal runing over the stoney bar on which I lay but did not see it; from the weight with which it ran I supposed it to be either an Elk or a brown bear. the latter are very abundant in this neighbourhood. the night was cool but I felt very little inconvenience from it as I had a large fire all night. Capt. Clark had proceeded on after I seperated from him and encamped on a islad. only about 2 miles below me but did not hear the report of my gun nor of my hooping.-I saw some deer and antelopes.

[Clark, July 30, 1805] July 30th Monday 1805 We Set out 8 oClock and proceeded on 131/2 miles up the N. fork the river verry rapid & Sholey the Channel entirely Corse gravel many Islands and a number of Chanels in different directions thro the bottom &c. passed the place the Squar interpretress was taken, one man with his Sholder Strained, 2 with Turners, we Camped on the Std. Side the evening Cool. Capt Lewis who walkd on Shore did not join me this evening

[Lewis, July 31, 1805] Wednesday July 31st 1805. This morning I waited at my camp very impatiently for the arrival of Capt. Clark and party; I observed by my watch that it was 7 A.M. and they had not come in sight. I now became very uneasy and determined to wait until 8 and if they did not arrive by that time to proceed on up the river taking it as a fact that they had passed my camp some miles last evening. just as I set out to pursue my plan I discovered Charbono walking up shore some distance below me and waited untill arrived I now learnt that the canoes were behind, they arrived shortly after. their detention had been caused by the rapidity of the water and the circuitous rout of the river. they halted and breakfasted after which we all set out again and I continued my walk on the Stard. shore the river now becomes more collected the islands tho numerous ar generally small. the river continues rapid and is from 90 to 120 yd. wide has a considerable quantity of timber in it's bottoms.

towards evening the bottoms became much narrower and the timber much more scant. high hills set in close on the Lard. and the plain high waivy or reather broken on the Stard. and approach the river closely for a shot distance vally above 1 1/2 M wd. About one mile above Capt. Clark's encampment of the last evening the principall entrance of a considerable river discharges itself into Jefferson's river. this stream is a little upwards of 30 yd. wide discharges a large quantity of very clear water it's bed like that of Jefferson's river is pebble and gravel. it takes it's rise in the snowclad mountains between Jefferson's and Madison's Rivers to the S. W. and discharges itself into the former by seven mouths it has some timber in it's bottoms and vas numbers of beaver and Otter. this stream we call River Philosophy. the rock of the clifts this evening is a hard black grannite like that of the clifts of most parts of the river below the limestone clifts at the 3 forks of the Missouri this evening just before we encamped Drewyer discovered a brown bear enter a small cops of bushes on the Lard. side; we surrounded the place an surched the brush but he had escaped in some manner unperceived but how we could not discover. nothing killed today and our fresh meat is out. when we have a plenty of fresh meat I find it impossible to make the men take any care of it, or use it with the least frugallity. tho I expect that necessity will shortly teach them this art. the mountains on both sides of the river at no great distance are very lofty. we have a lame crew just now, two with turners or bad boils on various parts of them, one with a bad stone bruise, one with his arm accidently dislocated but fortunately well replaced, and a fifth has streigned his back by sliping and falling backwards on the gunwall of the canoe. the latter is Sergt. Gass. it gives him great pain to work in the canoe in his present situation, but he thinks he can walk with convenience, I therefore scelected him as one of the party to accompany me tomorrow, being determined to go in quest of the Snake Indians. I also directed Drewyer and Charbono to hold themselves in readiness. Charbono thinks that his ankle is sufficiently recovered to stand the march but I entertain my doubts of the fact; he is very anxious to accompany me and I therefore indulge him. There is some pine on the hills on both sides of the river opposite to our encampment which is on the Lard. side upon a small island just above a run. the bull rush & Cat-tail flag grow in great abundance in the moist parts of the bottoms the dryer situations are covered with fine grass, tanzy, thistles, onions and flax. the bottom land fertile and of a black rich loam. the uplands poor sterile and of a light yellow clay with a mixture of small smooth pebble and gravel, poducing prickley pears, sedge and the bearded grass in great abundance; this grass is now so dry that it would birn like tinder.- we saw one bighorn today a few antelopes and deer.-

[Clark, July 31, 1805] July 31st Tuesday 1805 a fair Morning Capt Lewis out all night, we arrived at his Camp to brackfast, he was without a blanket, & he killed a Duck whiche Suped on &c. the river as yesterday Sholey & rapid, passed the lower mouth of a Small river on the Lard. in the morning & the upper mouth a _____ Miles above, this little river is the one I camped on the 26th & heads in the Snow mountains to the S W. proceeded on verry well and Camped on a Small Island a little above the place I Camped the 25th instant at the mouth of a run on the Lard. Side, the bottoms from the Mouth of the river extend to 2 1/2 Miles & enter a Short & high hill which is about 1 mile thro and, the river then passes thro a 2d value of about 1 1/2 Miles wide, Some Islands. below this Knobe the river is Crouded with Islands, we are out of fresh meet, & nothing killed to day The Mountains on either Side is high & rough we have two men with toumers and unable to work.

Capt Lewis deturmin to proceed on with three men in Serch of the Snake Indians, tomorrow

[Lewis, August 1, 1805] August 1st 1805 At half after 8 A.M. we halted for breakfast and as had been previously agreed on between Capt. Clark and myself I set out with 3 men in quest of the Snake Indians. the men I took were the two Interpreters Drewyer and Sharbono and Sergt. Gass who by an accedental fall had so disabled himself that it was with much pain he could work in the canoes tho he could march with convenience. the rout we took lay over a rough high range of mountains on the North side of the river. the rive entered these mountains a few miles above where we left it. Capt Clark recommended this rout to me from a belief that the river as soon as it past the mountains boar to the N. of W. he having a few days before ascended these mountains to a position from which he discovered a large valley passing betwen the mountains and which boar to the N. West. this however poved to be the inlet of a large creek which discharged itself into the river just above this range of mountans, the river bearing to the S. W. we were therefore thrown several miles out of our rout. as soon as we discovered our mistake we directed our course to the river which we at length gained about 2 P.M. much exhausted by the heat of the day the roughnes of the road and the want of water. the mountains are extreemly bare of timber and our rout lay through the steep valleys exposed to the heat of the sun without shade and scarcely a breath of air; and to add to my fatieque in this walk of about 11 miles I had taken a doze of glauber salts in the morning in consequence of a slight desentary with which I had been afflicted for several days; being weakened by the disorder and the opperation of the medecine I found myself almost exhausted before we reached the river. I felt my sperits much revived on our near approach to the river at the sight of a herd of Elk of which Drewyer and myself killed two. we then hurried to the river and allayed our thirst. I ordered two of the men to skin the Elk and bring the meat to the river while myself and the other prepared a fire and cooked some of the meat for our dinner. we made a comfortable meal of the Elk and left the ballance of the meat on the bank of the river the party with Capt. Clark. this supply was no doubt very acceptable to them as they had had no fresh meat for near two days except one beaver Game being very scarce and shy. we had seen a few deer and some goats but had not been fortunate enough to kill any of them. after dinner we resumed our march and encamped about 6 m. above on the Stard side of the river.

[Lewis, August 1, 1805] Thursday August 1st 1805. This morning we set out early and proceeded on tolerably well untill 8 OCT. by which time we had arrived within a few miles of a mountain through which the river passes. we halted on the Stard. side and took breakfast. after which or at 1/2 after 8 A.M. as had been previously concerted betwen Capt. Clark and myself I set out with three men in surch of the Snake Indians or Sosonees. our rout lay over a high range of mountains on the North side of the river. Capt C. recommended this rout to me no doubt from a beleif that the river as soon as it passed this chain of mountains boar to the N. of W. he having on the 26th ult. ascended these mountains to a position from whence he discoved a large valley passing between the mountains which boar to the N. W. and presumed that the river passed in that direction; this however proved to be the passage of a large creek which discharged itself into the river just above this range of mountains, the river bearing to the S. W. we were therefore thrown several miles out of our rout. as soon as we discovered our error we directed our course to the river which we at length gained about 2 P.M. much exhausted by the heat of the day, the roughness of the road and the want of water. the mountains are extreemly bare of timber, and our rout lay through the steep and narrow hollows of the mountains exposed to the intese heat of the midday sun without shade or scarcely a breath of air to add to my fatiegue in this walk of about 11 miles, I had taken a doze of glauber salts in the morning in consequence of a slight disentary with which I had been afflicted for several days. being weakened by the disorder and the operation of the medicine I found myself almost exhausted before we reached the river. I felt my sperits much revived on our near approach to the river at the sight of a herd of Elk, of which Drewyer and myself soon killed a couple. we then hurryed to the river and allayed our thirst. I ordered two of the men to skin the Elk and bring the meat to the river, while myself and the other prepared a fire and cooked some of the meat for our dinner. we made a comfortable meal on the Elk, and left the ballance of the meat and skins on the bank of the river for Capt. Clark and party. this supply will no doubt be acceptable to them, as they had had no fresh meat when I left them for almost 2 days except one beaver; game being very scarce and shy above the forks. we had seen a few deer and antelopes but had not been fortunate enough to kill any of them. as I passed these mountains I saw a flock of the black or dark brown phesants; the young phesant is almost grown we killed one of them. this bird is fully a third larger than the common phesant of the Atlantic states. it's form is much the same. it is booted nearly to the toes and the male has not the tufts of long black feathers on the sides of the neck which are so conspicuous in those of the Atlantic. their colour is a uniform dark brown with a small mixture of yellow or yelloish brown specks on some of the feathers particularly those of the tail, tho the extremities of these are perfectly black for about one inch. the eye is nearly black, the iris has a small dash of yellowish brown. the feathers of the tail are reather longer than that of our phesant or pattridge as they are Called in the Eastern States; are the same in number or eighteen and all nearly of the same length, those in the intermediate part being somewhat longest. the flesh of this bird is white and agreeably flavored. I also saw near the top of the mountain among some scattering pine a blue bird about the size of the common robbin. it's action and form is somewhat that of the jay bird and never rests long in any one position but constantly flying or hoping from sprey to sprey. I shot at one of them but missed it. their note is loud and frequently repeated both flying and when at rest and is char ah', char'ah, char ah', as nearly as letters can express it. after dinner we resumed our march and my pack felt much lighter than it had done about 2 hours before. we traveled about six miles further and encamped on the stard. bank of the river, making a distance of 17 miles for this day. the Musquetoes were troublesome but I had taken the precaution of bringing my bier.

Shortly after I left Capt. Clark this morning he proceed on and passed through the mountains; they formed tremendious clifts of ragged and nearly perpendicular rocks; the lower .part of this rock is of the black grannite before mentioned and the upper part a light coloured freestone. these clifts continue for 9 miles and approach the river very closely on either side. he found the current verry strong. Capt. C. killed a big horn on these clifts which himself and party dined on. after passing this range of mountains he entered this beautifull valley in which we also were it is from 6 to 8 miles wide. the river is crooked and crouded with islands, it's bottoms wide fertile and covered with fine grass from 9 inches to 2 feet high and possesses but a scant proportion of timber, which consists almost entirely of a few narrow leafed cottonwood trees distributed along the verge of the river. in the evening Capt. C. found the Elk I had left him and ascended a short distance above to the entrance of a large creek which falls in on Stard. and encamped opposite to it on the Lard. side. he sent out the two Fieldses to hunt this evening and they killed 5 deer, which with the Elk again gave them a plentifull store of fresh provisions. this large creek we called Field's Creek after Reubin Fields one our party. on the river about the mountains wich Capt. C. passed today he saw some large cedar trees and some juniper also just at the upper side of the mountain there is a bad rappid here the toe line of our canoe broke in the shoot of the rapids and swung on the rocks and had very nearly overset. a small distance above this rapid a large bold Creek falls in on Lard. side which we called Frazier's Creek after Robt. Frazier. They saw a large brown bear feeding on currants but could not get a shoot at him.

[Clark, August 1, 1805] August 1st Wednesday 1805 A fine day Capt. Lewis left me at 8 oClock just below the place I entered a verrey high mountain which jutted its tremedious Clifts on either Side for 9 Miles, the rocks ragide Some verry dark & other part verry light rock the light rocks is Sand Stone. The water Swift & very Sholey. I killed a Ibix on which the whole party Dined, after passing through the Mountain we entered a wide extesive vallie of from 4 to 8 Miles wide verry leavell a Creek falls in at the Commencement of this Vallie on the Lard Side, the river widens & spreds into Small Chanels. We encamped on the Lard Side opposit a large Creek I sent out Jo. & R fields to hunt this evening they killed 5 Deer, I saw a large Bear eateing Currents this evining The river so rapid that the greatest exertion is required by all to get the boats on wind S W Murckery at sun rise 50° Ab. 0

[Lewis, August 2, 1805] August 2nd 1805. We resumed our march this morning at sunrise the weather was fair and wind from N. W. finding that the river still boar to the south I determined to pass it if possible to shorten our rout this we effected about five miles above our camp of last evening by wading it. found the current very rappid about 90 yards wide and waist deep this is the first time that I ever dared to make the attempt to wade the river, tho there are many places between this and the three forks where I presume it migh be attempted with equal success. the valley though which our rout of this day lay and through which the river winds it's meandering course is a beatifull level plain with but little timber and that on the verge of the river. the land is tolerably fertile, consisting of a black or dark yellow loam, and covered with grass from 9 Inches to 2 feet high. the plain ascends gradually on either side of the river to the bases of two ranges of mountains which ly parrallel to the river and which terminate the width of the vally. the tops of these mountains were yet partially covered with snow while we in the valley. were suffocated nearly with the intense heat of the midday sun. the nights are so could that two blankets are not more than sufficient covering. we found a great courants, two kinds of which were red, others yellow deep purple and black, also black goosburies and service buries now ripe and in full perfection, we feasted suptuously on our wild fruit particularly the yellow courant and the deep purple servicebury which I found to be excellent the courrant grows very much like the red currant common to the gardens in the atlantic states tho the leaf is somewhat different and the growth taller. the service burry grows on a smaller bush and differs from ours only in colour and the superior excellence of it's flavor and size, it is of a deep purple. this day we saw an abundance of deer and goats or antelopes and a great number of the tracks of Elk; of the former we killed two. we continued our rout along this valley which is from six to eight Miles wide untill sun set when we encamped for the night on the river bank having traveled about 24 miles. I feel myself perfectly recovered of my indisposition and do not doubt being able to pursue my march with equal comfort in the morning.

[Lewis, August 2, 1805] Friday August 2cd 1805. We resumed our march this morning at sunrise; the day was fair and wind from N. W. finding that the river still boar to the South I determined to pass it if possible in order to shorten our rout; this we effected by wading the river about 5 miles above our encampment of the last evening. we found the current very rapid waist deep and about 90 yd. wide bottom smooth pebble with a small mixture of coarse gravel. this is the first time that I ever dared to wade the river, tho there are many places between this and the forks where I presume it might be attempted with equal success. The vally allong which we passed today, and through which the river winds it's meandering course is from 6 to 8 miles wide and consists of a beatifull level plain with but little timber and that confined to the verge of the river; the land is tolerably fertile, and is either black or a dark yellow loam, covered with grass from 9 inches to 2 feet high. the plain ascends gradually on either side of the river to the bases of two ranges of high mountains, which lye parallel to the river and prescribe the limits of the plains. the tops of these mountains are yet covered partially with snow, while we in the valley are nearly suffocated with the intense heat of the midday sun; the nights are so cold that two blankets are not more than sufficient covering. soon after passing the river this morning Sergt. Gass lost my tommahawk in the thick brush and we were unable to find it, I regret the loss of this usefull implement, however accedents will happen in the best families, and I consoled myself with the recollection that it was not the only one we had with us. the bones of the buffaloe and their excrement of an old date are to be met with in every part of this valley but we have long since lost all hope of meeting with that animal in these mountains. we met with great quantities of currants today, two species of which were red, others yellow, deep perple and black; also black goosberries and serviceberries now ripe and in great perfection. we feasted sumptuously on our wild fruits, particularly the yellow currant and the deep perple serviceberries, which I found to be excellent. the serviceberry grows on a small bush and differs from ours only in colour size and superior excellence of it's flavour. it is somewhat larger than ours. on our way we saw an abundance of deer Antelopes, of the former we killed 2. we also saw many tracks of the Elk and bear. no recent appearance of Indians. the Indians in this part of the country appear to construct their lodges with the willow boughs and brush; they are small of a conic figure and have a small aperture on one side through which they enter. we continued our rout up this valley on the Lard. side of the river untill sunset, at which time we encamped on the Lard. bank of the river having traveled 24 miles. we had brought with us a good stock of venison of which we eat a hearty supper. I feel myself perfectly recovered of my indisposition, and do not doubt being able to pursue my rout tomorrow with the same comfort I have done today.- we saw some very large beaver dams today in the bottoms of the river several of which wer five feet high and overflowed several acres of land; these dams are formed of willow brush mud and gravel and are so closely interwoven that they resist the water perfectly. the base of this work is thick and rises nearly perpendicularly on the lower side while the upper side or that within the dam is gently sloped. the brush appear to be laid in no regular order yet acquires a strength by the irregularity with which they are placed by the beaver that it would puzzle the engenuity of man to give them.

Capt. Clark continued his rout early this morning. the rapidity of the current was such that his progress was slow, in short it required the utmost exertion of the men to get on, nor could they resist this current by any other means than that of the cord and pole. in the course of the day they passed some villages of burrowing squirrels, saw a number of beaver dams and the inhabitants of them, many young ducks both of the Duckanmallard and the redheaded fishing duck, gees, several rattle snakes, black woodpeckers, and a large gang of Elk; they found the river much crouded with island both large and small and passed a small creek on Stard. side which we called birth Creek. Capt. Clark discovers a tumor rising on the inner side of his ankle this evening which was painfull to him. they incamped in a level bottom on the Lard. side.-

[Clark, August 2, 1805] August 2nd Friday 1805 a fine day Set out early the river has much the Same kind of banks Chanel Current &c. as it had in the last vallie, I walked out this morning on Shore & Saw Several rattle Snakes in the plain, the wind from the S W we proceeded on with great dificuelty from the rapidity of the current & rapids, abt. 15 miles and Encamped on the Lard Side, saw a large Gangue of Elk at Sunset to the S W. passed a Small Creek on the Stard Side and maney large and Small Islands. Saw a number of young Ducks as we have also Seen everry Day, Some geese I saw Black woodpeckers- I have either got my foot bitten by Some poisonous insect or a turner is riseing on the inner bone of my ankle which is painfull

[Lewis, August 3, 1805] August the 3rd 1805. Set out this morning at sunrise and continued our rout through the valley on the Lard. side of the river. at eleven A.M. Drewyer killed a doe and we halted and took breakfast. the mountains continue high on either side of the valley, and are but skantily supplyed with timber; small pine appears to be the prevalent growth. there is no timber in the valley except a small quantity of the narrow leafed cottonwood on the verge of the river. the underwood consists of the narrowleafed or small willow, honeysuckle rosebushes, courant, goosbury and service bury bushes allso a small quantity of a species of dwarf burch the leaf of which, oval, deep green, finely indented and very small. we encamped this evening after sunset having traveled by estimate 23 miles. from the width and appearance of the valley at this place I concieved that the river forked not far above me and therefore resolved the next morning to examine the adjacent country more minutely.

[Lewis, August 3, 1805] Saturday August 3rd 1805. Set out early this morning, or before sunrise; still continued our march through the level valley on the lard. side of the river. the valley much as yesterday only reather wider; I think it 12 Miles wide, tho the plains near the mountains rise higher and are more broken with some scattering pine near the mountain. in the leaveler parts of the plain and river bottoms which are very extensive there is no timber except a scant proportion of cottonwood neat the river. the under wood consists of the narrow leafed or small willow, the small honeysuckle, rosebushes, currant, serviceberry, and goosbery bushes; also a small species of berth in but small quantities the leaf which is oval finely, indented, small and of a deep green colour. the stem is simple ascending and branching, and seldom rises higher than 10 or 12 feet. the Mountains continue high on either side of the valley, and are but scantily supplyed with timber; small pine apears to be the prevalent growth; it is of the pith kind, with a short leaf. at 11 A.M. Drewyer killed a doe and we halted about 2 hours and breakfasted, and then continued our rout untill night without halting, when we arrived at the river in a level bottom which appeared to spread to greater extent than usual. from the appearance of the timber I supposed that the river forked above us and resolved to examine this part of the river minutely tomorrow. this evening we passed through a high plain for about 8 miles covered with prickley pears and bearded grass, tho we found this even better walking than the wide bottoms of the river, which we passed in the evening; these altho apparently level, from some cause which I know not, were formed into meriads of deep holes as if rooted up by hogs these the grass covered so thick that it was impossible to walk without the risk of falling down at every step. some parts of these bottoms also possess excellent terf or peat, I beleive of many feet deep. the mineral salts also frequently mentioned on the Missouri we saw this evening in these uneven bottoms. we saw many deer, Antelopes ducks, gees, some beaver and great appearance of their work. also a small bird and the Curlooe as usual. we encamped on the river bank on Lard. side having traveled by estimate 23 Miles. The fish of this part of the river are trout and a species of scale fish of a white colour and a remarkable small long mouth which one of our men inform us are the same with the species called in the Eastern states bottlenose. the snowey region of the mountains and for some distance below has no timber or herbage of any kind; the timber is confined to the lower and middle regions. Capt. Clark set out this morning as usual. he walked on shore a small distance this morning and killed a deer. in the course of his walk he saw a track which he supposed to be that of an Indian from the circumstance of the large toes turning inward. he pursued the track and found that the person had ascended a point of a hill from which his camp of the last evening was visible; this circumstance also confirmed the beleif of it's being an Indian who had thus discovered them and ran off. they found the river as usual much crouded with islands, the currant more rapid & much more shallow than usual. in many places they were obliged to double man the canoes and drag them over the stone and gravel. this morning they passed a small creek on Stard. at the entrance of which Reubin Fields killed a large Panther. we called the creek after that animal Panther Creek. they also passed a handsome little stream on Lard. which is form of several large springs which rise in the bottoms and along the base of the mountains with some little rivulets from the melting snows. the beaver have formed many large dams on this stream. they saw some deer Antelopes and the common birds of the country. in the evening they passed a very bad rappid where the bed of the river is formed entrely of solid rock and encamped on an island just above. the Panther which Fields killed measured seven and 1/2 feet from the nose to the extremity of the tail. it is precisely the same animal common to the western part of our country. the men wer compelled to be a great proportion of their time in the water today; they have had a severe days labour and are much fortiegued.

[Clark, August 3, 1805] August 3rd Saturday1805 a fine morning wind from the N E I walked on Shore & killed a Deer in my walk I saw a fresh track which I took to be an Indian from the Shape of the foot as the toes turned in, I think it probable that this Indian Spied our fires and Came to a Situation to view us from the top of a Small knob on the Lard Side. the river more rapid and Sholey than yesterday one R. F. man killed a large Panthor on the Shore we are oblige to haul over the Canoes Sholey in maney places where the Islands are noumerous and bottom Sholey, in the evening the river more rapid and Sholey we encamped on an Island avove a part of the river which passed thro a rockey bed enclosed on both sides with thick willow current & red buries &c &c passed a bold Stream which heads in the mountains to our right and the drean of the minting Snow in the Montn. on that side ar in View- at 4 oClock passed a bold Stream which falls from a mountn in three Channels to our left, the Greater portion of the Snow on this mountain is melted, but little remaining near us Some Deer Elk & antelopes & Bear in the bottoms. but fiew trees and they Small the Mountains on our left Contain pine those on our right but verry partially Supplied and what pine & cedar it has is on the Lower region, no wood being near the Snow. great numbers of Beaver Otter &c. Some fish trout & and bottle nose. Birds as usial. Geese young Ducks & Curlows

[Lewis, August 4, 1805] August 4th 1805. Set out very early this morning and steered S. E. by E. about 4 Miles when we passed a bould runing creek about 12 yards wide the water could and remarkably clear, we then changed our course to S. E. passing obliquely across a valley which boar nearly E leaving the valley which we had pursued for the 2 preceeding days. at the distance of 3 miles we passed a handsome little river which passes through this valley; it is about 30 yards wide affords a considerable quantity of water and I believe it may be navigated some miles. I then changed my rout to S. W. passed a high plain which lyes between the vallies and returned to the S. valley, in passing which I fell in with a river about 45 yards wide which I waideg and then continued my rout down to it's junction with the river just mentioned, and from thence to the entrance of the creek which falls in about 2 miles below; still continuing my rout down this stream about three miles further and about 2 M. below our encampment of the last evening this river forms a junction with a river 50 yards wide which comes from the N. W. and falling into the S. valley runs parrallel with the middle fork about 12 miles. this is a bould rapid & clear stream it's bed so broken and obstructed by gravel bars and Islands that it appeared to me impossible to navigate it with safety. the middle fork is gentle and possesses about 2/3ds as much water as this rapid stream, it's cours so far as I can observe it is about S. W. and it appears to be navigable; its water is much warmer than that of the rappid fork and somewhat turbid, from which I concluded that it had it's source at a greater distance in the mountains and passed through an opener country than the other. under this impression I wrote a note to Capt. Clark recommending his taking the middle fork provided he should arrive at this place before my return which I expect will be the day after tomorrow. the note I left on a pole at the forks of the river and having refreshed ourselves and eat heartily of some venison we killed this morning I continued my rout up the Stard side of the N. W. fork, determining to pursue it untill 12 OC. the next day and then pass over to the middle fork and return to their junction or untill I met Capt. Clark. we encamped this evening near the point where the river leaves the valley and enters the mountains, having traveled about 20 miles.-

[Lewis, August 4, 1805] Sunday August 4th 1805. Set out very early this morning and Steered S. E. by E. 4 M. when we pased a bold runing Creek 12 yds. wide, the water of which was clear and very cold. it appears to be formed by four dranes from the snowey mountains to our left. after passing this creek we changed our direction to S. E. passing obliquely across a valley which boar E leaving the valley we had pursued for the two peceeding days. at the distance of 3 Ms. we passed a handsome little river which meanders through this valley; it is about 30 yds wide, affords a considerable quantity of water and appears as if it might be navigated some miles. the currant is not rapid nor the water very clear; the banks are low and the bed formed of stone and gravel. I now changed my rout to S. W. passed a high plain which lies between the valleies and returned to the South valley, in passing which I fell in with a river about 45 yds. wide gravley bottom gentle currant waist deep and water of a whitish blue tinge. this stream we waded and continued our rout down it to the entrance of the river just mentioned about 3/4 of a mile. still continuing down we passed the entrance of the creek about 2 miles lower down; and at the distance of three miles further arrived at it's junction with a river 50 yds. wide which Comes from the S. W. and falling into the South valley runs parallel with the middle fork about 12 miles before it forms a junction. I now found that our encampment of the last evening was about 11/2 miles above the entrance of this large river on Stard. this is a bold rappid and Clear Stream, it's bed so much broken and obstructed by gravley bars and it's waters so much subdivided by Islands that it appears to me utterly impossible to navigate it with safety. the middle fork is gentle and possesses about 2/3rds as much water as this stream. it's course so far as I can observe it is about S. W., and from the opening of the valley I beleive it still bears more to the West above it may be safely navigated. it's water is much warmer then the rapid fork and it's water more turbid; from which I conjecture that it has it's sources at a greater distance in the mountains and passes through an opener country than the other. under this impression I wrote a note to Capt Clark, recommending his taking the middle fork povided he should arrive at this place before my return, which I expect will be the day after tomorrow. this note I left on a pole at the forks of the river, and having refreshed ourselves and eat heartily of some venison which we killed this morning we continued our rout up the rapid fork on the Stard side, resolving to pursue this stream untill noon tomorrow and then pass over to the middle fork and come down it to their junction or untill I meet Capt Clark. I have seen no recent Indian sign in the course of my rout as yet. Charbono complains much of his leg, and is the cause of considerable detention to us. we encamped on the river bank near the place at which it leaves the valley and enters the mountain having traveled about 23 miles. we saw some Antelopes deer Grains, gees, and ducks of the two species common to this country. the summer duck has ceased to appear, nor do I beleive it is an inhabitant of this part of the country. the timber &c is as heretofore tho there is more in this valley on the rapid fork than we have seen in the same extent on the river since we entered this valley. the Indians appear on some parts of the river to have distroyed a great proportion of the little timber which there is by seting fire to the bottoms. This morning Capt. Clark set out at sunrise, and sent two hunters ahead to kill some meat. at 8 A.M. he arrived at my camp of the 2ed inst. where he breakfasted; here he found a note which I had left for him at that place informing him of the occurences of my rout &c. the river continued to be crouded with Islands, rapid and shoaly. these shoals or riffles succeeded each other every 3 or four hundred yards; at those places they are obliged to drag the canoes over the stone there not being water enough to float them, and betwen the riffles the current is so strong that they are compelled to have cecourse to the cord; and being unable to walk on the shore for the brush wade in the river along the shore and hawl them by the cord; this has increased the pain and labour extreemly; their feet soon get tender and soar by wading and walking over the stones. these are also so slipry that they frequently get severe falls. being constantly wet soon makes them feble also. their hunters killed 2 deer today and some gees and ducks wer killed by those who navigated the canoes. they saw deer antelopes Grains beaver Otter &c. Capt. Clark's ancle became so painfull to him that he was unable to walk.- This evening they encamped on the Stard. side in a bottom of cottonwood timber all much fatiegued.

[Clark, August 4, 1805] August 4th Sunday 1805 a fine morning cool proceeded on verry early and Brackfast at the Camp Capt Lewis left yesterday morning, at this Camp he left a note informing that he discovered no fresh Sign of Indians &c. The river continued to be crouded with Islands Sholey rapid & clear, I could not walk on Shore to day as my ankle was Sore from a turner on that part. the method we are compelled to take to get on is fatigueing & laborious in the extreen, haul the Canoes over the rapids, which Suckceed each other every two or three hundred yards and between the water rapid oblige to towe & walke on Stones the whole day except when we have poleing men wet all day Sore feet &c. &c Murcury at Sun rise 49 a. 0,

[Lewis, August 5, 1805] Monday August 5th 1805 As Charbono complained of being unable to march far today I ordered him and Sergt. Gass to pass the rappid river near our camp and proceed at their leasure through the level bottom to a point of high timber about seven miles distant on the middle fork which was in view; I gave them my pack that of Drewyer and the meat which we had, directing them to remain at that place untill we joined them. I took Drewyer with me and continued my rout up the stard. side of the river about 4 miles and then waded it; found it so rapid and shallow that it was impossible to navigate it. continued up it on the Lard. side about 11/2 miles further when the mountains put in close on both sides and arrose to great hight, partially covered with snow. from hence the course of the river was to the East of North. I took the advantage of a high projecting spur of the mountain which with some difficulty we ascended to it's summit in about half an hour. from this eminance I had a pleasing view of the valley through which I had passed many miles below and the continuation of the middle fork through the valley equally wide above me to the distance of about 20 miles when that also appeared to enter the mountains and disappeared to my view; however the mountains which termineate the valley in this direction appeared much lower than those up either of the other forks. on the rapid fork they appeared still to rise the one range towering above another as far as I could perceive them. the middle fork as I suspected dose bear considerably to the West of South and the gap formed by it in the mountains after the valley terminates is in the same direction. under these circumstances I did not hesitate in beleiving the middle fork the most proper for us to ascend. about South from me, the middle fork approached within about 5 miles. I resolved to pass across the plains to it and return to Gass and Charbono, accordingly we set out and decended the mountain among some steep and difficult precipices of rocks. here Drewyer missed his step and had a very dangerous fall, he sprained one of his fingers and hirt his leg very much. in fifteen or

20 minutes he was able to proceed and we continued our rout to the river where we had desighned to interscept it. I quenched my thirst and rested a few minutes examined the river and found it still very navigable. an old indian road very large and plain leads up this fork, but I could see no tracks except those of horses which appeared to have passed early in the spring. as the river mad a great bend to the South East we again ascended the high plain and steered our course as streight as we could to the point where I had directed Gass and Sharbono to remain. we passed the plain regained the bottom and struck the river about 3 miles above them; by this time it was perfectly dark & we hooped but could hear no tidings of them. we had struck the river at the point of timber to which I had directed them, but having mistaken a point of woods lower down, had halted short of the place. we continued our rout after dark down the bottom through thick brush of the pulppy leafed thorn and prickly pears for about 2 hours when we arrived at their camp. they had a small quantity of meat left which Drewyer and myself eat it being the first we had taisted today. we had traveled about 25 miles. I soon laid down and slept very soundly untill morning. I saw no deer today nor any game except a few Antelopes which were very shy. the soil of the plains is a light yellow clay very meager and intermixed with a large proportion of gravel, producing nothing except the twisted or bearded grass, sedge and prickly pears. the dryer parts of the bottoms are also much more indifferent in point of soil to those below and are covered with the southernwood pulpy leafed thorn and prickley pears with but little grass. the moist parts are fertile and covered with fine grass and sand rushes.

This morning Capt. Clark set out at sunrise and dispatched Joseph & Reubin Fields to hunt. they killed two deer on one of which the party breakfasted. the river today they found streighter and more rapid even than yesterday, and the labour and difficulty of the navigation was proportionably increased, they therefore proceeded but slowly and with great pain as the men had become very languid from working in the water and many of their feet swolen and so painfull that they could scarcely walk. at 4 P.M. they arrived at the confluence of the two rivers where I had left the note. this note had unfortunately been placed on a green pole which the beaver had cut and carried off together with the note; the possibility of such an occurrence never one occurred to me when I placed it on the green pole. this accedent deprived Capt. Clark of any information with ripect to the country and supposing that the rapid fork was most in the direction which it was proper we should pursue, or West, he took that stream and asscended it with much difficulty about a mile and encamped on an island that had been lately overflown and was yet damp; they were therefore compelled to make beds of brush to keep themselves out of the mud. in ascending this stream for about a quarter of a mile it scattered in such a maner that they were obliged to cut a passage through the willow brush which leant over the little channels and united their tops. Capt. Clarks ankle is extreemly painfull to him this evening; the tumor has not yet mature, he has a slight fever.- The men were so much fortiequed today that they wished much that navigation was at an end that they might go by land.-

[Clark, August 5, 1805] August 5th Monday 1805 a Cold Clear morning the wind from the S. E. the river Streight & much more rapid than yesterday, I Sent out Jo. & R. Fields to kill Some meat they killed 2 Deer & we brackfast on one of them and proceeded on with great dificuelety from the rapidity of the Current, and numerable rapids we had to encounter, at 4 oClock P M Murcury 49 ab. 0, passed the mouth of principal fork which falls in on the Lard. Side, this fork is about the Size of the Stard. one less water reather not so rapid, its Course as far as can be Seen is S. E & appear to pass through between two mountains, the N W. fork being the one most in our course i. e. S 25 W. as far as I can See, deturmind me to take this fork as the principal and the one most proper the S E fork is of a Greenish Colour & contains but little timber. The S W fok contains more timber than is below for Some distance, we assended this fork about one mile and Encamped on an Island which had been laterly overflown & was wet we raised our bead on bushes, we passed a part of the river above the forks which was divided and Scattered thro the willows in Such a manner as to render it dificult to pass through for a 1/4 of a mile, we wer oblige to Cut our way thro the willows- Men much fatigued from their excessive labours in hauling the Canoes over the rapids &c. verry weak being in the water all day. my foot verry painfull

Assended the N W Fork 9 miles on a Course S. 30° W. to a Bluff on the
Stard. Side passed Several Bayous & Islands

[Lewis, August 6, 1805] Tuesday August 6th 1805. We set out this morning very early on our return to the forks. having nothing to eat I set Drewyer to the woodlands to my left in order to kill a deer, sent Sergt. Gass to the right with orders to keep sufficiently near to discover Capt. C. and the party should they be on their way up that stream, and with Sharbono I directed my course to the main forks through the bottom directing the others to meet us there. about five miles above the forks I head the hooping of the party to my left and changed my rout towards them; on my arrival found that they had taken the rapid fork and learnt from Capt. Clark that he had not found the note which I had left for him at that place and the reasons which had induced him to ascend this stream. it was easeist & more in our direction, and apd. to contain as much water he had hoever previously to my comeing up with him, met Drewyer who informed him of the state of the two rivers and was on his return. one of their canoes had just overset and all the baggage wet, the medecine box among other articles and several articles lost a shot pouch and horn with all the implements for one rifle lost and never recovered. I walked down to the point where I waited their return. on their arrival found that two other canoes had filled with water and wet their cargoes completely. Whitehouse had been thrown out of one of the canoes as she swing in a rapid current and the canoe had rubed him and pressed him to the bottom as she passed over him and had the water been 2 inches shallower must inevitably have crushed him to death. our parched meal, corn, Indian preasents, and a great part of our most valuable stores were wet and much damaged on this ocasion. to examine, dry and arrange our stores was the first object; we therefore passed over to the lard. side opposite to the entrance of the rapid fork where there was a large gravly bar that answered our purposes; wood was also convenient and plenty. here we fixed our camp, and unloaded all our canoes and opened and exposed to dry such articles as had been wet. a part of the load of each canoe consisted of the leaden canestirs of powder which were not in least injured, tho some of them had remained upwards of an hour under water. about 20 lbs. of powder which we had in a tight Keg or at least one which we thought sufficiently so got wet and intirely spoiled. this would have been the case with the other had it not have been for the expedient which I had fallen on of securing the powder by means of the lead having the latter formed into canesters which were filled with the necessary proportion of poder to discharge the lead when used, and those canesters well secured with corks and wax. in this country the air is so pure and dry that any vessel however well seasoned the timber may be will give way or shrink unless it is kept full of some liquid. we found that three deer skins which we had left at a considerable hight on a tree were taken off which we supposed had been done by a panther. we sent out some men to hunt this evening, they killed 3 deer and four Elk which gave us a plentifull supply of meat once more. Shannon had been dispatched up the rapid fork this morning to hunt, by Capt Clark before he met with Drewyer or learnt his mistake in the rivers. when he returned he sent Drewyer in surch of him, but he rejoined us this evening and reported that he had been several miles up the river and could find nothing of him. we had the trumpet sounded and fired several guns but he did not join us this evening. I am fearful he is lost again. this is the same man who was seperated from us 15 days as we came up the Missouri and subsisted 9 days of that time on grapes only. Whitehouse is in much pain this evening with the injury one of his legs sustained from the canoe today at the time it upset and swing over him. Capt Clarks ankle is also very painfull to him.- we should have given the party a days rest some where near this place had not this accedent happened, as I had determined to take some observations to fix the Latitude and longitude of these forks. our merchandize medecine &c are not sufficiently dry this evening we covered them securely for the evening. Capt Clark had ascended the river about 9 miles from this place on a course of S 30° W. before he met with Drewyer.

we beleive that the N. W. or rapid fork is the dane of the melting snows of the mountains, and that it is not as long as the middle fork and dose not at all seasons of the year supply any thing like as much water as the other and that about this season it rises to it's greatest hight. this last appears from the apparent bed of the river which is now overflown and the water in many plases spreads through old channels which have their bottoms covered with grass that has grown this season and is such as appears on the parts of the bottom not innundated. we therefore determined that the middle fork was that which ought of right to bear the name we had given to the lower portion or River Jefferson and called the bold rapid an clear stream Wisdom, and the more mild and placid one which flows in from the S. E. Philanthrophy, in commemoration of two of those cardinal virtues, which have so eminently marked that deservedly selibrated character through life.

[Clark, August 6, 1805] August 6th Tuesday 1805 a Clear morning Cool wind from the S W we proceeded on with much dificuelty and fatigue over rapids & Stones; river about 40 or 50 yards wide much divided by Islands and narrow Bayoos to a low bluff on the Stard Side & Brackfast, dureing the time of Brackfast Drewyer Came to me from Capt. Lewis and informed me that they had explored both forks for 30 or 40 miles & that the one we were assending was impractiabl much further up & turned imediately to the north, The middle fork he reported was jintle and after a Short distanc turned to the S. W. and that all the Indian roades leades up the middle fork. this report deturmind me to take the middle fork, accordingly Droped down to the forks where I met with Capt Lewis & party, Capt Lewis had left a Letter on a pole in the forks informing me what he had discovered & the course of the rivers &c. this lettr was Cut down by the beaver as it was on a green pole & Carried off. Three Skins which was left on a tree was taken off by the Panthers or wolvers. In decending to the Point one Canoe Struck & turned on a rapid & Sunk, and wet every thing which was in her, this misfortune obliged us to halt at the forks and dry those articles, one other Canoe nearly turning over, filled half full of water & wet our medison & Some Goods Corn &c. Several hunters out to day & killed a young Elk, Antilope, & 3 Deer, one man Shannon did not return to night- This evening Cool my anckle much wors than it has been- this evening a Violent wind from the N. W accompanied with rain which lasted half an hour wind N. W

[Lewis, August 7, 1805] Wednesday August 7th 1805. The morning being fair we spread our stores to dry at an early hour. Dispatched Reubin Fields in surch of Shannon. our stores were now so much exhausted that we found we could proceed with one canoe less. we therefore drew out one of them into a thicket of brush and secured her in such manner that the water could not take her off should the river rise to the hight where she is. The creek which falls in above us we called turf creek from the cercustance of it's bottoms being composed of excellent turf. my air gun was out of order and her sights had been removed by some accedent I put her in order and regulated her. she shot again as well as she ever did. The clouds last night prevented my taking any lunar observations this day I took Equal Altitudes of the 0 with Sextant.

At one oclock all our baggage was dry we therefore packed it up reloaded the canoes and the party proceeded with Capt. Clark up Jefferson's river. I remained with Sergt. Gass to complete the observation of equal altitudes and joined them in the evening at their camp on the Lard. side just above the entrance of turf creek. we had a shower of rain wich continued about 40 minutes attended with thunder and lightning. this shower wet me perfectly before I reached the camp. the clouds continued during the night in such manner that I was unable to obtain any lunar observations. This evening Drewyer brought in a deer which he had killed. we have not heard any thing from Shannon yet, we expect that he has pursued Wisdom river upwards for som distance probably killed some heavy animal and is waiting our arrival. the large biteing fly or hare fly as they sometimes called are very troublesome to us. I observe two kinds of them a large black species and a small brown species with a green head. the musquetoes are not as troublesome as they were below, but are still in considerable quantities. the eye knats have disappeared. the green or blowing flies are still in swarms.

r the courses from the entrance of Wisdom river to the forks of Jefferson's river are taken directly to the objects mentioned and the distance set down is that by land on a direct line between the points; the estimated distances by water is also added in the body of the remarks on each course.

[Clark, August 7, 1805] August 7th Wednesday 1805 a fine morning put out our Stores &c. to dry & took equal altitudes with the Sextant,- as our Store were a little exorsted and one Canoe became unnecessary deturmind to leave one. we Hauled her up in the bushes on the lower Side of the main fork & fastened her So that the water could not flote her off. The Countrey in this quarter is as follows i, e a Vallie of 5 or 6 miles wide Inclosed between two high Mountains, the bottom rich Some Small timber on the Islands & bushes on the edges of the river Some Bogs & verry good turf in different places in the vallie, Some scattering Pine & ceder on the mountains in places, other Parts nacked except grass and Stone The Lattitude of the Mouth of Wisdom River is 45° 2' 21.6" North, we proceeded up the Main Middle or S. E. fork, passed a Camped on the Lard. Side above the mouth of a bold running Stream 12 yards wide, which we call turf Creek from the number of bogs & quanty of turf in its waters. this Creek runs thro a open Plain for Several miles, takeing its rise in a high mountain to the N E. The river Jefferson above Wisdom is gentle Crooked and about 40 yards wide, Containing but little timber, Some few Cotton willow Willow & Birch, and the Srubs common to the countrey and before mentioned at 5 oClock a thunder Storm from the N. W. accompanied with rain which lasted about 40 minits.- despatched R Fields to hunt Shannon, who was out huntg. on Wisdom river at the time I returned down that Stream, and has made on up the river expecting us to follow him up that river one Deer killed this evening. all those Streams Contain emence number of Beaver orter Muskrats &c.

[Lewis, August 8, 1805] Thursday August 8th 1805. We had a heavy dew this morning. as one canoe had been left we had now more hads to spear for the chase; game being scarce it requires more hunters to supply us. we therefore dispatched four this morning. we set out at sunrise and continued our rout up the river which we find much more gentle and deep than below the entrance of Wisdom river it is from 35 to 45 yards wide very crooked many short bends constituteing large and general bends; insomuch that altho we travel briskly and a considerable distance yet it takes us only a few miles on our general course or rout. there is but very little timber on this fork principally the under brush frequently mentioned. I observe a considerable quantity of the buffaloe clover in the bottoms. the sunflower, flax, green swoard, thistle and several species of the rye grass some of which rise to the hight of 3 or 4 feet. there is a grass also with a soft smooth leaf that bears it's seeds very much like the timothy but it dose not grow very luxouriant or appear as if it would answer so well as the common timothy for meadows. I preserved some of it's seeds which are now ripe, thinking perhaps it might answer better if cultivated, at all events is at least worth the experi-ment. it rises about 3 feet high. on a direct line about 2 miles above our encampment of this morning we passed the entrance of Philanthrophy River which discharges itself by 2 channels a small distance assunder. this river from it's size and S. Eastwardly course no doubt heads with Madisons river in the snowey mountains visible in that direction. at Noon Reubin Fields arrived and reported that he had been up Wisdom river some miles above where it entered the mountain and could find nothing of Shannon, he had killed a deer and an Antelope. great quantity of beaver Otter and musk-rats in these rivers. two of the hunters we sent out this morning returned at noon had killed each a deer and an Antelope. we use the seting poles today almost altogether. we encamped on the Lard sides where there was but little timber were obliged to use willow brush for fuel; the rosebushes and bryers were very thick. the hunters brought in another deer this evening. to tumor on Capt. Clarks ankle has discharged a considerable quantity of matter but is still much swolen and inflamed and gives him considerable pain. saw a number of Gees ducks and some Crains today. the former begin to fly.

the evening again proved cloudy much to my mortification and prevented my making any lunar observations. the Indian woman recognized the point of a high plain to our right which she informed us was not very distant from the summer retreat of her nation on a river beyond the mountains which runs to the west. this hill she says her nation calls the beaver's head from a conceived remblance of it's figure to the head of that animal. she assures us that we shall either find her people on this river or on the river immediately west of it's source; which from it's present size cannot be very distant. as it is now all important with us to meet with those people as soon as possible, I determined to proceed tomorrow with a small party to the source of the principal stream of this river and pass the mountains to the Columbia; and down that river untill I found the Indians; in short it is my resolusion to find them or some others, who have horses if it should cause me a trip of one month. for without horses we shall be obliged to leave a great part of our stores, of which, it appears to me that we have a stock already sufficiently small for the length of the voyage before us.

[Clark, August 8, 1805] August 8th Thursday 1805 We proceeded on early wind from the S W. The Thermometer at 52 a 0 at Sunrise at 5 miles by water & 41/2 on a derect line from the forks we passed a River on the Lard Side 30 yards wide and navagable for Some distance takeing its rise in the Mountains Easterly & with the waters of Madisons River, passes thro an extensive vallie open & furtill &c. this river we call Philanthophy- above this river (which has but little timber) Jeffersons R is crooked with Short bends a fiew Islands and maney gravelly Sholes, no large timber, Small willow Birch & Srubs &c. Encamped on the Lard Side, R Fields joined us this eveng. & informes that he could not find Shannon my foot yet verry Swore

[Lewis, August 9, 1805] Friday August 9th 1805. The morning was fair and fine; we set out at an early hour and proceeded on very well. some parts of the river more rapid than yesterday. I walked on shore across the land to a point which I presumed they would reach by 8 A.M. our usual time of halting. by this means I acquired leasure to accomplish some wrightings which I conceived from the nature of my instructions necessary lest any accedent should befall me on the long and reather hazardous rout I was now about to take. the party did not arrive and I returned about a mile and met them, here they halted and we breakefasted; I had killed two fine gees on my return. while we halted here Shannon arrived, and informed us that having missed the party the day on which he set out he had returned the next morning to the place from whence he had set out or furst left them and not finding that he had supposed that they wer above him; that he then set out and marched one day up wisdom river, by which time he was convinced that they were not above him as the river could not be navigated; he then returned to the forks and had pursued us up this river. he brought the skins of three deer which he had killed which he said were in good order. he had lived very plentifully this trip but looked a good deel worried with his march. he informed us that Wisdom river still kept it's course obliquely down the Jefferson's river as far as he was up it. immediately after breakfast I slung my pack and set out accompanyed by Drewyer Shields and McNeal who had been previously directed to hold themselves in readiness for this service. I directed my course across the bottom to the Stard. plain led left the beaver's head about 2 miles to my left and interscepted the river about 8 miles from the point at which I had left it; I then waded it and continued my rout to the point where I could observe that it entered the mountain, but not being able to reach that place, changed my direction to the river which I struck some miles below the mountain and encamped for the evening having traveled 16 M. we passed a handsom little stream formed by some large spring which rise in this wide bottom on the Lard. side of the river. we killed two Antelopes on our way and brought with us as much meat as was necessary for our suppers and breakfast the next morning. we found this bottom fertile and covered with taller grass than usual. the river very crooked much divided by islands, shallow rocky in many plases and very rapid; insomuch that I have my doubts whether the canoes could get on or not, or if they do it must be with great labour.- Capt. Clark proceeded after I left him as usual, found the current of the river increasing in rapidity towards evening. his hunters killed 2 antelopes only. in the evening it clouded up and we experienced a slight rain attended with some thunder and lightning. the musquetoes very troublesome this evening. there are some soft bogs in these vallies covered with turf. the earth of which this mud is composed is white or bluish white and appears to be argillacious.

[Clark, August 9, 1805] August 9th Friday 1805 a fine morning wind from the N. E we proceeded on verry well rapid places more noumerous than below, Shannon the man whome we lost on Wisdom River Joined us, haveing returned to the forks & prosued us up after prosueing Wisdom River one day

Capt Lewis and 3 men Set out after brackft. to examine the river above, find a portage if possible, also the Snake Indians. I Should have taken this trip had I have been able to march, from the rageing fury of a turner on my anckle musle, in the evening Clouded up and a fiew drops of rain Encamped on the Lard Side near a low bluff, the river to day as yesterday. the three hunters Could kill only two antelopes to day, game of every kind Scerce

[Lewis, August 10, 1805] Saturday August 10th 1805. We set out very early this morning and continued our rout through the wide bottom on the Lard. side of the river after passing a large creek at about 5 miles we fel in with a plain Indian road which led towards the point that the river entered the mountain we therefore pursued the road I sent Drewyer to the wright to kill a deer which we saw feeding and halted on the river under an immencely high perpendicular clift of rocks where it entered the mountain here we kindled a fire and waited for Drewyer. he arrived in about an hour and a half or at noon with three deer skins and the flesh of one of the best of them, we cooked and eat a haisty meal and departed, returning a shot distance to the Indian road which led us the best way over the mountains, which are not very high but ar ruggid and approach the river closely on both sides just below these mountains I saw several bald Eagles and two large white headed fishinghawks boath these birds were the same common to our country.

from the number of rattle snakes about the Clifts at which we halted we called them the rattle snake clifts. this serpent is the same before discribed with oval spots of yellowish brown. the river below the mountains is rapid rocky, very crooked, much divided by islands and withal shallow. after it enters the mountains it's bends are not so circuetous and it's general course more direct, but it is equally shallow les divided more rocky and rapid. we continued our rout along the Indian road which led us sometimes over the hills and again in the narrow bottoms of the river till at the distance of fifteen Ms. from the rattle snake Clifts we arrived in a hadsome open and leavel vally where the river divided itself nearly into two equal branches; here I halted and examined those streams and readily discovered from their size that it would be vain to attempt the navigation of either any further. here also the road forked one leading up the vally of each of these streams. I therefore sent Drewer on one and Shields on the other to examine these roads for a short distance and to return and compare their information with respect to the size and apparent plainness of the roads as I was now determined to pursue that which appeared to have been the most traveled this spring. in the mean time I wrote a note to Capt. Clark informing him of the occurrences which had taken place, recommending it to him to halt at this place untill my return and informing him of the rout I had taken which from the information of the men on their return seemed to be in favour of the S W or Left hand fork which is reather the smallest. accordingly I put up my note on a dry willow pole at the forks, and set out up the S. E. fork, after proceeding about 1 1/2 miles I discovered that the road became so blind that it could not be that which we had followed to the forks of Jefferson's river, neither could I find the tracks of the horses which had passed early in the spring along the other; I therefore determined to return and examine the other myself, which I did, and found that the same horses had passed up the West fork which was reather largest, and more in the direction that I wished to pursue; I therefore did not hesitate about changing my rout but determined to take the western road. I now wrote a second note to Capt C. informing him of this change and sent Drewyer to put it with the other at the forks and waited untill he returned. there is scarcely any timber on the river above the R. Snake Clifts, nor is there anything larger than willow brush in sight of these forks. immediately in the level plain between the forks and about 1/2 a mile distance from them stands a high rocky mountain, the base of which is surrounded by the level plain; it has a singular appearance. the mountains do not appear very high in any direction tho the tops of some of them are partially covered with snow. this convinces me that we have ascended to a great hight since we have entered the rocky Mountains, yet the ascent has been so gradual along the vallies that it was scarcely perceptable by land. I do not beleive that the world can furnish an example of a river runing to the extent which the Missouri and Jefferson's rivers do through such a mountainous country and at the same time so navigable as they are. if the Columbia furnishes us such another example, a communication across the continent by water will be practicable and safe. but this I can scarcely hope from a knowledge of its having in it comparitively short course to the ocean the same number of feet to decend which the Missouri and Mississippi have from this point to the Gulph of Mexico.

The valley of the west fork through which we passed for four miles boar a little to N of West and was about 1 mile wide hemned in on either side by rough mountain and steep Clifts of rock at 4 1/2 miles this stream enters a beatifull and extensive plain about ten miles long and from 5 to six in width. this plain is surrounded on all sides by a country of roling or high wavy plains through which several little rivulets extend their wide vallies quite to the Mountains which surround the whole in an apparent Circular manner; forming one of the handsomest coves I ever saw, of about 16 or 18 miles in diameter. just after entering this cove the river bends to the N. W. and runs close under the Stard. hills. here we killed a deer and encamped on the Stard.,side and made our fire of dry willow brush, the only fuel which the country produces. there are not more than three or four cottonwood trees in this extensive cove and they are but small. the uplands are covered with prickly pears and twisted or bearded grass and are but poor; some parts of the bottom lands are covered with grass and tolerably fertile; but much the greater proportion is covered with prickly pears sedge twisted grass the pulpy leafed thorn southernwood wild sage &c and like the uplands is very inferior in point of soil. we traveled by estimate 30 Ms. today, that is 10 to the Rattle snake Clift, 15 to the forks of Jefferson's river and 5 to our camp in the cove. at the apparent extremity of the bottom above us two perpendicular clifts of considerable hight stand on either side of the river and appers at this distance like a gate, it is about 10 M. due West.

Capt Clark set out at sunrise this morning and pursued his rout; found the river not rapid but shallow also very crooked. they were obliged to drag the canoes over many riffles in the course of the day. they passed the point which the natives call the beaver's head. it is a steep rocky clift of 150 feet high near the Stard. side of the river, opposite to it at the distance of 300 yards is a low clift of about 50 feet which is the extremity of a spur of the mountains about 4 miles distant on Lard. at 4 P.M. they experienced a heavy shower of rain attended with hail thunder and Lightning which continued about an hour. the men defended themselves from the hail by means of the willow bushes but all the party got perfectly wet. after the shower was over they pursued their march and encamped on the stard side only one deer killed by their hunters today. tho they took up another by the way which had been killed three days before by Jos. Fields and hung up near the river.

[Clark, August 10, 1805] August 10th Satturday 1805 Some rain this morning at Sun rise and Cloudy we proceeded on passed a remarkable Clift point on the Stard. Side about 150 feet high, this Clift the Indians Call the Beavers head, opposit at 300 yards is a low clift of 50 feet which is a Spur from the Mountain on the Lard. about 4 miles, the river verry Crooked, at 4 oClock a hard rain from the S W accompanied with hail Continued half an hour, all wet, the men Sheltered themselves from the hail with bushes We Encamped on the Stard Side near a Bluff, only one Deer killed to day, the one killed Jo Fields 3 Days past & hung up we made use of river narrow, & Sholey but not rapid.

[Lewis, August 11, 1805] Sunday August 11th 1805. We set out very early this morning; but the track which we had pursued last evening soon disappeared. I therefore resolved to proceed to the narrow pass on the creek about 10 miles West in hopes that I should again find the Indian road at the place, accordingly I passed the river which was about 12 yards wide and bared in several places entirely across by beaver dams and proceeded through the level plain directly to the pass. I now sent Drewyer to keep near the creek to my right and Shields to my left, with orders to surch for the road which if they found they were to notify me by placing a hat in the muzzle of their gun. I kept McNeal with me; after having marched in this order for about five miles I discovered an Indian on horse back about two miles distant coming down the plain toward us. with my glass I discovered from his dress that he was of a different nation from any that we had yet seen, and was satisfyed of his being a Sosone; his arms were a bow and quiver of arrows, and was mounted on an eligant horse without a saddle, and a small string which was attatched to the underjaw of the horse which answered as a bridle. I was overjoyed at the sight of this stranger and had no doubt of obtaining a friendly introduction to his nation provided I could get near enough to him to convince him of our being whitemen. I therefore proceeded towards him at my usual pace. when I had arrived within about a mile he mad a halt which I did also and unloosing my blanket from my pack, I mad him the signal of friendship known to the Indians of the Rocky mountains and those of the Missouri, which is by holding the mantle or robe in your hands at two corners and then throwing up in the air higher than the head bringing it to the earth as if in the act of spreading it, thus repeating three times. this signal of the robe has arrisen from a custom among all those nations of spreading a robe or skin for ther gests to set on when they are visited. this signal had not the desired effect, he still kept his position and seemed to view Drewyer an Shields who were now comiming in sight on either hand with an air of suspicion, I wold willingly have made them halt but they were too far distant to hear me and I feared to make any signal to them least it should increase the suspicion in the mind of the Indian of our having some unfriendly design upon him. I therefore haistened to take out of my sack some beads a looking glas and a few trinkets which I had brought with me for this purpose and leaving my gun and pouch with McNeal advanced unarmed towards him. he remained in the same stedfast poisture untill I arrived in about 200 paces of him when he turn his hose about and began to move off slowly from me; I now called to him in as loud a voice as I could command repeating the word tab-ba-bone, which in their language signifyes white man. but loking over his sholder he still kept his eye on Drewyer and Sheilds who wer still advancing neither of them haveing segacity enough to recollect the impropriety of advancing when they saw me thus in parley with the Indian. I now made a signal to these men to halt, Drewyer obeyed but Shields who afterwards told me that he did not observe the signal still kept on the Indian halted again and turned his horse about as if to wait for me, and I beleive he would have remained untill I came up whith him had it not been for Shields who still pressed forward. whe I arrived within about 150 paces I again repepeated the word tab-ba-bone and held up the trinkits in my hands and striped up my shirt sieve to give him an opportunity of seeing the colour of my skin and advanced leasure towards him but he did not remain untill I got nearer than about 100 paces when he suddonly turned his hose about, gave him the whip leaped the creek and disapeared in the willow brush in an instant and with him vanished all my hopes of obtaining horses for the preasent. I now felt quite as much mortification and disappointment as I had pleasure and expectation at the first sight of this indian. I fet soarly chargrined at the conduct of the men particularly Sheilds to whom I principally attributed this failure in obtaining an introduction to the natives. I now called the men to me and could not forbare abraiding them a little for their want of attention and imprudence on this occasion. they had neglected to bring my spye-glass which in haist I had droped in the plain with the blanket where I made the signal before mentioned. I sent Drewyer and Shields back to surche it, they soon found it and rejoined me. we now set out on the track of the horse hoping by that means to be lead to an indian camp, the trail of inhabitants of which should they abscond we should probably be enabled to pursue to the body of the nation to which they would most probably fly for safety. this rout led us across a large Island framed by nearly an equal division of the creek in this bottom; after passing to the open ground on the N. side of the creek we observed that the track made out toward the high hills about 3 m. distant in that direction. I thought it probable that their camp might probably be among those hills & that they would reconnoiter us from the tops of them, and that if we advanced haistily towards them that they would become allarmed and probably run off; I therefore halted in an elivated situation near the creek had a fire kindled of willow brush cooked and took breakfast. during this leasure I prepared a small assortment of trinkits consisting of some mockkerson awls a few strans of several kinds of beads some paint a looking glass &c which I attatched to the end of a pole and planted it near our fire in order that should the Indians return in surch of us they might from this token discover that we were friendly and white persons. before we had finised our meal a heavy shower of rain came on with some hail wich continued abot 20 minutes and wet us to the skin, after this shower we pursued the track of the horse but as the rain had raised the grass which he had trodden down it was with difficulty that we could follow it. we pursued it however about 4 miles it turning up the valley to the left under the foot of the hills. we pas several places where the Indians appeared to have been diging roots today and saw the fresh tracks of 8 or ten horses but they had been wandering about in such a confused manner that we not only lost the track of the hose which we had been pursuing but could make nothing of them. in the head of this valley we passed a large bog covered with tall grass and moss in which were a great number of springs of cold pure water, we now turned a little to the left along the foot of the high hills and arrived at a small branch on which we encamped for the night, having traveled in different directions about 20 Miles and about 10 from the camp of last evening on a direct line. after meeting with the Indian today I fixed a small flag of the U'S. to a pole which I made McNeal carry. and planted in the ground where we halted or encamped.

This morning Capt Clark dispatched several hunters a head; the morning being rainy and wet did not set out untill after an early breakfast. he passed a large Island which he called the 3000 mile Island from the circumstance of it's being that distance from the entrance of the Missouri by water. a considerable proportion of the bottom on Lard. side is a bog covered with tall grass and many parts would afford fine turf; the bottom is about 8 Ms. wide and the plains which succeed it on either side extend about the same distance to the base of the mountains. they passed a number of small Islands and bayous on both sides which cut and intersect the bottoms in various directions. found the river shallow and rapid, insomuch that the men wer compelled to be in the water a considerable proportion of the day in drageing the canoes over the shoals and riffles. they saw a number of geese ducks beaver & otter, also some deer and antelopes. the men killed a beaver with a seting pole and tommahawked several Otter. the hunters killed 3 deer and an Antelope. Capt. C. observed some bunches of privy near the river. there are but few trees in this botom and those small narrow leafed Cottonwood. the principal growth is willow with the narrow leaf and Currant bushes. they encamped this evening on the upper point of a large Island near the Stard. shore.-

[Clark, August 11, 1805] August 11th Sunday 1805. a Shower of rain this morning at Sun rise, Cloudy all the morning wind from the S W passed a large Island which I call the 3000 mile Island as it is Situated that distance from the mouth of the Missouri by water, a number of Small Bayoes running in different directions thro the Bottom, which is about 5 miles wide, then rises to an ellivated plain on each Side which extends as far. passed Several Small Islands and a number of Bayoes on each Side and Encamped on the upper point of a large Island, our hunters killed three Deer, one antelope, and Tomahawked Several Orter to day killed one Beaver with a Setting pole. I observed Some bunches of Privey on the banks

[Lewis, August 12, 1805] Monday August 12th 1805 This morning I sent Drewyer out as soon as it was light, to try and discover what rout the Indians had taken. he followed the track of the horse we had pursued yesterday to the mountain wher it had ascended, and returned to me in about an hour and a half. I now determined to pursue the base of the mountains which form this cove to the S. W. in the expectation of finding some Indian road which lead over the Mountains, accordingly I sent Drewyer to my right and Shields to my left with orders to look out for a road or the fresh tracks of horses either of which we should first meet with I had determined to pursue. at the distance of about 4 miles we passed 4 small rivulets near each other on which we saw som resent bowers or small conic lodges formed with willow brush. near them the indians had geathered a number of roots from the manner in which they had toarn up the ground; but I could not discover the root which they seemed to be in surch of. I saw several large hawks that were nearly black near this place we fell in with a large and plain Indian road which came into the cove from the N. E. and led along the foot of the mountains to the S. W. oliquely approaching the main stream which we had left yesterday. this road we now pursued to the S. W. at 5 miles it passed a stout stream which is a principal fork of the man stream and falls into it just above the narrow pass between the two clifts before mentioned and which we now saw below us. here we halted and breakfasted on the last of our venison, having yet a small peice of pork in reseve. after eating we continued our rout through the low bottom of the main stream along the foot of the mountains on our right the valley for 5 mes. further in a S. W. direction was from 2 to 3 miles wide the main stream now after discarding two stream on the left in this valley turns abruptly to the West through a narrow bottom betwen the mountains. the road was still plain, I therefore did not dispair of shortly finding a passage over the mountains and of taisting the waters of the great Columbia this evening. we saw an animal which we took to be of the fox kind as large or reather larger than the small wolf of the plains. it's colours were a curious mixture of black, redis-brown and yellow. Drewyer shot at him about 130 yards and knocked him dow bet he recovered and got out of our reach. it is certainly a different animal from any that we have yet seen. we also saw several of the heath cock with a long pointed tail and an uniform dark brown colour but could not kill one of them. they are much larger than the common dunghill fowls, and in their habits and manner of flying resemble the growse or prarie hen. at the distance of 4 miles further the road took us to the most distant fountain of the waters of the mighty Missouri in surch of which we have spent so many toilsome days and wristless nights. thus far I had accomplished one of those great objects on which my mind has been unalterably fixed for many years, judge then of the pleasure I felt in allying my thirst with this pure and ice cold water which issues from the base of a low mountain or hill of a gentle ascent for 1/2 a mile. the mountains are high on either hand leave this gap at the head of this rivulet through which the road passes. here I halted a few minutes and rested myself. two miles below McNeal had exultingly stood with a foot on each side of this little rivulet and thanked his god that he had lived to bestride the mighty & heretofore deemed endless Missouri. after refreshing ourselves we proceeded on to the top of the dividing ridge from which I discovered immence ranges of high mountains still to the West of us with their tops partially covered with snow. I now deceded the mountain about 3/4 of a mile which I found much steeper than on the opposite side, to a handsome bold running Creek of cold Clear water. here I first tasted the water of the great Columbia river. after a short halt of a few minutes we continued our march along the Indian road which lead us over steep hills and deep hollows to a spring on the side of a mountain where we found a sufficient quantity of dry willow brush for fuel, here we encamped for the night having traveled about 20 Miles. as we had killed nothing during the day we now boiled and eat the remainder of our pork, having yet a little flour and parched meal. at the creek on this side of the mountain I observed a species of deep perple currant lower in its growth, the stem more branched and leaf doubly as large as that of the Missouri. the leaf is covered on it's under disk with a hairy puberscence. the fruit is of the ordinary size and shape of the currant and is supported in the usual manner, but is ascid & very inferior in point of flavor.

this morning Capt. Clark set out early. found the river shoally, rapid shallow, and extreemly difficult. the men in the water almost all day. they are geting weak soar and much fortiegued; they complained of the fortiegue to which the navigation subjected them and wished to go by land Capt. C. engouraged them and passifyed them. one of the canoes was very near overseting in a rapid today. they proceeded but slowly. at noon they had a thunderstorm which continued about half an hour. their hunters killed 3 deer and a fawn. they encamped in a smoth plain near a few cottonwood trees on the Lard. side.-

[Clark, August 12, 1805] August 12th Monday 1805 We Set out early (Wind N E) proceeded on passed Several large Islands and three Small ones, the river much more Sholey than below which obliges us to haul the Canoes over those Sholes which Succkeed each other at Short intervales emencely laborious men much fatigued and weakened by being continualy in the water drawing the Canoes over the Sholes encamped on the Lard Side men complain verry much of the emence labour they are obliged to undergo & wish much to leave the river. I passify them. the weather Cool, and nothing to eate but venison, the hunters killed three Deer to day

[Lewis, August 13, 1805] Tuesday August 13th 1805. We set out very early on the Indian road which still led us through an open broken country in a westerly direction. a deep valley appeared to our left at the base of a high range of mountains which extended from S. E. to N. W. having their sides better clad with pine timber than we had been accustomed to see the mountains and their tops were also partially covered with snow. at the distance of five miles the road after leading us down a long decending valley for 2 Ms. brought us to a large creek about 10 yds. wide; this we passed and on rising the hill beyond it had a view of a handsome little valley to our left of about a mile in width through which from the appearance of the timber I conjectured that a river passed. I saw near the creek some bushes of the white maple, the shumate of the small species with the winged rib, and a species of honeysuckle much in it's growth and leaf like the small honeysuckle of the Missouri only reather larger and bears a globular berry as large as a garden pea and as white as wax. this berry is formed of a thin smooth pellicle which envellopes a soft white musilagenous substance in which there are several small brown seed irregularly scattered or intermixed without any sell or perceptable membranous covering.- we had proceeded about four miles through a wavy plain parallel to the valley or river bottom when at the distance of about a mile we saw two women, a man and some dogs on an eminence immediately before us. they appeared to vew us with attention and two of them after a few minutes set down as if to wait our arrival we continued our usual pace towards them. when we had arrived within half a mile of them I directed the party to halt and leaving my pack and rifle I took the flag which I unfurled and advanced singly towards them the women soon disappeared behind the hill, the man continued untill I arrived within a hundred yards of him and then likewise absconded. tho I frequently repeated the word tab-ba-bone sufficiently loud for him to have heard it. I now haistened to the top of the hill where they had stood but could see nothing of them. the dogs were less shye than their masters they came about me pretty close I therefore thought of tying a handkerchief about one of their necks with some beads and other trinkets and then let them loose to surch their fugitive owners thinking by this means to convince them of our pacific disposition towards them but the dogs would not suffer me to take hold of them; they also soon disappeared. I now made a signal fror the men to come on, they joined me and we pursued the back tarck of these Indians which lead us along the same road which we had been traveling. the road was dusty and appeared to have been much traveled lately both by men and horses. these praries are very poor the soil is of a light yellow clay, intermixed with small smooth gravel, and produces little else but prickly pears, and bearded grass about 3 inches high. the prickley pear are of three species that with a broad leaf common to the missouri; that of a globular form also common to the upper part of the Missouri and more especially after it enters the Rocky Mountains, also a 3rd peculiar to this country. it consists of small circular thick leaves with a much greater number of thorns. these thorns are stronger and appear to be barbed. the leaves grow from the margins of each other as in the broad leafed pear of the missouri, but are so slightly attatched that when the thorn touches your mockerson it adhears and brings with it the leaf covered in every direction with many others. this is much the most troublesome plant of the three. we had not continued our rout more than a mile when we were so fortunate as to meet with three female savages. the short and steep ravines which we passed concealed us from each other untill we arrived within 30 paces. a young woman immediately took to flight, an Elderly woman and a girl of about 12 years old remained. I instantly laid by my gun and advanced towards them. they appeared much allarmed but saw that we were to near for them to escape by flight they therefore seated themselves on the ground, holding down their heads as if reconciled to die which the expected no doubt would be their fate; I took the elderly woman by the hand and raised her up repeated the word tab-babone and strip up my shirt sieve to sew her my skin; to prove to her the truth of the ascertion that I was a white man for my face and hads which have been constantly exposed to the sun were quite as dark as their own. they appeared instantly reconciled, and the men coming up I gave these women some beads a few mockerson awls some pewter looking-glasses and a little paint. I directed Drewyer to request the old woman to recall the young woman who had run off to some distance by this time fearing she might allarm the camp before we approached and might so exasperate the natives that they would perhaps attack us without enquiring who we were. the old woman did as she was requested and the fugitive soon returned almost out of breath. I bestoed an equvolent portion of trinket on her with the others. I now painted their tawny cheeks with some vermillion which with this nation is emblematic of peace. after they had become composed I informed them by signs that I wished them to conduct us to their camp that we wer anxious to become acquainted with the chiefs and warriors of their nation. they readily obeyed and we set out, still pursuing the road down the river. we had marched about 2 miles when we met a party of about 60 warriors mounted on excellent horses who came in nearly full speed, when they arrived I advanced towards them with the flag leaving my gun with the party about 50 paces behind me. the chief and two others who were a little in advance of the main body spoke to the women, and they informed them who we were and exultingly shewed the presents which had been given them these men then advanced and embraced me very affectionately in their way which is by puting their left arm over you wright sholder clasping your back, while they apply their left cheek to yours and frequently vociforate the word ah-hi'-e, &h-hi'-e that is, I am much pleased, I am much rejoiced. bothe parties now advanced and we wer all carresed and besmeared with their grease and paint till I was heartily tired of the national hug. I now had the pipe lit and gave them smoke; they seated themselves in a circle around us and pulled of their mockersons before they would receive or smoke the pipe. this is a custom among them as I afterwards learned indicative of a sacred obligation of sincerity in their profession of friendship given by the act of receiving and smoking the pipe of a stranger. or which is as much as to say that they wish they may always go bearfoot if they are not sincere; a pretty heavy penalty if they are to march through the plains of their country. after smoking a few pipes with them I distributed some trifles among them, with which they seemed much pleased particularly with the blue beads and vermillion. I now informed the chief that the object of our visit was a friendly one, that after we should reach his camp I would undertake to explain to him fully those objects, who we wer, from whence we had come and wither we were going; that in the mean time I did not care how soon we were in motion, as the sun was very warm and no water at hand. they now put on their mockersons, and the principal chief Ca-me-ah-wait made a short speach to the warriors. I gave him the flag which I informed him was an emblem of peace among whitemen and now that it had been received by him it was to be respected as the bond of union between us. I desired him to march on, which did and we followed him; the dragoons moved on in squadron in our rear. after we had marched about a mile in this order he halted them ang gave a second harang; after which six or eight of the young men road forward to their encampment and no further regularity was observed in the order of march. I afterwards understood that the Indians we had first seen this morning had returned and allarmed the camp; these men had come out armed cap a pe for action expecting to meet with their enemies the Minnetares of Fort de Prarie whome they Call Rah'-kees. they were armed with bows arrow and Shield except three whom I observed with small pieces such as the N. W. Company furnish the natives with which they had obtained from the Rocky Mountain Indians on the yellow stone river with whom they are at peace. on our arrival at their encampmen on the river in a handsome level and fertile bottom at the distance of 4 Ms. from where we had first met them they introduced us to a londge made of willow brush and an old leather lodge which had been prepared for our reception by the young men which the chief had dispatched for that purpose. Here we were seated on green boughs and the skins of Antelopes. one of the warriors then pulled up the grass in the center of the lodge forming a smal circle of about 2 feet in diameter the chief next produced his pipe and native tobacco and began a long cerimony of the pipe when we were requested to take of our mockersons, the Chief having previously taken off his as well as all the warriors present. this we complyed with; the Chief then lit his pipe at the fire kindled in this little magic circle, and standing on the oposite side of the circle uttered a speach of several minutes in length at the conclusion of which he pointed the stem to the four cardinal points of the heavens first begining at the East and ending with the North. he now presented the pipe to me as if desirous that I should smoke, but when I reached my hand to receive it, he drew it back and repeated the same cremony three times, after which he pointed the stern first to the heavens then to the center of the magic circle smoked himself with three whifs and held the pipe untill I took as many as I thought proper; he then held it to each of the white persons and then gave it to be consumed by his warriors. this pipe was made of a dense simitransparent green stone very highly polished about 2 1/2 inches long and of an oval figure, the bowl being in the same direction with the stem. a small piece of birned clay is placed in the bottom of the bowl to seperate the tobacco from the end of the stem and is of an irregularly rounded figure not fitting the tube purfectly close in order that the smoke may pass. this is the form of the pipe. their tobacco is of the same kind of that used by the Minnetares Mandans and Ricares of the Missouri. the Shoshonees do not cultivate this plant, but obtain it from the Rocky mountain Indians and some of the bands of their own nation who live further south. I now explained to them the objects of our journey &c. all the women and children of the camp were shortly collected about the lodge to indulge themselves with looking at us, we being the first white persons they had ever seen. after the cerimony of the pipe was over I distributed the remainder of the small articles I had brought with me among the women and children. by this time it was late in the evening and we had not taisted any food since the evening before. the Chief informed us that they had nothing but berries to eat and gave us some cakes of serviceberries and Choke cherries which had been dryed in the sun; of these I made a hearty meal, and then walked to the river, which I found about 40 yards wide very rapid clear and about 3 feet deep. the banks low and abrupt as those of the upper part of the Missouri, and the bed formed of loose stones and gravel. Cameahwait informed me that this stream discharged itself into another doubly as large at the distance of half a days march which came from the S. W. but he added on further enquiry that there was but little more timber below the junction of those rivers than I saw here, and that the river was confined between inacessable mountains, was very rapid and rocky insomuch that it was impossible for us to pass either by land or water down this river to the great lake where the white men lived as he had been informed. this was unwelcome information but I still hoped that this account had been exagerated with a view to detain us among them. as to timber I could discover not any that would answer the purpose of constructing canoes or in short more than was bearly necessary for fuel consisting of the narrow leafed cottonwood and willow, also the red willow Choke Cherry service berry and a few currant bushes such as were common on the Missouri. these people had been attacked by the Minetares of Fort de prarie this spring and about 20 of them killed and taken prisoners. on this occasion they lost a great part of their horses and all their lodges except that which they had erected for our accomodation; they were now living in lodges of a conic figure made of willow brush. I still observe a great number of horses feeding in every direction around their camp and therefore entertain but little doubt but we shall be enable to furnish ourselves with an adiquate number to transport our stores even if we are compelled to travel by land over these mountains. on my return to my lodge an indian called me in to his bower and gave me a small morsel of the flesh of an antelope boiled, and a peice of a fresh salmon roasted; both which I eat with a very good relish. this was the first salmon I had seen and perfectly convinced me that we were on the waters of the Pacific Ocean. the course of this river is a little to the North of west as far as I can discover it; and is bounded on each side by a range of high Mountains. tho those on the E. side are lowest and more distant from the river.

This evening the Indians entertained us with their dancing nearly all night. at 12 O'Ck. I grew sleepy and retired to rest leaving the men to amuse themselves with the Indians. I observe no essential difference between the music and manner of dancing among this nation and those of the Missouri. I was several times awoke in the course of the night by their yells but was too much fortiegued to be deprived of a tolerable sound night's repose.

This morning Capt Clark set out early having previously dispatched some hunters ahead. it was cool and cloudy all the forepart of the day. at 8 A.M. they had a slight rain. they passed a number of shoals over which they were obliged to drag the canoes; the men in the water 3/4ths of the day, they passed a bold runing stream 7 yds. wide on the Lard. side just below a high point of Limestone rocks. this stream we call McNeal's Creek after Hugh McNeal one of our party. this creek heads in the Mountains to the East and forms a handsome valley for some miles between the mountains. from the top of this limestone Clift above the creek The beaver's head boar N 24° E. 12 Ms. the course of Wisdom river or that which the opening of it's valley makes through the mountains is N. 25 W. to the gap through which Jefferson's river enters the mountains above is S 18° W 10 M. they killed one deer only today. saw a number of Otter some beaver Antelopes ducks gees and Grains. they caught a number of fine trout as they have every day since I left them. they encamped on Lrd. in a smooth level prarie near a few cottonwood trees, but were obliged to make use of the dry willow brush for fuel.

[Clark, August 13, 1805] August 13th Tuesday 1805 a verry Cool morning the Thermometer Stood at 52 a 0 all the fore part of the day. Cloudy at 8 oClock a mist of rain we proceeded on passed inumerable Sholes obliged to haul the boat 3/4 of the Day over the Shole water. passed the mouth of a bold running Stream 7 yards wide on the Lard Side below a high Point of Limestone rocks on the Stard Side this Creek heads in the mountains to the easte and forms a Vallie between two mountains. Call this stream McNeal Creek From the top of this rock the Point of the Beaver head hill bears N. 24° E 12 ms.

The Course of the Wisdom river is- N. 25 W

The gap at the place the river passes thro a mountain in advance is- S. 18° W. 10 ms.

proceeded on and Encamped on the Lard side no wood except dry willows and them Small, one Deer killed to day. The river obliges the men to undergo great fatigue and labour in hauling the Canoes over the Sholes in the Cold water naked.

[Lewis, August 14, 1805] Wednesday August 14th In order to give Capt. Clark time to reach the forks of Jefferson's river I concluded to spend this day at the Shoshone Camp and obtain what information I could with rispect to the country. as we had nothing but a little flour and parched meal to eat except the berries with which the Indians furnished us I directed Drewyer and Shields to hunt a few hours and try to kill something, the Indians furnished them with horses and most of their young men also turned out to hunt. the game which they principally hunt is the Antelope which they pursue on horseback and shoot with their arrows. this animal is so extreemly fleet and dureable that a single horse has no possible chance to overtake them or run them down. the Indians are therefore obliged to have recorce to strategem when they discover a herd of the Antelope they seperate and scatter themselves to the distance of five or six miles in different directions arround them generally scelecting some commanding eminence for a stand; some one or two now pursue the herd at full speed over the hills values gullies and the sides of precipices that are tremendious to view. thus after runing them from five to six or seven miles the fresh horses that were in waiting head them and drive them back persuing them as far or perhaps further quite to the other extreem of the hunters who now in turn pursue on their fresh horses thus worrying the poor animal down and finally killing them with their arrows. forty or fifty hunters will be engaged for half a day in this manner and perhaps not kill more than two or three Antelopes. they have but few Elk or black tailed deer, and the common red deer they cannot take as they secrete themselves in the brush when pursued, and they have only the bow and arrow wich is a very slender dependence for killing any game except such as they can run down with their horses. I was very much entertained with a view of this indian chase; it was after a herd of about 10 Antelope and about 20 hunters. it lasted about 2 hours and considerable part of the chase in view from my tent. about 1 A.M. the hunters returned had not killed a single Antelope, and their horses foaming with sweat. my hunters returned soon after and had been equally unsuccessfull. I now directed McNeal to make me a little paist with the flour and added some berries to it which I found very pallateable.

The means I had of communicating with these people was by way of Drewyer who understood perfectly the common language of jesticulation or signs which seems to be universally understood by all the Nations we have yet seen. it is true that this language is imperfect and liable to error but is much less so than would be expected. the strong parts of the ideas are seldom mistaken.

I now prevailed on the Chief to instruct me with rispect to the geography of his country. this he undertook very cheerfully, by delienating the rivers on the ground. but I soon found that his information fell far short of my expectation or wishes. he drew the river on which we now are to which he placed two branches just above us, which he shewed me from the openings of the mountains were in view; he next made it discharge itself into a large river which flowed from the S. W. about ten miles below us, then continued this joint stream in the same direction of this valley or N. W. for one days march and then enclined it to the West for 2 more days march, here he placed a number of beeps of sand on each side which he informed me represented the vast mountains of rock eternally covered with snow through which the river passed. that the perpendicular and even juting rocks so closely hemned in the river that there was no possibilyte of passing along the shore; that the bed of the river was obstructed by sharp pointed rocks and the rapidity of the stream such that the whole surface of the river was beat into perfect foam as far as the eye could reach. that the mountains were also inaccessible to man or horse. he said that this being the state of the country in that direction that himself nor none of his nation had ever been further down the river than these mountains. I then enquired the state of the country on either side of the river but he could not inform me. he said there was an old man of his nation a days march below who could probably give me some information of the country to the N. W. and refered me to an old man then present for that to the S. W.- the Chief further informed me that he had understood from the persed nosed Indians who inhabit this river below the rocky mountains that it ran a great way toward the seting sun and finally lost itself in a great lake of water which was illy taisted, and where the white men lived. I next commenced my enquiries of the old man to whom I had been refered for information relative the country S W. of us. this he depicted with horrors and obstructions scarcely inferior to that just mentioned. he informed me that the band of this nation to which he belonged resided at the distance of 20 days march from hence not far from the white people with whom they traded for horses mules cloth metal beads and the shells which they woar as orniment being those of a species of perl oister. that the course to his relations was a little to the West of South. that in order to get to his relations the first seven days we should be obliged to climb over steep and rocky mountains where we could find no game to kill nor anything but roots such as a ferce and warlike nation lived on whom he called the broken mockersons or mockersons with holes, and said inhabited those mountains and lived like the bear of other countries among the rocks and fed on roots or the flesh of such horses as they could take or steel from those who passed through their country. that in passing this country the feet of our horses would be so much wounded with the stones many of them would give out. the next part of the rout was about 10 days through a dry and parched sandy desert in which no food at this season for either man or horse, and in which we must suffer if not perish for the want of water. that the sun had now dryed up the little pools of water which exist through this desert plain in the spring season and had also scorched all the grass. that no animal inhabited this plain on which we could hope to subsist. that about the center of this plain a large river passed from S. E. to N. W. which was navigable but afforded neither Salmon nor timber. that beyond this plain thee or four days march his relations lived in a country tolerable fertile and partially covered with timber on another large river which ran in the same direction of the former. that this last discharged itself into a large river on which many numerous nations lived with whom his relations were at war but whether this last discharged itself into the great lake or not he did not know. that from his relations it was yet a great distance to the great or stinking lake as they call the Ocean. that the way which such of his nation as had been to the Stinking lake traveled was up the river on which they lived and over to that on which the white people lived which last they knew discharged itself into the Ocean, and that this was the way which he would advise me to travel if I was determined to proceed to the Ocean but would advise me to put off the journey untill the next spring when he would conduct me. I thanked him for his information and advise and gave him a knife with which he appeared to be much gratifyed. from this narative I was convinced that the streams of which he had spoken as runing through the plains and that on which his relations lived were southern branches of the Columbia, heading with the rivers Apostles and Collorado, and that the rout he had pointed out was to the Vermillion Sea or gulph of Callifornia. I therefore told him that this rout was more to the South than I wished to travel, and requested to know if there was no rout on the left of this river on which we now are, by means of which, I could intercept it below the mountains through which it passes; but he could not inform me of any except that of the barren plain which he said joined the mountain on that side and through which it was impossible for us to pass at this season even if we were fortunate enough to escape from the broken mockerson Indians. I now asked Cameahwait by what rout the Pierced nosed indians, who he informed me inhabited this river below the mountains, came over to the Missouri; this he informed me was to the north, but added that the road was a very bad one as he had been informed by them and that they had suffered excessively with hunger on the rout being obliged to subsist for many days on berries alone as there was no game in that part of the mountains which were broken rockey and so thickly covered with timber that they could scarcely pass. however knowing that Indians had passed, and did pass, at this season on that side of this river to the same below the mountains, my rout was instantly settled in my own mind, povided the account of this river should prove true on an investigation of it, which I was determined should be made before we would undertake the rout by land in any direction. I felt perfectly satisfyed, that if the Indians could pass these mountains with their women and Children, that we could also pass them; and that if the nations on this river below the mountains were as numerous as they were stated to be that they must have some means of subsistence which it would be equally in our power to procure in the same country. they informed me that there was no buffaloe on the West side of these mountains; that the game consisted of a few Elk deer and Antelopes, and that the natives subsisted on fish and roots principally. in this manner I spent the day smoking with them and acquiring what information I could with respect to their country. they informed me that they could pass to the Spaniards by the way of the yellowstone river in 10 days. I can discover that these people are by no means friendly to the Spaniard their complaint is, that the Spaniards will not let them have fire arms and amunition, that they put them off by telling them that if they suffer them to have guns they will kill each other, thus leaving them defenceless and an easy prey to their bloodthirsty neighbours to the East of them, who being in possession of fire arms hunt them up and murder them without rispect to sex or age and plunder them of their horses on all occasions. they told me that to avoid their enemies who were eternally harrassing them that they were obliged to remain in the interior of these mountains at least two thirds of the year where the suffered as we then saw great heardships for the want of food sometimes living for weeks without meat and only a little fish roots and berries. but this added Cameahwait, with his ferce eyes and lank jaws grown meager for the want of food, would not be the case if we had guns, we could then live in the country of buffaloe and eat as our enimies do and not be compelled to hide ourselves in these mountains and live on roots and berries as the bear do. we do not fear our enimies when placed on an equal footing with them. I told them that the Minnetares Mandans & Recares of the Missouri had promised us to desist from making war on them & that we would indevour to find the means of making the Minnetares of fort d Prarie or as they call them Pahkees desist from waging war against them also. that after our finally returning to our homes towards the rising sun whitemen would come to them with an abundance of guns and every other article necessary to their defence and comfort, and that they would be enabled to supply themselves with these articles on reasonable terms in exchange for the skins of the beaver Otter and Ermin so abundant in their country. they expressed great pleasure at this information and said they had been long anxious to see the whitemen that traded guns; and that we might rest assured of their friendship and that they would do whatever we wished them.

I now told Cameahwait that I wished him to speak to his people and engage them to go with me tomorrow to the forks of Jeffersons river where our baggage was by this time arrived with another Chief and a large party of whitemen who would wait my return at that place. that I wish them to take with them about 30 spare horses to transport our baggage to this place where we would then remain sometime among them and trade with them for horses, and finally concert our future plans for geting on to the ocean and of the traid which would be extended to them after our return to our homes. he complyed with my request and made a lengthey harrangue to his village. he returned in about an hour and a half and informed me that they would be ready to accompany me in the morning. I promised to reward them for their trouble. Drewyer who had had a good view of their horses estimated them at 400. most of them are fine horses. indeed many of them would make a figure on the South side of James River or the land of fine horses.- I saw several with Spanish brands on them, and some mules which they informed me that they had also obtained from the Spaniards. I also saw a bridle bit of spanish manufactary, and sundry other articles which I have no doubt were obtained from the same source. notwithstanding the extreem poverty of those poor people they are very merry they danced again this evening untill midnight. each warrior keep one ore more horses tyed by a cord to a stake near his lodge both day and night and are always prepared for action at a moments warning. they fight on horseback altogether. I observe that the large flies are extreemly troublesome to the horses as well as ourselves.

The morning being cold and the men stif and soar from the exertions of yesterday Capt. Clark did not set out this morning untill 7 A.M. the river was so crooked and rapid that they made but little way at one mile he passed a bold runing stream on Stard. which heads in a mountain to the North, on which there is snow. this we called track Creek. it is 4 yard wide and 3 feet deep at 7 Ms. passed a stout stream which heads in some springs under the foot of the mountains on Lard. the river near the mountain they found one continued rapid, with was extreemly laborious and difficult to ascend. this evening Charbono struck his indian Woman for which Capt. C. gave him a severe repremand. Joseph and Reubin Fields killed 4 deer and an Antelope, Capt. C. killed a buck. several of the men have lamed themselves by various accedents in working the canoes through this difficult part of the river, and Capt. C. was obliged personally to assist them in this labour. they encamped this evening on Lard. side near the rattlesnake clift

[Clark, August 14, 1805] August 14th Wednesday 1805. a Cold morning wind from the S. W. The Thermometer Stood at 51° a 0, at Sunrise the morning being cold and men Stiff. I deturmind to delay & take brackfast at the place we Encamped. we Set out at 7 oClock and proceeded on river verry Crooked and rapid as below Some fiew trees on the borders near the mountain, passed a bold running Stream at 1 mile on the Stard. Side which heads in a mountain to the North on which there is Snow passed a bold running Stream on the Lard. Side which heads in a Spring undr. a mountain. the river near the mountain is one continued rapid, which requres great labour to push & haul the Canoes up. We Encamped on the Lard Side near the place the river passes thro the mountain. I checked our interpreter for Strikeing his woman at their Dinner.

The hunters Jo. & R. Fields killed 4 Deer & a antilope, I killed a fat
Buck in the evening, Several men have hurt themselves pushing up the
Canoes. I am oblige to a pole occasionally.

[Lewis, August 15, 1805] Thursday August 15th 1805. This morning I arrose very early and as hungary as a wolf. I had eat nothing yesterday except one scant meal of the flour and berries except the dryed cakes of berries which did not appear to satisfy my appetite as they appeared to do those of my Indian friends. I found on enquiry of McNeal that we had only about two pounds of flour remaining. this I directed him to divide into two equal parts and to cook the one half this morning in a kind of pudding with the hurries as he had done yesterday and reserve the ballance for the evening. on this new fashoned pudding four of us breakfasted, giving a pretty good allowance also to the Chief who declared it the best thing he had taisted for a long time. he took a little of the Hour in his hand, taisted and examined very scrutinously and asked me if we made it of roots. I explained to him the manner in which it grew. I hurried the departure of the Indians. the Chief addressed them several times before they would move they seemed very reluctant to accompany me. I at length asked the reason and he told me that some foolish persons among them had suggested the idea that we were in league with the Pahkees and had come on in order to decoy them into an ambuscade where their enimies were waiting to receive them. but that for his part he did not believe it. I readily perceived that our situation was not entirely free from danger as the transision from suspicion to the confermation of the fact would not be very difficult in the minds of these ignorant people who have been accustomed from their infancy to view every stranger as an enimy. I told Cameahwait that I was sorry to find that they had put so little confidence in us, that I knew they were not acquainted with whitemen and therefore could forgive them. that among whitemen it was considered disgracefull to lye or entrap an enimy by falsehood. I told him if they continued to think thus meanly of us that they might rely on it that no whitemen would ever come to trade with them or bring them arms and amunition and that if the bulk of his nation still entertained this opinion I still hoped that there were some among them that were not affraid to die, that were men and would go with me and convince themselves of the truth of what I had asscerted. that there was a party of whitemen waiting my return either at the forks of Jefferson's river or a little below coining on to that place in canoes loaded with provisions and merchandize. he told me for his own part he was determined to go, that he was not affraid to die. I soon found that I had touched him on the right string; to doubt the bravery of a savage is at once to put him on his metal. he now mounted his horse and haranged his village a third time; the perport of which as he afterwards told me was to inform them that he would go with us and convince himself of the truth or falsity of what we had told him if he was sertain he should be killed, that he hoped there were some of them who heard him were not affraid to die with him and if there was to let him see them mount their horses and prepare to set out. shortly after this harange he was joined by six or eight only and with these I smoked a pipe and directed the men to put on their packs being determined to set out with them while I had them in the humour at half after 12 we set out, several of the old women were crying and imploring the great sperit to protect their warriors as if they were going to inevitable distruction. we had not proceeded far before our party was augmented by ten or twelve more, and before we reached the Creek which we had passed in the morning of the 13th it appeared to me that we had all the men of the village and a number of women with us. this may serve in some measure to ilustrate the capricious disposition of those people who never act but from the impulse of the moment. they were now very cheerfull and gay, and two hours ago they looked as sirly as so many imps of satturn. when we arrived at the spring on the side of the mountain where we had encamped on the 12th day I insited on halting to let the horses graize with which I complyed and gave the Indians smoke. they are excessively fond of the pipe; but have it not much in their power to indulge themselves with even their native tobacco as they do not cultivate it themselves.- after remaining about an hour we again set out, and by engaging to make compensation to four of them for their trouble obtained the previlege of riding with an indian myself and a similar situation for each of my party. I soon found it more tiresome riding without tirrups than walking and of course chose the latter making the Indian carry my pack. about sunset we reached the upper part of the level valley of the Cove which now called Shoshone Cove. the grass being birned on the North side of the river we passed over to the south and encamped near some willow brush about 4 miles above the narrow pass between the hills noticed as I came up this cove the river was here about six yards wide, and frequently darned up by the beaver. I had sent Drewyer forward this evening before we halted to kill some meat but he was unsuccessfull and did not rejoin us untill after dark I now cooked and among six of us eat the remaining pound of flour stired in a little boiling water.- Capt. Clark delayed again this morning untill after breakfast, when he set out and passed between low and rugged mountains which had a few pine trees distributed over them the clifts are formed of limestone and a hard black rock intermixed. no trees on the river, the bottoms narrow river crooked shallow shoaly and rapid. the water is as coald as that of the best springs in our country. the men as usual suffered excessively with fatiegue and the coldness of the water to which they were exposed for hours together. at the distance of 6 miles by water they passed the entrance of a bold creek on Stard. side 10 yds. wide and 3 f. 3 i. deep which we called Willard's Creek after Alexander Willard one of our party. at 4 miles by water from their encampment of las evening passed a bold branch which tumbled down a steep precipice of rocks from the mountains on the Lard. Capt Clark was very near being bitten twice today by rattlesnakes, the Indian woman also narrowly escaped. they caught a number of fine trout. Capt. Clark killed a buck which was the only game killed today. the venison has an uncommon bitter taist which is unpleasent. I presume it proceeds from some article of their food, perhaps the willow on the leaves of which they feed very much. they encamped this evening on the Lard. side near a few cottonwood trees about which there were the remains of several old Indian brush lodges.

[Clark, August 15, 1805] August 15th Thursday 1805 a Cool windey morning wind from the S W we proceeded on thro a ruged low mountain water rapid as usial passed a bold running Stream which falls from the mountain on the Lard. Side at 4 miles, also a bold running Stream 10 yards wide on the Stard Side 8 feet 3 In. Deep at 6 miles, Willards Creek the bottoms narrow, the Clifs of a Dark brown Stone Some limestone intermixed- an Indian road passes on the Lard Side latterly used. Took a Meridian altitude at the Comsnt. of the Mountain with Octent 65° 47' 0". The Latd. 44° 0' 48 1/10" proceeded on with great labour & fatigue to the Mouth of a Small run on the Lard. Side

passed Several Spring runs, the men Complain much of their fatigue and being repetiedly in the water which weakens them much perticularly as they are obliged to live on pore Deer meet which has a Singular bitter taste. I have no accounts of Capt Lewis Sence he Set out

In walking on Shore I Saw Several rattle Snakes and narrowly escaped at two different times, as also the Squar when walking with her husband on Shore- I killed a Buck nothing else killed to day- This mountn. I call rattle Snake mountain. not one tree on either Side to day

[Lewis, August 16, 1805] Friday August 16th 1805. I sent Drewyer and Shields before this morning in order to kill some meat as neither the Indians nor ourselves had any thing to eat. I informed the Ceif of my view in this measure, and requested that he would keep his young men with us lest by their hooping and noise they should allarm the game and we should get nothing to eat, but so strongly were there suspicions exited by this measure that two parties of discovery immediately set out one on ech side of the valley to watch the hunters as I beleive to see whether they had not been sent to give information of their approach to an enemy that they still preswaided themselves were lying in wait for them. I saw that any further effort to prevent their going would only add strength to their suspicions and therefore said no more. after the hunters had been gone about an hour we set out. we had just passed through the narrows when we saw one of the spies comeing up the level plain under whip, the chief pawsed a little and seemed somewhat concerned. I felt a good deel so myself and began to suspect that by some unfortunate accedent that perhaps some of there enimies had straggled hither at this unlucky moment; but we were all agreeably disappointed on the arrival of the young man to learn that he had come to inform us that one of the whitemen had killed a deer. in an instant they all gave their horses the whip and I was taken nearly a mile before I could learn what were the tidings; as I was without tirrups and an Indian behind me the jostling was disagreeable I therefore reigned up my horse and forbid the indian to whip him who had given him the lash at every jum for a mile fearing he should loose a part of the feast. the fellow was so uneasy that he left me the horse dismounted and ran on foot at full speed, I am confident a mile. when they arrived where the deer was which was in view of me they dismounted and ran in tumbling over each other like a parcel of famished dogs each seizing and tearing away a part of the intestens which had been previously thrown out by Drewyer who killed it; the seen was such when I arrived that had I not have had a pretty keen appetite myself I am confident I should not have taisted any part of the venison shortly. each one had a peice of some discription and all eating most ravenously. some were eating the kidnies the melt and liver and the blood runing from the corners of their mouths, others were in a similar situation with the paunch and guts but the exuding substance in this case from their lips was of a different discription. one of the last who attacted my attention particularly had been fortunate in his allotment or reather active in the division, he had provided himself with about nine feet of the small guts one end of which he was chewing on while with his hands he was squezzing the contents out at the other. I really did not untill now think that human nature ever presented itself in a shape so nearly allyed to the brute creation. I viewed these poor starved divils with pity and compassion I directed McNeal to skin the deer and reserved a quarter, the ballance I gave the Chief to be divided among his people; they devoured the whole of it nearly without cooking. I now boar obliquely to the left in order to interscept the creek where there was some brush to make a fire, and arrived at this stream where Drewyer had killed a second deer; here nearly the same seene was encored. a fire being kindled we cooked and eat and gave the ballance of the two deer to the Indians who eat the whole of them even to the soft parts of the hoofs. Drewyer joined us at breakfast with a third deer. of this I reserved a quarter and gave the ballance to the Indians. they all appeared now to have filled themselves and were in a good humour. this morning early soon after the hunters set out a considerable part of our escort became allarmed and returned 28 men and three women only continued with us. after eating and suffering the horses to graize about 2 hours we renued our march and towads evening arrived at the lower part of the cove Shields killed an Antelope on the way a part of which we took and gave the remainder to the Indians. being now informed of the place at which I expected to meat Capt C. and the party they insisted on making a halt, which was complyed with. we now dismounted and the Chief with much cerimony put tippets about our necks such as they temselves woar I redily perceived that this was to disguise us and owed it's origine to the same cause already mentioned. to give them further confidence I put my cocked hat with feather on the chief and my over shirt being of the Indian form my hair deshivled and skin well browned with the sun I wanted no further addition to make me a complete Indian in appearance the men followed my example and we were son completely metamorphosed. I again repeated to them the possibility of the party not having arrived at the place which I expected they were, but assured them they could not be far below, lest by not finding them at the forks their suspicions might arrise to such hight as to induce them to return precipitately. we now set out and rode briskly within sight of the forks making one of the Indians carry the flag that our own party should know who we were. when we arrived in sight at the distance of about 2 miles I discovered to my mortification that the party had not arrived, and the Indians slackened their pace. I now scarcely new what to do and feared every moment when they would halt altogether, I now determined to restore their confidence cost what it might and therefore gave the Chief my gun and told him that if his enimies were in those bushes before him that he could defend himself with that gun, that for my own part I was not affraid to die and if I deceived him he might make what uce of the gun he thought proper or in other words that he might shoot me. the men also gave their guns to other indians which seemed to inspire them with more confidence; they sent their spies before them at some distance and when I drew near the place I thought of the notes which I had left and directed Drewyer to go with an Indian man and bring them to me which he did. the indian seeing him take the notes from the stake on which they had been plased I now had recource to a stratagem in which I thought myself justifyed by the occasion, but which I must confess set a little awkward. it had it's desired effect. after reading the notes which were the same I had left I told the Chief that when I had left my brother Chief with the party below where the river entered the mountain that we both agreed not to bring the canoes higher up than the next forks of the river above us wherever this might happen, that there he was to wait my return, should he arrive first, and that in the event of his not being able to travel as fast as usual from the difficulty of the water, that he was to send up to the first forks above him and leave a note informing me where he was, that this note was left here today and that he informed me that he was just below the mountains and was coming on slowly up, and added that I should wait here for him, but if they did not beleive me that I should send a man at any rate to the Chief and they might also send one of their young men with him, that myself and two others would remain with them at this place. this plan was readily adopted and one of the young men offered his services; I promised him a knife and some beads as a reward for his confidence in us. most of them seemed satisfyed but there were several that complained of the Chief's exposing them to danger unnecessarily and said that we told different stories, in short a few were much dissatisfyed. I wrote a note to Capt. Clark by the light of some willow brush and directed Drewyer to set out early being confident that there was not a moment to spare. the chief and five or six others slept about my fire and the others hid themselves in various parts of the willow brush to avoid the enimy whom they were fearfull would attack them in the course of the night. I now entertained various conjectures myself with rispect to the cause of Capt. Clarks detention and was even fearful I that he had found the river so difficult that he had halted below the Rattlesnake bluffs. I knew that if these people left me that they would immediately disperse and secrete themselves in the mountains where it would be impossible to find them or at least in vain to pursue them and that they would spread the allarm to all other bands within our reach & of course we should be disappointed in obtaining horses, which would vastly retard and increase the labour of our voyage and I feared might so discourage the men as to defeat the expedition altogether. my mind was in reallity quite as gloomy all this evening as the most affrighted indian but I affected cheerfullness to keep the Indians so who were about me. we finally laid down, and the Chief placed himself by the side of my musquetoe bier. I slept but little as might be well expected, my mind dwelling on the state of the expedition which I have ever held in equal estimation with my own existence, and the fait of which appeared at this moment to depend in a great measure upon the caprice of a few savages who are ever as fickle as the wind. I had mentioned to the chief several times that we had with us a woman of his nation who had been taken prisoner by the Minnetares, and that by means of her I hoped to explain myself more fully than I could do by signs. some of the party had also told the Indians that we had a man with us who was black and had short curling hair, this had excited their curiossity very much. and they seemed quite as anxious to see this monster as they wer the merchandize which we had to barter for their horses.

at 7 A M. Capt. C. set out after breakfast. he changed the hands in some of the canoes; they proceeded with more ease than yesterday, yet they found the river still rapid and shallow insomuch that they were obliged to drag the large canoes the greater part of the day. the water excessively cold. in the evening they passed several bad rapids. considerable quantities of the buffaloe clover grows along the narrow bottoms through which they passed. there was no timber except a few scatiring small pine on the hills. willow service berry and currant bushes were the growth of the river bottoms. they geatherd considerable quantities of service berries, and caught some trout. one deer was killed by the hunters who slept out last night. and did not join the party untill 10 A.M.

Capt. Clark sent the hunters this evening up to the forks of the river which he discovered from an eminence; they mus have left this place but a little time before we arrived. this evening they encamped on the Lard. side only a few miles below us. and were obliged like ourselves to make use of small willow brush for fuel. the men were much fatigued and exhausted this evening.

[Clark, August 16, 1805] August 16th Friday 1805 as this morning was cold and the men fatigued Stiff and Chilled deturmined me to detain & take brackfast before I Set out. I changed the hands and Set out at 7 oClock proceeded on Something better than yesterday for the fore part of the Day passed Several rapids in the latter part of the day near the hills river passed between 2 hills I saw a great number of Service berries now ripe. the Yellow Current are also Common I observe the long leaf Clover in great plenty in the vallie below this vallie- Some fiew tres on the river no timber on the hills or mountn. except a fiew Small Pine & Cedar. The Thmtr. Stood at 48° a. 0 at Sunrise wind S W. The hunters joined me at 1 oClock, I dispatched 2 men to prosue an Indian roade over the hills for a fiew miles, at the narrows I assended a mountain from the top of which I could See that the river forked near me the left hand appeared the largest & bore S. E. the right passed from the West thro an extensive Vallie, I could See but three Small trees in any Direction from the top of this mountain. passed an Isld. and Encamped ion the Lard. Side the only wood was Small willows

[Lewis, August 17, 1805] Saturday August 17th 1805. This morning I arrose very early and dispatched Drewyer and the Indian down the river. sent Shields to hunt. I made McNeal cook the remainder of our meat which afforded a slight breakfast for ourselves and the Cheif. Drewyer had been gone about 2 hours when an Indian who had straggled some little distance down the river returned and reported that the whitemen were coming, that he had seen them just below. they all appeared transported with joy, & the chef repeated his fraturnal hug. I felt quite as much gratifyed at this information as the Indians appeared to be. Shortly after Capt. Clark arrived with the Interpreter Charbono, and the Indian woman, who proved to be a sister of the Chif Cameahwait. the meeting of those people was really affecting, particularly between Sah cah-gar-we-ah and an Indian woman, who had been taken prisoner at the same time with her, and who had afterwards escaped from the Minnetares and rejoined her nation. At noon the Canoes arrived, and we had the satisfaction once more to find ourselves all together, with a flattering prospect of being able to obtain as many horses shortly as would enable us to prosicute our voyage by land should that by water be deemed unadvisable.

We now formed our camp just below the junction of the forks on the Lard. side in a level smooth bottom covered with a fine terf of greensward. here we unloaded our canoes and arranged our baggage on shore; formed a canopy of one of our large sails and planted some willow brush in the ground to form a shade for the Indians to set under while we spoke to them, which we thought it best to do this evening. accordingly about 4 P.M. we called them together and through the medium of Labuish, Charbono and Sah-cah-gar-weah, we communicated to them fully the objects which had brought us into this distant part of the country, in which we took care to make them a conspicuous object of our own good wishes and the care of our government. we made them sensible of their dependance on the will of our government for every species of merchandize as well for their defence & comfort; and apprized them of the strength of our government and it's friendly dispositions towards them. we also gave them as a reason why we wished to petrate the country as far as the ocean to the west of them was to examine and find out a more direct way to bring merchandize to them. that as no trade could be carryed on with them before our return to our homes that it was mutually advantageous to them as well as to ourselves that they should render us such aids as they had it in their power to furnish in order to haisten our voyage and of course our return home. that such were their horses to transport our baggage without which we could not subsist, and that a pilot to conduct us through the mountains was also necessary if we could not decend the river by water. but that we did not ask either their horses or their services without giving a satisfactory compensation in return. that at present we wished them to collect as many horses as were necessary to transport our baggage to their village on the Columbia where we would then trade with them at our leasure for such horses as they could spare us.- They appeared well pleased with what had been said. the chief thanked us for friendship towards himself and nation & declared his wish to serve us in every rispect; that he was sorry to find that it must yet be some time before they could be furnished with firearms but said they could live as they had done heretofore untill we brought them as we had promised. he said they had not horses enough with them at present to remove our baggage to their village over the mountain, but that he would return tomorrow and encourage his people to come over with their horses and that he would bring his own and assist us. this was complying with all we wished at present. we next enquired who were chiefs among them. Cameahwait pointed out two others whom he said were Chiefs we gave him a medal of the small size with the likeness of Mr. Jefferson the President of the U States in releif on one side and clasp hands with a pipe and tomahawk on the other, to the other Chiefs we gave each a small medal which were struck in the Presidency of George Washing Esqr. we also gave small medals of the last discription to two young men whom the 1st Chief informed us wer good young men and much rispected among them. we gave the 1st Chief an uniform coat shirt a pair of scarlet legings a carrot of tobacco and some small articles to each of the others we gave a shirt leging handkerchief a knife some tobacco and a few small articles we also distributed a good quantity paint mockerson awls knives beads lookingglasses &c among the other Indians and gave them a plentifull meal of lyed corn which was the first they had ever eaten in their lives. they were much pleased with it. every article about us appeared to excite astonishment in ther minds; the appearance of the men, their arms, the canoes, our manner of working them, the back man york and the segacity of my dog were equally objects of admiration. I also shot my air-gun which was so perfectly incomprehensible that they immediately denominated it the great medicine. the idea which the indians mean to convey by this appellation is something that eminates from or acts immediately by the influence or power of the great sperit; or that in which the power of god is manifest by it's incomprehensible power of action. our hunters killed 4 deer and an Antelope this evening of which we also gave the Indians a good proportion. the cerimony of our council and smoking the pipe was in conformity of the custom of this nation perfomed bearfoot. on those occasions points of etiquet are quite as much attended to by the Indians as among scivilized nations. To keep indians in a good humour you must not fatiegue them with too much business at one time. therefore after the council we gave them to eat and amused them a while by shewing them such articles as we thought would be entertaining to them, and then renewed our enquiries with rispect to the country. the information we derived was only a repetition of that they had given me before and in which they appeared to be so candid that I could not avoid yealing confidence to what they had said. Capt. Clark and myself now concerted measures for our future operations, and it was mutually agreed that he should set out tomorrow morning with eleven men furnished with axes and other necessary tools for making canoes, their arms accoutrements and as much of their baggage as they could carry. also to take the indians Carbono and the indian woman with him; that on his arrival at the Shoshone camp he was to leave Charbono and the Indian woman to haisten the return of the Indians with their horses to this place, and to proceede himself with the eleven men down the Columbia in order to examine the river and if he found it navigable and could obtain timber to set about making canoes immediately. In the mean time I was to bring on the party and baggage to the Shoshone Camp, calculating that by the time I should reach that place that he would have sufficiently informed himself with rispect to the state of the river &c. as to determine us whether to prosicute our journey from thence by land or water. in the former case we should want all the horses which we could perchase, the latter only to hire the Indians to transport our baggage to the place at which we made the canoes. in order to inform me as early as possible of the state of the river he was to send back one of the men with the necessary information as soon as he should satisfy himself on this subject. this plan being settled we gave orders accordingly and the men prepared for an early march. the nights are very cold and the sun excessively hot in the day. we have no fuel here but a few dry willow brush. and from the appearance of country I am confident we shall not find game here to subsist us many days. these are additional reasons why I conceive it necessary to get under way as soon as possible.- this morning Capt. Clark had delayed untill 7 A.M. before he set out just about which time Drewyer arrived with the Indian; he left the canoes to come on after him, and immediately set out and joined me as has been before mentioned.The sperits of the men were now much elated at the prospect of geting horses.

[Clark, August 17, 1805] August 17th Satturday 1805 a fair Cold morning wind S. W. the Thermometer at 42 a. 0 at Sunrise, We Set out at 7 oClock and proceeded on to the forks I had not proceeded on one mile before I saw at a distance Several Indians on horsback Comeing towards me, The Intertrepeter & Squar who were before me at Some distance danced for the joyful Sight, and She made signs to me that they were her nation, as I aproached nearer them descovered one of Capt Lewis party With them dressed in their Dress; the met me with great Signs of joy, as the Canoes were proceeding on nearly opposit me I turned those people & joined Capt Lewis who had Camped with 16 of those Snake Indians at the forks 2 miles in advance. those Indians Sung all the way to their Camp where the others had provd. a cind of Shade of Willows Stuck up in a Circle the Three Chiefs with Capt. Lewis met me with great cordialliaty embraced and took a Seat on a white robe, the Main Chief imedeately tied to my hair Six Small pieces of Shells resembling perl which is highly Valued by those people and is prcured from the nations resideing near the Sea Coast. we then Smoked in their fassion without Shoes and without much cerimoney and form.

Capt Lewis informed me he found those people on the Columbia River about 40 miles from the forks at that place there was a large camp of them, he had purswaded those with him to Come and See that what he said was the truth, they had been under great apprehension all the way, for fear of their being deceived. The Great Chief of this nation proved to be the brother of the Woman with us and is a man of Influence Sence & easey & reserved manners, appears to possess a great deel of Cincerity. The Canoes arrived & unloaded- every thing appeared to asstonish those people. the appearance of the men, their arms, the Canoes, the Clothing my black Servent. & the Segassity of Capt Lewis's Dog. we Spoke a fiew words to them in the evening respecting our rout intentions our want of horses &c. & gave them a fiew presents & medals- we made a number of inquires of those people about the Columbia River the Countrey game &c. The account they gave us was verry unfavourable, that the River abounded in emence falls, one perticularly much higher than the falls of the Missouri & at the place the mountains Closed So Close that it was impracticable to pass, & that the ridge Continued on each Side of perpendicular Clifts inpenetratable, and that no Deer Elk or any game was to be found in that Countrey, aded to that they informed us that there was no timber on the river Sufficiently large to make Small Canoes, This information (if true is alarming) I deturmined to go in advance and examine the Countrey, See if those dificueltes presented themselves in the gloomey picture in which they painted them, and if the river was practiable and I could find timber to build Canoes, those Ideas & plan appeard to be agreeable to Capt Lewis's Ideas on this point, and I selected 11 men, directed them to pack up their baggage Complete themselves with amunition, take each an ax and Such tools as will be Soutable to build Canoes, and be ready to Set out at 10 oClock tomorrow morning. Those people greatly pleased our hunters killed three Deer & an antilope which was eaten in a Short time the Indians being so harrassed & compelled to move about in those rugid mountains that they are half Starved liveing at this time on berries & roots which they geather in the plains. Those people are not begerley but generous, only one has asked me for anything and he for powder.

This nation Call themselves Cho-shop-ne the Chief is name
Too-et-te-con'l Black Gun is his war name Ka-me-ah-wah- or Come &
Smoke. this Chief gave me the following name and pipe Ka-me-ah-wah.

[Lewis, August 18, 1805] Sunday August 18th 1805. This morning while Capt Clark was busily engaged in preparing for his rout, I exposed some articles to barter with the Indians for horses as I wished a few at this moment to releive the men who were going with Capt Clark from the labour of carrying their baggage and also one to keep here in order to pack the meat to camp which the hunters might kill. I soon obtained three very good horses for which I gave an uniform coat, a pair of legings, a few handkerchiefs, three knives and some other small articles the whole of which did not cost more than about 20$ in the U States. the Indians seemed quite as well pleased with their bargin as I was. the men also purchased one for an old checked shirt a pair of old legings and a knife. two of those I purchased Capt. C. took on with him. at 10 A.M. Capt. Clark departed with his detatchment and all the Indians except 2 men and 2 women who remained with us. Two of the inferior chiefs were a little displeased at not having received a present equivolent to that given the first Chief. to releive this difficulty Capt. Clark bestoed a couple of his old coats on them and I promised that if they wer active in assisting me over the mountains with horses that I would give them an additional present; this seemed perfectly to satisfy them and they all set out in a good humour. Capt. Clark encamped this evening near the narrow pass between the hills on Jefferson's river in the Shoshone Cove. his hunters killed one deer which the party with the aid of the Indians readily consumed in the course of the evening.- after there departure this morning I had all the stores and baggage of every discription opened and aired. and began the operation of forming the packages in proper parsels for the purpose of transporting them on horseback. the rain in the evening compelled me to desist from my operations. I had the raw hides put in the water in order to cut them in throngs proper for lashing the packages and forming the necessary geer for pack horses, a business which I fortunately had not to learn on this occasion. Drewyer Killed one deer this evening. a beaver was also caught by one of the party. I had the net arranged and set this evening to catch some trout which we could see in great abundance at the bottom of the river. This day I completed my thirty first year, and conceived that I had in all human probability now existed about half the period which I am to remain in this Sublunary world. I reflected that I had as yet done but little, very little indeed, to further the hapiness of the human race, or to advance the information of the succeeding generation. I viewed with regret the many hours I have spent in indolence, and now soarly feel the want of that information which those hours would have given me had they been judiciously expended. but since they are past and cannot be recalled, I dash from me the gloomy thought and resolved in future, to redouble my exertions and at least indeavour to promote those two primary objects of human existence, by giving them the aid of that portion of talents which nature and fortune have bestoed on me; or in future, to live for mankind, as I have heretofore lived for myself.

[Clark, August 18, 1805] August 18th Sunday 1805 Purchased of the Indians three horses for which we gave a Chiefs Coat Some Handkerchiefs a Shirt Legins & a fiew arrow points &c. I gave two of my coats to two of the under Chiefs who appeared not well Satisfied that the first Chief was dressed so much finer than themselves. at 10 oClock I Set out accompanied by the Indians except 3 the interpreter and wife, the fore part of the day worm, at 12 oClock it became hasey with a mist of rain wind hard from the S. W. and Cold which increased untill night the rain Seased in about two hours. We proceeded on thro a wide leavel vallie without wood except willows & Srubs for 15 miles and Encamped at a place the high lands approach within 200 yards in 2 points the River here only 10 yards wide Several Small Streams branching out on each Side below. all the Indians proceeded on except the 3 Chiefs & two young men. my hunters killed two Deer which we eate. The Course from the forks is West 9 miles N. 60° W. 6 miles. The Laid. of the forks agreeable to observations is 43° 30' 43" North-

[Lewis, August 19, 1805] Monday August 19th 1805. This morning I arrose at dylight. and sent out three hunters. some of the men who were much in want of legings and mockersons I suffered to dress some skins. the others I employed in repacking the baggage, making pack saddles &c. we took up the net this morning but caugt no fish. one beaver was caught in a trap. the frost which perfectly whitened the grass this morning had a singular appearance to me at this season. this evening I made a few of the men construct a sein of willow brush which we hawled and caught a large number of fine trout and a kind of mullet about 16 Inhes long which I had not seen before. the scales are small, the nose is long and obtusely pointed and exceedes the under jaw. the mouth is not large but opens with foalds at the sides, the colour of it's back and sides is of a bluish brown and belley white; it has the faggot bones, from which I have supposed it to be of the mullet kind. the tongue and pallate are smooth and it has no teeth. it is by no means as good as the trout. the trout are the same which I first met with at the falls of the Missouri, they are larger than the speckled trout of our mountains and equally as well flavored.- The hunters returned this evening with two deer. from what has been said of the Shoshones it will be readily perceived that they live in a wretched stait of poverty. yet notwithstanding their extreem poverty they are not only cheerfull but even gay, fond of gaudy dress and amusements; like most other Indians they are great egotists and frequently boast of heroic acts which they never performed. they are also fond of games of wrisk. they are frank, communicative, fair in dealing, generous with the little they possess, extreemly honest, and by no means beggarly. each individual is his own sovereign master, and acts from the dictates of his own mind; the authority of the Cheif being nothing more than mere admonition supported by the influence which the propiety of his own examplery conduct may have acquired him in the minds of the individuals who compose the band. the title of cheif is not hereditary, nor can I learn that there is any cerimony of instalment, or other epoh in the life of a Cheif from which his title as such can be dated. in fact every man is a chief, but all have not an equal influence on the minds of the other members of the community, and he who happens to enjoy the greatest share of confidence is the principal Chief. The Shoshonees may be estimated at about 100 warriors, and about three times that number of woomen and children. they have more children among them than I expected to have seen among a people who procure subsistence with such difficulty. there are but few very old persons, nor did they appear to treat those with much tenderness or rispect. The man is the sole propryetor of his wives and daughters, and can barter or dispose of either as he thinks proper. a plurality of wives is common among them, but these are not generally sisters as with the Minnetares & Mandans but are purchased of different fathers. The father frequently disposes of his infant daughters in marriage to men who are grown or to men who have sons for whom they think proper to provide wives. the compensation given in such cases usually consists of horses or mules which the father receives at the time of contract and converts to his own uce. the girl remains with her parents untill she is conceived to have obtained the age of puberty which with them is considered to be about the age of 13 or 14 years. the female at this age is surrendered to her sovereign lord and husband agreeably to contract, and with her is frequently restored by the father quite as much as he received in the first instance in payment for his daughter; but this is discretionary with the father. Sah-car-gar-we-ah had been thus disposed of before she was taken by the Minnetares, or had arrived to the years of puberty. the husband was yet living and with this band. he was more than double her age and had two other wives. he claimed her as his wife but said that as she had had a child by another man, who was Charbono, that he did not want her. They seldom correct their children particularly the boys who soon become masters of their own acts. they give as a reason that it cows and breaks the Sperit of the boy to whip him, and that he never recovers his independence of mind after he is grown. They treat their women but with little rispect, and compel them to perform every species of drudgery. they collect the wild fruits and roots, attend to the horses or assist in that duty cook dreess the skins and make all their apparal, collect wood and make their fires, arrange and form their lodges, and when they travel pack the horses and take charge of all the baggage; in short the man dose little else except attend his horses hunt and fish. the man considers himself degraded if he is compelled to walk any distance, and if he is so unfortunately poor as only to possess two horses he rides the best himself and leavs the woman or women if he has more than one, to transport their baggage and children on the other, and to walk if the horse is unable to carry the additional weight of their persons- the chastity of their women is not held in high estimation, and the husband will for a trifle barter the companion of his bead for a night or longer if he conceives the reward adiquate; tho they are not so importunate that we should caress their women as the siouxs were and some of their women appear to be held more sacred than in any nation we have seen I have requested the men to give them no cause of jealousy by having connection with their women without their knowledge, which with them strange as it may seem is considered as disgracefull to the husband as clandestine connections of a similar kind are among civilized nations. to prevent this mutual exchange of good officies altogether I know it impossible to effect, particularly on the part of our young men whom some months abstinence have made very polite to those tawney damsels. no evil has yet resulted and I hope will not from these connections.- notwithstanding the late loss of horses which this people sustained by the Minnetares the stock of the band may be very safely estimated at seven hundred of which they are perhaps about 40 coalts and half that number of mules.these people are deminutive in stature, thick ankles, crooked legs, thick flat feet and in short but illy formed, at least much more so in general than any nation of Indians I ever saw. their complexion is much that of the Siouxs or darker than the Minnetares mandands or Shawnees. generally both men and women wear their hair in a loos lank flow over the sholders and face; tho I observed some few men who confined their hair in two equal cues hanging over each ear and drawnn in front of the body. the cue is formed with throngs of dressed lather or Otterskin aternately crossing each other. at present most of them have cut short in the neck in consequence of the loss of their relations by the Minnetares. Cameahwait has his cut close all over his head. this constitutes their cerimony of morning for their deceased relations. the dress of the men consists of a robe long legings, shirt, tippet and Mockersons, that of the women is also a robe, chemise, and Mockersons; sometimes they make use of short legings. the ornaments of both men and women are very similar, and consist of several species of sea shells, blue and white beads, bras and Iron arm bands, plaited cords of the sweet grass, and collars of leather ornamented with the quills of the porcupine dyed of various colours among which I observed the red, yellow, blue, and black. the ear is purforated in the lower part to receive various ornaments but the nose is not, nor is the ear lasserated or disvigored for this purpose as among many nations. the men never mark their skins by birning, cuting, nor puncturing and introducing a colouring matter as many nations do. there women sometimes puncture a small circle on their forehead nose or cheeks and thus introduce a black matter usually soot and grease which leaves an indelible stane. tho this even is by no means common. their arms offensive and defensive consist in the bow and arrows sheild, some lances, and a weapon called by the Cippeways who formerly used it, the pog-gal'-mag-gon'. in fishing they employ wairs, gigs, and fishing hooks. the salmon is the principal object of their pursuit. they snair wolves and foxes. I was anxious to learn whether these people had the venerial, and made the enquiry through the intrepreter and his wife; the information was that they sometimes had it but I could not learn their remedy; they most usually die with it's effects. this seems a strong proof that these disorders bothe gonaroehah and Louis venerae are native disorders of America. tho these people have suffered much by the small pox which is known to be imported and perhaps those other disorders might have been contracted from other indian tribes who by a round of communication might have obtained from the Europeans since it was introduced into that quarter of the globe. but so much detatched on the other had from all communication with the whites that I think it most probable that those disorders are original with them. from the middle of May to the firt of September these people reside on the waters of the Columbia where they consider themselves in perfect security from their enimies as they have not as yet ever found their way to this retreat; during this season the salmon furnish the principal part of their subsistence and as this firsh either perishes or returns about the 1st of September they are compelled at this season in surch of subsistence to resort to the Missouri, in the vallies of which, there is more game even within the mountains. here they move slowly down the river in order to collect and join other bands either of their own nation or the Flatheads, and having become sufficiently strong as they conceive venture on the Eastern side of the Rockey mountains into the plains, where the buffaloe abound. but they never leave the interior of the mountains while they can obtain a scanty subsistence, and always return as soon as they have acquired a good stock of dryed meat in the plains; when this stock is consumed they venture again into the plains; thus alternately obtaining their food at the risk of their lives and retiring to the mountains, while they consume it.- These people are now on the eve of their departure for the Missouri, and inform us that they expect to be joined at or about the three forks by several bands of their own nation, and a band of the Flatheads. as I am now two busily engaged to enter at once into a minute discription of the several articles which compose their dress, impliments of war hunting fishing &c I shall pursue them at my leasure in the order they have here occurred to my mind, and have been mentioned. This morning capt. Clark continued his rout with his party, the Indians accompanying him as yesterday; he was obliged to feed them. nothing remarkable happened during the day. he was met by an Indian with two mules on this side of the dividing ridge at the foot of the mountain, the Indian had the politeness to offer Capt. C. one of his mules to ride as he was on foot, which he accepted and gave the fellow a waistcoat as a reward for his politeness. in the evening he reached the creek on this side of the Indian camp and halted for the night. his hunters killed nothing today. The Indians value their mules very highly. a good mule can not be obtained for less than three and sometimes four horses, and the most indifferent are rated at two horses. their mules generally are the finest I ever saw without any comparison.- today I observed time and distance of sun's and moon's nearest limbs with sextant sun East.

[Clark, August 19, 1805] August 19th Monday 1805 A verry Cold morning Frost to be Seen we Set out at 7 oClock and proceeded on thro a wide leavel Vallie the Chief Shew me the place that a number of his nation was killed about 1 years past this Vallie Continues 5 miles & then becoms narrow, the beaver has Darned up the River in maney places we proceeded on up the main branch with a gradial assent to the head and passed over a low mountain and Decended a Steep Decent to a butifull Stream, passed over a Second hill of a verry Steep assent & thro a hilley Countrey for 8 miles an Encamped on a Small Stream the Indians with us we wer oblige to feed- one man met one with a mule & Spanish Saddle to ride, I gave him a wistoat a mule is considered a of great value among those people we proceeded on over a verry mountanious Countrey across the head of hollows & Springs

[Lewis, August 20, 1805] Tuesday August 20th 1805. This morning I sent out the two hunters and employed the ballance of the party pretty much as yesterday. I walked down the river about - 3/4 of a mile and scelected a place near the river bank unperceived by the Indians for a cash, which I set three men to make, and directed the centinel to discharge his gun if he pereceived any of the Indians going down in that direction which was to be the signal for the men at work on the cash to desist and seperate, least these people should discover our deposit and rob us of the baggage we intend leaving here. by evening the cash was completed unperceived by the Indians, and all our packages made up. the Pack-saddles and harries is not yet complete. in this operation we find ourselves at a loss for nails and boards; for the first we substitute throngs of raw hide which answer verry well, and for the last to cut off the blades of our oars and use the plank of some boxes which have heretofore held other articles and put those articles into sacks of raw hide which I have had made for the purpose. by this means I have obtained as many boards as will make 20 saddles which I suppose will be sufficient for our present exegencies. The Indians with us behave themselves extreemly well; the women have been busily engaged all day making and mending the mockersons of our party. In the evening the hunters returned unsuccessfull. Drewyer went in search of his trap which a beaver had taken off last night; he found the beaver dead with the trap to his foot about 2 miles below the place he had set it. this beaver constituted the whole of the game taken today. the fur of this animal is as good as I ever saw any, and beleive that they are never out of season on the upper part of the Missouri and it's branches within the Mountains. Goodrich caught several douzen fine trout. today. I made up a small assortment of medicines, together with the specemines of plants, minerals, seeds &c. which, I have collected betwen this place and the falls of the Missouri which I shall deposit here. the robe woarn by the Shoshonees is the same in both sexes and is loosly thrown about their sholders, and the sides at pleasure either hanging loose or drawn together with the hands, sometimes if the weather is cold they confine it with a girdel around the waist; they are generally about the size of a 2 1/2 point blanket for grown persons and reach as low as the middle of the leg. this robe forms a garment in the day and constitutes their only covering at night. with these people the robe is formed most commonly of the skins of Antelope, Bighorn, or deer, dressed with the hair on, tho they prefer the buffaloe when they can procure them. I have also observed some robes among them of beaver, moonax, and small wolves. the summer robes of both sexes are also frequently made of the Elk's skin dressed without the hair. The shirt of the men is really a commodious and decent garment. it roomy and reaches nearly half way the thye, there is no collar, the apperture being sufficiently large to admit the head and is left square at top, or most frequently, both before and behind terminate in the tails of the animals of which they are made and which foald outwards being frequently left entire or somtimes cut into a fring on the edges and orniment with the quills of the Porcupine. the sides of the shirt are sewed deeply fringed, and ornamented in a similar manner from the bottom upwards, within six or eight inches of the sieve from whence it is left open as well as the sieve on it's under side to the elbow nearly. from the elbow the sieve fits the arm tight as low as the wrist and is not orniminted with a fringe as the sides and under parts of the sieve are above the elbow. the sholder straps are wide and on them is generally displayed the taste of the manufacterer in a variety of figures wrought with the quills of the porcupine of several colours; beads when they have them are also displayed on this part. the tail of the shirt is left in the form which the fore legs and neck give it with the addition of a slight fringe. the hair is usually left on the tail, & near the hoofs of the animal; part of the hoof is also retained to the skin and is split into a fring by way of orniment. these shirts are generally made of deer's Antelope's, Bighorn's, or Elk's skins dressed without the hair. the Elk skin is less used for this purpose than either of the others. their only thread used on this or any other occasion is the sinews taken from the back and loins of the deer Elk buffaloe &c. Their legings are most usually formed of the skins of the Antelope dressed without the hair. in the men they are very long and full each leging being formed of a skin nearly entire. the legs, tail and neck are also left on these, and the tail woarn upwards; and the neck deeply fringed and orniminted with porcupine qulls drags or trails on the ground behind the heel. the skin is sewn in such manner as to fit the leg and thye closely; the upper part being left open a sufficient distance to permit the legs of the skin to be dran underneath a girdle both before and behind, and the wide part of the skin to cover the buttock and lap before in such manner that the breechcloth is unnecessary. they are much more decent in concealing those parts than any nation on the Missouri the sides of the legings are also deeply fringed and orniminted. sometimes this part is orniminted with little fassicles of the hair of an enimy whom they have slain in battle. The tippet of the Snake Indians is the most eligant peice of Indian dress I ever saw, the neck or collar of this is formed of a strip of dressed Otter skin with the fur. it is about four or five inches wide and is cut out of the back of the skin the nose and eyes forming one extremity and the tail the other. begining a little behind the ear of the animal at one edge of this collar and proceeding towards the tail, they attatch from one to two hundred and fifty little roles of Ermin skin formed in the following manner. the skin is first dressed with the fur on it and a narrow strip is cut out of the back of the skin reaching from the nose and imbracing the tail. this is sewed arround a small cord of the silk-grass twisted for the purpose and regularly tapering in such manner as to give it ajust proportion to the tail which is to form the lower extremity of the stran. thus arranged they are confined at the upper point in little bundles of two-three, or more as the disign may be to make them more full; these are then attatched to the collars as before mentioned, and to conceal the connection of this part which would otherwise have a course appearance they attatch a broad fringe of the Ermin skin to the collar overlaying that part. little bundles of fine fringe of the same materials is fastened to the extremity of the tails in order to shew their black extremities to greater advantage. the center of the otterskin collar is also ornamented with the shells of the perl oister. the collar is confined arond the neck and the little roles of Ermin skin about the size of a large quill covers the solders and body nearly to the waist and has the appearance of a short cloak and is really handsome. these they esteem very highly, and give or dispose of only on important occasions. the ermin whic is known to the traiders of the N. W. by the name of the white weasel is the genuine ermine, and might no doubt be turned to great advantage by those people if they would encourage the Indians to take them. they are no doubt extreemly plenty and readily taken, from the number of these tippets which I have seen among these people and the great number of skins employed in the construction of each timppet. scarcely any of them have employed less than one hundred of these skins in their formation.- This morning Capt. Clark set out at 6 in the morning and soon after arrived near their camp they having removed about 2 miles higher up the river than the camp at which they were when I first visited them. the chief requested a halt, which was complyed with, and a number of the indians came out from the village and joined them after smoking a few pipes with them they all proceeded to the village where Capt C. was conducted to a large lodge prepared in the center of the encampment for himself and party. here they gave him one salmon and some cakes of dryed berries. he now repeated to them what had been said to them in council at this place which was repeated to the village by the Cheif. when he had concluded this address he requested a guide to accompany him down the river and an elderly man was pointed out by the Cheif who consented to undertake this task. this was the old man of whom Cameahwait had spoken as a person well acquainted with the country to the North of this river. Capt. C. encouraged the Indians to come over with their horses and assist me over with the baggage. he distrubuted some presents among the Indians. about half the men of the village turned out to hunt the antelope but were unsuccessfull. at 3 P.M. Capt. Clark departed, accompanyed by his guide and party except one man whom he left with orders to purchase a horse if possible and overtake him as soon as he could. he left Charbono and the indian woman to return to my camp with the Indians. he passed the river about four miles below the Indians, and encamped on a small branch, eight miles distant. on his way he met a rispectable looking indian who returned and continued with him all night; this indian gave them three salmon. Capt. C. killed a cock of the plains or mountain cock. it was of a dark brown colour with a long and pointed tail larger than the dunghill fowl and had a fleshey protuberant substance about the base of the upper chap, something like that of the turkey tho without the snout.

[Clark, August 20, 1805] August 20th Tuesday 1805 Set out at half past 6 oClock and proceeded on (met maney parties of Indians) thro a hilley Countrey to the Camp of the Indians on a branch of the Columbia River, before we entered this Camp a Serimonious hault was requested by the Chief and I Smoked with all that Came around for Several pipes, we then proceeded on to the Camp & I was introduced into the only Lodge they had which was pitched in the Center for my party all the other Lodges made of bushes, after a fiew Indian Seremonies I informed the Indians the object of our journey our good intentions towards them my consern for their distressed Situation, what we had done for them in makeing a piece with the Minitarras Mandans Rickara &c. for them-. and requested them all to take over their horses & assist Capt Leiwis across &c. also informing them the oject of my journey down the river and requested a guide to accompany me, all of which was repeited by the Chief to the whole village.

Those pore people Could only raise a Sammon & a little dried Choke Cherris for us half the men of the tribe with the Chief turned out to hunt the antilopes, at 3 oClock after giveing a fiew Small articles as presents I set out accompanied by an old man as a Guide (I endevered to procure as much information from thos people as possible without much Suckcess they being but little acquainted or effecting to be So-) I lef one man to purchase a horse and overtake me and proceeded on thro a wide rich bottom on a beaten Roade 8 miles Crossed the river and encamped on a Small run, this evening passed a number of old lodges, and met a number of men women children & horses, met a man who appeared of Some Consideration who turned back with us, he halted a woman & gave us 3 Small Sammon, this man continued with me all night and partook of what I had which was a little Pork verry Salt. Those Indians are verry attentive to Strangers &c. I left our interpreter & his woman to accompany the Indians to Capt Lewis tomorrow the Day they informed me they would Set out I killed a Pheasent at the Indian Camp larger than a dungal fowl with feshey protuberances about the head like a turkey. Frost last night

[Lewis, August 21, 1805] Wednesday August 21st 1805. This morning was very cold. the ice 1/4 of an inch thick on the water which stood in the vessels exposed to the air. some wet deerskins that had been spread the grass last evening are stiffly frozen. the ink feizes in my pen. the bottoms are perfectly covered with frost insomuch that they appear to be covered with snow. This morning early I dispatched two hunters to kill some meat if possible before the Indians arrive; Drewyer I sent with the horse into the cove for that purpose. The party pursued their several occupations as yesterday. by evening I had all the baggage, saddles, and harness completely ready for a march. after dark, I made the men take the baggage to the cash and deposit it. I beleve we have been unperceived by the Indians in this movement. notwithstanding the coldness of the last night the day has proved excessively warm. neither of the hunters returned this evening and I was obliged to issue pork and corn. The mockersons of both sexes are usually the same and are made of deer Elk or buffaloe skin dressed without the hair. sometimes in the winter they make them of buffaloe skin dressed with the hair on and turn the hair inwards as the Mandans Minetares and most of the nations do who inhabit the buffaloe country. the mockerson is formed with one seem on the outer edge of the foot is cut open at the instep to admit the foot and sewed up behind. in this rispect they are the same with the Mandans. they sometimes orniment their mockersons with various figures wrought with the quills of the Porcupine. some of the dressey young men orniment the tops of their mockersons with the skins of polecats and trale the tail of that animal on the ground at their heels as they walk.the robe of the woman is generally smaller than that of the man but is woarn in the same manner over the sholders. the Chemise is roomy and comes down below the middle of the leg the upper part of this garment is formed much like the shirt of the men except the sholder strap which is never used with the Chemise. in women who give suck, they are left open at the sides nearly as low as the waist, in others, close as high as the sleeve. the sleeve underneath as low as the elbow is open, that part being left very full. the sides tail and upper part of the sleeves are deeply fringed and sometimes ornimented in a similar manner with the shirts of the men with the addition of little patches of red cloth about the tail edged around with beads. the breast is usually ornament with various figures of party colours rought with the quills of the Porcupine. it is on this part of the garment that they appear to exert their greatest ingenuity. a girdle of dressed leather confines the Chemise around the waist. when either the man or woman wish to disengage their arm from the sleeve they draw it out by means of the opening underneath the arm an throw the sleeve behind the body. the legings of the women reach as high as the knee and are confined with a garter below. the mockerson covers and confins it's lower extremity. they are neither fringed nor ornamented. these legings are made of the skins of the antelope and the Chemise usually of those of the large deer Bighorn and the smallest elk.- They seldom wear the beads they possess about their necks at least I have never seen a grown person of either sex wear them on this part; some their children are seen with them in this way. the men and women were them suspen from the ear in little bunches or intermixed with triangular peices of the shells of the perl oister. the men also were them attached in a similar manner to the hare of the fore part of the crown of the head; to which they sometimes make the addition of the wings and tails of birds. the nose in neither sex is pierced nor do they wear any ornament in it. they have a variety of small sea shells of which they form collars woarn indiscriminately by both sexes. these as well as the shell of the perl oister they value very highly and inform us that they obtain them from their friends and relations who live beyond the barren plain towards the Ocean in a S. Westerly direction. these friends of theirs they say inhabit a good country abounding with Elk, deer, bear, and Antelope, and possess a much greater number of horses and mules than they do themselves; or using their own figure that their horses and mules are as numerous as the grass of the plains. the warriors or such as esteem themselves brave men wear collars made of the claws of the brown bear which are also esteemed of great value and are preserved with great care. these claws are ornamented with beads about the thick end near which they are peirced through their sides and strung on a throng of dressed leather and tyed about the neck commonly with the upper edge of the tallon next the breast or neck but sometimes are reversed. it is esteemed by them an act of equal celebrity the killing one of these bear or an enimy, and with the means they have of killing this animal it must really be a serious undertaking. the sweet sented grass which grows very abundant on this river is either twisted or plaited and woarn around the neck in ether sex, but most commonly by the men. they have a collar also woarn by either sex. it generally round and about the size of a man's finger; formed of leather or silk-grass twisted or firmly rolled and covered with the quills of the porcupine of different colours. the tusks of the Elk are pierced strung on a throng and woarn as an orniment for the neck, and is most generally woarn by the women and children. the men frequently wear the skin of a fox or a broad strip of that of the otter around the forehead and head in form of a bando. they are also fond of the feathers of the tail of the beautifull eagle or callumet birds with which they ornament their own hair and the tails and mains of their horses. The dress of these people is quite as desent and convenient as that of any nation of Indians I ever saw.

This morning early Capt. C. resumed his march; at the distance of five miles he arrived at some brush lodges of the Shoshones inhabited by about seven families here he halted and was very friendly received by these people, who gave himself and party as much boiled salmon as they could eat; they also gave him several dryed salmon and a considerable quantity of dryed chokecherries. after smoking with them he visited their fish wear which was abut 200 yds. distant. he found the wear extended across four channels of the river which was here divided by three small islands. three of these channels were narrow, and were stoped by means of trees fallen across, supported by which stakes of willow were driven down sufficiently near each other to prevent the salmon from passing. about the center of each a cilindric basket of eighteen or 20 feet in length terminating in a conic shape at it's lower extremity, formed of willows, was opposed to a small apperture in the wear with it's mouth up stream to receive the fish. the main channel of the water was conducted to this basket, which was so narrow at it's lower extremity that the fish when once in could not turn itself about, and were taken out by untying the small ends of the longitudinal willows, which frormed the hull of the basket. the wear in the main channel was somewhat differently contrived. there were two distinct wears formed of poles and willow sticks, quite across the river, at no great distance from each other. each of these, were furnished with two baskets; the one wear to take them ascending and the other in decending. in constructing these wears, poles were first tyed together in parcels of three near the smaller extremity; these were set on end, and spread in a triangular form at the base, in such manner, that two of the three poles ranged in the direction of the intended work, and the third down the stream. two ranges of horizontal poles were next lashed with willow bark and wythes to the ranging poles, and on these willow sticks were placed perpendicularly, reaching from the bottom of the river to about 3 or four feet above it's surface; and placed so near each other, as not to permit the passage of the fish, and even so thick in some parts, as with the help of gravel and stone to give a direction to the water which they wished.- the baskets were the same in form of the others. this is the form of the work, and disposition of the baskets.

After examining the wears Capt. C. returned to the lodges, and shortly continued his rout and passed the river to the Lard. side a little distance below the wears. he sent Collins with an Indian down the Lard. side of the river to the forks 5 me. in surch of Cruzatte who was left at the upper camp yesterday to purchase a horse and had followed on today and passed them by another road while they were at the lodges and had gone on to the forks. while Capt. Clark was at these lodges an Indian brought him a tomehawk which he said he found in the grass near the lodge where I had staid at the upper camp when I was first with his nation the tommahawk was Drewyer's he missed it in the morning before we had set out and surched for it but it was not to be found I beleive the young fellow stole it, but if he did it is the only article they have pilfered and this was now returned. Capt. C. after traveling about 20 miles through the valley with the course of the river nearly N. W. encamped on the Stard. side in a small bottom under a high Clift of rocks. on his way one of the party killed a very large Salmon in a creek which they passed at the distance of 14 ms. he was joined this evening by Cruzatte and Collins who brought with them five fresh salmon which had been given them by the Indians at the forks. the forks of this river is famous as a gig fishery and is much resorted by the natives.- They killed one deer today. The Guide apeared to be a very friendly intelligent old man, Capt. C. is much pleased with him.

[Clark, August 21, 1805] August 21st Wednesday 1805 Frost last night proceeded on with the Indians I met about 5 miles to there Camp, I entered a lodge and after Smokeing with all who Came about me I went to See the place those people take the fish, a wear across the Creek in which there is Stuk baskets Set in different derections So as to take the fish either decending or assending on my return to the Camp which was 200 yards only the different lodges (which is only bushes) brought in to the lodge I was introduced into, Sammon boiled, and dried Choke Chers. Sufficent for all my party.- one man brought me a tomahawk which we expected they had Stolen from a man of Capt Lewis's party, this man informed me he found the tomk in the grass near the place the man Slept. Crossed the River and went over a point of high land & Struck it again near a Bluff on the right Side the man I left to get a horse at the upper Camp missed me & went to the forks which is about five miles below the last Camp.

I sent one man by the forks with derections to join me to night with the one now at that place, those two men joined me at my Camp on the right Side below the 1st Clift with 5 Sammon which the Indians gave them at the forks, the place they gig fish at this Season. Their method of takeing fish with a gig or bone is with a long pole, about a foot from one End is a Strong String attached to the pole, this String is a little more than a foot long and is tied to the middle of a bone from 4 to 6 inches long, one end Sharp the other with a whole to fasten on the end of the pole with a beard to the large end, the fasten this bone on one end & with the other, feel for the fish & turn and Strike them So hard that the bone passes through and Catches on the opposit Side, Slips off the End of the pole and holds the Center of the bone Those Indians are mild in their disposition appear Sincere in their friendship, punctial, and decided. kind with what they have, to Spare. They are excessive pore, nothing but horses there Enemies which are noumerous on account of there horses & Defenceless Situation, have Deprived them of tents and all the Small Conveniances of life. They have only a few indifferent Knives, no ax, make use of Elk's horn Sharpened to Spit ther wood, no clothes except a Short Legins & robes of different animals, Beaver, Bear, Buffalow, wolf Panthor, Ibex, Sheep Deer, but most commonly the antilope Skins which they ware loosely about them- Their ornements are Orter Skin dcurated with See Shells & the Skins & tales of the white weasel, Sea Shels of different size hung to their Ears hair and breast of their Shirts, beeds of Shells platted grass, and Small Strings of otter Skin dressed, they are fond of our trinkets, and give us those ornements as the most valueable of their possession. The women are held Sacred and appear to have an equal Shere in all Conversation, which is not the Case in any othe nation I have Seen. their boeys & Girls are also admited to Speak except in Councils, the women doe all the drugery except fishing and takeing care of the horses, which the men apr. to take upon themselves.- The men ware the hair loose flowing over ther Sholders & face the women Cut Short, orniments of the back bones of fish Strung plated grass grains of Corn Strung Feathers and orniments of Birds Claws of the Bear encurcling their necks the most Sacred of all the orniments of this nation is the Sea Shells of various Sizes and Shapes and colours, of the bassterd perl kind, which they inform us they get from the Indians to the South on the other Side of a large fork of this river in passing to which they have to pass thro Sandy & barron open plains without water to which place they can travel in 15 or 20 days- The men who passed by the forks informed me that the S W. fork was double the Size of the one I came down, and I observed that it was a handsom river at my camp I shall injustice to Capt Lewis who was the first white man ever on this fork of the Columbia Call this Louis's river. one Deer killed this morning, and a Sammon in the last Creek 21/2 feet long The Westerley fork of the Columbia River is double the Size of the Easterley fork & below those forks the river is about the Size Jeffersons River near its mouth or 100 yards wide, it is verry rapid & Sholey water Clear but little timber. This Clift is of a redish brown Colour the rocks which fall from it is a dark brown flint tinged with that Colour. Some Gullies of white Sand Stone and Sand fine & as white as Snow. The mountains on each Side are high, and those on the East ruged & Contain a fiew Scattering pine, those on the West contain pine on ther tops & high up the hollows- The bottoms of this is wide & rich from some distance above the place I struck the East fork they are also wide on the East Passed a large Creek which fall in on the right Side 6 miles below the forks a road passes up this Creek & to the Missouri.

[Lewis, August 22, 1805] Thursday August 22ed 1805 This morning early I sent a couple of men to complete the covering of the cash which could not be done well last night in the dark, they soon accomplished their work and returned. late last night Drewyer returned with a fawn he had killed and a considerable quantity of Indian plunder. the anecdote with rispect to the latter is perhaps worthy of relation. he informed me that while hunting in the Cove yesterday about 12 OCk. he came suddonly upon an Indian Camp, at which there were a young man an Old man a boy and three women, that they seemed but little supprised at seeing him and he rode up to them and dismounted turning horse out to graize. these people had just finished their repast on some roots, he entered into conversation with them by signs, and after about 20 minutes one of the women spoke to the others of the party and they all went immediately and collected their horses brought them to camp and saddled them at this moment he thought he would also set out and continue his hunt, and accorgingly walked to catch his horse at some little distance and neglected to take up his gun which, he left at camp. the Indians perceiving him at the distance of fifty paces immediately mounted their horses, the young man took the gun and the whole of them left their baggage and laid whip to their horses directing their course to the pass of the mountains. finding himself deprived of his gun he immediately mounted his horse and pursued; after runing them about 10 miles the horses of two of the women nearly gave out and the young fellow with the gun from their frequent crys slackened his pace and being on a very fleet horse road around the women at a little distance at length Drewer overtook the women and by signs convinced them that he did not wish to hirt them they then halted and the young fellow approached still nearer, he asked him for his gun but the only part of the answer which he could understand was pah kee which he knew to be the name by which they called their enimies. watching his opportunity when the fellow was off his guard he suddonly rode along side of him seized his gun and wrest her out of his hands. the fellow finding Drewyer too strong for him and discovering that he must yeald the gun had pesents of mind to open the pan and cast the priming before he let the gun escape from his hands; now finding himself devested of the gun he turned his horse about and laid whip leaving the women to follow him as well as they could. Drewyer now returned to the place they had left their baggage and brought it with him to my camp. it consisted of several dressed and undressed skins; a couple of bags wove with the fingers of the bark of the silk-grass containing each about a bushel of dryed service berries some checherry cakes and about a bushel of roots of three different kinds dryed and prepared for uce which were foalded in as many parchment hides of buffaloe. some flint and the instrument of bone for manufactureing the flint into arrow points. some of this flint was as transparent as the common black glass and much of the same colour easily broken, and flaked off much like glass leaving a very sharp edge. one speceis of the roots were fusiform abot six inches long and about the size of a man's finger at the larger end tapering to a small point. the radicles larger than in most fusiform roots. the rind was white and thin. the body or consistence of the root was white mealy and easily reduced by pounding to a substance resembleing flour which thickens with boiling water something like flour and is agreeably flavored. this rout is frequently eaten by the Indians either green or in it's dryed state without the preparation of boiling. another speceis was much mutilated but appeared to be fibrous; the parts were brittle, hard of the size of a small quill, cilindric and as white as snow throughout, except some small parts of the hard black rind which they had not seperated in the preperation. this the Indians with me informed were always boiled for use. I made the exprement, found that they became perfectly soft by boiling, but had a very bitter taste, which was naucious to my pallate, and I transfered them to the Indians who had eat them heartily. a third speceis were about the size of a nutmeg, and of an irregularly rounded form, something like the smallest of the Jerusalem artichoke, which they also resemble in every other appearance. they had become very hard by being dryed then I also boiled agreeably to the instruction of the Indians and found them very agreeable. they resemble the Jerusalem Artichoke very much in their flavor and I thought them preferable, however there is some allowance to be made for the length of time I have now been without vegitable food to which I was always much attatched. these are certainly the best root I have yet seen in uce among the Indians. I asked the Indians to shew me the plant of which these roots formed a part but they informed me that neither of them grew near this place. I had set most of the men at work today to dress the deerskin belonging to those who had gone on command with Capt. Clark. at 11 A.M. Charbono the Indian Woman, Cameahwait and about 50 men with a number of women and children arrived. they encamped near us. after they had turned out their horses and arranged their camp I called the Cheifs and warriors together and addressed them a second time; gave them some further presents, particularly the second and third Cheifs who it appeared had agreeably to their promise exerted themselves in my favour. having no fresh meat and these poor devils half starved I had previously prepared a good meal for them all of boiled corn and beans which I gave them as soon as the council was over and I had distributed the presents. this was thankfully received by them. the Chief wished that his nation could live in a country where they could provide such food. I told him that it would not be many years before the whitemen would put it in the power of his nation to live in the country below the mountains where they might cultivate corn beans and squashes. he appeared much pleased with the information. I gave him a few dryed squashes which we had brought from the Mandans he had them boiled and declared them to be the best thing he had ever tasted except sugar, a small lump of which it seems his sister Sah-cah-gar Wea had given him. late in the evening I made the men form a bush drag, and with it in about 2 hours they caught 528 very good fish, most of them large trout. among them I now for the first time saw ten or a douzen of a whte speceis of trout. they are of a silvery colour except on the back and head, where they are of a bluish cast. the scales are much larger than the speckled trout, but in their form position of their fins teeth mouth &c they are precisely like them they are not generally quite as large but equally well flavored. I distributed much the greater portion of the fish among the Indians. I purchased five good horses of them very reasonably, or at least for about the value of six dollars a peice in merchandize. the Indians are very orderly and do not croud about our camp nor attempt to disterb any article they see lying about. they borrow knives kettles &c from the men and always carefully return them. Capt. Clark says, "we set out early and passed a small creek at one mile, also the points of four mountains which were high steep and rocky. the mountains are so steep that it is almost incredible to mention that horses had passed them. our road in many places lay over the sharp fragments of rocks which had fallen from the mountains and lay in confused heaps for miles together; yet notwithstanding our horsed traveled barefoot over them as fast as we could and did not detain us. passed two bold runing streams, and arrived at the entrance of a small river" where some Indian families resided. they had some scaffoalds of fish and burries exposed to dry. they were not acquainted with the circumstance of any whitemen being in their country and were therefore much allarmed on our approach several of the women and children fled in the woods for shelter. the guide was behind and the wood thick in which their lodges were situated we came on them before they had the least notice of us. those who remained offered us every thing they had, which was but little; they offered us collars of elks tusks which their children woar Salmon beries &c. we eat some of their fish and buries but returned them the other articles they had offered with a present of some small articles which seemed to add much to their pacification.

The guide who had by this time arrived explained to them who we were and our object in visiting them; but still there were some of the women and Children inconsoleable, they continued to cry during our stay, which was about an hour. a road passes up this river which my guide informed me led over the mountains to the Missouri. from this place I continued my rout along the steep side of a mountain for about 3 miles and arrived at the river near a small Island on the lower point of which we encamped in the evening we attempted to gig fish but were unsuccessfull only obtaining one small salmon. in the course of the day we had passed several women and children geathering burries who were very liberal in bestoing us a part of their collections. the river is very rapid and shoaly; many rocks lie in various derections scattered throughout it's bed. There are some few small pine scattered through the bottoms, of which I only saw one which appeared as if it would answer for a canoe and that was but small. the tops of the mountains on the Lard. side are covered with pine and some also scattered on the sides of all the mountains. I saw today a speceis of woodpecker, which fed on the seeds of the pine. it's beak and tail were white, it's wings were black, and every other part of a dark brown. it was about the size of a robin-

[Clark, August 22, 1805] August 22d Thursday 1805 We Set out early passed a Small Creek on the right at 1 mile and the points of four mountains verry Steap high & rockey, the assent of three was So Steap that it is incredible to describe the rocks in maney places loose & Sliped from those mountains and is a bed of rugid loose white and dark brown loose rock for miles. the Indian horses pass over those Clifts hills Sids & rocks as fast as a man, the three horses with me do not detain me any on account of those dificulties, passed two bold rung. Streams on the right and a Small river at the mouth of Which Several families of Indians were encamped and had Several Scaffolds of fish & buries drying we allarmed them verry much as they knew nothing of a white man being in their Countrey, and at the time we approached their lodges which was in a thick place of bushes- my guiedes were behind.- They offered every thing they possessed (which was verry littl) to us, Some run off and hid in the bushes The first offer of theirs were Elks tuskes from around their Childrens necks, Sammon &c. my guide attempted passifyed those people and they Set before me berres, & fish to eate, I gave a fiew Small articles to those fritened people which added verry much to their pasification but not entirely as Some of the women & Childn. Cried dureing my Stay of an hour at this place, I proceeded on the Side of a verry Steep & rockey mountain for 3 miles and Encamped on the lower pt. of an Island. we attempted to gig fish without Suckcess. caught but one Small one.The last Creek or Small river is on the right Side and "a road passes up it & over to the Missouri" in this day passed Several womin and Children gathering and drying buries of which they were very kind and gave us a part. the river rapid and Sholey maney Stones Scattered through it in different directions. I Saw to day Bird of the wood pecker kind which fed on Pine burs its Bill and tale white the wings black every other part of a light brown, and about the Size of a robin. Some fiew Pine Scattered in the bottoms & Sides of the Mountains (the Top of the Motn. to the left Covered & inaxcessable) I Saw one which would make a Small Canoe.

[Lewis, August 23, 1805] Friday August 23rd 1805. This morning I arrose very early and despatched two hunters on horseback with orders to extend their hunt to a greater distance up the S. E. fork than they had done heretofore, in order if possible to obtain some meet for ourselves as well as the Indians who appeared to depend on us for food and our store of provision is growing too low to indulge them with much more corn or flour. I wished to have set out this morning but the cheef requested that I would wait untill another party of his nation arrived which he expected today, to this I consented from necessity, and therefore sent out the hunters as I have mentioned. I also laid up the canoes this morning in a pond near the forks; sunk them in the water and weighted them down with stone, after taking out the plugs of the gage holes in their bottoms; hoping by this means to guard against both the effects of high water, and that of the fire which is frequently kindled in these plains by the natives. the Indians have promised to do them no intentional injury and beleive they are too lazy at any rate to give themselves the trouble to raise them from their present situation in order to cut or birn them. I reminded the chief of the low state of our stores of provision and advised him to send his young men to hunt, which he immediately recommended to them and most of them turned out. I wished to have purchased some more horses of them but they objected against disposing of any more of them untill we reach their camp beyond the mountains. the Indians pursued a mule buck near our camp I saw this chase for about 4 miles it was really entertaining, there were about twelve of them in pursuit of it on horseback, they finally rode it down and killed it. the all came in about 1 P.M. having killed 2 mule deer and three goats. this mule buck was the largest deer of any kind I had ever seen. it was nearly as large as a doe Elk. I observed that there was but little division or distribution of the meat they had taken among themselves. some familes had a large stock and others none. this is not customary among the nations of Indians with whom I have hitherto been acquainted I asked Cameahwait the reason why the hunters did not divide the meat among themselves; he said that meat was so scarce with them that the men who killed it reserved it for themselves and their own families. my hunters arrived about 2 in the evening with two mule deer and three common deer. I distributed three of the deer among those families who appeared to have nothing to eat. at three P.M. the expected party of Indians arrived, about 50 men women and Children. I now learnt that most of them were thus far on their way down the valley towards the buffaloe country, and observed that there was a good deel of anxiety on the part of some of those who had promised to assist me over the mountains to accompany this party, I felt some uneasiness on this subject but as they still said they would return with me as they had promised I said nothing to them but resolved to set out in the morning as early as possible. I dispatched two hunters this evening into the cove to hunt and leave the meat they might kill on the rout we shall pass tomorrow.

The metal which we found in possession of these people consited of a few indifferent knives, a few brass kettles some arm bands of iron and brass, a few buttons, woarn as ornaments in their hair, a spear or two of a foot in length and some iron and brass arrow points which they informed me they obtained in exchange for horses from the Crow or Rocky Mountain Indians on the yellowstone River. the bridlebits and stirrips they obtained from the Spaniards, tho these were but few. many of them made use of flint for knives, and with this instrument, skined the animals they killed, dressed their fish and made their arrows; in short they used it for every purpose to which the knife is applyed. this flint is of no regular form, and if they can only obtain a part of it, an inch or two in length that will cut they are satisfyed, they renew the edge by fleaking off the flint by means of the point of an Elk's or deer's horn. with the point of a deer or Elk's horn they also form their arrow points of the flint, with a quickness and neatness that is really astonishing. we found no axes nor hatchets among them; what wood they cut was done either with stone or Elk's horn. the latter they use always to rive or split their wood. their culinary eutensils exclusive of the brass kettle before mentioned consist of pots in the form of ajar made either of earth, or of a white soft stone which becomes black and very hard by birning, and is found in the hills near the three forks of the Missouri betwen Madison's and Gallitin's rivers they have also spoons made of the Buffaloe's horn and those of the Bighorn. Their bows are made of ceader or pine and have nothing remarkable about them. the back of the bow is covered with sinues and glue and is about 2 1/2 feet long. much the shape of those used by the Siouxs Mandans Minnetares &c. their arrows are more slender generally than those used by the nations just mentioned but much the same in construction. Their Sheild is formed of buffaloe hide, perfectly arrow proof, and is a circle of 2 feet 4 I. or 2 F. 6 I. in diameter. this is frequently painted with varios figures and ornamented around the edges with feather and a fringe of dressed leather. they sometimes make bows of the Elk's horn and those also of the bighorn. those of the Elk's horn are made of a single peice and covered on the back with glue and sinues like those made of wood, and are frequently ornamented with a stran wrought porcupine quills and sinues raped around them for some distance at both extremities. the bows of the bighorn are formed of small peices laid flat and cemented with gleue, and rolled with sinews, after which, they are also covered on the back with sinews and glew, and highly ornamented as they are much prized. forming the sheild is a cerimony of great importance among them, this implement would in their minds be devested of much of its protecting power were it not inspired with those virtues by their old men and jugglers. their method of preparing it is thus, an entire skin of a bull buffaloe two years old is first provided; a feast is next prepared and all the warriors old men and jugglers invited to partake. a hole is sunk in the ground about the same in diameter with the intended sheild and about 18 inches deep. a parcel of stones are now made red hot and thrown into the hole water is next thrown in and the hot stones cause it to emit a very strong hot steem, over this they spread the green skin which must not have been suffered to dry after taken off the beast. the flesh side is laid next to the groround and as many of the workmen as can reach it take hold on it's edges and extend it in every direction. as the skin becomes heated, the hair seperates and is taken of with the fingers, and the skin continues to contract untill the whoe is drawn within the compas designed for the shield, it is then taken off and laid on a parchment hide where they pound it with their heels when barefoot. this operation of pounding continues for several days or as long as the feast lasts when it is delivered to the propryeter and declared by the jugglers and old men to be a sufficient defence against the arrows of their enimies or even bullets if feast has been a satisfactory one. many of them beleive implisitly that a ball cannot penitrate their sheilds, in consequence of certain supernaural powers with which they have been inspired by their jugglers.- The Poggamoggon is an instrument with a handle of wood covered with dressed leather about the size of a whip handle and 22 inches long; a round stone of 2 pounds weight is also covered with leather and strongly united to the leather of the handle by a throng of 2 inches long; a loop of leather united to the handle passes arond the wrist. a very heavy blow may be given with this instrument. They have also a kind of armor which they form with many foalds of dressed Atelope's skin, unite with glue and sand. with this they cover their own bodies and those of their horses. these are sufficient against the effects of the arrow.- the quiver which contains their arrows and implements for making fire is formed of various skins. that of the Otter seems to be prefered. they are but narrow, of a length sufficent to protect the arrow from the weather, and are woarn on the back by means of a strap which passes over the left sholder and under the wright arm. their impliments for making fire is nothing more than a blunt arrow and a peice of well seasoned soft spongey wood such as the willow or cottonwood. the point of this arrow they apply to this dry stick so near one edge of it that the particles of wood which are seperated from it by the friction of the arrow falls down by it's side in a little pile. the arrow is held between the palms of the hand with the fingers extended, and being pressed as much as possible against the peice is briskly rolled between the palms of the hands backwards and forwards by pressing the arrow downwards the hands of course in rolling arrow also decend; they bring them back with a quick motion and repeat the operation till the dust by the friction takes fire; the peice and arrow are then removed and some dry grass or Boated wood is added. it astonished me to see in what little time these people would kindle fire in this way. in less than a minute they will produce fire.

Capt. Clark set out this morning very early and poroceeded but slowly in consequence of the difficulty of his road which lay along the steep side of a mountain over large irregular and broken masses of rocks which had tumbled from the upper part of the mountain. it was with much wrisk and pain that the horses could get on. at the distance of four miles he arrived at the river and the rocks were here so steep and juted into the river such manner that there was no other alternative but passing through the river, this he attempted with success tho water was so deep for a short distance as to swim the horses and was very rapid; he continued his rout one mile along the edge of the river under this steep Clift to a little bottom, below which the whole current of the river beat against the Stard. shore on which he was, and which was formed of a solid rock perfectly inaccessible to horses. here also the little track which he had been pursuing, terminated. he therefore determined to leave the horses and the majority of the party here and with his guide and three men to continue his rout down the river still further, in order more fully to satisfy himself as to it's practicability. accordingly he directed the men to hunt and fish at this place untill his return. they had not killed anything today but one goose, and the ballance of the little provision they had brought with them, as well as the five salmon they had procured yesterday were consumed last evening; there was of tours no inducement for his halting any time, at this place; after a few minutes he continued his rout clambering over immence rocks and along the sides of lofty precepices on the border of the river to the distance of 12 miles, at which place a large creek discharged itself on the Norh side 12 yds. wide and deep. a short distance above the entrance of this creek there is a narrow bottom which is the first that he had found on the river from that in which he left the horses and party. a plain indian road led up this creek which the guide informed him led to a large river that ran to the North, and was frequented by another nation who occasionally visited this river for the purpose of taking fish. at this place he saw some late appearance of Indians having been encamped and the tracks of a number of horses. Capt. C. halted here about 2 hours, caught some small fish, on which, with the addition of some berries, they dined. the river from the place at which he left the party to his present station was one continued rapid, in which there were five shoals neither of which could be passed with loaded canoes nor even run with empty ones. at those several places therefore it would be necessary to unload and transport the baggage for a considerable distance over steep and almost inacassable rocks where there was no possibility of employing horses for the releif of the men; the canoes would next have to be let down by cords and even with this precaution Capt. C. conceived there would be much wriske of both canoes and men. at one of those shoals the lofty perpendicular rocks which from the bases of the mountains approach the river so nearly on each side, as to prevent the possibility of a portage, or passage for the canoes without expending much labour in removing rocks and cuting away the earth in some places. to surmount These difficulties, precautions must be observed which in their execution must necessarily consume much time and provision, neither of which we can command. the season is now far advanced to remain in these mountains as the Indians inform us we shall shortly have snow; the salmon have so far declined that they are themselves haistening from the country and not an animal of any discription is to be seen in this difficult part of the river larger than a pheasant or a squirrel and they not abundant; add to this that our stock of provision is now so low that it would not support us more than ten days. the bends of the river are short and the currant beats from side to side against the rocks with great violence. the river is about 100 yds. wide and so deep that it cannot be foarded but in a few places, and the rocks approach the river so near in most places that there is no possibility of passing between them and the water; a passage therefore with horses along the river is also impracticable. The sides of these mountains present generally one barren surface of confused and broken masses of stone. above these are white or brown and towards the base of a grey colour and so hard that when struck with a steel, yeald fire like flint. those he had just past were scarcely releived by the appearance of a tree; but those below the entrance of the creek were better covered with timber, and there were also some tall pine near the river. The sides of the mountains are very steep, and the torrents of water which roll down their sides at certain seasons appear to carry with them vast quantities of the loose stone into the river. after dinner Capt. C. continued his rout down the river and at 1/2 a mile passed another creek not so large as that just mentioned, or about 5 yards wide. here his guide informed him that by ascending this creek some distance they would have a better road and would cut off a considerable bend which the river made to the south; accordingly he pursued a well beaten Indian track which led up this creek about six miles, then leaving the creek on the wright he passed over a ridge, and at the distance of a mile arrived at the river where it passes through a well timbered bottom of about eighty acres of land; they passed this bottom and asscended a steep and elivated point of a mountain, from whence the guide shewed him the brake of the river through the mountains for about 20 miles further. this view was terminated by one of the most lofty mountains, Capt. C. informed me, he had ever seen which was perfectly covered with snow. the river directed it's course immediately to this stupendous mountain at the bace of which the gude informe him those difficulties of which himself and nation had spoken, commenced. that after the river reached this mountain it continued it's rout to the North for many miles between high and perpendicular rocks, roling foaming and beating against innumerable rocks which crouded it's channel; that then it penetrated the mountain through a narrow gap leaving a perpendicular rock on either side as high as the top of the mountain which he beheld. that the river here making a bend they could not see through the mountain, and as it was impossible to decend the river or clamber over that vast mountain covered with eternal snow, neither himself nor any of his nation had ever been lower in this direction, than in view of the place at which the river entered this mountain; that if Capt. C. wished him to do so, he would conduct him to that place, where he thought they could probably arrive by the next evening. Capt. C. being now perfictly satisfyed as to the impractability of this rout either by land or water, informed the old man, that he was convinced of the varacity of his assertions and would now return to the village from whence they had set out where he expected to meet myself and party. they now returned to the upper part of the last creek he had passed, and encamped. it was an hour after dark before he reached this place. a small river falls into this fork of the Columbia just above the high mountain through which it passes on the south side.

[Clark, August 23, 1805] August 23rd Friday 1805 We Set out early proceed on with great dificuelty as the rocks were So Sharp large and unsettled and the hill sides Steep that the horses could with the greatest risque and dificulty get on, no provisions as the 5 Sammons given us yesterday by the Indians were eaten last night, one goose killed this morning; at 4 miles we came to a place the horses Could not pass without going into the river, we passed one mile to a verry bad riffle the water Confined in a narrow Channel & beeting against the left Shore, as we have no parth further and the Mounts. jut So close as to prevent the possibiley of horses proceeding down, I deturmined to delay the party here and with my guide and three men proceed on down to examine if the river continued bad or was practiable. I Set out with three men directing those left to hunt and fish until my return. I proceeded on Somtims in a Small wolf parth & at other times Climeing over the rocks for 12 miles to a large Creek on the right Side above the mouth of this Creek for a Short distance is a narrow bottom & the first, below the place I left my partey, a road passes down this Creek which I understoode passed to the water of a River which run to Th North & was the ground of another nation, Some fresh Sign about this Creek of horse and Camps. I delayd 2 hours to fish, Cought Some Small fish on which we dined.

The River from the place I left my party to this Creek is almost one continued rapid, five verry Considerable rapids the passage of either with Canoes is entirely impossable, as the water is Confined betwen hugh Rocks & the Current beeting from one against another for Some distance below &c. &c. at one of those rapids the mountains Close So Clost as to prevent a possibility of a portage with great labour in Cutting down the Side of the hill removeing large rocks &c. &c. all the others may be passed by takeing every thing over Slipery rocks, and the Smaller ones Passed by letting down the Canoes empty with Cords, as running them would certainly be productive of the loss of Some Canoes, those dificuelties and necessary precautions would delay us an emince time in which provisions would be necessary. (we have but little and nothing to be precured in this quarter except Choke Cheres & red haws not an animal of any kind to be seen and only the track of a Bear) below this Creek the lofty Pine is thick in the bottom hill Sides on the mountains & up the runs. The river has much the resemblance of that above bends Shorter and no passing, after a few miles between the river & the mountains & the Current So Strong that is dangerous crossing the river, and to proceed down it would rendr it necessarey to Cross almost at every bend This river is about 100 yards wide and can be forded but in a few places. below my guide and maney other Indians tell me that the Mountains Close and is a perpendicular Clift on each Side, and Continues for a great distance and that the water runs with great violence from one rock to the other on each Side foaming & roreing thro rocks in every direction, So as to render the passage of any thing impossible. those rapids which I had Seen he said was Small & trifleing in comparrison to the rocks & rapids below, at no great distance & The Hills or mountains were not like those I had Seen but like the Side of a tree Streight up-Those Mountains which I had passed were Steep Contain a white, a brown, & low down a Grey hard stone which would make fire, those Stone were of different Sises all Sharp and are continuly Slipping down, and in maney places one bed of those Stones inclined from the river bottom to the top of the mountains, The Torrents of water which come down aftr a rain carries with it emence numbers of those Stone into the river about 1/2 a mile below the last mentioned Creek another Creek falls in, my guide informed me that our rout was up this Creek by which rout we would Save a considerable bend of the river to the South. we proceeded on a well beeten Indian parth up this Creak about 6 miles and passed over a ridge 1 mile to the river in a Small vally through which we passed and assended a Spur of the Mountain from which place my guide Shew me the river for about 20 miles lower & pointed out the dificulty we returned to the last Creek & camped about one hour after dark.

There my guide Shewed me a road from the N Which Came into the one I was in which he Said went to a large river which run to the north on which was a Nation he called Tushapass, he made a map of it

[Lewis, August 24, 1805] Saturday August 24th 1805. As the Indians who were on their way down the Missouri had a number of spare hoses with them I thought it probable that I could obtain some of them and therefore desired the Cheif to speak to them and inform me whether they would trade. they gave no positive answer but requested to see the goods which I was willing to give in exchange. I now produced some battle axes which I had made at Fort Mandan with which they were much pleased. knives also seemed in great demand among them. I soon purchased three horses and a mule. for each horse I gave an ax a knife handkercheif and a little paint; & for the mule the addition of a knife a shirt handkercheif and a pair of legings; at this price which was quite double that given for the horses, the fellow who sold him made a merit of having bestoed me one of his mules. I consider this mule a great acquisition. These Indians soon told me that they had no more horses for sale and I directed the party to prepare to set out. I had now nine horses and a mule, and two which I had hired made twelve these I had loaded and the Indian women took the ballance of the baggage. I had given the Interpreter some articles with which to purchase a horse for the woman which he had obtained. at twelve Oclock we set out and passed the river below the forks, directing our rout towards the cove along the track formerly mentioned. most of the horses were heavily laden, and it appears to me that it will require at least 25 horses to convey our baggage along such roads as I expect we shall be obliged to pass in the mountains. I had now the inexpressible satisfaction to find myself once more under way with all my baggage and party. an Indian had the politeness to offer me one of his horses to ride which I accepted with cheerfullness as it enabled me to attend better to the march of the party. I had reached the lower part of the cove when an Indian rode up and informed me that one of my men was very sick and unable to come on. I directed the party to halt at a small run which falls into the creek on Lard. at the lower part of the Cove and rode back about 2 Miles where I found Wiser very ill with a fit of the cholic. I sent Sergt. Ordway who had remained with him for some water and gave him a doze of the essence of Peppermint and laudinum which in the course of half an hour so far recovered him that he was enabled to ride my horse and I proceeded on foot and rejoined the party. the sun was yet an hour high but the Indians who had for some time impatiently waited my return at length unloaded and turned out their horses and my party had followed there ex-ample. as it was so late and the Indians had prepared their camp for the night I thought it best to acquiess and determined also to remain. we had traveled only about six miles. after we encamped we had a slight shower of rain. Goodrich who is our principal fisherman caught several fine trout. Drewyer came to us late in the evening and had not killed anything. I gave the Indians who were absolutely engaged in transporting the baggage, a little corn as they had nothing to eat. I told Cameahwait that my stock of provision was too small to indulge all his people with provision and recommended it to him to advise such as were not assisting us with our baggage to go on to their camp to morrow and wait our arrival; which he did accordingly. Cameahwait literally translated is one who never walks. he told me that his nation had also given him another name by which he was signalized as a warrior which was Too-et'-te-con'-e or black gun. these people have many names in the course of their lives, particularly if they become distinguished characters. for it seems that every important event by which they happen to distinguish themselves intitles them to claim another name which is generally scelected by themselves and confirmed by the nation. those distinguishing acts are the killing and scalping an enemy, the killing a white bear, leading a party to war who happen to be successfull either in destroying their enemies or robing them of their horses, or individually stealing the horses of an enemy. these are considered acts of equal heroism among them, and that of killing an enemy without scalping him is considered of no importance; in fact the whole honour seems to be founded in the act of scalping, for if a man happens to slay a dozen of his enemies in action and others get the scalps or first lay their hand on the dead person the honor is lost to him who killed them and devolves on those who scalp or first touch them. Among the Shoshones, as well as all the Indians of America, bravery is esteemed the primary virtue; nor can any one become eminent among them who has not at some period of his life given proofs of his possessing this virtue. with them there can be no preferment without some warelike achievement, and so completely interwoven is this principle with the earliest Elements of thought that it will in my opinion prove a serious obstruction to the restoration of a general peace among the nations of the Missouri. while at Fort Mandan I was one day addressing some cheifs of the Minetares wo visited us and pointing out to them the advantages of a state of peace with their neighbours over that of war in which they were engaged. the Chiefs who had already geathered their havest of larals, and having forceably felt in many instances some of those inconveniences attending a state of war which I pointed out, readily agreed with me in opinon. a young fellow under the full impression of the Idea I have just suggested asked me if they were in a state of peace with all their neighhours what the nation would do for Cheifs?, and added that the cheifs were now oald and must shortly die and that the nation could not exist without cheifs. taking as granted that there could be no other mode devised for making Cheifs but that which custom had established through the medium of warlike acievements.

The few guns which the Shoshones have are reserved for war almost exclusively and the bow and arrows are used in hunting. I have seen a few skins among these people which have almost every appearance of the common sheep. they inform me that they finde this animals on the high mountains to the West and S. W. of them. it is about the size of the common sheep, the wool is reather shorter and more intermixed with long hairs particularly on the upper part of the neck. these skins have been so much woarn that I could not form a just Idea of the animal or it's colour. the Indians however inform me that it is white and that it's horns are lunated comprest twisted and bent backward as those of the common sheep. the texture of the skin appears to be that of the sheep. I am now perfectly convinced that the sheep as well as the Bighorn exist in these mountains.

The usual caparison of the Shoshone horse is a halter and saddle. the 1st consists either of a round plated or twisted cord of six or seven strands of buffaloe's hair, or a throng of raw hide made pliant by pounding and rubing. these cords of bufaloe's hair are about the size of a man's finger and remarkably strong. this is the kind of halter which is prefered by them. the halter of whatever it may be composed is always of great length and is never taken from the neck of the horse which they commonly use at any time. it is first attatched at one end about the neck of the horse with a knot that will not slip, it is then brought down to his under jaw and being passed through the mouth imbaces the under jaw and tonge in a simple noose formed by crossing the rope inderneath the jaw of the horse. this when mounted he draws up on the near side of the horse's neck and holds in the left hand, suffering it to trail at a great distance behind him sometimes the halter is attatched so far from the end that while the shorter end serves him to govern his horse, the other trails on the grond as before mentioned. they put their horses to their full speed with those cords trailing on the ground. when they turn out the horse to graze the noose is mearly loosed from his mouth. the saddle is made of wood and covered with raw hide which holds the parts very firmly together. it is made like the pack saddles in uce among the French and Spaniards. it consists of two flat thin boards which fit the sides of the horses back, and are held frirm by two peices which are united to them behind and before on the outer side and which rise to a considerable hight terminating sometimes in flat horizontal points extending outwards, and alwas in an accute angle or short bend underneath the upper part of these peices. a peice of buffaloe's skin with the hair on, is usually put underneath the saddle; and very seldom any covering on the saddle. stirrups when used are made of wood and covered with leather. these are generally used by the elderly men and women; the young men scarcely ever use anything more than a small pad of dressed leather stuffed with hair, which is confined with a leather thong passing arond the body of the horse in the manner of a girth. they frequently paint their favorite horses, and cut their ears in various shapes. they also decorate their mains and tails, which they never draw or trim, with the feathers of birds, and sometimes suspend at the breast of the horse the finest ornaments they possess. the Spanish bridle is prefered by them when they can obtain them, but they never dispence with the cord about the neck of the horse, which serves them to take him with more ease when he is runing at large. They are excellent horsemen and extreemly expert in casting the cord about the neck of a horse. the horses that have been habituated to be taken with the cord in this way, however wild they may appear at first, surrender the moment they feel the cord about their necks.- There are no horses in this quarter which can with propriety be termed wild. there are some few which have been left by the indians at large for so great a length of time that they have become shye, but they all shew marks of having been in possession of man. such is that one which Capt. Clark saw just below the three forks of the Missouri, and one other which I saw on the Missouri below the entrance of the Mussle shell river.- Capt. Clark set out very early this morning on his return, he traveled down the creek to it's entrance by the same Indian track he had ascended it; at the river he marked his name on a pine tree, then ascended to the bottom above the second creek, and brekfasted on burries, which occupied them about one hour. he now retraced his former track and joined the party where he had left them at 4 P.M. on his way Capt. C. fell from a rock and injured one of his legs very much. the party during his absence had killed a few pheasants and caught a few small fish on which together with haws and Serviceburies they had subsisted. they had also killed one cock of the Mountains Capt. Clark now wrote me a discription of the river and country, and stated our prospects by this rout as they have been heretofore mentioned and dispatched Colter on horseback with orders to loose no time reaching me. he set out late with the party continued his rout about two miles and encamped. Capt Clark had seen some trees which would make small canoes but all of them some distance below the Indian Caps which he passed at the entrance of fish Creek.

[Clark, August 24, 1805] August 24th Satturday 1805 Set out verry early this morning on my return passed down the Creek at the mouth marked my name on a pine Tree, proceed on to the bottom above the Creek & Brackfast on buries & delayed 1 hour, then proceed on up the river by the Same rout we decended to the place I left my party where we arrived at 4 oClock, (I Sliped & bruised my leg verry much on a rock) the party had killed Several phesents and Cought a fiew Small fish on which they had Subsisted in my absence. also a heath hen, near the Size of a Small turkey.

I wrote a letter to Capt Lewis informing him of the prospects before us and information recved of my guide which I thought favourable &c. & Stating two plans one of which for us to pursue &c. and despatched one man & horse and directed the party to get ready to march back, every man appeared disheartened from the prospects of the river, and nothing to eate, I Set out late and Camped 2 miles above, nothing to eate but Choke Cherries & red haws which act in different ways So as to make us Sick, dew verry heavy, my beding wet in passing around a rock the horses were obliged to go deep into the water.

The plan I stated to Capt Lewis if he agrees with me we shall adopt is to procure as many horses (one for each man) if possible and to hire my present guide who I sent on to him to interegate thro the Intprtr. and proceed on by land to Some navagable part of the Columbia River, or to the Ocean, depending on what provisions we can procure by the gun aded to the Small Stock we have on hand depending on our horses as the last resort.

a second plan to divide the party one part to attempt this deficuet river with what provisions we had, and the remaindr to pass by Land on hose back Depending on our gun &c for Provisions &c. and come together occasionally on the river.

the 1s of which I would be most pleased with &c.

I saw Several trees which would make Small Canoes and by putting 2 together would make a Siseable one, all below the last Indian Camp Several miles

[Lewis, August 25, 1805] Sunday August 25th 1805. This morning loaded our horses and set out a little after sunrise; a few only of the Indians unengaged in assisting us went on as I had yesterday proposed to the Cheif. the others flanked us on each side and started some Antelope which they pursued for several hours but killed none of them. we proceeded within 2 Ms. of the narrow pass or seven miles from our camp of last evening and halted for dinner. Our hunters joined us at noon with three deer the greater part of which I gave the indians. sometime after we had halted, Charbono mentioned to me with apparent unconcern that he expected to meet all the Indians from the camp on the Columbia tomorrow on their way to the Missouri. allarmed at this information I asked why he expected to meet them. he then informed me that the 1st Cheif had dispatched some of his young men this morning to this camp requesting the Indians to meet them tomorrow and that himself and those with him would go on with them down the Missouri, and consequently leave me and my baggage on the mountain or thereabouts. I was out of patience with the folly of Charbono who had not sufficient sagacity to see the consequences which would inevitably flow from such a movement of the indians, and altho he had been in possession of this information since early in the morning when it had been communicated to him by his Indian woman yet he never mentioned it untill the after noon. I could not forbear speaking to him with some degree of asperity on this occasion. I saw that there was no time to be lost in having those orders countermanded, or that we should not in all probability obtain any more horses or even get my baggage to the waters of the Columbia. I therefore Called the three Cheifs together and having smoked a pipe with them, I asked them if they were men of their words, and whether I could depent on the promises they had made me; they readily answered in the affermative; I then asked them if they had not promised to assist me with my baggage to their camp on the other side of the mountains, or to the place at which Capt. Clark might build the canoes, should I wish it. they acknowledged that they had. I then asked them why they had requested their people on the other side of the mountain to meet them tomorrow on the mountain where there would be no possibility of our remaining together for the purpose of trading for their horses as they had also promised. that if they had not promised to have given me their assistance in transporting my baggage to the waters on the other side of the mountain that I should not have attempted to pass the mountains but would have returned down the river and that in that case they would never have seen anymore white men in their country. that if they wished the white men to be their friends and to assist them against their enemies by furnishing them with arms and keeping their enemies from attacking them that they must never promis us anything which they did not mean to perform. that when I had first seen them they had doubted what I told them about the arrival of the party of whitemen in canoes, that they had been convinced that what I told them on that occasion was true, why then would they doubt what I said on any other point. I told them that they had witnessed my liberality in dividing the meat which my hunters killed with them; and that I should continue to give such of them as assisted me a part of whatever we had ourselves to eat. and finally concluded by telling them if they intended to keep the promises they had made me to dispatch one of their young men immediately with orders to their people to remain where they were untill our arrival. the two inferior cheifs said that they wished to assist me and be as good as their word, and that they had not sent for their people, that it was the first Chief who had done so, and they did not approve of the measure. Cameahwait remained silent for some time, at length he told me that he knew he had done wrong but that he had been induced to that measure from seeing all his people hungary, but as he had promised to give me his assistance he would not in future be worse than his word. I then desired him to send immediately and countermand his orders; acordingly a young man was sent for this purpose and I gave him a handkerchief to engage him in my interest. this matter being arranged to my satisfaction I called all the women and men together who had been assisting me in the transportation of the baggage and gave them a billet for each horse which they had imployed in that service and informed them when we arrived at the plaice where we should finally halt on the river I would take the billet back and give them merchandize for it. every one appeared now satisfyed and when I ordered the horses loaded for our departure the Indians were more than usually allert. we continued our march untill late in the evening and encamped at the upper part of the cove where the creek enters the mountains; here our hunters joined us with another deer which they had killed, this I gave to the women and Children, and for my own part remained supperless. I observed considerable quantities of wild onions in the bottom lands of this cove. I also saw several large hares and many of the cock of the plains.

Capt. Clark set out early this morning and continued his rout to the indian camp at the entrance of fish Creek; here he halted about an hour; the indians gave himself and party some boiled salmon and hurries. these people appeared extreemly hospitable tho poor and dirty in the extreem. he still pursued the track up the river by which he had decended and in the evening arrived at the bluff on the river where he had encamped on the 21st Inst. it was late in the evening before he reached this place. they formed their camp, and Capt. C. sent them in different directions to hunt and fish. some little time after they halted a party of Indians passed by on their way down the river, consisting of a man a woman and several boys; from these people the guide obtained 2 salmon which together with some small fish they caught and a beaver which Shannon killed furnished them with a plentifull supper. the pine grows pretty abundantly high up on the sides of the mountains on the opposite side of the river. one of the hunters saw a large herd of Elk on the opposite side of the river in the edge of the timbered land.- Winsor was taken very sick today and detained Capt C. very much on his march. three hunters whom he had sent on before him this morning joined him in the evening having killed nothing; they saw only one deer.

The course and the distances, of Capt. Clark's rout down this branch of the Columbia below this bluff, commencing opposite to an Island, are as follow.

This morning while passing through the Shoshone cove Frazier fired his musquet at some ducks in a little pond at the distance of about 60 yards from me; the ball rebounded from the water and pased within a very few feet of me. near the upper part of this cove the Shoshonees suffered a very severe defeat by the Minnetares about six years since. this part of the cove on the N. E. side of the Creek has lately been birned by the Indians as a signal on some occasion.

[Clark, August 25, 1805] August 25th Sunday 1805 Set out verry early and halted one hour at the Indian Camp, they were kind gave us all a little boiled Sarnmon & dried buries to eate, abt. half as much as I could eate, those people are kind with what they have but excessive pore & Durtey.- we proceeded on over the mountains we had before passed to the Bluff we Encamped at on the 21s instant where we arrived late and turned out to hunt & fish, Cought Several Small fish, a party of Squars & one man with Several boys going down to guathe berries below, my guide got two Sammon from this party (which made about half a Supper for the party), after Dark Shannon came in with a beaver which the Party suped on Sumptiously- one man verry Sick to day which detained us verry much I had three hunters out all day, they saw one Deer, killed nothing. one of the Party Saw 9 Elk on a Mountain to our right assending, amongst the Pine timber which is thick on that side

[Lewis, August 26, 1805] Monday August 26th 1805. This morning was excessively cold; there was ice on the vessels of water which stood exposed to the air nearly a quarter of an inch thick. we collected our horses and set out at sunrise. we soon arrived at the extreem source of the Missouri; here I halted a few minutes, the men drank of the water and consoled themselves with the idea of having at length arrived at this long wished for point. from hence we proceeded to a fine spring on the side of the mountain where I had lain the evening before I first arrived at the Shoshone Camp. here I halted to dine and graize our horses, there being fine green grass on that part of the hillside which was moistened by the water of the spring while the grass on the other parts was perfectly dry and parched with the sun. I directed a pint of corn to be given each Indian who was engaged in transporting our baggage and about the same quantity to each of the men which they parched pounded and made into supe. one of the women who had been assisting in the transportation of the baggage halted at a little run about a mile behind us, and sent on the two pack horses which she had been conducting by one of her female friends. I enquired of Cameahwait the cause of her detention, and was informed by him in an unconcerned manner that she had halted to bring fourth a child and would soon overtake us; in about an hour the woman arrived with her newborn babe and passed us on her way to the camp apparently as well as she ever was. It appears to me that the facility and ease with which the women of the aborigines of North America bring fourth their children is reather a gift of nature than depending as some have supposed on the habitude of carrying heavy burthens on their backs while in a state of pregnancy. if a pure and dry air, an elivated and cold country is unfavourable to childbirth, we might expect every difficult incident to that operation of nature in this part of the continent; again as the snake Indians possess an abundance of horses, their women are seldom compelled like those in other parts of the continent to carry burthens on their backs, yet they have their children with equal convenience, and it is a rare occurrence for any of them to experience difficulty in childbirth. I have been several times informed by those who were conversant with the fact, that the indian women who are pregnant by whitemen experience more difficulty in childbirth than when pregnant by an Indian. if this be true it would go far in suport of the opinion I have advanced.

the tops of the high and irregular mountains which present themselves to our view on the opposite side of this branch of the Columbia are yet perfectly covered with snow; the air which proceeds from those mountains has an agreeable coolness and renders these parched and South hillsides much more supportable at this time of the day it being now about noon. I observe the indian women collecting the root of a speceis of fennel which grows in the moist grounds and feeding their poor starved children; it is really distressing to witness the situation of those poor wretches. the radix of this plant is of the knob kind, of a long ovate form terminating in a single radicle, the whole bing about 3 or four inches in length and the thickest part about the size of a man's little finger. it is white firm and crisp in it's present state, when dryed and pounded it makes a fine white meal; the flavor of this root is not unlike that of annisseed but not so pungent; the stem rises to the hight of 3 or four feet is jointed smooth and cilindric; from r to 4 of those knobed roots are attatched to the base of this stem. the leaf is sheathing sessile, & pultipartite, the divisions long and narrow; the whole is of a deep green. it is now in blame; the flowers are numerous, small, petals white, and are of the umbellaferous kind. several small peduncles put forth from the main stock one at each joint above the sheathing leaf. it has no root leaves. the root of the present year declines when the seeds have been matured and the succeeding spring other roots of a similar kind put fourth from the little knot which unites the roots and stem and grow and decline with the stem as before mentioned. The sunflower is very abundant near the watercourses the seeds of this plant are now rip and the natives collect them in considerable quantities and reduce them to meal by pounding and rubing them between smooth stones. this meal is a favorite food their manner of using it has been beforementiond. after dinner we continued our rout towards the village. on our near approach we were met by a number of young men on horseback. Cameahwait requested that we would discharge our guns when we arrived in sight of the Village, accordingly when I arrived on an eminence above the village in the plain I drew up the party at open order in a single rank and gave them a runing fire discharging two rounds. they appeared much gratified with this exhibition. we then proceeded to the village or encampment of brush lodges 32 in number. we were conducted to a large lodge which had been prepared for me in the center of their encampmerit which was situated in a beautifull level smooth and extensive bottom near the river about 3 miles above the place I had first found them encamped. here we arrived at 6 in the evening arranged our baggage near my tent and placed those of the men on either side of the baggage facing outwards. I found Colter here who had just arrived with a letter from Capt. Clark in which Capt. C. had given me an account of his peregrination and the description of the river and country as before detailed from this view of the subject I found it a folly to think of attemping to decend this river in canoes and therefore to commence the purchase of horses in the morning from the indians in order to carry into execution the design we had formed of passing the rocky Mountains. I now informed Cameahwait of my intended expedition overland to the great river which lay in the plains beyond the mountains and told him that I wished to purchase 20 horses of himself and his people to convey our baggage. he observed that the Minnetares had stolen a great number of their horses this spring but hoped his people would spear me the number I wished. I also asked a guide, he observed that he had no doubt but the old man who was with Capt. C. would accompany us if we wished him and that he was better informed of the country than any of them. matters being thus far arranged I directed the fiddle to be played and the party danced very merily much to the amusement and gratification of the natives, though I must confess that the state of my own mind at this moment did not well accord with the prevailing mirth as I somewhat feared that the caprice of the indians might suddenly induce them to withhold their horses from us without which my hopes of prosicuting my voyage to advantage was lost; however I determined to keep the indians in a good humour if possible, and to loose no time in obtaining the necessary number of horses. I directed the hunters to turn out early in the morning and indeavor to obtain some meat. I had nothing but a little parched corn to eat this evening.

This morning Capt. C. and party

[Clark, August 26, 1805] August 26th Monday 1805 a fine morning Despatched three men a head to hunt, our horses missing Sent out my guide and four men to hunt them, which detained me untill 9 oClock a.m. at which time I Set out and proceeded on by the way of the forks to the Indian Camps at the first were not one mouthfull to eate untill night as our hunters could kill nothing and I could See & catch no fish except a few Small ones. The Indians gave us 2 Sammon boiled which I gave to the men, one of my men Shot a Sammon in the river about Sunset those fish gave us a Supper. all the Camp flocked about me untill I went to Sleep- and I beleve if they had a Sufficency to eate themselves and any to Spare they would be liberal of it I derected the men to mend their Mockessons to night and turn out in the morning early to hunt Deer fish birds &c. &c. Saw great numbers of the large Black grass hopper. Some bars which were verry wild, but few Birds. a number of ground Lizards; Some fiew Pigions

[Clark, August 27, 1805] August 27th Tuesday 1805 Some frost this morning every Man except one, out hunting, a young man Came from the upper Village & informed me that Capt Lewis would join me abt. 12 oClock to day. one man killed a Small Sammon, and the Indians gave us another which afforded us a Sleight brackfast. Those Pore people are here depending on what fish They Can Catch, without anything else to depend on; and appere Contented, my party hourly Complaining of their retched Situation and doubts of Starveing in a Countrey where no game of any kind except a fiew fish can be found, an Indian brough in to the Camp 5 Sammon, two of which I purchased which afforded us a Supper.

[Clark, August 28, 1805] August 28th Wednesday 1805 a frost this morning. The Inds. Cought out of their traps Several Sammon and gave us two, I purchased two others which we made last us to day. Several a Camp of about 40 Indians came from the West fork and passed up to day, nothing killed by my party with every exertion in all places where game probably might be found. I dispatched one man to the upper camps to enquire if Cap. Lewis was comeing &c. he returned after night with a letter from Capt. Lewis informing me of his Situation at the upper Village, and had precured 22 horses for our rout through by land on the plan which I had preposed in which he agreed with me in; and requsted me to ride up and get the horses the Indian informed him they had reserved for me &c. I purchased Some fish roe of those pore but kind people with whome I am Encamped for which I gave three Small fish hooks, the use of which they readily proseved, one Indian out all day & killed only one Sammon with his gig; my hunters killed nothing, I had three pack Saddles made to day for our horses which I expected Capt Lewis would purchase &c. Those Sammon which I live on at present are pleasent eateing, not with standing they weaken me verry fast and my flesh I find is declineing

[Clark, August 29, 1805] August 29th Thursday 1805 a Cold morning Some frost. the Wind from the South, I left our baggage in possession of 2 men and proceeded on up to join Capt Lewis at the upper Village of Snake Indians where I arrived at 1 oClock found him much engaged in Counceling and attempting to purchase a fiew more horses. I Spoke to the Indians on various Subjects endeavoring to impress on theire minds the advantaje it would be to them for to Sell us horses and expedite the our journey the nearest and best way possibly that we might return as Soon as possible and winter with them at Some place where there was plenty of buffalow,- our wish is to get a horse for each man to Carry our baggage and for Some of the men to ride occasionally, The horses are handsom and much acustomed to be changed as to their Parsture; we cannot Calculate on their carrying large loads & feed on the Grass which we may Calculate on finding in the Mountain Thro which we may expect to pass on our rout made Some Selestial observations, the Lard. of this Part the Columbia River is _____ North. Longtd. _____ W

I purchased a horse for which I gave my Pistol 100 Balls Powder & a Knife. our hunters Killed 2 Deer near their Camp to day. 2 yesterday & 3 The Day before, this meet was a great treat to me as I had eate none for 8 days past

[Clark, August 30, 1805] August 30th Friday 1805 a fine Morning, finding that we Could purchase no more horse than we had for our goods &c. (and those not a Sufficint number for each of our Party to have one which is our wish) I Gave my Fuzee to one of the men & Sold his musket for a horse which Completed us to 29 total horses, we Purchased pack Cords Made Saddles & Set out on our rout down the river by land guided by my old guide one other who joined him, the old gude's 3 Sons followed him before we Set out our hunters killed three Deer proceded on 12 miles and encamped on the river South Side- at the time we Set out from the Indian Camps the greater Part of the Band Set out over to the waters of the Missouri. we had great attention paid to the horses, as they were nearly all Sore Backs and Several pore, & young Those horses are indifferent, maney Sore backs and others not acustomed to pack, and as we Cannot put large loads on them are Compelled to purchase as maney as we Can to take our Small propotion of baggage of the Parties. (& Eate if necessary) Proceeded on 12 miles to day

[Clark, August 31, 1805] August 31st 1805 Satturday A fine morning Set out before Sun rise, as we passed the lodges at which place I had encamped for thre nights and left 2 men, Those 2 men joined us and we proceeded on in the Same rout I decended the 21st Instant, halted 3 hours on Sammon Creek to Let our horses graze the wind hard from the S. W. I met an Indian on horse back who fled with great Speed to Some lodges below & informed them that the Enemis were Coming down, armd with guns &c. the inhabitents of the Lodges indisceved him, we proceeded on the road on which I had decended as far as the 1st run below & left the road & Proceeded up the Run in a tolerable road 4 miles & Encamped in Some old lodjes at the place the road leaves the Creek and assends the high Countrey Six Indians followed us four of them the Sons of our guide; our hunters killed one Deer a goose & Prarie fowl. This day warm and Sultrey, Praries or open Valies on fire in Several places- The Countrey is Set on fire for the purpose of Collecting the different bands, and a Band of the Flatheads to go to the Missouri where They intend passing the winter near the Buffalow Proceeded on 22 miles to Day, 4 miles of which up a run

[Clark, September 1, 1805] September 1st Sunday 1805 a fine morning Set out early and proceeded on over high ruged hills passing the heads of the Small runs which fall into the river on our left to a large Creek which falls into the river 6 miles to our left and encamped in the bottom, Some rain to day at 12 and in the evening which obliges us to Continu all night despatched 2 men to the mouth of the Creek to purchase fish of the Indians at that place, They returned with Some dried, we giged 4 Sammon & killed one Deer to Day. the Countrey which we passed to day is well watered & broken Pore Stoney hilly country except the bottoms of the Creek which is narrow, all the Indians leave us except our Guide, one man Shot two bear this evining unfortunately we Could git neither of them

[Clark, September 2, 1805] September 2nd Monday 1805 a Cloudy Mornin, raind Some last night we Set out early and proceeded on up the Creek, Crossed a large fork from the right and one from the left; and at 8 miles left the roade on which we were pursuing and which leads over to the Missouri; and proceeded up a West fork without a roade proceded on thro thickets in which we were obliged to Cut a road, over rockey hill Sides where our horses were in pitial danger of Slipping to Ther certain distruction & up & Down Steep hills, where Several horses fell, Some turned over, and others Sliped down Steep hill Sides, one horse Crippeled & 2 gave out. with the greatest dificuley risque &c. we made five miles & Encamped on The left Side of the Creek in a Small Stoney bottom after night Some time before the rear Came up, one Load left, about 2 miles back, the horse on which it was Carried Crippled. Some rain at night

[Clark, September 3, 1805] September 3rd Tuesday 1805 A Cloudy morning, horses verry Stiff Sent 2 men back with the horse on which Capt Lewis rode for the load left back last night which detained us until) 8 oClock at which time we Set out. The Country is timbered with Pine Generally the bottoms have a variety of Srubs & the fur trees in Great abundance. hills high & rockey on each Side, in the after part of the day the high mountains closed the Creek on each Side and obliged us to take on the Steep Sides of those Mountains, So Steep that the horses Could Screcly keep from Slipping down, Several Sliped & Injured themselves verry much, with great dificuelty we made _____ miles & Encamped on a branh of the Creek we assended after Crossing Several Steep points & one mountain, but little to eate I killed 5 Pheasents & The huntes 4 with a little Corn afforded us a kind of Supper, at dusk it began to Snow at 3 oClock Some rain. the mountains to the East Covered with Snow. we met with a great misfortune, in haveing our last Thmometer broken by accident, This day we passed over emence hils and Some of the worst roade that ever horses passed our horses frequently fell Snow about 2 inches deep when it began to rain which termonated in a Sleet our genl. Courses nearly North from the R

[Clark, September 4, 1805] September 4th Wednesday 1805 a verry cold morning every thing wet and frosed, we detained untill 8 oClock to thaw the covering for the baggage &c. &c. groun covered with Snow, we assended a mountain & took a Divideing ridge which we kept for Several Miles & fell on the head of a Creek which appeared to run the Course we wished to go, I was in front, & Saw Several of the Argalia or Ibex decended the mountain by verry Steep decent takeing the advantage of the points and best places to the Creek, where our hunter killed a Deer which we made use of and prosued our Course down the Creek to the forks about 5 miles where we met a part of the Flat head nation of 33 Lodges about 80 men 400 Total and at least 500 horses, those people recved us friendly, threw white robes over our Sholders & Smoked in the pipes of peace, we Encamped with them & found them friendly but nothing but berries to eate a part of which they gave us, those Indians are well dressed with Skin Shirts & robes, they Stout & light complected more So than Common for Indians, The Chiefs harangued untill late at night, Smoked our pipe and appeared Satisfied. I was the first white man who ever wer on the waters of this river.

[Clark, September 5, 1805] September 5th Thursday 1805 a Cloudy morning we assembled the Chiefs & warriers and Spoke to them (with much dificuely as what we Said had to pass through Several languajes before it got in to theirs, which is a gugling kind of languaje Spoken much thro the fhrought) we informed them who we were, where we Came from, where bound and for what purpose &c. &c. and requsted to purchase & exchange a fiew horses with them, in the Course of the day I purchased 11 horses & exchanged 7 for which we gave a fiew articles of merchendize. those people possess ellegant horses.- we made 4 Chiefs whome we gave meadels & a few Small articles with Tobacco; the women brought us a few berries & roots to eate and the Principal Chief a Dressed Brarow, otter & two Goat & antilope Skins

Those people wore their hair the men Cewed with otter Skin on each Side falling over the Sholrs forward, the women loose promisquisly over ther Sholdrs & face long Shirts which Coms to the anckles & tied with a belt about their waste with a roabe over, the have but fiew ornaments and what they do were are Similar to the Snake Indians, They Call themselves Eoote-lash-Schute and consist of 450 Lodges in all and divided into Several bands on the heads of Columbia river & Missouri, Some low down the Columbia River

[Clark, September 6, 1805] September 6th Friday 1805 Some little rain, purchased two fine horses & took a Vocabiliary of the language litened our loads & packed up, rained contd. Untill 12 oClock we Set out at 2 oClock at the Same time all the Indians Set out on Ther way to meet the Snake Indians at the 3 forks of the Missouri. Crossed a Small river from the right we call _____ Soon after Setting out, also a Small Creek from the North all three forks Comeing together below our Camp at which place the Mountains Close on each Side of the river, We proceeded on N 30 W. Crossed a Mountain and Struck the river Several miles down, at which place the Indians had Encamped two days before, we Proceeded on Down the River which is 30 yds. wide Shallow & Stoney. Crossing it Several times & Encamped in a Small bottom on the right side. rained this evening nothing to eate but berries, our flour out, and but little Corn, the hunters killed 2 pheasents only- all our horses purchased of the oote lash Shutes we Secured well for fear of their leaveing of us, and watched them all night for fear of their leaving us or the Indians prosuing & Steeling them.

[Clark, September 7, 1805] September 7th Satturday 1805 A Cloudy & rainie Day the greater Part of the Day dark & Drisley we proceedd on down the river thro a Vallie passed Several Small Runs on the right & 3 creeks on the left The Vallie from 1 to 2 miles wide the Snow top mountains to our left, open hilley Countrey on the right. Saw 2 horses left by the Indians Those horses were as wild a Elk. One of our hunters Came up this morning without his horse, in the course of the night the horse broke loose & Cleared out- we did not make Camp untill dark, for the want of a good place, one of our hunters did not join us this evening. he haveing killed an elk packed his horses & could not overtake us

[Clark, September 8, 1805] September 8th Sunday 1805 a Cloudy morning Set out early and proceeded on through an open vallie for 23 miles passed 4 Creeks on the right Some runs on the left, The bottoms as also the hills Stoney bad land. Some pine on the Creeks and mountains, an partial on the hills to the right hand Side. two of our hunters came up with us at 12 oClock with an Elk, & Buck- the wind from the N. W. & Cold. The foot of the Snow mountains approach the River on the left Side. Some Snow on The mountain to the right also proceeded on down the Vallie which is pore Stoney land and encamped on the right Side of the river a hard rain all the evening we are all Cold and wet. on this part of the river on the head of Clarks River I observe great quantities of a peculiar Sort of Prickly peare grow in Clusters ovel & about the Size of a Pigions egge with Strong Thorns which is So birded as to draw the Pear from the Cluster after penetrateing our feet. Drewyer killed a Deer. I killed a prarie fowl we found 2 mears and a Colt the mears were lame, we ventered to let our late purchase of horses loose to night

[Lewis, September 9, 1805] Monday September 9th 1805. Set out at 7 A M. this morning and proceeded down the Flathead river leaving it on our left, the country in the valley of this river is generally a prarie and from five to 6 miles wide the growth is almost altogether pine principally of the longleafed kind, with some spruce and a kind of furr resembleing the scotch furr. near the wartercourses we find a small proportion of the narrow leafed cottonwood some redwood honeysuckle and rosebushes form the scant proportion of underbrush to be seen. at 12 we halted on a small branch which falls in to the river on the E. side, where we breakfasted on a scant proportion of meat which we had reserved from the hunt of yesterday added to three geese which one of our hunters killed this morning. two of our hunters have arrived, one of them brought with him a redheaded woodpecker of the large kind common to the U States. this is the first of the kind I have seen since I left the Illinois. just as we were seting out Drewyer arrived with two deer. we continued our rout down the valley about 4 miles and crossed the river; it is hear a handsome stream about 100 yards wide and affords a considerable quantity of very clear water, the banks are low and it's bed entirely gravel. the stream appears navigable, but from the circumstance of their being no sammon in it I believe that there must be a considerable fall in it below. our guide could not inform us where this river discharged itself into the columbia river, he informed us that it continues it's course along the mountains to the N. as far as he knew it and that not very distant from where we then were it formed a junction with a stream nearly as large as itself which took it's rise in the mountains near the Missouri to the East of us and passed through an extensive valley generally open prarie which forms an excellent pass to the Missouri. the point of the Missouri where this Indian pass intersects it, is about 30 miles above the gates of the rocky mountain, or the place where the valley of the Missouri first widens into an extensive plain after entering the rockey mountains. the guide informed us that a man might pass to the missouri from hence by that rout in four days. we continued our rout down the W. side of the river about 5 miles further and encamped on a large creek which falls in on the West as our guide informes that we should leave the river at this place and the weather appearing settled and fair I determined to halt the next day rest our horses and take some scelestial Observations. we called this Creek Travellers rest. it is about 20 yards wide a fine bould clear runing stream the land through which we passed is but indifferent a could white gravley soil. we estimate our journey of this day at 19 M.

[Clark, September 9, 1805] September 9th Monday 1805 a fair morning Set out early and proceeded on thro a plain as yesterday down the valley Crossed a large Scattering Creek on which Cotton trees grew at 11/2 miles, a Small one at 10 miles, both from the right, the main river at 15 miles & Encamped on a large Creek from the left which we call Travelers rest Creek. killed 4 deer & 4 Ducks & 3 prarie fowls. day fair Wind N. W. See Suplement

[Lewis, September 10, 1805] Tuesday September 10th 1805. The morning being fair I sent out all the hunters, and directed two of them to procede down the river as far as it's junction with the Eastern fork which heads near the missouri, and return this evening. this fork of the river we determined to name the Valley plain river. I think it most probable that this river continues it's course along the rocky Mts. Northwardly as far or perhaps beyond the scources of Medecine river and then turning to the West falls into the Tacootchetessee. The Minetares informed us that there was a large river west of, and at no great distance from the sources of Medecine river, which passed along the Rocky Mountains from S. to N.this evening one of our hunters returned accompanyed by three men of the Flathead nation whom he had met in his excurtion up travellers rest Creek. on first meeting him the Indians were allarmed and prepared for battle with their bows and arrows, but he soon relieved their fears by laying down his gun and advancing towards them. the Indians were mounted on very fine horses of which the Flatheads have a great abundance; that is, each man in the nation possesses from 20 to a hundred head. our guide could not speake the language of these people but soon engaged them in conversation by signs or jesticulation, the common language of all the Aborigines of North America, it is one understood by all of them and appears to be sufficiently copious to convey with a degree of certainty the outlines of what they wish to communicate. in this manner we learnt from these people that two men which they supposed to be of the Snake nation had stolen 23 horses from them and that they were in pursuit of the theaves. they told us they were in great hast, we gave them some boiled venison, of which the eat sparingly. the sun was now set, two of them departed after receiving a few small articles which we gave them, and the third remained, having agreed to continue with us as a guide, and to introduce us to his relations whom he informed us were numerous and resided in the plain below the mountains on the columbia river, from whence he said the water was good and capable of being navigated to the sea; that some of his relation were at the sea last fall and saw an old whiteman who resided there by himself and who had given them some handkerchiefs such as he saw in our possession.- he said it would require five sleeps wich is six days travel, to reach his relations. the Flatheads are a very light coloured people of large stature and comely form.

[Clark, September 10, 1805] September 10th Tuesday 1805 A fair morning Concluded to Delay to day and make Some observations, as at this place the rout which we are to prosue will pass up the Travelers rest Creek, The day proved fair and we took equal altitudes & Some Inner observations. The Latd. 46° 48' 28" as the guide report that no game is to be found on our rout for a long ways, ads an addition to the cause of our delay to precure Some meat, despatched all our hunters in different directions, to hunt the Deer which is the only large game to be found they killed 4 deer a Beaver & 3 Grouse which was divided, one of the hunters Colter, met with 3 Tushapaw Indians who were in pursuit of 2 Snake Indians that bade taken from ther Camps on the head of Kooskooske River 21 horses, Those Indians came with Colter to our Camp & informed by Signs of their misfortune & the rout to ther villages &c. &c. one of them Concluded to return with us. we gave them a ring fish hook & tied a pece of ribin in the hare of each which appeared to please them verry much, Cap Lewis gave them a Steel & a little Powder to make fire, after eating 2 of them proceeded on in pursute of their horses. men all much engaged preparing mockersons &c. &c. The Countrey about this place is already described in that above.

[Clark, September 11, 1805] September 11th Wednesday 1805 A fair morning wind from the N W we Set out at 3 oClock and proceeded on up the Travelers rest Creek, accompanied by the flat head or Tushapaws Indians about 7 miles below this Creek a large fork comes in from the right and heads up against the waters of the Missouri below the Three forks, this river has extensive Vallies of open leavel land, "and passes in its Whole Course thro a Valie" they call it our Guide tels us a fine large roade passes up this river to the Missouri- The loss of 2 of our horses detained us util. 3 oClock. P.M. our Flathead Indian being restless thought proper to leave us and proceed on alone, Sent out the hunters to hunt in advance as usial. (we have Selected 4 of the best hunters to go in advance to hunt for the party. This arrangement has been made long sinc) we Proceeded on up the Creek on the right Side thro a narrow valie and good road for 7 miles and Encamped at Some old Indian Lodges, nothing killed this evening hills on the right high & ruged, the mountains on the left high & Covered with Snow. The day Verry worm

[Clark, September 12, 1805] September 12th Thursday 1805 a white frost Set out at 7 oClock & proceeded on up the Creek, passed a Fork on the right on which I saw near an old Indian encampment a Swet house Covered wthh earth, at 2 miles assended a high hill & proceeded through a hilley and thickly timbered Countrey for 9 miles & on the Right of the Creek, passing Several branches from the right of fine clear water and Struck at a fork at which place the road forks, one passing up each fork. The Timber is Short & long leaf Pine Spruce Pine & fur. The road through this hilley Countrey is verry bad passing over hills & thro Steep hollows, over falling timber &c. &c. continued on & passed Some most intolerable road on the Sides of the Steep Stoney mountains, which might be avoided by keeping up the Creek which is thickly covered with under groth & falling timber Crossed a mountain 8 miles with out water & encamped on a hill Side on the Creek after Decending a long Steep mountain, Some of our Party did not git up untill 10 oClock P M. I mad camp at 8 on this roade & particularly on this Creek the Indians have pealed a number of Pine for the under bark which they eate at certain Seasons of the year, I am told in the Spring they make use of this bark our hunters Killed only one Pheasent this after noon. Party and horses much fatigued.

[Clark, September 13, 1805] September 13th Wednesday 1805 a cloudy morning Capt Lewis and one of our guides lost their horses, Capt Lewis & 4 men detained to hunt the horses, I proceeded on with the partey up the Creek at 2 miles passed Several Springs which I observed the Deer Elk &c. had made roads to, and below one of the Indians had made a whole to bathe, I tasted this water and found it hot & not bad tasted The last _____ in further examination I found this water nearly boiling hot at the places it Spouted from the rocks (which a hard Corse Grit, and of great size the rocks on the Side of the Mountain of the Same texture) I put my finger in the water, at first could not bare it in a Second-as Several roads led from these Springs in different derections, my Guide took a wrong road and took us out of our rout 3 miles through intolerable rout, after falling into the right road I proceeded on thro tolerabl rout for abt. 4 or 5 miles and halted to let our horses graze as well as waite for Capt Lewis who has not yet Come up, The pine Countrey falling timber &c. &c. Continue. This Creek is verry much darned up with the beaver, but we can See none, dispatched two men back to hunt Capt Lewis horse, after he came up, and we proceeded over a mountain to the head of the Creek which we left to our left and at 6 miles from the place I nooned it, we fell on a Small Creek from the left which Passed through open glades Some of which 1/2 a mile wide, we proceeded down this Creek about 2 miles to where the mountains Closed on either Side crossing the Creek Several times & Encamped.

One Deer & Some Pheasants killed this morning, I shot 4 Pheasents of the Common Kind except the taile was black. The road over the last mountain was thick Steep & Stoney as usial, after passing the head of Travelers rest Creek, the road was verry fine leavel open & firm Some mountains in view to the S E & S W. Covered with Snow.

[Clark, September 14, 1805] September 14th Thursday 1805 a Cloudy day in the Valies it rained and hailed, on the top of the mountains Some Snow fell we Set out early and Crossed a high mountn on the right of the Creek for 6 miles to the forks of the Glade Creek the right hand fork which falls in is about the Size of the other, we Crossed to the left Side at the foks, and Crossd a verry high Steep mountain for 9 miles to a large fork from the left which appears to head in the Snow toped mountains Southerley and S. E. we Crossd. Glade Creek above its mouth, at a place the Tushepaws or Flat head Indians have made 2 wears across to Catch Sammon and have but latterly left the place I could see no fish, and the grass entirely eaten out by the horses, we proceeded on 2 miles & Encamped opposit a Small Island at the mouth of a branch on the right side of the river which is at this place 80 yards wide, Swift and Stoney, here we wer compelled to kill a Colt for our men & Selves to eat for the want of meat & we named the South fork Colt killed Creek, and this river we Call Flathead River- The Mountains which we passed today much worst than yesterday the last excessively bad & Thickly Strowed with falling timber & Pine Spruc fur Hackmatak & Tamerack, Steep & Stoney our men and horses much fatigued, The rain

---

[Clark, September 15, 1805] Wednesday Septr. 15th 1805 We set out early. the morning Cloudy and proceeded on Down the right Side of River over Steep points rockey & buschey as usial for 4 miles to an old Indian fishing place, here the road leaves the river to the left and assends a mountain winding in every direction to get up the Steep assents & to pass the emence quantity of falling timber which had falling from dift. causes i e. fire & wind and has deprived the Greater part of the Southerley Sides of this mountain of its gren timber, 4 miles up the mountain I found a Spring and halted for the rear to come up and to let our horses rest & feed, about 2 hours the rear of the party came up much fatigued & horses more So, Several horses Sliped and roled down Steep hills which hurt them verry much The one which Carried my desk & Small trunk Turned over & roled down a mountain for 40 yards & lodged against a tree, broke the Desk the horse escaped and appeared but little hurt Some others verry much hurt, from this point I observed a range of high mountains Covered with Snow from S E. to S W with Their top bald or void of timber. after two hours delay we proceeded on up the mountain Steep & ruged as usial, more timber near the top, when we arrived at the top As we Conceved we could find no water and Concluded to Camp and make use of the Snow we found on the top to cook the remnt. of our Colt & make our Supe, evening verry Cold and Cloudy. Two of our horses gave out, pore and too much hurt to proceed on and left in the rear- nothing killed to day except 2 Phests.

From this mountain I could observe high ruged mountains in every direction as far as I could See. with the greatest exertion we Could only make 12 miles up this mountain and encamped on the top of the mountain near a Bank of old Snow about 3 feet deep lying on the Northern Side of the mountain and in Small banks on the top & leavel parts of the mountain, we melted the Snow to drink, and Cook our horse flesh to eat.

[Clark, September 16, 1805] Saturday Septr. 16th 1805 began to Snow about 3 hours before Day and Continud all day the Snow in The morning 4 Inches deep on The old Snow, and by night we found it from 6 to 8 Inches deep I walked in front to keep the road and found great dificuelty in keeping it as in maney places the Snow had entirely filled up the track, and obliged me to hunt Several minits for the track at 12 oClock we halted on the top of the mountain to worm & dry our Selves a little as well as to let our horses rest and graze a little on Some long grass which I observed, (on) The South Steep hills Side & falling timber Continue to day, and a thickly timbered Countrey of 8 different kinds of pine, which are So covered with Snow, that in passing thro them we are continually covered with Snow, I have been wet and as cold in every part as I ever was in my life, indeed I was at one time fearfull my feet would freeze in the thin mockersons which I wore, after a Short delay in the middle of the Day, I took one man and proceeded on as fast as I could about 6 miles to a Small branch passing to the right, halted and built fires for the party agains their arrival which was at Dusk verry cold and much fatigued we Encamped at this Branch in a thickly timbered bottom which was Scercely large enough for us to lie leavil, men all wet cold and hungary. Killed a Second Colt which we all Suped hartily on and thought it fine meat.

I saw 4 Black tail Deer to day before we Set out which came up the mountain and what is Singular Snaped 7 tims at a large buck. it is Singular as my gun has a Steel frisen and never Snaped 7 times before in examining her found the flint loose to describe the road of this day would be a repitition of yesterday excpt the Snow which made it much wors to proseed as we had in maney places to derect our Selves by the appearence of the rubbings of the Packs against the trees which have limbs quiet low and bending downwards

[Clark, September 17, 1805] Sunday 17th Septr. 1805 Cloudy morning our horses much Scattered which detained us untill one oClock P.M. at which time we Set out the falling Snow & Snow from the trees which kept us wet all the after noon passed over Several high ruged Knobs and Several dreans & Springs passing to the right, & passing on the ridge devideing the waters of two Small rivers. road excessively bad Snow on the Knobs, no Snow in the vallies Killed a fiew Pheasents which was not Sufficient for our Supper which compelled us to kill Something. a coalt being the most useless part of our Stock he fell a Prey to our appetites. The after part of the day fare, we made only 10 miles to day two horses fell & hurt themselves very much. we Encamped on the top of a high Knob of the mountain at a run passing to the left. we proceed on as yesterday, & with dificulty found the road

[Lewis, September 18, 1805] Wednesday September 18th 1805. Cap Clark set out this morning to go a head with six hunters. there being no game in these mountains we concluded it would be better for one of us to take the hunters and hurry on to the leavel country a head and there hunt and provide some provision while the other remained with and brought on the party the latter of these was my part; accordingly I directed the horses to be gotten up early being determined to force my march as much as the abilities of our horses would permit. the negligence of one of the party Willard who had a spare horse not attending to him and bringing him up last evening was the cause of our detention this morning untill 1/2 after 8 A M when we set out. I sent willard back to serch for his horse, and proceeded on with the party at four in the evening he overtook us without the horse, we marched 18 miles this day and encamped on the side of a steep mountain; we suffered for water this day passing one rivulet only; we wer fortunate in finding water in a steep raviene about 1/2 maile from our camp. this morning we finished the remainder of our last coult. we dined & suped on a skant proportion of portable soupe, a few canesters of which, a little bears oil and about 20 lbs. of candles form our stock of provision, the only recources being our guns & packhorses. the first is but a poor dependance in our present situation where there is nothing upon earth exept ourselves and a few small pheasants, small grey Squirrels, and a blue bird of the vulter kind about the size of a turtle dove or jay bird. our rout lay along the ridge of a high mountain course S. 20 W. 18 in. used the snow for cooking.

[Clark, September 18, 1805] Monday 18th Septr. 1805 a fair morning cold I proceded on in advance with Six hunters to try and find deer or Something to kill we passed over a countrey Similar to the one of yesterday more falling timber passed Several runs & Springs passing to the right from the top of a high part of the mountain at 20 miles I had a view of an emence Plain and leavel Countrey to the S W. & West at a great distance a high mountain in advance beyond the Plain, Saw but little Sign of deer and nothing else, much falling timber, made 32 miles and Encamped on a bold running Creek passing to the left which I call Hungery Creek as at that place we had nothing to eate. I halted only one hour to day to let our horses feed on Grass and rest

[Lewis, September 19, 1805] Thursday September 19th 1805. Set out this morning a little after sun rise and continued our rout about the same course of yesterday or S. 20 W. for 6 miles when the ridge terminated and we to our inexpressable joy discovered a large tract of Prairie country lying to the S. W. and widening as it appeared to extend to the W. through that plain the Indian informed us that the Columbia river, in which we were in surch run. this plain appeared to be about 60 Miles distant, but our guide assured us that we should reach it's borders tomorrow the appearance of this country, our only hope for subsistance greately revived the sperits of the party already reduced and much weakened for the want of food. the country is thickly covered with a very heavy growth of pine of which I have ennumerated 8 distinct species. after leaving the ridge we asscended and decended several steep mountains in the distance of 6 miles further when we struck a Creek about 15 yards wide our course being S. 35 W. we continued our rout 6 miles along the side of this creek upwards passing 2 of it's branches which flowed in from the N. 1st at the place we struck the creek and the other 3 miles further. the road was excessively dangerous along this creek being a narrow rockey path generally on the side of steep precipice, from which in many places if ether man or horse were precipitated they would inevitably be dashed in pieces. Fraziers horse fell from this road in the evening, and roled with his load near a hundred yards into the Creek. we all expected that the horse was killed but to our astonishment when the load was taken off him he arose to his feet & appeared to be but little injured, in 20 minutes he proceeded with his load. this was the most wonderfull escape I ever witnessed, the hill down which he roled was almost perpendicular and broken by large irregular and broken rocks. the course of this Creek upwards due W. we encamped on the Stard. side of it in a little raviene, having traveled 18 miles over a very bad road. we took a small quantity of portable soup, and retired to rest much fatiegued. several of the men are unwell of the disentary. brakings out, or irruptions of the Skin, have also been common with us for some time.

[Clark, September 19, 1805] Tuesday 19th Septr. 1805 Set out early proceeded on up the Creek passing through a Small glade at 6 miles at which place we found a horse. I derected him killed and hung up for the party after takeing a brackfast off for our Selves which we thought fine after Brackfast proceed on up the Creek two miles & left it to our right passed over a mountain, and the heads of branch of hungary Creek, two high mountains, ridges and through much falling timber (which caused our road of to day to be double the derect distance on the Course) Struck a large Creek passing to our left which I Kept down for 4 miles and left it to our left & passed over a mountain bad falling timber to a Small Creek passing to our left and Encamped. I killed 2 Pheasents, but fiew birds Blue jay, Small white headed hawk, Some Crows & ravins & large hawks. road bad.

[Lewis, September 20, 1805] Friday September 20th 1805. This morning my attention was called to a species of bird which I had never seen before. It was reather larger than a robbin, tho much it's form and action. the colours were a blueish brown on the back the wings and tale black, as wass a stripe above the croop 3/4 of an inch wide in front of the neck, and two others of the same colour passed from it's eyes back along the sides of the head. the top of the head, neck brest and belley and butts of the wing were of a fine yellowish brick reed. it was feeding on the buries of a species of shoemake or ash which grows common in country & which I first observed on 2d of this month. I have also observed two birds of a blue colour both of which I believe to be of the haulk or vulter kind. the one of a blue shining colour with a very high tuft of feathers on the head a long tale, it feeds on flesh the beak and feet black. it's note is cha-ah, cha-ah. it is about the size of a pigeon; and in shape and action resembles the jay bird.- another bird of very similar genus, the note resembling the mewing of the cat, with a white head and a light blue colour is also common, as are a black species of woodpecker about the size of the lark woodpecker Three species of Pheasants, a large black species, with some white feathers irregularly scattered on the brest neck and belley a smaller kind of a dark uniform colour with a red stripe above the eye, and a brown and yellow species that a good deel resembles the phesant common to the Atlantic States. we were detained this morning untill ten oclock in consequence of not being enabled to collect our horses. we had proceeded about 2 miles when we found the greater part of a horse which Capt Clark had met with and killed for us. he informed me by note that he should proceed as fast as possible to the leavel country which lay to the S. W. of us, which we discovered from the hights of the mountains on the 19th there he intended to hunt untill our arrival. at one oclock we halted and made a hearty meal on our horse beef much to the comfort of our hungry stomachs. here I larnt that one of the Packhorses with his load was missing and immediately dispatched Baptiest Lapage who had charge of him, to surch for him. he returned at ;3 OC. without the horse. The load of the horse was of considerable value consisting of merchandize and all my stock of winter cloathing. I therefore dispatched two of my best woodsmen in surch of him, and proceeded with the party. Our rout lay through a thick forrest of large pine the general course being S. 25 W. and distance about 15 miles. our road was much obstructed by fallen timber particularly in the evening we encamped on a ridge where ther was but little grass for our horses, and at a distance from water. however we obtained as much as served our culinary purposes and suped on our beef. the soil as you leave the hights of the mountains becomes gradually more fertile. the land through which we passed this evening is of an excellent quality tho very broken, it is a dark grey soil. a grey free stone appearing in large masses above the earth in many places. saw the hucklebury, honeysuckle, and alder common to the Atlantic states, also a kind of honeysuckle which bears a white bury and rises about 4 feet high not common but to the western side of the rockey mountains. a growth which resembles the choke cherry bears a black bury with a single stone of a sweetish taste, it rises to the hight of 8 or 10 feet and grows in thick clumps. the Arborvita is also common and grows to an immence size, being from 2 to 6 feet in diameter.

[Clark, September 20, 1805] Wednesday 20th September 1805 I Set out early and proceeded on through a Country as ruged as usial passed over a low mountain into the forks of a large Creek which I kept down 2 miles and assended a Steep mountain leaveing the Creek to our left hand passed the head of Several dreans on a divideing ridge, and at 12 miles decended the mountain to a leavel pine Countery proceeded on through a butifull Countrey for three miles to a Small Plain in which I found maney Indian lodges, at the distance of 1 mile from the lodges I met 3 boys, when they Saw me ran and hid themselves searched found gave them Small pieces of ribin & Sent them forward to the village a man Came out to meet me with ;great Caution & Conducted us to a large Spacious Lodge which he told me (by Signs) was the Lodge of his great Chief who had Set out 3 days previous with all the Warriers of the nation to war on a South West derection & would return in 15 or 18 days. the fiew men that were left in the Village aged, great numbers of women geathered around me with much apparent Signs of fear, and apr. pleased they gave us a Small piece of Buffalow meat, Some dried Salmon beries & roots in different States, Some round and much like an onion which they call quamash the Bread or Cake is called Passhe-co Sweet, of this they make bread & Supe they also gave us the bread made of this root all of which we eate hartily, I gave them a fiew Small articles as preasents, and proceeded on with a Chief to his Village 2 miles in the Same Plain, where we were treated kindly in their way and continued with them all night Those two Villages consist of about 30 double lodges, but fiew men a number of women & children; They call themselves Cho pun-nish or Pierced Noses; " their dialect appears verry different from the Tushapaws altho orignealy the Same people" They are darker than the Tushapaws Their dress Similar, with more beads white & blue principally, brass & Copper in different forms, Shells and ware their haire in the Same way. they are large Portley men Small women & handsom fetued Emence quantity of the quawmash or Pas-shi-co root gathered & in piles about the plains, those roots grow much an onion in marshey places the seed are in triangular Shell on the Stalk. they Sweat them in the following manner i. e. dig a large hole 3 feet deep Cover the bottom with Split wood on the top of which they lay Small Stones of about 3 or 4 Inches thick, a Second layer of Splited wood & Set the whole on fire which heats the Stones, after the fire is extinguished they lay grass & mud mixed on the Stones, on that dry grass which Supports the Pash-Shi-co root a thin Coat of the Same grass is laid on the top, a Small fire is kept when necessary in the Center of the kite &c.

I find myself verry unwell all the evening from eateing the fish & roots too freely. Sent out the hunters they killed nothing Saw Some Signs of deer.

[Lewis, September 21, 1805] Saturday September 21st 1805. We were detained this morning untill 11 OCk. in consequence of not being able to collect our horses. we then set out and proceeded along the ridge on which we had encamped, leaving which at 11/2 we passed a large creek runing to the left just above it's junction with another which run parrallel with and on the left of our road before we struck the creek; through the level wide and heavy timbered bottom of this creek we proceeded about 21/2 miles when bearing to the right we passed a broken country heavily timbered great quantities of which had fallen and so obstructed our road that it was almost impracticable to proceed in many places. though these hills we proceeded about 5 Ms. when we passed a small creek on which Capt Clark encamped on the 19th passing this creek we continued our rout 5 Ms thro a similar country when we struck a large creek at the forks, passed the Northen branch and continued down it on the West side 1 mile and encamped in a small open bottom where there was tolerable food for our horses. I directed the horses to be hubbled to prevent delay in the morning being determined to make a forced march tomorrow in order to reach if possible the open country. we killed a few Pheasants, and I killd a prarie woolf which together with the ballance of our horse beef and some crawfish which we obtained in the creek enabled us to make one more hearty meal, not knowing where the next was to be found. the Arborvita increases in quantity and size. I saw several sticks today large enough to form eligant perogues of at least 45 feet in length.- I find myself growing weak for the want of food and most of the men complain of a similar deficiency and have fallen off very much. the general course of this day S 30 W 15M.

[Clark, September 21, 1805] Septr. 21st Saturday 1805 a fine morning Sent out all the hunters early in different directions to Kill Something and delayed with the Indians to prevent Suspicion & to acquire as much information as possible. one of them Drew me a Chart of the river & nations below informed of one falls below which the white men lived from whome they got white beeds cloth &c. &c. The day proved warm, 2 Chifs of Bands visited me to-day- the hunters all returned without any thing, I collected a horse load of roots & 3 Sammon & Sent R Fields with one Indian to meet Capt Lewis at 4 oClock Set out with the other men to the river, passed thro a fine Pine Country deceded a Steep ruged hill verry long to a Small river which comes from our left and I suppose it to be _____ River passed down the river 2 miles on a Steep hill side at r r oClock P.M. arrived at a camp of 5 Squars a boy & 2 Children those people were glad to See us & gave us drid Sammon one had formerly been taken by the Minitarries of the north & Seen white men, our guide called the Chief who was fishing on the other Side of the river, whome I found a Cherfull man of about 65 I gave him a Medal.

[Clark, September 21, 1805] Thursday 21st Septr. 1805 A fine morning Sent out all the hunters in different directions to hunt deer, I myself delayd with the Chief to prevent Suspission and to Collect by Signs as much information as possible about the river and Countrey in advance. The Cheif drew me a kind of chart of the river, and informed me that a greater Cheif than himself was fishing at the river half a days march from his village called the twisted hare, and that the river forked a little below his Camp and at a long distance below & below 2 large forks one from the left & the other from the right the river passed thro'gh the mountains at which place was a great fall of the water passing through the rocks, at those falls white people lived from whome they preceured the white Beeds & Brass &c. which the womin wore; a Chief of another band visit me to day and Smoked a pipe, I gave my handkerchief & a Silver Cord with a little Tobacco to those Chiefs, The hunters all return without any thing, I purchased as much Provisions as I could with what fiew things I chaned to have in my Pockets, Such a Salmon Bread roots & berries, & Sent one man R. Fields with an Indian to meet Capt. Lewis, and at 4 oClock P M. Set out to the river, met a man at dark on his way from the river to the village, whome I hired and gave the neck handkerchief of one of the men, to polit me to the Camp of the twisted hare we did not arrive at the Camp of the Twisted hare but oppost, untill half past 11 oClock P M. found at this Camp five Squars & 3 Children. my guide called to the Chief who was Encamped with 2 others on a Small Island in the river, he Soon joind me, I found him a Chearfull man with apparant Siencerity, I gave him a medal &c. and Smoked untill 1 oClock a.m. and went to Sleep. The Countrey from the mountains to the river hills is a leavel rich butifull Pine Countrey badly watered, thinly timbered & covered with grass- The weather verry worm after decending into the low Countrey,- the river hills are verry high & Steep, Small bottoms to this little river which is Flat head & is 160 yards wide and Sholey This river is the one we killed the first Coalt on near a fishing were I am verry Sick to day and puke which relive me.

[Lewis, September 22, 1805] Sunday September 22cd 1805. Notwithstanding my positive directions to hubble the horses last evening one of the men neglected to comply. he plead ignorance of the order. this neglect however detained us untill 1/2 after eleven OCk at which time we renewed our march, our course being about west. we had proceeded about two and a half miles when we met Reubin Fields one of oure hunters, whom Capt. Clark had dispatched to meet us with some dryed fish and roots that he had procured from a band of Indians, whose lodges were about eight miles in advance. I ordered the party to halt for the purpose of taking some refreshment. I divided the fish roots and buries, and was happy to find a sufficiency to satisfy compleatly all our appetites. Fields also killed a crow after refreshing ourselves we proceeded to the village due West 71/2 Miles where we arrived at 5 OCk. in the afternoon our rout was through lands heavily timbered, the larger wood entirely pine. the country except the last 3 miles was broken and decending the pleasure I now felt in having tryumphed over the rocky Mountains and decending once more to a level and fertile country where there was every rational hope of finding a comfortable subsistence for myself and party can be more readily conceived than expressed, nor was the flattering prospect of the final success of the expedition less pleasing. on our approach to the village which consisted of eighteen lodges most of the women fled to the neighbouring woods on horseback with their children, a circumstance I did not expect as Capt. Clark had previously been with them and informed them of our pacific intentions towards them and also the time at which we should most probably arrive. the men seemed but little concerned, and several of them came to meet us at a short distance from their lodges unarmed.

[Clark, September 22, 1805] September 22nd Sunday 1805 a fine morning, I proceed on down the little river to about 11/2 a mile & found the Chif in a Canoe Comeing to meet me I got into his Canoe & Crossed over to his Camp on a Small Island at a rapid Sent out the hunters leaving one to take care of the baggage, & after eating a part of a Samn. I Set out on my return to meet Capt. Lewis with the Chief & his Son at 2 miles met Shields with 3 Deer, I took a Small peice & Changed for his horse which was fresh & proced on this horse threw me 3 times which hurt me Some. at Dark met Capt Lewis Encamped at the first Village men much fatigued & reduced, the Supply which I sent by R Flds. was timely, they all eate hartily of roots & fish, 2 horses lost 1 Days journey back

[Clark, September 22, 1805] Friday 22nd Septr. 1805 a verry worm day the hunters Shild killed 3 Deer this morning. I left them on the Island and Set out with the Chief & his Son on a young horse for the Village at which place I expected to meet Capt Lewis this young horse in fright threw himself & me 3 times on the Side of a Steep hill & hurt my hip much, Cought a Coalt which we found on the roade & I rode it for Several miles untill we saw the Chiefs horses, he cought one & we arrived at his Village at Sunset, & himself and myslf walked up to the 2d Village where I found Capt Lewis & the party Encamped, much fatigued, & hungery, much rejoiced to find something to eate of which They appeared to partake plentifully. I cautioned them of the Consequences of eateing too much &c.

The planes appeared covered with Spectators viewing the White men and the articles which we had, our party weacke and much reduced in flesh as well as Strength, The horse I left hung up they receved at a time they were in great want, and the Supply I Sent by R. Fields proved timely and gave great encouragement to the party with Captn. Lewis. he lost 3 horses one of which belonged to our guide. Those Indians Stole out of R. F. Shot pouch his knife wipers Compas & Steel, which we Could not precure from them, we attempted to have Some talk with those people but Could not for the want of an Interpreter thro which we Could Speake, we were Compelled to converse Altogether by Signs- I got the Twisted hare to draw the river from his Camp down which he did with great cherfullness on a white Elk Skin, from the 1s fork which is a few seven miles below, to the large fork on which the So So ne or Snake Indians fish, is South 2 Sleeps; to a large river which falls in on the N W. Side and into which The Clarks river empties itself is 5 Sleeps from the mouth of that river to the falls is 5 Sleeps at the falls he places Establishments of white people &c. and informs that great numbers of Indians reside on all those foks as well as the main river; one other Indian gave me a like account of the Countrey, Some few drops of rain this evening. I precured maps of the Country & river with the Situation of Indians, To come from Several men of note Seperately which varied verey little.

[Clark, September 23, 1805] Septr. 23rd Sunday Traded with the Indians, made 3 Chiefs and gave them meadels & Tobacco & Handkerchif & knives, and a flag & left a Flag & hand kerches for the great Chief when he returns from war, in the evening proceeded to the 2d Vilg 2 miles, a hard wind and rain at dark, traded for Some root Bread & Skins to make Shirts. hot day

[Clark, September 23, 1805] Saturday 23rd Septr 1805. We assembled the principal Men as well as the Chiefs and by Signs informed them where we came from where bound our wish to inculcate peace and good understanding between all the red people &c. which appeared to Satisfy them much, we then gave 2 other Medals to other Chefs of bands, a flag to the twisted hare, left a flag & Handkerchief to the grand Chief gave, a Shirt to the Twisted hare & a knife & Handkerchif with a Small pece of Tobacco to each. Finding that those people gave no provisions to day we deturmined to purchase with our Small articles of merchindize, accord we purchased all we could, Such as roots dried, in bread, & in ther raw State, Berris of red Haws & Fish and in the evening Set out and proceeded on to the 2d Village 2 miles dist. where we also purchased a few articles all amounting to as much as our weak horses Could Carry to the river Capt. Lewis & 2 men verry Sick this evening, my hip verry Painfull, the men trade a few old tin Canisters for dressed Elk Skin to make themselves Shirts, at dark a hard wind from The S W accompaned with rain which lasted half an hour. The twisted hare envited Capt Lewis & myself to his lodge which was nothin more than Pine bushes & bark, and gave us Some broiled dried Salmon to eate, great numbers about us all night at this village the women were busily employed in gathering and drying the Pas-she co root of which they had great quantites dug in piles

[Clark, September 24, 1805] Septr. 24th Monday 1805 Set out early for the river and proceeded on the Same road I had prevsly gorn to the Island at which place I had found the Chief & formed a Camp several 8 or 9 men Sick, Capt Lewis Sick all Complain of a Lax & heaviness at the Stomack, I gave rushes Pills to Several hot day maney Indians & thier gangues of horses follow us hot day Hunter had 5 Deer

[Clark, September 24, 1805] Sunday 24th Septr. 1805 a fine morning collected our horses despatched J. Colter back to hunt the horses lost in the mountains & bring up Some Shot left behind, and at 10 oClock we all Set out for the river and proceeded on by the Same rout I had previously traveled, and at Sunset We arrived at the Island on which I found the Twisted hare and formed a Camp on a large Island a littl below, Capt Lewis Scercely able to ride on a jentle horse which was furnishd by the Chief, Several men So unwell that they were Compelled to lie on the Side of the road for Some time others obliged to be put on horses. I gave rushes Pills to the Sick this evening. Several Indians follow us.

[Clark, September 25, 1805] Septr. 25th I with th Chief & 2 young men went down to hunt timber for Canoes- proceeded on down to the forks 4 miles N 70° W 2 miles S. 75°W 2 miles, halted young men Cought 6

Sammon, the forks nearly the Same Size, Crossed the South fork & found Timber large Pine in a bottom Proceeded up the South Side 3 parts of Party Sick Capt Lewis verry Sick hot day

[Clark, September 25, 1805] Monday 25th of September 1805 a verry hot day most of the Party Complaining and 2 of our hunters left here on the 22nd verry Sick they had killed only two Bucks in my absence. I Set out early with the Chief and 2 young men to hunt Some trees Calculated to build Canoes, as we had previously determined to proceed on by water, I was furnished with a horse and we proceeded on down the river Crossed a Creek at 1 mile from the right verry rockey which I call rock dam Creek & Passed down on the N side of the river to a fork from the North which is about the Same Size and affords about the Same quantity of water with the other forks we halted about an hour, one of the young men took his guilt and killed 6 fine Salmon two of them were roasted and we eate, two Canoes Came up loaded with the furnitur & provisions of 2 families, those Canoes are long Stedy and without much rake I crossed the South fork and proceeded up on the South Side, the most of the way thro a narrow Pine bottom in which I Saw fine timber for Canoes one of the Indian Canoes with 2 men with Poles Set out from the forks at the Same time I did and arrived at our Camp on the Island within 15 minits of the Same time I did, not withstanding 3 rapids which they had to draw the Canoe thro in the distance, when I arrived at Camp found Capt Lewis verry Sick, Several men also verry Sick, I gave Some Salts & Tarter emetic, we deturmined to go to where the best timbr was and there form a Camp

[Clark, September 26, 1805] Septr. 26th Set out early and proceeded down the river to the bottom on the S Side opposit the forks & formed a Camp had ax handled ground &c. our axes all too Small, Indians caught Sammon & Sold us, 2 Chiefs & thir families came & camped near us, Several men bad, Capt Lewis Sick I gave Pukes Salts &c. to Several, I am a little unwell. hot day

[Clark, September 26, 1805] Tuesday 26th Septr. 1805 Set out early and proceeded on down the river to a bottom opposit the forks of the river on the South Side and formed a Camp. Soon after our arrival a raft Came down the N. fork on which was two men, they came too, I had the axes distributed and handled and men apotned. ready to commence building canoes on tomorrow, our axes are Small & badly Calculated to build Canoes of the large Pine, Capt Lewis Still very unwell, Several men taken Sick on the way down, I administered Salts Pils Galip, Tarter emetic &c. I feel unwell this evening, two Chiefs & their families follow us and encamp near us, they have great numbers of horses. This day proved verry hot, we purchase fresh Salmon of the Indians

[Clark, September 27, 1805] Septr. 27th Thursday 1805 Set all the men able to work abt. building Canoes, Colter returned and found one horse & the Canister of Shot left in the mountains he also killed a Deer 1/2 of which he brought hot day- men Sick

[Clark, September 27, 1805] 27th Septr. Wednesday 1805 all the men able to work comened building 5 Canoes, Several taken Sick at work, our hunters returned Sick without meet. J. Colter returned he found only one of the lost horses, on his way killed a deer, half of which he gave the Indians the other proved nourishing to the Sick The day verry hot, we purchase fresh Salmon of them Several Indians Come up the river from a Camp Some distance below Capt Lewis very Sick nearly all the men Sick. our Shoshonee Indian Guide employed himself makeing flint points for his arrows

[Clark, September 28, 1805] Septr. 28th Friday Several men Sick all at work which is able, nothing killed to day. Drewyer Sick maney Indians visit us worm day

[Clark, September 28, 1805] Thursday 28th Septr. 1805 Our men nearly all Complaining of ther bowels, a heaviness at the Stomach & Lax, Some of those taken first getting better, a number of Indians about us gazeing &c. &c. This day proved verry worm and Sultery, nothing killed men complaining of their diat of fish & roots. all that is able working at the Canoes, Several Indians leave us to day, the raft continue on down the river, one old man informed us that he had been to the White peoples fort at the falls & got white beeds &c his Story was not beleved as he Could explain nothing.

[Clark, September 29, 1805]
Septr. 29th Satterday Drewyer killed 2 deer Collins 1 der men Conte
Sickly at work all able to work.

[Clark, September 29, 1805] Sunday 29th Septr. 1805 a Cool morning wind from the S. W. men Sick as usial, all The men that are able to at work, at the Canoes Drewyer killed 2 Deer Colter killed 1 Deer, the after part of this day worm Cap Lewis very Sick, and most of the men complaning very much of ther bowels & Stomach

[Clark, September 30, 1805] Sunday 30th Septr. 1805 Forks a fine morning our men recruting a little cool, all at work doing Something except 2 which are verry Sick, Great run of Small duck passing down the river this morning.

[Clark, September 30, 1805] Septr. 30th Saturday (Monday) 1805 a fine fair morning a the men recruiting a little, all at work which are able. Great number of Small Ducks pass down the river this morning. maney Indians passing up and down the river.

[Clark, October 1, 1805] October 1st 1805 Tuesday a cool morning wind from the N. E. I examine & Dry all our article Cloths &. nothing to eate except Drid fish verry bad diet Capt Lewis getting much better than for Several days past Several Indians visit us from the different villages below and on the main fork S. nothing killed

[Clark, October 1, 1805] October 1st Tuesday 1805 A cool morning wind from the East had Examined and dried all our clothes and other articles and laid out a Small assortment of Such articles as those Indians were fond of to trade with them for Some provisions (they are remarkably fond of Beeds) nothin to eate except a little dried fish which they men complain of as working of them as as much as a dost of Salts. Capt Lewis getting much better. Several Indians visit us from the different tribes below Some from the main South fork our hunters killed nothing to day worm evening

[Clark, October 2, 1805] Oct. 2nd 1805 Wednesday dispatch 2 men & an Indian up to the villages we first Came too to purchase roots fish &c. nothing to eate but roots. gave a small pice of Tobacco to the Indians, 3 broachs & 2 rings with my Handkerchif divided between 5 of them. I walked on the hills to hunt to day, Saw only one deer, Could kill nothing day excesively hot in the river bottom wind North, Burning out the holler of our canoes, men Something better nothing except a Small Prarie wolf Killed to day, our Provisions all out except what fiew fish we purchase of the Indians with us; we kill a horse for the men at work to eate &c. &c.

[Clark, October 2, 1805] October 2nd Wednesday 1805 Despatched 2 men Frasure & S. Guterich back to the village with 1 Indian & 6 horses to purchase dried fish, roots &c. we have nothing to eate but roots, which give the men violent pains in their bowels after eating much of them. To the Indians who visited us yesterday I gave divided my Handkerchief between 5 of them, with a Small piece of tobacco & a pece of riebin & to the 2 principal men each a ring & brooch. I walked out with my gun on the hills which is verry Steep & high could kill nothing. day hot wind N. Hunters killed nothing excep a Small Prarie wolf. Provisions all out, which Compells us to kill one of our horses to eate and make Suep for the Sick men.

[Clark, October 3, 1805] October 3rd Thursday 1805 Canoe Camp a fair cool morning wind from the East all our men getting well and at work at the canoes &c.

[Clark, October 3, 1805] October 3rd Thursday 1805 a fine morning cool wind East all our men getting better in helth, and at work at the Canoes &. The Indians who visited us from below Set out on their return early. Several others Came from different directions

[Clark, October 4, 1805] October 4th 1805 Friday This morning is a little cool wind from the East. displeased an Indian by refuseing to let him have a pice of Tobacco. thre Inds. from the S. fork visit us Frasur and Guterich return from the village with fish roots &c. which they purchased

[Clark, October 4, 1805] October 4th Friday 1805 a Cool wind from off the Eastern mountains I displeased an Indian by refuseing him a pice of Tobacco which he tooke the liberty to take out of our Sack Three Indians visit us from the Grat River South of us. The two men Frasure and Guterich return late from the Vllage with Fish roots &c. which they purchased as our horse is eaten we have nothing to eate except dried fish & roots which disagree with us verry much. The after part of this day verry warm. Capt Lewis Still Sick but able to walk about a little.

[Clark, October 5, 1805] October 5th Saturday 1805 a Cool morning wind from the East, Collected all our horses, & Branded them 38 in No. and delivered them to the men who were to take Charge of them, each of which I gave a Knife & one a wampom Shell gorget, The Lattd. of this place the mean of 2 observations is 46° 34' 56.3" North. nothing to eate but dried roots & Dried fish, Capt Lewis & my Self eate a Supper of roots boiled, which filled us So full of wind, that we were Scercely able to Breathe all night felt the effects of it. Lanced 2 Canoes to day one proved a little leakey the other a verry good one

[Clark, October 5, 1805] October 5th Saty 1805 Wind Easterley and Cool, had all our horses 38 in number Collected and branded Cut off their fore top and delivered them to the 2 brothers and one Son of one of the Chiefs who intends to accompany us down the river to each of those men I gave a Knife & Some Small articles &c. they promised to be attentive to our horses untill we Should return.

Lattitude of this place from the mean of two observations is 46° 34' 56.3" North

Nothing to eate except dried fish & roots. Capt Lewis & myself eate a Supper of roots boiled, which Swelled us in Such a manner that we were Scercely able to breath for Several hours- finished and lanced 2 of our Canoes this evening which proved to be verry good our hunters with every diligence Could kill nothing. The hills high and ruged and woods too dry to hunt the deer which is the only game in our neighbourhood. Several Squars

Came with Fish and roots which we purchased of them for Beeds, which they were fond of- Capt Lewis not So well to day as yesterday

[Clark, October 6, 1805] October 6th Sunday 1805 A Col Easterley wind which Spring up in the latter part of the night and Continues untill about 7 or 8 oClock A.M. had all our Saddles Collected a whole dug and in the night buried them, also a Canister of powder and a bag of Balls at the place the Canoe which Shields made was cut from the body of the tree- The Saddles were buried on the Side of a bend about 1/2 a mile below- all the Canoes finished this evening ready to be put into the water. I am taken verry unwell with a paine in the bowels & Stomach, which is certainly the effects of my diet-which last all night-.

The winds blow cold from a little before day untill the Suns gets to Some hight from the Mountans East as they did from the mountans at the time we lay at the falls of Missouri from the West The river below this forks is Called Kos kos keel it is Clear rapid with Shoals or Swift places The open Countrey Commences a fiew miles below This on each side of the river, on the Lard Side below the 1st Creek. with a few trees Scattered near the river. passd maney bad rapids, one Canoe that in which I went in front Sprung a Leak in passing the 3rd rapid

Set out at 3 oClock P M & proceeded on

[Clark, October 7, 1805] October 7th Monday 1805 I continu verry unwell but obliged to attend every thing all the Canoes put into the water and loaded, fixed our Canoes as well as possible and Set out as we were about to Set out we missd. both of the Chiefs who promised to accompany us; I also missed my Pipe Tomahawk which Could not be found.

The after part of the day Cloudy proceded on passed 10 rapids which wer danjerous the Canoe in which I was Struck a rock and Sprung a leak in the 3rd rapid, we proceeded on 20 miles and Encamped on a Stard point oppost a run. passed a Creek Small on the Lard. Side at 9 miles, a Short distanc from the river at 2 feet 4 Inches N. of a dead toped pine Treee had burid 2 Lead Canisters of Powder

Had the Canoes unloaded examined and mended a Small leake which we discovered in a thin place in her Side passed Several Camps of Indians to day our Course and distance Shall be given after I get to the forks. &c.which the Indians Say is the last of the bad water untill we get to the great falls 10 day below, where the white people live &c. The Lodges are of Sticks set in a form of roof of a house & covered with mats and Straw

[Clark, October 8, 1805] 8th Octr. 1805 Tuesday a cloudy morning Changed Canoes and buried 2 Lead canisters of Powder 2 foot 4 In. North of a dead toped pine opposit our Camp & opposit the mouth of a run after repareing leaks in the Canoes Sprung Coming over the rapids yesterday Set out at 9 oClock

[Clark, October 8, 1805] October 8th Tuesday 1805 A Cloudy morning loaded our Canoes which was unloaded last night and Set out at 9 oClock passed 15 rapids four Islands and a Creek on the Stard Side at 16 miles just below which one canoe in which Serjt. Gass was Stearing and was nearle turning over, She Sprung a leak or Split open on one Side and Bottom filled with water & Sunk on the rapid, the men, Several of which Could not Swim hung on to the Canoe, I had one of the other Canoes unloaded & with the assistance of our Small Canoe and one Indian Canoe took out every thing & toed the empty Canoe on Shore, one man Tompson a little hurt, every thing wet perticularly the greater part of our Small Stock of merchindize, had every thing opened, and two Sentinals put over them to keep off the Indians, who are enclined to theave haveing Stole Several Small articles those people appeared disposed to give us every assistance in their power dureing our distress- We passed Several Encampments of Indians on the Islands and those near the rapids in which places they took the Salmon, at one of Those Camps we found our two Chiefs who had promised to accompany us, we took them on board after the Serimony of Smokeing

[Clark, October 9, 1805] Octo. 9th all day drying our roots good & articles which got wet in the Canoe last night. our 2 Snake Indian guides left us without our knowledge, The Indians troublesom Stole my Spoon which they returned. men merry at night & Singular acts of a Ind. woman

[Clark, October 9, 1805] October 9th Wednesday 1805 The morning Cool as usial the greater part of the day proved to be Cloudy, which was unfavourable for drying our things &c. which got wet yesterday. In examoning our canoe found that by putting Knees & Strong peces pined to her Sides and bottom &c. She Could be made fit for Service in by the time the goods dried, Set 4 men to work at her, Serjt. Pryor & Gass, Jo Fields & Gibson, others to Collect rosin, at 1 oClock She was finished Stronger than ever The wet articles not Sufficiently dried to pack up obliged us to delay another night dureing the time one man was tradeing for fish for our voyage, at Dark we were informed that our old guide & his Son had left us and had been Seen running up the river Several miles above, we Could not account for the Cause of his leaveing us at this time, without receiving his pay for the Services he had rendered us, or letting us know anything of his intention.

we requested the Chief to Send a horseman after our old guide to come back and recive his pay &c. which he advised us not to do as his nation would take his things from him before he passed their camps The Indians and our party were very mery this after noon a woman faind madness &c. &c. Singular acts of this woman in giveing in Small potions all She had & if they were not received She would Scarrify her Self in a horid manner &c. Capt Lewis recovring fast.

a verry worm day, Indians continue all day on the banks to view us as low as the forks. Two Indians come up in a Canoe, who means to accompany us to the Great rapids, Could get no observations, worm night The water of the South fork is of a bluish green colour

[Clark, October 10, 1805] October 10th Wednesday Thursday a fine Morning loaded and Set out at 7 oClock at 2 1/2 miles passed a run on the Stard. Side haveing passed 2 Islands and two bad rapids at 3 miles lower passed a Creek on the Lard. with wide Cotton willow bottoms haveing passed an Island and a rapid an Indian Camp of three Lodgs below the Creek at 8 1/2 miles lower we arrived at the heade of a verry bad riffle at which place we landed near 8 Lodges of Indians on the Lard Side to view the riffle, haveing passed two Islands & Six rapids Several of them verry bad-after view'g this riffle two Canoes were taken over verry well; the third Stuck on a rock which took us an hour to get her off which was effected without her receving a greater injurey than a Small Split in her Side which was repared in a Short time, we purchased fish & dogs of those people, dined and proceeded on- here we met with an Indian from the falls at which place he Sais he Saw white people, and expressd an inclination to accompany us, we passd. a fiew miles above this riffle 2 Lodges and an Indian batheing in a hot bath made by hot Stones thrown into a pon of water. at this riffle which we Call ragid rapid took meridian altitude of the Suns upper Limb with Sextt. 74° 26' 0" Latd. produced _____ North at five miles lower and Sixty miles below the forks arived at a large Southerly fork which is the one we were on with the Snake or So-So-nee nation (haveing passed 5 rapids) This South fork or Lewis's River which has two forks which fall into it on the South the ist Small the upper large and about 2 days march up imediately parrelal to the first villages we Came to and is called by those Indians Par-nash-te on this fork a little above its mouth resides a Chief who as the Indian Say has more horses than he can Count and further Sayeth that Louises River is navagable about 60 miles up with maney rapids at which places the Indians have fishing Camps and Lodjes built of an oblong form with flat ruffs. below the 1st river on the South Side there is ten established fishing places on the 1st fork which fall in on the South Side is one fishing place, between that and the Par nash to River, five fishing places, above two, and one on that river all of the Cho-pun-nish or Pierced Nose Nation many other Indians reside high up those rivers The Countrey about the forks is an open Plain on either Side I can observe at a distance on the lower Stard. Side a high ridge of Thinly timbered Countrey the water of the South fork-is a greenish blue, the north as clear as cristial

Imediately in the point is an Indian Cabin & in the South fork a Small Island, we came to on the Stard. Side below with a view to make some luner observations the night proved Cloudy and we were disapointed The Indians Came down all the Couses of this river on each Side on horses to view us as we were desending,- The man whome we saw at the ruged rapid and expressed an inclination to accompany us to the great rapids, came up with his Son in a Small Canoe and procisted in his intentions- worthey of remark that not one Stick of timber on the river near the forks and but a fiew trees for a great distance up the River we decended I think Lewis's River is about 250 yards wide, the Koos koos ke River about 150 yards wide and the river below the forks about 300 yards wide. a miss understanding took place between Shabono one of our interpreters, and Jo. & R Fields which appears to have originated in just- our diet extremely bad haveing nothing but roots and dried fish to eate, all the Party have greatly the advantage of me, in as much as they all relish the flesh of the dogs, Several of which we purchased of the nativs for to add to our Store of fish and roots &c. &c.-

The Cho-pun-nish or Pierced nose Indians are Stout likeley men, handsom women, and verry dressey in their way, the dress of the men are a white Buffalow robe or Elk Skin dressed with Beeds which are generally white, Sea Shells-i e the Mother of Pirl hung to ther hair & on a pice of otter Skin about their necks hair Cewed in two parsels hanging forward over their Sholders, feathers, and different Coloured Paints which they find in their Countrey Generally white, Green & light Blue. Some fiew were a Shirt of Dressed Skins and long legins, & Mockersons Painted, which appears to be their winters dress, with a plat of twisted grass about their necks.

The women dress in a Shirt of Ibex, or Goat Skins which reach quite down to their anckles with a girdle, their heads are not ornemented, their Shirts are ornemented with quilled Brass, Small peces of Brass Cut into different forms, Beeds, Shells & curios bones &c. The men expose those parts which are generally kept from view by other nations but the women are more perticular than any other nation which I have passed in Screting the parts

Their amusements appear but fiew as their Situation requires the utmost exertion to prcure food they are generally employed in that pursute, all the Summer & fall fishing for the Salmon, the winter hunting the deer on Snow Shoes in the plains and takeing care of ther emence numbers of horses, & in the Spring cross the mountains to the Missouri to get Buffalow robes and meet &c. at which time they frequent meet with their enemies & lose their horses & maney of ther people

Ther disorders are but fiew and those fiew of a Scofelous nature. they make great use of Swetting. The hot and cold baethes, They are verry Selfish and Stingey of what they have to eate or ware, and they expect in return Something for everything give as presents or the Survices which they doe let it be however Small, and fail to make those returns on their part.

[Clark, October 11, 1805] October 11th 1805 a cloudy morning wind from the East We Set out early and proceeded on passed a rapid at two miles, at 6 miles we came too at Some Indian lodges and took brackfast, we purchased all the fish we could and Seven dogs of those people for Stores of Provisions down the river. at this place I saw a curious Swet house under ground, with a Small whole at top to pass in or throw in the hot Stones, which those in threw on as much water as to create the temporature of heat they wished- at 9 mile passed a rapid at 15 miles halted at an Indian Lodge, to purchase provisions of which we precred some of the Pash-he-quar roots five dogs and a few fish dried, after takeing Some dinner of dog &c we proceeded on. Came to and encamped at 2 Indian Lodges at a great place of fishing here we met an Indian of a nation near the mouth of this river.

we purchased three dogs and a fiew fish of those Indians, we Passed today nine rapids all of then great fishing places, at different places on the river saw Indian houses and Slabs & Spilt timber raised from the ground being the different parts of the houses of the natives when they reside on this river for the purpose of fishing at this time they are out in the Plain on each side of the river hunting the antilope as we are informed by our Chiefs, near each of those houses we observe Grave yards picketed, or pieces of wood stuck in permiscuesly over the grave or body which is Covered with earth, The Country on either Side is an open plain leavel & fertile after assending a Steep assent of about 200 feet not a tree of any kind to be Seen on the river The after part of the day the wind from the S. W. and hard. The day worm.

[Clark, October 12, 1805] October 12th 1805 Saturday a fair cool morning wind from E after purchasing all the drid fish those people would Spear from their hole in which they wer buried we Set out at 7 oClock and proceeded on

[Clark, October 12, 1805] October 12th Saturday 1805 A fair Cool morning wind from the East. after purchaseing every Speces of the provisions those Indians could Spare we Set out and proceeded on at three miles passed four Islands Swift water and a bad rapid opposit to those Islands on the Lard. Side. at 141/2 miles passed the mouth of a large Creek on the Lard Side opposit a Small Island here the Countrey assends with a gentle assent to the high plains, and the River is 400 yards wide about 1 mile below the Creek on the Same Side took meridian altitude which gave 72° 30' 00" Latitude produced _____ North in the afternoon the wind Shifted to the S. W. and blew hard we passed to day _____ rapids Several of them very bad and came to at the head of one (at 30 miles) on the Stard. Side to view it before we attemptd. to dsend through it. The Indians had told us was verry bad- we found long and dangerous about 2 miles in length, and maney turns necessary to Stear Clare of the rocks, which appeared to be in every direction. The Indians went through & our Small Canoe followed them, as it was late we deturmined to camp above untill the morning. we passed Several Stoney Islands today Country as yesterday open plains, no timber of any kind a fiew Hack berry bushes & willows excepted, and but few drift trees to be found So that fire wood is verry Scerce- The hills or assents from the water is faced with a dark ruged Stone. The wind blew hard this evening.-

[Clark, October 13, 1805] October 13th Sunday 1805 rained a little before day, and all the morning, a hard wind from the S West untill 9 oClock, the rained Seased & wind luled, and Capt Lewis with two Canoes Set out & passed down the rapid The others Soon followed and we passed over this bad rapid Safe. We Should make more portages if the Season was not So far advanced and time precious with us

The wife of Shabono our interpetr we find reconsiles all the Indians, as to our friendly intentions a woman with a party of men is a token of peace

[Clark, October 13, 1805] October 13th Sunday 1805 a windey dark raney morning The rain commenced before day and Continued moderately until) near 12 oClock- we took all our Canoes through This rapid without any injurey. a little below passed through another bad rapid at _____ miles passed the Mo. of a large Creek little river in a Stard. bend, imediately below a long bad rapid; in which the water is Confined in a Chanel of about 20 yards between rugid rocks for the distance of a mile and a half and a rapid rockey Chanel for 2 miles above. This must be a verry bad place in high water, here is great fishing place, the timbers of Several houses piled up, and a number of wholes of fish, and the bottom appears to have been made use of as a place of deposit for their fish for ages past, here two Indians from the upper foks over took us and continued on down on horse back, two others were at this mouth of the Creek- we passed a rapid about 9 mile lower. at dusk came to on the Std. Side & Encamped. The two Inds. on horse back Stayed with us. The Countery Thro which we passed to day is Simlar to that of yesterday open plain no timber passed Several houses evacuated at established fishing places, wind hard from The S. W. in the evening and not very cold

[Clark, October 14, 1805] October 14th Monday 1805 a verry Cool morning wind from the West Set out at 8 oClock proceeded on

at this rapid the Canoe a Stern Steared by drewyer Struck a rock turned the men got out on a rock the Stern of the Canoe took in water and She Sunk the men on the rock hel her, a number of articles floated all that Could be Cought were taken by 2 of the othr Canoes, Great many articles lost among other things 2 of the mens beding Shot pouches Tomahaws &c. &c. and every article wet of which we have great Cause to lament as all our loose Powder two Canisters, all our roots prepared in the Indian way, and one half of our goods, fortunately the lead canisters which was in the canoe was tied down, otherwise they must have been lost as the Canoe turned over we got off the men from the rock toed our canoe on Shore after takeing out all the Stores &c. we Could & put them out to dry on the Island on which we found Some wood which was covered with Stones, this is the Parts of an Indian house, which we used for fire wood, by the wish of our two Chiefs- Those Chees, one of them was in the Canoe, Swam in & Saved Some property, The Inds. have buried fish on this Isld. which we are Cautious not to touch. our Small Canoe & three Indians in another was out of Sight at the time our missfortune hapined, and did not join us. wind hard S W.

[Clark, October 14, 1805] October 14th Monday 1805 a Verry Cold morning wind from the West and Cool untill about 12 oClock When it Shifted to the S. W. at 21/2 miles passed a remarkable rock verry large and resembling the hull of a Ship Situated on a Lard point at Some distance from the assending Countrey passed rapids at 6 and 9 miles. at 12 miles we Came too at the head of a rapid which the Indians told me was verry bad, we viewed the rapid found it bad in decending three Stern Canoes Stuk fast for Some time on the head of the rapid and one Struk a rock in the worst part, fortunately all landed Safe below the rapid which was nearly 3 miles in length. here we dined, and for the first time for three weeks past I had a good dinner of Blue wing Teel, after dinner we Set out and had not proceded on two miles before our Stern Canoe in passing thro a Short rapid opposit the head of an Island, run on a Smoth rock and turned broad Side, the men got out on the rock all except one of our Indian Chiefs who Swam on Shore, The Canoe filed and Sunk a number of articles floated out, Such as the mens bedding clothes & Skins, the Lodge &c. &c. the greater part of which were cought by 2 of the Canoes, whilst a 3rd was unloading & Steming the Swift Current to the relief of the men on the rock who could with much dificuelty hold the Canoe. however in about an hour we got the men an Canoe to Shore with the Loss of Some bedding Tomahaws Shot pouches Skins Clothes &c &c. all wet we had every articles exposed to the Sun to dry on the Island, our loss in provisions is verry Considerable all our roots was in the Canoe that Sunk, and Cannot be dried Sufficint to Save, our loose powder was also in the Canoe and is all wett This I think, we Shall saved.- In this Island we found some Split timber the parts of a house which the Indians had verry Securely covered with Stone, we also observed a place where the Indians had buried there fish, we have made it a point at all times not to take any thing belonging to the Indians even their wood. but at this time we are Compelled to violate that rule and take a part of the Split timber we find here bured for fire wood, as no other is to be found in any direction. our Small Canoe which was a head returned at night with 2 ores which they found floating below. The wind this after noon from the S. W. as usial and hard way of the forks to the Indian Camps at the first were not one mouthfull to eate untill night as our hunters could kill nothing and I could See & catch no fish except a few Small ones. The Indians gave us 2 Sammon boiled which I gave to the men, one of my men Shot a Sammon in the river about Sunset those fish gave us a Supper. all the Camp flocked about me untill I went to Sleep- and I beleve if they had a Sufficency to eate themselves and any to Spare they would be liberal of it I detected the men to mend their Mockessons to night and turn out in the morning early to hunt Deer fish birds &c. &c. Saw great numbers of the large Black grass hopper. Some bars which were verry wild, but few Birds. a number of ground Lizards; Some fiew Pigions plainly See a rainge of mountains which bore S. E. & N. W. the nearest point south about 60 miles, and becoms high toward the N. W. The plaines on each Side is wavering. Labiesh killed 2 gees & 2 Ducks of the large kind. at two oClock we loaded & Set out, our Powder & Provisions of roots not Sufficently dry. we Shall put them out at the forks or mouth of this river which is at no great distance, and at which place we Shall delay to make Some Selestial observations &c. passed Eleven Island and Seven rapids to day. Several of the rapids verry bad and dificuelt to pass. The Islands of different Sizes and all of round Stone and Sand, no timber of any kind in Sight of the river, a fiew Small willows excepted; in the evening the countrey becomes lower not exceding 90 or 100 feet above the water and back is a wavering Plain on each Side, passed thro narrows for 3 miles where the Clifts of rocks juted to the river on each Side compressing the water of the river through a narrow chanel; below which it widens into a kind of bason nearly round without any proceptiable current, at the lower part of this bason is a bad dificuelt and dangerous rapid to pass, at the upper part of this rapid we over took the three Indians who had Polited us thro the rapids from the forks. those people with our 2 Chiefs had proceeded on to this place where they thought proper to delay for us to warn us of the difficulties of this rapid. we landed at a parcel of Split timber, the timber of a house of Indians out hunting the Antilope in the plains; and raised on Scaffolds to Save them from the Spring floods. here we were obliged for the first time to take the property of the Indians without the consent or approbation of the owner. the night was cold & we made use of a part of those boards and Split logs for fire wood. Killed two teel this evening. Examined the rapids which we found more dificuelt to pass than we expected from the Indians information. a Suckcession of Sholes, appears to reach from bank to bank for 3 miles which was also intersepted with large rocks Sticking up in every direction, and the chanel through which we must pass crooked and narrow. we only made 20 miles today, owing to the detention in passing rapids &c.

[Clark, October 16, 1805] Oar. 16th 1805 Wednesday a cool morning Set out early passed the rapid with all the Canoes except Sgt. Pryors which run on a rock near the lower part of the rapid and Stuck fast, by the assistance of the 3 other Canoes She was unloaded and got off the rock without any further injorey than, the wetting the greater part of her loading- loaded and proceeded on I walked around this rapid

We halted a Short time above the Point and Smoked with the Indians, & examined the Point and best place for our Camp, we Camped on the Columbia River a little above the point I Saw about 200 men Comeing down from their villages & were turned back by the Chief, after we built our fires of what wood we Could Collect, & get from the Indians, the Chief brought down all his men Singing and dancing as they Came, formed a ring and danced for Some time around us we gave them a Smoke, and they returned the village a little above, the Chief & Several delay untill I went to bead. bought 7 dogs & they gave us Several fresh Salmon & Som horse dried

[Clark, October 16, 1805] October 16th Wednesday 1805 A cool morning deturmined to run the rapids, put our Indian guide in front our Small Canoe next and the other four following each other, the canoes all passed over Safe except the rear Canoe which run fast on a rock at the lower part of the Rapids, with the early assistance of the other Canoes & the Indians, who was extreamly ellert every thing was taken out and the Canoe got off without any enjorie further than the articles which it was loaded all wet. at 14 miles passed a bad rapid at which place we unloaded and made a portage of 3/4 of a mile, haveing passd. 4 Smaller rapids, three Islands and the parts of a house above, I Saw Indians & Horses on the South Side below. five Indians came up the river in great haste, we Smoked with them and gave them a piece of tobacco to Smoke with their people and Sent them back, they Set out in a run & continued to go as fast as They Could run as far as we Could See them. after getting Safely over the rapid and haveing taken Diner Set out and proceeded on Seven miles to the junction of this river and the Columbia which joins from the N. W. passd. a rapid two Islands and a graveley bare, and imediately in the mouth a rapid above an Island. In every direction from the junction of those rivers the Countrey is one Continued plain low and rises from the water gradually, except a range of high Countrey which runs from S. W & N E and is on the opposit Side about 2 miles distant from the Collumbia and keeping its detection S W untill it joins a S W. range of mountains.

We halted above the point on the river Kimooenim to Smoke with the Indians who had collected there in great numbers to view us, here we met our 2 Chiefs who left us two days ago and proceeded on to this place to inform those bands of our approach and friendly intentions towards all nations &c. we also met the 2 men who had passed us Several days ago on hors back, one of them we observed was a man of great influence with those Indians, harranged them; after Smokeing with the Indians who had collected to view us we formed a camp at the point near which place I Saw a fiew pieces of Drift wood after we had our camp fixed and fires made, a Chief came from their Camp which was about 1/4 of a mile up the Columbia river at the head of about 200 men Singing and beeting on their drums Stick and keeping time to the musik, they formed a half circle around us and Sung for Some time, we gave them all Smoke, and Spoke to their Chiefs as well as we could by Signs informing them of our friendly disposition to all nations, and our joy in Seeing those of our Children around us, Gave the principal chief a large Medal Shirt and Handkf. a 2nd Chief a Meadel of Small Size, and to the Cheif who came down from the upper villages a Small Medal & Handkerchief.

The Chiefs then returned with the men to their camp; Soon after we purchased for our Provisions Seven Dogs, Some fiew of those people made us presents of fish and Several returned and delayed with us untill bedtime- The 2 old Chiefs who accompanied us from the head of the river precured us Some full Such as the Stalks of weed or plant and willow bushes- one man made me a present of a about 20 lb. of verry fat Dried horse meat.

Great quantities of a kind of prickley pares, much worst than any I have before Seen of a tapering form and attach themselves by bunches.

[Clark, October 17, 1805]
October 17th Thursday 1805 Forks of Columbia
This morning after the Luner observations, the old chief came down, and
Several men with dogs to Sell & womin with fish &c. the Dogs we
purchased the fish not good.

I took 2 men and Set out in a Small Canoe with a view to go as high up the Columbia river as the 1st forks which the Indians made Signs was but a Short distance, I set out at 2 oClock firs course was N. 83° W 6 miles to the lower point of a Island on the Lard. Side, passed an Island in the middle of the river at 5 miles, at the head of which is a rapid not bad at this rapid 3 Lodges of mats on the Lard emenc quantites of dried fish, then West 4 miles to the Lower point of an Island on the Stard. Side, 2 lodges of Indians large and built of mats- passed 3 verry large mat lodges at 2 mile on the Stard Side large Scaffols of fish drying at every lodge, and piles of

Salmon lying. the Squars engaged prepareing them for the Scaffol- a Squar gave me a dried Salmon from those lodes on the Island an Indian Showed me the mouth of the river which falls in below a high hill on the Lard. N. 80° W. 8 miles from the Island. The river bending Lard.- This river is remarkably Clear and Crouded with Salmon in maney places, I observe in assending great numbers of Salmon dead on the Shores, floating on the water and in the Bottoms which can be seen at the debth of 20 feet. the Cause of the emence numbers of dead Salmon I can't account for So it is I must have seen 3 or 400 dead and maney living the Indians, I believe make use of the fish which is not long dead as, I Struck one nearly dead and left him floating, Some Indians in a canoe behind took the fish on board his canoe

The bottoms on the South Side as high as the Tarcouche tesse is from 1 to 2 miles wide, back of the bottoms rises to hilly countrey, the Plain is low on the North & Easte for a great distance no wood to be Seen in any direction.

The Tarcouche tesse bears South of West, the Columbia N W above range of hills on the West Parrelel a range of mountains to the East which appears to run nearly North & South distance not more than 50 miles- I returned to the point at Dusk followed by three canoes of Indians 20 in number- I killed a Fowl of the Pheasent kind as large as a turkey. The length from his Beeck to the end of its tail 2 feet 6- 3/4 Inches, from the extremity of its wings across 3 feet 6 Inches. the tail feathers 13 Inches long, feeds on grass hoppers, and the Seed of wild Isoop 6

Those Indians are orderly, badly dressed in the Same fashions of those above except the women who wore Short Shirts and a flap over them 22 Fishing houses of Mats robes of Deer, Goat & Beaver.

[Clark, October 17, 1805] October 17th Thursday 1805 A fair morning made the above observations during which time the principal Chief came down with Several of his principal men and Smoked with us. Several men and woman offered Dogs and fish to Sell, we purchased all the dogs we could, the fish being out of Season and dieing in great numbers in the river, we did not think proper to use them, Send out Hunters to Shute the Prarie Cock a large fowl which I have only Seen on this river; Several of which I have killed, they are the Size of a Small turkey, of the pheasant kind, one I killed on the water edge to day measured from the Beek to the end of the toe 2 feet 6 & 3/4 Inches; from the extremities of its wings 3 feet 6 inches; the tale feathers is 13 inches long; they feed on grasshoppers and the Seed of the wild plant which is also peculiar to this river and the upper parts of the Missoury somewhat resembling the whins-. Capt. Lewis took a vocabelary of the Language of those people who call themselves So hulk, and also one of the language of a nation resideing on a Westerly fork of the Columbia which mouthes a fiew miles above this place who Call themselves Chim na pum Some fiew of this nation reside with the So kulks nation, Their language differ but little from either the Sokulks or the Cho-pun-nish (or pierced nose) nation which inhabit the Koskoskia river and Lewis's R below.

I took two men in a Small Canoe and assended the Columbia river 10 miles to an Island near the Stard. Shore on which two large Mat Lodges of Indians were drying Salmon, (as they informed me by Signs for the purpose of food and fuel, & I do not think at all improbable that those people make use of Dried fish as fuel,) The number of dead Salmon on the Shores & floating in the river is incrediable to Say and at this Season they have only to collect the fish Split them open and dry them on their Scaffolds on which they have great numbers, how far they have to raft their timber they make their Scaffolds of I could not lern; but there is no timber of any Sort except Small willow bushes in Sight in any directionfrom this Island the natives showed me the enterance of a large Westerly fork which they Call Tapetett at about 8 miles distant, the evening being late I deturmined to return to the forks, at which place I reached at Dark. from the point up the Columbia River is N. 83° W. 6 miles to the lower point of an Island near the Lard. Side passed a Island in the middle of the river at 5 miles at the head of which is a rapid, not dangerous on the Lard Side opposit to this rapid is a fishing place 3 Mat Lodges, and great quants. of Salmon on Scaffolds drying. Saw great numhers of Dead Salmon on the Shores and floating in the water, great numbers of Indians on the banks viewing me and 18 canoes accompanied me from the point- The Waters of this river is Clear, and a Salmon may be Seen at the deabth of 15 or 20 feet. West 4 miles to the lower point of a large Island near the Stard. Side at 2 Lodges, passed three large lodges on the Stard Side near which great number of Salmon was drying on Scaffolds one of those Mat lodges I entered found it crouded with men women and children and near the enterance of those houses I saw maney Squars engaged Splitting and drying Salmon. I was furnished with a mat to Sit on, and one man Set about prepareing me Something to eate, first he brought in a piece of a Drift log of pine and with a wedge of the elks horn, and a malet of Stone curioesly Carved he Split the log into Small pieces and lay'd it open on the fire on which he put round Stones, a woman handed him a basket of water and a large Salmon about half Dried, when the Stones were hot he put them into the basket of water with the fish which was Soon Suflicently boiled for use. it was then taken out put on a platter of rushes neetly made, and Set before me they boiled a Salmon for each of the men with me, dureing those preperations, I Smoked with those about me who Chose to Smoke which was but fiew, this being a custom those people are but little accustomed to and only Smok thro form. after eateing the boiled fish which was delicious, I Set out & halted or came too on the Island at the two Lodges. Several fish was given to me, in return for Which I gave Small pieces of ribbond from those Lodges the natives Showed me the mouth of Tap teel River about 8 miles above on the west Side this western fork appears to beare nearly West, The main Columbia river N W.- a range of high land to the S W and parralal to the river and at the distance of 2 miles on the Lard. Side, the countrey low on the Stard. Side, and all Coverd. with a weed or plant about 2 & three feet high and resembles the whins. I can proceive a range of mountains to the East which appears to bare N. & South distant about 50 or 60 miles. no wood to be Seen in any derection- On my return I was followd. by 3 canoes in which there was 20 Indians I shot a large Prairie Cock Several Grouse, Ducks and fish. on my return found Great Numbr. of the nativs with Capt Lewis, men all employd in dressing ther Skins mending their clothes and putting ther arms in the best order the latter being always a matter of attention with us. The Dress of those natives differ but little from those on the Koskoskia and Lewis's rivers, except the women who dress verry different in as much as those above ware long leather Shirts which highly ornimented with heeds Shells &c. &c. and those on the main Columbia river only ware a truss or pece of leather tied around them at their hips and drawn tite between ther legs and fastened before So as barly to hide those parts which are So Sacredly hid & Scured by our women. Those women are more inclined to Copulency than any we have yet Seen, with low Stature broad faces, heads flatened and the foward compressed so as to form a Streight line from the nose to the Crown of the head, their eyes are of a Duskey black, their hair of a corse black without orniments of any kind braded as above, The orniments of each Sects are Similar, Such as large blue & white beeds, either pendant from their ears or encircling their necks, or wrists & arms. they also ware bracelets of Brass, Copper & horn, and trinkets of Shells, fish bones and curious feathers. Their garments Consists of a short Shirt of leather and a roabe of the Skins of Deer or the Antilope but fiew of them ware Shirts all have Short robes. Those people appears to live in a State of comparitive happiness; they take a greater Share labor of the woman, than is common among Savage tribes, and as I am informd. Content with one wife (as also those on the Ki moo e nim river) Those people respect the aged with veneration, I observed an old woman in one of the Lodges which I entered She was entirely blind as I was informed by Signs, had lived more than 100 winters, She occupied the best position in the house, and when She Spoke great attention was paid to what She Said-. Those people as also those of the flat heads which we had passed on the Koskoske and Lewis's rivers are Subject to Sore eyes, and maney are blind of one and Some of both eyes. this misfortune must be owing to the reflections of the Sun &c. on the waters in which they are continually fishing during the Spring Summer & fall, & the Snows dureing the, winter Seasons, in this open countrey where the eye has no rest. I have observed amongst those, as well in all other tribes which I have passed on these waters who live on fish maney of different Sectes who have lost their teeth about middle age, Some have their teeth worn to the gums, perticelar those of the upper jaws, and the tribes generally have bad teeth the cause of it I cannot account sand attachd. to the roots &c the method they have of useing the dri'd Salmon, which is mearly worming it and eating the rine & Scales with the flesh of the fish, no doubt contributes to it

The Houses or Lodges of the tribes of the main Columbia river is of large mats made of rushes, Those houses are from 15 to 60 feet in length generally of an Oblong Squar form, Suported by poles on forks in the iner Side, Six feet high, the top is covered also with mats leaveing a Seperation in the whole length of about 12 or 15 inches wide, left for the purpose of admitting light and for the Smok of the fire to pass which is made in the middle of the house.- The roughfs are nearly flat, which proves to me that rains are not common in this open Countrey

Those people appeare of a mild disposition and friendly disposedThey have in their huts independant of their nets gigs & fishing tackling each bows & large quivers of arrows on which they use flint Spikes. Theire ammusements are Similar to those of the Missouri. they are not beggerley and receive what is given them with much joy.

I saw but flew horses they appeared make but little use of those animals principally useing Canoes for their uses of procureing food &c.

[Clark, October 18, 1805]
October 18th Friday 1805
a cold morning faire & wind from S E Several Heath hens or large
Pheasents lit near us & the men killed Six of them.

Took one altitude of the Suns upper Limb 28° 22' 15" at h m s 8 1 24 A.M.

Several Indian Canoes Come down & joind those with us, made a Second Chief by giveing a meadel & wampom I also gave a String of wampom to the old Chief who came down with us and informed the Indians of our views and intentions in a council

Measured the width of the Columbia River, from the Point across to a
Point of view is S 22° W from the Point up the Columa to a Point of view

is N. 84° W. 148 poles, thence across to the 1st point of view is S 28 1/2
E

Measured the width of Ki moo e nim River, from the Point across to an object on the opposit side is N. 41 1/2 E from the Point up the river is N. 8 E. 82 poles thence accross to the Point of view is N. 79° East

Distance across the Columbia 960 3/4 yds water

Distance across the Ki-moo-e nim 575 yds water

Names of this nation above the mouth of the Ki-moo-e-nim is So-Kulk Perced noses The Names of the nation on the Kimoenim River is Chopun-nish Piercd noses at the Prarie the name of a nation at the Second forks of the Tape tele River, or Nocktock fork Chim-na-pum, Some of which reside with the So kulkc above this-at and a few miles distance,- 4 men in a Canoe come up from below Stayed a fiew minits and returned.

Took a meridian altitude 68° 57' 30" the Suns upper Limb. The Lattitudes produced is 46° 15' 13 9/10" North, Capt Lewis took a vocabillary of the So kulk or Pierced noses Language and Chim-nd-pum Language whic is in Some words different but orriginally the Same people The Great Chief Cuts-Sa.h nim gave me a Sketch of the rivers & Tribes above on the great river & its waters on which he put great numbers of villages of his nation & friends, as noted on the Sketch

The fish being very bad those which was offerd to us we had every reason to believe was taken up on the Shore dead, we thought proper not to purchase any, we purchased forty dogs for which we gave articles of little value, Such as beeds, bell, & thimbles, of which they appeard verry fond, at 4 OClock we Set out down the Great Columbia accompand by our two old Chiefs, one young man wished to accompany us, but we had no room for more, & he could be of no Service to us

The Great Chief Continued with us untill our departure.

we Encamped a little below & opsd. the lower point of the Island on the Lard. Side no wood to be found we were obliged to make use Small drid willows to Cook- our old Chief informed us that the great Chief of all the nations about lived at the 9 Lodges above and wished us to land &c. he Said he would go up and Call him over they went up and did not return untill late at night, about 20 came down & built a fire above and Stayed all night. The chief brought a basket of mashed berries.

[Clark, October 18, 1805] October 18th Friday 1805 This morning Cool and fare wind from the S. E. Six of the large Prarie cock killed this morning. Several canoes of Indians Came down and joined those with us, we had a council with those in which we informed of our friendly intentions towards them and all other of our red children; of our wish to make a piece between all of our red Children in this quarter &c. &c. this was conveyed by Signs thro our 2 Chiefs who accompanied us, and was understood, we made a 2d Chief and gave Strings of wompom to them all in remembrance of what we Said- four men in a Canoe came up from a large encampment on an Island in the River about 8 miles below, they delayed but a fiew minits and returned, without Speaking a word to us.

The Great Chief and one of the Chim-na pum nation drew me a Sketch of the Columbia above and the tribes of his nation, living on the bank, and its waters, and the Tape tett river which falls in 18 miles above on the westerly side See Sketch below for the number of villages and nations &c. &c.

We thought it necessary to lay in a Store of Provisions for our voyage, and the fish being out of Season, we purchased forty dogs for which we gave articles of little value, Such as bells, thimbles, knitting pins, brass wire & a few beeds all of which they appeared well Satisfied and pleased.

every thing being arranged we took in our Two Chiefs, and Set out on the great Columbia river, haveing left our guide and the two young men two of them enclined not to proceed on any further, and the 3rd could be of no Service to us as he did not know the river below

Took our leave of the Chiefs and all those about us and proceeded on down the great Columbia river passed a large Island at 8 miles about 3 miles in length, a Island on the Stard. Side the upper point of which is opposit the center of the last mentioned Island and reaches 3 1/2 miles below the 1st. Island and opposit to this near the middle of the river nine Lodges are Situated on the upper point at a rapid which is between the lower point of the 1st Island and upper point of this; great numbers of Indians appeared to be on this Island, and emence quantites of fish Scaffold we landed a few minits to view a rapid which Commenced at the lower point, passd this rapid which was verry bad between 2 Small Islands two Still Smaller near the Lard. Side, at this rapid on the Stard. Side is 2 Lodges of Indians Drying fish, at 2 1/2 miles lower and 14 1/2 below the point passed an Island Close under the Stard. Side on which was 2 Lodges of Indians drying fish on Scaffolds as above at 16 miles from the point the river passesinto the range of high Countrey at which place the rocks project into the river from the high clifts which is on the Lard. Side about 2/3 of the way across and those of the Stard Side about the Same distance, the Countrey rises here about 200 feet above The water and is bordered with black rugid rocks, at the Commencement of this high Countrey on Lard Side a Small riverlet falls in which appears to passed under the high County in its whole cose Saw a mountain bearing S. W. Conocal form Covered with Snow. passed 4 Islands, at the upper point of the 3rd is a rapid, on this Island is two Lodges of Indians, drying fish, on the fourth Island Close under the Stard. Side is nine large Lodges of Indians Drying fish on Scaffolds as above at this place we were called to land, as it was near night and no appearance of wood, we proceeded on about 2 miles lower to Some willows, at which place we observed a drift log formed a Camp on the Lard Side under a high hill nearly opposit to five Lodges of Indians; Soon after we landed, our old Chiefs informed us that the large camp above "was the Camp of the 1st Chief of all the tribes in this quarter, and that he had called to us to land and Stay all night with him, that he had plenty of wood for us &" This would have been agreeable to us if it had have been understood perticelarly as we were compelled to Use drid willows for fuel for the purpose of cooking, we requested the old Chiefs to walk up on the Side we had landed and call to the Chief to come down and Stay with us all night which they did; late at night the Chief came down accompanied by 20 men, and formed a Camp a Short distance above, the chief brought with him a large basket of mashed berries which he left at our Lodge as a present. I saw on the main land opposit those Lodges a number of horses feeding, we made 21 miles to day.

[Clark, October 19, 1805] October 19th Saturday, The Great Chief 2d Chief and a Chief of a band below Came and Smoked with us we gave a Meadel a String of Wampom & handkerchef to the Great Chief by name Yel-leppit The 2d Chief we gave a String of wampom, his name is _____ The 3d who lives below a String of Wampom his name I did not learn. the Chief requested us to Stay untill 12 we excused our Selves and Set out at 9 oClock

P. Crusat played on the Violin which pleasd and astonished those reches who are badly Clad, 3/4 with robes not half large enough to cover them, they are homeley high Cheeks, and but fiew orniments. I Suped on the Crane which I killed to day.

[Clark, October 19, 1805] October 19th Saturday 1805 The great chief Yel-lep-pit two other chiefs, and a Chief of Band below presented themselves to us verry early this morning. we Smoked with them, enformed them as we had all others above as well as we Could by Signs of our friendly intentions towards our red children Perticular those who opened their ears to our Councils. we gave a Medal, a Handkercheif & a String of Wompom to Yelleppit and a String of wompom to each of the others. Yelleppit is a bold handsom Indian, with a dignified countenance about 35 years of age, about 5 feet 8 inches high and well perpotiond. he requested us to delay untill the Middle of the day, that his people might Come down and See us, we excused our Selves and promised to Stay with him one or 2 days on our return which appeared to Satisfy him; great numbers of Indians Came down in Canoes to view us before we Set out which was not untill 9 oClock A M. we proceeded on passed a Island, close under the Lard Side about Six miles in length opposit to the lower point of which two lsds. are situated on one of which five Lodges vacent & Saffolds drying fish at the upper point of this Island Swift water. a Short distance below passed two Islands; one near the middle of the river on which is Seven lodges of Indians drying fish, at our approach they hid themselves in their Lodges and not one was to be seen untill we passed, they then Came out in greater numbers than is common in Lodges of their Size, it is probable that, the inhabitants of the 5 Lodges above had in a fright left their lodges and decended to this place to defend them Selves if attackted there being a bad rapid opposit the Island thro which we had to pass prevented our landing on this Island and passifying those people, about four miles below this fritened Island we arrived at the head of a verry bad rapid, we came too on the Lard Side to view the rapid before we would venter to run it, as the Chanel appeared to be close under the oppd. Shore, and it would be necessary to liten our canoe, I deturmined to walk down on the Lard Side, with the 2 Chiefs the interpreter & his woman, and derected the Small canoe to prcede down on the Lard Side to the foot of the rapid which was about 2 miles in length I Sent on the Indian Chiefs &c. down and I assended a high clift about 200 feet above the water from the top of which is a leavel plain extending up the river and off for a great extent, at this place the Countrey becoms low on each Side of the river, and affords a prospect of the river and country below for great extent both to the right and left; from this place I descovered a high mountain of emence hight covered with Snow, this must be one of the mountains laid down by Vancouver, as Seen from the mouth of the Columbia River, from the Course which it bears which is West I take it to be Mt. St. Helens, destant 156 miles a range of mountains in the Derection crossing, a conacal mountain S. W. toped with Snow This rapid I observed as I passed opposit to it to be verry bad interseped with high rock and Small rockey Islands, here I observed banks of Muscle Shells banked up in the river in Several places, I Delayed at the foot of the rapid about 2 hours for the Canoes which I Could See met with much dificuley in passing down the rapid on the oposit Side maney places the men were obliged to get into the water and haul the canoes over Sholes- while Setting on a rock wateing for Capt Lewis I Shot a Crain which was flying over of the common kind. I observed a great number of Lodges on the opposit Side at Some distance below and Several Indians on the opposit bank passing up to where Capt. Lewis was with the Canoes, others I Saw on a knob nearly opposit to me at which place they delayed but a Short time before they returned to their Lodges as fast as they could run, I was fearfull that those people might not be informed of us, I deturmined to take the little Canoe which was with me and proceed with the three men in it to the Lodges, on my aproach not one person was to be Seen except three men off in the plains, and they Sheared off as I aproached near the Shore, I landed in front of five Lodges which was at no great distance from each other, Saw no person the enteranc or Dores of the Lodges wer Shut with the Same materials of which they were built a mat, I approached one with a pipe in my hand entered a lodge which was the nearest to me found 32 persons men, women and a few children Setting permiscuesly in the Lodg, in the greatest agutation, Some crying and ringing there hands, others hanging their heads. I gave my hand to them all and made Signs of my friendly dispotion and offered the men my pipe to Smok and distributed a fiew Small articles which I had in my pockets,-this measure passified those distressed people verry much, I then Sent one man into each lodge and entered a Second myself the inhabitants of which I found more fritened than those of the first lodge I destributed Sundrey Small articles amongst them, and Smoked with the men, I then entered the third 4h & fifth Lodge which I found Somewhat passified, the three men, Drewer Jo. & R. Fields, haveing useed everey means in their power to convince them of our friendly disposition to them, I then Set my Self on a rock and made Signs to the men to come and Smoke with me not one Come out untill the Canoes arrived with the 2 Chiefs, one of whom spoke aloud, and as was their Custom to all we had passed the Indians came out & Set by me and Smoked They said we came from the clouds &c &c and were not men &c. &c. this time Capt. Lewis came down with the Canoes rear in which the Indian, as Soon as they Saw the Squar wife of the interperters they pointed to her and informed those who continued yet in the Same position I first found them, they imediately all came out and appeared to assume new life, the sight of This Indian woman, wife to one of our interprs. confirmed those people of our friendly intentions, as no woman ever accompanies a war party of Indians in this quarter- Capt Lewis joined us and we Smoked with those people in the greatest friendship, dureing which time one of our Old Chiefs informed them who we were from whence we Came and where we were going giveing them a friendly account of us, those people do not Speak prosisely the Same language of those above but understand them, I Saw Several Horses and persons on hors back in the plains maney of the men womin and children Came up from the Lodges below; all of them appeared pleased to See us, we traded some fiew articles for fish and berries, Dined, and proceeded on passed a Small rapid and 15 Lodges below the five, and Encamped below an Island Close under the Lard Side, nearly opposit to 24 Lodges on an Island near the middle of the river, and the Main Stard Shor Soon after we landed which was at a fiew willow trees about 100 Indians Came from the different Lodges, and a number of them brought wood which they gave us, we Smoked with all of them, and two of our Party Peter Crusat & Gibson played on the violin which delighted them greatly, we gave to the principal man a String of wompon treated them kindly for which they appeared greatfull, This Tribe can raise about 350 men their Dress are Similar to those at the fork except their robes are Smaller and do not reach lower than the waste and 3/4 of them have Scercely any robes at all, the women have only a Small pece of a robe which Covers their Sholders neck and reaching down behind to their wastes, with a tite piece of leather about the waste, the brests are large and hang down verry low illy Shaped, high Cheeks flattened heads, & have but fiew orniments, they are all employed in fishing and drying fish of which they have great quantites on their Scaffolds, their habits customs &c. I could not lern. I killed a Duck that with the Crain afforded us a good Supper. the Indians continued all night at our fires

This day we made 36 miles.

[Clark, October 20, 1805] October 20th 1805 Sunday a very cold morning wind S. W. about 100 Indians Came over this morning to See us, after a Smoke, a brackfast on Dogs flesh we Set out. about 350 men

Killed 2 large speckle guts 4 Duck in Malade Small ducks the flavour of which much resembles the Canvis back no timber of any kind on the river, we Saw in the last Lodges acorns of the white oake which the Inds. inform they precure above the falls The men are badly dressed, Some have scarlet & blue cloth robes. one has a Salors jacket, The women have a Short indiferent Shirt, a Short robe of Deer or Goat Skins, & a Small Skin which they fastend. tite around their bodies & fastend. between the legs to hide the

[Clark, October 20, 1805] October 20th Sunday 1805 A cool morning wind S. W. we concluded to delay untill after brackfast which we were obliged to make on the flesh of dog. after brackfast we gave all the Indian men Smoke, and we Set out leaveing about 200 of the nativs at our Encampment; passd. three Indian Lodges on the Lard Side a little below our Camp which lodges I did not discover last evening, passed a rapid at Seven miles one at a Short distance below we passed a verry bad rapid, a chane of rocks makeing from the Stard. Side and nearly Chokeing the river up entirely with hugh black rocks, an Island below close under the Stard. Side on which was four Lodges of Indians drying-fish,- here I Saw a great number of pelicons on the wing, and black Comerants. at one oClock we landed on the lower point of an Island at Some Indian Lodges, a large Island on the Stard Side nearly opposit and a Small one a little below on the Lard Side on those three Island I counted Seventeen Indian Lodges, those people are in every respect like those above, prepareing fish for theire winter consumption here we purchased a fiew indifferent Dried fish & a fiew berries on which we dined- (On the upper part of this Island we discovered an Indian vault) our curiosity induced us to examine the methot those nativs practicd in diposeing the dead, the Vault was made by broad poads and pieces of Canoes leaning on a ridge pole which was Suported by 2 forks Set in the ground Six feet in hight in an easterly and westerly direction and about 60 feet in length, and 12 feet wide, in it I observed great numbers of humane bones of every description perticularly in a pile near the Center of the vault, on the East End 21 Scul bomes forming a circle on Mats-; in the Westerley part of the Vault appeared to be appropriated for those of more resent death, as many of the bodies of the deceased raped up in leather robes lay on board covered with mats, &c we observed, independant of the canoes which Served as a Covering, fishing nets of various kinds, Baskets of different Sizes, wooden boles, robes Skins, trenchers, and various Kind of trinkets, in and Suspended on the ends of the pieces forming the vault; we also Saw the Skeletons of Several Horses at the vault & great number of bones about it, which Convinced me that those animals were Sacrefised as well as the above articles to the Deceased.) after diner we proceeded on to a bad rapid at the lower point of a Small Island on which four Lodges of Indians were Situated drying fish; here the high countrey Commences again on the Stard. Side leaveing a vallie of 40 miles in width, from the mustle Shel rapid. examined and passed this rapid close to the Island at 8 miles lower passed a large Island near the middle of the river a brook on the Stard. Side and 11 Islds. all in view of each other below, a riverlit falls in on the Lard. Side behind a Small Island a Small rapid below. The Star Side is high rugid hills, the Lard. Side a low plain and not a tree to be Seen in any Direction except a fiew Small willow bushes which are Scattered partially on the Sides of the bank

The river to day is about 1/4 of a mile in width; this evening the Countrey on the Lard. Side rises to the hight of that on the Starboard Side, and is wavering- we made 42 miles to day; the current much more uniform than yesterday or the day before. Killed 2 Speckle guls Severl. ducks of a delicious flavour.

[Clark, October 21, 1805]
October 21st 1805 Monday
a verry Cold morning we Set out early wind from the S W. we Could not
Cook brakfast before we embarked as usial for the want of wood or
Something to burn.-

[Clark, October 21, 1805] October 21st Monday 1805 A verry cool morning wind from the S. W. we Set out verry early and proceeded on, last night we could not Collect more dry willows the only fuel, than was barely Suffient to cook Supper, and not a Sufficency to cook brackfast this morning, passd. a Small Island at 5 1/2 miles a large one 8 miles in the middle of the river, Some rapid water at the head and Eight Lodges of nativs opposit its Lower point on the Stard. Side, we came too at those lodges, bought some wood and brackfast. Those people recived us with great kindness, and examined us with much attention, their employments custom Dress and appearance Similar to those above; Speak the Same language, here we Saw two Scarlet and a blue cloth blanket, also a Salors Jacket the Dress of the men of this tribe only a Short robe of Deer or Goat Skins, and that of the womn is a Short piece of Dressed Skin which fall from the neck So as to Cover the front of the body as low as the waste, a Short robe, which is of one Deer or antilope Skin, and a Hap, around their waste and Drawn tite between their legs as before described, their orniments are but fiew, and worn as those above.

we got from those people a fiew pounded rotes fish and Acorns of the white oake, those Acorns they make use of as food, and inform us they precure them of the nativs who live near the falls below which place they all discribe by the term Timm at 2 miles lower passed a rapid, large rocks Stringing into the river of large Size opposit to this rapid on the Stard. Shore is Situated two Lodges of the nativs drying fish here we halted a fiew minits to examine the rapid before we entered it which was our constant Custom, and at all that was verry dangerous put out all who could not Swim to walk around, after passing this rapid we proceeded on passed anoothe rapid at 5 miles lower down, above this rapid on five Lodges of Indians fishing &c. above this rapid maney large rocks on each Side at Some distance from Shore, one mile passed an Island Close to the Stard. Side, below which is two Lodge of nativs, a little below is a bad rapid which is bad crouded with hugh rocks Scattered in every Direction which renders the pasage verry Difficuelt a little above this rapid on the Lard. Side emence piles of rocks appears as if Sliped from the Clifts under which they lay, passed great number of rocks in every direction Scattered in the river 5 Lodges a little below on the Stard. Side, and one lodge on an Island near the Stard. Shore opposit to which is a verry bad rapid, thro which we found much dificuelty in passing, the river is Crouded with rocks in every direction, after Passing this dificult rapid to the mouth of a Small river on the Larboard Side 40 yards wide descharges but little water at this time, and appears to take its Sourse in the Open plains to the S. E. from this place I proceved Some fiew Small pines on the tops of the high hills and bushes in the hollars. imediately above & below this little river comences a rapid which is crouded with large rocks in every direction, the pasage both crooked and dificuelt, we halted at a Lodge to examine those noumerous Islands of rock which apd. to extend maney miles below,-. great numbs. of Indians came in Canoes to View us at this place, after passing this rapid which we accomplished without loss; winding through between the hugh rocks for about 2 miles-. (from this rapid the Conocil mountain is S. W. which the Indians inform me is not far to the left of the great falls; this I call the Timm or falls mountain it is high and the top is covered with Snow) imediately below the last rapids there is four Lodges of Indians on the Stard. Side, proceeded on about two miles lower and landed and encamped near five Lodges of nativs, drying fish those are the relations of those at the Great falls, they are pore and have but little wood which they bring up the river from the falls as they Say, we purchased a little wood to cook our Dog meat and fish; those people did not recive us at first with the same cordiality of those above, they appear to be the Same nation Speak the Same language with a little curruption of maney words Dress and fish in the Same way, all of whome have pierced noses and the men when Dressed ware a long taper'd piece of Shell or beed put through the nose-this part of the river is furnished with fine Springs which either rise high up the Sides of the hills or on the bottom near the river and run into the river. the hills are high and rugid a fiew scattering trees to be Seen on them either Small pine or Scrubey white oke.

The probable reason of the Indians residing on the Stard. Side of this as well as the waters of Lewis's River is their fear of the Snake Indians who reside, as they nativs Say on a great river to the South, and are at war with those tribes, one of the Old Chiefs who accompanies us pointed out a place on the lard. Side where they had a great battle, not maney years ago, in which maney were killed on both Sides-, one of our party J. Collins presented us with Some verry good beer made of the Pashi-co-quar-mash bread, which bread is the remains of what was laid in as Stores of Provisions, at the first flat heads or Cho-punnish Nation at the head of the Kosskoske river which by being frequently wet molded & Sowered &c. we made 33 miles to day.

[Clark, October 22, 1805] October 22nd Tuesday 1805 a fine morning Calm. we Set out at 9 oClock and on the Course S. 52° W. 10 miles passed lodges & Inds. and rapids as mentioned in the Cours of yesterday, from the expiration of

Took our Baggage & formed a Camp below the rapids in a cove on the Stard Side the distance 1200 yards haveing passed at the upper end of the portage 17 Lodges of Indians, below the rapids & above the Camp 5 large Loges of Indians, great numbers of baskets of Pounded fish on the rocks Islands & near their Lodges thos are neetly pounded & put in verry new baskets of about 90 or 100 pounds wight. hire Indians to take our heavy articles across the portage purchased a Dog for Supper Great numbers of Indians view us, we with much dificuelty purchd. as much wood as Cooked our dogs this evening, our men all in helth- The Indians have their grave yards on an Island in the rapids. The Great Chief of those Indians is out hunting. no Indians reside on the Lard Side for fear of the Snake Indians with whome they are at war and who reside on the large fork on the lard. a little above

[Clark, October 22, 1805] October 22d Tuesday 1805 A fine morning calm and fare we Set out at 9 oClock passed a verry bad rapid at the head of an Island close under the Stard. Side, above this rapid on the Stard Side is Six Lodges of nativs Drying fish, at 9 mls. passed a bad rapid at the head of a large Island of high, uneaven rocks, jutting over the water, a Small Island in a Stard. Bend opposit the upper point, on which I counted 20 parcels of dryed and pounded fish; on the main Stard Shore opposit to this Island five Lodges of Indians are Situated Several Indians in Canoes killing fish with gigs, &c. opposit the center of this Island of rocks which is about 4 miles long we discovered the enterence of a large river on the Lard. Side which appeared to Come from the S. E.- we landed at Some distance above the mouth of this river and Capt. Lewis and my Self Set out to view this river above its mouth, as our rout was intersepted by a deep narrow Chanel which runs out of this river into the Columbia a little below the place we landed, leaveing a high dry rich Island of about 400 yards wide and 800 yards long here we Seperated, I proceeded on to the river and Struck it at the foot of a verry Considerable rapid, here I beheld an emence body of water Compressd in a narrow Chanel of about 200 yds in width, fomeing over rocks maney of which presented their tops above the water, when at this place Capt. Lewis joined me haveing delayed on the way to examine a root of which the nativs had been digging great quantities in the bottoms of this River. at about two miles above this River appears to be confined between two high hils below which it divided by numbers of large rocks, and Small Islands covered with a low groth of timber, and has a rapid as far as the narrows three Small Islands in the mouth of this River, this River haveing no Indian name that we could find out, except "the River on which the Snake Indians live," we think it best to leave the nameing of it untill our return.

we proceeded on pass the mouth of this river at which place it appears to discharge 1/4 as much water as runs down the Columbia. at two miles below this River passed Eight Lodges on the Lower point of the Rock Island aforesaid at those Lodges we saw large logs of wood which must have been rafted down the To war-ne hi ooks River, below this Island on the main Stard Shore is 16 Lodges of nativs; here we landed a fiew minits to Smoke, the lower point of one Island opposit which heads in the mouth of Towarnehiooks River which I did not observe untill after passing these lodges about 1/2 a mile lower passed 6 more Lodges on the Same Side and 6 miles below the upper mouth of Towarnehiooks River the comencement of the pitch of the Great falls, opposit on the Stard. Side is 17 Lodges of the nativs we landed and walked down accompanied by an old man to view the falls, and the best rout for to make a portage which we Soon discovered was much nearest on the Stard. Side, and the distance 1200 yards one third of the way on a rock, about 200 yards over a loose Sand collected in a hollar blown by the winds from the bottoms below which was disagreeable to pass, as it was Steep and loose. at the lower part of those rapids we arrived at 5 Large Lodges of nativs drying and prepareing fish for market, they gave us Philburts, and berries to eate, we returned droped down to the head of the rapids and took every article except the Canoes across the portag where I had formed a camp on ellegable Situation for the protection of our Stores from Thieft, which we were more fearfull of, than their arrows. we despatched two men to examine the river on the opposit Side, and reported that the Canoes could be taken down a narrow Chanel on the opposit Side after a Short portage at the head of the falls, at which place the Indians take over their Canoes. Indians assisted us over the portage with our heavy articles on their horses, the waters is divided into Several narrow chanels which pass through a hard black rock forming Islands of rocks at this Stage of the water, on those Islands of rocks as well as at and about their Lodges I observe great numbers of Stacks of pounded Salmon neetly preserved in the following manner, i e after Suffiently Dried it is pounded between two Stones fine, and put into a speces of basket neetly made of grass and rushes of better than two feet long and one foot Diamiter, which basket is lined with the Skin of Salmon Stretched and dried for the purpose, in theis it is pressed down as hard as is possible, when full they Secure the open part with the fish Skins across which they fasten tho the loops of the basket that part very Securely, and then on a Dry Situation they Set those baskets the Corded part up, their common Custom is to Set 7 as close as they can Stand and 5 on the top of them, and secure them with mats which is raped around them and made fast with cords and Covered also with mats, those 12 baskets of from 90 to 100 w. each form a Stack. thus preserved those fish may be kept Sound and Sweet Several years, as those people inform me, Great quantities as they inform us are Sold to the whites people who visit the mouth of this river as well as to the nativs below.

on one of those Island I saw Several tooms but did not visit them The principal Chiefs of the bands resideing about this Place is out hunting in the mountains to the S. W.- no Indians reside on the S. W.side of this river for fear (as we were informed) of the Snake Indians, who are at war with the tribes on this river— they represent the Snake Indians as being verry noumerous, and resideing in a great number of villages on Towarnehiooks River which falls in 6 miles above on the Lard. Side and is reaches a great ways and is large a little abov its mouth at which part it is not intersepted with rapids, they inform that one considerable rapid & maney Small ones in that river, and that the Snake live on Salmon, and they go to war to their first villages in 12 days, the Couse they pointed is S. E. or to the S of S. E. we are visited by great numbers of Indians to Day to view us, we purchased a Dog for Supper, Some fish and with dificuelty precured as much wood as Cooked Supper, which we also purchased we made 19 miles to day

[Clark, October 23, 1805] October 23rd (Saturday) Wednesday 1805 Took the Canoes over the Portage on the Lard. Side with much dificuelty, description on another Paper one Canoe got loose & cought by the Indians which we were obliged to pay. our old Chiefs over herd the Indians from below Say they would try to kill us & informed us of it, we have all the arm examined and put in order, all th Inds leave us early, Great numbers of flees on the Lard Side- Shot a Sea Oter which I did not get, Great Numbers about those rapids we purchased 8 dogs, Small & fat for our party to eate, the Indians not verry fond of Selling their good fish, compells us to make use of dogs for food Exchanged our Small canoe for a large & a very new one built for riding the waves obsd Merdn. altd. 66° 27' 30" Latd. prodsd. 45° 42' 57 3/10" North

[Clark, October 23, 1805] October 23d Wednesday 1805 a fine morning, I with the greater part of the men Crossed in the Canoes to opposit Side above the falls and hauled them across the portage of 457 yards which is on the Lard. Side and certainly the best side to pass the canoes I then decended through a narrow chanel of about 150 yards wide forming a kind of half circle in it course of a mile to a pitch of 8 feet in which the chanel is divided by 2 large rocks at this place we were obliged to let the Canoes down by Strong ropes of Elk Skin which we had for the purpose, one Canoe in passing this place got loose by the Cords breaking, and was cought by the Indians below. I accomplished this necessary business and landed Safe with all the Canoes at our Camp below the falls by 3 oClock P.M. nearly covered with flees which were So thick amongst the Straw and fish Skins at the upper part of the portage at which place the nativs had been Camped not long Since; that every man of the party was obliged to Strip naked dureing the time of takeing over the canoes, that they might have an oppertunity of brushing the flees of their legs and bodies- Great numbers of Sea Otters in the river below the falls, I Shot one in the narrow chanel to day which I could not get. Great numbers of Indians visit us both from above and below— one of the old Chiefs who had accompanied us from the head of the river, informed us that he herd the Indians Say that the nation below intended to kill us, we examined all the arms &c. complete the amunition to 100 rounds. The nativs leave us earlyer this evening than usial, which gives a Shadow of Confirmation to the information of our Old Chief, as we are at all times & places on our guard, are under no greater apprehention than is common.

we purchased 8 Small fat dogs for the party to eate the nativs not being fond of Selling their good fish, compells us to make use of Dog meat for food, the flesh of which the most of the party have become fond of from the habits of useing it for Some time past. The Altitude of this day 66° 27' 30" gave for Latd. 45° 42' 57 1/10 N.

I observed on the beach near the Indian Lodges two Canoes butiful of different Shape & Size to what we had Seen above wide in the midde and tapering to each end, on the bow curious figures were Cut in the wood &c.

Capt. Lewis went up to the Lodges to See those Canoes and exchanged our Smallest Canoe for one of them by giveing a Hatchet & few trinkets to the owner who informed that he purchased it of a white man below for a horse, these Canoes are neeter made than any I have ever Seen and Calculated to ride the waves, and carry emence burthens, they are dug thin and are suported by cross pieces of about 1 inch diamuter tied with Strong bark thro holes in the Sides. our two old Chiefs appeared verry uneasy this evening.

[Clark, October 24, 1805] October 24th Thursday 1805 a fine morning the Indians approached us with caution. our 2 old Chiefs deturmin to return home, Saying they were at war with Indians below and they would kill them we pursuaded them to Stay 2 nights longer with us, with a view to make a peace with those Indians below as well as to have them with us dureing our Delay with this tribe. Capt Lewis went to view the falls I Set out with the party at 9 oClock a m at 2 1/2 miles passed a rock which makes from the Stard Side 4 Lodges above 1 below and Confined the river in a narrow channel of about 45 yards this continued for about 1/4 of a mile & widened to about 200 yards, in those narrows the water was agitated in a most Shocking manner boils Swell & whorl pools, we passed with great risque It being impossible to make a portage of the Canoes, about 2 miles lower passed a verry Bad place between 2 rocks one large & in the middle of the river here our Canoes took in Some water, I put all the men who Could not Swim on Shore; & Sent a fiew articles Such as guns & papers, and landed at a village of 20 houses on the Stard Side in a Deep bason where the river ap-prd. to be blocked up with emence rocks I walked down and examined the pass found it narrow, and one verry bad place a little in the narrows I pursued this Chanel which is from 50 to 100 yards wide and Swels and boils with a most Tremendeous manner; prosued this channel 5 ms & returned found Capt Lewis & a Chief from below with maney of his men on a visit to us, one of our Party Pete Crusat played on the violin which pleased the Savage, the men danced, Great numbers of Sea Orter Pole Cats about those fishories. the houses of those Indians are 20 feet Square and Sunk 8 feet under ground & Covered with bark with a Small door round at top rose about 18 Inches above ground, to keep out the Snow I saw 107 parcels of fish Stacked, and great quantites in the houses

[Clark, October 24, 1805] October 24th Thursday 1805 The morning fare after a beautifull night, the nativs approached us this morning with great caution. our two old chiefs expressed a desire to return to their band from this place, Saying "that they Could be of no further Service to us, as their nation extended no further down the river than those falls, and as the nation below had expressed hostile intentions against us, would Certainly kill them; perticularly as They had been at war with each other;" we requested them to Stay with us two nights longer, and we would See the nation below and make a peace between them, they replied they "were anxious to return and See our horses" we insisted on their Staying with us two nights longer to which they agreed; our views were to detain those Chiefs with us untill we Should pass the next falls, which we were told was verry bad, and at no great distance below, that they might inform us of any designs of the nativs, and if possible to bring about a peace between them and the tribes below.

The first pitch of this falls is 20 feet perpendicular, then passing thro a narrow Chanel for 1 mile to a rapid of about 18 feet fall below which the water has no perceptable fall but verry rapid See Sketch No. 1. It may be proper here to remark that from Some obstruction below, the cause of which we have not yet learned, the water in high fluds (which are in the Spring) rise below these falls nearly to a leavel with the water above the falls; the marks of which can be plainly trac'd around the falls. at that Stage of the water the Salmon must pass up which abounds in Such great numbers above- below those falls are Salmon trout and great numbers of the heads of a Species of trout Smaller than the Salmon. those fish they catch out of the Salmon Season, and are at this time in the act of burrying those which they had drid for winter food. the mode of buring those fish is in holes of various Sizes, lined with Straw on which they lay fish Skins in which they inclose the fish which is laid verry close, and then Covered with earth of about 12 or 15 inches thick. Capt Lewis and three men crossed the river and on the opposit Side to view the falls which he had not yet taken a full view of- At 9 oClock a.m. I Set out with the party and proceeded on down a rapid Stream of about 400 yards wide at 2 1/2 miles the river widened into a large bason to the Stard. Side on which there is five Lodges of Indians. here a tremendious black rock Presented itself high and Steep appearing to choke up the river nor could I See where the water passed further than the Current was drawn with great velocity to the Lard Side of this rock at which place I heard a great roreing. I landed at the Lodges and the natives went with me to the top of this rock which makes from the Stard. Side; from the top of which I could See the dificulties we had to pass for Several miles below; at this place the water of this great river is compressed into a Chanel between two rocks not exceeding forty five yards wide and continues for a 1/4 of a mile when it again widens to 200 yards and continues this width for about 2 miles when it is again intersepted by rocks. This obstruction in the river accounts for the water in high floods riseing to Such a hite at the last falls. The whole of the Current of this great river must at all Stages pass thro this narrow chanel of 45 yards wide. as the portage of our canoes over this high rock would be impossible with our Strength, and the only danger in passing thro those narrows was the whorls and Swills arriseing from the Compression of the water, and which I thought (as also our principal watermen Peter Crusat) by good Stearing we could pass down Safe, accordingly I detur mined to pass through this place notwithstanding the horrid appearance of this agitated gut Swelling, boiling & whorling in every direction (which from the top of the rock did not appear as bad as when I was in it;) however we passed Safe to the astonishment of all the Inds. of the last Lodges who viewed us from the top of the rock. passed one Lodge below this rock and halted on the Stard. Side to view a verry bad place, the Current divided by 2 Islands of rocks the lower of them large and in the middle of the river, this place being verry bad I Sent by land all the men who could not Swim and Such articles as was most valuable to us Such as papers Guns & amunition, and proceeded down with the Canoes two at a time to a village of 20 wood housies in a Deep bend to the Stard. Side below which a rugid black rock about 20 feet biter than the Common high fluds of the river with Several dry Chapels which appeared to Choke the river up quite across; this I took to be the 2d falls or the place the nativs above call timm, The nativs of this village reived me verry kindly, one of whome envited me into his house, which I found to be large and comodious, and the first wooden houses in which Indians have lived Since we left those in the vicinty of the Illinois, they are scattered permiscuisly on a elivated Situation near a mound of about 30 feet above the Common leavel, which mound has Some remains of houses and has every appearance of being artificial- those houses are about the Same Shape Size and form 20 feet wide and 30 feet long with one Dore raised 18 Inches above ground, they are 29 1/2 inches high & 14 wide, forming in a half Circle above those houses were Sunk into the earth Six feet, the roofs of them was Supported by a ridge pole resting on three Strong pieces of Split timber three one of which the dore was cut that and the walls the top of which was just above ground Suported a certain number of Spars which are Covered with the Bark of the white Ceadar, or Arber Vitea; and the whole attached and Secured by the fibers of the Cedar. the eaves at or near the earth, the gable ends and Side walls are Secured with Split boards which is Seported on iner Side with Strong pieces of timber under the eves &c. to keep those pieces errect & the earth from without pressing in the boards, Suported by Strong posts at the Corners to which those poles were attached to give aditional Strength, Small openings were left above the ground, for the purpose, as I conjectured, of dischargeing Their arrows at a besiegeing enimey; Light is admited Thro an opening at top which also Serves for the Smoke to pass through. one half of those houses is apropriated for the Storeing away Dried & pounded fish which is the principal food The other part next the dore is the part occupied by the nativs who have beds raised on either Side, with a fire place in the center of this Space each house appeared to be occupied by about three families; that part which is apropriated for fish was crouded with that article, and a fiew baskets of burries- I dispatched a Sufficent number of the good Swimers back for the 2 canoes above the last rapid and with 2 men walked down three miles to examine the river Over a bed of rocks, which the water at verry high fluds passes over, on those rocks I Saw Several large Scaffols on which the Indians dry fish; as this is out of Season the poles on which they dry those fish are tied up verry Securely in large bundles and put upon the Scaffolds, I counted 107 Stacks of dried pounded fish in different places on those rocks which must have contained io,ooo w. of neet fish, The evening being late I could not examine the river to my Satisfaction, the Chanel is narrow and compressed for about 2 miles, when it widens into a deep bason to the Stard. Side, & again contracts into a narrow chanel divided by a rock I returned through a rockey open countrey infested with pole-cats to the village where I met with Capt. Lewis the two old Chiefs who accompanied us & the party & canoes who had all arrived Safe; the Canoes haveing taken in Some water at the last rapids. here we formed a Camp near the Village, The principal Chief from the nation below with Several of his men visited us, and afforded a favourable oppertunity of bringing about a Piece and good understanding between this chief and his people and the two Chiefs who accompanied us which we have the Satisfaction to Say we have accomplished, as we have every reason to believe and that those two bands or nations are and will be on the most friendly terms with each other. gave this Great Chief a Medal and Some other articles, of which he was much pleased, Peter Crusat played on the violin and the men danced which delighted the nativs, who Shew every civility towards us. we Smoked with those people untill late at night, when every one retired to rest.

[Clark, October 25, 1805] October 25th Friday 1805 A Cold morning, we deturmined to attempt the Chanel after brackfast I took down all the party below the bad places with a load & one Canoe passed well, a 2d passed well I had men on the Shore with ropes to throw in in Case any acidence happened at the Whirl &c- the Inds on the rocks veiwing us the 3rd Canoe nearly filled with water we got her Safe to Shore. The last Canoe Came over well which to me was truly gratifying Set out and had not passed 2 mils before 3 Canoes run against a rock in the river with great force no damg. met with a 2d Chief of the nation from hunting, we Smoked with him and his party and gave a medal of The Small Size & Set out passed great numbers of rocks, good water and Came to at a high point of rocks below the mouth of a Creek which falls in on the Lard Side and head up towards the high Snow mountain to the S W. this Creek is 20 yards wide and has Some beaver Signs at its mouth river about 1/2 a mile wide and Crouded with Sea otters, & drum was Seen this evening we took possession of a high Point of rocks to defend our Selves in Case the threts of those Indians below Should be put in execution against us. Sent out Some hunters to look if any Signs of game, one man killed a Small deer & Several others Seen I killed a goose, and Suped hartily on venison & goose. Camped on the rock guard under the hill.

[Clark, October 25, 1805] October 25th Friday 1805 a cool morning Capt Lewis and my Self walked down to See the place the Indians pointed out as the worst place in passing through the gut, which we found difficuelt of passing without great danger, but as the portage was impractiable with our large Canoes, we Concluded to Make a portage of our most valuable articles and run the canoes thro accordingly on our return divided the party Some to take over the Canoes, and others to take our Stores across a portage of a mile to a place on the Chanel below this bad whorl & Suck, with Some others I had fixed on the Chanel with roapes to throw out to any who Should unfortunately meet with difficuelty in passing through; great number of Indians viewing us from the high rocks under which we had to pass, the 3 firt Canoes passed thro very well, the 4th nearly filled with water, the last passed through by takeing in a little water, thus Safely below what I conceved to be the worst part of this Chanel, felt my Self extreamly gratified and pleased. we loaded the Canoes & Set out, and had not proceeded, more than two mile before the unfortunate Canoe which filled crossing the bad place above, run against a rock and was in great danger of being lost, This Chanel is through a hard rough black rock, from 50-100 yards wide. Swelling and boiling in a most tremendious maner Several places on which the Indians inform me they take the Salmon as fast as they wish; we passed through a deep bason to the Stard Side of 1 mile below which the River narrows and divided by a rock The Curent we found quit jentle, here we met with our two old Chiefs who had been to a village below to Smoke a friendly pipe, and at this place they met the Cheif & party from the village above on his return from hunting all of whome were then crossing over their horses, we landed to Smoke a pipe with this Chief whome we found to be a bold pleasing looking man of about 50 years of age dressd. in a war jacket a cap Legins & mockersons. he gave us Some meat of which he had but little and informed us he in his rout met with a war party of Snake Indians from the great river of the S. E. which falls in a few miles above and had a fight. we gave this Chief a Medal, &c. a parting Smoke with our two faithful friends the Chiefs who accompanied us from the head of the river, (who had purchased a horse each with 2 robes and intended to return on horse back) we proceeded on down the water fine, rocks in every derection for a fiew miles when the river widens and becoms a butifull jentle Stream of about half a mile wide, Great numbers of the Sea Orter about those narrows and both below and above. we Came too, under a high point of rocks on the Lard. Side below a creek of 20 yards wide and much water, as it was necessary to make Some Selestial observations we formed our Camp on the top of a high point of rocks, which forms a kind of fortification in the Point between the river & Creek, with a boat guard, this Situation we Concieve well Calculated for defence, and Conveniant to hunt under the foots of the mountain to the West & S. W. where timber of different kinds grows, and appears to be handsom Coverts for the Deer, in oke woods, Sent out hunters to examine for game G. D. Killed a Small Deer & other Saw much Sign, I killed a goose in the creek which was verry fat- one of the guard saw a Drum fish to day as he Conceved our Situation well Calculated to defend our Selves from any designs of the natives, Should They be enclined to attack us.

This little Creek heads in the range of mountains which run S S W & N W for a long distance on which is Scattering pine white Oake &c. The Pinical of the round toped mountain which we Saw a Short distance below the forks of this river is S. 43° W. of us and abt 37 miles, it is at this time toped with Snow we called this the falls mountain or Timm mountain. The face of the Countrey, on both Side of the river above and about the falls, is Steep ruged and rockey open and contain but a Small preportion of erbage, no timber a fiew bushes excepted, The nativs at the upper falls raft their timber down Towarnehooks River & those at the narrows take theirs up the river to the lower part of the narrows from this Creek, and Carry it over land 3 miles to their houses &c. at the mouth of this creek Saw Some beaver Sign, and a Small wolf in a Snare Set in the willows The Snars of which I saw Several made for to catch wolves, are made as follows vz: a long pole which will Spring is made fast with bark to a willow, on the top of this pole a String

[Clark, October 26, 1805] October 26th 1805 Saturday a fine morning Sent out Six men to hunt deer & Collect rozin to Pitch our Canoes, had all our articles put out to dry- Canoes drawed out and repaired, the injories recved in drawing them over the rocks, every article wet in the Canoe which nearly Sunk yesterday-

In the evening 2 Chief and 15 men came over in a Single Canoe, those Chf's proved to be the 2 great Chiefs of the tribes above, one gave me a dressed Elk Skin, and gave us Som deer meet, and 2 Cakes of white bread made of white roots, we gave to each Chief a Meadel of the Small Size a red Silk handkerchief & a knife to the 1st a arm ban & a pin of Paint & a Comb to his Son a Piece of riben tied to a tin gorget and 2 hams of Venison They deturmined to Stay with us all night, we had a fire made for them & one man played on the violin which pleased them much my Servent danced- our hunters killed five Deer, 4 verry large gray Squirrels, a goose & Pheasent, one man giged a Salmon trout which we had fried in a little Bears oil which a Chief gave us yesterday and I think the finest fish I ever tasted, Saw great numbers of white Crams flying in Different directions verry high. The river has rose nearly 8 Inches to day and has every appearance of a tide, from what Cause I can't Say- our hunters Saw Elk & bear signs to day in the white oake woods the Country to the Lard is broken Country thinly timbered with pine and white oake, a mountain which I must call Timm or falls Mountain rises verry high and bears to S W the Course it has bore Sinc we first Saw it. our men danced to night. dried all our wet articles and repaired our Canoes

The flees my Self and the men got on them in passing thro the plains the Indians had lately lived in Lodges on the Lard. Side at the falls, are very troublesom and with every exertion the men Can't get rid of them, perticilarly as they have no clothes to change those which they wore Those Indians are at Ware with the Snake

Indians on the river which falls in a few miles above this and have lately had a battle with them, their loss I cannot lern.

[Clark, October 26, 1805] October 26th Saturday 1805 A fine morning Sent Six men out to hunt Deer, and Collect rozin to pitch the Canoes which has become verry leakey, by frequently hauling them over rocks &c as well Striking rocks frequently in passing down. all our articles we have exposed to the Sun to Dry; and the Canoes drawn out and turned up- maney of our Stores entirely Spoiled by being repeetedly wet; A number of Indians came to the Oposit Side of the river in the fore part of the day and Shew that they were anxious to Cross to us, we did not think proper to cross them in our Canoes and did not Send for them. in the evening two Chiefs and 15 men came over in a Small Canoe, those two Chiefs proved to be the two Principal Chiefs of the tribes above at the falls, and above, who was out hunting at the time we passed their bands; one of those Chiefs made Capt Lewis and my Self each a Small present of Deer meat, and Small Cakes of white bread made of roots. we gave to each Chief a Meadel of the Small Size a red Silk handkerchief, arm band, Knife & a piece of Paint, and acknowledged them as chiefs; as we thought it necessary at this time to treat those people verry friendly & ingratiate our Selves with them, to insure us a kind & friendly reception on our return, we gave Small presents to Several, and half a Deer to them to eate. we had also a fire made for those people to Sit around in the middle of our Camp, and Peter Crusat Played on the violin, which pleased those nativs exceedingly. the two Chiefs and Several men deturmined to delay all night (yorked Danced for the Inds) with us all the others returned, leaving the horses for those who Staied on the opposit Side. our hunters returned in the evening Killed five Deer, four verry large grey Squirels and a grouse. one of the guard at the river guiged a Salmon Trout, which we had fried in a little Bears Oil which the Chief we passed below the narrows gave us; this I thought one of the most delicious fish I have ever tasted Great numbers of white Crain flying in different Directions verry high- The river rose 8 Inches today from what cause I cannot Say certainly, as the tides cannot effect the river here as there is a falls below, I conjecture that the rise is owing to the winds which has Set up the river for 24 hours past. our hunters inform that the countrey back is broken, Stoney and thinly timbered with pine and White Oake. They Saw Elk & Bear Sign in the mountains. Dried all our wet articles and repared our Canoes to day, and the Party amused themselves at night danceing. The Flees which the party got on them at the upper & great falls, are very troublesom and dificuelt to get rid of, perticularly as the men have not a Change of Clothes to put on, they Strip off their Clothes and kill the flees, dureing which time they remain neckid.

The nations in the vicinity of this place is at War with the Snake Indians who they Say are noumerous and live on the river we passed above the falls on the Same Side on which we have encamped, and the nearest town is about four days march they pointed nearly S. E. and informed that they had a battle with those Inds. laterly, their loss I could not assertain

[Clark, October 27, 1805] October 27th Sunday 1805 a verry windy night and morning wind from the West and hard, Send out hunters and they killed 4 deer 1 pheasent and a Squirel the 2 Chiefs and party Continue with us, we treat them well give them to eate & Smoke, they were joined by Seven others, from below who Stayed about 3 hours and returned down the river in a pet, Soon after the Chiefs deturmined to go home we had them put across the river the wind verry high, we took a vocabelary of the Languages of the 2 nations, the one liveing at the Falls call themselves E-nee-shur The other resideing at the levels or narrows in a village on the Std. Side call themselves E-chee-lute not withstanding those people live only 6 miles apart, but fiew words of each others language- the language of those above having great Similarity with those tribes of flat heads we have passed- all have the Clucking tone anexed which is predomint. above, all flatten the heads of their female children near the falls, and maney above follow the Same Custom The language of the Che-luc-it-to-quar a fiew miles below is different from both in a Small degree. The wind increased in the evening and blew verry hard from the Same point W. day fair and Cold- The Creek at which we are Encamped is Called by the natives-Que-nett Some words with Shabono about his duty- The pinical of Falls mountain bears S 43° W. about 35 miles

[Clark, October 27, 1805] October 27th Sunday 1805 Wind hard from the west all the last night and this morning. Some words with Shabono our interpreter about his duty. Sent out Several hunters who brought in four Deer, one Grouse & a Squirel. The two Chiefs & party was joined by Seven others from below in two canoes, we gave them to eate & Smoke Several of those from below returned down the river in a bad humer, haveing got into this pet by being prevented doeing as they wished with our articles which was then exposed to dry- we took a Vocabelary of the Languages of those two chiefs which are verry different notwithstanding they are Situated within Six miles of each other, Those at the great falls Call themselves E-nee-shur and are understood on the river above. Those at the Great Narrows Call themselves Eche-lute and is understood below, maney words of those people are the Same, and Common to all the flat head Bands which we have passed on the river, all have the clucking tone anexed which is prodomonate above. all the Bands flatten the heads of the female Children, and maney of the male children also. Those two Chief leave us this evening and returned to their bands, the wind verry high & from the West, day proved fair and Cool.

The nativs Call this Creek near which we are encamped-Que-nett.

[Clark, October 28, 1805]
October 28th Monday 1805
a windey morning loaded our Canoes and Set out at 9 oClock a m 3 Canoes
Came down from the Village above & 2 from that below in one of those
Canoes a Indian wore his hair cued, and had on a round hat. Wind from
West

Those Indians have a musket a Sword, and Several Brass Tea kitties which they appear to be verry fond of we
purchased of those people five Small dogs, and Some Dried beries & white bread of roots, the wind rose and
we were obliged to lie by about 1 mile below on the Lard. Side North 1 mile to a rock Island on the Stard. Side.
we had not landed long eer an Indian Canoe Came from below with 3 Indians in it, those Indians make verry
nice Canoes of Pine. Thin with aporns & Carve on the head imitation of animals & other heads; The Indians
above Sacrafise the property of the Deceased to wit horses Canoes, bowls Basquets of which they make great
use to hold water boil their meet &c. &c. great many Indians came down from the uppr Village & Sat with us,
Smoked, rained all the evenig & blew hard from the West encamped on the Lard Side opsd. an Rock in a verry
Bad place

[Clark, October 28, 1805] October 28th Monday 1805 A cool windey morning we loaded our Canoes and Set
out at 9 oClock, a.m. as we were about to Set out 3 canoes from above and 2 from below came to view us in
one of those Canoes I observed an Indian with round hat jacket & wore his hair cued we proceeded on river
inclosed on each Side in high Clifts of about 90 feet of loose dark coloured rocks at four miles we landed at a
village of 8 houses on the Stard. Side under Some rugid rocks, Those people call themselves Chil-luckit-tequaw,
live in houses Similar to those described, Speake Somewhat different language with maney words the Same &
understand those in their neighbourhood Cap Lewis took a vocabilary of this Language I entered one of the
houses in which I Saw a British musket, a cutlass and Several brass Tea kittles of which they appeared verry
fond Saw them boiling fish in baskets with Stones, I also Saw figures of animals & men Cut & painted on boards
in one Side of the house which they appeared to prize, but for what purpose I will not venter to Say,-. here we
purchased five Small Dogs, Some dried buries, & white bread made of roots, the wind rose and we were obliged
to lie by all day at 1 mile below on the Lard. Side. we had not been long on Shore before a Canoe came up with
a man woman & 2 children, who had a fiew roots to Sell, Soon after maney others joined them from above, The
wind which is the cause of our delay, does not retard the motions of those people at all, as their canoes are
calculated to ride the highest waves, they are built of white cedar or Pine verry light wide in the middle and
tapers at each end, with aperns, and heads of animals carved on the bow, which is generally raised. Those
people make great use of Canoes, both for transpotation and fishing, they also use of bowls & baskets made of
Grass & Splits to hold water and boil their fish & meat. Maney of the nativs of the last Village Came down Set
and Smoke with us, wind blew hard accompanied with rain all the evening, our Situation not a verry good one
for an encampment, but Such as it is we are obliged to put up with, the harbor is a Safe one, we encamped on
the Sand wet and disagreeable one Deer killed this evening, and another wounded near our Camp.

[Clark, October 29, 1805] October 29th Tuesday 1805 a Cloudy morning wind Still from th West not hard, we
Set out at day light proceeded on about 5 miles and Came too at a Lodge of a Chief which we made at the
upper village at th falls about his house there is Six others This chief gave us to eate Sackacommis burries
Hasel nuts fish Pounded, and a kind of Bread made of roots- we gave to the Women pices of ribon, which they
appeared pleased with- those houses are large 25 feet Sqr and contain abt. 8 men, Say 30 inhabitents-

Those people are friendly gave us to eate fish Beries, nuts bread of roots & Drid beries and we Call this the
friendly Village We purchased 12 dogs of them & 4 Sacks of Pounded fish, and Some fiew Dried Berries and
proceeded on at 4 miles further we landed to Smoke a pipe with the people of a village of 11 houses we found
those people also friendly Their Village is Situated imediately below the mouth of a River of 60 yards water
which falls in on the Stard. Side and heads in the mountains to the N. & N, E, the Indians inform us that this
river is long and full of falls no Salmon pass up it. They also inform that 10 nations lives on this river by
hunting and on buries &c. The Countrey begin to be thinly timbered with Pine & low white oake verry rocky and
hilley- We purchased at this vilg 4 dogs- at the end of this Course is 3 rocks, in the river and a rock point from
the Lard. the middle rock is large and has a number of graves on it we call it the Sepulchar Island. The last
River we call Caterack River from the number of falls which the Indians inform is on it The Indians are afraid to
hunt or be on th Lard Side of this Columbia river for fear of the Snake Ind. who reside on a fork of this river
which falls in above the falls a good Situation for winter quarters if game can be had is just below Sepulchar
rock on the Lard Side, high & pine and oake timber the rocks ruged above, good hunting Countrey back, as it
appears from the river Indian village opsd. Of 2 Lodgs river 1/2 mile wide at rocks

The robes of those Indians are, of wolf deer Elk, wild cats, Some fox, & Deer I saw one of the mountain Sheep,
th wool thick and long Corse hair on the back, resembling bristles- those animals live among the rocks in those

mountains below, orter is much valued by those people they Cew their hair on each Side with it and ware it about the necks with the tail in front

Came too at 3 miles on this Course at 3 Houses of flatheads and Encamped on the Stard. Side, a Pond lies back of those people in which we Saw great numbers of the Small Swan. we Purchased of those people 3 Dogs they gave us High bush cramburies, bread of roots and roots, they were pleased with musick of th violin.

[Clark, October 29, 1805] October 29th Tuesday 1805 A cloudy morning wind from the West but not hard, we Set out at day light, and proceeded on about five miles Came too on the Stard. Side at a village of 7 houses built in the Same form and materials of those above, here we found the Chief we had Seen at the long narrows named _____

we entered his lodge and he gave us to eate Pounded fish, bread made of roots, Filberts nuts, & the berries of Sackecomme. we gave to each woman of the lodge a brace of Ribon of which they were much pleased. each of those houses may be calculated to contain 8 men and 30 Soles, they are hospitable and good humered Speak the Same language of the inhabitants of the last village, we call this the friendly village. I observed in the lodge of the Chief Sundery articles which must have been precured from the white people, Such a Scarlet & blue Cloth Sword Jacket & hat. I also observed two wide Split boards with images on them Cut and painted in emitation of a man; I pointed to this image and asked a man to what use he put them to, he Said Something the only word I understood was "good," and then Steped to the image and took out his Bow & quiver to Show me, and Some other of his war emplemints, from behind it.

The Chief then directed his wife to hand him his medison bag which he opened and Showed us 14 fingers which he Said was the fingers of his enemies which he had taken in war, and pointed to S. E. from which direction I concluded they were Snake Indians; this is the first Instance I ever knew of the Indians takeing any other trofea of their exploits off the dead bodies of their Enimies except the Scalp.- The Chief painted those fingers with Several other articles which was in his bag red and Securely put them back, haveing first mad a Short harrang which I Suppose was bragging of what he had done in war. we purchased 12 Dogs and 4 Sacks of fish, & Some fiew ascid berries, after brackfast we proceeded on, the mountains are high on each Side, containing Scattering pine white oake & under groth, hill Sides Steep and rockey; at 4 miles lower we observed a Small river falling in with great rapidity on the Stard. Side below which is a village of 11 houses, here we landed to Smoke a pipe with the nativs and examine the mouth of the river, which I found to be 60 yards wide rapid and deep, The inhabitants of the village are friendly and Chearfull; those people inform us also those at the last village that this little river is long and full of falls, no Salmon pass up it, it runs from N. N. E. that ten nations live on this river and its waters, on buries, and what game they Can kill with their Bow & arrows

we purchased 4 dogs and Set out- (this village is the of the Same nation of the one we last passed) and proceeded on The Countrey on each side begin to be thicker timbered with Pine and low white Oake; verry rockey and broken. passed three large rocks in The river the middle rock is large long and has Several Squar vaults on it. we call this rockey Island the Sepulchar- The last river we passed we Shall Call the Cataract River from the number of falls which the Indians say is on it- passed 2 Lodges of Indians a Short distance below the Sepulchar Island on the Stard. Side river wide, at 4 mile passed 2 houses on the Stard. Side, Six miles lower passed 4 houses above the mouth of a Small river 40 yards wide on the Lard. Side a thick timbered bottom above & back of those houses; those are the first houses which we have Seen on the South Side of the Columbia River, (and the axess to those dificuelt) for fear of the approach of their common enemies the Snake Indians, passed 14 houses on the Std. Side Scattered on the bank- from the mouth of this little river which we shall Call Labeasche River, the falls mountain is South and the top is covered with Snow. one mile below pass the mouth of a large rapid Stream on the Stard. Side, opposit to a large Sand bar, in this creek the Indians above take their fish, here we Saw Several canoes, which induced us to call this Canoe Creek it is 28 yards wide, about 4 miles lower and below the Sand bar is a butifull cascade falling over a rock of about 100 feet, a Short distance lower passed 4 Indian houses on the Lard. Side in a timbered bottom, a fiew miles further we came too at 3 houses on Stard. Side, back of which is a pond in which I Saw Great numbers of Small Swan, Capt. Lewis and I went into the houses of those people who appeared Somewhat Surprised at first Their houses are built on the Same Construction of those above, Speak the Same language and Dress in the Same way, robes of the Skins of wolves Deer, Elk, wild cat, or Loucirvia & fox, also Saw a mountain Sheap Skin the wool of which is long, thick, & corse with long corse hare on the top of the neck and back Something resembling bristles of a goat, the skin was of white hare, those animals these people inform me by Signs live in the mountains among the rocks, their horns are Small and Streight, Orter Skins are highly prised among those people as well as those on the river above, They Cue their hare which is divided on each Sholder, and also ware Small Strips about their necks with the tale hanging down in front.- Those people gave us, High bush cram berries, bread made of roots, and roots; we purchased three dogs for the party to eate; we Smoked with the men, all muche pleased with the violin-. Here the mountains are high on each Side, those to the Lard. Side has Some Snow on them at this time, more timber than above and of greater variety.

[Clark, October 30, 1805] October 30th Wednesday 1805 A Cloudy morning. Some little rain all night, after eating a Slight brackfast of venison we Set out.

The rocks project into the river in maney places and have the appearance of haveing fallen from the highe hills those projected rocks is common & Small Bays below & nitches in the rocks passed 4 Cascades or Small Streams falling from the mountains on Lard. This part of the river resembles a pond partly dreaned leaving many Stumps bare both in & out of the water, current about 1 mil pr. Hour

The bottom above the river is about 3/4 of a mile wide and rich, Some deer & bear Sign- rained moderately all day we are wet and cold. Saw Several Specis of wood which I never Saw before, Some resembling Beech & others Poplar.- Day dark and disagreeable

I with 2 men proceeded down the river 2 miles on an old Indian parth to view the rapids, which I found impassable for our canoes without a portage, the roade bad at 1 mile I saw a Town of Houses laterly abandoned on an elevated Situation opsd. a 2d Shute, returned at dark. Capt. Lewis and 5 men went to the Town found them kind they gave Beries & nuts, but he cd. get nothin from them in the way of Information, the greater part of those people out collecting roots below, rained all the evining Those people have one gun & maney articles which they have purchased of the white people their food is principally fish

[Clark, October 30, 1805] October 30th Wednesday 1805 A cool morning, a moderate rain all the last night, after eating a partial brackfast of venison we Set out passed Several places where the rocks projected into the river & have the appearance of haveing Seperated from the mountains and fallen promiscuisly into the river, Small nitches are formed in the banks below those projecting rocks which is comon in this part of the river, Saw 4 Cascades caused by Small Streams falling from the mountains on the Lard. Side, a remarkable circumstance in this part of the river is, the Stumps of pine trees are in maney places are at Some distance in the river, and gives every appearance of the rivers being darned up below from Some cause which I am not at this time acquainted with, the Current of the river is also verry jentle not exceeding 11/2 mile pr. hour and about 3/4 of a mile in width. Some rain, we landed above the mouth of a Small river on the Stard. Side and Dined J. Shields Killed a Buck & Labiech 3 Ducks, here the river widens to about one mile large Sand bar in the middle, a Great rock both in and out of the water, large Stones, or rocks are also permiscuisly Scattered about in the river, this day we Saw Some fiew of the large Buzzard Capt. Lewis Shot at one, those Buzzards are much larger than any other of ther Spece or the largest Eagle white under part of their wings &c. The bottoms above the mouth of this little river is rich covered with grass & firn & is about 3/4 of a mile wide rich and rises gradually, below the river (which is 60 yards wide above its mouth) the Countery rises with Steep assent. we call this little river New Timbered river from a Speces of Ash which grows on its banks of a verry large and different from any we had before Seen, and a timber resembling the beech in bark but different in its leaf which is Smaller and the tree smaller. passed maney large rocks in the river and a large creek on the Stard. Side in the mouth of which is an Island, passed on the right of 3 Islands near the Stard. Side, and landed on an Island close under the Stard. Side at the head of the great Shute, and a little below a village of 8 large houses on a Deep bend on the Stard. Side, and opposit 2 Small Islands imediately in the head of the Shute, which Islands are covered with Pine, maney large rocks also, in the head of the Shute. Ponds back of the houses, and Countrey low for a Short distance. The day proved Cloudy dark and disagreeable with Some rain all day which kept us wet. The Countary a high mountain on each Side thickly Covered with timber, Such as Spruc, Pine, Cedar, Oake Cotton &c. &c. I took two men and walked down three miles to examine the Shute and river below proceeded along an old Indian path, passd. an old village at 1 mile on an ellevated Situation of this village contained verry large houses built in a different form from any I had Seen, and laterly abandoned, and the most of the boads put into a pond of water near the village, as I conceived to drown the flees, which was emencely noumerous about the houses-. I found by examanation that we must make a portage of the greater perpotion of our Stores 21/2 miles, and the Canoes we Could haul over the rocks, I returned at Dark Capt Lewis and 5 men had just returned from the village, Cap L. informed me that he found the nativs kind, they gave him berries, nuts & fish to eate; but he could get nothing from them in the way of information. The greater part of the inhabitants of this village being absent down the river Some distance Colecting roots Capt. L. Saw one gun and Several articles which must have been precured from the white people. a wet disagreeable evening, the only wood we could get to burn on this little Island on which we have encamped is the newly discovered Ash, which makes a tolerable fire. we made fifteen miles to daye.

[Clark, October 31, 1805] October 31st Thursday 1805 a cloudey raney morning I proceed down the river to view it more at leasure, I took Jos. Fields & Peter Crusat and proceeded on down, Send Crusat back at 2 ms. to examine the rapid near the shore & I proceeded on down about 10 miles to a very high rock in a bottom on the Stard. opsd. 2 Islands covered with timber on which I saw Inds. at a distance; found the river rocky for 6 miles, after which the Current became uniform- at 1 mile I passed an old deserted village on a Pond on a high Situation of 8 Houses- at 31/2 miles one house the only remt. of an antient Village 1/2 a mile lower I saw 8 Vaults for the Dead which was nearly Square 8 feet Closely Covered with broad boads Curiously engraved, the bones in Some of those vaults wer 4 feet thick, in others the Dead was yet layed Side of each other nearly East & west, raped up & bound Securley in robes, great numbers of trinkets Brass Kittle, Sea Shells, Iron, Pan Hare &c. &c. was hung about the vaults and great many wooden gods, or Images of men Cut in wood, Set up round the vaults, Some of those So old and worn by time that they were nearly worn out of Shape, and Some of those vaults So old that they were roted entirely to the ground- notwithstanding they wood is of Pine & _____ or Seder as also the wooden gods

I can not learn certainly if those people worship those woden emiges, they have them in conspicuous parts of their houses at 5 miles I passed 4 large houses on the Stard Side a little above the last rapid and opposit a large Island which is Situated near the Lard. Side- The enhabitents of those houses had left them closely Shut up, they appeared to Contn. a great deel of property and Provisions Such as those people use, I did not disturb any thing about those houses, but proceed on down below the rapid which I found to be the last, a large village has at Some period been on the Stard. Side below this rapid The bottom is high Stoney and about 2 miles wide covered with grass, here C is the head of a large Island in high water, at this time no water passes on the Stard. Side I walked thro this Island which I found to be verry rich, open & covered with Strawberry vines, and has greatly the appearance of having at Some period been Cultivated, The natives has dug roots in Some parts of this Isld. which is about 3 miles long & 1 Wide, a Small Island covered with timber opposit the lower point no water runs on the Stard. Side. of it. below and in the middle of the river is a large Island Covered with tall trees opposit the Strawberry Island on its Stard. Side a creek falls in which has no running water at present, it has the appearanc of throwing out emense torents- I saw 5 Indians in a canoe below- Jo. killed a Sand hill Crane & we returned by the same rout to camp at the grand Shute where I found Several Indians, I Smoked. Two canoes loaded with fish for the Trade below Came down & unloaded the after noon fare

Those Indians Cut off the hands of those they kill & proserve the fingers.

[Clark, October 31, 1805] October 31st Thursday 1805 A Cloudy rainey disagreeable morning I proceeded down the river to view with more attention we had to pass on the river below, the two men with me Jo. Fields & Peter Crusat proceeded down to examine the rapids the Great Shute which commenced at the Island on which we encamped Continud with great rapidity and force thro a narrow chanel much compressd. and interspersed with large rocks for 1/2 a mile, at a mile lower is a verry Considerable rapid at which place the waves are remarkably high, and proceeded on in a old Indian parth 21/2 miles by land thro a thick wood & hill Side, to the river where the Indians make a portage, from this place I dispatched Peter Crusat (our principal waterman) back to follow the river and examine the practibility of the Canoes passing, as the rapids appeared to continue down below as far as I could See, I with Jo. Fields proceeded on, at 1/2 a mile below the end of the portage passed a house where there had been an old town for ages past as this house was old Decayed and a plat of flees I did not enter it, about 1/2 a mile below this house in a verry thick part of the woods is 8 vaults which appeared Closely Covered and highly deckerated with orniments. Those vaults are all nearly the Same Sise and form 8 feet Square, 5 feet high, Sloped a little So as to convey off the rain made of Pine or Cedar boards Closely Connected & Scurely Covered with wide boards, with a Dore left in The East Side which is partially Stoped with wide boards curiously engraved. In Several of those vaults the dead bodies wre raped up verry Securely in Skins tied around with cords of grass & bark, laid on a mat, all east & west and Some of those vaults had as maney as 4 bodies laying on the Side of each other. the other Vaults Containing bones only, Some contained bones for the debth of 4 feet. on the tops and on poles attached to those vaults hung Brass kitties & frying pans pearced thro their bottoms, baskets, bowls of wood, Sea Shels, Skins, bits of Cloth, Hair, bags of Trinkets & Small peices of bone &c and independant of the curious ingraveing and Paintings on the boards which formed the vaults I observed Several wooden Images, cut in the figure of men and Set up on the Sides of the vaults all round. Some of those So old and worn by time, that they were nearly out of Shape, I also observed the remains of Vaults rotted entirely into the ground and covered with moss. This must bee the burrying place for maney ages for the inhabitants of those rapids, the vaults are of the most lasting timber Pine & Cedar- I cannot Say certainly that those nativs worship those wooden idols as I have every reason to believe they do not; as they are Set up in the most conspicious parts of their houses, and treated more like orniments than objects of aderation. at 2 miles lower & 5 below our Camp I passed a village of 4 large houses abandend by the nativs, with their Bores bared up, I looked into those houses and observed as much property as is usial in the houses of those people which induced me to conclude that they wre at no great distance, either hunting or Colecting roots, to add to their winter Subsistance. from a Short distance below the vaults the mountain which is but low on the Stard. Side leave the river, and a leavel Stoney open bottom Suckceeds on the Said Std. Side for a great Distance down, the mountains high and rugid on the Lard Side this open bottom is about 2 miles a Short distance below this village is a bad Stoney rapid and appears to be the last in view I observed at this lower rapid the remains of a large and antient Village which I could plainly trace by the Sinks in which they had formed their houses, as also those in which they had buried their fish- from this rapid to the lower end of the portage the river is Crouded with rocks of various Sizes between which the water passes with great velocity createing in maney places large Waves, an Island which is Situated near the Lard. Side occupies about half the distance the lower point of which is at this rapid. immediately below this rapid the high water passes through a narrow Chanel through the Stard. Bottom forming an Island of 3 miles Long & one wide, I walked through this Island which I found to be verry rich land, and had every appearance of haveing been at Some distant period Cultivated. at this time it is Covered with grass intersperced with Strawberry vines. I observed Several places on this Island where the nativs had dug for roots and from its lower point I observed 5 Indians in a Canoe below the upper point of an Island near the middle of the river Covered with tall timber, which indued me to believe that a village was at no great distanc below, I could not See any rapids below in the extent of my view which was for a long distance down the river, which from the last rapids widened and had everry appearance of being effected by the tide,- I deturmind to return to Camp 10 miles distant, a remarkable high detached rock Stands in a bottom on the Stard Side near the lower point of this Island on the Stard. Side about 800 feet high and 400 paces around, we call the Beaten rock. a Brook falls into the narrow Chanel which forms the Strawberry Island, which at this time has no running water, but has every appearance of dischargeing emence torrents &c. &c. Jo. Fields Shot a Sand hill Crane. I returned by the Same rout on an Indian parth passing up on the N W. Side of the river to our Camp at the Great Shute. found Several Indians from the village, I Smoked with them; Soon after my return two Canoes loaded with fish & Bear grass for the trade below, came down ,from the village at the mouth of the Catterack River, they unloaded and turned their Canoes up Side down on the beech, & camped under a Shelveing rock below our Camp

one of the men Shot a goose above this Great Shute, which was floating into the Shute when an Indian observed it, plunged into the water & Swam to the Goose and brought in on Shore, at the head of the Suck, as this Indian richly earned the goose I Suffered him to keep it which he about half picked and Spited it up with the guts in it to roste.

This Great Shute or falls is about 1/2 a mile with the water of this great river Compressed within the Space of 150 paces in which there is great numbers of both large and Small rocks, water passing with great velocity forming & boiling in a most horriable manner, with a fall of about 20 feet, below it widens to about 200 paces and current gentle for a Short distance. a Short distance above is three Small rockey Islands, and at the head of those falls, three Small rockey Islands are Situated Crosswise the river, Several rocks above in the river & 4 large rocks in the head of the Shute; those obstructions together with the high Stones which are continually brakeing loose from the mountain on the Stard Side and roleing down into the Shute aded to those which brake loose from those Islands above and lodge in the Shute, must be the Cause of the rivers darning up to Such a distance above, where it Shows Such evidant marks of the Common current of the river being much lower than at the present day

[Clark, November 1, 1805] November 1st Friday 1805 a verry cold morning wind from N. E and hard Set all hands packing the loading over th portage which is below the Grand Shutes and is 940 yards of bad way over rocks & on Slipery hill Sides The Indians who came down in 2 Canoes last night packed their fish over a portage of 21/2 miles to avoid a 2d Shute. four of them took their canoes over the 1st portage and run the 2d Shute, Great numbers of Sea otters, they are So Cautious that I with deficuelty got a Shute at one to day, which I must have killed but Could not get him as he Sunk

We got all our Canoes and baggage below the Great Shute 3 of the canoes being Leakey from injures recved in hauling them over the rocks, obliged us to delay to have them repaired a bad rapid just below us three Indian canoes loaded with pounded fish for the &c. trade down the river arrived at the upper end of the portage this evening. I Can't lern whether those Indians trade with white people or Inds. below for the Beeds & copper, which they are So fond of- They are nearly necked, prefuring beeds to anything- Those Beeds they trafick with Indians Still higher up this river for Skins robes &c. &c. The Indians on those waters do not appear to be Sickly, Sore eyes are Common and maney have lost their eyes, Some one and, maney both, they have bad teeth, and the greater perpotion of them have worn their teeth down, maney into the gums, They are rather Small high Cheeks, women Small and homely, maney of them had Sweled legs, large about the knees,-owing to the position in which they Set on their hams, They are nearly necked only a piece of leather tied about their breech and a Small robe which generally comes to a little below their wastes and Scercely Sufficely large to cover arround them when confined- they are all fond of Clothes but more So of Beeds perticularly blue & white beeds. They are durty in the extreme both in their Coockery and in their houses.

Those at the last Village raise the beads about five feet from the earth-under which they Store their Provisions- Their houses is about 33 feet to 50 feet Square, the Bore of which is about 30 Inc. high and 16 Inches wide in this form cut in a wide pine board they have maney imeges Cut in wood, generally, in the figure of a man- Those people are high with what they have to Sell, and Say the white people below Give them great Prices for what they Sell to them. Their nose are all Pierced, and the wear a white Shell maney of which are 2 Inch long pushed thro the nose- all the women have flat heads pressed to almost a point at top The press the female childrens heads between 2 bords when young-untill they form the Skul as they wish it which is generally verry flat. This amongst those people is considered as a great mark of butyand is practised in all the tribes we have passed on this river more or less. men take more of the drugery off the women than is common with Indians

[Clark, November 1, 1805] November 1st Friday 1805 A verry Cool morning wind hard from the N. E. The Indians who arrived last evining took their Canoes on ther Sholders and Carried them below the Great Shute, we Set about takeing our Small Canoe and all the baggage by land 940 yards of bad Slippery and rockey way The Indians we discoverd took ther loading the whole length of the portage 21/2 miles, to avoid a Second Shute which appears verry bad to pass, and thro which they passed with their empty canoes. Great numbers of Sea Otters, they are So cautious that I with dificuelty got a Shot at one to day, which I must have killed, but could not get him as he Sunk

we got all our baggage over the Portage of 940 yards, after which we got the 4 large Canoes over by Slipping them over the rocks on poles placed across from one rock to another, and at Some places along partial Streams of the river. in passing those canoes over the rocks &c. three of them recived injuries which obliged us to delay to have them repared.

Several Indian Canoes arrived at the head of the portage, Some of the men accompanied by those from the village came down to Smoke with us, they appear to Speak the Same language with a little different axcent

I visited the Indian Village found that the Construction of the houses Similar to those abov described, with this difference only that they are larger Say from 35 to 50 feet by 30 feet, raised about 5 feet above the earth, and nearly as much below The Dores in the Same form and Size cut in the wide post which Supports one end of the ridge pole and which is carved and painted with different figures & Hieroglyphics Those people gave me to eate nuts berries & a little dried fish, and Sold me a hat of ther own taste without a brim, and baskets in which they hold their water- Their beads are raised about 41/2 feet, under which they Store away their dried fish, between the part on which they lie and the back wall they Store away their roots burries nuts and valuable articles on mats, which are Spread also around the fire place which is Sunk about one foot lower than the bottom fore of the house, this fire place is about 8 feet long and Six feet wide Secured with a fraim those houses are calculated for 4, 5 & 6 families, each familey haveing a nice painted ladder to assend up to their beads. I Saw in those houses Several wooden Images all cut in imitation of men, but differently fasioned and placed in the most conspicious parts of the houses, probably as an orniment I cannot lern certainly as to the traffick those Inds. carry on below, if white people or the indians who trade with the Whites who are either Settled or visit the mouth of this river. I believe mostly with the latter as their knowledge of the white people appears to be verry imperfect, and the articles which they appear to trade mostly i e Pounded fish, Beargrass, and roots; cannot be an object of comerce with furin merchants- however they git in return for those articles Blue and white beeds copper Tea Kitties, brass arm bands, some Scarlet and blue robes and a fiew articles of old clothes, they prefer beeds to any thing and will part with the last mouthfull or articles of clothing they have for a fiew of those beeds, those beeds the trafick with Indians Still higher up this river for roabs, Skins, cha-pel-el bread, beargrass &c. who in their turn trafick with those under the rockey mountains for Beargrass, Pashico roots & robes &c.

The nativs of the waters of the Columbia appear helthy, Some have turners on different parts of their bodies, and Sore and weak Eyes are common, maney have lost their Sight entirely great numbers with one eye out and frequently the other verry weak; This misfortune I must again asscribe to the water &c. They have bad teeth, which is not common with indians, maney have worn their teeth down and Some quite into their gums, this I cannot Satisfactorily account for it, do ascribe it in some measure to their method of eateing, their food, roots pertiulary, which they make use of as they are taken out of the earth frequently nearly covered with Sand, I have not Seen any of their long roots offered for Sale clear of Sand. They are rether below the Common Size high cheeks womin Small and homely, and have Swelled legs and thighs, and their knees remarkably large which I ascribe to the method in which they Sit on their hams-go nearly necked wareing only a piece of leather tied about their breast which falls down nearly as low as the waste, a Small roabe about 3 feet Square, and a piece of leather tied about their breach, They have all flat heads in this quarter They are tirty in the extream, both in their person and cooking, ware their hare loose hanging in every direction. They asc high prices for what they Sell and Say that the white people below give great prices for every thing &c.

The noses are all pierced and when they are dressed they have a long tapered piece of white shell or wampum put through the nose, Those Shells are about 2 inches in length. I observed in maney of the villeages which I have passed, the heads of the female children in the press for the purpose of compressing their heads in their infancy into a certain form, between two boards

[Clark, November 2, 1805] Novr. 2d Saturday 1805 Meridian altitude 59° 45' 45" made a portage of about 11/2 miles with half of the Baggage, and run the rapid with the Canoes without much damage, one Struck a rock & Split a little, and 3 others took in Some water 7 Squars Came over the portage loaded with Dried fish & Beargrass, Soon after 4 men Came down in a Canoe after takeing brackfast, & after taking a meridian altitude we Set out Passed 2 bad rapids one at 2 & the other at 4 mile below the Isd on Lard. and upper end of Strawberry Island on the Stard. Side from the Creek end of last Course

We Labiech killed 14 Geese & a Brant, Collins one Jos. Fields & R 3 those gees are much Smaller than Common, and have white under their rumps & around the tale, The tide rises here a fiew 9 Inches, I cannot assertain the prosise hite it rises at the last rapid or at this placeof Camp.

The Indians we left at the portage passed us this evening one other Canoe Come up

[Clark, November 2, 1805] November 2nd Saturday 1805 Examined the rapid below us more pertcelarly the danger appearing too great to Hazzard our Canoes loaded, dispatched all the men who could not Swim with loads to the end of the portage below, I also walked to the end of the portage with the carriers where I delayed untill everry articles was brought over and canoes arrived Safe. here we brackfast and took a Meridn. altitude 59°45'45" about the time we were Setting out 7 Squars came over loaded with Dried fish, and bear grass neetly bundled up, Soon after 4 Indian men came down over the rapid in a large canoe. passed a rapid at 2 miles & 1 at 4 miles opposit the lower point of a high Island on the Lard Side, and a little below 4 Houses on the Stard. Bank, a Small Creek on the Lard Side opposit Straw berry Island, which heads below the last rapid, opposit the lower point of this Island passed three Islands covered with tall timber opposit the Beatin rock Those Islands are nearest the Starboard Side, imediately below on the Stard. Side passed a village of nine houses, which is Situated between 2 Small Creeks, and are of the Same construction of those above; here the river widens to near a mile, and the bottoms are more extensive and thickly timbered, as also the high mountains on each Side, with Pine, Spruce pine, Cotton wood, a Species of ash, and alder. at 17 miles passed a rock near the middle of the river, about 100 feet high and 80 feet Diamuter, proceed on down a Smoth gentle Stream of about 2 miles wide, in which the tide has its effect as high as the Beaten rock or the Last rapids at Strawberry Island,- Saw great numbers of waterfowl of Different kinds, Such as Swan, Geese, white & grey brants, ducks of various kinds, Guls, & Pleaver. Labeach killed 14 brantjoseph Fields 3 & Collins one. we encamped under a high projecting rock on the Lard. Side, here the mountains leave the river on each Side, which from the great Shute to this place is high and rugid; thickly Covered with timber principalley of the Pine Species. The bottoms below appear extensive and thickly Covered with wood. river here about 2 1/2 miles wide. Seven Indians in a Canoe on their way down to trade with the nativs below, encamp with us, those we left at the portage passed us this evening and proceeded on down The ebb tide rose here about 9 Inches, the flood tide must rise here much higher- we made 29 miles to day from the Great Shute-

[Clark, November 3, 1805] November 3rd Sunday 1805 The fog So thick this morning we did not think it prudent to Set out untill 10 oClock we Set out and proceeded on verry well, accompanied by our Indian friends-This morning Labich killed 3 Geese flying Collins killed a Duck- The water rose Inches last night the effects of tide. The Countrey has a handsom appearance in advance no mountains extensive bottoms- the water Shallow for a great distance from Shore-. The fog continued thick untill 12 oClock, we Coasted, and halted at the mouth of a large river on the Lard Side, This river throws out emence quanty of Sand and is verry Shallow, th narrowest part 200 yards wide bold Current, much resembling the river Plat, Several Islands about 1 mile up and has a Sand bar of 3 miles in extent imedeately in its mouth, discharging it waters by 2 mouths, and Crowding its Corse Sands So as to throw the Columbian waters on its Nothern banks, & confdg it to 1/2 ms. in width Passed a Small Prarie on the Stard. Side above, a large Creek opposit qk Sand River on the Stard. Side, extensive bottoms and low hilley Countrey on each Side (good wintering Place) a high peaked mountain Suppose to be Mt. Hood is on the Lard Side S. 85 E. 40 miles distant from the mouth of quick Sand river.-

[Clark, November 3, 1805] November 3rd Sunday 1805 The Fog So thick this morning that we could not See a man 50 Steps off, this fog detained us untill 10 oClock at which time we Set out, accompanied by our Indian friends who are from a village near the great falls, previous to our Setting out Collins killed a large Buck, and Labiech killed 3 Geese flying. I walked on the Sand beech Lard. Side, opposit the canoes as they passed allong. The under groth rushes, vines &c. in the bottoms too thick to pass through, at 3 miles I arrived at the enterance of a river which appeared to Scatter over a Sand bar, the bottom of which I could See quite across and did not appear to be 4 Inches deep in any part; I attempted to wade this Stream and to my astonishment found the bottom a quick Sand, and impassable- I called to the Canoes to put to Shore, I got into the Canoe and landed below the mouth, & Capt Lewis and my Self walked up this river about 1 1/2 miles to examine this river which we found to be a verry Considerable Stream Dischargeing its waters through 2 Chanels which forms an Island of about 3 miles in length on the river and 1 1/2 miles wide, composed of Corse Sand which is thrown out of this quick Sand river Compressing the waters of the Columbia and throwing the whole Current of its waters against its Northern banks, within a Chanel of 1/2 a mile wide, Several Small Islands 1 mile up this river, This Stream has much the appearance of the River Plait; roleing its quick Sands into the bottoms with great velocity after which it is divided into 2 Chanels by a large Sand bar before mentioned, the narrowest part of this River is 120 yards-on the Opposit Side of the Columbia a falls in above this Creek on the Same Side is a Small prarie. extensive low country on each Side thickly timbered.

The Quick Sand river appears to pass through the low countrey at the foot of those high range of mountains in a Southerly direction,- The large Creeks which fall into the Columbia on the Stard. Side rise in the Same range of mountains to the N. N. E. and pass through Some ridgey land- A Mountain which we Suppose to be Mt. Hood is S. 85 E about 47 miles distant from the mouth of quick sand river This mtn. is Covered with Snow and in the range of mountains which we have passed through and is of a Conical form but rugid- after takeing dinner at the mouth of this river we proceeded on passed the head of a Island near the lard Side back of which on the Same Side and near the head a large Creek falls in, and nearly opposit & 3 miles below the upper mouth of quick Sand river is the lower mouth, This Island is 3 1/2 miles long, has rocks at the upper point, Some timber on the borders of this Island in the middle open and ponney. Some rugid rocks in the middle of the Stream opposit this Island. proceeded in to Center of a large Island in the middle of the river which we call Dimond Isld. from its appearance, here we met 15 Indn men in 2 canoes from below, they informed us they Saw 3 vestles below &c. &c. we landed on the North Side of this Dimond Island and Encamped, Capt. L walked out with his gun on the Island, Sent out hunters & fowlers- below quick Sand River the Countery is low rich and thickly timbered on each Side of the river, the Islands open & Some ponds river wide and emence numbers of fowls flying in every direction Such as Swan, geese, Brants, Cranes, Stalks, white guls, comerants & plevers &c. also great numbers of Sea Otter in the river- a Canoe arrived from the village below the last rapid with a man his wife and 3 children, and a woman whome had been taken prisoner from the Snake Inds. on Clarks River I Sent the Interpreters wife who is a So So ne or Snake Indian of the Missouri, to Speake to this Squar, they Could not understand each other Sufficiently to Converse. This familey and the Inds. we met from below continued with us Capt Lewis borrowed a Small Canoe of those Indians & 4 men took her across to a Small lake in the Isld. Cap L. and 3 men Set out after night in this Canoe in Serch of the Swans, Brants Ducks &c. &c. which appeared in great numbers in the Lake, he Killed a Swan and Several Ducks which made our number of fowls this evening 3 Swan, 8 brant and 5 Ducks, on which we made a Sumptious Supper. We gave the Indian-who lent the Canoe a brant, and Some meat to the others. one of those Indians, the man from the village near the lower Rapids has a gun with a brass barrel & Cock of which he prises highly- note the mountain we Saw from near the forks proves to be Mount Hood

[Clark, November 4, 1805] Novr. 4th Monday 1805 A Cloudy Cool morning, wind West, we Set out at 1/2 past 8 oClock having dispatched 4 men in the Small canoe to hunt

(Those people men & women heads are flat)

We landed at a village 200 men of Flatheads of 25 houses 50 canoes built of Straw, we were treated verry kindly by them, they gave us round root near the Size of a hens egg roasted which they call Wap-to to eate

I walked out on the Stard. Side found the country fine, an open Prarie for 1 mile back of which the wood land comence riseing back, the timber on the edge of the Prarie is white oke, back is Spruce pine & other Species of Pine mixed Some under groth of a wild crab & a Specis of wood I'm not acquainted, a Specis of maple & Cotton wood grow near this river, Some low bushes

Indians continue to be with us, Several Canoes Continue with us, The Indians at the last village have more Cloth and uriopian trinkets than above I Saw Some Guns, a Sword, maney Powder flasks, Salers jackets, overalls, hats & Shirts, Copper and Brass trinkets with few Beeds only. dureing the time I was at Dinner the Indians Stold my tomahawk which I made use of to Smoke I Serched but Could not find it, a Pond on the Stard Side, off from the river. Raspberries and _____ are also in the bottoms- met a large and Small canoe with 12 men from below the men were dressed with a variety of articles of European manufactory the large Canoe had emeges on the bow & Stern handsomly Carved in wood & painted with the figur of a Bear in front & man in a Stern. Saw white geese with black wings- Saw a Small Crab-apple with all the taste & flavor of the Common- Those Indians were all armed with Pistols or bows and arrows ready Sprung war axes &c.

Mount Hellen bears N. 25° E about 80 miles, this is the mountain we Saw near the foks of this river. it is emensely high and covered with Snow, riseing in a kind of Cone perhaps the highest pinecal from the common leavel in america passed a village of 4 hs. on the Stard Side at 2 mils, one at 3 mls.

One deer 2 Ducks & Brant killed

[Clark, November 4, 1805] November 4th Monday 1805 A cloudy cool morning wind from the West we Set out at 1/2 past 8 oClock, one man Shannon Set out early to walk on the Island to kill Something, he joined us at the lower point with a Buck. This Island is 6 miles long and near 3 miles wide thinly timbered (Tide rose last night 18 inches perpndicular at Camp) near the lower point of this dimond Island is The head of a large Island Seperated from a Small one by a narrow chanel, and both Situated nearest the Lard Side, those Islands as also the bottoms are thickly Covered with Pine &c. river wide, Country low on both Sides; on the Main Lard Shore a Short distance below the last Island we landed at a village of 25 Houses; 24 of those houses were thached with Straw, and covered with bark, the other House is built of boards in the form of those above, except that it is above ground and about 50 feet in length and covered with broad Split boards This village contains about 200 men of the Skil-loot nation I counted 52 canoes on the bank in front of this village maney of them verry large and raised in bow. we recognised the man who over took us last night, he invited us to a lodge in which he had Some part and gave us a roundish roots about the Size of a Small Irish potato which they roasted in the embers until they became Soft, This root they call Wap-pa-to which the Bulb of the Chinese cultivate in great quantities called the Sa-git ti folia or common arrow head-. it has an agreeable taste and answers verry well in place of bread. we purchased about 4 bushels of this root and divided it to our party, at 7 miles below this village passed the upper point of a large Island nearest the Lard Side, a Small Prarie in which there is a pond opposit on the Stard. here I landed and walked on Shore, about 3 miles a fine open Prarie for about 1 mile, back of which the countrey rises gradually and wood land comencies Such as white oake, pine of different kinds, wild crabs with the taste and flavour of the common crab and Several Species of undergroth of which I am not acquainted, a few Cottonwood trees & the Ash of this countrey grow Scattered on the river bank, Saw Some Elk and Deer Sign and Joined Capt. Lewis at a place he had landed with the party for Diner. Soon after Several Canoes of Indians from the village above came down dressed for the purpose as I Supposed of Paying us a friendly visit, they had Scarlet & blue blankets Salors jackets, overalls, Shirts and Hats independant of their Usial dress; the most of them had either war axes Spears or Bows Sprung with quivers of arrows, Muskets or pistols, and tin flasks to hold their powder; Those fellows we found assumeing and disagreeable, however we Smoked with them and treated them with every attention & friendship.

dureing the time we were at dinner those fellows Stold my pipe Tomahawk which They were Smoking with, I imediately Serched every man and the canoes, but Could find nothing of my Tomahawk, while Serching for the Tomahawk one of those Scoundals Stole a Cappoe of one of our interpreters, which was found Stufed under the root of a treer, near the place they Sat, we became much displeased with those fellows, which they discovered and moved off on their return home to their village, except 2 canoes which had passed on down- we proceeded on met a large & a Small Canoe from below, with 12 men the large Canoe was orniminted with Images carved in wood the figures of a Bear in front & a man in Stern, Painted & fixed verry netely on the the of the Canoe, rising to near the hight of a man two Indians verry finely Dressed & with hats on was in this canoe passed the lower point of the Island which is nine miles in length haveing passed 2 Islands on the Stard Side of this large Island, three Small Islands at its lower point. the Indians make Signs that a village is Situated back of those Islands on the Lard. Side and I believe that a Chanel is Still on the Lrd, Side as a Canoe passed in between the Small Islands, and made Signs that way, probably to traffick with Some of the nativs liveing on another Chanel, at 3 miles lower, and 12 Leagues below quick Sand river passed a village of four large houses on The Lard. Side, near which we had a full view of Mt. Helien which is perhaps the highest pinical in America from their base it bears N. 25° E about 90 miles- This is the mountain I Saw from the Muscle Shell rapid on the 19th of October last Covered with Snow, it rises Something in the form of a Sugar lofe- about a mile lower passed a Single house on the Lard. Side, and one on the Stard. Side, passed a village on each Side and Camped near a house on the Stard. Side we proceeded on untill one hour after dark with a view to get clear of the nativs who was constantly about us, and troublesom, finding that we could not get Shut of those people for one night, we landed and Encamped on the Stard. Side Soon after 2 canoes Came to us loaded with Indians, we purchased a fiew roots of them.

This evening we Saw vines much resembling the raspberry which is verry thick in the bottoms. A range of high hills at about 5 miles on the Lard Side which runs S. E. & N W. Covered with tall timber the bottoms below in this range of hills and the river is rich and leavel, Saw White geese with a part of their wings black. The river here is 11/2 miles wide, and current jentle. opposit to our camp on a Small Sandy Island the brant & geese make Such a noise that it will be impossible for me to Sleap. we made 29 miles to day Killed a Deer and Several brant and ducks. I Saw a Brarow tamed at the 1st village to day The Indians which we have passd to day of the Scil-loot nation in their language from those near & about the long narrows of the Che-luc-it-te-quar or E-chee-lute, their dress differ but little, except they have more of the articles precured from the white traders, they all have flatened heads both men and women, live principally on fish and Wap pa toe roots, they also kill Some fiew Elk and Deer, dureing the Short time I remained in their village they brought in three Deer which they had killed with their Bow & arrows. They are thievishly inclined as we have experienced.

[Clark, November 5, 1805] Novr. 5th Tuesday 1805 a Cloudy morning Som rain the after part of last night & this morning. I could not Sleep for the noise kept by the Swans, Geese, white & black brant, Ducks &c. on a opposit base, & Sand hill Crane, they were emensely numerous and their noise horrid. We Set out at Sun rise & our hunters killed 10 Brant 4 of which were white with black wings 2 Ducks, and a Swan which were divided, we Came too and Encamped on the Lard. Side under a high ridgey land, the high land come to the river on each Side. the river about 11/2 mile wide. those high lands rise gradually from the river & bottoms- we are all wet Cold and disagreeable, rain Continues & encreases. I killed a Pheasent which is very fat- my feet and legs cold. I saw 17 Snakes to day on a Island, but little appearance of Frost at this place.

[Clark, November 5, 1805] November 5th Tuesday 1805 Rained all the after part of last night, rain continues this morning, I slept but verry little last night for the noise Kept dureing the whole of the night by the Swans,

Geese, white & Grey Brant Ducks &c. on a Small Sand Island close under the Lard. Side; they were emensely noumerous, and their noise horid- we Set out early here the river is not more than 3/4 of a mile in width, passed a Small Prarie on the Stard. Side passed 2 houses about 1/2 a mile from each other on the Lard. Side a Canoe came from the upper house, with 3 men in it mearly to view us, passed an Isld. Covered with tall trees & green briers Seperated from the Stard. Shore by a narrow Chanel at 9 miles I observed on the Chanel which passes on the Stard Side of this Island a Short distance above its lower point is Situated a large village, the front of which occupies nearly 1/4 of a mile fronting the Chanel, and closely Connected, I counted 14 houses in front here the river widens to about 11/2 miles. Seven canoes of Indians came out from this large village to view and trade with us, they appeared orderly and well disposed, they accompanied us a fiew miles and returned back. about 111/2 miles below this village on the Lard Side behind a rockey Sharp point, we passed a Chanel 1/4 of a mile wide, which I take to be the one the Indian Canoe entered yesterday from the lower point of Immage Canoe Island a Some low clifts of rocks below this Chanel, a large Island Close under the Stard Side opposit, and 2 Small Islands, below, here we met 2 canoes from below,- below those Islands a range of high hills form the Stard. Bank of the river, the Shore bold and rockey, Covered with a thick groth of Pine an extensive low Island, Seperated from the Lard side by a narrow Chanel, on this Island we Stoped to Dine I walked out found it open & covered with grass interspersed with Small ponds, in which was great numbr. of foul, the remains of an old village on the lower part of this Island, I saw Several deer our hunters killed on this Island a Swan, 4 white 6 Grey brant & 2 Ducks all of them were divided, below the lower point of this Island a range of high hills) which runs S. E. forms the Lard. bank of the river the Shores bold and rockey & hills Covered with pine, The high hills leave the river on the Stard. Side a high bottom between the hill & river. We met 4 Canoes of Indians from below, in which there is 26 Indians, one of those Canoes is large, and orniminted with Images on the bow & Stern. That in the Bow the likeness of a Bear, and in Stern the picture of a man- we landed on the Lard. Side & camped a little below the mouth of a creek on the Stard. Side a little below the mouth of which is an Old Village which is now abandaned-; here the river is about one and a half miles wide, and deep, The high Hills which run in a N W. & S E. derection form both banks of the river the Shore boald and rockey, the hills rise gradually & are Covered with a thick groth of pine &c. The valley which is from above the mouth of Quick Sand River to this place may be computed at 60 miles wide on a Derect line, & extends a great Distanc to the right & left rich thickly Covered with tall timber, with a fiew Small Praries bordering on the river and on the Islands; Some fiew Standing Ponds & Several Small Streams of running water on either Side of the river; This is certainly a fertill and a handsom valley, at this time Crouded with Indians. The day proved Cloudy with rain the greater part of it, we are all wet cold and disagreeable- I Saw but little appearance of frost in this valley which we call Wap-pa-loo Columbia from that root or plants growing Spontaneously in this valley only In my walk of to Day I saw 17 Striped Snakes I killed a grouse which was verry fat, and larger than Common. This is the first night which we have been entirely clear of Indians Since our arrival on the waters of the Columbia River. We made 32 miles to day by estimation-

[Clark, November 6, 1805] November 6th Wednesday a cold wet morning. rain Contd. untill _____ oClock we Set out early & proceeded on the Corse of last night &c.

[Clark, November 6, 1805] November 6th Wednesday 1805 A cool wet raney morning we Set out early at 4 miles pass 2 Lodges of Indians in a Small bottom on the Lard Side I believe those Indians to be travelers. opposit is the head of a long narrow Island close under the Starboard Side, back of this Island two Creeks fall in about 6 miles apart, and appear to head in the high hilley countrey to the N. E. opposit this long Island is 2 others one Small and about the middle of the river. the other larger and nearly opposit its lower point, and opposit a high clift of Black rocks on the Lard. Side at 14 miles: here the Indians of the 2 Lodges we passed to day came in their canoes with Sundery articles to Sell, we purchased of them Wap-pa-too roots, Salmon trout, and I purchased 2 beaver Skins for which I gave 5 Small fish hooks. here the hills leave the river on the Lard. Side, a butifull open and extensive bottom in which there is an old Village, one also on the Stard. Side a little above both of which are abandened by all their inhabitents except Two Small dogs nearly Starved, and an unreasonable portion of flees- The Hills and mountains are covered with Sever kinds of Pine-Arber Vitea or white Cedar, red Loril, alder and Several Species of under groth, the bottoms have common rushes, nettles, & grass the Slashey parts have Bull rushes & flags- Some willow on the waters edge, passed an Island 3 miles long and one mile wide, close under the Stard. Side below the long narrow Island below which the Stard Hills are verry from the river bank and Continues high and rugid on that Side all day, we over took two Canoes of Indians going down to trade one of the Indians Spoke a fiew words of english and Said that the principal man who traded with them was Mr. Haley, and that he had a woman in his Canoe who Mr. Haley was fond of &c. he Showed us a Bow of Iron and Several other things which he Said Mr. Haley gave him. we came too to Dine on the long narrow Island found the woods So thick with under groth that the hunters could not get any distance into the Isld. the red wood, and Green bryors interwoven, and mixed with pine, alder, a Specis of Beech, ash &c. we killed nothing to day The Indians leave us in the evening, river about one mile wide hills high and Steep on the Std. no place for Several Miles suffcently large and leavil for our camp we at length Landed at a place which by moveing the Stones we made a place Suffcently large for the party to lie leavil on the Smaller Stones Clear of the Tide Cloudy with rain all day we are all wet and disagreeable, had large fires made on the Stone and dried our bedding and Kill the flees, which collected in our blankets at every old village we encamped near I had like to have forgotten a verry remarkable Knob riseing from the edge of the water to about 80 feet high, and about 200 paces around at its Base and Situated on the long narrow Island above and nearly opposit to the 2 Lodges we passed to day, it is Some distance from the high land & in a low part of the Island

[Clark, November 7, 1805] November 7th Thursday 1805 a Cloudy fogey morning, a little rain. Set out at 8 oClock proceeded on

The womens peticoat is about 15 Inches long made of arber vita or the white Cedar bark wove to a String and hanging down in tossles and tied So as to cover from their hips as low as the peticoat will reach and only Covers them when Standing, as in any other position the Tosels Seperate. Those people Sold us otter Skins for fish hooks of which they wer fond

We delayed 1 1/2 hour & Set out the tide being up in & the river So Cut with Islands we got an Indian to pilot us into the main chanel one of our Canoes Seperated from us this morning in the fog- great numbers of water fowls of every descriptn. common to this river

[Clark, November 7, 1805] November 7th Thursday 1805 A cloudy foggey morning Some rain. we Set out early proceeded under the Stard Shore under a high rigid hills with Steep assent the Shore boalt and rockey, the fog So thick we could not See across the river, two Canos of Indians met and returned with us to their village which is Situated on the Stard Side behind a cluster of Marshey Islands, on a narrow chanl. of the river through which we passed to the Village of 4 Houses, they gave us to eate Some fish, and Sold us, fish, Wap pa to roots three dogs and 2 otter Skins for which we gave fish hooks principally of which they were verry fond.

Those people call themselves War-ci-a-cum and Speake a language different from the nativs above with whome they trade for the Wapato roots of which they make great use of as food. their houses differently built, raised entirely above ground eaves about 5 feet from the ground Supported and covered in the same way of those above, dotes about the Same size but in the Side of the house in one Corner, one fire place and that near the opposit end; around which they have their beads raised about 4 feet from the fore which is of earth, under their beads they Store away baskets of dried fish Berries & wappato, over the fire they hang the flesh as they take them and which they do not make immediate use. Their Canoes are of the Same form of those above. The Dress of the men differ verry little from those above, The womin altogether different, their robes are Smaller only Covering their Sholders & falling down to near the hip- and Sometimes when it is Cold a piec of fur curiously plated and connected So as to meet around the body from the arms to the hips The garment which occupies the waist and thence as low as the knee before and mid leg behind, cannot properly be called a petticoat, in the common acception of the word; it is a Tissue formed of white Cedar bark bruised or broken into Small Straps, which are interwoven in their center by means of Several cords of the Same materials which Serves as well for a girdle as to hold in place the Straps of bark which forms the tissue, and which Strans, Confined in the middle, hang with their ends pendulous from the waiste, the whole being of Suffcent thickness when the female Stands erect to conceal those parts useally covered from familiar view, but when she stoops or places herself in any other attitudes this battery of Venus is not altogether impervious to the penetrating eye of the amorite. This tissue is Sometims formed of little Strings of the Silk grass twisted and knoted at their ends &c. Those Indians are low and ill Shaped all flat heads

after delaying at this village one hour and a half we Set out piloted by an Indian dressed in a Salors dress, to the main Chanel of the river, the tide being in we Should have found much dificuley in passing into the main Chanel from behind those islands, without a pilot, a large marshey Island near the middle of the river near which Several Canoes Came allong Side with Skins, roots fish &c. to Sell, and had a temporey residence on this Island, here we See great numbers of water fowls about those marshey Islands; here the high mountainous Countrey approaches the river on the Lard Side, a high mountn. to the S W. about 20 miles, the high mountans. Countrey Continue on the Stard Side, about 14 miles below the last village and 18 miles of this day we landed at a village of the Same nation. This village is at the foot of the high hills on the Stard Side back OF 2 Small Islands it contains 7 indifferent houses built in the Same form of those above, here we purchased a Dog Some fish, wappato roots and I purchased 2 beaver Skins for the purpose of makeing me a roab, as the robe I have is rotten and good for nothing. opposit to this Village the high mountaneous Countrey leave the river on the Lard Side below which the river widens into a kind of Bay & is Crouded with low Islands Subject to be Covered by the tides- we proceeded on about 12 miles below the Village under a high mountaneous Countrey on the Stard. Side. Shore boald and rockey and Encamped under a high hill on the Stard. Side opposit to a rock Situated half a mile from the Shore, about 50 feet high and 20 feet Diamieter, we with dificuly found a place Clear of the tide and Sufficiently large to lie on and the only place we could get was on round Stones on which we lay our mats rain Continud. moderately all day & Two Indians accompanied us from the last village, they we detected in Stealing a knife and returned, our Small Canoe which got Seperated in the fog this morning joined us this evening from a large Island Situated nearest the Lard Side below the high hills on that Side, the river being too wide to See either the form Shape or Size of the Islands on the Lard Side.

Great joy in camp we are in View of the Ocian, this great Pacific Octean which we been So long anxious to See. and the roreing or noise made by the waves brakeing on the rockey Shores (as I Suppose) may be heard distictly

we made 34 miles to day as Computed

[Clark, November 8, 1805]
Novr. 8th Friday 1805 a cloudy morning Some rain and wind we Changed our Clothes and Set out at 9 oClock proceeded on Close under the Stard. Side

R. Fields Killed a goose & 2 Canvis back Ducks in this bay after Dinner we took the advantage of the returning tide & proceeded on to the 2d point, at which place we found the Swells too high to proceed we landed and drew our canoes up So as to let the tide leave them. The three Indians after Selling us 4 fish for which we gave Seven Small fishing hooks, and a piece of red Cloth. Some fine rain at intervales all this day. the Swells Continued high all the evening & we are Compelled to form an Encampment on a Point Scercely room Sufficent for us all to lie Clear of the tide water. hills high & with a Steep assent, river wide & at this place too Salt to be used for Drink. we are all wet and disagreeable, as we have been Continually for Severl. days past, we are at a loss & cannot find out if any Settlement is near the mouth of this river.

The Swells were So high and the Canoes roled in Such a manner as to cause Several to be verry Sick. Reuben fields, Wiser McNeal & the Squar wer of the number

[Clark, November 8, 1805] November 8th Friday 1805 A Cloudy morning Some rain, we did not Set out untill 9 oClock, haveing Changed our Clothing- proceeded on Close under the Stard. Side, the hills high with Steep assent, Shore boald and rockey Several low Islands in a Deep bend or Bay to the Lard Side, river about 5 or 7 miles wide. three Indians in a Canoe overtook us, with Salmon to Sell, passed 2 old villages on the Stard. Side and at 3 miles entered a nitch of about 6 miles wide and 5 miles deep with Several Creeks makeing into the Stard Hills, this nitch we found verry Shallow water and Call it the Shallow nitch we came too at the remains of an old village at the bottom of this nitch and dined, here we Saw great numbers of fowl, Sent out 2 men and they killed a Goose and two Canves back Ducks here we found great numbers of Hees which we treated with the greatest caution and distance; after Diner the Indians left us and we took the advantage of a returning tide and proceeded on to the Second point on the Std. here we found the Swells or waves So high that we thought it imprudent to proceed; we landed unloaded and drew up our Canoes. Some rain all day at intervals; we are all wet and disagreeable, as we have been for Several days past, and our present Situation a verry disagreeable one in as much; as we have not leavel land Sufficient for an encampment and for our baggage to lie Cleare of the tide, the High hills jutting in So Close and Steep that we cannot retreat back, and the water of the river too Salt to be used, added to this the waves are increasing to Such a hight that we cannot move from this place, in this Situation we are compelled to form our Camp between the hite of the Ebb and flood tides, and rase our baggage on logs- We are not certain as yet if the whites people who trade with those people or from whome they precure ther goods are Stationary at the mouth, or visit this quarter at Stated times for the purpose of trafick &c. I believe the latter to be the most probable conjucture- The Seas roled and tossed the Canoes in Such a manner this evening that Several of our party were Sea Sick.

[Clark, November 9, 1805] Novr. 9th Saturday 1805 The tide of last night obliged us to unload all the Canoes one of which Sunk before She was unloaded by the high waves or Swells which accompanied the returning tide, The others we unloaded, and 3 others was filled with water Soon after by the Swells or high Sees which broke against the Shore imediately where we lay, rained hard all the fore part of the day, the tide which rose untill 2 oClock P M to day brought with it Such emence Swells or waves, added to a hard wind from the South which Loosened the Drift trees which is verry thick on the Shores, and tossed them about in Such a manner, as to endanger our Canoes very much, with every exertion and the Strictest attention by the party was Scercely Suffient to defend our Canoes from being Crushed to pieces between those emensely large trees maney of them 200 feet long and 4 feet through. The tide of this day rose about _____ feet & 15 Inches higher than yesterday this is owing to the wind which Sets in from the ocian, we are Compelled to move our Camp from the water, as also the loading every man as wet all the last night and this day as the rain Could make them which Contind. all day. at 4 oClock the wind Shifted about to the S. W imediately from the ocian and blew a Storm for about 2 hours, raised the tide verry high all wet & cold Labiech killed 4 Ducks very fat & R. Fields Saw Elk Sign.

not withstanding the disagreeable time of the party for Several days past they are all Chearfull and full of anxiety to See further into the ocian. the water is too Salt to Drink, we use rain water. The Salt water has acted on some of the party already as a Pergitive. rain continus.

[Clark, November 9, 1805] November 9th Saturday 1805 The tide of last night did not rise Sufficiently high to come into our camp, but the Canoes which was exposed to the mercy of the waves &c. which accompanied the returning tide, they all filled, and with great attention we Saved them untill the tide left them dry- wind Hard from the South and rained hard all the fore part of the day, at 2 oClock P M the flood tide came in accompanied with emence waves and heavy winds, floated the trees and Drift which was on the point on which we Camped and tosed them about in Such a manner as to endanger the Canoes verry much, with every exertion and the Strictest attention by every individual of the party was Scercely Sufficient to Save our Canoes from being crushed by those monsterous trees maney of them nearly 200 feet long and from 4 to 7 feet through. our camp entirely under water dureing the hight of the tide, every man as wet as water could make them all the last night and to day all day as the rain Continued all day, at 4 oClock P M the wind Shifted about to the S. W. and blew with great violence imediately from the Ocian for about two hours, notwithstanding the disagreeable Situation of our party all wet and Cold (and one which they have experienced for Several days past) they are chearfull and anxious to See further into the Ocian, The water of the river being too Salt to use we are obliged to make use of rain water- Some of the party not accustomed to Salt water has made too free a use of it on them it acts as a pergitive.

at this dismal point we must Spend another night as the wind & waves are too high to proceed.

[Clark, November 10, 1805] November 10th Sunday 1805 rained verry hard the greater part of the last night & Continus this morning, the wind has layed and the Swells are fallen. we loaded our Canoes and proceeded on, passed a Deep Bay on the Stard. Side I Call _____ The wind rose from the N W. and the Swells became So high, we were Compelled to return about 2 miles to a place where we Could unld. our Canoes, which was in a Small Bay on Driftwood, on which we had also to make our fires to dry our Selves as well as we could the Shore being either a Clift of Purpendicular rocks or Steep assents to the hight of 4 or 500 feet, we continued on this drift wood untill about 3 oClock when the evening appearing favourable we loaded & Set out in hopes to turn the Point below and get into a better harber, but finding the waves & Swells continue to rage with great fury below, we got a Safe place for our Stores & a much beter one for the Canoes to lie and formed a Campment on Drift logs in the Same little Bay under a high hill at the enterence of a Small drean which we found verry convt. on account of its water, as that of the river is Brackish- The logs on which we lie is all on flote every high tide- The rain Continud all day- we are all wet, also our beding and many other articles. we are all employed untill late drying our bedding. nothing to eate but Pounded fish

[Clark, November 10, 1805] November 10th Sunday 1805 Rained verry hard the greater part of last night and continues this morning. the wind has luled and the waves are not high; we loaded our canoes and proceeded on passed Several Small and deep nitch on the Stard. Side, we proceeded on about 10 miles Saw great numbers of Sea Guls, the wind rose from the N. W. and the waves became So high that we were compelled to return about 2 miles to a place we Could unload our Canoes, which we did in a Small nitch at the mouth of a Small run on a pile of drift logs where we Continued untill low water, when the river appeared calm we loaded and Set out; but was obliged to return finding the waves too high for our Canoes to ride, we again unloaded the Canoes, and Stoed the loading on a rock above the tide water, and formed a camp on the Drift Logs which appeared to be the only Situation we could find to lie, the hills being either a perpendicular Clift, or Steep assent, riseing to about 500 feet- our Canoes we Secured as well as we could- we are all wet the rain haveing continued all day, our beding and maney other articles, employ our Selves drying our blankets- nothing to eate but dried fish pounded which we brought from the falls. we made 10 miles today

[Clark, November 11, 1805] November 11th Monday 1805 a hard rain all the last night we again get wet the rain continue at intervals all day. Wind verry high from S W and blew a Storm all day Sent out Jo. Fields & Collins to hunt. at 12 oClock at a time the wind was verry high and waves tremendeous five Indians Came down in a Canoe loaded with fish of Salmon Spes. Called Red Charr, we purchased of those Indians 13 of these fish, for which we gave, fishing hooks & some trifling things, we had Seen those Indians at a village behind Some marshey Islands a few days ago. they are on their way to trade those fish with white people which they make Signs live below round a point, those people are badly Clad, one is dressd. in an old Salors Jacket & Trouses, the others Elk Skin robes. we are truly unfortunate to be Compelled to lie 4 days nearly in the Same place at a time that our day are precious to us, The Wind Shifted to _____ the Indians left us and Crossed the river which is about 5 miles wide through the highest Sees I ever Saw a Small vestle ride, their Canoe is Small, maney times they were out of Sight before the were 2 miles off Certain it is they are the best canoe navigators I ever Saw The tide was 3 hours later to day than yesterday and rose much higher, the trees we camped on was all on flote for about 2 hours from 3 untill 5 oClock P M, the great quantities of rain which has fallen losenes the Stones on the Side of the hill & the Small ones fall on us, our Situation is truly a disagreeable one our Canoes in one place at the mercy of the waves our baggage in another and our Selves & party Scattered on drift trees of emense Sizes, & are on what dry land they can find in the Crevices of the rocks & hill Sides

[Clark, November 11, 1805] November 11th Monday 1805 A hard rain all the last night, dureing the last tide the logs on which we lay was all on float Sent out Jo Fields to hunt, he Soon returned and informed us that the hills was So high & Steep, & thick with undergroth and fallen Timber that he could not get out any distance; about 12 oClock 5 Indians came down in a canoe, the wind verry high from the S. W. with most tremendious waves brakeing with great violence against the Shores, rain falling in torrents, we are all wet as usial and our Situation is truly a disagreeable one; the great quantites of rain which has loosened the Stones on the hill Sides, and the Small Stones fall down upon us, our canoes at one place at the mercy of the waves, our baggage in another and our Selves and party Scattered on floating logs and Such dry Spots as can be found on the hill Sides, and Crivices of the rocks. we purchased of the Indians 13 red chary which we found to be an excellent fish we have Seen those Indians above and are of a nation who reside above and on the opposit Side who call themselves Call-har-ma they are badly clad & illy made, Small and Speak a language much resembling the last nation, one of those men had on a Salors Jacket and Pantiloons and made Signs that he got those Clothes from the white people who lived below the point &c. those people left us and Crossed the river (which is about 5 miles wide at this place) through the highest waves I ever Saw a Small vestles ride. Those Indians are Certainly the best Canoe navigaters I ever Saw. rained all (lay

[Clark, November 12, 1805] November 12th Tuesday 1805 a tremendious thunder Storm abt. 3 oClock this morning accompanied by wind from the S W. and Hail, this Storm of hard Clap's thunder Lighting and hail untill about 6 oClock at intervals it then became light for a Short time when the heavens became darkined by a black Cloud from the S, W, & a hard rain Suckceeded which lasted untill 12 oClock with a hard wind which raised the Seas tremendiously high braking with great force and fury against the rocks & trees on which we lie, as our Situation became Seriously dangerous, we took the advantage of a low tide & moved our Camp around a point a Short distance to a Small wet bottom at the mouth of a Small Creek, which we had not observed when we first Came to this Cove, from its being very thick and obscured by drift trees & thick bushes, Send out men to hunt they found the woods So thick with Pine & timber and under Broth that they could not get through, Saw Some Elk tracks, I walked up this creek & killed 2 Salmon trout, the men killd. 13 of the Salmon Species, The Pine of fur Specs, or Spruc Pine grow here to an emense Size & hight maney of them 7 & 8 feet through and upwards of 200 feet high. It would be distressing to a feeling person to See our Situation at this time all wet and cold with our bedding &c. also wet, in a Cove Scercely large nough to Contain us, our Baggage in a Small holler about 1/2 a mile from us, and Canoes at the mercy of the waves & drift wood, we have Scured them as well as it is possible by Sinking and wateing them down with Stones to prevent the emence waves dashing them to pices against the rocks- one got loose last night & was left on a rock by the tide Some distance below without recving much damage. fortunately for us our Men are helthy. It was clear at 12 for a Short time. I observed the Mountains on the opposit Side was covered with Snowour party has been wet for 8 days and is truly disagreeable, their robes & leather Clothes are rotten from being Continually wet, and they are not in a Situation to get others, and we are not in a Situation to restore them- I observe great numbers of Sea guls, flying in every derection- Three men Gibson Bratten & Willard attempted to decend in a Canoe built in the Indian fashion and abt. the Size of the one the Indians visited us in yesterday, they Could not proceed, as the waves tossed them about at will, they returned after proceeding about 1 mile- we got our Selves tolerable Comfortable by drying our Selves & bedding Cought 3 salmon this evining in a Small branch above about 1 mile

[Clark, November 12, 1805] November 12th Tuesday 1805 A Tremendious wind from the S. W. about 3 oClock this morning with Lightineng and hard claps of Thunder, and Hail which Continued untill 6 oClock a.m. when it became light for a Short time, then the heavens became Sudenly darkened by a black Cloud from the S. W. and rained with great violence untill 12 oClock, the waves tremendious brakeing with great fury against the rocks and trees on which we were encamped. our Situation is dangerous. we took the advantage of a low tide and moved our camp around a point to a Small wet bottom at the mouth of a Brook, which we had not observed when we Came to this cove; from it being verry thick and obscured by drift trees and thick bushes It would be distressing to See our Situation, all wet and Colde our bedding also wet, (and the robes of the party which Compose half the bedding is rotten and we are not in a Situation to supply their places) in a wet bottom Scercely large enough to contain us, our baggage half a mile from us and Canoes at the mercy of the waves, altho Secured as well as possible, Sunk with emence parcels of Stone to wate them down to prevent their dashing to pieces against the rocks; one got loose last night and was left on a rock a Short distance below, without rciving more daminage than a Split in her bottom- Fortunately for us our men are healthy. 3 men Gibson Bratten & Willard attempted to go aroud the point below in our Indian Canoe, much Such a canoe as the Indians visited us in yesterday, they proceeded to the point from which they were oblige to return, the waves tossing them about at will I walked up the branch and giged 3 Salmon trout. the party killed 13 Salmon to day in a branch about 2 miles above. rain Continued

[Clark, November 13, 1805] November 13th Wednesday 1805 Some intervales of fair weather last night, rain and wind Continue this morning, as we are in a Cove & the Mountains verry high & Pine Spruce verry high & thick Cannot determine the procise course of the winds. I walked to the top of the first part of the mountain with much fatigue as the distance was about 3 miles thro intolerable thickets of Small Pine, arrow wood a groth much resembling arrow wood with briers, growing to 10 & 15 feet high interlocking with each other & Furn, aded to this difficulty the hill was So Steep that I was obliged to drawing my Self up in many places by the bowers, the Countrey Continues thick and hilley as far back a I could See. Some Elk Sign, rained all day moderately. I am wet &c. &c. The Hail which fell 2 night past is yet to be Seen on the mountain on which I was to day. I Saw a Small red Berry which grows on a Stem of about 6 or 8 Inches from the Ground, in bunches and in great quantity on the Mountains, the taste insiped. I saw a number of verry large Spruce Pine one of which I measured 14 feet around and verry tall. My principal objects in assdg. this mountain was to view the river below, the weather being So Cloudey & thick that I could not See any distance down, discovered the wind high from the N. W. and waves high at a Short distance below our Encampment, (Squar displeased with me for not sin &c &c. Wap-lo a excellent root which is rosted and tastes like a potato I Cut my hand despatched 3 men in a Indian canoe (which is calculated to ride high Swells) down to examine if they can find the Bay at the mouth & good barbers below for us to proceed in Safty. The fides at every Hud come in with great Swells & Breake against the rocks & Drift trees with great fury- the rain Continue all the evening nothing to eate but Pounded fish which we have as a reserve See Store, and what Pore fish we can kill up the branch on which we are encamped our canoe and the three men did not return this evening- if we were to have cold weather to accompany the rain which we have had for this 6 or 8 days passed we must eneviatilbly Suffer verry much as Clothes are Scerce with us.

[Clark, November 13, 1805] November 13th Wednesday 1805 Some intervales of fair weather last night, rain continue this morning. I walked up the Brook & assended the first Spur of the mountain with much fatigue, the distance about 3 miles, through an intolerable thickets of Small pine, a groth much resembling arrow wood on the Stem of which there is thorns; this groth about 12 or 15 feet high inter lockd into each other and Scattered over the high fern & fallen timber, added to this the hills were So Steep that I was compelled to draw my Self up by the assistance of those bushes- The Timber on those hills are of the pine Species large and tall maney of them more than 200 feet high & from 8 to 10 feet through at the Stump those hills & as far back as I could See, I Saw Some Elk Sign, on the Spur of the mountain tho not fresh. I killed a Salmon trout on my return. The Hail which fell 2 nights past is yet to be Seen on the mountains; I Saw in my ramble to day a red berry resembling Solomons Seal berry which the nativs call Sol-me and use it to eate. my principal object in assending this mountain was to view the countrey below, the rain continuing and weather proved So Cloudy that I could not See any distance on my return we dispatched 3 men Colter, Willard and Shannon in the Indian canoe to get around the point if possible and examine the river, and the Bay below for a god barber for our Canoes to lie in Safty &c. The tide at every floot tide Came with great swells brakeing against the rocks & Drift trees with great fury The rain Continue all day. nothing to eate but pounded fish which we Keep as a reserve and use in Situations of this kind.

[Clark, November 14, 1805] Novr. 14th Thursday 1805 Rained last night without intermission and this morning the wind blew hard from the _____ We Could not move, one Canoe was broken last night against the rocks, by the waves dashing her against them in high tide about 10 oClock 5 Indians Come up in a Canoe thro emence waves & Swells, they landed and informed us they Saw the 3 men we Sent down yesterday, at Some distance below Soon after those people Came Colter one of the 3 men returned and informed us that he had proceeded with his Canoe as far as they Could, for the waves and Could find no white people, or Bay, he Saw a good Canoe barber & 2 Camps of Indians at no great distance below and that those with us had taken his gig & knife &c. which he forcably took from them & they left us, after our treating them well. The rain Continue all day all wet as usial, killed only 2 fish to day for the whole Party, at 3 oClock Capt. Lewis Drewyer Jo. & R. Fields & Frasure Set out down on the Shore to examine if any white men were below within our reach, they took a empty Canoe & 5 men to Set them around the Point on a Gravelley Beech which Colter informed was at no great distance below. The Canoe returned at dusk half full of water, from the waves which dashed over in passing the point Capt Lewis is object is also to find a Small Bay as laid down by Vancouver just out of the mouth of the Columbia River. rained as usial all the evening, all wet and disagreeable Situated

[Clark, November 14, 1805] November 14th Thursday 1805 rained all the last night without intermition, and this morning. wind blows verry hard but our Situation is Such that we Cannot tell from what point it comes- one of our Canoes is much broken by the waves dashing it against the rocks- 5 Indians Came up in a Canoe, thro the waves, which is verry high and role with great fury- They made Signs to us that they Saw the 3 men we Sent down yesterday. only 3 of those Indians landed, the other 2 which was women played off in the waves, which induced me to Suspect that they had taken Something from our men below, at this time one of the men Colter returnd by land and informed us that those Indians had taken his Gigg & basket, I called to the Squars to land and give back the gigg, which they would not doe untill a man run with a gun, as if he intended to Shute them when they landed, and Colter got his gig & basket I then ordered those fellows off, and they verry readily Cleared out they are of the War-ci-a-cum N. Colter informed us that "it was but a Short distance from where we lay around the point to a butifull Sand beech, which continud for a long ways, that he had found a good harber in the mouth of a creek near 2 Indian Lodgesthat he had proceeded in the Canoe as far as he could for the waves, the other two men Willard & Shannon had proceeded on down"

Capt Lewis concluded to proceed on by land & find if possible the white people the Indians Say is below and examine if a Bay is Situated near the mouth of this river as laid down by Vancouver in which we expect, if there is white traders to find them &c. at 3 oClock he Set out with 4 men Drewyer Jos. & Reu. Fields & R. Frasure, in one of our large canoes and 5 men to Set them around the point on the Sand beech. this canoe returned nearly filled with water at Dark which it receved by the waves dashing into it on its return, haveing landed Capt. Lewis & his party Safe on the Sand beech. The rain Continues all day all wet. The rain &c. which has continued without a longer intermition than 2 hours at a time for ten days past has distroyd. the robes and rotted nearly one half of the fiew Clothes the party has, perticularley the leather Clothes,- fortunately for us we have no very Cold weather as yet and if we have Cold weather before we Can kill & Dress Skins for Clothing the bulk of the party will Suffer verry much.

[Clark, November 15, 1805] November 15th Friday 1805 Rained all the last night at intervales of Sometimes of 2 hours, This morning it became Calm & fair, I prepared to Set out at which time the wind sprung up from the S. E. and blew down the River & in a fiew minits raised Such Swells and waves brakeing on the Rocks at the point as to render it unsafe to proceed. I went to the point in an empty canoe and found it would be dangerous to proceed even in an empty Canoe The Sun Shown untill 1 oClock p.m.which gave an oppertunity for us to dry Some of our bedding, & examine our baggage, the greater Part of which I found wet Some of our Pounded fish Spoiled I had all the arms put in order & amunition examined.

The rainey weather Continued without a longer intermition than 2 hours at a time from the 5th in the morng. untill the 16th is eleven days rain, and the most disagreeable time I have experienced Confined on a tempiest Coast wet, where I can neither get out to hunt, return to a better Situation, or proceed on: in this Situation have we been for Six days past.- fortunately the wind lay about 3 oClock we loaded I in great haste and Set out passed the blustering Point below which is a Sand beech, with a Small marshey bottom for 3 miles on the Stard. Side, on which is a large village of 36 houses deserted by the Inds. & in full possession of the flees, a Small Creek fall in at this village, which waters the Country for a few miles back; Shannon & 5 Indians met me here, Shannon informed me he met Capt. Lewis Some distance below & he took willard with him & Sent him to meet me, the Inds with him wer rogues, they had the night before Stold both his and Willards guns from under their heads, Capt. Lewis & party arrived at the Camp of those Indians at So Timely a period that the Inds. were allarmed & delivered up the guns &c. The tide meeting of me and the emence Swells from the main Ocean (imedeately in front of us) raised to Such a hite that I concluded to form a Camp on the highest Spot I could find in the marshey bottom, and proceed no further by water as the Coaste becomes verry dangerous for Crafts of the Size of our Canoes-and as the Ocian is imedeately in front and gives us an extensive view of it from Cape disapointment to Point addams, my Situation is in the upper part of Haley Bay S. 86° W. _____ miles Course five to Cape Disapt. and S. 35° W. Course _____ miles from point Addams

The River here at its mouth from Point addams to the enterance of Haley Bay above is _____ Miles or thereabouts, a large Isd. the lower point of which is immediately in the mouth above

4 Indians in a Canoe Came down with papto roots to Sell, for which they asked, blankets or robes, both of which we could not Spare I informed those Indians all of which understood Some English that if they Stole our guns &c the men would Certainly Shute them, I treated them with great distance, & the Sentinal which was over our Baggage allarmed them verry much, they all Promised not to take any thing, and if any thing was taken by the Squars & bad boys to return them &c. the waves became very high Evening fare & pleasent, our men all Comfortable in the Camps they have made of the boards they found at the Town above

[Clark, November 15, 1805] November 15th Friday 1805 Rained all the last night, this morning it became Calm and fair, I preposed Setting out, and ordered the Canoes Repared and loaded; before we could load our canoes the wind Sudenly Sprung up from the S. E and blew with Such violence, that we could not proceed in Safty with the loading. I proceeded to the point in an empty Canoe, and found that the waves dashed against the rocks with Such violence that I thought it unsave to Set out with the loaded Canoes- The Sun Shown untill 1 oClock P M which afford us time to Dry our bedding and examine the baggage which I found nearly all wet, Some of our pounded fish Spoiled in the wet; I examined the amunition and Caused all the arms to be put in order.

About 3 oClock the wind luled, and the river became calm, I had the canoes loaded in great haste and Set Out, from this dismal nitich where we have been confined for 6 days passed, without the possibility of proceeding on, returning to a better Situation, or get out to hunt, Scerce of Provisions, and torents of rain poreing on us all the time- proceeded on passed the blustering point below which I found a butifull Sand beech thro which runs a Small below the mouth of this Stream is a village of 36 houses uninhabited by anything except flees, here I met G. Shannon and 5 Indians. Shannon informed me that he met Capn. Lewis at an Indian Hut about 10 miles below who had Sent him back to meet me, he also told me the Indians were thievish, as the night before they had Stolen both his and Willards rifles from under their heads, that they Set out on their return and had not proceeded far up the beech before they met Capt Lewis, whose arival was at a timely moment and alarmed the Indians So that they instantly produced the Guns- I told those Indians who accompanied Shannon that they

Should not Come near us, and if any one of their nation Stold anything from us, I would have him Shot, which they understoot verry well. as the tide was Comeing in and the Seas became verry high imediately from the Ocian (imediately faceing us) I landed and formed a camp on the highest Spot I could find between the hight of the tides, and the Slashers in a Small bottom this I could plainly See would be the extent of our journey by water, as the waves were too high at any Stage for our Canoes to proceed any further down. in full view of the Ocian from Point Adams to Cape Disapointment, I could not See any Island in the mouth of this river as laid down by Vancouver. The Bay which he laies down in the mouth is imediately below me. This Bay we call Haleys bay from a favourate Trader with the Indians which they Say comes into this Bay and trades with them Course to Point adams is S. 35°W. about 8 miles To Cape Disapointment is S. 86°W. about 14 miles 4 Indians of the War-ki a cum nation Came down with pap-pa-too to Sell &c. The Indians who accompanied Shannon from the village below Speake a Different language from those above, and reside to the north of this place The Call themselves Chin nooks, I told those people that they had attempted to Steal 2 guns &c. that if any one of their nation stole any thing that the Sentinl. whome they Saw near our baggage with his gun would most certainly Shute them, they all promised not to tuch a thing, and if any of their womin or bad boys took any thing to return it imediately and Chastise them for it. I treated those people with great distance. our men all Comfortable in their Camps which they have made of boards from the old Village above. we made 3 miles to day.

[Clark, November 16, 1805] November 16th Saturday 1805 a fine morning cool the latter part of the night, I had all our articles of every discription examined, and found much wet, had all put out & dried, The 5 Indians Theves left me. I took a meriden altd. with Sextt. 50° 36 15 the Shakeing emige below- I Sent out Several hunters Some to kill fowl others to hunt deer or Elk. The Sea is fomeing and looks truly dismal to day, from the wind which blew to day from the S. W. an Indian Canoe passed down to day, loaded with roots &c. three Indians Came up from below I gave them Smoke but allowed then no kind of Priveleges what ever, they camped with the 4 which Came down yesterday, near us, The evening provd. Cloudy & I could make no lunar observations. one man Sick with a violent Cold, Caught by lying in his wet Clothes, Several nights Course from Stormey point to Cape Disapointment is _____ Miles, passd a Small Creek and an old village at 2 miles on the Stard Side a Small Creek at 1 mile we Encamped just above a Point in a Deep bay to the Stard. Side into which falls 2 Small rivers Std. Grat many Indians liveing on the Bay & those two rivers, the the Countrey on the Stard. Side high broken & thickly timbered, that on the Lard. at Some distance from Point Adms high and mountains on a Pinecal of a which is Snow at this time- near the Point is Low bottom land

our hunters and fowlers killd 2 Deer 1 Crane & 2 ducks, my Servt. York killed 2 Geese & 8 white, black and Speckle Brants, The White Brant, with part of their wings black is much the largest, the black brant is verry Small, a little larger than a large Duck- the deer pore but large

[Clark, November 16, 1805] November 16th Saturday 1805 Cool the latter part of the last night this morning Clear and butifull; I had all our articles of every discription examined and put out to Dry. The 5 Chin nooks left us I took a meridenal altitude with the Sextn. 50° 36' 15 which gave for Lattitude 46° 19' 11 1/10" North. I Sent out Several hunters and fowlers in pursute Elk, Deer, or fowls of any kind. wind hard from the S W The Waves high & look dismal indeed breaking with great fury on our beech an Indian canoe pass down to day loaded with Wap-pa-toe roots; Several Indians came up to day from below, I gave them Smoke but allowed them no kind of privilage whatever in the camp, they with the 4 which came down yesterday encamped a Short distance from us. The evening proved Cloudy and I could not take any Luner observations- One man Sick with a violent cold, Caught by laying in his wet leather Clothes for maney nights past.

The Countrey on the Stard Side above Haley Bay is high broken and thickley timbered on the Lard Side from Point Adams the Contrey appears low for 15 or 20 miles back to the mountains, a pinical of which now is Covered with Snow or hail, as the opposit is too far distant to be distinguished well, I Shall not attempt to describe any thing on that Side at present. our hunters and fowlers killed 2 Deer 1 Crain & 2 Ducks, and my man York killed 2 geese and 8 Brant, 3 of them white with a part of their wings black and much larger than the Grey brant which is a Sise larger than a Duck.

[Clark, November 17, 1805] November 17th Sunday 1805 a fair cool windey morning wind from the East. every tide which rises 8 feet 6 Inches at this place, comes in with high Swells which brake on the Sand Shore with great fury.

I Sent out 6 men to kill deer & fowls this morning at half past 1 oClock Capt. Lewis and his Party returned haveing around passd. Point Disapointment and Some distance on the main Ocian to the N W. Several Indians followed him & Soon after a canoe with wapto roots, & Lickorish boiled, which they gave as presents, in return for which we gave more than the worth to Satisfy, them a bad practice to receive a present of Indians, as they are never Satisfied in return. our hunters killed 3 Deer & th fowler 2 Ducks & q brant I Surveyed a little on the corse & made Some observns. The Chief of the nation below us Came up to See us the name of the nation is Chin-nook and is noumerous live principally on fish roots a fiew Elk and fowls. they are well armed with good Fusees. I directed all the men who wished to See more of the Ocean to Get ready to Set out with me on tomorrow day light. the following men expressed a wish to accompany me i'e Seri. Nat Pryor Serjt. J. Ordway, Jo. Fields R. Fields, Jo. Shannon, Jo Colter, William Bratten, Peter Wiser, Shabono & my Servant York. all others being well Contented with what part of the Ocean & its curiosities which Could be Seen from the vicinity of our Camp.

[Clark, November 17, 1805] November 17th Sunday 1805 A fair cool morning wind from the East. The tide rises at this place 8 feet 6 inches and comes in with great waves brakeing on the Sand beech on which we lay with great fury Six hunters out this morning in serch of Deer & fowl.

At half past 1 oClock Capt Lewis returned haveing travesed Haleys Bay to Cape Disapointment and the Sea Coast to the North for Some distance. Several Chinnook Indians followed (,apt L- and a Canoe came up with roots mats &c. to Sell. those Chinnooks made us a present of a rute boiled much resembling the common liquorice in taste and Size; in return for this root we gave more than double the value to Satisfy their craveing dispostn. It is a bad practice to receive a present from those Indians as they are never Satisfied for what they reive in return if ten time the value of the articles they gave. This Chin nook Nation is about 400 Souls inhabid the Countrey on the Small rivrs which run into the bay below us and on the Ponds to the N W of us, live principally on fish and roots, they are well armed with fusees and Sometimes kill Elk Deer and fowl. our hunters killed to day 3 Deer, 4 brant and 2 Ducks, and inform me they Saw Some Elk Sign. I directed all the men who wished to See more of the main Ocian to prepare themselves to Set out with me early on tomorrow morning. The principal Chief of the Chinnooks & his familey came up to See us this evening-

[Clark, November 18, 1805] Novr. 18th Monday 1805 a little Cloudy this morning I set out at day light with 10 men & my Sevent, Shabono, Sergt. Pryer odderway Jos. & R. Fields Shannon Colter, wiser, Lebiech & york proceeded on Down the Shore from the 1st point

At a run & Island near the Shore here the Traders ancher & trade? we passed at each point a Soft Clifts of yellow, brown & dark Soft Stones here Capt Lewis myself & Severl. of the men marked our names day of the month & by Land &c. &c. from this S. W. 3 miles to the Iner pt. of Cape Disapointmt passed a point & 2 Small nitches (Reuben Fields killed a Vulter) we found a Curious fiat fish Shaped like a turtle, with fins on each side, and a tale notched like a fish, the Internals on one Sid and tale & fins flat wise This fish Flownder has a white on one Side & lies flat to the Ground- passed from last hitch across to the ocean 1/2 a mile low land the Cape is a high Partly bald hill, founded on rock, I assencled a high Seperate bald hill Covered with long corse grass & Seperated from the hight of Country by a Slashey bottom 2 miles S. 60 W of the Cape- thence to a 2d Grassey pt is N. 50° W. 2 miles, Those hills are founded on rocks & the waves brake with great fury against them, the Coast is Sholey for Several miles of this Cape & for Some distance off to the N W a Sand bar in the mouth. Sholey Some distance out from the mouth The Coast from the Cape N W is open for a Short distance back then it becomes thick piney Countrey intersperced with ponds

Point addams is S 20° W about 20 miles the Course on that Side bears S 45 W. I cannot assertain the prosise Course of the Deep water in the mouth of the river, the Channel is but narrow. I proceeded on up above the 2d point and Encamped on the Shore above the high tide, evening Clear, for a Short time. Supd. on Brant and pounded fish men all Chearfull, express a Desire to winter near the falls this winter.

[Clark, November 18, 1805] November 18h Monday 1805 A little cloudy this morning I Set out with to men and my man York to the Ocian by land. i. e. Seijt. Ordway & Pryor, Jos. & Ru. Fields, Go. Shannon, W. Brattin, J. Colter, P. Wiser, W. Labieche & P. Shabono one of our interpreters & York. I Set out at Day light and proceeded on a Sandy beech from Cape Disapointment to a high point of a Mountn. which we shall call Clarke's Point of View beares S. 20° W. about 40 miles, point adams is verry low and is Situated within the direction between those two high points of land, the water appears verry Shole from off the mouth of the river for a great distance, and I cannot assertain the direction of the deepest Chanel, the Indians point nearest the opposit Side. the waves appear to brake with tremendious force in every direction quite across a large Sand bar lies within the mouth nearest to point Adams which is nearly covered at high tide. I suped on brant this evening with a little pounded fish. Some rain in the after part of the night. men appear much Satisfied with their trip beholding with estonishment the high waves dashing against the rocks & this emence ocian

[Clark, November 19, 1805] November 19th Tuesday 1805 began to rain a little before day and Continued raining untill 11 oClock I proceeded on thro emencely bad thickets & hills crossing 2 points to a 3rd on which we built a fire and Cooked a Deer which Jos. Field Killd. from this point I can See into a Deep bend in the coast to the N. E. for 10 miles. after Brackfast I proceeded on N. 20 E. 5 miles to Comcement a large Sand bar at a low part ponds a little off from the Coast here the high rockey hills end and a low marshey Countrey Suckceed. I proceeded up the Course N. 10° W. 4 miles & marked my name & the Day of the Month on a pine tree, the waters which Wash this Sand beach is tinged with a deep brown Colour for Some distance out. The Course Contd. is N. 20° W. low Coast and Sand beech, Saw a Dead Sturgen 10 feet long on the Sand, & the back bone of a Whale, as I conceived raind I then returned to the Cape & dined, Some curious Deer on this Course darker large boded Shorte legs Pronged horns & the top of the tale black under part white as usial passed a nitch in the rocks below into which falls a Stream, after Dinner I Set out on my return S. E. passed over a low ridge & thro a piney countrey 21 Vs miles to the Bay, thence up the Bay to the mouth of the Chen-nook River Crossed in the Canoe we had left there & Encamped on the upper Side The Hills in the point of this bay are not high, & imedeately below this River the present yellow Bluffs above the River and up for about 2 miles the land is low Slashey and Contains much drift wood, the Countrey up this Creek is low with Copse of high land or as I may Say elevated. The Buzzard which Ruben Fields killed diameter of one feather is- 11/4 & 1 Line from the tip of one to the tip of the other wing is 9 feet 0 Inches, from the point of the Bill to the tale is 3 feet 101/4 Ins. middle Toe 51/2 Inches, Toe nale 1 Inches wing feather 2 feet 1/2 In. Tale feathers 141/4 In. Head is 61/4 Inch long including the beek

[Clark, November 19, 1805] November 19th Tuesday 1805 a Cloudy rainey day proceeded up the Coast which runs from my camp 11/4 miles west of the iner extry of the Cape N. 20° W. 5 miles through a rugged hilley countrey thickly off the Sea coast to the Comencment of an extencive Sand beech which runs N. 10° W. to point Lewis about 20 miles distance. I proceeded up this coast 4 miles and marked my name on a low pine. and returned 3 miles back (The Countrey opsd. this Sand Coast is low and Slashey,) Crossed the point 2 miles to the bay and encamped on Chinnook river- See another book for perticulars

[Clark, November 19, 1805] Tuesday November the 19th 1805 I arose early this morning from under a wet blanket caused by a Shower of rain which fell in the latter part of the last night and Sent two men on a head with directions to proceed on near the Sea Coast and Kill Something for brackfast and that I Should follow my Self in about half an hour. after drying our blankets a little I Set out with a view to proceed near the Coast the direction of which induced me to conclude that at the distance of 8 or 10 miles, the Bay was at no great distance across. I overtook the hunters at about 3 miles, they had killed a Small Deer on which we brackfast it comened raining and Continud moderately untill 11 oClock A M.

after takeing a Sumptious brackfast of venison which was rosted on Stiks exposed to the fire, I proceeded on through ruged Country of high hills and Steep hollers on a course from the Cape N 20° W. 5 miles on a Direct line to the Commencement of a Sandy Coast which extended N. 10° W. from the top of the hill above the Sand Shore to a Point of high land distant near 20 miles. this point I have taken the Liberty of Calling after my particular friend Lewis- at the commencement of this Sand beech the high lands leave the Sea coast in a Direction to Chinnook river, and does not touch the Sea Coast again below point Lewis leaveing a low pondey countrey, maney places open with small ponds in which there is great numbr. of fowl I am informed that the Chinnook Nation inhabit this low countrey and live in large wood houses on a river which passes through this bottom Parrilal to the Sea coast and falls into the Bay

I proceeded on the Sandy Coast 4 miles, and marked my name on a Small pine, the Day of the month & year, &c. and returned to the foot of the hill, from which place I intended to Strike across to The Bay, I saw a Sturgeon which had been thrown on Shore and left by the tide 10 feet in length, and Several joints of the back bone of a whale which must have foundered on this part of the Coast. after Dineing on the remains of our Small Deer I proceeded through over a land S E with Some Ponds to the bay distance about 2 miles, thence up to the mouth of Chinnook river 2 miles, crossed this little river in the Canoe we left at its mouth and Encamped on the upper Side in an open Sandy bottom- The hills next to the bay Cape disapointment to a Short distance up the Chinnook river is not verry high thickly Coverd. with different Species of pine &c. maney of which are large, I observed in maney places pine of 3 or 4 feet through growing on the bodies of large trees which had fallen down, and covered with moss and yet part Sound. The Deer of this Coast differ materially from our Common deer in a much as they are much darker deeper bodied Shorter ledged horns equally branched from the beem the top of the tail black from the rute to the end Eyes larger and do not lope but jump-.

[Clark, November 20, 1805] Novr. 20 Wednesday 1805 Some rain last night despatchd. 3 men to hunt Jo. Fields & Cotter to hunt Elk & Labich to kill some Brant for our brackfast The Morning Cleared up fare and we proceeded on by the Same rout we went out, at the River we found no Indians. made a raft & Ruben Fields Crossed and took over a Small Canoe which lay at the Indian Cabin- This Creek is at this time of high tide 300 yards wide & the marshes for Some distance up the Creek Covered with water. not an Indian to be Seen near the Creek. I proceeded on to Camp & on my way was over taken by 3 Indians one gave us Sturgeon & Wapto roots to eate I met Several parties on way all of them appeared to know me & was distant, found all well at Camp, maney Indians about one of which had on a robe made of 2 Sea Orter Skins. Capt Lewis offered him many things for his Skins with others a blanket, a coat all of which he refused we at length purchased it for a belt of Blue Beeds which the Squar had- The tide being out we walked home on the beech

[Clark, November 20, 1805] Wednesday November the 20th 1805 Some rain last night dispatched Labiech to kill Some fowl for our brackfast he returned in about 2 hours with 8 large Ducks on which we brackfast I proceeded on to the enterance of a Creek near a Cabin no person being at this cabin and 2 Canoes laying on the opposit Shore from us, I deturmined to have a raft made and Send a man over for a canoe, a Small raft was

Soon made, and Reuben Fields Crossed and brought over a Canoe- This Creek which is the outlet of a number of ponds, is at this time (high tide) 300 yds wide- I proceeded on up the Beech and was overtaken by three Indians one of them gave me Some dried Sturgeon and a fiew wappato roots, I employd Those Indians to take up one of our Canoes which had been left by the first party that Came down, for which Service I gave them each a fishing hook of a large Size- on my way up I met Several parties of Chinnooks which I had not before Seen they were on their return from our Camp. all those people appeard to know my deturmonation of keeping every individual of their nation at a proper distance, as they were guarded and resurved in my presence &c. found maney of the Chin nooks with Capt. Lewis of whome there was 2 Cheifs Com com mo ly & Chil-lar-la-wil to whome we gave Medals and to one a flag. one of the Indians had on a roab made of 2 Sea Otter Skins the fur of them were more butifull than any fur I had ever Seen both Capt. Lewis & my Self endeavored to purchase the roab with different articles at length we precured it for a belt of blue beeds which the Squar-wife of our interpreter Shabono wore around her waste. in my absence the hunters had killed Several Deer and fowl of different kinds

[Clark, November 21, 1805]
November 21st Thursday 1805
a Cloudy morning most of the Indians left us, The nation on the opposit
Side is Small & Called Clap-soil, Their great chief name Stil-la-sha
The nation liveing to the North is Called Chieltz. The chief is name
Malaugh not large nation and wore his beards as informed by the Inds.
In my absence the hunters Kild. 7 Deer, 4 brants & a Crane.

Great numbers of the dark brant passing Southerley, the white yet Stationary, no gees & Swan to be Seen. The wind blew hard from the S. E. which with the addition of the flood tide raised emence Swells & waves which almost entered our Encampment morng. dark & Disagreeable, a Supriseing Climent. We have not had One cold day Since we passed below the last falls or great Shute & Some time before the Climent is temperate, and the only change we have experienced is from fair weather to rainey windey weather- I made a chief & gave a medel this man is name Tow-wall and appears to have Some influence with the nation and tells me he lives at the great Shute-we gave the Squar a Coate of Blue Cloth for the belt of Blue Beeds we gave for the Sea otter Skins purchased of an Indian. at 12 oClock it began to rain, and continued moderately all day, Some wind from the S. E., waves too high for us to proceed on our homeward bound journey. Lattitude of this place is 46° 19' 11 1/10" North Several Indians and Squars came this evening I beleave for the purpose of gratifying the passions of our men, Those people appear to View Sensuality as a necessary evile, and do not appear to abhore this as Crime in the unmarried females. The young women Sport openly with our men, and appear to receive the approbation of their friends & relations for So doing maney of the women are handsom.

They are all low both men and women, I saw the name of J. Bowmon marked or picked on a young Squars left arm. The women of this nation Pick their legs in different figures as an orpiment. they were their hair loose, Some trinkets in their ears, none in the nose as those above, their Dress is as follows, i,e the men, were a roabe of either the skins of _____ a Small fured animal, & which is most common, or the Skins of the Sea orter, Loon, Swan, Beaver, Deer, Elk, or blankets either red, blu, or white, which roabes cover the sholders arms & body, all other parts are nakd.

The women were a Short peticoat of the iner bark of the white Ceder or Arber Vita, which hang down loose in Strings nearly as low as the knee, with a Short Robe which fall half way down the Thigh. no other part is Covered. The orniments are beeds, Blue principally, large Brass wire around their rists Som rings, and many men have Salors Clothes, many have good fusees & Ball & Powder. The women ware a String of Something curious tied tight above the anckle, all have large Swelled legs & thighs The men Small legs & thighs and Generally badly made- They live on Elk Deer fowls, but principally fish and roots of 3 Kinds, Lickorish, Wapto &c. The women have more privalages than is Common amongst Indians- Pocks & Venerial is Common amongst them I Saw one man & one woman who appeared to be all in Scabs, & Several men with the venereal, their other Disorders and the remides for them I could not lern we divided Some ribin between the men of our party to bestow on their favourite Lasses, this plan to Save the knives & more valueable articles.

Those people gave me Sturgion Salmon & wapto roots, & we bought roots, Some mats &c. &c. for which we were obliged to give emence prices- we also purchased a kind of Cranberry which the Indians Say the geather in the low lands, off of Small either vines or bushes just abov the ground- we also purchased hats made of Grass &c. of those Indians, Some very handsom mats made of flags-Some fiew curious baskets made of a Strong weed & willow or _____ Splits-, also a Sweet Soft black root, about th Sise & Shape of a Carrot, this root they Value verry highly- The Wapto root is Scerce, and highly valued by those people, this root they roste in hot ashes like a potato and the outer Skin peals off, tho this is a trouble they Seldom perform.

[Clark, November 21, 1805] Thursday November 21st 1805 a cloudy morning most of the Chinnooks leave our Camp and return home, great numbers of the dark brant passing to the South, the white Brant have not yet commenced their flight. The wind blew hard from the S. E. which with the addition of the flood tide raised verry high waves which broke with great violence against the Shore throwing water into our Camp- the fore part of this day Cloudy at 12 oClock it began to rain and Continud all day moderately, Several Indians Visit us to day of differant nations or Bands Some of the Chiltz Nation who reside on the Sea Coast near Point Lewis, Several of the Clotsops who reside on the opposit Side of the Columbia imediately opposit to us, and a Chief from the Grand rapid to whome we gave a Medal.

An old woman & wife to a Cheif of the Chinnooks came and made a Camp near ours She brought with her 6 young Squars I believe for the purpose of gratifying the passions of the men of our party and receving for those indulgiences Such Small as She (the old woman) thought proper to accept of, Those people appear to view Sensuality as a Necessary evel, and do not appear to abhor it as a Crime in the unmarried State- The young females are fond of the attention of our men and appear to meet the sincere approbation of their friends and connections, for thus obtaining their favours; the womin of the Chinnook Nation have handsom faces low and badly made with large legs & thighs which are generally Swelled from a Stopage of the circulation in the feet (which are Small) by maney Strands of Beeds or curious Strings which are drawn tight around the leg above the anckle, their legs are also picked with different figures, I Saw on the left arm of a Squar the following letters,. Bowmon, all those are Considered by the natives of this quarter as handsom deckerations, and a woman without those deckorations is Considered as among the lower Class they ware their hair lose hanging over their back and Sholders maney have blue beeds threaded & hung from different parts of their ears and about ther neck and around their wrists, their dress other wise is prosisely like that of the Nation of Wa ci a cum as already discribed. a Short roab, and tissue or kind of peticoat of the bark of Cedar which fall down in Strings as low as the knee behind and not So low before maney of the men have blankets of red blue or Spotted Cloth or the common three & 2 1/2 point blankets, and Salors old Clothes which they appear to prise highly, they also have robes of Sea Otter, Beaver, Elk, Deer, fox and Cat common to this countrey, which I have never Seen in the U States. They also precure a roabe from the nativs above, which is made of the Skins of a Small animal about the Size of a Cat, which is light and dureable and highly prized by those people- the greater numbers of the men of the Chinnooks have Guns and powder and Ball- The Men are low homely and badly made, Small Crooked legs large feet, and all of both Sects have flattened heads- The food of this nation is principally fish & roots the fish they precure from the river by the means of nets and gigs, and the Salmon which run up the Small branches together with what they collect drifted up on the Shores of the Sea coast near to where they live

The roots which they use are Several different kinds, the Wappato which they precure from the nativs above, a black root which they call Shaw-na tah que & the wild licquorish is the most Common, they also kill a fiew Elk Deer & fowl- maney of the Chinnooks appear to have venerious and pustelus disorders. one woman whome I saw at the beech appeared all over in Scabs and ulsers &c.

we gave to the men each a pece of ribin We purchased Cramberies Mats verry netely made of flags and rushes, Some roots, Salmon and I purchased a hat made of Splits & Strong grass, which is made in the fashion which was common in the U States two years ago also Small baskets to hold Water made of Split and Straw, for those articles we gave high prices-.

[Clark, November 22, 1805] Novr. 22nd Friday 1805 Some little rain all the last night with wind, before day the wind increased to a Storm from the S. S. E. and blew with violence throwing the water of the river with emence waves out of its banks almost over whelming us in water, O! how horriable is the day- This Storm Continued all day with equal violence accompanied with rain, Several Indians about us, nothing killed the waves & brakers flew over our Camp, one Canoe Split by the Tossing of those waves- we are all Confined to our Camp and wet. purchased some Wapto roots for which was given, brass armbans & rings of which the Squars were fond. we find the Indians easy ruled and kept in order by a Stricter indifference towards them

[Clark, November 22, 1805] Friday November 22nd 1805 a moderate rain all the last night with wind, a little before Day light the wind which was from the S S. E. blew with Such violence that we wer almost overwhelmned with water blown from the river, this Storm did not Sease at day but blew with nearly equal violence throughout the whole day accompaned with rain. O! how horriable is the day waves brakeing with great violence against the Shore throwing the Water into our Camp &c. all wet and Confind to our Shelters, Several Indian men and women Crouding about the mens Shelters to day, we purchased a fiew wappato roots for which we gave armbans, & rings to the old Squar, those roots are equal to the Irish potato, and is a tolerable Substitute for bread

The threat which I made to the men of this nation whome I first Saw, and an indifference towards them, is I am fulley Convinced the Cause of their Conducting themselves with great propriety towards ourselves & Party.

[Clark, November 23, 1805] November 23rd Saturday 1805 The Cloudy and Calm, a moderate rain the greater part of the last night, Sent out men to hunt this morning and they Killed 3 Bucks, rained at intervales all day. I marked my name the Day of the month & year on a Beech trees & (By Land) Capt Lewis Branded his and the men all marked their nams on trees about the Camp. one Indian Came up from their village on some lakes near Haleys bay. In the Evening 7 Indians of the Clatt Sopp nation, opposit Came over, they brought with them 2 Sea orter Skins, for which the asked Such high prices we were uneabled to purchase, without reduceing our Small Stock of merchindize on which we have to depend in part for a Subsistance on our return home, Kiled 4 brant & 3 Ducks to day

[Clark, November 23, 1805] Saturday November 22rd 1805. A calm Cloudy morning, a moderate rain the greater part of the last night, Capt Lewis Branded a tree with his name Date &c. I marked my name the Day & year on a Alder tree, the party all Cut the first letters of their names on different trees in the bottom. our hunters killed 3 Bucks, 4 Brant & 3 Ducks to day.

in the evening Seven indians of the Clot Sop Nation Came over in a Canoe, they brought with them 2 Sea otter Skins for which they asked blue beads &c. and Such high pricies that we were unable to purchase them without reducing our Small Stock of merchindize, on which we depended for Subcistance on our return up this river-mearly to try the Indian who had one of those Skins, I offered him my Watch, handkerchief a bunch of red beads and a dollar of the American Coin, all of which he refused and demanded "ti-a, co-mo-shack" which is Chief beads and the most common blue beads, but fiew of which we have at this time

This nation is the remains of a large nation destroyed by the Small pox or Some other which those people were not acquainted with, they Speak the Same language of the Chinnooks and resemble them in every respect except that of Stealing, which we have not Cought them at as yet.

[Clark, November 24, 1805] November 24th Sunday 1805 Several of the Chenn nook N. Came, one of them brought an Sea orter Skin for which we gave Some blue Beeds- This day proved to be fair and we dried our wet articles bedding &c. The hunters killed only 1 brant no Deer or any thing else

The old chief of Chinn-nook nation and Several men & women Came to our camp this evening & Smoked the pipe

Serjt J. Ordway Cross & examine S Serjt. N. Pryor do do S Sgt. P. Gass do do S Jo. Shields proceed to Sandy R

Go. Shannon Examn. Cross falls T. P. Howard do do falls P. Wiser do do S. R J. Collins do do S. R Jo Fields do do up Al. Willard do do up R Willard do do up J. Potts do do falls R. Frasure do do up Wm. Bratten do do up R. Fields do do falls J. B. Thompson do do up J. Colter do do up H. Hall do do S. R. Labeech do do S R Peter Crusatte do do S R J. B. Depage do do up Shabono - - - S. Guterich do do falls W. Werner do do up Go. Gibson do do up Jos. Whitehouse do do up Geo Drewyer Examn other side falls McNeal do do up York " " lookout

falls Sandy River lookout up 6 10 12

Janey in favour of a place where there is plenty of Potas.

Cp L Proceed on to morrow & examine The other side if good hunting to winter there, as Salt is an objt. if not to proceed on to Sandy it is probable that a vestle will come in this winter, & that by proceeding on at any distance would not inhance our journey in passing the Rockey mountains, &c.

W C. In favour of proceding on without delay to the opposit Shore & there examine, and find out both the disposition of the Indians, & probibilaty of precureing Subsistance, and also enquire if the Tradeing vestles will arrive before the time we Should depart in the Spring, and if the Traders, Comonly arive in a Seasonable time, and we Can Subsist without a depends. on our Stores of goods, to Continue as the Climent would be more favourable on the Sea Coast for our naked men than higher up the Countrey where the Climate must be more Severe- The advantage of the arival of a vestle from whome we Can precure goods will be more than an over ballance, for the bad liveing we Shall have in liveing on Pore deer & Elk we may get in this neighbourhood. If we Cannot subsist on the above terms to proceed on, and make Station Camps, to neighbourhood of the Frendly village near the long narrows & delay untill we Can proceed up the river. Salt water I view as an evil in as much as it is not helthy- I am also of opinion that one two or three weeks Exemination on the opposide if the propects are any wise favourable, would not be too long

Variation of the Compass is 16° East

[Clark, November 24, 1805] Sunday November 24th 1805. A fair morning Sent out 6 hunters, and we proceeded to make the following observations a Chief and Several men of the Chin nook nation Came to Smoke with us this evening one of the men brought a Small Sea otter Skin for which we gave Some blue beads- this day proved fair which gave us an oppertunity of drying our wet articles, bedding &c. &c. nothing killed to day except one Brant. the variation of the Compass is 16° East.

being now determined to go into Winter quarters as Soon as possible, as a convenient Situation to precure the Wild animals of the forest which must be our dependance for Subsisting this Winter, we have every reason to believe that the nativs have not provisions Suffient for our Consumption, and if they had, their price's are So high that it would take ten times as much to purchase their roots & Dried fish as we have in our possesion, encluding our Small remains of merchindz and Clothes &c. This Certinly enduces every individual of the party to make diligient enquiries of the nativs the part of the Countrey in which the wild Animals are most plenty. They generaly agree that the most Elk is on the opposit Shore, and that the greatest numbers of Deer is up the river at Some distance above.

The Elk being an animal much larger than Deer, easier to kiled better meat (in the winter when pore) and Skins better for the Clothes of our party; added to-, a convenient Situation to the Sea coast where we Could make Salt, and a probibility of vessels Comeing into the mouth of Columbia ("which the Indians inform us would return to trade with them in 3 months") from whome we might precure a fresh Supply of Indian trinkets to purchase provisions on our return home; together with the Solicitations of every individual, except one of our party induced us Conclude to Cross the river and examine the opposit Side, and if a Suffcent quantity of Elk could probebly be precured to fix on a Situation as convenient to the Elk & Sea Coast as we Could find- added to the above advantagies in being near the Sea Coast one most Strikeing one occurs to me i e, the Climate which must be from every appearance much milder than that above the 1st range of Mountains, The Indians are Slightly Clothed and give an account of but little Snow, and the weather which we have experiened Since we arrived in the neighbourhood of the Sea Coast has been verry warm, and maney of the fiew days past disagreeably So. if this Should be the Case it will most Certainly be the best Situation of our naked party dressed as they are altogether in leather.

[Clark, November 25, 1805] November 25th Munday 1805 a fine day Several Indians Come up from below, we loaded and Set out up the river, and proceeded on to the Shallow Bay, landed to dine, The Swells too high to cross the river, agreeabley to our wish which is to examine if game Can be precured Suffcent for us to winter on that Side, after dinner which was on Drid pounded fish we proceeded on up on the North Side to near the place of our Encampment of the 7th Instant and encamped after night The evening cloudy wind of to day Generally from the E S. E, Saw from near of last Campment Mount Ranier bearing _____

[Clark, November 25, 1805] Monday 25th November 1805 The Wind being high rendered it impossible for us to Cross the river from our Camp, we deturmind to proceed on up where it was narrow, we Set out early accompanied by 7 Chit Sops for a fiew miles, they left us and Crossed the river through emence high waves; we Dined in the Shallow Bay on Dried pounded fish, after which we proceeded on near the North Side of the Columbia, and encamp a little after night near our Encampment of the 7th instant near a rock at Some distance in the river. evening Cloudy the Winds of to day is generally E. S. E which was a verry favourable point for us as the highlands kept it from us Mt. St. Hilians Can be Seen from the mouth of this river.

[Clark, November 26, 1805] November 26th Tuesday 1805 Cloudy and Some rain this morning at daylight wind blew from the E N. E, we Set out and proceeded on up on the North Side of this great river to a rock in the river from thence we Crossed to the lower point of an _____ Island passed between 2 Islands to the main Shore, and proceeded down the South Side, passed 2 Inlets & halted below the 2d at a Indian village of 9 large houses- those Indians live on an emenence behind a Island or a Channel of the river not more than 300 yds wide, they live on fish & Elk and Wapto roots, of which we bought a few at a high price they Call them Selves Cat-tar-bets description

We proceeded on about 8 miles and Encamped in a deep bend to the South, we had not been Encamped long ere 3 Indians Came in a Canoe to trade the Wapto roots- we had rain all the day all wet and disagreeable a bad place to Camp all around this great bend is high land thickly timbered brushey & almost impossible to penetrate we Saw on an Island below the village a place of deposit for the dead in Canoes

Great numbers of Swan Geese Brant Ducks & Gulls in this great bend which is Crouded with low Islands covered with weeds grass &c. and overflowed every flood tide The people of the last village is-_____ they ask emence prices for what they have to Sel Blue Beeds is their great trade they are fond of Clothes or blankits of Blue red or brown We are now decending to see if a favourable place should offer on the So Side to winter &c.

from a high Point opsd. a high Isd down the South Side is S. 30° W 6 mis to a point of low land opsd. upr. pt of Isd. passed lowr. pt. 1st Isd. marshey. at the upr. pt. Of 2 low Isd. opsd. each other at 4 miles

[Clark, November 26, 1805] Tuesday 26th November 1805 Cloudy and Some rain this morning from 6 oClock. wind from the E. N. E, we Set out out early and crossed a Short distance above the rock out in the river, & between Some low marshey Islands to the South Side of the Columbia at a low bottom about 3 miles below Point Samuel and proceeded near the South Side leaveing the Seal Islands to our right and a marshey bottom to the left 5 Miles to the Calt-har-mar Village of 9 large wood houses on a handsom elivated Situation near the foot of a Spur of the high land behind a large low Island Seperated from the Southerly Shore by a Chanel of about 200 yards Wide, This nation appear to differ verry little either in language, Customs dress or appearance from the Chin nooks & War-ci a cum live principally on fish and pappato they have also other roots, and Some Elk meat.

We purchased Some green fish, & wap pa to for which we gave Imoderate pricie's. after dining on the fresh fish which we purchased, we proceeded on through a Deep bend to the South and encamped under a high hill, where we found much difficuelty in precureing wood to burn, as it was raining hard, as it had been the greater part of the day. Soon after we encamped 3 Indians of the last town Came in a Canoe with wappato roots to Sell to us Some of which we purchased with fish hooksfrom the Village quite around this bend to the West the land is high and thickly timbered with pine balsom &c. a Short distance below the Calt har mer Village on the Island which is Opposit I observed Several Canoes Scaffold in which Contained their dead, as I did not examine this mode of deposing the dead, must refer it to a discription hereafter.

[Clark, November 27, 1805] November 27th Wednesday 1805 Some rain all the last night & this morning at day light 3 Canoes and 11 men Came down with roots meat, Skins &c. to Sill, they asked Such high prices we were unable to purchase any thing, and as we were about Setting out, discovered that one of those Indians had Stole an ax, we Serched and found it under the roabe of one man whome we Shamed verry much

we proceeded on, around Point William th Swells became high and rained so hard we Concluded to halt and dry our Selves, Soon after our landing the wind rose from the East and blew hard accompanied with rain, this rain obliged us to unload & draw up our Canoes, one of which was Split to feet before we got her out of the river, this place the Peninsoley is about 50 yards and 3 miles around this point of Land. water Salt below not Salt above.

[Clark, November 27, 1805] Wednesday 27th November 1805 Rained all the last night and this morning it Continues moderatelyat day light 3 Canoes and 11 Indians Came from the Village with roots mats, Skins &c. to Sell, they asked Such high prices that we were unable to purchase any thing of them, as we were about to Set out missed one of our axes which was found under an Indians roab I shamed this fellow verry much and told them they should not proceed with us- we proceded on between maney Small Islands passing a Small river of _____ yds wide which the Indians Call _____ and around a verry remarkable point which projects about 1 1/2 Miles directly towards the Shallow bay the isthmus which joins it to the main land is not exceding 50 yards and about 4 Miles around. we call this Point William

below this point the waves became So high we were Compelled to land unload and traw up the Canoes, here we formed a Camp on the neck of Land which joins Point William to the main at an old indian hut. The rain Continued hard all day we are all Wet and disagreeable. one Canoe Split before we Got her out of the Water 2 feet- The water at our Camp Salt that above the isthmus fresh and fine

[Clark, November 28, 1805] November 28th Thursday 1805 Wind Shifted about to the S. W. and blew hard accompanied with hard rain all last night, we are all wet bedding and Stores, haveing nothing to keep our Selves or Stores dry, our Lodge nearly worn out, and the pieces of Sales & tents So full of holes & rotten that they will not keep any thing dry, we Sent out the most of the men to drive the point for deer, they Scattered through the point; Some Stood on the pensolu, we Could find no deer, Several hunters attempted to penetrate the thick woods to the main South Side without Suckcess, the Swan & gees wild and Cannot be approached, and wind to high to go either back or forward, and we have nothing to eate but a little Pounded fish which we purchasd. at the Great falls, This is our present Situation,! truly disagreeable. aded to this the robes of our Selves and men are all rotten from being Continually wet, and we Cannot precure others, or blankets in their places. about 12 oClock the wind Shifted about to the N. W and blew with great violence for the remainder of the day at maney times it blew for 15 or 20 minits with Such violence that I expected every moment to See trees taken up by the roots, Some were blown down. Those Squals were Suckceeded by rain, ! O how Tremendious is the day. This dredfull wind and rain Continued with intervales of fair weather, the greater part of the evening and night.

[Clark, November 28, 1805] Thursday 28th November 1805 Wind Shifted about to the S. W. and blew hard accompanied with hard rain. rained all the last night we are all wet our bedding and Stores are also wet, we haveing nothing which is Sufficient to keep ourselves bedding or Stores dry Several men in the point hunting deer without Suckcess, the Swan and brant which are abundant Cannot be approached Sufficently near to be killed, and the wind and waves too high to proceed on to the place we expect to find Elk, & we have nothing to eate except pounded fish which we brought from the Great falls, this is our present Situation; truly disagreeable. about 12 oClock the wind Shifted around to the N W. and blew with Such violence that I expected every moment to See trees taken up by the roots, maney were blown down. This wind and rain Continued with Short intervales all the latter part of the night. O! how disagreeable is our Situation dureing this dreadfull weather.

[Lewis, November 29, 1805] November 29th 1805. the wind being so high the party were unable to proceed with the perogues. I determined therefore to proceed down the river on it's E. side in surch of an eligible place for our winters residence and accordingly set out early this morning in the small canoe accompanyed by 5 men. drewyer R. Fields, Shannon, Colter & labiesh. proceeded along the coast.

send out the hunters they killed 4 deer 2 brant a goos and seven ducks, it rained upon us by showers all day. left three of these deer and took with us one encamped at an old Indian hunting lodge which afforded us a tolerable shelter from the rain, which continued by intervales throughout the night.

[Clark, November 29, 1805] November 29th Friday 1805 Blew hard and rained the greater part of the last night and this morning, Capt Lewis and 5 men Set out in our Small Indian canoe (which is made in the Indian fashion Calculated ride the waves) down the South Side of the river to the place the Indians informed us by Signs that numbers of Elk were to be found near the river- The Swells and waves being too high for us to proceed down in our large Canoes, in Safty

I Sent out two hunters to hunt deer, & one to hunt fowl, all the others employed in drying their leather and prepareing it for use, as but fiew of them have many other Clothes to boste of at this time, we are Smoked verry much in this Camp The Shore on the Side next the Sea is Covered with butifull pebble of various Colours- our diat at this time and for Severall days past is the dried pounded fish we purchased at the falls boiled in a little Salt water

[Clark, November 29, 1805] Friday 29th of November 1805 The wind and rain Continued all the last night, this morning much more moderate. the waves Still high and rain Continues. Capt Lewis and 5 hunters Set out in our Indian Canoe (which is Calculated to ride wave) dow to the place we expected to find Elk from the Inds. information, they pointed to a Small Bay which is yet below us- I Sent out 2 men to hunt Deer which I expected might be on the open hill Sides below, another to hunt fowl in the deep bend above the point, all the others engaged drying their leather before the fire, and prepareing it for usethey haveing but fiew other Species of Clothing to ware at this time

The winds are from Such points that we cannot form our Camp So as to provent the Smoke which is emencely disagreeable, and painfull to the eyes- The Shore below the point at our Camp is formed of butifull pebble of various colours. I observe but fiew birds of the Small kind, great numbers of wild fowls of Various kinds, the large Buzzard with white wings, grey and bald eagle's, large red tailed Hawks, ravens & Crows in abundance, the blue Magpie, a Small brown bird which frequents logs & about the roots of trees- Snakes, Lizards, Small bugs, worms, Spiders, flyes & insects of different kinds are to be Seen in abundance at this time.

[Lewis, November 30, 1805] November 30th 1805. cloudy morning set out before sun rise and continued our rout up the bey

Sent out three men to examin the country to the S. & W. they returned after about 2 hours and informed me that the wood was so thick and obstructed by marrasses & lakes that they were unable to proceed to the ocean which could not be at any considerable distance fom the apparent sound of the waves breaking on the Coast. we now returned and asscended the inlet which we had last passd no fresh appearance of Elk or deer in our rout so far. asscend the inlet as we intended about 1 m. found it became much smaller and that it did not keep it's direction to the high land which boar S. 10 W. but inclined West. therefore returned to the large arm of the bay which we passed this morning. here we expect to meet with the Clat-sop Indians, who have tantilized us with there being much game in their neighbourhood. this information in fact was the cause of my present resurch, for where there is most game is for us the most eligible winter station.- continued our rout up the large arm of the bay about 6 miles and encamped on the Stard. side on the highland. the water was quite sweet. therefore concluded that it must be supplyed from a large crick. at our camp it is 120 yds. wide, tho it gets narrower above. it rained but little on us today tho it was cloudy generally.- Wind from N. E.- saw a great abundance of fowls, brant, large geese, white brant sandhill Cranes, common blue crains, cormarants, haulks, ravens, crows, gulls and a great variety of ducks, the canvas back, duckinmallard, black and white diver, brown duck- &c &c

[Clark, November 30, 1805] November 30th Saturday 1805 Some rain and hail with intervales of fair weather for 1 and 2 hours dureing the night and untill 9 oClock this morning at which time it Cleared up fair and the Sun Shown, I Send 5 men in a Canoe in the Deep bend above the Peninsulear to hunt fowles, & 2 men in the thick woods to hunt Elk had all our wet articles dried & the men all employed dressing their Skins, I observe but few birds in this Countrey of the Small kindsgreat numbers of wild fowl, The large Buzzard with white under their wings Grey & Bald eagle large red tailed hawk, ravins, Crows, & a small brown bird which is found about logs &c. but fiew small hawks or other smaller birds to be seen at this time Snakes, Lizzards, Snales bugs worms Spiders, flies & insects of different kinds are to be Seen in plenty at this time. The Squar, gave me a piece of Bread to day made of Some flower She had Cearfully kept for her child, and had unfortunately got wet The hunters killed only 3 hawks, saw 3 Elk but Could not git a Shot at them, The fowlers, killed 3 black ducks, with white Sharp bills, a brown Spot in their foward, Some white under the tail, which Short, and a fiew of the tips of the wing feathers white, Their toes are long Seperated and flaped, no Craw, keep in emence large flocks in the Shallow waters & feed on Grass &c.- Several men Complaining of being unwell to day- a Broock comes in to the bend above the 1st point above, and a river falls in the next nitch above this river is Small,- I observe rose bushes Pine, a kind of ash a Species of Beech and a Species of Maple, in addition to the pine Lorrel and under groth Common to the woods in this Lower Countrey the hills are not high & Slope to the river

[Clark, November 30, 1805] Saturday 30th of November 1805 Some rain and hail with intervales of fair weather for the Space of one or two hours at a time dureing the night untill 9 oClock this morning, at which time it Cleared away and the Sun Shewn for _____ hours, Several men out hunting I Send 5 men in the bend above to hunt fowl &c. in a Canoe, employ all the others in drying our wet articles by the fire Several men Complain of a looseness and gripeing which I contribute to the diet, pounded fish mixed with Salt water, I derect that in future that the party mix the pounded fish with fresh water- The Squar gave me a piece of bread made of flour which She had reserved for her child and carefully Kept untill this time, which has unfortunately got wet, and a little Sour- this bread I eate with great Satisfaction, it being the only mouthfull I had tasted for Several months past. my hunters killed three Hawks, which we found fat and delicious, they Saw 3 Elk but Could not get a Shot at them. The fowlers killed 3 black Ducks with Sharp White beeks keep in large flocks & feed on Grass, they have no Craw and their toes are Seperate, Common in the U. States

The Chinnooks Cath ldh mah & others in this neighbourhood bury their dead in their Canoes. for this purpose 4 pieces of Split timber are Set erect on end, and sunk a fiew feet in the ground, each brace having their flat Sides opposit to each other and Sufficiently far assunder to admit the width of the Canoe in which the dead are to be deposited; through each of those perpindicular posts, at the hight of 6 feet a mortice is Cut, through which two bars of wood are incerted; on those Cross bars a Small Canoe is placed, in which the body is laid after beaing Carefully roled in a robe of Some dressed Skins; a paddle is also deposited with them; a larger Canoe is now reversed, overlaying and imbracing the Small one, and resting with its gunnals on the Cross bars; one or more large mats of flags or rushes are then rold. around the Canoe and the whole Securely lashed with a long Cord usially made of the bark of the arbar vita or white Cedar. on the Cross bars which Support the Canoes is frequently hung or laid various articles of Clothing Culinary utensils &c. we cannot understand them Sufficiently to make any enquiries relitive to their religious opinions, from their depositing Various articles with their dead, beleve in a State of future ixistance.

I walked on the point and observed rose bushes different Species of pine, a Spcies of ash, alder, a Species of wild Crab Loral and Several Species of under Broth Common to this lower part of the Columbia river- The hills on this Coast rise high and are thickly covered with lofty pine maney of which are 10 & 12 feet through and more than 200 feet high. hills have a Steep assent.

[Lewis, December 1, 1805] December 1st 1805 Cloudy morning wind from the S. E. sent out the men to hunt and examin the country, they soon returned all except Drewyer and informed me that the wood was so thick it was almost impenetrable and that there was but little appearance of game; they had seen the track of one deer only and a few small grey squirrels. these suirrels are about the size of the red squirrel of the lakes and eastern Atlantic States, their bellies are of a redish yellow, or tanners ooze colour the tale flat and as long as the body eyes black and moderately large back and sides of a greyish brown the brier with a brown bark and three laves which put forth at the extremety of the twigs like the leaves of the blackbury brier, tho is a kind of shrub and rises sometimes to the hight of 10 feet the green brier yet in leaf; the ash with a remarkable large leaf; the large black alder. the large elder with skey blue buries. the broad leave shrub which grows something like the quill wood but has no joints, the leaf broad and deeply indented the bark peals hangs on the stem and is of a yelowish brown colour. the seven bark is also found here as is the common low cramburry-there is a wild crab apple which the natives eat this growth differs but little in appearance from that of the wild crab of the Atlantic States. but the fruit consists of little oval hurries which grow in clusters at the extremities of the twigs like the black haws. the fruit is of a brown colour, oval form and about double as large as the black haw; the rind is smoth and tough somewhat hard; the seed is like that of the wild crab and nearly as large; the pulp is soft of a pale yellow coulour; and when the fruit has been touched by the frost is not unpleasant, being an agreeable assed. the tree which bears a red burry in clusters of a round form and size of a red haw. the leaf like that of the small magnolia, and brark smoth and of a brickdust red coulour it appears to be of the evergreen kind.- half after one oclock Drewyer not yet arrived. heard him shoot 5 times just above us and am in hopes he has fallen in with a gang of elk.

[Clark, December 1, 1805] December 1st Sunday 1805 Cloudy windey morning wind from the East, Sent out 2 hunters in the woods, I intended to take 5 men in a Canoe and hunt the marshey Islands above, found the wind too high & returned to partake of the dried fish, The day Some what Cooler than usial, but Scercely perceveable. began to rain at Sun Set and Continued half the night. my hunters returned without any thing Saw 2 gang of Elk a disagreeable Situation, men all employed in mending their leather Clothes, Socks &c. and

Dressing Some Leather. The Sea which is imedeately in front roars like a repeeted roling thunder and have rored in that way ever Since our arrival in its borders which is now 24 Days Since we arrived in Sight of the Great Western Ocian, I cant Say Pasific as Since I have Seen it, it has been the reverse. Elegant Canoes

[Clark, December 1, 1805] Sunday December 1st 1805 A cloudy windey morning wind from the East, dispatched two hunters, I deturmined to take a Canoe & a fiew men and hunt the marshey Islands above Point William, the Wind rose So high that I could not proceed, and returned to partake the dried fish, which is our Standing friend, began to rain hard at Sun Set and Continud. my hunters returned without any thing haveing Seen 2 parcels of elk men all employed to day in mending their leather Clothes, Shoes &c. and Dressing leather.

The emence Seas and waves which breake on the rocks & Coasts to the S W. & N W roars like an emence fall at a distance, and this roaring has continued ever Since our arrival in the neighbourhood of the Sea Coast which has been 24 days Since we arrived in Sight of the Great Western; (for I cannot Say Pacific) Ocian as I have not Seen one pacific day Since my arrival in its vicinity, and its waters are forming and petially perpetually breake with emenc waves on the Sands and rockey Coasts, tempestous and horiable. I have no account of Capt. Lewis Since he left me.

[Clark, December 2, 1805] December 2nd Monday 1805 Cloudy and Some little rain this morning I despatched 3 men to hunt and 2 and my Servent in a Canoe to a Creek above to try & Catch Some fish- I am verry unwell the drid fish which is my only diet does not agree with me and Several of the men Complain of a lax, and weakness- I expect Capt. Lewis will return to day with the hunters and let us know if Elk or deer Can be found Sufficent for us to winter on, If he does not come I Shall move from this place, to one of better prospects for game &c. Joseph Fields came home with the marrow bones of an Elk which he had killed 6 miles distant, I sent out 6 men in a canoe for the meat, the evening being late they did not return this night, which proved fair moon Shineing night- This is the first Elk we have killed on this Side the rockey mounts a great deal of Elk Sign in the neighbourhood

[Clark, December 2, 1805] Monday 2nd December 1805 Cloudy with Some rain this morning I Send out three men to hunt & 2 & my man york in a Canoe up the Ke-ke-mar-que Creek in Serch of fish and fowl- I feel verry unwell, and have entirely lost my appetite for the Dried pounded fish which is in fact the cause of my disorder at present- The men are generally Complaining of a lax and gripeing- In the evening Joseph Field came in with the Marrow bones of a elk which he killed at 6 miles distant, this welcome news to us. I dispatched Six men in a empty Canoe with Jo. mediately for the elk which he Said was about 3 miles from the water this is the first Elk which has been killd. on this Side of the rockey mountains- Jo Fields givs me an account of a great deel of Elk Sign & Says he Saw 2 Gangs of those Animals in his rout, but it rained So hard that he could not Shoot them- The party up the Creek returned without any thing and informs me they could not See any fish in the Creek to kill and the fowls were too wild to be killed, this must

[Clark, December 3, 1805] December 3rd Tuesday 1805 a fair windey morning wind from the East, the men Sent after an Elk yesterday returnd. with an Elk which revived the Sperits of my men verry much, I am unwell and cannot Eate, the flesh O! how disagreeable my Situation, a plenty of meat and incaple of eateing any- an Indian Canoe Came down with 8 Indians in it from the upper village, I gave a fish hook for a fiew Wap-e-to roots, which I eate in a little Elk Supe, The Indians proceeded on down. wind Confines to blow, and Serjt. Pryor & Gibson who went to hunt yesterday has not returnd. as yet I marked my name & the day of the month and year on a large Pine tree on this Peninsella & by land Capt William Clark December 3rd 1805. By Land. U States in 1804 & 1805"- The Squar Broke the two Shank bones of the Elk after the marrow was taken out, boiled them & extracted a Pint of Greese or tallow from them- Serjt. Pryor & Gibson returned after night and informed me they had been lost the greater part of the time they were out, and had killed 6 Elk which they left lying haveing taken out their interals. Some rain this afternoon

[Clark, December 3, 1805] Tuesday 3d December 1805 a fair windey morning wind from the East the men returned with the Elk which revived the Spirits of my party verry much I am Still unwell and Can't eate even the flesh of the Elk. an Indian Canoe of 8 Indians Came too, those Inds. are on their way down to the Chit Sops with Wap pa to to barter with that nation, I purchasd. a fiew of those roots for which I gave Small fish hooks, those roots I eate with a little Elks Soupe which I found gave me great relief I found the roots both nurishing and as a check to my disorder. The Indians proceeded on down through emence high waves maney times their Canoe was entirely out of Sight before they were 1/2 a mile distance. Serjt. Pryor & Gibson who went hunting yesterday has not returned untill after night, they informed me that they had killed 6 Elk at a great distance which they left lying, haveing taken out their interals that they had been lost and in their ramble saw a great deel of Elk Sign. after eateing the marrow out of two Shank bones of an Elk, the Squar choped the bones fine boiled them and extracted a pint of Grease, which is Superior to the tallow of the animal. Some rain this evening I marked my name on a large pine tree imediately on the isthmus William Clark December 3rd 1805. By Land from the U. States in 1804 & 1805.

[Clark, December 4, 1805]
December 4th Wednesday 180151
Some little rain all the last night and this morning after day the rain
increased and Continued

I despatched Serjt. Pryer & 6 men to the Elk which he had killed yesterday, with directions to Save the meet
and take loads to the River below in the next great bend- a Spring tide which rose 2 feet higher than Common
flud tides, and high water at 11 oClock to-day- wind from the S. E in the after noon hard wind from South-
rained all day, moderately the Swells too high for me to proceed down, as I intended, I feel my self Something
better and have an appetite to eate Something

[Clark, December 4, 1805] Wednesday 4th December 1805 Some rain all the last night, this morning it
increased with the wind from the S. E. I Set out Sergiant Pryor and 6 men to the Elk he had killed with
directions to Carry the meat to a bay which he informed me was below and as he believed at no great distance
from the Elk, and I Should proceed on to that bay as Soon as the wind would lay a little and the tide went out in
the evening- the Smoke is exceedingly disagreeable and painfull to my eyes, my appetite has returned and I
feel much better of my late complaint- a Spring tide to day rose 2 feet higher than Common flood tides and
high water at 11 oClock- Hard wind from the South this evening, rained moderately all day and the waves too
high for me to proceed in Safty to the bay as I intended, in Some part of which I expected would be convenient
for us to make winter quarters, the reports of seven huntes agreeing that elke were in great abundance about
the Bay below. no account of Capt. Lewis. I fear Some accident has taken place in his craft or party

[Clark, December 5, 1805] December 5th Thursday 1805 Som hard Showers of rain last night, this morn Cloudy
and drisley rain, in the bay above the Showers appear harder. High water to day at 12 oClock this tide is 2 Ins.
higher than that of yesterday all our Stores again wet by the hard Showers of last night Capt Lewis's long delay
below has been the cause of no little uneasiness on my part for him, a 1000 conjectures has crouded into my
mind respecting his probable Situation & Safty— rained hard. Capt Lewis returned haveing found a good
Situation and Elk Suffient to winter on, his party killed 6 Elk & 5 Deer in their absence in Serch of a Situation
and game

Rain continued all the after pt. of the day accompanied with hard wind from the S W. which provents our
moveing from this Camp.

[Clark, December 5, 1805] Thursday 5th of December 1805 Some hard Showers of rain last night, this morning
Cloudy and drisley at Some little distant above the isthmus the rain is much harder. high water to day at 12 this
tide is 2 inches higher than that of yesterday. all our Stores and bedding are again wet by the hard rain of last
night. Capt. Lewis's long delay below, has been the Sorce of no little uneasiness on my part of his probable
Situation and Safty, the repeeted rains and hard winds which blows from the S, W. renders it impossible for me
to move with loaded Canoes along an unknown Coast we are all wet & disagreeable; the party much better of
indispositions-. Capt. Lewis returned with 3 men in the Canoe and informs me that he thinks that a Sufficient
number of Elk may be prcured Convenient to a Situation on a Small river which falls into a Small bay a Short
distance below, that his party had Killed 6 Elk & 5 Deer in his rout, two men of his party left behind to Secure
the Elk this was verry Satisfactory information to all the party. we accordingly deturmined to proceed on to the
Situation which Capt. Lewis had Viewed as Soon as the wind and weather Should permit and Comence building
huts &c.

[Clark, December 6, 1805] December 6th Friday 1805 Wind blew hard all the last night, and a moderate rain,
the waves verry high, This morning the wind which is Still from the S W increased and rained Continued all day,
at Dusk wind Shifted to the North and it Cleared up and became fare, High water to day at 12 oClock & 13
Inches higher than yesterday. we were obliged to move our Camp out of the Water on high grown all wet.

[Clark, December 6, 1805] Friday 6th of December 1805 The wind blew hard all the last night with a moderate
rain, the waves verry high, the wind increased & from the S. W. and the rain Continued all day, about Dark the
wind Shifted to the North cleared away and became fair weather.

The high tide of today is 13 inches higher than yesterday, and obliged us to move our Camp which was in a low
Situation, on higher ground Smoke exceedingly disagreeable.

[Clark, December 7, 1805] December 7th Saturday 1805 Some rain from 10 to 12 last night this morning fair,
we Set out at 8 oClock down to the place Capt Lewis pitched on for winter quarters, when he was down
proceeded on against the tide at the point No. 2 we met our men Sent down after meet

To point Adams is West

To pt. Disapointment N 75 W

They informed me that they found the Elk after being lost in the woods for one Day and part of another, the most of the meat was Spoiled, they distance was So great and uncertain and the way bad, they brought only the Skins, york was left behind by Some accident which detained us Some time eer he Came up after passing round the pt. No. 2 in verry high swells, we Stopd & Dined in the commencement of a bay, after which proceeded on around the bay to S E. & assended a Creek 8 miles to a high pt. & Camped haveing passed arm makeing up to our left into the countrey

Mt. St. Helens is the mountain we mistook for Mt. Reeaneer

receved 2 Small Brooks on the East, extencive marshes at this place of Encampment We propose to build & pass the winter, The situation is in the Center of as we conceve a hunting Countrey- This day is fair except about 12 oClock at which time Some rain and a hard wind imedeately after we passed the point from the N. E which Continued for a about 2 hours and Cleared up. no meat

[Clark, December 7, 1805] Saturday 7th of December 1805 Some rain from 10 to 12 last night, this morning fair, have every thing put on board the Canoes and Set out to the place Capt Lewis had viewed and thought well Situated for winter quarters- we proceeded on against the tide to a point about _____ miles here we met Sergt Pryor and his party returning to the Camp we had left without any meat, the waves verry verry high, as much as our Canoes Could bear rendered it impossible to land for the party, we proceeded on around the point into the bay and landed to take brackfast on 2 Deer which had been killed & hung up, one of which we found the other had been taken off by some wild animal probably Panthors or the Wildcat of this Countrey here all the party of Serjt Pryors joined us except my man york, who had Stoped to rite his load and missed his way, Sergt Pryor informed us that he had found the Elk, which was much further from the bay than he expected, that they missed the way for one day and a half, & when he found the Elk they were mostly Spoiled, and they only brought the Skins of 4 of the Elk after brackfast I delayed about half an hour before York Came up, and then proceeded around this Bay which I have taken the liberty of calling Meriwethers Bay the Cristian name of Capt. Lewis who no doubt was the 1st white man who ever Surveyed this Bay, we assended a river which falls in on the South Side of this Bay 3 miles to the first point of high land on the West Side, the place Capt. Lewis had viewed and formed in a thick groth of pine about 200 yards from the river, this situation is on a rise about 30 feet higher than the high tides leavel and thickly Covered with lofty pine. this is certainly the most eligable Situation for our purposes of any in its neighbourhood.

Meriwethers Bay is about 4 miles across deep & receves 2 rivers the Kil how-d-nah-kle and the Ne tul and Several Small Creeks- we had a hard wind from the N. E. and Some rain about 12 oClock to day which lasted 2 hours and Cleared away. From the Point above Meriwethers Bay

to Point Adams is West

to point Disapointment is N. 75° W

[Clark, December 8, 1805] December 8th Sunday 1805 a Cloudy morning, I took 5 men and Set out to the Sea to find the nearest place & make a way, to prevent our men getting lost and find a place to make Salt, Steered S 62° W at 2 miles passed the head of a Brook running to the right, the lands good roleing much falling timber, lofty Pine of the Spruce kind, & Some fur, passed over a high hill & to a Creek which we kept down 11/2 miles and left it to our right, Saw fish in this Creek & Elk & Bear tracks on it, passed over a ridge to a low marshey bottom which we Crossed thro water & thick brush for 1/2 a mile to the Comencement of a Prarie which wavers, Covered with grass & Sackay Commis, at 1/2 Crossed a marsh 200 yds wide, boggey and arrived at a Creek which runs to the right. Saw a gange of Elk on the opposit Side below, rafted the Creek, with much dificulty & followed the Elk thro, emence bogs, & over 4 Small Knobs in the bogs about 4 miles to the South & Killed an Elk, and formed a Camp, Covered our Selves with the Elk Skins. the left of us Bogs & a lake or pond those bogs Shake, much Cramberry growing amongst the moss. Some rain this evening we made a harty Supper of the Elk & hung up the balsa

[Clark, December 8, 1805] Sunday December 8th 1805 Fort Clatsop We haveing fixed on this Situation as the one best Calculated for our Winter quarters I deturmin'd to go as direct a Course as I could to the Sea Coast which we Could here roar and appeared to be at no great distance from us, my principal object is to look out a place to make Salt, blaze the road or rout that they men out hunting might find the direction to the fort if they Should get lost in cloudy weather-and See the probibillity of game in that direction, for the Support of the Men, we Shall Send to make Salt, I took with me five men and Set out on a Course S 60 W proceeded on a dividing ridge through lofty piney land much falling timber. passed the heads of 2 brooks one of them had wide bottoms which was over flown & we waded to our knees crossed 2 Slashes and arrived at a Creek in a open ridgey prarie covered with Sackacomma this Creek we were obliged to raft, which is about 60 yards over and runs in a direction to Point adams, we discovered a large gange of Elk in the open lands, and we prosued them through verry bad Slashes and Small ponds about 3 miles, Killed one and camped on a Spot Scercely large enough to lie Clear of the Water. it is almost incredeable to assurt the bogs which those animals Can pass through, I prosue'd this gang of Elk through bogs which the wate of a man would Shake for 1/2 an Acre, and maney places I Sunk into the mud and water up to my hips without finding any bottom on the trale of those Elk. Those bogs are Covered with a kind of moss among which I observe an ebundance of Cramberries. in those Slashes Small Knobs are promisquisly Scattered about which are Steep and thickly Covered with pine Common to the Countrey & Lorel. we made a Camp of the Elk Skin to keep off the rain which Continued to fall, the Small Knob on which we Camped did not afford a Sufficiency of dry wood for our fire, we collected what dry wood we Could and what Sticks we Could Cut down with the Tomahawks, which made us a tolerable fire.

[Clark, December 9, 1805] December 9th Monday 1805 rained all the last night we are all wet, Send 2 men in pursute of the Elk & with the other 3 I Set out with a view to find the Ocian in our first direction, which Can be at no great Distance, I crossed 3 Slashes by wadeing to my knees & was prevented proceeding by the 4th which was a pond of 200 yds. we. I went around, and was Stoped by a 5th which apd. to be a rung Stream to the right. I then returned to the raft and recrossd. & proceeded down the Stream I first Struck about 2 miles & met 3 Indians, who informed me they lived on the See cost at a Short distance, I de-termd. to accompany them to their vilg. & we Set out, crossed the Stream, and 2 of the Indians took the Canoe over the wavering open rich plains for 1/2 a mile and we Crossed the same stream which run to the left, we then left the canoe and proceeded to the Same Stream which runs to the right and empties its Self into the See here I found their vilg. 4 Lodges on the west bank of this little river which is here 70 yards wide, Crossed in a Canoe & was invited to a lodge by a young Chief was treated great Politeness, we had new mats to Set on, and himself and wife produced for us to eate, fish, Lickorish, & black roots, on neet Small mats, and Cramberries & Sackacomey berris, in bowls made of horn, Supe made of a kind of bread made of berries common to this Countrey which they gave me in a neet wooden trencher, with a Cockle Shell to eate it with It began to rain and with a tremendious storm from the S. W. which lasted untill 10 oClock P M- when I was disposd to go to Sleep 2 neet mats was produced & I lay on them but the flees were So troublesom that I Slept but little Those people has 2 plays which they are fond of one is with a Been which they pass from one hand into the other, and the oponent guess on this game the resquist nubr of the white Beeds which is the principal property- they other game is with round Pieces of wood much the Shape of the _____ Backgammon which they role thro between 2 pins.

[Clark, December 9, 1805] Monday 9th December 1805 rained all the last night we are all wet, I directed 2 hunters Drewyer & Shannon to go in pursute of the Elk, with the other 3 men I determined to proceed on to the Ocian, & Set out on a Westerley direction Crossed 3 Slashes and arived at a Creek which I could not Cross as it was deep and no wood to make a raft, I proceeded down this Creek a Short distance and found that I was in a fork of the Creek, I then returned to raft on which we had Crossed the day. crossed and kept down about one mile and met 3 Indians loaded with fresh Salmon which they had Giged in the Creek I crossed yesterday in the hills, those indians made Signs that they had a town on the Seacoast at no great distance, and envited me to go to their town which envitation I axcepted and accompand. them, they had a Canoe hid in the Creek which I had just before rafted which I had not observed, we crossed in this little Canoe just large enough to carry 3 men an their loads after Crossing 2 of the Indians took the Canoe on theire Sholders and Carried it across to the other Creek about 1/4 of a mile, we Crossed the 2d Creek and proceeded on to the mouth of the Creek which makes a great bend above the mouth of this Creek or to the S. is 3 houses and about 12 families of the Clat Sop Nation, we cross to those houses, which were built on the S. exposur of the hill, Sunk into the ground about 4 feet the walls roof & gable ends are of Split pine boards, the dotes Small with a ladder to decend to the iner part of the house, the fires are 2 in the middle of the house their beads ar all around raised about 2 1/2 feet from the bottom flore all covered with mats and under those beads was Stored their bags baskets and useless mats, those people treated me with extrodeanary friendship, one man attached himself to me as Soon as I entered the hut, Spred down new mats for me to Set on, gave me fish berries rutes &c. on Small neet platteers of rushes to eate which was repeated, all the Men of the other houses Came and Smoked with me Those people appeared much neeter in their diat than Indians are Comonly, and frequently wash theer faces and hands- in the eveng an old woman presented a bowl made of a light Coloured horn a kind of Surup made of Dried berries which is common to this Countrey which the natives Call Shele wele this Surup I though was pleasent, they Gave me Cockle Shells to eate a kind of Seuip made of bread of the Shele well berries mixed with roots in which they presented in neet trenchers made of wood. a flock of Brant lit in the Creek which was 70 yds wide I took up my Small rifle and Shot one which astonished those people verry much, they plunged into the Creek and brought the brant on Shorein the evening it began to rain and Continud accompanied with a Violent wind from the S. W. untill 10 oClock P.M. those people have a Singular game which they are verry fond of and is performed with Something about the Size of a large been which they pass from, one hand into the other with great dexterity dureing which time they Sing, and ocasionally, hold out their hands for those who Chuse to risque their property to guess which hand the been is in-; the individual who has the been is a banker & opposed to all in the room. on this game they risque their beeds & other parts of their most valuable effects- this amusement has occupied about 3 hours of this evening, Several of the lodge in which I am in have lost all the beeds which they had about them- they have one other game which a man attempted to Show me, I do not properly understand it, they make use of maney peces about the Shape and size of Backgammon Pices which they role through between two pins Stuck up at certain distancies &.- when I was Disposed to go to Sleep the man who had been most attentive named Cus-ka-lah producd 2 new mats and Spred them near the fire, and derected his wife to go to his bead which was the Signal for all to retire which they did emediately. I had not been long on my mats before I was attacked most violently by the flees and they kept up a close Siege dureing the night

[Clark, December 10, 1805] December 10th 1805 Tusday A Cloudey rainy morning those people was Some what astonished, at three Shot I made with my little riffle to day, a gangu of Brant Set in the little river, I Killd. 2 of them as they Set, and on my return Saw a Duck which I took the head off of, the men plunged into the water like Spaniards Dogs after those fowls, after eateing a brackfast which was Similar to my Suppar, I attempted to purchase Some fiew roots which I offered red beeds for, they would give Scercely any thing for Beeds of that Colour, I then offered Small fish hooks which they were fond of and gave me Some roots for them, I then Set out on my return by the Same road I had went out accompd. by my young Chief by name Cus-ca-lar who Crossed me over the 3 Creek, and returned I proceeded on to my Camp thro a heavy Cold rain, Saw no game- at the Sea Cost near those Indins I found various kinds of Shells, a kind of Bay opsd. those people with a high pt. about 4 miles below, out from which at Some dists I Saw large rocks, as the day was Cloudy I could not See distinctly- found Capt Lewis with all hands felling trees, to build with, rained nearly all day, in my absence they men had bt. in the 6 Elk which was Killed Some days past 4 men complaining of being unwell from various causes

[Clark, December 10, 1805] Tuesday 10th December 1805 a Cloudy rainey morning verry early I rose and walked on the Shore of the Sea coast and picked up Several Curious Shells. I Saw Indians walking up and down the beech which I did not at first understand the Cause of, one man came to where I was and told me that he was in Serch of fish which is frequently thrown up on Shore and left by the tide, and told me the "Sturgion was verry good" and that the water when it retired left fish which they eate this was Conclusive evedance to me that this Small band depended in Some Measure for their winters Subsistance on the fish which is thrown on Shore and left by the tide- after amuseing my Self for about an hour on the edge of the rageing Seas I returned to the houses, one of the Indians pointed to a flock of Brant Sitting in the creek at Short distance below and requested me to Shute one, I walked down with my Small rifle and killed two at about 40 yds distance, on my return to the houses two Small ducks Set at about 30 Steps from me the Indians pointed at the ducks they were near together, I Shot at the ducks and accidently Shot the head of one off, this Duck and brant was Carried to the house and every man Came around examined the Duck looked at the gun the Size of the ball which was 100 to the pound and Said in their own language Clouch Musket, wake, com ma-tax Musket which is, a good Musket do not under Stand this kind of Musket &c. I entered the Same house I Slept in, they imediately Set before me their best roots, fish and Surup-, I attempted to purchase a Small Sea otter Skin for read beeds which I had in my pockets, they would not trade for those beeds not priseing any other Colour than Blue or White, I purchased a little of the berry bread and a fiew of their roots for which I gave Small fish hooks, which they appeared fond of- I then Set out on my return by the Same rout I had Come out accompanied by Cus-ka lah and his brother as far as the 3d Creek, for the purpose of Setting me across, from which place they returned, and I proceeded on through a heavy rain to the Camp at our intended fort, Saw a bears track & the tracks of 2 Elk in the thick woods- found Capt Lewis with all the men out Cutting down trees for our huts &c. in my absence the Men brought in the Six Elk which was killed Several days ago-. 4 men Complaining of violent Coalds. three Indians in a Canoe Came up from the Clat Sop Village yesterday and returned to day. The Sea Coast is about 7 miles distant Nearly West about 5 miles of the distance through a thick wood with reveens hills and Swamps the land, rich black moald 2 miles in a open wavering Sandy prarie, ridge runing parrelal to the river, Covered with Green Grass.

[Clark, December 11, 1805] December 11th Wednesday rained all last night moderately, we are all employed putting up the huts, rained at intervales all day moderately employed in putting up Cabins for our winter quarters, one man with Turners, one with a Strained Knee, one Sick with Disentary & Serjt. Pryor unwell from haveing his Sholder out of place

[Clark, December 11, 1805] Wednesday 11th December 1805 rained all the last night moderately we are all employed putting up huts or Cabins for our winters quarters. Sergeant Pryor unwell from a dislocation of his Sholder, Gibson with the disentary, Jo. Fields with biles on his legs, & Werner with a Strained Knee. The rained Continued moderately all day.

[Clark, December 12, 1805] December 12th Thursday 1805 Some moderate Showers last night and this morning all hands who are well employed in building Cabins, despatched 2 men to get board timber, The flees so bad last night that, I made but a broken nights rest we can't get them out of our robes & Skins, which we are obliged to make use of for bedding Some rain to day at Intervales- all at work, in the evening 2 Canoe of Indians Came from the 2 villages of Clotsop below, & brought Wapitoo roots a black root they call Si-ni-tor and a Small Sea orter Skin all of which we purchased for a fiew fishing hooks & Some Snake Indian Tobacco. Those

Indians appeare well disposed, I made a Chief of one & gave him a Small medel, his name is Conyear we treated those people well- they are tite Deelers, value Blu & white beeds verry highly, and Sell their roots also highly as they purchase them from the Indians abov for a high price

[Clark, December 12, 1805] Thursday 12th December 1805 All hands that are well employ'd in Cutting logs and raising our winter Cabins, detached two men to Split boards- Some rain at intervales all last night and to day- The flees were So troublesom last night that I made but a broken nights rest, we find great dificuelty in getting those trouble insects out of our robes and blankets- in the evening two Canoes of Chit Sops Visit us they brought with them Wap pa to, a black Sweet root they Call Sha-na toe qua, and a Small Sea Otter Skin, all of which we purchased for a fiew fishing hooks and a Small Sack of Indian tobacco which was given by the Snake Inds.

Those Indians appear well disposed we gave a Medal to the principal Chief named Con-ny-au or Com mo-wol and treated those with him with as much attention as we could- I can readily discover that they are Close deelers, & Stickle for a verry little, never close a bargin except they think they have the advantage Value Blue beeds highly, white they also prise but no other Colour do they Value in the least- the Wap pa to they Sell high, this root the purchase at a high price from the nativs above.

[Clark, December 13, 1805] December 13th Friday 1805 The Indians left us to day after brackfast, haveing Sold us 2 of the robes of a Small animal for which I intend makeing a Capot, and Sold Capt Lewis 2 Loucirvia Skins for the Same purpose. Drewyer & Shannon returned from hunting havg. killed 18 Elk and butchered all except 2 which they Could not get as night provented ther finding them & they Spoild.

3 Indians in a Canoe Came and offered us for Sale Sinutor roots, fish & 2 Sea otter Skins for Sale none of which we Could purchase. Some rain last night and this day at Several times, light Showers. we Continue building our houses of the Streightest & _____ logs, Sent out 2 men to Split timber to Covet the Cabins, and I am glad to find the timber Splits butifully, and of any width

[Clark, December 13, 1805] Friday 13th December 1805 The Clatsops leave us to day after a brackfast on Elk which they appeared to be very fond of before they left us they Sold me two robes of the Skins of a Small animal about the Size of a Cat, and to Captain Lewis 2 Cat or Loucirva Skins for the purpose of makeing a Coat. Drewyer & Shannon returned from hunting, haveing killed 18 Elk & left them boochered in the woods near the right fork of the river about 6 miles above this place- in the evining 3 Indians came in a Canoe, and offered to us for Sale roots & 2 Sea otter Skins, neither of which we Could purchase this evening. Some Showers of rain last night, and to day Several verry hard Showers- we Continue to put up the Streight butifull balsom pine on our houses-and we are much pleased to find that the timber Splits most butifully and to the width of 2 feet or more.

[Clark, December 14, 1805] December 14th Saturday 1805 a cloudy day & rained moderately all day we finish the log works of our building, the Indians leave us to day after Selling a Small Sea otter Skin and a roabe, Send 4 men to Stay at the Elk which is out in the woods &c.

[Clark, December 14, 1805] Saturday 14th December 1805 The Day Cloudy and rained moderately all day we finish the log work of our building, the Indians leave us to day after Selling a Small Sea otter Skin and a roab, dispatch 4 men to the Elk out in the woods with derections to delay untill the party goes up tomorrow. all employd in finishing a house to put meat into. all our last Supply of Elk has Spoiled in the repeeted rains which has been fallen ever Since our arrival at this place, and for a long time before, Scerce one man in Camp Can host of being one day dry Since we landed at this point, the Sick getting better, my man York Sick with Cholick & gripeing

[Clark, December 15, 1805] December 15th Sunday 1805 I Set out with 16 men in 3 Canoes for the Elk proced up the 1st right hand fork 4 miles & pack the meat from the woods to the Cano from 4 mile to 3 miles distance all hands pack not one man exempted from this labour I also pack my Self Some of this meat, and Cook for those out in packing Some rain in the evening Cloudy all day, the last load of meat all the party got out of the road or Direction and did not get to the Canoe untill after night, 5 did not join to night

[Clark, December 15, 1805] Sunday the 15th December 1805. I Set out early with 16 men and 3 Canoes for the Elk, proceed up the River three miles and thence up a large Creek from the right about 3 miles the hite of the tide water drew up the Canoes and all hands went out in three different parties and brought in to the Canoe each Man a quarter of Elk, I Sent them out for a Second load and had Some of the first Cooked against their return, after eateing a harty diner dispatched the party for a third and last load, about half the men missed their way and did not get to the Canoes untill after Dark, and Serjt. Ordway Colter, Colins Whitehouse & McNeal Staid out all night without fire and in the rain- Cloudy all day Some rain in the evening.

[Clark, December 16, 1805] December 16th Monday 1805 rained all the last night we Covered our Selves as well as we Could with Elk Skins, & Set up the greater part of the night, all wet I lay in the water verry Cold, the 5 men who Stayed out all night joined me this morning Cold & wet, Ordway Colter Collens, Jo Whitehouse J McNeal, I had the two Canoes loaded with the 11 Elk which was brought to the Canoes, despatched 12 men to meet me below with 2 Elk, The rain Contines, with Tremendious gusts of wind, which is Tremds. I proceeded on and took in the 2 Elk which was brought to the Creek, & Send back 7 men to Carrey to the Canoe & take down to Camp 3 Elk which was left in the woods, and I proceeded on to Camp thro the Same Chanel I had assd. The winds violent Trees falling in every derection, whorl winds, with gusts of rain Hail & Thunder, this kind of weather lasted all day, Certainly one of the worst days that ever was! I found 3 Indeans with Capt Lewis in camp they had brought fish to Sell, we had a house Covered with Punchen & our meat hung up. Several men Complaining of hurting themselves Carry meet, &c.

[Clark, December 16, 1805] Monday 16th December 1805 I as also the party with me experiencd a most dreadfull night rain and wet without any Couvering, indeed we Set up the greater part of the Night, when we lay down the water Soon Came under us and obliged us to rise. the five men who Stayed out all night joind me this morning wet and Cold, haveing Stayed out without fire or Shelter and the rain poreing down upon them all night their appearance was truly distressingthey had left all their loads near the place they Spent the night- I dispatched 12 men for 2 Elk which was reather below on the opposit Side of the Creak, with directions to meet me at the 2d bend in the Creek below, had all the meat which had been brought in yesterday put into 2 Canoes and proceeded down to the 2d bend where I met the 12 men with the 2 Elk, dispatchd 6 men with one of those who Staid out last night for the meet left in the woods & the remainder an elk at Some distance and proceeded on my Self with 3 Canoes to the fort. wind violent from the S E

trees falling, rain and hail, we with Some risque proceeded on thro the high waves in the river, a tempestious disagreeable day.

I found 3 indians at our Camp, they brought fish to Sell which were pore & not fit for use, had the meet house coverd and the meat all hung up, Several men complain of haveing hurt themselves heavy loads of meat.

[Clark, December 17, 1805] December 17th Tuesday 1805 rained Some last night and this morning, all hands at work about the huts Chinking them, The 7 men left to bring in the Elk left in the woods Come with 2 the 3rd they Could not find, as it was that left by the party that got lost night before last

The after part of the Day fair & Cool, fore part of the Day rain hailed & blew hard, The mountain which lies S. E of this is covered with Snow to day we fleece all the meat and hang it up over a Small Smoke The trees are hard to Split for Punchens to Cover our houses &c.

[Clark, December 17, 1805] Tuesday 17th of December 1805 Some rain last night and a continuation of it this morning. all the men at work about the houses, Some Chinking, Dobbing Cutting out dores &c. &c. The 7 men left to bring in the Elk arrived and informed that they Could not find the meat that the party who Stayed out all night had left- the forepart of this day rained hailed and blew hard, the after part is fair and Cool- a Mountain which is S. _____° E. about 10 miles distant has got Snow on its top which is ruged and uneavin

Cause a Small fire & Smoke to be made under the meat which is hung up in Small peaces. The trees which our men have fallen latterly Split verry badly into boards. The most of our Stores are wet. our Leather Lodge has become So rotten that the Smallest thing tares it into holes and it is now Scrcely Sufficent to keep off the rain off a Spot Sufficiently large for our bead.

[Clark, December 18, 1805] December 18th Wednesday 1805 rained and Snowed alturnitely all the last night and the gusts of Snow and hail continue untill 12 oClock, Cold and a dreadfull day wind hard and unsettled, we continue at work at our huts, the men being but thinly dressed, and no Shoes causes us to doe but little- at 12 the Snow & hail Seased & the after part of the day was Cloudy with Some rain.

[Clark, December 18, 1805]
Wednesday 18th December 1805
rained and Snowed alternely all the last night, and Spurts of Snow and
Hail Continued untill 12 oClock, which has chilled the air which is
Cool and disagreeable, the wind hard & unsettled- The men being thinly
Dressed and mockersons without Socks is the reason that but little can
be done at the Houses to day- at 12 the Hail & Snow Seased, and rain
Succeeded for the latter part of the day

[Lewis, December 18, 1805] Fort Clatsop, December 18th 1805. This day one of the men shot a bird of the Corvus genus, which was feeding on some fragments of meat near the camp. this bird is about the size of the kingbird or bee martin, and not unlike that bird in form. the beak is 3/4 of an inch long, wide at the base, of a convex, and cultrated figure, beset with some small black hairs near it's base. the chaps are of nearly equal lengths tho the upper exceeds the under one a little, and has a small nich in the upper chap near the extremity perceptable only by close examineation. the colour of the beak is black. the eye is large and prominent, the puple black, and iris of a dark yellowish brown. the legs and feet are black and imbricated. has four toes on each foot armed with long sharp tallons; the hinder toe is nearly as long as the middle toe in front and longer than the two remaining toes. the tale is composed of twelve fathers the longest of which are five inches, being six in number placed in the center. the remaining six are placed 3 on either side and graduly deminish to four inches which is the shortest and outer feathers. the tail is half the length of the bird, the whole length from the extremity of the beak to the extremity of the tale being 10 Inches. the head from it's joining the nect forward as far as the eyes nearly to the base of the beak and on each side as low as the center of the eye is black. arround the base of the beak the throat jaws, neck, brest and belley are of a pale bluish white. the wings back and tale are of a bluish black with a small shade of brown. this bird is common to this piny country are also found in the rockey mountains on the waters of the columbia river or woody side of those mountains, appear to frequent the highest sumits of those mountains as far as they are covered with timber. their note is que, quit-it, que-hoo; and tah, tah, &- there is another bird of reather larger size which I saw on the woddy parts of the rockey mountains and on the waters of the Missouri, this bird I could never kill tho I made several attempts, the predominate colour is a dark blue the tale is long and they are not crested; I believe them to be of the corvus genus also. their note is char, char, char-ar, char; the large blue crested corvus of the Columbia river is also

[Lewis, December 19, 1805] Discription of the blue Crested corvus bird common to the woody and western side of the Rockey mountains, and all the woody country from thence to the Pacific Ocean It's beak is black convex, cultrated, wide at its base where it is beset with hairs, and is 11 inches from the opening of the chaps to their extremity, and from the joining of the head to the extremity of the upper chap 1 1/8 Inches, the upper exceeds the under chap a little; the nostrils are small round unconnected and placed near the base of the beak where they lye concealed by the hairs or hairy feathers which cover the base of the upper chap. the eye reather large and full but not prominent and of a deep bluefish black, there being no difference in the colour of the puple and the iris. the crest is very full the feathers from 1 to 11/2 Inches long and occupye the whole crown of the head. the head neck, the whole of the body including the coverts of the wings, the upper disk of the tail and wings are of a fine gossey bright indigo blue Colour the under disk of the tail and wings are of a dark brown nearly black. the leg and first joint of the tye are 41/4 In. long, the legs and feet are black and the front covered with 6 scales the hinder part smothe, the toes are also imbrecated, four in number long and armed with long sharp black tallons. the upper disk of the first four or five feathers of the wing next to the boddy, are marked with small transverse stripes of black as are also the upper side of the two center feathers of the tail; the tail is five inches long & is composed of twelve feathers of equal length. the tail 1 & 1/2 as long as the boddy. the whole length from the point of the beak to extremity of the tail 1 Foot 1 Inch; from the tip of one to the tip of the other wing 1 Foot 51/2 Inches. the Conta. the size & the whole Contour of this bird resembles very much the blue jay or jaybird as they are called in the U States. like them also they seldom rest in one place long but are in constant motion hoping from spra to spray. what has been said is more immediately applicable to the male, the colours of the female are somewhat different in her the head crest neck half the back downwards and the converts of the wings are of a dark brown, but sometimes there is a little touch of the Indigo on the short feathers on the head at the base of the upper chap. this bird feeds on flesh when they can procure it, also on bugs flies and buries. I do not know whether they distroy little birds but their tallons indicate their capacity to do so if nature, has directed it. their note is loud and frequently repeated cha' -a cha' -a' &c.- also twat twat twat, very quick

[Clark, December 19, 1805] December 19th Thursday 1805 Some rain with intervales of fair weather last night, The morning Clear and wind from S W. I despatched Sjt. Pryer with 8 men in 2 Canoes across the bay for the boads of an Indian house which is abandoned, the other part of the men continue to doe a little at the huts, the after part of the day Cloudy with hail & rain, Sgt. Pryer and party returned with 2 Canoe loads of Boards, two Indians Came & Stayed but a Short time

[Clark, December 19, 1805] Thursday 19th December 1805 Some rain with intervales of fair weather last night, this morning Clear & the wind from the S, W. we dispatched Sjt. Pryor with 8 men in 2 Canoes across Meriwethers Bay for the boards of an old Indian house which is vacant, the residue of the men at work at their huts- the after part of the Day Cloudy with Hail and rain, Serjt. Pryor & party returned in the evening with a load of old boards which was found to be verry indifferent

2 Indians Cam and Stayed a Short time to day

[Clark, December 20, 1805] December 20th Friday 1805 Some rain and hail last night and this morning it rained hard untill 10 oClock, men all employd Carrying Punchens and Covering Cabins 4 of which we had Covered, & Set Some to Dobing- the after part of the day Cloudy and Some Showers of rain. 3 Indians came with Lickorish Sackacomie berries & mats to Sell, for which they asked Such high prices that we did not purchase any of them,- Those people ask double & tribble the value of everry thing they have to Sell, and never take less than the full value of any thing, they prise only Blue & white heeds, files fish hooks and Tobacco- Tobacco and Blue beeds principally

[Clark, December 20, 1805] Friday 20th of December 1805 Some rain and hail last night and the rained Continued untill 10 oClock a,m, Men all employd in Carrying punchens or boards & Covering the houses, 4 of which were Covered to day, the after part of the day Cloudy with Several Showers of rain- 3 Indians arrive in a Canoe. they brought with them mats, roots & Sackacome berries to Sell for which they asked Such high prices that we did not purchase any of them. Those people ask generally double and tribble the value of what they have to Sell, and never take less than the real value of the article in Such things as is calculated to do them Service. Such as Blue & white heeds, with which they trade with the nativs above; files which they make use of to Sharpen their tools, fish hooks of different Sises and tobacco- Tobacco and blue beeds they do prefur to every thing.

[Clark, December 21, 1805] December 21st Saturday 1805 rain as usial last night and all day to day moderately. we Continued at the Cabins dobbing & Shinking of them, fall Several trees which would not Split into punchins- the Indians were detected in Stealing a Spoon & a Bone, and left us, our Sackey Commy out Send 2 men to gather Some at the ocian, Saw Elk Sign

[Clark, December 21, 1805] Saturday 21st December 1805 rained as useal all the last night, and contd. moderately all day to day without any intermition, men employd at the houses. one of the indians was detected Stealing a horn Spoon, and leave the Camp. dispatched two men to the open lands near the Ocian for Sackacome, which we make use of to mix with our tobacco to Smoke which has an agreeable flavour.

[Clark, December 22, 1805] December 22nd Sunday 1805 rained all the last night & to day without much intermition we finish dobbig 4 huts which is all we have Covered, the Punchin floor & Bunks finished Drewyer go out to trap- Sjt. J. Ordway, Gibson & my Servent Sick Several with Biles on them & bruses of different kinds, much of our meat Spoiled.

[Clark, December 22, 1805] Sunday 22nd December 1805 rained Continued all the last night and to day without much intermition, men employd doeing what they can at the houses. Drewyer Set out up the Creek to Set his traps for beaver, Sergt. ordway, Gibson & my Servent Sick, Several men Complain of biles and bruses of differant kinds.

We discover that part of our last Supply of meat is Spoiling from the womph of the weather not withstanding a constant Smoke kept under it day and night.

[Clark, December 23, 1805] December 23rd Monday 1805 rained without intermition all last night, and this day much Thunder in the morning and evening with rain and Some hail to day, we are all employd about our huts have ours Covered and Dobed & we move into it, 2 Canoes of Indians Came up to day. I purchased 3 mats verry neetly made, 2 bags made with Flags verry neetly made, those the Clotsops Carry ther fish in. also a Panthor Skin and Some Lickorish roots, for which I gave a worn out file, 6 fish hooks & Some Pounded fish which to us was Spoiled, but those people were fond of- in the evining those people left us I also gave a String of wompom to a Chief, and Sent a Small pice of Simimon to a Sick Indian in the Town who had attached himself to me

[Clark, December 23, 1805] Monday 23rd December 1805 Rained without intermition all the last night and to day with Thunder and Hail the fore and after part of this day Capt Lewis and my Self move into our hut to day unfinished- two Canoes with Indians of the Clat Sop nation Came up to day. I purchased 3 mats and bags all neetly made of flags and rushes, those bags are nearly Square of different size's open on one Side, I also purchased a panthor Skin 71/2 feet long including the tail, all of which I gave 6 Small fish hooks, a Small worn out file & Some pounded fish which we Could not use as it was So long wet that it was Soft and molded, the Indians of this neighbourhood prize the pound'd fish verry highly, I have not observed this method of Secureing fish on any other part of the Columbian waters then that about the Great falls. I gave a 2d Chief a String of wampom, and Sent a little pounded fish to Cus-ca-lah who was Sick in the village & could not come to See us.

[Clark, December 24, 1805] December 24th Tuesday-5 Some hard rain at different times last night, and moderately this morning without intermition all hands employed in Carrying Punchens & finishing Covering the huts, and the greater part of the men move into them a hard rain in the evening.

Cuscalar the young Clot Sop Chief Came with a young brother and 2 young Squar, they gave or laid before Capt Lewis and my Self a mat and each a large Parsel of roots, Some time after he demanded 2 files for his Present we returned the present as we had no files to Speare which displeased them a little they then offered a woman to each which we also declined axcpting which also displeased them. Jo Fields finish for Capt Lewis and my Self each a wide Slab hued to write on, I gave a handkerchief &c

[Clark, December 24, 1805] Tuesday 24th December 1805 hard rain at Different times last night and all this day without intermition. men all employd in finishing their huts and moveing into them.

Cuscalah the Indian who had treated me So politely when I was at the Clatsops village, come up in a Canoe with his young brother & 2 Squars he laid before Capt Lewis and my Self each a mat and a parcel of roots Some time in the evening two files was demanded for the presents of mats and roots, as we had no files to part with, we each returned the present which we had received, which displeased Cuscalah a little. he then offered a woman to each of us which we also declined axcepting of, which displeased the whole party verry much- the female part appeared to be highly disgusted at our refuseing to axcept of their favours &c.

our Store of Meat entirely Spoiled, we are obliged to make use of it as we have nothing else except a little pounded fish, the remains of what we purchased near the great falls of the Columbia, and which we have ever found to be a convenient resort, and a portable method of curing fish

[Clark, December 25, 1805] December 25th Christmas 1805 Wednesday Some rain at different times last night and Showers of hail with intervales of fair Starr light, This morning at day we were Saluted by all our party under our winders, a Shout and a Song- after brackfast we divided our tobacco which amounted to 2 Carrots, one half we gave to the party who used Tobacco those who did not we gave a Handkerchief as a present, The day proved Showery all day, the Inds. left us this eveningall our party moved into their huts. we dried Some of our wet goods. I rcved a present of a Fleeshe Hoserey vest draws & Socks of Capt Lewis, pr. Mockerson of Whitehouse, a Small Indian basket of Guterich, & 2 Doz weasels tales of the Squar of Shabono, & Some black roots of the Indians G. D. Saw a Snake passing across the parth

Our Diner to day Consisted of pore Elk boiled, Spilt fish & Some roots, a bad Christmass diner worm Day

[Clark, December 25, 1805] Christmas Wednesday 25th December 1805 at day light this morning we were awoke by the discharge of the fire arm of all our party & a Selute, Shoute and a Song which the whole party joined in under our windows, after which they retired to their rooms were Chearfull all the morning- after brackfast we divided our Tobacco which amounted to 12 carrots one half of which we gave to the men of the party who used tobacco, and to those who doe not use it we make a present of a handkerchief, The Indians leave us in the evening all the party Snugly fixed in their huts- I recved a presnt of Capt L. of a fleece hosrie Shirt Draws and Socks-, a pr. mockersons of Whitehouse a Small Indian basket of Gutherich, two Dozen white weazils tails of the Indian woman, & Some black root of the Indians before their departure- Drewyer informs me that he Saw a Snake pass across the parth to day. The day proved Showerey wet and disagreeable.

we would have Spent this day the nativity of Christ in feasting, had we any thing either to raise our Sperits or even gratify our appetites, our Diner concisted of pore Elk, So much Spoiled that we eate it thro mear necessity, Some Spoiled pounded fish and a fiew roots.

[Clark, December 26, 1805] December 26th Thursday 1805 rained and blew hard last night Some hard Thunder, The rain continued as usial all day and wind blew hard from the S. E, Joseph Fields finish a Table & 2 Seats for us. we dry our wet articles and have the blankets fleed, The flees are So troublesom that I have Slept but little for 2 nights past and we have regularly to kill them out of our blankets every day for Several past- maney of the men have ther Powder wet by the horns being repeetdly wet, hut Smoke verry bad.

[Clark, December 26, 1805] Thursday 26th December 1805 rained and blew with great Violence S E all the last night, Some hard Claps of Thunder, the rain as usial Continued all day- we dry our wet articles before the fire, and have our blankets fleed, great numbers were Caught out of the blankets, those trouble insects are So abundant that we have to have them killd. out of our blankets every day or get no Sleep at night- The powder in maney of the mens horns are wet from their being so long exposed to the rain &c.

[Clark, December 27, 1805] December 27th Friday 1805. rained last night as usial and the greater part of this day, the men Complete Chimneys & Bunks to day, in the evening a Chief and 4 men Come of the Clotsop nation, Chief Co-ma wool we Sent out R. Fields & Collins to hunt and order Drewyer, Shannon & Labiach to Set out early to morrow to hunt,- Jo Fields, Bratten, & Gibson to make Salt at Point Addams,- Willard & Wiser, to assist them in carrying the Kitties &c to the Ocian, and all the others to finish the Pickets and gates. worm weather I Saw a Musquetor which I Showed Capt. Lewis- Those Indians gave is, a black root they Call Shan-na-tah que a kind of Licquerish which they rost in embers and Call Cul ho-mo, a black berry the Size of a Cherry & Dried which they call Shel-well,- all of which they prise highly and make use of as food to live on, for which Capt Lewis gave the chief a Cap of Sheep Skin and I his Son, ear bobs, Piece of riben, a pice of brass, and 2 Small fishing hooks, of which they were much pleased Those roots & berres, are greatfull to our Stomcks as we have nothing to eate but Pore Elk meet, nearly Spoiled; & this accident of Spoiled meet, is owing to wormth & the repeeted rains, which cause the meet to tante before we Can get it from the woods Musquetors troublesorn

[Clark, December 27, 1805] Friday 27th December 1805 rained last night as usial and the greater part of this day. In the evening Co-mo wool the Chief and 4 men of the Clat Sop nation they presented us a root which resembles the licquirish in Size and taste, which they roste like a potato which they Call Cul ho-mo, also a black root which is cured in a kill like the pash-a-co above; this root has a Sweet taste and the natives are verry fond of it- they Call this root Shaw-na-tah-que. also a dried berry about the size of a Chery which they Call Shele well all those roots those Indians value highly and give them verry Spearingly. in return for the above roots Capt Lewis gave the Chief a Small piece of Sheap Skin to Ware on his head, I gave his Son a par of ear bobs and a pece of ribon, and a Small piece of brass for which they were much pleased.

Those roots and berries are timely and extreamly greatfull to our
Stomachs, as we have nothing to eate but Spoiled Elk meat, I Showed
Capt L. 2 Musquetors to day, or an insect So much the Size Shape and
appearance of a Musquetor that we Could observe no kind of differance.

[Clark, December 28, 1805] December 28th Saturday 1805 rained as usial, a great part of the last night, and this morning rained and the wind blew hard from the S. E. Sent out the hunters and Salt makers, & employd the baleanc of the men Carrying the Pickets &c. &c. hunters Sent out yesterday returned, haveing killed one deer near the Sea cost, my boy york verry unwell from violent Colds & Strains Carrying in meet and lifting logs on the huts to build them, This day is worm, and rained all day moderately without intermition.

[Clark, December 28, 1805] Saturday the 28th December 1805 rained as usial the greater part of the last night and a continuation this morning accompanied with wind from the S East Derected Drewyer, Shannon, Labeash, Reuben Field, and Collins to hunt; Jos. Fields, Bratten, Gibson to proceed to the Ocean at Some Convenient place form a Camp and Commence makeing Salt with 5 of the largest Kittles, and Willard and Wiser to assist them in Carrying the Kittles to the Sea Coastall the other men to be employed about putting up pickets & makeing the gates of the fort. my man Y. verry unwell from a violent Coald and Strain by Carrying meet from the woods and lifting the heavy logs on the works &c. rained all Day without intermition. the Weather verry worm.

[Clark, December 29, 1805] December 29th Sunday 1805 rained last night as usial, this morning Cloudy without rain a hard wind from the S. E. The Inds. left us this morning and returned to their village, after begging for maney things which they did not secure as we Could not Spare them I gave the Chief Canio a Razor, Sent out 3 men across the river to hunt, all others employd putting up pickets Pete Crusat Sick with a violent Cold My Servent better- we are told by the Indians that a whale has foundered on the Coast to the N. W and that nations is collecting fat of him, the wind is too high for us to See it, Capt Lewis is been in readiness 2 days to go and Collect Some of the whale oyle the wind has proved too high as yet for him to Set out in Safty In the evening a young Chief 4 men and 2 womin of the War-ci-a-cum tribe came in a large canoe with Wapto roots, Dressed Elk Skins &c. to Sell, the Chief made me a present of about a half a bushel of those roots- we gave him a medal of a Small Size and a piece of red ribin to tie around the top of his Hat which was made with a double Cone, the diameter of the upper about 3 Inches the lower a about 1 foot

We purchased about 11/2 bushels of those roots for which we gave Some few red beeds, Small pices of brass wire and old Check- those roots proved greatfull to us as we are now liveing on Spoiled Elk which is extreamly disagreeable to the Smel. as well as the taste, I can plainly discover that a considerable exchange of property is Continually Carried on between the Tribes and villages of those people they all dress litely ware nothing below the waste, a pice of fur abt. around the body, and a Short robe which Composes the total of their dress, except a few Split hats, and heeds around ther necks wrists and ancles, and a few in their ears. They are small and not handsom generally Speaking women perticulary.

The Chin nook womin are lude and Carry on Sport publickly the Clotsop and others appear deffidend, and reserved The flees are So noumerous in this Countrey and difficult to get Cleare of that the Indians have difft. houses & villages to which they remove frequently to get rid of them, and not withstanding all their precautions, they never Step into our hut without leaveing Sworms of those troublesom insects. Indeed I Scercely get to Sleep half the night Clear of the torments of those flees, with the precaution of haveing my blankets Serched and the flees killed every day- The 1 s of those insects we Saw on the Collumbia River was at the 1 s Great falls- I have the Satisfaction to Say that we had but little rain in the Course of this day, not as much as would wet a person. but hard wind and Cloudy all day.

[Clark, December 29, 1805] Sunday 29th December 1805 rained all the last night a usial, this morning Cloudy without rain, a hard wind from the S. E I gave the Cheif a razor, and himself and party left us after begging us for maney articles none of which they recvied as we Could not Spare the articles they were most in want of. Peter Crusat

Sick with a violent Cold, my man Y. better. all hands employed about the Pickets & gates of the fort. we were informed day before yesterday that a whale had foundered on the coast to the S. W. near the Kil a mox N. and that the greater part of the Clat Sops were gorn for the oile & blubber, the wind proves too high for us to proceed by water to See this monster, Capt Lewis has been in readiness Since we first heard of the whale to go and see it and collect Some of its Oil, the wind has proved too high as yet for him to proceed- this evining a young Chief 4 Men and 2 womin of the War ci a cum Nation arrived, and offered for Sale Dressed Elk Skins and Wap pa to, the Chief made us a preasent of about 1/2 a bushel of those roots. and we purchased about 11/2 bushels of those roots for which we gave Some fiew red beeds Small peaces of brass wire & old Check those roots proved a greatfull addition to our Spoiled Elk, which has become verry disagreeable both to the taste & Smell we gave this Chief a Medal of a Small Size and a piece of red riben to tie around the top of his hat which was of a Singular Construction Those people will not Sell all their Wap pa to to us they inform us that they are on their way to trade with the Chit Sops. The nations above Carry on a verry Considerable interchange of property with those in this neighbourhood. they pass altogether by water, they have no roads or pathes through the Countrey which we have observed, except across portages from one Creek to another, all go litely dressed ware nothing below the waste in the Coaldest of weather, a piece of fur around their bodies and a Short roabe Composes the Sum total of their dress, except a few hats, and heeds about their necks arms and legs Small badly made and homely generally. The flees are So noumerous and hard to get rid of; that the Indians have different houses which they resort to occasionally, not withstanding all their precautions they never Step into our house without leaveing Sworms of those tormenting insects; and they torment us in Such a manner as to deprive us of half the nights Sleep frequently- the first of those insects which we saw on the Columbian waters was at the Canoe portage at the great falls. Hard winds & Cloudy all day but verry little rain to day.

[Clark, December 30, 1805] December 30th Monday 1805 Hard wind and Some rain last night, this morning fair and the Sun Shown for a Short time 4 Indians Came from the upper Villages they offered us roots which we did not Chuse to axcept of, as their expectations for those presents of a fiew roots is 3 or 4 times their real worth, those Indians with those of yesterday Continued all day. Drewyer & party of hunters returned and informed they had killed 4 Elk, a party of 6 men was imediately Sent for the meet, they returned at Dusk, with the 4 Elk, of which we had a Sumptious Supper of Elk Tongues & marrow bones which was truly gratifying.

The fort was Completed this evening and at Sun Set we let The Indians know that, our Custom will be to Shut the gates at Sun Set, at which time, they must all go out of the fort those people who are verry foward and disegreeable, left the huts with reluctiance- This day proved the best we have had Since at this place, only 3 Showers of rain to day, Cloudy nearly all day, in the evening the wind luled and the fore part of the night fair and clear. I Saw flies & different kinds of insects in motion to day Snakes are yet to be seen, and Snales without Cover is Common and large, fowls of every kind Common to this quarter abound in the Creek & Bay near us

[Clark, December 30, 1805] Monday 30th December 1805 Hard wind and Some rain last night. this morning the Sun Shown for a Short time- four Indians came down from the War cia cum Village, they offered us roots which we did not think proper to accept of as in return they expect 3 or 4 times as much as the roots as we Could purchase the Roots for, and are never Satisfied with what they receive, those 4 Indians & these that Came yesterday Stayed all day. Drewyer returned and informed that he had killed 4 Elk at no great distance off, a party of 6 men was imediately dispatched for the meat, and returned at Dusk with the 4 Elk- we had a Sumptious Supper of Elks tongues & marrow bones which was truly gratifying- our fortification is Completed this evening-and at Sun Set we let the nativs know that our Custom will be in future, to Shut the gates at Sun Set at which time all Indians must go out of the fort and not return into it untill next morning after Sunrise at which time the gates will be opened, those of the War ci a cum Nation who are very foward left the houses with reluctianc this day proved to be the fairest and best which we have had since our arrival at this place, only three Showers dureing this whole day, wind the fore part of the day.

[Clark, December 31, 1805] December 31st Tuesday 1805 A Cloudy night & Some rain, this day proved Cloudy and Some Showers of rain to day all the Indians Continued at their Camp near us, 2 others Canoes Came one from the War-ci-a-cum Village, with three Indians, and the other from higher up the river of the Skil-lute nation with three men and a Squar; Those people brought with them Some Wapto roots, mats made of flags, & rushes, dried fish and Some fiew Shene-tock-we (or black) roots & Dressed Elk Skins, all of which they asked enormous prices for, particularly the Dressed Elk Skins; I purchased of those people Some Wapto roots, two mats and a Small pouch of Tobacco of their own manufactory- for which I gave large fish hooks, which they were verry fond, those Indians are much more reserved and better behaved to day than yesterday- the Sight of our Sentinal who walks on his post, has made this reform in those people who but yesterday was verry impertenant and disagreeable to all- This evening they all Cleared out before the time to Shut the gates, without being derected to doe So- I derected Sinks to be dug and a Sentinal Box which was accomplished one of those Indeans brought a Musquet to be repared, which only wanted a Screw flattened, for which he gave me a Peck of Wapto roots, I gave him a flint and a pice of Sheep Skin of which he was pleased

[Clark, December 31, 1805] Tuesday 31st December 1805 last night was Cloudy and Some rain, this day prove Cloudy and Showerry all day, all the Indians Continue at their Camp near us, two other Canoes arrived, one from the War ci a cum Village with 3 indians and the other of 3 men & a Squar from higher up the river and are of the Skil-lute nation, those people brought with them Some Wappato roots, mats made of flags and rushes dried fish, and a fiew Shaw-na tah-que and Dressed Elk Skins, all of which they asked enormous prices for, perticularly the dressed Elk Skins, I purchased of those people Some Wap pa to two mats and about 3 pipes of their tobacco in a neet little bag made of rushes- This tobacco was much like what we had Seen before with the So So ne or Snake indians, for those articles I gave a large fishing hook and Several other Small articles, the fishinghooks they were verry fond of. Those Skit lutes are much better behaved than the War ci a cum indeed we found a great alteration in the Conduct of them all this morning, the Sight of our Sentinal on his post at the gate, together with our deturmined proseedure of putting all out at Sun Set has made this reform in those War ci a corns who is foward impertinant an thieveish.

The nativs all leave us the fort this evening before Sun Set without being told or desired to do So- we had Sinks dug & a Sentinal box made- a Skit lute brought a gun which he requested me to have repared, it only wanted a Screw flattened So as to Catch, I put a flint into his gun & he presented me in return a peck of Wappato for payment, I gave him piece of a Sheap Skin and a Small piece of blue Cloth to Cover his lock for which he was much pleased and gave me in return Some roots &c.

I Saw flies and different kinds of insects in motion to-day- Snakes are yet to be Seen and Snales without Covers is Common and verry large water fowls of various kinds are in great numbers in the rivers and Creeks and the sides of Meriwethers Bay near us but excessively wild- the fore part of this night fair and Clear

With the party of Clat Sops who visited us last was a man of much lighter Coloured than the nativs are generaly, he was freckled with long duskey red hair, about 25 years of age, and must Certainly be half white at least, this man appeared to understand more of the English language than the others of his party, but did not Speak a word of English, he possessed all the habits of the indians

[Lewis, January 1, 1806] Fort Clatsop 1806. January 1st Tuesday. This morning I was awoke at an early hour by the discharge of a volley of small arms, which were fired by our party in front of our quarters to usher in the new year; this was the only mark of respect which we had it in our power to pay this celebrated day. our repast of this day tho better than that of Christmass, consisted principally in the anticipation of the 1st day of January 1807, when in the bosom of our friends we hope to participate in the mirth and hilarity of the day, and when with the zest given by the recollection of the present, we shall completely, both mentally and corporally, enjoy the repast which the hand of civilization has prepared for us. at present we were content with eating our boiled Elk and wappetoe, and solacing our thirst with our only beverage pure water. two of our hunters who set out this morning reterned in the evening having killed two bucks elk; they presented Capt. Clark and myself each a marrow-bone and tonge, on which we suped. visited today by a few of the Clotsops who brought some roots and burries for the purpose of trading with us. we were uneasy with rispect to two of our men, Willard and Wiser, who were dispatched on the 28th ulto. with the saltmakers, and were directed to return immediately; their not having returned induces us to believe it probable that they have missed their way.- our fourtification being now completed we issued an order for the more exact and uniform dicipline and government of the garrison. (see orderly book 1st January 1806).-

[Clark, January 1, 1806] January 1st Wednesday 1806 This morning proved cloudy with moderate rain, after a pleasent worm night during which there fell but little rain- This morning at Day we wer Saluted from the party without, wishing us a "hapy new year" a Shout and discharge of their arms- no Indians to be Seen this morning- they left the place of their encampment dureing the last night The work of our houses and fort being now Complete, we Ishued an order in which we pointed out the rules & regulations for the government of the Party in respect to the Indians as also for the Safty and protection of our Selves &c.

two Clotsops Came with a mat and Some fiew roots of Cut wha mo, for which they asked a file they did not trade but Continued all night

Sent out 2 hunters this morning who returned, haveing killed 2 Elk about 3 miles distant, Some fiew Showers of rain in the Course of this day. Cloudy all the day.

[Clark, January 1, 1806] Fort Clatsop 1806 Wednesday the 1st of January This morning I was awoke at an early hour by the discharge of a Volley of Small arms, which were fired by our party in front of our quarters to usher in the new year, this was the only mark of respect which we had it in our power to pay this Selibrated day. our repast of this day tho better than that of Christmas Consisted principally in the anticipation of the 1st day of January 1807, when in the bosom of our friends we hope to participate in the mirth and hilarity of the day, and when with the relish given by the recollection of the present, we Shall Completely, both mentally and Corparally, the repast which the hand of Civilization has produced for us. at present we were Content with eating our boiled Elk and Wappato, and Solacing our thirst with our only beverage pure water. two of our hunters who Set out this morning returned in the evening haveing killed two Buck Elks; they presented Capt. Lewis and my Self each a marrow bone and tongue on which we Suped- we are visited to day by a fiew of the Clatsops by water they brought some roots and berries for the purpose of tradeing with us. our fortification being now Complete we issue an order for the more exact and uniform dicipline and government of the garrison. (See orderly book Jany 2d 1806)

[Lewis, January 1, 1806] Fort Clatsop, January 1st 1806 The fort being now completed, the Commanding officers think proper to direct that the guard shall as usual consist of one Sergeant and three privates, and that the same be regularly relieved each morning at sun rise. The post of the new guard shall be in the room of the Sergeants respectivly commanding the same. the centinel shall be posted, both day and night, on the parade in front of the commanding offercers quarters; tho should he at any time think proper to remove himself to any other part of the fort, in order the better to inform himself of the desighns or approach of any party of savages, he is not only at liberty, but is hereby required to do so. It shall be the duty of the centinel also to announce the arrival of all parties of Indians to the Sergeant of the Guard, who shall immediately report the same to the Commanding officers.

The Commanding Officers require and charge the Garrison to treat the natives in a friendly manner; nor will they be permitted at any time, to abuse, assault or strike them; unless such abuse assault or stroke be first given by the natives. nevertheless it shall be right for any individual, in a peaceable manner, to refuse admittance to, or put out of his room, any native who may become troublesome to him; and should such native refuse to go when requested, or attempt to enter their rooms after being forbidden to do so; it shall be the duty of the Sergeant of the guard on information of the same, to put such native out of the fort and see that he is not again admitted during that day unless specially permitted; and the Sergeant of the guard may for this purpose imploy such coercive measures (not extending to the taking of life) as shall at his discretion be deemed necessary to effect the same.

When any native shall be detected in theft, the Sergt. of the guard shall immediately inform the Commanding offercers of the same, to the end that such measures may be pursued with rispect to the culprit as they shall think most expedient.

At sunset on each day, the Sergt. attended by the interpreter Charbono and two of his guard, will collect and put out of the fort, all Indians except such as may specially be permitted to remain by the Commanding offercers, nor shall they be again admitted untill the main gate be opened the ensuing morning.

At Sunset, or immediately after the Indians have been dismissed, both gates shall be shut, and secured, and the main gate locked and continue so untill sunrise the next morning; the water-gate may be used freely by the Garrison for the purpose of passing and repassing at all times, tho from sunset, untill sunrise, it shall be the duty of the centinel, to open the gate for, and shut it after all persons passing and repassing, suffering the same never to remain unfixed long than is absolutely necessary.

It shall be the duty of the Sergt. of the guard to keep the kee of the Meat house, and to cause the guard to keep regular fires therein when the same may be necessary; and also once at least in 24 hours to visit the canoes and see that they are safely secured; and shall further on each morning after he is relieved, make his report verbally to the Commandg officers.

Each of the old guard will every morning after being relieved furnish two loads of wood for the commanding offercers fire.

No man is to be particularly exempt from the duty of bringing meat from the woods, nor none except the Cooks and Interpreters from that of mounting guard.

Each mess being furnished with an ax, they are directed to deposit in the room of the commanding offercers all other public tools of which they are possessed; nor shall the same at any time hereafter be taken from the said deposit without the knoledge and permission of the commanding officers; and any individual so borrowing the tools are strictly required to bring the same back the moment he has ceased to use them, and no case shall they be permited to keep them out all night.

Any individual selling or disposing of any tool or iron or steel instrument, arms, accoutrements or ammunicion, shall be deemed guilty of a breach of this order, and shall be tryed and punished accordingly.the tools loaned to John Shields are excepted from the restrictions of this order.

Meriwether Lewis
Capt. 1st U.S. Regt.
Wm. Clark
Capt. &c

[Lewis, January 2, 1806] Thursday, January 2nd 1806 Sent out a party of men and brought in the two Elk which were killed yesterday. Willard and Wiser have not yet returned nor have a party of hunters returned who set out on the 26th Ulto. the Indians who visited yesterday left us at 1 P M today after having disposed of their roots and berries for a few fishinghooks and some other small articles. we are infested with swarms of flees already in our new habitations; the presumption is therefore strong that we shall not devest ourselves of this intolerably troublesome vermin during our residence here. The large, and small or whistling swan, sand hill Crane, large and small gees, brown and white brant, Cormorant, duckan mallard, Canvisback duck, and several other species of ducks, still remain with us; tho I do not think that they are as plenty as on our first arrival in the neighbourhood. Drewyer visited his traps and took an otter. the fur of both the beaver and otter in this country are extreemly good; those annamals are tolerably plenty near the sea coast, and on the small Creeks and rivers as high as the grand rappids, but are by no means as much so as on the upper part of the Missouri.

[Clark, January 2, 1806] January 2nd Thursday 1806. A Cloudy rainey morning after a wet night. dispatched 12 Men for the two Elk Killed yesterday which they brought in at 11 oClock. the day proved Cloudy and wet, the Indians left us at 1 oClock P. M, Drewyer visited his traps which had one otter in one of them. The flees are verry troublesom, our huts have alreadey Sworms of those disagreeable insects in them, and I fear we Shall not get rid of them dureing our delay at this place.

[Clark, January 2, 1806] Thursday 2nd of January 1806. Sent out a party of men and brought in the two Elk which was killed yesterday. Willard & Wiser have not yet returned nor have a party of hunters who Set out on the 26th ulto the Indians who visited us yesterday left us at 1 P. M to day after haveing disposed of their roots and berries for a fiew fishing hooks and Some other Small articles. we are infestd. with Sworms of flees already in our new habatations; the presumption is therefore Strong that we Shall not devest our Selves of this intolerably troublesom vermin dureing our residence here. The large, & Small or whistling Swan, Sand hill crane, large & Small Gees, brown and white brant, Comorant, Duckanmallard, canvis back duck, and Several other Species of Ducks Still remain with us; tho I doe not think they are as plenty as on our first arrival in the neighbourhood. Drewyer visit his traps at took out an otter. the fur of both the beaver and otter as also the rackoon in this countrey are extreemly good; those animals are tolerably plenty near the Sea coast, on the Small creeks and rivers as high as the grand Rapids.

[Lewis, January 3, 1806] Friday January 3d 1806. At 11 A.M. we were visited by our near neighbours, Chief or Tia, Como-wool; alias Conia and six Clatsops. they brought for sale some roots buries and three dogs also a small quantity of fresh blubber. this blubber they informed us they had obtained from their neighbours the Callamucksz who inhabit the coast to the S. E. near whose vilage a whale had recently perished. this blubber the Indians eat and esteeme it excellent food. our party from necessaty having been obliged to subsist some lenth of time on dogs have now become extreemly fond of their flesh; it is worthy of remark that while we lived principally on the flesh of this anamal we were much more healthy strong and more fleshey than we had been since we left the Buffaloe country. for my own part I have become so perfectly reconciled to the dog that I think it an agreeable food and would prefer it vastly to lean Venison or Elk. a small Crow, the blue crested Corvus and the smaller corvus with a white brest, the little brown ren, a large brown sparrow, the bald Eagle and the beatifull Buzzard of the columbia still continue with us.- Sent Sergt. Gass and George Shannon to the saltmakers who are somewhere on the coast to the S. W. of us, to enquire after Willard and Wiser who have not yet returned. Reubin Fields Collins and Pots the hunters who set out on the 26th Ulto. returned this evening after dark. they reported that they had been about 15 Miles up the river at the head of the bay just below us and had hunted the country from thence down on the East side of the river, even to a considerable distance from it and had proved unsuccessful) having killed one deer and a few fowls, barely as much as subsisted them. this reminded us of the necessity of taking time by the forelock, and keep out several parties while we have yet a little meat beforehand. I gave the Chief Comowooll a pare of sattin breechies with which he appeared much pleased.

[Clark, January 3, 1806] January 3rd Friday 1806 The Sun rose fair this morning for the first time for Six weeks past, the Clouds Soon obscure it from our view, and a Shower of rain Suckceededlast night we had Sharp lightening a hard thunder Suckceeded with heavy Showers of hail, and rain, which Continud with intervales of fair moon Shine dureing the night. Sent out Sergt. Gass & 2 men to the Salt makers with a vew to know what is the Cause of the delay of 2 of our party Willard & Wiser who we are uneasy about, as they were to have been back 6 days ago.

[Clark, January 3, 1806] Friday the 3rd January 1806 At 11 A. m. we were visited by our near neighbour Chief (or Tia) Co mo wool alias Conia and Six Clat sops. they brought for Sale Some roots berries and 3 Dogs also a Small quantity of fresh blubber. this blubber they informed us they had obtained from their neighbours the Cal la mox who inhabit the coast to the S. E near one of their Villages a Whale had recently perished. this blubber the Indians eat and esteem it excellent food. our party from necescity have been obliged to Subsist Some length of time on dogs have now become extreamly fond of their flesh; it is worthey of remark that while we lived principally on the flesh of this animal we wer much more helthy Strong and more fleshey then we have been Sence we left the Buffalow Country. as for my own part I have not become reconsiled to the taste of this animal as yet. a Small Crow, the blue Crested Corvus and the Smaller Corvus with a white breast, the little brown ren, and a large brown Sparrow, the bald Eagle, and the butiful Buzzard of the Columbia Still Continue with us, Send Sarjt. Gass and G. Shannon to the Salt makers who are on the Sea Coast to the S, W. of us, to enquire after Willard & Wiser who have not yet returned. R. Field, potts & Collins the hunters who Set out on the 28th ulto. returned this evening after dark. they reported that they had been about 15 miles up the river which falls into Meriwethers Bay to the East of us, and had hunted the Country a considerable distance to East, and had proved unsucksesfull haveing killed one Deer and a fiew fowls, bearly as much as Subsisted them. this reminded us of the necessity of takeing time by the forelock, and keep out Several parties while we have yet a little meat beforehand. Capt Lewis gave the Cheif Cania a par of Sattin breechies with which he appeared much pleased.

[Lewis, January 4, 1806] Saturday January 4th 1806. Comowooll and the Clatsops who visited us yesterday left us in the evening. These people the Chinnooks and others residing in this neighbourhood and speaking the same language have been very friendly to us; they appear to be a mild inoffensive people but will pilfer if they have an opportuny to do so where they conceive themselves not liable to detection. they are great higlers in trade and if they conceive you anxious to purchase will be a whole day bargaining for a handfull of roots; this I should have thought proceeded from their want of knowledge of the comparitive value of articles of merchandize and the fear of being cheated, did I not find that they invariably refuse the price first offered them and afterwards very frequently accept a smaller quantity of the same article; in order to satisfy myself on this subject I once offered a Chinnook my watch two knives and a considerable quantity of beads for a small inferior sea Otter's skin which I did not much want, he immediately conceived it of great value, and refused to barter except I would double the quantity of beads; the next day with a great deal of importunity on his part I received the skin in exchange for a few strans of the same beads he had refused the day before. I therefore believe this trait in their character proceeds from an avaricious all grasping disposition. in this rispect they differ from all Indians I ever became acquainted with, for their dispositions invariably lead them to give whatever they are possessed off no matter how usefull or valuable, for a bauble which pleases their fancy, without consulting it's usefullness or value. nothing interesting occurred today, or more so, than our wappetoe being all exhausted.

[Clark, January 4, 1806] Saturday 4th January 1806 Comowool and the Clatsops who visited us yesterday left us in the morning. Those people the Chinnook and others resideing in this neighbourhood and Speaking the Same language have been very friendly to us; they appear to be a mild inoffensive people but will pilfer if they have an oppertunity to do So when they Conceive themselves not liable to detection. they are great higlers in trade and if they Conceive you anxious to purchase will be a whole day bargaining for a hand full of roots; this I Should have thought proceeded from their want of Knowledge of the Comparitive value of articles of merchandize and the fear of being Cheated, did I not find that they invariably refuse the price first offered them and afterwards very frequently accept a Smaller quantity of the Same article; in order to Satisfy myself on this point, I once offered a Clatsop man my watch a knife, a Dollar of the Coin of U State and hand full of beeds, for a Small Sea otter Skin, which I did not much want, he immediately Conceived it of great value, and refused to Sell unless I would give as maney more beads; the next day with a great deel of importunity on his part we receved the Skin in exchange for a fiew Strans of the Same beeds he had refused the day before. I therefore beleive this treat in their Charector proceeds from an avericious all grasping dis-position. in this respect they differ from all Indians I ever became acquainted with, for their dispositions invariably lead them to give what ever they are possessed off no matter how usefull or valueable, for a bauble which pleases their fancy, without Consulting its usefullness or value. nothing occured to day, or more So, than our wappato being all exhausted.

[Lewis, January 5, 1806] Sunday January 5th 1806. At 5 P.M. Willard and Wiser returned, they had not been lost as we apprehended. they informed us that it was not untill the fifth day after leaving the Fort that they could find a convenient place for making salt; that they had at length established themselves on the coast about 15 Miles S. W. from this, near the lodge of some Killamuck families; that the Indians were very friendly and had given them a considerable quantity of the blubber of a whale which perished on the coast some distance S. E. of them; part of this blubber they brought with them, it was white & not unlike the fat of Poark, tho the texture was more spongey and somewhat coarser. I had a part of it cooked and found it very pallitable and tender, it resembled the beaver or the dog in flavour. it may appear somewhat extraordinary tho it is a fact that the flesh of the beaver and dog possess a very great affinity in point of flavour. These lads also informed us that J. Fields, Bratton and Gibson (the Salt makers) had with their assistance erected a comfortable camp killed an Elk and several deer and secured a good stock of meat; they commenced the making of salt and found that they could obtain from 3 quarts to a gallon a day; they brought with them a specemine of the salt of about a gallon, we found it excellent, fine, strong, & white; this was a great treat to myself and most of the party, having not had any since the 20th ultmo.; I say most of the party, for my friend Capt. Clark declares it to be a mear matter of indifference with him whether he uses it or not; for myself I must confess I felt a considerable inconvenience from the want of it; the want of bread I consider as trivial provided, I get fat meat, for as to the species of meat I am not very particular, the flesh of the dog the horse and the wolf, having from habit become equally formiliar with any other, and I have learned to think that if the chord be sufficiently strong, which binds the soul and boddy together, it dose not so much matter about the materials which compose it. Colter also returned this evening unsuccessfull from the chase, having been absent since the 1st Inst.- Capt. Clark determined this evening to set out early tomorrow with two canoes and 12 men in quest of the whale, or at all events to purchase from the Indians a parcel of the blubber, for this purpose he prepared a small assortment of merchandize to take with him.

[Clark, January 5, 1806] Sunday 5th of January 1806 At 5 p.m.Willard and Wiser returned, they had not been lost as we expected. they informd us that it was not untill the 5th day after leaveing the fort, that they Could find a Convenient place for makeing Salt; that they had at length established themselves on the Sea Coast about 15 miles S. W. from this, near the houses of Some Clat Sop & Kil a mox families; that the Indians were very friendly and had given them a considerable quantity of the blubber of the whale which perished on the Coast Some distance S. E. of them, it was white and not unlike the fat of Pork, tho the texture was more Spungey and Somewhat Coarser. we had part of it Cooked and found it very pallitable and tender, it resembles the beaver in flavour. those men also informed us that the Salt makers with their assistance had erected a Comfortable Camp, had killed an Elk and Several Deer and Secured a good Stock of Meat; they Commenced the makeing of Salt and found that they Could make from 3 quarts to a gallon a day; they brought with them a Specimen of the Salt, of about a gallon, we found it excellent white & fine, but not So Strong as the rock Salt or that made in Kentucky or the Western parts of the U, States- this Salt was a great treat to most of the party, haveing not had any Since the 20th ulto. as to my Self I care but little whether I have any with my meat or not; provided the meat fat, haveing from habit become entirely cearless about my diat, and I have learned to think that if the Cord be Sufficiently Strong which binds the Soul and boddy together, it does not So much matter about the materials which Compose it.

Colter returned this evening unsecksessfull from the Chase, haveing been absent since the 1st inst.

I determine to Set out early tomorrow with two canoes & 12 men in quest of the whale, or at all events to purchase from the indians a parcel of the blubber, for this purpose I made up a Small assortment of merchindize, and directed the men to hold themselves in readiness &c.

[Lewis, January 6, 1806] Monday January 6th 1806. Capt Clark set out after an early breakfast with the party in two canoes as had been concerted the last evening; Charbono and his Indian woman were also of the party; the Indian woman was very impotunate to be permited to go, and was therefore indulged; she observed that she had traveled a long way with us to see the great waters, and that now that monstrous fish was also to be seen, she thought it very hard she could not be permitted to see either (she had never yet been to the Ocean).

The Clatsops, Chinnooks, Killamucks &c. are very loquacious and inquisitive; they possess good memories and have repeated to us the names capasities of the vessels &c of many traders and others who have visited the mouth of this river; they are generally low in stature, proportionally small, reather lighter complected and much more illy formed than the Indians of the Missouri and those of our frontier; they are generally cheerfull but never gay. with us their conversation generally turns upon the subjects of trade, smoking, eating or their women; about the latter they speak without reserve in their presents, of their every part, and of the most formiliar connection. they do not hold the virtue of their women in high estimation, and will even prostitute their wives and daughters for a fishinghook or a stran of beads. in common with other savage nations they make their women perform every species of domestic drudgery. but in almost every species of this drudgery the men also participate. their women are also compelled to geather roots, and assist them in taking fish, which articles form much the greatest part of their subsistance; notwithstanding the survile manner in which they treat their women they pay much more rispect to their judgment and oppinions in many rispects than most indian nations; their women are permitted to speak freely before them, and sometimes appear to command with a tone of authority; they generally consult them in their traffic and act in conformity to their opinions. I think it may be established as a general maxim that those nations treat their old people and women with most differrence and rispect where they subsist principally on such articles that these can participate with the men in obtaining them; and that, that part of the community are treated with.least attention, when the act of procuring subsistence devolves intirely on the men in the vigor of life. It appears to me that nature has been much more deficient in her filial tie than in any other of the strong affections of the human heart, and therefore think, our old men equally with our women indebted to civilization for their ease and comfort. Among the Siouxs, Assinniboins and others on the Missouri who subsist by hunting it is a custom when a person of either sex becomes so old and infurm that they are unable to travel on foot from camp to camp as they rome in surch of subsistance, for the children or near relations of such person to leave them without compunction or remose; on those occasions they usually place within their reach a small peace of meat and a platter of water, telling the poor old superannuated wretch for his consolation, that he or she had lived long enough, that it was time they should dye and go to their relations who can afford to take care of them much better than they could. I am informed that this custom prevails even among the Minetares Arwerharmays and Recares when attended by their old people on their hunting excurtions; but in justice to these people I must observe that it appeared to me at their vilages, that they provided tolerably well for their aged persons, and several of their feasts appear to have principally for their object a contribution for their aged and infirm persons.

This day I overhalled our merchandize and dryed it by the fire, found it all damp; we have not been able to keep anything dry for many days together since we arrived in this neighbourhood, the humidity of the air has been so excessively great. our merchandize is reduced to a mear handfull, and our comfort during our return the next year much depends on it, it is therefore almost unnecessary to add that we much regret the reduced state of this fund.

[Clark, January 6, 1806] 2 3 4 5 & all Day 6t of January 1805 all last night rained without intermition, & the morning. I sat out with 12 men in 2 Canoes to around thro the bay and up a Creek to an old landing at which place the Indians have a roade across thro Shashes West I landed made the Canoes fast and Set out up the Cree on a road passed thro 3 Stashes to a pond, then up & around th bend along a bad thick way, took an Indian path which took us to a Creek which runs into the Sand bay at which place we found a Canoe which took over 3 men at a time crossed and on the top of a rise Saw Elk prosued & Killed one and encamped at the forks of a Creek the West Eate th Elk all up. a fine Butifull moon Shining night unto _____, Swan Geese, Brand &c.

[Clark, January 6, 1806] Monday 6th of January 1806 The last evening Shabono and his Indian woman was very impatient to be permitted to go with me, and was therefore indulged; She observed that She had traveled a long way with us to See the great waters, and that now that monstrous fish was also to be Seen, She thought it verry hard that She Could not be permitted to See either (She had never yet been to the Ocian). after an early brackfast I Set out with two Canoes down the Ne tel R into Meriwether Bay with a view to proced on to the Clatsop town, and hire a guide to conduct me through the Creeks which I had every reason to beleeve Comunicated both with the Bay and a Small river near to which our men were making Salt. Soon after I arrived in the Bay the wind Sprung up from the N. W and blew So hard and raised the waves so high that we were obliged to put into a Small Creek Short of the Village. finding I could not proceed on to the Village in Safty, I deturmined to assend this Creek as high as the Canoes would go; which from its directions must be near the open lands in which I had been on the 10th ulto., and leave the Canoes and proceed on by land. at the distance of about 3 miles up this Creek I observed Some high open land, at which place a road Set out and had every appearance of a portage, here I landed drew up the Canoes and Set out by land, proceeded on through 3 deep Slashes to a pond about a mile in length and 200 yards wide, kept up this pond leaving it to the right, and passing the head to a Creek which we Could not Cross, this Creek is the one which I rafted on the 8th & 9 ultimo. and at no great distance from where I crossed in Cus ca lars Canoe on the 10th ulto. to which place I expected a find a canoe, we proceeded on and found a Small Canoe at the place I expected, calculated to Carry 3 men, we crossed and from the top of a ridge in the Prarie we Saw a large gange of Elk feeding about 2 miles below on our direction. I divided the party So as to be Certain of an elk, Several Shot were fired only one Elk fell, I had this Elk butchered and carried to a Creak in advance at which place I intended to encamp, two other Elk were badly Shot, but as it was nearly dark we Could not pursue them, we proceeded on to the forks of the Creek which we had just Crossed turning around to the S W. and meeting one of equal Size from the South, the two makeing a little river 70 yards wide which falls into the Ocian near the 3 Clat Sop houses which I visited on the 9th ulto. in the forks of this Creek we found Some drift pine which had been left on the Shore by the tide of which we made fires. the evening a butifull Clear moon Shiney night, and the 1st fair night which we have had for 2 months

[Lewis, January 7, 1806] Monday January 7th 1806. Last evening Drewyer visited his traps and caught a beaver and an otter; the beaver was large and fat we have therefore fared sumptuously today; this we consider a great prize for another reason, it being a full grown beaver was well supplyed with the materials for making bate with which to catch others. this bate when properly prepared will intice the beaver to visit it as far as he can smell it, and this I think may be safely stated at a mile, their sense of smelling being very accute. To prepare beaver bate, the castor or bark stone is taken as the base, this is gently pressed out of the bladderlike bag which contains it, into a phiol of 4 ounces with a wide mouth; if you have them you will put from four to six stone in a phiol of that capacity, to this you will add half a nutmeg, a douzen or 15 grains of cloves and thirty grains of cinimon finely pulverized, stir them well together and then add as much ardent sperits to the composition as will reduce it the consistency mustard prepared for the table; when thus prepared it resembles mustard precisely to all appearance. when you cannot procure a phiol a bottle made of horn or a tight earthen vessel will answer, in all cases it must be excluded from the air or it will soon loose it's virtue; it is fit for uce immediately it is prepared but becomes much stronger and better in about four or five days and will keep for months provided it be perfectly secluded from the air. when cloves are not to be had use double the quantity of Allspice, and when no spice can be obtained use the bark of the root of sausafras; when sperits cannot be had use oil stone of the beaver adding mearly a sufficient quantity to moisten the other materials, or reduce it to a stif past. it appears to me that the principal uce of the spices is only to give a variety to the scent of the bark stone and if so the mace vineller and other sweetsmelling spices might be employed with equal advantage. The male beaver has six stones, two which contain a substance much like finely pulvarized bark of a pale yellow colour and not unlike tanner's ooz in smell, these are called the bark stones or castors; two others, which like the bark stone resemble small bladders, contain a pure oil of a strong rank disagreeable smell, and not unlike train oil, these are called the oil stones; and 2 others of generation. the Barkstones are about two inches in length, the others somewhat smaller all are of a long oval form; and lye in a bunch together between the skin and the root of the tail, beneath or behind the fundament with which they are closely connected and seem to communicate. the pride of the female lyes on the inner side much like those of the hog. they have no further parts of generation that I can perceive and therefore beleive that like the birds they copulate with the extremity of the gut. The female have from two to four young ones at a birth and bring fourth once a year only, which usually happens about the latter end of may and begining of June. at this stage she is said to drive the male from the lodge, who would otherwise destroy the young.- dryed our lodge and had it put away under shelter; this is the first day during which we have had no rain since we arrived at this place. nothing extraordinary happened today.

[Clark, January 7, 1806] Jany 7th Tuesday 1806 Set out at Day light, porceded up the Creek about 2 mile and crossed on a tree trunk the Salt makers have fallen across, then proceeded on to the Ocean 3/4 mile & proceded up 3 miles to the mouth of Colimex River about 80 or 100 yds verry rapid & Cuts its banks, here we found an old Village of 3 houses, one only inhabited by one familey, I gave the man a fish hook to put the party across, on the bank found a Skeet fish which had been lef by the tide proceded on 2 miles on the bank opposit a kind of bay the river Cross to the Sea Cost to 2 Inds Indians Lodges at which place I found our Salt makers near the foot of a mountain which form the Shore. Brackfast and hirired an Indian to pilot me to the Ca le mix nation where the whale is for which I gave a file, we proceded on the Stone under a high hill on our right bluff. Soft Stone Sees verry high, Several parts of this hill recently Sliped in, about 3/4 of a mile abov the Houses Saw a Canoe in which the Dead was buried at 2 1/2 miles assended a Steep mountain, as Steep at it is possible places for 1500 feet we hauled our Selves up by the assistence of the bushes if one had Given way we must have fallen a great distant the Steepest worst & highest mountain I ever assended I think it at least 1500 feet highr than the Sea imidiately under on the riht. we met 14 Indians loaded with blubber proceded on thro an unusual bad way falling timber bendig under logs &c. and encamped on a Creek which runs to my left find Day and night, the timber Spruc White Cedar & &.

[Clark, January 7, 1806] Tuesday 7th of January 1806 Some frost this morning. It may appear Somewhat incredible, but So it is that the Elk which was killed last evening was eaten except about 8 pounds, which I directed to be taken along with the Skin, I proceeded up the South fork of the Creek about 2 miles and crossed on a pine tree which had been fallen by the Saltmakers on their first going out, on this tree we crossed the deepest of the water and waded on the opposit Side for 30 yards, from thence to the ocian 3/4 of a mile through a Continuation of open ridgey Prarie, here the Coast is Sandy, we proceeded on the Sandy beech nearly South for 3 miles to the mouth of butifull river with bold and rapid Current of 85 yards wide and 3 feet deep in the Shallowest place, a Short distance up this river on the N E Side is the remains of an old village of Clatsops. I entered a house where I found a Man 2 Womn & 3 Children, they appeared retchedly pore & dirty, I hired the man to Set us across the River which I call after the Nation Clat Sop river for which I gave 2 fishing hooks- at this place the Creek over which I crossed on a tree passes within 100 yards of the Clat Sop river over which the nativs have a portage which affords them an easy Communication with the villages near point adams, and at the mouth of the Creek, on which we lay last night. in walking on the Sand after crossing the river I Saw a Singular Species of fish which I had never before Seen one of the men Call this fish a Skaite, it is properly a Thornback. I proceeded on about 2 miles to near the base of high Mountain where I found our Salt makers, and with them Sergt. Gass, Geo. Shannon was out in the woods assisting Jo Field and gibson to kill Some meat, the Salt makers had made a neet Close Camp, Convenient to wood Salt water and the fresh water of the Clat Sop river which at this place was within 100 paces of the Ocian they wer also Situated near 4 houses of Clatsops & Killamox, who they informed me had been verry kind and attentive to them. I hired a young Indian to pilot me to the whale for which Service I gave him a file in hand and promised Several other Small articles on my return, left Sergt. Gass and one man of my party Werner to make Salt & permited Bratten to accompany me, we proceeded on the round Slipery Stones under a high hill which projected into the ocian about 4 miles further than the direction of the Coast. after walking for 2 1/2 miles on the Stones my guide made a Sudin halt, pointed to the top of the mountain and uttered the word Pe Shack which means bad, and made Signs that we could not proceed any further on the rocks, but must pass over that mountain, I hesitated a moment & view this emence mountain the top of which was obscured in the clouds, and the assent appeard. to be almost perpindecular; as the Small Indian parth allong which they had brought emence loads but a fiew hours before, led up this mountain and appeared to assend in a Sideling direction, I thought more than probable that the assent might be torerably easy and therefore proceeded on, I soon found that the _____ become much worst as I assended, and at one place we were obliged to Support and draw our Selves up by the bushes & roots for near 100 feet, and after about 2 hours labour and fatigue we reached the top of this high mountain, from the top of which I looked down with estonishment to behold the hight which we had assended, which appeared to be 10 or 12 hundred feet up a mountain which appeared to be almost perpindicular, here we met 14 Indians men and women loaded with the oil & Blubber of the whale. In the face of this tremendeous precipic imediately below us, there is a Strater of white earth (which my guide informed me) the neighbouring indians use to paint themselves, and which appears to me to resemble the earth of which the French Porcelain is made; I am confident that this earth Contains argill, but whether it also Contains Silex or magnesia, or either of those earths in a proper perpotion I am unable to deturmine. we left the top of the precipice and proceeded on a bad road and encamped on a Small run passin g to the left. all much fatiagued

[Lewis, January 8, 1806] Tuesday January 8th 1806. Our meat is begining to become scarse; sent Drewyer and Collins to hunt this morning. the guard duty being hard on the men who now remain in the fort I have for their relief since the departure of Capt. Clark made the Cooks mount guard. Sergt. Gass and Shannon have not yet returned, nor can I immajen what is the cause of their detention. In consequence of the clouds this evening I lost my P.M. observation for Equal Altitudes, and from the same cause have not been able to take a single observation since we have been at this place. nothing extraordinary happened today.

The Clatsops Chinnooks and others inhabiting the coast and country in this neighbourhood, are excessively fond of smoking tobacco. in the act of smoking they appear to swallow it as they dran it from the pipe, and for many draughts together you will not perceive the smoke which they take from the pipe; in the same manner also they inhale it in their lungs untill they become surcharged with this vapour when they puff it out to a great distance through their nostils and mouth; I have no doubt the smoke of the tobacco in this manner becomes much more intoxicating and that they do possess themselves of all it's virtues in their fullest extent; they freequently give us sounding proofs of it's creating a dismorallity of order in the abdomen, nor are those light matters thought indelicate in either sex, but all take the liberty of obeying the dictates of nature without reserve. these people do not appear to know the uce of sperituous liquors, they never having once asked us for it; I presume therefore that the traders who visit them have never indulged them with the uce of it; from what ever cause this may proceede, it is a very fortunate occurrence, as well for the natives themselves, as for the quiet and safety of thos whites who visit them.

[Clark, January 8, 1806] Jany 8 Wedned Set out at Day a fine morning wind hard from S. E at 1 1/2 miles arived at a Open where I had a view of the Seas Coast for a long Distance rocks in every direction. Struck a branch and come down to the Sea at which place an old village between 2 Creeks of the Colemix Nation which inhabits this Coast, grave yard deposed of in Canoes in which the bodies are laid in boxes in the Canoe, Paddles &c thos poople must use thos Canoes in the higher Seas of which then ever I Saw on a Cost ruding Countrey Crossed 3 points rocks great Distanc in the Sea, hill Sides Sliping from emins ravins which appears to _____ proceeded on to the mouth of a Creek about 80 yards wide at which Place I saw 5 Lodges of Indian of the Ca la mix nation, boiling whale in a trough of about 20 gallons with hot Stones, and the oyle they put into a Canoe I proceded on a Short distance to the whales which was nothing more than the Sceleton, of 105 feet long, we took out a few bones and returned to the Cabins at the mouth of the Creek, and attempted to trade with thos people who I found Close and Capricious, would not trade the Smallest piece except they thought they got an advantage of the bargain, their disposition is averitious, & independant in trade, they offered to trade for Elk of which we had not I purchased some oile and about 120 w of Blubber after rendered, finding they would not trade I Deturmined to return home with what we have The Houses of these people appear temporary a ridge pole on 2 forks Supported a Certain number of Split boards of the red Cedar & pine, Set on the end the gable ends of the Same materials and Calculated for 2 families first, The Dress and appearenc of the nativs as also the language is procisely that of the Clopsots & Chinnooks, those people Save their oile in bladder Guts &c.

Their food is principally fish that is thrown on the Shores by the Seas & left by the tide, This Cost is rockey, the mountains high & rugged, They inform me that their nation lives in 5 villages to the S E of this place at the mouths of Creek in which they catch Samn. in the Season, I got of those people a few roots Some Sturgeon whale-_____ &. They Call a whale E cu-la a Creek Shu man, they have Some fiew Sea ortter for which they ask Such prices I could not purchase any of them

Th party much fatigued in crossing 1 mountain & 4 high Points Steep & Slipery, also Stony Beach Slippery and tiresom The high tide obliged me to delay untill late before the tide put out, I Shot a raven & a gul with my Small riffle which Suppised these people a little They are fond of blue & white large beed only, files & fish Hooks which are large- after Diner we Set out Crossed the Creek in a Small Canoe The tide out and Encamped on the opposit Side, I was asked for ferrage and paid a pin, one hut on the Side in which I Camped & Village a Short distance above which I did not See last night, all the men came over & Smoked with me, about bed time I herd a hollowing on the opposit Side of the river which allarnied all the Indian men about me, they run across the Creek, I Suspected perhaps Some of my party was over after the Squars, by exemening found that McNeal was not in Camp, my guide who Staid with me told me Some body throat was Cut. I emediately Sent Serjt Pryor & 2 men across for McNeal, they Soon returned haveing met the person I was anxious to find out the Cause of the allarm, McNeal Said that a man envited him to go across and get Some fish, locked arms of which he Contd to hold he took him into a lodge and the woman gave him a Small piec the man then invited him to another, the woman of the lodge puled his blanket, & Sent out a Squar to hollow across, to inform of Something which aid. McNeal I Sent over Sergt. Pryor to Know the Cause of the allarm which he was informed that a Plot was laid to kill McNeal for his Blanket & Clothes by this Indian who was from another Villg at Some distance, and that She had attempted to Stop McNeal & findeing She Could not that She then allarmed the men, Several of the mans Band was with me who imedeately Cleared out, 2 men Came over & Slept at my feet. I kept a guard & Sentinel all night a fair night wind blew from S. E. during the evening I acquired all the information possiable respecting the Coast to the S. E. got the name of many nations & the Nos. of their houses, a map of the Coast in their way. I am very pore & weak for want of Sufficient food and fear much that I shall require more assistance to get back than I had to get to this place. a deturmined purcistance will as it has done carry me through

[Clark, January 8, 1806] Wednesday 8th January 1805 The last night proved fair and Cold wind hard from the S. E. we Set out early and proceeded to the top of the mountain next to the which is much the highest part and that part faceing the Sea is open, from this point I beheld the grandest and most pleasing prospects which my eyes ever surveyed, in my frount a boundless Ocean; to the N. and N. E. the coast as as far as my sight Could be extended, the Seas rageing with emence wave and brakeing with great force from the rocks of Cape Disapointment as far as I could See to the N. W. The Clatsops Chinnooks and other villagers on each Side of the Columbia river and in the Praries below me, the meanderings of 3 handsom Streams heading in Small lakes at the foot the high Country; The Columbia River for a Some distance up, with its Bays and Small rivers and on the other Side I have a view of the Coast for an emence distance to the S. E. by S. the nitches and points of high land which forms this Corse for a long ways aded to the inoumerable rocks of emence Sise out at a great distance from the Shore and against which the Seas brak with great force gives this Coast a most romantic appearance. from this point of View my guide pointed to a village at the mouth of a Small river near which place he Said the whale was, he also pointed to 4 other places where the princpal Villages of the Kil la mox were Situated, I could plainly See the houses of 2 of those Villeges & the Smoke of a 3rd which was two far of for me to disern with my naked eye- after taking the Courses and computed the Distances in my own mind, I proceeded on down a Steep decent to a Single house the remains of an old Kil a mox Town in a nitch imediately on the Sea Coast, at which place great no. of eregular rocks are out and the waves comes in with great force. Near this old Town I observed large Canoes of the neetest kind on the ground Some of which appeared nearly decayed others quit Sound, I examoned those Canoes and found they were the repository of the dead- This Custom of Secureing the Dead differs a little from the Chinnooks. the Kil a mox Secure the dead bodies in an oblong box of Plank, which is placed in an open Canoe resting on the ground, in which is put a paddle and Sundery other articles the property of the disceased. The Coast in the neighbourhood of this old village is slipping from the Sides of the high hills, in emence masses; fifty or a hundred acres at a time give way and a great proportion of an instant precipitated into the Ocean. those hills and mountains are principally composed of a yellow Clay; their Slipping off or Spliting assunder at this time is no doubt Caused by the incessant rains which has fallen within the last two months. the mountans Covered with a verry heavy Croth of pine & furr, also the white Cedar or arbor vita and a Small proportion of the black alder, this alder grows to the hight of Sixty or Seventy feet and from 2 to 3 feet in diamiter. Some Species of pine on the top of the Point of View rise to the emmence hight of 210 feet and from 8 to 12 feet in diameter, and are perfectly Sound and Solid. Wind hard from the S. E and See looked _____ in the after part of the Day breaking with great force against the Scattering rocks at Some distance from Shore, and the ruged rockey points under which we wer obleged to pass and if we had unfortunately made one false Stet we Should eneviateably have fallen into the Sea and dashed against the rocks in an instant, fortunately we passed over 3 of those dismal points and arived on a butifull Sand Shore on which we Continued for 2 miles, Crossed a Creek 80 yards near 5 Cabins, and proceeded to the place the whale had perished, found only the Skelleton of this monster on the Sand between 2 of the villages of the Kil a mox nation; the Whale was already pillaged of every valuable part by the Kil a mox Inds. in the vecinity of whose village's it lay on the Strand where the waves and tide had driven up & left it. this Skeleton measured 105 feet. I returned to the village of 5 Cabins on the Creek which I shall call E co-la or whale Creek, found the nativs busily engaged boiling the blubber, which they performed in a large Squar wooden trought by means of hot Stones; the oil when extracted was Secured in bladders and the Guts of the whale; the blubber from which the oil was only partially extracted by this process, was laid by in their Cabins in large flickes for use; those flickes they usially expose to the fire on a wooden Spit untill it is prutty well wormed through and then eate it either alone or with roots of the rush, Shaw na tdk we or diped in the oil. The Kil a mox although they possessed large quantities of this blubber and oil were so prenurious that they disposed of it with great reluctiance and in Small quantities only; insomuch that my utmost exertion aided by the party with the Small Stock of merchindize I had taken with me were not able to precure more blubber than about 300 wt. and a fiew gallons of oil; Small as this Stock is I prise it highly; and thank providence for directing the whale to us; and think him much more kind to us than he was to jonah, having Sent this monster to be Swallowed by us in Sted of Swallowing of us as jonah's did. I recrossed E co la Creek and Encamped on the bank at which place we observed an ebundance of fine wood the Indian men followed me for the purpose of Smokeing. I enquired of those people as well as I could by

Signs the Situation, mode of liveing & Strength of their nation They informed me that the bulk of their nation lived in 3 large villages Still further along the Sea coast to the S, S, W. at the enterence Of 3 Creek which fell into a bay, and that other houses were Scattered about on the Coast, Bay and on a Small river which fell into the Bay in which they Cought Salmon, and from this Creek (which I call Kil a mox River) they crossed over to the Wappato I. on the Shock-ah-lil com (which is the Indian name for the Columbia river) and purchased Wappato &c. that the nation was once verry large and that they had a great maney houses, In Salmon Season they Cought great numbers of that fish in the Small Creeks, when the Salmon was Scerce they found Sturgion and a variety of other fish thrown up by the waves and left by the tide which was verry fine, Elk was plenty in the mountains, but they Could not Kill maney of them with their arrows. The Kil d mox in their habits Customs manners dress & language differ but little from the Clatsops, Chinnooks and others in this neighbourhood are of the Same form of those of the Clatsops with a Dore at each end & two fire places i, e the house is double as long as wide and divided into 2 equal parts with a post in the middle Supporting the ridge pole, and in the middle of each of those divisions they make their fires, dotes Small & houses Sunk 5 feet

[Lewis, January 9, 1806] Friday January 9th 1806. Our men are now very much engaged in dressing Elk and Deer skins for mockersons and cloathing. the deer are extreemly scarce in this neighbourhood, some are to be found near the praries and open grounds along the coast. this evening we heard seven guns in quick succession after each other, they appeared to be on the Creek to the South of us and several miles distant; I expect that the hunters Drewyer and Collins have fallen in with a gang of Elk. some marrow bones and a little fresh meat would be exceptable; I have been living for two days past on poor dryed Elk, or jurk as the hunters term it.

The Clatsops Chinnooks &c. bury their dead in their canoes. for this purpose four pieces of split timber are set erect on end, and sunk a few feet in the grown, each brace having their flat sides opposite to each other and sufficiently far assunder to admit the width of the canoes in which the dead are to be deposited; through each of these perpendicular posts, at the hight of six feet a mortice is cut, through which two bars of wood are incerted; on these cross bars a small canoe is placed in which the body is laid after being carefully roled in a robe of some dressed skins; a paddle is also deposited with them; a larger canoe is now reversed, overlaying and imbracing the small one, and resting with it's gunwals on the cross bars; one or more large mats of rushes or flags are then roled around the canoes and the whole securely lashed with a long cord, usually made of the bark of the Arbor vita or white cedar. on the cross bars which support the canoes is frequently hung or laid various articles of cloathing culinary eutensels &c. I cannot understand them sufficiently to make any enquiries relitive to their religeous opinions, but presume from their depositing various articles with their dead, that they believe in a state of future existence.

The persons who usually visit the entrance of this river for the purpose of traffic or hunting I believe are either English or Americans; the Indians inform us that they speak the same language with ourselves, and give us proofs of their varacity by repeating many words of English, as musquit, powder, shot, nife, file, damned rascal, sun of a bitch &c. whether these traders are from Nootka sound, from some other late establishment on this coast, or immediately from the U States or Great Brittain, I am at a loss to determine, nor can the Indians inform us. the Indians whom I have asked in what direction the traders go when they depart from hence, or arrive here, always point to the S. W. from which it is presumeable that Nootka cannot be their destination; and as from Indian information a majority of these traders annually visit them about the beginning of April and remain with them six or seven Months, they cannot come immediately from Great Britain or the U States, the distance being too great for them to go and return in the ballance of the year. from this circumstance I am sometimes induced to believe that there is some other establishment on the coast of America south West of this place of which little is but yet known to the world, or it may be perhaps on some Island in the pacific ocean between the Continents of Asia and America to the South West of us. This traffic on the part of the whites consists in vending, guns, (principally old british or American musquits) powder, balls and Shot, Copper and brass kettles, brass teakettles and coffee pots, blankets from two to three point, scarlet and blue Cloth (coarse), plates and strips of sheet copper and brass, large brass wire, knives, beads and tobacco with fishinghooks buttons and some other small articles; also a considerable quantity of Sailor's cloaths, as hats coats, trowsers and shirts. for these they receive in return from the natives, dressed and undressed Elkskins, skins of the sea Otter, common Otter, beaver, common fox, spuck, and tiger cat; also dryed and pounded sammon in baskets, and a kind of buisquit, which the natives make of roots called by them shappelell. The natives are extravegantly fond of the most common cheap blue and white beads, of moderate size, or such that from 50 to 70 will weigh one penneyweight. the blue is usually pefered to the white; these beads constitute the principal circulating medium with all the indian tribes on this river; for these beads they will dispose any article they possess.- the beads are strung on strans of a fathom in length and in that manner sold by the bredth or yard.-

[Clark, January 9, 1806] January 9th Thursday 1806 a fine morning wind N E Set out at day lighte every man Some meat of the whale and a little oile proceded on the track we Came out to a house at a branch where we halted 1/2 an hour to rest this house is at at place an old village has formerly been, on the Coast at the

Comencment _____ 27 foot wide 35 feet long Sunk in the ground 5 feet 2 Dotes & 2 fire places dotes 29 Ins. high & 141/4 wide handsom Steps to decend down a post in the middle Coverede with boards Split thin an 2 feet wide, old grave in Canoes of 3 feet 8 Inches wide & 5 feet long neetly made high at bow proceded on to the top of the hill Passing 3 bad points rockey &. from the Point Clarks Point of view Cape Disapt. bears S. 12° E passing a Great point at 15 miles one at 40 miles rocks out to the 1st large point from the Creek 4 points, between the 1st large Point and 2d a point of many large rocks, Day Clouded up, I can See a point Bearing N 5° East along way just in Sight. from Clarks View Point to Cape Disapointment is N 20° W. To point adams &the open Slope point is North and a Sharp point, met a party of Chinnooks going to get whale blubber to eate & oile each of which they eate together, we also over took Several parties of the Clot Sops loaded with imence laods of the blubber and oile maney of those loads I with difficuelty raised, Estonishing what custom will do. at 2 oClock we arrived at the Camp of our Salt makers verry much fatigued, more So than I ever was before, the Indians all proceeded on, I concluded to Stay all night, as the party was much fatigued, and Send out 2 men which I had left here to hunt Ducks up the little river, Jo. Fields had killed an Elk and brought in a quarter on which we Dined he also had killed & brought in a Deer. The Indians with the oile & bluber tole me they had to purchase of the Ca-le nixx and would Come to the fort & Sell to us in 3 Days time, this I incouraged, as I expect to purchase at the fort as cheep as at the village at which I was, day proved fine. rained the greater part of the night I went into an Indian Lodge they were pore Durty and the house full of flees. he offered me roots which they geather on the Sea Cost a kind of rush, of which they offered me to eate,

[Clark, January 9, 1806] Thursday 9th of January 1806 a fine morning wind from the N. E. last night about 10 oClock while Smokeing with the nativ's I was alarmed by a loud Srile voice from the Cabins on the opposite Side, the Indians all run immediately across to the village, my guide who Continued with me made Signs that Some one's throat was Cut, by enquiry I found that one man McNeal was absent, I imediately Sent off Sergt. N. Pryor & 4 men in quest of McNeal who they met comeing across the Creak in great hast, and informed me that the people were alarmed on the opposit Side at Something but what he could not tell, a man had verry friendly envited him to go and eate in his lodge, that the Indian had locked armes with him and went to a lodge in which a woman gave him Some blubber, that the man envited him to another lodge to get Something better, and the woman held him by the blanket which he had around him another ran out and hollow'd and his pretended friend disapeared- I emediately ordered every man to hold themselves in a State of rediness and Sent Sergt. Pryor & 4 men to know the cause of the alarm which was found to be a premeditated plan of the pretended friend of McNeal to assanate for his Blanket and what fiew articles he had about him, which was found out by a Chin nook woman who allarmed the men of the village who were with me in time to prevent the horred act. this man was of another band at Some distance and ran off as Soon as he was discovered. we have now to look back and Shudder at the dreadfull road on which we have to return of 45 miles S E of Point adams & 35 miles from Fort Clatsop. I had the blubber & oil divided among the party and Set out about Sunrise and returned by the Same rout we had went out, met Several parties of men & womin of the Chinnook and Clatsops nations, on their way to trade with the Kil a mox for blubber and oil; on the Steep decent of the Mountain I overtook five men and Six womin with emence loads of the Oil and blubber of the Whale, those Indians had passed by Some rout by which we missed them as we went out yesterday; one of the women in the act of getting down a Steep part of the mountain her load by Some means had Sliped off her back, and She was holding the load by a Strap which was fastened to the mat bag in which it was in, in one hand and holding a bush by the other, as I was in front of my party, I endeavored to relieve this woman by takeing her load untill She Could get to a better place a little below, & to my estonishment found the load as much as I Could lift and must exceed 100 wt. the husband of this woman who was below Soon came to her releif, those people proceeded on with us to the Salt works, at which place we arrived late in the evening, found them without meat, and 3 of the Party J. Field Gibson & Shannon out hunting. as I was excessively fatigued and my party appeared verry much so, I determined to Stay untill the morning and rest our Selves a little. The Clatsops proceeded on with their lodes- The Clatsops, Chin nooks Kil a mox &c. are verry loquacious and inquisitive; they possess good memories and have repeeted to us the names capasities of the Vessels &c of maney traders and others who have visited the mouth of this river; they are generally low in Statue, proportionably Small, reather lighter complected and much more illy formed than the Indians of the Missouri and those of our fronteers; they are generally Chearfull but never gay. with us their Conversation generally turns upon the subject of trade, Smokeing, eating or their womin; about the latter, they Speak without reserve in their presence, of their every part, and of the most farmiliar Connection. they do not hold the virtue of their womin in high estimation, and will even prostitute their wives and Daughters for a fishing hook or a Stran of beeds. in Common with other Savage nations they make their womin perform every Species of domestic drugery; but in almost every Species of this drugery the men also participate. their woman are compelled to gather roots, and assist them in takeing fish; which articles form much the greater part of their Subsistance; notwithstanding the Survile manner in which they treat their womin they pay much more respect to their judgement and oppinion in maney respects than most indian nations; their womin are permited to Speak freely before them, and Sometimes appear to command with a tone of authority; they generally consult them in their traffic and act conformably to their opinions.

I think it may be established as a general maxim that those nations treat their old people and women with most defference and respect where they Subsist principally on Such articles that these can participate with the men in obtaining them; and that, that part of the Community are treated with least attention, when the act of precureing subsistance devolves intirely on the men in the vigor of life. It appears to me that nature has been much more deficient in her filial ties than in any others of the Strong effections of the humane heart, and therefore think our old men equally with our woman indebted to Sivilization for their ease and Comfort. I am told among the Sioux's, Assinniboins and others on the Missouri who Subsist by hunting it is a Custom when a person of either Sex becoms So old and infirm that they are unable to travel on foot, from Camp to Camp as they rove in serch of Subsistance, for the Children or near relations of Such person to leave them without Compunction or remorse; on those occasions they usially place within their reach a Small piece of meat and a platter of water, telling the poor old Superannuated retch for their Consolation, that he or She had lived long enough, and that it was time they Should die and go to their relations who Can afford to take Care of them, much better than they Could. I am informed that the Me ne tar es Ar war har mays and Ricares when attended by their old people on their hunting expedition prosued the Same Custom; but injustice to those people I must observe that it appeared to me at their villages, that they provided tolerably well for their aged persons, and Several of their feasts appear to have principally for their object a contribution for their aged and infirm persons. In one of the Mandan villages I Saw an old man to whome I gave a knife and enquired his age, he Said he had Seen more than 100 winters, and that he Should Soon go down the river to their old village- he requested I would give him Something to prevent the pain in his back his grand Son a Young man rebuked the old man and Said it was not worth while, that it was time for the old man to die. the old man occupied one Side of the fire and was furnished with plenty of Covouring and food, and every attention appeared to be paid him &c. Jo. Field in my absence had killed an Elk and a Deer, brought in the Deer and half of the Elk on a part of which we Suped, Some rain a little after dark. I visited a house near the Salt boilers found it inhabited by 2 families, they were pore dirty and their house Sworming with flees.-

[Lewis, January 10, 1806] Saturday January 10th 1806. About 10 A.M. I was visited by Tia Shah-har-war-cap and eleven of his nation in one large canoe; these are the Cuth'-lah-mah nation who reside first above us on the South side of the Columbia river; this is the first time that I have seen the Chief, he was hunting when we past his vilage on our way to this place. I gave him a medal of the smallest size; he presented me with some indian tobacco and a basquit of wappetoe, in return for which I gave him some thread for making a skiming net and a small piece of tobacco. these people speak the same language with the Chinnooks and Catsops whom they also resemble in their dress customs manners &c. they brought some dryed salmon, wappetoe, dogs, and mats made of rushes and flags, to barter; their dogs and a part of their wappetoe they disposed off, an remained all night near the fort. This morning Drewyer and Collins returned having killed two Elk only, and one of those had died in their view over a small lake which they had not the means of passing it being late in the evening and has of course spoiled, as it laid with the entrals in it all night; as the tide was going out we could not send for the elk today, therefore ordered a party to go for it early in the morning and George and Collins to continue their hunt; meat has now become scarce with us.

Capt Clark returned at to P.M. this evening with the majority of the party who accompanyed him; having left some men to assist the saltmakers to bring in the meat of two Elk which they had killed, and sent 2 others through by land to hunt. Capt. Clark found the whale on the Coast about 45 Miles S. E. of Point Adams, and about 35 Miles from Fort Clatsop by the rout he took; The whale was already pillaged of every valuable part by the Killamucks, in the vicinity of one of whose villages it lay on the strand where the waves and tide had driven up and left it. this skelleton measured one hundred and five feet. Capt. C. found the natives busily engaged in boiling the blubber, which they performed in a large wooden trought by means of hot stones; the oil when extracted was secured in bladders and the guts of the whale; the blubber, from which the oil was only partially extracted by this process, was laid by in their lodges in large fliches for uce; this they usually expose to the fire on a wooden spit untill it is pretty well warmed through and then eat it either alone or with the roots of the rush, squawmash, fern wappetoe &c. The natives although they possessed large quantities of this blubber and oil were so penurious that they disposed of it with great reluctance and in small quantities only; insomuch that the utmost exertions of Capt. C. and the whole party aided by the little stock of merchandize he had taken with him and some small articles which the men had, were not able to procure more blubber than about 300 lb. and a few gallons of the oil; this they have brought with them, and small as the store is, we prize it highly, and thank providence for directing the whale to us, and think him much more kind to us than he was jonah, having sent this monster to be swallowed by us in stead of swallowing of us as jona's did. Capt. C. found the road along the coast extreemly difficult of axcess, lying over some high rough and stoney hills, one of which he discribes as being much higher than the others, having it's base washed by the Ocean over which it rares it's towering summit perpendicularly to the hight of 1500 feet; from this summit Capt. C. informed me that there was a delightfull and most extensive view of the Ocean, the coast and adjacent country; this Mout. I have taken the liberty of naming Clark's Mountain and point of view; it is situated about 30 M. S. E. of Point Adams and projects about 2 1/2 miles into the Ocean; Killamucks river falls in a little to the N. W. of this mountain; in the face of this tremendious precepice there is a stra of white earth (see specimen No. _____) which the neighbouring Indians use to paint themselves, and which appears to me to resemble the earth of which the French Porcelain is made; I am confident this earth contains Argill, but wether it also contains Silex or magnesia, or either of those earths in a proper proportion I am unable to determine.- Shannon and Gass were found with the Salt makers and ordered to return McNeal was near being assassinated by a Killamuck Indian, but fortunately escaped in consequence of a Chinnook woman giving information to Capt. C., the party and Indians with them before the villain had prepaired himself to execute his purposes. The party returned excessively fortiegued and tired of their jaunt. Killamucks river is 85 yards wide, rappid and 3 feet deep in the shallowest part. The Killamucks in their habits customs manners dress and language differ but little from the Clatsops & Chinnooks. they place their dead in canoes resting on the ground uncovered, having previously secured the dead bodies in an oblong box of plank.

The coast in the neighbourhood of Clarks Mountain is sliping off & falling into the Ocean in immence masses; fifty or a hundred Acres at a time give way and a great proportion in an instant precipitated into the Ocean. these hills and mountains are principally composed of a yellow clay; there sliping off or spliting assunder at this time is no doubt caused by the incessant rains which have fallen within the last two months. the country in general as about Fort Clatsop is covered with a very heavy growth of several species of pine & furr, also the arbor vita or white cedar and a small proportion of the black Alder which last sometimes grows to the hight of sixty or seventy feet, and from two to four feet in diameter. some species of the pine rise to the immence hight of 210 feet and are from 7 to 12 feet in diameter, and are perfectly sound and solid.

[Clark, January 10, 1806] Jany 10 Friday 1806 I left Sergt. Gass here and Set out at Sun rise, Crossed the little river which I waded 85 yards wide & 3 feet Deep Swift, at which place I Saw Several Indians one of which had 2 butifull Sea orter Skins on as a roabe, here the Creek which I crossed at a tree and on which I camped the 6th inst. came within 200 yds of the river & they Inds. make a portage here, Continued on a place 3 miles Crossed this Creek in a Small Canoe. here I expected to find Shannon and gibson with meet to furnish the Salt makers, but did not, divided the party Sent 2 men to my right to try and kill Elk, Soon after met Gibson & Shannon with meat, they had killed 2 Elk 2 miles to my right, I divided the meat between the party, and the load of 3 men whome I Send with gibson & Shannon to help Carrey the 2 Elk to the Salt makers, and I my Self and the party returned by the Same rout we went out to the Canoes Rd. Frasure behaved very badly, and mutonous- he also lost his large Knife. I Sent him back to look for his knife, with Directions to return with the party of Serjt Gass, I proceded on, here is a portage of 1/4 of a mile from this Creck to a branch which falls into the Bay, we proceeded on a much bette road than we went out across a Deep Slash and found our Canoes Safe, and Set out at Sunset, and arived at the foart, wet and Cold at 9 oClock P.M. found a Cheif & number of Indians both Encamped on the Shore, and at the fort of the Cath la-hur Tribe which lives at no great distance above this back of an Island Close under the South Side of the Columbia River

Those people Speake the Same Language of the Clotsops dress nearly alike the men of both Cut their hair in the neck. use blankets of the manifactory of the nativs near the falls of the Sheep Wool-fond of brass arm bands and Check, They bring Wap-pa-to root (which is Sagittifolia or the Common arrow head which is Cultivated by the Chinees) to Sell.

[Clark, January 10, 1806] Friday the 10th of January 1806 I derected Serjt. Gass to Continue with the Salt makers untill Shannon return from hunting, and then himself and Shannon to return to the Fort, I Set out at Sunrise with the party waded the Clat Sop river which I found to be 85 Steps across and 3 feet deep, on the opposite Side a Kil a mox Indian Came to and offered to Sell Some roots of which I did not want, he had a robe made of 2 large Sea otter Skins which I offered to purchase, but he would not part with them, we returned by nearly the Same rout which I had Come out, at four miles, I met Gibson & Shannon each with a load of meat, they informed me that they had killed Elk about 2 miles off, I directed 3 men to go with the hunters and help them pack the meat to the place they were makeing Salt, and return to the fort with Serjt. Gass, the balance of the party took the load of the 3 men, after crossing the 2d Creek frasure informed me that he had lost his big knife, here we Dined, I put frasurs load on my guide who is yet with me, and Sent him back in Serch of his knife with directions to join the other men who were out packing meat & return to the fort all together. I arrived at the Canoes about Sunset, the tides was Comeing in I thought it a favourable time to go on to the fort at which place we arrived at 10 oClock P M, found Several inidians of the Cath'-lah-mah nation the great Chief Shahhar-wah cop who reside not far above us on the South Side of the Columbia River, this is the first time I have Seen the Chief, he was hunting when we passed his village on our way to this place, we gave him a medal of the Smallest Size, he presented me with a basquet of Wappato, in return for which I gave him a fish hook of a large Size and Some wire, those people Speak the Same language with the Chinnooks and Clatsops, whome they all resemble in Dress, Custom, manners &c. they brought Some Dried Salmon, Wappato, Dogs, and mats made of rushes & flags to barter; their Dogs and part of their wappato they disposed of, and remained in their Camp near the fort all night.

In my absence the hunters from the fort killed only two Elk which is yet out in the woods. Capt. Lewis examined our Small Stock of merchendize found Some of it wet and Dried it by the fire. Our merchindize is reduced to a mear handfull, and our Comfort, dureing our return next year, much depends on it, it is therefore almost unnecessary to add that it is much reduced The nativs in this neighbourhood are excessively fond of Smokeing tobacco. in the act of Smokeing they appear to Swallow it as they draw it from the pipe, and for maney draughts together you will not perceive the Smoke they take from the pipe, in the Same manner they inhale it in their longs untill they become Surcharged with the vapour when they puff it out to a great distance through their norstils and mouth; I have no doubt that tobacco Smoked in this manner becomes much more intoxicating, and that they do possess themselves of all its virtues to the fullest extent; they frequently give us Sounding proofs of its createing a dismorallity of order in the abdomen, nor are those light matters thought indelicate in either Sex, but all take the liberty of obeying the dicktates of nature without reserve. Those people do not appear to know the use of Speritious licquors, they never haveing once asked us for it; I prosume therefore that the traders who visit them have never indulged them with the use of it; of whatever Cause this may proceed, it is a verry fortunate occurrence, as well for the nativs themselves, as for the quiet and Safty of those whites who visit them. George Drewyer visited this traps in my absence and caught a Beaver & a otter; the beaver was large and fat, and Capt. L. has feested Sumptiously on it yesterday; this we Consider as a great prize, it being a full grown beaver was well Supplyed with the materials for makeing bate with which to Catch others. this bate when properly prepared will entice the beaver to visit it as far as he can Smell it, and this I think may be Safely Stated at 1/2 a mile, their Sence of Smelling being verry accute. To prepare beaver bate, the Caster or bark Stone is taken as the base, this is generally pressed out of the bladder like bag which Contains it, into a phiol of 4 ounces with a wide mouth; if you have them you will put from 4 to 6 Stone in a phial of that Capacity, to this you will add half a nutmeg, a Dozen or 15 grains of Cloves and 30 grains of Sinimon finely pulverised, Stur them well together, and then add as much ardent Sperits to the Composition as will reduce it to the Consistancey of mustard prepared for the table, when thus prepared it resembles mustard precisely to all appearance. When you cannot precure a phial a bottle made of horn or a light earthern vessel will answer, in all Cases it must be excluded from the air or it will Soon lose its Virtue; it is fit for use imediately it is prepared but becoms much Stronger and better in 4 or 5 days and will keep for months provided it be purfectly Secluded from the air. when Cloves are not to be had use double the quantity of allspice, and when no Spices can be obtained use the bark of the root of the Sausafras; when Sperits cannot be had use oil Stone of the beaver adding mearly a Sufficent quantity to moisten the other materials, or reduce it to a Stiff paste. it appears to me that the principal use of the Spices is only to give a variety to the Scent of the bark Stone and if So the mace vineller, and other Sweet Smelling Spices might be employd with equal advantage. The Male Beaver has Six stones, two which Contanes a Substance much like finely pulverised bark of a pale yellow Colour and not unlike tanner's ooz in Smell, these are Called the bark Stones or castors; two others, which like the bark stone resemble Small blatters, contain a pure oil of a Strong rank disagreable Smell, and not unlike train Oil, these are Called the Oil Stones, and two others of Generation. The bark stones are about 2 inches in length, the others Somewhat Smaller, all are of a long Oval form, and lye in a bunch together between the skin and the root of the tail beneath or behind the fundiment with which they are Closely Connected and Seam to Communicate, the pride of the female lye on the inner Side much like those of the hog they have no further parts of Generation that I can proceive, and therefore believe that like the birds they Coperate with the extremity of the gut. The female have from 2 to 4 young ones at a birth and bring forth once a year only which usially happins about the Latter end of May and beginning of June. at this Stage She is Said to drive the Mail from the lodge, who would otherwise distroy the young

[Lewis, January 11, 1806] Sunday January 11th 1806. Sent a party early this morning for the Elk which was killed on the 9th. they returned with it in the evening; Drewyer and Collins also returned without having killed anything. this morning the Sergt. of the guard reported the absence of our Indian Canoe, on enquiry we found that those who came in it last evening had been negligent in securing her and the tide in the course of the night had taken her off; we sent a party down to the bay in surch of her, they returned unsuccessfull, the party also who went up the river and Creek in quest of the meat were ordered to lookout for her but were equally unsuccessfull; we ordered a party to resume their resurches for her early tomorrow; this will be a very considerable loss to us if we do not recover her; she is so light that four men can carry her on their sholders a mile or more without resting; and will carry three men and from 12 to 15 hundred lbs. the Cuthlahmahs left us this evening on their way to the Catsops, to whom they purpose bartering their wappetoe for the blubber and oil of the whale, which the latter purchased for beads &c. from the Killamucks; in this manner there is a trade continually carryed on by the natives of the river each trading some article or other with their neighbours above and below them; and thus articles which are vended by the whites at the entrance of this river, find their way to the most distant nations enhabiting it's waters.

[Clark, January 11, 1806] Saturday 11th of January 1806 Sent a party early this morning for the Elk which was killed on the 9th they returned with it in the evining; This morning the Serjt. of the guard reported that our Indian Canoe had gone a Drift, on enquiry we found that those who Came in it last evening had been negligent in Secureing her, and the tide in Corse of the night had taken her off; we Sent a party down to the bay in Serch of her, they returned unsecksessfull, the party who went up the river and Creek after meat were derected to look out for her but were equally unsecksessfull; this will be a verry considerable loss to us if we do not recover her, She is so light that 4 men Can Carry her on their Sholders a mile or more without resting, and will Carry four men and from 10 to 12 hundred pounds. The Cath IA mahs left us this evening on their way to the Clatsops, to whome they perpose bartering their wappato for the blubber & Oil of the whale, which the latter purchased for Beeds &c. from the Kil a mox; in this manner there is a trade Continually Carried on by the nativs of the river each tradeing Some articles or other with their neighbours above and below them, and those articles which are Vended by the whites at their enterance of this river, find their way to the most distant nations inhabiting its waters.

[Lewis, January 12, 1806] Monday January 12th 1806. The men who were sent in surch of the canoe returned without being able to find her, we therefore give her over as lost. This morning sent out Drewyer and one man to hunt, they returned in the evening, Drewyer having killed seven Elk; I scarcely know how we should subsist were it not for the exertions of this excellet hunter. At 2 P.M. the ballance of the party who had been left by Capt. C. arrived; about the same time the two hunters also arrived who had been dispatched by Capt C. for the purpose of hunting on the 9th inst.; they had killed nothing. We have heretofore usually divided the meat when first killed among the four messes into which we have divided our party leaving to each the care of preserving and the discretion of using it, but we find that they make such prodigal use of it when they hapen to have a tolerable stock on hand that we have determined to adapt a different system with our present stock of seven Elk; this is to jerk it & issue it to them in small quantities.

[Clark, January 12, 1806] Sunday the 12th January 1806 This morning Sent out Drewyer and one man to hunt, they returned in the evening Drewyer haveing killed 7 Elk; I scercely know how we Should Subsist, I beleive but badly if it was not for the exertions of this excellent hunter; maney others also exert themselves, but not being accquainted with the best method of finding and killing the elk and no other wild animals is to be found in this quarter, they are unsucksessfull in their exertions. at 2 P. M Serjt. Gass and the men I left to assist the Salt makers in Carrying in their meat arrived also the hunters which I directed to hunt in the point, they killed nothing-. We have heretofore devided the meat when first killed among the four messes, into which we have divided our party, leaveing to each the Care of preserving and distribution of useing it; but we find that they make such prodigal use of it when they happen to have a tolerable Stock on hand, that we are determined to adapt a Different System with our present stock of Seven Elk; this is to jurk it and issue it to them in Small quantities

[Lewis, January 13, 1806] Tuesday January 13th 1806. This morning I took all the men who could be spared from the Fort and set out in quest of the flesh of the seven Elk that were killed yesterday, we found it in good order being untouched by the wolves, of which indeed there are but few in this country; at 1 P.M. we returned having gotten all the meat to the fort. this evening we exhausted the last of our candles, but fortunately had taken the precaution to bring with us moulds and wick, by means of which and some Elk's tallow in our possession we do not yet consider ourselves destitute of this necessary article; the Elk we have killed have a very small portion of tallow.

The traders usually arrive in this quarter, as has been before observed, in the month of April, and remain untill October; when here they lay at anchor in a bay within Cape Disappointment on the N. side of the river; here they are visited by the natives in their canoes who run along side and barter their comodities with them, their being no houses or fortification on shore for that purpose. the nations who repare thither are fist, those of the sea coast S. E. of the entrance of the river, who reside in the order in which their names are mentioned, begining at the entrance of the river (viz) The Clatsop, Killamuck, Ne-cost, Nat-ti, Nat-chies, Tarl-che, E-slitch, You-cone and So-see. secondly those inhabiting the N. W. coast begining at the entrance of the river and mentioned in the same order; the Chinnook and Chiltch the latter very numerous; and thirdly the Cath-lah-mah, and Skil-lutes, the latter numerous and inhabiting the river from a few miles above the marshey Islands, where the Cuth-lahmahs cease, to the grand rappids. These last may be esteemed the principal carryers or intermediate traders betwen the whites and the Indians of the Sea Coast, and the E-ne-shurs, the E-chee-lutes, and the Chil-luckkit-te quaws, who inhabit the river above, to the grand falls inclusive, and who prepare most of the pounded fish which is brought to market. The bay in which this trade is carryed on is spacious and commodious, and perfectly secure from all except the S. and S. E. winds, these however are the most prevalent and strong winds in the Winter season. fresh water and wood are very convenient and excellent timber for refiting and reparing vessels.

[Clark, January 13, 1806] Monday 13th January 1806 Capt. Lewis took all the men which Could be Speared from the Fort and Set out in quest of the flesh of the Seven Elk which were killed yesterday they found the meat all Secure untouched by the Wolves, of which indeed there are but fiew in this Countrey; at 1 P.M. the party returned with the 2d and Last load of meat to the fort. this evening we finished all last of our Candles, we brought with us, but fortunately had taken the precaution to bring with us moulds and wick, by means of which and Some Elk tallow in our possession we do not think our Selves distitute of this necessary article, the Elk which have been killed have a verry Small portion of tallow. The Traders usially arrive in this quarter, in the month of april, and remain until October; when here they lay at anchor in a Bay within Cape Disapointent on the N. Side of the river; here they are visited by the nativs in their Canoes who run along Side and barter their Comodities with them, their being no houses or fortification on Shore for that purpose.

The nations who repare thither ar first those of the Sea Coast S. E & N W of the enterance of the river, who reside in the order in which their names are mentioned to the S E. the Clat Sops, Kil-a-mox, and those to the N W. the Chin nooks, and Chiltch; and Secondly the Cath-lah-mah, War-ki-a-cum, and Skil-lutes, the latter noumerous and inhabiting those last may be considered or intermedeate traders between the whites and nations on the Sea Coast, and the E-ne-churs, the E-chee-lutes, and the Chil-luck-kitte-quaws, who inhabit the river up to the great falls inclusive, and who prepare most of the pounded fish which is brought to Market.

The Bay in which the trade is Carried on is Spacious and Commodious, and perfectly Secure from all except the S. & S E Winds and those blow but Seldom the most prevalent & Strong winds are from the S W & N W in the Winter Season. fish water and wood are very Convenient and excellent timber for refitting and repareing vessels.-.

[Lewis, January 14, 1806] Wednesday January 14th 1806. This morning the Sergt. of the Guard reported the absence of one of the large perogues, it had broken the chord by which it was attatched and the tide had taken it off; we sent a party immediately in surch of her, they returned in about 3 hours having fortunately found her. we now directed three of the perogues to be drawn up out of reach of the tide and the fourth to be mored in the small branch just above the landing and confined with a strong rope of Elk-skin. had we lost this perogue also we should have been obliged to make three small ones, which with the few tools we have now left would be a serious undertaking. a fatiegue of 6 men employed in jerking the Elk beaf.

From the best estimate we were enabled to make as we dscended the Columbia we conceived that the natives inhabiting that noble stream, for some miles above the great falls to the grand rappids inclusive annually prepare about 30,000 lbs. of pounded sammon for market. but whether this fish is an article of commerce with the whites or is exclusively sold to and consumed by the natives of the sea Coast, we are at a loss to determine. the first of those positions I am disposed to credit most, but, still I must confess that I cannot imagine what the white merchant's object can be in purchasing this fish, or where they dispose of it. and on the other hand the Indians in this neighbourhood as well as the Skillutes have an abundance of dryed sammon which they take in the creeks and inlets, and I have never seen any of this pounded fish in their lodges, which I pesume would have been the case if they purchased this pounded fish for their own consumption. the Indians who prepared this dryed and pounded fish, informed us that it was to trade with the whites, and shewed us many articles of European manufacture which they obtained for it. it is true they obtain those articles principally for their fish but they trade with the Skillutes for them and not immediately with the whites; the intermediate merchants and carryers, the Skillutes, may possibly consume a part of this fish themselves and dispose of the ballance of it the natives of the sea coast, and from them obtain such articles as they again trade with the whites.

[Clark, January 14, 1806] Tuesday 14th January 1806 This morning the Serjt. of the guard reported the absence of one of our Canoes it had broken the Cord by which it was attached and the tide had taken her off; we Sent a party imediately in Serch of her, they returned in about 3 hours haveing fortunately found her. we now derect that 3 of the canoes be drawed up out of reach of the tide and the 4th to be tied with a long Strong Cord of Elk Skins, ready for use. had we lost this large Canoe we Should have been obliged to make 3 other Small ones, which with the fiew tools we have now left would be a Serious undertakeing. a fatiege of Six men employd in jurking the Elk beef. From the best estermate we were enabled to make as we decended the Columbia we Conceived that the nativs inhabiting that noble Stream (from the enterance of Lewis's river to the neighbourhood of the falls the nativs Consume all the fish they Catch either for food or fuel) From Tow ar ne hi ooks River or a fiew mils above the Great falls to the grand rapids inclusive anually prepare about 30,000 lbs of pounded fish (Chiefly Salmon) for market, but whether this fish is an article of Commerce with their neighbours or is exclusively Sold to, and Consumed by the nativs of the Sea coast, we are at a loss to determine the latter of those positions I am dispose to credit most, as I cannot imagine what the white merchents objet Could be in purchaseing fish, or where they Could dispose of it. on the other hand the Indians in this neighbourhood as well as the Skillutes and those above have an abundance of Dryed Salmon which they take in the Creeks and inlets. they are excessively fond of the pounded fish haveing frequently asked us for Some of it-. the Indians who prepared this pounded fish made Signs that they traded it with people below them for Beeds and trinkets &c and Showed us maney articles of European manufacture which they obtained for it; The Skillutes and Indians about the great rapids are the intermediate merchants and Carryers, and no doubt Consume a part of this fish themselves and dispose of the ballance of it to the nativs of the Sea coast, and from this obtain Such articles as they again trade with the whites.

The persons who usially visit the enterence of this river for the purpose of traffic or hunting, I believe is either English or Americans; the Indians inform us that they Speak the Same language with our Selves, and gave us proofs of their varacity by repeating maney words of English, Sun of a pitch &c. whether those traders are from Nootka Sound, from Some other late establishment on this Coast, or imediately from the U States or Great Brittain, I am at a loss to determine, nor Can the Indians inform us. the Indians whome I have asked in what direction the traders go when they depart from hence, allways point to the S. W. from which it is prosumeable that Nootka cannot be their distination, and from Indian information a majority of those traders annually visit them about the beginning of April and remain Some time and either remain or revisit them in the fall of which I cannot properly understand, from this Circumstance they Cannot Come directly from the U States or Great Brittain, the distance being to great for them to go and return in the ballance of a year. I am Sometimes induced to believe that there is Some other Establishment on the Coast of America South of this place of which little is but yet known to the world, or it may be perhaps on Some Island in the Pacific Ocian between the Continant of America & Asia to the S. W. of us. This traffic on the part of the whites Consist in vending, guns, principally old British or American Musquets, powder, balls and Shote, brass tea kettles, Blankets from two to three points, Scarlet and blue Cloth (Coarse), plates and Strips of Sheet Copper and brass, large brass wire Knives Beeds &Tobacco with fishing hooks, buttons and Some other Small articles; also a considerable quantity of Salors Clothes, as hats, Coats, Trouses and Shirts. for those they receive in return from the nativs Dressed and undressed Elk Skins, Skins of the Sea otter, Common Otter, beaver, common fox, Speck, and tiger Cat, also Some Salmon dried or pounded and a kind of buisket, which the nativs make of roots called by them Shappelell. The nativs are extravigantly fond of the most Common Cheap Blue and white beeds, of moderate Size, or Such that from 50 to 70 will way one pennyweight, the blue is usially prefured to the white; those beeds Constitute the principal Circulating medium with all the Indian tribes on this river; for those beeds they will dispose of any article they possess-. the beeds are Strung on Straps of a fathom in length & in that manner Sold by the breth or yard-.

[Lewis, January 15, 1806] Thursday January 15th 1806. Had a large coat completed out of the skins of the Tiger Cat and those also of a small animal about the size of a squirrel not known to me; these skins I procured from the Indians who had previously dressed them and formed them into robes; it took seven of these robes to complete the coat. we had determined to send out two hunting parties today but it rained so incessantly that we posponed it. no occurrence worthy of relation took place today.

The implyments used by the Chinnooks Clatsops Cuthlahmahs &c in hunting are the gun the bow & arrow, deadfalls, pitts, snares, and spears or gigs; their guns are usually of an inferior quality being oald refuse American & brittish Musquits which have been repared for this trade. there are some very good peices among them, but they are invariably in bad order; they apear not to have been long enouh accustomed to fire arms to understand the management of them. they have no rifles. Their guns and amunition they reserve for the Elk, deer and bear, of the two last however there are but few in their neighbourhood. they keep their powder in small japaned tin flasks which they obtain with their amunition from the traders; when they happen to have no ball or shot, they substitute gravel or peices of potmettal, and are insensible of the damage done thereby to their guns. The bow and arrow is the most common instrument among them, every man being furnished with them whether he has a gun or not; this instrument is imployed indiscriminately in hunting every species of anamal on which they subsist. Their bows are extreamly neat and very elastic, they are about two and a half feet in length, and two inches in width in the center, thence tapering graduly to the extremities where they are half an inch wide they are very flat and thin, formed of the heart of the arbor vita or white cedar, the back of the bow being thickly covered with sinews of the Elk laid on with a gleue which they make from the sturgeon; the string is made of sinues of the Elk also. the arrow is formed of two parts usually sha sometime entire; those formed of two parts are unequally divided that part on which the feathers are placed occupyes four fifths of it's length and is formed of light white pine reather larger than a swan's quill, in the lower extremity of this is a circular mortice secured by sinues roled arround it; this mortice receives the one end of the 2nd part which is of a smaller size than the first and about five inches long, in the end of this the barb is fixed and confined with sinue, this barb is either stone, iron or copper, if metal in this form forming at it's point a greater angle than those of any other Indians I have observed. the shorter part of the arrow is of hearder wood as are also the whole of the arrow when it is of one piece only. as these people live in a country abounding in ponds lakes &c and frequently hunt in their canoes and shoot at fowl and other anamals where the arrow missing its object would be lost in the water they are constructed in the manner just discribed in order to make them float should they fall in the water, and consequently can again he recovered by the hunter; the quiver is usually the skin of a young bear or that of a wolf invariably open at the side in stead of the end as the quivers of other Indians generally are; this construction appears to answer better for the canoe than if they were open at the end only. maney of the Elk we have killed since we have been here, have been wounded with these arrows, the short piece with the barb remaining in the animal and grown up in the flesh.- the deadfalls and snares are employed in taking the wolf the raccoon and fox of which there are a few only. the spear or gig is used to take the sea otter, the common otter, spuck, and beaver. their gig consists of two points or barbs and are the same in their construction as those discribed before as being common among the Indians on the upper part of this river. their pits are employed in taking the Elk, and of course are large and deep, some of them a cube of 12 or 14 feet. these are usually placed by the side of a large fallen tree which as well as the pit lye across the toads frequented by the Elk. these pitts are disguised with the slender boughs of trees and moss; the unwary Elk in passing the tree precipitates himself into the pitt which is sufficiently deep to prevent his escape, and is thus taken.

[Clark, January 15, 1806] Friday 15th of January 1806 Capt. Lewis had a large Coat finished made of the Skins of the tiger Cat, and those of the Small animal about the Size of Small Cat not known to me; those Skins were precured from the Indians who had previously dressed them and formed them into robes; it took Seven of those robes to Complete the Coat. no occurrence worthey of remark took place. rained hard all day. The imployments used by the Chinnooks Clatsops, Cath lah mahs Kil a mox &c. in hunting are the gun the bow & arrow, dead falls, Pitts, Snares, and Spears or gigs; their guns are usially of an inferior quallity being old refuse american or brittish muskets which have been repared for this trade there are Some verry good pieces among them, but they are invariably in bad order they appear not to be long enough acquainted with fire arms to understand the management of them. They have no rifles. Their guns and amunition they reserve for the Elk, Deer, and Bear, of the two last however there are but fiew in their neighbourhoods. they keep their powder in Small japaned tin flasks which they obtain with their amunition from the traders; when they happen to have no Ball or Shot they Substitute Gravel and are insenceable of the dammage done thereby to their Guns.

The Bow and arrow is the most common instrement among them, every man being furnished with them whether he has a gun or not, this instrement is imployed indiscreminately in hunting every Species of animal on which they Subsist, Their bows are extreemly meet neat and very elastic, they are about two feet Six inches long and two inches wide in the Center, thence tapering gradually to the extremities, where they ar 3/4 of an Inch wide, they are very flat and thin, formed of the heart of the arbor vita or white Cedar, the back of the Bow being thickly Covered with Sinues of the Elk laid on with a Gleue which they make from the Sturgeon; the String is made of the Sinues of the Elk also, the arrow is formed of two parts usually tho Sometimes entire; those formed of 2 parts are unequailly devided, the part on which the feathers are placed occupie 4/5 of it's length and is formed of light white pine rather larger than a Swans quill, in the lower extremity of this is a Circular mortice Secured by Sinues raped around it; this mortice recives the one end of the 2d part which is of Smaller Size than the first and about five inches long, in the end of this the barb is fixed and Confined with Sinues, the berb is either Iron Copper or Stone- in this form forming at its point a greater angle than those of any other Indians I have observed. The Shorter part of the arrow is of harder wood, as are also the whole of the arrow where it is of one piece only. as these people live in a Countrey abounding in Ponds lakes &c. and frequently hunt in their Canoes and Shoot at fowls and other animals where the arrow missing its object would be lost in the water they are constructed in the Manner just discribed in order to make them flote Should they fall in the water, and Consequently Can again be recovered by the hunter; the quiver is useally the Skin of a young bear or that of a wolf invariably open at the Side in Sted of the end, as the quiver of other Indians generally are, this Construction appears to answer better for the Canoe, than if they were open at the end only. maney of the Elk which our hunters have killd. Sence we have been here have been wounded with those arrows, the Short piece with the barbe remaining in the Animal and grown up in the flesh.- the Deadfalls & Snares are employd in takeing the Wolf, the racoon and fox of which there are a fiew. the Spear or gig is used to take the Sea otter, Spuck, & Beaver. The gig consists of two points or birbs and are the Same in their Construction as those which are Common among the Indians on the upper part of this river and before discribed. Their pitts are employed in takeing the Elk, and of Course are large and Deep, Some of them a Cube of 12 or 14 feet, those ar commonly placed by the Side of a large fallen tree which as well as the pitt lie across the roads frequented by the Elk, these pitts are disguised with the Slender bows of trees & moss; the unwarry Elk in passing the tree precipates himself into the Pitt which is Sufficiently deep to prevent his escape.-

[Lewis, January 16, 1806] Friday January 16th 1806. This evening we finished curing the meat. no occurrence worthy of relation took place today. we have plenty of Elk beef for the present and a little salt, our houses dry and comfortable, and having made up our minds to remain until the 1st of April, every one appears content with his situation and his fare. it is true that we could even travel now on our return as far as the timbered country reaches, or to the falls of the river; but further it would be madness for us to attempt to proceede untill April, as the indians inform us that the snows lye knee deep in the plains of Columbia during the winter, and in these plains we could scarcely get as much fuel of any kind as would cook our provision as we descended the river; and even were we happyly over these plains and again in the woody country at the foot of the Rocky Mountains we could not possibly pass that immence barrier of mountains on which the snows ly in winter to the debth in many places of 20 feet; in short the Indians inform us that they are impracticable untill about the 1st of June, at which time even there is an abundance of snow but a scanty subsistence may be obtained for the horses.- we should not therefore forward ourselves on our homeward journey by reaching the rocky mountains early than the 1st of June, which we can easily effect by seting out from hence on the 1st of April.

The Clatsops Chinnooks &c. in fishing employ the common streight net, the scooping or diping net with a long handle, the gig, and the hook and line. the common net is of different lengths and debths usually employed in taking the sammon, Carr and trout in the inlets among the marshey grounds and the mouths of deep creeks. the skiming or scooping net to take small fish in the spring and summer season; the gig and hook are employed indiscriminately at all seasons in taking such fish as they can procure by their means. their nets and fishing lines are made of the silk-grass or white cedar bark; and their hooks are generally of European manufactary, tho before the whites visited them they made hooks of bone and other substances formed in the following manner A C, and C. B. are two small pieces of bone about the size of a strong twine, these are flattened and leveled off of their extremities near C. where they are firmly attatched together with sinues and covered with rosin. C A. is reduced to a sharp point at A where it is also bent in a little; C B. is attatched to the line, for about half it's length at the upper extremity B. the whole forming two sides of an accute angled triangle.

[Clark, January 16, 1806] Saturday 16th January 1806 This evening we finished cureing the meat. no occurrence worthey of relation took place to day. we have a plenty of Elk beef for the present and a little Salt, our houses dry and Comfortable, haveing made up our minds to Stay untill the 1st of April every one appears contented with his Situation, and his fair. it is true we Could travel even now on our return as far as the timbered Country reaches, or to the falls of the river, but further it would be madness for us to attempt to proceed untill april, as the indians inform us that the Snows lyes knee deep in the Columbian Plains dureing the winter, and in those planes we could not git as much wood as would Cook our provisions untill the drift wood comes down in the Spring and lodges on the Shore &c. and even were we happily over those plains and in the woodey countrey at the foot of the rockey mountains, we could not possibly pass that emence bearier of mountains on which the Snow lyes in winter to the debth in maney placs of 20 feet; in Short the Indians tell us they impassable untill about the 1s of June, at which time even then is an abundance of snow but a Scanty Subsistance may be had for the horses- we Should not foward our homeward journey any by reaching the Rocky mountains earlier than the 1st of June which we can effect by Setting out from hence by the 1st of April

The Clatsops, Chinnooks &c. in fishing employ the Common Streight net, the Scooping or dipping net with a long handle, the gig, and the hook and line. the Common nets are of different lengths and debths usually employd in takeing the Salmon, Carr and trout in the inlets among the marshey grounds and the mouths of deep Creeks,- the Skiming or scooping nets to take Smaller fish in the Spring and Summer Season; the gig and hook are employed indiscreminately at all Seasons in takeing Such fish as they Can precure by these means. their nets and fishing lines are made of the Silk Grass or white Cedar bark; and their hooks are generally of European manufactory, tho before the whites visited them they made their Hooks of bone and other Substances formed in the following manner A C and B C are two Small pieces of bone about the Size of a Strong twine, these are flattened & beaveled off to their extremites at C, where they are firmley attached together and Covered with rozin C A is reduced to a Sharp point at A where it is also bent in a little; C B is attached to the line, at the upper extremity B. the whole forming two Sides of an accute angled triangle. the line has a loop at D which it is anexed to a longer line and taken off at pleasure. Those Hooks are yet common among the nativs on the upper parts of the Columbia river for to Catch fish in Deep places.

[Lewis, January 17, 1806] Saturday January 17th 1806 This morning we were visited by Comowool and 7 of the Clatsops our nearest neighbours, who left us again in the evening. They brought with them some roots and buries for sale, of which however they disposed of but very few as they asked for them such prices as our stock in trade would not license us in giving. the Chief Comowool gave us some roots and buries for which we gave him in return a mockerson awl and some thread; the latter he wished for the purpose of making a skiming net. one of the party was dressed in three very eligant Sea Otter skins which we much wanted; for these we offered him many articles but he would not dispose of them for any other consideration but blue beads, of these we had only six fathoms left, which being 4 less than his price for each skin he would not exchange nor would a knife or an equivalent in beads of any other colour answer his purposes, these coarse blue beads are their favorite merchandiz, and are called by them tia Commashuck or Chiefs beads. the best wampum is not so much esteemed by them as the most inferior beads. Sent Coalter out to hunt this morning, he shortly after returned with a deer, venison is a rarity with us we have had none for some weeks. Drewyer also set out on a hunting excertion and took one man with him. he intends both to hunt the Elk and trap the beaver.

The Culinary articles of the Indians in our neighbourhood consist of wooden bowls or throughs, baskets, wooden spoons and woden scures or spits. Their wooden bowls and troughs are of different forms and sizes, and most generally dug out of a solid piece; they are ither round or simi globular, in the form of a canoe, cubic, and cubic at top terminating in a globe at bottom; these are extreemly well executed and many of them neatly carved the larger vessels with hand-holes to them; in these vessels they boil their fish or flesh by means of hot stones which they immerce in the water with the article to be boiled. they also render the oil of fish or other anamals in the same manner. their baskets are formed of cedar bark and beargrass so closely interwoven with the fingers that they are watertight without the aid of gum or rosin; some of these are highly ornamented with strans of beargrass which they dye of several colours and interweave in a great variety of figures; this serves them the double perpose of holding their water or wearing on their heads; and are of different capacites from that of the smallest cup to five or six gallons; they are generally of a conic form or reather the segment of a cone of which the smaller end forms the base or bottom of the basket. these they make very expediciously and dispose off for a mear trifle. it is for the construction of these baskets that the beargrass becomes an article of traffic among the natives this grass grows only on their high mountains near the snowey region; the blade is about 3/8 of an inch wide and 2 feet long smoth pliant and strong; the young blades which are white from not being exposed to the sun or air, are those most commonly employed, particularly in their neatest work. Their spoons are not remarkable nor abundant, they are generally large and the bole brawd. their meat is roasted with a sharp scure, one end of which is incerted in the meat with the other is set erect in the ground. the spit for roasting fish has it's upper extremity split, and between it's limbs the center of the fish is inscerted with it's head downwards and the tale and extremities of the scure secured with a string, the sides of the fish, which was in the first instance split on the back, are expanded by means of small splinters of wood which extend crosswise the fish. a small mat of rushes or flags is the usual plate or dish on which their fish, flesh, roots or burries are served. they make a number of bags and baskets not watertight of cedar bark, silk-grass, rushes, flags and common coarse sedge. in these they secure their dryed fish, rooots, buries, &c.

[Clark, January 17, 1806] Sunday 17th January 1806 This morning we weere visited by Comowool and 7 of the Clatsops our nearest neighbours, who left us again in the evening. They brought with them Some roots and beries for Sale, of which however they disposed of very fiew as they asked for them Such prices as our Stock in trade would not licence us in giveing. The Chief Comowool gave us Some roots and berries, for which we gave him in return a mockerson awl and Some thread; the latter he wished for the purpose of makeing a Skiming Net. one of the party was dressed in three verry elegant Sea otter Skins which we much wanted; for these we offered him maney articles but he would not dispose of them for aney other Consideration but Blue beeds, of those we had only Six fathoms left, which being 4 less than his price for each Skin he would not exchange nor would a Knife or any other equivolent in beeds of aney other Colour answer his purpose; these Coarse blue beeds are their favourite merchandize and are Called by them Tia com ma shuck or Chief beeds, the best Wampom is not as much esteemed by them as the most indifferent beeds. Sent Colter out to hunt he Shortly after returned with a Deer, Venison is a rarity with us we have had none for Some weeks. Drewyer Set out on a hunting expedition one man went with him. he intends to hunt the Elk and trap the beaver.

The Culinary articles of the Indians in our neighbourhood Consists of wooden bowls or troughs, Baskets, Shell and wooden Spoons and wooden Scures or Spits, their wooden Bowles and troughs are of different forms and Sizes, and most generally dug out of Solid piecies; they are either round, Square or in the form of a canoe; those are extreemly well executed and maney of them neetly covered, the larger vessels with handholes to them; in these vessels they boil their fish or flesh by means of hot Stones which they immerce in the water with the articles to be boiled. They also render the Oil of the fish, or other animals in the Same manner. Their baskets are formed of Cedar bark and bargrass So closely interwoven withe hands or fingers that they are watertight without the aid of gum or rozin; Some of those are highly ornimented with the Straps of bargrass which they dye of Several Colours and interweave in a great variety of figures; this Serves a double purpose of holding the Water or wareing on their heads; and are of different Capacities, from that of a Smallest Cup to five or Six gallons, they are generally of a Conic form or reather the Segment of a Cone of which the Smaller end forms the base or bottom of the basket. these they make verry expediciously and dispose of for a mear trifle. it is for the Construction of those baskets that Bargrass becoms an article of traffic among the nativs of the Columbia. this grass grows only on their mountains near the Snowey region; the blade is about 3/8 of an inch wide and 2 feet long Smothe plient & Strong; the young blades which are white from not being exposed to the Sun or air, are those which are most Commonly employ'd, particularly in their neatest work. Their wooden Spoons are not remarkable nor abundant, they are large & the bowls broad. their meat is roasted with a Sharp Scure, one end of which is incerted in the meat while the other is Set erect in the ground. The Spit for roasting fish has its upper extremity Split, and between its limbs the Center of the fish is incerted with its head downwards, and the tale and the extremities of the Scure Secured with a String, the Side of the fish, which was in the first instance Split in the back, are expanded by means of Small Splinters of wood which extend Crosswise the fish. a Small mat of rushes or flags is the usual plate, or Dish on which their fish, flesh, roots & berries are Served. they make a number of Bags and Baskets not water tight of Cedar bark Silk Grass, rushes, flags, and common Gorse Sedge-. in those they Secure their dried fish, roots berries &.-

[Lewis, January 18, 1806] Sunday January 18th 1806. Two of the Clatsops who were here yesterday returned today for a dog they had left; they remained with us a few hours and departed. no further occurrence worthy of relation took place. the men are still much engaged in dressing skins in order to cloath themselves and prepare for our homeward journey. The Clatsops Chinnooks &c construct their houses of timber altogether. they are from 14 to 20 feet wide and from 20 to 60 feet in length, and acommodate one or more families sometimes three or four families reside in the same room. thes houses are also divided by a partition of boards, but this happens only in the largest houses as the rooms are always large compared with the number of inhabitants. these houses are constructed in the following manner; two or more posts of split timber agreeably to the number of divisions or partitions are furst provided, these are sunk in the ground at one end and rise perpendicularly to the hight of 14 or 18 feet, the tops of them are hollowed in such manner as to receive the ends of a round beam of timber which reaches from one to the other, most commonly the whole length of the building, and forming the upper part of the roof; two other sets of posts and poles are now placed at proper distances on either side of the first, formed in a similar manner and parrallel to it; these last rise to the intended hight of the eves, which is usually about 5 feet. smaller sticks of timber are now provided and are placed by pares in the form of rafters, resting on, and reaching from the lower to the upper horizontal beam, to both of which they are attatched at either end with the cedar bark; two or three ranges of small poles are now placed horizontally on these rafters on each side of the roof and are secured likewise with strings of the Cedar bark. the ends sides and partitions are then formed with one range of wide boards of abut two inches thick, which are sunk in the ground a small distance at their lower ends and stand erect with their upper ends Taping on the outside of the eve poles and end rafters to which they are secured by an outer pole lying parallel with the eve poles and rafters being secured to them by chords of cedar bark which pass through wholes made in the boards at certain distances for that purpose; the rough roof is then covered with a double range of thin boards, and an aperture of 2 by 3 feet left in the center of the roof to permit the smoke to pass. these houses are sometimes sunk to the debth of 4 or 5 feet in which cace the eve of the house comes nearly to the surface of the earth. in the center of each room a space of six by eight feet square is sunk about twelve inches lower than the floor having it's sides secured with four sticks of squar timber, in this space they make their fire, their fuel being generally pine bark. mats are spread arround the fire on all sides, on these they set in the day and frequently sleep at night. on the inner side of the hose on two sides and sometimes on three, there is a range of upright peices about 4 feet removed from the wall; these are also sunk in the ground at their lower ends, and secured at top to the rafters, from these other peices ar extended horizontally to the wall and are secured in the usual method by bark to the upright peices which support the eve poles. on these short horizontal pieces of which there are sometimes two ranges one above the other, boards are laid, which either form ther beads, or shelves on which to put their goods and chattles of almost every discription. their uncured fish is hung on sticks in the smoke of their fires as is also the flesh of the Elk when they happen to be fortunate enough to procure it which is but seldom.

[Clark, January 18, 1806] Monday 18th January 1806 Two of the Clatsops that were here yesterday returned to day for a Dog they had left; they remained with us a fiew hours and departed. no further accounts worthey of relation took place. the men are much engaged dressing Skins in order to Cloath themselves and prepare for the homeward journey.

The Clatsops Chinnooks &c. construct their Houses of timber altogether. they are from 14 to 20 feet wide, and from 20 to 60 feet in length, and accomodate one or more families Sometimes three or four families reside in the Same room. this house is also devided by petitions of Boards, but this happens only in the largest houses, as the rooms are always large Compared with the number of inhabitents. those houses are Constructed in the following manner; two or more posts of Split timber agreeably to the number of devisions or partitions are first provided, these are Sunk in the ground at one end and raised pirpindicular to the hight of 12 or 14 feet, the top of them are hollowed So as to recive the end of a round beem of timber which reaches from one to the other or the entire length of the house; and forming the ridge pole; two other Sets of posts and poles are then placed at proper distancies on either Side of the first, formed in a Similar manner and parrelal to it; those last rise to the intended hight of the eves, which is usially about 5 feet,- Smaller Sticks of timber is then previded and are placed by pears in the form of rafters, resting on, and reaching from the lower to the upper horizontial beam, to both of which they are atached at either end with the Cedar bark; two or 3 ranges of Small poles are then placed Horizontially on these rafters on each Side of the roof & are Secured likewise with Cedar bark. the ends, Sides, and partitions are then formed, with one range of wide boards of about 2 inches thick, which are Sunk in the ground a Small distance at their lower ends & Stands erect with their upper ends lapping on the out Side of the eve poles and end rafters to which they are Secured by a outer pole lyeing parrelal with the eve pole and rafters being Secured to them by Cords of Cedar bark which pass through wholes made in the bods at Certain distances for that purpose; the rough roof is then Covered with a double range of thin boards, and an aperture of 2 by 3 feet left in the Center of the roof to admit the Smoke to pass. These houses are commonly Sunk to the debth of 4 or 5 feet in which Case the eve of the house comes nearly to the Surface of the earth. in the Center of each room a Space of from 6 by 8 feet is Sunk about 12 inches lower than the Hoar haveing its Sides Secured by four thick boards or Squar pieces of timber, in this Space they make their fire, their fuel being generally dry pine Split Small which they perform with a peice of an Elks horn Sharpened at one end drove into the wood with a Stone. mats are Spred around the fire on all Sides, on these they Sit in the day and frequently Sleep at night. on the inner Side of the house on two Sides and Sometimes on three, there is a range of upright pieces about 4 feet removed from the wall; these are also Sunk in the ground at their lower end, and Secured at top to the rafters, from those, other pieces are extended horozontially to the wall and are Secured in the usial manner with bark to the upright pieces which Support the eve pole. on these Short horizontial peics of which there are Sometimes two ranges one above the other, boards are laid, which either form their beads, or Shelves on which to put their goods and Chattles, of almost every discription. their uncured fish is hung on Sticks in the Smoke of their fires as is also the flesh of the Elk when they happen to be fortunate enough to precure it which is but Seldom

[Lewis, January 19, 1806] Monday January 19th 1806. This morning sent out two parties of hunters, consisting of Collins and Willard whom we sent down the bay towards point Adams, and Labuish and Shannon whom we sent up Fort River; the fist by land and the latter by water. we were visited today by two Clatsop men and a woman who brought for sale some Sea Otter skins of which we purchased one, giving in exchange the remainder of our blue beads consisting of 6 fathoms and about the same quantity of small white beads and a knife. we also purchased a small quantity of train oil for a pair of Brass armbands and a hat for some fishinghooks. these hats are of their own manufactory and are composed of Cedar bark and bear grass interwoven with the fingers and ornimented with various colours and figures, they are nearly waterproof, light, and I am convinced are much more durable than either chip or straw. These hats form a small article of traffic with the Clatsops and Chinnooks who dispose of them to the whites. the form of the hat is that which was in vogue in the Ued States and great Britain in the years 1800 & 1801 with a high crown reather larger at the top than where it joins the brim; the brim narrow or about 2 or 21/2 inches.

Several families of these people usually reside together in the same room; they appear to be the father & mother and their sons with their son's wives and children; their provision seems to be in common and the greatest harmoney appears to exist among them. The old man is not always rispected as the head of the family, that duty most commonly devolves on one of the young men. They have seldom more than one wife, yet the plurality of wives is not denyed them by their customs. These families when ascociated form nations or bands of nations each acknoledging the authority of it's own chieftain who dose not appear to be heriditary, nor his power to extend further than a mear repremand for any improper act of an individual; the creation of a chief depends upon the upright deportment of the individual & his ability and disposition to render service to the community; and his authority or the deference paid him is in exact equilibrio with the popularity or voluntary esteem he has acquired among the individuals of his band or nation. Their laws like those of all uncivilized Indians consist of a set of customs which have grown out of their local situations. not being able to speak their language we have not been able to inform ourselves of the existence of any peculiar customs among them.

[Clark, January 19, 1806] Tuesday 19th of January 1806 This morning Sent out two parties of hunters, one party towards Point adams and the other party up Ne tel River by water. we were visited to day by two Clatsop men and a woman who brought for Sale Some Sea otter Skins of which we purchased one gave in exchange the remainder of our blue heeds Consisting of 6 fathoms, and the Same quantity of Small white beids and a knife. we also purchased a Small quantity of train oil for a par of Brass arm bands, and a hat for Som fishinghooks. these hats are of their own manufactory and are Composed of Cedar bark and bear grass interwoven with the fingers and ornimented with various Colours and figures, they are nearly water proof, light, and I am Convinced are much more dureable than either Chip or Straw,- These hats form a article of traffic with Clatsops an Chinnooks who dispose of them to the whites, the form of the Hats is that which was in voge in the U States and Great Britain in 1800 & 1801 with a high Crown rather larger at the top than where it joins the brim, the brim narrow about 2 or 21/2 inches.

Several families of those people usially reside together in the Same room; they appear to be the father mother with their Sons and their Sons wives and children; their provisions appears to be in common and the greatest harmoney appears to exist among them. the old man is not always respected as the head of the family that duty generally devolves on one of the young men. They have Sildom more than one wife, yet plurality of wives are not denyed them by their Customs. those families when associated form bands of nations each acknowledgeing the authority of its own Chieftains, who does not appear to be herittary, or has power to extend further than a mear repremand for any improper deportment of the indevidual; the Creation of a Chief depends upon the upright Conduct of the individual his abiltity and disposition to render Service to the Comunity, and his authority and the defference paid him is in extent equilibrio with the popolarity or volintary esteem he has acquired among the individuals of his band, or nation. Their Laws like all uncivilized Indians Consist of a Set of customs which has grown out of their local Situations. not being able to Speak their language we have not been able to inform ourselves of the existance of any peculiar Customs among them.

[Lewis, January 20, 1806] Tuesday January 20th 1806. Visited this morning by three Clatsops who remained with us all day; the object of their visit is mearly to smoke the pipe. on the morning of the eighteenth we issued 6 lbs. of jirked Elk pr. man, this evening the Sergt. repoted that it was all exhausted; the six lbs. have therefore lasted two days and a half only. at this rate our seven Elk will last us only 3 days longer, yet no one seems much concerned about the state of the stores; so much for habit. we have latterly so frequently had our stock of provisions reduced to a minimum and sometimes taken a small touch of fasting that three days full allowance excites no concern. In those cases our skill as hunters afford us some consolation, for if there is any game of any discription in our neighbourhood we can track it up and kill it. most of the party have become very expert with the rifle. The Indians who visited us today understood us sufficiently to inform us that the whites did not barter for the pounded fish; that it was purchased and consumed by the Clatsops, Chinnooks, Cathlahmah's and Skillutes. The native roots which furnish a considerable proportion of the subsistence of the indians in our neighbourhood are those of a species of Thistle, fern and rush; the Liquorice, and a small celindric root the top of which I have not yet seen, this last resembles the sweet pittatoe very much in it's flavor and consistency.

[Clark, January 20, 1806] Wednesday 20th January 1806 Visited this morning by three Clapsots who remained with us all day; the object of their visit is mearly to Smoke the pipe. on the morning of the 18 inst. we issued 6 wt. of jurked meat pr. man, this evening the Serjt. reports that is all exhosted; the 6 w. have therefore lasted 2 days and a half only. at this rate our Seven Elk will only last us 3 days longer, yet no one appears much concerned about the State of the Stores; So much for habet. we have latterly so frequently had our Stock of provisions reduced to a minimum and Sometimes taken a Small tuck of fasting that 3 days full allowance exites no concern. In those Cases our Skill as hunters affords us Some Consolation, for if there is any game of any discription in our neighbourhood we can track it up and kill it. most of the party have become very expert with the rifle. The Indians who visit us to day understood us Sufficiently to inform us that the white who visit them did not barter for the pounded fish; that it was purchased and Consumed by the Clatsops, Chin nooks, Cath lah mahs and Skil lutes, and Kil a moxs.

The native roots which furnish a considerable proportion of the Subsistance of the indians in our neighbourhoodd are those of a Species of Thistle, fern, and rush; the Licquorice, and a Small celindric root the top of which I have not yet Seen, this last resembles the Sweet potato verry much in its flavour and Consistency.

[Lewis, January 21, 1806] Wednesday January 21st 1806. Two of the hunters Shannon & Labuish returned having killed three Elk. Ordered a party to go in quest of the meat early tomorrow morning and the hunters to return and continue the chase. the Indians left us about 12 O'Clk. The root of the thistle, called by the natives shan-ne-tahque is a perpendicular fusiform and possesses from two to four radicles; is from 9 to 15 Inces in length and about the size a mans thumb; the rhind somewhat rough and of a brown colour; the consistence when first taken from the earth is white and nearly as crisp as a carrot; when prepared for uce by the same process before discribed of the white bulb or pashshequo quawmash, it becomes black, and is more shugary than any fuit or root that I have met with in uce among the natives; the sweet is precisely that of the sugar in flavor; this root is sometimes eaten also when first taken from the ground without any preperation; but in this way is vastly in-ferior. it delights most in a deep rich dry lome which has a good mixture of sand. the stem of this plant is simple ascending celindric and hisped. the root leaves yet possess their virdure and are about half grown of a plale green. the cauline leaf as well as the stem of the last season are now dead, but in rispect to it's form &c. it is simple, crenate, & oblong, reather more obtuse at it's apex than at the base or insertion; it's margin armed with prickles while it's disks are hairy, it's insertion decurrent and position declining. the flower is also dry and mutilad. the pericarp seems much like that of the common thistle. it rises to the hight of from 3 to 4 feet.-

[Clark, January 21, 1806] Thursday 21st of January 1806 Two of the hunters Shannon & Labieche returned haveing killed three Elk, ordered a party to go in quest of the meat early tomorrow morning and the hunters to return and continue the chase-. the Indians left us about 12 oClock.

The root of the thistle called by the nativs Chan-ne-tak-que is pirpendicular and possesses from two to 4 radicles; is from 9 to 15 inches in length and is Commonly about the Size of a mans thum the rhine Somewhat rough and of a brown Colour; the Consistence when first taken from the earth is white and nearly as Crisp as a Carrot, when prepared for use by the Same process before discribed of the white bulb or gash she quo, qua-mosh, it becomes black and is more Sugary than any root I have met with among the nativs; the Sweet is prosisely that of the Sugar in flavor, this root is Sometimes eaten when first taken from the ground without any preperation, in this way it is well tasted but soon weathers and becoms hard and insipped. it delights most in a deep rich moist lome which has a good mixture of Sand- The Stems of this plant is Simple ascending celindric and hisped. the root leaves, posses their virdure and are about half grown of a deep Green. the Cauline leaf as well as the Stem of the last Season are now dead, but in respect to it's form &c. it is Simple Crenated and oblong, rather more obtuce at it's apex than the base or insertion, it's margin armed with prickles while it's disks are hairy, its insertion decurrent and position declineing. the flower is also dry and mutilated the pericarp seems much like that of the Common thistle it rises to the hight of from 3 to 4 feet.

[Lewis, January 22, 1806] Thursday January 22nd 1806. The party sent for the meat this morning returned with it in the Evening; it was in very inferior order, in short the animals were poor. Reubin Fields also remained with the other hunters Shannon & Labuish our late supply of salt is out. we have not yet heared a sentence from the other two parties of hunter's who are below us towards Point Adams and the Praries.

There are three species of fern in this neighbourhood the root one of which the natves eat; this grows very abundant in the open uplands and praries where the latter are not sandy and consist of deep loose rich black lome. the root is horizontal sometimes a little deverging or obliquely descending, frequently dividing itself as it procedes into two equal branches and shooting up a number of stems; it lies about 4 Inces beneath the surface of the earth. the root is celindric, with few or no radicles and from the size of a goose quill to that of a man's finger; the center of the root is divided into two equal parts by a strong flat & white ligament like a piece of thin tape on either side of this there is a white substance which when the root is roasted in the embers is much like wheat dough and not very unlike it in flavour, though it has also a pungency which becomes more visible after you have chewed it some little time; this pungency was disagreeable to me, but the natives eat it very voraciously and I have no doubt but it is a very nutricious food. the bark of the root is black, somewhat rough, thin and brittle, it easily seperates in flakes from the part which is eaten as dose also the internal liggament. this root perennil. in rich lands this plant rises to the hight of from 4 to five feet. the stem is smooth celindric, slightly groved on one side erect about half it's hight on the 2 first branches thence reclining backwards from the grooved side; it puts forth it's branches which are in reallyty long footstalks by pares from one side only and near the edges of the groove, these larger footstalks are also grooved cilindric and gradually tapering towards the extremity, puting forth alternate footstalks on either side of the grove near it's edge; these lesser footstalks the same in form as the first put forth from forty to fifty alternate pinate leaves which are sessile, horizontal, multipartite for half their length from the point of insertion and terminating in a long shaped apex, and are also revolute with the upper disk smoth and the lower slightly cottanny. these alternate leaves after proceeding half the length of the footstalk cease to be partite and assume the tongue like form altogether. this plant produces no flower or fruit whatever, is of a fine green colour in summer and a beautiful) plant. the top is annual and is of course dead at present.-

[Clark, January 22, 1806] Friday 22nd January 1806 The party Sent for the meat this morning returned with it in the evening; it was in verry inferior order, in Short the animals were pore. Rieuben Field Shannon and Labiech remained in the woods to hunt. our late Supply of Salt is out. we have not heard a word of the other hunters who are below us towards point adams and the Praries. Some rain this day at intervales

There are three Species of fern in this neighbourhood the root one of which the nativs eate; that of which the nativs eate produce no flowers whatever or fruit of a fine green Colour and the top is annual, and in Course dead at present.

I observe no difference between the licorice of this Countrey and that Common to maney parts of the United States where it is sometimes Cultivated in our gardins-. this plant delights in a deep lose Sandy Soil; here it grows verry abundant and large; the nativs roste it in the embers and pound it Slightly with a Small Stick in order to make it Seperate more readily from the Strong liggaments which forms the center of the root; this they discard and chew and Swallow the ballance of the root; this last is filled with a number of thin membrencies like network, too tough to be masticated and which I find it necessary also to discard. This root when roasted possesses an agreeable flavour not unlike the Sweet potato. The root of the thistle (described yesterday) after undergoing the process of Sweting or bakeing in a kiln is Sometimes eaten with the train oil also, at other times pounded fine and mixed with Cold water, untill reduced to the Consistancy of Gruel; in this way I think it verry agreeable. but the most valuable of all their roots is foreign to this neighbourhood I mean the Wappetoe.

The Wappetoe, or bulb of the Sagitifolia or common arrow head, which grows in great abundance in the marshey grounds of that butifull and fertile vally on the Columbia commenceing just above the quick Sand River and extending downwards for about 70 miles. this bulb forms a principal article of trafic between the inhabitents of the vally and those of their neighbourhood or Sea coast.

[Lewis, January 23, 1806] Friday January 23rd 1806. This morning dispatched Howard and Warner to the Camp of the Saltmakes for a supply of salt. The men of the garison are still busily employed in dressing Elk's skins for cloathing, they find great difficulty for the want of branes; we have not soap to supply the deficiency, nor can we procure ashes to make the lye; none of the pines which we use for fuel affords any ashes; extrawdinary as it may seem, the greene wood is consoomed without leaving the residium of a particle of ashes.

The root of the rush used by the natives is a sollid bulb about one inch in length and usually as thick as a man's thumb, of an ovate form depressed on two or more sides, covered with a thin smothe black rind. the pulp is white brittle and easily masticated either raw or roasted the latter is the way in which it is most usually prepared for uce. this root is reather insipid in point of flavour, it grows in greatest abundance along the sea coast in the sandy grounds and is most used by the Killamucks and those inhabiting the coast. each root sends up one stock only which is annual, the root being perenniel. the bulb is attatched to the bottom of the caulis or stem by a firm small and strong radicle of about one Inch long; this radicle is mearly the prolongation of the caulis and decends perpendicilarly; a little above the junction of this radicle with the caulis, the latter is surrounded in a whorl with a set of small radicles from 6 to 9 inches long which are obliquely descending. the caulis is celindric erect hollow and jointed, and is about the size or reather larger than the largest quill. it rises to the hight of 3 or 4 feet, not branching nor dose it either bear flower or seed that I can discover tho I am far from denying that it dose so sometimes, but I have not been able to discover it. the stem is rough like the sand rush and is much like it when green or in it's succulent state. at each joint it puts out from twenty to thirty long lineal stellate or radiate & horizontal leaves which surround the stem. above each joint about half an inch the stem is sheathed like the sand rush.

[Clark, January 23, 1806] Saturday 23rd of January 1806 This morning dispatched Howard & Werner to the Camp of the Salt makers for a Supply of Salt. the men of the garrison are Still busily employed in dressing Elk Skins for cloathing, they fine great dificuelty for the want of branes; we have not Soap to Supply the deficiency, nor can we precure ashes to make the lye; none of the pine which we use for fuel afford any ashes; extrawdinary as it may seem, the green wood is cosumed without leaveing the risiduem of a particle of ashes.-

The root of the rush used by the nativs is a Solid bulb about one inch in length and usially as thick as a mans thumb, of an ovel form depressed on two or more Sides, covered with a thin black rine. the pulp is white brittle and easily masticated either raw or rosted, the latter is the way it is most commonly prepared for use. this root is reather insippid in point of flavour, it grows in the Greatest abundance along the Sea coast in the wet Sandy grounds and is most used by the Kil a mox and those inhabiting the Sea coast. each root Sends up its Stalk which is annual, the root being perennial. the bulb is atached to the bottom of the Stem by a firm Small and Strong radicle which is mearly the prolongation of the Stem which is hollow and jointed and is rather larger than the largest quill. it rises to the hight of 3 or 4 feet, not branching no does it either bear flower or Seed that I could discover tho I am far from denying that it does So Sometimes, and perhaps every year, but I have not been able to discover it, the Stem is rough like the Sand rush, and it's much like it when green, at each joint it puts out from 20 to 30 radiate & horizontal leaves which Surrounds the Stem. above each joint about half an inch the Stem is Shethed like the Sand rush.

The instruments used by the nativs in digging their roots is a Strong Stick of three feet and a half long Sharpened at the lower end and its upper inserted into a part of an Elks or buck's horn which Serves as a handle; Standing transvirsely in the Stick- or it is in this form as thus A is the lower part which is a little hooked B is the upper part or handle of Horn.

[Lewis, January 24, 1806] Saturday January 24th 1806. Drewyer and Baptiest La Paage returned this morning in a large Canoe with Comowooll and six Clatsops. they brought two deer and the flesh of three Elk & one Elk's skin, having given the flesh of one other Elk which they killed and three Elk's skins to the Indians as the price of their assistance in transporting the ballance of the meat to the Fort; these Elk and deer were killed near point Adams and the Indians carryed them on their backs about six miles, before the waves were sufficiently low to permit their being taken on board their canoes. the Indians remained with us all day. The Indians witnissed Drewyer's shooting some of those Elk, which has given them a very exalted opinion of us as marksmen and the superior excellence of our rifles compared with their guns; this may probably be of service to us, as it will deter them from any acts of hostility if they have ever meditated any such. My Air-gun also astonishes them very much, they cannot comprehend it's shooting so often and without powder; and think that it is great medicine which comprehends every thing that is to them incomprehensible.

I observe no difference between the liquorice this country and that common to many parts of the United states where it is also sometimes cultivated in our gardens. this plant delights in a deep loose sandy soil; here it grows very abundant and large; the natives roast it in the embers and pound it slightly with a small stick in order to make it seperate more readily from the strong liggament which forms the center of the root; this the natives discard and chew and swallow the ballance of the root; this last is filled with a number of thin membrenacious lamela like net work, too tough to be masticated and which I find it necessary also to discard. this root when roasted possesses an agreeable flavour not unlike the sweet pittaitoe. beside the small celindric root mentioned on the 20th inst., they have also another about the same form size and appearance which they use much with the train oil, this root is usually boiled; to me it possesses a disagreeable bitterness. the top of this plant I have never yet seen. The root of the thistle after undergoing the prossess of sweating or baking in a kiln is sometimes eaten with the train oil also, and at other times pounded fine and mixed with could water untill reduced to the consistency of sagamity or indian mush; in this way I think it very agreeable. but the most valuable of all their roots is foreign to this neighbourhood I mean the Wappetoe, or the bulb of the Sagitifolia or common arrow head, which grows in great abundance in the marshey grounds of that beatifull and firtile valley on the Columbia commencing just above the entrance of Quicksand River, and extending downwards for about 70 Miles. this bulb forms a principal article of traffic between the inhabitants of the valley and those of this neighbourhood or sea coast. The instrument used by the natives in diging their roots is a strong stick of 31/2 feet long sharpened at the lower end and it's upper inscerted into a part of an Elks or buck's horn which serves as a handle, standing transversely with the stick or it is in this form A the lower point, B the upper part or handle.

[Clark, January 24, 1806] Sunday 24th of January 1806 Drewyer and Bapteist laPage returned this morning in a large Canoe with Commowol and six Clatsops. they brought two Deer and three Elk and one elk Skin, haveing given the flesh of one other Elk they killed and three Elk skins to the Indians as the price of their assistance in transporting the ballance of the meat to the Fort; these Deer and Elk were killed near pt. Adams and those Indians Carried them on their Backs near 4 miles, before the waves were Sufficiently low to permit their being taken on board their Canoes. The indians remain'd with us all day. The Clapsots witnessed Drewyers Shooting Some of those Elk, which has given them a very exolted opinion of us as marksmen and the Superior excellency of our rifles Compared with their guns; this may probably be of service to us, as it will deter them from any acts of hostility if they have ever meditated any such.

our air gun also astonishes them very much, they Cannot Comprehend its Shooting So often and without powder, and think that it is great medison which Comprehends every thing that is to them incomprehensible.

The nativs of this neighbourhood ware no further Covering than a light roabe, their feet legs & every other part exposed to the frost Snow & ice &c.

[Lewis, January 25, 1806] Sunday January 25th 1806. Commowooll and the Clatsops departed early this morning. At meridian Colter returned and repoted that his comrade hunter Willard had continued his hunt from point Adams towards the salt makers; and that they had killed only those two deer which the Indians brought yesterday. In the evening Collins one of the saltmakers returned and reported that they had mad about one bushel of salt & that himself and two others had hunted from the salt camp for five days without killing any thing and they had been obliged to subsist on some whale which they procured from the natives.

The native fruits and buries in uce among the Indians of this neighbourhood are a deep purple burry about the size of a small cherry called by them Shal-lun, a small pale red bury called Sol'-me; the vineing or low Crambury, a light brown bury reather larger and much the shape of the black haw; and a scarlet bury about the size of a small cherry the plant called by the Canadin Engages of the N. W. sac a commis produces this bury; this plant is so called from the circumstance of the Clerks of those trading companies carrying the leaves of this plant in a small bag for the purpose of smokeing of which they are excessively fond. the Indians call this bury
———

I have lately learned that the natives whome I have heretofore named as distinct nations, living on the sea coast S. E. of the Killamucks, are only bands of that numerous nation, which continues to extend itself much further on that coast than I have enumerated them, but of the particular appellations of those distant bands I have not yet been enabled to inform myself; their language also is somewhat different from the Clatsops Chinnooks and Cathlahmahs; but I have not yet obtaind a vocabulary which I shall do the first oportunity which offers.

[Clark, January 25, 1806] Monday 25th of January 1806 Commowol and the Clatsops departed early this morning. Colter returned and reported that his comrade hunter Willard had Continued his hunt from Point Adams towards the Saltmakers; and that they had killed only those two deer which the indians brought yesterday; in the evening Collins one of the Saltmakers returned and reported that they had made about one bushel of Salt and that himself and two others had hunted from the Salt Camp for five days without killing any thing and they had been obliged to Subsist on Some whale which they purchased from the nativs-.

The native fruits and berries in use among the Indians of this neighbourhood are a Deep purple about the Size of a Small cherry called by them Shal lun, a Small pale red berry called Sol me; the vineing or low brown berry, a light brown berry rather larger and much the Shape of a black haw; and a Scarlet berry about the Size of a Small Chirry the plant Called by the Canadian Engages of the N. W. Sac a commis produces this berry; this plant is So Called from the circumstances of the Clerks of these tradeing Companies Carrying the leaves of this plant in a Small bag for the purpose of Smokeing of which they are excessively fond the Indians Call this berry _____

[Lewis, January 26, 1806] Monday January 26th 1806. Werner and Howard who were sent for salt on the 23rd have not yet returned, we are apprehensive that they have missed their way; neither of them are very good woodsmen, and this thick heavy timbered pine country added to the constant cloudy weather makes it difficult for even a good woodsman to steer for any considerable distance the course he wishes. we ordered Collins to return early in the morning and rejoin the salt makers, and gave him some small articles of merchandize to purchase provisions from the Indians, in the event of their still being unfortunate in the chase. The Shallun or deep purple berry is in form much like the huckkleberry and terminates bluntly with a kind of cap or cover at the end like that fruit; they are attatched seperately to the sides of the boughs of the shrub by a very short stem hanging underneath the same and are frequently placed very near each other on the same bough; it is a full bearer. the berry is easily geathered as it seperates from the bough readily, while the leaf is strongly affixed. the shrub which produces this fruit rises to the hight of 6 or 8 feet sometimes grows on the high lands but moste generally in the swampy or marshey grounds; it is an evergreen. the stem or trunk is from three to 10 Inches in circumference irregularly and much branched, seldom more than one steem proceding from the same root, tho they are frequently associated very thickly. the bark is somewhat rough and of a redish brown colour. the wood is very firm and hard. the leaves are alternate declining and attatched by a short fotstalk to the two horizontal sides of the boughs; the form is a long oval, reather more accute towards its apex than at the point of insertion; it's margin slightly serrate, it's sides colapsing or partially foalding upwards or channelled; it is also thick firm smothe and glossey, the upper surface of a fine deep green, while the under disk is of a pale or whiteish green. this shrub retains it's virdure very perfectly during the winter and is a beautifull shrub.- the natives either eat these berrys when ripe immediately from the bushes or dryed in the sun or by means of their sweating kilns; very frequently they pound them and bake then in large loaves of 10 or fifteen pounds; this bread keeps very well during one season and retains the moist jeucies of the fruit much better than by any other method of preservation. this bread is broken and stired in could water until it be sufficiently thick and then eaten; in this way the natives most generally use it.

[Clark, January 26, 1806] Tuesday 26th of January 1806 We order Collins to return early in the morning and join the Salt makers, and gave him Some Small articles of merchendize to purchase Some provisions from the indians in the event of their Still being unfortunate in the chase.

The or deep purple berry is in form much like the huckleberry and termonate bluntly with a kind of Cap or cover at the end like that fruit; they are attached Seperately to the Sides of the boughes of the shrub by a very Short Stem ganging under neath the Same, and are frequently placed verry near each other on the Same bough it is a full bearer; the berry is easily gathered as it Seperates from the bough, readily, while the leaf is Strongly affixed. the Shrub which produces this fruit rises to the hight of 6 or 8 feet Sometimes grows on high lands but most frequently in Swampy or marshey grounds; it is an ever green. the Stem or trunk is from 3 to 10 inches in circumferance irrigularly and much branched, Seldom more than one Stem proceeding from the Same root, tho they are frequently associated very thickly. the bark is Somewhat rough and of a redish brown Colour. the wood is very firm and hard. the leaves are alternate declining and attachd by a Short fotstalk to the two horozontal Sides of the bough's; the form is a long oval, reather more accute towards its apex that at the point of insertion; it's Sides partially folding upwards; or Channeled, it is also thick Smothe and glossy, the upper Surfice of a fine deep green, while the under disk is of a pale or whiteish green. this Shrub retains its verdure verry perfectly dureing the winter and is a butifull Shrub-. the nativs either eate those berries ripe imediately from the bushes, or dried in the Sun or by means of the Swetting kiln; verry frequently they pound them and bake them in large loaves 10 or 15 pounds weight; this bread keeps verry well dureing one Season and retains the moist jouicies of the frute much better than any other method of preperation. The bread is broken and Stured in Coald water untill it be Sufficiently thick and then eaten, in this way the nativ's most generally use it-.-

[Lewis, January 27, 1806] Tuesday January 27th 1806. This morning Collins set out for the Salt works. in the evening Shannon returned and reported that himself and party had killed ten Elk. he left Labuche and R. fields with the Elk. two of those Elk he informed us were at the distance of nine miles from this place near the top of a mountain, that the rout by which they mus be brought was at least four miles by land through a country almost inaccessible from the fallen timber, brush and sink-holes, which were now disguised by the snow; we therefore concluded to relinquish those two Elk for the present, and ordered every man who could be speared from the fort to go early in the morning in surch of the other eight.

Goodrich has recovered from the Louis veneri which he contracted from an amorous contact with a Chinnook damsel. I cured him as I did Gibson last winter by the uce of murcury. I cannot learn that the Indians have any simples which are sovereign specifics in the cure of this disease; and indeed I doubt very much wheter any of them have any means of effecting a perfect cure. when once this disorder is contracted by them it continues with them during life; but always ends in decipitude, death, or premature old age; tho from the uce of certain simples together with their diet, they support this disorder with but little inconvenience for many years, and even enjoy a tolerable share of health; particularly so among the Chippeways who I believe to be better skilled in the uce of those simples than any nation of Savages in North America. The Chippeways use a decoction of the root of the Lobelia, and that of a species of sumac common to the Atlantic states and to this country near and on the Western side of the Rocky Mountains. this is the smallest species of the sumac, readily distinguished by it's winged rib, or common footstalk, which supports it's oppositely pinnate leaves. these decoctions are drank freely and without limitation. the same decoctions are used in cases of the gonnaerea and are effecatious and sovereign. notwithstanding that this disorder dose exist among the Indians on the Columbia yet it is witnessed in but few individuals, at least the males who are always sufficiently exposed to the observations or inspection of the phisician. in my whole rout down this river I did not see more than two or three with the gonnaerea and about double that number with the pox.

The beary which the natives call solme is the production of a plant about the size and much the shape of that common to the atlantic states which produces the berry commonly called Solloman's seal berry. this berry also is attatched to the top of the stem in the same manner; and is of a globelar form, consisting of a thin soft pellecle which encloses a soft pulp inveloping from three to four seeds, white, firm, smothe, and in the form of a third or quarter of a globe, and large in proportion to the fruit or about the size of the seed of the common small grape. this berry when grown and unripe is not speckled as that of the Solomon's seal berry is; this last has only one globular smoth white firm seed in each berry.the Solme grows in the woodlands among the moss and is an annual plant to all appearance.

[Clark, January 27, 1806] Wednesday 27th January 1806 This morning Collins Set out to the Saltmakers Shannon returned and reported that himself and party had killed 10 Elk. he lef Labiech & R Field with the Elk, two of those Elk he informed us was at the distance of 9 miles from this place near the top of a mountain, that the rout by which they must be brought was at least 5 miles by land thro a Countrey almost inexcessable, from the fallen timber brush, and Sink holes, which were now disguised by the Snow; we therefore Concluded to relinquish those two Elks for the present, and ordered every man that Could be Speared from the Fort to go early in the morning in Serch of the other Eight, which is at no great distance from the Netul river, on which we are. Goudrich has recoverd from the louis veneri which he contracted from a amorous Contact with a Chinnook damsel. he was Cured as Gibson was with murcury by _____ I cannot lern that the Indians have any Simples Sovereign Specifics in the cure of this disease; indeed I doubt verry much whether any of them have any means of effecting a perfect cure. when once this disorder is contracted by them it Continues with them dureing life; but always ends in deceputide, death; or premature old age; tho from the use of certain Simples together with their diet, they Support this disorder with but little inconveniance for maney years, and even enjoy a tolerable Share of health; particularly So among the Chippeways who I beleive to be better Skilled in the use of those Simples than any nation of Indians in North America. The Chippaways use a decoction of the root of the Labelia, and that of a Species of Sumac Common to the Atlantic States and to this countrey near and on the western Side of the Rocky mountains. This is the Smallest Specis of Sumake, readily distinguished by it's winged rib, or common footstalk, which Supports it's oppositly pinnate leaves. these decoctions are drank freely and without limatation. the Same decoctions are used also in cases of the gonnarea and are effecatious and sovereign. notwithstanding that this disorder does exist among the indians on the Columbia yet it is witnessed in but fiew individuals high up the river, or at least the males who are always Sufficiently exposed to the observation or inspection of the phisician. in my whole rout down this river I did not See more than two or three with Gonnarea and about double that number with the Pox.

The berry which the nativs Call Sol me is the production of a plant about the Size and much the Shape of that Common to the atlantic States which produces the berry Commonly Called Sollomons Seal berry this berry is also attached to the top of the Stem in the Same manner; and is of a globular form Consisting of a thin Soft Pellicle rine which encloses a Soft Pellicle pulp inveloping from 3 to 4 Seed, white firm, Smothe, and in the form of a third or a quarter of a Globe, and large in perportion to the fruit, or about the Size of the Seed of the Common Small grape. the berry when grown and unripe is not Specked as the Solomon's seal Berry is; this last haveing only one Globaler Smothe, ferm, white Seed in each berry-. the Sol me grows in the wood lands amonge the moss and on the high ridges. and is an annual plant to all appearance

[Lewis, January 28, 1806] Wednesday January 28th 1806. Drewyer and Baptiest La Page set out this morning on a hunting excurtion. about noon Howard and Werner returned with a supply of salt; the badness of the weather and the difficulty of the road had caused their delay. they inform us that the salt makers are still much straitened for provision, having killed two deer only in the last six days; and that there are no Elk in their neighbourhood. The party that were sent this morning up Netul river for the Elk returned in the even ing with three of them only; the Elk had been killed just before the snow fell which had covered them and so altered the apparent face of the country that the hunters could not find the Elk which they had killed. the river on which Fort Clatsop stands we now call Ne-tul, this being the name by which the Clatsops call it.

The Cranbury of this neighbourhood is precisely the same common to the U States, and is the production of marshey or boggy grounds. The light brown berry, is the fruit of a tree about the size shape and appearance in every rispect with that in the U. States called the wild crab apple; the leaf is also precisely the same as is also the bark in texture and colour. the berrys grow in clumps at the end of the small branches; each berry supported by a seperate stem, and as many as from 3 to 18 or 20 in a clump. the berry is ovate with one of it's extremities attatched to the peduncle, where it is in a small degre concave like the insertion of the stem of the crab apple. I know not whether this fruit can properly be denominated a berry, it is a pulpy pericarp, the outer coat of which is in a thin smoth, tho firm tough pillecle; the pericarp containing a membranous capsule with from three to four cells, each containing a seperate single seed in form and colour like that of the wild crab.

The wood of this tree is excessively hard when seasoned. the natives make great uce of it to form their wedges with which they split their boards of pine for the purpose of building houses. these wedges they also employ in spliting their fire-wood and in hollowing out their canoes. I have seen the natives drive the wedges of this wood into solid dry pine which it cleft without fracturing or injuring the wedg in the smallest degree. we have also found this wood usefull to us for ax handles as well as glutts or wedges. the native also have wedges made of the beams of the Elk's horns which appear to answer extremely well. this fruit is exceedingly assid, and resembles the flavor of the wild crab.

[Clark, January 28, 1806] Thursday 28th January 1806 Drewyer and Baptiest Lapage Set out this morning on a hunting excurtion. about noon Howard & Werner returned with a Supply of Salt; the badness of the weather and the dificuelty of the road had detained them. they informed us that the Salt makers are Still much Stratened for provisions haveing killed two deer only in the last Six days; and that there are no Elk in their neighbourhood.

The party that was Sent up the Netul river for the Elk returned this evening with three of them only; The Elk had been killed just before the Snow fell which had Covered them and So altered the apparant face of the Countrey that the hunters Could not find them. The River on which Fort Clat Sop Stands we now call Netul, this being the name by which the Clatsops Call it.

The Cranberry of this neighbourhood is precisely the Same Common to the united States, and is the production of boggy or mashey grounds.-.

The light-brown berry, is the fruit of a tree, about the Size Shape and appearance in every respect with that in the united States called the wild Crab apple; the leaf is also presisely the Same as is also the bark in textue and colour. the berry grows in Clumps at the ends of the Smaller branches; each berry Supported by a Stem, and as maney as from 3 to 18 or 20 in a Clump. the berry is oval with one of its extremitis attached to the peduncle, where it is in a Small degree Concave like the insersion of the Stem of the Crab apple. I know not whether this fruit Can properly be denomonated a berry, it is a pulpy pericarp, the outer coat of which is a thin Smothe, capsule with from three to four Cells, each containing a Seperate Single Seed in form and Colour like that of the wild Crab apple The wood of this tree is excessively hard when Seasoned. The nativs make great use of it to form their wedges of which they Split their boards of Pine for the purpose of building houses. those wedges they employ in common with those formed of the Elks horn, in Splitting their fire wood and in hollowing out their Canoes. I have Seen the nativs drive the wedges of this wood into a solid dry pine which it cleft without fractureing injuring the wedge in the Smallest degree. we have also found this wood usefull) to us for ax handles, as well as glutt or wedges. The bark of this tree is chewed by our party in place of tobacco.

The fruit is exceedingly ascid and resembles the flavor of the wild Crab.

[Lewis, January 29, 1806] Thursday January 29th 1806. Nothing worthy of notice occurred today. our fare is the flesh of lean elk boiled with pure water, and a little salt. the whale blubber which we have used very sparingly is now exhausted. on this food I do not feel strong, but enjoy the most perfect health;- a keen appetite supplys in a great degree the want of more luxurious sauses or dishes, and still render my ordinary meals not uninteresting to me, for I find myself sometimes enquiring of the cook whether dinner or breakfast is ready.-

The Sac a commis is the growth of high dry situations, and invariably in a piney country or on it's borders. it is generally found in the open piney woodland as on the Western side of the Rocky mountain but in this neighbourhood we find it only in the praries or on their borders in the more open wood lands; a very rich soil is not absolutely necessary, as a meager one frequently produces it abundantly. the natives on this side of the Rockey mountains who can procure this berry invariably use it; to me it is a very tasteless and insippid fruit. this shrub is an evergreen, the leaves retain their virdure most perfectly through the winter even in the most rigid climate as on lake Winnipic. the root of this shrub puts forth a great number of stems which seperate near the surface of the ground; each stem from the size of a small quill to that of a man's finger; these are much branched the branches forming an accute angle with the stem, and all more poperly pocumbent than creeping, for altho it sometimes puts forth radicles from the stem and branches which strike obliquely into the ground, these radicles are by no means general, equable in their distances from each other nor do they appear to be calculated to furnish nutriment to the plant but reather to hold the stem or branch in it's place. the bark is formed of several thin layers of a smoth thin brittle substance of a dark or redish brown colour easily seperated from the woody stem in flakes. the leaves with rispect to their position are scatered yet closely arranged near the extremities of the twigs particularly. the leaf is about 3/4 of an inch in length and about half that in width, is oval but obtusely pointed, absolutely entire, thick, smoth, firm, a deep green and slightly grooved. the leaf is supported by a small footstalk of proportionable length. the berry is attatched in an irregular and scattered manner to the small boughs among the leaves, tho frequently closely arranged, but always supported by seperate short and small peduncles, the insertion of which poduces a slight concavity in the bury while it's opposite side is slightly convex; the form of the berry is a spheroid; the shorter diameter being in a line with the peduncle.- this berry is a pericarp the outer coat of which is a thin firm tough pellicle, the inner part consists of a dry mealy powder of a yellowish white colour invelloping from four to six proportionably large hard light brown seeds each in the form of a section of a spheroid which figure they form when united, and are destitute of any membranous covering.- the colour of this fruit is a fine scarlet. the natives usually eat them without any preperation. the fruit ripens in september and remains on the bushes all winter. the frost appears to take no effect on it. these berries are sometimes geathered and hung in their lodges in bags where they dry without further trouble, for in their most succulent state they appear to be almost as dry as flour.

[Clark, January 29, 1806] Friday 29th January 1806 Nothing worthey of notice occured to day. our fare is the flesh of lean Elk boiled with pure water and a little Salt. the whale blubber which we have used very Spearingly is now exhosted. on this food I do not feel Strong, but enjoy tolerable health-. a keen appetite Supplies in a great degree the want of more luxurious Sauses or dishes, and Still renders my ordanary meals not uninteresting to me, for I find myself Sometimes enquireing of the Cook whether dinner Supper or Brackfast is readyindeed my appetite is but Seldom gratified, not even after I have eaten what I conceve a Sufficency.-

Maney of the nativs of the Columbia were hats & most commonly of a conic figure without a brim confined on the head by means of a String which passes under the chin and is attached to the two opposit Sides of a Secondary rim within the hat- the hat at top termonates in a pointed knob of a conic form, or in this Shape. these hats are made of the bark of Cedar and beargrass wrought with the fingers So closely that it Casts the rain most effectually in the Shape which they give them for their own use or that just discribed, on these hats they work various figures of different colours, but most commonly only black and white are employed. these figures are faint representations of the whales, the Canoes, and the harpooners Strikeing them. Sometimes Square dimonds triangle &c. The form of a knife which Seems to be prefured by those people is a double Edged and double pointed dagger the handle being near the middle, the blades of uneaquel length, the longest from 9 to 10 incs. and the Shorter one from 3 to 5 inches. those knives they Carry with them habitually and most usially in the hand, Sometimes exposed, when in Company with Strangers under their Robes with this knife they Cut & Clense their fish make their arrows &c. this is the form of the Knife A is a Small loop of a Strong twine throng through which they Sometimes they incert the thumb in order to prevent it being wrested from their hand.-.

[Lewis, January 30, 1806] Friday January 30th 1806. Nothing transpired today worthy of notice. we are agreeably disappointed in our fuel which is altogether green pine. we had supposed that it burn but illy, but we have found that by spliting it that it burns very well. The dress of the Clatsops and others in this neighbourhood differs but little from that discribed of the skillutes; they never wear leggins or mockersons which the mildness of this climate I presume has rendered in a great measure unnecessary; and their being obliged to be frequently in the water also renders those articles of dress inconvenient. they wear a hat of a conic figure without a brim confined on the head by means of a string which passes under the chin and is attatched to the two opsite sides of a secondary rim within the hat. the hat at top terminates in a pointed knob of a connic form also, or in this shape. these hats are made of the bark of cedar and beargrass wrought with the fingers so closely that it casts the rain most effectually in the shape which they give them for their own uce or that just discribed. on these hats they work various figures of different colours, but most commonly only black and white are employed. these figures are faint representations of whales the canoes and the harpoonneers striking them. sometimes squares dimonds triangles &c. The form of knife which seems to be prefered by these people is a double edged and double pointed daggar; the handle being in the middle, and the blades of unequal lengths, the longest usually from 9 to ten inches and the shorter one from four to five. these knives they carry with them habitually and most usually in the hand, sometimes exposed but most usually particularly when in company with strangers, under their robes with this knife they cut and clense their fish make their arrows &c. this is somewhat the form of the knife- A is a small loop of a strong twine through which they sometimes insert the thumb in order to prevent it's being wrested from their hand.

[Clark, January 30, 1806] Fort Clatsop on the Pacific Ocian on the South Side of the Columbia River Thursday 30th January 1806 Nothing transpired to day worthey of notice. we are agreeably disapointed in our fuel which is altogether green pine. we had Supposed that it burned badly, but we have found by Spliting it burns very well.

The dress of the Clatsops and others of the nativs in the neighbourhood differ but little from that described of the Skilutes and Wau ki a cums; they never ware ligins or mockersons which the mildness of the Climate I presume has rendered in a great measure unnecessary; and their being obliged to be frequently in the water also renders those articles of dress inconveniant.

The Sac-a commis is the groth of high dry Situations, and invariably in a piney Country, or on its borders; it is Generally found in the open piney woodlands as on the Western Side of the Rocky mountains but in this neighbourhood we find it in the praries or on the borders in the more open woodland's; a very rich Soil is not absolutely necessary, as a meager one frequently produces it abundantly. the nativs on the West side of the Rocky mountains who can precure this berry invariably use it; to me it is a very tasteless and insipid frute. This Shrub is an evergreen, the leaves retain their virdue most perfectly throughout the winter even in the most rigid climate as on Lake Winnipic. the root of this shrub puts foth a great number of Stems, which seperate near the surface of the ground; each Stem from the size of a Small quill, to that of a mans finger. These are much branched forming an accute angle with the Stem, and all more properly procumbent than crossing, for altho it sometimes puts foth radicles from the Stems and branches which Strike obliquely into the ground, those radicles are by no means general, equable in their distances from each other nor do they appear to be calculated to furnish nutriment to the plant but rather to hold the Stem or branch in its place. the bark is formed of several thin layers of a Smothe thin brittle substance of a redish brown colour easily seperated from the woody Stem in flakes. the leaves with respect to their possition are scatter'd yet closely arranged near the extremities of the twigs particularly. the leaves are about 3/4 of an inch in length and about half that in width, is oval but obtusely pointed, absolutely entire, thick, Smoth, firm, a deep green and slightly grooved. the leaf is Supported by a Small footstalk of preportionable length. the berry is attached in an irregular and Scattered manner to the Small boughs among the leaves, tho frequently Closely arranged, but always Supported by a Seperate Short and Small peduncles, the incersion of which produces a Small concavity in the berry while its opposit side is Slightly convex; the form of the berry is a Spheroid, the Shorter diameter being in a line with the peduncle or Stem-. this berry is a pericarp the outer Coat of which is a thin firm tough pellicle, the inner part consists of dry mealy powder of a yellowish white colour invelloping from four to six propotionably large hard light brown seeds each in the form of section of a spheroid which figure they form when united, and are distitute of any membranous covering.- the colour of this fruit is a fine scarlet. the nativs usually eat them without any preparation. the fruit ripens in September and remains on the bushes all winter. the frost appears to take no effects on it. these berries are Sometimes gathered and hung in their houses in bags where they dry without further trouble, for in their succulent State they appear to be almost as dry as flour.

[Lewis, January 31, 1806] Saturday January 31st 1806. Sent a party of eight men up the river this morning to renew their surch for the Elk and also to hunt; they proceded but a few miles before they found the river so obstructed with ice that they were obliged to return. Joseph Fields arrived this evening, informed us that he had been hunting in company with Gibson and Willard for the last five days in order to obtain some meat for himself and the other Salt makers, and that he had been unsuccessfull untill yesday evening when he had fortunately killed two Elk, about six miles distant from this place and about 8 from the salt works; he left Gibson and Willard to dry the meat of these Elk and had come for the assistance of some men to carry the meat to the salt camp; for this purpose we ordered four men to accompany him early in the morning. discovered that McNeal had the pox, gave him medecine. Charbono found a bird dead lying near the fort this morning and brought it to me I immediately recognized it to be of the same kind of that which I had seen in the Rocky mountains on the morning of the 20th of September last. this bird is about the size as near as may be of the robbin. it's contour also is precisely the same with that bird. it measures one foot 31/4 Inches from tip to tip of the wings when extended. 91/4 inches from the extremity of the beak to that of the tail. the tail is 33/4 inches in length, and composed of eleven feathers of the same length. The beak is smoth, black, convex and cultrated; one and 1/8 inches from the point to the opening of the chaps and 3/4 only uncovered with feathers; the upper chap exceeds the other a little in length. a few small black hairs garnish the sides of the base of the upper chap. the eye is of a uniform deep sea green or black, moderately large. it's legs feet and tallons are white; the legs are an inch and a 1/4 in length and smoth; four toes on each foot, of which that in front is the same length with the leg including the length of the tallon, which is 4 lines; the three remaining toes are 3/4 of an inch, each armed with proportionally long tallons. the toes are slightly imbricated. the tallons are curved and sharply pointed. The crown of the head from the beak back to the neck, the back of the neck imbracing reather more than half the circumpherence of the neck, the back and tale, are of bluish dark brown; the two outer feathers of the tale have a little dash of white near their tips not percemptible when the tail is foalded. a fine black forms the ground of the wings; two stripes of the same colour pass on either side of the head from the base of the beak along the side of the head to it's junction with the neck, and imbraces the eye to it's upper edge; a third stripe of the same colour 3/4 of an inch in width passes from the sides of the neck just above the butts of the wings across the croop in the form of a gorget. the throat or under part of the neck brest and belly is of a fine yellowish brick red. a narrow stripe of this colour also commences just above the center of each eye, and extends backwards to the neck as far as the black stripe reaches before discribed, to which, it appears to answer as a border. the feathers which form the 1st and second ranges of the coverts of the two joints of the wing next the body, are beautifully tiped with this brick red; as is also each large feather of the wing on the short side of it's plumage for 1/2 an inch in length commening at the extremity of the feathers which form the first or main covert of the wing. this is a beatifull little bird. I have never heard it's note it appears to be silent. it feeds on berries, and I beleive is a rare bird even in this country, or at least this is the second time only that I have seen it.- between the legs of this bird the feathers are white, and those which form the tuft underneath the tail are a mixture of white and a brick red.

[Clark, January 31, 1806] Friday January 31st 1806 Sent a party of Eight men with the hunters to renew their Serch for the Elk, and also to hunt; they proceeded but a fiew miles before they found the river So obstructed with ice that they were obliged to return. Jo. Field arrives this evening, informs us That he had been hunting in Company with gibson and willard for the last four days in order to obtain some meat for himself and the other Salt-makers, and that he had been unsucksessfull untill yesterday evening when he had fortunately killed two Elk, about six miles distant from this place and about 8 from the Salt works; he left gibson and willard to dry the meat of those Elk, and had come for assistance to carry the meat to the Salt Camp; for this purpose we ordered four men to accompany him early in the morning. discovered that McNeal had the pox, gave him medicine. Chabono found a bird dead lying near the Fort this morning and brought it in, I reconized it to be the Same kind of that which I had Seen in the Rocky Mountains at severl different times. this berd is about the Size as near as may be of the robin. it's contour is also presisely the Same with that bird. it measured one foot 3/4 inches from tip to tip of the wings when extended. 9 1/4 inches from the extremity of the beak to that of the tail. the tail is 3 3/4 inches in length, and Composed of 11 feathers of the Same length. The beak is Smoth, black, convex and cultrated; 1 1/8 inchs from the point to the opening of the Chaps and 3/4 only uncovered with feathers, the upper Chap exceeds the other a little in length. a fiew Small black hairs garnish the Side of the upper chap. The Eye is of a uniform deep Sea green or black, moderately large. it's legs feet and tallants are white; the legs are of 1 1/4 in length and Smoth; four toes on each foot, of which that in front is the Same length of the leg including the tallants, which is 4 lines; the 3 remaining toes are 3/4 of an inch, each armed with proportianably large tallons. the toes are Slightly imbricated. the tallons are curved and Sharply pointed. The Crown of the head from the beak back to the neck imbracing rather more than half the circumphrence of the neck, the Back and tail is of a bluish dark brown; the two outer feathers of the tail have a little dash of white near the tips, not proceivable when the tail is foalded. a fine black forms the ground of the wings; two Stripes of the same colour passes on either side of the Head from the base of the Back along the Side of the head to it's junction with the neck, and embraces the eye to its upper edge; a third Stripe of the Same Colour 3/4 of an inch in width passes from the Side of the neck just above the buts of the wings across the troop in the form of a gorget. the throat or under part of the neck brest and belly is of a fine Yellowish brick red. a narrow Stripe of this Colour also Commences just above the center of each eye, and extends backwards to the Neck as far as the black Spots reaches before discribed, to which it appears to answer as a border. the feathers which form the 1st and Second range of the coverts of the two joints of the wings next the body are butifully aped with this Brick red; as is also each large feather of the wing on the Short Side of its plumage for 1/2 an inch in length Comencing at the extremity of the feather which form the first or main Covert of the wing. This is a butifull little bird. I have never herd its notes it appears to be Silent. it feeds on berries, and I believe is a rare bird even in this country-. between the legs of this bird the feathers are white, and those which form the tuft underneath the tail are a mixture of white and Brick red.

[Lewis, February 1, 1806] Saturday February 1st 1806. This morning a party of four men set out with Joseph Fields; Sergt. Gass with a party of five men again set out up the Netul river in surch of the Elk which had been killed some days since, and which could not be found in consequence of the snow. The Canoes of the natives inhabiting the lower portion of the Columbia River make their canoes remarkably neat light and well addapted for riding high waves. I have seen the natives near the coast riding waves in these canoes with safety and apparently without concern where I should have thought it impossible for any vessel of the same size to lived a minute. they are built of whitecedar or Arborvita generally, but sometimes of the firr. they are cut out of a solid stick of timber, the gunwals at the upper edge foald over outwards and are about 5/8 of an inch thick and 4 or five broad, and stand horrizontally forming a kind of rim to the canoe to prevent the water beating into it. they are all furnished with more or less crossbars in proportion to the size of the canoe. these bars are round sticks about half the size of a man's arm, which are incerted through holes (just) made in either side of the canoe just below the rim of the gunwall and are further secured with strings of waytape; these crossbars serve to lift and manage the canoe on land. when the natives land they invariably take their canoes on shore, unless they are heavily laden, and then even, if they remain all night, they discharge their loads and take the canoes on shore. some of the large canoes are upwards of 50 feet long and will carry from 8 to 10 thousand lbs. or from 20 to thirty persons and some of them particularly on the sea coast are waxed painted and ornimented with curious images at bough and Stern; those images sometimes rise to the hight of five feet; the pedestals on which these immages are fixed are sometimes cut out of the solid stick with the canoe, and the imagary is formed of seperate small peices of timber firmly united with tenants and motices without the assistance of a single spike of any kind. when the natives are engaged in navigating their canoes one sets in the stern and steers with a paddle the others set by pears and paddle over the gunwall next them, they all kneel in the bottom of the canoe and set on their feet. their paddles are of a uniform shape of which this is an imitation these paddles are made very thin and the middle of the blade is thick and hollowed out siddonly and made thin at the sides while the center forms a kind of rib. the blade occupys about one third of the length of the paddle which is usually from 4 1/2 to 5 feet. I have observed four forms of canoe only in uce among the nations below the grand chatarac of this river they are as follow. this is the smallest size about 15 feet long and calculated for one or two persons, and are most common among the Cathlahmahs and Wack ki a cums among the marshey

Islands. A the bow; B, the stern; these are from twenty to thirty five feet and from two 1/2 to 3 feet in the beam and about 2 feet in the hole; this canoe is common to all the nations below the grand rappids. it is here made deeper and shorter in proportion than they really are.- the bowsprit from C, to D is brought to a sharp edge tapering gradually from the sides.

This is the most common forms of the canoe in uce among the Indians from; the Chil-luck-kit-te-quaw inclusive to the Ocean and is usually about 30 or 35 feet long, and will carry from ten to twelve persons. 4 men are competent to carry them a considerable distance say a mile without resting. A is the end which they use as the bow, but which on first sight I took to be the stern C. D. is a comb cut of the sollid stick with the canoe and projects from the center of the end of the canoe being about 1 inch thirck it's sides parallel and edge at C D. sharp. it is from 9 to 11 Inches in length and extends from the underpart of the bowsprit at A to the bottom of the canoe at D.- the stern B. is mearly rounding and gradualy ascending. 1 2 3 represents the rim of the gunwalls about 4 Inches wide, reather ascending as they recede from the canoe. 4 5 6 7 8 are the round holes through which the cross bars are inserted.

This form of canoe we did not meet with untill we reached tidewater or below the grand rappids. from thence down it is common to all the nations but more particularly the Killamucks and others of the coast. these are the largest canoes. B. is the bow and comb. C. the stern and comb. their immages are representations of a great variety of grotesque figures, any of which might be safely worshiped without committing a breach of the commandments.

They have but few axes among them, and the only too usually imployed in felling the trees or forming the canoe, carving &c is a chissel formed of an old file about an Inch or an Inch and a half broad. this chissel has sometimes a large block of wood for a handle; they grasp the chissel just below the block with the right hand holding the edge down while with the left they take hold of the top of the block and strike backhanded against the wood with the edge of the chissel. a person would suppose that the forming of a large canoe with an instrument like this was the work of several years; but these people make them in a few weeks. they prize their canoes very highly; we have been anxious to obtain some of them, for our journey up the river but have not been able to obtain one as yet from the natives in this neighbourhood.- today we opened and examined all our ammunition, which had been secured in leaden canesters. we found twenty seven of the best rifle powder, 4 of common rifle, three of glaized and one of the musqut powder in good order, perfectly as dry as when first put in the canesters, altho the whole of it from various accedents has been for hours under the water. these cannesters contain four lbs. of powder each and 8 of lead. had it not have been for that happy expedient which I devised of securing the powder by means of the lead, we should not have had a single charge of powder at this time. three of the canesters which had been accedentally bruized and cracked, one which was carelessly stoped, and a fifth that had been penetrated with a nail, were a little dammaged; these we gave to the men to make dry; however exclusive of those five we have an abundant stock to last us back; and we always take care to put a proportion of it in each canoe, to the end that should one canoe or more be lost we should still not be entirely bereft of ammunition, which is now our only hope for subsistence and defence in a rout of 4000 miles through a country exclusively inhabited by savages.

[Clark, February 1, 1806] Saturday February 1st 1806 This morning a party of four men Set out with Jo. Field; and Sergt. Gass with a party of five men again Set out up the Netul river in Serch of the Elk which had been killed Some days since, and which Could not be found in Consequence of the Snow.

The Canoes of the nativs inhabitting the lower part of the Columbia River from the Long narrows down make their canoes remarkably neat light and well addapted for rideing high waves. I have Seen the nativs near the Coast rideing waves in these Canoes in Safty and appearantly without Concern when I Should it impossible for any vessel of the Same Size to have lived or kept above water a minute. they are built of Arborvitia or white Cedar generally, but Sometimes of fir. they are cut out of a solid Stick of timber, the gunnals at the upper edge fold over outwards and are about 5/8 of an inch thick and 4 or 5 broad, and Stand out nearly Horizontially forming a kind of rim to the Canoe to prevent the water beating into it. they are all furnished with more or less Cross bars agreeably to thier sizes of the Canoe, those bars are round Sticks about 1 inch and 1/2 diameter which are atached to the iner Side of the canoes a little below the rim on either Side with throngs of Cedar bark which is incerted through holes and made fast to the ends of the Stick, which is made Smaller than the other part of the Stick to prevent the cord Slipping off these cross bears Serve to Strengthen the canoe, and by which they lift and manage her on land. when the nativs land they invariably take their Canoes on Shore unless they are heavily ladined, and then even, if they remain all night, they discharge their loads and take the Canoe on Shore.

Some of the large Canoes are upwards of 50 feet long and will Carry from 8 to 12 thousand lbs. or from 20 to 30 persons, and Some of them particularly on the Sea Coast are waxed painted and ornimented with curious images on bow and Stern; those images sometimes rise to the hight of five feet; the pedestile on which these images are fixed, are Sometimes cut out of the Solid Stick with the Canoe, and the image is formed of Seperate pieces of timber firmly united with tenants and mortices without the appearance of a Single Spike or nail of any kind. when the nativs are engaged in navigateing their Canoes, one Sets in the Stern and Stears with a paddle the others Set by pars and paddle over their gunnals next them, they all kneel in the bottom of the Canoe and Set on their feet. their paddles are of an uniform shape which this is an imitation those paddles are made verry thin and the middle of the blade is thick and hollowed out Suddenly, and made thin on the Sides, the center forming a kind of ridge. the handle occupies about 1/8 of the length of the paddle which is usually 4 to 41/2 feet in length. I have observed five forms of Canoes only in use among the nativs below the Grand Cataract of this river. they areas follows. this is the Smallest Size about 15 feet long, 12 and Calculated for one two men mearly to cross creeks, take over Short portages to navagate the ponds and Still water, and is mostly in use amongst the Clatsops and Chinnooks. this is the next Smallest and from 16 to 20 feet long and calculated for two or 3 persons and are most common among the Wau-ki-a-cums and Cath-lah-mahs among the marshey Islands, near their villages. A the bow; B the Stern; those are from 20 to 40 feet in length and from 21/2 to 31/2 feet in the beam and about 2 feet deep; this Canoe is common to all the nations below the grand Rapids it here made deeper and Shorter in pertotion than the Canoe realy is, the bow sprit from C. to D. is brought to a Sharp edge tapering gradually from the Sides. This is the most common form of the Canoes in use among the indians from the Chil-luck-kit-te quaw inclusive to the ocian and is commonly from about 30 to 35 feet long, and will carry from 10 to 12 persons. 4 men are competent to carry them a considerable distance Say a mile without resting. A is the end the nativs use as the bow, but which on first Sight I took to be the Stern c. d. is a comb cut of the solid wood with the Canoe, and projects from the Center of the end of the Canoe being about 1 inch thick, it's Sides parallel and edge at c, d, Sharp it is from 9 to 11 inches in debth and extends from the under part of the bow sprit at A to the bottom at, d,. the Stern B is nearly rounding and gradually assending. 1, 2, 3, represents the rim of the gunnals about 4 inches wide, reather ascending as they recede from the Canoe. 4, 5, 6, 7, 8, are the holes through which the String pass to fasten the round pieces which pass Crosswise the Canoe to Strengthen & lift her. This form of a canoe we did not meet with untill we reached tide water or below the Great Rapids. from thence down it is common to all the nations but more particularly the Kil a mox and others of the Coast. these are the largest Canoes, I measured one at the Kilamox villag S S W of us which was _____ feet long _____ feet wide and _____ feet deep, and they are most Commonly about that Size. B is the how, and Comb. C, the stern and Comb. Their images are representations of a great variety of grotesque figures, any of which might be Safely worshiped without commiting a breach of the Commandments.

They have but fiew axes among them, and the only tool usially employd in forming the Canoe, carveing &c is a chissel formed of an old file about an inch or 11/2 inchs broad, this chissel has Sometimes a large block of wood for a handle; they grasp the chissel just below the block with the right hand holding the top of the block, and Strikes backwards against the wood with the edge of the Chissel. a person would Suppose that forming a large Canoe with an enstriment like this was the work of Several years; but those people make them in a fiew weeks. They prize their Canoes very highly; we have been anxious to obtain Some of them, for our journy up the river but have not been able to obtain one as yet from the nativs in this neighbourhood.

To day we opened and examined all our Ammunition, which has been Secured in leaden Canistirs. we found twenty Sevin of the best Rifle powder, 4 of Common rifle, 3 of Glaize and one of Musquet powder in good order, perfectly as dry as when first put in the Canisters, altho the whole of it from various accidince have been for hours under the water. these Cannisters Contain 4 pounds of powder each and 8 of Lead. had it not been for that happy expedient which Capt Lewis devised of Securing the powder by means of the Lead, we Should have found great dificuety in keeping dry powder untill this time-; those Cannisters which had been accidently brused and cracked, one which was carelessly Stoped, and a fifth which had been penetrated with a nail; were wet and damaged; those we gave to the men to Dry; however exclusive of those 5 we have an abundant Stock to last us back; and we always take Care to put a purpotion of it in each canoe, to the end that Should one Canoe or more be lost we Should Still not be entirely bereft of ammunition, which is now our only hope for Subsistance and defences in the rout of 4,000 miles through a Country exclusively inhabited by Indians-many bands of which are Savage in every Sense of the word-.

[Lewis, February 2, 1806] Sunday February 2cd 1806. Not any occurrence today worthy of notice; but all are pleased, that one month of the time which binds us to Fort Clatsop and which seperates us from our friends has now elapsed. one of the games of amusement and wrisk of the Indians of this neighbourhood like that of the Sosones consists in hiding in the hand some small article about the size of a bean; this they throw from one hand to the other with great dexterity accompanying their opperations with a particular song which seems to have been addapted to the game; when the individul who holds the peice has amused himself sufficiently by exchanging it from one hand to the other, he hold out his hands for his compettitors to guess which hand contains the peice; if they hit on the hand which contains the peice they win the wager otherwise loose. the individual who holds the peice is a kind of banker and plays for the time being against all the others in the room; when he has lost all the property which he has to venture, or thinks proper at any time, he transfers the peice to some other who then also becoms banker. The Sosone and Minnetares &c have a game of a singular kind but those divide themselves in two parties and play for a common wager to which each individual contributes to form the stock of his party. one of them holdes the peice and some one of the opposite party gesses which hand contains if he hits on the hand which contains it the peice is transferred to the opposite party and the victor counts one, if he misses the party still retain the peice and score one but the individual tranfers the peice to some other of his own party; the game is set to any number they think proper, and like the natives of this quarter they always accompany their opperations with a particular song. the natives here have also another game which consists in bowling some small round peices about the size of Bacgammon men, between two small upright sticks placed a few inches asunder, but the principals of the game I have not learn not understanding their language sufficiently to obtain an explanation. their boys amuse themselves with their bows and arrows as those do of every Indian nation with which I am acquainted. these people are excessively fond of their games of risk and bet freely every species of property of which they are possessed. They have a smal dog which they make usefull only in hunting the Elk.

[Clark, February 2, 1806]
Sunday February 2nd 1806
Not any accurrence to day worthy of notice; but all are pleased, that
one month of the time which binds us to fort Clatsop, and which
Seperates us from our friends, has now alapsed.

The games of amusements of the natives of this neighbourhood are Several, one of which is verry similar to one which the Sosone's & Minatare's are verry fond of and frequently play. they devide themselves into two parties and play for a common wager to which each individual Contributes to form the Stock of his party, one of them holdes the piece which is usually about the Size of a Bean, and Some one of the oposit party gesses which hand Contains, if he hits on the hand which Contains it, the piece is transfired to the opposit party and the victor Counts one, if he misses the party Still retains the piece and scores one, but the individual transfirs the piece to Some one of his own party; the game is Set to any number they think proper. they always accompany their operations with a particular Song. The amusements of the boys of all nations which I am acquainted with are generally the Bows and arrows.

All nations of Indians with which I am acquainted are excessive fond of their games of risk, and bet away Species of property of which they are possessed.

The nativs of this neighbourhood have a Small Dog which they make usefull only in hunting the Elk.

[Lewis, February 3, 1806] Monday February 3rd 1806. About three o'clock Drewyer and La Page, returned; Drewyer had killed seven Elk in the point below us, several miles distant but can be approached with in 3/4 of a mile with canoes by means of a small creek which discharges itself into the bay on this side of the Clatsop village direct Sergt. pryor to go in quest of the meat, the wind was so high that they were unable to set out untill a little before sunset, when they departed; at 10 P.M. they return excessively could and informed us that they could not make land on this side of the bay nor get into the creek in consequence of the tide being out and much lower than usual. we are apprehensive that the Clatsops who know where the meat is will rob us of a part if not the whole of it. at half after 4 P.M. Sergt Gass returned with his party, they brought with them the flesh of four other Elk which the hunters had found, being a part of the ten which were killed up the Netul river the other day. he left R. Fields, Shannon and Labuish to continue the hunt and made an appointment to return to them on Friday. late in the evening the four men who had been sent to assist the saltmakers in transporting meat which they had killed to their camp, also returned, and brought with them all the salt which had been made, consisting of about one busshel only. with the means we have of boiling the salt water we find it a very tedious opperation, that of making salt, notwithstanding we keep the kettles boiling day and night. we calculate on three bushels lasting us from hence to our deposits of that article on the Missouri.

[Clark, February 3, 1806] Monday February 3rd 1806 About 3 oClock Drewyer & Lapage returned, Drewyer had killed Seven Elk in the point below us, Several miles distant, but Can be approached within 3/4 of a mile with Canoes by means of a Small Creak which discharges itself into the Bay, on this Sid of the Clatsop Village. Directed Serjt. Pryor to go in quest of the meat, the winds was So high that they were unable to Set out until) a little before Sunset, when they departed; at 10 P.M. they returned excessively Cold and informed us that they could not make land on this Side of the bay or get into the Creek in consequence of the tides being out and much lower than usial. we are apprehensive that the Clatsops knowing where the meat is, will rob us of a part if not the whole of it. at half after 4 P. M Sergt. Gass returned with his party they brought with them the flesh of 4 other Elk which the hunters had found, being part of the 10 which were killed up the Netul river the other day. He left Ro. Field, Shannon & Labiesh to Continue the hunt, and made an appointment to return to them on friday. late in the evening the four men who had been Sent to assist the Saltmakers in transporting meat which they had killed to their Camp also returned, and brought with them all the Salt which had been made, consisting of about one Sushel only. with the means we have of boiling the Salt water we find it a very tegious opperation that of makeing Salt, notwithstanding the Kitties are kept boiling day and night. we Calculate on three bushels lasting us from hiere to our deposit of that article on the Missouri.

[Lewis, February 4, 1806] Tuesday February 4th 1806. Sergt. Pryor with a party of five men set out again in quest of the Elk which Drewyer had killed. Drewyer and La Page also returned to continue the chase in the same quarter. the Elk are in much better order in the point near the praries than they are in the woody country arround us or up the Netul. in the praries they feed on grass and rushes, considerable quantities of which are yet green and succulet. in the woody country their food is huckle berry bushes, fern, and an evergreen shrub which resembles the lore) in some measure; the last constitutes the greater part of their food and grows abundantly through all the timbered country, particularly the hillsides and more broken parts of it. There are sveral species of fir in this neighbourhood which I shall discribe as well as my slender botanical skit will enable me and for the convenience of comparison with each other shal number them. (No 1.) a species which grows to immence size; very commonly 27 feet in the girth six feet above the surface of the earth, and in several instances we have found them as much as 36 feet in the girth or 12 feet diameter perfectly solid and entire. they frequently rise to the hight of 230 feet, and one hundred and twenty or 30 of that hight without a limb. this timber is white and soft throughout and rives better than any other species which we have tryed. the bark skales off in irregula rounded flakes and is of a redish brown colour particularly of the younger growth. the stem of this tree is simple branching, ascending, not very defuse, and proliferous. the leaf of this tree is acerose, 1/10th of an Inch in width, and 3/4 of an Inch in length; is firm, stif and accuminate; they are triangular, a little declining, thickly scattered on all sides of the bough, but rispect the three uppersides only and are also sessile growing from little triangular pedestals of soft spungy elastic bark. at the junction of the boughs, the bud-scales continue to incircle their rispective twigs for several yeas; at least three years is common and I have counted as many as the growth of four years beyond these scales. this tree affords but little rosin. it's cone I have not yet had an opportunity to discover altho I have sought it frequently; the trees of this kind which we have felled have had no cones on them.

[Clark, February 4, 1806] Tuesday February 4th 1806 Serjt. Pryor with a party of 5 men Set out again in quest of the Elk which Drewyer had Killed. Drewyer also returned to continue the Chase in the Same quarter. the Elk are in much better order in the point near the praries than they are in the woodey Country around us or up the Netul. in the praries they feed on grass and rushes, which are yet green. in the woddey Countrey their food is huckleberry bushes, fern, and the Shal-lon an evergreen Shrub, which resembles the Lorel in Some measure; the last constitutes the greater part of their food and grows abundant through all the timbered Country, particularly the hill Sides and more broken parts of it. There are Several Species of Fir in this neighbourhood which I shall discribe as well as my botanicale Skill will enable me, and for the Convenience of Comparrison with each other Shall number them. (No. i,) a Species which grows to an emence size; verry commonly 27 feet in Surcumferonce at 6 feet above the surface of the earth, and in Several instances we have found them as much as 36 feet in the Girth, or 12 feet Diameter perfectly Solid & entire. they frequently rise to the hight of 230 feet, and 120 or 30 of that hight without a limb. this timber is white and Soft throughout and rives better than any other Species we have tried the bark Shales off in arregular rounded flakes and is of a redish brown Colour, particularly of the younger growth, the Stem of this tree is simple branching, assending, not very defuse, and proliferous, the leaf of this tree is accerose 1/2 a line in width, and 3/4 of an inch in length; is firm Stiff and accuminate; they are triangular, little declineing, thickly scattered on all Sides of the Bough, but respect the three upper Sides only Growing from little triangular pedistals of Soft Spungy Elastic bark. at the junction of these bough's, the bud-scales continue to incircle the respective twigs for several years; at least 3 years is common and I have counted as maney as the groth of 4 years beyond these Scales. this tree affords but little rozin. it's cone I have not yet had an oppertunity to discover altho I have Sought it frequently; the trees of this kind which we have fell'd have had no cones on them.

[Lewis, February 5, 1806] Wednesday February 5th 1806. Late this evening one of the hunters fired his gun over the swamp of the Netul opposite to the fort and hooped. I sent sergt. Gass and a party of men over; the tide being in, they took advantage of a little creek which makes up in that direction nearly to the highlands, and in their way fortunately recovered our Indian Canoe, so long lost and much lamented. The Hunter proved to be Reubin Fields, who reported that he had killed six Elk on the East side of the Netul a little above us; and that yesterday he had heard Shannon and Labuishe fire six or seven shots after he had seperated from them and supposed that they had also killed several other Elk. Filds brought with him a phesant which differed but little from those common to the Atlantic states; it's brown is reather brighter and more of a redish tint. it has eighteen feathers in the tale of about six inches in length. this bird is also booted as low as the toes. the two tufts of long black feathers on each side of the neck most conspicuous in the male of those of the Atlantic states is also observable in every particular with this.- Fir No. 2 is next in dignity in point of size. it is much the most common species, it may be sad to constitute at least one half of the timber in this neighbourhood. it appears to be of the spruse kind. it rises to the hight of 160 to 180 feet very commonly and is from 4 to 6 feet in diameter, very streight round and regularly tapering. the bark is thin of a dark colour, and much divided with small longitudinal intersticies; that of the boughs and young trees is somewhat smoth but not so much so as the balsom fir nor that of the white pine of our country. the wood is white throughout and reather soft but very tough, and difficult to rive. The trunk of this tree is a simple branching diffused stem and not proliferous as the pines & firs usially are but like most other trees it puts forth buds from the sides of the small boughs as well as their extremities. the stem usually terminates in a very slender pointed top like the cedar. The leaves are petiolate, the footstalk small short and oppressed; acerose reather more than half a line in width and very unequal in length, the greatest length being little more than half an inch, while others intermixed on every part of the bough are not more than a 1/4 in length. flat with a small longitudinal channel in the upper disk which is of a deep green and glossey, while the uder disk is of a whiteish green only; two ranked, obtusely pointed, soft and flexable. this tree affords but little rosin. the cone is remarkably small not larger than the end of a man's thumb soft, flexable and of an ovate form, produced at the ends of the small twigs.

[Clark, February 5, 1806] Wednesday February 5th 1806 Late this evening one of the hunters fired off his gun over the marsh of the Netul opposit to the fort & hhoped. we Sent Sergt. Gass and a party of men over; the tide being in they took advantage of a little Creek which makes up in that direction nearly to the high lands, and in their way fortunately recovered our Indian Canoe So long lost and much lamented. The hunter provd. to be Reubin Field, who reported that he had killed Six Elk on the East Side of the Netul a little above us; and that he had parted with Shannon and Labiesh yesterday after he had herd them fire Six or Seven Shot after he had Seperated from them, and Supposed that they had also killed Several other Elk. Fields brought with him a Pheasant which differs but little from those Common to the United States- Fur No. 2 is next in dignity in point of Size. it is much the most common Species, it may be Said to Constitute one half of the timber of this neighbourhood. it appears to be of the Spruce kind. it rises to the higth of 160 or 180 feet very Commonly and is from 4 to 6 feet in diameter, very Streight round and regularly tapering. the bark is thin of a dark colour, and much divided with Small longitudinal interstices; that of the boughs and young trees are Somewhat Smoth but not So much so as the balsom fir, nor that of the white pine of our Countrey. the wood is white throughout and rather Soft but rather tough and dificult to rive. The trunk of this tree is Simple branching, deffused Stem and not proliferous as the pine and fir usially are, but like most other trees it puts foth buds from the Sides of the Small boughes as well as from their extremities. the Stem usially termonate in a very slender pointed top like the Cedar. The leaves are petiolate, the footstalk Small Short and oppressed; acerose reather more than 1/2 a line in wedth and very uneaqual in length, the greatest length being a little more than half an inch, while others intermixed on every part of the bough are not more than a 1/4 of an inch in length. flat with a Small longitudinal channel in the upper disk which is of a Deep green and glossy, while the under disk is of a whitish green only; two ranked, obtusely pointed, Soft and flexable. this tree affords but little rosin. the Cone is remarkably Small, not larger than the end of a mans thumb Soft, flexable and of an oval form, produced at the end of a Small twig.

[Lewis, February 6, 1806] Thursday February 6th 1806. Sent Sergts. Gass and Ordway this morning with R. Fields and a party of men to bring in the Elk which Field had killed. Late in the evening Sergt. Pryor returned with the flesh of about 2 Elk and 4 skins the Indians having purloined the ballance of seven Elk which Drewyer killed the other day. I find that there are 2 vilages of Indians living on the N. side of the Columbia near the Marshy Islands who call themselves Wackki-a-cum. these I have hertofore Considered as Cath-lah-mahs. they speak the same language and are the same in every other rispect.

No. 3 A species of fir which one of my men informs me is precisely the same with that called the balsam fir of Canada. it grows here to considerable size, being from 21/2 to 4 feet in diameter and rises to the hight of eighty or an hundred feet. it's stem is simple branching, ascending and proliferous. it's leaves are sessile, acerose, one 1/8 of an inch in 1/16th of an inch in width, thickly scattered on all sides of the twigs as far as the growth of four preceeding years and rispect the three undersides only the uper side being neglected and the under side but thinly furnished; gibbous, a little declining, obtusely pointed, soft flexible, and the upper disk longitudinally marked with a slight channel; this disk is of a glossy deep green, the under one green tho paler and not glossy. this tree affords considerable quantities of a fine clear arromatic balsam in appearance and taste like the Canadian balsam. smal pustules filled with this balsam rise with a blister like appearance on the body of the tree and it's branches; the bark which covers these pustules is soft thin smooth and easily punctured. the bark of the tree generally is thin of a dark brown colour and reather smooth tho not as much so as the white pine of our county. the wood is white and soft.- (No. 4) is a species of fir which in point of size is much that of No. 2. the stem simple branching ascending and proliferous; the bark of a redish dark brown and thicker than that of No. 3. it is divided with small longitudinal interstices, but these are not so much ramifyed as in species No. 2. the leaves with rispect to their position in regard to each other is the same with the balsam fir, as is the leaf in every other rispect except that it not more than 2/3ds the width and little more than half the length of the other, nor is it's upper disk of so deep a green nor so glossey. it affords no balsam and but little rosin. the wood also white soft and reather porus tho tough.- No 5. is a species of fir which arrives to the size of Nos. 2 and 4, the stem simple branching, diffuse and proliferous. the bark thin, dark brown, much divided with small longitudinal interstices and sometimes scaleing off in thin rolling flakes. it affords but little rosin and the wood is redish white 2/3ds of the diameter in the center, the ballance white, somewhat porus and tough. the twigs are much longer and more slender than in either of the other species. the leaves are acerose, 1/20th of an inch in width, and an inch in length, sessile, inserted on all sides of the bough, streight, their extremities pointing obliquely toward the extremities of the bough and more thickly placed than in either of the other species; gibbous and flexeable but more stif than any except No. 1 and more blontly pointed than either of the other species; the upper disk has a small longitudinal channel and is of a deep green tho not so glossy as the balsam fir, the under disk is of a pale green.- No. 65 the white pine; or what is usually so called in Virginia. I see no difference between this and that of the mountains in Virginia; unless it be the uncommon length of cone of this found here, which are sometimes 16 or 18 inches in length and about 4 inches in circumpherence. I do not recollect those of virginia perfectly but it strikes me that they are not so long. this species is not common I have only seen it but in one instance since I have been in this neighbourhood which was on the border of Haley's bay on the N. side of the Columbia near the Ocean.

[Clark, February 6, 1806] Thursday February 6th 1806 Sent Serjt. Gass and party this morning with Ru Field to bring in the Elk which Field had killed. late in the evening Serjt. Pryor returned with the fish of about 2 Elk and four skins the Indians haveing taken the ballance of Seven Elk which Drewyer killed the other day. I find that those people will all Steal.

No. 3 a Species of fir, which one of my men inform me is presisely the Same with that called the balsam fir of Canada. it grows here to considerable Size, being from 2 1/2 to 4 feet in diameeter and rises to the hight of 100 or 120 feet. it's Stem is Simple branching assending and proliferous-. it's leaves are cessile, acerose, 1/8 of an inch in length and 1/16 of an inch in width, thickly scattered on all Sides of the twigs as far as the groth of four proceeding years, and respects the three undersides only, the upper Side being neglected and the under Side but thinly furnished; gibbous a little declineing, obtusely pointed, Soft flexable, and the upper disk longitudinally marked with a Slight Channel; this disk is of a glossy deep green, the under one green tho paler and not glossy. This tree affords a considerable quantity of a fine Clear arromatic Balsom in appearance and taste like the Canadian balsom. Small pustuls filled with the balsom rise with a blister like appearance on the body of the tree and it's branches; the bark which covers these pustules is Soft thin Smothe and easily punctured. the bark of the tree is generally thin of a dark brown colour and reather Smooth tho not as much so as the white pine of the U. States the wood is white and Soft.

No. 4 a Species of fir which in point of Size is much that of No 2,-. the Stem Simple branching assending and proliferous; the bark of a redish dark brown and thicker than that of No. 3. it is devided with Small longitudinal interstices, but these are not So much ramefied as in the Specis No. 2. the leaves with respect to their possition in reguard to each other is the Same with the balsam fir, as is the leaf in every other respect than that, it is not more than 2/3ds the width and little more than half the length of the other, nor is it's upper disk of so deep a green nor glossy. it affords no balsam, and but little rosin. the wood also white Soft and reather porus tho tough-.- No. 5 is a species of fir which arives to the Size of No. 2, and No. 4. the Stem Simple branching, diffuse and proliferous. the bark thin dark brown, much divided with Small longitudinal interstices scaleing off in thin rolling flakes. it affords but little rosin and the wood is redish white 2/3ds the diamieter in the Center the ballance white Somewhat porus and tough. the twigs are much longer and more slender than in either of the other speceies. the leaves are acerose 1/20 of an inch in width, and an inch in length, sessile, inserted on all Sides of the bough, Streight, their extremities pointing obliquely towards the extremities of the bough and more thickly placed than in either of the other Species; gibbous and flexable but more stiff than any except No. 1 and more blontly pointed than either of the other Species; the upper disk has a Small longitudinal Channel and is of a deep green tho not so Glossy as the balsam fir, the under disk is of a pail green. No. 6 the White pine; or what is usially So Called in Virginia. I see no difference between this and that of the mountains in Virginia; unless it be the uncommon length of the cone of this found here, which are Sometimes 16 or 18 inches in length and about 4 inches in Surcumfrance. I do not recollect those of Virginia, but it Strikes me that they are not So long. this Species is not common I have Seen it only in three instances since I have been in this neighbourhood, I saw a few on Haleys bay on the North Side of the Columbia River, a fiew scattering on the Sea coast to the North on one of which I engraved my name-and Some on the S S E Side of E co la Creek near the Kil a mox nation, at which place I Saw the white & red Cedar

[Lewis, February 7, 1806] Friday February 7th 1806. This evening Sergt. Ordway and Wiser returned with a part of the meat which R. Fields had killed; the ballance of the party with Sergt. Gass remained in order to bring the ballance of the meat to the river at a point agreed on where the canoe is to meet them again tomorrow morning. This evening we had what I call an excellent supper it consisted of a marrowbone a piece and a brisket of boiled Elk that had the appearance of a little fat on it. this for Fort Clatsop is living in high stile. In this neighbourhood I observe the honeysuckle common in our country I first met with it on the waters of the Kooskooske near the Chopunnish nation, and again below the grand rappids In the Columbian Valley on tidewater. The Elder also common to our country grows in great abundance in the rich woodlands on this side of the rocky Mountains; tho it differs Here in the colour of it's berry, this being of a pale sky blue while that of the U States is a deep perple. The seven bark or nine-bark as it is called in the U States is also common in this quarter. There is a species of huckleberry common to the piny lands from the commencement of the Columbian valley to the seacoast; it rises to the hight of 6 or 8 feet. is a simple branching some what defuse stem; the main body or trunk is cilindric and of a dark brown, while the colateral branches are green smooth, squar, and put forth a number of alternate branches of the same colour and form from the two horizontal sides only. the fruit is a small deep perple berry which the natives inform us is very good. the leaf is thin of a pale green and small being 3/4 of an inch in length and 3/8 in width; oval terminateing more accutely at the apex than near the insertion of the footstalk which is at the base; veined, nearly entire, serrate but so slightly so that it is scarcely perceptible; footstalk short and there position with rispect to each other is alternate and two ranked, proceeding from the horizontal sides of the bough only. The small pox has distroyed a great number of the natives in this quarter. it prevailed about 4 years since among the Clatsops and distroy several hundred of them, four of their chiefs fell victyms to it's ravages. those Clatsops are deposited in their canoes on the bay a few miles below us. I think the late ravages of the small pox may well account for the number of remains of vilages which we find deserted on the river and Sea coast in this quarter.

[Clark, February 7, 1806] Friday February 7th 1806 This evening Serjt Ordway and wiser returned with a part of the meat which R. Field had killed; the balance of the Party with Serjt. Gass remained in order to bring the ballance of the meat to the river at a point agreed on, where the Canoe is to meet them again tomorrow morning. This evening we had what I call an excellent supper it consisted of a marrowbone, a piece of brisket of boiled Elk that had the appearance of a little fat on it. this for Fort Clatsop is liveing in high Stile, and in fact fiesting-.

In this neighbourhood I observe the honeysuckle common in the U States, I first met with it on the waters of the Kooskooske near the Chopunnish Nation, and again below the grand rapids in the Columbian Vally on tide water. The Elder also common to our Countrey grows in great abundance in the rich wood land on this Side of the rocky mountains, tho it differs here in the Colour of its berry, this being of a pale Sky blue while that of the U, States is a deep purple. The Seven or nine bark as it is called in the U, States is also Common in this quarter. There is a Species of huckkleberry Common to the piney lands from the Commencement of the Columbian Vally to the Sea coast; it rises to the hight of 6 or 8 feet, is a Simple branching, Somewhat defused Stem; the main body or trunk is cilindric branches are green Smothe squar, and put foth a number of alternet branches of the Same Colour and form from the two horizontal Sides only. the frute is a small deep purple berry which the nativs inform us is very good, the leaf is thin of a pale green and Small being 3/4 of an inch in length and 3/8 in width; oval terminateing more accutely at the apax, than near the insersion of the footstalk which is at the base vened nearly entire; footstalks Short and their position in respect to each other is alternate and too ranked, proceeding from the horizontal Side of the bough only.

The Small Pox had distroyed a great number of the nativs in this quarter. it provailed about 4 or 5 yrs Sinc among the Clatsops, and distroy'd Several hundreds of them, four of their Chiefs fell a victym to it's ravages. these Clatsops are Deposited in their Canoes on the bay a fiew miles below us. I think the late ravages of the Small Pox, may well account for the number of remains of villages which I Saw on my rout to the Kil a mox in Several places-.

[Lewis, February 8, 1806] Saturday February 8th 1806. Sent Sergt. Ordway and two men this morning to join the party with Sergt. Gass and bring the ballance of R. Fields's Elk. in the evening they returned with the balance of the flesh of five Elk, that of one of them having become tainted and unfit for uce. late in the evening Sergt. Pryor returned with Shannon Labuish and his party down the Netul. they brought with them the flesh of 4 Elk which those two hunters had killed. we have both dined and suped on Elk's tongues and marrow bones.

I have discovered that the shrub and fruit discribed on the 26th of January is not that which the Indians call the Shal-lon, but that is such as is there discribed, and the berry is estemed and used by the natives as there mentioned except that it is not like the shallon, baked in large loaves, but is simply dryed in the sun for winter uce, when they either eat them in thir dryed state or boil them in water. The Shallon is the production of a shrub which I have heretofore taken to be a speceis of loral and mentioned as abounding in this neighbourhood and that the Elk fed much on it's leaves. it generally rises to the hight of 3 feet but not unusualy attains to that of 5 feet. it grows very thick and is from the size of a goos quill to that of a man's thumb, celindric, the bark of the older or larger part of the stock is of a redish brown colour while that of the younger branches and succulent shoots are red where most exposed to the sun and green elsewhere. the stem is simple branching reclining, and partially fluxouse, or at least the smaler stocks or such parts of them and the boughs as produce the leaves, take a different direction at the insertion of every petiole. the leaf is oval four & 3/4 inches in length and 2 1/2 in width. petiolate, the petiole short only 3/8th of an inch in length, celindric with a slight channel on it's upper side where it is generally red; undivided or entire, slightly serrate, the apex termineating in an accute point; the upper disk of a glossey deep green, the under disk of a pale green; veined. the leaves are also alternate and two ranked. the root is horizontal puting forth perpendicular radicles. this shrub is an evergreen. the fruit is a deep perple berry about the size of a buck short or common black cherry, of an ovate form tho reather more bluntly pointed, than at the insertion of the peduncle; at the extremity, the thin coloured membranous pellicle, which forms the surface of the pericarp, is divided into five accute angular points, which meet in the center, and contains a soft pulp of the same colour invelloping a great number of small brown kidney formed seeds. each berry is supported by a seperate celindric peduncle of half an inch in length; these to the number of ten or twelve issue from a common peduncle or footstalk which is fuxouse and forms the termination of the twig of the present years growth; each peduncle supporting a berry is furnished with one oblong bracte placed at it's insertion on the common footstalk which when the fruit is ripe withers with the peduncle.

[Clark, February 8, 1806] Saturday February 8th 1806 Sent Serjt. Ordway and two men this morning to joint the party with Serjt. Gass, and bring the ballance of R. Field's Elk. in the evening they returned with the ballance of the flesh of five Elk, that of one of them having become tainted and unfit for use. late in the evening Serjt. Pryor returned with Shannon Labieshe and his party down the Netul. they brought with them the flesh of 4 Elk which those two hunters had killed.

we have both Dined and Suped on Elks tongues and marrowbones. a great Luxury for Fort Clatsop.

The Shat lon is a production of Shrub which I have taken heretofore to be a Species of Loral and mentioned as abounding in this neighbourhood, and that the Elk feed much on its leaves. it generally rises to the hight of 3 feet, and not unusially attain to that of 5 feet. it grows very thick and is from the size of that of a goose quil to that of a mans thumb, Celendric. the bark of the older or larger part of the Stalk is of a redish brown Colour, whilst that of the younger branches & succulent Shoots are red where most exposed to the Sun and green elsewhere. the Stem is Simple branching, reclineing and partially fuxouse, or at least the Smaller Stalks or Such parts of them and their boughs which produce the leaves, take a different direction at the insertion of every petiole. A, A, the leaves as they grow from the Stalk B. B. B the Stalk between each leaf.

The leaf is oval 4 and 3/4 inches in length, and 2 and a half in width. petiolate, the potiale Short only 3/8 of an inch in length cilindric with a Slight Channel on its upper Side where it is generally red; undevided, or entire, Slightly serrate, the apex termonateing in an accute point; the upper disk of a glossy deep Green, the under disk of a pail Green, veined. the leaves are also alternate and two ranked. the root is horozontal, putting foth pirpendicular radicles. This Shrub is an evergreen. the frute is a deep purple berry about the Size of a buck Shot or common black cherry, of an ovale form, tho reather more bluntly pointed than at the insertion of the peduncle, at the extremity, the thin coloured membranus pellicle, which forms the Surfice of the paricarp, is divided into 4 anguar points, which meet at the Center, and Contains a Soft pulp of the Same Colour invelloping a great number of Small brown kidney formed Seedeach berry is Supported by a Seperate celindric peduncle of half an inch in length, these to the number of 10 or 12 issue from a common peduncle of footstalk which forms the termination of the twig of the present years groth; each peduncle Supporting a berry is furnished with one oblong bracte placed at it's insertion on the common footstalk, which when the frute is ripe withers with the peduncle-.

[Lewis, February 9, 1806] Sunday February 9th 1806 This morning Collins and Wiser set out on a hunting excursion; they took our Indian canoe and passed the Netul a little above us. in the evening Drewyer returned; had killed nothing but one beaver. he saw one black bear, which is the only one which has been seen in this neighbourhood since our arrival; the Indians inform us that they are abundant but are now in their holes.

in the marshy ground frequently overflown by the tides there grows a species of fir which I take to be the same of No. 5 which it resembles in every particular except that it is more defusely branched and not so large, being seldom more than 30 feet high and 18 inches or 2 feet in diameter; it's being more defusely branched may proceed from it's open situation seldom growing very close. the cone is 2 1/2 inches in length and 3 3/4 in it's greatest circumpherence, which is near it's base, and from which it tapers regularly to a point. it is formed of imbricated scales of a bluntly rounded form, thin not very firm and smoth. a thin leaf is inserted into the pith of the cone, which overlays the center of and extends 1/2 an inch beyond the point of each scale. the form of this leaf is somewhat thus overlaying one of the imbricated scales.

The stem of the black alder of this country before mentioned as arriving to great size, is simply branching and defuse. the bark is smooth of a light colour with white coloured spreading spots or blotches, resembling much that of the beech; the leaf fructification &c is precisely that of the common alder of our country. these trees grow seperately from different roots and not in clusters or clumps as those of the Atlantic states. fearing that our meat would spoil we set six men to jurking it.

[Clark, February 9, 1806] Sunday February 9th 1806 This morning Collins & Wiser Set out on a hunting excursion; in the evening Drewyer returned; had Killed nothing but one Beaver. he Saw one black Bear, which is the only one which has been seen in the neighbourhood Since our arrival. the Indians inform us that they are abundant but are now in their holes.

In the marshey grounds frequently overflown by the tides there grows a Species of fir which I took to be the Same of No. 5. from examonation I find it a distinct species of fir. it is more perfusely branched. This tree

Seldom rises to a greater hight than 35 or 40 feet and is from 2 to 4 feet in Diamieter; the Bark the Same with that of No. 1. only reather more rugid. the leaf is acerose, 2/10 of an inch in width and 3/4 in length, they are firm Stiff and Somewhat accuminated, ending in a Short pointed hard tendril, gibbous thickly scattered on all Sides of the bough as respects the 3 upper Sides only; those which have their insertion on the underside incline side- wise with their points upwards gieveing the leaf the Shape of a Sythe. the others are perpindicular or pointing upwards, growing as in No. 1 from Small triangular pedestals of a Soft Spungy elastic bark. the under disk of these leaves or that which grows nearest to the Base of the bough is of a dark glossy green, while the upper or opposit side is of a whiteish pale green; in this respect differing from almost all leaves. The boughs retain their leaves as far back as almost to the Sixth year's groth. the peculiarity of the budscales observed in No. 1 is obsd. in this Species. The Cone is 31/2 Inches in length, and 3 in circumfranse, of an ovale figure being thickest in the middle and tapering and terminateing in two obtuce points. it composes several flexable, thin, obtusely jointed Smoth and redish brown imbricated scales. each scale Covering two small winged Seed and being itself Covered in the center by a small thin inferior scale accutely pointed. The Cone is Some what of this figure. they proceed from the sides as well as the extremities of the bough, but in the former case allways at or near the Commencement of Some one years groth which in Some instances are as far back as the third year

The Stem of the Black Alder of this couintery before mentioned as ariveing at great Size, is Simple branching and defuse. the bark is Smoth of a light Colour with white Coloured Spredding Spots or blotches, resembling much that of beech. the leaf is procisely that of the Common alder of the United States or Virginia. those trees grow Seperately from different roots and not in Clusters or Clumps, as those of the atlantic States, casts its folage about the 1st of December.

Fearing that our meat would Spoil we Set Six men to jurking it to day, which they are obliged to perform in a house under shelter from the repeated rains.

[Lewis, February 10, 1806] Monday February 10th 1806. Drewyer visited his traps today but caught no beaver. Collins and Wiser returned had killed no Elk. Willard arrived late in the evening from the Saltworks, had cut his knee very badly with his tommahawk. he had killed four Elk not far from the Salt works the day before yesterday, which he had butched and took a part of the meat to camp, but having cut his knee was unable to be longer ucefull at the works and had returned. he informed us that Bratton was very unwell, and that Gibson was so sick that he could not set up or walk alone and had desired him to ask us to have him brought to the Fort. Coalter also returned this evening. continue the operation of drying our meat.

There is a tree common to the Columbia river below the entrance of cataract river which in it's appearance when divested of it's foliage, much resembles the white ash; the appearance of the wood and bark is also that of the ash. it's stem is simple branching and diffuse. the leaf is petiolate, plane, scattered, palmate lobate, divided by four deep sinuses; the lobes are repand, or terminate in from 3 to 5 accute angular points, while their margins are indented with irregular and somewhat circular incissures. the petiole is celendric smooth and 7 inches long. the leaf 8 inches in length and 12 in bredth. this tree is frequently 3 feet in diameter and rises to 40 or 50 feet high. the fruit is a winged seed somewhate like the maple. in the same part of the country there is also another growth which resembles the white maple in it's appearance, only that it is by no means so large; seldom being more than from 6 to 9 inches in diamater, and from 15 to 20 feet high; they frequently grow in clusters as if from the same bed of roots spreading and leaning outwards. the twigs are long and slender. the stems simple branching. the bark smooth and in colour resembling that of the white maple. the leaf is petiolate, plane, scattered nearly circular, with it's margin cut with accute angular incissures of an inch in length and from six to 8 in number the accute angular points formed by which incissures are crenate, or cut with small accute angular incissures. or in this form. it is 3 inches in length, and 4 in width. the petiole celindric smooth and one and a 1/4 inches long. the fruit or flower not known.

[Clark, February 10, 1806] Monday February 10th 1806 Collins and Wiser returned without killing any Elk. Willard arrived late this evening from the Salt Camp, he had cut his knee very badly with his tomahawk. he had killed four Elk not far from the Salt Camp, the day before yesterday, which he had butchered and took a part of the meat to the Camp, but haveing Cut his Knee was unable to be longer Servisable at the works & had returned. he informed us that Bratten was very unwell, and that Gibson was So Sick that he could not Set up or walk alone, and had desired him to ask us to have him brought to the Fort. Colter also returnd. this evening. continue the opperation of dryin our meat.

There is a tree common to the Columbia river below the enterance of Cataract River which in its appearance when divested of its folage, much resembles the white ash; the appearance of the wood and bark is also that of the ash. it's Stem is Simple branching and diffuse. the lief is petiolate, plane, scattered palmate lobate, divided by four deep Sinusus; the lobes are repand or terminate in from 3 to 5 accute angular points, while their margins are indented with irregular and Somewhat Circular incissures. the peteole is Celindric Smoth and 7 inches long. the leaf 8 inches in length and 12 in bredth. this tree is frequently 2 & 3 feet in diameter, and rises to 50 or 60 feet high-the froot is a winged Seed Somewhat like the maple. In the Same part of the countrey there is also another groth, which resembles the white maple in its appearance, only that it is by no means so large, seldom being more than from 6 to 9 inches in diamieter, and from 20 to 30 feet high; they frequently grow in clusters as if from the same bed or root, Spreading and leaning outwards. the twigs are long and Slender. the Stems simple branching. the bark Smoth and in Colour resembles that of the white maple. the leaf is patiolate, plain, scattered nearly circular, with it's margin cut with accute anglar incissures of an inch in length and from 6 to 8 in number, the accute angular points formed, by which incissures, are crenate, or cut with small angular incissures. or in this form. it is 3 inches in length, and 4 in width. the petiole is cilendric smoth and 11/4 inches long. the froot or flour I have not as yet found out &c.

[Lewis, February 11, 1806] Tuesday February 11th 1806. This morning Sergt. Gass Reubin Fields and Thompson passed the Netul opposite to us on a hunting expedition. sent Sergt Pryor with a party of four men to bring Gibson to the fort. also sent Colter and Wiser to the Salt works to carry on the business with Joseph Fields; as Bratton had been sick we desired him to return to the Fort also if he thought proper; however in the event of his not coming Wiser was directed to return.

There is a shrub which grows commonly in this neighbourhood which is precisely the same with that in Virginia some times called the quillwood. also another which grows near the water in somewhat moist grounds & rises to the hight of 5 or 6 feet with a large, peteolate spreading plane, crenate and somewhat woolly leaf like the rose raspberry. it is much branched the bark of a redish brown colour and is covered with a number of short hooked thorns which renders it extreemly disagreeable to pass among; it dose not cast it's foliage untill about the 1st of December. this is also the case with the black alder. There is also found in this neighbourhood an evergreen shrub which I take to be another variety of the Shallun and that discribed under that name in mistake on the 26th of January. this shrub rises to the hight of from four to five feet, the stem simple branching, defuse and much branched. the bark is of a redish dark brown, that of the mane stein is somewhat rough while that of the boughs is smooth. the leaves are petiolate the petiole 1/40 of an inch long; oblong, obtuse at the apex and accute angular at the insertion of the petiole; 3/4 of an inch in length and Ysths in width; convex, somewhat revolute, serrate, smoth and of a paler green than the evergreens usually are; they are also opposite and ascending. the fruit is a small deep perple berry like the common huckleberry of a pleasent flavor. they are seperately scattered & attatched to the small boughs by short peduncles.-. the natives eat this berry when ripe but seldom collect it in such quantities as to dry it for winter uce.

[Clark, February 11, 1806] Tuesday February 11th 1806. This Morning Serjt. Gass R. Field and J. Thompson passed the Netul opposit to us on a hunting expedition. Sent Serjeant Natl. Pryor with 4 men in a Canoe to bring gibson to the Fort. also Sent Colter & P. Weser to the Salt works to carry on the business with Jos. Field; as bratten is also Sick we derected that he Should return to the fort if he continued unwell; There is Shrub which grows Commonly in this neighbourhood which grows on the Steep Sides of the hills and also in low moist grounds, and rise to the hight of 5 or 6 feet with a large peteolate, Spreading plain crenate and Somewhat woolly leaf like the rose raspberry. it is much branched the bark of a redish brown colour and is covered with a number of Short hooked thorns which renders it extreamly disagreeable to pass among, it does not cast its foliage untill about the 1st of December.

There is a Species of bryor which is common in this neighbourhood of a green colour which grows most abundant in the rich dry lands near the water courses, but is also found in Small quantities in the piney lands at a distance from the water Courses in the former Situations the Stem is frequently the Size of a mans finger and rise perpendicularly to the hight of 4 or 5 feet when it decends in an arch and becoms procumbent or rests on Some neighbouring plant or Srubs; it is Simple unbranched and celindric; in the latter Situation it is much Smaller, and usially procumbent. the Stem is armed with Sharp and hooked bryors. the leaf is peteolate, ternate and resembles in Shape and appearance that of the purple Raspberry common to the atlantic States. The frute is a berry resembling the Blackberry in every respect and is eaten when ripe and much esteemed by the nativs but is not dryed for winters Consumption. in the Countrey about the enterance of the quick Sand rivers I first discovered this bryor, it grows So abundantly in the furtile Vally of Columbia and on the Islands in that part of the river, that the Countrey near the river is almost impenitrable in maney places. This green Bryor retains its leaf or foliage and virdue untill late in December. The Briory bush with a wide leaf is also one of its ascociates.

[Lewis, February 12, 1806] Wednesday February 12th 1806. This morning we were visited by a Clatsop man who brought with him three dogs as a remuneration for the Elk which him self and nation had stolen from us some little time since, how ever the dogs took the alarm and ran off; we suffered him to remain in the fort all night.

There are two species of ever green shrubs which I first met with at the grand rappids of the Columbia and which I have since found in this neighbourhood also; they grow in rich dry ground not far usually from some watercourse. the roots of both species are creeping and celindric. the stem of the 1st is from a foot to 18 inches high and as large as a goosqull; it is simple unbranced and erect. it's leaves are cauline, compound and spreading. the leafets are jointed and oppositely pinnate, 3 pare & terminating in one, sessile, widest at the base and tapering to an accuminated point, an inch and a quarter the greatest width, and 3 inches & a 1/4 in length. each point of their crenate margins armed with a subulate thorn or spine and are from 13 to 17 in number. they are also veined, glossy, carinated and wrinkled; their points obliquely pointing towards the extremity of the common footstalk.- The stem of the 2nd is procumbent abot the size of the former, jointed and unbranched. it's leaves are cauline, compound and oppositely pinnate; the rib from 14 to 16 inches long celindric and smooth. the leafets 21/2 inches long and 1 inch wide. greatest width 1/2 inch from their base, to which they are regularly rounded, and from the same point tapering to an accute apex, wich is mostly, but not invariably tirminated with a small subulate thorn. they are jointed and oppositely pinnate, consisting of 6 pare and terminating in one, sessile serrate, or like the teeth of a whipsaw, each point terminating in a small subulate spine, being from 25 to 27 in number; veined, smooth, plane and of a deep green, their points tending obliquely towards the extremity of the rib or common footstalk. I do not know the fruit or flower of either. the 1st resembles the plant common to many parts of the U States called the mountain holley.

[Clark, February 12, 1806] Wednesday February 12th 1806. This morning we were visited by a Clatsop man who brought with him three dogs as a remuneration for the Elk which himself and Nation had Stolen from us Some little time Sence, however the dogs took the alarm and ran off; we suffered him to remain in the fort all night.

There are two Species of evergreen Shrubs. this is the leaf of one which I first met with at the grand rapids of the Columbia River, and which I have sence found in this neighbourhood also; they usially grow in rich dry ground not far from Some water course. the roots of both Species are creeping and celindric. the Stem of the first (as above) is from a foot to 18 inches high and as large as a Goose quil; it is Simple and erect. its leaves are cauline, and Spredding. the leafits are jointed & oppositly poinnate 3 par and termonateing in one, cessile widest at the base and tapering to an accuminated point, an inch and 1/4 the greatest width; & 31/4 inches in length. each point of their crenate margins armed with a thorn or Spine, and are from 13 to 17 in number. they are also veined, glossy, corinated and wrinkled; their points obliquely pointing towards the extremity of the Common footstalk.

The Stem of the 2nd is procumbent about the Size of the former, jointed and umbracated. it's leaves are Cauline, compound and oppositly pointed; the rib from 14 to 16 inches long Celendric and Smooth the leafits 21/2 inches long and 1 inch wide. the greatest width 1/2 inch from their base which they are regularly rounded, and from the Same point tapering to an accute apex, which is mostly but not entirely termonated with a Small Subulate thorn. they are jointed & oppositly pointed consisting of 6 par and termonateing in one (in this form) sessile, Serrate, or like the teeth of a whipsaw, each point terminateing in a small subulate spine, being from 25 to 27 in numbr; veined, Smoth, plane and of a deep green, their points tending obliquely towards the extremity of the rib or common footstalk. I do not know the fruit or flower of either. the 1st resembles a plant Common to maney parts of the United States Called the Mountain Holly

[Lewis, February 13, 1806] Thursday February 13th 1806. The Clatsop left us this morning at 11 A.M. not any thing transpired during the day worthy of notice. yesterday we completed the operation of drying the meat, and think we have a sufficient stock to last us this month. the Indians inform us that we shall have great abundance of a small fish in March which from their discription must be the herring. these people have also informed us that one More who sometimes touches at this place and trades with the natives of this coast, had on board of his vessel three Cows, and that when he left them he continued his course along the N. W. coast. I think this strong circumstancial proof that there is a stettlement of white persons at Nootka sound or some point to the N. W. of us on the coast.

There is a species of bryer which is common in this neighbourhood of a green colour which grows most abundant in the rich dry lands near the watercourses, but is also found in small quantities in the piny lands at a distance from the watercourses in the former situation the stem is frequently the size of a man's finger and rises perpendicularly to the hight of 4 or 5 feet when it decends in an arch and becomes procumbent or rests on some neighbouring plants or shrubs; it is simple unbranched and celindric; in the latter situation it is much smaller and usually procumbent. the stem is armed with sharp and hooked bryers. the leaf is peteolate ternate and resembles in shape and appearance that of the perple raspberry common to the Atlantic states. the fruit is a berry resembling the black berry in every rispect and is eaten when ripe and much esteemed by the natives but is not dryed for winter consumption. in the country about the entrance of the quicksand river I first discovered this bryer. it groows so abundantly in the fertile valley of Columbia and the Islands in that part of the river that the country near the river is almost impenitrable in many places. the briary bush with a wide leaf is also one of it's ascociates. the green bryer retains it's foliage and verdure untill late in December.- There are also two species of firn which are common to this country beside that formerly discribed of which the natives eat the roots. these from their disparity in point of size I shall designate the large and small firn. both species continue green all winter.- The large farn, rises to the height of 3 or four feet the stem is a common footstalk or rib which proceedes immediately from the radix wich is somewhat flat on two sides about the size of a man's arm and covered with innumerable black coarce capillary radicles which issue from every pat of it's surface; one of those roots or a collected bed of them will send fourth from twenty to forty of those common footstalks all of which decline or bend outwards from the common center. these ribs are cylindric and marked longitudinally their whole length with a groove or channel on their upper side. on either side of this grove a little below it's edge, the leafets are inserted, being shortly petiolate for about 2/3 ds of the length of the middle rib commencing at the bottom and from thence to the extremity sessile. the rib is terminated by a single undivided lanceolate gagged leaft. the leafets are lanceolate, from 2 to 4 inches in length gagged and have a small accute angular projection on the upper edge near the base where it is spuar on the side which has the projection and obliquely cut at the base on the other side of the rib of the leafet. or which will give a better idea in this form. the upper surface is Smooth and of a deep green the under disk of a pale green and covered with a brown bubersence of a woolly appearance particularly near the cental fiber or rib. these leafets are alternately pinnate. they are in number from 110 to 140; shortest at the two extremities of the common footstalk and longest in the center, gradduly lengthening and deminishing as they succeed each other.-

The small firn also rises with a common footstalk from the radix and are from four to eight in number. about 8 inches long; the central rib marked with a slight longitudinal groove throughout it's whole length. the leafets are oppositely pinnate about 1/3 rd of the length of the common footstalk from the bottom and thence alternately pinnate; the footstalk terminating in a simple undivided nearly entire lanceolate leafet. the leafets are oblong, obtuse, convex absolutely entire, marked on the upper disk with a slight longitudinal groove in place of the central rib, smooth and of a deep green. near the upper extremity these leafets are decursively pinnate as are also those of the large f rn. The grasses of this neighbourhood are generally coase harsh and sedge-like, and grow in large tufts. there is none except in the open grounds. near the coast on the tops of some of the untimbered hills there is a finer and softer species which resembles much the green sword. the salt marshes also produce a coarse grass, Bull rushes and the Cattail flagg. the two last the natives make great use in preparing their mats bags &c.

[Clark, February 13, 1806] Tuesday February 13th 1806. The Clatsop left us this morning at 11 A.M. not anything transpired dureing the day worthy of notice. yesterday we completed the opperation of drying the meat, and think we have a Sufficient Stock to last us this month. the Indians inform us that we shall have great abundance of Small fish in March. which from the discription must be the Herring. Those people have also informed us that one Moore who sometimes touches at this place and traded with the nativs of this Coast, had on board his Ship 3 Cows, and that when he left them he continued his course along the N W. Coast. I think this (if those Cows were not Coats) Strong circumstantial proof that their is a Settlement of white persons at Nootka Sound or Some place to the N W. of us on the coast.

There are also two Species of firn which are common to this Countrey besides that before mentioned of which the nativs eate the roots. these two from their disparity in point of Size I shall distinguish the large and Small firn. both species continue green all winter

The large fern, rise to the hight of 3 or 4 feet, the Stem is a Common footstalk or rib which proceeds imediately from the radix which is Somewhat flat on two Sides about the Size of a man's arm and covered with innumerable black coarse capillary radicles which issue from every part of its surface; one of those roots or a collected bead of them will Send forth from 20 to 40 of those Common footstalks all of which decline or bend outwards from the Common center. those ribs are cylindric and marked longitudinally their whole length with a groove or channel on their upper Side. on either Side of this groove a little below it's edge, the leafets are inserted, being partly petiolate for about 2/3ds of the length of the middle rib, commenceing at the bottom and from thence to the extremity Sessile. the rib is termonated by a Single undevided lanceolate gagged leafet. the leafets are lanceolate, from 2 to 4 inches in length gagged and have a Small accute angular projection and obliquely cut at the base on either Side of the rib of the leafet. upper Surface is Smooth and of a deep Green, the under disk of a pale Green and covered with a brown Substance of a woolly appearance particalarly near the center fiber or rib these leafets are alternately pointed they are in number from 110 to 140; shortest at the two extremities of the common footstalk and longest in the center, gradually lengthing and diminishing as they Succceed each other

The Small firn also rises with a Common footstalk from the radix and are from 4 to 8 in number, about 8 inches long; the Central rib marked with a Slight longitudinal Groove through out it's whole length. the leafets are oppositly pinnate about A of the length of the Common footstalk from the bottom and thence alternately pinnate; the footstalk termonating in a Simple undevided nearly entire lanceolate leafet. the leafets are oblong, obtuse, convex absolutely entire, marked on the upper disk with a Slight longitudinal grove in place of the central rib, smooth and of a deep green; near the upper extremity those lefets are decurscivly pinnate as are also those of the larg firn.

The Grass's of this neighbourhood are generally coarse harsh and Sedge like, and grow in large tufts. there is none except in the open grounds. near the Coast on the top of Some of the untimbered hills there is a finer and Softer Species which resembles much the Greensword. the Salt marshes also produce a Corse grass, Bullrushes and the Cattail flaggs. of the two last the nativs make great use in prepareing their mats bags &c. in those bags they Carry their fish Berries roots &c.

[Lewis, February 14, 1806] Friday February 14th 1806. We are very uneasy with rispect to our sick men at the salt works. Sergt. Pryor and party have not yet returned nor can we conceive what causes their delay. Drewyer visited his traps today and caught a very fine fat beaver on which we feasted this evening. on the 11th inst. Capt Clark completed a map of the country through which we have been passing from Fort Mandan to this place. in this map the Missouri Jefferson's river the S. E. branch of the Columbia, Kooskooske and Columbia from the entrance of the S. E. fork to the pacific Ocean as well as a part of Flathead river and our tract across the Rocky Mountains are laid down by celestial observation and survey. the rivers are also connected at their sources with other rivers agreeably to the information of the natives and the most probable conjecture arrising from their capacities and the relative positions of their rispective entrances which last have with but few exceptions been established by celestial observation. we now discover that we have found the most practicable and navigable passage across the Continent of North America; it is that which we traveled with the exception of that part of our rout from the neighbourhood of the entrance of Dearborn's River untill we arrived on Clarks river at the entrance of Traveler's rest creek; the distance between those two points would be traveled more advantageously by land as the navigation of the Missouri above the river Dearborn is laborious and 420 miles distant by which no advantage is gained as the rout which we are compelled to travel by land from the source of Jefferson's river to the entrance of Travelers rest Creek is 220 miles being further by 500 miles than that from the entrance of Dearborn's river to the last mentioned point and a much worse rout if Indian information is to be relyed on; from the same information the Flathead river like that of the S. E. fork of the Columbia which heads with Jefferson's and Maddison's Rivers can not be navigated through the Rocky Mountains in consequence of falls & rappids and as a confermation of this fact, we discovered that there were no salmon in the Flathead river, which is the case in the S. E. branch of the Columbia although it is not navigable. added to this, the Indians further inform us, that the Flathead river runs in the direction of the Rocky Mountains for a great distance to the North before it discharges itself into the Columbia river, which last from the same information from the entrance of the S. E. fork to that of Flathead river is obstructed with a great number of difficult and dangerous rappids. considering therefore the danger and difficulties attending the navigation of the Columbia in this part, as well as the circuitous and distant rout formed by itself and the Flathead river we conceive that even admitting the Flathead river contrary to information to be as navigable as the Columbia river below it's entrance, that the tract by land over the Rocky Mountains usually traveled by the natives from the Entrance of Traveller's-rest Creek to the forks of the Kooskooske is preferable; the same being a distance of 184 Miles. The inferrence therefore deduced from those premices are that the best and most Practicable rout across the Continent is by way of the Missouri to the entrance of Dearborn's river or near that place; from thence to flathead river at the entrance of Traveller's rest Creek, from thence up Traveller's rest creek to the forks, from whence you pursue a range of mounttains which divides the waters of the two forks of this creek, and which still continuing it's West wardly course divides the waters of the two forks of the Kooskooske river to their junction; from thence to decend this river by water to the S. E. branch of the Columbia, thence down that river to the Columbia and with the latter to the Pacific Ocean.

[Clark, February 14, 1806] Friday February 14th 1806 We are very uneasy with respect to our Sick men at the Salt works. Serjt. Pryor and party haveing not yet returneded, nor can we conceive what can be the Cause of their delay. Drewyer visited his traps & to day and Cought a fine fat beaver on which we feasted this evening and thought it a great delecessey.-.

I compleated a map of the Countrey through which we have been passing from the Mississippi at the Mouth of Missouri to this place. In the Map the Missouri Jefferson's river the S. E. branch of the Columbia or Lewis's river, Koos-koos-ke and Columbia from the enterance of the S. E fork to the pacific Ocian, as well as a part of Clark's river and our track across the Rocky Mountains are laid down by celestial observations and Survey. the rivers are also conected at their Sources with other rivers agreeably to the information of the nativs and the most probable conjecture arrising from their capacities and the relative positions of their respective enterances which last have with but fiew exceptions been established by celestial observations. We now discover that we have found the most practicable and navigable passage across the Continent of North America; it is that which we have traveled with the exception of that part of our rout from the foot of the Falls of the Missouri, or in neighbourhood of the enterance of the Rocky Mountains untill we arive on Clarks river at the enterence of Travelers-rest Creek; the distance between those two points would be traveled more advantagiously by land as the navigation of the Missouri above the Falls is crooked laborious and 521 miles distant by which no advantage is gained as the rout which we are compelled to travel by land from the Source of Jeffersons River to the enterance of Travellers rest Creek is 220 miles being further by At. 600 miles than that from the Falls of the Missourie to the last mentioned point (Travellers rest Creek) and a much worse rout if indian information is to be relied on which is from the So so nee or Snake Indians, and the Flatheads of the Columbia west of the rocky mountains. from the Same information Clarks river like that of the S. E. branch of the Columbia which heads with Jefferson's and Maddisons river's can not be navagated thro the rocky mountains in consequence of falls and rapids, and as a confirmation of the fact we discovered that there were no Salmon in Clark's river, which is not the Case in the S. E. branch of the Columbia altho it is not navagable. added to this, the Indians of different quartes further inform us, that Clark's river runs in the direction of the Rocky Mountains for a great distance to the north before it discharges itself into the Columbia river— from the Same information the Columbia from the enterance of the S. E. branch to the enterance of Clark's river is obstructed with a great number of dificuelt and dangerous rapids (and the place Clark's river comes out of the Rocky mountains is a tremendious falls &c which there is no possibillity of passing the mountains either by land or water.) Considering therefore the dangers and deficuelties attending the navigation of the Columbia in this part, as well as the circuitous and distant rout formed by itself and that of Clark's River we Conceive that even admitting that Clarks river contrary to information to be as navagable as the Columbia below it's enterance, that the tract by land over the Rocky Mountains usially traveled by the nativs from the enterance of Travellers rest Creek to the Forks of the Kooskooske is preferable; the Same being a distance of 184 miles. The inferrence therefore deduced from these premises are, that the best and most practicable rout across the Continent is by way of the Missouri to the Great Falls; thence to Clarks river at the enterance of Travellers rest Creek, from thence up travillers rest Creek to the forks, from whence you prosue a range of mountains which divides the waters of the two forks of this Creek, and which still Continues it's westwardly Course on the mountains which divides the waters of the two forks of the Kooskooske river to their junction; from thence to decend this river to the S. E. branch of the Columbia, thence down that river to the Columbia, and down the Latter to the Pacific Ocian-. There is a large river which falls into the Columbia on its South Side at what point we could not lern; which passes thro those extencive Columbian Plains from the South East, and as the Indians inform us head in the mountains South of the head of Jeffersons River and at no great distance from the Spanish Settlements, and that that fork which heads with the River Rajhone and waters of the Missouri passes through those extensive plains in which there is no wood, and the river Crowded with rapids & falls many of which are impassable. the other or westerly fork passes near a range of mountains and is the fork which great numbers of Indian Bands of the So sone or Snake Indians, this fork most probably heads with North River or the waters of Callifornia. This River may afford a practicable land Communication with New Mexico by means of its western fork. This river cannot be navagable as an unpracticable rapid is within one mile of its enterance into the Columbia, and we are fully purswaded that a rout by this river if practicable at all, would lengthen the distance greatly and incounter the Same dificuelties in passing the Rocky Mountains with the rout by way of Travellers rest Creek & Clarks river.

[Lewis, February 15, 1806] Saturday February 15th 1806. Drewyer and Whitehouse set out this morning on a hunting excurtion towards the praries of Point Adams. we have heard our hunters over the Netul fire several shot today, but have had no account from them as yet. about 3 P.M. Bratton arrived from the salt works and informed us that Sergt. Pryor and party were on their way with Gibson who is so much reduced that he cannot stand alone and that they are obliged to carry him in a litter. Bratton himself appears much reduced with his late indisposition but is now recovering fast. Bratton informed that the cause of Sergt. Pryor's delay was attributeable to the winds which had been so violent for several days as to render it impossible to get a canoe up the creek to the point where it was necessary to pass with Gibson. the S. W. winds are frequently very violent on the coast when we are but little sensible of them at Fort Clatsop. in consequence of the lofty and thickly timbered fir country which surrounds us on that quarter from the South to the North East.

after dark Sergt. Pryor arrived with Gibson. we are much pleased in finding him by no means as ill as we had expected. we do no conceive him in danger by any means, tho he has yet a fever and is much reduced. we beleive his disorder to have orriginated in a violent cold which he contracted in hunting and pursuing Elk and other game through the swams and marshes about the salt works. he is nearly free from pain tho a gooddeel reduced and very languid. we gave him broken dozes of diluted nitre and made him drink plentifully of sage tea, had his feet bathed in warm water and at 9 P.M. gave him 35 drops of laudanum.

The quadrupeds of this country from the Rocky Mountains to the pacific Ocean are 1st the domestic animals, consisting of the horse and the dog only; 2cdly the native wild animals, consisting of the Brown white or grizly bear, (which I beleive to be the same family with a mearly accedental difference in point of colour) the black bear, the common red deer, the black tailed fallow deer, the Mule deer, Elk, the large brown wolf, the small woolf of the plains, the large wolf of the plains, the tiger cat, the common red fox, black fox or fisher, silver fox, large red fox of the plains, small fox of the plains or kit fox, Antelope, sheep, beaver, common otter, sea Otter, mink, spuck, seal, racoon, large grey squirrel, small brown squirrel, small grey squirrel, ground squirrel, sewelel, Braro, rat, mouse, mole, Panther, hare, rabbit, and polecat or skunk. all of which shall be severally noticed in the order in which they occur as well as shuch others as I learn do exist and which not been here recapitulated. The horse is confined principally to the nations inhabiting the great plains of Columbia extending from Latitude 40° to 50° N. and occuping the tract of country lying between the rocky mountains and a range of Mountains which pass the columbia river about the great falls or from Longitude 116 to 121 West. in this extesive tract of principally untimbered country so far as we have leant the following nations reside (viz) the Sosone or snake Indians, the Chopunnish, sokulks, Cutssahnims, Chymnapums, Ehelutes, Eneshuh & Chilluckkittequaws. all of whom enjoy the bennefit of that docile, generous and valuable anamal the horse, and all of them except the three last have immence numbers of them. Their horses appear to be of an excellent race; they are lofty eligantly formed active and durable; in short many of them look like the fine English coarsers and would make a figure in any country. some of those horses are pided with large spots of white irregularly scattered and intermixed with the black brown bey or some other dark colour, but much the larger portion are of an uniform colour with stars snips and white feet, or in this rispect marked much like our best blooded horses in virginia, which they resemble as well in fleetness and bottom as in form and colours. the natives suffer them to run at large in the plains, the grass of which furnishes them with their only subsistence their masters taking no trouble to lay in a winters store for them, but they even keep fat if not much used on the dry grass of the plains during the winter. no rain scarcely ever falls in these plains and the grass is short and but thin. The natives appear to take no pains in scelecting their male horses from which they breed, in short those of that discription which I have noticed appeared much the most indifferent. whether the horse was orrigeonally a native of this country or not it is out of my power to determine as we can not understand the language of the natives sufficiently to ask the question. at all events the country and climate appears well adapted to this anamal. horses are said to be found wild in many parts of this extensive plain country. the several tribes of Sosones who reside towards Mexico on the waters of Clark's river or particularly one of them called Sh&-bo-bo-ah have also a great number of mules, which among the Indians I find are much more highly prized than horses. an eligant horse may be purchased of the natives in this country for a lew peads or other paltry trinkets which in the U States would not cost more than one or two dollars. This abundance and cheapness of horses will be extremely advantageous to those who may hereafter attemt the fir trade to the East Indies by way of the Columbia river and the Pacific Ocean.- the mules in the possession of the Indians are principally stolen from the Spaniards of Mexeco; they appear to be large and fine such as we have seen. Among the Sosones of the upper part of the S. E. fork of the Columbia we saw several horses with spanish brands on them which we supposed had been stolen from the inhabitants of Mexeco.

[Clark, February 15, 1806] Saturday February 15th 1806 Drewyer and Whitehouse Set out on a hunting excurtion towards the mountains Southwest of us. we have heard our hunters over the Netul fire Several Shot today, but have had no account of them as yet. 3 P.M. Bratten arived from the Saltworks, and informed us that Serjt. Pryor and party were on their way with gibson in a litter. he is verry bad and much reduced with his present indisposition. Wm. Bratten appears much reduced, and is yet verry unwell. he informs that the Cause of Sergt. Pryor's delay was attributiable to the winds which had been so violent for Several days as to render it impossible to get a Canoe up the Creek to the point where it was necessary to pass with Gibson. the S. W. winds are frequently very violent on the coast when we are but little Sensible of them at Fort Clatsop. in Consequence of the lofty and thickly timbered fir country which Surrounds us from that quarter, from the South to the N. East.-. After Dark Sergt. Pryor arrived with Gibson. we are much pleased in findeing him by no means as ill as we had expected. we do not conceive him in danger by any means, tho he has yet a fever and is much reduced. we believe his disorder to have originated in a violent Cold which he contracted in hunting and prosueing Elk and other game through the Swamps and marshes about the salt works. he is nearly free from pain tho a good deel reduced and very languid. we gave him double doses of diluted niter and made him drink plentifully of Sage tea, had his feat bathed in worm water and at 9 P.M. gave him 35 drops of laudanum.

The quadrupeds of this countrey from the Rocky Mountains to the Pacific Ocian are first the Domestic Animals, consisting of the Horses and Dogs only; 2ndly the Native Wild Animals, consisting of the White, brown, or Grizly bear (which I believe to be the same family with a mearly accidentail difference in point of Colour) The Black Bear, the Elk, the Common red Deer, the Mule deer, the black tailed fallow Deer, the large brown wolf, the Small wolf of the Plains, the large wolf of the Plains, Panther, the tiger cat, the common red fox, the black fox or fisher, the Silver fox, large red fox of the plains, Small fox of the plains or kit fox, Antelope, Sheep, beaver, Common Otter, Sea Otter, minks, Seals racoons, large Grey Squerrel, Small brown Squirrel, Small grey Squirrel, Ground Squirrel, Sewelel, Braro, rat, mouse, mole, hare, rabbet, and pole Cat or Skunk. all of which Shall be Severally noticed in the order in which they occur as well as Such others as I learn do exist, and which not been here recapitulated.

The Horse is principally Confined to the Nations inhabiting the great Plains of Columbia extending from Latitude 40° to 50° N. and occupying the tract of Countrey lying between the Rocky Mountains and a rang of mountains which pass the Columbia River about the Great Falls or from Longitude 116° to 121° West in this extensive tract of Principally untimbered countrey So far as we have lernt the following nations reside (viz) The Sosone, or Snake Indians inhabiting the South fork or _____ River, the Chopunnish, Sokulk's, Cutssahnims, Chym na pum, Ehelutes, Eneshuh & Chilluckkittequaws. all of whome enjoy the benifit of that docile generous and valueable Animal the Horse, and all of them except the three last have emence numbers of them. their horses appear to be of an excellent race; they are lofty eligantly formed active and durable; in Short maney of them look like the fine English coursers and would make a figure in any country. Some of those horses in pided with large spots of white irrigularly scattered and intermixed with black, brown, Bey or Some other dark colour, but much the larger portion are of a uniform Colour with Stars, snips, and white feet, or in this respect marked much like our best blooded horses in the U, States, which they resemble as well in fleetness and bottom as in form and Colour. the nativs Suffer them to run at large in the plains, the Grass of which furnish them with their only Subsistance, their owners takeing no trouble to lay in a winters Store for them, but they keep fat if not much used on the dry grass of the plains dureing the winter. rain scercely ever falls in those plains and the Grass is Short and but thin. the nativs appear to take no pains in Selecting their male horses from which they bread, in Short those of that discription which I have noticed appear much the most indifferent. whether the horses was originally a native of this Country or not, it is out of my power to determine as we cannot understand the language of the nativs Sufficiently to ask the question. at all events the Country and Climate appears well adapted to this Animal. Horses are Said to be found wild in maney parts of this extensive plain Country-. The Several tribes of Sosones who reside near Mexico on the waters of Clark's river, or particularly one of them called Shd-bo-bo-ah have also a great number of Mules, which among the Inds. I find are much more highly prized than horses. an eligant horse may be purchased of the nativs in this Country for a fiew beeds or other paltry trinkits which in the United states would not cost more than one or two dollars. This abundance and Cheepness of horses will be extremely advantagious to those who may hereafter attempt the fir trade to the East Indies by way of the Columbia and the Pacific Ocian.-. The mules in the possession of the Inds. are principally Stolen from the Spaniards of New Mexico; Such as we have Seen appear to be large with Spanish brands. among the Sosones of the upper part of Lewis's river we Saw Several horses with Spanish brands on them which the nativs informed us Came from the South most probably from the Settlement in New Mexico, on the heads of the North river or waters of the Bay of California.

[Lewis, February 16, 1806] Sunday February 16th 1806. By several trials made today in order to adjust my Octant and ascertain her error in the direct observation, I found that it was 2° 1' 45" + or additive beyond the fracture; this error was ascertained by a comparison with my sextant the error of which had been previously ascertained. the error of Octant in the direct observation on the broken limb next to 0 or below 55° 20 inclusive is 2° additive only.- Sent Shannon Labuish and Frazier this morning on a hunting excurtion up the Kil-haw'-a-nak-kle river which discharges itself into the head of the bay. no tidings yet of Sergt. Gass and party. Bratton is still very weak and complains of a pain in the lower part of the back when he moves which I suppose procedes from dability. I gave him barks. Gibson's fever still continues obstenate tho not very high; I gave him a doze of Dr. Rush's which in many instances I have found extreemly efficatious in fevers which are in any measure caused by the presence of boil. the nitre has produced a profuse perspiration this evening and the pills operated late at night his fever after which abated almost entirely and he had a good night's rest.

The Indian dog is usually small or much more so than the common cur. they are party coloured; black white brown and brindle are the most usual colours. the head is long and nose pointed eyes small, ears erect and pointed like those of the wolf, hair short and smooth except on the tail where it is as long as that of the curdog and streight. the natives do not eat them nor appear to make any other use of them but in hunting the Elk as has been before observed.- The brown white or grizly bear are found in the rocky mountains in the timbered parts of it or Westerly side but rarely; they are more common below the rocky Mountain on the borders of the plains where there are copses of brush and underwood near the watercouses. they are by no means as plenty on this side of the rocky mountains as on the other, nor do I beleive that they are found atall in the woody country, which borders this coast as far in the interior as the range of mountains which, pass the Columbia between the Great Falls and rapids of that river. the black bear differs not any from those common to the United states and are found under the rocky Mountains in the woody country on the borders of the great plains of columbia and also in this tract of woody country which lie between these plains and the Pacific Ocean. their oconimy and habits are also the same with those of the United States.

[Clark, February 16, 1806] Sunday February 16th 1806 Sent Shannon Labiesh and frazier on a hunting excurtion up the Kilhaw-a-nak-kle river which discharges itself into the head of Meriwethers Bay. no word yet of Sergt. Gass and party. Bratten is verry weak and complains of a pain in the lower part of the back when he moves which I suppose proceeds from debility. I gave him barks and Salt peter. Gibsons fever Still Continues obstinate tho not verry high; we gave him a dose of Dr. Rushes pills which in maney instancis I have found extreamly efficasious in fevers which are in any measure Caused by the presence of boil. the niter has produced a perfuse perspiration this evening and the pils opperated late at night his feaver after which abated almost intirely and he had a good nights rest.

The Indian Dogs are usually small or much more so than the common cur. they are party coloured; black white brown and brindle are the more usual colours. the head is long and nose pointed eyes Small, ears erect and pointed like those of the wolf, hair Short and Smooth except on the tail where it is as long as that of the Cur dog and streight. the nativs do not eate them, or make any further use of them than in hunting the Elk as has been before observed. Shannon an Labiesh brought in to us to day a Buzzard or Vulture of the Columbia which they had wounded and taken alive. I believe this to be the largest Bird of North America. it was not in good order and yet it wayed 25 lbs had it have been so it might very well have weighed 10 lbs. more or 35 lbs. between the extremities of the wings it measured 9 feet 2 Inches; from the extremity of the beak to that of the toe 3 feet 9 inches and a half. from hip to toe 2 feet, girth of the head 9 inches 3/4. Girth of the neck 71/2 inches; Girth of the body exclusive of the wings 2 feet 3 inches; girth of the leg 3 inches. the diameter of the eye 41/2 10ths of an inch, the iris of a pale scarlet red, the puple of a deep Sea green or black and occupies about one third of the diameter of the eye the head and part of the neck as low as the figures 12 is uncovered with feathers except that portion of it represented by dots foward and under the eye. (See likeness on the other Side of this leaf) the tail is Composed of twelve feathers of equal length, each 14 inches. the legs are 43/4 inches in length and of a whitefish colour uncovered with feathers, they are not entirely Smooth but not imbricated; the toes are four in number three of which are foward and that in the center much the longest; the fourth is Short and is inserted near the inner of the three other toes and reather projecting foward. the thye is covered with feathers as low as the Knee. the top or upper part of the toes are imbricated with broad scales lying transversly; the nails are black and in proportion to the Size of the bird comparitively with those of the Hawk or Eagle, Short and bluntly pointed— the under Side of the wing is Covered with white down and feathers. a white Stripe of about 2 inches in width, also marks the outer part of the wing, imbraceing the lower points of the feathers, which cover the joints of the wing through their whole length or width of that part of the wing. all the other feathers of whatever part are of a Glossy Shineing black except the down, which is not glossy, but equally black. the Skin of the beak and head to the joining of the neck is of a pale orrange Yellow, the other part uncovered with feathers is of a light flesh Colour. the Skin is thin and wrinkled except on the beak where it is Smooth. This bird fly's very clumsily. nor do I know whether it ever Seizes it's prey alive, but am induced to believe it does not. we have Seen it feeding on the remains of the whale and other fish which have been thrown up by the waves on the Sea Coast. these I believe constitute their principal food, but I have no doubt but that they also feed on flesh. we did not meet with this bird untille we had decended the Columbia below the great falls; and have found them more abundant below tide water than above. this is the Same Species of Bird which R. Field killed on the 18th of Novr. last and which is noticed on that day tho not fully discribed then I thought this of the Buzzard Specis. I now believe that this bird is reather of the Vulture genus than any other, tho it wants Some of their characteristics particularly the hair on the neck, and the feathers on the legs. this is a handsom bird at a little distance. it's neck is proportionably longer than those of the Hawks or Eagle. Shannon also brought a Grey Eagle which appeared to be of the Same kind common to the U, States. it weighed 15 pds. and measured 7 feet 7 inches between the extremities of the wings

Shannon and Labiesh informed us that when he approached this Vulture after wounding it, that it made a loud noise very much like the barking of a Dog. the tongue is long firm and broad, filling the under Chap and partakeing of its transvirs curvature, or its Sides forming a longitudinal Groove; obtuse at the point, the margin armed with firm cartelagenous prickkles pointed and bending inwards.

[Lewis, February 17, 1806] Monday February 17th 1806. Collins and Windsor were permited to hunt today towards the praries in Point Adams with a view to obtain some fresh meat for the sick. a little before noon Shannon LaBuishe & Frazier returned with the flesh and hide of an Elk which had been wouded by Sergt. Gass's party and took the water where they pursued it and caught it. they did not see Sergt. Gass or any of his party nor learn what further success they had had. continue the barks with Bratton, and commenced them with Gibson his fever being sufficiently low this morning to permit the uce of them. I think therefore that there is no further danger of his recovery.- at 2 P.M. Joseph Fields arrived from the Salt works and informed us that they had about 2 Kegs of salt on hand which with what we have at this place we suppose will be sufficient to last us to our deposits of that article on the Missouri. we there directed a party of six men to go with Fields in the morning in order to bring the salt and kettles to the fort. Shannon brought me one of the large carrion Crow or Buzzads of the Columbia which they had wounded and taken alive. I bleive this to be the largest bird of North America. it was not in good order and yet it weighed 25 lbs. had it have been so it might very well have weighed 10 lbs mor or 35 lbs. between the extremities of the wings it measured 9 feet 2 inches; from the extremity of the beak to that of the toe 3 F. 91/2 In. from hip to toe 2 feet, girth of head 93/4 In. girth of the neck 71/2 Inches; do. of body exclusive of the wings 2 feet 3 Inches; do of leg 3 inches. diameter of the eye 41/2/toths of an inch. the iris of a pale scarlet red, the puple of deep sea green or black and occupyed about one third of the diameter of the eye. the head and a part of the neck as low as the figures 12 is uncovered with feathers except that portion of it represented by dots (see likeness). the tail is composed of 12 feathers of equal length, each 14 inches. the legs are 43/4 inches in length and of a white colour un covered with feathers, they are not entirely smooth but not imbricated; the toes are four in number three of which are forward and that in the center much the longes; the fourth is short and is inserted near the inner of the three other toes and reather projecting forward. the thye is covered with feathers as low as the knee. the top or upper part of the toes are imbricated with broad scales lying transversly; the nails are blak and in proportion to the size of the bird comparitively with those of the halk or Eagle, short and bluntly pointed. the under side of the wing is covered with white down and feathers. a white stripe of about two inches in width, also marks the outer part of the wing, imbracing the lower points of the feathers, which cover the joints of the wing through their whole length or width of that part of the wing. all the other feathers of whatever part are glossey shining black except the down which is not glossey but equally black. the skin of the beak and head to the joining of the neck is of a pale orrange yellow the other part uncovered with feathers is of a light flesh colour. the skin is thin and wrinkled except on the beak where it is smooth. this bird flys very clumsily nor do I know whether it ever seizes it's prey alive, but am induced to beleive that it dose not. we have seen it feeding on the remains of the whale & other fish which have been thrown up by the waves on the sea coast. these I beleive constitute their prinsipal food, but I have no doubt but they also feed on flesh; we did not met with this bird untill we had decended the Columbia below the great falls, and have found them more abundant below tide-water than above. I beleive that this bird is reather of the Vulture genus than any other, tho it wants some of their charactaristics particularly the hair on the neck and feathers on the legs.- this is a handsome bird at a little distance. it's neck is proportionably longer than those of the hawks or Eagle. Shannon also brought me a grey Eagle which appeared to be of the same kind common to the U States; it weighed 15 lb. and measured 7 Feet 7 Inches between the extremities of the wings.- At 4 P.M. Sergt. Gass and party arrived; they had killed eight Elk. Drewyer and Whitehouse also returned late in the evening, had killed one Elk.- Labuishe informed me that when he approached this vulture, after wounding it, that it made a loud noise very much like the barking of a dog & the tongue is large firm and broad, filling the under chap and partaking of it's transverse curvature, or it's sides colapsing upwards forming a longitudinal groove; obtuse at the point, the margin armed with firm cartelaginous prickkles pointed and bending inwards.

[Clark, February 17, 1806] Monday February 17th 1806 Collins and Windser were permited to hunt to day towards the praries in point Adams with a view to obtain Some fresh meat for the Sick. a little before noon Shannon and Labiesh & frazier Came with the flesh and hide of an Elk which had been wounded by Serjt. Gasses party and took the water where they pursued it and cought it. they did not See Sergt. Gass or any of his party or learn what further Sucksess they have had. Continu the barks with Bratten, and Commenced them with gibson his feaver being Sufficiently low this morning to permit the use of them. I think therefore that there is no further danger of his recovery.— at 2 P.M. Joseph Field arrived from the Salt works and informd us that they had about 2 Kegs of Salt on hand (say 3 bushels) which with what we have at this place we suppose will be Sufficient to last us to our deposit of that article on the Missouri. we directed a party of Six men to go in the morning in order to bring the salt and Kittles to the Fort. at 4 P.M. Serjt. Gass and party arrive; they had killed 8 Elk. Drewyer and Whitehouse also return late in the evening, they had killed one Elk, part of the meat of which they brought in with them.

The Brown, White, or Grizly Bear are found in the rocky mountains in the timbered part of it or Westerly Side but rarely; they are more Common below or on the East Side of the Rocky Mountains on the borders of the plains where there are Copses of bushes and underwood near the water cources. they are by no means as plenty on this Side of the Rocky Mountains as on the other, nor do I believe they are found at all in the woody country which borders this coast as far in the interior as the range of mountains which pass the Columbia between the enterance of Clarks and the Quick sand Rivers or below the Great falls of Columbia.

The Black Bear differs not any from those Common to the U. States, and are found under the Rocky Mountains in the woody country on the borders of the Great Plain's of Columbia and also in this tract of woody country which lie between these plains and the Pacific Ocian. their econimy and habits are also the Same with those of the United States.-.

[Lewis, February 18, 1806] Tuesday February 18th 1806. This morning we dispatched a party to the Saltworks with Sergt. Ordway and a second with Sergt. Gass after the Elk killed over the Netul. in the evening Sergt. Ordway returned and reported that the waves ran so high in the bay that he could not pass to the entrance of the creek which we had directed him to assend with the canoe. Collins and Winsor returned this evening with one deer which they had killed. the deer are poor and their flesh by no means as good as that of the Elk which is also poor but appears to be geting better than some weeks past.- in the forenoon we were visited by eight Clasops and Chinnooks from whom we purchased a Sea Otter's skin and two hats made of waytape and white ceder bark. they remained untill late in the evening and departed for their village. these people are not readily obstructed by waves in their canoes.- Sergt. Ordway brought me a specemine of a species of pine peculiar to the swamps and marshes frequently overflown by the tide as this is a distinct species I shall call it No. 7. this tree seldom rises to a greater hight than 35 feet and is from 2 1/2 to 4 feet in diameter; the stem is simple branching diffuse and proliferous. the bark the same with that of No. 1 only reather more rugged. the leaf is acerose, 2/10ths of an inch in width and 3/4 in length. they are firm stif and somewhat accuminated, ending in a short pointed hard tendril, gibbous, thickly scattered on all sides of the bough but rispect the three upper sides only. those which have there insersion on the underside incline sidewise with their points upwards giving the leaf the figure of a sythe. the others are perpendicular or pointing upwards. is sessile growing as in No. 1 from small triangular pedestals of a soft spungy elastic bark. the under disk of these leaves or that which grows nearest towards the base of the bough is a deep glossey green while the upper or opposite side is of a mealy whiteish pale green; in this rispect differing from almost all leaves. the boughs retain their leaves as far back as to the sixth years growth. the peculiarity of the bud scales observed in No 1 is observed in this species. The cone is 31/2 inches in length and 3 in circumpherence, of an ovate figure being thickest in the middle and tapering and terminating in two obtuse points. it is composes of small, flexible, thin, obtusely pointed smooth and redish brown imbricated scales. each scale covering two small winged seeds and being itself covered in the center by a small thin inferior scale accutely pointed. the cone is somewhat of this figure. they proceede from the side as well as the extremities of the bough but in the former case always at or near the commencement of some one years growth which is some instances are as far back as the third year.

[Clark, February 18, 1806] Tuesday February 18th 1806 This morning we dispatched a party to the Salt works with Sergt. Ordway. and a Second party with Sergt. Gass after the Eight Elk killed over the Netul. in the evening Sergt. Ordway returned and reported that the waves ran So high in the Bay that he could not pass to the enterance of a Creek which we had directed him to assend with the Canoe. Collins & Windsir returned this evening with one Deer which they had Killed. the deer are pore and their flesh by no means as good as that of the Elk which is also poore but appears to be getting better than Some weeks past. in the forenoon we were visited by a Clatsop & Seven Chinnooks from whome I purchased a Sea otter's Skin and two hats made of way tape and Silk grass and white cedar bark. they remained untill late in the evening and departed for their village. those people are not readily obstructed by waves in their Canoes. Since their departure we have discovered that they have Stole an ax.- Whitehouse brought me a roab which he purchased of the Indians formed of three Skins of the Tiger Cat, this Cat differs from any which I have ever Seen. it is found on the borders of the plains and the woody Country lying along the Pacific Ocian. this animale is about the Size or reather larger than the wild Cat of our Countrey and is much the Same in form, agility and ferosity. the colour of the back, neck and Sides, is a redish brown irrigular varigated with Small Spots of dark brown the tail is about two inches long nearly white except the extremity which is black; it termonates abruptly as if it had been cut off. the belly is white with Small black spots. butifully varigated. the legs are of the Same Colour with the Sides and back marked with transvers stripes of black the ears are black on the outer Side Covered with fine black hair, Short except at the upper point which is furnished with a pencil of verry fine Streight black hair, 3/4 of an inch in length, the fur of this animale is long and fine. much more So than the wild Cat of the U States but less so than the Louserva of the N West. the nativs of this Country make great use of the skins of this Cat, to form the robes which they wear; three whole Skins is the complement usually employed, and Sometimes four in each roab. Those Cats are not marked alike maney of them have but fiew Spots of a darker Colour, particularly on the Back.

[Lewis, February 19, 1806] Wednesday February 19th 1806. Sergt. Ordway set out again this morning with a party for the salt works by land. in the evening Sergt. Gass returned with the flesh of eight Elk, and seven skins; having left one skin with Shannon and Labuishe who remained over the netul to continue the chase. we had the Elk skins divided among the messes in order that they might be prepared for covering our baggage when we set out in the spring. our sick are recovering but they appear to strengthen but slowly. The common red deer we found under the rocky mts. in the neighbourhood of the Chopunnish, and about the great falls of the Columbia river and as low down the same as the commencement of tide water. these do not appear to differ essentially from those of our country being about the same size shape and appearance in every rispect except their great length of tail which is more than half as long again as our deer I measured one of them which was 17 inches long. The Black tailed fallow deer are peculiar to this coast and are a distinct species of deer partaking equally of peculiarities of the mule deer and the common deer. their ears are reather larger and their winter coat darker than the common deer; the recepticle of the eye or drane is mor conspicuous; their legs shorter and body thicker and larger than the common deer; their tail is about the length of our deer or from 8 to 10 inches the hair on the underside of which is white, and that of it's sides and top quite black the horns resemble in form and colour those of the mule deer which it also resembles in it's gate; that is bounding with all four feet off the ground at the same time when runing at full speed and not loping as the common deer or antelope do. they are sometimes found in the woodlands but most frequently in the praries and open grounds. they may be said generally to be a size larger than the common deer and that less than the mule deer. they are very seldom found in good order, or fat, even in the season which the common deer are so, and their flesh is inferior to any species of deer which I have ever seen.-

[Clark, February 19, 1806] Wednesday February 19th 1806. Sergt. Ordway Set out again with a party to the Salt works by land. in the evening Sergt. Gass returned with the flesh of Eight Elk, and Seven Skins haveing left one Skin with Shannon and Labiche who remained over the Netul to Continue the chase. we devided the Skins between the messes in order that they might be prepared for Covering the baggage when we Set out in the Spring. our Sick appear to Strengthen but Slowly I gave Bratten 6 of Scotts pills which did not work him. he is very weak and Complains of his back.

The black Fox or as they are more frequently Called by the N West Trader Fisher is found in the woody country on this Coast. how this Animal obtained the name of fisher I know not, but certain it is, that the name is not appropriate, as it does not prey on or Seek it as a prey-. they are extreeinly active Strong and made for climbing which they do with great agility, and bound from tree to tree in pursute of the squirel or Rackoon, their natural and most usual food. their Colour is a jut Black except a Small Spot of white on the breast. the body is long, legs Short and formed Something like the turnspit Dog, with a remarkable long tail. it does not differ here from those of the United States.

The Silver Fox this animale is very rare even in the Countrey where it exists, I have never Seen more than the Skins of this Animal and those were in the possession of the nativs of the woody Country below the Great falls of the Columbia, from which I think it is most probably they are the inhabitants of the woody country exclusively. from the Skins, it appeard to be about the Size of the large red Fox of the plains and much of its form with a large tail. the legs I think somewhat longer it has a fine long deep fur poil. the poil is of a dark lead colour and the long hairs intermixed with it, are either white or black at the lower part, and white at top, the whole mixture forming a butifull Silver Grey. I think this the handsomest of all the Fox Species, except a Species of which I Saw one running, and Capt Lewis had a good view of another of the Same Species on the Missouri near the natural walls. The large red fox of the plains, and the Kit fox are the Same which we met with on the Missouri and are the inhabitants almost exclusively of the open plains, or of the copse of bushes within the plain country. the Common red or grey fox of the United States is also found in the woody country on this coast, nor does it appear to be altered in respect to it's fur colour or any other particular. we have Seen none of the large red fox.

[Lewis, February 20, 1806] Thursday February 20th 1806. Permited Collins to hunt this morning he returned in the evening unsuccessfull as to the chase but brought with him some cranberries for the sick. Gibson is on the recovery fast; Bratton has an obstenate cough and pain in his back and still appears to be geting weaker. McNeal from his inattention to his disorder has become worse.

This forenoon we were visited by Tdh-cum a principal Chief of the Chinnooks and 25 men of his nation. we had never seen this cheif before he is a good looking man of about 50 years of age reather larger in statue than most of his nation; as he came on a friendly visit we gave himself and party some thing to eat and plyed them plentifully with smoke. we gave this cheif a small medal with which he seemed much grati-fyed. in the evening at sunset we desired them to depart as is our custom and closed our gates. we never suffer parties of such number to remain within the fort all night; for notwithstanding their apparent friendly disposition, their great averice and hope of plunder might induce them to be treacherous. at all events we determined allways to be on our guard as much as the nature of our situation will permit us, and never place our selves at the mercy of any savages. we well know, that the treachery of the aborigenes of America and the too great confidence of our countrymen in their sincerity and friendship, has caused the distruction of many hundreds of us. so long have our men been accustomed to a friendly intercourse with the natives, that we find it difficult to impress on their minds the necessity of always being on their guard with rispect to them. this confidence on our part, we know to be the effect of a series of uninterupted friendly intercouse, but the well known treachery of the natives by no means entitle them to such confidence, and we must check it's growth in our own minds, as well as those of our men, by recollecting ourselves, and repeating to our men, that our preservation depends on never loosing sight of this trait in their character, and being always prepared to meet it in whatever shape it may present itself.-

The Mule deer are the same with those of the plains of the Missouri so frequently mentioned. we met with them under the Rocky mountains in the Neighbourhood of the Chopunnish nation on the Kooskooske river, but have not seen them since nor do we know whether they exist in the interior of the great plains of Columbia or on their lower border near the mountains which pass the river about the great falls. The Elk is the same with that found in much the greatest portion of North America, they are common to every part of this country, as well the timbered lands as the plains, but are much more abundant in the former than the latter The large brown woolf is like that of the Atlantic States and are found only in the woody country on the Pacific Ocean imbracing the mountains which pass the Columbia between the great falls and rapids of the same. the large and small woolves of the plains are the inhabitants principally of the open country and the woodlands on their borders and resemble in their habits and appearance those of the plains of the Missouri precisely. they are not abundant in the plains of Columbia because there is but little game on which for them to subsist.

[Clark, February 20, 1806] Thursday February 20th 1806. Permited Collins to hunt this morning he returned in the evening unsucksessfull as to the chase, but brought with him Some Cramberries for the Sick. Gibson is on the recovery fast; Bratten has an obstenate Cough and pain in his back and Still appears to be getting weaker. H. McNeal from his inattention to his disorder has become worse. Willard has a high fever and complains of the pain in his head and want of appetite.

The forenoon we were visited by Tfih-cum a principal chief of the Chinnooks and 25 men of his nation. we had never Seen this Chief before he is a good looking man of about 50 years of age reather larger in Statue than most of his nation; as he came on a friendly visit we gave himself and party something to eate and plyed them plenty fully with Smoke. we gave this cheif a small Medal with which he Seamed much pleased. in the evening at Sunset we desired them to depart as is our custom and Close our gates. we never Suffer parties of Such numbers to remain within the Fort all night; for not withstanding their apparent friendly disposition, their great averis and hope of plunder might induce them to ́be treacherous. at all events we are determined always to be on our guard, as much as the nature of our Situation will permit us, and never place our selves at the mercy of any Savages. we well know, that the treachery of the Aborigenes of America and the too great confidence of our country men in their friendship and fadility has caused the distruction of maney hundreds of us. so long has our men been accustomed to a friendly intercourse with the nativs, that we find it dificult to impress on their minds the necessity of always being on their Guard with respect to them. this confidence on our part we know to be the effect of a serious of a friendly and unintorupted intercourse. but the well Known treachery of the natives by no means entitle them to Such confidence, and we must check it's groth in our own minds as well as those of our men, by recollecting our selves, and repeating to our men, that our preservation depends on our never loseing Sight of this trate in their character, and being always prepared to meet it in whatever Shape it may present itself

The Mule Deer are the Same with those of the Plains of the Missouri So frequently mentioned. we met with them under the rocky mountains in the neighbourhood of the Chopunnish Nation on the Koskooske river, but have not Seen them Since nor do we know whether they exist in the interiors of the great Plains of Columbia, or on the lower border near the mountains which pass the river about the great falls. The Elk is the Same with that found in much the greater portion of North America, they are common to every part of this Country, as well the timbered lands as the plains. but are much more abundant in the former than the latter

[Lewis, February 21, 1806] Friday February 21st 1806. Visited this morning by 3 Clatsop who remained with us all day; they are great begers; I gave one of them a few nedles with which he appeared much gratifyed. in the evening late they departed. Drewyer and Collins went in pursuit of some Elk, the tracks of which Collins had discovered yesterday; but it rained so hard that they could not pursue them by their tracks and returned unsuccessfull. Drewyer saw a fisher black fox but it escaped from him among the fallen timber. Sergt. Ordway returned with the party from the salt camp which we have now evacuated. they brought with them the salt and eutensils. our stock of salt is now about 20 Gallons; 12 gallons of which we secured in 2 small iron bound kegs and laid by for our voyage. gave Willard and bratton each a doze of Scotts pills; on the former they operated and on the latter they (lid not. Gibson still continues the barks three times a day and is on the recovery fast.-

The tyger Cat is found on the borders of the plains and in the woody country lying along the Pacific Ocean. this animal is about the size or reather larger than the wild cat of our country and is much the same in form, agility and ferosity. the colour of the back neck and sides is a redish brown irregularly variegated with small spots of dark brown the tail is about two inches long nearly white except the extremity which is black; it terminates abruptly as if it had been cut off. the belly is white with small black spots, beautifully variagated. the legs are of the same colour with the sides and back marked with transverse stripes of black the ears are black on the outer side covered with fine short hair except at the upper point which furnished with a pensil of fine, streight, black hair, = 3/4 of an inch in length. the fur of this anamal is long and fine, much more so than the wild cat of the United States but less so than that of Louservea of the N. West. the natives in this quarter make great use of the skins of this Cat to form the robes which they wear; four skins is the compliment usuly employed in each robe. the Black fox, or as they most frequently called in the neighbourhood of Detroit, Fisher is found in the woody country on this coast. how this animal obtained the name of fisher I know not, but certain it is, that the name is not appropriate, as it dose not prey on fish or seek it as a prey. they are extreemly active strong and prepared for climbing, which they do with great agility, and bound from tree to tree in pursuit of the squirrel or Rackoon their natural and most usual food. their colour is a jut black except a small spot of white on the breast. the body is long, legs short and formed something like the ternspit dog with a remarkable long tail. it dose not differ here from those of the United States. The Silver fox this animal is very rare even in the country where it exists; I have never seen more than the Skins of this anamal and those were in the possession of the natives of the woody Country below the great falls of the Columbia from which I think that it is most probably the inhabtant of the woody country exclusively. from the skin it appeared to be about the size of the large red fox of the plains and much of it's form with a large tail. the legs I think somewhat longer. it has a fine long deep fur poll. the poil is of a dark lead colour and the long hairs intermixed with it are either white or black at the lower part and white at the top, the whole mixture forming a beatifull silver grey. I think thiss the most beautifull of all the Foxes except species of which I saw one only on the Missouri near the natural walls. the large red fox of the plains and the Kit fox are the same which we met with on the Missouri and are the inhabitants almost exclusively of the open plains, or of the cops of brush within the pain country. The common red fox of the United States is also found in the woody country on this coast nor dose it appear to be altered in rispect to it's fur colour or any other particular

[Clark, February 21, 1806] Friday February 21st 1806 Visited this morning by three Clatsops, who remained with us all day; they are great begers; Capt Lewis gave one of them a fiew nedles with which he appeared much gratified, in the evening late they departed.

Drewyer and Collins went in pursute of Some Elk the tracks of which Collins had discovered yesterday; but it rained So hard they Could not pursue them by the tracks, and returned unsucksessfull. Drewyer Saw a fisher but it escaped from him among the fallen timber. Sergt. Ordway returned with the party from the Salt Camp which we have now avacuated. they brought with them the Salt and utensels. our Stock of Salt is now about 20 Gallons; 12 Gallons we had Secured in 2 Small iron bound Kegs and laid by for our voyage. Gave Willard a dose of Scots pills; they opperated very well. Gibson Still Continus the bark 3 times a day and is on the recovery fast.

The large brown Wolf is like that of the atlantic States, and are found only in the woody Country on the Pacific Ocean embraceing the mountains which pass the Columbia between the Great Falls an Rapids of the same. The large and Small Wolves of the inhabitents principally of the open Country and the wood land on their borders, and resemble in their habits those of the plains of Missouri presisely they are not abundant in the Plains of Columbia because there is but little game on which for them to subsist-

[Lewis, February 22, 1806] Saturday February 22cd 1806. We were visited today by two Clatsop women and two boys who brought a parsel of excellent hats made of Cedar bark and ornamented with beargrass. two of these hats had been made by measures which Capt Clark and myself had given one of the women some time since with a request to make each of us a hat; they fit us very well, and are in the form we desired them. we purchased all their hats and distributed them among the party. the woodwork and sculpture of these people as well as these hats and their waterproof baskets evince an ingenuity by no means common among the Aborigenes of America. in the evening they returned to their village and Drewyer accompanied them in their canoe in order to get the dogs which the Clatsops have agreed to give us in payment for the Elk they stole from us some weeks since. these women informed us that the small fish began to run which we suppose to be herring from their discription. they also informed us that their Chief, Coma or Comowooll, had gone up the Columbia to the valley in order to purchase wappetoe, a part of which he in tended trading with us on his return. one of our canoes brake the cord by which it was attatched and was going off with the tide this evening; we sent Sergt. Pryor and a party after her who recovered and brought her back. our sick consisting of Gibson, Bratton, Sergt. Ordway, Willard and McNeal are all on the recovery. we have not had as may sick at any one time since we left Wood River. the general complaint seams to be bad colds and fevers, something I beleive of the influenza.

The Antelope is found in the great plains of Columbia and are the same of those on the Missouri found in every part of that untimbered country. they are by no means as plenty on this side of the Rocky Mountains as on the other. the natives here make robes of their skins dressed with the hair on them. when the salmon begin to decline in the latter end of the sunme and Autumn the natves leave the river, at least a majority and remove to the plains at some distance for the purpose of hunting the Antelope. they pursue them on horse back and shoot them with their arrows. The sheep is found in various parts of the Rocky mountains, but most commonly in those parts which are timbered and steep. they are also found in greater abundance on the Chain of mountains with form the commencement of the woody country on this coast and which pass the Columbia between the great falls and rapids we have never met with this anamal ourselves but have seen many of their skins in possession of the natives dressed with the wooll on them and aso seen the blankets which they manufacture of the wooll of this sheep. from the skin the animal appears to be about the size of the common sheep; of a white colour. the wooll is fine on most parts of the body but not so long as that of our domestic sheep. the wooll is also curled and thick. on the back and more particularly on the top of the neck the wooll is intermixed with a considerable proportion of long streight hairs. there is no wooll on a small part of the body behind the sholders on each side of the brisquit which is covered with a short fine hairs as in the domestic sheep. form the signs which the Indians make in discribing this animal they have herect pointed horns, tho one of our Engages La Page, assures us that he saw them in the black hills where the little Missouri passes them, and that they were in every rispect like the domestic sheep, and like them the males had lunated horns bent backwards and twisted. I should be much pleased at meeting with this animal, but have had too many proofs to admit a doubt of it's existing and in considerable numbers in the mountains near this coast. the Beaver and common Otter have before been mentioned in treating of the occupations of the natives in hunting fishing &c. these do not differ from those of other parts of the Continent.

[Clark, February 22, 1806] Saturday February 22nd 1806 We were visited to day by two Clatsops women and two boys who brought a parcel of excellent hats made of Cedar bark, and ornemented with bear grass. two of those hats had been made by measure which Capt Lewis and my Self had given a woman Some time Since, with a request to make each of us a hat; they fit us very well, and are in the form we desired them. we purchased the hats and distributed them among the party. the woodwork and sculpture of these people as well as those hats and the water proof baskits evince an ingenuity by no means common among the Aborigenes of America. in the evining they returned to their village and Drewyer accompanied them in order to get Some dogs &c. These women informed us that the Small fish began to run which we suppose to be herring from their discription. they also informed us that their Chief Conia Comawool, had gorn up the Columbia to the Vally in order to purchase Wappatoe, a part of which he entended tradeing with us on his return. our sick consisting of

Gibson, Bratten, Willard McNeal and Baptiest LaPage is Something better Serjt. Ordway is complaining of a Coald & head ake. we have not had as many Sick at one time Since we left the Settlements of the Illinois. the general Complaint appears to be bad colds and fevers, with a violent pain in the head, and back, something I believe of the influenza.

The Antelope is found in the great plains of Columbia and are the Same with those of the Missouri found in every part of that untimbered Country. they are by no means as plenty on this Side of the Rocky Mountains as on the other. the nativs here make robes of their Skins dressed withe the hair on them. when the Salmon begin to decline in the latter end of Summer and autumn, the nativs leave the river, at least a majority and move out into the plains at Some distance for the purpose of hunting the Antelope. they pursue them on hors back and Shute them with their arrows.

The Sheep is found in various parts of the Rocky Mountains, but most Commonly on those parts which are timbered and Steep. they are also found in greater abundance on the chain of mountains which forms the Commencement of the woody country on this Coast and which pass the Columbia between the great falls and rapids. we have never met with this animal ourselves but have Seen maney of their Skins in the possession of the nativs dressed with the wool on them and also Seen and have the blankets which they manufacture of the wool of this Sheep. from the Skin the animal appears to be about the Size of the common Sheep; of a white colour. the wool is fine on most parts of the body, but not so long as that of the domestic Sheep; the wool is also Curled and thick. on the back and more particularly on the top of the neck the wool is intermixed with a Considerable proportion of long Streight hair. there is no wool on a Small part of the body behind the Sholders on each Side of the brisquit which is covered with a Short fine hairs as in the domestic Sheep. from the Signs which the Indians make in discribing this animale they have herect pointed horns, tho one of our Engages Lapage, assures us that he Saw them in the Black hills where the Little Missouri river passes them, and that they were in every respect like our domestic Sheep, and like them the mail had lunated horns bent backwards and twisted. I should be much pleased at meeting with this animal. but have had too maney proofs to admit a doubt of it's existing and in considerable numbers in the mountains on this Coast. The Beaver and Common Otter have before been mentioned in treating of the Occupation of the nativs in hunting, fishing, &c. these do not differ from those of other parts of the Continent-.-.

[Lewis, February 23, 1806] Sunday February 23rd 1806. not anything transpired during this day worthy of particular notice. our sick are all on the recovery, except Sergt. Ordway who is but little wose and not very ill tho more so than any of the others. the men have provided themselves very amply with mockersons and leather cloathing, much more so indeed than they ever have since they have been on this voige.

The Sea Otter is found on the sea coast and in the salt water. this anamal when fully grown is as large as a common mastive dog. the ears and eyes are remarkaby small, particularly the former which is not an inch in length thick fleshey and pointed covered with short hair. the tail is about 10 inches in length thick where it joins the body and tapering to a very sharp point; in common with the body it is covered with a deep fir particularly on the upper side, on the under part the fur is not so long. the legs are remarkably short and the feet, which have five toes each are broad large and webbed. the legs are covered with fur and the feet with short hair. the body of this animal is long and nearly of the same thickness throughout. from the extremity of the tail to that of the nose they will measure 5 feet or upwards. the colour is a uniform dark brown and when in good order and season perfectly black and glossey. it is the riches and I think the most delicious fur in the world at least I cannot form an idea of any more so. it is deep thick silkey in the extreem and strong. the inner part of the fur when opened is lighter than the surface in it's natural position. there are some fine black and shining hairs intermixed with the fur which are reather longer and add much to it's beauty. the nose, about the eyes ears and forehead in some of these otter is of a lighter colour, sometimes a light brown. those parts in the young sucking Otter of this species is sometimes of a cream coloured white, but always much lighter than the other parts. the fur of the infant Otter is much inferior in point of colour and texture to that of the full grown otter, or even after it has been weaned. there is so great a difference that I have for some time supposed it a different animal; the Indians called the infant Otter Spuck, and the full grow or such as had obtained a coat of good fur, E-luck'-ke. this still further confirmed the opinion of their being distinct species; but I have since learned that the Spuck is the young Otter. the colour of the neck, body, legs and tail is a dark lead brown. The mink is found in the woody country on this coast, and dose not differ in any particu from those of the Atlantic coast. the seal are found here in great numbers, and as far up the Columbia river as the great falls above which there are none. I have reason to beleive from the information of the men that there are several species of the seal on this coast and in the river but what the difference is I am unable to state not having seen them myself sufficiently near for minute inspection nor obtained the different kinds to make a comparison. the skins of such as I have seen are covered with a short coarse stiff and glossey hair of a redish hey brown colour. tho the anamal while in the water or as we saw them frequently in the river appear to be black and spoted with white sometimes. when we first saw those animals at the great falls and untill our arrival at this place we conseived they were the Sea Otter. but the indians here have undeceived us.- I am not much acquainted with the Seal but suppose that they are the same common also to the Atlantic Ocean in the same parallel of latitude. the skins I have seen are precisely such as our trunks are frequently covered with.

[Clark, February 23, 1806] Sunday February 23rd 1806. Not any thing transpired desering particular notice. our Sick are all on the recovery. the men have provided themselves verry amply with mockersons & leather clothing, much more So indeed than they have ever been Since they have been on the voyage.

The Sea Otter is found only on the Sea Coast and in the Salt water. Those animals which I took to be the Sea Otter from the Great Falls of the Columbia to the mouth, proves to be the Phosia or Seal which at a little distance has every appearance of the Sea Otters. The Sea otter when fully grown is as large as the common mastif dog, the eail and Eyes are remarkably Small, particularly the former which is not an inch in length thick fleshey and pointed, Covered with short hair. the tail is about 10 inches in length thick where it joins the body and tapering to a very Sharp point; in common with the body it is covered with a deep fur particularly on the upper Side, on the under part the fur is not So long. the legs are remarkably Short and the feat which have five toes each are broad large and webbed. the legs are covered with fur and the feet with Short hair. the body of this Animal is long and nearly of the Same thickness throughout. from the extremity of the tail to that of the nose they will measure 5 feet or upwards. the colour is of a uniform dark brown, and when in good order and Season perfectly Black and Glossey. it is the richest and I think the most delightfull fur in the world at least I cannot form an idea of any more so. it is deep thick silky in the extream and Strong. the inner part of the fur when open is lighter than the surface in its natural position. there are Some fine black Shineing hairs intermixed with the fur which are reather longer and add much to its beauty. the nose, about the eyes, ears and forehead in Some of those otter is of a light Colour, Sometimes a light brown. those parts in the young Suckling otters of this Species is Sometimes of a creem colour'd white, but always much lighter than the other parts. the fur of the infant otter is much inferior in point of colour, and texture, to that of the full grown otter, or even after it has been weened-. there is so great a difference that I have for Some time Supposed it a different animal; the Indians Call the infant otter Spuck, and the full grown or such as had obtained a Coat of good fur, E luck'ko. this Still further confirmed the opinion of their being distinct Species; but I have Since lerned that the Spuck is the young otter. the Colour of the neck, body, legs and tail is a dark lead brown. The Mink is found in the woody Country on this Coast and does not differ in any particular from those of the Atlantic Coasts.

The Seal or Phoca are found here in great numbers, and as far up the Columbia as the great Falls, above which there are none. I have reasons to believe from the information of the men that there are Several Species of the Phoca on this Coast and in the river, but what the difference is I am unable to State not haveing Seen them myself Sufficiently near for manute inspection nor obtain the different kinds to make a comparison. the Skins of Such as I have Seen are covered with a Short thick Coarse Glossy hair of a redish bey brown Colour. tho the animal while in the water, or as we saw them frequently in the river appear to be black and Spoted with white sometimes. I am not much acquainted with the Seal, but Suppose that they are the Same common also to the atlantic Ocian in the Same parrelal of Latitude. the Skins, or those which I have Seen are presisely Such as trunks are frequently Covered with. the flesh of this animal is highly prised by the nativs who Swinge the hair off and then roste the flesh on Sticks before the fire.

[Lewis, February 24, 1806] Monday February 24th 1806. Our sick are still on the recovery. Shannon & Labuishe returned in the forenoon; they had killed no Elk and reported that they beleived the Elk have retired from their former haunts and gone further back in the country to a considerable distance from this place. this is very unwelcome information for poor and inferior as the flesh of this animal is it is our principal dependance for subsistence.

This evening we were visited by Comowooll the Clatsop Chief and 12 men women & children of his nation. Drewyer came a passenger in their canoe, and brought with him two dogs. The chief and his party had brought for sail a Sea Otter skin some hats, stergeon and a species of small fish which now begin to run, and are taken in great quantities in the Columbia R. about 40 miles above us by means of skiming or scooping nets. on this page I have drawn the likeness of them as large as life; it as perfect as I can make it with my pen and will serve to give a general idea of the fish. the rays of the fins are boney but not sharp tho somewhat pointed. the small fin on the back next to the tail has no rays of bone being a thin membranous pellicle. the fins next to the gills have eleven rays each. those of the abdomen have eight each, those of the pinna-ani are 20 and 2 half formed in front. that of the back has eleven rays. all the fins are of a white colour. the back is of a bluish duskey colour and that of the lower part of the sides and belley is of a silvery white. no spots on any part. the first bone of the gills next behind the eye is of a bluis cast, and the second of a light goald colour nearly white. the puple of the eye is black and the iris of a silver white. the underjaw exceeds the uper; and the mouth opens to great extent, folding like that of the herring. it has no teeth. the abdomen is obtuse and smooth; in this differing from the herring, shad anchovey &c of the Malacopterygious Order & Class Clupea, to which however I think it more nearly allyed than to any other altho it has not their accute and serrate abdomen and the under jaw exceeding the upper. the scales of this little fish are so small and thin that without minute inspection you would suppose they had none. they are filled with roes of a pure white colour and have scarcely any perceptable alimentary duct. I find them best when cooked in Indian stile, which is by roasting a number of them together on a wooden spit without any previous preperation whatever. they are so fat they require no additional sauce, and I think them superior to any fish I ever tasted, even more delicate and lussious than the white fish of the lakes which have heretofore formed my standart of excellence among the fishes. I have heard the fresh anchovey much extolled but I hope I shall be pardoned for beleiving this quite as good. the bones are so soft and fine that they form no obstruction in eating this fish. we purchased all the articles which these people brought us; we suffered these people to remain all night as it rained, the wind blew most violently and they had their women and children with them; the latter being a sure pledge of their pacific dispositions. the Sturgeon which they brought us was also good of it's kind. we determine to send a party up the river to procure some of those fish, and another in some direction to hunt Elk as soon as the weather will permit.

[Clark, February 24, 1806] Monday February 24th 1806 Our Sick are Still on the recovery. Shannon and Labiche returned in the forenoon, they had killed no Elk, and reported that they believe the Elk have returned from their former haunts and gorn further back in the mountains to a considerable distance from this place. this is very unwelcom information, for poore and inferior as the flesh of this animale is, it is our principal dependance for Subsistance.

The Rackoon is found in the woody Country on the Coast in considerable quantities. the nativs take a fiew of them in Snars, and deadfalls; tho appear not to value their Skins much, and but Seldom prepare them for robes. The large Grey Squirel appear to be a native of a narrow tract of Country on the upper Side of the mountains below the Great falls of Columbia which is pritty well covered in maney parts with a Species of white oak. this animal is much larger than the Gray Squirel of our Country, it resembles it much in form and colour. it is as large as the Fox Squirel of the South Atlantic States. the tail is reather larger than the whole of the body and head, the hair of which is long and tho inserted on all Sides reispect the horozontal one. the eyes are black, whiskers black and long. the back, Sides, head, tale and outer parts of the legs are of a blue lead colour grey. the breast, belly, and inner parts of the legs are of a pure white. the hair is Short as that of the Fox Squirel but is much finer and intermixed with a propotion of fur. the nativs make great use of those Skins in forming their robes. this Squirel Subsists principally on the acorn and filburts, which last also grow abundantly in the Oak Country-. The Small brown Squirel is a butifull little animal about the size of the red Squirel of the E. States or Something larger than the ground Squirel of the U States. the tail is as long as the body and neck formed Somewhat flat. the eyes black, whiskers long and black but not abundant. the back, Sides, head, neck and outer parts of the legs are of a redish dark brown. the throat, breast, belly and inner parts of the legs are of a pale brick red. the tail is a mixture of black and fox coloured red in which the black prodomonates in the middle, and the other on the edges and extremity. the hair of the body is about 1/2 inch long and So fine and soft that it has the appearance of fur. the hair of the tail is coarser and double as long. this animal Subsists principally on the Seeds of various Species of pine and are always found in the piney Country. they are common to the tract of woody country on this coast. they lodge in Clefts of rocks, holes in the Ground, old Stumps of trees and the hollow trunks of falling timber; in this respect resemble the rat always haveing their habitation in or near the earth. The Small Grey Squirel Common to every part of the Rocky Mountains which is timbered, differ from the dark brown squirel just discribed only in its colour.

it's back, neck, Sides, head, tail and outer Sides of the legs are of brown lead coloured Grey; the tail has a Slight touch of the fox colour near the extremity of some of the hairs. the throat, belly, breast, and inner part of the legs are of the Colour of tanners ooze and have a narrow Stripe of black commencing behing each Sholder and extending longitudinally for about 3 inches between the Colours of the Side & belly. their habits are also the Same with the dark brown Squirel of this neighbourhood, and like them are extreamly nimble and active. The Ground Squirel is found in various parts of the Countrey as well the Praries as wood lands, and is one of the fiew animals which we have Seen in every part of our voy-age. it differs not at all from those of the U, States.

The Barking Squirel and handsom Ground Squirel of the Plains on the East Side of the Rocky Mountains are not found in the plains of the Columbia.

This evening we were visited by Comowooll the Clatsop Chief and 14 men women and Children of his nation. Drewyer came a pasinger in their Canoe, and brought with him two dogs. the Chief and his party had brought for Sale a Sea otter Skin, Some hats, Sturgeon and a Species of fish which now begins to run and are taken in Great quantities in the Columbia River about 40 miles above us by means of Skiming or scooping nets. See likeness on the other Side of this leaf or page. Capt Lewis gave an old Coat and Vest for a Sea otter Skin, we purchased Several hads of the Indian manufactry and distributed them among the party. we also purchased a fiew of the Small fish which we found deliciously fine.

[Lewis, February 25, 1806] Tuesday February 25th 1806. It continued to rain and blow so violently that there was no movement of the party today. the Indians left us in the morning on their return to their village. Willard somewhat worse the other Invalledes on the ricovery. I am mortifyed at not having it in my power to make more celestial observations since we have been at Fort Clatsop, but such has been the state of the weather that I have found it utterly impracticable.-

The Rackoon is found in the woody country on this coast in considerable quantities. the natives take a few of them in snars and deadfalls; tho appear not to value their skins much, and but seldom prepare them for robes. The large grey squirrel appears to be a native of a narrow tract of country on the upper side of the mountains just below the grand falls of Columbia which is pretty well covered in many parts with a species of white oak. in short I beleive this squirrel to be coextensive with timber only, as we have not seen them in any part of the country where pine forms the majority of the timber, or in which the oak dose not appear. this animal is much larger than the grey squirrel of our country it resembles it much in form and colours. it is as large as the fox squirrel of the Southern Atlantic states. the tail is reather longer than the whole length of the body and head. the hair of which is long and tho inserted on all sides reispect the horizontal ones only. the eyes are black. whiskers black and long. the back, sides, head, tail and outer part of the legs are of a blue lead coloured grey. the breast belley and inner part of the legs are of a pure white. the hair is short as that of the fox-squirrel but is much finer and intermixed with a proportion of fur. the natives make great use of these skins in forming their robes. this squirrel subsists principally on the acorn and filbird which last also grows abundantly in the oak country.- The small brown squirrel is a beautifull little animal about the size and form of the red squirrel of the Eastern Atlantic states and western lakes. the tail is as long as the body and neck, formed like that of the red squirrel or somewhat flat. the eyes black. whiskers long and black but not abundant. the back, sides, head, neck and outer part of the legs are of a redish dark brown. the throat, breast, belley and inner part of the legs are of a pale brick red. the tail is a mixture of black and fox coloured red in which the black predominates in the midle and the other on the edges and extremity. the hair of the body is about 1/2 an inch long and so fine and soft that it has the appearance of fur. the hair of the tail is coarser and doubly as long. this animal subsists principally on the seeds of various species of pine, and are always found in the piny country they are common to the tract of wooddy country on this coast. they lodge in clifts of rocks, holes in the ground old stumps of trees and the hollow trunks of fallen timber; in this rispect resembling the rat, always having their habitatin in or near the earth. the small grey squirrel common to every part of the rocky mountain which is timbered, difirs from the dark brown squirrel just discribed only in it's colour. it's back, sides, neck, head tail and outer side of the legs are of a brown lead coloured grey; the tail has a slight touch of the fox colour near the extremity of some of the hairs. the throat, breast, belley, and inner parts of the legs are of the colour of tanner's ooze and have a narrow stripe of black, commencing just behide each sholder and extending longitudinaly for about 3 inches below the colours of the sides and belley. their habids are also the same of the dark brown squirrel of this neighbourhood and like them are extreemly nimble and active. the ground squirrel is found in every part of the country, as well the praries as woodlands, and is one of the few animals which we have seen in every part of our voyage. it differs not at all from those of the U States. the barking squirrel and handsome ground squirrel of the plains on the East side of the rocky mountains are not found in the plains of Columbia.

[Clark, February 25, 1806] Tuesday February 25th 1806 It continued to rain and blow So violently that there was no movement of the party to day. the Indians left us in the morning on their return to their village. Willard Somewhat worse the others are on the recovery. we are mortified at not haveing it in our power to make more Celestial observations since we have been at Fort Clatsop, but Such has been the State of the weather that we have found it utterly impractiable-. I purchased of the Clatsops this morning about half a bushel of Small fish which they had cought about 40 miles up the Columbia in their scooping nets. as this is an uncommon fish to me and one which no one of the party has ever Seen. on the next page I have drawn the likeness of them as large as life; it's as perfect as I can make it with my pen and will Serve to give a general idea of the fish. the rays of the fins are boney but not Sharp tho Somewhat pointed. the Small fin on the back next to the tail has no rays of bone being a thin membranous pellicle. the fins next to the gills have eleven rays each. those of the abdomen have Eight each, those of the pinna ani are 20 and 2 half formed in front. that of the back has eleven rays. all the fins are of a white colour. the back is of a blueish duskey colour and that of the lower part of the Sides and belly is of a Silvery White. no Spots on any part. the first of the gills next behind the eye is of a blueish cast, and the second of a light gold colour nearly white. the puple of the eye is black and the iris of a silver white. the under jaw exceeds the upper; and the mouth opens to great extent, folding like that of the Herring. it has no teeth. the abdomen is obtuse and Smooth; in this differing from the herring, Shad, anchovey &c. of the Malacapterygious Order and Class Clupea, to which however I think it more nearly allyed than to any other altho it has not their accute and Serrate abdomen and the under jaw exceeding the upper. the scales of this little fish are So small and thin that without manute inspection you would Suppose they had none. they are filled with roes of a pure white Colour and have Scercely any perceptable alimentary duct. I found them best when cooked in Indian Stile, which is by rosting a number of them together on a wooden spit without any previous preperation whatever. they are so fat that they require no aditional sauce, and I think them Superior to any fish I ever tasted, even more dilicate and lussious than the white fish of the Lakes which have heretofore formed my Standard of excellence among the fishes. I have herd the fresh anchovey much extoll'd but I hope I shall be pardened for believeing this quit as good. the bones are So Soft and fine that they form no obstruction in eating this fish.

[Lewis, February 26, 1806] Wednesday February 26th 1806. This morning we dispatched Drewyer and two men in our Indian canoe up the Columbia River to take sturgeon and Anchovey. or if they were unsuccessfull in fishing we directed them to purchase fish from the natives for which purpose we had furnished them with a few articles such as the natives are pleased with. we also Sent Shields, Joseph Fields and Shannon up the Netul to hunt Elk. and directed Reubin Fields and some others to hunt in the point towards the praries of Point Adams. thus we hope shortly to replenish our stock of provision which is now reduced to a mere minnamum. we have three days provision only in store and that of the most inferior dryed Elk a little tainted. a comfortable prospect for good living. Sewelel is the Chinnook and Clatsop name for a small animal found in the timbered country on this coast. it is more abundant in the neighbourhood of the great falls and rapids of the Columbia than immediately on the coast. the natives make great use of the skins of this animal in forming their robes, which they dress with the fur on them and attatch together with sinews of the Elk or deer. I have never seen the animal and can therefore discribe it only from the skin and a slight view which some of our hunters have obtained of the living animal. the skin when dressed is from 14 to 18 inches in length and from 7 to 9 in width; the tail is always severed from the skin in forming their robes I cannot therefore say what form or length it is. one of the men informed me that he thought it reather short and flat. that he saw one of them run up a tree like a squirrel and that it returned and ran into a hole in the ground. the ears are short thin pointed and covered with short fine hair. they are of a uniform colour, a redish brown; tho the base of the long hairs, which exceed the fur but little in length, as well as the fur itself is of a dark colour for at least two thirds of it's length next to the skin. the fur and hair are very fine, short, thickly set and silky. the ends of the fur and tips of the hair being of the redish brown that colour predominates in the ordinary appearance of the animal. I take this animal to be about the size of the barking squirrel of the Missouri. and beleive most probably that it is of the Mustela genus, or perhaps the brown mungo itself. I have indeavoured in many instances to make the indians sensible how anxious I was to obtain one of these animals entire, without being skined, and offered them considerable rewards to furnish me with one, but have not been able to make them comprehend me. I have purchased several of the robes made of these skins to line a coat which I have had made of the skins of the tiger cat. they make a very pleasant light lining. the Braro so called by the French engages is an animal of the civit genus and much resembles the common badger. this is an inhabitant of the open plains of the Columbia as they are of those of the Missouri but are sometimes also found in the woody country. they burrow in the hard grounds of the plains with surprising ease and dexterity an will cover themselves in the ground in a very few minutes. they have five long fixed nails on each foot; those of the forefeet are much the longest; and one of those on each hind foot is double like those of the beaver. they weigh from 14 to 18 lbs. the body is reather long in proportion to it's thickness. the forelegs remarkably large and muscular and are formed like the ternspit dog. they are short as are also the hind legs. they are broad across the sholders and brest. the neck short. the head is formed much like the common fist dog only that the skull is more convex. the mouth is wide and furnished with sharp streight teeth both above and below, with four sharp streight pointed tusks, two in the upper and two in the lower jaw. the eyes are black and small. whiskers are plased in four points on each side near the nose and on the jaws near the opening of the mouth. the ears are very short wide and appressed as if they had ben cut off. the apperture through them to the head is remarkably small. the tail is about 4 inches long; the hair longest on it at it's junction with the body and becoming shorter towards it's extremity where it ends in an accute point. the hairs of the body are much longer on the side and rump than any other part, which gives the body and apparent flatness, particularly when the animal rests on it's belley. this hair is upwards of 3 inches in length particularly on the rump where it extends so far towards the point of the tail that it almost conceals the shape of that part and gives to the whole of the hinder part of the body the figure of an accute angled triangle of which the point of the tail forms the accute angle. the small quantity of coarse fur which is intermixed with the hair is of a redish pale yellow. the hair of the back, sides, upper part of the neck and tail, are of a redish light or pale yellow for about 2/3rds of their length from the skin, next black, and then tiped with white; forming a curious mixture of grey and fox coloured red with a yellowish hue. the belley flanks and breast are of the foxcoloured redish yellow. the legs black. the nails white the head on which the hair is short, is varia gated with black and white. a narrow strip of white commences on the top of the nose about 1/2 an inch from it's extremity and extends back along the center of the forehead and neck nearly to the sholders- two stripes of black succeed the white on either side imbracing the sides of the nose, the eyes, and extends back as far as the ears. two other spots of black of a ramboidal figure are placed on the side of the head near the ears and between them and the opening of the mouth. two black spots also immediately behind the ears. the other parts of the head white. this animal feeds on flesh, roots, bugs, and wild fruits.- it is very clumsy and runs very slow. I have in two instances out run this animal and caught it. in this rispect they are not much more fleet than the porcupine.

[Clark, February 26, 1806] Wednesday February 26th 1806 This morning we dispatched Drewyer and two men in our indian canoe up the Columbia River to take Sturgion and Anchovey. or if they were unsucksessfull in fishing we directed them to purchase fish from the nativs, for which purpose we had furnished them with a fiew articles Such as the nativs are pleased with. we also Sent Shields Jo. Field and Shannon up the Netul to hunt Elk. and directed Reubin Field and Some other man to hunt in the point towards the Praries & point Adams. thus we hope Shortly to replenish our Stock of provisions which is now reduced to a mear minnamum. we have three days provisions only in Store and that of the most inferior dried Elk a little tainted. what a prospect for good liveing at Fort Clatsop at present.

Se we lel is the Clatsop and Chinnook name for a Small animal found in the timbered Country on this Coast. it is more abundant in the neighbourhood of the great falls and rapids of the Columbia than imediately on the Coast. the nativs make great use of the Skins of this animal in forming their robes, which they dress with the fur on them and attached together with the sinears of the Elk or Deer. I have never Seen the ammale and can therefore only discribe it from the Skin and a Slight view which Some of our party have obtained of the liveing animal. the Skin when dressed is from 14 to 18 inches in length, and from 7 to 9 in width; the tail is always Severed from the body in forming their robes, I cannot therefore Say in what form or length it is. one of the men informed me that he thought it reather Short and flat. that he saw one of them run up a tree like a squirel, and that it returned and ran into a hole in the ground. the ears are Short, thin, pointed and Covered with Short fine hair. they are of uniform Colour, a redish brown; tho the base of the long hairs, exceed the fur but little in length, as well as the fur itself is of a Dark colour for at least 2/3ds of it's length next to the Skin. the fur and hair are very fine, Short, thickly Set, and Silky. the ends of the fur and tips of the hair is of a redish brown, that colour prodominates in the ordinary appearance of the Animate. I took this animal to be about the Size of the barking Squirel of the Missouri. and believe most probably that it is of the Mustela genus, or perhaps the brown mungo itself I have in maney instances endeavured to make the nativs Sensiable how anxious I was to obtain one of those animals entire, without being Skined, and offered them rewards to furnish me with one, but have not been able to make them Comprehend me. we have purchased Several of the roabs made of those Skins to loin a westcoat of the Sea otter, which I have made and Capt Lewis a Tiger Cat Skin Coat loined with them also, they make a very pleasant light lighting.

The Rat in the rocky mountains on its west side are like those on the upper part of the Missouri in and near those Mountains and have the distingushing trait of possessing a tail covered with hair like other parts of the body; one of these we caught at the white bear Islands in the beginning of July last and then partially discribed.

There is rats in this neighbourhood but I have not seen them it is most probable that they are like those of the Atlantic States, or at least the native rat of our country which have no hair on their tail. this Specis we found on the Missouri as far up it as the woody country extended. it is as large as the Common European house rat or reather larger is of a lighter Colour bordering more on the lead or drab colour, the hair longer; and the female has only four tits which are placed far back near the hinder legs. this rat I have Seen in the Southern parts of the State of Kentucky & west of the Miami.

The Mouse and mole of this neighbourhood are the Same as those native animals with us.

The Panther is found indifferently either in the great Plains of Columbia the Western Side of the Rocky Mountains or on this coast in the timbered country. it is precisily the Same animal common to the Atlantic States, and most commonly met with on our frontiers or unsettled parts of the Country. this animal is Scerce in the Country where they exist and are So remarkable Shye and watchfull that it is extreamly dificuelt to kill them.

The Polecat is found in every part of the Country. they are very abundant on Some parts of the Columbia, particularly in the neighbourhood of the Great falls & Narrows of that river, where they live in the Clifts along the river & feed on the offal of the Indian fishing Shores. they are the Same as those of other parts of North America.

[Lewis, February 27, 1806] Thursday February 27th 1806. Reubin Fields returned this evening and had not killed anything. he reports that there are no Elk towards point Adams. Collins who had hunted up the Netul on this side returned in the evening having killed a buck Elk. Willard still continues very unwell the other sick men have nearly recovered. Gutridge and McNeal who have the pox are recovering fast, the former nearly well.

The rat in the Rocky mountain on it's West side are like those on the upper part of the Missouri in and near those mountains and have the distinguishing trait of possessing a tail covered with hair like other parts of the body; one of those we caught at the White bear Islands in the beginning of July last and was then discribed. I have seen the nests of those in this neighbourhood but not the animal. I think it most probable that they are like those of the Atlantic states or at least the native rat of our country which have no hair on the tail. this species we found on the Missouri as far up it as the woody country extended. it is as large as the common European house rat or reather larger, is of a lighter colour bordering more on the lead or drab colour, the hair longer; and the female has only four tits which are placed far back near the hinder legs. this rat I have observed in the Western parts of the State of Georgia and also in Madison's cave in the state of Virginia the mouse and mole of this neighbourhood are the same as those native animals with us. The Panther is found indifferently either in the Great Plains of Columbia, the Western side of the rocky mountains or on this coast in the timbered country. it is precisely the same animal common to the Atlantic coast, and most commonly met with on our frontiers or unsettled parts of the country. this animal is scarce in the country where they exist and are so remarkable shye and watchfull that it is extreemly difficult to kill them.

[Clark, February 27, 1806] Thursday February 27th 1806 Reubin Field returned this evening and had not killed anything, he reported that there were no Elk towards point Adams. Collins who had hunted up the Netul on this Side returned in the evening haveing killed a buck Elk. Willard Still Continue very unwell the other Sick men have nearly recovered. Goodrich & McNeal who have the Pox are recovering fast, the former nearly well. La Page complaining.

The Braro so called by the French engages is an animal of the Civit genus and much resembles the common badger. this is an enhabitent of the open plains of the Columbia as they are of those of the Missouri, but are Sometimes also found in the woody country. they burrow in the hard Grounds in the Plains with Surprising ease and dexterity and will cover themselves in the Ground in a very fiew minits. they have five long fixed nails on each foot; those of the fore feet are much the longest; and one of those on each hind foot is double like those of the beaver. they weigh from 14 to 20 lbs. the body is reather long in perportion to its thickness. the fore legs remarkably large and muscular and are formed like the turnspit dog. they are Short as also the hind legs. they are broad across the Sholders and breast. the neck Short, the head is formed much like the Common fist dog only that the Skull is more Convex, the mouth is wide and furnishid with long Sharp teeth, both above and below, and with four Sharp Streight Pointed tushes, two in the upper and two in the lower jaw. the eyes are black and Small. Whiskers are placed in four points on each Side near the nose and on the jaws near the opening of the mouth. the ears are very Short wide and appressed as if they had been cut off. the appertue through them to the head is remarkably Small; the tail is about 4 inches long; the hair longest on it at it's junction, with the body and becomeing Shorter towards it's extremity where it ends in an accute point. the hairs of the body are much longer on the Sides and rump than any other part, which givs the body an appearent flatness, particularly when the animal rests on it's belly. this hair is upwards of 3 inches in length, particularly on the rump where it extends so far towards the point of the tail, that it almost conceals the Shape of that part and givs to all the hinder part of the body an accute angled triangle, of which the point of the tail forms the accute angle. the Small quantity of fur which is intermixed with the hair is of a redish pale yellow. the hair of the back, Sides upper part of the neck and tail, are of redish light or pale yellow fox about two thirds of their length from the Skin, next black, and then tiped with white; forming a curious mixture of grey and fox colourd. red with a yellowish hue. the belly flanks and breast are of the fox coloured redish yellow. the legs black, the nails white. the head on which the hair is short is varigated with black and white. a narrow Strip of white Commences on the top of the nose about half an inch from its extremity and extends back along the Center of the forehead and neck nearly to the Sholders- two Stripes of black Suckceed the white on either Side, imbraceing the Side of the nose, the eyes, and extends back as far as the ears. two other Spots of black of a romboidal figure are placed on the Side of the head near the ears and between them and the opening of the mouth. two black Spots also imediately behind the ears. the other part of the head white. this animal feeds on flesh, roots, bugs and wild fruits.- it is very clumsy and runs very Slow, depending more on burring to Secure it Self than running. I have in Several instances out run and caught this animal. in this respect they are not much more fleet than the porcupine.

[Lewis, February 28, 1806] Friday February 28th 1806. Reubin Fields and Collins set out this morning early on a hunting excurtion. Kuskelar a Clatsop man and his wife visited us today. they brought some Anchovies, Sturgeon, a beaver robe, and some roots for sail tho they asked so high a price for every article that we purchased nothing but a part of a Sturgeon for which we gave a few fishing hooks. we suffered them to remain all night. Shields Jos. Fields and Shannon returned late this evening having killed five Elk tho two of them ar on a mountain at a considerable distance. we ordered these hunters to return early in the morning and continue their hunt, and Sergt. Gass to take a party and go in quest of the Elk which they had killed. the hunters inform us that the Elk are tolerable plenty near the mountains about 9 or ten miles distant. Kuskelar brought a dog which Cruzatte had purchased.

The hare on this side of the Rocky mountains is exclusively the inhabitant of the great Plains of Columbia, as they are of those of the Missouri East of these mountains. they weigh from 7 to eleven pounds. the measure of one which weighed ten lbs. was as follows. from the extremity of the hinder, to that of the fore feet when extended 3 F. length from nose to the extremity of the tail 2 F. 2 I. hight when standing erect 1 F. 3 I. girth of the body 1 F. 4 I. length of tail 61/2 I. length of ear 51/2 I. width of do 3 1/8 I. from the hip to the extremity of toe of the hind foot 1 F. 41/4 I.- the eye is large and prominent. the pupil is circular, of a deep sea green and occupys one third of the diameter of the eye, the iris is of a bright yellowish silver colour. the ears are placed far back on the head and very near each other, they are flexable and the animal moves them with great ease and quickness, and can dilate and throw them forward, or contract and fold them on his back at pleasure. the fold of the front of the ear is of a redish brown colour, the inner folds or those which lie together when the ears are thrown back, and which occupy 2/3ds of the width of the ears are of a pure white except the tips of the ears for about an inch. the hinder folds or those which lie on the back are of a light grey. the head neck, back, sholders, sides, & outer part of the legs and thyes are of a lead coloured grey; the sides as they approach the belley become gradually more white. the belley, brest, and inner part of the legs and thyes are white, with a slight shade of the lead colour. the tail is round and blontly pointed, covered with fine soft white fur not quite as long as on the other parts of the body. the body is covered with a deep fine soft close fur. the colours here discribed are those which the animal assumes from the middle of April to the middle of November, the ballance of the year they are of a pure white, except the black and redish brown of the ears which never changes. a few redish brown spots are sometimes seen intermixed with the white, at this season, on their heads and upper part of the neck and sholders. the body of this animal is smaller and longer in proportion to it's hight than the rabbit. when it runs it carrys it's tail streight behind in the direction of it's body. they appear to run with more ease and bound with greater agility than any animal I ever saw. they are extreemly fleet and never burrow or take sheter in the ground when pursued. it's teeth are like those of the rabbit as is also it's upper lip which is divided as high as the nose. it's food is grass, herbs, and in winter feeds much on the bark of several aromatic shrubs which grow in the plains and the young willow along the rivers and other wartercourses.- I have measured the leaps of this animal and find them commonly from 18 to 21 feet. they are generally found seperate, and never seen to asscociate in any number or more than two or three.- the rabbit are the same of our country and are found indifferently either in the praries or woodlands. they are not very abundant in this country. The Pole-cat is also found in every part of the country. they are very abundant on some parts of the columbia, particularly in the neighbourhood of the great falls and narrows of that river, where they live in the clifts along the river and feed on the offal of the Indian fishing shores. these are the same as those of other parts of North America.

[Clark, February 28, 1806] Friday February 28th 1806 Reuben Field and Collins Set out this morning early on a hunting excurtion up the Netul. Kus ke-lar a Clatsop man, his wife and a Small boy (a Slave, who he informed me was his Cook, and offerd to Sell him to me for beeds & a gun) visited us to day they brought Some anchovies, Sturgeon, a beaver robe, and Some roots for Sale tho they asked Such high prices for every article that we purchased nothing but a part of a Sturgeon for which we gave a fiew fishing hooks. we Suffered them to Stay all night. Shields Jos. Field and Shannon returned late this evening haveing killed five Elk tho two of them are of a mountain at a considerable distance. we ordered these hunters to return early in the morning and continue the hunt, and Sergt. Gass to take a party and go in quest of the Elk which they had killed. the hunters informed us that the Elk is tolerable plenty near the mountains about nine or ten miles distant. Kuskalaw brought a dog which Peter Crusat had purchased with his Capo which this fellow had on.

The Hare on this Side of the Rocky Mountains is exclusively the inhabitents of the Great Plains of Columbia, as they are of those of the Missouri East of the mountains. they weigh from 7 to 12 pounds. the measure of one which weighed 10 pounds, was as follows. from the extremity of the hinder, to that of the fore feet when extended 3 Feet. length from nose to the extremity of the tail 2 feet, 2 inches. Hight when Standing erect 1 foot, 3 inches-. Girth of the body 1 foot, 4 inches-. length of tail 61/2 inches-. length of ear 51/2 inches-. width of ear 3 inches and 1/8-. from the hip to the extremity of toe of the hind foot 1 foot 41/4 inches-. The eye is large and prominent. the pupil is circular, of a deep Sea Green and Occupies one third of the diamiter of the eye, the iris is of a bright yellowish silver colour. The ears are placed far back on the head and very near each other, they are flexable and the animal moves them with great ease and quickness and can dilate and throw them foward, or contract and fold them on his back at pleasure. the fold of the front of the ear is of a redish brown colour, the inner folds are those which lie together when the ears are thrown back, and which occupies 2/3ds of the width of the ears of a pure white except the tips of the ears for about an inch. the hinder folds or those which lie on the back are of a light grey; the Sides as they approach the belly become gradually more white, the belly brest, and inner part of the legs and thyes are white, with a Slight Shade of a lead Colour. The Head, neck, back Sholders, Sides, outer part of the legs and thyes are of a Lead Coloured Grey. the tail is bluntly pointed and round, covered with fine Soft white fur not quite as long as on the other parts of the body. the body is covered with a deep fine Soft close fur. the colours here discribed are those which the Animale assumes from the middle of April to the middle of November, the ballance of the year they are of a pure white, except the black and redish brown of the ears which never changes. a fiew redish brown spots are Sometimes Seen intermixed with the white, at this Season on the heads and upper parts of the neck an Sholders. The body of this animal is Smaller and longer in purpotion to it's hight than the Rabbit. when it runs it carrys its tail Streight behind in the direction of it's body. they appear to run with more ease and bound with greater agility than any animal I ever saw. they are extreemly fleet and never burrow or take Shelter in the grounds when pursued. it's teeth are like those of the rabit, as is also its upper lip which is divided as high as the nose. it's food is Grass, herbs, and in winter feeds much on the bark of Several arematic Shrubs which grow in the plains and the young willows along the rivers and other water courses.- I have measured the leaps of this animal and find them commonly from 18 to 22 feet. they are Generally found Seperate, and never Seen to associate in any number or more than two or three.

[Lewis, March 1, 1806] Saturday March 1st 1806. This morning Sergt. Gass and a party set out in quest of the Elk which had been killed by the hunters the day before yesterday. they returned with the flesh of three of them late in the evening. Thompson was left with the hunters in order to jurk and take care of the flesh of the remaining two. Kuskelar and wife left us about noon. he had a good looking boy of about 10 years of age with him who he informed us was his slave. this boy had been taken prisoner by the Killamucks from some nation on the Coast to the S. East of them at a great distance. like other Indian nations they adopt their slaves in their families and treat them very much as their own children. Reubin Fields and Collins who have been absent since yesterday morning returned without having killed any game. The birds of the Western side of the Rocky Mountain to the Pacific Ocean, for convenience I shall divide into two classes, which I shal designate from the habits of the birds, Terrestrial and Aquatic.

The Grouse or Prarie hen is peculiarly the inhabitant of the Grait Plains of Columbia they do not differ from those of the upper portion of the Missouri, the tail of which is pointed or the feathers in it's center much longer than those on the sides. this Species differs essentially in the construction of this part of their plumage from those of the Illinois which have their tails composed of fathers of equal length. in the winter season this bird is booted even to the first joint of it's toes. the toes are also curiously bordered on their lower edges with narrow hard scales which are placed very close to each other and extend horizontally about 1/8 of an inch on each side of the toes thus adding to the width of the tread which nature seems bountifully to have furnished them at this season for passing over the snow with more ease. in the summer season those scales fall off. They have four toes on each foot. Their colour is a mixture of dark brown redish and yellowish brown and white confusedly mixed in which the redish brown prevails most on the upper parts of the body wings and tail and the white underneath the belley and lower parts of the breast and tail. they associate in large flocks in autumn & winter and are frequently found in flocks of from five to six even in summer. They feed on grass, insects, the leaves of various shrubs in the plains and on the seeds of several species of spelts and wild rye which grow in the richer parts of the plains. in winter their food is the buds of the willow & Cottonwood also the most of the native berries furnish them with food. The Indians of this neighbourhood eat the root of the Cattail or Cooper's flag. it is pleasantly taisted and appears to be very nutricious. the inner part of the root which is eaten without any previous preperation is composed of a number of capillary white flexable strong fibers among which is a mealy or starch like substance which readily desolves in the mouth and separate from the fibers which are then rejected. it appears to me that this substance would make excellent starch; nothing can be of a purer white than it is.-

[Clark, March 1, 1806] Saturday March the 1st 1806 This morning we despatched Sergt. Gass with 12 men in two Canoes in quest of the Elk which had been killed by the hunters the day before yesterday. they returned with the flesh of three of them late in the evening. Thompson was left with the hunters in order to jurk and take care of the flesh of the remaining two. Kuskalar &c. left us about noon. The boy which this Indian offered to Sell to me is about 10 years of age. this boy had been taken prisoner by the Kit a mox from Some Nation on the Coast to the S. East of them at a great distance. like other Indian nations they adopt their Slaves in their famelies and treat them very much like their own Children. Reuben Field and Collins who had been absent Since yesterday morning returned without killing any thing.

The birds on the western Side of the Rocky Mountain's to the Pacific Ocian for Convenience I Shall devide into from the habit of the birds, Terrestrial and Aquatic. i e Fowls of the air, and fowls of the water.

The Prarie Hen sometimes called the Grouse is peculiarly the inhabitent of the Great Plains of Columbia. they do not differ from those of the upper portion of the Missouri, the tails of which is pointed or the feathers in its center much longer than those on the Sides. this Species differ assentially in the construction of this part of their plumage from those of the Illinois which have their tail composed of feathers of equal length. in the winter Season this berd is booted even to the first joint of it's toes. the toes are also curiously bordered on their lower edges with narrow hard scales which are placed very close to each other and extend horizontally about 1/8 of an inch on each Side of the toe, thus adding to the width of the tread which nature Seams bountifully to have furnished them with at this Season for passing over the Snow with more ease. in the Summer Season those Scales fall off. they have four toes on each foot. their colour is a mixture of dark brown redish and yellowish brown and white confusedly mixed in which the redish brown prevails most on the upper parts of the body wings and tail. and the white underneath the belley and lower parts of the breast and tail. they associate in large flocks in autumn & winter and are frequently found in flocks of from five to Six even in Summer. They feed on grass, insects, the leaves of various Shrubs in the Praries, and on the Seeds of Several Species of Spelts and wild rye which grow in the richer parts of the Plains. in the winter their food is the buds of the willow and

Cottonwood also the most of the native berries furnish them with food. they cohabit in flock & the Cocks fight verry much at those Seasons.

[Lewis, March 2, 1806] Sunday March 2cd The diet of the sick is so inferior that they recover their strength but slowly. none of them are now sick but all in a state of convalessence with keen appetites and nothing to eat except lean Elk meat. late this evening Drewyer arrived with a most acceptable supply of fat Sturgeon, fresh Anchovies and a bag containing about a bushel of Wappetoe. we feasted on Anchovies and Wappetoe.

The Cock of the Plains is found in the plains of Columbia and are in Great abundance from the entrance of the S. E. fork of the Columbia to that of Clark's river. this bird is about 2/3rds the size of a turkey. the beak is large short curved and convex. the upper exceeding the lower chap. the nostrils are large and the beak black. the colour is an uniform mixture of dark brown reather bordeing on a dove colour, redish and yellowish brown with some small black specks. in this mixture the dark brown prevails and has a slight cast of the dove colour at a little distance. the wider side of the large feathers of the wings are of a dark brown only. the tail is composed of 19 feathers of which that in the center is the longest, and the remaining 9 on each side deminish by pairs as they receede from the center; that is any one feather is equal in length to one equa distant from the center of the tail on the oposite side. the tail when foalded comes to a very sharp point and appears long in proportion to the body. in the act of flying the tail resembles that of a wild pigeon. tho the motion of the wings is much that of the pheasant and Grouse. they have four toes on each foot of which the hinder one is short. the leg is covered with feathers about half the distance between the knee and foot. when the wing is expanded there are wide opening between it's feathers the plumeage being so narrow that it dose not extend from one quill to the other. the wings are also proportionably short, reather more so than those of the pheasant or grouse. the habits of this bird are much the same as those of the grouse. only that the food of this fowl is almost entirely that of the leaf and buds of the pulpy leafed thorn; nor do I ever recollect seeing this bird but in the neighbourhood of that shrub. they sometimes feed on the prickley pear. the gizzard of it is large and much less compressed and muscular than in most fowls; in short it resembles a maw quite as much as a gizzard. when they fly they make a cackling noise something like the dunghill fowl. the following is a likeness of the head and beak. the flesh of the cock of the Plains is dark, and only tolerable in point of flavor. I do not think it as good as either the Pheasant or Grouse.- it is invariably found in the plains.The feathers about it's head are pointed and stif some hairs about the base of the beak. feathers short fine and stif about the ears.

[Clark, March 2, 1806] Sunday March 2nd 1806 The diet of the Sick is So inferior that they recover their Strength but Slowly. none of them are now Sick but all in a State of Covelessence with keen appetites and nothing to eate except lean Elk meat.

The nativs of this neighbourhood eate the root of the Cattail or Cooper's flag. it is pleasantly tasted and appears to be very nutrecious. the inner part of the root which is eaten without any previous preperation is Composed of a number of capellary white flexable Strong fibers among which is a mealy or Starch like Substance which readily disolves in the mouth and Seperates from the fibers which are then rejected. it appears to me that this Substance would make excellent Starch; nothing Can be of a pureer white than it is

This evening late Drewyer, Crusat & Wiser returned with a most acceptable Supply of fat Sturgen, fresh anchoves and a bag Containing about a bushel of Wappato. we feasted on the Anchovies and wappatoe.-.

The Heath Cock or cock of the Plains is found in the Plains of Columbia and are in great abundance from the enterance of Lewis's river to the mountains which pass the Columbia between the Great falls and Rapids of that river. this fowl is about 3/4ths the Size of a turkey. the beak is large Short Curved and convex. the upper exceeding the lower chap. the nostrils are large and the back black. the Colour is a uniform mixture of dark brown reather bordering on a dove colour, redish and yellowish brown with Some Small black Specks. in this mixture the dark brown provails and has a Slight cast of the dove colour at a little distance. the wider side of the larger feathers of the wings are of a dark brown only. the tail is composed of 19 feathers of which that in the center is the longest, and the remaining 9 on each Side deminish by pairs as they receede from the Center; that is any one feather is equal in length to one of an equal distance from the Center of the tail on the opposit Side. the tail when folded Comes to a very Sharp point and appears long in perpotion to the body in the act of flying the tail resembles that of a wild pigeon. tho the motion of the wings is much that of the Pheasant and Grouse. they have four toes on each foot of which the hinder one is Short. the leg is covered with feathers about half the distance between the knee and foot. when the wings is expanded there are wide opening between it's feathers, the plumage being So narrow that it does not extend from one quill to another. the wings are also propotionally Short, reather more So than those of the Pheasant or Grouse. the habits of this bird is much the Same as those of the Prarie hen or Grouse. only that the food of this fowl is almost entirely that of the leaf and buds of the pulpy leafed thorn, nor do I ever recollect Seeing this bird but in the neighbourhood of that Shrub. The gizzard of it is large and much less compressed and muscular than in most fowls, in Short it resembles a maw quite as much as a gizzard. When they fly they make a cackling noise Something like the dunghill fowl. the flesh of this fowl is dark and only tolerable in point of flavour. I do not think it as good as wth the Pheasant or Prarie hen, or Grouse. the feathers above it's head are pointed and Stiff Some hairs about the base of the beak. feathers Short fine and Stiff about the ears, and eye. This is a faint likeness of the Cock of the plains or Heath Cock the first of those fowls which we met with was on the Missouri below and in the neighbourhood of the Rocky Mountains and from to the mountain which passes the Columbia between the Great falls and Rapids they go in large gangues or Singularly and hide remarkably close when pursued, make Short flights, &c.

The large Black & White Pheasant is peculiar to that portion of the Rocky Mountains watered by the Columbia River. at least we did not See them untill we reached the waters of that river, nor Since we have left those mountains. they are about the Size of a well grown hen. the contour of the bird is much that of the redish brown Pheasant common to our country. the tail is proportionally as long and is composed of 18 feathers of equal length, of a uniform dark brown tiped with black. the feathers of the body are of a dark brown black and white. the black is that which most prodomonates, and white feathers are irregularly intermixed with those of the black and dark brown on every part but in greater perpotion about the neck breast and belly. this mixture gives it very much the appearance of that kind of dunghill fowl, which the henwives of our Countrey Call dommanicker. in the brest of Some of those birds the white prodominates most. they are not furnished with tufts of long feathers on the neck as other Pheasants are, but have a Space on each Side of the neck about 2 1/2 inches long and one inch in width on which no feathers grow, tho it is consealed by the feathers which are inserted on the hinder and front part of the neck, this Space Seams to Serve them to dilate or contract the feathers of the neck with more ease. the eye is dark, the beak black, uncovered Somewhat pointed and the upper exceeds the under chap. they have a narrow Strip of vermillion colour above each eye which consists of a fleshey Substance not protuberant but uneaven, with a number of minute rounded dots. it has four toes on each foot of which three are in front, it is booted to the toes. it feeds on wild fruits, particularly the berry of the Sac-a-com-mis, and much also on the Seed of the pine & fir. this fowl is usially found in Small numbers two and three & 4 together on the ground. when Supprised flies up & lights on a tree and is easily Shot their flesh is Superior to most of the Pheasant Species which we have met with. they have a gizzard as other Pheasants &c. feed also on the buds of the Small Huckleberry bushes

[Lewis, March 3, 1806] Monday March 3rd 1806. Two of our perogues have been lately injured very much in consequence of the tide leaving them partially on shore. they split by this means with their own weight. we had them drawn out on shore. our convalessents are slowly on the recovery. Lapage is taken sick, gave him a doze of Scots pills which did not operate. no movement of the party today worthy of notice. every thing moves on in the old way and we are counting the days which seperate us from the 1st of April and which bind us to fort Clatsop.- The large black and white pheasant is peculiar to that portion of the Rocky Mountain watered by the Columbia river. at least we did not see them in these mountains until I we reached the waters of that river nor since we have left those mountains. they are about the size of a well grown hen. the contour of the bird is much that of the redish brown pheasant common to our country. the tail is proportionally as long and is composed of eighteen feathers of equal length, of an uniform dark brown tiped with black. the feathers of the body are of a dark brown black and white. the black is that which most predominates, and white feathers are irregularly intermixed with those of the black and dark brown on every part, but in greater proportion about the neck breast and belley. this mixture gives it very much the appearance of that kind of dunghill fowl which the hen-wives of our country call dom-manicker. in the brest of some of these birds the white predominates most. they are not furnished with tufts of long feathers on the neck as our pheasants are, but have a space on each side of the neck about 2 1/2 inches long and 1 In. in width on which no feathers grow, tho tis concealed by the feathers which are inserted on the hinder and front part of the neck; this space seems to surve them to dilate or contract the feathers of the neck with more ease. the eye is dark, the beak black, curved somewhat pointed and the upper exceeds the under chap. they have a narrow stripe of vermillion colour above each eye which consists of a fleshey substance not protuberant but uneven with a number of minute rounded dots. it has four toes on each foot of which three are in front. it is booted to the toes. it feeds on wild fruits, particularly the berry of the sac-a-commis, and much also on the seed of the pine and fir.

The small speckled pheasant found in the same country with that above discribed, differs from it only in point of size and somewhat in colour. it is scarcely half the size of the other; ascociates in much larger flocks and is very gentle. the black is more predominant and the dark bron feathers less frequent in this than the larger species. the mixture of white is also more general on every part of this bird. it is considerably smaller than our pheasant and the body reather more round. in other particulars they differ not at all from the large black and white pheasant. this by way of distinction I have called the speckled pheasant. the flesh of both these species of party coloured phesants is of a dark colour and with the means we had of cooking them not very well flavored.

The small brown pheasant is an inhabitant of the same country and is of the size and shape of the specled pheasant which it also resembles in it's economy and habits. the stripe above the eye in this species is scarcely perceptable, and is when closely examined of a yellow or orrange colour instead of the vermillion of the outhers. it's colour is an uniform mixture of dark and yellowish brown with a slight mixture of brownish white on the breast belley and the feathers underneath the tail. the whol compound is not unlike that of the common quail only darker. this is also booted to the toes. the flesh of this is preferable to either of the others and that of the breast is as white as the pheasant of the Atlantic coast.the redish brown pheasant has been previously discribed.- The Crow raven and Large Blackbird are the same as those of our country only that the crow is here much smaller yet it's note is the same. I observe no difference either between the hawks of this coast and those of the Atlantic. I have observed the large brown hawk, the small or sparrow hawk, and the hawk of an intermediate size with a long tail and blewish coloured wings remarkably swift in flight and very firce. sometimes called in the U States the hen hawk. these birds seem to be common to every part of this country, and the hawks crows & ravens build their nests in great numbers along the high and inaccessible clifts of the Columbia river and it's S. E. branch where we passed along them.- we also met with the large hooting Owl under the Rocky mountain on the Kooskoskee river. it did not appear to differ materially from those of our country. I think it's colours reather deeper and brighter than with us, particularly the redish brown. it is the same size and form.

[Clark, March 3, 1806] Monday March 3rd 1806 Two of our Canoes have been lately injured very much in consequence of the tide leaveing them partially on Shore. they Split by this means with their own weight. we had them drawn out on Shore. our convalessents are Slowly on the recovery. La page is taken Sick. gave him Some of Scotts Pills which did not opperate. no movement of the party to day worthey of notice. every thing moves on in the old way and we are Counting the days which Seperate us from the 1st of April, & which bind us to Fort Clatsop.-.-.

The Small Speckled Pheasant found in the Rocky Mountains, and differ from the large black and white pheasant only in point of Size, and Somewhat in colour. it is scercely half the Size of the other; assosiates in much larger flocks and is also very gentle. the black is more predominate and the dark brown feathers less frequent in this than the larger Species. the mixture of white is also more general on every part of this bird. it is considerably Smaller than our Pheasant and the body reather more round. in other particulars they differ not at all, from the large black and white Pheasant. this by way of distinction I have called the Speckled Pheasant. the flesh of both these Species of party coloured Pheasant is of a dark colour, and with the means we had of cooking them were only tolerably flavoured tho these birds would be fine well cooked.

The small Brown Pheasant is an inhabitant of the Same Country and is of the Size and Shape of the Speckled Pheasant, which it also resembles in it's economy and habits, the Stripe above the eye in this Species is scercely preceptable and is when closely examined of a yellow or orrange colour in Sted of the vermillion of the others. it's colour is of a uniform mixture of dark and yellowish brown with a Slight mixture of brownish white on the breast belley and the feathers under the tail. the whole Compound is not unlike that of the Common quaile only darker. this is also booted to the toes. the flesh is tolerable and that of the breast is as white as the Pheasant of the atlantic coast. the redish brown Pheasant has been previously discribed.-.

The Crow Ravin and large Blackbird are the Same as those of our Country, only that the Crow here is much Smaller, yet its note is the Same. I observe no difference between the Hawk of this Coast and those of the Atlantic. I have observed the large brown Hawk, the Small or Sparrow hawk, and a hawk of an intermediate Size with a long tail and blewish coloured wings, remarkably Swift in flight and very ferce. Sometimes called in the Un. States the hen Hawk. those birds Seam to be common to every part of this Country in greater or smaller numbers, and the Hawks, Crows, and ravins build their nests in great numbers along the high & inaxcessable clifts of the Columbia, and Lewis's rivers when we passd along them. we also met with the large hooting Owl under the Rocky mountains on the Kooskooske R. it's Colour reather deeper than with us, but differ in no other respect from those of the U States.

[Lewis, March 4, 1806] Tuesday March 4th 1806. Not any occurrence today worthy of notice. we live sumptuously on our wappetoe and Sturgeon. the Anchovey is so delicate that they soon become tainted unless pickled or smoked. the natives run a small stick through their gills and hang them in the smoke of their lodges, or kindle a small fire under them for the purpose of drying them. they need no previous preperation of guting &c and will cure in 24 hours. the natives do not appear to be very scrupelous about eating them when a little feated.- the fresh sturgeon they keep for many days by immersing it in water. they coock their sturgeon by means of vapor or steam. the process is as follows. a brisk fire is kindled on which a parcel of stones are lad. when the fire birns down and the stones are sufficiently heated, the stones are so arranged as to form a tolerable level surface, the sturgeon which had been previously cut into large fletches is now laid on the hot stones; a parsel of small boughs of bushes is next laid on and a second course of the sturgeon thus repating alternate layers of sturgeon and boughs untill the whole is put on which they design to cook. it is next covered closely with matts and water is poared in such manner as to run in among the hot stones and the vapor arrising being confined by the mats, cooks the fish. the whole process is performed in an hour, and the sturgeon thus cooked is much better than either boiled or roasted.

The turtle dove and robbin are the same of our country and are found as well in the plain as open country. the Columbian robbin heretofore discribed seems to be the inhabitant of the woody country exclusively. the Magpy is most commonly found in the open country and are the same with those formerly discribed on the Missouri. the large woodpecker or log cock, the lark woodpeckers and the small white woodpecker with a read head are the same with those of the Atlantic states and are found exclusively in the timbered country. The blue crested Corvus and the small white breasted do have been previously discribed and are the natives of a piney country invariably, being found as well on the rocky mountains as on this coast.- the lark is found in the plains only and are the same with those before mentioned on the Missouri, and not very unlike what is called in Virginia the old field lark.- The large bluefish brown or sandhill Crain are found in the valley of the Rocky mountains in Summer and Autumn where they raise their young, and in the winter and begining of spring on this river below tidewater and on this coast. they are the same as those common to the Southern and Western States where they are most generally known by the name of the Sandhill crain. The vulture has also been discribed. there are two species of the flycatch, a small redish brown species with a short tail, round body, short neck and short pointed beak. they have some fine black specks intermixed with the uniform redish brown. this the same with that which remains all winter in Virginia where it is sometimes called the wren. the second species has lately returned and dose not remain here all winter. it's colours are a yellowish brown on the back head neck wings and tail the breast and belley of a yellowish white; the tail is in proportion as the wren but it is a size smaller than that bird. it's beak is streight pointed convex reather lage at the base and the chaps of equal length. the first species is the smallest, in short it is the smalest bird that I have ever seen in America except the humming bird. both these species are found in the woody country only or at least I have never seen them elsewhere.

[Clark, March 4, 1806] Tuesday March 4th 1806 Not any accurrance to day worthy of notice. we live Sumptiously on our wappatoe and Sturgeon. the Anchovey is so delicate that they Soon become tainted unless pickled or Smoked. the nativs run a Small Stick through their gills and hang them in the Smoke of their Lodges, or Kindle Small fires under them for the purpose of drying them. they need no previous preperation of gutting &c. and will Cure in 24 hours. the nativs do not appear to be very Scrupilous about eating them a little feated.

the fresh sturgeon they Keep maney days by immersing it in water. they Cook their Sturgeon by means of vapor or Steam. the process is as follows. a brisk fire is kindled on which a parcel of Stones are Sufficiently heated, the Stones are So arranged as to form a tolerable leavel Surface, the Sturgeon which had been previously cut into large flaetches is now laid on the hot Stones; a parcel of Small boughs of bushes is next laid on, and a Second course of the Sturgeon thus repeating alternate layers of Sturgeon & boughs untill the whole is put on which they design to Cook. it is next covered closely with mats and water is poared in Such manner as to run in among the hot Stones, and the vapor arriseing being confind by the mats, cooks the fish. the whole process is performd in an hour and the Sturgeon thus Cooked is much better than either boiled or roasted. in their usial way of bolting of other fish in baskets with hot Stones is not so good.

The turtle doves and robin are the Same of those of our countrey and are found as well as the plains as open countrey. the Columbia robin heretofore discribed Seams to be the inhabitent of the woody Country exclusively. the magpye is most commonly found in the open Country and are the Same with those formerly discribed on the Missouri.

The large wood pecker or log cock the lark woodpecker and the common wood pecker with a red head are the Same with those of the Atlantic States, and are found exclusively in the timbered Country. The Blue crested Corvus and the Small white brested corvus are the nativs of a piney country invariably, being found as well on the Rocky Mountains as on this coast-. The lark is found in the plains only and are the Same with those on the Missouri and the Illinois and not unlike what is Called in Virginia the old field Lark.

The large bluish brown or Sandhill Crain are found in the Vally's of the Rocky Mountain in Summer and autumn when they raise their young and in the winter and beginning of Spring on this river below tide water and on this coast. they are the Same as those Common to the Southern and Western States where they are most generally known by the name of the Sand hill Crain. The Vulture has already been discribed.

There are two Species of fly Catch, a Small redish brown with a Short tail, round body, Short neck, and Short pointed beak, and the Same as that with us sometimes called the Wren. the 2d Species does not remain all winter they have just returned and are of a Yellowish brown Colour.

[Lewis, March 5, 1806] Wednesday March 5th 1806. This morning we were visited by two parties of Clatsops. they brought some fish a hat and some skins for sale most of which we purchased. they returned to their village in the evening. late in the evening the hunters returned from the kil-haw-a-nack-kle River which discharges itself into the head of the bay. They had neither killed nor seen any Elk. they informed us that the Elk had all gone off to the mountains a considerable distance from us. this is unwelcome information and reather allarming we have only 2 days provision on hand, and that nearly spoiled. we made up a small assortment of articles to trade with the Indians and directed Sergt. Pryor to set out early in the morning in a canoe with 2 men, to ascend the Columbia to the resort of the Indian fishermen and purchase some fish; we also directed two parties of hunters to renew the Chase tomorrow early. the one up the Netul and the other towards Point Adams. if we find that the Elk have left us, we have determined to ascend the river slowly and indeavour to procure subsistence on the way, consuming the Month of March in the woody country. earlyer than April we conceive it a folly to attempt the open plains where we know there is no fuel except a few small dry shrubs. we shall not leave our quarters at fort Clatsop untill the first of April, as we intended unless the want of subsistence compels us to that measure. The common snipe of the marshes and the small sand snipe are the same of those common to the Atlantic Coast tho the former are by no means as abundant here. the prarrow of the woody country is also similar to ours but not abundant. those of the plains of Columbia are the same with those of the Missouri, tho they are by no means so abundant. I have not seen the little singing lark or the large brown Curloo so common to the plains of the Missouri, but I beleive that the latter is an inhabitant of this country during summer from Indian information. I have no doubt but what many species of birds found here in Autumn and Summer had departed before our arrival.

[Clark, March 5, 1806] Wednesday March 5th 1806. This morning we were visited by two parties of Clatsops they brought Some fish, a hat and Some Skins for Sale most of which we purchased, they returned to their Village in the evening with the returning tide. late in the evening the Hunters returned from the Kil-haw-d nack-kle River which discharges itself into the head of the Bay. They had neither killed nor Seen any Elk. they informed us that the Elk had all gorn off to the mountains a considerable distance from us. this is unwelcom information and reather alarming. we have only two days provisions on hand and that nearly Spoiled. we made up a Small assortment of Articles to trade with the Indians, and directed Sergt Natl. Pryor to Set out early in the morning in a canoe with two men, to assend the Columbia to the resort of the Indians fishermen and purchase Some fish; we also derected two parties of hunters to renew the chase tomorrow early. the one up the Netul, and the other towards point Adams. If we find that the Elk have left us, we have determined to assend the river slowly and endeaver to precure Subsistance on the way, Consumeing the month of March in the woody Country, earlyer than april we conceive it a folly to attempt the Open plains where we know there is no fuel except a fiew Small dry Shrubs. we Shall not leave our quarters at Fort Clatsop untill the 1st of April as we intended, unless the want of Subsistance compels us to that measure.

The common Snipe of the marshes and the Small sand snipe are the same of those Common to the atlantic coast tho the former are by no means as abundant here.

The Sparrow of the woody country is also Similar to ours but not abundant. those of the plains of Columbia are the Same with those of the Missouri. tho they are by no means So Abundant. I have not Seen the little Singing lark or the large brown Curloe So Common to the Plains of the Missouri. but believe the Curloe is an inhabitent of this Countrey dureing Summer from Indian information and their attemps to mimick the notes of this fowl. I have no doubt but what maney Species of birds found here in autumn and Summer had departed before our arrival.

The Aquatic Birds of this country or such as obtain their Subsistence from the water, are the large blue and brown heron, fishing Hawk, blue crested fisher, Gulls of Several Species of the Coast, the large grey Gull of the Columbia, Comorant, loons of two Species, white and the brown brant, Small and large Geese, small and large Swans, the Duckinmallard, canvis back Duck, red headed fishing Duck, black and white duck, little brown Duck, Black Duck, two Species of Divers, blue winged teal, 14 and Some other Species of Ducks, two Species of Plevers.

The hunters who were out last informed me that they discovered a very Considerable fall in the Kit-haw-a-nack-kle River on its main western fork at which place it falls abt. 100 feet from the Side of a mountain S. E. about 6 miles from Fort Clatsop and nearly 15 from its enterance into the bay by the Meanderings of this river a high mountain is Situated S 60° W. about 18 miles from Fort Clatsop on which there has been Snow Since Nov.

[Lewis, March 6, 1806] Thursday March 6th 1806. This morning the fishing and hunting parties set out agreeably to their instructions given them last evening. at 11 A.M. we were visited by Comowoll and two of his children. he presented us with some Anchovies which had been well cured in their manner. we foud them excellent. they were very acceptable particularly at this moment. we gave the old man some small articles in return. this we have found much the most friendly and decent savage that we have met with in this neighbourhood. Hall had his foot and ankle much injured yesterday by the fall of a large stick of timber; the bones were fortunately not broken and I expect he will be able to walk again shortly. Bratton is now weaker than any of the convalessants, all of whom recover slowly in consequence of the want of proper diet, which we have it not in our power to procure.-

The Aquatic birds of this country, or such as obtain their subsistence from the water, are the large blue and brown heron, fishing hawk, blue crested fisher, gulls of several species of the Coast, the large grey gull of the Columbia, Cormorant, loons of two species, white, and the brown brant, small and large geese, small and large

Swan, the Duckinmallard, canvis back duck, red headed fishing duck, black and white duck, little brown duck, black duck, two speceis of divers, blue winged teal, and some other speceis of ducks.

[Clark, March 6, 1806] Thursday March 6th 1806 This morning, the fishing and hunting party's Set out agreeably to their instructions given them last evening. At 11 a.m. we were visited by Commowoll and two boys Sons of his. he presented us with Some Anchovies which had been well Cured in their manner, we found them excellent. they were very acceptable perticularly at this moment. we gave the old mans Sones a twisted wire to ware about his neck, and I gave him a par of old glovs which he was much pleased with. this we have found much the most friendly and decent Indian that we have met with in this neighbourhood.

Hall had his foot and ankle much injured yesterday by the fall of a log which he had on his Sholder; the bones are fortunately not broken, I expect he will be able to walk again Shortly. Bratten is now weaker than any of the convalessants, and complains verry much of his back, all of them recovering Slowly in consequence of the want of proper diet, which we have it not in our power to precure.

The large Blue and brown Herons or crains as they are usialy called in the U States are found below tide water. they are the Same of those of the U, States. The Fishing Hawk with the Crown of the head white, and back of a milkey white, and the blue crested or king fisher are found on every part of the Columbia and its water Along which we passed and are the Same with those of the U, States. the fishing hawk is not abundant, particularly in the mountains. There are 4 Species of the larus or gull on this coast and river. 1st a Small Species the Size of a Pegion; white except some black spots about the head and the little bone on the but of the wing. 2d a Species Somewhat larger of a light brown colour, with a mealy coloured back. 3rd the large Grey Gull, or white larus with a greyish brown back, and light grey belly and breast, about the Size of a well grown pullet, the wings are remarkably long in perpotion to the Size of the body and it's under chap towards the extremity is gibbous and protuberant than in either of the other Species. a White Gull about the Size of the Second with a remarkable beak; adjoining the head and on the base of the upper Chap there is an elivated orning of the Same Substance with the beak which forms the nostriels at A; it is Somewhat in this form. the feet are webed and the legs and feet of a yellow colour. the form of the wings body &c are much that of the 2d Species this bird was Seen on Haleys bay.

The large Grey Gull is found on the Columbian waters as high as the enterence of the Koos koos ke and in common with the other Species on the coast; the others appear confined to the tidewater, and the 4th Species not So common as either of the others. The Comorant is a large black duck which feeds on fish; I proceive no difference between it & these found in the rivers of the Atlantic Coasts. we met with as high up the river as the enterance of the Chopunnish into the Kooskooske river. they increased in numbers as we decended, and formed much the Greatest portion of waterfowls which we saw on the Columbia untill we reached tidewater, where they also abound but do not bear a Similar proportion to the fowls found in this quarter. we found this bird fat and tolerably flavoured as we decended the Columbia.

[Lewis, March 7, 1806] Friday March 7th 1806. The wind was so high that Comowol did not leave us untill late this evening. Labuish and Drewyer returned at sunset having killed one Elk only. they report that there are some scattering male Elk in the neighbourhood of the place they killed this one or about 5 miles up the Netul on this side.- Bratton is much wose today, he complains of a violent pain in the small of his back and is unable in consequence to set up. we gave him one of our flanel shirts, applyed a bandage of flannel to the part and bathed and rubed it well with some vollatile linniment which I prepared with sperits of wine, camphor, castile soap and a little laudinum. he felt himself better in the evening.- the large blue and brown herons, or Crams as they are usually called in the U States are found on this river below tidewater. they are the same with those of the U States. the fishing hawk with the crown of the head White and back of a mealy white, and the blue crested or King fisher are found on every part of the Columbia and it's waters and are the same with those of the U States. the fishing hawk is not abundant particularly in the mountains. there are four speceis of larus or gull on this coast and river, 1st a small speceis about the size of a pigeon; white except some black spots about the head and a little brown on the but of the wings, 2nd a speceis somewhat larger of a light brown colour with a whitish or mealy coloured back. 3rd the large grey gull, or white larus with a greyish brown back and a light grey belley and breast, about the size of a well grown pullet or reather larger. the wings are remarkably long in proportion to the size of the body and it's under chap towards the extremity is more gibbous and protuberant than in either of the other speceis. 4th a white gull about the size of the second with a remarkable beak; adjoining the head and at the base of the uper Chap there is an elivated orning of the same substance with the beak which forms the nostrils; it is some what in this forma the feet are webbed and the legs and feet of a yellow colour. the form of the wings body &c are much that of the second species. the large grey gull is found on the river as high as the entrance of the Kooskooske and in common with the other speceis on the coast; the others appear to be confined to tidewater; and the fourth speceis not so common as either of the others. the cormorant is a large black duck which feeds on fish; I perceive no difference between it and those found in the Potomac and other rivers on the Atlantic Coast. tho I do not recollect seeing those on the atlantic so high up the rivers as those are found here. we first met with them on the Kooskooske at the entrance of Chopunnish river. they increased in quantity as we decended, and formed much the greatest portion of the waterfowl which we saw on the Columbia untill we reached tidewater where they also abound but do not bear a similar proportion to the other fowls found in this quarter.

There are two speceis of loons. 1st the Speckled loon found on every part of the rivers of this country. they are the same size colours and form with those of the Atlantic coast. the second speceis we first met with at the great falls of the Columbia and from thence down. this bird is not more than half the size of the speckled loon, it's neck is long, slender and white in front. the Colour of the body and back of the neck and head are of a dun or ash colour, the breast and belley are white. the beak is like that of the speckled loon and like them it cannot fly but flutters along on the top of the warter or dives for security when pursued.

[Clark, March 7, 1806] Friday March 7th 1806 The wind was So high that Comowol did not leave us untill late this evening. Drewyer & Labiesh returned at Sunset haveing killed one Elk only. they report that there are Some Scattering mail Elk in the neighbourhood of the place they killed this one or about 5 miles up the Netul river on the west Side-. Bratten is much worst to day he complains of a violent pain in the Small of his back, and is unable in consequence of it to Set up. we gave him one of our flanel Shirts. I applied a bandage of flanel to the part and rubed it well with Some volatile linniment which was prepared with Sperits of wine, camphire, Sastile Soap, and a little laudinum. he felt himself better in the evening at which time I repeated the linnement and bathed his feet to restore circulation which he complaind of in that part.

There are two Species of Loons. 1st the Speckled loon found on every part of the rivers of this quarter, they are the Same Size Colour and form with those of the Ohio, and atlantic coasts. the 2d Species we first met with at the great falls of the Columbia and from thence down. this bird is not more than half the Size of the Speckled loon, it's neck is long, Slender and white in front. the colour of the body and back of the neck and head are of a dun or ash Colour, the breast and belly are white. the back is like that of the Speckled loon, and like them it cannot fly, but flutters along on the top of the water or Dives for Security when pursued.

John Shields Reubin Fields & Robert frasure measured 2 trees of the fur kind one 37 feet around, appears sound, has but fiew limbs for 200 feet it is East of the Netul abt 280 feet high.

[Lewis, March 8, 1806] Saturday March 8th 1806. Bratton is much better today, his back gives him but little pain. Collins returned early in the morning and informed us that he had killed three Elk about five miles distant on the edge of the prarie in Point Adams. one of them fell in a deep pond of water and could not get it, the other two he butcherd and secured. he saw two large herds of Elk in that quarter. we sent Drewyer and Joseph Fields to hunt those Elk. a party were also sent with Labuish for the flesh of the Elk which Drewyer and himself had killed up the netul, they returned with it in the evening. Shields, R. Fields and Frazier returned this evening from the Kilhawanackkle unsuccessfull having seen no Elk. McNeal and Goodrich having recovered from the Louis veneri I directed them to desist from the uce of mercury. The white brant is very common in this country particularly below tidewater where they remain in vast quantities during the winter. they feed like the swan gees &c on the grass roots and seeds which they find in the marshes. this bird is about the size of the brown brant or a third less than the common Canadian or wild goose. the head is proportionably with the goose reather large; the beak also thicker shorter and of much the same form, being of a yellowish white colour except the edges of the chaps, which are frequently of a dark brown. the legs and feet are of the same form of the goose and are of a redish white or pale flesh colour. the tail is composed of sixteen feathers of equal length as those of the geese and brown brant are and bears about the same proportion in point of length. the eye is of a dark colour and nothing remarkable as to size. the wings are rether longer compared with those of the goose but not as much so as in the brown or pided brant. the colour of the plumage of this bird is unifomly a pure white except the large feathers of the extremities of the wings which are black. the large feathers of the 1st joint of the wing next to the body are white. the note of this bird differs essentially from that of the goose; it more resembles that of the brown brant but is somewhat different. it is like the note of young domestic goose which has not perfectly attained it's full note. the flesh of this bird is exceedingly fine, preferable to either the goose or pided brant.- The Brown or pided brant are much the same size and form of the white only that their wings are considerably longer and more pointed. the plumage of the upper part of the body neck head and tail is much the colour of the canadian goose but reather darker in consequence of som dark brown feathers which are distributed and irregularly scattered throughout. they have not the white on the neck and sides of the head as the goose has nor is the neck darker than the body. like the goose there are some white feathers on the rump at the joining of the tail. the beak is dark and the legs and feet also dark with a greenish cast; the breast and belley are of a lighter colour than the back and is also irregularly intermixed with dark brown and black feathers which give it a pided appearance. the flesh of this bird is dark and in my estimation reather better than that of the goose. the habits of this bird are the same nearly with the goose and white brant with this difference that they do not remain in this climate in such numbers during the winter as the others, and that it sets out earlier in the fall season on it's return to the south and arrives later in the spring than the goose. I see no difference between this bird and that called simply the brant, common to the lakes the Ohio and Mississippi &c. The small goose of this country is reather less than the brant; it's head and neck like the brant are reather larger than that of the goose in proportion; their beak is also thicker and shorter. their notes are more like those of our tame gees; in all other rispects they are the same with the large goose with which, they so frequently ascociate that it was some time after I first observed this goose before I could determine whether it was a distinct speceis or not. I have now no hesitation in declaring them a distinct speceis. the large goose is the same of that common on the Atlantic coast, and known by the appellation of the wild, or Canadian goose.

[Clark, March 8, 1806] Saturday March 8th 1806 Bratten is much better this morning, his back givs him but little pain. Collins returned early in the morning, and informed us that he had killed three Elk about five miles distance on the edge of the prarie in point Adams. one of them fell in a deep pond of water and he could not git to it. the other two he butchered and Saved. he saw two large herds of Elk in that quarter. we Sent Drewyer & Jos. Field to hunt these Elk, a party was also Sent with Labiesh for the flesh of the Elk which Drewyer and himself had killd up the Netul, they returned with it in the evening. Shields, R. Field and Frasure returned this evening from the Kilhawanackkle unsuccessfull haveing Seen no Elk. McNeal and Goodrich haveing recovered from the Louis veneri I detected them to desist from takeing the murcury or useing in future. willard is yet complaining and is low Spirited.

The White Brant is very common in this country particularly below tide water where they remain in vast quantities dureing the winter. they feed like the Swan Goose &c. on the grass and roots & Seeds which they find in the marshes this bird is a little larger than the brown brant and a fourth less than the common wild or Canadian goose. the head is proportionably with the goose reather large; the beak thicker Shorter and of the Same form, being of a yellowish white colour except the edges of the Chaps, which are frequently of a dark brown. the legs and feet are of the Same form of the goose and are of a redish white or pail flesh colour. the tail is composed of Sixteen feathers of equal length as those of the geese and brown brant are, and bears about the Same perpotion in point of length. the Eye is of a dark colour and nothing remarkable as to Size. the wings are reather longer compared with those of the goose, but not as much So as is the brown or pieded brant. the colour of the plumage of this bird is uniformly a pure white except the large feathers of the extremities of the wings which are black. The large feathers of the 1st joint of the wing next to the body are white. the note of this bird differs essentially from that of the goose; it more resembles that of the brown brant but is Somewhat different. it is like the note of a young domestic goose which has not perfectly attained its full note. the flesh of this bird is exceedingly fine, prefferable to either the goose or pieded brant. the neck is Shorter in prpotion than that of the goose.

The Brown or pieded brant are nearly the Size and much the Same form of the white brante only that their wings are considerably longer and more pointed. the plumage of the upper part of the body, neck, head and tail is much the Colour of the Common or Canadian Goose but rather darker in consequence of Some dark brown feathers which are distributed and irregularly scattered throughout. they have not the white on the neck and Sides of the head as the goose has nor is the neck darker than the body. like the goose there are Some white feathers on the rump at the junction of the tail. the beak, legs and feet are dark, with a greenish cast; the breast and belly are of a lighter colour than the back and is also intermixed, irregularly, with dark brown and black feathers which gives it a pieded appearance. the flesh of this bird is dark, and in my estimation reather better than that of the goose. the habits of this bird is nearly the same with the goose and white brant, with this difference that they do not remain in this Climate in Such numbers dureing the winter as the others. I See no difference between this bird and that Called Simpily the Brant Common to the Lakes and frequently Seen on the Ohio and Mississippi in large flocks &c.

The Small Goose of this country is reather less than the Brant; it's head and neck like the brant are reather larger than that of the goose in purpotion; their beak is also thicker and Shorter. their notes are more like those of our taim geese, in all other respect they are the Same with the large Goose with which, they So frequently ascoiete, that it was Some time after I first observed this goose before I could whether it was a distinct Speces or not. I have no hesitation now in declareing them a distinct Species. the large Goose is the Same as that common to the Ohio, and atlantic coast, and known by the appellation of the wild, or Canadian Goose.

[Lewis, March 9, 1806] Sunday March 9th 1806. This morning the men set out at daylight to go in gust of the Elk which Collins had killed, they returned with it at eleven A.M. Bratton complains of his back being very painfull to him today; I conceive this pain to be something of the rheumatism. we still apply the linniment and flannel; in the evening he was much better. Drewyer and Joseph Fields returned not having found any Elk. Sergt. Pryor and the fishing party not yet arrived, suppose they are detained by the winds. visited by 3 Clatsop men who brought a dog some fish and a Sea Otter skin for sale. we suffered them to remain all night. we set Shields at work to make some sacks of Elk skin to contain various articles. The large Swan is precisely the same common to the Atlantic States. the small swan differs only from the larger one in size and it's note. it is about one fourth less and it's note entirely different. the latter cannot be justly immetated by the sound of letters nor do I know any sounds with which a comparison would be pertinent. it begins with a kind of whistleing sound and terminates in a round full note which is reather louder than the whistleing, or former part; this note is as loud as that of the large swan. from the peculiar whistleing of the note of this bird I have called it the whistleing swan it's habits colour and contour appear to be precisely those of the large Swan. we first saw them below the great narrows of the Columbia near the Chilluckkittequaw nation. They are very abundant in this neighbourhood and have remained with us all winter. in number they are fully five for one of the large speceis. The duckinmallard or common large duck wich resembles the domestic duck are the same here with those of the U Sts. they are abundant and are found on every part of the river below the mountains. they remain here all winter but I beleive they do not continue during winter far above tidewater. a beautifull duck and one of the most delicious in the world is found in considerable quantities in this neighbourhood during the Autumn and winter. this is the same with that known in the Delliware, Susquehannah, and Potomac by the name of the Canvisback and in James River by that of shell-Drake; in the latter river; however I am informed that they have latterly almost entirely disappeared. to the epicure of those parts of the union where this duck abounds nothing need be added in praise of the exqusite flavor of this duck. I have frequently eaten of them in several parts of the Union and I think those of the Columbia equally as delicious. this duck is never found above tide-water; we did not meet with them untill after we reached the marshey Islands; and I beleive that they have already left this neighbourhood, but whether they have gone northwardly or Southwardly I am unable to determin; nor do I know in what part of the Continent they raise their young.- The read headed fishing duck is common to every part of the river and are found as well in the Rocky Mountains as elsewhere; in short this was the only duck we saw on the waters of the Columbia within the mountains. they feed principally on crawfish and are the same in every rispect as those on the rivers in the mountains of the Atlantic Ocean.

[Clark, March 9, 1806] Sunday Mach 9th 1806 This morning the men Set out at day light to go in quest of the Elk which Collins had killed, they returned at 11 A.M. Bratten complains of his backs being very painfull to him to day. we Still apply the linnement & flannel; in the evening he was much better. Jos. Field & Drewyer returned not haveing found any Elk. Sergt. Pryor and the fishing party not yet returned, Suppose they are detained by the winds. we are visited by 3 Clatsop men who brought a Dog, Some fish and a Sea otter Skin for Sale. we Suffered them to remain all night. we Set Shields at work to make Some Sacks of Elk Skin to contain my papers, and various articles which we wish kept Dry.

The large Swan is precisely the Same Common to the Missouri, Mississippi and the Atlantic States &c. The Small Swan differ only from the large one in Size and it's note. it is about 1/4th less, and its notes entirely different. the latter cannot be justly immetated by the Sound of letters nor do I know any Sound with which a comparison would be perti-nent. it begins with a kind of whistling Sound and terminates in a round full note which is reather louder than the whistling, or former part; this note is as loud as that of the large Swan. from the peculiar whistling of the note of this bird I have Called it the Whistleing Swan. it's habits colour and contour appear to be precisely those of the large swan. we first saw them below the great narrows of the Columbia near the Chilluckkittequaw Nation. they are very abundant in this neighbourhood and have remained with us all winter. in number they are fully five for one of the large Species of the Swan's.

The Duckinmallard are the Same here with those of the U, States. they are abundant and are found on every part of the river below the mountains. they remain here all winter, but I believe they do not remain all winter above tide water.- a butifull Duck and one of the most delicious in the world is found in Considerable quantities in this neighbourhood dureing the Autumn and winter. this is the Same as that known in the Dilliwar, Susquehannah and Potomac by the name of the Canvisback and James River by that of Shell-Drake; in the latter river I am informed that they have latterly almost entirely disapeared. the epicures of those parts of the Union where those Ducks abound nothing need be added in prais of the exquisit flavor of this duck. I have eaten of them in Several parts of the Union and I think those of the Columbia equally as delicious. this duck is never found above tide water; we did not meat with them untill after we reached the marshey Islands; and I believe that they have already left this neighbourhood; but whether they are gorn Northerly or Southerly, I am unable to deturmine; nor do I know in what part of the Country they rais their young

The red headed fishing duck is common to every part of the river and are found as well in the Rocky Mountains as elsewhere; in short this was the only duck we Saw within the Mountain on the Columbian waters. they feed principally on Crawfish; and are the Same in every respects as those on the Ohio and rivers in the mountains of the atlantic Ocian.

The black and white Duck are Small about the Size of the blue-winged teal, or reather larger. the mail is butifully varigated with black and white. the white occupies the Side of the head, breast and back. black the tail, large feathers of the wing, two tufts of feathers which cover the upper part of the wings when folded, the neck and head. the female is darker or has much less white about her. I take this to be the Same Species of duck common to the ohio, as also the atlantic Coast, and Sometimes called the butter box. the back is wide and Short, and as well as the legs of a dark Colour. the flesh of this duck is verry well flavored I think Superior to the Duckinmallard.

[Lewis, March 10, 1806] Monday March 10th 1806. About 1 P.M. it became fair and we sent out two parties of hunters on this side of the Netul the one below and the other above. we also directed a party to set out early in the morning and pass the bay and hunt beyond the Kilhowanackkle. from the last we have considerable hope as we have as yet hunted but little in that quarter. it blew hard all day. in the evening the Indians departed. The hunters who were over the Netull the other day informed us that they measured a pine tree, (or fir No 1) which at the hight of a man's breast was 42 feet in the girth about three feet higher, or as high as a tall man could reach, it was 40 feet in the girth which was about the circumpherence for at least 200 feet without a limb, and that it was very lofty above the commencement of the limbs. from the appearance of other trees of this speceis of fir and their account of this tree, I think it may be safely estimated at 300 feet. it had every appearance of being perfectly sound. The black and white duck are small abut the size of the blue-winged teal, or reather larger. the male is beautifully variagated with black and white. the white occupys the sides of the head, breast and back, black, the tail feathers of the wings two tufts of feathers which cover the upper part of the wings when foalded, the neck and head. the female is darker or has much less white about her. I take this to be the same speceis of duck common to the Atlantic coast, and frequently called the butterbox. the beak is wide and short, and as well as the legs, of a dark colour. the flesh of this duck is very well flavored. the brown duck is much in form like the duckinmallard, tho not much more than half it's size. the colour is an uniform mixture of yellowish and dark brown. there is nothing remarkable in the appearance of this duck it generally resorts the same kind of grassey marshes with the duckinmallard and feeds in a similar manner, on grass seed, and roots. both these ducks are common to the river for some distance above tide water as well as below. The black duck is about the size of the bluewinged teal. their colour is a duskey black the breast and belley somewhat lighter than the other parts, or a dark brown. the legs stand longitudinally with the body, and the bird when on shore stands of cours very erect. the legs and feet are of a dark brown, the toes are four on each foot, a short one at the heel and three long toes in front, which are unconnected with a web. the webs are attatched to each sides of the several joints of the toe, and divided by deep sinuses at each joint. the web assuming in the intermediate part an eliptical figure. the beak is about two inches long, streight, flated on the sides, and tapering to a sharp point. the upper chap somewhat longest, and bears on it's base at the joining of the head, a little conic protuberance of a cartelagenous substace, being redish brown at the point. the beak is of an ivory white colour. the eye dark. these ducks usually associate in large flocks, and are very noisey; their note being a sharp shrill whistle. they are usually fat and agreeably flavored; and feed principally on moss, and other vegitable productions of the water. we did not meet with them untill we reached tide-water, but I beleive them not exclusively confined to that district at all seasons, as I have noticed the same duck on many parts of the Rivers Ohio and Mississippi. the gizzard and liver are also remarkably large in this fowl. the divers are the same with those of the Atlantic States. the smaller species has some white feathers about the rump with no perceptable tail and is very active and cluck in it's motion; the body is of a redish brown. the beak sharp and somewhat curved like that of the pheasant. the toes are not connected but webed like those discribed of the black duck. the larger speceis are about the size of the teal and can flye a short distance which the small one scarcely ever attapts. they have a short tail. their colour is also an uniform brickredish brown, the beak is streight and pointed. the feet are of the same form of the other speceis and the legs are remarkably thin and flat one edge being in front. the food of both speceis is fish, and the flesh unfit for uce. the bluewinged teal are a very excellent duck, and are the same with those of the Atlantic coast.- There are some other speceis of ducks which shall be hereafter discribed as I may hereafter have an opportunity to examine them.

[Clark, March 10, 1806] Monday March 10th 1806 about 1 P.M. it became fair and we Sent out two parties of hunters on this Side of the Netul, one above and the other below, we also derected a party to Set out early in the morning and pass Meriwethers Bay and hunt beyond the Kilhow anak kle. from the last we have considerable hope, as we have as yet hunted but little in that quarter. it blew hard all day, in the evening the Indians departed. The Hunters, S. R. F. & F. who were over the netul the other day informed us that they measured a 2d tree of the fir Speces (No. i) as high as a man Could reach, was 39 feet in the girth; it tapered but very little for about 200 feet without any Considerable limbs, and that it was a very lofty above the Commmencement of the limbs. from the appearance of other Species of fir, and their account of this tree, I think it might safely estimated at 300 feet. it had every appearance of being perfectly Sound in every part

The brown Duck is much in form like the Duckinmallard, tho not much more than half it's Size. the colour is one uniform mixture of yellowish and dark brown. there is nothing remarkable in the colour of this duck; it resorts the Same kind of grassy marshes with the Duckinmallard, and feeds in a Similar manner, on grass, Seeds & roots. both these ducks are common to the river for Some distance above tide water as well as below. The black Duck is about the Size of the bluewinged teel. their colour is a duskey black the breast and belly Somewhat lighter than the other parts, or a dark brown. the legs Stand longitudianally with the body, and the Bird when on Shore Stands very erect. the legs and feet are of a dark brown, the toes are four on each foot, a short one on the heel and three long toes in front which are unconnected with a web. the web is atached to each Side of the Several joints of the toes, and devided by deep Sinuses at each joint. the web assumeing in the intermediate part an elipticle figure. the beak is about two inches long, Streight, flated on the Sides, and tapering to a Sharp point. the upper chap Somewhat longest and bears on its base at the joining of the head, a little conic protuberance of a cartelagenous Substance, being redish brown. the beak is of a ivery white colour. the eye dark. these ducks usially associate in large flocks, and are very noisey; their note being a Sharp shrill whistle. they are usially fat and tolerably flavoured; and feed on moss and other vegitable productions of the water. we did not meet with them untill we reached tide water, I have noticed the Same duck on maney parts of the ohio an Mississippi. the Gizzard and liver are also remarkably large in this fowl-. The Divers are the Same with those of the atlantic States. the Smaller Species has some white feathers about the rump and no perceptable tail and is very active and quick in its motion; the body is of a redish brown. the beak sharp and Somewhat curved like that of the Pheasant the toes are not connected but webd. like those discribed of the black duck. The large Species are about the Size of the teal &c. the food of both those Species is fish. and their flesh is unfit for use.

The bluewinged teal are a very excellent duck, and are the Same with those of the atlantic coast.- There are some other Species of ducks which Shall be hereafter discribd. as I may hereafter have an oppertunity of exameneing them.

[Lewis, March 11, 1806] Tuesday March 11th 1806. Early this morning Sergt. Pryor arrived with a small canoe loaded with fish which he had obtained from the Cathlahmah's for a very small part of the articles he had taken with him. the wind had prevented his going to the fisery on the opposite side of the river above the Wackiacums, and also as we had suspected, prevented his return as early as he would otherwise have been back.- The dogs at the Cathlahmahs had bitten the trong assunder which confined his canoe and she had gone a drift. he borrowed a canoe from the Indians in which he has returned. he found his canoe on the way and secured her, untill we return the Indians their canoe, when she can be brought back. Sent Sergt. Gass and a party in surch of a canoe which was reported to have been sunk in a small creek on the opposite side of the Netul a few miles below us, where she had been left by Shields R. Fields and Frazier when they were lately sent out to hunt over the Netul. They returned and reported that they could not find the canoe she had broken the cord by which she was attatched, and had been carried off by the tide. Drewyer Joseph Fields and Frazier set out by light this morning to pass the bay in order to hunt as they had been directed the last evening. we once more live in clover; Anchovies fresh Sturgeon and Wappetoe. the latter Sergt. Pryor had also procured and brought with him. The reptiles of this country are the rattlesnake garter snake and the common brown Lizzard. The season was so far advanced when we arrived on this side of the rocky mountains that but few rattlesnakes were seen I did not remark one particularly myself, nor do I know whether they are of either of the four speceis found in the different parts of the United states, or of that species before mentioned peculiar to the upper parts of the Missouri and it's branches. The garter snake so called in the United States is very common in this country; they are found in great numbers on the open and sometimes marshey grounds in this neighbourhood. they differ not at all from those of the U States. the black or dark brown lizzard we saw at the rock fort Camp at the commencement of the woody country below the great narrows and falls of the Columbia; they are also the same with those of the United States. The snail is numerous in the woody country on this coast; they are in shape like those of the United States, but are at least five times their bulk. There is a speceis of water lizzard of which I saw one only just above the grand rapids of the Columbia. it is about 9 inches long the body is reather flat and about the size of a mans finger covered with a soft skin of a dark brown colour with an uneven surface covered with little pimples the neck and head are short, the latter terminating in an accute angular point and flat. the fore feet each four toes, the hinder ones five unconnected with a web and destitute of tallons. it's tail was reather longer than the body and in form like that of the Musk-rat, first rising in an arch higher than the back and decending lower than the body at the extremity, and flated perpendicularly. the belley and under part of the neck and head were of a brick red every other part of the colour of the upper part of the body a dark brown. the mouth was smooth, without teeth.

[Clark, March 11, 1806] Tuesday March 11th 1806 Early this morning Sergt. Pryor arrived with a Small Canoe loaded with fish which he had obtained from the Cath-lah-mah's for a very Small part of the articles he had taken with him. the wind had prevented his going to the fishery on the opposit Side of the river above the Waukiecum's, and also as we had suspected, prevented his return as early as he otherwise would have been back. The dogs of the Cathlahmah's had bitten the throng assunder which confined his canoe and she had gorn adrift. he borrowed a Canoe from the Indians in which he has returned. he found his canoe on the way and Secured her, untill we return the Indians their Canoe- Sent Sergt. Gass and a party in Serch of one of our Canoes which was reported to have been lost from a hunting party of Shields R. Field & Frazier when they were last out on the opposit Side of the Netul. they returned and reported that they Could not find the Canoe which had broken the Cord with which it was attached, and was caried off by the tide. Drewyer Jo. Field & Frazier Set out by light this morning to pass the bay in order to hunt as they had been directed last evening. we once more live in Clover; Anchovies fresh Sturgeon and Wappatoe. the latter Sergt. Pryor had also procured a fiew and brought with him. The Deer of this Coust differ from the Common Deer, fallow Deer or Mule Deer as has beformentiond.

The Mule Deer we have never found except in rough Country; they prefer the Open Grounds and are Seldom found in the wood lands near the river; when they are met with in the wood lands or river bottoms and pursued, they imediately run to the hills or open country as the Elk do, the Contrary happens with the common Deer. there are Several differences between the mule and common deer as well as in form as in habits. they are fully a third larger in general, and the male is particularly large; think there is Somewhat greater disparity of Size between the Male and the female of this Species than there is between the male and female fallow Deer; I am Convinced I have Seen a Buck of this Species twice the volume a Buck of the Common Deer. the Ears are peculiarly large, I measured those of a large Buck which I found to be eleven inches long and 31/2 in width at the widest part; they are not so delicately formed, their hair in winter is thicker longer and of a much darker grey, in Summer the hair is Still coarser longer and of a paler red, more like that of the Elk; in winter they also have a Considerable quantity of very fine wool intermixed with the hair and lying next to the Skin as the Antelope has. the long hair which grows on the outer Side of the first joint of the hind legs, and which in the Common Deer do not usially occupy more than 2 inches in them occupy from 6 to 8; their horns also differ, those in the Common deer consist of two main beams gradually deminishing as the points proceed from it, with the mule deer the horns consist of two beams which at the distance of 4 or 6 inches from the head divide themselves into two equal branches which again either divide into two other equal branches or terminate in a Smaller, and two equal ones; haveing either 2, 4 or 6 points on a beam; the horn is not so rough about the base as the common deer, and are invariably of a much darker Colour. the most Strikeing difference of all, is the white rump and tail. from the root of the tail as a center there is a circular Spot perfectly white of about 31/2 inches radius, which occupy a part of the rump and the extremities of buttocks and joins the white of the belley underneath; the tail which is usially from 8 to 9 inches long for the first 4 or 5 inches from its upper extremity is covered with Short white hairs, much Shorter indeed than those hairs of the body; from hence for about one inch further, the hair is Still white but gradually becoms longer; the tail then termonates in a tissue of Black hair of about 3 inches long. from this black hair of the tail they have obtained among the French engages the appelation of the black tailed Deer, but this I conceive by no means Characteristic of the Animal as much the larger portion of the tail is white. the Ears and the tail of this Animale when Compared with those of the Common Deer, So well Comported with those of the Mule when compared with the Horse, that we have by way of distinction adapted the appelation of the mule Deer which I think much more appropriate. on the inner corner of each eye there is a drane (like the Elk) or large recepticle which Seams to Answer as a drane to the eye which givs it the appearance of weeping, this in the Common Deer of the Atlantic States is scercely proceptable but becoms more Conspicious in the fallow Deer, and Still more So in the Elk; this recepticle in the Elk is larger than any of the Pecora order with which I am acquainted.

I have Some reasons to believe that the Calumet Eagle is Sometimes found on this Side of the Rocky mountains from the information of the Indians in whose possession I have Seen their plumage. those are the Same with those of the Missouri, and are the most butifull of all the family of the Eagle of America it's colours are black and white with which it is butifully varigated. the feathers of the tail which is so highly prized by the Indians is composed of twelve broad feathers of equal length those are white except about two inches at the extremity which is of a jut black. their wings have each a large circular white Spot in the middle when extended. the body is variously marked with white and black. the form is much that of the Common bald Eagle, but they are reather Smaller and much more fleet. this Eagle is feared by all carnivarous birds, and on his approach all leave the carcase instantly on which they were feeding. it breads in the inaccessable parts of the Mountains where it Spends the Summer, and decends to the plains and low country in the fall and winter when it is usially Sought and taken by the nativs. two tails of this bird is esteemed by Mandans, Minnetares, Ricaras, &c. as the full value of a good horse, or Gun and accoutrements. with the Osage & Kanzas and those nations enhabiting Countrys where this bird is more rare, the price is even double of that mentioned. with these feathers the nativs deckerate the Stems of their Sacred pipes or Calumets; whence the name of Calumet Eagle, which has Generally obtained among the Engages. The Ricaras have domesticated this bird in many instances for the purpose of obtaining its plumage. the nativs in every part of the Continent who can precure those feathers attach them to their own hair and the mains and tail of their favorite horses by way of ornament. they also deckerate their own caps or bonnets with those feathers. The Leather winged bat is found &c.

[Lewis, March 12, 1806] Wednesday March 12th 1806 We sent a party again in surch of the perogue but they returned unsuccessful) as yesterday. Sent one hunter out on this side of the Netul, he did not return this evening. I beleive the Callamet Eagle is sometimes found on this side of the rocky mountains from the information of the Indians in whose possession I have seen their plumage. these are the same with those of the Missouri, and are the most beautiful) of all the family of the Eagles of America. it's colours are black and white with which it is beautifully variagated. the feathers of the tail which are so highly prized by the Indians is composed of twelve broad feathers of equal length. these are white except about 2 inches at the extremity which is of a jut black. there wings have each a large circular white spot in the middle when extended. the body is variously marked with white and black. the form is much that of the common bald Eagle, but they are reather smaller and much more fleet. this eagle is feared by all carnivorous birds, and on his approach all leave the carcase instantly on which they were feeding. it breads in the inaccessable parts of the mountains where it spends the summer, and decends to the plains and low country in the fall and winter when it is usually sought and taken by the natives. two tails of this bird is esteemed by the Mandans Minetares Ricares, &c as the full value of a good horse, or gun and accoutrements. with the Great and little Osages and those nations inhabiting countries where this bird is more rare the price is even double of that mentioned. with these feathers the natives decorate the stems of their sacred pipes or callamets; whence the name, of Callamet Eagle, which has generally obtained among the Engages. the Ricares have domesticated this bird in many instancies for the purpose of obtaining it's plumage. the natives in every part of the con tinent who can procure these feathers attatch them to their own hair and the mains and tails of their favorite horses by way of ornament. they also decorate their war caps or bonnets with those feathers.- The leather winged batt common to the United States is also found on this side of the Rocky mountains.- Beside the fish of this coast and river already mentioned we have met with the following speceis viz. the Whale, Porpus, Skaite, flounder, Salmon, red charr, two speceis of Salmon trout, mountain or speckled trout, and a speceis similar to one of those noticed on the Missouri within the mountains, called in the Eastern states, bottle-nose. I have no doubt but there are many other speceis of fish, which also exist in this quarter at different seasons of the year, which we have not had an oportunity of seeing. the shell fish are the Clam, perrewinkle, common mussle, cockle, and a speceis with a circular flat shell. The Whale is sometimes pursued harpooned and taken by the Indians of this coast; tho I beleive it is much more frequently killed by runing fowl on the rocks of the coast in violent storms and thrown on shore by the wind and tide. in either case the Indians preseve and eat the blubber and oil as has been before mentioned. the whalebone they also carefully preserve for sale.- Our party are now furnished with 358 pair of Mockersons exclusive of a good portion of dressed leather.-

[Clark, March 12, 1806] Wednesday March 12th 1806 We Sent a party again in Serch of the Canoe but they returned unsucksessfull as yesterday Sent one hunter out on this Side of the Netul he did not return this evening. Our party are now furnished with 358 par of Mockersons exclusive of a good portion of Dressed leather, they are also previded with Shirts Overalls Capoes of dressed Elk Skins for the homeward journey.

Besides the fish of this Coast and river already mentioned we have met with the following Species. viz. the Whale, Porpus, Skaite, flounder, Salmon, red-carr, two Specis of Salmon trout, mountain or Speckled trout, and a Speceis Similar to one of those noticed on the Missouri within the mountains, called in the Eastern States, bottle nose. I have no doubt but there are many other Species of fish which also exist in this quarter at different Seasons of the year, which we have not had an oppertunity of seeing. the Shell fish are the Clam, perriwinkle, common Muscle, cockle, and a Species with a circular flat Shell.

The Whale is Sometimes pursued harpooned and taken by the Indians of this Coast; tho I believe it is much more frequently killed by running on the rocks of the Coast to S. S. W. in violent Storms, and thrown on different parts of the Coast by the winds and tide-. in either case the Indians preserve and eat the blubber and Oil as has been before mentioned. the whale bone they also carefully preserve for Sale.

The Reptiles of this Country are the rattle snake, garter Snake a common brown Lizzard. The Season was so far advanced on this side of the Rocky Mountains that but fiew rattle Snakes were Seen, I did not remark one particularly my Self, nor do I know if they are of either of the four Species found in different parts of the United States, or of that Species before observed only on the upper parts of the Missouri & its branches.

The Garter Snake So Called in the U States is very common in this country, they are found in great numbers on the open and Sometimes marshy grounds in this neighbourhood. they differ not at all from those of the United States. the Black or Dark brown Lizzard we Saw at the long narrows or Commencement of the woody country on the Columbia; they are also the Same with those of the U, States. The Snail is noumerous in the woodey Country on this Coast, they are in Shape like those of the U, States, but are at least five times their bulk. there is a Specis of water Lizzard of which I only Saw one just above the grand rapid of the Columbia. it is about 9 inches long the body is reather flat and about the Size of a mans finger, covered with a Soft Skin of dark brown Colour with an uneaven sufice covered with little pimples, the neck and head are Short, the latter termonateing in an accute angular point and flat. the fore feet each have four toes, the hinder ones five unconnected with a web and destitute of tallons. it's tail was reather longer than the body, and in form like that of the muskrat, first riseing in an arch higher than the back, and decending lower than the body at the extremety, and flated perpindicularly. the belly and under part of the neck and head were of a Brick red every other part of the colour of the upper part of the body are dark brown. the mouth was Smooth without teeth.

The horns of Some of the Elk have not yet fallen off and those of others have Grown to the length of Six inches. the latter are in the best order, from which it would Seem that the pore Elk retain their horns longer.

[Lewis, March 13, 1806] Thursday March 13th 1806. This morning Drewyer Jos Feilds and Frazier returned; they had killed two Elk and two deer. visited by two Cathlahmahs who left us in the evening. we sent Drewyer down to the Clatsop village to purchase a couple of their canoes if possible. Sergt. Pryor and a party made another surch for the lost peroge but was unsuccessfull; while engaged in surching for the perogue Collins one of his party killed two Elk near the Netul below us. we sent Sergt. Ordway and a party for the flesh of one of the Elk beyond the bay with which they returned in the evening. the other Elk and two deer were at some distance. R. Fields and Thompson who set out yesterday morning on a hunting excurtion towards point Adams have not yet returned. The horns of some of the Elk have not yet fallen off, and those of others have shotten out to the length of six inches. the latter are in the best order, from which it would seem that the poor Elk retain their horns longest.

The Porpus is common on this coast and as far up the river as the water is brackish. the Indians sometimes gig them and always eat the flesh of this fish when they can procure it; to me the flavor is disagreeable. the Skaite is also common to the salt water, we have seen several of them that had perished and were thrown out on the beach by the tide. The flounder is also an inhabitant of the salt water, we have seen them also on the beach where they had been left by the tide. the Indians eat the latter and esteem it very fine. these several speceis are the same with those of the Atlantic coast. the common Salmon and red Charr are the inhabitants of both the sea and rivers. the former is usually largest and weighs from 5 to 15 lbs. it is this speceis that extends itself into all the rivers and little creeks on this side of the Continent, and to which the natives are so much indebted for their subsistence. the body of this fish is from 21/2 to 3 feet long and proportionably broad. it is covered with imbricated scales of a moderate size and is variegated with irregular black spots on it's sides and gills. the eye is large and the iris of a silvery colour the pupil black. the rostrum or nose extends beyond the under jaw, and both the upper and lower jaws are armed with a single series of long teeth which are subulate and infleted near the extremities of the jaws where they are also more closely arranged. they have some sharp teeth of smaller size and same shape placed on the tongue which is thick and fleshey. the fins of the back are two; the first is plaised nearer the head than the ventral fins and has _____ rays, the second is placed far back near the tail is small and has no rays. the flesh of this fish is when in order of a deep flesh coloured red and every shade from that to an orrange yellow, and when very meager almost white. the roes of this fish are much esteemed by the natives who dry them in the sun and preserve them for a great length of time. they are about the size of a small pea nearly transparent and of a redish yellow colour. they resemble very much at a little distance the common currants of our gardens but are more yellow. this fish is sometimes red along the sides and belley near the gills particularly the male. The red Charr are reather broader in proportion to their length than the common salmon, the skales are also imbricated but reather large. the nostrum exceeds the lower jaw more and the teeth are neither as large nor so numerous as those of the salmon. some of them are almost entirely red on the belley and sides; others are much more white than the salmon and none of them are variagated with the dark spots which make the body of the other. their flesh roes and every other particular with rispect to their form is that of the Salmon. this fish we did not see untill we decended below the grat falls of the Columbia; but whether they are exclusively confined to this portion of the river or not at all seasons, I am unable to determine.

[Clark, March 13, 1806] Thursday March 13th 1806. This morning Drewyer Jos. Fields and Frazer returned; they had killed two Elk and two deer. Visited by two Cath-lah-mars who left us in the evening. we Sent Drewyer down to the Clatsop Village to purchase a couple of their canoes if possible. Sergt. Pryor and a party made another Serch for the lost Canoe but was unsucksessfull; while engaged in Serching for the Canoe, Collins one of his party killed two Elk near the Netul below us. we Sent Sergt. Ordway and a party for the flesh of one of the Elk beyond the Bay with which they returned in the evening; the other Elk and 2 Deer were at Some distance- R. Field and Thompson who Set out on a hunting excursion yesterday morning towards point Adams have not yet returned. took equal altitudes to day this being the only fair day for Sometime past.

The Porpus is common on this coast and as far up the river as the water is brackish. the Indians Sometimes gig them and always eat the flesh of this fish when they Can precure it; to me the flavour is disagreeable. the Skaite is also common to the Salt water, I have Seen Several of them that had perished and were thrown out on the beach by the tide. The flounder is also an enhabitent of the Salt water. we have Seen them also on the beach where they had been left by the tide. the nativs eate the latter and esteem it very fine. these Several Species are the Same of those of the atlantic Coasts. The Common Salmon and red charr are the inhabitents of both the Sea and river. the former is usially largest and weighs from 5 to 15 lbs. it is this Species that extends itself into all the rivers and little creek on this Side of the Continent, and to which the nativs are So much indebted for their Subsistence. the body of this fish is from 21/2 to 3 feet long and perpotionably broad. it is covered with imbricated scales of a moderate Size and is varigated with errigular black Spots on its Side and gills. the eye is large and the iris of a Silvery colour the pupil black. the rostrum or nose extend beyond the under jaws, and both the upper and the lower jaw are armed with a Single Series of long teeth which are Subulate and infleted near the extremities of the jaws where they are more closely arranged. they have Some Sharp teeth of Smaller Size and Same Shape on the tongue which is thick and fleshey. the fins of the back are two; the first is placed nearer the head than the Venteral fins and has _____ rays, the Second is placed far back near the tail is small and has no rays. The flesh of this fish when in order of a deep flesh coloured red and every Shade from that to an orrange yellow, and when very meager almost white. the Roe of this fish are much esteemed by the nativs, who dry them in the Sun and preserve them for a great length of time. they are about the Size of a Small pea nearly transparrent and of a redish yellow colour. they resemble very much at a little distance the Common Current of our gardens but are more yellow. this fish is Sometimes red along the Sides and belly near the gills; particularly the male of this Species.

The Red Charr are reather broader in proportion to their length than the Common Salmon, the Skales are also embricated but reather large. the nostrum exceeds the lower jaw more and the teeth are neither So noumerous or large as those of the Salmon. Some of them are almost entirely red on the belly and Sides; others are much more white than the Salmon, and none of them are varigated with the dark Spots which mark the body of the other. their flesh roe and every other particular with respect to their is that of the Salmon. this fish we did not See untill we had decended below the Great falls of the Columbia; but whether they are exclusively confined to this portion of the river or not at all Seasons, I am unable to determine.

The Salmon Trout are Seldom more than two feet in length, they are narrow in purportion to their length, at least much more So than the Salmon & red charr. their jaws are nearly of the Same length, and are furnished with a Single Series of Subulate Streight teeth, not so long or so large as those of the Salmon, the mouth is wide, and the tongue is also furnished with Some teeth. the fins are placed much like those of the Salmon. at the Great Falls are met with this fish of a Silvery white colour on the belly and Sides, and a blueish light brown on the back and head. in this neighbourhood we have met with another Species which does not differ from the other in any particular except in point of Colour. this last is of a dark colour on the back, and its Sides and belley are yellow with transverse Stripes of dark brown. Sometimes a little red is intermixed with these Colours on the belly and Sides towards the head. the flesh & roe is like those described of the Salmon. the white Species which we found below the falls were in excellent order when the Salmon were entirely out of Season and not fit for use. The Species which we found here early in november on our arival in this quarter had declined considerably, reather more so than the Red charr with which we found them asociated in the little riverlets and creeks. I think it may be Safely asserted that the Red Charr and both Species of the Salmon trout remain in Season longer in the fall of the year than the common Salmon; but I have my doubt whether of the Species of the Salmon trout ever pass the Great falls of the Columbia. The Indians tell us that the Salmon begin to run early in the next month; it will be unfortunate for us if they do not, for they must form our principal dependance for food in assending the Columbia above the Falls and it's S. E. branch Lewis's river to the Mountains.

The Speckled or Mountain Trout are found in the waters of the Columbia within the Rocky mountains. they are the Same of those found in the upper part of the Missouri, but are not So abundent in the Columbian Waters as in that river. The bottle nose is also found on the waters of the Columbia within the mountains.

[Lewis, March 14, 1806] Friday March 14th 1806. This morning we sent a party after the two Elk which Collins killed last evening, they returned with them about noon. Collins, Jos. Fends and Shannon went in quest of the flock of Elk of which Collins had killed those two. this evening we heared upwards of twenty shot, and expect that they have fallen in with and killed a number of them. Reubin Fields and Thompson returned this evening unsuccessfull having killed one brant only. late in the evening Drewyer arrived with a party of the Clatsops who brought an indifferent canoe some hats and roots for sale. the hats and roots we purchased, but could not obtain the canoe without giving more than our stock of merchandize would lisence us. I offered him my laced uniform coat but he would not exchange. The Salmon Trout are seldom more than two feet in length they are narrow in proportion to their length, at least much more so than the Salmon or red charr. the jaws are nearly of the same length, and are furnished with a single series of small subulate streight teeth, not so long or as large as those of the Salmon. the mouth is wide, and the tongue is also furnished with some teeth. the fins are placed much like those of the salmon. at the great falls we met with this fish of a silvery white colour on the belley and sides, and a bluish light brown on the back and head. in this neighbourhood we have met with another speceis which dose not differ from the other in any particular except in point of colour. this last is of a dark colour on the back, and it's sides and belley are yellow with transverse stripes of dark brown. sometimes a little red is intermixed with these colours on the belley and sides towards the head. the eye, flesh, and roes are like those discribed of the Salmon. the white speceis which we found below the falls was in excellent order when the salmon were entirely out of season and not fit for uce. the speceis which we found here on our arrival early in November had declined considerably, reather more so inded than the red Charr with which we found them asociated in the little rivulets and creeks. I think it may be safely asserted that the red Charr and both speceis of the salmon trout remain in season longer in the fall of the year than the common Salmon; but I have my doubts whether either of them ever pass the great falls of the Columbia. The Indians tell us that the Salmon begin to run early in the next month; it will be unfortunate for us if they do not, for they must form our principal dependence for food in ascending the Columbia, above the falls and it's S. E. branch to the mountains. The mountain or speckled trout are found in the waters of the Columbia within the mountains. they are the same of those found in the upper part of the Missouri, but are not so abundant in the Columbia as on that river. we never saw this fish below the mountains but from the transparency and coldness of the Kooskooske I should not doubt it's existing in that stream as low as it's junction with the S E. branch of the Columbia.- The bottle nose is the same with that before mentioned on the Missouri and is found exclusively within the mountains.

[Clark, March 14, 1806] Friday March 14th 1806 This morning we dispatched a party after two Elk which Collins killed last evening, they returned with them about noon. Jos. Field, Collins, Go. Shannon & Labiesh went in quest of the Gang of Elk out of which Collins had killed the 2 yesterday. this evening we herd upwards of twenty Shot and expect they have fallen in with and killed Several of them. Reuben Field and Thompson returned this evening unsuksessfull haveing killed only one Brant. late in the evening Geo. Drewyer arrived with a party of the Clatsops who brought an indifferent Canoe, three hats and Some roots for Sale we could not purchase the Canoe without giveing more than our Stock of merchandize would lisence us. Capt Lewis offered his laced uniform Coat for a verry indiferent Canoe, agreeable to their usial way of tradeing his price was double. we are informed by the Clatsops that they have latterly Seen an Indian from the Quin-na-chart Nation who reside Six days march to the N. W and that four vessles were there and the owners Mr. Haley, Moore, Callamon & Swipeton were tradeing with that noumerous nation, whale bone Oile and Skins of various discription.

[Lewis, March 15, 1806] Saturday March 15th 1806. This morning at 11 OCk. the hunters arrived, having killed four Elk only. Labuish it seems was the only hunter who fell in with the Elk and having by some accedent lost the fore sight of his gun shot a great number of times but killed only the number mentioned. as the elk were scattered we sent two parties for them, they returned in the evening with four skins and the flesh of three Elk, that of one of them having become putrid from the liver and pluck having been carelessly left in the animal all night. we were visited this afternoon by Delashshelwilt a Chinnook Chief his wife and six women of his nation which the old baud his wife had brought for market. this was the same party that had communicated the venerial to so many of our party in November last, and of which they have finally recovered. I therefore gave the men a particular charge with rispect to them which they promised me to observe. late this evening we were also visited by Catel a Clatsop man and his family. he brought a canoe and a Sea Otter Skin for sale neither of which we purchased this evening. The Clatsops who had brought a canoe for sale last evening left us early this morning.- Bratton still sick.

There is a third speceis of brant in the neighbourhood of this place which is about the size and much the form of the pided brant. they weigh about 81/2 lbs. the wings are not as long nor so pointed as those of the common pided brant. the following is a likeness of it's head and beak. a little distance around the base of the beak is white and is suddonly succeeded by a narrow line of dark brown. the ballance of the neck, head, back, wings, and tail all except the tips of the feathers are of the bluish brown of the common wild goose. the breast and belly are white with an irregular mixture of black feathers which give that part a pided appearance. from the legs back underneath the tail, and arond the junction of the same with the body above, the feathers are white. the tail is composed of 18 feathers; the longest of which are in the center and measure 6 Inches with the barrel of the quill; those sides of the tail are something shorter and bend with their extremeties inwards towards the center of the tail. the extremities of these feathers are white. the beak is of a light flesh colour. the legs and feet which do not differ in structure from those of the goose or brant of the other speceis, are of an orrange yellow colour. the eye is small; the iris is a dark yellowish brown, and pupil black. the note of this brant is much that of the common pided brant from which in fact they are not to be distinguished at a distance, but they certainly are a distinct speis of brant. the flesh of this fowl is as good as that of the common pided brant. they not remain here during the winter in such numbers as the white brant do, tho they have now returned in considerable quantities. first saw them below tide-water.

[Clark, March 15, 1806] Saturday March 15th 1806 This morning at 11 oClock the hunters arived, haveing Killed four Elk only. Labiesh it Seams was the only Hunter who fell in with the Elk and haveing by some accident lost the foresight of his gun Shot a great number of times and only killed four. as the Elk were scattered we Sent two parties for them, they return in the evening with four Skins, and the flesh of three Elk, that of one of them haveing become putred from the liver and pluck haveing been carelessly left in the Animal all night. We were visited this Afternoon in a Canoe 4 feet 2 I. wide by De-lash-hel-wilt a Chinnook Chief his wife and Six women of his Nation, which the Old Boud his wife had brought for Market. this was the Same party which had communicated the venereal to Several of our party in November last, and of which.they have finally recovered. I therefore gave the men a particular Charge with respect to them which they promised me to observe. late this evening we were also visited by Ca-tel a Clatsop man and his family. he brought a Canoe and a Sea Otter Skin for Sale neither of which we could purchase of him. the Clatsops which had brought a Canoe for Sale last evening left us this morning. Bratten is still very weak and unwell.

There is a third Species of Brant in the neighbourhood of this place which is about the Size and much the form of the bided brant. they weigh about 81/2 lbs. the wings are not as long nor So pointed as the Common pided brant. the following is a likeness of its head and beak. a little distance arround the base of the beak is white and is Suddenly Succeeded by a narrow line of dark brown. the ballance of the neck, head, back, wings and tail all except the tips of the feathers are of the blueish brown of the Common wild goose, the breast and belly are white with an irregular mixture of black feathers which give that part a pided appearance. from the legs back underneath the tail, and around the junction of the Same with the body above, the feathers are white. the tail is composed of 18 feathers; the longest of which are in the center and measure 6 inches with the barrel of the quill; those on the Side of the tail are Something Shorter and bend with their extremities inwards towards the center of the tail. the extremities of these feathers are white. the beak is of a light flesh colour. the legs and feet which do not differ in Structure from those of the Goose or brant of the other Species, are of an orrange yellow Colour. the eye is Small; the iris is of a dark yellowish brown, and puple black. the note of this brant is much that of the common pided brant from which in fact they are not to be distinguished at a distance, but they Certainly are a distinct Species of brant. the flesh of this fowl is as good as that of the Common pided brant. they do not remain here dureing the winter in Such numbers as the white brant do, tho they have now returned in Considerable quantities. we first met with this brant on tide water.

The Clams of this coast are very Small. the Shells consist of two valves which open with a hinge, the Shell is Smooth thin and of an oval form or like that of the Common Muscle and of a Skye blue colour; it is of every Size under a Inch & 3/4 in length, and hangs in clusters to the moss of the rocks, the nativs Sometimes eate them.- The Periwinkle both of the river and Ocian are Similar to those found in the Same Situation on the Atlantic.- there is also an Animal which inhabits a Shell perfectly circular about 3 inches in diameetor, thin and entire on the marjin, convex and Smooth on the upper Side, plain on the under part and covered with a number of minute Capillary fibers by means of which it attaches itself to the Sides of the rocks. the Shell is thin and Consists of one valve. a Small circular opperture is formed in the Center of the under Shell the Animal is Soft and boneless &c.-.

[Lewis, March 16, 1806] Sunday March 16th 1806. Not any occurrence worthy of relation took place today. Drewyer and party did not return from the Cathlahmahs this evening as we expected. we suppose he was detained by the hard winds of today. the Indians remained with us all day, but would not dispose of their canoes at a price which it was in our power to give consistently with the state of our Stock of Merchandize. two handkercheifs would now contain all the small articles of merchandize which we possess; the ballance of the stock consists of 6 blue robes one scarlet do. one uniform artillerist's coat and hat, five robes made of our large flag, and a few old cloaths trimed with ribbon. on this stock we have wholy to depend for the purchase of horses and such portion of our subsistence from the Indians as it will be in our powers to obtain. a scant dependence indeed, for a tour of the distance of that before us. the Clam of this coast are very small. the shell consists of two valves which open with a hinge. the shell is smooth thin of an oval form or like that of the common mussle, and sky blue colour. it is about 11/2 inches in length, and hangs in clusters to the moss of the rocks. the natives sometimes eat them. the perewinkle both of the river and Ocean are similar to those found in the same situations on the Atlantic coast. the common mussle of the river are also the same with those in the rivers of the atlantic coast. the cockle is small and also much the same of the Atlantic. there is also an animal which inhabits a shell perfectly circular about 3 Inches in diameter, thin and entire on the margin, convex and smooth on the upper side, plain on the under part and covered with a number minute capillary fibers by means of which it attatches itself to the sides of the rocks. the shell is thin and consists of one valve. a small circular apperture is formed in the center of the under shell. the animal is soft & boneless.

The white Salmon Trout which we had previously seen only at the great falls of the Columbia has now made it's appearance in the creeks near this place. one of them was brought us today by an Indian who had just taken it with his gig. this is a likness of it; it was 2 feet 8 Inches long, and weighed 10 lbs. the eye is moderately large, the puple black and iris of a silvery white with a small addmixture of yellow, and is a little terbid near it's border with a yellowish brown. the position of the fins may be seen from the drawing, they are small in proportion to the fish. the fins are boney but not pointed except the tail and back fins which are a little so, the prime back fin and ventral ones, contain each ten rays; those of the gills thirteen, that of the tail twelve, and the small fin placed near the tail above has no bony rays, but is a tough flexable substance covered with smooth skin. it is thicker in proportion to it's width than the salmon. the tongu is thick and firm beset on each border with small subulate teeth in a single series. the teeth of the mouth are as before discribed. neither this fish nor the salmon are caught with the hook, nor do I know on what they feed.

[Clark, March 16, 1806] Sunday March 16th 1806 Not any occurrence worthy of relation took place today. Drewyer and party did not return from the Cath lah mah's this evening as we expected. we Suppose he was detained by the hard winds today. the Indians remain with us all day, but would not dispose of their Canoe at a price which it was in our power to give consistently with the State of our Stock of Merchandize. One handkerchief would contain all the Small articles of merchandize which we possess, the ballance of the Stock

Consists of 6 Small blue robes or Blankets one of Scarlet. one uniform Artillerist's Coat and hat, 5 robes made of our larg flag, and a fiew our old Clothes trimed with ribon. on this Stock we have wholy to depend for the purchase of horses and Such portion of our Subsistence from the Indians as it will be in our power to obtain. a scant dependence indeed for the tour of the distance of that before us.

The pellucid jelly like Substance, called the Sea nettle I found in great abundance along the Strand where it has been thrown up by the waves and tide, and adheres to the Sand.

There are two Species of the Fuci, or (Seawead) Seawreck which we also found thrown up by the waves. the 1st Specie at one extremity consists of a large sesicle or hollow vessale which would contain from one to 2 gallons, of a conic form, the base of which forms the extreem End and is convex and Globelar bearing on its center Some Short broad and irregular fibers. the Substance is about the consistancy of the rind of a citron Mellon and 3/4 of an inch thick, yellow celindrick, and regularly tapering the tube extends to 20 or 30 feet and is then termonated with a number of branches which are flat 1/2 inch in width, rough particularly on the edges, where they are furnished with a number of little oval vesicles or bags of the Size of a Pigions egg. this plant Seams to be calculated to float at each extremity, while the little end of the tube from whence the branches proceed, lies deepest in the water.

The white Salmon Trout which we had previously seen only at the Great Falls of the Columbia, or a little below the Great Falls, has now made its appearance in the creeks near this place. one of them was brought us to day by an indian who had just taken it with his gig. This is a likeness of it; it was 2 feet 8 inches long, and weighed ten pounds. the eye is moderately large, the puple black with a Small admixture of yellow and the iris of a Silvery white with a Small admixture of yellow and a little tirbed near its border with a yellowish brown. the position of the fins may be seen from the drawing, they are small in perpotion to the fish. the fins are honey but not pointed except the tail and back fins which are a little So, the prime back fin and venteral ones, contain each ten rays; those of the gills twelve, and the Small Finn placed near the tail above has no long rays, but is a tough flexable Substance covered with Smooth Skin. it is thicker in perpotion to it's width than the Salmons. the tongue is thick and firm beset on each border with small subulate teeth in a Single Series. the Teeth of the mouth are as before discribed. neither this fish nor the Salmon are cought with the hook, nor do I know on what they feed.-now begin to run &c. &c.

[Lewis, March 17, 1806] Monday March 17th 1806. Catel and his family left us this morning. Old Delashelwilt and his women still remain they have formed a camp near the fort and seem to be determined to lay close sege to us but I beleive notwithstanding every effort of their wining graces, the men have preserved their constancy to the vow of celibacy which they made on this occasion to Capt C. and myself. we have had our perogues prepared for our departer, and shal set out as soon as the weather will permit. the weather is so precarious that we fear by waiting untill the first of April that we might be detained several days longer before we could get from this to the Cathlahmahs as it must be calm or we cannot accomplish that part of our rout. Drewyer returned late this evening from the Cathlahmahs with our canoe which Sergt. Pryor had left some days since, and also a canoe which he had purchased from those people. for this canoe he gave my uniform laced coat and nearly half a carrot of tobacco. it seems that nothing excep this coat would induce them to dispose of a canoe which in their mode of traffic is an article of the greatest value except a wife, with whom it is equal, and is generally given in exchange to the father for his daughter. I think the U States are indebted to me another Uniform coat, for that of which I have disposed on this occasion was but little woarn.- we yet want another canoe, and as the Clatsops will not sell us one at a price which we can afford to give we will take one from them in lue of the six Elk which they stole from us in the winter.-

The pellucid jellylike substance, called the sea-nettle is found in great abundance along the strad where it has been thrown up by the waves and tide.

There are two speceis of the Fuci or seawreckwhich we also find thrown up by the waves. the 1st speceis at one extremity consists of a large vesicle or hollow vessell which would contain from one to two gallons, of a conic form, the base of which forms the extreem end and is convex and globelar bearing on it's center some short broad and irregular fibers. the substance is about the consistence of the rind of a citron mellon and 3/4 of an inch thick. the rihind is smooth. from the small extremity of the cone a long, hollow, celindrick, and regularly tapering tube extends to 20 or thirty feet and is then terminated with a number of branches which are flat 1/2 an inch in width rough particular on the edges where they are furnished with a number of little ovate vesicles or bags of the size of a pigeon's egg. this plant seems to be calculated to float at each extremity while the little end of the tube from whence the branches proceed, lies deepest in the water.

The other speceis I have never seen but Capt. Clark who saw it on the coast towards the Killamucks informed me that it resembled a large pumpkin, it is solid and it's specific gravity reather greater than the water, tho it is sometimes thrown out by the waves. it is of a yellowis brown colour. the rhind smooth and consistence harder than that of a pumpkin tho easily cut with a knife. there are some dark brown fibers reather harder than any other part which pass longitudinally through the pulp or fleshey substance wich forms the interior of this marine production.The following is a list of the names of the commanders of vessels who visit the entrance of the Columbia river in the spring and autumn fror the purpose of trading with the natives or hunting Elk. these names are spelt as the Indians pronounce them.

Mr. Haley, their favorite trader visits them in a vessel with three masts, and continues some time

Youens, visits in a 3 masted vessel- Trader Tallamon do. 3 do. no trader Callallamet do. 3 do. Trader. has a wooden leg. Swipton do. 3 do. Trader. Moore do. 4 do. do. Mackey do. 3 do. do. Washington do. 3 do. do. Mesship do. 3 do. do. Davidson do. 2

no trader hunts Elk Jackson do. 3 masted vessel Trader Bolch do. 3 do. do. Skelley do. 3 do. do. tho he has been gone some years. he has one eye.

[Clark, March 17, 1806] Monday March 17th 1806 Catel and his family left us this morning. Old Delashelwill and his women still remain, they have formed a Camp near the fort and Seam determined to lay Close Sege to us, but I believe notwithstanding every effort of their wining graces, the men have preserved their constancy to the vow of celibacy which they made on this Occasion to Capt L. and my self. we have had our Canoes prepared for our departure, and Shall Set out as Soon as the weather will permit. the weather is So precarious that we fear by waiting untill the first of April that we might be detained Several days longer before we could get from this to the Cath-lah-mahs, as it must be Calm or we cannot accomplish that part of the rout in our Canoes. Drewyer returned late this evening from the Cath-lah-mahs with our Indian Canoe which Sergt. Pryor had left Some days since, and also a Canoe, which he had purchased from those people. for this canoe he gave Captn. Lewis's uniform laced coat and nearly half a Carrot of to-bacco. it Seams that nothing except this Coat would induce them to dispose of a Canoe which in their mode of traffic is an article of the greatest value except a wife, with whome it is nearly equal, and is generally given in exchange to the father for his Daughter. I think that the United States are injustice indebted to Captn Lewis another uniform Coat for that of which he has disposed of on this ocasion, it was but little worn.

We yet want another Canoe as the Clatsops will not Sell us one, a proposition has been made by one of our interpt and Several of the party to take one in lieu of 6 Elk which they Stole from us this winter &c.

[Lewis, March 18, 1806] Tuesday March 18th 1806. Drewyer was taken last night with a violent pain in his side. Capt. Clark blead him. several of the men are complaining of being unwell. it is truly unfortunate that they should be sick at the moment of our departure. we directed Sergt. Pryor to prepare the two Canoes which Drewyer brought last evening for his mess. they wanted some knees to strengthen them and several cracks corked and payed. he completed them except the latter operation which the frequent showers in the course of the day prevented as the canoes could not be made sufficiently dry even with the assistance of fire. Comowooll and two Cathlahmahs visited us today; we suffered them to remain all night. this morning we gave Delashelwilt a certificate of his good deportment &c. and also a list of our names, after which we dispatched him to his village with his female band. These lists of our names we have given to several of the natives and also paisted up a copy in our room. the object of these lists we stated in the preamble of the same as follows (viz) "The object of this list is, that through the medium of some civilized person who may see the same, it may be made known to the informed world, that the party consisting of the persons whose names are hereunto annexed, and who were sent out by the government of the U States in May 1804 to explore the interior of the Continent of North America, did penetrate the same by way of the Missouri and Columbia Rivers, to the discharge of the latter into the Pacific Ocean, where they arrived on the 14th November 1805, and from whence they departed the ____ day of March 1806 on their return to the United States by the same rout they had come out."- on the back of some of these lists we added a sketch of the connection of the upper branches of the Missouri with those of the Columbia, particularly of it's main S. E. branch, on which we also delienated the track we had come and that we meant to pursue on our return where the same happened to vary. There seemed so many chances against our government ever obtaining a regular report, though the medium of the savages and the traders of this coast that we declined making any. our party are also too small to think of leaving any of them to return to the U States by sea, particularly as we shall be necessarily divided into three or four parties on our return in order to accomplish the objects we have in view; and at any rate we shall reach the United States in all human probability much earlier than a man could who must in the event of his being left here depend for his passage to the United States on the traders of the coast who may not return immediately to the U States or if they should, might probably spend the next summer in trading with the natives before they would set out on their return. this evening Drewyer went inquest of his traps, and took an Otter. Joseph Fields killed an Elk.- The Indians repeated to us the names of eighteen distinct tribes residing on the S. E. coast who spoke the Killamucks language, and beyound those six others who spoke a different language which they did not comprehend.

[Clark, March 18, 1806] Tuesday March 17th 1806 Drewyer was taken last night with a violent pain in his Side. I bled him. Several of the men are complaining of being unwell. it is truly unfortunate that they Should be Sick at the moment of our departure. Derected Sergt. Pryor to prepare the two Indian Canoes which we had purchased for his mess. they wanted Some knees to Strengthen them, and Several cracks corked and payed. he compleated them except paying. the frequent Showers of rain prevented the Canoes drying Sufficient to pay them even with the assistance of fire.

Commorwool and two Cathlahmahs visited us to day; we Suffered them to remain all night. this morning we gave Delashelwilt a certificate of his good deportment &c. and also a list of our names, after which we dispatched him to his village with his female band. Those list's of our Names we have given to Several of the nativs, and also pasted up a Copy in our room. the Object of these lists we Stated in the preamble of the Same as follows Viz: "The Object of this list is, that through the medium of Some civilized person who may See the Same, it may be made known to the informed world, that the party consisting of the persons whoes names are hereunto annexed, and who were Sent out by the Government of the United States in May 1804, to explore the interior of the Continent of North America, did penetrate the Same by way of the Missouri and Columbia rivers, to the discharge of the latter into the Pacific Ocian, where they arrived on the 14th of November 1805, and from whence they departed the _____ day of March 1806 on their return to the United States by the Same rout they had come out."

On the back of lists we added a Sketch of the continent of the upper branches of the Missouri with those of the Columbia, particularly of its upper N. E. branch or Lewis's River, on which we also delienated the track we had Came and that we ment to pursue on our return, when the Same happened to vary. There Seemes So many chances against our governments ever obtaining a regular report, through the medium of the Savages, and the traders of this Coast that we decline makeing any. Our party are too small to think of leaveing any of them to return to the Unt. States by Sea, particularly as we Shall be necessarily devided into two or three parties on our return in order to accomplish the Object we have in View; and at any rate we Shall reach the U, States in all humain probabillity much earlier than a man Could who must in the event of his being left here depend for his passage to the U, State on the traders of the Coast, who may not return imediately to the U, States. or if they should, might probably Spend the next Summer in tradeing with the nativs before they would Set out on their return. This evening Drewyer went in quest of his traps, and took an otter. Joseph Field killd and Elk.- The Indians repeated to us Eighteen distinct Nations resideing on the S S. E Coast who Speak the Kil a mox language or understand it. and beyond those Six other Nations which Speak a different language which they did not comprehend.

The 2d Species of Seawreck which I saw on the coast to the S. S. E. near the Kil a mox nation. it resembles a large pumpkin, it is Solid and it's Specific Gravity reather greater than the water, tho it is Sometimes thrown out by the waves. it is of a pale yellowish brown colour. the rhind Smooth and consistency harder than that of the pumpkin, tho easily cut with a knife. there are Some fibers of a lighter colour and much harder than any other part which pass Longitudinally through the pulp or fleshey Substance which forms the interior of this marine production—

[Lewis, March 19, 1806] Wednesday March 19th 1806. It continued to rain and hail today in such manner that nothing further could be done to the canoes. a pratry were sent out early after the Elk which was killed yesterday with which they returned in the course of a few hours. we gave Comowooll alias Connia, a cirtificate of his good conduct and the friendly intercourse which he has maintained with us during our residence at this place; we also gave him a list of our names.do not. The Killamucks, Clatsops, Chinnooks, Cathlahmahs and Wac-ki-a-cums resemble each other as well in their persons and dress as in their habits and manners.- their complexion is not remarkable, being the usual copper brown of most of the tribes of North America. they are low in statue reather diminutive, and illy shapen; possessing thick broad flat feet, thick ankles, crooked legs wide mouths thick lips, nose moderately large, fleshey, wide at the extremity with large nostrils, black eyes and black coarse hair. their eyes are sometimes of a dark yellowish brown the puple black. I have observed some high acqualine noses among them but they are extreemty rare. the nose is generally low between the eyes.- the most remarkable trait in their physiognomy is the peculiar flatness and width of forehead which they artificially obtain by compressing the head between two boards while in a state of infancy and from which it never afterwards perfectly recovers. this is a custom among all the nations we have met with West of the Rocky mountains. I have observed the heads of many infants, after this singular bandage had been dismissed, or about the age of 10 or eleven months, that were not more than two inches thick about the upper edge of the forehead and reather thiner still higher. from the top of the head to the extremity of the nose is one streight line. this is done in order to give a greater width to the forehead, which they much admire. this process seems to be continued longer with their female than their mail children, and neither appear to suffer any pain from the operation. it is from this peculiar form of the head that the nations East of the Rocky mountains, call all the nations on this side, except the Aliahtans or snake Indians, by the generic name of Flat heads. I think myself that the prevalence of this custom is a strong proof that those nations having originally proceeded from the same stock. The nations of this neighbourhood or those recapitulated above, wear their hair loosly flowing on the back and sholders; both men and women divide it on the center of the crown in front and throw it back behind the ear on each side. they are fond of combs and use them when they can obtain them; and even without the aid of the comb keep their hair in better order than many nations who are in other rispects much more civilized than themselves.- the large or apparently swolen legs particularly observable in the women are obtained in a great measure by tying a cord tight around the ankle. their method of squating or resting themselves on their hams which they seem from habit to prefer to siting, no doubt contributes much to this deformity of the legs by preventing free circulation of the blood. the dress of the man consists of a smal robe, which reaches about as low as the middle of the thye and is attatched with a string across the breast and is at pleasure turned from side to side as they may have occasion to disencumber the right or left arm from the robe entirely, or when they have occasion for both hands, the fixture of the robe is in front with it's corners loosly hanging over their arms. they sometimes wear a hat which has already been discribed. this robe is made most commonly of the skins of a small animal which I have supposed was the brown mungo, tho they have also a number, of the skins of the tiger cat, some of those of the Elk which are used principally on their war excursions, others of the skins of the deer panther and bear and a blanket wove with the fingers of the wool of the native sheep. a mat is sometimes temperarily thrown over the sholders to protect them from rain. they have no other article of cloathing whatever neither winter nor summer. and every part except the sholders and back is exposed to view. they are very fond of the dress of the whites, which they wear in a similar manner when they can obtain them, except the shoe which I have never seen woarn by any of them. they call us pah-shish'e-ooks, or cloth men. The dress of the women consists of a robe, tissue, and sometimes when the weather is uncommonly cold, a vest. their robe is much smaller than that of the men, never reaching lower than the waist nor extending in front sufficiently far to cover the body. it is like that of the men confined across the breast with a string and hangs loosly over the sholders and back. the most esteemed and valuable of these robes are made of strips of the skins of the Sea Otter net together with the bark of the white cedar or silk-grass. these strips are first twisted and laid parallel with each other a little distance assunder, and then net or wove together in such manner that the fur appears equally on both sides, and unites between the strands. it make a warm and soft covering. other robes are formed in a similar manner of the skin of the Rackoon, beaver &c. at other times the skin is dressed in the hair and woarn without any further preperation. in this way one beaver skin, or two of those of the Raccoon or tiger catt forms the pattern of the robe. the vest is always formed in the manner first discribed of their robes and covers the body from the armpits to the waist, and is confined behind, and destitute of straps over the sholder to keep it up. when this vest is woarn the breast of the woman is concealed, but without it which is almost always the case, they are exposed, and from the habit of remaining loose and unsuspended grow to great length particularly in aged women in many of whom I have seen the hubby reach as low as the waist. The garment which occupys the waist, and from thence as low as nearly to the knee before and the ham, behind, cannot properly be denominated a petticoat, in the common acceptation of that term; it is a tissue of white cedar bark, bruised or broken into small shreds, which are interwoven in the middle by means of several cords of the same materials, which serve as well for a girdle as to hold in place the shreds of bark which form the tissue, and which shreds confined in the middle hang with their ends pendulous from the waist, the whole being of sufficient thickness when the female stands erect to conceal those parts usually covered from formiliar view, but when she stoops or places herself in many other attitudes, this battery of Venus is not altogether impervious to the inquisitive and penetrating eye of the amorite. This tissue is sometimes formed of little twisted cords of the silk grass knoted at their ends and interwoven as discribed of the bark. this kind is more esteemed and last much longer than those of bark. they also form them of flags and rushes which are woarn in a similar manner. the women as well as the men sometimes cover themselves from the rain by a mat woarn over the sholders. they also cover their heads from the rain sometimes with a common water cup or basket made of the cedar bark and beargrass. these people seldom mark their skins by puncturing and introducing a colouring matter. such of them as do mark themselves in this manner prefer their legs and arms on which they imprint parallel lines of dots either longitudinally or circularly. the women more frequently than the men mark themselves in this manner.

The favorite ornament of both sexes are the common coarse blue and white beads which the men wear tightly wound arond their wrists and ankles many times untill they obtain the width of three or more inches. they also wear them in large rolls loosly arond the neck, or pendulous from the cartelage of the nose or rims of the ears which are purforated for the purpose. the women wear them in a similar manner except in the nose which they never purforate. they are also fond of a species of wampum which is furnished them by a trader whom they call Swipton. it seems to be the native form of the shell without any preperation. this shell is of a conic form somewhat curved, about the size of a raven's quill at the base, and tapering to a point which is sufficiently large to permit to hollow through which a small thred passes; it is from one to 11/2 Inches in length, white, smooth, hard and thin. these are woarn in the same manner in which the beads are; and furnish the men with their favorite ornament for the nose. one of these shells is passed horizontally through the cartilage of the nose and serves frequently as a kind of ring to prevent the string which suspends other ornaments at the same part from chafing and freting the flesh. the men sometimes wear collars of bears claws, and the women and children the tusks of the Elk variously arranged on their necks arms &c. both males and females wear braslets on their wrists of copper brass or Iron in various forms. I think the most disgusting sight I have ever beheld is these dirty naked wenches. The men of these nations partake of much more of the domestic drudgery than I had at first supposed. they collect and prepare all the fuel, make the fires, assist in cleansing and preparing the fish, and always cook for the strangers who visit them. they also build their houses, construct their canoes, and make all their wooden utensils. the peculiar provence of the woman seems to be to collect roots and manufacture various articles which are prepared of rushes, flags, cedar bark, bear grass or waytape. the management of the canoe for various purposes seems to be a duty common to both sexes, as also many other occupations which with most Indian nations devolves exclusively on the woman. their feasts which they are very fond are always prepared and served by the men.

Comowool and the two Cathlahmahs left us this evening. it continued to rain so constantly today that Sergt. Pryor could not pitch his canoes.

[Clark, March 19, 1806] Wednesday March 19th 1806 Inds. Descd. It continued to rain and hail in Such a manner that nothing Could be done to the Canoes. a party were Sent out early after the Elk which was killed last evening, with which they returned in the Course of a fiew hours, we gave Commorwool alias Cania, a Certificate of his good conduct and the friendly intercourse which he has maintained with us dureing our residence at this place; we also gave him a list of our names &c.- The Kilamox, Clatsops, Chinnooks, Cath lah mahs Wau ki a cum and Chiltz I-resemble each other as well in their persons and Dress as in their habits and manners.- their complexion is not remarkable, being the usial Copper brown of the tribes of North America. they are low in Statue reather diminutive, and illy Shaped, possessing thick broad flat feet, thick ankles, crooked legs, wide mouths, thick lips, noses Stuk out and reather wide at the base, with black eyes and black coarse hair.

I have observed Some high acqualine noses among them but they are extreemly reare. the most remarkable trate in their physiognamy is the peculiar flatness and width of the forehead which they Artificially obtain by compressing the head between two boards while in a State of infancy, and from which it never afterwards perfectly recovers. This is a custom among all the nations, we have met with West of the Rocky Mountains. I have observed the head of maney infants, after this Singular Bandage had been dismissed, or about the age of 11 or 12 months, that were not more than two inches thick about the upper part of the forehead and reather thiner Still higher. from the top of the head to the extremity of the nose is one Streight line. this is done in order to give a greater width to the forehead, which they much admire. This process seams to be continued longer with their female than their male children, and neither appears to Suffer any pain from the opperation. it is from this peculiar form of the head that the nations East of the Rocky Mountains, call all the nations on this Side, except Aliahtans, So-so-ne, or Snake Indians by the General name of Flat Heads. I think my Self that the provalence of this custom is a Strong proof of those nations haveing originally proceeded from the Same Stock. The nations of this neighbourhood or those recpitulated above, ware their hair loosly flowing on their back and Sholders; both men and women divide it on the Center of the Crown in front and throw it back behind the ear on each Side. they are fond of Combs and use them when they Can obtain them; and even without the aid of Combs keep their in better order, than inaney nations who are in other respects much more Civilized than themselves.

The large or apparently Sweled legs particularly observable in the women, are obtained in a great measure by tying a cord tight around the leg above the ancle bone. their method of Squating or resting themselves on their hams which they Seam from habit to prefer to Setting, no doubt contributes much to this deformity of the legs by preventing free circulation of the blood. This is also the Custom of the nations above.

The dress of the men like those above on the Columbia river Consists of a Small robe, which reaches about as low as the middle of the thye and is attatched with a String across the breast and is at pleasure turned from Side to Side as they may have an occasion to disincumber the right or left arm from the robe entirely, or when they have occasion for both hands, the fixture of the robe is in front with it's corner loosly hanging over their Arms. they Sometimes wear a hat which have already been discribed (See 29th Jany.) Their Robes are made most commonly of the Skins of a Small animal which I have Supposed was the brown mungo, tho they have also a number of the Skins of the tiger Cat, Some of those of the Elk which are used principally on their war excursions, others of the Skins of Deer, panthor, Bear, and the Speckle Loon, and blankets wove with the fingers of the wool of the native Sheep. and Some of those on the Sea Coast have robes of Beaver and the Sea Otter. a mat is Sometimes temperaly thrown over the Sholders to protect them from rain. they have no other article of Cloathing whatever neither winter nor Summer, and every part except the Sholders and back is exposed to view. they are very fond of the dress of the whites, which they ware in a Similar manner when they Can obtain them, except the Shoe or mockerson which I have never Seen worn by any of them. They Call us pah-shish-e-ooks or Cloath men. The dress of the women consists of a roab, tissue, and Sometimes when the weather is uncommonly Cold, a vest. their robe is much Smaller than that of the men, never reaching lower than the waist nor extending in front Sufficiently far to cover the body. it is like that of the men confined across the breast with a String and hangs loosely over the Sholders and back. the most esteemed & valuable of those robes are made of Strips of the Skin of the Sea Otter net together with the bark of the white Cedar or Silk grass. these fish are first twisted and laid parallel with each other a little distance asunder, and then net or wove together in Such a manner that the fur appears equally on both Sides, and united between the Strands. it makes a worm and Soft covering. other robes are formed in a Similar manner of the Skins of the rackoon, beaver &c. at other times the Skins is dressed in the hair and worn without any further preperation. in this way one beaver Skin or two of the rackoon or one of the tiger Cat forms a vest and Covers the body from the Armpits to the waist, and is confined behind, and destitute of Straps over the Sholder to keep it up. when this vest is worn the breast of the woman in consealed, but without it which is almost always the case, they are exposed, and from the habit of remaining loose and unsuspended grow to great length, particularly in aged women, on many of whome I have Seen the bubby reach as low as the waist. The petticoat or tissue which occupies the waiste has been already described (See 7th Novr. 1805) formd. of the Bark of white cedar, Silk grass, flags & rushes. The women as well as the men Sometimes cover themselves from the rain by a mat worn over the Sholders. They also Cover their heads from the rain Sometimes with a common water cup or basket made of Cedar bark and bear grass.

Those people Sometimes mark themselves by punctureing and introducing a Colouring matter. Such of them as do mark themselves in this manner prefur the legs and arms on which they imprint parallel lines of dots either longitudinally or circularly. the woman more frequently than the men mark themselves in this manner. The favorite orniments of both Sexes are the Common coarse blue and white beads as before discribed of the Chinnooks. Those beads the men wear tightly wound around their wrists and Ankles maney times untill they obtain the width of three or four inches. they also wear them in large rolls loosly around the neck, or pendulous from the cartelage of the nose or rims of the ears which are purfarated in different places round the extremities for the purpose. the woman wear them in a Similar manner except in the nose which they never purfarate. they are also fond of a Species of wompum, which is furnished by a trader whome they call Swipton. it seams to be the nativ form of the Shell without any preperation. this Shell is of a conic form Somewhat curved about the Size of a ravens quill at the base, and tapering to a point which is Sufficiently large to permit a hollow through which a Small thread passes; it is from 1 to 11/2 inches in length, white, Smooth, hard and thin these are worn in the Same manner in which the beeds are; and furnish the men with their favorite orniment for the nose. one of these Shells is passed horizontally through cartilage of the nose and Serves frequently as a kind of ring which prevents the string which Suspends other orniments at the Same part from Chafing and freting the flesh. The men Sometimes wear Collars of Bears Claws, and the women and children the tusks of the Elk variously arranged on their necks arms &c. both male and female wear bracelets on their wrists of Copper, Brass or Iron in various forms. The women Sometimes wash their faces & hands but Seldom. I think the most disgusting Sight I have ever beheld is those dirty naked wenches.

The men of those nations partake of much more of the domestic drudgery than I had at first Supposed. they Collect and prepare all the fuel, make the fires, cook for the Strangers who visit them, and assist in Cleaning and prepareing the fish. they also build their houses, construct their Canoes, and make all their wooden utensils. the peculiar province of the woman Seams to be to collect roots and manufacture various articles which are prepared of rushes, flags, Cedar bark, bear grass or way tape, also dress and manufacture the Hats & robes for Common use. the management of the Canoe for various purposes Seams to be a duty common to both Sexes, as are many other occupations which with most Indian nations devolve exclusively on the womin. their feasts of which they are very fond are always prepared and Served by the men.-.-.

it Continued to rain So constantly dureing the day that Sergt. Pryor Could not Pay his Canoes. The Clatsop Chief Commowool and the two Cath-lah-mahs left us this evening and returned to their village.

[Lewis, March 20, 1806] Thursday March 20th 1806. It continued to rain and blow so violently today that nothing could be done towards forwarding our departure. we intended to have Dispatched Drewyer and the two Fieldses to hunt near the bay on this side of the Cathlahmahs untill we jounded them from hence, but the rain rendered our departure so uncertain that we declined this measure for the present. nothing remarkable happened during the day. we have yet several days provision on hand, which we hope will be sufficient to subsist us during the time we are compelled by the weather to remain at this place.

Altho we have not fared sumptuously this winter and spring at Fort Clatsop, we have lived quite as comfortably as we had any reason to expect we should; and have accomplished every object which induced our remaining at this place except that of meeting with the traders who visit the entrance of this river. our salt will be very sufficient to last us to the Missouri where we have a stock in store.- it would have been very fortunate for us had some of those traders arrived previous to our departure from hence, as we should then have had it our power to obtain an addition to our stock of merchandize which would have made our homeward bound journey much more comfortable. many of our men are still complaining of being unwell; Willard and Bratton remain weak, principally I beleive for the want of proper food. I expect when we get under way we shall be much more healthy. it has always had that effect on us heretofore. The guns of Drewyer and Sergt. Pryor were both out of order. the first was repared with a new lock, the old one having become unfit for uce; the second had the cock screw broken which was replaced by a duplicate which had been prepared for the lock at Harpers ferry where she was manufactured. but for the precaution taken in bringing on those extra locks, and parts of locks, in addition to the ingenuity of John Shields, most of our guns would at this moment been untirely unfit for use; but fortunately for us I have it in my power here to record that they are all in good order.

[Clark, March 20, 1806] Thursday March 20th 1806 It continued to rain and blow so violently to day that nothing could be done towards fowarding our departure. we intended to have dispatched Drewyer & the 2 Field'es to hunt above Point William untill we joined them from hense but the rain renders our departure So uncertain that we decline this measure for the present. nothing remarkable happened dureing the day. we have yet Several days provisions on hand, which we hope will be Sufficient to Serve us dureing the time we are compell'd by the weather to remain at this place.-.

Altho we have not fared Sumptuously this winter & Spring at Fort Clatsop, we have lived quit as comfortably as we had any reason to expect we Should; and have accomplished every object which induced our remaining at this place except that of meeting with the traders who visit the enterance of this river. our Salt will be very sufficient to last us to the Missouri where we have a Stock in Store.- it would have been very fortunate for us had Some of those traders arrived previous to our departure from hence; as we Should then have had it in our power to obtain an addition to our Stock of merchandize, which would have made our homeward bound journey much more comfortable.

Maney of our men are Still Complaining of being unwell; Bratten and
Willard remain weak principally I believe for the want of proper food.
I expect when we get under way that we Shall be much more healthy. it
has always had that effect on us heretofore.

The Guns of Sergt. Pryor & Drewyer were both out of order. the first had a Cock screw broken which was replaced by a duplicate which had been prepared for the Locks at Harpers Ferry; the Second repared with a new Lock, the old one becoming unfit for use. but for the precaution taken in bringing on those extra locks, and parts of locks, in addition to the ingenuity of John Shields, most of our guns would at this moment been entirely unfit for use; but fortunate for us I have it in my power here to record that they are in good order, and Complete in every respect-

[Lewis, March 21, 1806] Friday March 21st 1806. As we could not set out we thought it best to send out some hunters and accordingly dispatched Sheilds and Collins on this side the Netul for that purpose with orders to return in the evening or sooner if they were successfull. The hunters returned late in the evening unsuccessfull. we have not now more than one day's provision on hand. we directed Drewyer and the Feildses to set out tomorrow morning early, and indevour to provide us some provision on the bay beyond point William. we were visited to day by some Clatsop indians who left us in the evening. our sick men Willard and bratton do not seem to recover; the former was taken with a violent pain in his leg and thye last night. Bratton is now so much reduced that I am somewhat uneasy with rispect to his recovery; the pain of which he complains most seems to be seated in the small of his back and remains obstinate. I beleive that it is the rheumatism with which they are both afflicted.

[Clark, March 21, 1806] Friday March 21st 1806 as we could not Set out we thought it best to Send out Some hunters and accordingly dispatched Shields and Collins on this Side of the Netul for that purpose with orders to return in the evening or Sooner if they were Successfull. they returned late in the evening unsuccessfull. we have not now more than two days provisions on hand. we derected Drewyer and the two Fieldses to Set out tomorrow morning early, and indevour to provide us Some provision on the Bay beyond point William. we were visited to day by Some Clatsops who left us in the evening. our sick men willard and Bratten do not Seem to recover; the former was taken with a violent pain in his leg and thye last night. Bratten is now so much reduced that I am Somewhat uneasy with respect to his recovery; the pain of which he complains most Seems to be Settled in the Small of his back and remains obstenate. I believe that it is the Rheumatism with which they are both affected.-.

[Lewis, March 22, 1806] Saturday March 22cd 1806. Drewyer and the Feildses departed this morning agreably to the order of the last evening. we sent out seven hunters this morning in different directions on this side the Netul. about 10 A.M. we were visited by 4 Clatsops and a killamucks; they brought some dried Anchoveis and a dog for sale which we purchased. the air is perefectly temperate, but it continues to rain in such a manner that there be is no possibility of geting our canoes completed.- at 12 OCk. we were visited by Comowooll and 3 of the Clatsops. to this Cheif we left our houses and funiture. he has been much more kind an hospitable to us than any other indian in this neighbourhood. the Indians departed in the evening. the hunters all returned except Colter, unsuccessfull. we determined to set out tomorrow at all events, and to stop the canoes temperarily with Mud and halt the first fair day and pay them. the leafing of the hucklebury riminds us of spring.

[Clark, March 22, 1806] Saturday March 22nd 1806 Drewyer and the two Fieldses departed this morning agreably to the order of last evening. we Sent out Six hunters this morning in different directions on both Sides of the Netul. about 10 A.M. we were visited by Que-ne-o alias Commorwool 8 Clatsops and a Kil-a-mox; they brought Some dried Anchovies, a common Otter Skin and a Dog for Sale all of which we purchased. the Dog we purchased for our Sick men, the fish for to add to our Small Stock of provision's, and the Skin to cover my papers. those Indians left us in the evening. the air is perfectly temperate, but it continues to rain in Such a manner that there is no possibillity of getting our canoes completed in order to Set out on our homeward journey. The Clatsops inform us that Several of their nation has the Sore throat, one of which has laterly died with this disorder. the Hunters Sent out to day all returned except Colter unsessfull.

[Lewis, March 23, 1806] Sunday March 23rd 1806. Half after 9 A.M. Colter arrived, having killed one Elk but so distant that we could not send for the meat and get arround Point William today, we therefore prefered seting out and depending on Drewyer and the hunters we have sent forward for meat. the wind is pretty high but it seems to be the common opinion that we can pass point William. we accordingly distributed the baggage and directed the canoes to be launched and loaded for our departure.- at 1 P.M. we bid a final adieu to Fort Clatsop. we had not proceeded more than a mile before we met Delashelwilt and a party of 20 Chinooks men and women. this Cheif leaning that we were in want of a canoe some days past, had brought us one for sale, but being already supplyed we did not purchase it. I obtained one Sea Otter skin from this party. at a 1/4 before three we had passed Meriwethers bay and commenced coasting the difficult shore; at 1/2 after five we doubled point William, and at 7 arrived in the mouth of a small creek where we found our hunters. they had killed 2 Elk, at the distance of a mile & 1/2. it was too late to send after it this evening. we therefore encamped on the Stard side of the Creek. the wind was not very hard.

[Clark, March 23, 1806] Sunday 23rd March 1806 This morning proved So raney and uncertain that we were undeturmined for Some time whether we had best Set out & risque the river which appeared to be riseing or not. Jo. Colter returned haveing killed an Elk about 3 miles towards Point Adams. the rained Seased and it became fair about Meridean, at which time we loaded our Canoes & at 1 P.M. left Fort Clatsop on our homeward bound journey. at this place we had wintered and remained from the 7th of Decr. 1805 to this day and have lived as well as we had any right to expect, and we can Say that we were never one day without 3 meals of Some kind a day either pore Elk meat or roots, not withstanding the repeeted fall of rain which has fallen almost Constantly Since we passed the long narrows on the _____ of Novr. last indeed we have had only _____ days fair weather since that time. Soon after we had Set out from Fort Clatsop we were met by De lash el wilt & 8 men of the Chinnooks, and Delashelwilts wife the old bond and his Six Girls, they had, a Canoe, a Sea otter Skin, Dried fish and hats for Sale, we purchased a Sea otter Skin, and proceeded on, thro Meriwethers Bay, there was a Stiff breese from the S. W. which raised Considerable Swells around Meriwethers point which was as much as our Canoes Could ride. above point William we came too at the Camp of Drewyer & the 2 Field's. they had killed 2 Elk which was about 11/2 miles distant. here we Encampd. for the night having made 16 miles.

[Lewis, March 24, 1806] Monday March 24th 1806. This morning we sent out a party of 15, at light, for the meat, and concluded to take breakfast before we set out. they soon returned. we breakfasted and set out at 1/2 after 9 A.M. Saw a white woodpecker with a red head of the small kind common to the United States; this bird has but lately returned. they do not remain during the winter. the country thick and heavily timbered. we saw very few waterfowl today, not a single swan, white brant nor a small goose is to be seen. a few Cormorant, duckinmallard, butterbox, and common large geese were only to be found the tide being out this morning we found some difficulty in passing through the bay below the Cathlahmah village; this side of the river is very shallow to the distance of 4 miles from the shore tho there is a channel sufficient for canoes near S. side. at 1 P.M. we arrived at the Cathlahmah village where we halted and purchased some wappetoe, a dog for the sick, and a hat for one of the men. on one of the seal Islands opposite to the village of these people thy have scaffolded their dead in canoes elivating them above tidewater mark. these people are very fond of sculpture in wood of which they exhibit a variety of specemines about their houses. the broad peices supporting the center of the roof and those through which the doors are cut, seem to be the peices on which they most display their taist. I saw some of these which represented human figures setting and supporting the burthen on their sholders. at half after 3 P.M. we set out and continued our rout among the seal Islands; not paying much attention we mistook our rout which an Indian perceiving pursued overtook us and put us in the wright channel. this Cathlahmah claimed the small canoe which we had taken from the Clatsops. however he consented very willingly to take an Elk's skin for it which I directed should be given him and he immediately returned. we continued our rout along the South side of the river and encamped at an old village of 9 houses opposite to the lower Wackkiacum village. the night was cold tho wood was abundant after dark two Chinnook men came to us in a small canoe. they remained with us all night. came 15 miles today.

[Clark, March 24, 1806] Monday 24th of March 1806 Sent out 15 men verry early this morning for the flesh of the two Elk killed by Drewyer and Fields yesterday. they returned at 8 oClock, after taking a Slight brackfast we Set out at half past 9 a.m. and proceeded to the Cath lah mah Village at 1 P.M. and remained untill 1/2 after 3 p.m.at this village we purchased a fiew wappato and a Dog for our Sick men Willard and Bratten who are yet in a weak State. at this Village I saw two very large elegant Canoes inlaid with Shills, those Shills I took to be teeth at first View, and the nativs informed Several of the men that they the teeth of their enemies which they had killed in War. in examineing of them Closely haveing taken out Several pices, we found that were Sea Shells which yet contained a part of the iner ____ they also deckerate their Smaller wooden vessles with those Shells which have much the appearance of humane teeth, Capt Cook may have mistaken those Shills verry well for humane teeth without a Close examination. The Village of these people is the dirtiest and Stinkingest place I ever Saw in any Shape whatever, and the inhabitants partake of the carrestick of the Village. we proceeded on through Some difficult and narrow Channels between the Seal Islands, and the South Side to an old village on the South Side opposit to the lower War ki a com village, and Encamped. to this old villg. a very considerable deposit of the dead at a Short distance below, in the usial and Customary way of the nativs of this Coast in Canoes raised from the ground as before described. Soon after we made our Camp 2 Indians visited us from the opposit Side, one of them Spoke Several words of English and repeeted the names of the traders, and maney of the Salors. made 16 Miles

[Lewis, March 25, 1806] Tuesday March 25th 1806. The morning being disagreeably cold we remained and took break-fast. at 7 A.M. we set out and continued our rout along the South Coast of the river against the wind and a strong current, our progress was of course but slow. at noon we halted and dined. here some Clatsops came to us in a canoe loaded with dryed anchovies, which they call Olthen, Wappetoe and Sturgeon. they informed us that they had been up on a trading voyage to the Skillutes.- I observe that the green bryer which I have previously mentioned as being common on this river below tide water retains it's leaves all winter.- the red willow and seven bark begin to put fourth their leaves.- after dinner we passed the river to a large Island 2 and continued our rout allong the side of the same about a mile when we arrived at a Cathlahmah fishing cam of one lodge; here we found 3 men 2 women and a couple of boys, who from appearances had remained here some time for the purpose of taking sturgeon, which they do by trolling. they had ten or douzen very fine sturgeon which had not been long taken. we offered to purchase some of their fish but they asked us such an extravegant price that we declined purchase. one of the men purchased a sea Otterskin at this lodge, for which he gave a dressed Elkskin and an handkercheif. near this lodge we met some Cathlahmahs who had been up the river on a fishing excurtion. they had a good stock of fish on board, but did not seem disposed to sell them. we remained at this place about half an hour and then continued our rout up the Island to it's head and passed to the south side. the wind in the evening was very hard. it was with some difficulty that we could find a spot proper for an encampment, the shore being a swamp for several miles back; at length late in the evening opposite to the place we had encamped on the 6th of November last; we found the entrance of a small creek which afforded us a safe harbour from the wind and encamped. the ground was low and moist tho we obtained a tolerable encampment. here we found another party of Cathlahmahs about 10 in number who had established a temperary residence for the purpose of fishing and taking seal. they had taken a fine parcel of sturgeon and some seal. they gave us some of the fleese of the seal which I found a great improvement to the poor Elk. here we found Drewyer and the Feildses who had been seperated from us since morning; they had passed on the North side of the large Island which was much nearer. the bottom lands are covered with cottonwood, the growth with a broad leaf which resembles ash except the leaf. the underbrush red willow, broad leafed willow, sevenbark, goosburry, green bryer & the larged leafed thorn; the latter is now in bloom; the natives inform us that it bears a freut about an inch in diameter which is good to eat.

[Clark, March 25, 1806] Tuesday 25th of March 1806 Last night and this morning are cool wend hard a head and tide going out, after an early brackfast we proceeded on about 4 miles and came too on the South Side to worm and dry our Selves a little. Soon after we had landed two Indians Came from a War kia cum village on the opposit Side with 2 dogs and a fiew Wappato to Sell neither of which we bought. Som Clatsops passed down in a Canoe loaded with fish and Wappato. as the wind was hard a head and tide against us we Concluded to delay untill the return of the tide which we expected at 1 oClock, at which hour we Set out met two Canoes of Clatsops loaded with dried anchovies and Sturgion which they had taken and purchased above we crossed over to an Island on which was a Cath lahmah fishing Camp of one Lodge; here we found 3 man two woman and a couple of boys who must have for Some time for the purpose of taking Sturgeon which they do by trolling. they had 10 or 12 very fine Sturgeon which had not been long taken; we wished to purchase some of their fish but they asked Such extravegant prices that we declined purchaseing. one of our Party purchased a Sea otter Skin at this Lodge for which he gave a dressed Elk Skin & a Handkerchief. we remained at this place about half an hour and then Continued our rout. the winds in the evening was verry hard, it was with Some dificulty that we Could find a Spot proper for an encampment, the Shore being a Swamp for Several miles back; at length late in the evening opposit to the place we had encamped on the 6th of Novr. last; we found the enterance of a Small Creek which offered us a Safe harbour from the Winds and Encamped. the Ground was low and moist tho we obtained a tolerable encampment. here we found another party of Cathlahmahs about 10 in number, who had established a temporary residence for the purpose of fishing and takeing Seal. they had taken about 12 Sturgeon and Some Seal. they gave us Some of the flesh of the Seal which I found a great improvement to the poor Elk. here we found Drewyer and the 2 Fields who had been Seperated from us Since Morning; they had passed on the North Side of the large Island which was much nearest. the bottom lands are Covered with a Species of Arspine, the Growth with a broad leaf which resembles ash except the leaf. the under brush red willow, broad leafed Willow, Seven bark, Goose berry, Green bryor, and the larged leaf thorn; the latter is Now in blume, the nativs inform us that it bears a fruit about an Inch in diamieter which is good to eate. the red willow and 7 bark begin to put foth their leaves. The green bryor which I have before mentioned retains leaves all winter. made 15 Miles

[Lewis, March 26, 1806] Wednesday March 26th 1806. The wind blew so hard this morning that we delayed untill 8 A.M. we gave a medal of small size to a man by the name of Wal-lal'-le, a principal man among the Cathlahmahs, he appeared very thankfull for the honour conferred on him and presented us a large sturgeon. we continued our rout up the river to an old village on the Stard. side where we halted for dinner. we met on the way the principal Cheif of the Cathlahmahs, Sah-hah-woh-cap, who had been up the river on a trading voyage. he gave us some Wappetoe and fish; we also purchased some of the latter. soon after we halted for dinner the two Wackiacums who have been pursuing us since yesterday morning with two dogs for sale, arrived. they wish tobacco in exchange for their dogs which we are not disposed to give as our stock is now reduced to a very few carrots. our men who have been accustomed to the use of this article Tobaco and to whom we are now obliged to deny the uce of this article appear to suffer much for the want of it. they substitute the bark of the wild crab which they chew; it is very bitter, and they assure me they find it a good substitute for tobacco. the smokers substitute the inner bark of the red willow and the sacacommis. here our hunters joined us having killed three Eagles and a large goose. I had now an oportunity of comparing the bald with the grey Eagle; I found that the greay Eagle was about 1/4 larger, it's legs and feet were dark while those of the bald Eagle wer of a fine orrange yellow; the iris of the eye is also of a dark yellowish brown while that of the other is of a bright silvery colour with a slight admixture of yellow. after dinner we proceeded on and passed an Elegant and extensive bottom on the South side and an island near it's upper point which we call Fanny's Island and bottom. the greater part of the bottom is a high dry prarie. near the river towards the upper point we saw a fine grove of whiteoak trees; we saw some deer and Elk at a distance in the prarie, but did not delay for the purpose of hunting them. we continued our rout after dinner untill late in the evening and encamped on the next island above fanny's Island. we found it difficult to obtain as much wood as answered our purposes. the hunters who had proceeded on before us after dinner did not join us this evening. some Indians visited us after dark, but did not remain long. agreeably to our estimate as we decended the river, we came 16 m. 23rd, 16 m. the 24th, 15 the 25th, and 18 m. the 26th, tho I now think that our estimate in decending the river was too short.

[Clark, March 26, 1806] Wednesday March 26th 1806 The wind blew So hard untill 8 A M. that we detained, we gave a Medal to a Man by the name of Wal-lal-le a principal man among the Cath lah mahs, he appeared very thankfull for the honor Confured on him and presented us with a large Sturgion. we Continued our rout up the river to an old Village on the South Side where we halted for dinner. we met on the way the principal Chief of the Cathlahmahs, Sah-hah-wah-cop, who had been up the river on a trading voyage, he gave us some Wappato and fish, we also purchased Some Wappato Soon after halted for dinner at an Old Village on the South point opposit the lower pt. of Fannys Island. The two Warkiacums who had been pursueing us Since yester day morning with two dogs for Sale, arrived. they wish Tobacco in exchange for their dogs which we are not disposed to give, as our Stock is now reduced to 3 carrots. our men who have been acustomed to the use of this article, and to Whome we are now obliged to deny the use of this article appear to Suffer Much for the want of it. they Substitute the bark of the wild Crab which they Chew; it is very bitter and they assure me they find it a good Substitute for tobacco. the Smokers Substitute the iner bark of the redwillow and the saccomis.

here our hunters joined us haveing killed 3 Eagles and a large Wild goose. I had now an oppertunity of Comparing the bald with the grey Eagle; I found the grey Eagle about 1/4 largest, its legs and feet were dark which those of the bald eagle were of a fine orrange yellow; the iris of the eye is also of a dark yellowish brown, while that of the Grey is of a light Silvery colour with a Slight admixture of yellow. after dinner I walked on Shore through an eligant bottom on the South Side opposit to Fannys Island.

This bottom we also Call fannys bottom it is extensive and an open leavel plain except near the river bank which is high dry rich oak land. I saw Some deer & Elk at a distance in the Prarie. we continued untill late in the evening and encamped on a Small Island near the Middle of the river haveing made 18 Miles. 2 Indians Visited us this evining

[Lewis, March 27, 1806] Thursday March 27th 1806. We set out early this morning and were shortly after joined by some of the Skillutes who came along side in a small canoe for the purpose of trading roots and fish.

at 10 A.M. we arrived at two houses of this nation on the Stard. side where we halted for breakfast. here we overtook our hunters, they had killed nothing. the natives appeared extreemly hospitable, gave us dryed Anchovies, Sturgeon, wappetoe, quamash, and a speceis of small white tuberous roots about 2 inches in length and as thick as a man's finger; these are eaten raw, are crisp, milkey, and agreeably flavored. most of the party were served by the natives with as much as they could eat; they insisted on our remaining all day with them and hunting the Elk and deer which they informed us were very abundant in their neighbourhood. but as the weather would not permit us to dry our canoes in order to pitch them we declined their friendly invitation, and resumed our voyage at 12 OCk. the principal village of these Skillutes reside on the lower side of the Cow-e-lis'-kee river a few miles from it's entrance into the columbia. these people are said to be numer-ous. in their dress, habits, manners and language they differ but little from the Clatsops Chinnooks &c. they have latterly been at war with Chinnooks but peace is said now to be restored between them, but their intercourse is not yet resumed. no Chinnooks come above the marshey islands nor do the Skillutes visit the mouth of the Columbia. the Clatsops, Cathlahmahs and Wackkiacums are the carriers between these nations being in alliance with both.- The Coweliskee is 150 yards wide, is deep and from indian Information navigable a very considerable distance for canoes. it discharges itself into the Columbia about three miles above a remarkable high rocky vole which is situated on the N. side of the river by which it is washed on the South side and is seperated from the Nothern hills of the river by a wide bottom of several miles to which it is united. I suspect that this river waters the country lying West of the range of mountains which pass the columbia between the great falls and rapids, and north of the same nearly to the low country which commences on the N. W. coast about Latitude _____ North. above the Skillutes on this river another nation by the name of the Hul-loo-et-tell reside, who are said also to be numerous. at the distance Of 2 m. above the village at which we breakfasted we passed the entrance of this river; we saw several fishing camps of the Skillutes on both sides of the Columbia, and were attended all the evening by parties of the natives in their canoes who visited us for the purpose of trading their fish and roots; we purchased as many as we wished on very moderate terms; they seemed perfectly satisfyed with the exchange and behaved themselves in a very orderly manner. late in the evening we passed our camp of the 5th of November and encamped about 41/2 above at the commencement of the bottom land on stard. below Deer Island. we had scarcely landed before we were visited by a large canoe with eight men; from them we obtained a dryed fruit which resembled the raspburry and which I beeive to be the fruit of the large leafed thorn frequently mentioned. it is reather ascid tho pleasently flavored. I preserved a specemine of this fruit I fear that it has been baked in the process of drying and if so the seed will not vegitate. saw the Cottonwood, sweet willow, oak, ash and the broad leafed ash, the growth which resembles the beach &c. these form the growth of the bottom lands while the hills are covered almost exclusively with the various speceis of fir heretofore discribed. the black Alder appears as well on some parts of the hills as the bottoms. before we set out from the Skillute village we sent on Gibson's canoe and Drewyers with orders to proceed as fast as they could to Deer island and there to hunt and wait our arrival. we wish to halt at that place to repair our canoes if possible. the indians who visited us this evening remained but a short time, they passed the river to the oposite side and encamped. the night as well as the day proved cold wet and excessively disagreeable. we came 20 miles today.

[Clark, March 27, 1806] Thursday March 27th 1806. a rainey disagreeable night rained the greater part of the night we Set out this morning verry early and proceeded on to two houses of the Skil-lute Indians on the South Side here we found our hunters who had Seperated from us last evening. the wind rose and the rain became very hard Soon after we landed here we were very friendly receved by the natives who gave all our party as much fish as they Could eate, they also gave us Wappato and pashaquaw roots to eate prepared in their own way. also a Species of Small white tuberous roots about 2 inches in length and as thick as a mans finger, these are eaten raw, or crips, milkey and agreeably flavoured; the nativs insisted on our remaining all day with them and hunt the Elk and deer which they informed us was very abundant in this neighbourhood. but as the weather would not permit our drying our Canoes in order to pitch them, we declined their friendly invertation, and resumed our voyage at 12 oClock. The principal village of the Skil-lutes is Situated on the lower Side of the Cow-e-lis kee river a fiew miles from it's enterance into the Columbia. those people are Said to be noumerous, in their dress, habits, manners and Language they differ but little from the Clatsops, Chinnooks &c. they have latterly been at war with the Chinnooks, but peace is Said to be now restored between them, but their inter Course is not yet restored. no Chinnook Come above the Warkiacums, nor do the Skillutes visit the Mouth of the Columbia. The Clatsops, Cath lahmahs & War kia coms are the Carriers between those nations being in alliance with both-. The Cow e lis kee river is 150 yards wide, is deep and from Indian information navigable a very considerable distance for canoes. it discharges itself into the Columbia about 3 miles above a remarkable knob which is high and rocky and Situated on the North Side of the Columbia, and Seperated from the Northern hills of the river by a Wide bottom of Several Miles, to which it united. I Suspect that this river Waters the Country lying west of a range of Mountains which passes the Columbia between the Great falls and rapids, and North of the Same nearly to the low country which Commences on the N W. Coast about Latitude 4° _____ North. above the Skil lutes on this river another nation by the name of the Hul-loo-et-tell reside who are Said also to be numerous. at the distance of 2 miles above the village at which we brackfast we passed the enterance of this river; we Saw Several fishing camps of the Skillutes on both Sides of the Columbia, and also on both Sides of this river. we were attended all the evening by parties of the nativs in their Canoes who visited us for the purpose of tradeing their fish and roots; we purchased as maney as we wished on very moderate terms; they Seamed perfectly Satisfied with the exchange and behaved themselves in a very orderly manner. late in the evening we passed the place we Camped the 5th of Novr. and Encamped about 4 miles above at the Commencement of the Columbian Vally on the Stard. Side below Deer Island. we had Scercily landed before we were visited by a large Canoe with 8 men; from them we obtained a dried fruit which resembled the raspberry and which I beleave is the fruit of the large leafed thorn frequently mentioned. it is reather ascide tho pleasently flavored. Saw Cotton wood, Sweet Willow, white oake, ash and the broad leafed ash the Growth which resembles the bark &c. these form the groth of the bottom lands, whilst the Hills are almost exclusively Covered with the various Species of fir heretofore discribed. the black alder appears on Maney parts of the hills Sides as on the bottoms. before we Set out from the 2 houses where we brackfast we Sent on two Canoes with the best hunters, with orders to pro ceed as fast as they Could to Deer island and there to hunt and wait our arrival. we wish to halt at that place and repare 2 of our Canoes if possible. the Indians that visited us this evining remained but a Short time, they passed over to an Island and encamped. the night as well as the day proved Cold wet and excessively disagreeable. we Came 20 miles in the Course of this day.

[Lewis, March 28, 1806] Friday March 28th 1806. This morning we set out very early and at 9 A.M. arrived at the old Indian Village on Lard side of Deer Island where we found our hunters had halted and left one man with the two canoes at their camp; they had arrived last evening at this place and six of them turned out to hunt very early this morning; by 10 A.M. they all returned to camp having killed seven deer. these were all of the common fallow deer with the long tail. I measured the tail of one of these bucks which was upwards of 17 Inches long; they are very poor, tho they are better than the black tailed fallow deer of the coast. these are two very distinct speceis of deer. the Indians call this large Island E-lal-lar or deer island which is a very appropriate name. the hunters informed us that they had seen upwards of a hundred deer this morning on this island. the interior part of the island is praries and ponds, with a heavy growth of Cottonwood ash and willow near the river. we have seen more waterfowl on this island than we have previously seen since we left Fort Clatsop, consisting of geese, ducks, large swan, and Sandhill crams. I saw a few of the Canvisback duck. the duckinmallard are the most abundant. one of the hunters killed a duck which appeared to be the male, it was a size less than the duckinmallard. the head neck as low as the croop, the back tail and covert of the wings were of a fine black with a small addmixture of perple about the head and neck, the belley & breast were white; some long feathers which lie underneath the wings and cover the thye were of a pale dove colour with fine black specks; the large feathers of the wings are of a dove colour. the legs are dark, the feet are composed of 4 toes each of which there are three in front connected by a web, the 4th is short Hat and placed high on the heel behind the leg. the tail is composed of 14 short pointed feathers. the beak of this duck is remarkably wide, and is 2 inches in length, the upper chap exceeds the under one in both length and width, insomuch that when the beak is closed the under is entirly concealed by the upper chap. the tongue, indenture of the margin of the chaps &c. are like those of the mallard. the nostrils are large longitudinal and connected. a narrow strip of white garnishes the upper part or base of the upper chap; this is succeeded by a pale skye blue colour which occupys about one inch of the chap, is again succeeded by a transverse stripe of white and the extremity is of a pure black. the eye is moderately large the puple black and iris of a fine orrange yellow. the feathers on the crown of the head are longer than those on the upper part of neck and other parts of the head; these feathers give it the appearance of being crested. at 1/2 after ten A.M. it became fair, and we had the canoes which wanted repairing hailed out and with the assistance of fires which we had kindled for the purpose dryed them sufficiently to receive the pitch which was immediately put on them; at 3 in the evening we had them compleat and again launched and reloaded. we should have set out, but as some of the party whom we had permitted to hunt since we arrived have not yet returned we determined to remain this evening and dry our beding baggage &c. the weather being fair. Since we landed here we were visited by a large canoe with ten natives of the quathlahpahtle nation who are numerous and reside about seventeen miles above us on the lard. side of the Columbia, at the entrance of a small river. they do not differ much in their dress from those lower down and speak nearly the same language, it is in fact the same with a small difference of accent. we saw a great number of snakes on this island they were about the size and much the form of the common garter snake of the Atlantic coast and like that snake are not poisonous. they have 160 scuta on the abdomen and 71 on the tail. the abdomen near the head, and jaws as high as the eyes, are of a bluefish white, which as it receedes from the head becomes of a dark brown. the field of the back and sides is black. a narrow stripe of a light yellow runs along the center of the back, on each side of this stripe there is a range of small transverse oblong spots of a pale brick ret which gradually deminish as they receede from the head and disappear at the commencement of the tail. the puple of the eye is black, with a narrow ring of white bordering it's edge; the ballance of the iris is of a dark yellowish brown.- the men who had been sent after the deer returned and brought in the remnent which the Vultures and Eagles had left us; these birds had devoured 4 deer in the course of a few hours. the party killed and brought in three other deer a goose some ducks and an Eagle. Drewyer also killed a tiger cat. Joseph Fields informed me that the Vultures had draged a large buck which he had killed about 30 yards, had skined it and broken the back bone. we came five miles only today.

[Clark, March 28, 1806] Friday March 28th 1806 This morning we Set out verry early and at 9 A.M. arived at an old Indian Village on the N E side of Deer island where we found our hunters had halted and left one man with the Canoes at their Camp, they arrived last evening at this place, and Six of them turned out very early to hunt, at 10 A.M. they all returned to camp haveing killed Seven Deer, those were all of the Common fallow Deer with a long tail. I measured the tail of one of these bucks which was upwards of 17 inches long; they are very poor, tho they are better than the black tail Species of the Sea coast. those are two very distinct Species of Deer. the Indians call this large Island E-lal-lar, or Deer Island, which is a very appropriate name. the hunters informed us that they had Seen upwards of a hundred Deer this morning on this island. the interior of this Island is a prarie & ponds, with a heavy growth of Cotton wood, ash & willow near the river. we have Seen more water fowl on this island than we have previously Seen Since we left Fort Clatsop, Consisting of Geese, Ducks, large Swan & Sand Hill crains. I saw a fiew of the Canvis back duck as I believe. at 1/2 after 10 A.M. it became fair and we had the Canoes which wanted repareing hauled out and with the assistance of fires which we had kindled for the purpose dryed them Sufficiently to receve the pitch which was imedeately put on them; at 3 in the evening we had them Compleated and lanced and reloaded. we should have Set out but some of the party whome we had permitid to hunt Since we arrived heve not yet returned. we determined to remain here this evening and dry our bedding &c. the weather being fair. Since we landed here we were visited by a large Canoe with ten nativs of the Quathlahpohtle nation who are numerous and reside about fourteen Miles above us on the N E. Side of the Columbia above the Enterance of a Small river which the Indians call Chfih-w&h-na-hi-ooks. we saw a great number of Snakes on this island; they were about the Size and much the form of the garter snake of the U. S. the back and Sides are black with a narrow Stripe of light yellow along the Center of the back, with small red spots on each Side they have _____ scuta on the abdomin & _____ on the tail and are not poisonous. The men who had been Sent after the deer returned with four only, the other 4 haveing been eaten entirely by the Voulturs except the Skin. The men we had been permitted to hunt this evening killed 3 deer 4 Eagles & a Duck. the deer are remarkably pore. Some rain in the after part of the day. we only made 5 miles to day-.

[Lewis, March 29, 1806] Saturday March 29th 1806. We set out early this morning and proceeded along the side of Deer Island; halted at 10 A.M. near its upper point and breakfasted. here we were joined by three men of the Clan-nah-min-na-mun nation. the upper point of this Island may be esteemed the lower side or commencement of the Columbian valley. after breakfast we proceeded on and at the distance of 14 miles from our encampment of the last evening we passed a large inlet 300 yds in width. this inlet or arm of the river extends itself to the South 10 or 12 M. to the hills on that side of the river and receives the waters of a small creek which heads with killamucks river, and that of a bayau which passes out of the Columbia about 20 miles above, the large Island thus formed we call wappetoe island. on this inlet and Island the following nations reside, (viz) Clan-nah-min-namun, Clacks-star, Cath-lah-cum-up, Clah-in-na-ta, Cath-lah-nah-qui-ah, and Cath-lah-cam-mah-tup. the two first reside on the inlet and the others on the bayau and island. observed a speceies of small wild onion growing among the moss on the rocks, they resemble the shives of our gardens and grow remarkably close together forming a perfect turf; they are quite as agreeably flavoured as the shives. on the North side of the columbia a little above the entrance of this inlet a considerable river discharges itself. this stream the natives call the Cah-wah-na-hi-ooks. it is 150 yards wide and at present discharges a large body of water, tho from the information of the same people it is not navigable but a short distance in consequence of falls and rappids a tribe called the Hul-lu-ettell reside on this river above it's entr.- at the distance of three miles above the entrance of the inlet on the N. side behind the lower point of an island we arrived at the village of the Cath-lah-poh-tle with consists of 14 large wooden houses. here we arrived at 3 P.M. the language of these people as well as those on the inlet and wappetoe Island differs in some measure from the nations on the lower part of the river. tho many of their words are the same, and a great many others with the difference only of accent. the form of their houses and dress of the men, manner of living habits customs &c as far as we could discover are the same. their women wear their ornaments robes and hair as those do below tho here their hair is more frequently braded in two tresses and hang over each ear in front of the body. in stead of the tissue of bark woarn by the women below, they wear a kind of leather breech clout about the width of a common pocket handkerchief and reather longer. the two corners of this at one of the narrow ends are confined in front just above the hips; the other end is then brought between the legs, compressed into a narrow foalding bundel is drawn tight and the corners a little spread in front and tucked at the groin over and arround the part first confind about the waist. the small robe which dose not reach the waist is their usual and only garment commonly woarn be side that just mentioned. when the weather is a litte warm this robe is thrown aside and the leather truss or breech-clout constitutes the whole of their apparel. this is a much more indecent article than the tissue of bark, and bearly covers the mons venes, to which it is drawn so close that the whole shape is plainly perceived. the floors of most of their houses are on a level with the surface of the earth tho some of them are sunk two or 3 feet beneath. the internal arrangement of their houses is the same with those of the nations below. they are also fond of sculpture. various figures are carved and painted on the peices which support the center of the roof, about their doors and beads. they had large quantities of dryed Anchovies strung on small sticks by the gills and others which had been first dryed in this manner, were now arranged in large sheets with strings of bark and hung suspended by poles in the roofs of their houses; they had also an abundance of sturgeon and wappetoe; the latter they take in great quantities from the neighbouring bonds, which are numerous and extensive in the river bottoms and islands. the wappetoe furnishes the principal article of traffic with these people which they dispose of to the nations below in exchange for beads cloth and various articles. the natives of the Sea coast and lower part of the river will dispose of their most valuable articles to obtain this root. they have a number of large symeters of Iron from 3 to 4 feet long which hang by the heads of their beads; the blade of this weapon is thickest in the center tho thin even there. all it's edges are sharp and it's greatest width which is about 9 inches from the point is about 4 inches. the form is thus. this is a formidable weapon. they have heavy bludgeons of wood made in the same form nearly which I presume they used for the same purpose before they obtained metal. we purchased a considerable quantity of wappetoe, 12 dogs, and 2 Sea otter skins of these people. they were very hospitable and gave us anchovies and wappetoe to eat. notwithstanding their hospitality if it deserves that appellation, they are great begers, for we had scarcely finished our repast on the wappetoe and Anchovies which they voluntarily set before us before they began to beg. we gave them some small articles as is our custom on those occasions with which they seemed perfectly satisfyed. we gave the 1st Cheif a small medal, which he soon transfered to his wife. after remaining at this place 2 hours we set out & continued our rout between this island, which we now call Cath-lah-poh-tle after the nation, and the Lard shore. at the distance of 2 miles we encamped in a small prarie on the main shore, having traveled 19 miles by estimate. the river rising fast. great numbers of both the large and small swans, gees and ducks seen today. the former are very abundant in the ponds where the wappetoe is found, they feed much on this bulb. the female of the duck which was described yesterday is of a uniform dark brown with some yellowish brown intermixed in small specks on the back neck and breast. the garter snakes are innumerable, & are seen entwined arround each other in large bundles of forty or fifty lying about in different directions through the praries. the frogs are croaking in the swams and marhes; their notes do not differ from those of the Atlantic States; they are not found in the salt marshes near the entrance of the river. heared a large hooting owl hollowing this evening. saw several of the crested fishers and some of the large and small black-birds.

[Clark, March 29, 1806] Saturday March 29th 1806 we Set out very early this morning and proceeded to the head of deer island and took brackfast. the morning was very cold wind Sharp and keen off the rainge of Mountains to the East Covered with snow. the river is now riseing very fast and retards our progress very much as we are compelled to keep out at Some distance in the Curent to clear the bushes, and fallin trees and drift logs makeing out from the Shore. dureing the time we were at Brackfast a Canoe with three Indians of the Clan-nar-min-na-mon Nation came down, one of those men was dressed in a Salors jacket & hat & the other two had a blanket each, those people differ but little either in their dress manners & Language from the Clatsops & Chinnooks they reside on Wappato Inlet which is on the S W. side about 12 miles above our encampment of the last night and is about 2 miles from the lower point, four other Tribes also reside on the inlet and Since which passes on the South W. Side of the Island, the first tribe from the lower point is the Clannarminamon, on the Island, the Clackster Nation on the main S. W. Shore. the next Cath-lah-cum-up, Clhh-in-na-ta, Cath-lah-nah-qui-ah and at Some distance further up is a tribe called Cath-lah-com-mah-up Those tribes all occupie Single Villages. we proceeded on to the lower point of the Said island accompanied by the 3 Indians, & were met by 2 canoes of nativs of the quath-lah-pah-tal who informed us that the chanel to the N E of the Island was the proper one. we prosued their advice and Crossed into the mouth of the Chahwah-na-hi-ooks River which is about 200 yards wide and a great portion of water into the columbia at this time it being high. The indians inform us that this river is crouded with rapids after Some distance up it. Several tribes of the Hul-lu-et-tell Nation reside on this river. at 3 oClock P.M. we arived at the Quath lah pah tie Village of 14 Houses on main Shore to the N E. Side of a large island. those people in their habits manners Customs and language differ but little from those of the Clatsops and others below. here we exchanged our deer Skins killed yesterday for dogs, and purchased others to the Number of 12 for provisions for the party, as the deer flesh is too poore for the Men to Subsist on and work as hard as is necessary. I also purchased a Sea Otter robe. we purchased wappatoe and Some pashaquar roots. gave a Medal of the Small Size to the principal Chief, and at 5 oClock reembarked and proceeded up on the N E. of an Island to an inlet about 1 mile above the village and encamped on a butiful grassy plat, where the nativs make a portage of their Canoes and Wappato roots to and from a large pond at a Short dis-tance. in this pond the nativs inform us they Collect great quantities of pappato, which the womin collect by getting into the water, Sometimes to their necks holding by a Small canoe and with their feet loosen the wappato or bulb of the root from the bottom from the Fibers, and it imedeately rises to the top of the water, they Collect & throw them into the Canoe, those deep roots are the largest and best roots. Great numbers of the whistling Swan, Gees and Ducks in the Ponds. Soon after we landed 3 of the nativs came up with Wappato to Sell a part of which we purchased. they Continued but a Short time. our men are recoverey fast. Willard quit well & Bratten much Stronger. we made 15 miles to day only.

[Lewis, March 30, 1806] Sunday March 30th 1806. We got under way very early in the morning, and had not reached the head of the island before we were met by three men of the Clan-nah-minna-mun nation one of whom we recognized being the same who had accompanied us yesterday, and who was very pressing in his entreaties that we should visit his nation on the inlet S. W. of Wappetoe island. at the distance of about 2 M. or at the head of the quathlahpahtle island we met a party of the Claxtars and Cathlahcumups in two canoes; soon after we were met by several canoes of the different nations who reside on each side of the river near this place. Wappetoe Island is about 20 miles long and from 5 to 10 in width; the land is high and extreemly fertile and intersected in many parts with ponds which produce great quantities of the sagittaria Sagittifolia, the bulb of which the natives call wappetoe. there is a heavy growth of Cottonwood, ash, the large leafed ash and sweet willow on most parts of this island. the black alder common on the coast has now disappeared. we passed several fishing camps on wappetoe island and at the distance of 5 miles above quathlahpotle Island on the N. E. side we halted for breakfast near the place we had encamped on the evening of the 4th of November last; here we were visited by several canoes which came off from two towns situated a little distance above us on wappetoe Island. the 1st of these tribes about 2 miles above us call themselves Clan-nah-quah, the other about a mile above them call themselves Mult-no-mah. from these visiters we purchased a sturgeon and some wappetoe and pashequa, for which we gave some small fishinghooks. these like the natives below are great higglers in dealing. at 10 A.M. we set out and had not proceeded far before we came to a landing place of the natives where there were several large canoes drawn out on shore and several natives seting in a canoe apparently waiting our arrival; they joined the fleet and continued with us some miles. we halted a few minutes at this landing and the Indians pointed to a village which was situated abut 2 miles from the river behid a pond lying parallel with it on the N. E. side nearly opposite to the Clan-nah-quah town. here they informed us that the Sho-toes resided. here we were joined by several other canoes of natives from the Island. most of these people accompanyed us untill 4 in the evening when they all returned; their principal object I beive was merely to indulge their curiossity in looking at us. they appeared very friendly, tho most had taken the precaution to bring with them their warlike implements. we continued our rout along the N. E. shore of the river to the place we had halted to dine on the 4th of Novembr opposite to the center of Immage canoe island where the Indians stole Capt. Clarks tomahawk. here we encamped a little before sunset in a beautifull prarie above a large pond having traveled 23 M. I took a walk of a few miles through the prarie and an open grove of oak timber which borders the prarie on the back part. I saw 4 deer in the course of my walk and much appearance of both Elk and deer. Joseph feields who was also out a little above me saw several Elk and deer but killed none of them; they are very shye and the annual furn which is now dry and abundant in the bottoms makes so much nois in passing through it that it is extreemly difficult to get within reach of the game. Fends killed and brought with him a duck. about 10 P.M. an indian alone in a small canoe arrived at our camp, he had some conversation with the centinel and soon departed. The natives who inhabit this valley are larger and reather better made than those of the coast. like those people they are fond of cold, hot, & vapor baths of which they make frequent uce both in sickness and in health and at all seasons of the year. they have also a very singular custom among them of baithing themselves allover with urine every morning. The timber and apearance of the country is much as before discribed. the up lands are covered almost entirely with a heavy growth of fir of several speceis like those discribed in the neighbourhood of Fort Clatsop; the white cedar is also found hereof large size; no white pine nor pine of any other kind. we had a view of mount St. helines and Mount Hood. the 1st is the most noble looking object of it's kind in nature. it's figure is a regular cone. both these mountains are perfectly covered with snow; at least the parts of them which are visible. the highlands in this valley are rolling tho by no means too steep for cultivation they are generally fertile of a dark rich loam and tolerably free of stones. this valley is terminated on it's lower side by the mountanous country which borders the coast, and above by the rainge of mountains which pass the Columbia between the great falls and rapids of the Columbia river. it is about 70 miles wide on a direct line and it's length I beleive to be very extensive tho how far I cannot determine. this valley would be copetent to the mantainance of 40 or 50 thousand souls if properly cultivated and is indeed the only desireable situation for a settlement which I have seen on the West side of the Rocky mountains.

[Clark, March 30, 1806] Sunday March 30th 1806 we got under way verry early and had not proceeded to the head of the island before we met with the three men of the Clan-nar-min-a-mon's who met us yesterday brackfast at the upper point of the Island we met Several of the Clackstar and Cath-lah-cum-up in two canoes. Soon after we were overtaken by Several Canoes of different tribes who reside on each Side of the river the three above Tribes and the Cldh-in-na-ta cath-lahnah-qui-up & Cath-lah-com-mah-tup reside on each Side of Wappato inlet and back of Wappato Island which Island is formed by a Small Chanel which passes from the Lower part of Image Canoe Island into an inlet which makes in from the S W. Side, and receves the water of a Creek which heads with the Kil a mox River. this wappato Island is about 18 or 20 Miles long and in places from 6 to 10 miles wide high & furtile with ponds on different parts of it in which the nativs geather Wappato. nearly opposit the upper point of the Isld. behing which we encamped last night, or on the Wappato Isld. is Several Camps of the nativs catching Sturgion. about 5 miles Still higher up and on the N E. Side we halted for brackfast at the place which We had encamped the 4th of November last. here we were visited by several canoes of Indians from two Towns a Short distance above on the Wappato Island. the 1st of those Tribes Call themselves Clan-nah-quah and Situated about 2 miles above us, the other about a mile above Call themselves Mult-no-mah we purchased of those visitors a Sturgion and Some Wappato & quarmarsh roots for which we gave Small fishing hooks. at 10 a.m. we Set out and had not proceeded far before we came to a landing place where there was Several large canoes hauled up, and Sitting in a canoe, appearantly waiting our arival with a view to join the fleet indian who was then along Side of us. this man informed he was a Shoto and that his nation resided a little distance from the river. we landed and one of the indians pointed to the Shoto village which is Situated back of Pond which lies parrelal with the river on the N E. Side nearly opposit the Clan-nah quah village. here we were also joined by Several Canoes loaded with the natives from the Island who Continued to accompany us untill about 4 oClock when they all returned and we proceeded on to the place the Indians Stole my Tomahawk 4th Novr. last and Encamped in a Small Prarie above a large Pond on N. E and oppost the Center of image Canoe Island. capt Lewis walked out and Saw Several deer. Jo. Field Shot at Elk he killed and brought in a fine duck. Soon after I had got into bead an Indian came up alone in a Small Canoe. Those tribes of Indians who inhabit this vally differ but little in either their dress, manners, habuts and language from the Clat Sops Chinnooks, and others on the Sea coast. they differ in a fiew words and a little in the accent. The men are Stouter and much better formed than those of the Sea Coast. more of their womin ware their hair braded in two tresses and hang over each ear. in Stead of the tissue of bark worn by the women below, they ware a kind of leather breech clout as before described as worn by the Womin at the enterance of Lewis's river-the width of a Common pocket Handkerchief or Something Smaller and longer. the two Corners of this at one of the narrow ends are confined in front just above the hips; the other Side is then brought between their legs, Compressed into a narrow folding bundle is drawn tight, and the Corners a little Spred in front tucked at the ends over and around the part first confined about the Waiste. a Small roab which does not reach the Waiste is their usial and only garment commonly worn besides this just mentioned. when the weather is a little worm the roab is thrown aside, and the latter truss or breach clout constitutes the whole of their apparreal. this is a much more indesant article than the tissue of bark, and bearly covers the Mons versus, to which it is drawn So close that the whole Shape is plainly perseived. The Houses are Similar to those already descrbed. they are fond of Sculpture. various figures are carved and painted on the pieces which Support the Center of the roof about their dotes and beads. They are well Supplied with anchoves Sturgion and Wappato. The latter furnishes the principal article of traffic with those Tribes which they despose of to the nativs below in exchange for beeds, Cloath and Various articles. the nativs of the Sea coast and lower part of this river will dispose of their most valueable articles to obtain this root. I saw in Several houses of the Cath lah poh tie Village large Symeters of Iron from 3 to 4 feet long which hangs by the heads of their beads; the blade of this weapon is thickest in the Center tho thin even there, all it's edges are Sharp and its greatest width which is about 9 inches from the point, is about 4 inches. the form is this this is a formable weapon. they have heavy bludgeons of wood made in the Same form nearly which I presume they use for the Same purpose before they obtained metal. we made 22 Miles only to day the wind and a Strong current being against us all day, with rain. discovered a high mountain S E. Covered with Snow which we call Mt. Jefferson.

[Lewis, March 31, 1806] Monday March 31st 1806 We set out early this morning and proceeded untill 8 A.M. when we Landed on the N. side opposite one large wooden house of the Shah-ha-la nation and took breakfast. when we decended the river in November last there were 24 other lodges formed of Straw and covered with bark near this house; these lodges are now distroyed and the inhabitants as the indians inform us have returned to the great rapids of this river which is their permanent residence; the house which remains is inhabited; soon after we landed two canoes came over from this house with 4 men and a woman. they informed us that their relations who were with them last fall usuly visit them at that season for the purpose of hunting deer and Elk and collecting wappetoe and that they had lately returned to the rapids I presume to prepare for the fishing season as the Salmon will begin to run shortly.- this morning we overtook the man who had visited our camp last night he had a fine sturgeon in his canoe which he had just taken. the Sagittaria Sagittifolia dose not grow on this river above the Columbian valley.- These indians of the rapids frequently visit this valley at every season of the year for the purpose of collecting wappetoe which is abundant and appears never to be out of season at any time of the year. at 10 A.M. we resumed our march accompanyed by three men in a canoe; one of these fellows appeared to be a man of some note among them; he was dressed in a salor's jacket which was decorated in his own fassion with five rows of large and small buttons in front and some large buttons on the pocket flaps. they are remarkably fond of large brass buttons. these people speak a different language from those below tho in their dress habits manners &c they differ but little from the quathlahpohtles. their women wear the truss as those do of all the nations residing from the quathlahpohtles to the entrance of Lewis's river. they differ in the manner of intering their dead. they lay them horizontally on boards and cover them with mats, in a valt formed with boards like the roof of a hose supported by forks and a single pole laid horizontally on those forks. many bodies are deposited in the same valt above ground. these are frequently laid one on the other, to the hight of three or for corps. they deposit with them various articles of which they die possessed, and most esteem while living. their canoes are frequently broken up to strengthen the vault.- these people have a few words the same with those below but the air of the language is intirely different, insomuch, that it may be justly deemed a different language. their women wear longer and larger robes generally, than those below; these are most commonly made of deer skins dressed with the hair on them. we continued our rout along the N. side of the river passed diamond Island and whitebrant island to the lower point of a handsom prarie opposite to the upper entrance of the Quicksand river; here we encamped having traveled 25 miles today. a little below the upper point of the White brant Island Seal river discharges itself on the N. side. it is about 80 yards wide, and at present discharges a large body of water. the water is very clear. the banks are low and near the Columbia overflow and form several large ponds. the natives inform us that it is of no great extent and heads in the mountains just above us. at the distance of one mile from the entrance of this stream it forks, the two branches being nearly of the same size. they are both obstructed with falls and innumerable rappids, insomuch that it cannot be navigated. as we could not learn any name of the natives for this stream we called it Seal river from the great abundance of those animals which we saw about it's entrance. we determined to remain at our present encampment a day or two for the several purposes of examining quicksand river making some Celestial observations, and procuring some meat to serve us as far as the falls or through the Western mountains where we found the game scarce as we decended.- the three indians who accompanied us last evening encamped a little distance above us and visited our camp where they remained untill 9 P.M. in the entrance of Seal river I saw a summer duck or wood duck as they are sometimes called. this is the same with those of our country and is the first I have seen since I entered the rocky mountains last summer.- our hunters who had halted a little below Seal river in consequence of the waves being too high for their small canoe did not join us untill after dark. Drewyer who was out below Seal river informed us that game was very scarce in that quarter, a circumstance which we did not expect.

[Clark, March 31, 1806] Monday March 31st 1806 we Set out this morning and proceeded untill 8 oClock when we landed on the N. Side opposit one large House of the Shah-ha-la Nation near this house at the time we passed on the 4th of November last was Situated 25 houses, 24 of them were built of Straw & Covered with bark as before mentioned. those of that description are all distroyed, the one built of wood only remains and is inhabited. we overtook the man whome came to our Camp last night and Soon after we landed two canoes Came over from the opposit Side with 5 men & a woman those people informed us that their relations who was with them last fall reside at the Great rapids, and were down with them last fall gathering Wappato which did not grow above, and also killing deer, that they Secured the bark of the houses which they then lived in against their return next fall. they also inform us that their relations also visit them frequently in the Spring to collect this root which is in great quantities on either Side of the Columbia. at 10 A. M we proceeded on accompanied by one Canoe and three men, one of them appeared to be a man of Some note, dressed in a Salors jacket which had 5 rows of large & Small buttons on it. Those people Speak a differant language from those below, with Some fiew Words the Same, the accent entirely different. their dress and Manners appear very Similar. the women ware the truss or breach clout and Short robes, and men roabs only passed up on the N. Side of White brant Island near the upper point of Which a Small river falls in about 80 yards wide and at this time discharges a great quantity of water. the nativs inform us that this river is very Short and heads in the range of mountains to the N E of its enterance into the Columbia the nativs haveing no name which we could learn for this little river we Call it Seal river from the great number of those Animals which frequents its mouth. this river forks into two nearly equal branches about 1 mile up and each branch is crouded with rapids & falls. we proceed on about 2 miles above the enterance of this Seacalf river and imedeately opposit the upper mouth of the quick Sand river we formed a Camp in a Small Prarie on the North Side of the Columbia where we intend to delay one or two days to make Some Selestial observations, to examine quick sand river, and kill Some meat to last us through the Western Mountains which Commences a fiew miles above us and runs in a N. N. W. & S. S. E. derection. The three Indians encamped near us and visited our fire we entered into a kind of a Conversation by signs, of the Country and Situation of the rivers. they informed us that Seal river headed in the mountains at no great distance. quick Sand river was Short only headed in Mt. Hood which is in view and to which he pointed. this is a circumstance we did not expect as we had heretofore deemed a considerable river. Mount Hood bears East from this place and is distant from this place about 40 miles. this information if true will render it necessary to examine the river below on the South Side behind the image canoe and Wappato islands for some river which must water the Country weste of the western mountains to the Waters of California. The Columbia is at present on a Stand and we with dificuelty made 25 miles to-day-.

[Lewis, April 1, 1806] Tuesday April 1st 1806. This morning early we dispatched Sergt. Pryar with two men in a small canoe up quicksand river with orders to proceed as far as he could and return this evening. we also sent a party of three hunters over the river to hunt a large bottom of woodland and prarie above the entrance of the Quicksand river; the ballance of the hunters we sent out in different directions on this side of the Columbia and employed those about camp in making a rope of Elkskin. the Indians who encamped near us last evening continued with us untill about midday. they informed us that the quicksand river which we have heretofore deemed so considerable, only extendes through the Western mountains as far as the S. Western side of mount hood where it takes it's source. this mountain bears E from this place and is distant about 40 miles. this information was corroborated by that of sundry other indians who visited us in the course of the day. we were now convinced that there must be some other considerable river which flowed into the columbia on it's south side below us which we have not yet seen, as the extensive valley on that side of the river lying between the mountainous country of the Coast and the Western mountains must be watered by some stream which we had heretofore supposed was the quicksand river. but if it be a fact that the quicksand river heads in Mount Hood it must leave the valley within a few miles of it's entrance and runs nearly parallel with the Columbia river upwards. we indeavoured to ascertain by what stream the southern portion of the Columbian valley was watered but could obtain no satisfactory information of the natives on this head. they informed us that the quicksand river is navigable a short distance only in consequence of falls and rapids; and that no nation inhabits it.- Sergt. Pryar returned in the evening and reported that he had ascended the river six miles; that above the point at which it divides itself into two channels it is about 300 yds wide tho the channel is not more than 50 yds and only 6 ft deep. this is a large vollume of water to collect in so short a distance; I therefore think it probable that there are some large creeks falling into it from the S. W. the bed of this stream is formed entirely of quicksand; it's banks are low and at preasent overflows. the water is turbid and current rapid.the following are the courses taken by Sergt. Pryor. S. 10° W. 1 M. to a point on the Lard. side passing a large Island on Stard. S. 24° E. 2 m. to the head of an Island near the Lard. shore. S 33° E. 4 m. to a stard. point passing several islands on the Lard. side and a creek 50 yds. wide on Stard at 11/2 miles. the river from hence appeared to bend to the East. he heard falls of water. several different tribes informed us that it heads at Mount Hood. We were visited by several canoes of natives in the course of the day; most of whom were descending the river with their women and children. they informed us that they resided at the great rapids and that their relations at that place were much streightened at that place for the want of food; that they had consumed their winter store of dryed fish and that those of the present season had not yet arrived. I could not learn wheather they took the Sturgeon but presume if they do it is in but small quantities as they complained much of the scarcity of food among them. they informed us that the nations above them were in the same situation & that they did not expect the Salmon to arrive untill the full of the next moon which happens on the 2d of May. we did not doubt the varacity of these people who seemed to be on their way with their families and effects in surch of subsistence which they find it easy to procure in this fertile valley.- This information gave us much uneasiness with rispect to our future means of subsistence. above falls or through the plains from thence to the Chopunnish there are no deer Antelope nor Elk on which we can depend for subsistence; their horses are very poor most probably at this season, and if they have no fish their dogs must be in the same situation. under these circumstances there seems to be but a gloomy prospect for subsistence on any terms; we therefore took it into serious consideration what measures we were to pursue on this occasion; it was at once deemed inexpedient to wait the arrival of the salmon as that would detain us so large a portion of the season that it is probable we should not reach the United States before the ice would close the Missouri; or at all events would hazard our horses which we lelft in charge of the Chopunnish who informed us that they intended passing the rocky mountains to the Missouri as early as the season would permit wich is as we believe about the begining of May. should these people leave their situation near kooskooske before our arrival we may probably find much difficulty in recovering our horses; without which there will be but little possibility of repassing the mountains; we are therefore determined to loose as little time as possible in geting to the Chopunnish Village. at 3 P.M. the hunters who were sent over the river returned having killed 4 Elk and two deer; the Elk were in good order but the deer extreemly poor. they informed us that game is very plenty in that quarter. the hunters on this side of the river also returned but had killed nothing; they saw a few Elk and deer. there was also much sign of the black bear seen on the other side of the river. we sent a party to bring in the flesh of the Elk and deer that were killed. they did not return this evening. I purchased a canoe from an Indian today for which I gave him six fathoms of wampum beads; he seemed satisfyed with his bargain and departed in another canoe but shortly after returned and canceled the bargain; took his canoe and returned the beads. this is frequently the case in their method of traiding and is deemed fair by them. The last evening and this morning were so cloudy that I could neither obtain any Lunar observations nor equal altitudes.-

[Clark, April 1, 1806] Tuesday April 1st 1806 This morning early we dispatched Sergt. Pryor, with two men in a Small canoe up quick sand river with orders to proceed as far as he Could and return this evening. we also Sent a party of three hunters over the river to hunt a large bottom of woodland and prarie above the enterance of Q. Sand River; the ballance of the hunters we Sent out in different directions on this Side of the Columbia, and employed those about Camp in makeing a rope of Elk Skin.

The information given by the indians to us last night respecting quick Sand river was corrobarated by Sundery other indians who visited us in the Course of this day. we were now convinced that if there information be just; that Some Considerable river which flowed into the Columbia on it's South Side below us which we have not yet Seen, as the extensive vally on that Side of the river lying between the mountanious Country of the Coast, and the western mountains must be watered by Some Stream, which we had heretofore Supposed was the quick Sand river. but if it be a fact that Quick Sand river heads in Mount Hood it must leave the vally within a fiew miles of it's enterance, and runs nearly parrilal with the Columbia River upwards. we indeavoured to assertained by what Stream the South portion of the Columbian Vally was watered, but could obtain no Satisfactory information of the waters on this head. they inform us that the quick Sand river is not naviagable any distance in consequence of falls and rapids; and that no nation inhabit it. Sergt. Pryor returned in the evening and reported that he had assended the river Six Miles; that above the point which it divides itself into two Chanels, it is about 300 yards wide tho the Chanel is not more than 50 yards, and only 6 feet deep. the other part of the river from 2 to 4 inches water, the bead of this river is formed entirely of quick Sand; its banks are low and at present overflown. the water is turbed and current rapid.- The following are the Courses taken by Sergt. Pryor.- "S. 10° W. 1 mile to a point on the Lard. Side passing a large island on Stard Side. S 24° E. 2 m. to the head of the island near the Lard Shore. S 33° E 4 m. to a Stard. point passing Several islands on the Lard Side and a Creek 50 yards wide on the Stard. Side at 11/2 miles. the river from hence upwards bend to the East. a fall of water heard at no great distance up this river." Several diffirent tribes of indians inform us that it heads at Mount Hood which is in view.

We were visited by Several Canoes of the nativs in the Course of this day; most of whome were decending the river with their womin and children. they inform us that they reside at the great rapids and that their relations at that place were much Streightened for the want of food; that they had consumed their winter Store of dryed fish and those of the present Season had not yet arived. I could not lern whether they took Sturgion but prosume if they do it is in but Small quantities as they complain much of the Scercity of food among them, they informed us that the nativs above them were in the Same Situation, and that they did not expect the Salmon to arrive untill the full of the next moon which happens on the 2nd of May. we did not doubt the veracity of those people who Seamed to be on their way with their families and effects in serch of Subsistence which they find it easy to precure in this fertile Vally-. This information givs us much uneasiness with respect to our future means of Subsistence, above the falls, on through the Plains from thence to the Chopunnish there are no Deer Antilopes or Elk on which we could depend for Subsistence; their horses are very poor most probably at this Season, and if they have no fish their dogs must be in the Same Situation. under these circumstances there Seams to be a gloomey prospect for Subsistence on any terms; we therefore took it into Serious Consideration what measure we were to pursue on this Occasion; it was at once deemed inexpedient to waite the arival of the Salmon as that would detain us So long a portion of the Season that it is probable we Should not reach the U States before the ice would close the Missouri; or at all events would hazard our horses which we left in charge of the Chopunnish who informed us that they intended passing the Rocky Mountains to the Missouri as early as the Season would permit them which is about the first of May. Should these people leave their Situation near Kooskooske before our arival we may probably find much dificulty in recovering our horses; without which there will be but little possibility of repassing the Mountains; we are therefore determined to lose as little time as possible in getting to the Cho punnish Village.

at 3 P.M. the hunters who were Sent over the river returned, haveing Killed 4 Elk and 2 Deer; the Elk were in good order but the deer extreemly poor. they informed us that game is very plenty in that quarter. the hunters on this Side of the river also returned but had killed nothing; they Saw a fiew Elk and Deer. there were also much Sign of the black bear Seen on the other Side of the river. we Sent a party to bring in the flesh of the Elk and Deer that were killed. they did not return this evening. We purchased a Canoe from an Indian today for Six fathoms of white wampom; he Seemed Satisfied with his bargin and departed in another Canoe but Shortly after returned and canseled the bargain, took his canoe and returned the beeds. this is frequently the case in their method of tradeing and is deemed fair by them. The last evening and this morning were So cloudy that we could neither obtain any Lunar observations nor equal altitudes

[Lewis, April 2, 1806] Wednesday April 2ed 1806. This morning we came to a resolution to remain at our present encampment or some where in this neighbourhood untill we had obtained as much dryed meat as would be necessary for our voyage as far as the Chopunnish. to exchange our perogues for canoes with the natives on our way to the great falls of the columbia or purchase such canoes from them for Elkskins and Merchandize as would answer our purposes. these canoes we intend exchanging with the natives of the plains for horses as we proceed untill we obtain as many as will enable us to travel altogether by land. at some convenient point, perhaps at the entrance of the S. E. branch of the Columbia, we purpose sending a party of four or five men a head to collect our horses that they may be in readiness for us by our arrival at the Chopunnish; calculating by thus acquiring a large stock of horses we shall not only sucure the means of transporting our baggage over the mountains but that we will also have provided the means of subsisting; for we now view the horses as our only certain resource for food, nor do we look forward to it with any detestation or borrow, so soon is the mind which is occupied with any interesting object reconciled to it's situation. The men who were sent in quest of the Elk and deer that were killed yesterday returned at 8 A.M. this morning. we now enformed the party of our intention of laying in a store of meat at this place, and immediately dispatched two parteis consisting of nine men to the opposite side of the river. five of those we sent below the Quicksand river and 4 above. we also sent out three others on this side, and those who remained in camp were employed in collecting wood making a scaffoald and cuting up the meat in order to dry it. about this time several canoes of the natives arrived at our camp and among others one from below which had on board eight men of the Shah-ha-la nation these men informed us that 2 young men whom they pointed out were Cash-hooks and resided at the falls of a large river which discharges itself into the Columbia on it's South side some miles below us. we readily prevailed on them to give us a sketch of this river which they drew on a mat with a coal. it appeared that this river which they called Mult-no-mah discharged itself behind the Island which we called the image canoe Island and as we had left this island to the S. both in ascending and decending the river we had never seen it. they informed us that it was a large river and run a considerable distance to the South between the mountains. Capt. Clark determined to return and examine this river accordingly he took a party of seven men and one of the perogues and set out 1/2 after 11 A.M., he hired one of the Cashhooks, for a birning glass, to pilot him to the entrance of the Multnomah river and took him on board with him. in their manners dress language and stature these people are the same with the quathlahpohtle nation and others residing in the neighbourhood of wappetoe Island. near the entrance of multnomah river a considerable nation resides on the lower side of that stream by the same name. as many as ten canoes with natives arrived at our camp in the course of the day; most of them were families of men women and children decencing the river. they all gave the same account of the scarcity of provision above. I shot my air gun, with which they were much astonished. one family consisting of ten or twelve persons remained near us all night. they conducted themselves in a very orderly manner. the three hunters on this side of the river returned in the evening they had killed two deer, tho they were so poor and at such a distance from camp that they brought in their skins only. the night and morning being cloudy I was again disappointed in making the observations I wished.

Fir is the common growth of the uplands, as is the cottonwood, ash; large leafed ash and sweet willow that of the bottom lands. the huckleburry, shallon, and the several evergreen shrubs of that speceis which bear burries have seased to appear except that speceis which has the leaf with a prickly margin. among the plants of this prarie in which we are encamped I observe the passhequo, Shannetahque, and compound firn the roots of which the natives eat; also the water cress, strawburry, flowering pea not yet in blume, the sinquefoil, narrow dock, sand rush which are luxuriant and abundant in the river bottoms; a speceis of the bearsclaw of which I preserved a specemine it is in blume. the large leafed thorn has also disappeared. the red flowering currant is found here in considerable quantities on the uplands. the hunters inform me that there are extensive praries on the highlands a few miles back from the river on this side. the land is very fertile.

[Clark, April 2, 1806] Wednesday April 2nd 1806 This morning we came to a resolution to remain at our present encampment or Some where in this neighbourhood untill we had obtained as much dried meat as would be necessary for our voyage as far as the Chopunnish. to exchange our large Canoes for Small ones with the nativs on our way to the great Falls of the Columbia or purchase Such canoes from them for Elk skins and Merchandize as would answer our purposes. these canoes we intend exchangeing with the nativs of the Plains for horses as we proceed untill we obtain as maney as will enable us to travel altogether by land. at Some convenient point, perhaps at the enterance of Lewis's River we intend Sending a party of 4 or 5 men ahead to Collect our horses that they may be in readiness for us by our arrival at the Chopunnish; Calculating by thus acquireing a large Stock of horses we shall not only Secure the means of transporting our baggage over the Mountains, but that we also have provided the means of Subsisting; for we now view the horses as our only Certain resource for food, nor do we look foward to it with any detestation or horrow, So Soon is the Mind which is occupied with any interesting object, reconsiled to it's Situation. The men who went in quest of the Elk and Deer which were killed yesterday returned at 8 A.M. this morning. we now informed the party of our intention of laying in a Store of meat at this place, and imediately dispatched two parties Consisting of nine men to the opposit Side of the river. 5 of them below and 4 above quick Sand River. we also Sent out 3 others on this Side, and those who remained in Camp were employd in Collecting wood makeing a Scaffold and Cutting up the meat in order to dry it. about this time Several Canoes of the nativs arived at our Camp among others two from below with Eight men of the Shah-ha-la Nation those men informed us that they reside on the opposit Side of the Columbia near Some pine trees which they pointed to in the bottom South of the Dimond Island, they Singled out two young men whome they informed us lived at the Falls of a large river which discharges itself into the Columbia on it's South Side Some Miles below us. we readily provailed on them to give us a Sketch of this river which they drew on a Mat with a coal, it appeared that this river which they Call Mult-no'-mah discharged itself behind the Island we call the image Canoe island, and as we had left this Island to the South both in decending & assending the river we had never Seen it. they informed us that it was a large river and runs a Considerable distance to the South between the Mountains. I deturmined to take a Small party and return to this river and examine its Size and Collect as much information of the nativs on it or near its enterance into the Columbia of its extent, the Country which it waters and the nativs who inhabit its banks &c. I took with me Six Men. Thompson J. Potts, Peter Crusat, P. Wiser, T. P. Howard, Jos. Whitehouse & my man York in a large Canoe, with an Indian whome I hired for a Sun glass to accompany me as a pilot. at half past 11 A.M. I Set out, and had not proceeded far eer I saw 4 large Canoes at Some distance above decending and bending their Course towards our Camp which at this time is very weak Capt. Lewis haveing only 10 men with him. I hisitated for a moment whether it would not be advisable for me to return and delay untill a part of our hunters Should return to add more Strength to our Camp. but on a Second reflection and reverting to the precautions always taken by my friend Capt Lewis on those occasions banished all apprehensions and I proceeded on down. at 8 miles passed a village on the South side at this place my Pilot informed me he resided and that the name of his tribe is Ne-cha-co-lee, this village is back or to the South of Dimond island, and as we passed on the North Side of the island both decending & assending did not See or know of this Village. I proceeded on without landing at this village. at 3 P.M. I landed at a large double house of the Ne-er-choki-oo tribe of the Shah-ha-la Nation. at this place we had Seen 24 aditional Straw Huts as we passed down last fall and whome as I have before mentioned reside at the Great rapids of the Columbia. on the bank at different places I observed Small Canoes which the women make use of to gather Wappato & roots in the Slashes. those Canoes are from 10 to 14 feet long and from 18 to 23 inches wide in the widest part tapering from the center to both ends in this form and about 9 inches deep and So light that a woman may with one hand haul them with ease, and they are Sufficient to Carry a woman an Some loading. I think 100 of those canoes were piled up and Scattered in different directions about in the Woods in the vecinity of this house, the pilot informed me that those Canoes were the property of the inhabitants of the Grand rapids who used them ocasionally to gather roots. I entered one of the rooms of this house and offered Several articles to the nativs in exchange for Wappato. they were Sulkey and they positively refused to Sell any. I had a Small pece of port fire match in my pocket, off of which I cut a pece one inch in length & put it into the fire and took out my pocket Compas and Set myself doun on a mat on one Side of the fire, and a magnet which was in the top of my ink Stand the port fire cought and burned vehemently, which changed the Colour of the fire; with the Magnit I turned the Needle of the Compas about very briskly; which astonished and alarmed these nativs and they laid Several parsles of Wappato at my feet, & begged of me to take out the bad fire; to this I consented; at this moment the match being exhausted was of course extinguished and I put up the magnet &c. this measure alarmed them So much that the womin and children took Shelter in their beads and behind the men, all this time a very old blind man was Speaking with great vehemunce, appearently imploreing his gode. I lit my pipe and gave them Smoke & gave the womin the full amount of the roots which they had put at my feet. they appeared Somewhat passified and I left them and proceeded on on the South Side of Image Canoe Island which I found to be two Islands hid from the opposit Side by one near the Center of the river. the lower point of the upper and the upper point of the lower cannot be Seen from the North Side of the Columbia on which we had passed both decending and ascending and had not observed the apperture between those islands. at the distance of 13 Miles below the last village and at the place I had Supposed was the lower point of the image Canoe island, I entered this river which the nativs had informed us of, Called Mult no mah River so called by the nativs from a Nation who reside on Wappato Island a little below the enterance of this river. Multnomah discharges itself in the Columbia on the S. E. and may be justly Said to be 1/4 the Size of that noble river. Multnomah had fallen 18 inches from it's greatest annual height. three Small Islands are situated in it's mouth which hides the river from view from the Columbia from the enterance of this river, I can plainly See Mt. Jefferson which is high and Covered with snow S. E. Mt. Hood East, Mt St. Helians a high humped Mountain to the East of Mt St. Helians. I also Saw the Mt. Raneer Nearly North. Soon after I arived at this river an old man passed down of the Clark a'mos Nation who are noumerous and reside on a branch of this river which receives it's waters from Mt.,Jefferson which is emensely high and discharges itself into this river one day and a half up, this distance I State at 40 Miles. This nation inhabits 11 Villages their Dress and language is very Similar to the Quath-lah-poh-tle and other tribes on Wappato Island.

The Current of the Multnomar is as jentle as that of the Columbia glides Smoothly with an eavin surface, and appears to be Sufficiently deep for the largest Ship. I attempted fathom it with a Cord of 5 fathom which was the only Cord I had, could not find bottom 1/3 of the distance across. I proceeded up this river 10 miles from it's enterance into the Columbia to a large house on the N E. Side and Encamped near the house, the flees being So noumerous in the house that we could not Sleep in it. this is the house of the Cush-hooks Nation who reside at the falls of this river which the pilot informs me they make use of when they Come down to the Vally to gather Wappato. he also informs me that a number of other Smaller houses are Situated on two Bayous which make out on the S. E. Side a little below the house. this house appears to have been laterly abandoned by its inhabitants in which they had left Sundery articles Such as Small Canoes mats, bladdles of Oil and baskits bowls & trenchers. and as my pilot informed me was gorn up this to the falls to fish which is 2 days or 60 miles up. this house is 30 feet wide & presisely 40 feet long. built in the usial form of broad boads Covered with bark.

The course and distance assending the Molt no mar R from it's enterance into the Columbia at the lower point of the 3rd Image Canoe island. viz.

S. 30°W. 2 Miles to the upper point of a Small island in the Middle of
Moltnomar river. thence

S. 10° W. 3 miles to a Sluce 80 yards wide which devides Wappato Island from the Main Stard. Side Shore passing a Willow point on the Lard. Side.

S. 60° E. 3 miles to a large Indian house on the Lard Side below Some high pine land. high bold Shore on the Starboard Side. thence

S. 30° E 2 miles to a bend under the high lands on the Stard Side

miles 10 passing a Larborad point.

thence the river bends to the East of S East as far as I could See. at this place I think the wedth of the river may be Stated at 500 yards and Sufficiently deep for a Man of War or Ship of any burthen.

[Lewis, April 3, 1806] Thursday April 3rd 1806. Early this morning Joseph Feilds came over and informed me that Reubin Feilds Drewyer and himself had killed four Elk. as the party with me were now but weak and the Indians constantly crouding about our camp, I thought it best to send a few men to dry the meat on the other side of the river; accordingly Sergt Pryor and two men returned with Jos. Fields for that purpose. the hunters were ordered to continue the chase; while the others were employed in drying the meat. I have had no account as yet from the party below the entrance of Quicksand river. The Indians continued to visit us today in considerable numbers most of them were decending the river with their families. these poor people appeared to be almost starved, they picked up the bones and little peices of refuse meat which had been thrown away by the party. they confirm the report of the scarcity of provision among the natives above. I observe some of the men among them who wear a girdle arround the waist between which and the body in front they confine a small skin of the mink or polecat which in some measure conceals the parts of generation, they also frequently wear a cap formed of the skin of the deer's head with the ears left on it, they have some collars of leather wrought with porcupine quills after the method of the Shoshonees. From this place Mount Hood bears S. 85 E. distant 40 miles. This evening we completed drying the flesh of the Elk which had been brought to camp. at 6 P.M. Capt. Clark returned, having completely succeeded in his expedition. he found the entrance of the large river of which the Indians had informed us, just at the upper part of wappetoe Island. the following is a sketch of the rivers furnished Capt C. by an old and inteligent Indian man.-

[Clark, April 3, 1806] Thursday April 3rd 1806 The water had fallen in the course of last night five inches. I Set out and proceeded up a Short distance and attempted a Second time to fathom the river with my cord of 5 fathom but could find no bottom. the mist was So thick that I could See but a Short distance up this river. where I left it, it was binding to the East of S. E. being perfectly Sati'fyed of the Size and magnitude of this great river which must Water that vast tract of Country betwen the Western range of mountains and those on the Sea coast and as far S. as the Waters of Callifornia about Latd. 37° North I deturmined to return. at 7 oClock A.M. Set out on my return. the men exirted themselves and we arived at the Ne er cho ki oo house in which the nativs were So illy disposed yesterday at 11 A.M. I entered the house with a view to Smoke with those people who Consisted of about 8 families, finding my presence alarmed them So much that the children hid themselves, womin got behind their men, and the men hung their heads, I detained but a fiew minits and returnd on board the canoe. My pilot who Continued in the Canoe informed me on my return that those people as well as their relations were very illy disposed and bad people. I proceeded on along the South Side met five canoes of the Shah-ha-la Nation from the Great rapids with their wives and Children decending the Columbia into this fertile Vally in pursute of provi-sions. my Pilot informed me in a low voice that those people were not good, and I did not Suffer them to come along Side of my Canoe which they appeared anxious to do. their numbers in those canoes who appeard anxious to come along Side was 21 men and 3 boys. at 3 P M. we arived at the residence of our Pilot which consists of one long house with Seven appartments or rooms in Square form about 30 feet each room opening into a passage which is quit through the house those passages are about 4 feet in width and formed of Wide boads Set on end in the ground and reaching to the Ruff which Serves also as divisions to the rooms. The ground plot is in this form 1 1 1 1 is the passages. 2 2 &c. is the apartments about 30 feet square. this house is built of bark of the White Cedar Supported on long Stiff poles resting on the ends of broad boads which form the rooms &c. back of this house I observe the wreck of 5 houses remaining of a very large Village, the houses of which had been built in the form of those we first Saw at the long narrows of the E-lute Nation with whome those people are connected. I indeavored to obtain from those people of the Situation of their nation, if scattered or what had become of the nativs who must have peopled this great town. an old man who appeared of Some note among them and father to my guide brought foward a woman who was badly marked with the Small Pox and made Signs that they all died with the disorder which marked her face, and which She was verry near dieing with when a Girl. from the age of this woman this Distructive disorder I judge must have been about 28 or 30 years past, and about the time the Clatsops inform us that this disorder raged in their towns and distroyed their nation. Those people Speak a different language from those below tho in their dress habits and manners &c. they differ but little from the Quathlahpohtles. theire women use the truss as those do of all the nations risideing from the quathlahpohtle to the enterance of Lewis's river and on the Columbia above for Some distance. those people have Some words the Same with those below but the air of their language is entirely different, their men are Stouter and much better made, and their womin ware larger & longer robes than those do below; those are most commonly made of Deer Skins dressed with the hair on them. they pay great attention to their aged Severall men and women whom I observed in this village had arived at a great age, and appeared to be helthy tho blind. I provailed on an old man to draw me a Sketch of the Multnomar River ang give me the names of the nations resideing on it which he readily done, See draft on the other Side and gave me the names Of 4 nations who reside on this river two of them very noumerous. The first is Clark a-mus nation reside on a Small river which takes its rise in Mount Jefferson and falls into the Moltnomar about 40 miles up. this nation is noumerous and inhabit 11 Towns. the 2d is the Cush-hooks who reside on the N E. Side below the falls, the 3rd is the Char-cowah who reside above the Falls on the S W. Side neether of those two are noumerous. The fourth Nation is the Cal-lar-po-e-wah which is very noumerous & inhabit the Country on each Side of the Multnomar from its falls as far up as the knowledge of those people extend. they inform me also that a high mountain passes the Multnomar at the falls, and above the Country is an open plain of great extent.

I purchased 5 dogs of those people for the use of their Oil in the Plains, and at 4 P M left the Village and proceeded on to Camp where I joind Capt. Lewis

The enterance of Multnomah river is 142 miles up the Columbia river from its enterance into the Pacific Ocean-. in my absence and Soon after I left camp Several Canoes of men women and Children came to the camp. and at one time there was about 37 of those people in Camp Capt Lewis fired his Air gun which astonished them in Such a manner that they were orderly and kept at a proper distance dureing the time they Continued with him- as maney as 10 Canoes arrived at Camp in the Course of this day. they all Seem to give the Same account of the Scercity of Provisions above. one family Continued all night and behaved themselves in a very orderly manner.

on the 3rd Joseph Field returned from the woods and informed the Drewyer Rubin & himself had killed four Elk. Capt L. Sent Sergt. Pryor and two men with Joseph Field to dry the flesh of the Elk in the woods on Scaffolds with fire. the party bilow quick Sand river did not return to day. The Indians continue to vist our Camp in Considerable number from above with their families. these pore people appeared half Starved. they picked up the bones and little refuse meat which had been thrown away by the party. Capt L had the flesh of the 4 Elk which was killed on the 1st inst. dried- Some of the men of the nativs who visited Capt Lewis wore a girdle, with a Small Skin in front and a Cap of the Skin of the deers head &c.

[Lewis, April 4, 1806] Friday April 4th 1806. This morning early we sent Sergt. Ordway in Surch of Sergt. Gass and party below the entrance of the Quicksand river fom whom we have yet had no report. in the course of a few hours both parties returned. Sergt. Gass and party brought the flesh of a bear and some venison. they informed us that they had killed an Elk and six deer tho the flesh of the greater part of those animals was so meagre that it was unfit for uce and they had therefore left it in the woods. Collins who had killed the bear, found the bed of another in which there were three young ones; and requested to be permitted to return in order to waylay the bed and kill the female bear; we permitted him to do so; Sergt. Gass and Windsor returned with him. Several parties of the natives visit us today as usual both from above and below; those who came from above were moving with their families, and those from below appeared to be empeled mearly by curiossity to see us. About noon we dispatched Gibson Shannon Howard and Wiser in one of the light canoes, with orders to proceed up the Columbia to a large bottom on the South side about six miles above us and to hunt untill our arrival. late in the evening Joseph Fields and Drewyer returned. they had killed two deer yesterday, and informed us that the meat would be dryed by midday tomorrow. we directed Drewyer and the two Feildses to ascend the river tomorrow to join Gibson and party, and hunt untill our arrival. this evening being fair I observed time and distance of Ys Eastern Limb from regulus with Sextant. k West.

[Clark, April 4, 1806] Friday April 4th 1806. Mouth of quick Sand River This morning early we Sent Sergt. Ordway in Serch of Sergt. Gass and party below the enterance of quick Sand river from whome we have yet had no report. in the Course of a fiew hours both parties returned. Sergt. Gass and party brought the Flesh of a Bear, and Some venison. they informed us they had killed an Elk and Six Deer tho the flesh of the greater part of those Animals were So Meagre that it was unfit for uce, and they had therefore left it in the woods. Collins who had killed the Bear, found the bead of another in which there was three young ones; and requested to be permited to return in order to waylay the bed and kill the female bear; we permited them to do So; Sergt. Gass and Windser returned with him. Several parties of the nativs visit us to day as usial both from above and below; those who came from above were moveing with their families, and those from below appeared to be impeled mearly by curiosity to See us. About noon we dispatched Gibson, Shannon, Howard & Wiser in one of the light Canoes, with orders to proceed up the Columbia to a large bottom on the South Side about Six Miles above us and there to hunt untill our arrival. late in the evening Jos Fields and Drewyer returned with a load of dried meat. they had killed two deer yesterday and informed us that the meat would be dryed by Mid-day tomorrow. We directed Drewyer and Field's to assend the river tomorrow and join Gibson & party, and hunt untill our arrival. this evening being fair observed time and distance of moon's Eastern Limb from regulus with Sextant * West

[Lewis, April 5, 1806] Saturday April 5th 1806. This morning was so cloudy that I could not obtain any lunar observations with a Aquila as I wished. Joseph Fields and Drewyer departed this morning agreeably to their orders of last evening. at 9 A.M. we Sent Sergt. Ordway and a party to assist Sergt. Pryor in bringing in the meat of four Elk which he had dried. at 1 P. M the party returned with the meat. it had been so illy dryed that we feared it would not keep. we therefore directed it to be cut thinner and redryed over a fire this evening, as we purpose setting out early in the morning. the deerskins which we have had cased for the purpose of containing our dryed meat are not themselves sufficiently dryed for that purpose, we directed them to be dryed by the fire also. the weather has been so damp that there was no possibility of pounding the meat as I wished.-

we were visited today by several parties of the natives as usual; they behaved themselves in a very orderly manner. Observed Magnetic Azimuth and altitude of the sun with Circumferenter and Sextant.

Saw the Log cock, the hummingbird, gees ducks &c today. the tick has made it's appearance it is the same with those of the Atlantic States. the Musquetoes have also appeared but are not yet troublesome.- this morning at 10 OClock Sergt. Gass returned with Collins and Windsor they had not succeeded in killing the female bear tho they brought the three cubs with them. the Indians who visited us today fancyed these petts and gave us wappetoe in exchange for them. Drewyer informed me that he never knew a female bear return to her young when they had been allarmed by a person and once compelled to leave them. The dogwood grows abundantly on the uplands in this neighbourhood. it differs from that of the United States in the appearance of it's bark which is much smoother, it also arrives here to much greater size than I ever observed it elsewhere sometimes the stem is nearly 2 feet in diameter. we measured a fallen tree of fir No 1 which was 318 feet including the stump which was about 6 feet high. this tree was only about 31/2 feet in diameter. we saw the martin, small gees, the small speckled woodpecker with a white back, the Blue crested Corvus, ravens, crows, eagles Vultures and hawks. the mellow bug and long leged spider have appeared, as have also the butterfly blowing fly and many other insects. I observe not any among them which appear to differ from those of our country or which deserve particular notice.

[Clark, April 5, 1806]
Saturday April 5th 1806.
This morning was So Cloudy that we could not obtain any lunar
observations with a Aquila as we wished.

Joseph Field & Drewrey left us this morning agreeably to their orders of last evening. at the Same time we Sent Sergt. Ordway and five men to assist Sergt. Pryor in bringing in the meat of four Elk which he had dried in the woods. at 1 p.m.the party returned with the meat. it was not Sufficiently dryed to keep. we had it cut thiner and redryed over a fire this evening, as we purpose Setting out early in the morning. the dear skins which we had cased for the purpose of holding our dried meat is not Sufficently dry for that purpose, we derected them to be dried by the fire also. the weather being So damp that there was no possibullity of pounding the meat as I wished.- We were visited by Several parties of the nativs to day; they behaved themselves in a very orderly manner.

Saw the Log cock, the humming bird, Geese, Ducks &c. to day. the tick has made it's appearance it is the Same with those of the Atlantic States. the Musquetors have also appeared, but are not yet much troublesom.- this morning at 10 A M Sergt. Gass returned with Collins and Windser they had not Succeeded in killing the female bear, tho they brought the three cub's with them. the Indians who visited us to day fancied those Petts and gave us wappato in exchange for them. Fir and White Cedar is the common growth of the up lands, as is the Cotton wood, ash, large leafed Ash and Sweet Willow that of the bottom lands. The Huckleberry, shallon, and the Several evergreen Shrubs, of that Speces that bears berries have Seased to appear, except that Species which has the leaf with a prickley Margin. among the plants of this prarie in which we are encamped I observe the pashequo, Shannetahque, and Compound firn, the root of which the nativs eate; also the water cress, Straw berry flowering pea not yet in blume, narrow dock, and rush which are luxuriant and abundent in the river bottoms. the large leafed thorn has also disappeard. The red flowering Current is found here in considerable quantities on the upland, and the Common Dog wood is found on either Side of the river in this neighbourhood and above Multnomah river. The Country on either Side is fertile, the bottom on the South Side is wide and inter sperced with Small ponds in which the nativs gather their Wappato. back of this bottom the Country rises to about 200 feet and the Soil is very rich as that also above q Sandy river quite to the Mountains. the Country on the N. Side from a fiew Miles above this place as low down as the enterance of Cah-wah-na-ki-ooks River rises to the hight generally of 150 or 200 feet is tolerably leavel, thickly timbered with Fir and White Cedar. the Soil of the richest quallity. Some Small Praries on the bank of the river. That portion of Country below as low down as the enterance of Cah-wah na ki ooks River is a broken rich Country. the hills are high, the bottom lands as before mentioned and fertile &c.-The Country a fiew miles up the Multnomah River rises from the river bottoms to the hight of from 2 to 300 feet and is rich & fertile. Some Plains can be Seen to the N. E. of our Camp of 10 or 12 miles in Secumference The Hunters & Serjt Pryor informed us that they had Measured a tree on the upper Side of quick Sand River 312 feet long and about 4 feet through at the Stump.

[Lewis, April 6, 1806] Sunday April 6th 1806. This morning we had the dryed meat secured in skins and the canoes loaded; we took breakfast and departed at 9 A.M. we continued up the N. side of the river nearly to the place at which we had encamped on the 3rd of Nov. when we passed the river to the south side in quest of the hunters we had sent up yesterday and the day before. from the appearance of a rock near which we had encamped on the 3rd of November last I could judge better of the rise of the water than I could at any point below. I think the flood of this spring has been about 12 feet higher than it was at that time; the river is here about 11/2 miles wide; it's general width from the beacon rock which may be esteemed the head of tide water, to the marshey islands is from one to 2 miles tho in many places it is still wider. it is only in the fall of the year when the river is low that the tides are persceptable as high as the beacon rock. this remarkable rock which stands on the North shore of the river is unconnected with the hills and rises to the hight of seven hundred feet; it has some pine or reather fir timber on it's nothern side, the southern is a precipice of it's whole hight. it rises to a very sharp point and is visible for 20 miles below on the river. at the distance of ten miles from our encampment we met with our hunters in the upper end of the bottom to which we had directed them on the South side of the river. they had killed three Elk this morning and wounded two others so badly that they expected to get them. we therefore determined to encamp for the evening at this place in order to dry the meat, in surch of which we sent a party immediately and employed others in preparing scaffoalds and collecting firewood &c against their return. we found some indians with our hunters when we arrived; these people are constantly hanging about us.- As has been before mentioned Capt C set out with a party of seven men on 2ed inst. in surch of the entrance of the Multnomah river. he departed at 1/2 after 11 A. M and directed his course along the Southern side of the river. at the distance of 8 miles he passed the village of the Na-cha-co-lee tribe of the E-lute Nation; this village is not large and being situated on the main shore opposite to and S. of the Diamond Island it was concealed by that island from our view both ascending and decending the Columbia as we passed near the Northern shore. Capt C. passed this village without halting and continued his rout untill 3 P.M. when he arrived at a large double house of the Ne-er-cho-ki-oo tribe of the Shah'ha-la nation; at this place we had seen 24 additional straw and bark huts as we passed down last fall, the inhabitants of which as I have before mentioned reside at the great rapids of the Columbia river. about this place in different directions Capt C. saw a great number of small canoes lying scattered on the bank. these small canoes are employed by the women in collecting wappetoe; with one of these a woman enters a pond where the Sagitaria Sagittifolia grows frequently to her breast in water and by means of her toes and feet breakes the bulb of this plant loos from the parent radicle and disincumbering it from the mud it immediately rises to the surface of the water when she seizes it and throws it into her canoe which she always keeps convenient to her. they will remain in the water for hours together in surch of this bulb in middle of winter. those canoes are from 10 to 14 feet in length, from 18 to 23 inches in width near the middle tapering or becoming narrower towards either extremity and 9 inches deep their form is thus. they are so light that a woman can draw them over land or take them with ease through the swamps in any direction, and are sufficient to carry a single person and several bushells of roots. Capt. Clarks pilot informed him that the small canoes which he saw in the vicinity of this lodge were the property of the Shah-ha-las who used them occasionally when they visit this neighbourhood for the purpose of collecting roots. while at this place Capt C. entered one of the appartments of the house and offered several articles to the natives in exchange for wappetoe, they appeared to be in an ill humour and positively refused to let him have any. Capt. C. sat himself down near the fire and having a part of a portfire match in his pocket cut of a small peice of it and threw it in the fire; at the same time he took out his pocket compass and by means of a magnet which he had in the top of his inkstand he turned the nedle of the compass about very briskly; the match took fire and birned vehemently; the indians astonished and allarmed at these exhibitions, ran and brought several parcels of wappetoe and laid at his feet and begged that he would put out the bad fire; to this he consented; at this moment the match being exhausted was of course extenguished and he put up his compass & magnet. they were now much more complisant, tho the women and children were yet so much allarmed that they took refuge in their beads and behing the men who were seting opposite to Capt. C. during the whole of this farcical seen an old man who was seting by continued to speak with great vehemence apparently imploring his god for protection. Capt. C. gave them an adiquate compensation for their roots and having lighted his pipe smoaked with the men. they appeared in a great measure to get the better of their allarm and he left them and continued his rout along the south side of Image canoe Island which he found to be three islands, the one in the center concealing the apperture between the two others in such manner that from the north side of the river where we have previously passed they all appeared to form one island only. at the distance of 13 miles below the village just mentioned, and at the lower point of what we have heretofore deemed the image canoe Island, Capt C. entered the Multnomah river so called by the natives from a nation of that name who reside on wappetoe island a little below the entrance of this river? Multnomah river discharges itself on the S. side of the Columbia 140 miles above the entrance of the latter into the Pacific Ocean, and may be justly esteemed one fourth of that noble river. Capt. C. found that this river had attained it's greatest annual hight and had now fallen about 18 inches. it has three small islands in it's mouth which conceal the river from the view of those who pass with the stream of the Columbia. from the Columbia at the entrance of the Multonomah river Mount Jefferson bears S. E. this is a noble mountain. I think equally as high as Mount St. Helines but it's distance being much greater than that of the latter, so great a portion of it dose not appear above the range of mountains which lie betwen boath those stupendious mountains and this point of view. like mount St. Heleans it's figure is a regular cone and is covered with eternal snow. M. St. Heleans from the same point boar N _____, Mount Hood due East, and Mount Raniei nearly North. there is also a very high humped mountain a little to the East of Mount St. Heleans which appears to lie in the same chain with those conic pointed mountains before mentioned. soon after Capt Clark entered the Multnomah river he was met by an old Indian man alone in a canoe decending the river, the pilot had some conversation with him and informed Capt.

C. that this was a man of the Clark-a'-mas nation who are numerous and inhabit eleven vilages on either side of a river of the same name which has it's source in Mount Jefferson and after tranversing a woody and fertile country discharges itself into the Multnomah river on it's E. side at the distance of about 40 miles from it's junction with the Columbia. the Clarkamas river is navigable for canoes a great distance, from the Indian account almost to the foot of mount, Jefferson. the nation who inhabit it's borders live principally on fish with which this stream abounds and also on roots which they procure on it's borders. they sometimes also come down to the Multnomah and Columbia in surch of Wappatoe. they do not differ essentially in their language dress &c from the Quathlahpohtles and others in the vicinity of wappetoe island. The current of the Multnomah river is as gentle as that of the Columbia, glides smoothly with an even surface, and appears to possess sufficient debth for the largest ship. Capt. C. attempted to sound it with a cord of 5 fathoms which was the longest in his possession but could not find bottom at this debth for at least one third of the width of the river. Capt. C. ascended this river ten miles to a large wood house on the East side of the river, near which he encamped for the evening; the house being infested with such swarms of flees that they could not remain in it. this his guide informed him was the house of the Cush-hooks nation who reside just below the falls of the Multnomah river and who occasionally reside at this place for the purpose of collecting wappetoe. at present this house appeared to have been lately abandoned by the natives who had left therein exposed to every visiter various articles such as small canoes, mats, bladders of train oil, baskets, bowls and trenchers. this is a strong evidence of the honesty of the natives with rispect to the property of each other, but they have given us several evidences that they do not pay the same rispect to the property of white men. his guide further informed him that there were a number of small houses belonging to the last mentioned nation situated on two bayous which make out of the river a little above this large hose on the East side; that the inhabitants of these as well as those of the large house had gone up to the falls of the Multnomah river for the purpose of taking fish. these falls are situated at the distance of 2 days travel from the junction of the Multnomah and Columbia rivers agreeably to the Indian account which we have estimated at 60 miles or 20 m. above the entrance of Clarkamus river. Capt C. took the dementions of the hose of the Ne-mal-quin-ner tribe of the Cushhooks nation near which he encamped on the 2ed inst. and found it presisely thirty feet by 40 squar constructed with broad boards and covered with the bark of the white cedar or arborvita; the floor is on a level with the surface of the earth and the internal arrangement is similar to those of the natives of the Sea coast.- these people carry on a trafic with the Killamucks of the coast across the mountains and by way of the Killamucks river from the Killamucks they obtain their train oil. The courses and distances taken by Capt. Clark in ascending the Multnomah river from it's junction with the Columbia river, commencing at the lower extremity of the Image canoe Islands are as follows. (viz) S. 30° W. 4 m. to the upper point of a small island in the center of Multnomah river. thence S 10° W. 3 m. to a sluce 80 yds. wide on Stard. which dividing wappetoe Island from the main land discharges itself into wappetoe inlet passed a willow point on Lard. S. 60° W. 3 ms. to a large indian house on the Lard. side, just below some high fir land the shore is bold and high on Stard. side. S 30° E. 2 ms. to the center of a bend under The highlands on Stard. side, passing a Lard. point; from hence the river directed it's course to the E. of S. E. as far as Capt. C. could perceive it.- at this place the Multnomah river is 500 yds. wide and sufficiently deep to admit the largest ship. the river appears to be washing away it's banks in some places, and has more sandbars and willow points than the Columbia.On the morning of the 3rd inst. Capt. Clark observed that the water had fallen in the course of the night about 5 inches. he set out early and proceeded up the river a short distance few miles and attempted a second time to fathom it but with the same success as before he could nt find bottom with his cord of 5 fathoms for the distance of half the width of the stream. Capt C. having fully satisfyed himself of the magnitude of this great river he set out on his return at 7 A.M. I have but little doubt but that this river waters a vast tract of country lying between the Western mountains and the mountainous country of the sea coast extending as far south as the waters of the gulph of Callifornia or about Latitude 37° North. at 11 A.M. Capt. C. arrived at the Ne-er-cho-ki-oo house where he had allarmed the inhabtants yesterday. he halted here a few minutes to smoke with these people who consisted of eight families. he found that his presents excited fresh allarm particularly among the women and children who hid themselves and took refuge behind the men as yesterday; the men held down their heads and seemed much conserned; he therefore remained in the house but a few minutes, returned to his canoe and pursued his rout. his pilot now informed him that these people as well as their relations at the falls of the Columbia were illy disposed bad men. soon after he set out he met five canoes on board of which there were as many families of the Shah-ha-la nation decending the river in surch of subsistence. they were extreemly anxious to come along side, but he forbid their doing so as their number was too considerable there being 21 men on board these canoes. his pilot told him that they were mischevous bad men. at 3 P.M. he arrived at the present residence of his pilot on the South side of the river opposite the Diamond Island. here he halted about an hour he found this house very large; it consisted of seven appartments in one range above ground each about 30 feet square. the entrances to these appartments were from passages which extended quite across the house, about 4 feet wide and formed like the walls of the hose of broad boards set on end extending from beneath the floor to the roof of the house. the apperture or hole through which they enter all those wooden houses are remarkably small not generally more than 3 feet high and about 22 inches wide. the ground plot of the Nechecolee house is thus 1 1 1 1 the passages of 4 feet and 2 2 &c. the appartments of 30 feet square. this house is covered with the bark of the white cedar, laid on in a double course, supported by rafters and longitudinal round poles attatched to the rafters with cores of this bark. the peices of the cedar bark extend the whole length of the side of the roof and jut over at the eve about 18 inches. at the distance of 18 inches transverse splinters of dry fir is inserted through the cedar bark in order to keep it smooth and prevent it's edges from colapsing by the heat of the sun; in this manner the natives make a very secure light and lasting roof of this bark. in the vicinity of this house Capt. Clark observed the remains of five other large houses which appeared to have been sunk in the ground several feet and built after the method of those of the Elutes nation at the great narrows of the columbia with whom these people claim affinity. their language is the same with the Elutes, tho in their habits, dress manners &c they differ but little from the Quathlahpohtles and others in this neighborhood. they make use of some words common to their neighbours but the air of their language is entirely different. they are much better formed and their men larger than the nations below. their women wear larger and longer robes which are made principally of deerskins dressed in the hair. they pay great rispect to their aged persons. Capt. C. observed several persons of both sexes who appeared to have arrived to great age yet they appeared perfectly healthy tho most of them perfectly blind. the loss of sight I have observed to be more common among all the nations inhabiting this river than among any people I ever observed. they have almost invariably soar eyes at all stages of life. the loss of an eye is very common among them; blindness in perdsons of middle age is by no means uncommon, and it is almost invariably a concommitant of old age. I know not to what cause to attribute this prevalent deficientcy of the eyes except it be their exposure to the reflection of the sun on the water to which they are constantly exposed in the occupation of fishing. Capt. C. enquired of the Nechecole the cause of the decline of their village. an old man who appeared to be of some note among them and the father of his guide brought forward a woman who was much marked with the small pox, and made signs that the inhabitants of those houses which he saw in ruins had all died with the disorder which marked the face of the woman and with which this woman was very near dying when a girl. from the apparent age of the woman Capt. C. supposed that it was about 28 or 30 years since this disorder had prevailed among these people. this is about the time which we have supposed that it prevailed among the Clatsops and others of the coast. Capt C. now prevailed on this old man to give him a sketch of the Multnomah river it's branches and the position and names of the Indian nations residing thereon this the old man son executed with his finger in the dust. (see scetch inserted on the 3rd inst.). he informed that the Cush-hooks and Char-cow-ah nations who reside at the falls of that river were not numerous; but that the Cal-lah-po-e-wah nation who inhabited both sides of this river above the falls as far as it was known to himself or his nation were very numerous. that the country they inhabited was level and wholy destitute of timber. that a high range of mountains passed the Multnomah river at the falls, on the upperside of which the country was one vast plain. the nations who inhabit this country reside on the rivers and subsist like those of the Columbia on fish and roots principally. Capt C. bought five dogs of these people and set out for my camp at 5 P.M. where he arrived a little before dark, on the evening of the third.- the party whom we sent for the flesh of the Elk which Shannon had killed returned in the evening with that of four, one had by some mistake been omitted. Drewyer and shannon found the two wounded Elk and had killed them. we set all hands at work to prepare the meat for the saffoald they continued their operations untill late at night. we directed Shannon to go out early in the morning with a party to bring in the Elk which had been left last evening in mistake. we also directed Drewyer and the two Feildses to ascend the river early in the morning to a small bottom a few miles above and hunt untill our arrival.-

[Clark, April 6, 1806] Sunday April 6th 1806. Two Indians Came last night very late to our Camp and continued all night. early we had all the meat packed up and our Canoes loaded ready for to Set out and after an early brackfast at which time all things were ready and we Set out and proceeded to the Camp of Gibson & party about 9 miles, they had killed 3 Elk at no great distance and Wounded two others so badly that we expect to precure them. Sent a party of Six men with Shannon who had killed the Elk to bring in the Elk, and formed a Camp, near which we had a Scaffold made ready to dry the meat as Soon as it Should arive. Reubin Field killed a bird of the Quail kind or Class which was whistleing near our Camp it is larger than the quail or partridge as they are Called Kentucky and Virginia. it's form is presisely that of our partridge tho its plumage differs in every part. the upper part of the head, Sides and back of the neck, including the Croop and about of the under part of the body is of a bright dove coloured blue, under neath the under beak, as high as the lower edge of the eye, and back as far as the hinder part of the eyes and thence comeing down to a point in the front of the neck about 2/3rd of it's length downwards, is of a fine dark brick red. between this brick red and the dove colour there runs a narrow Stripe of pure white. the ears are covered with some coarse dark brown feathers. just at the base of the under chap there is a narrow transvirce Stripe of white. from the crown of the head two long round feathers extend backwards nearly in the direction of the beak and are of a black Colour. the length of these feathers is 2 1/2 inches. one overlais and Conseals the other which is Somewhat Shorter and Seems to be raped in the plumage of that in front which folding backwards colapses behing and has a round appearance. the tail is composed of 12 dark brown feathers of nearly equal length. the large feathers of the wings are of a dark brown & are reather Short in purpotion to the body of the bird. in this respect very Similar to the partridge. the covert of the wings and back are of a dove Colour with a Slight admixture of redish brown. a wide Stripe which extends from Side to Side of the body and occupies the lower region of the breast is beautifully varigated with the brick red white & black which perdominates in the order they are mentioned and the Colours mark the feathers transversely. the legs are covered with feathers as low as the Knee; these feathers are of dark brown tiped with a dark brick red as are also those between and about the joining of the legs with the body. the foot is presisely that of the Common partridge except that they are as also the legs white. the upper beak is Short, wide at it's base, black, convex, curved downwards and reather obtusely pointed. it exceeds the under chap considerably which is of a white colour, also convex under neath and obtusely pointed. the nostrils are remarkably Small, placed far back and low down on the Sides of the beak. they are covered by a thin proterant elastic, black leather like Substance. the eyes are of a uniform pierceing black colour. this is a most butifull bird I preserved the Skin of this bird retaining the wings feet & head which I hope will give a just Idea of the bird. it's loud note is Single and Consists of a loud Squall, intirely different from the whistling of our partridge or quailes. it has a chiping note when allarmed like our partridge.- to day there was a Second of those birds killed which presisely resembles that just discribed. I believe those to be the mail bird the female, if so, I have not yet Seen.-.

at 6 P.M. Shannon and party returned with the flesh of five Elk. the two he had wounded in the morning he found dead near the place he had Shot them. we had the meat cut into thin pices and Scaffored with a fire under it to dry out, which we expect in the course of the night Can be effected. four Indians from the great rapids visited us to day and Continued all day. they give the Same account of the Scercity of provisions above the falls as has already been given by others. This Supply of Elk I think by useing economey and in addition of roots and dogs which we may probably precure from he Nativs on Lewis's river will be Sufficient to last us to the Chopunnish where we Shall Meet with our horses-. and near which place there is Some deer to be precured.

Frazer killed a pheasent of the Common kind. Jos. Field killed a vulture of that Speces already discribed. in the evening late the Indians left us and returned to their village. we detected that fires be kept under the meat all night. and tha Drewyer and the two Fields proceed on to the next bottom and hunt untill we Should arive. 9 miles

[Lewis, April 7, 1806] Monday April 7th 1806. This morning early the flesh of the remaining Elk was brought in and Drewyer with the Feildses departed agreeably to the order of the last evening. we employed the party in drying the meat today which we completed by the evening, and we had it secured in dryed Elkskins and put on board in readiness for an early departure. we were visited today by several parties of indians from a village about 8 miles above us of the Sahhalah nation. I detected one of them in steeling a peice of lead and sent him from camp. I hope we have now a sufficient stock of dryed meat to serve us as far the Chopunnish provided we can obtain a few dogs horses and roots by the way. in the neighbourhood of the Chopunnish we can procure a few deer and perhaps a bear or two for the mountains. last evening Reubin Fields killed a bird of the quail kind it is reather larger than the quail, or partridge as they are called in Virginia. it's form is precisely that of our patridge tho it's plumage differs in every part. the upper part of the head, sides and back of the neck, including the croop and about 1/3 of the under part of the body is of a bright dove coloured blue, underneath the under beak, as high as the lower edge of the eyes, and back as far as the hinder part of the eyes and thence coming down to a point in front of the neck about two thirds of it's length downwards, is of a fine dark brick red. between this brick red and the dove colour there runs a narrow stripe of pure white. the ears are covered with some coarse stiff dark brown feathers. just at the base of the under chap there is narrow transverse stripe of white. from the crown of the head two long round feathers extend backwards nearly in the direction of the beak and are of a black colour. the longest of these feathers is two inches and an half, it overlays and conceals the other which is somewhat shorter and seems to be raped in the plumage of that in front which folding backwards colapses behind and has a round appearance. the tail is composed of twelve dark brown feathers of nearly equal length. the large feathers of the wings are of a dark brown and are reather short in proportion to the body of the bird in that rispect very similar to our common partridge. the covert of the wings and back are of a dove colour with a slight admixture of redish brown. a wide stripe which extends from side to side of the body and occupyes the lower region of the breast is beautifully variagated with the brick red white and black which pedominate in the order they are mentioned and the colours mark the feathers transversely. the legs are covered with feathers as low as the knee; these feathers are of a dark brown tiped with the dark brick red as are also those between and about the joining of the legs with the body. they have four toes on each foot of which three are in front and that in the center the longest, those one each side nearly of a length; that behing is also of good length and are all armed with long and strong nails. the legs and feet are white and imbrecated with proportionably large broad scales. the upper beak is short, wide at it's base, black, convex, curved downwards and reather obtusely pointed. it exceeds the under chap considerably which is of a white colour, also convex underneath and obtusely pointed. the nostrils are remarkably small placed far back and low down on the sides of the beak. they are covered by a thin protuberant elastic, black leatherlike substance. the eyes are of a uniform piercing black colour. this is a most beautifull bird. I preserved the skin of this bird retaining the wings feet and head which I hope will give a just idea of the bird. it's loud note is single and consists of a loud squall, intirely different from the whistling of our quales or partridge. it has a cherping note when allarmed something like ours.- today there was a second of these birds killed by Capt C. which precisely resembled that just discribed. I believe these to be the male bird the female, if so, I have not yet seen.- the day has been fair and weather extreemly pleasant. we made our men exercise themselves in shooting today and regulate their guns found several of them that had their sights moved by accedent, and others that wanted some little alterations all which were compleatly rectifyed in the course of the day. in the evening all the Indians departed for their village.

[Clark, April 7, 1806] Monday April 7th 1806 This morning Drewyer & the two Fields Set out agreeably to their orders of last evening, the remainder of the party employed in drying the flesh of the five Elk killed by Shannon yesterday. which was completed and we had it Secured in dried Shaved Elk Skins and put on board in readiness for our early departure. we were visited by Several parties of Indians from a Village about 12 miles above us of the Sahhalah nation. one of them was detected in Stealing a piece of Lead. I Sent him off imedeately. I hope now we have a Sufficient Stock of dryed meat to Serve us as far as the Chopunnish provided we can obtain a fiew dogs, horses and roots by the way. in the neighbourhood of the Chopunnish under the Rocky Mountains we can precure a fiew deer, and perhaps a Bear or two for the Mountains.

The day has been fair and weather exceedingly pleasent. we made our men exersise themselves in Shooting and regulateing their guns, found Several of them that had their Sights moved by accident, and others that wanted Some little alterations all which were compleated rectified in the Course of the day except my Small rifle, which I found wanted Cutting out. about 4 oClock P M all the Indians left us, and returned to their Village. they had brought with them Wappato, & pashequa roots Chapellel cakes, and a Species of Raspberry for Sale, none of which they disposed of as they asked Such enormous prices for those articles that we were not able to purchase any. Drewyer returned down the river in the evening & informed us that the nativs had Sceared all the Elk from the river above. Joseph & reuben Fields had proceeded on further up the river in the canoe, he expected to the village.

I provaled on an old indian to mark the Multnomah R down on the Sand which hid and perfectly Corisponded with the Sketch given me by sundary others, with the addition of a circular mountain which passes this river at the falls and connects with the mountains of the Seacoast. he also lais down the Clark a mos passing a high Conical Mountain near it's mouth on the lower Side and heads in Mount Jefferson which he lais down by raiseing the Sand as a very high mountain and Covered with eternal Snow. the high mountain which this Indian lais down near the enterance of Clark a mos river, we have not Seen as the hills in it's diretion from this vally is high and obscures the Sight of it from us. Mt Jefferson we Can plainly See from the enterance of Multnomah from which place it bears S. E. this is a noble Mountain and I think equally as high or Something higher than Mt. St. Heleansa but its distance being much greater than that of the latter, So great a portion of it does not appear above the range of mountains which lie between both those Stupendious Mountains and the Mouth of Multnomah. like Mt. St. Heleans its figure is a regular Cone and is covered with eturnial Snow. that the Clarkamos nation as also those at the falls of the Multnomah live principally on fish of which those Streams abound and also on roots which they precure on it's borders, they also Sometimes Come down to the Columbia in Serch of Wappato. they build their houses in the Same form with those of the Columbian Vally of wide Split boads and Covered with bark of the White Cedar which is the entire length of the one Side of the roof and jut over at the eve about 18 inches. at the distance of about 18 inches transvers Spinters of dried pine is inserted through the Ceder bark inorder to keep it Smooth and prevent it's edge from Colapsing by the heat of the Sun; in this manner the nativs make a very Secure light and lasting roof of this bark. which we have observed in every Vilege in this Vally as well as those above. this Indian also informed me the multnomah above the falls was Crouded with rapids and thickly inhabited by indians of the Callah-po-e-wah Nation. he informed he had himself been a long way up that river &c.

[Lewis, April 8, 1806] Tuesday April 8th 1806. The wind blew so violently this morning that we were obliged to unlode our perogues and canoes, soon after which they filled with water. being compelled to remain during the day at our present station we sent out some hunters in order to add something to our stock of provision; and exposed our dryed meat to the sun and the smoke of small fires. in the evening the hunters returned having killed a duck only; they saw two bear and some of the blacktailed jumping or fallow deer, such as are found about Fort Clatsop; this kind of deer are scarce in this neighbourhood, the common longtailed fallow deer being most abundant. we have seen the black bear only in this quarter. the wind continued without intermission to blow violently all day. I took a walk today of three miles down the river; in the course of which I had an opportunity to correct an errow which I have heretofore made with rispect to the shrub I have hithertoo called the large leafed thorn. the leaf of this thorn is small being only abut 2 1/2 inches long, is petiolate, conjugate; the leafets are petiolate accutely pointed, having their margins cut with unequal angular insissures. the shrub which I have heretofore confounded with this grows in similar situations, has a stem precisely like it except the thorn and bears a large three loabed leaf. this bryer is of the class Polyandria and order Polygynia. the flowers are single, the peduncle long and celindric. the calix is a perianth, of one leaf, five cleft, & accutely pointed. the perianth is proper, erect, inferior with rispect to both petals and germen, and equal. the corolla consists of five accute pale scarlet petals, insirted in the recepticle with a short and narrow claw. the Corolla is smooth, moderately long, situated at the base of the germen, permanent, and cup shaped. of the stamens the filaments are subulate, inserted into the recepticle, unequal and bent inwards concealing the pistillum; anther two loabed and inflected situated on the top of the fillaments of the pistillum the germ is conical, imbricated, superior, sessile and short. the styles are short with rispect to the stamen, capillary smooth, obtuse, distributed over the serface of the germ and decid-uous. no perseptable stigma.- late at night the centinel detected an old indian man in attempting to creep into camp in order to pilfer; he allarmed the indian very much by presenting his gun at him; he gave the fellow a few stripes with a switch and sent him off. this fellow is one of a party of six who layed incamped a few hundred yards below us, they departed soon after this occurrence.

[Clark, April 8, 1806] Tuesday April 8th 1806 This morning about day light I heard a Considerable roreing like wind at a distance and in the Course of a Short time ways rose very high which appeared to come across the river and in the Course of an hour became So high that we were obliged to unload the canoes, at 7 oClock A.M. the winds Suelded and blew So hard and raised the Waves So emensely high from the N. E and tossed our Canoes against the Shore in Such a manner as to render it necessary to haul them up on the bank. finding from the appearance of the winds that it is probable that we may be detained all day, we Sent out Drewyer, Shannon Colter & Collins to hunt with derections to return if the Wind Should lul, if not to Continue the hunt all day except they killed Elk or bear Sooner &c. we had the dried meat which was cured at our last encampment below exposed to the Sun. John Shields Cut out my Small rifle & brought hir to Shoot very well. the party ows much to the injenuity of this man, by whome their guns are repared when they get out of order which is very often.

I observed an Indian Woman who visited us yesterday blind of an eye, and a man who was nearly blind of both eyes. the loss of Sight I have observed to be more Common among all the nations inhabiting this river than among any people I ever observed. they have almost invariably Sore eyes at all Stages of life. the loss of an eye is very Common among them; blindness in persons of middle age is by no means uncommon, and it is almost invariably a concammitant of old age. I Know not to what cause to attribute this prevalent deficientcy of the eye except it be their exposure to the reflection of the Sun on the water to which they are constantly exposed in the Occupation of fishing. about 1 P M Collins Shannon and Colter returned. Collins Saw 2 bear but could not get a Shot at them. neither Shannon nor Colter Saw any thing worth Shooting. Soon after Drewyer returned haveing only a Summer Duck. the Elk is gorn to the mountains as the hunters Suppose. in the evening late an old man his Son & Grand Son and their Wives &c. Came down dureing the time the waves raged with great fury. the wife of the Grand Son is a woman of differant appearance from any we have Seen on this river, she has a very round head and pierceing black eyes. Soon after those people arived the Old man was detected in Stealing a Spoon and he was ordered away, at about 200 yards below our Camp they built themselves a fire and did not return to our fires after-. The Wind Continued violently hard all day, and threw our Canoes with Such force against the Shore that one of them Split before we Could get it out.

[Lewis, April 9, 1806] Wednesday April 9th 1806. This morning early we commenced the operation of reloading our canoes; at 7 A.M. we departed and proceeded on to the Camp of Reubin and Joseph Fields they had not killed any game; we made no halt at this place but continued our rout to the Wah-clel-lah Village which is situated on the North side of the river about a mile below the beacon rock; here we halted and took breakfast. John Colter one of our party observed the tomehawk in one of the lodges which had been stolen from us on the 4th of November last as we decended this river; the natives attempted to wrest the tomahawk from him but he retained it. they indeavoured afterwards to exculpate themselves from the odium of having stolen it, they alledged that they had bought it from the natives below; but their neighbours had several days previously, informed us that these people had stolen the Tommehawk and then had it at their village. this village appears to be the winter station of the Wah-clel-lahs and Clahclellars, the greater part of the former have lately removed to the falls of the Multnomah, and the latter have established themselves a few miles above on the North side of the river opposite the lower point of brant island, being the commencement of the rapids, here they also take their salmon; they are now in the act of removing, and not only take with them their furniture and effects but also the bark and most of the boards which formed their houses. 14 houses remain entire but are at this time but thinly inhabited, nine others appear to have been lately removed, and the traces of ten or twelve others of ancient date were to be seen in the rear of their present village. they sometimes sink their houses in the earth, and at other times have their floors level with the surface of the earth; they are generally built with boards and covered with Cedar bark. most of them have a devision in their houses near the entrance wich is at the end or in the event of it's bing a double house is from the center of a narrow passage. several families inhabit one appartment. the women of these people pierce the cartelage of the nose in which they wear various ornaments in other rispects they do not differ from those in the neighbourhood of the Diamond island; tho most of the women brad their hair which hanges in two tresses one hanging over each ear. these people were very unfriendly, and seemed illy disposed had our numbers not detered them any acts of violence. with some difficuly we obtained five dogs from them and a few wappetoe. on our way to this village we passed several beautifull cascades which fell from a great hight over the stupendious rocks which cloles the river on both sides nearly, except a small bottom on the South side in which our hunters were encamped. the most remarkable of these casscades falls about 300 feet perpendicularly over a solid rock into a narrow bottom of the river on the south side. it is a large creek, situated about 5 miles above our encampment of the last evening. several small streams fall from a much greater hight, and in their decent become a perfect mist which collecting on the rocks below again become visible and decend a second time in the same manner before they reach the base of the rocks. the hills have now become mountains high on each side are rocky steep and covered generally with fir and white cedar. we saw some turkey buzzards this morning of the speceis common to the United states which are the first we have seen on this side the rocky mountains. during our halt at this village the grand Cheif and two inferior Cheifs of the Chil-luck-kit-to-quaw nation arrived with several men and women of their nation in two large canoes. these people were on their return up the river, having been on a trading voyage to the Columbean vally, and were loaded with wappetoe dryed anchovies, with some beads &c which they had received in exchange for dryed and pounded salmon shappelell beargrass &c. These people had been very kind to us as we decended the river we therefore smoked with them and treated them with every attention. at 2 P.M. we renewed our voyage; passed under the beacon rock on the north side, to the left of two small islands situated near the shore. at four P.M. we arrived at the Clah-clel-lah village; here we found the natives busily engaged in erecting their new habitations, which appear to be reather of a temperary kind; it is most probable that they only reside here during the salmon season. we purchased two dogs of these people who like those of the village blow were but sulky and illy disposed; they are great rogues and we are obliged to keep them at a proper distance from our bag-gage. as we could not ascend the rapid by the North side of the river with our large canoes, we passed to the oposite side and entered the narrow channel which seperates brant Island from the South shore; the evening being far spent and the wind high raining and very cold we thought best not to attempt the rapids this evening, we therefore sought a safe harbour in this narrow channel and encamped on the main shore. our small canoe with Drewer and the two feildses was unable to pass the river with us in consequence of the waves they therefore toed her up along the N. side of the river and encamped opposite the upper point of brant Island. after halting this evening I took a turn with my gun in order to kill a deer, but was unsuccessfull. I saw much fresh sign. the fir has been lately injured by a fire near this place and many of them have discharged considerable quantities of rozin. we directed that Collins should hunt a few hours tomorrow morning and that Gibson and his crew should remain at his place untill we returned and employ themselves in collectng rozin which our canoes are now in want of.

[Clark, April 9, 1806] Wednesday April 9th 1806 last night at a late hour the old amsiated Indian who was detected in Stealing a Spoon yesterday, Crept upon his belley with his hands and feet, with a view as I Suppose to take Some of our baggage which was in Several defferent parcels on the bank. the Sentinal observed the motions of this old amcinated retch untill he got with a fiew feet of the baggage at he hailed him and approached with his gun in a possion as if going to Shoote which allarmed the old retch in Such a manner that he ran with all his power tumbling over brush and every thing in his way. at 7 A.M. we Set out and proceeded on to the Camp of Joseph & Reubin Fields. they had killed nothing. here we did not delay but proceeded on to Wah-clel-lah Village on the North Side and brackfast here one the men Colter observed the Tomahawk which was Stolen from on the 4th of Novr. last as we decended the Columbia, he took the tomahawk the natives attempted to wrest it from him, he held fast the Tomahawk. Those people attempted to excuse themselves from odium of Stealing it, by makeing Signs that they had purchased the Tomahawk, but their nighbours informed me otherwise and made Signs that they had taken it. This Village appears to be the wintering Station of two bands of the Shah-ha-la Nation. One band has already moved the Falls of the Multnomah which is the place they take their Salmon. The other band is now moveing a fiew miles above to the foot of the first rapid on this river, at which place they take their Salmon. 14 houses only appear occupied and the inhabitants of those moveing off hourly, they take with them in their Canoes independent of all their houshold effects the bark of their houses, and boards. 9 houses has been latterly abandened and 14 others is yet is thinly inhabited at present, and the remains of 10 or 12 others are to be Seen and appears to have been enhabited last fall. those people were not hospital and with Some dificuelty we precured 5 dogs and a fiew Wappato of them. Soon after we arived at this Village the Grand Cheif and two others of the Chee-luck-kit-le-quaw Nation arived from below. they had with them 11 men and 7 womin and had been trading in the Columbia Vally for Wappato, beeds and dried Anchovies &c in exchange for which they had given pounded fish Shappalell, bear grass, acorns boiled berries &c. &c. and are now on their return to their village. as those people had been very Kind to us as we decended the river we gave them Smoke. at 2 oClock P. M we Set out and passed under the Beacon rock on the North Side of two Small Islds. Situated nearest the N. side. at 4 P.M. we arived at the first rapid at the head of Straw berry island at which place on the N W. Side of the Columbia here we found the nativs from the last village rebuilding their habitations of the bark of their old Village 16 Huts are already Compleated and appear only temporary it is most probable that they only reside here dureing the Season of the Salmon. as we Could not pass with the large Canoes up the N. W. Side for the rocks, the wind high and a rainey disagreeable evining. our Smallest Canoe being too low to cross through the high waves, we Sent her up on the N W. Side with Drewyer and the two Fields and after purchaseing 2 dogs Crossed and into the Sluce of a large high Island seperated from the S. E Side by a narrow chanel, in this chanel we found a good harbor and encamped on the lower Side. We Saw Some deer Sign and Collins to hunt in the mornig untill the Canoes were toed above the rapids. made 16 Miles to day. evening wet & disagreeable.

[Lewis, April 10, 1806] Thursday April 10th 1806. We set out early and droped down the channel to the lower end of brant Island from whence we drew them up the rapid by a cord about a quarter of a mile which we soon performed; Collins and Gibson not having yet come over we directed Sergt. Pryor to remain with the cord on the Island untill Gibson arrived and assist him with his crew in geting his canoe up the rapid, when they were to join us on the oposite side at a small village of six houses of the Clah-clah'lahs where we halted for breakfast. in passing the river which is here about 400 yds. wide the rapidity of the currant was such that it boar us down a considerable distance notwithstanding we employed five oars. on entering one of these lodges, the natives offered us a sheepskin for sail, than which nothing could have been more acceptable except the animal itself. the skin of the head of the sheep with the horns remaining was cased in such manner as to fit the head of a man by whom it was woarn and highly prized as an ornament. we obtained this cap in exchange for a knife, and were compelled to give two Elkskins in exchange for the skin. this appeared to be the skin of a sheep not fully grown; the horns were about four inches long, celindric, smooth, black, erect and pointed; they rise from the middle of the forehead a little above the eyes. they offered us a second skin of a full grown sheep which was quite as large as that of a common deer. they discovered our anxity to purchase and in order to extort a great plrice declared that they prized it too much to dispose of it. in expectation of finding some others of a similar kind for sale among the natives of this neighbourhood I would not offer him a greater price than had been given for the other which he refused. these people informed us that these sheep were found in great abundance on the hights and among the clifts of the adjacent mountains. and that they had lately killed these two from a herd of 36, at no great distance from their village. we could obtain no provision from those people except four white salmon trout. at ten oclock Sergt. Pryor and Gibson joined us with Collins who had killed 3 deer. these were all of the blacktailed fallow kind. we set out and continued our rout up the N. side of the river with great difficulty in consequence of the rapidity of the current and the large rocks which form this shore; the South side of the river is impassable. as we had but one sufficient toerope and were obliged to employ the cord in geting on our canoes the greater part of the way we could only take them one at a time which retarded our progress very much. by evening we arrived at the portage on the North side where we landed and conveyed our bagage to the top of the hill about 200 paces distant where we formed a camp. we had the canoes drawn on shore and secured. the small canoe got loose from the hunters and went a drift with a tin vessel and tommahawk in her; the Indians caught her at the last village and brought her up to us this evening for which service we gave them a couple of knives; the canoe overset and lost the articles which were in her.- Saw the white pine at this place.

[Clark, April 10, 1806] Thursday April 10th 1806 Collins went out in the bottom to hunt agreeable to the order of last evening, and gibsons Crew was derected to delay for Collins dureing which time they were derected to Collect rozin from the pines in the bottom near our Camp at 6 A M. we Set out and proceeded to the lower point of the Island from whence we were Compelled to draw our Canoes up a rapid for about 1/4 mile which we Soon performed. Collins & gibson haveing not yet Come over we derected Serjt. Pryor to delay on the Island untill Gibson Came over & assist him with the large toe roap which we also left and to join us at a village of four houses of the Clah-lah-lar Tribe which is opposit to this Island on North Side at which place we intened to brackfast. in crossing the River which at this place is not more than 400 yards wide we fell down a great distance owing to the rapidity of the Current. I entered one of the houses of those people and was Scercely Seated before they offered me a Sheep Skin for Sale nothing could be more acceptable except the Animal itself in examoning this Skin I found it was a young one, the Skin of the head was Cased So as to fit the head of a man and was esteemed as a great orniment and highly prised by them. we precured this Cased head for a knife and, the Skin we were obliged to give two Raw Elk Skins for. Soon after they offered a large one for Sall. after finding us anxious to purchase they declined silling this Skin. those people informed us that they killed those Animals among the rocks in the mountains under which they live; and that great numbers of those animals inhabit those mountains & that the lamb was killed out of a gange of 36 at a Short distance from their village. The wool of the full grown Sheep, or that on the Skin which we Saw was much Corser than that of the one which we purchased, the Skin was about the Size of that of a Common deer. The Skin we obtained appeared to be the Skin of a Sheep not fully grown, the wool fine, the Horns were abought 4 inches long, Celindric, Smooth, black, a little bending backwards and pointed; they rise from the Middle of the foeheard, and a little above the eyes, and appeared to possess all the marks of the Common Sheep as already discribed. We could precure no provisions from those people except four white Salmon trout. at 10 oClock Sergt. Pryor and Gibson joined us with Collins who had killed 3 deer. these were all of the blacktailed fallow kind. We Set out and Continued up on the N. Side of the river with great dificuelty in Consequence of the Rapidity of the Current and the large rocks which forms this Shore; the South Side of the river is impassable.

As we had but one Suffcent toe roap and were obliged to employ the Cord in getting on our Canoes the greater part of the way we could only take them one at a time which retarded our progress very much. by evening we arived at the portage on the N. Side where we landed and Conveyed our baggage to the top of the hill about 200 paces distant where we found a Camp. we had the Canoes drawn on Shore and Secured. the Small Canoe got loose from the hunters and went adrift with a tin cup & a tomahawk in her; the Indians Caught her at the last Village and brought her up to us this evening for which we gave them two knives; the Canoe overset and lost the articles which were in her.-.

[Lewis, April 11, 1806] Friday April 11th 1806. As the tents and skins which covered both our men and baggage were wet with the rain which fell last evening, and as it continued still raining this morning we concluded to take our canoes first to the head of the rapids, hoping that by evening the rain would cease and afford us a fair afternoon to take our baggage over the portage. this portage is two thousand eight hundred yards along a narrow rough and slipery road. the duty of getting the canoes above the rapid was by mutual consent confided to my friend Capt. C. who took with him for that purpose all the party except Bratton who is yet so weak he is unable to work, three others who were lamed by various accedents and one other to cook for the party. a few men were absolutely necessary at any rate to guard our baggage from the War-clel-lars who crouded about our camp in considerable numbers. these are the greates theives and scoundrels we have met with. by the evening Capt. C. took 4 of our canoes above the rapids tho with much difficulty and labour. the canoes were much damaged by being driven against the rocks in dispite of every precaution which could be taken to prevent it. the men complained of being so much fatiegued in the evening that we posponed taking up our 5th canoe untill tomorrow. these rapids are much worse than they were fall when we passed them, at that time there were only three difficult points within seven miles, at present the whole distance is extreemly difficult of ascent, and it would be impracticable to decend except by leting down the empty vessels by a cord and then even the wrisk would be greater than in taking them up by the same means. the water appears to be upwards of 20 feet higher than when we decended the river. the distance by way of the river between the points of the portage is 3 Msmany of the natives crouded about the bank of the river where the men were engaged in taking up the canoes; one of them had the insolence to cast stones down the bank at two of the men who happened to be a little detatched from the party at the time. on the return of the party in the evening from the head of the rapids they met with many of the natives on the road, who seemed but illy disposed; two of these fellows met with John Sheilds who had delayed some time in purchasing a dog and was a considerable distance behind the party on their return with Capt. C. they attempted to take the dog from him and pushed him out of the road. he had nothing to defend himself with except a large knife which he drew with an intention of puting one or both of them to death before they could get themselves in readiness to use their arrows, but discovering his design they declined the combat and instantly fled through the woods. three of this same tribe of villains the Wah-clel-lars, stole my dog this evening, and took him towards their village; I was shortly afterwards informed of this transaction by an indian who spoke the Clatsop language, and sent three men in pursuit of the theives with orders if they made the least resistence or difficulty in surrendering the dog to fire on them; they overtook these fellows or reather came within sight of them at the distance of about 2 miles; the indians discovering the party in pursuit of them left the dog and fled. they also stole an ax from us, but scarcely had it in their possession before Thompson detected them and wrest it from them. we ordered the centinel to keep them out of camp, and informed them by signs that if they made any further attempts to steal our property or insulted our men we should put them to instant death. a cheif of the Clah-clel-lah tribe informed us that there were two very bad men among the Wah-clel-lahs who had been the principal actors in these seenes of outradge of which we complained, and that it was not the wish of the nation by any means to displease us. we told him that we hoped it might be the case, but we should certainly be as good as our words if they presisted in their insolence. I am convinced that no other consideration but our number at this moment protects us. The Cheif appeared mortified at the conduct of his people, and seemed friendly disposed towards us. as he appeared to be a man of consideration and we had reason to beleive much rispected by the neighbouring tribes we thought it well to bestoe a medal of small size upon him. he appeared much gratifyed with this mark of distinction, and some little attention which we shewed him. he had in his possession a very good pipe tomahawk which he informed us he had received as a present from a trader who visited him last winter over land pointing to the N. W., whome he called Swippeton; he was pleased with the tommahawk of Capt. C. in consequence of it's having a brass bowl and Capt. C. gratified him by an exchange. as a further proof of his being esteemed by this white trader, he gave us a well baked saylor's bisquit which he also informed us he had received from Swippeton. from these evidences I have no doubt but the traders who winter in some of the inlets to the N. of us visit this part of the Columbia by land at certain seasons, most probably when they are confined to their winter harbour. and if so some of those inlets are probably at no great distance from this place, as there seems to be but little inducement to intice the trader hither from any considerable distance particularly as the difficulty in traveling on the borders of this mountainous country must be great at that season as the natives informed me their snows were frequently breast deep. I observe snowshoes in all the lodges of the natives above the Columbean vally. I hope that the friendly interposition of this chief may prevent our being compelled to use some violence with these people; our men seem well disposed to kill a few of them. we keep ourselves perefectly on our guard. This evening we send Drewyer and the two Feildses on a few miles up the river to the entrance of Cruzatt's river to hunt untill our arrival. The inhabitants of the Y-eh-huh Village on the North side immediately above the rapids have lately removed to the opposite side of the river, where it appears they usually take their salmon. like their relations the Wah-Clel-lars they have taken their houses with them. I observe that all the houses lately established have their floors on the surface of the earth, are smaller and of more temperary structure than those which are sunk in the ground. I presume the former are their spring and Summer dwellings and the latter those of the fall and winter. these houses are most generally built with boards and covered with bark. some of an inferior ore more temperary cast are built entirely of cedar bark, which is kept smooth and extended by inserting small splinters of wood through the bark crosswise at the distance of 12 or 14 inches assunder. several families inhabit the same appartment. their women as well as those of the 3 villages next below us pierce the cartelage of the nose and insert various ornaments. they very seldom imprint any figures on their skins; a few I observed had one or two longitudinal lines of dots on the front of the leg, reaching from the ankle upwards about midleg. most of their women braid their hair in two tresses as before mentioned. the men usually cew their hair in two parsels which like the braded tresses of the female hang over each ear in front of the sholder, and gives an additional width to the head and face so much admired by them. these cews are usually formed with throngs of dressed Otterskin crossing each other and not roled in our manner arrond the hair. in all other rispects I observe no difference in their dress habits manners &c. from those in the Neighbourhood of the diamond Island. today we recognized a man of the Elute nation who reside at the long narrows of the Columbia, he was on his return from a trading voyage to the Columbean valley with 10 or 12 others of his nation. many other natives from the villages above were employed in taking their roots &c over the portage on their return. I observed that the men equally with the women engage in the labour of carrying. they all left their canoes below the rapids and took others above which they had left as they decended. those which were left below were taken down the river by the persons from whom they had been hired or borrowed. the natives from above behaved themselves in a very orderly manner. The salmon have not yet made their appearance, tho the natives are not so much distressed for food as I was induced to believe. I walked down today about 3/4 of a mile below our encampment to observe the manner in which these people inter their dead. I found eight sepulchers near the north bank of the river built in the following manner. four strong forks are first sunk several feet in the ground and rise about six feet high, froming a parrallelogram of 8 by 10 feet. the intervals between these upright forks, on which four poles are laid, are filled up with broad erect boards with their lower ends sunk in the ground and their upper ends confined to the horizontal poles. a flat roof is formed of several layers of boards; the floors of these sepulchres are on a level with the surface of the earth. the human bodies are well rolled in dressed skins and lashed securely with chords and laid horizontaly on the back with the head to the west. in some of these sepulchres they are laid on each other to the debth of three or four bodies. in one of those sepulchers which was nearly decayed I observed that the human bones filled it perfectly to the hight of about three feet. many articles appear to be sacreficed to the dead both within and without the sepulcres. among other articles, I observed a brass teakettle, some scollep shells, parts of several robes of cloth and skins, with sticks for diging roots &c.- this appears to be the burying ground of the Wahclellahs, Clahclellahs and Yehhuhs.

[Clark, April 11, 1806] Friday April 11th 1806 rained the greater part of the last night and continued to rain this morning, as the Skins and the Covering of both the mend and loading were wet we determined to take the Canoes over first in hopes that by the evening the rain would Sease and afford us a fair afternoon to Carry our baggage over the portage which is 2 miles by land and a Slipery road. I therefore took all the men except three who had Sore feet and two to cook, and who were with the baggage; and with great dificuelty and much fatigue we drew up 4 of our canoes above the Rapids 3 miles in extent. the men became So fatigued that we deturmined to puspone takeing the 5th Canoe untill tomorrow. Those rapids are much worse than they were at the time we passed last fall at that time there was only three bad places in the distance of 7 miles. at this time the whole distance is a rapid and dificuelt of assent; and would be very dangerous at this Stage of the water (which is _____ feet higher than when we passed down) to decent in any kind of Craft. Great numbers of the nativs visited us and viewed us from the banks as we passed on with the Canoes, maney of those people were also about our baggage and on the portage road. two of those fellows insulted John Shields who had delayed in purchaseing a dog at the upper part of the rapids and was Some distance behind myself and the party on our return to camp. they attempted to take his dog and push him out of the road. he had nothing to defend himself except a large knife which he drew with a full deturmination to put one of them to death before he had an opportunity of dischargeing his arrow. the nativs obseveing his motion ran off. one other Indn. Stold an ax and was not in possession before he was detected by Thompson and the ax taken from him. one other fellow attempted to Steal Capt. Lewis's dog, and had decoyed him nearly half a mile we were informed of it by a man who Spoke the Clatsop language and imediately Sent three men with their guns who over took the Indians, who on their approach ran off and lift the dog- we informed the nativ's by Signs that if the indians insulted our men or Stold our property we Should Certainly put them to death a Chief of the Clah-clal-lahs Tribe informed us that there was two very bad men who had been guilty of those mischevious acts. that it was not the wish of their tribe that any thing should be done which might displese the white people. this Chief had a large fine pipe tomahawk which he informed me he got from a Trader he called Swippeton. I exchanged tomahawks with this Chief, and as he appeared to be a man of consideration among the tribes of this neighbourhood and much conserned for the ingiries offered us, we gave him a Medal of the Small Size which appeard. to please him verry much; and will I hope have a favourable tendincy, in as much as it will attach him to our interest, and he probably will harang his people in our favour, which may prevent any acts of violence being Commited, on either Side. nothing but the Strength of our party has prevented our being robed before this time. Sent Drewyer & 2 Fields on a head to hunt. The inhabitants of the Wyach-hich Tribe Village imediately above those rapids on the N W. Side have latterly moved their village to the opposit Side of the river, where they take their Salmon; they are now in the act of removeing and not only take their furniture and effects but also the bark and most of the boards which formed their houses. Those like the tribes below Sometimes Sink their houses in the earth, and at other times have their flowrs leavil with the Surface of the earth; they are Generally built of boards and Covered with bark. those which appear intended for temporary use are most generally built of the White Cedar bark. Most of those have a division in the houses near the enterance which is at the end, or in the event of it's being a double house is from the center of a narrow passage. Several families enhabit one appartment. the women of those people as well as those in the 3 villages below pierce the cartilage of the nose in which they ware Various orniments. in other respects they do not deffer from those of the Dimond Island. tho most of the women brad their hair which hangs in two tresses, one hanging over each ear. The yound men of all those tribes ware their hair plated, in two plats anging over each Sholder, maney of them also Cew their hair with otter Skin divided on the crown of the head and hanging over each ear. to day I recognised a man of the Elute nation who reside at the Long narrows, he was on his return from a tradeing voyage to the Columbian Vally with 10 or 12 of his tribe. maney others from the villages above this were takeing their roots &c. over the portage to day on their return home.

vegitation is rapidly progressing. Sarvis berry, Sackacommis and the large leafed ash is in blume. also fir N. _____ in bloom

[Lewis, April 12, 1806] Saturday April 12th 1806. It rained the greater part of last night and still continued to rain this morning. I therefore determined to take up the remaining perogue this morning for which purpose I took with me every man that could be of any service. a small distance above our camp there is one of the most difficult parts of the rapid. at this place the current sets with great violence against a projecting rock. in hawling the perogue arround this point the bow unfortunately took the current at too great a distance from the rock, she turned her side to the stream and the utmost exertions of all the party were unable to resist the forse with which she was driven by the current, they were compelled to let loose the cord and of course both perogue and cord went a drift with the stream. the loss of this perogue will I fear compell us to purchase one or more canoes of the indians at an extravegant price. after breakfast all hands were employed in taking our baggage over the portage. we caused all the men who had short rifles to carry them, in order to be prepared for the natives should they make any attempts to rob or injure them. I went up to the head of the rapids and left Capt. C. below. during the day I obtained a vocabulary of the language of the War-clel-lars &c. I found that their numbers were precisely those of the Chinnooks but the other parts of their language essentially different. by 5 P.M. we had brought up all our baggage and Capt. C. joined me from the lower camp with the Clahclellah cheif. there is an old village situated about halfway on the portage road the fraim of the houses, which are remarkably large one 160 by 45 feet, remain almost entire. the covering of the houses appears to have been sunk in a pond back of the village. this the chief informed us was the residence occasionally of his tribe. these houses are fraimed in the usual manner but consist of a double set as if oune house had been built within the other. the floors are on a level with the ground. the natives did not croud about us in such numbers today as yesterday, and behaved themselves much better; no doubt the precautions which they observed us take had a good effect. I employed sergt. Pryor the greater part of the day in reparing and corking the perogue and canoes. it continued to rain by showers all day. about 20 of the Y-eh-huhs remained with me the greater part of the day and departed in the evening. they conducted themselves with much propryety and contemned the conduct of their relations towards us. We purchased one sheepskin for which we gave the skin of an Elk and one of a deer. this animal was killed by the man who sold us the skin near this place; he informed us that they were abundant among the mountains and usually resorted the rocky parts. the big horned animal is also an inhabitant of these mountains. I saw several robes of their skins among the natives.as the evening was rainy cold and far advanced and ourselves wet we determined to remain all night. the mountains are high steep and rocky. the rock is principally black. they are covered with fir of several speceis and the white cedar. near the river we find the Cottonwood, sweet willow, broad leafed ash, a species of maple, the purple haw, a small speceis of cherry; purple currant, goosberry, red willow, vining and white burry honeysuckle, huckkle burry, sacacommis, two speceis of mountain holley, &common ash. for the three last days this inclusive we have made only 7 miles.

[Clark, April 12, 1806] Saturday April 12th 1806. rained the greater part of the last night and this morning untile 10 A.M. we employed all hands in attempting to take up the lost Canoe. in attempting to pass by a rock against which the Current run with emence force, the bow unfortunately took the Current at too great a distance from the rock, She turned broad Side to the Stream, and the exertions of every man was not Sufficient to hold her. the men were Compelled to let go the rope and both the Canoe and rope went with the Stream. the loss of this Canoe will I fear Compell us to purchase another at an extravigent price. after brackfast all hands who were employed in Carrying the baggage over the portage 1 1/2 miles which they performed by 4 P.M. the nativs did not visit us in Such Crouds to day as yesterday. we Caused all the men of the party who ha Short guns to carry them on the portage for fear of Some attempt on the part of the nativs to rob the party. The rain Continued at intervales all day. in the evening after everry thing was taken from the lower Camp I Set out myself accompanied by the Cheif of the Clah-clal lars to the head of the portage. as we passed the remains of an old Village about half way the portage, this Cheif informed me that this old Village had been the residence of his Tribe dureing the last Salmon Season. this village I mentiond in decending this river, but did not know the Tribes that had inhabited it that time. Capt. Lewis took a vocabulary of the languge of those people whilst I had all the baggage taken across the portage & we formed a Camp at the place we had encamped on our way down.

at my arival at the head of the portage found about 20 of the natives of the Wy ach hich tribe who reside above the rapids, with Capt Lewis. those people appeared much better disposed towards us than either the Clahclallah or Wahclellah and Condemn their Conduct much. Those tribes I believe to be all the Same Nation their Language habits manners dress &c. are presisely alike and differ but little from those below the Great Narrows of this river. I observed a woman with a Sheep Skin robe on which I purchased for one Elk and one deer Skin. the father of this woman informed me that he had killed the animal off of which he had taken this Skin on the mountains imediately above his village, and that on those mountains great numbers of those animals were to be found in large flocks among the Steep rocks. I also purchased 2 pieces of Chapellell and Some roots of those people. as the evening was rainey and ourselves and party wet we Concluded to delay untill the morning and dry our selves. The Indians left us about 6 P M and returned to their Village on the opposit Side. mountains are high on each Side and Covered with Snow for about 1/3 of the way down. the growth is principally fir and White Cedar. the bottoms and low Situations is Covered with a variety Such as Cotton, large leafed ash, Sweet willow a Species of beech, alder, white thorn, cherry of a Small Speces, Servis berry bushes, Huckleberries bushes, a Speces of Lorel &c. &c. I saw a turkey buzzard which is the 3rd which I have Seen west of the rocky mountains. the 1st was on the 7 inst. above quick Sand river. for the three last days this inclusive we have made 7 miles only.

[Lewis, April 13, 1806] Sunday April 13th 1806. The loss of one of our perogues rendered it necessary to distribute her crew and cargo among the 2 remaining perogues and 2 canoes, which being done we loaded and set out 8 A.M. we passed the village immediately above the rapids where only one house at present remains entire, the other 8 having been taken down and removed to the oposite side of the river as before mentioned. we found the additional laiding which we had been compelled to put on board rendered our vessels extreemly inconvenient to mannage and in short reather unsafe in the event of high winds; I therefore left Capt. C. with the two perogues to proceede up the river on the N. side, and with the two canoes and some additional hands passed over the river above the rapids to the Y-eh-huh village in order to purchase one or more canoes. I found the village consisting of 11 houses crouded with inhabitants; it appeared to me that they could have mustered about 60 fighting men then present. they appeared very friendly disposed, and I soon obtained two small canoes from them for which I gave two robes and four elkskins. I also purchased four paddles and three dogs from them with deerskins. the dog now constitutes a considerable part of our subsistence and with most of the party has become a favorite food; certain I am that it is a healthy strong diet, and from habit it has become by no means disagreeable to me, I prefer it to lean venison or Elk, and is very far superior to the horse in any state. after remaining about 2 hours at this Village I departed and continued my rout with the four canoes along the S. side of the river the wind being too high to pass over to the entrance of Cruzatts river where I expected to have overtaken Capt. C. not seing the perogues on the opposite side I ascended the river untill one oclock or about 5 ms. above the entrance of Cruzat's river. being convinced that the perogues were behind I halted and directed the men to dress the dogs and cook one of them for dinner; a little before we had completed our meal Capt. C. arrived with the perogues and landed opposite to us. after dinner I passed the river to the perogues and found that Capt. C. had halted for the evening and was himself hunting with three of the party. the men in formed me that they had seen nothing of the hunters whom we had sent on the 11th ints. to the Entrance of Cruzatt's Riv. I directed Sergt. ordway to take the two small canoes for his mess and the loading which he had formerly carried in the perogue we lost yesterday, and to have them dryed this evening and payed with rozin. Capt. Clark returned in about an hour and being convinced that the hunters were yet behind we dispatched Sergt. Pryor in surch of them with two men and an empty canoe to bring the meat they may have killed. John Sheilds returned a little after six P.M. with two deer which he had killed. these were also of the blacktailed fallow deer; there appears to be no other speceis of deer in these mountains. Capt. C. informed me that the wind had detained him several hours a little above Cruzatt's river; that while detained here he sent out some men to hunt; one of them wounded two deer but got neither of them. the wind having lulled in the evening and not seing anything of Drewyer and the Feildses he had proceeded on to this place where he intended waiting for me, and as he did not see my canoes when he landed had taken a hunt with some of the men as before mentioned.

[Clark, April 13, 1806] Sunday April 13th 1806 The loss of one of our large Canoes rendered it necessary to divide the loading and men of that Canoe between the remaining four, which was done and we loaded and Set out at 8 oClock A.M. passed the village imediately above the rapids, where only one house remains entire the other 8 haveing been taken down and moved to the opposit Side of the Columbia as already mentioned. the additional men and baggage in each Canoe renders them Crouded and unsafe. Capt. Lewis with 2 of the Smallest Canoes of Sergt. Pryor & gibson and Crossed above the Rapids to the Village on the S E Side with a view to purchase a Canoe of the nativs if possible. he took with him Some Cloth and a fiew Elk skins and Deer Skins. I with the two large Canoes proceeded on up the N. W. Side with the intention of gitting to the Encampment of our hunters who was derected to hunt in the bottom above Crusats River, and there wait the arival of Capt. Lewis. I proceeded on to the bottom in which I expected to find the hunters but Could See nothing of them. the wind rose and raised the ways to Such a hight that I could not proceed any further. we landed and I sent out Shields and Colter to hunt; Shields Shot two deer but Could get neither of them. I walkd. to Crusats river and up it 1/2 a mile on my return to the party found that the wind had lulled and as we Could See nothing of our hunters. I deturmined to proceed on to the next bottom where I thought it probable they had halted at 1/2 passed 2 P M Set out and proceeded on to the bottom 6 miles and halted at the next bottom formed a Camp and Sent out all the hunters. I also walked out my self on the hills but saw nothing. on my return found Capt. Lewis at Camp with two canoes which he had purchased at the Y-ep-huh village for two robes and four elkskins. he also purchased 4 paddles and three Dogs from the nativs with deer Skins. the dogs now constitutes a considerable part of our Subsistance & with most of the party has become a favourable food. Certain I am that is a helthy Strong diet, derected Serjt. ordway to take the 2 Small Canoes purchased by Capt. Lewis for his mess and the loading he had in his Canoe which we lost yesterday, and drawed up and paid with rozin.

I was convinced that the hunters must have been up River Cruzatt. despatched Sergt. Pryor with 2 men in a Canoe, with directions to assend Crusats River and if he found the hunters to assist them in with the meat. Jo. Shields returned about Sunset with two deer which he had killed, those were of the Black tail fallow Deer. there appears to be no other Species of Deer in those mountains. We proceeded on 12 miles.

[Lewis, April 14, 1806] Monday April 14th 1806. This morning at seven oCk. we were joined by Sergt. Pryor and the three hunters they brought with them 4 deer which Drewyer had killed yesterday. we took breakfast and departed. at 9 A.M. the wind arrose and continued hard all day but not so violent as to prevent our proceeding. we kept close along the N. shore all day. the river from the rapids as high as the commencement of the narrows is from 1/2 to 3/4 of a mile in width, and possesses scarcely any current. the bed is principally rock except at the entrance of Labuish's river which heads in Mount hood and like the quicksand river brings down from thence vast bodies of sand. the mountains through which the river passes nearly to the sepulchre rock, are high broken, rocky, partially covered with fir white cedar, and in many places exhibit very romantic seenes. some handsome cascades are seen on either hand tumbling from the stupendious rocks of the mountains into the river. near the border of the river I observed today the long leafed pine. this pine increases in quantity as you ascend the river and about the sepulchre rock where the lower country commences it superceeds the fir altogether. throughout the whole course of this river from the rapids as high as the Chilluckkittequaws, we find the trunks of many large pine trees sanding erect as they grew at present in 30 feet water; they are much doated and none of them vegetating; at the lowest tide of the river many of these trees are in ten feet water. certain it is that those large pine trees never grew in that position, nor can I account for this phenomenon except it be that the passage of the river through the narrow pass at the rapids has been obstructed by the rocks which have fallen from the hills into that channel within the last 20 years; the appearance of the hills at that place justify this opinion, they appear constantly to be falling in, and the apparent state of the decayed trees would seem to fix the era of their decline about the time men-tioned. at 1 P.M. we arrived at a large village situated in a narrow bottom on the N. side a little above the entrance of canoe creek. their houses are reather detatched and extent for several miles. they are about 20 in number. These people call themselves We-ock-sock, Wil-lacum. they differ but litte in appeance dress &c. from those of the rapids. Their men have some leging and mockersons among them. these are in the stile of Chopunnish. they have some good horses of which we saw ten or a douzen. these are the fist horses we have met with since we left this neighbourhood last fall, in short the country below this place will not permit the uce of this valuable animal except in the Columbian vally and there the present inhabitants have no uce for them as they reside immediately on the river and the country is too thickly timbered to admit them to run the game with horses if they had them. we halted at this village and dined. purchased five dogs some roots, shappalell, filberds and dryed burries of the inhabitants. here I observed several habitations entirely under grownd; they were sunk about 8 feet deep and covered with strong timber and several feet of earth in a conic form. these habitations were evacuated at present. they are about 16 feet in diameter, nearly circular, and are entered through a hole at the top which appears to answer the double purpose of a chimney and a door. from this entrance you decend to the floor by a ladder. the present habitations of these people were on the surface of the ground and do not differ from those of the tribes of the rapids. their language is the same with that of the Chilluckkittequaws. these people appeared very friendly. some of them informed us that they had lately returned from a war excurtion against the snake indians who inhabit the upper part of the Multnomah river to the S. E. of them. they call them To-wannah'-hi'-ooks. that they had been fortunate in their expedition and had taken from their enimies most of the horses which we saw in their possession. after dinner we pursued our voyage; Capt. Clark walked on shore with Charbono. I ascended the river about six miles at which place the river washed the base of high clifts on the Lard. side, here we halted a few minutes and were joined by Capt. C. and Charbono and proceeded on to the entrance of a small run on N. side a little below a large village on the same side opposite the sepulchre rock. this village can raise about an hundred fighting men they call themselves. they do not differ in any rispect from the village below. many of them visited our camp this evening and remained with us untill we went to bed. they then left us and retired to their quarters.-

[Clark, April 14, 1806] Monday April 14th 1806 This morning at 7 oClock we were joined by Sgt. Pryor and they three hunters they brought with them 4 deer which drewyer had killed yesterday. we took brackfast and departed at 9 A.M. the wind rose and Continued to blow hard all day but not so violent as to prevent our proceeding. we kept Close along the N. Shore all day. the river from the rapids to the Commencement of the narrows is from 1/2 to 3/4 of a Mile in wedth, and possesses but little Current. the bead is rock except at the enterence of Labiech's river which heads in Mt. Hood and like the quick Sand River brings down from thence Vast bodies of Sand the Mountains through which the river passes nearly to Cataract River are high broken rocky, particularly Covered with fir and white Cedar, and in maney places very romantic scenes. Some handsom Cascades are Seen on either Side tumbling from the Stupendious rocks of the mountains into the river. I observe near the river the long leafed Pine which increas as we assend and Superseeds the fir altogether about the Sepulchre rock. We find the trunks of maney large pine trees Standing erect as they grew, at present in 30 feet water; they are much doated and none of them vegitateing. at the lowest water of the river maney of those trees are in 10 feet water. the Cause I have attempted to account for as I decended. at 1 P M. we arrived at a large village Situated in a narrow bottom on the N. Side a little above the enterance of Canoe Creek. their houses are reather detached, and extend for Several Miles. they are about 20 in number. those people Call themselves Wil-la-cum. they differ but little in appearance dress &c. from those of the rapids. their men have Some legins and mockersons among them. those are in the Stile of Chopunnish. they have Some good horss of which we Saw 10 or 12 these are the first horses we have met with Since we left this neighbourhood last fall in Short the Country below this place will not permit the use of this valuable animal except in the Columbian vally, and there the present inhabitants have no use for them as they reside imediately on the river and the Country is too thickly timbd. We halted at this village Dined and purchased five dogs, Some roots Chappalell, Philberds and dried berries of the inhabitants. here I observed Several habitations under ground; they were Sunk about 8 feet deep and covered with Strong timber and Several feet of earth in a conic form. those habitations are avacuated at present. they are about 16 feet diamieter, nearly Circular, and are entered through a hole at top which appears to answer the double purpose of a Chimney and a dore. from this enterance you decend to the flore by a ladder. the present habitations of those people were on the Surface of the ground and do not differ from those of the tribes about the Rapids. their language is the Same with the Che luck kit to quaws. these people appeared very friendly. Some of them informed us that they had latterly returned from the War excurtion against the Snake Indians who inhabit the upper part of the Multnomah river to the S. E. of them they Call them To wan nah hi ooks. that they had been fortunate in the expidition and had taken from their enimies most of the horses which we Saw in their possession. after dinner we proceeded on our voyage. I walked on Shore with Shabono on the N. Side through a handsom bottom. met Several parties of women and boys in Serch of herbs & roots to Subsist on maney of them had parcels of the Stems of the Sunflower. I joined Capt Lewis and the party at 6 miles, at which place the river washed the bottom of high Clifts on the N. Side. Several Canoes over take us with families moveing up. we passed 3 encampments and came too in the mouth of a Small Creek on the N. Side imediately below a village and opposit the Sepulchar rock. this village Consists of about 100 fighting men of Several tribes from the plains to the North Collected here waiting for the Salmon. they do not differ in any respect from those below. many of them visited our Camp this evening and remaind. with us untill we went to bead. they then left us and returned to their quarters. made _____ miles.

[Lewis, April 15, 1806] Tuesday April 15th 1806 We delayed this morning untill after breakfast in order to purchase some horses of the Indians; accordingly we exposed some articles in exchange for horses the natives were unwilling to barter, we therefore put up our merchandize and at 8 A.M. we set out. we halted a few minutes at the sepulchre rock, and examined the deposits of the ded at that place. these were constructed in the same manner of those already discribed below the rapids. some of them were more than half filled with dead bodies. there were thirteen sepulchres on this rock which stands near the center of the river and has a surface of about 2 acres above highwater mark.- from hence we returned to the nothern shore and continued up it about four miles to another village of the same nation with whom we remained last night. here we halted and informed the natives of our wish to purchase horses; the produced us several for sale but would not take the articles which we had in exchange for them. they wanted an instrumet which the Northwest traders call an eye-dag which we had not. we procured two dogs of them and departed. a little below the entrance of Cataract river we halted at another village of the same people, at which we were equally unsuccessful) in the purchase of horses. we also halted at the two villages of the Chilluckkittequaws a few miles above with no better success. at three in the evening we arrived at the entrance of Quinnette creek which we ascended a short distance and encamped at the place we have called rockfort camp. here we were visited by some of the people from the villages at the great narrows and falls. we informed them of our wish to purchase horses, & agreed to meet them on the opposite or North side of the river tomorrow for the purpose of bartering with them. most of them returned to their villages this evening three only remained with us all night. these people are much better clad than any of the nations below; their men have generally leging mockersons and large robes, many of them wear shirts of the same form those of the Chopunnish and Shoshonees highly ornamented with the quills of the porcupine as are also their mockersons and legings. they conceal the parts of generation with the skin of a fox or some other small animal drawn underneath a girdle and hanging loosly in front of them like a narrow apron. the dress of their women differs very little from those about the rapids. both men and women cut their hair in the forehead which comes down as low as the eyebrows, they have long earlocks cut square at the end. the other part of their hair is dressed in the same manner as those of the rapids. after we landed and formed our camp this evening Drewyer and some others took a hunt and killed a deer of the longtailed kind. it was a buck and the young horns had shot fourth about 2 inches.

[Clark, April 15, 1806] Tuesday April 15th 1806 We delayed this morning untill after brackfast in order to purchase Some horses of the Indians; accordingly we exposed Some articles in exchange for horses the nativs were unwilling to exchange their horses, we put up our merchindize and at 8 A M. Set out. we halted a fiew minits at the Sepulchar rock and examined the deposit of the dead at that place. those were Constructed in the Same manner of those already described below the rapids. Some of them were more than half filled with dead bodies. there were 13 Sepulchers on this rock which Stands near the Center of the river, and has a Cerface of about two acres above the water.-. from hence we returned to the Northern Shore and Continued up it about 4 miles to a Village at the enterance of Cateract River, here we halted and informed the nativs of our wish to purchase horses; the produced Several for Sale but would not take the articles we had in exchange for them. they wanted an instriment which the Northw Traders call an eye dag which we had not. we precured two dogs and departed we also halted at the two villages of the Chil luck kitequaws a fiew Ms. above with no better Sucksess. at 3 in the evening we arivied at the enterance of Quinnett Creek which we assended a Short distance and Encamped at the place we had Called rock fort Camp. here we were visited by Some of the people from the Villages at the long Narrows & Falls. we informed them of our wish to purchase horses, and agreed to meet them on the opposit or north Side on tomorrow for the purpose of bartering with them. most of them returned to their village this evening three only remained with us all night. those people are much better Clad than the nativs below. their men have generaly Legins mockersons & large robes. Maney of them were Shirts of the Same form of those of the Chopunnish & Shoshonees highly ornamented with the quils of the purcupine, as are also their mockersons & Legins. they Conseal the parts of generation with the Skins of the Fox or Some other Small animal drawn under neath a girdle and hanging loosely in front of them like a narrow apron. The dress of their women differ verry little from those about the rapids. both men & women Cut their hair in the forehead which comes down as low as the Eyebrows, they have long ear locks Cut Square at the end. The other parts of their hair is dressed in the Same Manner as those of the rapids. after we landld and formed our Camp this evening Drewyer and some oths took a hunt and killed a Deer of the log tailed kind. it was a Buck and the young deer horns had Shot foth about two inches made _____ miles to day.

[Lewis, April 16, 1806] Wednesday April 16th 1806. About 8 A.M. Capt. Clark passed the river with the two interpreters, the indian woman and nine men in order to trade with the natives for their horses, for which purpose he took with him a good part of our stock of merchandize. I remained in camp; sent out the hunters very early in the morning, and set Sergts. Gass and Pryor with some others at work to make a parsel of packsaddles. twelve horses will be sufficient to transport our baggage and some pounded fish which we intend taking with us as a reserved store for the rocky mountains. I was visited today by several of the natives, and amused myself in making a collection of the esculent plants in the neighbourhood such as the Indians use, a specemine of which I preserved. I also met with sundry other plants which were strangers to me which I also preserved, among others there is a currant which is now in blume and has yellow blossom something like the yellow currant of the Missouri but is a different speceis. Reubin Feilds returned in the evening and brought with him a large grey squrrel and two others of a kind I had never before seen. they are a size less than the grey squrrel common to the middle atlantic states and of a pided grey and yellowish brown colour, in form it resembles our grey squrrel precisely. I had them skined leaving the head feet and tail to them and placed in the sun to dry. Joseph Feilds brought me a black pheasant which he had killed; this I found on examination to be the large black or dark brown pheasant I had met with on the upper part of the Missouri. it is as large as a well grown fowl the iris of the eye is of a dark yellowish brown, the puple black, the legs are booted to the toes, the tail is composed of 18 black feathers tiped with bluish white, of which the two in the center are reather shorter than the others which are all of the same length. over the eye there is a stripe of a 1/4 of an inch in width uncovered with feathers of a fine orrange yellow. the wide spaces void of feathers on the side of the neck are also of the same colour. I had some parts of this bird preserved. our present station is the last point at which there is a single stick of timber on the river for a great distance and is the commencement of the open plains which extend nearly to the base of the rocky Mts. Labuish returned this evening having killed two deer I sent and had them brought in. this evening Capt. C. informed me by some of the men whom he sent over that that he had obtained no horses as yet of the natives. that they promised to trade with him provided he would remove to their vil-lage. to this he had consented and should proceed to the Skillute village above the long narrows as soon as the men returned whom he had sent to me for some other articles. I dispatched the men on their return to capt. C. immediately with these articles and he set out with his party accompanyed by the natives to their village where he remained all night.- the natives who had spent the day with me seemed very well disposed, they left me at 6 in the evening and returned to their rispective villages. the hunters informed me that they saw some Antelopes, & the tracks of several black bear, but no appearance of any Elk. we were informed by the Indians that the river which falls in on the S. side of the Columbia just above the Eneshur village heads in Mount hood and dose not water the extensive country which we have heretofore calculated on. a great portion of that extensive tract of country to the S. and S. W. of the Columbia and it's S. E. branch, and between the same and the waters of Callifornia must be watered by the Multnomah river.-

[Clark, April 16, 1806] April 16th 1806 Crossed the river and Sent Drewyer & Goodrich to the Skil lute village to envite the Indians to trade horses with us, also sent Frazer & Shabono to the Che-luck-kit-ti-quar village for the same purpose a number of Indians came of both nations and delayed the greater part of the day without tradeing a Single horse the Great Chief of the Skillutes also came with Drewyer. he was lame and Could not walk he told me if I would go to his Town his people would trade with me. I Set out late and arrived at Sunset and informd. the natives that in the morning I would trade with them. he gave me onions to eate which had been Sweated. Peter played the violin and the men danced. Saw abt. 100 Stacks of fish. maney nations visit this place for trade. the discription of the houses, their dress habits &c. Smoked &c. I saw great numbers of horses

[Clark, April 16, 1806] Wednesday April 16th 1806 about 8 oClock this morning I passed the river with the two interpreters, and nine men in order to trade with the nativs for their horses, for which purpose I took with me a good part of our Stock of merchindize. Capt L. Sent out the hunters and Set Several men at work makeing pack Saddles. twelve horses will be Sufficient to trans port our baggage and Some pounded fish with our dried Elk. which we intend takeing with us as a reserved Store for the Plains & rocky mountains. I formed a Camp on the N. Side and Sent Drewyer & Goodrich to the Skillute Village, and Shabono & Frazer down to the Chilluckkitequaw Villages with derections to inform the nativs that I had Crossed the river for the purpose of purchaseing horses, and if they had horses to Sell us to bring them to my Camp. Great numbers of Indians came from both Villages and delayed the greater part of the day without tradeing a Single horse. Drewyer returned with the principal Chief of the Skillutes who was lame and Could not walk. after his arival Some horses were offered for Sale, but they asked nearly half the merchindize I had with me for one horse. this price I could not think of giveing. the Chief informed me if I would go to his town with him, his people would Sell me horses. I therefore Concluded to accompany him to his Village 7 miles distant. we Set out and arrived at the Village at Sunset. after Some Serimony I entered the house of the Chief. I then informed them that I would trade with them for their horses in the morning for which I would give for each horse the articles which I had offered yesterd. The Chief Set before me a large platter of Onions which had been Sweeted. I gave a part of those onions to all my party and we all eate of them, in this State the root is very Sweet and the tops tender. the nativs requested the party to dance which they very readily consented and Peter Cruzat played on the Violin and the men danced Several dances & retired to rest in the houses of the 1st and Second Cheif.

this village is moved about 300 yards below the Spot it Stood last fall at the time we passed down. they were all above grown and built in the Same form of those below already discribed. We observed maney stacks of fish remaining untouched on either Side of the river. The Inhabitants of this Village ware the robe of deer Elk Goat &c. and most of the men ware Legins and mockersons and Shirts highly orniminted with Porcupine quills & beeds. the women were the Truss most Commonly. tho Some of them have long Shirts all of those articles they precure from other nations who visit them for the purpose of exchangeing those articles for their pounded fish of which they prepare great quantities. This is the Great Mart of all this Country. ten different tribes who reside on Taptate and Catteract River visit those people for the purpose of purchaseing their fish, and the Indians on the Columbia and Lewis's river quite to the Chopunnish Nation Visit them for the purpose of tradeing horses buffalow robes for beeds, and Such articles as they have not. The Skillutes precure the most of their Cloth knivs axes & beeds from the Indians from the North of them who trade with white people who come into the inlets to the North at no great distance from the Tapteet. their horses of which I saw great numbers, they precure from the Indians who reside on the banks of the Columbia above, and what fiew they take from the To war ne hi ooks or Snake Indians. I smoked with all the principal men of this nation in the house of their great Cheif and lay my Self down on a Mat to Sleep but was prevented by the mice and vermin with which this house abounded and which was very troublesom to me.

[Lewis, April 17, 1806] Thursday April 17th 1806. This morning early I sent out the hunters, and set several additional hands about the packsaddles. I find that the sturgeon is not taken by any of the natives above the Columbean vally. the inhabitants of the rapids at this time take a few of the white salmon trout and considerable quantities of a small indifferent mullet on which they principally subsist. I have seen none except dryed fish of the last season in the possession of the people above that place, they subsist on roots principally with some dryed and pounded fish. the salmon not having made their appearance proves a serious inconvenience to us. but few of the natives visited my camp today and those only remained a few hours. even at this place which is merely on the border of the plains of Columbia the climate seems to have changed the air feels dryer and more pure. the earth is dry and seems as if there had been no rain for a week or ten days. the plain is covered with a rich virdure of grass and herbs from four to nine inches high and exhibits a beautiful) seen particularly pleasing after having been so long imprisoned in mountains and those almost impenetrably thick forrests of the seacoast. Joseph Feilds brought me today three eggs of the party coloured corvus, they are about the size and shape of those of the pigeon. they are bluish white much freckled with dark redish brown irregular spots, in short it is reather a mixture of those colours in which the redish brown predominates, particularly towards the larger end.- This evening Willard and Cruzatte returned from Capt. Clark and brought me a note in which Capt. C. informed me that he had sill been unsuccessful) having not obtained a single horse as yet from the natives and the state of our stores are so low that I begin to fear we shall not be enabled to obtain as many horses at this place as will convey our baggage and unless we do obtain a sufficient number for that purpose we shall not hasten our progress as a part of our baggage must still be conveyed by water. Capt. C. informed me that he should proceed as far as the Eneshur village today and would return tomorrow and join me at the Skillute village to which place I mean to proceed with the party tomorrow. I dispatched Shannon with a note to Capt. Clark in which I requested him to double the price we have heretofore offered for horses and if possible obtain as many as five, by this means we shall be enabled to proceed immediately with our small canoes and those horses to the villages in the neighbourhood of the mussel shell rapid where horses are more abundant and cheaper; with the remainder of our merchandize in addition to the canoes we can no doubt obtain as many horses there as will answer our purposes. delay in the villages at the narrows and falls will be expensive to us inasmuch as we will be compelled to purchase both fuel and food of the indians, and might the better enable them to execute any hostile designh should they meditate any against us.- all the hunters returned in the evening. Sheilds had killed one deer which he brought with him. the packsaddles were completed this evening. I had some Elkskins put in the water today make harnes for the packhorses but shall not cut them untill I know the number we can obtain.- there is a species of hiasinth in these plains the bulb of which the natives eat either boiled baked or dryed in the sun. this bulb is white, not entirely solid, and of a flat form; the bulb of the present year overlays, or crowns that of the last, and seems to be pressed close to it, the old bulb is withered much thiner equally wide with that of the present year and sends fourth from it's sides a number of small radicles.- this hiasinth is of a pale blue colour and is a very pretty flower. I preserved a specemine of it.

[Clark, April 17, 1806] April 17th 1806 I rose early and took a position near to the village and exposed the artiles I had for Sale Great numbers of Indians Came from different derections, Some from below Some above and others across the Countrey from the Tapteet river See description of the Nations &c.- I obtained a Sketch of the Columbia as also Clarks river. See sketch I made a bargin with the Chief who has more horses than all the village besides for 2 horses. Soon after he Canseled his bargin, and we again bargined for 3 horses, they were brought forward, and only one fit for Service, the others had Such intolerable backs as to render them entirely unfit for Service. as I would not take the 3 he would not Sell the good one to me, and we were off the bargin. I then packed up and was about Setting out for the Falls when one Indian Sold me 2 horses and one other one horse, and Some others Said they wished to trade which caused me to conclude to delay here one other night. Maney of the natives from above Come and Said they would trade, but asked a higher price than I thought I could give or reather more than this nation asked.- Great numbers of Men.- I hed to purchase 3 dogs for the men to eate & Some Shap-per-lell. I Sent Crusat, Wiser, Willard and McNeal back to Capt Lewis informing him of my ill Suck'sess, and adviseing him to proceed on to this place as Soon as possible, and my intention of proceededing on to the falls to purchase horses if possible Several Indians arived late this evening. Capt. Lewis Sent me a note by Shannon informing me that he would Set early on tomorrow morning early &c. &c. I sleped in house of the 2d Chief and they had not any thing except fish to eate and no wood for fire. those people have a number of buffalow robes. They have great number of Skimming nets

[Clark, April 17, 1806] Thursday 17th of April 1806 I rose early after bad nights rest, and took my merchindize to a rock which afforded an elegable Situation for my purpose, and at a Short distance from the houses, and divided the articles of merchindize into parsels of Such articles as I thought best Calculated to pleas the Indians, and in each parcel I put as many articles as we could afford to give, and thus exposed them to view, informing the Indians that each parcel was intended for a horse. they tanterlised me the greater part of the day, Saying that they had Sent out for their horses and would trade as Soon as they Came. Several parcels of merchindize was laid by for which they told me they would bring horses. I made a bargin with the Chief for 2 horses, about an hour after he canseled the bargin and we again bargained for 3 horses which were brought foward, only one of the 3 could be possibly used the other two had Such intolerable backs as to render them entirely unfit for Service. I refused to take two of them which displeased him and he refused to part with the 3rd. I then packed up the articles and was about Setting out for the Village above when a man Came and Sold me two horses, and another man Sold me one horse, and Several others informed me that they would trade with me if I would Continue untill their horses could be drove up. this induced me to Continue at this Village another day. Maney of the nativs from different villages on the Columbia above offered to trade, but asked Such things as we had not and double as much of the articles which I had as we could afford to give. this was a very unfavourable circumstance as my dependance for precureing a Sufficiency of horses rested on the Suckcess above where I had reasons to believe there were a greater abundance of those animals, and was in hopes of getting them on better terms. I purchased 3 dogs for the party with me to eate and Some Chap-pa-lell for my Self. before precureing the 3 horses I dispatched Crusat, Willard & McNeal and Peter Wiser to Capt Lewis at the Rock fort Camp with a note informing him of my ill Suckcess in precureing horses, and advised him to proceed on to this place as Soon as possible. that I would in the mean time proceed on to the Enesher Nation above the Great falls and try to purchase Some horses of that people. Soon after I had dispatched this party the Chief of the Enesher's and 15 or 20 of his people visited me and appeared to be anxious to See the articles I offered for the horses. Several of them agreeed to let me have horses if I would add Sundery articles to those I offered which I agreeed to, and they lay'd those bundles by and informed me they would deliver me the horses in the morning. I proposed going with them to their Town. the Chief informed me that their horses were all in the plains with their womin gathering roots. they would Send out and bring the horses to this place tomorrow. this entilligence was flattering, tho I doubted the Sincerity of those people who had Several times disapointed me in a Similar way. however I deturmined to Continue untill tomorrow. in the mean time industously employd. our Selves with the great multitude of indians of differant Nations about us trying to purchase horses. Shabono purchased a verry fine Mare for which he gave Hurmen, Elks Teeth, a belt and Some other articles of no great value. no other purchase was made in the Course of this day. in the evening I recved a note from Capt L- by Shannon informing me that he Should Set out early on tomorrow morning and Should proceed up to the bason 2 miles below the Skillute Village. and adviseing me to give double the prices which we had first agreed on for each horse. I observe at every house Scooping Nets with which they take the Salmon.

I was envited into the house of the 2nd Chief where Concluded to Sleep. this man was pore nothing to eat but dried fish, and no wood to burn. altho the night was Cold they Could not rase as much wood as would make a fire

[Lewis, April 18, 1806] Friday April 18th 1806. Late last evening we were visited by the principal cheif of Chilluckkittaquaws and 12 of his nation they remained with us untill 9 OC. when they all departed except the Cheif and two others who slept at my feet. we loaded our vessels and set out after an early breakfast this morning. we gave the indians a passage to the N. shore on which they reside and pursued our rout to the foot of the first rapid at the distance of 4 ms. here we found it necessary to unload the perogues and canoes and make a portage of 70 paces over a rock; we then drew our vessels up by a cord and the assistance of setingpoles. from hence we proceeded to the bason below the long narrows 5 ms. further and landed on the Lard. side at 1/2 after 3. the Cheif when he left me this morning promised to bring some horses to barter with me at the bason.- the long narrows are much more formidable than they were when we decended them last fall there would be no possibility of passind either up or down them in any vessel.- after unloading the canoes and arranging the camp I walked up to the Skillute Village and jouined Capt. he had procured four horses only for which a high price had been given, at least more than double that which we had formerly given for those which we purchased from the Shoshonees and the first band of Flatheads. they have a great abundance of horses but will not dispose of them. we determined to make the portage to the head of the long narrows with our baggage and five small canoes. the 2 perogues we could take no further and therefore cut them up for fuel. in the evening Capt. C. and myself returned to the camp at the bason and left Drewyer and three others with the merchandize at the village, three parsels of which had been laid by at the request of individuals who promised to give us horses for them in the morning.- I shot my airgun in the presents of the natives at the village which excited great astonishment.

[Clark, April 18, 1806] April 18th 1806 early this morning I was awoke by a Indian from the nieghbourhood of our horses, he had he arived here yesterday & this morning found a Small bag of powder and ball which had been left when we exposed our goods yesterday and brought it to me. I had a fire made out and exposed the articles &c. having increased the articles for each horse, and Sent out 2 men to hunt the horses bought yesterday. after Colecting them Sent Shabono and Frazer with the 4 I had purchased down to Capt Lewis. and was tanterlised with the expectation of purchaseing more imediately. Great numbers of the Indians from the falls and both above and below. none of them appeared anxious to part with their horses but told me that Several were Comeing from the plains about 1 or 2 P M. and laid by 2 parcels of merchindize and told me that they had Sent for their horses. among other Tribes was those of the Skad-datts who bantered the Skillutes to play with them at a Singular Kind of game which was Soon Made up and 9 of aside Sat down they were Some time making up their bets of Beeds, brass thimbles or tubes robes &c. &c. when the bets were all made up the nine on each Side took opposides faceing each other at the distance of about 12 feet. in front of each party was placed a long pole on which they Struck with a Stick and Sung. they made use of 2 Small pices of bone in this form and Size a bone was given to 2 men of the Same party who changed it from hand to hand with great dexterity one hand above the other looking down, and when he was ready for the opposit party to guess he Seperated his hands Swinging them around the breast looking at the opposit party who waved their hand to the Side the bone was in. if the opposit party guessed the hand of each man the bone was given to them. if neither it was nothing. if they guessed one which they might single out if they pleased they recived his bone, and lost on the other as they hapened to fail in guessing the also lose one if they fail guessing both The game is plaid at different numbers & each party has 5 sticks. Several of those games were played to day in which the Skillute won, indeed the won all the beeds and Som robes of the Skad datts which they _____ one other game which they also played _____ 2 by men with 4 Sticks. 2 black & 2 White under a kind of hat made of bark. as this is a very intrecut game I cannot describe it: the one who holds the Sticks places them in different positions, and the opposit party, guess the position of the black Sticks by a motion of either one or both of the hands. each man has 4 Sticks. this as also the other is accompanied with a kind of Song. This hat is about 12 inches diamuter and the Sticks about 5 inches long— at 3 P M Sergt Ordway arived with 3 men from Capt Lewis with elk skins and Some fiew articles Such as a Coat & robes. I had 3 dogs purchased, Soon after Capt. Lewis Came up with J. Fields he had assended the river with much dificuelty to the bason 2 Miles below. I left Drewyer, Warner, Shannon & Goodrich with the articles and went down with Capt Lewis to the bason, Cut up 2 of our canoes for fire wood no horses more maney nations resort here for trade

[Clark, April 18, 1806] Friday 18th April 1806 Early this Morning I was awoke by an indian man of the Chopunnish Nation who informed me that he lived in the neighbourhood of our horses. this man delivered me a bag of powder and ball which he had picked up this morning at the place the goods were exposed yesterday I had a fire made of Some poles purchased of the nativs at a Short distance from the houses and the articles exposed as yesterday. Collected the 4 horses purchased yesterday and Sent Frazier and Shabono with them to the bason where I expected they would meet Cap L-s and Commence the portage of the baggage on those horses. about 10 A.M. the Indians Came down from the Eneesher Villages and I expected would take the articles which they had laid by yesterday. but to my estonishment not one would make the exchange to-day-. two other parcels of good were laid by and the horses promised at 2 P.M. I payed but little attention to this bargain however Suffered the bundles to lye. I dressed the Sores of the principal Chief gave Some Small things to his children and promised the Chief Some Medicine for to Cure his Sores. his wife who I found to be a Sulky Bitch and was Somewhat efflicted with pains in her back. this I thought a good oppertunity to get her on my Side giveing here Something for her back. I rubed a little Camphere on her temples and back, and applyed worm flannel to her back which She thought had nearly restored her to her former feelings. this I thought a favourable time to trade with the Chief who had more horses than all the nation besides. I accordingly made him an offer which he excepted and Sold me two horses. Great numbers of Indians from defferent derections visited me at this place to day, none of them appeared willing to part with their horses, but told me that Several were Comeing from the plains this evening. among other Nations who visit this place for the purpose of trade is the Skad-datt's. those people bantered the Skillutes to play at a Singular kind of game. in the Course of the day the Skillutes won all their beeds Skins arrows &c. This game was Composed of 9 men on a Side. they Set down opposit to each other at the distance of about 10 feet. in front of each party a long pole was placed on which they Struck with a Small Stick to the time of their Songs. after the bets were made up which was nearly half an hour after they Set down, two round bones was producd about the Size of a mans little finger or Something Smaller and 2 1/4 inches in length. which they held in their hand Changeing it from one hand to the other with great dexterity. 2 men on the Same Side performed this part, and when they had the bone in the hand they wished, they looked at their advosarys Swinging arms around their Sholders for their advosary Guess which they pirformed by the motion the hand either to the right or left. if the opposit party guessed the hand of both of the men who had the bone, the bones were given to them. if neither the bones was retained and nothing Counted. if they guessed one and not the other, one bone was dilivered up and the party possessing the other bone Counted one. and one for every time the advosary miss guessed untill they guessed the hand in which the bone was in-in this game each party has 5 Sticks. and one Side wins all the Sticks, once twice or thrice as the game may be Set. I observed another game which those people also play and is played by 2 persons with 4 Sticks about the Size of a mans finger and about 7 inches in length. two of those Sticks are black and the other 2 White and Something larger than the black ones. those Sticks they place in defferent positions which they perform under a kind of trencher made of bark round and about 14 inches diamiter. this is a very intricate game and I cannot Sufficiently understand to discribe it. the man who is in possession of the Sticks &c places them in defferent positions, and the opposit party tels the position of the black Sticks by a motion of either or both of his hands &c. this game is Counted in the Same way as the one before mentioned. all their games are accompanied with Songs and time. at 3 P. M Sergt. Ordway & three men arived from Cap Lewis they brought with them Several Elk Skins, two of my Coats and 4 robes of the party to add to the Stores I had with me for the purchase of horses. Sgt. O. informed me that Cap L. had arived with all the Canoes into the bason 2 miles below and wished Some dogs to eate. I had 3 dogs purchased and Sent down. at 5 P.M. Capt. Lewis Came up. he informed me that he had the river to the bason with much difecuelty and danger, haveing made one portage. as I had not Slept but very little for the two nights past on account of mice & virmen with which those indian houses abounded, and haveing no blanket with me, and the means of keeping a fire Sufficent to keep me worm out was too Expensive I deturmined to proceed with Capt L. down to Camp at the bason. I left the Articles of Merchendize &c. with Drewyer, Werner, Shannon & Goodrich untill the morning— at the bason we Cut up two of our Canoes for fire wood verry much to the Sagreen of the nativs not with standing they would give us nothing for them. In my absence Several Inds. visited Capt. Lewis at his camp among others was the great Cheif of the Chilluckkitquaw who Continued with him untill he left Rock fort Camp. Capt L. had 12 pack Saddles Completed and Strings prepared of the Elk skins for Lashing the loads he also kept out all the hunters who killed just deer enough for the party with him to Subsist on. The Cheif who had Visited Capt Lewis promised him that he would bring Some horses to the bason and trade with him. but he was not as good as his word. Capt Lewis gave a large Kittle for a horse which was offered to him at the bason this evening.

[Lewis, April 19, 1806] Saturday Aprl. 19th 1806. This morning early we had our small canoes drawn out, and employed all hands in transporting our baggage on their backs and by means of the four pack horses, over the portage. This labour we had accomplished by 3 P.M. and established our camp a little above the present Skillute village which has been removed a few hundred yards lower down the river than when we passed them last fall and like others below have the floors of their summer dwellings on the surface of the earth instead of those cellars in which they resided when we passed them. there was great joy with the natives last night in consequence of the arrival of the salmon; one of those fish was caught; this was the harbinger of good news to them. they informed us that these fish would arrive in great quantities in the course of about 5 days. this fish was dressed and being divided into small peices was given to each child in the village. this custom is founded in a supersticious opinon that it will hasten the arrival of the salmon. with much difficulty we obtained four other horses from the Indians today, we wer obliged to dispence with two of our kettles in order to acquire those. we have now only one small kettle to a mess of 8 men. in the evening Capt. Clark set out with four men to the Enesher village at the grand falls in order to make a further attempt to procure horses. these people are very faithless in their contracts. they frequently receive the merchandize in exchange for their horses and after some hours insist on some additional article being given them or revoke the exchange. they have pilfered several small articles from us this evening.- I directed the horses to be hubbled & suffered to graize at a little distance from our camp under the immediate eye of the men who had them in charge. one of the men Willard was negligent in his attention to his horse and suffered it to ramble off; it was not to be found when I ordered the others to be brought up and confined to the picquits. this in addition to the other difficulties under which I laboured was truly provoking. I repremanded him more severely for this peice of negligence than had been usual with me. I had the remaining horses well secured by picquits; they were extreemly wrestless and it required the attention of the whole guard through the night to retain them notwithstanding they were bubbled and picquted. they frequently throwed themselves by the ropes by which they were confined. all except one were stone horse for the people in this neighbourhood do not understand the art of gelding them, and this is a season at which they are most vicious. many of the natives remained about our camp all night.

[Clark, April 19, 1806] April 19th 1806 this morning early Some rain had the Small Canoes hauled out to dry every man Capable of Carrying a load Comencd the portage and by 5 P. M had every part of our baggage and canoes across the portage. I then took Sgt. Pryor, G. Shannon & Crusat & Labiech and went up to the falls at which place I arivd. about 8 P.M. in the Course of this day I purchased 4 horses at the town & Capt Lewis purchased one. the nativs finding that we were about to proceed on by water Sold us those fiew horses for which we were Compd. to pay them emence prices and the horses were indefferent. Several Showers of rain this day. description of those people &c narrows bad

[Clark, April 19, 1806] Saturday 19th April 1806. We deturmined to make the portage to the head of the long narrows with our baggage and 5 Small Canoes, the 2 large Canoes we Could take no further and therefore Cut them up for fuel. we had our Small Canoes drawn up very early and employed all hands in transporting our baggage on their backs and by means of 4 pack horses, over the portage. This labour we had accomplished by 3 P.M. and established our Camp a little above the present Skillute village which has been removed as before observed a fiew hundred yards lower down the river than when we passed it last fall. I left Capt L. at the bason and proceeded to the village early this morning with a view to recive the horses which were promised to be brought this morning for articles laid by last evining. in the Course of this day I purchased four horses at the Village, and Capt Lewis one at the bason before he left it. after the baggage was all Safely landed above the portage, all hands brought over the Canoes at 2 lodes which was accomplished by 5 P.M. as we had not a Sufficiency of horses to transport our baggage we agreed that I should proceed on to the Enesher villages at the great falls of the Columbia and if possible purchase as maney horses as would transport the baggage from that place, and rid us of the trouble and dificuelty of takeing our Canoes further. I set out with Serjt Pryor, Geo Shannon Peter Crusat & Labiech at half past 5 P.M. for the Enesher Village at which place I arrived at 8 P.M. Several Showers of rain in the after part of to day, and the S W wind very high. there was great joy with the nativs last night in consequence of the arrival of the Salmon; one of those fish was cought, this was the harbenger of good news to them. They informed us that those fish would arive in great quantities in the Course of about 5 days. this fish was dressed and being divided into Small pieces was given to each Child in the village. this Custom is founded on a Supersticious opinion that it will hasten the arrival of the Salmon.

we were oblige to dispence with two of our kitties in order to acquire two of the horses purchasd. to day. we have now only one Small kittle to a mess of 8 men. These people are very fathless in Contracts; they frequently reive the merchindize in exchange for their horses and after Some hours insist on Some additional article being given them or revoke the exchange.

The long narrows are much more formadable than they were when we decended them last fall, there would be no possibility of passing either up or down them in any vessle at this time.

I entered the largest house of the Eneeshers village in which I found all the enhabitents in bead. they rose and made a light of Straw, they haveing no wood to burn. many men Collected. we Smoked and I informed them that I had come to purchase a fiew horses of them. they promused to Sell me Some in the morning.

[Lewis, April 20, 1806] Sunday April 20th 1806. some frost this morning. The Enesher an Skillutes are much better clad than they were last fall, there men have generally legings mockersons and large robes; many of them wear shirts of the same form with those of the Shoshone Chopunnish &c highly ornamented with porcupine quills. the dress of their women differs very little from those of the great rapids and above. their children frequently wear robes of the large grey squirrel skins, those of the men and women are principally deer skins, some wolf, elk, bighorn and buffaloe; the latter they procure from the nations who sometimes visit the Missouri. indeed a considerable poportion of their wearing apparel is purchased from their neighbours to the N. W. in exchange for pounded fish copper and beads. at present the principal village of the Eneshur is below the falls on the N. side of the river. one other village is above the falls on the S. side and another a few miles above on the N. side. the first consists of 19, the 2cd of 11, and the 3rd of 5 lodges. their houses like those of the Skillutes have their floors on the surface of the ground, but are formed of sticks and covered with mats and straw. they are large and contain usually several families each for fuel they use straw, small willows and the southern wood. they use the silk grass in manufacturing their fishing nets and bags, the bear grass and cedar bark are employed in forming a variety of articles. they are poor, dirty, proud, haughty, inhospitable, parsimonious and faithless in every rispect, nothing but our numbers I beleive prevents their attempting to murder us at this moment.

This morning I was informed that the natives had pilfered six tommahawks and a knife from the party in the course of the last night. I spoke to the cheif on this subject. he appeared angry with his people and addressed them but the property was not restored. one horse which I had purchased and paid for yesterday and which could not be found when I ordered the horses into close confinement yesterday I was now informed had been gambled away by the rascal who had sold it to me and had been taken away by a man of another nation. I therefore took the goods back from this fellow. I purchased a gun from the cheif for which I gave him 2 Elkskins. in the course of the day I obtained two other indifferent horses for which I gave an extravigant price. I found that I should get no more horses and therefore resolved to proceed tomorrow morning with those which I had and to convey the baggage in two small canoes that the horses could not carry. for this purpose I had a load made up for seven horses, the eighth Bratton was compelled to ride as he was yet unable to walk. I barted my Elkskins old irons and 2 canoes for beads. one of the canoes for which they would give us but little I had cut up for fuel. These people have yet a large quantity of dryed fish on hand yet they will not let us have any but for an exorbitant price. we purchased two dogs and some shappellel from them. I had the horses graized untill evening and then picquited and bubbled within the limits of our camp. I ordered the indians from our camp this evening and informed them that if I caught them attempting to perloin any article from us I would beat them severely. they went off in reather a bad humour and I directed the party to examine their arms and be on their guard. they stole two spoons from us in the course of the day. The Scaddals, Squan-nan-os, Shan-wah-purrs and Shallattas reside to the N. W. of these people, depend on hunting deer and Elk and trade with these people for ther pounded fish.

[Clark, April 20, 1806] April 20th 1806 This morning very Cold hills covered with Snow. I Showed the nativs what I had to give for their horses and attempted to purchase them. they informed me that they would not Sell any horses to me, that their horses were at a long ways off and they would not trade them. my offer was a blue robe, Callico Shirt, a handkerchef, 5 parcels of paint a Knife, a wampom moon 4 braces of ribin, a pice of Brass and about 6 braces of yellow heeds; and to that amount for what I had I also offered my large blue blanket for one, my Coat Sword & Plume none of which Seem to entice those people to give horses if they had any. they Set in their huts which is of mats Supported on poles without fire. at night when they wish a light they burn dry Straw & Some fiew Small dry willows. they Speak defferent from those below, have but little to eate. Some roots & Dryed fish is to be found in their houses. I am half frozed at this inhospitable Village which is moved from its position above the falls to one below and Contains 19 large houses, a village is also established on the other Side imedeately above the falls. all the natives who was established above the Falls for Some distance has removed Those people are much better dressed than they were at the time we went down the river. They have all new, Deer, Elk, Ibex Goat & wolf Skin robes, their Children also the large squirel Skin robes, maney of them have Legins and mockersons, all of which they precure of the Indians at a distance in exchange for their pounded fish & Beeds, they also purchase Silk grass, of which they make their nets & Sales for takeing fish they also purchase Bear grass and maney other things for their fish. those people gave me roots and berries prepared in different ways for which I gave some Small articles in return.-Great numbers of Skiming knets on their houses. Those people are Pore and Kind durty & indolt. They ware their hair loose flowing the men cut in the foward which the Skilloots do not &c. &c.

I could not precure a Single horse of those people, dureing this day at any price, they offered me 2 for 2 kittles of which we Could not spear. I used every artifice decent & even false Statements to enduce those pore devils to Sell me horses. in the evening two different men offered to Sell me three horses which they informed me was a little distance off and they would bring them imediately. those two persons as I found went imediately off up the river to their tribe without any intention to find or Sell their horses. a little before Sunset 3 men arived from Some distance above and informed me that they Came to See me. at Sunset finding no probability of Capt Lewis arival, packed up the articles and took them into the lodge in which I lay last night. Great numbers of those people geathered around me to Smoke. I gave them 2 pipes and lay down in the back part of the house with Sgt. P. & the men with our arms in a Situation as to be ready in case of any alarm. those pore people appear entirely harmless- I purchased a dog and Some wood with a little pounded fish and Chappaless. made a fire on the rocks and Cooked the dogs on which the men breckfast & Dined. wind hard all day cold from N W.

[Clark, April 20, 1806] Sunday 20th April 1806 a very cold morning the western mountains Covered with Snow I Shewed the Eneshers the articles I had to give for their horses. they without hezitation informed me that they would not Sell me any for the articles I had, if I would give them Kitties they would let me have horses, and not without. that their horses were at a long ways off in the planes and they would not Send for them &c. my offer was a blue robe, a Calleco Shirt, a Silk handkerchief, 5 parcels of paint, a knife, a Wampom moon, 8 yards of ribon, Several pieces of Brass, a mockerson awl and 6 braces of yellow beeds; and to that amount for each horse which is more than double what we gave either the Sohsohne or first flat heads we met with on Clarks river I also offered my large blue blanket, my Coat Sword & plume none of which Seamed to entice those people to Sell their horses. not with standing every exertion not a Single horse Could be precured of those people in the Course of the day. Those people are much better Clad than they were last fall, their men have generally legins mockersons and large robes. maney of them ware Shirts of the Same form of those of the Chopunnish and Shoshone highly ornimented with porcupine quills. the dress of their winen differs verry little from those above the great rapids. their Children have Small robes of the Squirel Skins. those of the men & women are principally deer, Some elk, wolf, Ibix & buffalow which they precure from distant nations who purchase their Pounded fish in exchange for those robes & Beeds. The principal village of the Enesher nation is imedeately below the falls on the N. Side. one other village of the Same nation above the falls on the opposit Side and one other a few miles above on the North Side.- The Houses of those people like the Skillutes have the flores of their Summer dwelling on the Surface of the earth in Sted of those Sellers in which they resided when we passed them last fall. those houses are Covered with mats and Straw are large and Contain Several families each. I counted 19 at this Village & 11 on the opposit Side. those people are pore durty haughty. they burn Straw and Small willows. have but little to eate and deer with what they have. they precure the Silk grass of which they make their nets, the bear grass for makeing their mats and Several other necessary of the Indians of the following nations who trade with them as also the Skillutes for their pounded fish. Viz. Skad-dats, Squan-nun-os, Shan-wappoms, Shall-lat-tos, who reside to the north and Several bands who reside on the Columbia above.- I precured a Sketch of the Columbia and its branches of those people in which they made the river which falls into the Columbia imediately above the falls on the South Side to branch out into 3 branches one of which they make head in Mt.jefferson, one in mount Hood and the other in the S W. range of Mountains and does not water that extensive Country we have heretofore Calculated on. a great portion of that extensive tract of Country to the S. and S. W. of the Columbia and Lewis's river and between the Same and the waters of Callifornia must be watered by the Multnomah river.- See Sketch in the latter part of this book (No. 5). Those people are great jokies and deciptfull in trade.

at Sunset finding that Capt Lewis would not arrive this evening as I expected, I packed up all the articles which I had exposed, at a Situation I had pitched on to Encamp, and at which place we had bought as maney fishing poles as made a fire to Cook a dog which I had purchased for the men to eate, and returned to the lodge which I had Slept in last night. great number gathered around me to Smoke, I gave them two pipes, and then lay my self down with the men to Sleep, haveing our merchendize under our heads and guns &c in our arms, as we always have in Similar Situations

[Lewis, April 21, 1806] Monday April 21st 1806. Notwithstanding all the precautions I had taken with rispect to the horses one of them had broken his cord of 5 strands of Elkskin and had gone off spanseled. I sent several men in surch of the horse with orders to return at 10 A.M. with or without the horse being determined to remain no longer with these villains. they stole another tomahawk from us this morning I surched many of them but could not find it. I ordered all the spare poles, paddles and the ballance of our canoe put on the fire as the morning was cold and also that not a particle should be left for the benefit of the indians. I detected a fellow in stealing an iron socket of a canoe pole and gave him several severe blows and mad the men kick him out of camp. I now informed the indians that I would shoot the first of them that attempted to steal an article from us. that we were not affraid to fight them, that I had it in my power at that moment to kill them all and set fire to their houses, but it was not my wish to treat them with severity provided they would let my property alone. that I would take their horses if I could find out the persons who had stolen the tommahawks, but that I had reather loose the property altogether than take the hose of an inosent person. the chiefs were present hung their heads and said nothing. at 9 A.M. Windsor returned with the lost horse, the others who were in surch of the horse soon after returned also. the Indian who promised to accompany me as far as the Chopunnish country produced me two horses one of which he politely gave me the liberty of packing. we took breakfast and departed a few minutes after 10 OClock. having nine horses loaded and one which Bratton rode not being able as yet to march; the two canoes I had dispatched early this morning. at 1 P.M. I arrived at the Enesher Village where I found Capt Clark and party; he had not purchased a single horse. he informed me that these people were quite as unfriendly as their neighbours the Skillutes, and that he had subsisted since he left me on a couple of platters of pounded roots and fish which an old man had the politeness to offer him. his party fared much better on dogs which he purchased from those people. the man resided here from whom I had purchased the horse which ran off from me yesterday. I had given him a large kettle and a knife in exchange for that horse which I informed him should be taken from him unles he produced me the lost horse or one of equal value in his stead, the latter he prefered and produced me a very good horse which I very cheerfully received. we soon made the portage with our canoes and baggage and halted about 1/2 a mile above the Village where we graized our horses and took dinner on some dogs which we purchased of these people. after dinner we proceeded on about four miles to a village of 9 mat lodges of the Enesher a little below the entrance of Clark's river and encamped; one of the canoes joined us the other not observing us halt continued on. we obtained two dogs and a small quantity of fuel of these people for which we were obliged to give a higher price than usual. our guide continued with us, he appears to be an honest sincere fellow. he tells us that the indians a little above will treat us with much more hospitality than those we are now with. we purchased another horse this evening but his back is in such a horid state that we can put but little on him; we obtained him for a trifle, at least for articles which might be procured in the U States for 10 shillings Virga Cory.- we took the precaution of piquting and spanseling our horses this evening near our camp.

[Clark, April 21, 1806] April 21st 1806 a fair Cold morning. I find it useless to offer any articles or attempt to trade at this village and therefore deturmine to _____ before I rose the house was Crouded with Indians to Smoke I gave them none. they are well Supplied with Straw & bark bags ready to hold their pounded fish. at 12 oClock the advance of the party from below arived and Soon after the Canoes all things were taken above the falls & 2 Canoes, turned out the horss and Cooked & Eat 2 dogs which we purchased of the nativs, purchased one horse for Which we are to give a Kittle which was given by us to a man for a horse 3 days past &c. the horse was either taken or Strayed off. The Chief from below Came up and appeared Concerned for what had been done at his Village (See Journal)

a 4 P M loaded up & Set out the Canoes also proceed on about 3 miles opposit to the Mouth of Clarks river, and an Indian man who has attached himself to us and who has lent us a horse to pack & lives near the Rocky mountains. he told us that as the day was far Spent we had better Camp at a village of 9 Lodges a little off the road opsd. the River CClarks This river has a great falls above 2 forks on its West Side. we formed a Camp purchased Some wood & 3 dogs for which we gave pewter buttons which buttons we had made &c. but fiew Indians with us this evining purchased an old horse and tied up all the horses when we went to bed

Those are the Same people with those below at the falls. See journal for the next day-

Skad data ill looking people reside to the N about 18 or 20 miles they played against the Skillutes a game they Call _____ 9 of a Side and lost all the beeds & other articles

also a Single game with 2 black & 2 white Sticks under a kind of hat. 2 men played this game is intricit and each party has 4 pegs to count it

The former game is played with 2 bones or Sticks about the Size of a large quill and 2 inches long passing from one hand to the other and the adverse party guess. See description before mentioned. The nations abov at the falls also play this game and bet high

[Clark, April 21, 1806] Monday 21st April 1806 A fair Cold morning I found it useless to make any further attempts to trade horses with those unfriendly people who only Crouded about me to view and make their remarks and Smoke, the latter I did not indulge them with to day. at 12 oClock Capt Lewis and party Came up from the Skillutes Village with 9 horses packed and one which bratten who was yet too weak to walk, rode, and Soon after the two Small Canoes also loaded with the residue of the baggage which Could not be taken on horses. we had everry thing imedeately taken above the falls, in the mean time purchased 2 Dogs on which the party dined- whilst I remained at the Enesher Village I Subsisted on 2 platters of roots, Some pounded fish and

Sun flour Seed pounded which an old man had the politeness to give me. in return for which I gave him Several Small articles-.

Capt Lewis informed me that imedeately after I left him the nativs began to Steal and had Stolen Tomahawks of the party, and in the Course of the night had let our horses loose he had burnt one and Sold 2 of the largest Canoes for beeds, the other 2 brought on. an indian was detected in Stealing a socket and was kicked out of Camp. Capt L. informed the Indians that the next man who attempted to steal Should be Shot and thretened them and informed them that he could kill them in a moment and Set their town on fire if he pleased. but it was not his desire to hurt them Severly if they would let the property of the party alone. the Chiefs hung their heads and Said nothing. he lost the horse that was given for a large kittle, and a Chopunnish man lent a horse to carry a load and accompanied the party- The man who we had reason to believe had Stolen the horse he had given for the Kittle we thretend a little and he produced a very good horse in the place of that one which we Chearfully receved.

after dinner we proceeded on about 4 Miles to a Village of 9 Mat Lodges of the Enesher, a little below the enterance of To war nah hi ooks river and encamped. one of the Canoes joined us, the other not haveing observed us halt continued on. We obtained 2 Dogs and a Small quantity of fuel of those people for which we were obliged to give a higher price than usial. our guide continued with us, he appears to be an honest fellow. he tels us that the indians above will treat us with much more hospitallity than those we are now with. we purchased another horse this evening but his back is in Such a horrid State that we Can put but little on him; we obtained him for a triffle, at least for articles which might be precured in the U. States for 10/-virga. Currency- we took the precaution of picqueting and Spancelling our horses this evening near our Camp. the evening Cold and we Could afford only one fire.

[Lewis, April 22, 1806] Tuesday April 22cd 1806. Last night two of our horses broke loos from the picquits and straggled off some little distance, the men who had charge of them fortunately recovered them early. at 7 A.M. we set out having previously sent on our small Canoe with Colter and Potts. we had not arrived at the top of a hill over which the road leads opposite the village before Charbono's horse threw his load, and taking fright at the saddle and robe which still adhered, ran at full speed down the hill, near the village he disengaged himself from the saddle and robe, an indian hid the robe in his lodge. I sent our guide and one man who was with me in the rear to assist Charbono in retaking his horse which having done they returned to the village on the track of the horse in surch of the lost articles they found the saddle but could see nothing of the robe the indians denyed having seen it; they then continued on the track of the horse to the place from whence he had set out with the same success. being now confident that the Indians had taken it I sent the Indian woman on to request Capt. C. to halt the party and send back some of the men to my assistance being determined either to make the indians deliver the robe or birn their houses. they have vexed me in such a manner by such repeated acts of villany that I am quite disposed to treat them with every severyty, their defenseless state pleads forgivness so far as rispects their lives. with this resolution I returned to their village which I had just reached as Labuish met me with the robe which he informed me he found in an Indian lodg hid behind their baggage. I now returned and joined Capt Clark who was waiting my arrival with the party. the Indian woman had not reached Capt C. untill about the time I arrived and he returned from a position on the top of a hill not far from where he had halted the party. from the top of this emmenense Capt. C. had an extensive view of the country. he observed the range of mountains in which Mount Hood stands to continue nearly south as far as the eye could reach. he also observed the snow clad top of Mount Jefferson which boar S. 10 W. Mount Hood from the same point boar S. 30 W. the tops of the range of western mountains are covered with snow. Capt C. also discovered some timbered country in a Southern direction from him at no great distance. Clarks river which mouths immediately opposite this point of view forks at the distance of 18 or 20 miles from hence, the wright hand fork takes it rise in mount Hood, and the main branch continues it's course to the S. E.

we now made the following regulations as to our future order of march (viz) that Capt. C. & myself should devide the men who were disencumbered by horses and march alternately each day the one in front and the other in rear. haveing divided the party agreeably to this arrangement, we proceeded on through an open plain country about 8 miles to a village of 6 houses of the Eneshur nation, here we observed our 2 canoes passing up on the opposite side; the wind being too high for them to pass the river they continued on. we halted at a small run just above the village where we dined on some dogs which we purchased of the inhabitants and suffered our horses to graize about three hours. there is no timber in this country we are obliged to purchase our fuel of the natives, who bling it from a great distance. while we halted for dinner we purch a horse. after dinner we proceeded on up the river about 4 miles to a village of 7 mat lodges of the last mentioned nation. here our Chopunnish guide informed us that the next village was at a considerable distance and that we could not reach it tonight. the people at this place offered to sell us wood and dogs, and we therefore thought it better to remain all night. a man blonging to the next village abovd proposed exchanging a horse for one of our canoes, just at this moment one of our canoes was passing. we hailed them and ordered them to come over but the wind continued so high that they could not join us untill after sunset and the Indian who wished to exchange his horse for the canoe had gone on. Charbonoe purchased a horse this evening. we obtained 4 dogs and as much wood as answered our purposes on moderate terms. we can only afford ourselves one fire, and are obliged to lie without shelter, the nights are cold and days warm.- Colter and Pots had passed on with their canoe.

[Clark, April 22, 1806] Tuesday 22nd of April 1806 last night 2 of our horses broke loose and Strayed of at a Short dis-tance. at 7 oClock we loaded up and Set out, haveing previously Sent off the Canoe with Colter and Potts we had not arived at the top of the hill which is 200 feet before Shabonos horse threw off his load and went with great Speed down the hill to the Village where he disengaged himself of his Saddle & the robe which was under it, the Indians hid the robe and delayed Capt. Lewis and the rear party Some time before they found the robe which was in a lodge hid behind their baggage, and took possession of it. dureing the time the front of the party was waiting for Cap Lewis, I assended a high hill from which I could plainly See the range of Mountains which runs South from Mt. Hood as far as I could See. I also discovered the top of Mt. Jefferson which is Covered with Snow and is S to W. Mt. Hood is S. 30° W. the range of mountains are Covered with timber and also Mt Hood to a sertain bite. The range of Mountains has Snow on them. I also discovered some timbered land in a S. detection from me, Short of the mountains. Clarks river which mouthes imedeately opposit to me forks at about 18 or 20 miles, the West fork runs to the Mt Hood and the main branch Runs from S. E. after Capt Lewis Came up we proceeded on through a open ruged plain about 8 miles to a Village of 6 Houses on the river. here we observed our 2 Canoes passing up on the opposit Side and the Wind too high for them to join us. I halted at the mouth of a run above the village near Some good grass to let the horses graze and for the party to dine. Sent to the huts and purchased a dog & Some wood. dureing the time the party was takeing diner we purchased one horse. after we proceeded on up the river about 4 miles to a village of 7 mat Lodges. here our Chopunnish guide informed me that the next villg. was at Some distance and that we Could not get to it to night, and that there was no wood to be precured on this Side. a man offered to Sell us a horse for a Canoe. just at the moment we discovered one of our Canoes on the opposit Side. we concluded to Camp here all night with the expectation of precureing some horses. Sent and purchased Some wood and 4 dogs & Shapillele. Shabono purchased a hors for which he gave a red rapper, Shirt, ploom & Tomahawk &c. the party purchased a great quantity of Chapellell and Some berries for which they gave bits of Tin and Small pieces of Cloth & wire &c. had our horses led out and held to grass untill dusk when they were all brought to Camp, and pickets drove in the ground and the horses tied up. we find the horses very troublesom perticularly the Stud which Compose 10/13 of our number of horses. the air I find extreemly Cold which blows Continularly from Mt. Hoods Snowey regions. those Indians reside in Small Lodges built of the mats of Grass, flags &c. and Crouded with inhabitents, who Speak a language Somewhat different from those at the falls. their dress habits and appearance appear to be very much the Same with those below. we made 14 miles to day with the greatest exirtion. Serjt. Gass & R. Fields joined us with one Canoe this evening. the other Canoe with Colter & pots is a head.

[Lewis, April 23, 1806] Wednesday April 23rd 1806. At day light this morning we were informed that the two horses of our Interpreter Charbono were absent; on enquiry it appeared that he had neglected to confine them to picquts as had been directed last evening. we immediately dispatched Reubin Feilds and Labuish to assist Charbono in recovering his horses. one of them was found at no great distance and the other was given over as lost. at 8 A.M. Reuben Feilds and Sergt. Gass proceeded in the canoe. at 10 Labuish and Charbono returned unsuccessfull, they had gone back on the road nearly to the last village and suched the plains on either hand to a considerable distance. our remaining longer would have prevented our making a timely stage which in our situation is all important; we therefore determined to proceed immediately to the next village which from the information of our guide will occupy the greater part of the day to reach at eleven OCk. we loaded our horses and set out. during the time we were detained this morning we had two packsaddles made. we continued our march along a narrow rocky bottom on the N. side of the river about 12 miles to the Wah-how-pum Village of 12 temperary mat lodges near the Rock rapid. these people appeared much pleased to see us, sold us 4 dogs and some wood for our small articles which we had previously prepared as our only resource to obtain fuel and food through those plains. these articles conisted of pewter buttons, strips of tin iron and brass, twisted wire &c. we also obtained some shap-pe-lell newly made from these people. here we met with a Chopunnish man on his return up the river with his family and about 13 head of horses most of them young and unbroken. he offered to hire us some of them to pack as far a his nation, but we prefer bying as by hireing his horses we shal have the whole of his family most probably to mentain. at a little distance below this village we passed five lodges of the same people who like those were waiting the arrival of the salmon. after we had arranged our camp we caused all the old and brave men to set arround and smoke with us. we had the violin played and some of the men danced; after which the natives entertained us with a dance after their method. this dance differed from any I have yet seen. they formed a circle and all sung as well the spectators as the dancers who performed within the circle. these placed their sholders together with their robes tightly drawn about them and danced in a line from side to side, several parties of from 4 to seven will be performing within the circle at the same time. the whole concluded with a premiscuous dance in which most of them sung and danced. these people speak a language very similar to the Chopunnish whome they also resemble in their dress their women wear long legings mockersons shirts and robes. their men also dress with legings shirts robes and mockersons. after the dance was ended the Indians retired at our request and we retired to rest. we had all our horses side bubbled and turned out to graize; at this village, a large creek falls in on the N. side which we did not observe as we decended the river. the river is by no means as rapid as when we decended or at least not obstructed with those dangerous rapids the water at present covers most of the rocks in the bed of the river. the natives promised to barter their horses with us in the morning we therefore entertained a hope that we shall be enabled to proceede by land from hence with the whole of our party and baggage. came 12 miles by land. the sands made the march fatieguing.-

[Clark, April 23, 1806] Wednesday 23rd 1806 at day light this morning we were informed that the two horses of our interpreter Shabono were missing on enquirey we were informed that he had neglected to tie up his horses as derected last evening. we imedeately dispatch him, R. Fields & Labiech in Serch of the horses, one of them were found at no great distance. the other was not found. R. Fields retd. without finding the horse Set out with Sergt Gass in the Small Canoe at about 8 A M. at 10 Shabono and Labiech returned also unsucksessfull they had went on the back trail nearly to the last Village and took a circle around on the hills. as our Situation was Such that we Could not detain for a horse, which would prevent our makeing a timely Stage which is a great object with us in those open plains, we Concluded to give up the horse and proceed on to the next village which we were informed was at Some distance and would take us the greater part of the day. at 11 A.M. we packed up and Set out and proceeded up on the N. Side of the Columbia on a high narrow bottom and rockey for 12 miles to the Wah-how-pum village near the rock rapid of 12 temporary mat Lodges, those people appeared pleased to See us. they Sold us 4 dogs Some Shapollell and wood for our Small articles Such as awls pieces of Tin and brass. we passed Several Lodges on the bank of the river where they were fixed waiting for the Salmon. I over took a Choponish man whome I had Seen at the long, and who had found a bag of our powder and brought it to me at that place. this man had his family on the _____ and about 3 head of horses which appeared young and unbroke. his spous as also that of the other gave me a Cake of Chapellell and proceeded on with me to the Wah howpum Village and formed his Camp near us. we Caused all the old & brave men to Set around and Smoke with us. we Caused the fiddle to be played and Some of the men danced. after them the nativs danced. they dance different from any Indians I have Seen. they dance with their Sholders together and pass from Side to Side, defferent parties passing each other, from 2 to 7. and 4 parties danceing at the Same time and Concluding the dance by passing promiscuisly throu & beetween each other. after which we Sent of the Indians and retired to bed. Those people Speak a language verry Similal to the Chopunish and with a very inconsiderable difference. their dress and appearance is more like those of the Great falls of the Columbia. we had all our horses Side hobbled and let us out to feed. at this village a large Creek falls in on the N. Side which I had not observed as I decended the river. the river is by no means as rapid as it was at the time we decended. The nativs promised to give is a horse for one of our Canoes. and offer to Sell us another for a Scarlet robe which we have not at present. Shabono made a bargin with one of the Indian men going with us, for a horse for Which he gave his Shirt. and two of the leather Sutes of his wife. The Sand through which we walked to day is So light that renders the march verry fatigueing. made 12 miles by land.

[Lewis, April 24, 1806] Thursday April 24 th 1806. We were up early this morning and dispatched the men in surch of our horses, they were all found in a little time except McNeal's. we hired an indian to surch for this horse it was one in the evening before he returned with him. in the intermediate time we had 4 packsaddles made purchased three horses of the Wah-howpums, and hired three others of the Chopunnish man who accompanys us with his family and horses. we now sold our canoes for a few strands of beads, loaded up and departed at 2 P.M. the natives had tantalized us with an exchange of horses for our canoes in the first instance, but when they found that we had made our arrangements to travel by land they would give us nothing for them I determined to cut them in peices sooner than leave them on those terms, Drewyer struck one of the canoes and split of a small peice with his tommahawk, they discovered us determined on this subject and offered us several strands of beads for each which were accepted. we proceeded up the river between the hills and it's Northen shore. the road was rocky and sandy alternately, the road difficult and fatiegu-ing. at 12 ms. we arrived at a village of 5 lodges of the Met-cow-wes, having passed 4 lodges at 4 and 2 at 2 Ms. further. we ramined all night near the Met-cow-we lodges about 2 miles below our encampment of the _____ of October last; we purchased three dogs and some shappelel of these people which we cooked with dry grass and willow boughs. many of the natives pased and repassed us today on the road and behaved themselves with distant rispect towards us. most of the party complain of the soarness of their feet and legs this evening; it is no doubt caused by walking over the rough stones and deep sands after bing for some months passed been accustomed to a soft soil. my left ankle gives me much pain. I baithed my feet in cold water from which I experienced considerable releif. The curloos are abundant in these plains and are now laying their eggs. saw the Kildee, the brown lizzard, and a Moonax which the natives had petted. the winds which set from Mount Hood or in a westerly direction are much more cold than those from the opposite quarter. there are now no dews in these plains, and from the appearance of the earth there appears to have been no rain for several weeks.- we derected that the three horses which we purchased yesterday should be bubbled and confined to a picqut, and that the others should be disposed of in the same manner they were last evening.

[Clark, April 24, 1806] Thursday 24th April 1806 rose early this morning and Sent out after the horses all of which were found except McNeals which I hired an Indian to find and gave him a Tomahawk had 4 pack Saddles made ready to pack the horses which we may purchase. we purchased 3 horses, and hired 3 others of the Chopunnish man who accompanies us with his family, and at 1 P.M. Set out and proceeded on through a open Countrey rugid & Sandy between Some high lands and the river to a village of 5 Lodges of the Met-cow-we band haveing passed 4 Lodges at 4 miles and 2 Lodges at 6 miles. Great numbers of the nativs pass us on hors back maney meet us and Continued with us to the Lodges. we purchased 3 dogs which were pore, but the fattest we Could precure, and Cooked them with Straw and dry willow. we Sold our Canoes for a fiew Strands of beeds. the nativs had tantelized us with an exchange of horses for our Canoes in the first instance, but when they found that we had made our arrangements to travel by land they would give us nothing for them. we Sent Drewyer to Cut them up, he Struck one and Split her they discovered that we were deturmined to destroy the Canoes and offered us Several Strans of beeds which were acceptd most of the party Complain of their feet and legs this evening being very Sore. it is no doubt Causd. by walking over the rough Stone and deep Sand after being accustomed to a Soft Soil. my legs and feet give me much pain. I bathed them in Cold water from which I experienced Considerable relief. we directed that the 3 horses purchased yesterday should be hobbled and confined to pickquets and that the others Should be Hobbled & Spancled, and Strictly attended to by the guard made 12 miles to day.-

[Lewis, April 25, 1806] Friday April 25th 1806. This morning we collected our horses and set out at 9 A.M. and proceeded on 11 ms. to the Village of the Pish-quit-pahs of 51 mat lodges where we arrived at 2 P.M. purchased five dogs and some wood from them and took dinner. this village contains about 7 hundred souls. most of those people were in the plains at a distance from the river as we passed down last fall, they had now therefore the gratification of beholding whitemen for the first time. while here they flocked arround us in great numbers tho treated us with much rispect. we gave two medals of the small size to their two principal Cheifs who were pointed out to us by our Chopunnish fellow traveller and were acknowledged by the nation. we exposed a few old clothes my dirk and Capt. C's swoard to barter for horses but were unsuccessfull these articles constitute at present our principal stock in trade. the Pish-quit-pahs insisted much on our remaining with them all night, but sudry reasons conspired to urge our noncomplyance with their wishes. we passed one house or reather lodge of the Metcowwees about a mile above our encampment of the _____th of October last the Pish-quit-pahs, may be considered hunters as well as fishermen as they spend the fall and winter months in that occupation. they are generally pleasently featured of good statue and well proportioned. both women and men ride extreemly well. their bridle is usually a hair rope tyed with both ends to the under jaw of the horse, and their saddle consists of a pad of dressed skin stuffed with goats hair with wooden stirups. almost all the horses which I have seen in possession of the Indians have soar backs. the Pishquitpah women for the most part dress with short shirts which reach to their knees long legings and mockersons, they also use large robes; some of them weare only the truss and robe they brade their hair as before discribed but the heads of neither male nor female of this tribe are so much flattened as the nations lower down on this river. at 4 P.M. we set out accompanyed by eighteen or twenty of their young men on horseback. we continued our rout about nine miles where finding as many willows as would answer our purposes for fuel we encamped for the evening. the country we passed through was much as that of yesterday. the river hills are about 250 feet high and generally abrupt and craggey in many places faced with a perpendicular and solid rock. this rock is black and hard. leve plains extend themselves from the tops of the river hills to a great distance on either side of the river. the soil is not as fertile as about the falls, tho it produces a low grass on which the horses feed very conveniently. it astonished me to seed the order of their horses at this season of the year when I knew that they had wintered on the dry grass of the plains and at the same time road with greater severity than is common among ourselves. I did not see a single horse which could be deemed poor and many of them were as fat as seals. their horses are generally good. this evining after we had encamped, we traded for two horses with nearly the same articles we had offered at the village; these nags Capt. C. and myself intend riding ourselves; haveing now a sufficiency to transport with ease all our baggage and the packs of the men.- we killed six ducks in the course of the day; one of them was of a speceis which I had never before seen I therefore had the most material parts of it reserved as a specimine, the leggs are yellow and feet webbed as those of the duckandmallard. saw many common lizzards, several rattlesnakes killed by the party, they are the same as those common to the U States. the horned Lizzard is also common.- had the fiddle played at the request of the natives and some of the men danced. we passed five lodges of the Walldh wolldhs at the distance of 4 miles above the Pishquitpahs.

[Clark, April 25, 1806] Friday 25th of April 1806 This morning we Collected our horses very conveniently and Set out at 9 A M and proceeded on to a village of Pish-quit-pahs of 52 mat Lodges 11 miles this village Contains about 700 Soles here we turned out our horses and bought 5 dogs & some wood and dined here we met with a Chief and gave him a Medal of the Small Size. we passed a house a little above the place we encamped on the 20th of Octr. 1805. we offered to purchase with what articles we had Such as old Clothes &c.

emence numbers of those Indians flocked about us and behaved with distant respect towards us. we attempted to purchase Some horses without Suckcess. at 4 P. M Set out. I was in the rear and had not proceeded verry far before one of the horses which we had hired of the Chopunnish, was taken from Hall who I had directed to ride. he had fallen behind out of my sight at the time. we proceeded on about 9 miles through a Country Similar to that of yesterday and encamped below the mouth of a Small Creek we passed at 4 miles a Village of 5 Mat Lodges of the War-war-wa Tribe. We made a Chief and gave a medal to a Chief of each of those two tribes. great numbers of the nativs accompanied us to our encampmt. The Curloos are abundant in those plains & are now laying their eggs. Saw the Kildee the brown Lizzard, and a moonax which the nativs had petted. the Winds which Set from mount hood or in a westwardly direction are much more cold than those from any other quarter. there are no dews in these plains, and from the appearance of the earth there appears to have been no rain for Several Weeks. The pish-quit pahs may be considered as hunters as well as fishermen as they Spend the fall & winter months in that occupation. they are generally pleasently featured of good Statue and well proportiond. both women and men ride extreamly well. their bridle is usially a hair rope tied with both ends to the under jaw of the horse, and their Saddles Consist of a pad of dressed Skin Stuffed with goats hair with wooden Sturreps. almost all the horses I have Seen in the poss ession of the Indians have Sore backs.

The pishquitpahs women for the most part dress with Short Shirts which reach to their knees long legins, and mockersons, they also use long robes; Some of them weare only the truss and robe, they brade their hair as before discribed but the heads of neither the male nor female of this tribe are So much flattend as the nativs lower down on this river. we were accompd. by 18 or 20 young men on horseback. we Continued our rout about 9 miles, where finding as maney Willows as would answer our purpose for fuel we encamped for the night. the Country we passed through was Sandy indifferent rocky and hills on the left. proceeded up on the North Side the river hills are about 250 feet high & generally abrupt and Craggey in maney places faced with a pirpendicular and Solid rock. this rock is black and hard. leavel plains extend themselves from the top of the river hills to a great distance on either Side of the river. the Soil is not as fertile as about the falls tho it produces low grass on which the horses feed very Conveniently. it astonished me to See the order of their horses at this Season of the year when I know they had wintered on dry grass of the plains and at the Same time rode with greater Severity than is Common among ourselves. I did not See a Single horse which Could be deemed pore, and maney of them were verry fat. their horses are generally good. this evening after we had encamped we traded for two horses with nearly the Same articles we had offered at the Village. these Nags Capt. L-s and myself intend rideing ourselves; haveing now a Sufficency to transport with ease all our baggage and the packs of the men.- we killed 6 ducks in the course of the day; one of them were of a Species I had never before Seen. the legs yellow and feet wibbed as those of the duckinmallard. Saw great numbers of Common Lizzard. Several rattle Snakes, killed by the party, they are the Same as those Common to the U. States. the Horned Lizzard is also Common.- a Chief over took us. we had the fiddle played by the request of the nativs and Some of the men danced. I think those plains are much more Sandy than any which I have Seen and the road is a bed of loose Sand. made 20 miles.

[Lewis, April 26, 1806] Saturday April 26th 1806. This morning early we set forward and at the distance of three miles entered a low level plain country of great extent. here the river hills are low and receede a great distance from the river this low country commenced on the S. side of the river about 10 miles below our encampment of last evening. these plains are covered with a variety of herbatious plants, grass, and three speceis of shrubs specimens of which I have preserved. at the distance of twelve miles we halted near a few willows which afforded us a sufficient quantity of fuel to cook our dinner which consisted of the ballance of the dogs we had purchased yesterday evening and some jirked Elk. we were overtaken today by several families of the natives who were traveling up the river with a number of horses; they continued with us much to our annoyance as the day was worm the roads dusty and we could not prevent their horses from crouding in and breaking our order of mach without using some acts of severity which we did not wish to commit. after dinner we continued our march through the level plain near the river 16 Ms. and encamped about a mile below three lodges of the Wollah wollah nation, and about 7 Ms. above our encampment of the 19 of October last. after we encamped a little Indian boy caught several chubbs with a bone in this form which he substituted for a hook. these fish were of about 9 inches long small head large abdomen, small where the tail joined the body, the tail wide long in proportion and forked. the back and ventral fins were equadistant from the head and had each 10 bony rays, the fns next the gills nine each and that near the tail 12. the upper exceeded the under jaw, the latter is truncate at the extremity and the tonge and pallet are smooth. the colour is white on the sides and belley and a blewish brown on the back. the iris of the eye is of a silvery colour and puple black.- we covered ourselves partially this evening from the rain by means of an old tent.

[Clark, April 26, 1806] Saturday April 26th 1806 This morning early we proceeded on and at the distance of three miles entered a low leavel plain Country of great extent. here the river hills are low and receed a great distance from the river this low Country Comenced on the South Side about 10 miles below our Encampment of the last night, those plains are Covered with a variety of herbatious plants, Grass and 3 Species of Shrubs. at the distance of 12 miles halted near Some willows which afforded us a Suffcent quantity of fuel to cook our dinner which Consisted of the ballance of the dogs we had purchased yesterday evening and Some jerked Elk. we were over taken to day by Several families of the nativs who were traveling up the river with a Numr. of horses; they Continued with us much to our ennoyance as the day was worm the roads dusty and we Could not prevent their horses Crouding in and breaking our order of March without useing Some acts of Severty which we did not wish to Commit. after dinner we Continued our march through a leavel plain near the river 16 miles and encamped about a mile below 3 Lodges of the fritened band of the Wallah wallah nation, and about 7 miles above our encampment of the 19th of Octr. last. after we encamped a little Indian boy Cought Several Chubbs with a bone in this form which he Substituted for a hook. those fish were of about 9 inches long. we Covered our Selves perfectly this evening from the rain by means of an old tent. Saw a Goat and a Small wolf at a distance to day. made 28 miles

[Lewis, April 27, 1806] Sunday April 27th 1806. This morning we were detained untill 9 A.M. in consequence of the absence of one of Charbono's horses. the horse at length being recovered we set out and at the distance of fifteen miles passed through a country similar to that of yesterday; the hills at the extremity of this distance again approach the river and are rocky abrupt and 300 feet high. we ascended the hill and marched through a high plain for 9 miles when we again returned to the river, I now thought it best to halt as the horses and men were much fatiegued altho had not reached the Wallah wollah village as we had been led to beleive by our guide who informed us that the village was at the place we should next return to the river, and the consideration of our having but little provision had been our inducement to make the march we had made this morning. we collected some of the dry stalks of weeds and the stems of a shrub which resembles the southern wood; made a small fire and boiled a small quantity of our jerked meat on which we dined; while here the principal Cheif of the Wallahwallahs joined us with six men of his nation. this Cheif by name Yel-lept had visited us on the morning of the 19 of October at our encampment a little below this place; we gave him at that time a small medal, and promised him a larger one on our return. he appeared much gratified at seeng us return, invited us to remain at his village three or four days and assured us that we should be furnished with a plenty of such food as they had themselves; and some horses to assist us on our journey. after our scanty repast we continued our march accompanyed by Yellept and his party to the village which we found at the distance of six miles situated on the N. side of the river at the lower side of the low country about 12 ms. below the entrance of Lewis's river. This Cheif is a man of much influence not only in his own nation but also among the neighbouring tribes and nations.- This Village consists of 15 large mat lodges. at present they seem to subsist principally on a speceis of mullet which weigh from one to three lbs. and roots of various discriptions which these plains furnish them in great abundance. they also take a few salmon trout of the white kind.- Yellept haranged his village in our favour intreated them to furnish us with fuel and provision and set the example himself by bringing us an armfull of wood and a platter of 3 roasted mullets. the others soon followed his example with respect to fuel and we soon found ourselves in possession of an ample stock. they birn the stems of the shrubs in the plains there being no timber in their neighbourhood of any discription. we purchased four dogs of these people on which the party suped heartily having been on short allowance for near two days. the indians retired when we requested them this evening and behaved themselves in every rispect extreemly well. the indians informed us that there was a good road which passed from the columbia opposite to this village to the entrance of the Kooskooske on the S. side of Lewis's river; they also informed us, that there were a plenty of deer and Antelopes on the road, with good water and grass. we knew that a road in that direction if the country would permit would shorten our rout at least 80 miles. the indians also informed us that the country was level and the road good, under these circumstances we did not hesitate in pursuing the rout recommended by our guide whos information was corroberated by Yellept & others. we concluded to pass our horses over early in the morning.

[Clark, April 27, 1806] Sunday April 27th 1806. This morning we were detained untill 9 A M in consequence of the absence of one of Shabono's horses. the horse being at length recovered we Set out and to the distance of 15 miles passed through a Country Similar to that of yesterday. (passed Muscle Shell rapid) and at the experation of this distance again approached the river, and are rocky abrupt and 300 feet high. we assended the hill and marched through a high plain 10 miles where we again returned to the river. we halted altho we had not reached the Wal-lah-lal-lah village as we had been led to believe by our guide who informed us that the village was at the place we Should next return to the river, and the considiration of our haveing but little provisions had been our inducement to make the march we had made this morning. we collected Some of the dry stalks of weeds and the Stems of Shrubs or weeds which resemble the Southern wood; made a Small fire and boiled a Small quantity of our jurked meat on which we dined; while here we were met by the principal Chief of the Wal lah wal lah Nation and Several of his nation. this chief by name Yel lep-pet had visited us on the morning of the 19th of Octr. at our encampment imedeately opposit to us; we gave him at that time a Small Medal, and promised him a large one on our return. he appeared much gratified at Seeing us return. he envited us to remain at his village 3 or 4 days and assured us that we Should be furnished with a plenty of Such food as they had themselves, and Some horses to assist us on our journey. after our Scanty repast we Continued our March accompanied by Yelleppit and his party to the Village which we found at the distance of Six miles,

Situated on the North Side of the river. about 16 miles below the enterance of Lewis's river. This Chief is a man of much influence not only in his own nation but also among the neighbouring tribes and nations.- the village Consists of 15 large mat Lodges. at present they Seam to Subsist principally on a Species of Mullet which weighs from one to 3 pds. and roots of various discriptions which those plains furnish them in great abundance. They also take a fiew Salmon trout of the white kind. Yelleppet haranged his village in our favor intreated them to furnish us with fuel & provisions and Set the example himself by bringing us an armfull of wood, and a platter with 3 rosted mullets. the others Soon followed his example with respect to fuel and we Soon found ourselves in possession of an ample Stock, they burn the Stems of the Shrubs in the plains, there being no timber in this neighbourhood of any description. we purchased 4 dogs of those people on which the party Suped hartily haveing been on Short allowance for near 2 days. the Indians retired when we requested them this evening and behaved themselves in every respect very well. the Indians informed us that there was a good road Which passed from the Columbia opposit to this Village to the enterance of Kooskooske on the S. Side of Lewis's river, they also informed us, there were a plenty of Deer and Antilopes on the road with good water and grass. we knew that a road in that direction if the Country would permit it would Shorten the rout at least 80 miles. the Indians also inform us that the County was leavel and the road good, under those circumstances we did not hesitate in pursueing the rout recommended by our guide and Corroberated by Yetleppit and others. we Concluded to pass our horses over early in the morning.- made 31 miles to day

[Lewis, April 28, 1806] Monday April 28th 1806. This morning early Yellept brought a very eligant white horse to our camp and presented him to Capt. C. signifying his wish to get a kettle but on being informed that we had already disposed of every kettle we could possibly spear he said he was content with whatever he thought proper to give him. Capt. C. gave him his ssword a hundred balls and powder and some sail articles with which he appeared perfectly satisfied. it was necessary before we entered on our rout through the plains where we were to meet with no lodges or resident indians that we should lay in a stock of provision and not depend altogether on the gun. we directed Frazier to whom we have intrusted the duty of makeing those purchases to lay in as many fat dogs as he could procure; he soon obtained ten. being anxious to depart we requested the Cheif to furnish us with canoes to pass the river, but he insisted on our remaining with him this day at least, that he would be much pleased if we would conset to remain two or three, but he would not let us have canoes to leave him today. that he had sent for the Chym nap'-pos his neighbours to come down and join his people this evening and dance for us. we urged the necessity of our going on immediately in order that we might the sooner return to them with the articles which they wished but this had no effect, he said that the time he asked could not make any considerable difference. I at length urged that there was no wind blowing and that the river was consequently in good order to pass our horses and if he would furnish us with canoes for that purpose we would remain all night at our present encampment, to this proposition he assented and soon produced us a couple of canoes by means of which we passed our horses over the river safely and bubbled them as usual. we found a Shoshone woman, prisoner among these people by means of whome and Sahcahgarweah we found the means of conversing with the Wollahwollahs. we conversed with them for several hours and fully satisfyed all their enquiries with rispect to ourselves and the objects of our pursuit. they were much pleased. they brought several diseased persons to us for whom they requested some medical aid. one had his knee contracted by the rheumatism, another with a broken arm &c to all of which we administered much to the gratification of those poor wretches. we gave them some eye-water which I beleive will render them more essential service than any other article in the medical way which we had it in our power to bestoe on them. soar eyes seem to be a universal complaint amonge these people; I have no doubt but the fine sand of these plains and river contribute much to this disorder. ulsers and irruptions of the skin on various parts of the body are also common diseases among them. a little before sunset the Chymnahpos arrived; they were about 100 men and a few women; they joined the Wallahwollahs who were about the same number and formed a half circle arround our camp where they waited very patiently to see our party dance. the fiddle was played and the men amused themselves with dancing about an hour. we then requested the Indians to dance which they very cheerfully complyed with; they continued their dance untill 10 at night. the whole assemblage of indians about 550 men women and children sung and danced at the same time. most of them stood in the same place and merely jumped up to the time of their music. some of the men who were esteemed most brave entered the space arrond which the main body were formed in solid column, and danced in a circular manner sidewise. at 10 P.M. the dance concluded and the natives retired; they were much gratifyed with seeing some of our party join them in their dance.

[Clark, April 28, 1806] Monday April 28th 1806 This morning early the Great Chief Yel lip pet brought a very eligant white horse to our Camp and presented him to me Signifying his wish to get a kittle but being informed that we had already disposed of every kittle we could possibly Spare he Said he was Content with what ever I thought proper to give him. I gave him my Sword, 100 balls & powder and Some Small articles of which he appeared perfectly Satisfied. it was necessary before we entered on our rout through the plains where we were to meet with no lodges or resident Indians that we Should lay in a Stock of provisions and not depend altogether on the gun. we derected R. Frazer to whome we have intrusted the duty of makeing the purchases, to lay in as maney fat dogs as he could procure; he Soon obtained 10. being anxious to depart we requested the Chief to furnish us with Canoes to pass the river, but he insisted on our remaining with him this day at least, that he would be much pleased if we would consent to remain two or 3 days, but he would not let us have Canoes to leave him this day. that he had Sent for the Chim-na-pums his neighbours to come down and join his people this evening and dance for us. We urged the necessity of our proceeding on imediately in order that we might the Sooner return to them, with the articles which they wishd. brought to them but this had no effect, he Said that the time he asked Could not make any Considerable difference. I at length urged that there was no wind blowing and that the river was consequently in good order to pass our horses and if he would furnish us with Canoes for that purpose

we would remain all night at our present encampment, to this proposition he assented and Soon produced a Canoe. I Saw a man who had his knee Contracted who had previously applyed to me for Some Medisene, that if he would fournish another Canoe I would give him Some Medisene. he readily Consented and went himself with his Canoe by means of which we passed our horses over the river Safely and hobbled them as usial-. We found a Sho Sho ne woman, prisoner among those people by means of whome and Sah-cah gah-weah, Shabono's wife we found means of Converceing with the Wallahwallfirs. we Conversed with them for Several hours and fully Satisfy all their enquiries with respect to our Selves and the Object of our pursute. they were much pleased. they brought Several disordered persons to us for whome they requested Some Medical aid. one had his knee contracted by the Rhumitism (whome is just mentioned above) another with a broken arm &c. to all of whome we administered much to the gratification of those pore wretches, we gave them Some eye water which I believe will render them more esential Sirvece than any other article in the Medical way which we had it in our power to bestow on them Sore eyes Seam to be a universial Complaint among those people; I have no doubt but the fine Sands of those plains and the river Contribute much to the disorder. The man who had his arm broken had it loosely bound in a peice of leather without any thing to Surport it. I dressed the arm which was broken Short above the wrist & Supported it with broad Sticks to keep it in place, put in a Sling and furnished him with Some lint bandages &c. to Dress it in future. a little before Sun Set the Chim nah poms arrived; they were about 100 men and a fiew women; they joined the Wallah wallahs who were about 150 men and formed a half Circle arround our camp where they waited verry patiently to See our party dance. the fiddle was played and the men amused themselves with danceing about an hour. we then requested the Indians to dance which they very Chearfully Complyed with; they Continued their dance untill 10 at night. the whole assemblage of Indians about 350 men women and Children Sung and danced at the Same time. most of them danced in the Same place they Stood and mearly jumped up to the time of their musick. Some of the men who were esteemed most brave entered the Space around which the main body were formed in Solid Column and danced in a Circular manner Side wise. at 10 P M. the dance ended and the nativs retired; they were much gratified in Seeing Some of our Party join them in their dance. one of their party who made himself the most Conspicious Charecter in the dance and Songs, we were told was a Medesene man & Could foretell things. that he had told of our Comeing into their Country and was now about to Consult his God the moon if what we Said was the truth &c. &c.

[Lewis, April 29, 1806] Tuesday April 29th 1806. This morning Yellept furnished us with two canoes and we began to transport our baggage over the river; we also sent a party of the men over to collect the horses. we purchased some dogs and shappellell this morning. we had now a store of 12 dogs for our voyage through the plains. by 11 A.M. we had passed the river with our party and baggage but were detained several hours in consequence of not being able to collect our horses. our guide now informed us that it was too late in the evening to reach an eligible place to encamp; that we could not reach any water before night. we therefore thought it best to remain on the Wallahwollah river about a mile from the Columbia untill the morning, and accordingly encamped on that river near a fish wear. this wear consists of two curtains of small willow switches matted together with four lines of withs of the same materials extening quite across the river, parralel with eah other and about 6 feet assunder. those are supported by several parsels of poles placed in the manner before discribed of the fishing wears. these curtains of willow are either roled at one end for a few feet to permit the fish to pass or are let down at pleasure. they take their fish which at present are a mullet only of from one to five lbs., with small seines of 15 or 18 feet long drawn by two persons; these they drag down to the wear and raise the bottom of the seine against the willow curtain. they have also a small seine maniaged by one person it bags in the manner of the scooping net; the one side of the net is confined to a simicircular bow of half the size of a man's arm and about 5 feet long; the other side is confined to a strong string which being attatched to the extremities of the bow forms the cord line to the simicircle. The Wallahwollah river discharges itself into the Columbia on it's S. side 15 miles below the entrance of Lewis's river or the S. E. branch. a high range of hills pass the Columbia just below the entrance of this river. this is a handsome stream about 41/2 feet deep and 50 yds. wide; it's bed is composed of gravel principally with some sand and mud; the banks are abrupt but not high, tho it dose not appear to overflow; the water is clear. the indians inform us that it has it's surces in the range of mountains in view of us to the E and S. E. these mountains commence a little to the south of Mt. Hood and extending themselves in a N. Eastwardly direction terminate near a Southen branch of Lewis's river short of the Rocky mountains. The Towannahiooks river, river LaPage and the Wollah-wollah rivers all take their rise on the N side of these mountains; two principal branches of the first of these take their rise in Mountains Jefferson and hood. these mountains are covered with snow at present tho do not appear high; they seperate the waters of the Multnomah from those of the Columbia river. they appear to be about 65 or 70 miles distant from hence. The Snake indian prisoner informed us that at some distance in the large plains to the South of those mountains there was a large river runing to the N. W. which was as wide as the Columbia at this place which is nearly one mile. this account is no doubt some what exagerated but it serves to evince the certainty of the Multnomah being a very large river and that it's waters are seperated from the Columbia by those mountains and that with the aid of a southwardly branch of Lewis's river which passes arrond the eastern extremity of those mountains, it must water that vast tract of country extending from those mountains to the waters of the gulph of California. and no doubt it heads with the Yellowstone river and the del Nord. we gave small medals to two inferior cheifs of this nation and they each presented us a fine horse in return we gave them sundry articles and among others one of my case pistols and several hundred rounds of amunition. there are 12 other lodges of the Wollahwollah nation on this river a little distance below our camp. 12 these as well as those beyond the Columbia appear to depend on this fishing wear for their subsistence. these people as well as the Chymnahpos are very well dressed, much more so particularly their women than they were as we decended the river last fall most of them have long shirts and leggings, good robes and mockersons. their women wear the truss when they cannot procure the shirt, but very few are seen with the former at this moment. I presume the success of their winters hunt has produced this change in their attire. they all cut their hair in their forehead and most of the men wear the two cews over each sholder in front of the body; some have the addition of a few small plats formed of the earlocks and others tigh a small bundle of the docked foretop in front of the forehead. their ornaments are such as discribed of the nations below and are woarn in a similar manner. they insisted on our dancinq this evening but it rained a little the wind blew hard and the weather was cold, we therefore did not indulge them.

[Clark, April 29, 1806] Tuesday April 29th 1806 This Morning Yelleppit furnished us with 2 Canoes, and We began to transport our baggage over the river; we also Sent a party of the men over to collect our horses. we purchased Some deer and chappellell this morning. we had now a Store of 12 dogs for our voyage through the plains. by 11 A.M. we had passed the river with our party and baggage but were detained Several hours in consequence of not being able to Collect our horses. our guide now informed us that it was too late in the evening to reach an eligible place to encamp; that we Could not reach any water before night. we therefore thought it best to remain on the Wallah wallah river about a mile from the Columbia untill the morning, accordingly encampd on the river near a fish Wear. this weare Consists of two Curtains of Small willows wattled together with four lines of withes of the Same Materials extending quite across the river, parralal with each other and about 6 feet asunder. those are Supported by Several parrelals of poles placed in this manner those Curtains of willows is either roled at one end for a fiew feet to permit the fish to pass or are let down at pleasure. they take their fish which at present are a Mullet only of from one to 5 pounds Wt. with Small Seines of 15 or 18 feet long drawn by two persons; these they drag down to the Wear and rase the bottom of the seine against the willow Curtain. they have also a Small Seine managed by one person, it bags in the manner of the Scooping Nets; the one Side of the Net is Confined to a Simicircular bow of half the Size of a mans arm and about 5 feet long, the other Side is confined to a Strong String which being attatched to the extremities of the bow forms the Cord line to the Simicurcle. The Wallah wallah River discharges it's Self into the Columbia on it's South Side 15 miles below the enterance of Lewis's River, or the S. E. branch. a range of hills pass the Columbia just below the enterance of this river. this is a handsom Stream about 4 1/2 feet deep and 50 yards wide; it's bead is composed of gravel principally with Some Sand and Mud; the banks are abrupt but not high, tho it does not appear to overflow; the water is Clear. the Indians inform us that it has it's Source in the range of Mountains in view of us to the E. and S. E. these Mountains commence a little to the South of Mt. Hood and extend themselves in a S Eastwardly direction terminateing near the Southern banks of Lewis's river Short of the rockey Mountains. Ta wan nahiooks river, river Lapage and _____ River all take their rise on those Mountains. the two principal branches of the first of those take their rise in the Mountain's, Jefferson and Hood. those Mountains are Covered at present with Snow. those S W. Mountains are Covered with Snow at present tho do not appear high. they Seperate the Waters of the Multnomah from those of the Columbia river. they appear to be 65 or 70 miles distant from hence. The Snake indian prisoner informed us that at Some distance in the large plains to the South of those Mountains there was a large river running to the N. W. which was as wide as the Columbia at this place, which is nearly 1 mile. this account is no doubt Somewhat exagurated but it Serves to evince the Certainty of the Multnomah being a very large River and that it's waters are Seperated from the Columbia by those Mountains, and that with the aid of a Southwardly branch of Lewis's river which pass around the Eastern extremity of those mountains, it must water that vast tract of Country extending from those Mountains to the Waters of the Gulf of Callifornia. and no doubt it heads with the Rochejhone and Del Nord.

We gave Small Medals to two inferior Chiefs of this nation, and they each furnished us with a fine horse, in return we gave them Sundery articles among which was one of Capt Lewis's Pistols & Several hundred rounds of

Amunition. there are 12 other Lodges of the Wallahwallah Nation on this river a Short distance below our Camp. those as well as those beyond the Columbia appear to depend on their fishing weres for their Subsistance. those people as well as the Chym na poms are very well disposed, much more So particular their women than they were when we decended the river last fall. Most of them have long Shirts and leggins, good robes and Mockersons. their women were the truss when they Cannot precure the Shirt, but very fiew are Seen with the former at the present. I presume the Suckcess of their Winters hunt has produced this change in their attere. they all Cut their hair in the fore head, and most of the men ware the two Cews over each Sholder in front of the body; Some have the addition of a fiew Small plats formed of the eare locks, and others tigh a Small bundle of the docked foretop in front of the fore head. their orniments are Such as discribed of the nativs below, and are worn in a Similar manner. they insisted on our danceing this evening but it rained a little the wind blew hard and the weather was Cold, we therefore did not indulge them.- Several applyed to me to day for medical aides, one a broken arm another inward fever and Several with pains across their loins, and Sore eyes. I administered as well as I could to all. in the evining a man brought his wife and a horse both up to me. the horse he gave me as a present. and his wife who was verry unwell the effects of violent Coalds was placed before me. I did not think her Case a bad one and gave Such medesine as would keep her body open and raped her in flannel. left Some Simple Medesene to be taken. we also gave Some Eye water 1 G. of Ela v V. & 2 grs. of Sacchm Stry. to an ounce of water and in that perpotion. Great No. of the nativs about us all night.

[Lewis, April 30, 1806] Wednesday April 30th 1806. This morning we had some difficulty in collecting our horses notwithstanding we had bubbled and picquited those we obtained of these people. we purchased two other horses this morning and several dogs. we exchanged one of our most indifferent horses for a very good one with the Chopunnish man who has his family with him. this man has a daughter new arrived at the age of puberty, who being in a certain situation is not permitted to associate with the family but sleeps at a distance from her father's camp and when traveling follows at some distance behind. in this state I am informed that the female is not permitted to eat, nor to touch any article of a culinary nature or manly occupation. at 10 A.M. we had collected all our horses except the white horse which Yellept had given Capt. C. the whole of the men soon after returned without being able to find this horse. I lent my horse to Yellept to surch Capt. C's about half an hour after he set out our Chopunnish man brought up Capt. C's horse we now determined to leave one man to bring on my horse when Yellept returned and to proceed on with the party accordingly we took leave of these friendly honest people the Wollahwollahs and departed at 11 A.M. accompanyed by our guide and the Chopunnish man and family. we continued our rout N. 30 E. 14 ms. through an open level sandy plain to a bold Creek 10 yds. wide. this stream is a branch of the Wallahwollah river into which it discharges itself about six miles above the junction of that river with the Columbia. it takes it's rise in the same range of mountains to the East of the sources of the main branch of the same. it appears to be navigable for canoes; it is deep and has a bold current. there are many large banks of pure sand which appear to have been drifted up by the wind to the hight of 15 or 20 feet, lying in many parts of the plain through which we passed today. this plain as usual is covered with arromatic shrubs hurbatious plants and a short grass. many of those plants produce those esculent roots which form a principal part of the subsistence of the natives. among others there is one which produces a root somewhat like the sweet pittaitoe.- we encamped at the place we intersepted the creek where we had the pleasure once more to find an abundance of good wood for the purpose of making ourselves comfortable fires, which has not been the case since we left rock fort camp. Drewyer killed a beaver and an otter; a pan of the former we reserved for ourselves and gave the indians the ballance. these people will not eat the dog but feast heartily on the otter which is vastly inferior in my estimation, they sometimes also eat their horses, this indeed is common to all the indians who possess this annimal in the plains of Columbia; but it is only done when necessity compells them.- the narrow bottom of this creek is very fertile, tho the plains are poor and sandy. the hills of the creek are generally abrupt and rocky. there is a good store of timber on this creek at least 20 fold more than on the Columbia river itself. it consists of Cottonwood, birch, the crimson haw, redwillow, sweetwillow, chokecherry yellow currants, goosberry, whiteberryed honeysuckle rose bushes, seven bark, and shoemate. I observed the corngrass and rushes in some parts of the bottom. Reubin Feilds overtook us with my horse. our stock of horses has now encresed to 23 and most of them excellent young horses, but much the greater portion of them have soar backs. these indians are cruell horse-masters; they ride hard, and their saddles are so illy constructed that they cannot avoid wounding the backs of their horses; but reguardless of this they ride them when the backs of those poor annimals are in a horrid condition.

[Clark, April 30, 1806] Wednesday April 30th 1806. This morning we had Some dificuelty in Collecting our horses notwithstanding we had hobbled & Picqueted those we obtained of those people. we purchased two other horses this morning and 4 dogs. we exchanged one of our most indeferent horses for a very good one with the Choponnish man who has his family with him. this man has a doughter now arived at the age of puberty who being in a certain Situation-is not permited to acoiate with the family but Sleeps at a distance from her father's Camp, and when traveling follows at Some distance be-hind. in this State I am informed that the female is not permited to eat, nor to touch any article of a culinary nature or manly occupation. at 10 A.M. we had Collected all our horses except the White horse which Yelleppit the Great Chief had given me. the whole of the men haveing returned without being able to find this hors. I informed the chief and he mounted Capt Lewis's horse and went in Serch of the horse himself. about half an hour after the Chopunnish man brought my horse. we deturmined to proceed on with the party leaving one man to bring up Capt L.-s horse when Yelleppit Should return. We took leave of those honest friendly people the Wallah wallahs and departed at 11 A.M. accompanied by our guide and the Chopunnish man and family. we Continued our rout N. 30° E. 14 ms. through an open leavel Sandy Plain to a bold Creek 10 yards wide. this stream is a branch of the Wallahwallah river, and takes it's rise in the same range of mountains to the East of the main branch. deep and has a bold Current. there are maney large banks of pure Sand which appear to have been drifted up by the wind to the hight of 20 or 30 feet, lying in maney parts of the plains through which we passed to day. This plain as usial is covered with arromatic Shrubs, hurbatious plants and tufts of Short grass. Maney of those plants produce those esculent roots which forms a principal part of the Subsistance of the Nativs. among others there is one which produce a root Somewhat like the Sweet potato. We encamped at the place we intersepted the Creek where we had the pleasure once more to find a Sufficency of wood for the purpose of makeing ourselves comfortable fires, which has not been the Case Since we left Rock fort Camp below the falls. Drewyer killed a beaver and an otter. the narrow bottoms of this Creek is fertile. tho the plains are pore & Sandy. the hills of the Creek are generaly abrupt and rocky. there is Some timber on this Creek. it consists of Cotton wood, birch, the Crimson haw, red willow, Sweet willow, Choke Cherry, yellow Current, goose berry, white berried honey suckle, rose bushes, Seven bark, Shoemate &c. &c. rushes in Some parts of the bottoms.

R. Fields over took us with Capt Lewis's horse our Stock of horses have now increased to 23 and most of them excellent young horses, but much the greatest part of them have Sore backs. those Indians are cruel horse masters; they ride hard and their Saddles illey constructed. &c. &c.

[Lewis, May 1, 1806] Thursday May 1st 1806. We collected our horses tolerably early this morning took and set out a little after 7 A.M. we pursued the indian road which led us up the creek about nine miles, here the Chopunnish man wo was in front with me informed that an old unbeaten tract which he pointed out to the left was our nearest rout. we halted the party and directed them to unload and let their horses graize untill our guide came up who was at some distance behind. I wished to obtain good information of this newly recommended tract before I could consent to leave the present road which seemed to lead us in the proper direction was level and furnished with wood and water. when the guide arrived he seemed much displeased with the other, he assured us that the rout up the creek was the nearest, and much the best, that if we took the other we would be obliged to remain here untill tomorrow morning, and then travel a whole day before we could reach water, and that there was no wood; the other agreed that this was the case. we therefore did not hesitate to pursue the rout recommended by the guide. the creek, it's bottom lands, and the appearance of the plains were much as those of esterday only with this difference that the latter were not so sandy. we had sent out four hunters this morning two on foot and 2 on horseback they joined us while we halted here. Drewyer had killed a beaver. at 1 P.M. we resumed our march, leaving the Chopunnish man and his family; he had determined to remain at that place untill the next morning and then pursue the rout he had recommended to us. he requested a small quantity of powder and lead which we gave him. we traveled 17 miles this evening, making a total of 26 Ms. and encamped. the first 3 miles of our afternoons march was through a similar country with that of the forenoon; the creek bottoms then became higher and widened to the extent of from 2 to 3 Ms. the hills on the N. side were low but those on the opposite side retained their hight. we saw a number of deer of which Labuish killed one. the timber on the creek becomes more abundant and it's extensive bottoms affords a pleasent looking country. the guide informs us that we shall now find a plenty of wood water and game quite to the Kooskooske. we saw a great number of the Curloos, some Grains, ducks, prarie larks and several speceis of sparrows common to the praries. I see very little difference between the apparent face of the country here and that of the plains of the Missouri only that these are not enlivened by the vast herds of buffaloe Elk &c which ornament the other. the courses and distances of this day are N. 45 E. 9 M. and N. 75 E. 17 M. along the Northern side of this creek to our encampment. some time after we had encamped three young men arrived from the Wallahwollah village bringing with them a steel trap belonging to one of our party which had been neglegently left behind; this is an act of integrity rarely witnessed among indians. during our stay with them they several times found the knives of the men which had been carelessly lossed by them and returned them. I think we can justly affirm to the honor of these people that they are the most hospitable, honest, and sincere people that we have met with in our voyage.

[Clark, May 1, 1806] Thursday May 1st 1806. This morning we collected our horses and made an early Start, haveing preveously Sent a hed 4 hunters with derections to proceed up the Creek and kill every Species of game which they might meet with. the Small portion of rain which fell last night Caused the road to be much furmer and better than yesterday. the morning Cloudy and Cool. we proceeded up the Creek on the N. E. Side through a Countrey of less sand and Some rich bottoms on the Creek which is partially Supplyed with Small Cotton trees, willow, red willow, choke Cherry, white thorn, birch, elder, _____ rose & honey suckle. Great portion of these bottoms has been latterly burnt which has entirely distroyed the timbered growth. at the distance of nine miles we over took our hunters, they had killed one bever only at this place the road forked, one leaveing the Creek and the Corse of it is nearly North. the Chopunnish who had accompanied us with his family informed us that this was our best way. that it was a long distance without water. and advised us to Camp on the Creek at this place and in the morning to Set out early. This information perplexed us a little, in as much as the idea of going a days march without water thro an open Sandy plain and on a Course 50° out of our derection. we deturmined to unlode and wate for our Guide, or the Chopunnish man who had accompanied us from the long Narrows, who was in the rear with Drewyer our interpreter. on his arrival we enquired of him which was the best and most direct roade for us to take. he informed us that the road pointed out by his cumerade was through a open hilly and Sandy Countrey to the river Lewis's River, and was a long ways around, and that we Could not git to any water to day. the other roade up the creek was a more derect Course, plenty of water wood and only one hill in the whole distance and the road which he had always recomended to us. Some words took place between those two men the latter appeared in great pation Mounted his horse and Set out up the Creek. we Sent a man after him and brought him back informed him that we believed what he Said and Should imedeately after dinner proceed on the road up the Creek with him. we gave the former man Some powder and ball which had been promised him, and after an early dinner Set out up the Creek with our guide leaveing the Chopunnish man and his family encamped at the forks of the road where they intended to Stay untill the morning and proceed on the rout he had recommended to us. we traviled 17 miles this evening makeing a total of 26 mls. and encamped. the first 3 miles of our afternoons march was through a Simaler Country of that of the fore noon; the Creek bottoms then became higher and wider; to the extent of from 2 to 3 miles. we Saw Several Deer of which Labiech killed one. the timber on the Creek become more abundant and less burnt, and its extensive bottoms afford a pleasent looking Country. we Saw a Great number of Curloos, Some Crains, Ducks, prarie cocks, and Several Species of Sparrows common to the praries. I See Very little difference between the apparant face of the Country here and that of the plains of the Missouri. only that those are not enlivened by the vast herds of Buffalow, Elk &c. which animated those of the Missouri. The Courses & distances of this day are N. 45° E. 9 mls. & N. 75° E. 17 Miles along the North Side of this Creek to our encampment. Sometime after we had encamped three young men arrived from the Wallah wallah Village bringing with them a Steel trap belonging to one of our party which had been negligently left behind; this is an act of integrity rearly witnessed among Indians. dureing our Stay with them they Several times found the knives of the men which had been Carefully lossed by them and returned them. I think we can justly affirm to the honor of those people that they are the most hospitable, honist and Sencere people that we have met with on our Voyage.-

[Lewis, May 2, 1806] Friday May 2cd 1806. This morning we dispatched two hunters a head. we had much difficulty in collecting our horses. at 8 A.M. we obtained them all except the horse we obtained from the Chopunnish man whom we seperated from yesterday. we apprehended that this horse would make some attempts to rejoin the horses of this man and accordingly had him as we thought securely bubbled both before and at the side, but he broke the strings in the course of the night and absconded. we sent several men in different directions in surch of him. I engaged one of the young indians who overtook us last evening to return in surch of him. at half after 1 P.M. The indian and Joseph Feilds returned with the horse, they had found him on his way back about 17 Ms. I paid the indian the price stipulated for his services and we immediately loaded up and set forward. steered East 3 M. over a hilly road along the N. side of the Creek, wide bottom on S. side. a branch falls in on S. side which runs south towards the S. W. mountains which appear to be about 25 Ms. distant low yet covered with snow N. 75 E. 7 through an extensive level bottom. more timber than usual on the creek, some pine of the long leafed kind appears on the sides of the creek hills, also about 50 acres of well timbered pine land where we passed the creek at 4 m. on this course N. 45 E. 9 ms. repassed the creek at 4 M. and continued up a N. E. branch of the same which falls in about a mile below where we passed the main creek. the bottoms though which we passed were wide. the main creek boar to the S. and heads in the Mountains; it's bottoms are much narrower above where we passed it and the hills appear high. we passed the small creek at 83/4 from the commencement of this course and encamped on the N. side in a little bottom, having traveled 19 miles today. at this place the road leaves the creek and takes the open high plain. this creek is about 4 yds. wide and bears East as far as I could observe it. I observed considerable quantities of the qua-mash in the bottoms through which we passed this evening now in blume. there is much appearance of beaver and otter along these creeks. saw two deer at a distance; also observed many sandhill crains Curloos and other fowls common to the plains. the soil appears to improve as we advance on this road. our hunters killed a duck only. the three young men of the Wollahwollah nation continued with us. in the course of the day I observed them eat the inner part of the young and succulent stem of a large coarse plant with a ternate leaf, the leafets of which are three loabed and covered with a woolly puberscence. the flower and fructification resembles that of the parsnip this plant is very common in the rich lands on the Ohio and it's branches the Mississippi &c. I tasted of this plant found it agreeable and eat heartily of it without feeling any inconvenience.

[Clark, May 2, 1806] Friday May 2nd 1806 This morning we dispatched two hunters a head. we had much dificuelty in Collecting our horses. at 8 A.M. we obtained them all except the horse we obtained from the Chopunnish man whome we Seperated from yesterday. we apprehended that this horse would make Some attempts to rejoin the horses of this man and accordingly had him as we thought Scurely hobbled both before and at the Side, but he broke the Strings in the Course of the night and absconded. we Sent Several men in different directions in Serch of him. and hired one of the men who joined us last night to prosue him and over take us & at 4 after 1 P.M. the indian and Joseph Fields returned with the horse they had found him on his way back about 17 miles. I paid the Indian the price Stipulated for his Services and we imediately loaded up and Set forward. East 3 miles over a hilly road along the N. Side of the Creek. wide bottoms on the S. Side. a branch falls in on the S. side which runds from the S W. Mountains, which appear to be about 25 m. distant low yet Covered with Snow. N. 75° E. 7 m. through an extencive leavel bottom. more timber than usial on the Creek. Some pine of the long leaf kind appear on the Creek hills. also about 50 acres of well timbered pine land where we passed the Creek at 4 m. on the Course. N. 45° E. 9 m. passed the Creek at 4 M. and Continued up on the N. E. Side. the bottoms wide. the main creek bear to the S. and head in the Mountains. we passed a Small Creek at 83/4 m. from the Commencement of this Course and encamped on the N. Side in a little bottom. haveing traviled 19 miles to day. at this place the road leaves the Creek and passes through the open high plains. this creek is 5 yds wide and bears East towards the Mts. I observed a Considerable quantity of the qua mash in the bottoms through which we passed this evening now in blume. there is much appearance of beaver & otter along these creeks. Saw two deer at a distance, also Sand hill Cranes, Curloos and fowls common to the plains. the Soil appears to improve as we advance on this road. our hunters killed a deer only. The three young men of the Wallah wallah nation Continue with us in the Course of this day. I observed them cut the inner part of the young and succulent Stem of a large Corse plant with a ternate leaf, the leafets of which are three loabes and Covered with woolly pubersence. the flower and fructification resembles that of the parsnip. this plant is very common in the rich lands on the Ohio and its branches. I tasted of this plant found it agreeable and eate hartily of it without feeling any inconveniance.

[Lewis, May 3, 1806] Saturday May 3rd 1806. This morning we set out at 7 A.M. steered N. 25 E 12 ms. to Kimooenem Creek through a high level plain. this creek is about 12 yds. wide pebbly bottom low banks and discharges a considerable body of water it heads in the S. W. mountains and discharges itself into Lewis's river a few miles above the narrows. the bottoms of this creek are narrow with some timber principally Cottonwood and willow. the under brush such as mentioned on N. East Creek. the hills are high and abrupt. the land of the plains is much more fertile than below, less sand and covered with taller grass; very little of the aromatic shrubs appear in this part of the plain. we halted and dined at this creek; after which we again proceeded N. 45 E. 3 M. through the high plain to a small creek 5 yds. wide branch of the Kimooenem C. this stream falls into the creek some miles below. the hills of this creek like those of the Kimooenem are high it's bottoms narrow and possess but little timber, lands of a good quality, a dark rich loam. we continued our rout up this creek, on it's N. side. N. 75 E 7 Ms. the timber increases in quantity the hills continue high. East 4 Ms. up the creek. here we met with We-ark-koomt whom we have usually distinguished by the name of the bighorn Cheif from the circumstance of his always wearing a horn of that animal suspended by a cord to he left arm. he is the 1st Cheif of a large band of the Chopunnish nation. he had 10 of his young men with him. this man went down Lewis's river by land as we decended it by water last fall quite to the Columbia and I beleive was very instrumental in procuring us a hospitable and friendly reception among the natives. he had now come a considerable distance to meet us. after meeting this cheif we continued still up the creek bottoms N. 75. E. 2 m to the place at which the road leaves the creek and ascends the hills to the plain here we encamped in small grove of cottonwood tree which in some measure broke the violence of the wind. we came 28 ms. today. it rained hailed snowed and blowed with great violence the greater portion of the day. it was fortunate for us that this storm was from the S. W. and of course on our backs. the air was very cold. we divided the last of our dryed meat at dinner when it was consumed as well as the ballance of our dogs nearly we made but a scant supper and had not anything for tomorrow; however We-arkkoomt consoled us with the information that there was an indian lodge on the river at no great distance where we might supply ourselves with provision tomorrow. our guide and the three young Wallahwollahs left us this morning reather abruptly and we have seen nothing of them since. the S. W. mountains appear to become lower as they proceede to the N. E. this creek reaches the mountains. we are nearer to them than we were last evening

[Clark, May 3, 1806] Saturday 3rd May 1806 This morning we Set out at 7 A.M. Steared N. 25° E 12 m. to Kimoo e nimm Creek through a high leavel plain this Creek is 12 yds. wide pebbly bottom low banks and discharges a Considerable quanty of water it head in the S W. Mountains and discharges it Self into Lewis's river a fiew miles Above the narrows. the bottoms of this Creek is narrow with Some timber principally Cotton wood & Willow. the under brush Such as mentioned in the N. E. Creek. The hills are high and abrupt. the lands of the plains is much more furtile than below, less Sand and Covered with taller grass; very little of the aramatic Shrubs appear in this part of the plain. we halted and dined at this Creek. after which we again proceeded N. 45° E. 3 mes. through a high plain to a Small Creek 5 yds. wide, a branch of the Kimooenimm Creek. the hills of this Stream like those of the Ki moo enimm are high its bottoms narrow and possess but little timber. the land of a good quallity dark rich loam. we Continued our rout up this Creek on it's N. Side N. 75° E 7 mes. the timber increas in quantity the hills continue high. we met with the We arh koont whome we have usially distinguished by the name of the big horn Chief from the circumstance of his always wareing a horn of that animal Suspended by a Cord to his left arm. he is a 1st Chief of a large band of the Chopunnish Nation. he had ten of his young men with him. this man Went down Lewis's river by Land as we decended it by water last fall quite to the Columbia, and I believe was very instremental in precureing us a hospital and friendly reception among the nativs. he had now come a Considerable distance to meet us. after meeting this Cheif we Continued Still up the Creek bottoms N. 75° E. 2 m. to the place at which the roade leaves the Creek and assends the hill to the high plains: here we Encamped in a Small grove of Cotton trees which in some measure broke the violence of the wind. we Came 28 miles today. it rained, hailed, Snowed & blowed with Great Violence the greater portion of the day. it was fortunate for us that this Storm was from the S. W. and of Course on our backs. the air was very cold. we devided the last of our dried meat at dinner when it was Consumed as well as the ballance of our Dogs nearly we made but a Scant Supper, and had not any thing for tomorrow; however We-ark-koomt Consoled us with the information that there was an Indian Lodge on the river at no great distance where we might Supply our Selves with provisions tomorrow. our Guide and the three young Wallah wallah's left us this morning reather abruptly and we have Seen nothing of them Sence. the S W. Mountains appear to become lower as they receed to the N, E. This Creek reaches the mountains. we are much nearer to them than we were last evening. they are Covered with timber and at this time Snow.

[Lewis, May 4, 1806] Sunday May 4th 1806. Collected our horses and set out early; the morning was cold and disagreeable. we ascended the Lard. hills of the creek and steered N. 60° E. 4 miles through a high level plain to a ravine which forms the source of a small creek, thence down this creek N. 75° E. 8 ms. to it's entrance into Lewis's river 71/2 ms. below the entrance of the Kooskooske. on the river a little above this creek we arrived at a lodge of 6 families of which Weark-koomt had spoken. we halted here for breakfast and with much difficulty purchase 2 lean dogs. the inhabitants were miserably poor. we obtained a few large cakes of half cured bread made of a root which resembles the sweet potatoe, with these we made some scope and took breakfast. the lands through which we passed today are fertile consisting of a dark rich loam the hills of the river are high and approach it nearly on both sides. no timber in the plains. the S. W. Mountains which appear to be about 15 Ms. above us still continue to become lower they are covered with snow at present nearly to their bases. Lewis's river appeas to pass through these mots. near their N. Eastern extremity. these hills terminate in a high level plain between the Kooskooske and Lewis's river. these plains are in many places well covered with the Longleafed pine, with some Larch and balsom fir. the soil is extreemly fertile no dose it appear so thisty as that of the same apparent texture of the open plains. it produces great quantities of the quawmash a root of which the natives are extreemly fond. a great portion of the Chopunnish we are informed are now distributed in small vilages through this plain collecting the quawmash and cows; the salmon not yet having arrived to call them to the river. the hills of the creek which we decended this morning are high and in most parts rocky and abrupt. one of our pack horses sliped from one of those hights and fell into the creek with it's load consisting principally of ammunition but fortunately neith the horse nor load suffered any material injury. the amunition being secured in canesters the water did not effect it.- after dinner we continued our rout up the West side of the river 3 Ms. opposite to 2 lodges the one containing 3 and the other 2 families of the Chopunnish nation; here we met with Te-toh, ar sky, the youngest of the two cheifs who accompanied us last fall the great falls of the Columbia here we also met with our pilot who decended the river with us as far as the Columbia. these indians recommended our passing the river at this place and ascending the Kooskooske on the N. E. side. they said it was nearer and a better rout to the forkes of that river where the twisted hair resided in whose charge we had left our horses; thither they promised to conduct us. we determined to take the advice of the indians and immediately prepared to pass the river which with the assistance of three indian canoes we effected in the course of the evening, purchased a little wood and some bread of cows from the natives and encamped having traveled 15 Ms. only today. We-ark-koomt whose people resided on the West side of Lewis's river above left us when we determined to pass the river and went on to his lodg. the evening was cold and disagreeable, and the natives crouded about our fire in great numbers insomuch that we could scarcely cook of keep ourselves warm. at all these lodges of the Chopunnish I observe an appendage of a small lodg with one fire which seems to be the retreat of their women in a certain situation. the men are not permitted to approach this lodge within a certain distance and if they have any thing to convey to the occupants of this little hospital they stand at the distance of 50 or 60 paces and throw it towards them as far as they can and retire.

[Clark, May 4, 1806] Sunday May 4th 1806 Collected our horses and Set out early; the morning was Cold and disagreeable. we assended the Larboard Hill of the Creek and Steared N 60° E 4 M. through a high leavil plain to a revine which forms the Source of a small creek, thence down the Creek N 75° E. 8 Ms. to it's enterance into Lewis's river 71/2 ms. below the enterance of Koos koos ke. on the river a little above this Creek we arived at a lodge of 6 families of which We-ark'-koomt had Spoken. We halted here for brackfast and with much dificuelty purchased 2 lean dogs. the inhabitants were miserably pore. we obtained a fiew large cakes of half cured bread made of a root which resembles the Sweet potatoe, with these we made Some Soope and took brackfast. the lands through which we passed to day are fertile consisting of a dark rich loam. the hills of the river are high and abrupt approaching it nearly on both Sides. no timber in the plains. the S. W. Mountains which appear to be about 15 Miles from us Still Continue to become lower, they are Covered with Snow at present nearly to their bases. Lewis's river appear to pass through those Mountains near the N Eastern extremity. those hills termonate in a high leavil plain between the Kooskoske & Lewis's river. these plains are in maney places well covered with the long leafed pine and Some balsom fir. the Soil is extreamly fertile. no does it appear So thirsty as that of the Same apparrant texture of the open plains. it produces great quantities of the quawmash a root of which the nativs are extreemly fond. a Great portion of the Chopunnish we are informed are now distributed in Small villages through this plain Collecting the Cowse a white Meley root which is very fine in Soup after being dried and pounded; the Salmon not yet haveing arived to Call them to the river-. The hills of the Creek which we decended this morning are high and in most parts rocky and abrupt. one of our pack horses Sliped from one of those hights and fell into the Creek with it's load Consisting principally of amunition, but fortunately neither the horse nor load Suffered any Matereal injury. the ammunition being Secured in Canesters the water did not effect it.

after dinner we Continued our rout up the West Side of the river 3 ms. opposit 2 Lodges the one Containing 3 and the other 2 families of the Chopunnish Nation; here we met with Te-toh-ar-sky the oldest of the two Chiefs who accompanied us last fall to the Great falls of the Columbia. here we also met with our old pilot who decended the river with us as low as the Columbia these indians recommended our passing the river at this place and going up on the N E Side of the Kooskoske. they Sayed it was nearer and a better rout to the forks of that river where the twisted hair resided in whose charge we had left our horses; thither they promised to Conduct us. we determined to take the advise of the indians and imediately prepared to pass the river which with the assistance of three indian Canoes we effected in the Course of the evening, purchased a little Wood, Some Cows bread and encamped, haveing traveled 15 miles to day only. We ark koomt whose people reside on the West Side of Lewis's river above left us when we deturmined to pass the river. before he left us he expressed his concern that his people would be deprived of the pleasure of Seeing us at the forks at which place they had assimbled to Shew us Sivilities &c. I gave him a Small piece of tobacco and he went off Satisfied. the evening was Cold and disagreeable, and the nativs Crouded about our fire in great numbers in so much that we Could Scercely Cook or keep ourselves worm. at all those Lodges of the Chopunnish I observe an appendage of a Small lodge with one fire, which Seames to be the retreat of their women in a certain Situation. the men are not permited to approach this Lodge within a certain distance, and if they have any thing to Convey to the Occupents of this little hospital they Stand at the distance of 50 or 60 paces and throw it towards them as far as they Can and retire.

[Lewis, May 5, 1806] Monday May 5th 1806. Collected our horses and set out at 7 A.M. at 41/2 miles we arrived at the entrance of the Kooskooske, up the N. Eastern side of which we continued our march 12 ms. to a large lodge of 10 families having passed two other large mat lodges the one at 5 and the other at 8 Ms. from the mouth of the Kooskooske but not being able to obtain any provision at either of those lodges continued our march to the third where we arrived at 1 P.M. & with much difficulty obtained 2 dogs and a small quanty of root bread and dryed roots. at the second lodge we passed an indian man gave Capt. C. a very eligant grey mare for which he requested a phial of eye-water which was accordingly given him. while we were encamped last fall at the entrance of the Chopunnish river Capt. C. gave an indian man some volitile linniment to rub his kee and thye for a pain of which he complained, the fellow soon after recovered and has never ceased to extol the virtues of our medecines and the skill of my friend Capt C. as a phisician. this occurrence added to the benefit which many of them experienced from the eyewater we gave them about the same time has given them an exalted opinion of our medicine. my friend Capt. C. is their favorite phisician and has already received many applications. in our present situation I think it pardonable to continue this deseption for they will not give us any provision without compensation in merchandize and our stock is now reduced to a mere handfull. we take care to give them no article which can possibly oinjure them. we foud our Chopunnish guide at this lodge with his family. the indians brought us Capt. Clark's horse from the oposite side of the river and delivered him to us while here. this horse had by some accedent seperated from our other horses above and had agreeably to indian information been in this neighbourhood for some weeks. while at dinner an indian fellow verry impertinently threw a poor half starved puppy nearly into my plait by way of derision for our eating dogs and laughed very heartily at his own impertinence; I was so provoked at his insolence that I caught the puppy and thew it with great violence at him and struk him in the breast and face, siezed my tomahawk and shewed him by signs if he repeated his insolence I would tommahawk him, the fellow withdrew apparently much mortifyed and I continued my repast on dog without further molestation. after dinner we continued our rout 4 miles to the entrance of Colter's Creek about 1/2 a mile above the rapid where we sunk the 1st canoe as we decended the river last fall. we encamped on the lower side of this creek at a little distance from two lodges of the Chopunnish nation having traveled 201/2 ms. today. one of these lodges contained eight families, the other was much the largest we have yet seen. it is 156 feet long and about 15 wide built of mats and straw. in the form of the roof of a house having a number of small doors on each side, is closed at the ends and without divisions in the intermediate space this lodge contained at least 30 families. their fires are kindled in a row in the center of the house and about 10 feet assunder.

all the lodges of these people are formed in this manner. we arrived here extreemly hungry and much fatiegued, but no articles of merchandize in our possession would induce them to let us have any article of provision except a small quantity of bread of cows and some of those roots dryed. we had several applications to assist their sick which we refused unless they would let us have some dogs or horses to eat. a man whose wife had an absess formed on the small of her back promised a horse in the morning provided we would administer to her accordingly Capt. C. opened the absess introduced a tent and dressed it with basilicon; I prepared some dozes of the flour of sulpher and creem of tarter which were given with directions to be taken on each morning. a little girl and sundry other patients were offered for cure but we posponed our operations untill morning; they produced us several dogs but they were so poor that they were unfit for use. This is the residence of one of 4 principal Cheifs of the nation whom they call Neesh-ne,-park-ke-ook or the cut nose from the circumstance of his nose being cut by the snake indians with a launce in battle. to this man we gave a medal of the small size with the likeness of the President. he may be a great cheif but his countenance has but little inteligence and his influence among his people seems but inconsiderable. a number of indians beside the inhabitants of these lodges geathered about us this evening and encamped in the timbered bottom on the creek near us. we met with a snake indian man at this place through whome we spoke at some length to the natives this evening with rispect to the objects which had induced us to visit their country. this address was induced at this moment by the suggestions of an old man who observed to the natives that he thought we were bad men and had come most probably in order to kill them. this impression if really entertained I beleive we effaced; they appeared well satisfyed with what we said to them, and being hungry and tired we retired to rest at 11 oClock.- We-ark-koomt rejoined us this evening. this man has been of infinite service to us on several former occasions and through him we now offered our address to the natives.

[Clark, May 5, 1806] Monday May 5th 1806 Collected our horses and Set out at 7 A M. at 41/2 ms. we arived at the enterance of Kooskooske, up the N E. Side of which we continued our March 12 Miles to a large lodge of 10 families haveing passed two other large mat lodges the one at 5 and the other at 8 Miles from the Mouth of the Kooskooske, but not being able to obtain provisions at either of those Lodges continued our March to the 3rd where we arived at 1 P.M. and with much dificuelty obtained 2 dogs and a Small quantity of bread and dryed roots. at the Second Lodge of Eight families Capt L. & my self both entered Smoked with a man who appeared to be a principal man. as we were about to leave his lodge and proceed on our journey he brought foward a very eligant Gray mare and gave her to me, requesting Some eye water. I gave him a phial of Eye water a handkerchief and some Small articles of which he appeared much pleased-. While we were encamped last fall at the enterance of Chopunnish river, I gave an Indian man some volitile leniment to rub his knee and thye for a pain of which he Complained. the fellow Soon after recovered and have never Seased to extol the virtue of our medicines. near the enterance of the Kooskooske, as we decended last fall I met with a man, who Could not walk with a tumure on his thye. this had been very bad and recovering fast. I gave this man a jentle pirge cleaned & dressed his Sore and left him Some Casteel Soap to wash the Sore which Soon got well. this man also assigned the restoration of his leg to me. those two cures has raised my reputation and given those nativs an exolted oppinion of my Skill as a phician. I have already received maney applications. in our present Situation I think it pardonable to continue this deception for they will not give us any provisions without Compensation in merchendize, and our Stock is now reduced to a mear handfull. we take Care to give them no article which Can possibly injure them. and in maney Cases can administer & give Such Medicine & Sergical aid as will effectually restore in Simple Cases &c. We found our Chopunnish Guide with his family. the Indians brought my horse which was left at the place we made Canoes, from the opposit Side and delivered him to me while here. this horse had by Some accident Seperated from our other horses above, and agreeably to indian information had been in this neighbourhood Some weeks. while at dinner an indian fellow very impertinently threw a half Starved puppy nearly into the plate of Capt. Lewis by way of derision for our eating dogs and laughed very heartily at his own impertinence; Capt L.- was So provoked at the insolence that he cought the puppy and threw it with great violence at him and Struck him in the breast and face, Seazed his tomahawk, and Shewed him by Sign that if he repeeted his insolence that he would tomahawk him, the fellow withdrew apparently much mortified and we continued our Dinner without further Molestation. after dinner we continued our rout 4 miles to the enterance of Colter's Creek about 1/2 a mile above the rapid where we Sunk the 1st Canoe as we decended the river last fall. We encamped on the lower Side of this Creek a little distance from two Lodges of the Chopunnish nation haveing traviled 201/2 miles to day one of those Lodges Contained 8 families, the other was much the largest we have yet seen. it is 156 feet long and about 15 feet wide built of mats and Straw, in the form of the roof of a house haveing a number of Small dores on each Side, is closed at the ends and without divisions in the intermediate Space. this lodge at least 30 families. their fires are kindled in a row in the Center of the Lodge and about 10 feet assunder. all the Lodges of these people are formed in this manner. we arrived here extreemly hungary and much fatigued, but no articles of merchindize in our possession would induce them to let us have any article of Provisions except a Small quantity of bread of Cows and some of those roots dryed. We had Several applications to assist their Sick which we refused unless they would let us have Some dogs or horses to eat. a man whose wife had an absess formed on the Small of her back promised a horse in the morning provided we would administer to her, I examined the absess and found it was too far advanced to be cured. I told them her case was desperate. agreeably to thir request I opened the absess. I then introduced a tent and dressed it with bisilican; and prepared Some dozes of the flour of Sulpher and Creem of tarter which were given with directions to be taken on each morning. a little girl and Sundery other patients were brought to me for Cure but we posponed our opperations untill the morning; they produced us Several dogs but they were So pore that they were unfit to eat. This is the residence of one of four principal Cheafs of the nation whome they call Neesh-ne-park-ke-ook or the Cut nose from the circumstance of his nose being Cut by the Snake Indians with a launce in battle. to this man we gave a Medal of the Small Size with a likeness of the President. he may be a great Chief but his Countinance has but little inteligence and his influence among his people appears very inconsiderable. a number of Indians besides the inhabitents of these Lodges gathered about us this evening and encamped in the timbered bottom on the Creek near us. We met with a Snake indian man at this place through whome we Spoke at Some length to the nativs this evening with respect to the object which had enduced us to visit their Country. this address was induced at this moment by the Suggestions of an old man who observed to the nativs that he thought we were bad men and had Come most probably in order to kill them.- this impression if really entertained I believe we effected; they appeared well Satisfied with what we Said to them, and being hungary and tired we retired to rest at 11 oClock.- We-ark-koomt rejoined us this evening. this man has been of infinate Service to us on Several former occasions and through him we now offered our address to the nativs-.

[Lewis, May 6, 1806] Tuesday May 6th 1806. This morning the husband of the sick woman was as good as his word, he produced us a young horse in tolerable order which we immediately killed and butchered. the inhabitants seemed more accomodating this morning; they sold us some bread. we received a second horse for medecine and prescription for a little girl with the rheumatism. Capt. C. dressed the woman again this morning who declared that she had rested better last night than she had since she had been sick. sore eyes is an universal complaint with all the natives we have seen on the west side of the Rocky mountains. Capt. C. was busily engaged for several hours this morning in administering eye-water to a croud of applicants. we once more obtained a plentifull meal, much to the comfort of all the party. I exchanged horses with We-ark'-koomt and gave him a small flag with which he was much gratifyed. the sorrel I obtained is an eligant strong active well broke horse perfictly calculated for my purposes. at this place we met with three men of a nation called the Skeets-so-mish who reside at the falls of a large river disharging itself into the Columbia on it's East side to the North of the entrance of Clark's river. this river they informed us headed in a large lake in the mountains and that the falls below which they resided was at no great distance from the lake. these people are the same in their dress and appearance with the Chopunnish, tho their language is intirely different a circumstance which I did not learn untill we were about to set out and it was then too late to take a vocabulary. The river here called Clark's river is that which we have heretofore called the Flathead river, I have thus named it in honour of my worthy friend and fellow traveller Capt. Clark. for this stream we know no indian name and no whiteman but ourselves was ever on it's principal branches. the river which Fidler calls the great lake river may possibly be a branch of it but if so it is but a very inconsiderable branch and may as probably empty itself into the Skeetssomish as into that river. the stream which I have heretofore called Clark's river has it's three principal sources in mountains Hood, Jefferson & the Northern side of the S. W. Mountains and is of course a short river. this river I shall in future call the To-wannahiooks river it being the name by which it is called by the Eneshur nation. The Kooskooske river may be safely navigated at present all the rocks of the shoals and rapids are perfectly covered; the current is strong, the water clear and cold. this river is rising fast.The timber of this river which consists principally of the long leafed pine commences about 2 miles below our present camp on Colter's Creek. it was two oclock this evening before we could collect our horses. at 3 P.M. we set out accompanyed by the brother of the twisted hair and We arkkoomt. I directed the horse which we had obtained for the purpose of eating to be led as it was yet unbroke, in performing this duty a quarrel ensued between Drewyer and Colter. we continued our march this evening along the river 9 miles to a lodge of 6 families, built of sticks mats & dryed hay in the same form of those heretofore discribed. we passed a lodge of 3 families at 4 ms. on the road. no provision of any discription was to be obtained of these people. a little after dark our young horse broke the rope by which he was confined and made his escape much to the chagrine of all who recollected the keenness of their appetites last evening. the brother of the twisted hair and Wearkkoomt with 10 or 12 others encamped with us this evening.-

the natives have a considerable salmon fishery up Colter's Creek. this stream extends itself to the pirs of the rocky mountain and in much the greater part of it's course passes through a well timbered pine country it is 25 yds. wide and discharges a large body of water. the banks low and bed formed of pebbles.- had a small shower of rain this evening.

[Clark, May 6, 1806] Tuesday May 6th 1806 This morning the Susband of the Sick woman was as good as his word. he produced us a young horse in tolerable order which we imedeately had killed and butchered. the inhabitants Seemed more accommodating this morning. they Sold us Some bread. we received a Second horse for Medecine & procription to a little girl with the rhumitism whome I had bathed in worm water, and anointed her a little with balsom Capivia. I dressed the woman again this morning who declared that She had rested better last night than She had Since She had been sick. Sore Eyes is an universal Complaint among all the nations which we have Seen on the West Side of the rocky Mountains. I was busily imployed for several hours this morning in administering eye water to a Croud of applicants. we once more obtained a plentiful meal, much to the Comfort of all the party. Capt Lewis exchanged horses with We ark koomt and gave him a small flag with which he was much pleased and gratifyed. the Sorrel which Cap L. obtained is a Strong active well broke horse-. At this place we met with three men of a nation Called the Skeetsso-mish who reside at the falls of a Small river dischargeing itself into the Columbia on its East Side to the South of the enterance of Clarks river. this river they informed us headed in a large lake in the mountains and that the falls below which they reside was at no great distance from the lake. these people are the Same in their dress and appearance with the Chopunnish, tho their language is entirely different. one of them gave me his whip which was a twisted Stick 18 Ins. in length at one end a pice of raw hide Split So as to form two Strings about 20 inches in length as a lash, to the other end a String passed through a hole and fastened at each end for a loope to Slip over the wrist. I gave in return for this whip a fathom of narrow binding. The River here Calld. Clarks river is that which we have heretofore Called Flathead river. Capt. Lewis has thought proper to Call this after myself for this Stream we know no Indhan name and no white man but our Selves was ever on this river. The river which Fiddler call's the great Lake river may possibly be a branch of it, but if So it is but a very inconsiderable branch, and may as probably empty itself into the Columbia above as into Clarks river. the Stream which the party has heretofore Called Clarks river imedeately above the great falls, has it's three principal branches in Mountains Jefferson, Hood and the Northern Side of the S. W. Mountains and is of course a Short river. this river is Called by the Skillutes & Eneshure Nations Towannahhiooks which is also the name they Call those bands of Snake indians who Come on this river every Spring to Catch the Salmon-. The Kooskooske river may be Safely navigated at present all the rocks of the Sholes and rapids are perfectlly Covered; the Current is Strong, the water Clear and Cold. this river is riseing fast-. The timber of this river which consists principally of the long leafed pine which commences about 2 miles below our present encampment on Colters Creek. it was 2 P.M. this evening before we could collect our horses. at 3 P.M. we Set out accompanied by the brother of the twisted hair and We-ark-koomt. we derected the horse which I had obtained for the purpose of eateing to be led as it was unbroke, in performing this duty a quarrel ensued between Drewyer and Colter-. We Continued our march along the river on its North Side 9 miles to a lodge of 6 families built of Sticks mats and dryed Hay. of the Same form of those heretofore discribed. we passed a Lodge of 3 families at 4 ms. on the river, no provisions of any discription was to be obtained of these people. a little after dark our young horse broke the rope by which he was Confined and made his escape much to the chagrine of all who recollected the keenness of their appetites last evening. the brother of the twisted hair & wearkkoomt with 10 others encamped with us this evening

The nativs have a Considerable Salmon fishery up Colters Creek. this Stream extends itself to the Spurs of the Rocky Mountain and in much the greater part of its Course passes through a well timbered pine Country. it is 25 yds. wide and discharges a large body of water. the banks low and bead formed of pebbles-. had a Small Shower of rain this evening. The Chopunnish about the Mouth of the Kooskooske bury their dead on Stoney hill Sides generally, and as I was informed by an Indian who made Signs that they made a hole in the Grown by takeing away the Stones and earth where they wished to deposit the dead body after which they laid the body which was previously raped in a robe and Secured with Cords. over the body they placed Stones So as to form a Sort of arch on the top of which they put Stones and earth So as to Secure the body from the wolves and birds &c. they Sometimes inclose the grave with a kind of Sepulcher like the roof of a house formed of the canoes of the disceased. they also Sacrifice the favorite horses of the disceased. the bones of many of which we See on and about the graves.

[Lewis, May 7, 1806] Wednesday May 7th 1806. This morning we collected our horses and set out early accompanyed by the brother of the twisted hair as a guide; Wearkkoomt and his party left us. we proceeded up the river 4 miles to a lodge of 6 families just below the entrance of a small creek, here our guide recommended our passing the river. he informed us that the road was better on the South side and that game was more abundant also on that side near the entrance of the Chopunnish river. we determined to pursue the rout recommended by the guide and accordingly unloaded our horses and prepared to pass the river which we effected by means of one canoe in the course of 4 hours. a man of this lodge produced us two canisters of powder which he informed us he had found by means of his dog where they had been buried in a bottom near the river some miles above, they were the same which we had buryed as we decended the river last fall. as he had kept them safe and had honesty enough to return them to us we gave him a fire steel by way of compensation. during our detention at the river we took dinner, after which or at 3 P.M. we renewed our march along the river about 2 ms. over a difficult stony road, when we left the river and asscended the hills to the wright which are here mountains high. the face of the country when you have once ascended the river hills is perfectly level and partially covered with the longleafed pine. the soil is a dark rich loam thickly covered with grass and herbatious plants which afford a delightfull pasture for horses. in short it is a beautifull fertile and picteresque country. Neeshneparkeeook overtook us and after riding with us a few miles turned off to the wright to visit some lodges of his people who he informed me were geathering roots in the plain at a little distance from the road. our guide conducted us through the plain and down a steep and lengthey hill to a creek which we called Musquetoe Creek in consequence of being infested with swarms of those insects on our arrival at it. this is but an inconsiderable stream about 6 yds. wide heads in the plains at a small distance and discharges itself into the Kooskooke 9 miles by water below the entrance of the Chopunnish river. we struck this creek at the distance of 5 ms. from the point at which we left the river our cours being a little to the S. of East. ascending the creek one mile on the S. E. side we arrived at an indian incampment of six lodges which appeared to have been recently evacuated. here we remained all night having traveled 12 miles only. the timbered country on this side of the river may be said to commence near this creek, and on the other side of the river at a little distance from it the timber reaches as low as Colter's Creek. the earth in many parts of these plains is thrown up in little mounds by some animal whose habits are similar to the Sallemander, like that animal it is also invisible; notwithstanding I have observed the work of this animal thoughout the whole course of my long tract from St. Louis to the Pacific ocean I have never obtained a view of this animal. the Shoshone man of whom I have before made mention evertook us this evening with Neeshneparkeeoook and remained with us this evening.- we suped this evening as we had dined on horse-beef. we saw several deer this evening and a great number of the tracks of these animals we determined to remain here untill noon tomorrow in order to obtain some venison and accordingly gave orders to the hunters to turn out early in the morning. -he Spurs of the rocky Mountains which were in view from the high plain today were perfectly covered with snow. the Indians inform us that the snow is yet so deep on the mountains that we shall not be able to pass them untill the next full moon or about the first of June; others set the time at still a more distant period. this unwelcom inteligence to men confined to a diet of horsebeef and roots, and who are as anxious as we are to return to the fat plains of the Missouri and thence to our native homes. The Chopunnish bury their dead in Sepulchres formed of boards like the roofs of houses. the corps is rolled in skins and laid on boards above the surface of the earth. they are laid in several teer one over another being seperated by a board only above and below from other corps. I did observe some instances where the body was laid in an indifferent woden box which was placed among other carcased rolled in skin in the order just mentioned. they sacrifice horses canoes and every other speceis of property to their ded. the bones of many horses are seen laying about those sepulchres. this evening was cold as usual.

[Clark, May 7, 1806] Wednesday May 7th 1806 This morning we collected our horses and Set out early accompanied by the brother of the twisted hair as a guide; Wearkkoomt and his party left us. we proceeded up the river 4 miles to a lodge of 6 families just below the enterance of a Small Creek, here our guide recommended our passing the river, he informed us that the road was better on the South Side, and that game was more abundant also on that Side near the enterance of Chopunnish river. we deturmined to pursue the rout recommended by the guide, and accordingly unloaded our horses and prepared to pass the river which we effected by means of one Canoe in the Course of 4 hours. a man of this lodge produced us two Canisters of Powder which he informed us he had found by means of his dog where they had been berried in the bottom near the river a fiew miles above. they were the Same which we had buried as we decended the river last fall. as he had kept them Safe and had honisty enough to return them to us, we gave him a fire Steel by way of Compensation. dureing our detention at the river we took dinner. after which we renewed our march along the S. E. Side of the river about 2 miles over a dificuelt Stoney road, when we left the river and assended the hills to the right which are here mountains high. the face of the Country when you have once assended the river hills, is perfectly level and partially Covered with the long leafed pine. the Soil is a dark rich loam, thickly Covered with grass and herbatious plants which afford a delightfull pasture for horses. in Short it is a butifull fertile picteresque Country. Neeshneparkeeook over took us and after rideing with us a fiew miles turned off to the right to visit some lodges of his people who he informed us were gathering roots in the plains at a little distance from the road. our guide Conducted us through the plain and down a Steep and lengthy hill to a Creek which we Call Musquetoe Creek in consequence of being infested with Sworms of those insects on our arival at it. this is but an inconsiderable Stream about 6 yards wide heads in the plains at a Short distance and discharges itself into the Kooskooke 9 ms. by water below the forks. we Struck this Creek at the distance of 5 miles from the point at which we left the river our course being a little to the S. of East. we proceeded up the Creek one Mile and on the S. E. Side we arived at an old Indian incampment of Six Lodges which appeared to have been recently evacuated. here we remained all night haveing traveled 12 ms. only. the timbered Country on this Side of the river may be Said to Commence a Short distance below this Creek, and on the other Side of the river at a little distance from it the timber reaches as low as Colter's Creek. the earth in maney parts of those plains is thown up in little mounds by Some animal whose habits are Similar to the Sallemander, like that animal it is also invisible; notwithstanding I have observed the work of this animal throughout the whole course of my trail from St. Louis to the Pacific Ocian, I have never obtained a View of this animal. The Shoshone man of whome I have before mentioned over took us this evening with Neesh neparkeeook or Cut nose and remained with us this evening. we Suped this evening as we had done on horse beef. we Saw Several deer this evening, and a great number of the tracks of these animals we deturmined to remain here untill noon tomorrow in order to obtain some venison, and accordingly gave orders to the hunters to turn out early in the morning. The Spurs of the rocky mountains which were in view from the high plain to day were perfectly Covered with Snow. The

Indians inform us that the Snow is yet So deep on the Mountains that we Shall not be able to pass them untill after the next full moon or about the first of June. others Set the time at a more distant period. this unwelcom intiligence to men confined to a diet of horsebeef and roots, and who are as anxious as we are to return to the fat plains of the Missouri, and thence to our native homes. The Chopunnish bury their dead in different ways as I have obseved, besides that already discribed they scaffold Some and deposit others in Sepulchers, those are rearly to be Seen in this upper part of the Columbian Waters. the one already discribed is the most Common. they all Sacrifice horses, Canoes and every Species of property to the dead. the bones of maney horses are Seen lyeing about those repositaries of the dead &c.-.

I observed in all the Lodges which we have passed Since we Crossed Lewis's river decoys, or Stocking heads as they are Sometimes called. these decoys are for the deer and is formed of the Skin of the head and upper portion of the neck of that animale extended in the nateral Shape by means of a fiew little Sticks placed within. the hunter when he Sees a deer conseals himself and with his hand givs to the decoy the action of a deer at feed, and this induces the deer within arrowshot; in this mode the Indians near the woody country hunt on foot in Such places where they cannot pursue the deer with horses which is their favourite method when the grounds will permit-.-. The orniments worn by the Chopunnish are, in their nose a Single Shell of wampom, the pirl & beeds are Suspended from the ears. beads are worn arround their wrists, neck and over their Sholders crosswise in the form of a double Sash-. the hair of the men is Cewed in two rolls which hang on each side in front of the body. Collars of bears Claws are also Common; but the article of dress on which they appear to bestow most pains and orniments is a kind of collar or brestplate; this is most Commonly a Strip of otter skins of about Six inches Wide taken out of the Center of the Skin it's whole length including the head. this is dressed with the hair on, this is tied around the neck & hangs in front of the body the tail frequently reaching below their knees; on this Skin in front is attatched pieces of pirl, beeds, wampom, pices of red Cloth and in Short whatever they conceive most valuable or ornamental-.-.

[Lewis, May 8, 1806] Thursday May 8th 1806. Most of the hunters turned out by light this morning a few others remained without our permission or knoledge untill late in the morning, we chid them severely for their indolence and inattention to the order of last evening. about 8 OCk. Sheilds returned with a small deer on which we breakfasted. by 11 A.M. all our hunters returned, Drewyer and Cruzatte brought each a deer, Collins wounded another which my dog caught at a little distance from the camp. our stock of provision now consisted of 4 deer and the remnant of the horse which we killed at Colter's Creek. Sheilds killed a duck of an uncommon kind. the head beak and wing of which I preserved. the beak is remarkably wide and obtusely pointed, on it's edges it is furnished with a sceries of teeth very long and fine not unlike the teeth of a comb. the belley is of a brick red, the lower part of the neck white, the upper part or but of the wing is a sky blue, underneath which a narrow stripe of white succeeds marking the wing transversly, the large feathers are of a dark colour. tail short and pointed and consists of 12 dark brown feathers. the back is black and sides white; legs yellow and feet formed like the Duckinmallard which it also resembles in size and form. the eye is moderately large, puple black and iris of an orrange colour. the colours and appearance of the female is precisely that of the duckinmallard only, reather smaller. we are informed that the natives in this quarter were much distressed for food in the course of the last winter; they were compelled to collect the moss which grows on the pine which they boiled and eat; near this camp I observed many pine trees which appear to have been cut down about that season which they inform us was done in order to collect the seed of the longleafed pine which in those moments of distress also furnishes an article of food; the seed of this speceis of pine is about the size and much the shape of the seed of the large sunflower; they are nutricious and not unpleasent when roasted or boiled, during this month the natives also peal this pine and eat the succulent or inner bark. in the creek near our encampment I observed a falling trap constructed on the same plan with those frequent seen in the atlantic states for catching the fish decending the stream Capt. C. took several small trout from this trap. Neesh-ne-park-kee-ook and several other indians joined us this morning. we gave this cheif and the indians with us some venison, horsebeef, the entrels of the four deer, and four fawns which were taken from two of the does that were killed, they eat none of their food raw, tho the entrals had but little preperation and the fawns were boiled and consumed hair hide and entrals. these people sometimes eat the flesh of the horse tho they will in most instances suffer extreem hunger before they will kill their horses for that purpose, this seems reather to proceede from an attachment to this animal, than a dislike to it's flesh for I observe many of them eat very heartily of the horsebeef which we give them. The Shoshone man was displeased because we did not give him as much venison as he could eat and in consequence refused to interpret, we took no further notice of him and in the course of a few hours he became very officious and seemed anxious to reinstate himself in our good opinons. the relation of the twisted hair and Neeshneparkkeook gave us a sketch of the principall watercourses West of the Rocky Mountains a copy of which I preserved; they make the main Southwardly branch of Lewis's river much more extensive than the other, and place many villages of the Shoshonees on it's western side. at half after 3 P.M. we departed; for the lodge of the Twisted hair accompanyed by the Cheif and sundry other indians. the relation of the twisted hair left us. the road led us up a steep and high hill to a high and level plain mostly untimbered, through which we passed parrallel with the river about 4 miles when we met the Twisted hair and a party of six men. to this Cheif we had confided the care of our horses and a part of our saddles when we decended the river last fall. the Twisted hair received us very coolly an occurrence as unexpected as it was unaccountable to us. he shortly began to speak with a loud voice and in a angry manner, when he had ceased to speak he was answered by the Cutnose Cheif or Neeshneparkkeook; we readily discovered that a violet quarrel had taken place between these Cheifs but at that instant knew not the cause; we afterwards learnt that it was on the subject of our horses. this controversy between the cheifs detained us about 20 minutes; in order to put an end to this dispute as well as to releive our horses from the embarasment of their loads, we informed the Cheifs that we should continue our march to the first water and encamp accordingly we moved on and the Indians all followed. about two miles on the road we arrived at a little branch which run to the wright. here we encamped for the evening having traveled 6 miles today. the two cheifs with their little bands formed seperate camps at a short distance from ours, they all appeared to be in an ill humour. we had been informed some days since that the natives had discovered the deposit of our saddles and taken them away and that our horses were much scattered. we were very anxious to learn the particulars or truth of these reports from the twisted hair, as it must in some measure govern us in the establishment of our perminent camp which in consequence of our detention by the snow of the mountains has become necessary. to obtain our horses and saddles as quickly as possible is our wish, and we are somewhat apprehensive that this difference which has taken place between these Chiefs may millitate against our operations in this rispect. we were therefore desireous to bring about a good understanding between them as soon as possible. The Shoshone boy refused to speak, he aledged it was a quarrel between two Cheifs and that he had no business with it; it was in vain that we urged that his interpreting what we said on this subject was not taking the responsibil ity of the inteference on himself, he remained obstenately silent. about an hour after we had encamped Drewyer returned from hunting we sent him to the Twisted hair to make some enquiries relative to our horses and saddles and to ask him to come and smoke with us. The Twisted hair accepted the invitation and came to our fire. The twisted hair informed us that accordingly to the promis he had made us when he seperated from us at the falls of the Columbia he collected our horses on his return and took charge of them, that about this time the Cutnose or Neeshneparkkeook and Tun-nach'-emoo-tools or the broken arm returned from a war excurtion against the Shoshonees on the South branch of Lewis's river which had caused their absence when we were in this neighbourhood. that these men became dissatisfyed with him in consequence of our having confided the horses to his care and that they were eternally quarreling with him insomuch that he thought it best as he was an old man to relinquish any further attention to the horses, that they had consequently become scattered; that most of the horses were near this place, a part were in the forks between the Chopunnish and Kooskooske rivers and three or four others were at the lodge of the broken Arm about half a days march higher up the river. he informed us with rispect to our saddles that on the rise of the water this spring the earth had fallen from the door of the cash and exposed the saddles, he being informed of their situation had taken them up and placed them in another cash where they were at this time; he said it was probable that a part of them had fallen into the water but of this he was not certain. The Twisted hair said if we would spend the day tomorrow at his lodge which was a few miles only from hence and on the road leading to the Broken arm's lodge, he would collect such of our horses as were near this place and our saddles, that he would also send some young men over the Kooskooske to collect those in the forks and bring them to the lodge of the broken Arm to met us. he advised us to go to the lodge of the broken Arm as he said he was a Cheif of great emenence among them, and promised to accompany us thither if we wished him. we told him that we should take his advice in every particular, that we had confided the horses to his care and expected that he would collect them and deliver them to us which when he performed we should pay him the two guns and amunition we had promised him for that service. he seemed much pleased and promised his utmost exertions. we sent Drewyer to the Cutnose who also came to our fire and smoked with ourselves and the Twisted hair we took occasion in the course of the evening to express our regret that there should be a misunderstanding between these Cheifs; the Cutnose told us in the presents of the Twisted hair that he the twisted hair was a bad old man that he woar two faces, that in stead of taking care of our horses as he had promised us that he had suffered his young men to ride them hunting and had injured them very much; that this was the cause why himself and the Broken arm had forbid his using them. the other made no reply. we informed the Cutnose of our intention of spending tomorrow at the Twisted hair's lodge in order to collect our horses and saddles and that we should proceede the next day to the Broken Arm's lodge, he appeared well satisfyed with this arrangement and said he would continue with us, and would give us any assistance in his power; he said he knew the broken arm expected us at his lodge and that he had two bad horses for us, metaphorically speaking a present of two good horses. he said the broken arm had learnt our want of provision and had sent four of his young men with a supply to meet us but that they had taken a different road and had missed us.- about 10 P.M. our guests left us and we layed down to rest.

[Clark, May 8, 1806] Thursday 8th of May 1806. This morning our hunters was out by the time it was light. about 8 oClock Shields brought in a Small deer, on which we brackfast by 11 A.M. all our hunters returned Drewyer & P. Crusat brought in a Deer each & Collins wounded one which our Dog Caught near our Camp. Total of our Stock of provisions 4 deer & Some horse flesh. on the Small Creek which passes our Camp, the nativs have laterly encamped and as we are informed have been much distressed for provisions, they have fallen a number of Small pine in the vicinity of this Encampment for the Seed which is in the bur of which they eate. we are informed that they were Compelled to Collect the moss off the pine boil & eate it in the latter part of the last Winter. on the Creek near our Camp I observed a kind of trap which was made with great panes to catch the Small fish which pass down with the Stream This was a dam formed of Stone So as to Collect the water in a narrow part not exceeding 3 feet wide from which place the water Shot with great force and Scattered through Some Small willows Closely connected and fastened with bark. this mat of willow Switches was about 4 feet wide and 6 long lying in a horozontal position, fastened at the extremety. the Small fish which fell on those willows was washed on the Willows where they untill taken off &c. I cought or took off those willows 9 Small trout from 3 to 7 Inches in length. Soon after I returned from the fishery an Indian came from a fishery of a Similar kind a little above with 12 Small fish which he offered me which I declined accepting as I found from his Signs that his house was a Short distance above, and that those fisheries afforded the principal part of the food for his Children. The Great Chief of the Bands below who has a cut nose joined us this morning. we gave the interals with 4 young fauns which was in two of the deer killed to day to the Indians also some of our deer & horse flesh. the Paunch of the deer they eate without any preperation further than washing them a little. the fauns they boiled and eate every part of them even the Skins with the hair. The Snake Indian was much displeased that he was not furnished with as much Deer as he could eate. he refused to Speake to the wife of Shabono, through whome we Could understand the nativs. we did not indulge him and in the after part of the day he Came too and Spoke verry well. one of the Indians drew me a Sketch of the river (See the latter part of this book) in this Sketch he makes the 1st large Southerly fork of Lewis's river much the longest and on which great numbers of the Snake Indians reside &c. at _____ P.M. we loaded up and Set on on the roade leading as we were informed to the lodge of the twisted hair, the Chief in whoes Care we had left our horses. we were accompanied by the Cut nose Chief our old Chief who had accompanied us down the river and Several men. we assended the hills which was Steep and emencely high to a leavel rich Country thinly timbered with pine. we had not proceeded more than 4 miles before we met the twisted hair and Several men meeting of us. we were verry coolly recved by the twisted hair. he Spoke aloud and was answered by the Cut Nose. we Could not learn what they Said. but plainly discovered that a missunderstanding had taken place between them. we made Signs to them that we Should proceed on to the next water and encamp. accordingly I set out and they all followed. we had not proceeded far before the road Crossed a Small handsom Stream on which we encamped. The parties of those two Chiefs took different positions at Some distance from each other and all appeared Sulkey. after we had formed our Camp we Sent Drewyer with a pipe to Smoke with the twisted hair and lern the Cause of the dispute between him and the Cut nose, and also to invite him to our fire to Smoke with us. The twisted hair came to our fire to Smoke we then Sent drewyer to the Cut Noses fire with the Same directions. he returned and informed us that the Cut nose Said he would join us in a fiew minits. it appears that the Cause of the quarrel between those two men is about our horses. and we cannot lern the particulars of this quarrel which probably originated through jelousy on the part of the Cut nose who blames the twisted hair for Suffer our horses to be rode, and want water dureing the Winter &c. twisted hair Says the horses were taken from him &c. The Cut nose joined us in a Short time We Smoked with all the party of both Chiefs, and told them that we were Sorry to find them at varience with each other the cut nose said that the twisted hair was a bad man and wore two fases, that he had not taken care of our horses as was expected. that himself an the broken arm had Caused our horses to be Watered in the winter and had them drove together, and that if we would proceed on to the village of the great Chief whome we had left a flag last fall the broken arm he would Send for our horses, that he had himself three of them. he also informed us that the great Chief hering of our distressed Situation had Sent his Son and 4 men to meet us and have us furnished on the way &c. that the young men had missed us and Could never over take us untill this time. that the great chief had 2 bad horses for us and expected us to go to his lodge which was near the river and about half a days march above &c. The twisted hair told us that he wished to Smoke with us at his lodge which was on the road leading to the Great Chiefs lodge, and but a fiew miles a head. if we would delay at his lodge tomorrow he would go after our Saddles and horses which was near the place we made our Canoes last fall. we deturmined to Set out early in the morning and proceed on to the lodge of the twisted hair and Send for our Saddles and powder which we had left burried mear the forks. and the day after tomorrow to proceed on to the lodge of the Grand Chief. accordingly we informed the Indians of our intentions. we all Smoked and conversed untill about 10 P M. the Indians retired and we lay down. Derected 5 hunters to turn out early in the morning to hunt and meet us at the twisted hair's lodge.

[Lewis, May 9, 1806] Friday May 9th 1806. We sent out several hunters early this morning with instructions to meet us at the lodge of the Twisted hair. Collecting our horses detained us untill 9 A.M. when we charged our packhorses and set out. our rout lay through a level rich country similar to that of yesterday; at the distance of 6 miles we arrived at the lodge of the twisted hair; this habitation was built in the usual form with sticks mats and dryed hay, and contained 2 firs and about 12 persons. even at this small habitation there was an appendage of the soletary lodge, the retreat of the tawny damsels when nature causes them to be driven into coventry; here we halted as had been previously concerted, and one man with 2 horses accompaed the twisted hair to the canoe camp, about 4 ms. in quest of the saddles. the Twisted hair sent two young men in surch of our horses agreeably to his promis. The country along the rocky mountains for several hundred miles in length and about 50 in width is level extreemly fertile and in many parts covered with a tall and open growth of the longleafed pine. near the watercouses the hills are steep and lofty tho are covered with a good soil not remarkably stony and possess more timber than the level country. the bottom lands on the watercourses are reather narrow and confined tho fertile & seldom inundated. this country would form an extensive settlement; the climate appears quite as mild as that of similar latitude on the Atlantic coast if not more so and it cannot be otherwise than healthy; it possesses a fine dry pure air. the grass and many plants are now upwards of knee high. I have no doubt but this tract of country if cultivated would produce in great abundance every article essentially necessary to the comfort and subsistence of civillized man. to it's present inhabitants nature seems to have dealt with a liberal hand, for she has distributed a great variety of esculent plants over the face of the country which furnish them a plentiful) store of provision; these are acquired with but little toil, and when prepared after the method of the natives afford not only a nutricious but an agreeable food. among other roots those called by them the Quawmash and Cows are esteemed the most agreeable and valuable as they are also the most abundant. the cows is a knobbed root of an irregularly rounded form not unlike the Gensang in form and consistence. this root they collect, rub of a thin black rhind which covers it and pounding it expose it in cakes to the sun. these cakes ate about an inch and 1/4 thick and 6 by 18 in width, when dryed they either eat this bread alone without any further preperation, or boil it and make a thick muselage; the latter is most common and much the most agreeable. the flavor of this root is not very unlike the gensang.- this root they collect as early as the snows disappear in the spring and continue to collect it until) the quawmash supplys it's place which happens about the latter end of June. the quawmash is also collected for a few weaks after it first makes it's appearance in the spring, but when the scape appears it is no longer fit for use untill the seed are ripe which happens about the time just mentioned, and then the cows declines. the latter is also frequently dryed in the sun and pounded afterwards and then used in making soope.- I observed a few trees of the larch and a few small bushes of the balsam fir near the lodge of the Twisted hair. at 2 P.M. our hunters joined us Drewyer killed a deer but lost it in the river. a few pheasants was the produce of the hunt. we procured a few roots of cows of which we made scope. late in the evening The Twisted hair and Willard returned; they brought about half of our saddles, and some powder and lead which had been buried at that place. my saddle was among the number of those which were lost. about the same time the young men arrived with 21 of our horses. the greater part of our horses were in fine order. five of them appeared to have been so much injured by the indians riding them last fall that they had not yet recovered and were in low order. three others had soar backs. we had these horses caught and hubbled. the situation of our camp was a disagreeable one in an open plain; the wind blew violently and was cold. at seven P.M. it began to rain and hail, at 9 it was succeeded by a heavy shower of snow which continued untill the next morning.- several indians joined us this evening from the village of the broken arm or Tunnachemootoolt and continued all night. The man who had imposed himself on us as a relation of the twisted hair rejoined us this evening we found him an impertinent proud supercilious fellow and of no kind of rispectability in the nation, we therefore did not indulge his advances towards a very intimate connection. The Cutnose lodged with the twisted hair I beleive they have become good friends again. several indians slept about us.

[Clark, May 9, 1806] Friday 9th May 1806 The hunters Set out very early agreeable to their derections. we were detained untill 9 A.M. for our horses which were much Scattered at which time we Collected our horses and Set out and proceeded on through a butifull open rich Country for 6 miles to the Camp of the twisted hair. this Campment is formed of two Lodges built in the usial form of mats and Straw. the largest and principal Lodge is Calculated for 2 fires only and Contains about _____ persons. the Second lodge is Small & appears to be intended for the Sick women who always retire to a Seperate lodge when they have the _____ this Custom is Common to all the nations on this river as well as among all other Indian nations with whom I am acquainted. at the distance of 2 miles we passd. a lodge of 2 fires on a fork of the road which leads to the right Situated on a Small branch which falls into Musquetor Creek. before 2 P M all our hunters joined us haveing killed only one deer which was lost in the river and a pheasent. Soon after we halted at the lodge of the twisted hair he Set out with two boys and Willard with a pack horse down to the river near the place we made the Canoes for our Saddles and a Cannister of powder and Some lead buried there, also a part of our horses which resorted near that place. late in the evening they returned with 21 of our horse and about half of our Saddles with the powder and ball. The greater part of the horses were in fine order, tho five of them had been rode & worsted in Such a manner last fall by the Inds. that they had not recovered and are in very low order, and 3 with Sore backs. we had all the recovered horses Cought & hobbled. we precured Some pounded roots of which a Supe was made thick on which we Suped. the wind blew hard from the S. W. accompanied with rain untill from 7 oClock untill 9 P.M. when it began to Snow and Continued all night. Several Indians Came from the village of the Chief with whome we had left a flag and Continued with us all night. they slept in the house of the twisted hair and two of them along Side of us.

[Lewis, May 10, 1806] Saturday May 10th 1806. This morning the snow continued falling 1/2 after 6 A.M. when it ceased, the air keen and cold, the snow 8 inches deep on the plain; we collected our horses and after taking a scant breakfast of roots we set out for the village of Tunnachemootoolt; our rout lay through an open plain course S. 35 E. and distance 16 ms. the road was slippery and the snow clogged to the horses feet, and caused them to trip frequently. the mud at the sources of the little ravines was deep black and well supplyed with quawmash. Drewyer turned off to the left of the road in order to hunt and did not join us this evening. at 4 in the afternoon we decended the hills to Commearp Creek and arrived at the Village of Tunnachemootoolt, the cheeif at whos lodge we had left a flag last fall. this flag was now displayed on a staff placed at no great distance from the lodge. underneath the flag the Cheif met my friend Capt. C. who was in front and conducted him about 80 yds. to a place on the bank of the creek where he requested we should encamp; I came up in a few minutes and we collected the Cheifs and men of consideration smoked with them and stated our situation with rispect to provision. the Cheif spoke to his people and they produced us about 2 bushels of the Quawmas roots dryed, four cakes of the bread of cows and a dryed salmon trout. We thanked them for this store of provision but informed them that our men not being accustomed to live on roots alone we feared it would make them sick, to obviate which we proposed exchangeing a good horse in reather low order for a young horse in tolerable order with a view to kill. the hospitality of the cheif revolted at the aydea of an exchange, he told us that his young men had a great abundance of young horses and if we wished to eat them we should by furnished with as many as we wanted. accordingly they soon produced us two fat young horses one of which we killed, the other we informed them we would pospone killing untill we had consumed the one already killed. This is a much greater act of hospitality than we have witnessed from any nation or tribe since we have passed the Rocky mountains. in short be it spoken to their immortal honor it is the only act which deserves the appellation of hospitallity which we have witnessed in this quarter. we informed these people that we were hungry and fatiegued at this moment, that when we had eaten and refreshed ourselves we would inform them who we were, from whence we had come and the objects of our resurches. a principal Cheif by name Ho-hast,- ill-pilp arrived with a party of fifty men mounted on eligant horses. he had come on a visit to us from his village which is situated about six miles distant near the river. we invited this man into our circle and smoked with him, his retinue continued on horseback at a little distance. after we had eaten a few roots we spoke to them as we had promised; and gave Tinnachemootoolt and Hohastillpilp each a medal; the former one of the small size with the likeness of Mr. Jefferson and the latter one of the sewing medals struck in the presidency of Washington, we explained to them the desighn and the importance of medals in the estimation of the whites as well as the red men who had been taught their value. The Cheif had a large conic lodge of leather erected for our reception and a parsel of wood collected and laid at the door after which he invited Capt. C. and myself to make that lodge our home while we remained with him. we had a fire lighted in this lodge and retired to it accompanyed by the Cheifs and as many of the considerate men as could croud in a circcle within it. here after we had taken a repast on some horsebeef we resumed our council with the indians which together with smoking the pipe occupyed the ballance of the evening. I was surprised to find on decending the hills of Commearp Cr. to find that there had been no snow in the bottoms of that stream. it seems that the snow melted in falling and decended here in rain while it snowed on the plains. the hills are about six hundred feet high about one fourth of which distance the snow had decended and still lay on the sides of the hills. as these people had been liberal with is with rispect to provision I directed the men not to croud their lodge surch of food in the manner hunger has compelled them to do at most lodges we have passed, and which the Twisted hair had informed me was disgreeable to the natives. but their previous want of hospitality had induced us to consult their enclinations but little and suffer our men to obtain provision from them on the best terms they could. The village of the broken arm as I have heretofore termed it consists of one house only which is 150 feet in length built in the usual form of sticks matts and dry grass. it contains twenty four fires and about double that number of families. from appearances I presume they could raise 100 fighting men. the noise of their women pounding roots reminds me of a nail factory. The indians seem well pleased, and I am confident that they are not more so than our men who have their somachs once more well filled with horsebeef and mush of the bread of cows.- the house of coventry is also seen here.-

[Clark, May 10, 1806] Saturday 10th of May 1806 This morning the Snow continued falling untill 1/2 past 6 A M when it Seased. the air keen and Cold the Snow 8 inches deep on the plain. we Collected our horses and after takeing a Scanty brackfast of roots, we Set out for the Village of the Chief with a flag, and proceeded on through an open plain. the road was Slipry and the Snow Cloged and caused the horses to trip very frequently. the mud at heads of the Streams which we passed was deep and well Supplied with the Car mash. Drewyer turned off the road to hunt near the river to our lef and did not join us to day. at 4 P M we arrived at the Village of Tin nach-e-moo-toolt the Chief whome We had left a flag. this flag was hoisted on a pole unde the flag the Chief met me and Conducted me to a Spot near a Small run about 80 paces from his Lodges where he requested me to halt which I did. Soon after Cap Lewis who was in the rear Came up and we Smoked with and told this Chief our Situation in respect to provisions. they brought foward about 2 bushels of quawmash 4 Cakes of bread made of roots and a dried fish. we informed the Chief that our Party was not accustomed to eate roots without flesh & proposed to exchange Some of our oald horses for young ones to eate. they Said that they would not exchange horses, but would furnish us with Such as we wished, and produced 2 one of which we killed and informd. them that we did not wish to kill the other at this time. we gave Medals to the broken arm or Tin-nach-e-moo tolt and Hoh-halt-ill-pitp two principal Chiefs of the Chopunnish Natn. and was informed that there was one other Great Chief (in all 4) who had but one eye. he would be here tomorrow. a large Lodge of Leather was pitched and Capt. Lewis and my Self was envited into it. we entered and the Chief and principal men came into the lodge and formed a Circle a parcel of wood was Collected and laid at the dore and a fire made in this Conic lodge before we entered it. the Chief requested that we might make the Lodge our homes while we remained with him. here after we had taken a repast on roots & horse beef we resumed our Council with the indians which together with Smokeing took up the ballance of the evening. I was Supprised to find decending the hill to Commearp Creek to find that there had been no snow in the bottoms of that Stream. it seams that the Snow melted in falling and decended here in rain while it snowed in the plain. the hills are about Eight hundred feet high about 1/4 of which distance the Snow had decended and Still lay on the Sides of the hill. as those people had been liberal I directed the men not to croud their Lodge in serch of food the manner hunger has Compelled them to do, at most lodges we have passed, and which the Twisted Hair had informed us was disagreeable to the nativs. but their previous want of hospitality had enduced us to consult their enclinations but little and Suffer our men to obtain provisions from them on the best terms they could.

The Village of the broken Arm consists of one house or Lodge only which is 150 feet in length built in the usial form of Sticks, Mats and dry grass. it contains 24 fires and about double that number of families. from appearance I prosume they could raise 100 fighting men. the noise of their women pounding the cows roots remind me of a nail factory. The Indians appear well pleased, and I am Confident that they are not more so than our men who have their Stomach once more well filled with horse beef and the bread of cows. Those people has Shewn much greater acts of hospitallity than we have witnessed from any nation or tribe Since we have passed the rocky Mountains. in Short be it Spoken to their immortal honor it is the only act which diserves the appelation of hospitallity which we have witnessed in this quarter.

[Lewis, May 11, 1806] Sunday May 11th 1806. The last evening we were much crouded with the indians in our lodge, the whole floor of which was covered with their sleeping carcases. we arrose early and took breakfast. at 8 A.M. a Cheif of great note among these people arrived from his village or lodge on the S. side of Lewis's River. this is a stout fellow of good countenance about 40 years of age and has lost the left eye. his name is Yoom-park'-kar-tim. to this man we gave a medal of the smal kind. those with the likeness of Mr. Jefferson have all been disposed of except one of the largest size which we reserve for some great Cheif on the Yellow rock river. we now pretty fully informed ourselves that Tunnachemootoolt, Neeshneparkkeeook, Yoomparkkartim and Hohastillpilp were the principal Cheif of the Chopunnish nation and ranked in the order here mentioned; as all those cheifs were present in our lodge we thought it a favourable time to repeat what had been said yesterday and to enter more minutely into the views of our government with rispect to the inhabitants of this western part of the continent, their intention of establishing trading houses for their releif, their wish to restore peace and harmony among the natives, the strength power and wealth of our nation &c. to this end we drew a map of the country with a coal on a mat in their way and by the assistance of the snake boy and our interpretters were enabled to make ourselves understood by them altho it had to pass through the French, Minnetare, Shoshone and Chopunnish languages. the interpretation being tedious it ocupyed nearly half the day before we had communicated to them what we wished. they appeared highly pleased. after this council was over we amused ourselves with shewing them the power of magnetism, the spye glass, compass, watch, air-gun and sundry other articles equally novel and incomprehensible to them. they informed us that after we had left the Minnetares last spring that three of their people had visited that nation and that they had informed them of us and had told them that we had such things in our possession but that they could not place confidence in the information untill they had now witnessed it themselves.- A young man, son of a conspicuous Cheif among these people who was killed not long since by the Minnetares of Fort de Prarie, brought and presented us a very fine mare and colt. he said he had opened his ears to our councils and would observe them strictly, and that our words had made his heart glad. he requested that we would accept this mear and colt which he gave in token of his determination to pursue our advise.- about 3 P.M. Drewyer arrived with 2 deer which he had killed. he informed us that the snow still continued to cover the plain. many of the natives apply to us for medical aid which we gave them cheerfully so far as our skill and store of medicine would enable us. schrofela, ulcers, rheumatism, soar eyes, and the loss of the uce of their limbs are the most common cases among them. the latter case is not very common but we have seen thee instances of it among the Chopunnish. it is a very extraordinary complaint. a Cheif of considerable note at this place has been afflicted with it for three years, he is incapable of moving a single limb but lies like a corps in whatever position he is placed, yet he eats heartily, digests his food perfectly, injoys his understanding, his pulse are good, and has retained his flesh almost perfectly, in short were it not that he appears a little pale from having lain so long in the shade he might well be taken for a man in good health. I suspect that their confinement to a diet of roots may give rise to all those disorders except the rheumatism & soar eyes, and to the latter of these, the state of debility incident to a vegetable diet may measureably contribute.- The Chopunnish notwithstanding they live in the crouded manner before mentioned are much more clenly in their persons and habitations than any nation we have seen since we left the Ottoes on the river Platte.- The Twisted hair brought us six of our horses.

[Clark, May 11, 1806] Sunday 11th May 1806 Some little rain last night. we were Crouded in the Lodge with Indians who continued all night and this morning Great numbers were around us. The One Eyed Chief Yoom-park-kar-tim arived and we gave him a medal of the Small Size and Spoke to the Indians through a Snake boy Shabono and his wife. we informed them who we were, where we Came from & our intentions towards them, which pleased them very much. a young man Son to the great Chief who was killed not long Sence by the Indians from the N. E. brought an elegant mare and Coalt and Gave us. and Said he had opend. his ears to what we had Said and his heart was glad and requested us to take this mare and Coalt as a token of his deturmination to pursue our Councels &c. The twisted hair brough Six of our horses all in fine order. Great numbers of Indians apply to us for medical aide which we gave them Cherfully So far as our Skill and Store of Medicine would enable us. Schrofla, ulsers, rhumitism, Sore eyes, and the loss of the use of their Limbs are the most common cases among them. the latter Case is not very common but We have Seen 3 instances of it among the Chopunnish. a very extroadinery complnt. about 3 P.M. Geo. drewyer arived with 2 deer which he had killed. he informed us that the Snow Still Continued to cover the plains. We are now pretty well informed that Tunnachemootoolt, Hohastillpilp, Neshneparkkeeook, and Yoomparkkartim were the principal Chiefs of the Chopunnish Nation and ranked in the order here mentioned; as all those chiefs were present in our lodge we thought it a favourable time to repeet what had been said and to enter more minutely into the views of our government with respect to the inhabitents of this Western part of the Continent, their intention of establishing tradeing houses for their relief, their wish to restore peace and harmony among the nativs, the Strength welth and powers of our Nation &c. to this end we drew a map of the Country with a coal on a mat in their way, and by the assistance of the Snake boy and our intrepeters were enabled to make ourselves under stood by them altho it had to pass through French, Minnetare, Shoshone and Chopunnish languages. the interpretation being tegious it occupied the greater part of the day, before we had communicated to them what we wished. they appeared highly pleased. after this Council was over we amused ourselves with Shewing them the power of Magnetism, the Spye glass, compass, watch, air gun and Sundery other articles equally novel and incomprehensible to them. they informed us that after we left the Menetares last Spring that 3 of their people had visited that nation, and that they had informed them of us, and had told them that we had Such things in our possession but that they Could not place Confidence in the information untill they had now witnessed it themselves

In the evening a man was brought in a robe by four Indians and laid down near me. they informed me that this man was a Chief of Considerable note who has been in the Situation I see him for 5 years. this man is incapable of moveing a single limb but lies like a corps in whatever position he is placed, yet he eats hartily, dejests his food perfectly, enjoys his under standing, his pulse are good, and has retained his flesh almost perfectly; in Short were it not that he appears a little pale from having been So long in the Shade, he might well be taken for a man in good health. I Suspect that their Confinement to a deet of roots may give rise to all the disordes of the Nativs of this quarter except the Rhumitism & Sore eyes, and to the latter of those, the State of debility incident to a vegitable diet may measureably contribute.-. The Chopunnish not withstanding they live in the Crouded manner before mentioned are much more clenly in their persons and habitations than any nation we have Seen Sence we left the Illinois. These nativs take their fish in the following manner to wit. a Stand Small Stage or warf consisting of Sticks and projecting about 10 feet into the river and about 3 feet above the water on the extremity of this the fisherman stands with his guilt or a Skooping Net which differ but little in their form those Commonly used in our Country it is formed thus with those nets they take the Suckers and also the Salmon trout and I am told the Salmon also.

[Lewis, May 12, 1806] Monday May 12th 1806. This morning a great number of indians collected about us as usual. we took an early breakfast and Capt. C. began to administer eyewater to a croud of at least 50 applicants. The Indians held a council among themselves this morning with rispect to the subjects on which we had spoken to them yesterday. the result as we learnt was favourable. they placed confidence in the information they had received and resolved to pusue our advise. after this council was over the principal Cheif or the broken Arm, took the flour of the roots of cows and thickened the scope in the kettles and baskets of all his people, this being ended he made a harangue the purport of which was making known the deliberations of their council and impressing the necessity of unanimity among them and a strict attention to the resolutions which had been agreed on in councill; he concluded by inviting all such men as had resolved to abide by the decrees of the council to come and eat and requested such as would not be so bound to shew themselves by not partaking of the feast. I was told by one of our men who was present, that there was not a dissenting voice on this great national question, but all swallowed their objections if any they had, very cheerfully with their mush. during the time of this loud and animated harangue of the Cheif the women cryed wrung their hands, toar their hair and appeared to be in the utmost distress. after this cerimony was over the Cheifs and considerate men came in a body to where we were seated at a little distance from our tent, and two young men at the instance of the nation, presented us each with a fine horse. we caused the cheifs to be seated and gave them each a flag a pound of powder and fifty balls. we also gave powder and ball to the two young men who had presented the horses. Neeshneeparkkeeook gave Drewyer a good horse. The band of Ten-nach-e-mootoolt have six guns which they acquired from the Minnetaries and appear anxious to obtain arms and amunition. after they had received those presents the Cheifs requested we would retire to the tent whither they accompanied us, they now informed us that they wished to give an answer to what we had said to them the preceeding day, but also informed us that there were many of their people waiting in great pain at that moment for the aid of our medecine. it was agreed between Capt. C. and myself that he should attend the sick as he was their favorite phisician while I would here and answer the Cheifs. The father of Hohastillpilp was the orrator on this occasion. he observed that they had listened with attention to our advise and that the whole nation were resolved to follow it, that they had only one heart and one tongue on this subject. he said they were fully sensible of the advantages of peace and that the ardent desire which they had to cultivate peace with their neighbours had induced his nation early last summer to send a pipe by 3 of their brave men to the Shoshonees on the S. side of Lewis's river in the Plains of Columbia, that these people had murdered these men, which had given rise to the war expedition against that nation last fall; that their warriors had fallen in with the shoshonees at that time and had killed 42 of them with the loss of 3 only on their part; that this had satisfyed the blood of their disceased friends and that they would never again make war against the Shoshonees, but were willing to receive them as friends. that they valued the lives of their young men too much to wish them to be engaged in war. That as we had not yet seen the black foot Indians and the Minnetares of Fort de Prarie they did not think it safe to venture over to the Plains of the Missouri, where they would fondly go provided those nations would not kill them. that when we had established our forts on the Missouri as we had promised, they would come over and trade for arms Amunition &c. and live about us. that it would give them much pleasure to be at peace with these nations altho they had shed much of their blood. he said that the whitemen might be assured of their warmest attattchment and that they would alwas give them every assistance in their power; that they were poor but their hearts were good. he said that some of their young men would go over with us to the Missouri and bring them the news as we wished, and that if we could make a peace between themselves and their enimies on the other side of the mountain their nation would go over to the Missouri in the latter end of the summer. on the subject of one of their cheifs accompanying us to the Land of the whitemen they could not yet determine, but that they would let us know before we left them. that the snow was yet so deep in the mountain if we attempted to pass we would certainly perish, and advised us to remain untill after the next full moon when the said the snow would disappear and we could find grass for our horses.- when the oald man had concluded I again spoke to them at some length with which they appeared highly gratifyed. after smoking the pipe which was about 2 P.M. they gave us another fat horse to kill which was thankfully received by the party. Capt C. now joined us having just made an end of his medical distrabution. we gave a phiol of eyewater to the Broken Arm, and requested that he would wash the eyes of such as might apply for that purpose, and that when it was exhausted we would replenish the phiol. he was much pleased with this present. we now gave the Twisted hair one gun and a hundred balls and 2 lbs. of powder in part for his attention to our horses and promised the other gun and a similar quantity of powder and lead when we received the ballance of our horses. this gun we had purchased of the indians below for 2 Elkskins. this evening three other of our original stock of horses were produced, they were in fine order as well as those received yesterday. we have now six horses out only, as our old guide Toby and his son each took a horse of ours when they returned last fall. these horses are said to be on the opposite side of the river at no great distance from this place. we gave the young men who had delivered us the two horses this morning some ribbon, blue wampum and vermillion, one of them gave me a hansome pare of legings and the Broken Arm gave Capt. C. his shirt, in return for which we gave him a linin shirt.- we informed the indians of our wish to pass the river and form a camp at some proper place to fish, hunt, and graize our horses untill the snows of the mountains would permit us to pass. they recommended a position a few miles distant from hence on the opposite side of the river, but informed us that there was no canoe at this place by means of which we could pass our baggage over the river, but promised to send a man early in the morning for one which they said would meet us at the river by noon the next day. The indians formed themselves this evening into two large parties and began to gamble for their beads and other ornaments. the game at which they played was that of hiding a stick in their hands which they frequently changed acompanying their operrations with a song. this game seems common to all the nations in this country, and dose not differ from that before discribed of the Shoshonees on the S. E. branch of Lewis's river. we are anxious to procure some guides to accompany us on the different routs we mean to take from Travellers rest; for this purpose we have turned our attention to the Twisted hair who has several sons grown who are well acquainted as well as himself with the various roads in those mountains. we invited the old fellow to remove his family and live near us while we remained; he appeared gratified with this expression of our confidence and promised to do so.- shot at a mark with the indians, struck the mark with 2 balls. distn. 220 yds.

[Clark, May 12, 1806] Monday 12th May 1806 a fine Morning great number of Indians flock about us as usial. after brackfast I began to administer eye water and in a fiew minits had near 40 applicants with Sore eyes, and maney others with other Complaints most Common Rhumatic disorders & weaknesses in the back and loins perticularly the womin. the Indians had a grand Council this morning after which we were presented each with a horse by two young men at the instance of the nation. we caused the chiefs to be Seated and gave then each a flag a pint of Powder and 50 balls to the two young men who had presented the horses we also gave powder and ball. The broken arm or Tun na the mootoolt pulled off his leather Shirt and gave me. I in return gave him a Shirt. we retired into the Lodge and the natives Spoke to the following purpote, i e they had listened to our advice and that the whole nation were deturmined to follow it, that they had only one heart and one tongue on this Subject. explained the Cause of the War with the Shoshones. they wished to be at peace with all nations & Some of their Men would accompany us to the Missouri &c. &c. as a great number of men women & Children were wateing and requesting medical assistance maney of them with the most Simple Complaints which Could be easily releived, independent of maney with disorders intirely out of the power of Medison all requesting Some thing, we agreed that I Should administer and Capt L- to here and answer the Indians. I was closely employed until 12 P.M. administering eye water to about 40 grown persons. Some Simple Cooling Medicenes to the disabled Chief, to Several women with rhumatic effections & a man who had a Swelled hip &c. &c-. in the evening three of our horses were brought all in fine order. we have now only Six remaining out. we gave to each a Chief a pint of Powder and 50 Balls a Small flag and to the two young men who delivered us the horses we gave also powder & Ball and Some blue wompom & ribin. all appeared much pleased-. Those people are much affraid of the black foot indians, and the Big bellies of Fort deprarie establishment. those indians kill great numbers of this nation whenever they pass over to hunt on the Missouri. one of our men bought a horse for a fiew Small articles of an Indian. The Indians brought up a fat horse and requested us to kill and eate it as they had nothing else to offer us to eate. The Cut nose made a present of a horse to Drewyer at the Same time the two horses were offered to Capt. Lewis & my self. The horses of those people are large well formed and active. Generally in fine order. Sore backs Caused by rideing them either with out Saddles, or with pads which does not prevent the wate of the rider pressing imedeately on the back bone, and weathers of the horse. the Indians formed two partis and plaied for their heeds. we gave the twisted hair a gun, powder & 100 ball in part for takeing care of our horses &c.

and wish him to Camp near us untill we Crossed the Mountains which he agreeed to do, and was much pleased we have now turned our attentions towards the twisted hair who has Several Sons grown who are well acquainted as well as himself with the various roads through the rocky Mountains and will answer very well as guides to us through those Mountains-In the Council to day the father of Hohastillpelp Said the Chopunnish were fully Convinced of the advantages of peace and ardently wished to cultivate peace with their neighbours. early last Summer 3 of their brave men were Sent with a pipe to the Shoshones on the S E. fork of Lewis's river in the Plains of Columbia, their pipe was disreguarded and their 3 men murdered, which had given rise to the War expedition against that nation last fall; that their warriers had fallen in with and killed 42 of the Shoshones with the loss of 3 men only on their part; that this had Satisfied the blood of the deceased friends and they would never again make war against the Shoshones, but were willing to receve them as friends-. That as we had not Seen the Indians towards Fort de prere they did not think it Safe to venture over to the Plains of the Missouri, where they would fondly go provided those nations would not kill them. I gave a vial of eye water to the Broken arm for to wash the eyes of all who applied to him and told him when it was out we would replenish it again

[Lewis, May 13, 1806] Tuesday May 13th 1806. This morning Capt. C. as usual was busily engaged with his patients untill eleven OCk. at 1 P.M. we collected our horses and set out for the river escorted by a number of the natives on horseback. we followed the creek downwards about two miles, passing a stout branch at 1 m. which flowed in on the wright. our course S. E. we now entered an extensive open bottom of the Kooskooske R. through which we passed nearly N. about 1 1/2 miles and halted on the bank of the river at the place appointed to meet the canoe. the man had set out early this morning for the purpose but had not yet arrived with the canoe we therefore unloaded our horses and turned them out to graize. as the canoe did not arrive untill after sunset we remained here all night; a number of the natives continued with us. in the evening we tryed the speed of several of our horses. these horses are active strong and well formed. these people have immence numbers of them 50, 60 or a hundred hed is not unusual for an individual to possess. The Chopunnish are in general stout well formed active men. they have high noses and many of them on the acqueline order with cheerfull and agreeable countenances; their complexions are not remarkable. in common with other savage nations of America they extract their beards but the men do not uniformly extract the hair below, this is more particularly confined to the females. I observed several men among them whom I am convinced if they had shaved their beards instead of extracting it would have been as well supplyed in this particular as any of my countrymen. they appear to be cheerfull but not gay; they are fond of gambling and of their amusements which consist principally in shooting their arrows at a bowling target made of willow bark, and in riding and exercising themselves on horseback, racing &c. they are expert marksmen and good riders. they do not appear to be so much devoted to baubles as most of the nations we have met with, but seem anxious always to obtain articles of utility, such as knives, axes, tommahawks, kettles blankets and mockerson alls. blue beads however may form an exception to this remark; this article among all the nations of this country may be justly compared to goald or silver among civilized nations. They are generally well cloathed in their stile. their dress consists of a long shirt which reaches to the middle of thye, long legings which reach as high as the waist, mockersons, and robes. these are formed of various skins and are in all rispects like those particularly discribed of the

Shoshones. their women also dress like the Shoshones. their ornaments consist of beads shells and peices of brass variously attatched to their dress, to their ears arrond their necks wrists arms &c. a bando of some kind usually surrounds the head, this is most frequently the skin of some fir animal as the fox otter &c. tho they have them also of dressed skin without the hair. the ornament of the nose is a single shell of the wampum. the pirl and beads are suspended from the ears. beads are woarn arround their wrists necks and over their sholders crosswise in the form of a double sash. the hair of the men is cewed in two rolls which hang on each side in front of the body as before discribed of other inhabitants of the Columbia. collars of bears claws are also common; but the article of dress on which they appear to bstow most pains and ornaments is a kind of collar or brestplate; this is most commonly a strip of otterskin of about six inches wide taken out of the center of the skin it's whole length including the head. this is dressed with the hair on; a hole is cut lengthwise through the skin near the head of the animal sufficiently large to admit the head of the person to pass. thus it is placed about the neck and hangs in front of the body the tail frequently reaching below their knees; on this skin in front is attatched peices of pirl, beads, wampum peices of red cloth and in short whatever they conceive most valuable or ornamental. I observed a tippet woarn by Hohastillpilp, which was formed of human scalps and ornamented with the thumbs and fingers of several men which he had slain in battle. their women brade their hair in two tresses which hang in the same position of those of the men. they also wear a cap or cup on the head formed of beargrass and cedar bark. the men also frequently attatch some small ornament to a small plat of hair on the center of the crown of their heads.

[Clark, May 13, 1806] Tuesday 13th May 1806. a fine morning I administered to the Sick and gave directions. we collected all our horses and Set out at 1 P.M. and proceeded down the Creek to the Flat head River a Short distance below the enterance of the Creek at the distance of 3 miles from the Village. at this place we expected to have met the Canoe which was promised to be furnished us, and for which an indian Set out very early this morning. we halted at the Flat Head River unloaded our horses and turnd. them out to feed. Several Indians accompanied us to the river and Continued untill evening. The man who Set out early this morning to the forks of this river for a Canoe and was to meet us at this place. as the Canoe did not arive untill after Sun set we remained all night; in the evening we tried the Speed of Several of our horses. these horses are strong active and well formed. Those people have emence numbers of them 50 or 60 or a Hundred head is not unusial for an individual to possess.

The Chopunnish are in general Stout well formd active men. they have high noses and maney of them on the acqueline order with chearfull and agreeable countinances; their complexions are not remarkable. in common with other Indian Nations of America they extract their beard, but the men do not uniformly extract the hair below, this is more particularly confined to the females. they appear to be cheerfull but not gay; they are fond of gambling and of their amusements which consists principally in shooting their arrows at a targit made of Willow bark, and in rideing and exersiseing themselves on horsback, raceing &c. they are expirt marks men & good riders. they do not appear to be So much devoted to baubles as most of the nations we have met with, but Seen anxious always to riceve articles of utility, Such as knives, axes, Kittles, blankets & Mockerson awls. blue beeds however may form an exception to this remark; This article among all the nations of this Country may be justly compared to gold and Silver among civilized nations. They are generally well clothed in their Stile. their dress Consists of a long shirt which reaches to the middle of leg, long legins which reach as high as the waist, mockersons & robe. those are formed of various skins and are in all respects like those of the Shoshone. Their orniments consists of beeds, Shells and peices of brass variously attached to their dress, to their ears arround theire necks wrists arms &c. a band of Some kind usially Serounds the head, this is most frequently the Skin of Some fer animal as the fox otter &c.; I observed a tippet worn by Hohastillpilp, which was formed of Humane Scalps and ornemented with the thumbs and fingers of Several men which he had Slain in battle. they also were a coller or breast plate of otter Skin orniminted with Shells beeds & quills. the women brade their hair in two tresses which hang in the same position of those of the men, which ar Cewed and hang over each sholder. &c

[Lewis, May 14, 1806] Wednesday May 14th 1806. The morning was fair, we arrose early and dispatched a few of our hunters to the opposite side of the river, and employed a part of the men in transporting our baggage to the opposite shore wile others were directed to collect the horses; at 10 A.M. we had taken our baggage over and collected our horses, we then took breakfast, after which we drove our horses into the river which they swam without accedent and all arrived safe on the opposite shore. the river is 150 yds. wide at this place and extreemly rapid. tho it may be safely navigated at this season, as the water covers all the rocks which lie in it's bed to a considerable debth. we followed our horses and again collected them, after which we removed our baggage to a position which we had previously selected for our permanent camp about half a mile below. this was a very eligible spot for defence it had been an ancient habitation of the indians; was sunk about 4 feet in the ground and raised arround it's outer edge about three 1/2 feet with a good wall of eath. the whole was a circle of about 30 feet in diameter. arround this we formed our tents of sticks and grass facing outwards and deposited our baggage within the sunken space under a shelter which we constructed for the purpose. our situation was within 40 paces of the river in an extentsive level bottom thinly timbered with the longleafed pine.

here we are in the vicinity of the best hunting grounds from indian information, are convenient to the salmon which we expect daily and have an excellent pasture for our horses. the hills to the E and North of us are high broken and but partially timbered; the soil is rich and affords fine grass. in short as we are compelled to reside a while in this neighbourhood I feel perfectly satisfyed with our position.immediately after we had passed the river Tunnachemootoolt and Hosastillpilp arrived on the south side with a party of a douzen of their young men; they began to sing in token of friendship as is their custom, and we sent the canoe over for them. they left their horses and came over accompanyed by several of their party among whom were the 2 young men who had presented us with two horses in behalf of the nation; one of these was the son of Tunnachemootoolt and the other the son of the Cheif who was killed by the Minnetares of Fort de Prarie last year and the same who had given us the mare and Colt. we received them at our camp and smoked with them; after some hours Hohastillpilp with much cerimony presented me with a very eligant grey gelding which he had brought for that purpose. I gave him in return a handkercheif 200 balls and 4 lbs. of powder. with which he appeared perfectly satisfyed. Collins killed two bear this morning and was sent with two others in quest of the meat; with which they returned in the evening; the mail bear was large and fat the female was of moderate size and reather meagre. we had the fat bear fleaced in order to reserve the oil for the mountains. both these bear were of the speceis common to the upper part of the missouri. they may be called white black grzly brown or red bear for they are found of all those colours. perhaps it would not be unappropriate to designate them the variagated bear. we gave the indians who were about 15 in number half the female bear, with the sholder head and neck of the other. this was a great treat to those poor wretches who scarcely taist meat once a month. they immediately prepared a brisk fire of dry wood on which they threw a parsel of smooth stones from the river, when the fire had birnt down and heated the stones they placed them level and laid on a parsel of pine boughs, on these they laid the flesh of the bear in flitches, placing boughs between each course of meat and then covering it thickly with pine boughs; after this they poared on a small quantity of water and covered the whoe over with earth to the debth of four inches. in this situation they suffered it to remain about 3 hours when they took it out. I taisted of this meat and found it much more tender than that which we had roasted or boiled, but the strong flavor of the pine distroyed it for my pallate. Labuish returned late in the evening and informed us that he had killed a female bear and two large cubbs, he brought with him several large dark brown pheasants which he had also killed. Shannon also returned with a few pheasants and two squirrells. we have found our stone horses so troublesome that we indeavoured to exchange them with the Chopunnish for mears or gelings but they will not exchange altho we offer 2 for one; we came to a resolution to castrate them and began the operation this evening one of the indians present offered his services on this occasion. he cut them without tying the string of the stone as is usual, and assures us that they will do much better in that way; he takes care to scrape the string very clean and to seperate it from all the adhereing veigns before he cuts it. we shall have an opportunity of judging whether this is a method preferable to that commonly practiced as Drewyer has gelded two in the usual way. The indians after their feast took a pipe or two with us and retired to rest much pleased with their repast. these bear are tremendious animals to them; they esteem the act of killing a bear equally great with that of an enimy in the field of action.- I gave the claws of those which Collins killed to Hohastillpilp.

[Clark, May 14, 1806] Wednesday 14th of May 1806 a fine day. we had all our horses Collected by 10 a.m. dureing the time we had all our baggage Crossed over the Flat head River which is rapid and about 150 yards wide. after the baggage was over to the North Side we Crossed our horss without much trouble and hobbled them in the bottom after which we moved a Short distance below to a convenient Situation and formed a Camp around a very convenian Spot for defence where the Indiands had formerly a house under ground and hollow circler Spot of about 30 feet diamieter 4 feet below the Serfce and a Bank of 2 feet above this Situation we Concluded would be Seffiently convenient to hunt the wood lands for bear & Deer and for the Salmon fish which we were told would be here in a fiew days and also a good Situation for our horses. the hills to the E. & N. of us are high broken & but partially timbered; the soil rich and affords fine grass. in Short as we are Compelled to reside a while in this neighbourhood I feel perfectly Satisfied with our position. imediately after we had Crossed the river the Chief Called the broken Arm or Tin nach-e-moo toll another principal Chief Hoh-host'-ill-pitp arived on the opposite Side and began to Sing. we Sent the Canoe over and those Chiefs, the Son of the broken arm and the Sone of a Great Chief who was killed last year by the Big bellies of Sas kas she win river. those two young men were the two whome gave Capt Lewis and my self each a horse with great serimony in behalf of the nation a fiew days ago, and the latter a most elligant mare & colt the morning after we arived at the Village. Hohast ill pilt with much Serimoney presented Capt. Lewis with an elegant Gray horse which he had brought for that purpose. Capt Lewis gave him in return a Handkerchief two hundred balls and four pouds of powder with which he appeared perfictly Satisfyed, and appeared much pleased.

Soon after I had Crossed the river and during the time Cap Lewis was on the opposit Side John Collins whome we had Sent out verry early this morning with Labiech and Shannon on the North Side of the river to hunt, Came in and informed me, that he had killed two Bear at about 5 miles distant on the up lands. one of which was in good order. I imediately depatched Jo. Fields & P. Wiser with him for the flesh. we made Several attempts to exchange our Stalions for Geldings or mars without success we even offered two for one. those horses are troublesom and Cut each other very much and as we Can't exchange them we think it best to Castrate them and began the opperation this evening one of the Indians present offered his Services on this occasion. he Cut them without tying the String of the Stone as is usial. he Craped it very Clean & Seperate it before he Cut it. about Meredian Shannon Came in with two Grows & 2 Squireles Common to this Country. his mockersons worn out obliged to come in early.

Collins returned in the evening with the two bears which he had killed in the morning one of them an old hee was in fine order, the other a female with Cubs was Meagure. we gave the Indians about us 15 in number two Sholders and a ham of the bear to eate which they cooked in the following manner. to wit on a brisk fire of dryed wood they threw a parcel of Small Stones from the river, when the fire had burnt down and heated the Stone, they placed them level and laid on a parsel of pine boughs, on those they laid the flesh of the bear in flitches, placeing boughs between each course of meat and then Covering it thickly with pine boughs; after this they poared on a Small quantity of water, and Covered the whole over with earth to the debth of 4 inches. in this Situation they Suffered it to remain about 3 hours when they took it out fit for use. at 6 oClock P M Labiech returned and informed us that he had killed a female Bear and two Cubs, at a long distance from Camp towards the mountains. he brought in two large dark brown pheasents which he had also killed Shannon also returned also with a few black Pheasents and two squirels which he had killed in the wood land towards Collins Creek. This nation esteem the Killing of one of those tremendeous animals (the Bear) equally great with that of an enemy in the field of action-. we gave the Claws of those bear which Collins had killed to Hohastillpelp.

[Lewis, May 15, 1806] Thursday May 15th 1806. This morning early Reubin Fields in surching for his horse saw a large bear at no great distance from camp; several men went in pursuit of the bear, they followed his trail a considerable distance but could not come up with him. Labuish and Shannon set out with a view to establish a hunting camp and continuing several days, two others accompanyed them in order to bring in the three bear which Labuish had killed. Drewyer and Cruzatte were sent up the river; Sheilds R. Feilds and Willard hunted in the hills near the camp they returned in the evening with a few pheasents only and reported that there was much late appearance of bear, but beleived that they had gone off to a greater distance. at 11 A.M. the men returned with the bear which Labuich had killed. These bear gave me a stronger evidence of the various coloured bear of this country being one speceis only, than any I have heretofore had. The female was black with a considerable proportion of white hairs intermixed and a white spot on the breast, one of the young bear was jut black and the other of a light redish brown or bey colour. the poil of these bear were infinitely longer finer and thicker than the black bear their tallons also longer and more blont as if woarn by diging roots. the white and redish brown or bey coloured bear I saw together on the Missouri; the bey and grizly have been seen and killed together here for these were the colours of those which Collins killed yesterday. in short it is not common to find two bear here of this speceis precisely of the same colour, and if we were to attempt to distinguish them by their collours and to denominate each colour a distinct speceis we should soon find at least twenty. some bear nearly white have also been seen by our hunters at this place. the most striking differences between this speceis of bear and the common black bear are that the former are larger, have longer tallons and tusks, prey more on other animals, do not lie so long nor so closely in winter quarters, and will not climb a tree tho eversoheardly pressed. the variagated bear I beleive to be the same here with those on the missouri but these are not as ferocious as those perhaps from the circumstance of their being compelled from the scarcity of game in this quarter to live more on roots and of course not so much in the habit of seizing and devouring living animals. the bear here are far from being as passive as the common black bear they have attacked and faught our hunters already but not so fiercely as those of the Missouri. there are also some of the common black bear in this neighbourhood. Frazier, J. Fields and Wiser complain of violent pains in their heads, and Howard and York are afflicted with the cholic. I attribute these complaints to their diet of roots which they have not been accustomed. Tunnachemootoolt and 12 of his young men left us this morning on their return to their village. Hohastillpilp and three old men remained untill 5 in the evening when they also departed. at 1 P.M. a party of 14 natives on horseback passed our camp on a hunting excurtion; they were armed with bows and arrows and had decoys for the deer these are the skins of the heads and upper portions of the necks of the deer extended in their natural shape by means of a fraim of little sticks placed within. the hunter when he sees a deer conceals himself and with his hand gives to the decoy the action of a deer at feed; and thus induces the deer within arrowshot; in this mode the indians hunt on foot in the woodlands where they cannot pursue the deer with horses which is their favorite method when the ground will permit.- we had all of our horses driven together today near our camp, which we have directed shall be done each day in order to familiarize them to each other. several of the horses which were gelded yesterday are much swolen particularly those cut by Drewyer, the others bled most but appear much better today than the others.

we had our baggage better secured under a good shelter formed of grass; we also strengthened our little fortification with pine poles and brush, and the party formed themselves very comfortable tents with willow poles and grass in the form of the orning of a waggon, these were made perfectly secure as well from the heat of the sun as from rain. we had a bower constructed for ourselves under which we set by day and sleep under the part of an old sail now our only tent as the leather lodge has become rotten and unfit for use. about noon the sun shines with intense heat in the bottoms of the river. the air on the tom of the river hills or high plain forms a distinct climate, the air is much colder, and vegitation is not as forward by at least 15 or perhaps 20 days. the rains which fall in the river bottoms are snows on the plain. at the distance of fifteen miles from the river and on the Eastern border of this plain the Rocky Mountains commence and present us with winter it it's utmost extreem. the snow is yet many feet deep even near the base of these mountains; here we have summer spring and winter within the short space of 15 or 20 miles.- Hohastillpilp and the three old men being unable to pass the river as the canoe had been taken away, returned to our camp late in the evening and remained with us all night.

[Clark, May 15, 1806] Thursday 15th of May 1806 This morning Reubin Fields went out to hunt his horse very early and Saw a large bear and no great distance from Camp. Several men went in pursute of the bear, and prosued his trail Some time without gitting Sight of this Monster. Shannon went out with Labeach to hunt and continue out 3 days, Gibson and Hall accompanied them for the meat Labeech killed yesterday which they brought in by 11 A.M. this Morning the female was black with white hares intermixed and a white Spot on the breast the Cubs were about the Size of a dog also pore. one of them very black and the other a light redish brown or bey colour. These bear give me a Stronger evidence of the various Coloured bear of this Country being one Specie only, than any I have heretofore had. Several other Colours have been seen. Drewyer and Peter Crusat went up the river. John Shields, R. Fields and Willard hunted in the hills near Camp and returned before 2 P.M without killing any thing except a fiew Grows. they saw but few deer. Some bear Sign. Frazur Jo. Fields and Peter Wizer Complain of a violent pain in their heads. Howard and York with violent Cholicks. the Cause of those disorders we are unable to account for. their diet and the Sudin Change of Climate must contribute. The Great Chief Tin nach-e-moo-tolt (or broken Arm) and 12 of the young men of his nation left us today about 11 oClock and Crossed the river to his Village Hoh-hast-ill-pilt and 3 old men Continued with us untill about 5 P.M when they left us and returnd. to their Village. a party of 14 Indians passed our Camp about 1 P.M. on their way to the leavel uplands to run and kill the deer with their horses and Bows and arrows. Some of them were also provided with deers heads Cased for the purpose of decoying the deer. those men continued withus but a fiew minits and proceeded on. Those people hunt most Commonly on horse back Seround the Deer or Goat which they find in the open plains & kill them with their arrows. tho they Sometimes hunt the deer on foot & decoy them. we had all of our horses drove together to day with a view to fermilurize them to each other. those that were Cut yesterday are Stiff and Several of them much Swelled. we had all our baggage Secured and Covered with a rouf of Straw. our little fortification also completely Secured with brush around which our Camp is formed. the Greater part of our Security from the rains &c. is the grass which is formed in a kind of ruff So as to turn the rain Completely and is much the best tents we have. as the days are worm &c. we have a bowry made to write under which we find not only comfortable but necessary, to keep off the intence heet of the Sun which has great effect in this low bottom. on the high plains off the river the Climate is entirely different cool. Some Snow on the north hill Sides near the top and vegetation near 3 weeks later than in the river bottoms. and the rocky Mountains imedeately in view covered Several say 4 & 5 feet deep with Snow. here I behold three different Climats within a fiew miles a little before dark Hoh-hast-ill-pilt and the 3 old men & one other returned to our Camp and informed us the Canoe was a great way off and they could not cross this evening.

[Lewis, May 16, 1806] Friday May 16th 1806. Drewyer's horse left his camp last night and was brought to us this morning by an indian who informed us he had found him a considerable distance towards the mountains. Hohastillpilp and all the natives left us about noon and informed us that they were going up the river some distance to a place at which they expected to fine a canoe, we gave them the head and neck of a bear, a part of which they eat and took the ballance with them. these people sometimes kill the variagated bear when they can get them in the open plain where they can pursue them on horseback and shoot them with their arrows. the black bear they more frequently kill as they are less ferocious. our sick men are much better today. Sahcargarmeah geathered a quantity of the roots of a speceis of fennel which we found very agreeable food, the flavor of this root is not unlike annis seed, and they dispell the wind which the roots called Cows and quawmash are apt to create particularly the latter. we also boil a small onion which we find in great abundance, with other roots and find them also an antidote to the effects of the others. the mush of roots we find adds much to the comfort of our diet.- we sent out several hunters this morning but they returned about 11 A.M. without success; they killed a few pheasants only. at 5 P.M. Drewyer and Cruzatte returned having killed one deer only. Drewyer had wounded three bear which he said were as white as sheep but had obtained neither of them. they informed us that the hunting was but bad in the quarter they had been, the Country was broken and thickly covered in most parts with underbrush. a little after dark Shannon and Labuish returned with one deer; they informed us that game was wild and scarce, that a large creek (Collins Creek) ran parallel with the river at the distance of about 5 or 6 miles which they found impracticable to pass with their horses in consequence of the debth and rapidity of it's current. beyond this creek the Indians inform us that there is great abundance of game. Sergt. Pryor and Collins who set out this morning on a hunting excurtion did not return this evening.- I killed a snake near our camp, it is 3 feet 11 Inches in length, is much the colour of the rattlesnake common to the middle atlantic states, it has no poisonous teeth. it has 218 scutae on the abdomen and fifty nine squamae or half formed scutae on the tail. the eye is of moderate size, the iris of a dark yellowish brown and puple black. there is nothing remarkable in the form of the head which is not so wide across the jaws as those of the poisonous class of snakes usually are.- I preserved the skin of this snake.

[Clark, May 16, 1806] Friday 16th May 1806 a cloudy morning with Some rain which continued untill Meridean at intervales, but very moderately. a man and boy Came to our Camp at 11 A. M with Drewyers Horse which he informed us he found at a long distance towards the Mtns. this horse must have Strayed from Drewyers Camp last night. Hohhastillpelt and all the nativs left us at merdn. and went up the river with a view to Cross at Some distance above where they expected to find a Canoe.

we gave those people a head and Neck of the largest bear a part of which they eate and the balance they Carefully took with them for their children. The Indians of this Country Seldom kill the bear they are very much afraid of them and the killing of a white or Grzley bear, is as great a feet as two of their enimy. the fiew of those Animals which they Chance to kill is found in the leavel open lands and pursued on horses & killed with their Arrows. they are fond of the flesh of this animal and eate emoderately of it when they have a Sufficiency to indulge themselves. The men who were complaining of the head ake and Cholicks yesterday and last night are much better to day. Shabonos Squar gatherd a quantity of fenel roots which we find very paleatiable and nurishing food. the Onion we also find in abundance and boil it with our meat. Shields rode out and hunted in the morning without Suckcess he returned at 11 A.M. having killed only a black wood pecker with a red breast as discribed hereafter. A snake which resembles the rattle Snake in colour and Spots on the Skin, longer and inosent. at 5 P M Drewyer and Crusat returned haveing killed only one Deer only. D. Shot 3 White bear but Could get neither of them. they inform us that the hunting in the derection they were is very bad. the country hilly & brushey. a little after dark Shannon & Labiech came in from the Chass. Shannon killed one deer which he brought in. this deer being the only animal they Could kill. they informed that a large Creek (Collens's Creek) run parrelal with the river at about 5 or 6 miles distant between which there was but little game, and the Creek being high rapid and the Smothe rocks in the bottom rendered it impossible for them to pass it on hors back. Sergt. Pryor and Collins who Set out early this morning hunting have not returned. we derected that the horses be drove up in future at 12 oClock on each day

[Lewis, May 17, 1806] Saturday May 17th 1806. It rained the greater part of the last night and this morning untill 8 OCk. the water passed through flimzy covering and wet our bed most perfectly in shot we lay in the water all the latter part of the night. unfortunately my chronometer which for greater security I have woarn in my fob for ten days past, got wet last night; it seemed a little extraordinary that every part of my breechies which were under my head, should have escaped the moisture except the fob where the time peice was. I opened it and founded it nearly filled with water which I carefully drained out exposed it to the air and wiped the works as well as I could with dry feathers after which I touched them with a little bears oil. several parts of the iron and steel works were rusted a little which I wiped with all the care in my power. I set her to going and from her apparent motion hope she has sustained no material injury.- at 9 A.M. Sergt. Pryor and Collins returned, Sergt. Pryor brought the Skin and flesh of a black bear which he had killed; Collins had also killed a very large variegated bear but his horse having absconded last evening was unable to bring it. they had secured this meat perfectly from the wolves or birds and as it was at a considerable distance we did not think proper to send for it today. neither of these bear were in good order. as the bear are reather ferocious and we are obliged to depend on them pincipally for our subsistence we thought it most advisable to direct at least two hunters to go together, and they accordingly peared themselves out for this purpose. we also apportioned the horses to the several hunters in order that they should be equally rode and thereby prevent any horse being materially injured by being too constantly hunted. we appointed the men not hunters to take charge of certain horses in the absence of the hunters and directed the hunters to set out in different directions early in the morning and not return untill they had killed some game. it rained moderately the greater part of the day and snowed as usual on the plain. Sergt. Pryor informed me that it was shoe deep this morning when he came down. it is somewhat astonishing that the grass and a variety of plants which are now from a foot to 18 inches high on these plains sustain no injury from the snow or frost; many of those plants are in blume and appear to be of a tender susceptable texture. we have been visited by no indians today, and occurrence which has not taken place before since we left the Narrows of the Columbia.- I am pleased at finding the river rise so rapidly, it now doubt is attributeable to the meting snows of the mountains; that icy barier which seperates me from my friends and Country, from all which makes life esteemable.- patience, patience

[Clark, May 17, 1806] Saturday 17th May 1806 rained moderately all the last night and this morning untill we are wet. The little river on which we are encamped rise Sepriseingly fast. at 9 A.M. Sergt. Pryor and Collins returned with the flesh and Skin of a Black bear on Sgt. Pryors horse. Collins's horse haveing run off from him yesterday. they informed us that they had each killed a Bear neither of which were fat. the one which they left in the woods was of the white Species and very large we did not think it necessary in the cours of this day to

Send for the flesh of the bear left in the woods. the rains of the last night unfortunately wet the Crenomuter in the fob of Capt. L. breaches. which has never before been wet Since we Set out on this expedition. her works were cautiously wiped and made dry by Capt. L. and I think She will recive no injury from this misfortune &c. we arranged the hunters and horses to each hunter and directed them to turn out in the morning early and continue out untill they Killed Something. others arranged so as to take care of the hunters horses in their absence. rained moderately all day. at the Same time Snowed on the mountains which is in to the S. E. of us. no Indians visit us to day which is a Singular circumstance as we have not been one day without Indians Since we left the long narrows of the Columbia. the fiew worm days which we have had has melted the Snows in the Mountains and the river has rose considerably. that icy barier which Seperates me from my friends and Country, from all which makes life estimable, is yet white with the Snow which is maney feet deep. I frequently Consult the nativs on the subject of passing this tremendious barier which now present themselves to our view for great extent, they all appear to agree as to the time those Mountains may be passed which is about the Middle of June.

Sergt. pryor informs me that the Snow on the high plains from the river was Shoe deep this morning when he Came down. it is somewhat estonishing that the grass and a variety of Plants Sustain no injurey from the Snow or frost; Maney of those plants are in blume and appear to be of tender susceptable texture. At the distance of 18 Miles from the river and on the Eastern border of the high Plain the Rocky Mountain Commences and presents us with Winter here we have Summer, Spring and Winter in the Short Space of twenty or thirty miles

[Lewis, May 18, 1806] Sunday May 18th 1806. Twelve hunters turned out this morning in different directions agreeably to the order of last evening. Potts and Whitehouse accompanied Collins to the bear he had killed on the 16th inst. with which they returned in the afternoon. the colours of this bear was a mixture of light redish brown white and dark brown in which the bey or redish brown predominated, the fur was bey as well as the lower pertion of the long hairs, the white next succeeded in the long hairs which at their extremites were dark brown, this uncommon mixture might be termed a bey grizzle.

our indian woman was busily engaged today in laying in a store of the fennel roots for the Rocky mountains. these are called by the Shoshones year-pah. at 2 P.M. 3 Indians who had been hunting towards the place at which we met with Chopunnish last fall, called by them the quawmash grounds, called at our camp; they informed us that they had been hunting several days and had killed nothing; we gave them a small peice of meat which they told us they would reserve for their small children who were very hungary; we smoked with them and they shortly after departed. early this morning the natives erected a lodge on the opposite side of the river near a fishing stand a little above us. no doubt to be in readiness for the salmon, the arrival of which they are so ardently wishing as well as ourselves. this stand is a small stage are warf constructed of sticks and projecting about 10 feet into the river and about 3 feet above the surface of the water on the extremity of this the fisherman stands with his scooping net, which differ but little in their form from those commonly used in our country it is formed thus. the fisherman exercised himself some hours today but I believe without success. at 3 P.M. J. Fields returned very unwell having killed nothing. shortly after an old man and woman arrived; the former had soar eyes and the latter complained of a lax and rheumatic effections. we gave the woman some creem of tartar and flour of sulpher, and washed the old man's eyes with a little eyewater. a little before dark Drewyer R. Fields and LaPage returned having been also unsuccessfull they had killed a hawk only and taken the part of a salmon from an Eagle, the latter altho it was of itself not valuable was an agreeable sight as it gave us reason to hope that the salmon would shortly be with us. these hunters had scowered the country between the Kooskooske and Collins's Creek from hence to their junction about 10 miles and had seen no deer or bear and but little sign of either. shortly after dark it began to rain and continued raining moderately all night. the air was extreemly cold and disagreeable and we lay in the water as the preceeding night.

[Clark, May 18, 1806] Sunday 18th May 1806 Cloudy morning 12 hunters turned out this morning in different directions agreeably to the order of yesterday. Potts and Whitehouse accompanied Collins to the bear which he had killed on the 16th and brought in the flesh and Skin. this bear was not large but remarkably light coloured the hair of it as also the hair of all those which has been killed is very thick and long. The Squar wife to Shabono busied her Self gathering the roots of the fenel Called by the Snake Indians Year-pah for the purpose of drying to eate on the Rocky mountains. those roots are very paliatiable either fresh rosted boiled or dried and are generally between the Size of a quill and that of a mans fingar and about the length of the latter. at 2 P.M. 3 Indians who had been out hunting towards the place we met with the Chopunnish last fall, which place they Call the quarmash grounds. those men had been out Several days and killed nothing. we gave them a Small piece of meat which they told us they would reserve for their Small Children who was very hungary. we Smoked with them and they departed. The nativs made a lodge on the opposit bank of the river a little above us at a fishing place. as all communication is cut off between us and the nativs on the opposit Side of the river, we cannot Say by whome or for what service that lodge has been errected as no one has been near it Since it was errected this morning. at 3 P M Jo. Field returned from the chase without killing any thing he complains of being unwell. Son after an old man and a woman arived the man with Sore eyes, and the woman with a gripeing and rhumatic effections. I gave the woman a dose of creme of tarter and flour of Sulphur, and the man Some eye water. a little before night Rueben Field Drewyer and LaPage returned haveing killed nothing but a large hawk they had hunted in the point between the Kooskooske and Collins's Creek and Saw but little Sign of either deer or Bear. the evening Cloudy, Soon after dark it began to rain and rained moderately all night-. LaPage took a Salmon from an Eagle at a Short distance below our Camp. this is induces us to believe that the Salmon is in this river and most probably will be here in great numbers in the Course of a fiew days.

[Lewis, May 19, 1806] Monday May 19th 1806. It continued to rain this morning untill 8 OCk. when it became fair. We sent Charbono, Thompson, Potts, Hall and Wiser over the river to a village above in order to purchase some roots to eat with our lean bear meat. for this purpose we gave them a few awls, Kniting pins and Armbands. we were informed that there was a canoe at the village in which they could pass the river. I sent Joseph and R. Feilds up the river in surch of the horse which I rode over the Rocky mountains last fall. he had been seen yesterday with a parse) of indian horses and has become almost wild. at 11 A.M. Thompson returned from the village accompanied by a train of invalids consisting of 4 men 8 women and a child. The men had soar eyes and the women in addition to soar eyes had a variety of other complaints principally rheumatic; a weakness and pain in the loins is a common complaint with their women. eyewater was administered to all; to two of the women cathartics were given, to a third who appeared much dejected and who from their account of her disease we supposed it to be histerical, we gave 30 drops of Laudanum. the several parts of the others where the rheumatic pains were seated were well rubed with volitile linniment. all of those poor wretches thought themselves much benefited and all returned to their village well satisfyed. at 5 P.M. or marketers returned with about 6 bushels of the cows roots and a considerable quanty of bread of the same materials. late in the evening Reubin and Joseph Feilds returned with my horse; we had him immediately castrated together with two others by Drewyer in the ordinary. we amused ourselves about an hour this afternoon in looking at the men running their horses. several of those horses would be thought fleet in the U States. a little after dark Sheilds and Gibson returned unsuccessful) from the chase. they had seen some deer but no bear.

[Clark, May 19, 1806] Monday 19th May 1806 Rained this morning untill 8 oClock when it Cleared off and became fair-. we Sent Shabono, Thomson, Potts, Hall & Wizer over to the Villages above to purchase Some roots to eate with our pore bear meat, for which purchase we gave them a fiew Awls, Knitting pins, & arm bans and directed them to proceed up on this Side of the river opposit to the Village and Cross in the Cano which we are informed is at that place. Sent Jo. & Reuben Field up the river a Short distance after the horse which Capt. Lewis rode over the mountains last fall, which horse was Seen yesterday with a gangue of Indian horses, and is Very wild-. about 11 oClock 4 men and 8 Women Came to our Camp with Thompson who went to the Village very early this morning. those Men applyed for Eye water and the Women had a Variety of Complaints tho the most general Complaint was the Rhumitism, pains in the back and the Sore eyes, they also brought fowd. a very young Child whome they Said had been very Sick-. I administered eye water to all, two of the women I gave a carthartic, one whose Spirets were very low and much hipedz I gave 30 drops of Lodomem, and to the others I had their backs hips legs thighs & arms well rubed with Volitile leniment all of those pore people thought themselves much benifited by what had been done for them, and at 3 P.M. they all returned to their Villages well satisfied. at 5 P.M. Potts, Shabono &c. returned from the Village with about 6 bushels of the root the nativs Call Cowse and Some bread of the Same root. Rubin & Jos. Fields returned with the horse Capt. Lewis rode across the rocky mountains we had this horse imedeately Cut with 2 others which we had not before thought proper to Castrate. we amused ourselves about an hour this after noon looking at the men run their horses, Several of them would be thought Swift horses in the atlantic States. a little after dark John Shields and Gibson returned haveing killed nothing. they Saw Some deer but Saw no bear.

[Lewis, May 20, 1806] Tuesday May 20th 1806. It rained the greater part of last night and continued this morning untill noon when it cleared away about an hour and then rained at intervals untill 4 in the evening. our covering is so indifferent that Capt C. and myself lay in the water the greater part of the last night. Drewyer, and the two Feildses set out on a hunting excurtion towards the mountains. Shannon and Colter came in unsuccessfull, they had wounded a bear and a deer last evening but the night coming on they were unable to pursue them, and the snow which fell in the course of the night and this morning had covered the blood and rendered all further pursuit impracticable. at 2 P.M. Labuish arrived with a large buck of the Mule deer speceis which he had killed on Collins's Creek yesterday. he had left Cruzatte and Collins on the Creek where they were to wait his return. he informed us that it was snowing on the plain while it was raining at our camp in the river bottom. late in the evening Labuish and LaPage set out to join Collins and Cruzatte in order to resume their hunt early tomorrow morning. this evening a party of indians assembled on the opposite bank of the river and viewed our camp with much attention for some time and retired.- at 5 P.M. Frazier who had been permitted to go to the village this morning returned with a pasel of Roots and bread which he had purchased. brass buttons is an article of which these people are tolerably fond, the men have taken advantage of their prepossession in favour of buttons and have devested themselves of all they had in possesson which they have given in exchange for roots and bread.

[Clark, May 20, 1806] Tuesday 20th May 1806 rained the greater part of the last night and this morning untill meridean when it Cleared away for an hour and began to rain and rained at entervals untill 4 P.M. our Covering was so indefferent that Capt Lewis and my self was wet in our bed all the latter part of the night. Drewyer, Jos. & R. Fields Set out to towards the mountains. Shannon & Colter Came in without any thing. they had Seen and Shot at a Bear and a Deer neither of which they Could get. both of those Animals they must have Wounded Mortally, but the night Comeing on prevented their following them, and this morning the Snow had Covered the tracks and hid the blood and prevented their getting either of them.

at 2 P.M. Labiech Came in with a large Buck of the Mule Deer Speces which he had killed on Collins's Creek yesterday. he left Collins and Peter Crusat on the Creek at which place they would Continue untill his return. he informd. us that it was Snowing on the leavel plains on the top of the hill all the time it was raining in the bottom at our Camp. Labiech & Lapage returned to Collins & Crusat in the evening late for the purpose of Pursueing the hunt in the Morning early. Several Indians came to the opposit side of the River and viewed us some time. at 5 P M Frazur who had leave to go to the Village returned with Some roots which he had purchased. cloudy &c.

[Lewis, May 21, 1806] Wednesday May 21st 1806. It rained a few hours this morning. Sheilds and Gibson set out to hunt towards the mountains. Collins came to camp at noon and remained about 2 hours; he has killed nothing since he left us last. we set five men at work to make a canoe for the purpose of fishing and passing the river. the Indians have already promised us a horse for this canoe when we have no longer any uce for her. as our tent was not sufficient to shelter us from the rain we had a lodge constructed of willow poles and grass in the form of the orning of a waggon closed at one end. this we had made sufficiently large to sleep in and to shelter the most important part of our baggage. it is perfectly secure against the rain sun and wind and affords us much the most comfortable shelter we have had since we left Fort Clatsop. today we divided the remnant of our store of merchandize among our party with a view that each should purchase therewith a parsel of roots and bread from the natives as his stores for the rocky mountains for there seems but little probability that we shall be enabled to make any dryed meat for that purpose and we cannot as yet form any just idea what resource the fish will furnish us. each man's stock in trade amounts to no more than one awl, one Kniting pin, a half an ounce of vermillion, two nedles, a few scanes of thead and about a yard of ribbon; a slender stock indeed with which to lay in a store of provision for that dreary wilderness. we would make the men collect these roots themselves but there are several speceis of hemlock which are so much like the cows that it is difficult to discriminate them from the cows and we are affraid that they might poison themselves. the indians have given us another horse to kill for provision which we keep as a reserved store. our dependence for subsistence is on our guns, the fish we may perhaps take, the roots we can purchase from the natives and as the last alternative our horses. we eat the last morsel of meat which we had for dinner this evening, yet nobody seems much conserned about the state of provision. Willard, Sergt. Ordway and Goodrich were permitted to visit the village today; the former returned in the evening with some roots and bread, the two last remaining all night. one of our party brought in a young sandhill crain it was about the size of a pateridge and of a redish brown colour, it appeared to be about 5 or six days old; these crains are abundant in this neighbourhood.

[Clark, May 21, 1806] Wednesday 21st May 1806 rained this morning. Shields and Gibson Set out to hunt towards the mountains. Collins Came in to day and Stayed in about two hours, he has killed nothing Since he went out last. we Set 5 Men at work to build a Canoe for the purpose of takeing fish and passing the river and for which we can get a good horse. as our tent is not Sufficient to keep off the rain we are Compelled to have Some other resort for a Security from the repeeted Showers which fall. we have a small half circular place made and Covered with grass which makes a very Secure Shelter for us to Sleep under. We devided our Store of merchindize amongst our party for the purpose of precureing Some roots &c. of the nativs to each mans part amounted to about an awl Knitting pin a little paint and Some thread & 2 Needles which is but a Scanty dependance for roots to take us over those Great Snowey Barriers (rocky mountains) which is and will be the Cause of our Detention in this neighbourhood probably untill the 10 or 15 of June. they are at this time Covered deep with Snow. the plains on the high Country above us is also covered with Snow. Serjt. Ordway, Goodrich, & Willard went to the village to day to precure a fiew roots. we eate the last of our meat for Dinner to day, and our only Certain dependance is the roots we Can precure from the nativs for the fiew articles we have left those roots with what Game we Can precure from the wods will probably last us untill the arival of the Salmon. if they Should not; we have a horse in Store ready to be killed which the indians have offered to us. Willard returned from the Village. Sergt. Ordway and Goodrich Continued all night. one of the men brought me a young Sandhill Crain which was about 5 or 6 days old it was of a yellowish brown Colour, about the Size of a partridge. Those Crains are very abundant in every part of this country in pars of two, and Sometimes three together.

the party had gathered roots with leaves still attached they probably could have been sorted with Indian assistance. However, the parsley family (Apiaceae) is one of the most diverse and confusing plant families in the region, and Lewis could not be sure that the men would not bring back some other poisonous species not well known to the Indians. The decision to purchase roots was probably prudent.

[Lewis, May 22, 1806] Thursday May 22ed 1806. A fine morning we exposed all our baggage to air and dry as well as our store of roots and bread purchased from the natives. permited Windsor and McNeal to go to the indian village. Sergt. Ordway and Goodrich returned this morning with a good store of roots and bread. about noon 2 indian men came down the river on a raft and continued at our camp about 3 hours and returned to their village. we.sent out Shannon and Colter to hunt towards the mountains. we sent Sergt. Pryor down to the entrance of Collins's Creek to examine the country and look out for a good position for an encampment on the river below that Creek, having determined to remove our camp below that crek if it continues high, as soon as we have completed our canoe, as the country to which we are confined to hunt at present is limited by this creek and river to a very narrow tract, and game have already become scarce. if we can obtain a good situation below the entrance of this creek it will be much more eligible as the hunting country is more extensive and game more abundant than above. The horse which the indians have given us to kill was driven away yesterday by the natives with a gang of their horses I presume in mistake; being without meat at noon we directed one of the largest of our colts to be killed. we found the flesh of this animal fat tender and by no means illy flavoured. we have three others which we mean to reserve for the rocky mountains if we can subsist here without them. my horse which was castrated the day before yesterday wounded his thigh on the inner side with the rope by which he was confined that evening and is now so much swolen with the wound the castraiting and the collection of vermen that he cannot walk, in short he is the most wretched specticle; I had his wounds clensed of the vermen by washing them well with a strong decoction of the bark of the roots & leaves of elder but think the chances are against his recovery. at 3 P.M. we observed a large party of Indians on horseback in pursuit of a deer which they ran into the river opposite to our camp; Capt. C. Myself & three of our men shot and killed the deer in the water; the indians pursued it on a raft and caught it. it is astonishing to see these people ride down those steep hills which they do at full speed. on our return to camp we found Drewyer the Two Feildses Gibson and Sheilds just arrived with five deer which they had killed at a considerable distance towards the mountains. they also brought with them two red salmon trout which they had purchased from some indians whom they had met with on their return to camp.- Two Indians who were just arrived at our camp informed us that these salmon trout remained in this river the greater part of the winter, that they were not good at this season which we readily discovered, they were very meagre. these indians also informed us that there were at this time a great number of salmon at no great distance from hence in Lewis's river which had just arrived and were very fat and fine, they said it would be some yet before they would ascend this river as high as this place. a party of the natives on the opposite shore informed those with us that a party of the Shoshones had two nights past surrounded a lodge of their nation on the South side of Lewis's river, that the inhabitants having timely discovered the enimy effected their retreat in the course of the night and escaped. Charbono's Child is very ill this evening; he is cuting teeth, and for several days past has had a violent lax, which having suddonly stoped he was attacked with a high fever and his neck and throat are much swolen this evening. we gave him a doze of creem of tartar and flour of sulpher and applyed a poltice of boiled onions to his neck as warm as he could well bear it. Sergt. Pryor returned late in the evening and informed us that he had been down the river eight miles and that the clifts set in so abruptly to the river he could get no further without returning several miles back and ascending the hills and that he had thought it best to return and ride down tomorrow on the high plain as he believed the mouth of the creek was a considerable distance. Drewyer who has been at the place informs us that it is about 10 ms. and that there is no situation on the river for some distance below this creek which can possibly answer our purposes.- we dryed our baggage &c perfectly and put it up.-

[Clark, May 22, 1806] Thursday 22nd May 1806 a fine day we exposed all our baggage to the Sun to air and dry, also our roots which we have precured of the nativs. gave promission to Windser & McNeal to go to the Indian Villages. Sergt. Ordway and goodrich returned at 11 A.M. Soon after 2 Indian men Came down on a raft and Continued with us about 3 hours and then returned to their Village. Shannon & Colter went out to day to hunt towards the mountains. Sergt. Pryor went out to hunt down the river, and examine the mouth of Collins Creek, if a good Situation was below that Creek for a Camp. this Creek which Cannot be passed owing to it's debth & rapidity is a great beariore in our way to the best hunting Country. it confines us to a narrow scope between this Creek and the river on which we are Camped. If a Situation can be found imedeately below the Creek it will answer us better than our present one as from thence we Can get out to Some distance to hunt, and be convenient also to the fish Should they pass up &c. The horse the Indian's left with us to kill has been drove to their village with a gang of horses which I suppose belonged to another man. as the greater part of our men have not had any Meat to eate for 2 days, and the roots they Complain of, not being accustiomed to live on them altogether we derected a large Coalt which was given to us by a young man with an elegant mare on the _____ instant. this Coalt was fat and was handsom looking meat. late in the evening we were informed that the horse which Capt L. rode over the rocky mountains and which was Cut day before yesterday had his hip out of place Since that time, and Could not walk. Capt. Lewis examined him and thought he Could not recover. at 3 P.M. we observed a number of Indians in chase of a deer on their horses on the opposit hill Sides. Soon after the deer took the water I Capt L. and 3 men run down on this Side, and killed the deer in the water, the deer floated down and the Indians took it by means of a raft which they had ready. on my return to Camp found Drewyer Jos. & Reuben Fields, Shields and gibson just arrived from the Chass with 5 Deer which they had killed on the high lands toward the mountains. they also brought with them two Salmon trout which they had purchased of Indians which they Saw on their return to Camp. at 5 p. M. two young men highly decurated in their way Came to our camp and informed us that the fat fish were in great numbers in Lewis's river. that those Salmon trout which our hunters brought were pore and Such as were Cought in the Winter in this river and were not the kind which Comes up in the Spring of the year. great number of Indians Come to the opposit bank and inform those on this Side that the Snake Indians had come to a Lodge on Lewis's river at night. the inhabitents previously discovering them abandened the house. Shabonoes Son a Small child is, dangerously ill. his jaw and throat is much Swelled. we apply a poltice of Onions. after giveing him Some creem of tarter &c. this day proved to be fine fair which afforded us an oppertunety of drying our baggage which had got a little wet.

[Lewis, May 23, 1806] Friday May 23rd 1806. Sergt. Pryor wounded a deer early this morning in a lick near camp; my dog pursud it into the river; the two young Indian men who had remained with us all night mounted their horses swam the river and drove the deer into the water again; Sergt. Pryor killed it as it reached the shore on this side, the indians returned as they had passed over. we directed half this deer to be given to the indians, they immediately made a fire and cooked their meat, 4 others joined them from the village with the assistance of whom they consumed their portion of the spoil in less than 2 hours and took their leave of our camp. The Creem of tartar and sulpher operated several times on the child in the course of the last night, he is considerably better this morning, tho the swelling of the neck has abated but little; we still apply polices of onions which we renew frequently in the course of the day and night. at noon we were visited by 4 indians who informed us they cad come from their village on Lewis's river at the distance of two days ride in order to see us and obtain a little eyewater, Capt. C. washed their eyes and they set out on their return to their village. our skill as phisicans and the virture of our medecines have been spread it seems to a great distance. I sincerely wish it was in our power to give releif to these poor afficted wretches. at 1 P.M. Shannon, Colter, Labuish, Cruzatte, Collins, and LaPage returned from hunting without having killed anything except a few pheasants of the dark brown kind, which they brought with them.These hunters informed us that they had hunted the country deligently between the river and Creek for some distance above and below our camp and that there was no game to be found. all the horses which have been castrated except my poor unfortunate horse appear as if they would do very well. I am convinced that those cut by the indians will get well much soonest and they do not swell nor appear to suffer as much as those cut in the common way.

[Clark, May 23, 1806] Friday 23rd May 1806 a fair morning. Sergt. Pryor wounded a Deer at a lick near our Camp and our dog prosued it into the river. two Indians which happened to be at our Camp Mounted their horses and Swam across the river chased the deer into the water again and pursued it across to the Side on which we were, and as the Deer Came out of the Water Sgt. Pryor killed it. we derected half of this deer to be given to those two indians. they imediately made a fire and Cooked the meat. 4 others joined them from the Village and they Soon consumed their portion. The Child is Something better this morning than it was last night. we apply a fresh poltice of the wild Onion which we repeeted twice in the Course of the day. the Swelling does not appear to increas any Since yesterday. The 4 Indians who visited us to day informed us that they Came from their village on Lewis's river two days ride from this place for the purpose of Seeing of us and getting a little eye water I washed their eyes with Some eyewater and they all left us at 2 P.M. and returned to the Villages on the opposit Side of this river. at 1 oClock Shannon, Colter, Labiech, Crusatt Lapage and Collins all returned from hunting without haveing killed any thing except a fiew heath hens & black Pheasants two of which they brought with them. Labiech also brought a whisteling squerel which he had killed on it's hole in the high plains. this squerel differs from those on the Missouri in their Colour, Size, food and the length tal and from those found near the falls of Columbia

Our hunters brought us a large hooting owl which differ from those of the atlantic States. The plumage of this owl is an uniform mixture of dark yellowish brown and white, in which the dark brown prodominates. it's Colour may be properly termed a dark Iron gray. the plumage is very long and remarkably Silky and Soft. those have not the long feathers on the head which give it the appearance of ears, or horns, remarkable large eyes

the hunters informed us that they had hunted with great industry all the Country between the river and for Some distance above and below without the Smallest Chance of killing any game. they inform us that the high lands are very cold with snow which has fallen for every day or night for Several past. our horses which was Cut is like to doe well.

[Lewis, May 24, 1806] Saturday May 24th 1806. The child was very wrestless last night; it's jaw and the back of it's neck are much more swolen than they were yesterday tho his fever has abated considerably. we gave it a doze of creem of tartar and applyed a fresh poltice of onions. we ordered some of the hunters out this morning and directed them to pass Collins's creek if possible and hunt towards the quawmash feilds. William Bratton still continues very unwell; he eats heartily digests his food well, and his recovered his flesh almost perfectly yet is so weak in the loins that he is scarcely able to walk nor can he set upwright but with the greatest pain. we have tryed every remidy which our engenuity could devise, or with which our stock of medicines furnished us, without effect. John Sheilds observed that he had seen men in a similar situation restored by violent sweats. Bratton requested that he might be sweated in the manner proposed by Sheilds to which we consented. Sheilds sunk a circular hole of 3 feet diamiter and four feet deep in the earth. he kindled a large fire in the hole and heated well, after which the fire was taken out a seat placed in the center of the hole for the patient with a board at bottom for his feet to rest on; some hoops of willow poles were bent in an arch crossing each other over the hole, on these several blankets were thrown forming a secure and thick orning of about 3 feet high. the patient being striped naked was seated under this orning in the hole and the blankets well secured on every side. the patient was furnished with a vessell of water which he sprinkles on the bottom and sides of the hole and by that means creates as much steam or vapor as he could possibly bear, in this situation he was kept about 20 minutes after which he was taken out and suddonly plunged in cold water twise and was then immediately returned to the sweat hole where he was continued three quarters of an hour longer then taken out covered up in several blankets and suffered to cool gradually. during the time of his being in the sweat hole, he drank copious draughts of a strong tea of horse mint. Sheilds says that he had previously seen the tea of Sinnecca snake root used in stead of the mint which was now employed for the want of the other which is not be found in this country.- this experiment was made yesterday; Bratton feels himself much better and is walking about today and says he is nearly free from pain.- at 11 A.M. a canoe arrived with 3 of the natives one of them the sick man of whom I have before made mentions as having lost the power of his limbs. he is a cheif of considerable note among them and they seem extreemly anxious for his recovery. as he complains of no pain in any particular part we conceive it cannot be the rheumatism, nor do we suppose that it can be a pareletic attack or his limbs would have been more deminished. we have supposed that it was some disorder which owed it's origine to a diet of particular roots perhaps and such as we have never before witnessed. while at the village of the broken arm we had recommended a diet of fish or flesh for this man and the cold bath every morning. we had also given him a few dozes of creem of tarter and flour of sulpher to be repeated every 3rd day. this poor wretch thinks that he feels himself of somewhat better but to me there appears to be no visible alteration. we are at a loss what to do for this unfortunate man. we gave him a few drops of Laudanum and a little portable soup. 4 of our party pased the river and visited the lodge of the broken Arm for the purpose of traiding some awls which they had made of the links of small chain belonging to one of their steel traps, for some roots. they returned in the evening having been very successfull, they had obtained a good supply of roots and bread of cows.- this day has proved warmer than any of the preceeding since we have arrived here.

[Clark, May 24, 1806] Saturday 24th May 1806 a fine morning the Child was very restless last night its jaw and back of its neck is much more Swelled than it was yesterday. I gave it a dost of Creme of Tarter and a fresh Poltice of Onions. ordered Shields, Gibson, Drewyer, Crusat, Collins, and Jo. & rubin Fields to turn out hunting and if possible Cross Collins Creek and hunt towards the quar mash fields. W. Brattin is yet very low he eats hartily but he is So weak in the Small of his back that he Can't walk. we have made use of every remidy to restore him without it's haveing the desired effect. one of our party, John Shields observed that he had Seen men in Similar Situations restored by Violent Swets. and bratten requested that he might be Swetted in the way Sheilds purposed which we agreed to. Shields dug a round hole 4 feet deep & 3 feet Diamuter in which he made a large fire So as to beet the hole after which the fire was taken out a Seet placed in the hole. the patent was then Set on the Seat with a board under his feet and a can of water handed him to throw on the bottom & Sides of the hole So as to create as greate a heat as he Could bear. and the hole covered with blankets supported by hoops. after about 20 minits the patient was taken out and put in Cold water a few minits, & returned to the hole in which he was kept about 1 hour. then taken out and Covered with Several blankets, which was taken off by degrees untill he became Cool. this remedy took place yesterday and bratten is walking about to day and is much better than he has been. at 11 A.M. a canoe came down with the Indian man who had applyed for medical assistance while we lay at the broken arms village. this man I had given a fiew doses of Flower of Sulpher & Creme of Tarter and derected that he Should take the Cold bath every morning. he Conceited himself a little better than he was at that time. he had lost the use of all his limbs and his fingers are Contracted. We are at a loss to deturmine what to do for this unfortunate man. I gave him a few drops of Lodman and Some portable Supe as medisine. 4 of our men Crossed the river and went to the broken arms Village and returned in the evening with a Supply of bread and roots which they precured in exchange for Awls which were made of pieces of a chane- we were visited to day by the 2 young men who gave Capt. L. and my Self a horse each at the village. those men Stayed about two hours and returned to their village. this day proved to be very worm.

[Lewis, May 25, 1806] Sunday May 25th 1806. It rained the greater part of last night and continued untill 6 A.M. our grass tent is impervious to the rain. the Child is more unwell than yesterday. we gave it a doze of creem of tartar which did not operate, we therefore gave it a clyster in the evening. we caused a sweat to be prepared for the indian Cheif in the same manner in which Bratton had been sweated, this we attempted but were unable to succeed, as he was unable to set up or be supported in the place. we informed the indians that we knew of no releif for him except sweating him in their sweat houses and giving him a plenty of the tea of the horsemint which we shewed them. and that this would probably nos succeed as he had been so long in his present situation. I am confident that this would be an excellent subject for electricity and much regret that I have it not in my power to supply it.- Drewyer Labuish and Cruzatte set out this morning to hunt towards the quawmash grounds if they can possibly pass Collins's Creek. Joseph and Reuben Feilds passed the river in order to hunt on the opposite side some miles above where the natives inform us that there is an abundance of bear and some deer. Goodrich visited a village about 8 ms. above on the opposite side of the river and returned in the evening; he procured but few roots, he informed us that there were but 8 persons at home; the others were either hunting, diging roots or fishing on Lewis's river. he saw several salmon in their lodges which they informed him came from that river these fish were remarkably fat and fine. Gibson and shields returned this evening having killed a Sandhill Crain only. they had wounded a female bear and a deer but got neither of them. Gibson informed me that the bear had two cubbs one of which was white and other as black as jett. four indians remained with us this evening.-

[Clark, May 25, 1806] Sunday 25th May 1806 rained moderately the greater part of last night and this morning untill 6 A.M. The child is not So well to day as yesterday. I repeeted the Creem of tarter and the onion poltice. I caused a Swet to be prepared for the Indn. in the Same hole which bratten had been Sweeten in two days past Drewyer Labiech and Peter crusatt Set out hunting towards the quarmash grounds if they can cross the Creek which is between this and that place, which has been the bearrer as yet to our hunters. Jos. & R Fields crossed the river to hunt on the opposit side. Goodrich went to the 2d village to purchase roots a fiew of which he precured. he informed us that only 8 persons remained in the Village. the men were either hunting on Lewis's river fishing, & the women out digging roots. he saw Several fresh Salmon which the nativs informed him Came from Lewis's river and were fat and fine. one of our men purchased a Bear Skin of the nativs which was nearly of a Cream Coloured white. this Skin which was the Skin of an animal of the middle Size of bears together with the defferent Sizes colours &c. of those which have been killed by our hunters give me a Stronger evidence of the various Coloured bear of this country being one Species only, than any I have heretofore had. the poil of these bear were infinately longer finer & thicker than the black bear their tallons also longer & more blunt as worn by digging roots. the white redish brown and bey Coloured bear I saw together on the Missouri; the bey & Grizly have been Seen and killed together here. for these were the Colours of those which Collins killed on the 14th inst. in short it is not common to find two bear here of this Species presisely of the same colour, and if we were to attempt to distinguish them by their colours and to denomonate each colour a distinct Species we Should Soon find at least twenty. the most Strikeing difference between this Species of bear and the Common black bear are that the former are large and have longer tallons, hair, and tushes, prey more on other animals, do not lie so long or so closely in winter quarters, and will not Climb a tree, tho ever so hardly pursued. the varigated bear I believe to be the Same here with those of the Missouri but these are not so ferocious as those on the Missouri perhaps from the Circumstance of their being compeled from the scercity of game in this quarter to live more on roots and of course not so much in the habit of Seizing and debowering liveing animals. the bear here is far from being as passive as the common black bear, they have atacked and fought our hunters already but not so feircely as those of the Missouri. There are also some of the Common black bear in this neghbourhood tho no So Common as the other Species.

we attempted to swet the sick indian but could not Suckceed. he was not able either to Set up or be Supported in the place prepared for him. I therefore deturmined to inform the Nativs that nothing but Sefere Swetts would restore this disabled man, and even that doubtfull in his present Situation. in the evening Shields & gibson returned haveing killed a Sandhill Crane only. they Saw a female bear, & 2 Cubs & Several deer. they Shot the bear and a deer both of which made their escape. Gibson told me that the Cubs were of different Colours one jut black and the other of a whiteish Colour-. 4 indians Continue with us, one return to their village to daey

[Lewis, May 26, 1806] Monday May 26th 1806. Had frequent showers in the course of the last night. Collins, Shannon and Colter set out to hunt on the high lands some distance up on the N. E. side of Collins's Creek. The Clyster given the Child last evening operated very well. it is clear of fever this evening and is much better, the swelling is considerably abated and appears as if it would pass off without coming to a head. we still continue fresh poltices of onions to the swolen part. we directed the indians in what manner to treat the dieased Cheif, gave him a few dozes of flour of sulpher and Creem of tartar & some portable soupe and directed them to take him home. they seemed unwilling to comply with the latter part of the injunction for they consumed the day and remained with us all night. at 1 P.M. Joseph and R. Feilds returned, accompanyed by Hohastillpilp several other inferior Cheifs and some young men. These hunters informed us they were unable to reach the grounds to which they had been directed in consequence of the debth and rapidity of a large creek which falls in about 10 Ms. above. they passed Commearp Creek at about 1 1/2 Ms. and a second creek reather larger at 3 Ms. further. at the distance of 4 Ms. up this last creek on their return they called at a village which our traders have never yet visited, here they obtained a large quantity of bread and roots of Cows on very moderate terms. we permitted Sergt. Pryor and four men to pass the river tomorrow morning with a view to visit this village we also directed Charbono York and LePage to set out early for the same place and procure us some roots. our meat is again exhausted, we therefore directed R. Fields to hunt the horse in the morning which the Indians have given us to kill. one of our men saw a salmon in the river today. in the afternoon we compleated our canoe and put her in the water; she appears to answer very well and will carry about 12 persons.- the river still rising fast and snows of the mountains visibly diminish

[Clark, May 26, 1806] Monday 26th May 1806 Some Small Showers of rain last night, and continued Cloudy this morning untill 7 A. M when it Cleared away and became fair and worm. Collins Shannon & Colter set out to hunt on the high lands to the N E of us towards Collins Creek. The Child Something better this morning tho the Swelling yet continues. we Still apply the onion poltice. I detected what Should be done for the disabled man, gave him a fiew doses of Creem of tarter & flour Sulphur, and Some portable Supe and directed that he Should be taken home & Swetted &c. at 1 P.M. Joseph & R. Fields returned accompanied by Hoh hast ill pilt and an Second Chief and 4 men Several young men also rode down on this Side. Jo & R Fields informed us that they were at a village 4 Miles up the 2nd Creek from this place on the opposit side above at which place on the opposit side above at which place they precured roots on very reasonable terms. they Could not proceed higher up to hunt as the creeks were too high for them to Cross, &c. we gave permission to Serjt. Pryor and 4 men to cross the river and trade with nativs of the village the Field's were at yesterday for roots &c. we also directed Shabono & york to proceed on to the Same Village and precure Some roots for our Selves if possible. one of our men Saw a Salmon in the river to day. and two others eat of Salmon at the near Village which was brought from Lewis's river. our Canoe finished and put into the water. it will Carry 12 men. the riseing very fast and Snow appear to melt on the Mountains.

[Lewis, May 27, 1806] Tuesday May 27th 1806. Early this morning we sent Reubin Fields in surch of the horse which the indians had given us to kill. at 10 in the morning he returned with the horse and we killed and butchered him; he was large and in good order. Hohastillpilp told us that most of the horses we saw runing at large in this neighbourhood belonged to himself and his people, and whenever we were in want of meat he requested that we would kill any of them we wished; this is a peice of liberallity which would do honour to such as host of civilization; indeed I doubt whether there are not a great number of our countrymen who would see us fast many days before their compassion would excite them to a similar act of liberallity. Sergt. Pryor and the party ordered to the indian Village set out early this morning. in the evening he returned with Gibson and Sheilds. the others remained at the village all night; they brought a good store of roots and bread. we also sent Sergt. ordway and 2 men this morning over to Lewis's river for salmon, which the indians inform us may be procured in abundance at that place, and that it is but half a days ride, nearly south.- Drewyer, Cruzatte, and Labuish returned at 4 P.M. with five deer which they had killed at some distance up Collins's Creek on this side; that stream still continues so high that they could not pass it.- Charbono's son is much better today, tho the swelling on the side of his neck I beleive will terminate in an ugly imposthume a little below the ear . the indians were so anxious that the sick Cheif should be sweated under our inspection that they requested we would make a second attept today; accordingly the hole was somewhat enlarged and his father a very good looking old man, went into the hole with him and sustained him in a proper position during the operation; we could not make him sweat as copiously as we wished. after the operation he complained of considerable pain, we gave him 30 drops of laudanum which soon composed him and he rested very well.- this is at least a strong mark of parental affection. they all appear extreemly attentive to this sick man nor do they appear to relax in their asceduity towards him notwithstand he has been sick and helpless upwards of three years. the Chopunnish appear to be very attentive and kind to their aged people and treat their women with more rispect than the nations of the Missouri.- There is a speceis of Burrowing squirrel common in these plains which in their habits somewhat resemble those of the missouri but are a distinct speceis. this little animal measures one fot five and 1/2 inches from the nose to the extremity of the tail, of which the tail occupys 21/4 inches only; in the girth it is 11 In. the body is proportionably long, the neck and legs short; the ears are short, obtusely pointed, and lie close to the head; the aperture of the ear is larger proportionably than most animals which burrow. the eyes are of moderate size, the puple black and iris of a dark sooty brown. the teeth are like those of the squirrel as is it's whole contour. the whiskers are full, long and black; it also has some long black hairs above the eyes. it has five toes on each foot; the two inner toes of the fore feet are remarkably short, and have short blont nails. the remaining toes on those feet are long, black, slightly curved, and sharply pointed. the outer and inner toes of the hind feet are not short yet they are by no means as long as the three toes in the center of the foot which are remarkably long but the nails are not as long as those of the fore feet tho of the same form and colour. the hair of the tail tho of the same form and colour. the hair of the tail tho thickly inserted on every part rispects the two sides only. this gives it a flat appearance and a long ovol form. the tips of the hair which form the outer edges of the tail are white. the base of the hairs are either black or a fox red. the under disk of the tail is an iron grey, the upper a redish brown. the lower part of the jaws, under part of the neck, legs and feet from the body down and belley are of a light brick red. the nose as high as the eyes is of a darker brick red. the upper part of the head neck and body are of a curious brownish grey colour with a cast of the brick red. the longer hair of these parts being of a redish white colour at their extremities, fall together in such manner as to give it the appearance of being speckled at a little distance. these animals form large ascociations as those of the Missouri, occupying with their burroughs one or sometimes 200 acres of land. the burrows are seperate and are each occupied perhaps by ten or 12 of those animals. there is a little mound in front of the hole formed of the earth thrown out of the burrow and frequently there are three or four distinct holes forming what I term one burrow with their mouths arround the base of this little mound which seems to be occupied as a watch-tower in common by the inhabitants of those several holes. these mounds are sometimes as much as 2 feet high and 4 feet in diameter, and are irregularly distributed over the tract they occupy at the distance of from ten to thirty or 40 yds. when you approach a burrow the squirrels, one or more, usually set erect on these mounds and make a kind of shrill whistleing nois, something like tweet, tweet, tweet, &c. they do not live on grass as those of the missouri but on roots. one which I examined had in his mouth two small bulbs of a speceis of grass, which resemble very much what is sometimes called the grassnut. the intestins of those little animals are remarkably large for it's size. fur short and very fine.- the grass in their villages is not cut down as in those of the plains of the missouri. I preserved the skins of several of these animals with the heads feet and legs entire. The Black woodpecker which I have frequently mentioned and which is found in most parts of the roky Mountains as well as the Western and S. W. mountains. I had never an opportunity of examining untill a few days since when we killed and preserved several of them. this bird is about the size of the lark woodpecker of the turtle dove, tho it's wings are longer than either of those birds. the beak is black, one inch long, reather wide at the base, somewhat curved, and sharply pointed; the chaps are of equal length. arround the base of the beak including the eye and a small part of the throat is of a fine crimson red. the neck and as low as the croop in front is of an iron grey. the belly and breast is a curious mixture of white and blood reed which has much the appearance of having been artifically painted or stained of that colour. the red reather predominates. the top of the head back, sides, upper surface of the wings and tail are black, with a gossey tint of green in a certain exposure to the light. the under side of the wings and tail are of a sooty black. it has ten feathers in the tail, sharply pointed, and those in the center reather longest, being 2 1/2 inches in length. the tongue is barbed, pointed, and of an elastic cartelaginous substance. the eye is moderately large, puple black and iris of a dark yellowish brown. this bird in it's actions when flying resembles the small redheaded woodpecke common to the Atlantic states; it's note also somewhat resembles that bird. the pointed tail seems to assist it in seting with more eas or retaining it its resting position against the perpendicular side of a tree. the legs and feet are black and covered with wide imbricated scales. it has four toes on each foot of which two are in rear and two in front; the nails are much curved long and remarkably keen or sharply pointed. it feeds on bugs worms and a variety of insects.

[Clark, May 27, 1806] Tuesday 27th May 1806 A cloudy morning Serjt. Pryor and party Set out at 7 A.M. Serjt. Ordway and two men are ordered to cross this river and proceed on through the plains to Lewis's and precure Some Salmon on that river, and return tomorrow if possible he Set out at 8 A.M. we Sent Rub. Field in Serch of the horse which the indians had given us to kill. at 10 A. M he returned with the horse and he was killed and butchered; he was large and in good order. hohastillpilp told us that most of the horses which we Saw running in those plains in this neighbourhood at large belonged to himself and his people, and whenever we were in want of meet, he requested that would kill any of them we wished; this is a piece of liberallity which would do honour to Such as host of civilization. Serjt. Pryor, Gibson & Shields returned from the Village with a good Stock of roots and bread. Shabono Lapage & Yourk whome we had Sent to purchase roots for ourselves remained at the Village all night. Drewyer, Labiech & Crusat return at 4 P.M. with 5 Deer which they had killed at Some distance up Collin's Creek on this Side, that Stream Still continue So high that they could not pass it.

Shabono's child is much better to day; tho the Swelling on the Side of his neck I believe will termonate in an ugly imposthume a little below the ear. The Indians were so anxious that the Sick Chief (who has lost the use of his limbs) Should be Sweted under our inspection they requested me to make a 2d attempt to day; accordingly the hole was enlargened and his father a very good looking old man performed all the drugery &c. we could not make him Swet as copously as we wished. being compelled to keep him erect in the hole by means of Cords. after the oppiration he complained of Considerable pain, I gave him 30 drops of Laudnom which Soon composed him and he rested very well-. I observe the Strongest marks of parental affection. they all appear extreemly attentive to this Sick man, no do they appear to relax in their ascituity towards him not withstanding he has been Sick and helpless for near 5 years. The Chopunnish appear to be very attentive & kind to their aged people and treat their women with more respect than the nativs on the Missouri.

There is a Species of whistleing Squirel common in these plains which in their habit Somewhat resembles those of the Missouri but are a distinct Species. this little animale measures 1 foot 5 inches & a half from the nose to the extremity of the tail, of which the tail occupies 2 1/4 inches only; in the girth it is 11 inches the body is perpotionably long, the neck and legs Short; the ears are Short, obtusely pointed, and lye close to the head; the aperture of the ear is larger proportionably than most animals which burrow. the eyes are of Moderate Size, the puple black and iris of a dark dusky brown. the teeth are like those of the Squirel as is it's whole contour. the whiskers are full, long and black; it has also Some long black hars above the eye-. it has five toes on each foot; the 2 iner toes of the fore feet are remarkably Short, and have Short blunt nails. the remaining toes on these feet are long Slightly Curved, black and Sharply pointed. the outer and inner toes of the hind feet are not Short yet they are by no means as long as the three toes in the Center of the foot which are remarkably long but the nails are not as long as those of the fore feet tho of the Same form and colour. the bars of the tail tho thickly inserted on every part respects the two Sides only. this givs it a flat appearance and a long oval form. the tips of the hair which forms the outer edges of the tail are white. the bace of the hair are either black or a fox red. the under disk of the tail is an iron gray, the upper a redish brown. the lower part of the jaws, under part of the neck, legs and feet from the body down and belly are of a light brick red. the nose as high as the eyes is of a darker brick red. the upper part of the head neck and body are of a curious brownish gray colour with a cast of the brick red. the longer hairs of these parts being of a redish white colour at their extremities fall together in Such a Manner as to give it to the appearance of being Spekled at a little distance. these animals form large ascoations as those of the Missouri, occupying with their burroughs one or Sometimes 200 acres of Land. the burrows are Seperate and are each occupyed perhaps by 10 or 12 of those Animals. there is a little Mound in front of the hole formed of the earth thrown out of the burrow and frequently there are three or four distinct holes forming what I call one burrow, around the base of the mound, which Seams to be occupied as a watch tower in common by the inhabitents of those Several holes. these Mounds are Sometimes as much as 2 feet high, and 4 feet in diameter, and are irregularly distributed over the tract they occupy at the distance of from ten to 30 or forty yards. When you approach a burrow the Squirels one, or more, usially Set erect on these Mounds and make a kind of Shrill whistleing nois, Something like tweet, tweet, tweet &c. they do not live on grass as those of the Missouri but on roots. one which I examoned had in his mouth two Small bulbs of a Species of grass, which resembles very much what is Sometimes Called the Grass Nut. the intestins of these little animals are remarkably large for it's Size; fur Short and very fine. the grass in their village is not Cut down as in these of the plains of the Missouri. I preserved the Skins of Several of these animals with the heads feet and legs entire-.-. The Black Wood pecker which is found in most parts of the rocky Mountains as will as the Western and S W. mountains, I had never an oppertunity of examineing, untill a fiew days Since when we killed and preserved Several of them. this bird is about the Size of the lark woodpecker or the turtle dove, tho it's wings are longer than either of these birds. the beak is black, one inch long reather wide at the base, Somewhat cirved, and Sharply pointed; the chaps are of equal length. around the bace of the beak including the eye and a Small part of the throat is of a crimson red. the neck and as low as the croop in front is of an iron gray. the belly and breast is of a curious mixture of white and blood red which has much the appearance of haveing been artifically painted or Stained of that colour, the red reather predominates. the top of the head, back, Sides, upper Surface of the wings and tail are black, the under Side of the wings and tail are black. it has ten feathers in the tail, Sharply pointed, and those in the center reather longest, being 2 1/2 inches in length. the tongue is barbed, pointed, and of an elastic cartalaginous Substance. the eye is moderately large, puple black and iris of a dark yellowish brown. this bird in it's actions when flying resemble the Small redish woodpecker common to the altantic States; it's note also Somewhat resembles that bird. the pointed tail Seems to assist it in sitting with more ease or retaining it, in it's resting position against the perpendicular Side of a tree. the legs and feet are black, and covered with imbricated scales. it has four toes on each foot, of which two are in rear and two in front; the nails are much curved long and remarkably Keen or Sharply pointed. it feeds on bugs, worms and a variety of insects.-.

[Lewis, May 28, 1806] Wednesday May 28th 1806. We sent Goodrich to the village of the broken arm this morning he returned in the evening with some roots bread and a parsel of goats-hair for making our saddle pads. Reubin and Joseph Feilds set out this morning to hunt high up on a creek which discharges itself into this river about 8 miles above us. at Noon Charbono, York and Lapage returned; they had obtained four bags of the dryed roots of Cows and some bread. in the evening Collins Shannon and Colter returned with eight deer. they had fortunately discovered a ford on Collins's Creek where they were enabled to pass it with their horses and had hunted at the quawmash ground where we first met with the Chopunnish last fall. deer were very abundant they informed us, but there were not many bear. The sick Cheif was much better this morning he can use his hands and arms and seems much pleased with the prospect of recovering, he says he feels much better than he has for a great number of months. I sincerely wish these sweats may restore him; we have consented that he should still remain with us and repeat these sweats. he set up a great proportion of the day.- The Child is also better, he is free of fever, the imposthume is not so large but seems to be advancing to maturity.- since my arrival here I have killed several birds of the corvus genus of a kind found only in the rocky mountains and their neighbourhood. I first met with this bird above the three forks of the Missouri and saw them on the hights of the rocky Mountains but never before had an opportunity of examining them closely. the small corvus discribed at Fort Clatsop is a different speceis, tho untill now I had taken it to be the same, this is much larger and has a loud squawling note something like the mewing of a cat. the beak of this bird is 1 1/2 inches long, is proportionably large, black and of the form which characterizes this genus. the upper exceeds the under chap a little. the head and neck are also proportionably large. the eye full and reather prominent, the iris dark brown and puple black. it is about the size and somewhat the form of the Jaybird tho reather rounder or more full in the body. the tail is four and a half inches in length, composed of 12 feathers nearly of the same length. the head neck and body of this bird are of a dove colour. the wings are black except the extremities of six large fathers ocupying the middle joint of the wing which are white. the under disk of the wing is not of the shining or grossy black which marks it's upper surface. the two feathers in the center of the tail are black as are the two adjacent feathers for half their width the ballance are of a pure white. the feet and legs are black and imbricated with wide scales. the nails are black and remarkably long and sharp, also much curved. it has four toes on each foot of which one is in the rear and three in front. the toes are long particularly that in the rear. this bird feeds on the seed of the pine and also on insects. it resides in the rocky mountains at all seasons of the year, and in many parts is the only bird to be found.- our hunters brought us a large hooting Owl which differs considerably from those of the Atlantic States which are also common here. the plumage of this owl is an uniform mixture of dark yellowish brown and white, in which the dark brown predominates. it's colour may be properly termed a dark iron grey. the plumage is very long and remarkably silky and soft. these have not the long feathers on the head which give it the appearance of ears or horns. the leathers of the head are long narrow and closely set, they rise upwright nearly to the extremity and then are bent back sudonly as iff curled. a kind of ruff of these feathers incircle the thoat. the head has a flat appearance being broadest before and behind and is 1 foot 10 Is. in circumference. incircling the eyes and extending from them like rays from the center a tissue of open hairy long feathers are placed of a light grey colour, these conceal the ears which are very large and are placed close to the eyes behind and extending below them. these feathers meet over the beak which they nearly conceal and form the face of the owl. they eyes are remarkably large and prominant, the iris of a pale goald colour and iris circular and of a deep sea green. the beak is short and wide at it's base. the upper chap is much curved at the extremity and comes down over and in front of the under chap. this bird is about the size of the largest hooting Owl. the tail is composed of eleven feathers, of which those in the center are reather the longest. it is booted to the extremity of the toes, of which it has four on each foot, one in the rear one on the outer side and two in front. the toes are short particularly that in rear, but are all armed with long keen curved nails of a dark brown colour. the beak is white and nostrils circular large and unconnected. the habits and the note of this owl is much that of the common large hooting owl.

[Clark, May 28, 1806] Wednesday May 28th 1806 We sent Goodrich to the Village of the broken Arm for hair to Stuff Saddle pads. Jo. & R. Fields Set out this morning to hunt towards the mountains. at noon Shabono York and Lapage returned. they had obtained 4 bags of the dried roots of Cowse and Some bread. in the evening Collins, Shannon & Cotter returned with 8 deer. they fortunately discovered a ford on Collin's Creek where they were enable to pass it with there horses and had hunted at the quawmash Grounds where we first met with the Chopunnish last fall. deer were verry abundant they informed us, but there was not many bear. The Sick Chief is much better this morning he can use his hands and arms and Seems much pleased with the prospects of recovering, he Says he feels much better than he has done for a great Number of Months. I Sincerly wish that the Swetts may restore him. I have Consented to repeet the Sweets.

The Country along the rocky mountains for Several hundred Miles in length and about 50 in width is leavel extremely fertile and in many parts Covered with a tall and opult. growth of the long leafed pine. near the Watercourses the hills are lofty tho are covered with a good Soil and not remarkably Stoney and possess more timber than the leavel country. the bottom lands on the Water courses are reather narrow and confined tho fertile and Seldom inundated. this Country would form an extensive Settlement; the Climate appears quit as mild as that of a Similar latitude on the Atlantic Coast; & it cannot be otherwise than healthy; it possesses a fine dry pure air. the grass and maney plants are now upwards of Knee high. I have no doubt that this tract of Country if Cultivated would produce in great abundance every article esentially necessary to the comfort and Subsistence of civillized man. to it's present inhabitants nature Seems to have dealt with a liberal hand, for she has distributed a great variety of esculent plants over the face of the Country which furnish them a plentiful Store of provisions; those are acquired but little toil; and when prepared after the method of the nativs afford not only a nutricious but an agreeable food. among other roots those Called by them the Quawmash and Cows are esteemd. the most agreeable and valuable as they are also the most abundant in those high plains.

The Cows is a knobbed root of an erregularly rounded form not unlike the Gensang in form and Consistence; this root they Collect, rub off a thin black rhind which Covers it and pounding it exposes it in cakes to the Sun. these Cakes are about an inch and 1/4 thick and 6 by 18 in wedth, when dry they either eat this bread alone without any further preperation, or boil it and make a thick Musilage; the latter is most common & much the most agreeable. the flower of this root is not very unlike the gensang-. this root they Collect as early as the Snow disappears in the Spring, and Continues to collect it untill the Quawmash Supplies it's place which happins about the Middle of June. the quawmash is also Collected for a fiew weeks after it first makes it's appearance in the Spring, but when the scape appears it is no longer fit for use untill the Seed are ripe which happens about the time just mentioned. and then the Cows declines. The Cows is also frequently dried in the Sun and pounded afterwards and used in thickening Supe and Makeing Mush.

The Chopunnish held a Council in the morning of the 12th among themselves in respect to the Subject on which we had Spoken to them the day before, the result as we learnt was favourable, they placed Confidence in the information they had recived and resolved to pursue our advise. after this Council was over the principal Chief or the broken arm, took the flour of the roots of Cows and thickened the Soup in the Kitiles and baskets of all his people, this being ended he made a harangue the purpote of which was makeing known the deliberations of their councils and impressing the necessity of unanimity among them, and a strict attention to the resolution which had been agreed on in Councell; he concluded by enviting all such men as had resolved to abide by the decree of the councill to come and eat, and requested Such as would not be So bound to Show themselves by not partakeing of the feast. I was told by one of our men who was present in the house, that there was not a decenting voice on this great National question, but all Swallowed their objections if any they had, very cheerfully with their mush-. dureing the time of this loud animated harangue of the Chief the women Cryed wrung their hands, tore their hair and appeared to be in the utmost distress. after this cerimoney was over, the Chiefs and considerate men came in a body to where we were Seated at a little distance from our tent, and two young men at the instance of the nation presented Capt L. and myself each a fine horse. and informed us that they had listened with attentioned to what we had Said and were resolved to pursue our Counsels &c.- That as we had not seen the Black foot Indians and the Minetarries of Fort dePrarie they did not think it safe to venter over to the plains of the Missouri, where they would fondly go provided those nations would not kill them. that when we had established a tradeing house on the Missouri as we had promised they would Come over and trade for arms Amunition &c. and live about us. that it would give them much pleasure to be at peace with those nations altho they had Shed much of their blood-. They Said that they were pore but their hearts were good. we might be assured of their sincerety. Some of their brave men would go over with us to the Missouri and bring them the news as we wished, and if we Could make a peace between them and their enimies on the other Side of the mountains their nation would go over to the Missouri in the latter end of the Summer. on the Subject of one of their Chiefs accompanying us to the land of the White men they Could not yet determine, but that they would let us know before we left them. that the Snow was yet so deep in the Mountains that if we attempted to pass, we would Certainly perish, and advised us to remain untill after the next full Moon when the Snow would disappear on the South hill sides and we would find grass for our horses.-. Shabonos Child is better this day that he was yesterday. he is free from fever. the imposthume is not So large but Seems to be advanceing to meturity-.

[Lewis, May 29, 1806] Thursday May 29th 1806. No movement of the party today worthy of notice. we have once more a good stock of meat and roots. Bratton is recovering his strength very fast; the Child and the Indian Cheif are also on the recovery. the cheif has much more uce of his hands and arms. he washed his face himself today which he has been unable to do previously for more than twelvemonths. we would have repeated the sweat today had not been cloudy and frequently raining. a speceis of Lizzard called by the French engages prarie buffaloe are native of these plains as well as of those of the Missouri. I have called them the horned Lizzard. they are about the size and a good deel the figure of the common black lizzard. but their bellies are broader, the tail shorter and their action much slower; they crawl much like the toad. they are of brown colour with yellowish and yellowishbrown spots. it is covered with minute scales intermixed with little horny prosesses like blont prickles on the upper surface of the body. the belley and throat is more like the frog and are of a light yelowish brown colour. arround the edge of the belley is regularly set with little horney projections which give to those edges a serrate figure the eye is small and of a dark colour. above and behind the eyes there are several projections of the bone which being armed at their extremities with a firm black substance has the appearance of horns sprouting out from the head. this part has induced me to distinguish it by the apppellation of the horned Lizzard. I cannot conceive how the engages ever assimilated this animal with the buffaloe for there is not greater analogy than between the horse and the frog. this animal is found in greatest numbers in the sandy open parts of the plains, and appear in great abundance after a shower of rain; they are sometimes found basking in the sunshine but conceal themselves in little holes in the earth much the greater preportion of their time. they are numerous about the falls of the Missouri and in the plains through which we past lately above the Wallahwallahs.- The Choke Cherry has been in blume since the 20th inst. it is a simple branching ascending stem. the cortex smooth and of a dark brown with a redish cast. the leaf is scattered petiolate oval accute at its apex finely serrate smooth and of an ordinary green. from 11/2 to 3 inches in length and 13/4 to 2 in width. the peduncles are common, cilindric, and from 4 to 5 inches in length and are inserted promiscuously on the twigs of the preceeding years growth. on the lower portion of the common peduncle are frequently from 3 to 4 small leaves being the same in form as those last discribed. other peduncles 1/4 of an inch in length are thickly scattered and inserted on all sides of the common peduncle at wright angles with it each elivating a single flower, which has five obtuse short patent white petals with short claws inserted on the upper edge of the calyx. the calyx is a perianth including both stamens and germ, one leafed fine cleft entire simiglobular, infrior, deciduous. the stamens are upwards of twenty and are seated on the margin of the flower cup or what I have called the perianth. the filaments are unequal in length subulate inflected and superior membranous. the anthers are equal in number with the filaments, they are very short oblong & flat, naked and situated at the extremity of the filaments, is of a yelow colour as is also the pollen. one pistillum. the germen is ovate, smooth, superior, sessile, very small; the Style is very short, simple, erect, on the top of the germen, deciduous. the stigma is simple, flat very short.-

[Clark, May 29, 1806] Thursday 29th of May 1806 No movement of the party to day worthy of notice. we have once more a good Stock of Meat and roots. Bratten is recovering his Strength very fast. the Child, and the Indian Cheaf are also on the recovery. the Chief has much more use of his hands and arms. he washed his face himself today. Which he has not been able to do previously for more than twelve months past. I would have repeeted the Sweat to day had it not been Cloudy and frequently raining.-. Sence my arrival here I have killed Several birds of the Corvus genus of a kind found only in the rocky mountains and their neighbourhood. I first met with bird on Jeffersons River. and Saw them on the hights of the rocky mountains. but never before had an oppertunity of examineing them Closely. the Small Corvus discribed at Fort Clatsop is a different Species, tho untill now I had taken it to be the Same, this is much larger and has a loud squaling note something like the newing of a Cat. the beak of this bird is 1 1/2 inches long, is proportionably large, black and of the form which characterize this genus. the upper exeeds the under Chap a little. the head and neck are also propotionably large, the eyes full and reather prominant, the iris dark brown and purple black. it is about the Size and Some what the form of the jay bird, tho reather rounder and more full in the body. the tail is four and a half inches in length, composed of 12 feathers nearly of the Same length. the head, neck and body of this bird is of a dove Colour. the wings are black except the extremities of Six large feathers occupying the middle joint of the wings which are White. the under disk of the wings are not of the shineing or glossy black which mark it's upper Surface. the two feathers in the Center of the tail are black as are the two adjacent feathers for half their wedth, the ballance are of a pure White. the feet and legs are black, and imbricated with wide Scales, the nails are black and remarkably long and Sharp, also much Curved, it has four toes on each foot of which one is in the rear and 3 in front. the toes are long particular that in the rear. this bird feeds on the Seeds of the pine and also on insects. it resides in the rocky Mountains at all Seasons of the year, and in many parts is the only bird to be found. a Species of Lizzard Called by the French engages, Prarie buffaloe are nativs of these plains as well as those of the Missouri. I have Called them the horned Lizzard. they are about the Size and a good deel the figure of the Common black lizzard. but their bellies are broader, the tail Shorter and their action much Slower; they Crawl much like the toad. they are of a brown Colour with yellowish and yellowish brown Spots. it is covered with minute scales intermixed with little horney like blunt prickkles on the upper Surface of the body. the belly and throat is more like the frog and are of a light yellowish brown Colour. around the edge of the belly is regularly Set with little horney prejections which give to those edges a Serrate figure, the eye is Small and of a dark colour. above and behind the eyes there are Several Projections of the bone which being armed at their extremities with a firm black Substance has the appearance of horns Sprouting out from the head. this part has induced me to distinguish it by the appellation of the Horned Lizard. I cannot conceive how the engagees ever assimilated this animal withe Buffalow for there is not grater anology than between the Horse and the frog. this Animal is found in greatest numbers in the Sandy open parts of the Plains, and appear in great abundance after a rain; they are Sometimes found basking in the Sunshine but conceal themselves in little holes under the tufts of grass or herbs much the greater proportion of their time. they are noumerous about the Falls of Missouri, and in the plains through which we passed lately above the Falls of Columbia

The Choke Cherry has been in blume Since the 20th inst. it is a Simple branching ascending Stem. the Cortex Smooth and of a dark brown with a redish Cast. the leaf is scattered petiolate oval accute at it's apex finely Serated Smooth and of an ordinary green, from 2 1/2 to 3 inches in length and from 1 1/4 to 2 in width. the Peduncles cilindric and Common from 4 to 5 inches in length and are inserted promiscuisly on the twigs of the proceeding years growth. on the lower portion of the Common peduncle are frequently from 3 to 4 Small leaves, being the same in form as those last discribed. other peduncles 1/4 of an inch in length are Scattered and thickly inserted on all sides of the Common peduncle at right-angles with it, each elivateing a Single flower, which has five obtuse Short patent white petals with Short claws incerted on the upper edge of the calyx. the Calyx is a perianth including both Stemes & germ, one leafed five cleft entire, Semi globular. the Stamons are upwards of twenty and are Seated on the Margin of the flower Cup or what I have Called the perianth. the filaments are unequal in length Subulate inflected and Superior membranous. the anthers are equal in number with the filaments, they are very Short oblong and flat, naked and Situated at the extremity of the filaments. is of a yellowish colour asis also the pollen. one pistillum. the germin is ovate, Smooth, Superior, sessile, very Small; the Style is very Short, Simple, erect, on the top of the germen deciduous. the Stigma is Simple, flat very Short. This Shrub rises to the hight of from 6 to 8 feet generally but Sometimes rich Situations much higher. it is not confined to any particular Situation Capt. L-s met with a singular plant in blume of which we preserved a Specimene. it grows on the Steep fertile hill Sides near this place the radix is fibrous, not much branched, annual, woody, white and nearly Smooth. the Stem is Simple branching ascending 2 1/2 feet high. Celindric, villose and of a pale red Colour. the branches are but fiew and those near it's upper extremity. the extremities of the branches are flexable and are bent down near their extremities with the weight of the flowers. the leaf is sessile, scattered thinly, nearly lineor tho Somewhat widest in the middle, two inches in length, absolutely entire, villose, obtusely pointed and of an Ordinary green. above each leaf a Small Short branch protrudes, Supporting a tissue of four or five Small leaves of the Same appearance of those discribed. a leaf is placed under neath each branch and each flower. the Calyx is one flowered Spatha. the corolla Superior, consists of four pale perple petals which are tripartite, the Central lobe largest and all terminate obtusely; they are inserted with a long and narrow claw on the top of the germ, are long, Smooth and deciduous. there are two distinct Sets of Stamens the first or principal Consists of four, the filaments which are capillary, erect, inserted on the top of the germ alternately with the petals, equal short, membranus; the anthers are also four each being elivated with it's fillaments; they are reather flat, erect sessile, cohering to the base, membranous, longitudinally furrowed, twise as long as the fillament naked, and of a pale purple colour, the Second Set of Stamens are very minute, are also four and placed within and opposit to the petals, those are Scercely precptable while the first are large & Conspicious, the fillaments are capillary equal, very Short white and Smooth. the anthers are four, oblong, beaked, erect Cohering at the base, membanous, Shorter than the fillaments, White naked and appear not to form pollen, there is one pistillum; the germ of which is also one, celindric, villous, inferior, Sessile, as long as the first Stamuns, and grooved. the Single Style and Stigma form a perfect mono petallous corolla only with this difference that the Style which elivates the Stigma or limb is not a tube but solid tho it's outer appearance is that of a tube of a Monopetallous corolla swelling as it ascends and gliding in such manner into the limb that it Cannot be Said where the Style ends or the Stigma begins, jointly they are as long as the Gorilla, while the limb is four cleft, Sauser Shaped, and the margin of the lobes entire and rounded. this has the appearance of a monopetallous flower growing from the Center of the four petalled corollar which is rendered more conspicuous in consequence of the first being white and the latter of a pale purple. I regret very much that the Seed of this plant are not ripe as yet and it is probable will not be so dureing our residence in this neighbourhood-. our Horses maney of them have become So wild that we Cannot take them without the assistance of the indians who are extreemly dextrous in throwing a Rope and takeing them with a noose about the neck; as we frequently want the use of our horses when we cannot get the use of the indians to take them, we had a Strong pound formed to day in order to take them at pleasure-

[Lewis, May 30, 1806] Friday May 30th 1806. Lapage and Charbono set out to the indian vilages early this morning for the purpose of trading with them for roots; Sergt. Gass was sent this morning to obtain some goats hair to stuff the padds of our saddles. he ascended the river on this side and being unable to pass the river opposite to the village he wished to visit, returned in the evening unsuccessfull. Shannon and Collins were permitted to pass the river in order to trade with the natives and lay in a store of roots and bread for themselves with their proportion of the merchandize as the others had done; in landing on the opposite shore the canoe was driven broad side with the full forse of a very strong current against some standing trees and instantly filled with water and sunk. Potts who was with them is an indifferent swimer, it was with much difficulty he made the land. they lost three blankets a blanket coat and their pittance of merchandize. in our bear state of clootheing this was a serious loss. I sent Sergt. Pryor and a party over with the indian canoe in order to raise and secure ours but the debth of the water and the strength of the current baffled every effort. I fear that we have also lost our canoe. all our invalides are on the recovery. we gave the sick Cheif a severe sweat today, shortly after which he could move one of his legs and thyes and work his toes pretty well, the other leg he can move a little; his fingers and arms seem to be almost entirely restored. he seems highly delighted with his recovery. I begin to entertain strong hope of his restoration by these sweats. in the evening Joseph Feild returned in surch of his horses which had left them last evening and returned to camp. Feilds informed us that himself and his brother whom he had left at their camp 6 ms. distant on Collin's creek, had killed 3 deer. The reptiles which I have observed in this quarter are the Rattlesnake of the speceis discribed on the Missouri, they are abundant in every part of the country and are the only poisonous snake which we have yet met with since we left St. Louis. the 2 speceis of snakes of an inosent kind already discribed. the common black lizzard, the horned lizzard, a smal green tree frog, the smal frog which is common to our country which sings in the spring of the year, a large speceis of frog which resorts the water considerably larger than our bull frog, it's shape seems to be a medium between the delicate and lengthy form of our bull frog and that of our land frog or toad as they are sometimes called in the U States. like the latter their bodies are covered with little pustles or lumps, elivated above the ordinary surface of the body; I never heard them make any sound or nois. the mockerson snake or coperhead, a number of vipers a variety of lizzards, the toad bullfrog &c common to the U States are not to be found in this country. most of the insects common to the U States are found here. the butterflies, common house and blowing flies, the horse flies, except the goald coloured ear fly, tho in stead of this fly we have a brown coloured fly about the same size which attatches itself to that part of the horse and is equally as troublesome. the silkworm is also found here. a great variety of beatles common to the Atlantic states are found here likewise. except from this order the large cow beatle and the black beatle usually alled the tumble bug which are not found here. the hornet, the wasp and yellow wasp or yellow jacket as they are frequently called are not met with in this quarter. there is an insect which much resembles the latter only a vast deel larger which are very numerous particularly in the rocky mountains on the waters of the Columbia; these build in the ground where they form a nest like the hornet with an outer covering to the comb in which they deposit their eggs and raise their young. the sheets of this comb are attatched to each other as those of the hornets are. their wings are four of a dark brown colour. the head is black, the body and abdomen are yellow incircled with transverse rings of black, they are ferce and sting very severely, we found them troublesome in frightening our horses as we passed those mountains. the honey bee is not found here. the bumble bee is. one of the men brought me today some onions from the high plain of a different speceis from those near the borders of the river as they are also from the shive or small onion noticed below the falls of the Columbia. these onions were as large as a nutmeg, they generally grow double or two bulbs connected by the same tissue of radicles; each bulb has two long liniar flat solid leaves. the peduncle is solid celindric and crowned with an umbal of from 20 to 30 flowers. this onion is exceedingly crisp and delicately flavoured indeed I think more sweet and less strong than any I ever taisted. it is not yet perfectly in blow, the parts of the flower are not distinct.

[Clark, May 30, 1806] Friday May 30th 1806. Lapage and Shabono Set out early this morning to the Indian Village in order to trade with them for roots; Serjt. Gass was Sent this morning to obtain Some goats hair to Stuf the pads of our Saddles; he assended the river on this Side and being unable to pass the river to the village he wished to visit returned in the evening unsucksessfull. Shannon and Collins were permited to pass the river in order to trade with the nativs and lay in a Store of roots and bread for themselves with their proportion of the merchendize as others had done; on landing on the opposit Shore the Canoe was driven broad Side with the full force of a very Strong Current against Some Standing trees and instantly filled with water and Sunk. Potts who was with them is an indifferent Swimer, it was with dificuelty he made the land. they lost three blankets and a Blanket Cappo and their pittance of Merchindize. in our bear State of Clothing this was a Serious loss. I Sent Serjt. Pryor and a party over in the Indian Canoe in order to raise and Secure ours but the debth of the water and the Strength of the Current baffled every effort. I fear that we have also lost our Canoe. all our involedes are on the recovery. we gave the Sick Chief a Severe Swet to day, Shortly after which he could move one of his legs and thy's and work his toes pritty well, the other leg he can move a little; his fingers and arms Seem to be almost entirely restored. he Seems highly delighted with his recovery. I begin to entertain Strong hope of his recovering by these Sweats in the evening Joseph Fields returned in serch of his horses which had left them last evening and returned to Camp. Field informed us that himself and his brother whome he had left at their Camp 6 ms. distant on Collins Creek had killed 3 Deer.- The reptiles which I have observed in this quarter are the Rattle Snake of the Species discribed on the Missouri, they are abundant in every part of the Country and are the only poisonous Snake which we have met with Since we left St. Louis. the Second Species of Snake of an inosent kind already discribd. the Common black Lizzard, the horned Lizzard, a small green tree-frog; the Same frog which is common to our Country which Sings in the Spring of the year. a large Species of frog which resorts the water considerably larger than our bull-frog, it's Shape Seems to be a Medium between the delicate and lengthy form of our bullfrogs and that of our land frog or toad as they are Sometimes called in the United States. like the latter their bodies are covered with little pustles or lumps, elevated above the ordinary Surface of the body; I never heard them make any Sound or noise, the Mockerson Snake or Copper head, a number of vipers, a variety of Lizzards, the toad bullfrog &c. common to the U. States are not to be found in this Country. Most of the insects common to the U States are found here. the butterfly, common house and blowing flies, the horse flies, except the gold coloured ear fly. tho in Stead of this fly we have a brown coloured fly about the same Size which attatches itself to that part of the horse and is equally as troublesom. the Silk worm is also found here. a great variety of beatles common to the atlantic States are Seen here likewise. except from this order the large Cow beatle and the black beatle usially termed tumble bug which are not found here. the hornet, the Wasp and yellow Wasp or yellow jacket as they are frequently Called are not met with in this quarter. there is an insect which much resembles the latter only a vast deel larger which are very noumerous particular in the Rocky mountains on the waters of the Columbia, those build in the ground where they form a nest like the hornet with an outer covering to the Comb in which they deposit their eggs and raise their young. the Sheets of this Comb are attatched to each other as those of the hornets are. their wings are four of a dark brown Colour— the head is black, the body and abdomin are yellow insercled with transverce rings of black, they are firce and Sting very Severely; we found them troublesom in frightening our horses as we passed through mountains. the honey bee is not found here. the bumblebee is. one of the men brought me to day Some Onions from the high plains of a different Species from those near the borders of the river as they are also from the Shive or Small Onion noticed below the Falls of Columbia. these Onions were as large as an nutmeg, they generally grow double or two bulbs connected by the same tissue of radicles; each bulb has two long liner flat solid leaves. the pedencle is solid celindric and cround with an umble of from 20 to 30 flowers. this Onion is exceedingly crisp and delicately flavoured indeed. I think more Sweet and less strong than any I ever tasted, it is not yet perfectly in blume, the parts of the flower are not distinct

[Lewis, May 31, 1806] Saturday May 31st 1806. Goodrich and Willard visited the indian Villages this morning and returned in the evening. Willard brought with him the dressed skin of a bear which he had purchased for Capt. C. this skin was an uniform pale redish brown colour, the indians informed us that it was not the Hoh-host or white bear, that it was the Yack-kah. this distinction of the indians induced us to make further enquiry relative to their opinons of the several speceis of bear in this country. we produced the several skins of the bear which we had killed at this place and one very nearly white which I had purchased. The white, the deep and plale red grizzle, the dark bron grizzle, and all those which had the extremities of the hair of a white or frosty colour without regard to the colour of the ground of the poil, they designated Hoh-host and assured us that they were the same with the white bear, that they ascosiated together, were very vicisious, never climbed the trees, and had much longer nails than the others. the black skins, those which were black with a number of intire white hairs intermixed, the black with a white breast, the uniform bey, brown and light redish brown, they designated the Yack-kah;-said that they climbed the trees, had short nails and were not vicious, that they could pursue them and kill them with safety, they also affirmed that they were much smaller than the white bear. I am disposed to adopt the Indian distinction with rispect to these bear and consider them two distinct speceis. the white and the grizzly of this neighbourhood are the same of those found on the upper portion of the Missouri where the other speceis are not, and that the uniform redish brown black &c of this neighbourhood are a speceis distinct from our black bear and from the black bear of the Pacific coast which I believe to be the same with those of the Atlantic coast, and that the common black bear do not exist here. I had previously observed that the claws of some of the bear which we had killed here had much shorter tallons than the variagated or white bear usually have but supposed that they had woarn them out by scratching up roots, and these were those which the indians called Yak-kah. on enquiry I found also that a cub of an uniform redish brown colour, pup to a female black bear intermixed with entire white hairs had climbed a tree. I think this a distinct speceis from the common black bear, because we never find the latter of any other colour than an uniform black, and also that the poil of this bear is much finer thicker and longer with a greater proportion of fur mixed with the hair, in other ispects they are much the same.- This evening Joseph and R. Feilds returned with the three deer which they had killed. The Indians brought us another of our origional Stock of horses; there are only two absent now of those horses, and these the indians inform us that our shoshone guide rode back when he returned. we have sixty five horses at this time, most of them in excellent order and fine strong active horses.-

The Indians pursued a mule deer to the river opposite to our camp this evening; the deer swam over and one of our hunters killed it. there being a large party of indians assembled on this occasion on the opposite side, Hohast-ill-pilp desired them to raise our canoe which was sunk on that side of the river yesterday; they made the attempt but were unable to effect it.

[Clark, May 31, 1806] Saturday May 31st 1806 Goodrich and Willard visited the indian Village this morning and returned in the evening Willard brought with him the dressed Skin of a bear which he had purchased for me. this Skin was of a uniform pale redish brown colour, the indians inform us that it was not the Hoh-host or white bear, that it was the Yack-kah this distinction of the indians induced us to make further enquiry relitive to their oppinions of the defferent Species of bear in this country. We produced the Several Skins of the bear which our hunters had killed at this place and one very nearly white which Capt Lewis had purchased. the White, the deep and pale red grizzle, the dark brown grizzle, and all those that had the extremities of the hair of a White or frosty Colour without reguard to the Colour of the ground of the poil, they designated Hoh-host and assured us that they were the Same with the White bear, that they associated together, were very vicisious, never climb the trees, and had much longer nails than the others. The black skins, those which were black with a number of entire white hairs intermixed, the black with a White breast, the uniform bey, brown and light redish brown, they disignated the Yack-kah-; Said that they Climb the trees had Short nails and were not viscisious, that they could prosue them and kill them in Safty, they also affirmed that they were much Smaller than the white bear. I am disposed to adopt the Indians distinction with respect to these bear and consider them two distinct Species. the White and the Grizzly of this neighbourhood are the Same as those found on the upper part of the Missouri where the other Species are not, and that the uniform redish brown black &c. of this neighbourhood are a Species distinct from both Species of our black bear and from the black bear of the Pacific Coast which I believe to be the Same with those of the Atlantic Coast, and that the Common black bear do not exist here. I had previously observed that the claws of Some of the bear which we had killed here had much Shorter tallons than the varigated or White bear usially have but Supposed that they had worn them out by scratching out roots, and these were those which the indians call Yahkah. on enquiry I found also that a Cub of a uniform redish brown Colour pup to a female black bear intermixed with entire white hairs, had climbed a tree. I think this a distinct Species from the common black bear becaus we never find the latter of any other Colour than a uniform black, and also that the poil of this bear is much finer thicker and longer with a greater proportion of fur mixed with the hair, in other respects they are much the same

This evening, Joseph and Reuben Fields returned with the three deer they had killed. The indians brought us another of our Original Stock of Horses; there are only two Absent now of these horses, and these the indians inform us that our Sho-Sho-ne guide rode back when he returned. we have Sixty five horses at this time, most of them in excellent order and fine Strong active horses

The Indians pursued a Mule deer to the river opposit to our Camp this evening; the deer Swam over and one of our hunters killed it. there being a large party of indians assembled on this Occasion on the opposit Side with Tin-nach-e-moo-tolt they attempted to rais our Canoe which was Sunk on that Side of the river yesterday; they made the attempt but were unable to effect it-.

[Lewis, June 1, 1806] Sunday June 1st 1806. Yesterday evening Charbono an LaPage returned, having made a broken voyage. they ascended the river on this side nearly opposite to a village eight miles above us, here their led horse which had on him their merchandize, feell into the river from the side of a steep clift and swam over; they saw an indian on the opposite side whom they prevailed on to drive their horse back again to them; in swiming the river the horse lost a dressed Elkskin of LaPages and several small articles, & their paint was destroyed by the water. here they remained and dryed their articles the evening of the 30th Ult. the indians at the village learning their errand and not having a canoe, made an attempt esterday morning to pass the river to them on a raft with a parsel of roots and bread in order to trade with them; the indian raft struck a rock, upset and lost thir cargo; the river having fallen heir to both merchandize and roots, our traders returned with empty bags. This morning Drewyer accompanyed by Hohastillpilp set out in surch of two tomahawks of ours which we have understood were in the possession of certain indians residing at a distance in the plains on the South side of the Kooskoske; the one is a tomahawk which Capt. C. left at our camp on Musquetoe Creek and the other was stolen from us while we lay at the forks of this and the Chopunnish rivers last fall. Colter and Willard set out this morning on a hunting excurtion towards the quamash grounds beyond Collins's Creek. we begin to feel some anxiety with rispect to Sergt. Ordway and party who were sent to Lewis's river for salmon; we have received no inteligence of them since they set out. we desired Drewyer to make some enquiry after the Twisted hair; the old man has not been as good as his word with rispect to encamping near us, and we fear we shall be at a loss to procure guides to conduct us by the different routs we wish to pursue from Traveller's rest to the waters of the Missouri.- I met with a singular plant today in blume of which I preserved a specemine; it grows on the steep sides of the fertile hills near this place, the radix is fibrous, not much branched, annual, woody, white and nearly smooth. the stem is simple branching ascending, 21/2 feet high celindric, villose and of a pale red colour. the branches are but few and those near it's upper extremity. the extremities of the branches are flexable and are bent down near their extremities with the weight of the flowers. the leaf is sissile, scattered thinly, nearly linear tho somewhat widest in the middle, two inches in length, absolutely entire, villose, obtusely pointed and of an ordinary green. above each leaf a small short branch protrudes, supporting a tissue of four or five smaller leaves of the same appearance with those discribed. a leaf is placed underneath eah branch, and each flower. the calyx is a one flowered spathe. the corolla superior consists of four pale perple petals which are tripartite, the central lobe largest and all terminate obtusely; they are inserted with a long and narrow claw on the top of the germ, are long, smooth, & deciduous. there are two distinct sets of stamens the 1st or principal consist of four, the filaments of which are capillary, erect, inserted on the top of the germ alternately with the petals, equal short, membranous; the anthers are also four each being elivated with it's fillament, they are linear and reather flat, erect sessile, cohering at the base, membranous, longitudinally furrowed, twise as long as the fillament naked, and of a pale perple colour. the second set of stamens are very minute are also four and placed within and opposite to the petals, these are scarcely persceptable while the 1st are large and conspicuous; the filaments are capillary equal, very short, white and smooth. the anthers are four, oblong, beaked, erect, cohering at the base, membranous, shorter than the fillaments, white naked and appear not to form pollen. there is one pistillum; the germ of which is also one, cilindric, villous, inferior, sessile, as long as the 1st stamens, and marked with 8 longitudinal furrows. the single style and stigma form a perfict monapetallous corolla only with this difference, that the style which elivates the stigma or limb is not a tube but solid tho it's outer appearance is that of the tube of a monopetallous corolla swelling as it ascends and gliding in such manner into the limb that it cannot be said where the style ends, or the stigma begins; jointly they are as long as the corolla, white, the limb is four cleft, sauser shaped, and the margins of the lobes entire and rounded. this has the appearance of a monopetallous flower growing from the center of a four petalled corollar, which is rendered more conspicuous in consequence of the 1st being white and the latter of a pale perple. I regret very much that the seed of this plant are not yet ripe and it is proble will not be so during my residence in this neighbourhood.

[Clark, June 1, 1806] Sunday June 1st 1806. Late last evening Shabono & Lapage returnd. haveing made a broken voyage. they assended the river on this Side nearly opposit to the Village Eight miles above us, here their led horse who had on him their Stock of Merchindize fell into the river from the Side of a Steep Clift and swam over, they Saw an indian on the opposit side whome they prouailed on to drive their horse back again to them; in swiming the horse lost a dressed Elk skin of LaPages and Several small articles, and their paint was distroyed by the water. here they remained and dryed their articles the evening of the 30th ulto. the indians at the village learned their errand and not haveing a canoe, made an attempt Yesterday morning made an attempt to pass the river to them on a raft with a parcel of roots and bread in order to trade with them; the indian raft Struck a rock upset and lost their Cargo; the river haveing Swallowed both Merchindize & roots, our traders returned with empty bags. This morning Geo. Drewyer accompanied by Hohastillpilp Set out in Serch of two tomahawks of ours which we have understood were in the possession of certain indians resideing at a distance in the Plains on the South Side of Flat Head river; one is a pipe tomahawk which Capt L. left at our Camp on Musquetor Creek and the other was stolen from me whilst we lay at the forks of this and Chopunnish rivers last fall. Colter and Willard Set out this morning on a hunting excurtion towards the quawmash grounds beyond Colins creek. we begin to feel Some anxiety with respect to Sergt. Ordway and party who were Sent to Lewis's river for salmon; we have receved no intillegence of them Since they Set out. we desired Drewyer to make Some enquiry after the Twisted hair; the old man has not been as good as his word with respect to encamping near us, and we fear we Shall be at a loss to procure guides to conduct us by the different routs we wish to pursue from Travillers rest to the waters of the Missouri

[Lewis, June 2, 1806] Monday June 2cd 1806. McNeal and york were sent on a trading voyage over the river this morning. having exhausted all our merchandize we are obliged to have recourse to every subterfuge in order to prepare in the most ample manner in our power to meet that wretched portion of our journy, the Rocky Mountain, where hungar and cold in their most rigorous forms assail the waried traveller; not any of us have yet forgotten our sufferings in those mountains in September last, and I think it probable we never shall. Our traders McNeal and York were furnished with the buttons which Capt. C. and myself cut off our coats, some eye water and Basilicon which we made for that purpose and some Phials and small tin boxes which I had brought out with Phosphorus. in the evening they returned with about 3 bushels of roots and some bread having made a successful) voyage, not much less pleasing to us than the return of a good cargo to an East India Merchant.- Collins, Sheilds, R & J. Feilds and Shannon set out on a hunting excurtion to the Quawmash grounds on the lower side of Collins's Creek. our horses many of them have become so wild that we cannot take them without the assistance of the Indians who are extreemly dextrous in throwing a rope and taking them with a noose about the neck; as we frequently want the use of our horses when we cannot get the assistance of the indians to take them, we had a strong pound formed today in order to take them at pleasure. Drewyer arrived this evening with Neeshneparkkeeook and Hohastillpilp who had accompanyed him to the lodges of the persons who had our tomahawks. he obtained both the tomahawks principally by the influence of the former of these Cheifs. the one which had been stolen we prized most as it was the private property of the late Sergt. Floyd and Capt. C. was desireous of returning it to his friends. the man who had this tomahawk had purchased it from the Indian that had stolen it, and was himself at the moment of their arrival just expiring. his relations were unwilling to give up the tomehawk as they intended to bury it with the disceased owner, but were at length induced to do so for the consideration of a hadkerchief, two strands of beads, which Drewyer gave them and two horses given by the cheifs to be killed agreeably to their custom at the grave of the disceased. The bands of the Chopunnish who reside above the junction of Lewis's river and the Kooskooske bury their dead in the earth and place stones on the grave. they also stick little splinters of wood in betwen the interstices of the irregular mass of stone piled on the grave and afterwards cover the whole with a roof of board or split timber. the custom of sacreficing horses to the disceased appears to be common to all the nations of the plains of Columbia. a wife of Neeshneeparkkeeook died some short time since, himself and hir relations saceficed 28 horses to her. The Indians inform us that there are a plenty of Moos to the S. E. of them on the East branch of Lewis's river which they call Tommanamah R. about Noon Sergt. Ordway Frazier and Wizer returned with 17 salmon and some roots of cows; the distance was so great from which they had brought the fish that most of them were nearly spoiled. these fish were as fat as any I ever saw; sufficiently so to cook themselves without the addition of grease; those which were sound were extreemly delicious; their flesh is of a fine rose colour with a small admixture of yellow. these men set out on the 27th ult. and in stead of finding the fishing shore at the distance of half a days ride as we had been informed, they did not reach the place at which they obtained their fish untill the evening of the 29th having travelled by their estimate near 70 miles. the rout they had taken however was not a direct one; the Indians conducted them in the first instance to the East branch of Lewis's river about 20 miles above it's junction with the South branch, a distance of about 50 Ms. where they informed them they might obtain fish; but on their arrival at that place finding that the salmon had not yet arrived or were not taken, they were conducted down that river to a fishery a few miles below the junction of the forks of Lewis's river about 20 Ms. further, here with some difficulty and remaining one day they purchased the salmon which they brought with them. the first 20 Ms. of their rout was up Commeap Creek and through a plain open country, the hills of the creek continued high and broken with some timber near it's borders. the ballance of their rout was though a high broken mountanous country generally well timbered with pine the soil fertile in this quarter they met with an abundance of deer and some bighorned animals. the East fork of Lewis's river they discribe as one continued rapid about 150 Yds. wide it's banks are in most places solid and perpendicular rocks, which rise to a great hight; it's hills are mountains high. on the tops of some of those hills over which they passed, the snow had not entirely disappeared, and the grass was just springing up. at the fishery on Lewis's river below the forks there is a very considerable rapid nearly as great from the information of Segt. Ordway as the great falls of the Columbia the river 200 Yds. wide. their common house at this fishery is built of split timber 150 feet long and 35 feet wide flat at top. The general course from hence to the forks of Lewis's river is a little to the West of south about 45 Ms.- The men at this season resort their fisheries while the women are employed in collecting roots. both forks of Lewis's river above their junction appear to enter a high Mountainous country.- my sick horse being much reduced and apearing to be in such an agoni of pain that there was no hope of his recovery I ordered him shot this evening. the other horses which we casterated are all nearly recovered, and I have no hesitation in declaring my beleif that the indian method of gelding is preferable to that practiced by ourselves.

[Clark, June 2, 1806] Monday June 2nd 1806 McNeal and York were Sent on a tradeing voyage over the river this morning. having exhosted all our Merchendize we were obliged to have recourse to every Subterfuge in order to prepare in the most ample manner in our power to meet that wretched portion of our journy, the Rocky Mountains, where hungar and Cold in their most regorous form assail the waried traveller; not any of us have yet forgotten our those mountains in September last, I think it probable we never Shall. Our traders McNeal and York are furnished with the buttons which Capt L-. and my Self Cut off of our Coats, Some eye water and Basilicon which we made for that purpose and Some phials of eye water and Some tin boxes which Capt L. had brought from Philadelphia. in the evening they returned with about 3 bushels of roots and Some bread haveing made a Suckcessfull voyage, not much less pleasing to us than the return of a good Cargo to an East India merchant.

Shields, Collins, Reuben & Joseph Field & Shannon Set out on a hunting excurtion to the quaw mash the lower side of Collins Creek & towards the Mountains.

Drewyer arived this evening with Neeshneparkkeeook and Hohashillpilp who had accompanied him to the lodge of the person who had our tomahawks. he obtained both the tomahawks principally by the influence of the former of those Chiefs. the one which had been Stolen we prized most as it was the private property of the late Serjt. Floyd and I was desireous of returning it to his friends. The man who had this tomahawk had purchased it from the man who had Stolen it, and was himself at the moment of their arival just expireing. his relations were unwilling to give up the tomahawk as they intended to bury it with the deceased owner, but were at length to do so for the Consideration of a handkerchief, two Strands of heeds, which drewyer gave them and two horses given by the Chiefs to be Killed agreeable to their custom at the grave of the deceased. The custom of Sacrificeing horses to the disceased appears to be Common to all the nations of the plains of the Columbia. a Wife of Neeshneeparkkeeook died Some Short time Sence, himself and her relations sacrificed horses to her. The Indians inform us that there is a plenty of Moos to the S. E. of them on the East branch of Lewis's river which they Call Tommawamah River. About noon Sergt. Ordway Frazier and Wiser returnd. with 17 Salmon and Some roots of the Cows; the distance was So great from whence they brought the fish, that most of them were nearly Spoiled. those fish were as fat as any I ever saw; Sufficiently So to cook themselves without the addition of Grease or butter; those which were Sound were extreemly delicious; their flesh is of a fine rose colour with a Small admixture of yellow. these men Set out on the 27th ulto. and in Sted of finding the fishing Shore at the distance of half a days ride as we had been informed, they did not reach the place at which they obtained their fish untill the evening of the 29th haveing traveled near 70 miles. the rout they had taken however was not a direct one; the Indians Conducted them in the first instance to the East fork of Lewis's river about 10 miles above it's junction with the South branch, a distance of about 50 miles where they informed them they might obtain fish; but on their arival at that place finding that the Salmon had not arived or were not taken, they were Conducted down that river to a fishery a fiew miles below the junction of the forks of Lewis's River about 20 miles further, here they remained one day and with some dificulty, they purchased the Salmon which they brought with them. the first 20 ms. Of their rout was up Commeap Creek and through a plain open Country, the hills of the Creek Continued high and broken with Some timber near it's borders, the ballance of their rout was through a high broken Mountanious Country. generally well timbered with pine the soil fertile. in this quarter the meet with abundance of deer and Some big-horned Animals. The East fork of Lewis's river they discribe as one Continued rapid of about 150 yards wide, it's banks are in most places Solid and perpindicular rocks, which rise to a great hight; it's hills are mountanious high. on the top of Some of those hills over which they passed, the Snow had not entirely disappeared, and the grass was just springing up. at the fishery on Lewis's river below the forks there is a very Considerable rapid, nearly as Great from the information of Sergt. Ordway as the Great falls of the Columbia the river 200 yards wide. their common house at this fishery is built of Split timber 150 feet long and 35 feet in width, flat at top. the general Course from here to the forks of Lewis's river is a little to the west of South about 45 ms. The men at this Season resort their fisheries while the womin are employed in collecting roots-. both forks above the junction of Lewis's river appear to enter a high Mountainious Country. our horses are all recovering & I have no hesitation in declareing that I believe that the Indian Method of guilding preferable to that practised by ourselves.

[Lewis, June 3, 1806] Tuesday June 3rd 1806. Our invalids are all on the recovery; Bratton is much stronger and can walk about with considerable ease. the Indian Cheif appears to be gradually recovering the uce of his limbs, and the child is nearly well; the imposthume on his neck has in a great measure subsided and left a hard lump underneath his left ear; we still continue the application of the onion poltice. at 2 P.M. The Broken arm and 3 of his wariars visited us and remained all night. Colter, Jo. Fields and Willard returned this evening with five deer and one bear of the brown speceis; the hair of this was black with a large white spot on the breast containing a small circular black spot. today the Indians dispatched an express over the mountains to travellers rest or the neighbourhood of that Creek on Clark's river in order to learn from the Oote-lash-shoots a band of the Flatheads who have wintered there, the occurrences that have taken place on the East side of the mountains during that season. this is the band which we first met with on that river. the mountains being practicable for this express we thought it probable that we could also pass, but the indians informed us that several of the creeks would yet swim our horses, that there was no grass and that the roads were extreemly deep and slipery; they inform us that we may pass conveniently in twelve or fourteen days. we have come to a resolution to remove from hence to the quawmash grounds beyond Collins's creek on the 10th to hunt in that neighbourhood a few days, if possible lay in a stock of meat and then attempt the mountains about the middle of this month. I begin to lose all hope of any dependance on the Salmon as this river will not fall sufficiently to take them before we shall leave it, and as yet I see no appearance of their runing near the shores as the indians informed us they would in the course of a few days. I find that all the salmon which they procure themselves they obtain on Lewis's river, and the distance thither is too great for us to think of sending after them even had we merchandize with which to purchase.

[Clark, June 3, 1806] Tuesday June 3rd 1806 Our invalids are all on the recovery; bratten is much Stronger and can walk about with Considerable ease. the Indian Chief appears to be gradually recovering the use of his limbs, and the child is nearly well; the inflomation on his neck Continus but the Swelling appears to Subside. we Still Continue the application of the onion poltice. at 3 P.M. the broken arm and three wariors visited us and remained all night. Colter, Jos. Fields and Willard returned this evening with five deer and one bear of the brown Species; the hair of this was black with a large white Spot on the breast containing a Small circular black Spot. (this Species of bear is Smaller than our Common black bear) this was a female bear and as our hunters informed us had cubs last year, this they judged from the length and Size of her tits &c. this bear I am Confident is not larger than the yerlin Cubs of our Country. To day the Indians dispatched an express over the mountains to Travellers rest or to the neighbourhood of that Creek on Clark's river in order to learn from a band of Flat-Heads who inhabit that river and who have probably Wintered on Clarks river near the enterance of travellers rest Creek, the occurences which have taken place on the East Side of the mountains dureing the last winter. this is the band which we first met with on that river. the Mountains being practicable for this express we thought it probable that we could also pass, but the Chiefs informs us that Several of the Creek's would yet swim our horses, that there was no grass and that the road was extreemly deep and slipery; they inform us that we may pass Conveniently in twelve or fourteen days. we have come to a resolution to remove from hence to the Quawmash Grounds beyond Colins Creek on the 10th to hunt in that neighbourhood a fiew days, if possible lay in a Stock of Meat, and then attempt the Mountains about the Middle of this month. I begin to lose all hope of any dependance on the Salmon as this river will not fall Sufficiently to take them before we Shall leave it, and as yet I see no appearance of their running near the Shore as the indians informed us they would in the course of a fiew days. I find that all the Salmon which they precure themselves they obtain on Lewis's river, and the distance thither is too great for us to think of Sending after them, even had we merchendize with which to purchase the salmon.-.

[Lewis, June 4, 1806] Wednesday June 4th 1806. about noon The 3 Cheifs left us and returned to their vilages. while they were with us we repeated the promises we had formerly made them and invited them to the Missouri with us, they declined going untill the latter end of the summer and said it was there intention to spend the ensuing winter on the East side of the Rocky mountains. they gave us no positive answer to a request which we made, that two or three of their young men should accompany me to the falls of the Missouri and there wait my return from the upper part of Maria's river where it was probable I should meet with some of the bands of the Minnetares from Fort de Prarie; that in such case I should indeavor to bring about a good understanding between those indians and themselves, which when effected they would be informed of it though the young men thus sent with me, and that on the contrary should I not be fortunate enough to meet with these people nor to prevail on them to be at peace they would equally be informed through those young men, and they might still remain on their guard with respect to them untill the whites had it in their power to give them more effectual releif. The Broken Arm invited us to his village and said he wished to speak to us before we set out, and that he had some roots to give us for our journey over the mountains; Capt. C. promised to visit him as he wished the day after tomorrow.- Sheilds returned this evening from the quawmash grounds with 2 deer which he had killed.

[Clark, June 4, 1806] Wednesday June 4th 1806 about noon the 3 chiefs left us and returned to their villages. While they were with us we repeated the promisces we had formerly made them and envited them to the Missouri with us, they declined going untill the latter end of the Summer, and Said it was their intintion to Spend the insiewing winter on the East Side of the Rocky Mountains, they gave us no positive answer to a request which we made, that two or three of their young men Should accompany Capt L. to the falls of Missouri and there wait his return from the upper part of Maria's river where it was probable he Should meet with Some of the bands of the Blakfoot Indians and Minitarres of Fort dePrarie, that in Such Case Capt L. would indeavor to bring about a good understanding between those indians and themselves, which when effected they would be informed of it through the young men thus Sent with him. and that on the contrary Should he not be fortunate enough to meet with those people, nor to provaile on them to be at peace they would equally be informed through those young men, and they might Still remain on their guard with respect to them, untill the Whites had it more in their Power to give them more effectual relief. I also urged the necessaty of Sending one or two of their Considerate men to accompany me by way of the Shoshonees on the head of Jeffersons river and about the three forks of the Missouri which whome there is most probably Some of the Chiefs of those bands of Shoshones with whome they are at war, and by which means a message Sent to that nation & good understanding brought about between the Shoshones and the Chopunnish Nations which appears to be the wish of both Nations. The Broken Arm envited us to his Village and Said he wished to Speak to us before we Set out, and that he had Some roots to give us for our journey over the mountains; I promised to visit him as he wished the day after tomorrow-. Shields returned this evining from the Quawmash grounds with two Deer which he had killed

[Lewis, June 5, 1806] Thursday June 5th 1806. Colter and Bratton were permitted to visit the indian villages today for the purpose of trading for roots and bread, they were fortunate and made a good return. we gave the indian cheif another sweat today, continuing it as long as he could possibly bear it; in the evening he was very languid but appeared still to improve in the use of his limbs. the child is recovering fast the inflamation has subsided intirely, we discontinued the poltice, and applyed a plaster of basilicon; the part is still considerably swolen and hard. in the evening R. Feilds Shannon and Labuish return from the chaise and brought with them five deer and a brown bear. among the grasses of this country I observe a large speceis which grows in moist situations; it rises to the hight of eight or ten feet, the culm is jointed, hollow, smooth, as large as a goos quill and more firm than ordinary grasses; the leaf is linnear broad and rough; it has much the appearance of the maden cain as it is called in the state of Gergia, and retains it's virdure untill late in the fall. this grass propegates principally by the root which is horizontal and perennial. a second speceis grows in tussucks and rises to the hight of six or eight feet; it seems to delight in the soil of the river bottoms which possess a greater mixture of sand than the hills in this neighbourhood. this is also a harsh course grass; it appears to be the same which is called the Corn grass in the Southern states, and the foxtail in Virginia. a third speceis resembles the cheet, tho the horses feed on it very freely. a fourth and most prevalent speceis is a grass which appears to be the same called the blue grass common to many parts of the United States; it is common to the bottom as well as the uplands, is now seeding and is from 9 inches to 2 feet high; it affords an excellent pasture for horses and appears to bear the frosts and snow better than any grass in our country; I therefore regret very much that the seed will not be ripe before our probable departure. this is a fine soft grass and would no doubt make excellent hay if cultivated. I do not find the greenswoard here which we met with on the lower part of the Columbia. there are also several speceis of the wild rye to be met with in the praries. among the plants and shrubs common to our contry I observe here the seven bark, wild rose, vining honeysickle, sweet willow, red willow, longleafed pine, Cattail or cooper's flag, lamsquarter, strawberry, raspberry, tonge grass, musterd, tanzy, sinquefield, horsemint, coltsfoot, green plantin, cansar weed, elder, shoemate and several of the pea blume flowering plants.-

[Clark, June 5, 1806] Thursday June 5th 1806 Colter and Bratten were permitted to visit the Indian Village to day for the purpose of tradeing for roots and bread, they were fortunate and made a good return. we gave the Indian Cheif another Sweat to-day, continuing it as long as he could bear it. in the evening he was very languid but Still to improve in the use of his limbs. the Child is revovereing fast. I applied a plaster of Sarve made of the Rozen of the long leafed pine, Beas wax and Beare oil mixed, which has Subsided the inflomation entirely, the part is Considerably Swelled and hard-. in the evening Reuben Fields, G. Shannon, Labiech, & Collins returned from the chaise and brought with them five deer and a brown Bear.

Among the Grasses of this Country I observe a large Species which grows in moist Situations; it rises to the hight of Eight or ten feet, the Culm is jointed, hollow, Smooth, as large as a goose quill, and more firm than ordinary grass; the leaf is linner broad and rough; it has much the appearance of the Meadin Cain as it is Called in the Southern parts of the U States, and retains it's virdue untill late in the fall. this grass propegates principally by the Root which is horozontal and perennial.-. a Second Species grows in tussucks and rises to the hight of Six or Eight feet; it Seams to delight in the Soil of the river bottoms which possess agreater mixture of Sand than the hills in this neighbourhood. this is also a harsh Course grass; it appears to be the Same which is Called the Corn grass in the Southern States, and the Foxtail in Virginia. a third Species resembles the cheet, tho the horses feed on it very freely. a fouth and most prevalent Species is a grass which appears to be the Same Called the blue Grass common to maney parts of the United States; it is common to the bottoms as well as the uplands, is now Seeding and is from 9 inches to 2 feet high; it affords an excellent paterage for horses and appears to bear the frost and Snow better than any grass in our Country; I therefore regrete very much that the Seed will not be ripe before our probable departure. this is a fine Soft grass and would no doubt make excellent hay if cultivated. I do not find the Green Sword here which we met with on the lower part of the Columbia. There are also Several Species of the wild Rye to be met with in the praries. among the plants and Shrubs common to our Country I observe here the Seven bark, Wild rose, vineing honey suckle, Sweet willow, red willow, long leafed pine, Cattail or Coopers Flag. Lambs quarter, Strawberries, Raspberries, Goose berries, tongue grass, Mustard, tanzy, Sinquefield, horse mint, water penerial, elder, Coalts foot, Green Plantin, canser weed, Shoemate, and Several of the pea blume flowering plants.-. Frazier who had permission to visit the Twisted Hairs Lodge at the distance of ten or twelve miles did not return this evening-. The river falls in course of the day and rises Some at night as will be Seen by the remarks in the Diary of the weather. this most probably is the melding of the Snows dureing the day &c.

[Lewis, June 6, 1806] Friday June 6th 1806. This morning Frazier returned having been in quest of some roots and bread which had left at the lodg of the Twisted hair when on his way to the fishery on Lewis's river. the Twisted hair came with him but I was unable to converse with him for the want of an interpreter, Drewyer being absent with Capt. C. This Cheif left me in the evening and returned to his village. Capt C. Visited the Broken Arm today agreeably to his promise; he took with him Drewyer and several others. they were received in a friendly manner. The Broken Arm informed Capt. C. that the nation would not pass the mountain untill the latter end of the summer, and that with rispect to the young men whom we had requested should accompany us to the falls of the Missouri, were not yet scelected for that purpose nor could they be so untill there was a meeting of the nation in counsil. that this would happen in the course of ten or twelve days as the whole of the lodges were about to remove to the head of the Commeap Creek in the plain near Lewis's river, that when they had assembled themselves they would hold a council and scelect the young men. that if we set out previously to that period the men would follow us. we therefore do not calculate on any assistance from them as guides, but depend more upon engageing some of the Ootlashshoots in the neighborhood of Travellers rest C. for that purpose. The broken arm gave Capt. C. a few dryed Quawmas roots as a great present, but in our estimation those of cows are much better, I am confident they are much more healthy. The men who were with Capt. C. obtained a good store of roots and bread in exchange for a number of little notions, using the Yanke phrase, with which their own enginuity had principally furnished them. on examination we find that our whole party have an ample store of bread and roots for our voyage, a circumstance not unpleasing. They retuned at 5 P.M. shortly after which we were visited by Hohastillpilp the two young Cheifs who gave us the horses in behalf of the nation some time since and several others, who remained all night. The Kooskooske is about 150 Yds. wide at this place and discharges a vast body of water; notwithstanding it high state the water remains nearly transparent, and it's temperature appeas to be quite as cold as that of our best springs. we meet with a beautifull little bird in this neighbourhood about the size and somewhat the shape of the large spar-row. it is reather longer in proportion to it's bulk than the sparrow. it measures 7 inches from the extremity of the beek to that of the tail, the latter occupying 21/2 inches. the beak is reather more than half an inch in length, and is formed much like the Virginia nitingale; it is thick and large for a bird of it's size; wide at the base, both chaps convex, and pointed, the uper exceeds the under chap a little is somewhat curved and of a brown colour; the lower chap of a greenish yellow. the eye full reather large and of a black colour both puple and iris. the plumage is remarkably delicate; that of the neck and head is of a fine orrange yellow and red, the latter predominates on the top of the head and arround the base of the beak from whence it graduly deminishes & towards the lower part of the neck, the orrange yellow prevails most; the red has the appearance of being laid over a ground of yellow. the breast, the sides, rump and some long feathers which lie between the legs and extend underneath the tail are of a fine orrange yellow. the tail, back and wings are black, ecept a small stripe of yellow on the outer part of the middle joint of the wing, 1/4 of an inch wide and an inch in length. the tail is composed of twelve feathers of which those in the center are reather shortest, and the plumage of all the feathers of the tail is longest on that side of the quill next the center of the tail. the legs and feet are black, nails long and sharp; it has four toes on each foot, of which three are forward and one behind; that behind is as long as the two outer of the three toes in front.

[Clark, June 6, 1806] Friday June 6th 1806 I visited the Broken Arm to day agreeable to my promis of the 4th inst. and took with me Drewyer & three other men I was receved in a friendly manner. The broken Arm informed me that maney of the Small chiefs of the different Bands of his nation had not heard our word from our own mouths, Several of them were present and was glad to See me &c. I repeeted in part what had been Said in Council before. The Broken arm told me that the nation would not pass the mountains untill the latter part of the Summer, and with respect to the young men who we had requested to accompany us to the falls of Missouri, were not yet Selected for that purpose nor could they be So untill they had a Meeting of the Nation in Council. that this would happen in the Course of ten or 12 days as the whole of the Lodges were about to Move to the head of Commeap Creek in the Plain of Lewis's river, that when they held a council they would Select two young men. that if we Set out previously to that time the men would follow us. we therefore do not Calculate any assistance from them as guides, but depend more upon engageing Some of the Oatlash-shoots on Clarks river in the neighbouringhood of Travellers rest C. for that purpose. The Broken Arm gave me a fiew Quawmash roots as a great preasent, but in my estimation those of Cows is much better. I am Confident they are much more healthy. The Broken Arm informed me that they had latterly been informed that a party of the Shoshones had arived at the Ye-E-al-po Nation who reside to the South of the enterance of Kooskooske into Lewis's river. and had informed that people that their nation (the Shoshones) had received the talk which was given their relations on the head of the East fork of Lewis's river last fall, and were resolved to pursue our Councils, and had came foward for the purpose of makeing peace with them, and allso with the Chopunnish &c. that they had Sent Several men in Serch of those people with a view to bring them to Lewis's river at which place the Broken Arm informed me he Should meet them and Smoke the pipe of peace. which he Should afterwards Send by with Some of his Chiefs in company with those Shoshones to their nation and confirm a piece which never Should be broken on his part. he produced two pipes one of which he said was as a present to me the other he intended to Send to the Shoshones &c. and requested me to take one, I receved the one made in the fascion of the

Country, the other which was of Stone curiously inlaid with Silver in the common form which he got from the Shoshones. I deckorated the Stem of this pipe with blue ribon and white wampom and informed the Chief this was the emblem of peace with us.

The men who accompanied me obtained a good Store of roots and bread in exchange for a number of little notions, useing the Yanke phrase, with which their own enginuiety had principally furnished them. on examonation we find our whole party have a Sufficient Store of bread and roots for our Voyage. a Circumstance not unpleasing-.

I returned at 4 P. M followed by Hohastillpilp the 2 young Chiefs who gave us the horses in behalf of the nation Some time Sence, the young man who gave us the horse at Collins Creek to kill as we Came up, and Several others. I met the twisted hair and two other indians with Frazier on the opposit bank from our Camp this Morning & Sent him over to our Camp. I met him this evening on his return home. he informed me he could not accompany us across the mountains as his brother was Sick &c.-.

[Clark, June 6, 1806]
The Chopunnish call the Crow Indians Up-shar-look-kar

Chopunnish name for Sin-sho-cal Dearbourne R ditto- do- Cal la mar-Sha mosh Meddesons ditto- do- Co-ma win-nim Maria River ditto ditto- Ta-ki-a-ki-a Mescle Shell R ditto- ditto Wah-wo-ko-ye-o-cose is th _____ ditto do- Rockejhone- Elk river

ditto do- Koos-koos-an-nim-a the little Missouri ditto- do- Walch-Nim-mah- Knife R ditto- do Ni-hi-Sir-te- C. R

[Lewis, June 7, 1806] Saturday June 7th 1806. The two young Cheifs who visited last evening returned to their village on Commeap C. with some others of the natives. Sergt. Gass, McNeal, Whitehouse and Goodrich accompanyed them with a view to procure some pack or lash ropes in exchange for parts of an old sain, fish giggs, peices of old iron, old files and some bullets. they were also directed to procure some bags for the purpose of containing our roots & bread. in the evening they all returned except Whitehouse and Goodrich who remained all night. they procured a few strings but no bags. Hohastillpilp passed the river today and brought over a horse which he gave Frazier one of our party who had previously made him a present of a pair of Cannadian shoes or shoe-packs. Drewyer set out on a hunting excurtion up Collins's Creek this evening. we wish to leave the deer in the neighbourhood of the quawmash plains undisturbed untill the 10th when we intend removing thither to lay in some meat for our voyage over the Mountains. our party are much engaged in preparing their saddles arranging their loads provisions &c for our departure. There is a speceis of cherry which grows in this neighbourhood in sitations like the Choke cherry or near the little rivulets and wartercouses. it seldom grows in clumps or from the same cluster of roots as the choke cherry dose. the stem is simple branching reather diffuse stem the cortex is of a redish dark brown and reather smooth. the leaf is of the ordinary dexture and colour of those of most cherries, it is petiolate; a long oval 1 1/4 inhes in length and 1/2 an inch in width, obtuse, margin so finely serrate that it is scarcely perseptable & smooth. the peduncle is common 1 inch in length, branch proceeding from the extremities as well as the sides of the branches, celindric gradually tapering; the secondary peduncles are about 1/2 an inch in length scattered tho proceeding more from the extremity of the common peduncle and are each furnished with a small bracted. the parts of fructification are much like those discribed of the choke cherry except that the petals are reather longer as is the calix reather deeper. the cherry appears to be half grown, the stone is begining to be hard and is in shape somewhat like that of the plumb; it appears that when ripe it would be as large as the Kentish cherry, which indeed the growth of the bush somewhat resembles; it rises about 6 or 8 feet high

[Clark, June 7, 1806] Saurday June 7th 1806. The two young cheafs and other Indians who accompanied them Crossed the river and returned to their Village this morning after brackfast; Shabono Sergt Gass McNeal, Whitehouse & Goodrich accompanied them for the purpose of purchaseing or exchangeing old peces of Sane, fish gig, peces of iron, bullets, and old files and Such articles as they Could raise for ropes and Strings for to lash their loads, and bags to Cary their roots in Sergt. Gass, Shabono & McNeal returned at 2 P M haveing precured a String each only. Whitehouse and Goodrich continued at the Village all night. Hohastillpilp crossed the river to day and brought over a horse and gave it to Frazier one of our party who had made him a present previously of a Par of Canidian Shoes. one of our men informed me one of the young Chiefs who had given us two horses already was in Serch of one which he intended to give to me. George Drewyer Set out on a hunting excurtion up Collins's Creek alone. our party are all much engaged in prepareing Sadles and packing up their Stores of Provisions &c.- The Flat Head river is about 150 yards wide at this place and discharges a vast body of water; notwithstanding it's high State the water remains nearly transparent, and it's temperature appears to be quit as cold as that of our best Springs. we met with a butifull little bird in this neighbourhood about the Size and Somewhat the Shape of the large Sparrow. it measures 7 inches from the extremity of the beak to that of the tail, the latter Occupying 2 1/2 inches. the beak is reather more than half an inch in length, and is formed much like the Virginia Nightingal; red bd. it is thick and large for a bird of it's size, wide at the base, both Chaps convex, and pointed, the upper exceeds the under chap a little is Somewhat cirved and of a brown Colour; the lower chap of a Greenish yellow. the eye full reather large and of a black colour both puple and iris. the plumage is remarkably delicate; that of the neck and head is of a fine orrange yellow and red. the latter predomonates on the top of the head and around the base of the beak from whence it gradually diminishes towards the lower part of the Neck, the orring yellow prevails most, the red has the Appearance of haveing been laid over a Ground of yellow. the breast, the Sides, rump and some long feathers which lie between the legs extend underneath the tail is of a fine orrange yellow. the tail, back and wings are black, except a Small Strip of yellow on the outer part of the Middle joint of the wing, 1/4 of an inch wide and an inch in length. the tail is composed of 12 feathers of which those in the Center are reather Shortest, and the plumage of all the feathers of the tail is longest on that Side of the quill next to the Center of the tail. the legs and feet are black, nails long and Sharp; it has four toes on each foot, of which three are forward and one behind; that behind is as long as the two outer of the three toes in front

[Lewis, June 8, 1806] Sunday June 8th 1806. Drewyer returned this morning from the chase without having killed anything. his hose left him last night, he pursued him but did not overtake him untill he had nearly reached our camp. The sick Cheif is fast on the recovery, he can bear his weight on his legs, and has acquired a considerable portion of strength. the child is nearly well; Bratton has so far recovered that we cannot well consider him an invalid any longer, he has had a tedious illness which he boar with much fortitude and firmness.- The Cutnose visited us today with ten or twelve warriors; two of the latter were Y-e-let-pos a band of the Chopunnish nation residing on the South side of Lewis's river whom we have not previously seen. the band with which we have been most conversent call themselves pel-late-pal-ler. one of the yeletpos exchanged his horse for an indifferent one of ours and received a tomahawk to boot; this tomahawk was one for which Capt. C. had given another in exchange with the Clahclel-lah Chief at the rapids of the Columbia. we also exchanged two other of our indifferent horses with unsound backs for much better horses in fine order without any consideration but the horse itself. several foot rarces were run this evening between the indians and our men. the indians are very active; one of them proved as fleet as Drewer and R. Fields, our swiftest runners. when the racing was over the men divided themselves into two parties and played prison base, by way of exercise which we wish the men to take previously to entering the mountain; in short those who are not hunters have had so little to do that they are geting reather lazy and slouthfull.- after dark we had the violin played and danced for the amusement of ourselves and the indians.- one of the indians informed us that we could not pass the mountains untill the full of the next moon or about the first of July, that if we attempted it sooner our horses would be at least three days travel without food on the top of the mountain; this information is disagreable inasmuch as it causes some doubt as to the time at which it will be most proper for us to set out. however as we have no time to loose we will wrisk the chanches and set out as early as the indians generally think it practicable or the middle of this month

[Clark, June 8, 1806] Sunday June 8th 1806 Drewyer returned this morning from the chase without killing any thing. his horse left him last night and he prosued him near our camp before he cought him. The Sick Chief is much mended, he can bear his weight on his legs and recovers Strength. the Child has nearly recovered. The Cut nose and ten or 12 came over today to visit us, two of those were of the tribes from the plains of Lewis's river whome we had not before Seen; one of those men brought a horse which I gave a tomahawk which I had exchanged for with the Chief of the Clahclahlah's Nation below the Great rapids of Columbia, and broken-down horse which was not able to Cross the mountains. we also exchanged 2 of our inedefent horses for Sound back horses. in the evening Several foot races were run by the men of our party and the Indians; after which our party divided and played at prisoners base untill night. after dark the fiddle was played and the party amused themselves in danceing. one of those Indians informed us that we could not cross the mountains untill the full of the next moon, or about the 1st of July. if we attempted it Sooner our horses would be three days without eateing, on the top of the Mountns. this information is disagreeable to us, in as much as it admits of Some doubt, as to the time most proper for us to Set out. at all events we Shall Set out at or about the time which the indians Seem to be generally agreed would be the most proper. about the middle of this month

[Lewis, June 9, 1806] Monday June 9th 1806. This morning we had all our horses brought up and indeavoured to exchange five or shix with the Indians in consequence of their having unsound backs but succeeded in exchanging one only. Hohastillpilp with several of the natives who visited us yesterday took leave of us and set out for the plains near Lewis's river where the nation are about to assemble themselves. The broken arm made us a short visit this morning and took leave of us, being about to set out with his village today in order to join the nation at their rendezvouz on Lewis's R. The Cutnose or Neeshneeparkkeeook borrowed a horse and rode down the Kooskooske River a few miles this morning in quest of some young eagles which he intends raising for the benifit of their feathers; he returned soon after with a pair of young Eagles of the grey kind; they were nearly grown and pretty well feathered. in the evening the young Chief who gave both Capt. C. and myself a horse some time since, came to our camp with a party of young men and remained all night. this evening one of our party obtained a very good horse for an indifferent one by giving the indian an old leather shirt in addition. we eat the last of our meat yesterday evening and have lived on roots today. our party seem much elated with the idea of moving on towards their friends and country, they all seem allirt in their movements today; they have every thing in readiness for a move, and notwithstanding the want of provision have been amusing themselves very merrily today in runing footraces pitching quites, prison basse &c. the river has been falling for several days and is now lower by near six feet than it has been; this we view as a strong evidence that the great body of snow has left the mountains, though I do not conceive that we are as yet loosing any time as the roads is in many parts extreemly steep rocky and must be dangerous if wet and slippry; a few days will dry the roads and will also improve the grass.

[Clark, June 9, 1806] Moday June 9th 1806 We had all of our horses brought up and attempted to exchange our Sore back and most indifferent horses with the indians for Sound back horses, we exchanged one only. Hohasillpilp took his leave of us and Set out for the Plains of Lewises river, with Several of the nativs who Visited us yesterday. The broken arm came over and continued a fiew minits with us this morning, and also took his leave of us & Set out with his Village for the plains of Lewis's river. The Cut nose borrowed a horse and rode down the flathead river a fiew miles to take Some young Eagles, which he intends to raise for their feathers. in the evening one of the young Cheifs who had given both Capt Lewis and my Self a horse came to our camp accompanied by 10 of his people and continued with us all night. one of our men exchanged a very indefferent horse for a very good one. our party exolted with the idea of once more proceeding on towards thier friends and Country are elert in all their movements and amuse themselves by pitching quates, Prisoners bast running races &c-.

The flat head river is Still falling fast and nearly as low as it was at the time we arrived at this place. this fall of water is what the nativs have informed us was a proper token for us. when this river fell the Snows would be Sufficiently melted for us to Cross the Mountains. the greater length of time we delayed after that time, the higher the grass would grow on th Mountains-.

[Lewis, June 10, 1806] Tuesday June 10th 1806. This morning we arrose early and had our horses collected except one of Cruzatt's and one of Whitehouse's, which were not to be found; after a surch of some hours Cruzatt's horse was obtained and the indians promised to find the other and bring it to us at the quawmash flatts where we purpose encamping a few days. at 11 A.M. we set out with the party each man being well mounted and a light load on a second horse, beside which we have several supenemary horses in case of accedent or the want of provision, we therefore feel ourselves perfectly equiped for the mountains. we ascended the river hills which are very high and about three miles in extent our sourse being N. 22° E. thence N. 15 W. 2 m to Collins's creek . thence due North 5 m. to the Eastern border of the quawmash flatts where we encamped near the place we first met with the Chopunnish last fall. the pass of Collins's Creek was deep and extreemly difficult tho we passed without sustaining further injury than weting some of our roots and bread. the country through which we passed is extreemly fertile and generally free of stone, is well timbered with several speceis of fir, long leafed pine and larch. the undergrowth is chooke cherry near the water courses, black alder, a large speceis of redroot now in blume, a growth which resembles the pappaw in it's leaf and which bears a burry with five valves of a deep perple colour, two speceis of shoemate sevenbark, perple haw, service berry, goosburry, a wild rose honeysuckle which bears a white berry, and a species of dwarf pine which grows about ten or twelve feet high. bears a globular formed cone with small scales, the leaves are about the length and much the appearance of the common pitch pine having it's leaves in fassicles of two; in other rispects they would at a little distance be taken for the young plants of the long leafed pine. there are two speceis of the wild rose both quinqui petallous and of a damask red but the one is as large as the common red rose of our gardens. I observed the apples of this speceis last fall to be more than triple the size of those of the ordinary wild rose; the stem of this rose is the same with the other tho the leaf is somewhat larger. after we encamped this evening we sent out our hunters; Collins killed a doe on which we suped much to our satisfaction. we had scarcely reached Collins's Creek before we were overtaken by a party of Indians who informed us that they were going to the quawmash flatts to hunt; their object I beleive is the expectation of bing fed by us in which how ever kind as they have been we must disappoint them at this moment as it is necessary that we should use all frugallaty as well as employ every exertion to provide meat for our journey. they have encamped with us. we find a great number of burrowing squirels about our camp of which we killed several; I eat of them and found them quite as tender and well flavored as our grey squirel. saw many sand hill crains and some ducks in the slashey glades about this place.

[Clark, June 10, 1806] Tuesday June 10th 1806. rose early this morning and had all the horses Collected except one of Whitehouses horses which could not be found, an Indian promised to find the horse and bring him on to us at the quawmash fields at which place we intend to delay a fiew days for the laying in Some meat by which time we Calculate that the Snows will have melted more off the mountains and the grass raised to a sufficient hight for our horses to live. we packed up and Set out at 11 A M we Set out with the party each man being well mounted and a light load on a 2d horse, besides which we have several supernumary horses in case of accident or the want of provisions, we therefore feel ourselves perfectly equiped for the Mountains. we assended the hills which are very high and about three miles in extent our course being N. 22° E, thence N.

15° W 2 ms. to Collins Creek. Thence North 5 Miles to the Eastern boarders of the Quawmash flatts where we encamped near the place I first met with the Chopunnish Nation last fall. the pass of Collins Creek was deep and extreemly difficult tho we passed without sustaining further injury than wetting some of our roots and bread. The Country through which we passed is extreemly fertile and generally free from Stone, is well timbered with several Species of fir, long leafed pine and Larch . the undergrowth is choke cherry near the watercourses, black alder, a large species of red root now in blume, a Growth which resembles the poppaw in it's leaf and which bears a berry with five valves of a deep purple colour, two species of Shoemate, Seven bark, perple haw, Service berry, Goose berry, wildrose, honey suckle which bears a white berry, and a Species of dwarf pine which grows about 10 or 12 feet high, bears a globarlar formed cone with Small Scales, the leaf is about the length and much the appearance of the pitch pine haveing it's leaves in fassicles of two; in other respects they would at a little distance be taken for the young plants of the long leafed pine. There are two Species of the wild rose both quinque petallous and of a damask red, but the one is as large as the common red rose of our guardens. I observed the apples of these Species last fall to be more than triple the Size of those of the ordinary wild rose; the Stem of this rose is the Same with the other tho the leaf is somewhat larger. after we encamped this evening we Sent out our hunters; Collins killed a doe on which we Suped much to our Satisfaction, we had not reached the top of the river hills before we were overtaken by a party of 8 Indians who informed me that they were gowing to the quawmash flatts to hunt; their object I belive is the expectation of being fed by us in which however kind as they have been we must disappoint them at this moment as it is necessary that we Should use all frugallaty as well as employ every exertion to provide meat for our journey. they have encamped with us. we find a great number of burrowing Squirels about our camp of which we killed Several; I eate of them and found them quit as tender and well flavd. as our grey squirel. Saw many Sand hill crains and Some ducks in the Slashey Glades about this place-.

[Lewis, June 11, 1806] Wednesday June 11th 1806. All our hunters were out this morning by daylight; Labuish and Gibson only proved successfull, the former killed a black bear of the brown speceis and a very large buck, the latter also killed a fine fat buck. five of the Indians also turned out and hunted untill noon, when they returned without having killed anything; at three P.M. the left us on their return to ther villages. previous to their departure one of our men exchanged an indifferent horse with one of them for a very good one. in the evening our hunters resumed the chase; as game has become scarce and shye near our camp they were directed to hunt at a greater distance and therefore set out prepared to remain all night and make a mornings hunt in grounds not recently frequented. Whitehouse returned this morning to our camp on the Kooskooske in surch of his horse.- As I have had frequent occasion to mention the plant which the Chopunnish call quawmash I shall here give a more particular discription of that plant and the mode of preparing it for food as practiced by the Chopunnish and others in the vicinity of the Rocky Mountains with whom it forms much the greatest portion of their subsistence. we have never met with this plant but in or adjacent to a piny or fir timbered country, and there always in the open grounds and glades; in the Columbian vally and near the coast it is to be found in small quantities and inferior in size to that found in this neighbourhood and in the high rich flatts and vallees within the rocky mountains. it delights in a black rich moist soil, and even grows most luxuriantly where the land remains from 6 to nine inches under water untill the seed are nearly perfect which in this neighbourhood or on these flats is about the last of this month. neare the river where I had an opportunity of observing it the seed were begining to ripen on the 9th inst. and the soil was nearly dry. it seems devoted to it's particular soil and situation, and you will seldom find it more than a few feet from the inundated soil tho within it's limits it grows very closely in short almost as much so as the bulbs will permit; the radix is a tunicated bulb, much the consistence shape and appearance of the onion, glutanous or somewhat slymy when chewed and almost tasteless and without smell in it's unprepared state; it is white except the thin or outer tunicated scales which are few black and not succulent; this bulb is from the size of a nutmeg to that of a hens egg and most commonly of an intermediate size or about as large as an onion of one years growth from the seed. the radicles are numerous, reather large, white, flexable, succulent and diverging. the foliage consists of from one to four seldom five radicale, linear sessile and revolute pointed leaves; they are from 12 to 18 inches in length and from 1 to 3/4 of an inch in widest part which is near the middle; the uper disk is somewhat groved of a pale green and marked it's whole length with a number of small longitudinal channels; the under disk is a deep glossy green and smooth. the leaves sheath the peduncle and each other as high as the surface of the earth or about 2 inches; they are more succulent than the grasses and less so than most of the fillies hyesinths &c.- the peduncle is soletary, proceeds from the root, is columner, smooth leafless and rises to the hight of 2 or 21/2 feet. it supports from 10 to forty flowers which are each supported by seperate footstalk of 1/2 an inch in length scattered without order on the upper portion of the peduncle. the calix is a partial involucret situated at the base of the footstalk of each flower on the peduncle; it is long thin and begins to decline as soon as the corolla expands. the corolla consists of six long oval, obtusly pointed skye blue or water coloured petals, each about 1 inch in length; the corolla is regular as to the form and size of the petals but irregular as to their position, five of them are placed near ech other pointing upward while one stands horizantally or pointing downwards, they are inserted with a short claw on the extremity of the footstalk at the base of the germ; the corolla is of course inferior; it is also shriveling, and continues untill the seeds are perfect. The stamens are perfect, six in number; the filaments each elivate an anther, near their base are flat on the inside and rounded on the outer terminate in a subulate point, are bowed or bent upwards, inserted on the inner side and on the base of the claws of the petals, below the germ, are equal both with rispect to themselves and the corolla, smooth & membraneous. the Anther is oblong, obtusely pointed, 2 horned or forked at one end and furrowed longitudinally with four channels, the upper and lower of which seem almost to divide it into two loabs, incumbent patent, membranous, very short, naked, two valved and fertile with pollen, which last is of a yellow colour— the anther in a few hours after the corolla unfolds, bursts, discharges it's pollen and becomes very minute and shrivled; the above discription of the anther is therefore to be understood of it at the moment of it's first appearance. the pistillum is only one, of which, the germ is triangular reather swolen on the sides, smooth superior, sessile, pedicelled, short in proportion to the corolla atho wide or bulky; the style is very long or longer than the stamens, simple, cilindrical, bowed or bent upwards, placed on the top of the germ, membranous shrivels and falls off when the pericarp has obtained its full size. the stigma is three cleft very minute, & pubescent. the pericarp is a capsule, triangular, oblong, obtuse, and trilocular with three longitudinal valves. the seed so far as I could judge are numerous not very minute and globelar.- soon after the seeds are mature the peduncle and foliage of this plant perishes, the grownd becomes dry or nearly so and the root encreases in size and shortly becomes fit for use; this happens about the middle of July when the natives begin to collect it for use which they continue untill the leaves of the plant attain some size in the spring of the year. when they have collected a considerable quantity of these roots or 20 30 bushels which they readily do by means of stick sharpened at one end, they dig away the surface of the earth forming a circular concavity of 21/2 feet in the center and 10 feet in diameter; they next collect a parsel of split dry wood with which they cover this bason in the grown perhaps a foot thick, they next collect a large parsel of stones of about 4 or 6 lbs. weight which are placed on the dry wood; fire is then set to the wood which birning heats the stones; when the fire has subsided and the stones are sufficiently heated which are nearly a red heat, they are adjusted in such manner in the whole as to form as level a surface as pissible, a small quantity of earth is sprinkled over the stones and a layer of grass about an inch thick is put over the stones; the roots, which have been previously devested of the black or outer coat and radicles which rub off easily with the fingers, are now laid on in a conical pile, are then covered with a layer of grass about 2 or 3 inches thick; water is now thrown on the summit of the pile and passes through the roots and to the hot stones at bottom; some water is allso poared arround the edges of the hole and also finds its way to the hot stones; as soon as they discover from the quantity of steem which issues that the water has found its way generally to the hot stones, they cover the roots and grass over with earth to the debth of four inches and then build a fire of dry wood all over the connical mound which they continue to renew through the course of the night or for ten or 12 hours after which it is suffered to cool two or three hours when the earth and grass are removed and the roots thus sweated and cooked with steam are taken out, and most commonly exposed to the sun on scaffoalds untill they become dry, when they are black and of a sweet agreeable flavor. these roots are fit for use when first taken from the pitt, are soft of a sweetish tast and much the consistency of a roasted onion; but if they are suffered to remain in bulk 24 hour after being cooked they spoil. if the design is to make bread or cakes of these roots they undergo a second process of baking being previously pounded after the fist baking between two stones untill they are reduced to the consistency of dough and then rolled in grass in cakes of eight or ten lbs are returned to the sweat intermixed with fresh roots in order that the steam may get freely to these loaves of bread. when taken out the second time the women make up this dough into cakes of various shapes and sizes usually from 1/2 to 3/4 of an inch thick and expose it on sticks to dry in the sun, or place it over the smoke of their fires.- the bread this prepared if kept free from moisture will keep sound for a great length of time. this bread or the dryed roots are frequently eaten alone by the natives without further preparation, and when they have them in abundance they form an ingredient in almost every dish they prepare. this root is pallateable but disagrees with me in every shape I have ever used it.

[Clark, June 11, 1806] Wednesday June 11th 1806 All of our hunters were out by daylight this Morning. Labeech and Shann was the only Suckcessull hunters, Labeech killed a Black bear and a large buck, and Gibson killed a very fat Buck. five of the indians also turned out and hunted untill near Meridn. without having killed any thing. at 3 P M they all packed up and returned to their village. one of our men exchanged an indifferent horse for a verey good one with those people before they left us. in the evening all our hunters turned out in different directions with a view to find some probable Spot of killing deer and were directed to lay out all night and hunt in the morning early. Whitehouse returned this morning to our camp on the Kooskooske in Serch of his horse.

As I have had frequent occasion to mention the plant which the Chopunnish and other nations of the Columbia call Quawmash I Shall here give a more particular discription of that plant and the mode of prepareing it for food as practiced by the Chopinnish and others in the vicinity of the Rocky Mountains with whome it forms much the greatest portion of their Subsistence. we have never met with this plant but in or adjacent to a piney or fir timbered Country, and there always in the open grounds and glades; in the Columbian Vally and near the Coast it is to be found in small quantities and inferior in Size to that found in this neighbourhood or on those high rich flatts and vallies within the rocky moun-tains. it delights in a black rich moist Soil, and even grows most luxuriently where the lands remain from 6 to 9 inches under water untill the seed are nearly perfect, which in this neighbourhood or on those flatts is about the last of this month. near the river where I had an oppertunity of observing it, the Seed were beginning to ripen on the 9th inst. and the Soil was nearly dry. it seems devoted to it's particular Soil and Situation, and you will Seldom find more than a fiew feet from an inundated Soil tho within it's limits it grows very closely. in short almost as much so as the bulbs will permit. the radix is a tumicated bulb, much the consistence Shape and appearance of the Onion, glutinous or somewhat Slymey when chewed and almost tasteless and without smell in it's unprepared state; it is white except the thin or outer tumicated scales which are flew black and not Suculent; this bulb is from the Size of a nutmeg to that of a hen egg and most commonly of an intermediate size or about as large as a common onion of one years growth from the Seed. the radicles are noumerous, reather large, white, flexeable, Succulent and deviding the foliage consists of from one to four seldom five radicals, liner Sessile and revolute pointed leaves; they are from 12 to 18 inches in length and from 1 to 3/4 of an inch in widest part which is nearest the middle; the upper disk is Somewhat groved of a pale green and marked it's whole length with a number of Small longitudinal channels; the under disk is of a deep glossy green and Smooth. the leaves sheath the peduncle and each other as high as the Surface of the earth or about 2 inches; they are more succulent than the grasses and less so than most of the lillies hyisinths &c.- the peduncle is soletary, proceeds from the root, is columner, smooth and leafless and rises to the hight of 2 or 21/2 feet. it supports from 10 to 40 flowers which are each surported by a Seperate footstalk of 1/2 an inch in length scattered without order on the upper portion of the peduncle. the calix is a partial involucre or involucret Situated at the base of the footstalk of each flower on the peduncle; it is long thin and begins to decline as soon as the corrolla expands. the corolla consists of five long oval obtusely pointed Skye blue or water coloured petals, each about 1 inch in length; the Corolla is regular as to the form and size of the petals but irregular as to their position, five of them are placed near each other pointing upwards while one stands horozontially, or pointing downwards, they are inserted with a Short Claw on the extremity of the footstalk at the base of the germ; the corolla is of course inferior; it is also shriveling, and continues untill the Seed are perfect. The Stamens are perfect, Six in number; the falaments each elivate an anther, near their base are flat on the inner side and rounded on the outer, termonate in a subulate point, and bowed or bent upwards inserted on the inner Side and on the base of the Claws of the petals, below the germ, are equal both with respect to themselves and the Corolla, Smooth membranous. the Anther is oblong obtusely pointed, 2 horned or forked at one end and furrowed longitudinally with four channels, the upper and lower of which Seem almost to divide it into two loabs, incumbent, patent, membranous, very short, necked, two valved and fertile with pollen, which last is of a yellow colour. the Anther in a fiew hours after the Corolla unfoalds, bursts discharges it's pollen and becomes very manute and chrivled; the above discription of the Anther is therefore to be understood of it, at the moment of it's first appearance. the pistillum is only one, of which the Germ is triangular reather Swolen on the Sides, Smooth, Superior, Sessile, pedicelled, Short in proportion to the Corolla tho wide or bulky; the Style is very long or longer than the stamens, simple, cilindrical, bowed or bent upwards, placed on the top of the germ, membranous shrivels and falls off when the pericarp has obtained it's full Size.

the Stigma is three clefts very manute and pubescent. the pericarp is a capsule, triangular, oblong, obtuse, and trilocular with three longitudinal valves. the Seed So far as I could judge are noumerous not very manute and globilar.- Soon after the seed are mature the peduncle and foliage of this plant perishes, the ground becoms dry or nearly so and the root increases in size and shortly become fit for use; this happens about the middle of July when the nativs begin to collect it for use which they continue untill the leaves of the plant obtain Some Size in the Spring of the year. when they have Collected a considerable quantity of these roots or 20 or 30 bushels which they readily do by means of Sticks Sharpened at one end, they dig away the surface of the earth forming a cercular concavity of 21/2 feet in the center and 10 feet in diameter; they next collect a parcel of dry split wood with which they cover this bason from the bottom perhaps a foot thick, they next collect a parcel of Stones from 4 to 6 lb. weight which are placed on the dry wood; fire is then Set to the wood which burning heats the Stones; when the fire has subsided and the Stones are sufficiently heated which are nearly a red heat, they are adjusted in such manner in the hole as to form as leavel a Surface as possible, a small quantity of earth is Sprinkled over the Stones, and a layer of grass about an inch thick is laid over the Stone; the roots which have been previously devested of the black or outer coat and radicles which rub off easily with the fingers, are now laid on in a circular pile, are then covered with a layer of grass about 2 or 3 inches thick; water is then thrown on the Summit of the pile and passes through the roots and to the hot Stones at bottom; Some water is also pored around the edges of the hole, and also find it's way to the hot Stones. they cover the roots and grass over with earth to the debth of four inches and then build a fire of dry wood all over the Connical mound which they Continue to renew through the course of the night or for 10 or 12 hours, after which it is Suffered to cool, 2 or three hours, when the earth and grass are removed. and the roots thus Sweated are cooled with Steam or taken out, and most commonly exposed to the Sun on Scaffolds untill they become dry. when they are black and of a Sweet agreeable flavor. these roots are fit for use when first taken from the pitt, are Soft of a Sweetish taste and much the consistancy of a roasted onion; but if they are Suffered to remain in bulk 24 hours after being cooked they Spoil. if the design is to make bread or cakes of those roots they undergo a Second preperation of baking being previously pounded after the first baking between two Stones untill they are reduced to the consistancy of dough and then rolled in grass in cakes of 8 or 10 pounds, are returned to the Sweat intermixes with fresh roots in order that the steam may get freely to those loaves of bread. when taken out the Second time the Indn. woman make up this dough into cakes of various Shapes and Sizes, usually from 1/2 to 3/4 of an inch thick and expose it on sticks to dry in the Sun, or place it over the smoke of their fires.- The bread thus prepared if kept free from moisture will Sound for a great length of time. this bread or the dryed roots are frequently eaten alone by the nativs without further preperation, and when they have them in abundance they form an ingrediant in almost every dish they prepare. this root is palateable but disagrees with us in every shape we have ever used it. the nativs are extreemly fond of this root and present it their visiters as a great treat. when we first arrived at the Chopunnish last fall at this place our men who were half Starved made So free a use of this root that it made them all Sick for Several days after.

[Lewis, June 12, 1806] Thursday June 12th 1806. All our hunters except Gibson returned about noon; none of them had killed anything except Sheilds who brought with him two deer. in the evening they resumed their hunt and remained out all night. an indian visited us this evening and spent the night at our camp. Whitehouse returned with his horse at 1 P.M. the days are now very warm and the Musquetoes our old companions have become very troublesome. The Cutnose informed us on the 10th before we left him that two young men would overtake us with a view to accompany me to the falls of the Missouri. nothing interesting occurred in the course of this day. our camp is agreeably situated in a point of timbered land on the eastern border of an extensive level and beautiful) prarie which is intersected by several small branches near the bank of one of which our camp is placed. the quawmash is now in blume and from the colour of its bloom at a short distance it resembles lakes of fine clear water, so complete is this deseption that on first sight I could have swoarn it was water.

[Clark, June 12, 1806] Thursday June 12th 1806. All our hunters except Gibson returned about noon; none of them had killed any thing except Shields who brought with him two deer. in the evening they resumed their hunt and remained out all night. an Indian visited us this evening and Spent the night at our Camp. Whitehouse returned with his horse at 1 P.M. the days are very worm and the Musquetors our old Companions have become very troublesom.

The Cutnose informed us on the 10th before we left him that two young Chiefs would overtake us with a view to accompany us to the Falls of the Missouri and probably to the Seat of our Governmt. nothing interesting occured in the course of this day. our camp is agreeably Situated in a point of timbered land on the eastern borders of an extensive leave) and butifull prarie which is intersected by Several Small branches near the bank of one of which our Camp is placed. the quawmash is now in blume at a Short distance it resembles a lake of fine clear water, So complete is this deseption that on first Sight I could have Sworn it was water.

[Lewis, June 13, 1806] Friday June 13th 1806. Reubin Feilds and Willard were ordered to proceed on our road to a small prarie 8 miles distant on this side of Collins's Creek and there hunt until our arrival; they departed at 10 A.M. about noon seven of our hunters returned with 8 deer; they had wounded several others and a bear but did not get them. in the evening Labuish and Cruzatte returned and reported that the buzzards had eaten up a deer which they had killed butchered and hung up this morning. The indian who visited us yesterday exchanged his horse for one of ours which had not perfectly recovered from the operation of castration and received a small ax and a knife to boot, he seemed much pleased with his exchange and set out immediately to his village, as if fearfull that we would cansel the bargain which is customary among themselves and deemed only fair. we directed the meat to be cut thin and exposed to dry in the sun. we made a digest of the Indian Nations West of the Rocky Mountains which we have seen and of whom we have been repeated informed by those with whom we were conversant. they amount by our estimate to 69,000

[Clark, June 13, 1806] Friday June 13th 1806. Ordered Rubin Fields and Willard to proceed on to a Small prarie in the Mountains about 8 miles and there hunt untill we arrive the Set out at 10 A.M. Soon after they Set out all of our hunters returned each with a deer except Shields who brought two in all 8 deer. Labeech and P. Crusatt went out this morning killed a deer & reported that the buzzds. had eate up the deer in their absence after haveing butchered and hung it up. The indian who visited us yesterday exchanged his horse with one of our party for a very indiferant one in which exchange he rcived a Small ax a Knife &c. Soon after he had exchanged he returned to his village well Satisfied. we caused the meat to be cut thin and dried in the sun. I make a list of the Indian Nations their place of residence, and probable number of Soles of each nation from estimation and indian information &c.

[Lewis, June 14, 1806] Saturday June 14th 1806. Sent our hunters out early this morning. Colter killed a deer and brought it in by 10 A.M. the other hunters except Drewyer returned early without having killed anything. Drewyer returned. we had all our articles packed up and made ready for an early departure in the morning. our horses were caught and most of them hubbled and otherwise confined in order that we might not be detained. from hence to traveller's rest we shall make a forsed march; at that place we shal probably remain one or two days to rest ourselves and horses and procure some meat. we have now been detained near five weeks in consequence of the snows; a serious loss of time at this delightfull season for traveling. I am still apprehensive that the snow and the want of food for our horses will prove a serious imbarrassment to us as at least four days journey of our rout in these mountains lies over hights and along a ledge of mountains never intirely destitute of snow. every body seems anxious to be in motion, convinced that we have not now any time to delay if the calculation is to reach the United States this season; this I am detirmined to accomplish if within the compass of human power.

[Clark, June 14, 1806] Saturday June 14th 1806 Sent out Hunters this morning Colter killed a deer and brought it in by 10 A M Drewyer did not return untill night he wounded deer but could get none &c _____ neither of the other hunters killed nothing. we had our articles packed up ready for a Start in the morning, our horses Collected and hobble that they may not detain us in the morning. we expect to Set out early, and Shall proceed with as much expedition as possible over those Snowey tremendious mountains which has detained us near five weeks in this neighbourhood waiting for the Snows to melt Suffecent for us to pass over them. and even now I Shudder with the expectation with great dificuelties in passing those Mountains, from the debth of Snow and the want of grass Sufficient to Subsist our horses as about 4 days we Shall be on the top of the Mountain which we have every reason to beleive is Covered with Snow the greater part of the year.

[Lewis, June 15, 1806] Sunday June 15th 1806. We had some little difficulty in collecting our horses this morning they had straggled off to a greater distance than usual. it rained very hard in the morning and after collecting our horses we waited for it to abait, but as it had every appearance of a settled rain we set out at 10 A.M. we passed a little prarie at the distance of 81/2 me. to which we had previously sent R. Feilds and Willard. we found two deer which they had killed and hung up. at the distance of 21/2 miles further we arrived at Collins's Creek where we found our hunters; they had killed another deer, and had seen two large bear together the one black and the other white . we halted at the creek, dined and graized our horses. the rains have rendered the road very slippery insomuch that it is with much difficulty our horses can get on several of them fell but sustained no injury. after dinner we proceeded up the creek about 1/2 a mile, passing it three times, thence through a high broken country to an Easterly fork of the same creek about 101/2 miles and incamped near a small prarie in the bottom land the fallen timber in addition to the slippry roads made our march slow and extreemly laborious on our horses. the country is exceedingly thickly timbered with long leafed pine, some pitch pine, larch, white pine, white cedar or arborvita of large size, and a variety of firs. the undergrowth principally reed root from 6 to 10 feet high with all the other speceis enumerated the other day. the soil is good; in some plaices it is of a red cast like our lands in Virginia about the S. W. mountains. Saw the speckled woodpecker, bee martin and log cock or large woodpecker. found the nest of a humming bird, it had just began to lay its eggs.- Came 22 Miles today.

[Clark, June 15, 1806] Sunday June 15th 1806 Collected our horses early with the intention of makeing an early Start. Some hard Showers of rain detained us untill _____ A M at which time we took our final departure from the quawmash fields and proceeded with much dificuelty owing to the Situation of the road which was very Sliprey, and it was with great dificulty that the loaded horses Could assend the hills and Mountains they frequently Sliped down both assending and deceding those Steep hills. at g miles we passed through a Small prarie in which was quawmash in this Prarie Reubin Fields & Willard had killed and hung up two deer at 2 miles further we arrived at the Camp of R. Fields & Willard on Collin's Creek, they arrived at this Creek last evening and had killed another Deer near the Creek. here we let our horses graze in a Small glade and took dinner. the rain Seased and Sun Shown out. after detaining about 2 hours we proceeded on passing the Creek three times and passing over Some ruged hills or Spurs of the rocky Mountain, passing the Creek on which I encamped on the 17th Septr. last to a Small glade of about 10 acres thickly Covered with grass and quawmash, near a large Creek and encamped. we passed through bad fallen timber and a high Mountain this evening. from the top of this Mountain I had an extensive view of the rocky Mountains to the South and the Columbian plains for great extent also the S W. Mountains and a range of high Mountains which divides the waters of Lewis's & Clarks rivers and seems to termonate nearly a West Cours. Several high pts. to the N & N. E. Covered with Snow. a remarkable high rugd mountain in the forks of Lewis's river nearly South and covered with Snow. The vally up the Chopunnish river appears extensive tolerably leavel and Covered with timber. The S W. Mountain is very high in a S S W. derection.

[Lewis, June 16, 1806] Monday June 16th 1806. We collected our horses very readily this morning, took breakfast and set out at 6 A.M.; proceeded up the creek about 2 miles through some handsom meadows of fine grass abounding with quawmash, here we passed the creek & ascended a ridge which led us to the N. E. about seven miles when we arrived at a small branch of hungry creek. the difficulty we met with from the fallen timber detained us untill 11 oC before we reached this place. here is a handsome little glade in which we found some grass for our horses we therefore halted to let them graize and took dinner knowing that there was no other convenient situation for that purpose short of the glaids on hungry creek where we intended to encamp, as the last probable place, at which we shall find a sufficient quantity of grass for many days. this morning Windsor busted his rifle near the muzzle. before we reached this little branch on which we dined we saw in the hollows and N. hillsides large quatities of snow yet undisolved; in some places it was from two to three feet deep. vegetation is proportionably backward; the dogtooth violet is just in blume, the honeysuckle, huckburry and a small speceis of white maple are begining to put fourth their leaves; these appearances in this comparatively low region augers but unfavourably with rispect to the practibility of passing the mountains, however we determined to proceed, accordingly after taking a haisty meal we set out and continued our rout though a thick wood much obstructed with fallen timber, and intersepted by many steep ravines and high hills. the snow has increased in quantity so much that the greater part of our rout this evening was over the snow which has become sufficiently firm to bear our horshes, otherwise it would have been impossible for us to proceed as it lay in immence masses in some places 8 or ten feet deep. we found much difficulty in pursuing the road as it was so frequently covered with snow. we arrived early in the evening at the place that Capt. C. had killed and left the flesh of a horse for us last September. here is a small glade in which there was some grass, not a sufficiency for our horses but we thought it most advisable to remain here all night as we apprehended if we proceeded further we should find less grass. the air is pleasent in the course of the day but becomes very cold before morning notwithstanding the shortness of the nights. Hungry creek is but small at this place but is deep and runs a perfect torrent; the water is perfectly transparent and as cold as ice. the pitch pine, white pine some larch and firs constite the timber; the long leafed pine extends a little distance on this side of the main branch of Collins's creek, and the white cedar not further than the branch of hungry creek on which we dined. I killed a small brown pheasant today, it feeds on the tender leaves and buds of the fir and pitch pine. in the fore part of the day I observed the Cullumbine the blue bells and the yelow flowering pea in blume. there is an abundance of a speceis of anjelico in these mountains, much stonger to the taist and more highly scented than that speceis common to the U States. know of no particular virtue or property it possesses; the natives dry it cut it in small peices which they string on a small cord and place about their necks; it smells very pleasantly. we came 15 miles today.

[Clark, June 16, 1806] Monday June 16th 1806 Collected our horses early and Set Out 7 A M proceeded on up the Creek through a gladey Swompy bottom with grass and quawmash Crossed the Creek to the East and proceeded on through most intolerable bad fallen timber over a high Mountain on which great quantity of Snow is yet lying premisquissly through the thick wood, and in maney places the banks of snow is 4 feet deep. we noned it or dined on a Small Creek in a small open Vally where we found Some grass for our horses to eate, altho Serounded by Snow no other Convenient Situation Short of the glades on Hungery Creek where we intended to encamp, as the last probable place, at which we Shall find a Suffecient quantity of grass for maney days. This morning Windsor bursted his rifle near the Muzzle. Vigitation is propotionable backward; the dog tooth Violet is just in blume, the honeysuckle, huckleberry and a Small Species of white maple are beginning to put foth their leaves, where they are clear of the Snow, those appearances in this comparitively low region augers but unfavourably with respect to the practibility of passing the Mountains, however we deturmine to proceed, accordingly after takeing a hasty meal we Set out and Continued our rout through a thick wood much obstructed with fallen timber, and interupted by maney Steep reveins and hills which wer very high. the Snow has increased in quantity So much that the great part of our rout this evening was over the Snow which has become Suffecently firm to bear our horses, otherwise it would have been impossible for us to proceed as it lay in emince masses in Some places 8 or ten feet deep. We found much dificulty in finding the road, as it was So frequently covered with Snow. we arived early in the evening at the place I had killed and left the flesh of a horse for the party in my rear last Septr. here is a Small glade in which there is Some grass, not a Sufficency of our horses, but we thought it adviseable to remain here all night as we apprehended if we proceeded further we should find less grass. The air is pleasant in the Course of the day, but becomes very cold before morning not withstanding the Shortness of the night. Hungary Creek is but Small at this place but is deep and runs a perfect torrent; the water is perfectly transparent and as Cold as ice. the titch pine, white pine Some Larch and firs consists the timber, the long leafed pine extends but a Short distance on the Mts. Capt. L. killed a Small brown pheasant today, it feeds on the tender leaves and buds of the fir and pitch pine. in the forepart of the day I observed the Cullumbine the blue bells and the Yellow flowering pea in blume. there is an abundance of a Species of Anjelico in the mountains much Stronger to the taiste, and more highly Scented than that Species common to the U States. I know of no particular virtue or property it possesses the nativs dry it Cut it in Small pieces which they string on a Small Cord and place about the necks; it Smells pleasently. we Come 15 Ms. today.

[Lewis, June 17, 1806] Tuesday June 17th 1806. we collected our horses and set out early; we proceeded down hungry creek about seven miles passing it twice; we found it difficult and dangerous to pass the creek in consequence of its debth and rapidity; we avoided two other passes of the creek by ascending a very steep rocky and difficult hill. beyond this creek the road ascends the mountain to the hight of the main leading ridges which divides the Waters of the Chopunnish and Kooskooske rivers. this hill or reather mountain we ascended about 3 miles when we found ourselves invelloped in snow from 12 to 15 feet deep even on the south sides of the hills with the fairest exposure to the sun; here was winter with all it's rigors; the air was cold, my hands and feet were benumbed. we knew that it would require five days to reach the fish wears at the entrance of Colt Creek, provided we were so fortunate as to be enabled to follow the proper ridges of the mountains to lead us to that place; short of that point we could not hope for any food for our horses not even underwood itself as the whole was covered many feet deep in snow. if we proceeded and should get bewildered in these mountains the certainty was that we should loose all our horses and consequently our baggage instruments perhaps our papers and thus eminently wrisk the loss of the discoveries which we had already made if we should be so fortunate as to escape with life. the snow boar our horses very well and the travelling was therefore infinitely better that the obstruction of rocks and fallen timber which we met with in our passage over last fall when the snow lay on this part of the ridge in detached spots only. under these circumstances we conceived it madnes in this stage of the expedition to proceed without a guide who could certainly conduct us to the fish wears on the Kooskooske, as our horses could not possibly sustain a journey of more than five days without food. we therefore came to the resolution to return with our horses while they were yet strong and in good order and indevour to keep them so untill we could procure an indian to conduct us over the snowey mountains, and again to proceed as soon as we could procure such a guide, knowing from the appearance of the snows that if we remained untill it had desolved sufficiently for us to follow the road that we should not be enabled to return to the United States within this season. having come to this resolution, we ordered the party to make a deposit for all the baggage which we had not immediate use for, and also all the roots and bread of cows which they had except an allowance for a few days to enable them to return to some place at which we could subsist by hunting untill we procured a guide. we left our instruments papers &c beleiving them safer here than to wrisk them on horseback over the roads and creeks which we had passed. our baggage being laid on scaffoalds and well covered we began our retrograde march at 1 P.M. having remained about 3 hours on this snowey mountain. we returned by the rout we had come to hungry creek, which we ascended about 2 miles and encamped. we had here more grass for our horses than the preceeding evening yet it was but scant. the party were a good deel dejected tho not so as I had apprehended they would have been. this is the first time since we have been on this long tour that we have ever been compelled to retreat or make a retrograde march. it rained on us most of this evening.

[Clark, June 17, 1806] Tuesday June 17th 1806 We Collected our horses and Set out early; we proceeded down hungary Creek about 7 miles passing it twice; we found it dificuelt and dangerous to pass the creek in consequence of it's debth and rapidity; we avoided two other passes of the creek, by assending a Steep rockey and difficuelt hill. beyond this Creek the road assends the mountain to the hight of the main leading ridges, which divides the waters of the Kooskooske and Chopunnish Riv's. This mountain we ascended about 3 miles when we found ourselves invelloped in snow from 8 to 12 feet deep even on the South Side of the mountain. I was in front and Could only prosue the derection of the road by the trees which had been peeled by the nativs for the iner bark of which they Scraped and eate, as those pealed trees were only to be found Scattered promisquisley, I with great difficulty prosued the direction of the road one mile further to the top of the mountain where I found the Snow from 12 to 15 feet deep, but fiew trees with the fairest exposure to the Sun; here was Winter with all it's rigors; the air was Cold my hands and feet were benumed. we knew that it would require four days to reach the fish weare at the enterance of Colt Creek, provided we were So fortunate as to be enabled to follow the poper ridge of the mountains to lead us to that place; of this all of our most expert woodsmen and principal guides were extreemly doubtfull; Short of that point we could not hope for any food for our horses not even under wood itself as the whole was covered many feet deep in Snow. if we proceeded and Should git bewildered in those Mountains the Certainty was that we Should lose all of our horses and consequencely our baggage enstruments perhaps our papers and thus eventially resque the loss of our discoveries which we had already made if we Should be So fortunate as to escape with life. the Snow bore our horses very well and the traveling was therefore infinately better than the obstruction of rocks and fallen timber which we met with in our passage over last fall when the Snow lay on this part of the ridge in detached spops only. under these Circumstances we Conceived it madness in this stage of the expedition to proceed without a guide who Could Certainly Conduct us to the fishwears on the Kooskooske, as our horses could not possibly Sustain a journey of more than 4 or 5 days without food. we therefore Come to the resolution to return with our horses while they were yet strong and in good order, and indeaver to keep them So untill we could precure an indian to conduct us over the Snowey Mountains, and again to proceed as soon as we could precure Such a guide, knowing from the appearance of the snows that if we remained untill it had disolved Sufficiently for us to follow the road that we Should not be enabled to return to the United States within this Season. having come to this resolution, we ordered the party to make a deposit of all the baggage which we had not imediate use for, and also all the roots and bread of Cows which they had except an allowance for a fiew days to enable them to return to Some place at which we could Subsist by hunting untill we precured a guide. we left our instrements, and I even left the most of my papers believing them Safer here than to Wrisk them on horseback over the road, rocks and water which we had passed. our baggage being laid on Scaffolds and well covered, we began our retragrade march at 1 P.M. haveing remain'd about three hours on this Snowey mountain. we returned by the rout we had advanced to hungary Creek, which we assended about 2 miles and encamped. we had here more grass for our horses than the proceeding evening, yet it was but scant. the party were a good deel dejected, tho not as much So as I had apprehended they would have been. this is the first time Since we have been on this long tour that we have ever been compelled to retreat or make a retragrade march. it rained on us the most of this evening. on the top of the Mountain the Weather was very fluctiating and uncertain snowed cloudy & fair in a few minets.

[Lewis, June 18, 1806] Wednesday June 18th 1806. This morning we had considerable difficulty in collecting our horses they having straggled off to a considerable distance in surch of food on the sides of the mountains among the thick timber; at 9 OCk. we collected them all except one of Drewyers and one of Sheildes; we set out leaving Sheilds and LaPage to collect the two lost horses and follow us. We dispatched Drewyer and Shannon to the Chopunnish Indians in the plains beyond the Kooskooske in order to hasten the arrival of the indians who had promised to accompany us or to procure a gude at all events and rejoin us as soon as possible. we sent by them a rifle which we offered as a reward to any of them who would engage to conduct us to traveller's rest; we also dirrected them if they found difficulty in induciny any of them to accompany us to offer the reward of two other guns to be given them immediately and ten horses at the falls of Missouri. we had not proceeded far this morning before Potts cut his leg very badly with one of the large knives; he cut one of the large veigns on the inner side of the leg; I found much difficulty in stoping the blood which I could not effect untill I applyed a tight bandage with a little cushon of wood and tow on the veign below the wound. Colter's horse fel with him in passing hungry creek and himself and horse were driven down the creek a considerable distance rolling over each other among the rocks. he fortunately escaped without injury or the loss of his gun. by 1 P.M. we returned to the glade on the branch of hungry Creek where we had dined on the 16th inst. here we again halted and dined. as there was much appearance of deer about this place we left R. and J. Feilds with directions to hunt this evening and tomorrow morning at this place and to join us in the evening at the meadows of Collin's creek where we intend remaining tomorrow in order to rest our horses and hunt. after dinner we proceeded on to Collin's Creek and encamped in a pleasant situation at the upper part of the meadows about 2 ms. above our encampment of the 15th inst. we sent out several hunters but they returned without having killed anything. they saw a number of salmon in the creek and shot at them several times without success. we directed Colter and Gibson to fix each of them a gigg in the morning and indevour to take some of the salmon. the hunters saw much fresh appearance of bear but very little of deer. we hope by means of the fish together with what deer and bear we can kill to be enabled to subsist untill our guide arrives without the necessity of returning to the quawmash flats. there is a great abundance of good food here to sustain our horses.

[Clark, June 18, 1806] Wednesday June 18th 1806 This morning we had considerable dificuelty in collecting our horses they haveing Strageled of to a considerable distance in Serch of food on the Sides of the mountains among the thick timber, at 9 oClock we Collected them all except 2 one of Shields & one of Drewyer's. we Set out leaving Shields and LePage to collect the two lost horses and follow us.

We dispatched Drewyer and Shannon to the Chopunnish Indians in the plains beyond the Kooskooske in order to hasten the arrival of the Indians who promised to accompany us, or to precure a guide at all events and rejoin us as Soon as possible. We Sent by them a riffle which we offered as a reward to any of them who would engage to conduct us to Clarks river at the entrance of Travellers rest Creek; we also directed them if they found difficuelty in induceing any of them to accompany us to offer the reward of two other guns to be given them immediately and ten horses at the falls of Missouri. we had not proceeded far this morning before J. Potts cut his leg very badly with one of the large knives; he cut one of the large veins on the iner side of the leg; Colters horse fell with him in passing hungary creek and himself and horse were driven down the Creek a considerable distance roleing over each other among the rocks. he fortunately escaped without much injurey or the loss of his gun. he lost his blanket. at 1 P. M we returned to the glade on a branch of hungary Creek where we had dined on the 16th instant. here we again halted and dined. as there was some appearance of deer about this place we left J. & R Field with directions to hunt this evening and tomorrow morning at this place and join us in the evening in the Meadows on Collin's Creek where we intended to remain tomorrow in order to restour horses and hunt. after dinner we proceeded on to the near fork of Collins Creek and encamped in a pleasant Situation at the upper part of the Meadows about 2 miles above our encampment of the 15th inst. we Sent out Several hunters but they returned without having killed any thing-. they saw a number of large fish in the Creek and Shot at them Several times without Suckcess. we Gibson and Colter to fix each of themselves a gigg in the morning and indeaver to take Some of those fish. the hunters Saw much fresh appearance of Bear, but very little deer Sign. we hope by the means of the fish together with what deer and bear we can kill to been abled to Subsist untill our guide arives without the necessaty of returning to the quawmash flats. there is great abundance of good food here to Sustain our horses. we are in flattering expectations of the arrival of two young chiefs who informed us that they intended to accompany us to the U. States, and Should Set out from their village in 9 nights after we left them on the 19th inst. if they Set out at that time Drewyer & Shannon will meet them, and probably join us on the 20th or 21st-. Musquetors Troublesome.

[Lewis, June 19, 1806] Thursday June 19th 1806. Our hunters were out very early this morning, they returned before noon with one deer only. the Fishermen had been more unsuccessfull, they returned without a single fish and reported they could find but few and those they had tryed to take in vain. they had broke both their giggs which were of indian fabrication made of bone. I happened to have a pointed peice of iron in my pouch which answered by cuting in two peices to renew boath giggs. they took one fish this evening which proved to be a salmon trout much to our mortification, for we had hoped that they were the salmon of this spring arrival and of course fat and fine. these trout are of the red kind they remain all winter in the upper parts of the rivers and creeks and are generally poor at this season. At 2 P.M. J & R Feilds arived with two deer; John Sheilds and LaPage came with them, they had not succeeded in finding their horses. late in the evening Frazier reported that my riding horse that of Capt Clark and his mule had gone on towards the Quawmash flatts and that he had pursued their tracks on the road about 2 1/2 miles. we determined to send out all the hunters in the morning in order to make a fair experiment of the pactability of our being able to subsist at this place and if not we shall move the day after to the Quawmash flatts. the musquetoes have been excessively troublesome to us since our arrival at this place particularly in the evening. Cruzatte brought me several large morells which I roasted and eat without salt pepper or grease in this way I had for the first time the true taist of the morell which is truly an insippid taistless food. our stock of salt is now exhausted except two quarts which I have reserved for my tour up Maria's River and that I left the other day on the mountain.-

[Clark, June 19, 1806] Thursday June 19th 1806 This morning early Collins Labeesh & Crusat turned out to hunt, and Gibson & Colter fixed two Indian giggs and went in Serch of fish in the Creek. I took my gun and walked up the Creek about 4 Miles Saw some bear Sign and one fish only. Gibson killed only one fish which we found to be the Salmon Trout of the dark Species. this fish was of the common Size pore, and indifferently flavoured. Labeesh killed one Deer neither of the others killed any thing. about 1 P.M. Jo. & R Fields Shields & LaPage came up. Reubin &Joseph Fields brought two Deer which R. had killed in the Small glade on a branch of Hungary Creek where we had left them yesterday. Shields & LaPage did not find the two horses which we lost yesterday morning. they report that they hunted with great diligence in the vicinity of our camp of the 17th without suckcess. in my walk of this day up the Creek I observed a great abundance of fine grass sufficient to Sustain our horses any length of time we chose to Stay at this place. Several glades of quawmash. the S W. Sides of the hills is fallen timber and burnt woods, the N. E. Sides of the hills is thickly timbered with lofty pine, and thick under growth This evening Several Salmon trout were Seen in the Creek, they hid themselves under the banks of the Creek which jutted over in Such a manner as to secure them from the Stroke of our giggs nets and spears which were made for the purpose of taking those Salmon trout. we concluded to delay at this place another day with a view to give time to the two young Chiefs to arrive in case they set out on the 19th inst. as they informed us they Should they will have Sufficient time to join us tomorrow or early the next day. Should we get a guide from this place it will Save us two days march through some of the worst road through those Mountains, crouded with fallin timber mud holes and steep hills &c. we directed all the hunters to turn out early and kill something for us to live on &c. Musquetors troublesom

[Lewis, June 20, 1806] Friday June 20th 1806. Our hunters set out early this morning; most of them returned before noon. R. Feilds killed a brown bear the tallons of which were remarkably short broad at their base and sharply pointed this was of the speceis which the Chopunnish call Yah-kar. it was in very low order and the flesh of the bear in this situation is much inferior to lean venison or the flesh of poor Elk. Labush and Cruzatte returned late in the evening with one deer which the former had killed. we also caught seven salmon trout in the course of the day. the hunters assured us that their greatest exertions would not enable them to support us here more than one or two days longer from the great scarcity of game and the difficult access of the country, the under brush being very thick and great quantities of fallen timber. as we shall necessarily be compelled to remain more than two days for the return of Drewyer and Shannon we determined to return in the morning as far as the quawmash flatts and indeavour to lay in another stock of meat for the mountains, our former stock being now nearly exhausted as well as what we have killed on our return. by returning to the quawmash flatts we shall sooner be informed whether or not we can procure a guide to conduct us through the mountains; should we fail in procuring one, we have determined to wrisk a passage on the following plan immediately, because should we wait much longer or untill the snow desolves in such manner as to enable us to follow the road we cannot hope to reach the United States this winter; this is that Capt. C. or myself shall take four of our most expert woodsmen with three or four of our best horses and proceed two days in advance taking a plentiful) supply of provision. for this party to follow the road by the marks which the baggage of the indians has made in many places on the sides of the trees by rubing against them, and to blaize the trees with a tomahawk as they proceeded. that after proceeding two days in advance of hungary creek two of those men would be sent back to the main party who by the time of their return to Hungary Creek would have reached that place. the men so returning would be enabled to inform the main party of the probable success of the preceeding party in finding the road and of their probable progress, in order that should it be necessary, the main party by the delay of a day or two at hungary creek, should give the advance time to mark the road through before the main party could overtake them, and thus prevent delay on the part of the rout where no food is to be obtained for our horses. should it so happen that the advance could not find the road by the marks on the trees after attempting it for two days, the whole of then would return to the main party. in which case we wold bring back our baggage and attempt a passage over these mountains through the country of the Shoshones further to the South by way of the main S. Westerly fork of Lewis's river and Madison or Gallatin's rivers, where from the information of the Chopunnish there is a passage which at this season of the year is not obstructed by snow, though the round is very distant and would require at least a month in it's performance. The Shoshones informed us when we first met with them that there was a passage across the mountains in that quarter but represented the difficulties arrising from steep high and rugged mountains and also an extensive and barren plain which was to be passed without game, as infinitely more difficult than the rout by which we came. from the circumstance of the Chopunnish being at war with that part of the Shoshones who inhabit the country on this side of the Mountains through which the road passes I think it is highly probable that they cannot be well informed with rispect to the road, and further, had there been a better road in that quarter the Shoshones on the East fork of Lewis's river who knew them both would not have recommended that by which we came to this country. the travelling in the mountains on the snow at present is very good, the snow bears the horses perfictly; it is a firm coase snow without a crust, and the horses have good foot hold without sliping much; the only dificulty is finding the road, and I think the plan we have devised will succeed even should we not be enabled to obtain a guide. Although the snow may be stated on an average at 10 feet deep yet arround the bodies of the trees it has desolved much more than in other parts not being generally more than one or two feet deep immediately at the roots of the trees, and; of course the marks left by the rubing of the indian baggage against them is not concealed. the reason why the snow is comparitively so shallow about the roots of the trees I presume proceeds as well from the snow in falling being thrown off from their bodies by their thick and spreading branches as from the reflection of the sun against the trees and the warmth which they in some measure acquire from the earth which is never frozen underneath these masses of snow. Bratton's horse was also discovered to be absent this evening. I presume he has also returned to the flatts.

[Clark, June 20, 1806] Friday June 20th 1806 The hunters turned out early in different directions, our guiggers also turned out with 2 guigs a Bayonet fixed on a pole, a Scooping nett and a Snar made of horse. near the ford of the Creek in a deep hole we killed Six Salmon trout & 2 others were killed in the Creek above in the evening. Reubin Field killed a redish brown bear which was very meagure. the tallons of this bear was remarkably Short broad at their base and Sharply pointed, this was of the Species the Chopunnish call Yahkar. as it was in very low order the flesh was indifferent. Labiesh & Crusat returned late in the evening with one deer which the former had killed. the hunters assured us that, their greatest exertions would not enable them to support us here more than one or two days longer, from the great scercity of game and the dificuelt access of the Country, the under brush being very thick and great quantities of fallen timber. as we shall necessarily be compelled to remain more than two days for the return of Drewyer & Shannon we determine to return in the morning as far as the quawmash flatts, and endeavor to lay in another Stock of meat for the mountains, our former Stock now being nearly exhosted as well as what we have killed on our rout. by returning to the quawmash flatts we Shall Sooner be informed wheather or not we can precure a guide to conduct us through the Mountains; Should we fail in precureing one, we are deturmined to wrisk a passage on the following plan immediately, because Should we wait much longer, or untill the Snow disolves in Such manner as to enable us to follow the road we cannot expect to reach the U States this Winter; this is that Capt. L. or myself shall take four of our most expert woods men with 3 or four of our best horses and proceed two days in advance takeing a plentiful Supply of provisions. for this party to follow the road by the mark the indins have made in many places with their baggage on the Sides of the trees by rubbing against them, and to blaize the trees with a tomahawk as they proceed. that after proceeding two days in advance of Hungary Creek, two of those men would be sent back to the party who by the time of their return to hungary Creek would have reached that place. the men So returning would be enabled to inform the main party of the probable Suckcess of the proceeding party in finding the road and of their probable progress, in order that Should it be necessary, the main party by a delay of a day or two a hungary Creek, should give the advance time to make the road through before the main party could overtake them, and thus prevent delay on that part of the rout where no food is to be obtained for our horses. Should it So happen that the advance Should not find the road by the marks of the trees after attempting it for two days, the whole of them would return to the main party. in which Case we would bring back our baggage and attempt a passage over the Mountains through the Country of the Shoshones further to the South, by way of the main S Westerly fork of Lewis's river and Madisons or Gallitins river's, where from the information of the Chopunnish, there is a passage where at this season of the year is not obstructed by snow, though the round is very distant and would require at least a month in it's preformance. The Shoshones informed us when we first met with them that there was a passage across the Mountains in that quarter but represented the dificuelties arriseing from Steep ruggid high mountains, and also an extensive and barren plain which was to be passed without game, as infinitely more difficuelt than the rout by which we Came. from the Circumstance of the Chopunnish being at war with that part of the Shoshones who inhabit the Country on this side of the Mountains through which the road passes, I think it is highly probable they cannot be well informed with respect to the road, and further, had there been a better road in that quarter the Shoshones on the East fork of Lewis's river who knew them boath would not have recommend'd that by which we came to this country. The travelling in the Mountains on the Snow, at present is very good, the Snow bears the horses perfectly; it is a firm coase Snow without a crust, and the horses have good foot hold without slipping much; the only dificuelty is finding the road, and I think the plan we have devised will Suckceed even Should we not be enabled to obtain a guide. altho the Snow may be Stated on an average at 10 feet deep, yet arround the body of the trees it has disolved much more than in other parts, not being generally more than one or two feet deep imediately at the roots of the trees, and of course the marks made by the rubbing of the Indian baggage against them is not Concealed. The reason why the Snow is compiritively So Shallow about the roots of the trees, 1 prosume proceeds as well from the Snow in falling being thrown off from their bodies by the thick and Spreading branches, as from the reflection of the Sun against the trees and the warmth which they in Some measure acquire from the earth which is never frozen underneath those masses of Snow. 4 of our horses are absent.

[Lewis, June 21, 1806] Saturday June 21st 1806. We collected our horses early set out on our return to the flatts. we all felt some mortification in being thus compelled to retrace our steps through this tedious and difficult part of our rout, obstructed with brush and innumerable logs of fallen timber which renders the traveling distressing and even dangerous to our horses. one of Thompson's horses is either choked this morning or has the distemper very badly I fear he is to be of no further service to us. an excellent horse of Cruzatte's snagged himself so badly in the groin in jumping over a parsel of fallen timber that he will evidently be of no further service to us. at the pass of Collin's Creek we met two indians who were on their way over the mountain; they had brought with them the three horses and the mule that had left us and returned to the quawmash grounds. these indians returned with us about 1/2 a mile down the creek where we halted to dine and graize our horses at the same place I had halted and remained all night with the party on the _____ of Septembr last. as well as we could understand the indians they informed us that they had seen Drewyer and Shannon and that they would not return untill the expiration of two days; the cause why Drewyer and Shannon had not returned with these men we are at a loss to account for. we pressed these indians to remain with us and to conduct us over the mountain on the return of Drewyer and Shannon. they consented to remain two nights for us and accordingly deposited their store of roots and bread in the bushes at no great distance and after dinner returned with us, as far as the little prarie about 2 miles distant from the creek, here they halted with their horses and informed us they would remain untill we overtook them or at least two nights. they had four supenumery horses with them. we sent on four hunters a head to the quawmash flatts to take an evenings hunt; they so far succeeded as to kill one deer. we left Reubin and J. Feilds at the Creek where we dined together with Sergt Gass in order to hunt about that place untill our return. at seven in the evening we found ourselves once more at our old encampment where we shall anxiously await the return of Drewyer and Shannon.

[Clark, June 21, 1806] Saturday June 21st 1806 We collected our horses early and Set out on our return to the flatts. we all felt Some mortification in being thus compelled to retrace our Steps through this tedious and dificuelt part of our rout, obstructed with brush and innumerable logs and fallen timber which renders the traveling distressing and even dangerous to our horses. one of Thompsons horses is either choked this morning or has the distemper badly. I fear he is to be of no further Survice to us. an excellent horse of Cruzatt's snagged himself So badly in the groin in jumping over a parcel of fallen timber that he will eventually be of no further Survice to us. at the pass of Collin's Creek we met two indians who were on their way over the mountains, they had brought with them the three horses and the Mule which had left us and returned to the quawmash ground. those indians returned with us about 1/2 a mile down the Creek where we halted to dine and graze our horses. as well as we Could understand the indians they informed us they had Seen Geo Drewyer & Shannon, and that they would not return untill the expiration of two days. the cause why Drewyer & Shannon did not return with these men we are at a loss to account for. we pressed those indians to remain with us and conduct us over the Mountains on the return of Drewyer & Shannon. they consented to remain two nights for us and accordingly deposited their Stores of roots & Bread in the bushes at no great distance and after Dinner returned with us, as far as the little prarie about 2 Miles distance from the Creek, here they halted with their horses and informed us they would remain untill we overtook them or at least 2 nights. they had four Supernoumery horses with them. We Sent on four hunters a head to the quawmash flatts to make an evening hunt; they So far Suckceeded as to kill one deer. We left R. and Jo. Fields at the Creek where we dined, and Sergt. Gass in order to hunt about that place untill our return. at 7 in the evening we found ourselves once more at our old encampment where we Shall anxiously await the return of Drewyer & Shannon.

[Lewis, June 22, 1806] Sunday June 22nd 1806. this morning by light all hands who could hunt were sent out; the result of this days perfomance was greater than we had even hoped for. we killed eight deer and three bear. we dispatched Whitehouse to the Kooskooske near our old encampment above Collins's Creek in order to procure some Salmon which we have understood the natives are now taking in considerable quantities near that place. we gave Whitehouse a few beads which Capt. C. had unexpectedly found in one of his waistcoat pockets to purchase the fish. nothing further worthy of notice occurred in the course of this day. the last evening was cool but the day was remarkably pleasent with a fine breize from the N. W. neither Drewyer Shannon nor

Whitehouse returned this evening.- Potts's legg is inflamed and very painfull to him. we apply a poltice of the roots of Cows.-

[Clark, June 22, 1806] Sunday June 22nd 1806 This morning by light all hands who Could hunt were Sent out, the result of the days performance was greater than we had even hopes for. we killed eight Deer and three Bear. we despatched whitehouse to the Kooskooke near our old encampment above Collins Creek in order to precure Some Salmon which we understood the nativs are now takeing in considerable quantities near that place. we gave whitehouse a fiew beeds which I unexpectedly found in one of my waistcoat pockets to purchase the fish. nothing further occured in the Course of this day. the last evening was Cool but the day was remarkably pleasant with a fine breeze from the N. W. neither Shannon Drewyer nor whitehouse returned this evening.- Potts legg is inflamed and very painfull to him. we apply a poltice of the root of Cowes

[Lewis, June 23, 1806] Monday June 23rd 1806. Apprehensive from Drewyer's delay that he had met with some difficulty in procuring a guide, and also that the two indians who had promised to wait two nights for us would set out today, we thought it most advisable to dispatch Frazier and Wiser to them this morning with a vew if possible to detain them a day or two longer; and directed that in the event of their not being able to detain the indians, that Sergt. Gass, R & J. Feilds and Wiser should accompany the indians by whatever rout they might take to travellers rest and blaize the trees well as they proceeded and wait at that place untill our arrivall with the party. the hunters as usual wer dispatched early this morning. the does now having their fawns the hunters can bleat them up and in that manner kill them with more facility and ease. the indians pursue the game so much on horseback in this neighbourhood that it is very shye. our hunters killed 4 deer and a bear today. at 4 P.M. Drewyer Shannon and Whitehouse returned. Drewyer brought with him three indians who had consented to accompany us to the falls of the Missouri for the compensation of two guns. one of those men is the brother of the cutnose and the other two are the same who presented Capt. Clark and myself each with a horse on a former occasion at the Lodge of the broken arm. these are all young men of good character and much respected by their nation. we directed the horses to be brought near camp this evening and secured in such manner that they may he readily obtained in the morning being determined to make an early start if possible.- Colter one of our hunters did not return this evening.

[Clark, June 23, 1806] Monday June 23rd 1806 Apprehensive from Drewyer & Shannons delay that they had met with Some dificuelty in precureing a guide, and also that the two indians who had promised to wait two nights for us would Set out today, we thought it most adviseable to dispatch Wizer & Frazier to them this morning with a view if possible to detain them a day or two longer; and directed that in the event of their not being able to detain the indians, that Sergt. Gass, Jo. & R. Field & Wiser Should accompany the Indians by whatever rout they might take to travellers rest and blaize the trees well as they proceeded, and wait at that place untill our arival with the party. the hunters as usial were dispatched early this morning. The does now haveing their young the hunters can blait them up, and in that manner kill them with more facillity and ease. the indians pursue the game So much on horse back in this neighbourhood that it is very Shye. our hunters killed _____ deer today. at 4 P.M. Shannon Drewyer & Whitehouse returned. Shannon & Drewyer brought with them three indians who had consented to accompany us to the falls of the Missouri for the Compensation of 2 guns. one of those men is the brother of the Cutnose and the other two are the Same who presented Capt L. and myself with a horse on a former occasion at the Lodge of the broken arm, and the two who promised to pursue us in nine nights after we left the river, or on the 19th inst. Those are all young men of good Charrector and much respected by their nation. those men infor us that thir nation as well as the Wallar-wallars have made peace with the Shoshones agreeable to our late advice to them. they also inform us that they have heard by means of the Skeetsomis Nation & Clarks river that the Big bellies of Fort de Prarie Killed great numbers of the Shoshons and Otte lee Shoots which we met with last fall on the East fork of Lewis's river and high up the West fork of Clarks river &c.

We directed the horses to be brought near Camp and secured in Such a manner that they may be readily obtained in the morning being deturmined to make an early Start if possible-.- Colter one of our hunters did not return this evening

[Lewis, June 24, 1806] Tuesday June 24th 1806. We collected our horses early this morning and set out accompanyed by our three guides. Colter joined us this morning having killed a bear, which from his discription of it's poverty and distance we did not think proper to send after. we nooned it as usual at Collins's Creek where we found Frazier, solus; the other four men having gone in pursuit of the two indian men who had set out from Collins's Creek two hours before Frazier and Wizer arrived. after dinner we continued our rout to Fish Creek a branch of Collins's Creek where we had lain on the 19th & 20th inst. here we found Sergt. Gass Wiser and the two indians whom they had prevailed on to remain at that place untill our arrival; R. & J. Feilds had only killed one small deer only while they lay at Collins's Creek and of this they had been liberal to the indians insomuch that they had no provision; they had gone on to the branch of hungary Creek at which we shall noon it tomorrow in order to hunt. we had fine grass for our horses this evening.

[Clark, June 24, 1806] Tuesday June 24th 1806 We collected our horses early this morning and Set out accompanied by our 3 guides. Colter joined us this morning haveing killed a Bear, which from his discription of it's poverty and distance we did not think proper to send after. We nooned it as usial at Collins's Creek where we found Frazier, solus; the other four men haveing Born in pursute of the two indians who had Set out from Collin's Creek two hours before Fraziers arrival Wiser arrived there. after dinner we Continued our rout to fish Creek a branch of Collin's creek where we had lain the 15th 18th 19th & 20th inst. here we found Sargt. Gass, Wiser and the two indian men whome they had prevaild on to remain at that place untill our arival; Jos. & R. Field had killed one Small deer only while they lay at Collins creek, and of this they had been liberal to the indians insomuch that they had no provisions; they had gone on to the branch of hungary Creek at which we shall noon it tomorrow in order to hunt. we had fine grass for our horses this evening.

[Lewis, June 25, 1806] Wednesday June 25th 1806. last evening the indians entertained us with seting the fir trees on fire. they have a great number of dry lims near their bodies which when set on fire creates a very suddon and immence blaze from bottom to top of those tall trees. they are a beatiful object in this situation at night. this exhibition reminded me of a display of fireworks. the natives told us that their object in seting those trees on fire was to bring fair weather for our journey.- We collected our horses readily and set out at an early hour this morning. one of our guides complained of being unwell, a symptom which I did not much like as such complaints with an indian is generally the prelude to his abandoning any enterprize with which he is not well pleased. we left them at our encampment and they promised to pursue us in a few hours. at 11 A.M. we arrived at the branch of hungary creek where we found R. & J. Feilds. they had not killed anything. here we halted and dined and our guides overtook us. at this place I met with a plant the root of which the shoshones eat. it is a small knob root a good deel in flavor an consistency like the Jerusalem Artichoke. it has two small oval smooth leaves placed opposite on either side of the peduncle just above the root. the scape is only about 4 inches long is round and smooth. the roots of this plant formed one of those collections of roots which Drewyer took from the Shoshones last summer on the head of Jefferson's river. after dinner we continued our rout to hungary Creek and encamped about one and a half miles below our encampment of the 16th inst.- the indians continued with us and I beleive are disposed to be faithfull to their engagement. I gave the sik indian a buffaloe robe he having no other covering except his mockersons and a dressed Elkskin without the hair. Drewyer and Sheilds were sent on this morning to hungry Creek in surch of their horses which they fortunately recovered.

[Clark, June 25, 1806] Wednesday June 25th 1806 last evening the indians entertained us with Setting the fir trees on fire. they have a great number of dry limbs near their bodies which when Set on fire create a very Sudden and eminence blaize from bottom to top of those tail trees. they are a boutiful object in this Situation at night. this exhibition remide me of a display of firewoks. the nativs told us that their object in Setting those trees on fire was to bring fair weather for our journey-. We Collected our horses and Set out at an early hour this morning. one of our guides Complained of being unwell, a Symptom which I did not much like as such complaints with an indian is generally the prelude to his abandoning any enterprize with which he is not well pleased. we left 4 of those indians at our encampment they promised to pursue us in a fiew hours. at 11 A.M. we arrived at the branch of hungary Creek where we found Jo. & R. Fields. they had not killed anything. here we halted and dined and our guides overtook us. at this place the squaw Collected a parcel of roots of which the Shoshones Eat. it is a Small knob root a good deel in flavour and Consistency like the Jerusolem artichoke. it has two Small Smooth oval leaves placed opposit on either Side of the peduncle just above the root. the scope is only about 4 inches long is round and Smooth. the roots of this plant forms one of the Colection of roots which D-. took from the Shoshones last fall on the head of Jefferson river. after dinner we continued our rout to hungary creek and encamped about one and a half miles below our Encampment of the 16th inst.- The indians all continue with us and I beleive are disposed to be faithfull to their engagements. Capt. L. gave the Sick indian a Small buffalow robe which he brought from the Missouri, this indian having no other Covering except his mockersons and a dressed Elk Skin without the hair-. Drewyer & Shields were sent on this morning to hungary Creek in serch of their horses which they fortunately recovered.— came _____ miles to daye.

[Lewis, June 26, 1806] Thursday June 26th 1806. This morning we collected our horses and set out after an early breakfast or at 6 A.M. we passed by the same rout we had travelled on the 17th inst. to our deposit on the top of the snowey mountain to the N. E. of hungary Creek. here we necessarily halted about 2 hours to arrange our baggage and prepare our loads. we cooked and made a haisty meal of boiled venison and mush of cows. the snow has subsided near four feet since the 17th inst. we now measured it accurately and found from a mark which we had made on a tree when we were last here on the 17th that it was then 10 feet 10 inches which appeared to be about the common debth though it is deeper still in some places. it is now generally about 7 feet. on our way up this mountain about the border of the snowey region we killed 2 of the small black pheasant and a female of the large dommanicker or speckled pheasant, the former have 16 fathers in their tail and the latter 20 while the common pheasant have only 18. the indians informed us that neither of these speceis drumed; they appear to be very silent birds for I never heared either of them make a noise in any situation. the indians haistened to be off and informed us that it was a considerable distance to the place which they wished to reach this evening where there was grass for our horses. accordingly we set out with our guides who lead us over and along the steep sides of tremendious mountains entirely covered with snow except about the roots of the trees where the snow had sometimes melted and exposed a few square feet of the earth. we ascended and decended severall lofty and steep hights but keeping on the dividing ridge between the Chopunnish and Kooskooske rivers we passed no stream of water. late in the evening much to the satisfaction of ourselves and the comfort of our horses we arrived at the desired spot and encamped on the steep side of a mountain convenient to a good spring. having passed a few miles our camp of 18 Sepr 1805 here we found an abundance of fine grass for our horses. this situation was the side of an untimbered mountain with a fair southern aspect where the snows from appearance had been desolved about 10 days. the grass was young and tender of course and had much the appearance of the greensoward. there is a great abundance of a speceis of bear-grass which grows on every part of these mountains it's growth is luxouriant and continues green all winter but the horses will not eat it. soon after we had encamped we were overtaken by a Chopunnish man who had pursued us with a view to accompany me to the falls of the Missouri. we were now informed that the two young men whom we met on the 21st and detained several days are going on a party of pleasure mearly to the Oote-lash-shoots or as they call them Sha-lees a band of the Tush-she-pah nation who reside on Clark's river in the neighbourhood of traveller's rest. one of our guides lost 2 of his horses, which he returned in surch of; he found them and rejoined us a little before dark.

[Clark, June 26, 1806] Thursday June 26th 1806 We collected our horses and Set out early and proceeded on Down hungary Creek a fiew miles and assended to the Summit of the mountain where we deposited our baggage on the 17th inst. found every thing Safe and as we had left them. the Snow which was 10 feet 10 inches deep on the top of the mountain, had sunk to 7 feet tho perfectly hard and firm. we made Some fire Cooked dinner and dined, while our horses Stood on snow 7 feet deep at least. after dinner we packed up and proceeded on. about the borders of the Snowey region we killed 2 Small black pheasents and a female of the large dommanicker or Speckled pheasent, the former have 16 feathers in the tail and the latter 20 while the common Pheasent have 18. the indians informed us that neither of these Speces drumed; they appear to be very Silent birds for I never heard any of them make any noise. the Indians hastened us off and informed us that it was a considerable distance to the place they wished to reach this evening where there was grass for our horses. accordingly we Set out with our guides who led us over and along the Steep Sides of tremendious Mountains entirely covered with Snow except about the roots of the trees where the Snow was partially melted and exposed a Small Spot of earth. we assended and decended Several Steep lofty hights but keeping on the dividing ridge of the Chopunnish & Kooskooske river we passed no Stream of water. late in the evening much to the Satisfaction of ourselves and the Comfort of the horses we arived at the desired Spot and Encamped on the Steep Side of a Mountain Convenient to a good Spring. here we found an abundance of fine grass for our horses. this Situation was the Side of an untimbered mountain with a fair Southern aspect where the Snow from appearance had been disolved about 10 days, the grass was young and tender of course and had much the appearance of the Green Sword. there is a great abundance of Species of bear grass which grows on every part of those Mountains, its growth is luxurient and continues green all winter but the horses will not eate it. Soon after we had encamped we were over taken by a Chopunnish man who had pursued us with a view to accompany Capt Lewis to the falls of Missouri. we were now informed that the two young men we met on the 21st and detained Several days were going on a party of pleasure mearly to the Oat-lash-shoots or as they call them Sha-lees a band of the Tush-she-pah Nation who reside on Clarks river in the neighbourhood of the Mouth of Travelers rest. one of our Guides lost 2 of his horses, he returned in Serch of them he found them & rejoined us at Dark. all of the Indians with us have two & 3 horses each. I was taken yesterday with a violent pain in my head which has tormented me ever Since, most violently

[Lewis, June 27, 1806] Friday June 27th 1806. We collected our horses early and set out. the road still continued on the heights of the same dividing ridge on which we had traveled yesterday for nine miles or to our encampment of the 18th of September last. about one mile short of this encampment on an elivated point we halted by the request of the Indians a few minutes and smoked the pipe. on this eminence the natives have raised a conic mound of stones of 6 or eight feet high and on it's summit erected a pine pole of 15 feet long from hence they informed us that when passing over with their familes some of the men were usually sent on foot by the fishery at the entrance of Colt Creek in order to take fish and again met the main party at the Quawmash glade on the head of the Kooskooske river. from this place we had an extensive view of these stupendous mountains principally covered with snow like that on which we stood; we were entirely surrounded by those mountains from which to one unacquainted with them it would have seemed impossible ever to have escaped; in short without the assistance of our guides I doubt much whether we who had once passed them could find our way to Travellers rest in their present situation for the marked trees on which we had placed considerable reliance are much fewer and more difficult to find than we had apprehended. these fellows are most admireable pilots; we find the road wherever the snow has disappeared though it be only for a few hundred paces. after smoking the pipe and contemplating this seene sufficient to have damp the sperits of any except such hardy travellers as we have become, we continued our march and at the distance of 3 ms.

decended a steep mountain and passed two small branches of the Chopunnish river just above their forks and again ascended the ridge on which we passed several miles and at a distance of 7 ms. arrived at our encampment of September near which we passed 3 small branches of the Chopunnish river and again ascended to the dividing ridge on which we continued nine miles when the ridge became lower and we arrived at a situation very similar to our encampment of the last evening tho the ridge was somewhat higher and the snow had not been so long desolved of course there was but little grass. here we encamped for the night having traveled 28 miles over these mountains without releiving the horses from their packs or their having any food. the indians inform us that there is an abundance of the mountain sheep or what they call white buffaloe. we saw three black-tailed or mule deer this evening but were unable to get a shoot at them. we also saw several tracks of those animals in the snow. the indians inform that there is great abundance of Elk in the vally about the Fishery on the Kooskooske River. our meat being exhausted we issued a pint of bears oil to a mess which with their boiled roots made an agreeable dish. Potts's legg which has been much swolen and inflamed for several days is much better this evening and gives him but little pain. we applyed the pounded roots and leaves of the wild ginger & from which he found great relief.- neare our encampment we saw a great number of the yellow lilly with reflected petals in blume; this plant was just as forward here at this time as it was in the plains on the 10th of may.

[Clark, June 27, 1806] Friday June 27th 1806 We collected our horses early and Set out. the road Still Continue on the hights of the Dividing ridge on which we had traveled yesterday for 9 Ms. or to our encampment of the 16th Septr. last. about 1 m. Short of the encampment we halted by the request of the Guides a fiew minits on an ellevated point and Smoked a pipe on this eminance the nativs have raised a conic mound of Stons of 6 or 8 feet high and erected a pine pole of 15 feet long. from hence they informed us that when passing over with their families some of the men were usually Sent on foot by the fishery at the enterance of Colt Creek in order to take fish and again meet the party at the quawmash glade on the head of Kooskoske river. from this place we had an extencive view of these Stupendeous Mountains principally Covered with Snow like that on which we Stood; we were entirely Serounded by those mountains from which to one unacquainted with them it would have Seemed impossible ever to have escaped, in short without the assistance of our guides, I doubt much whether we who had once passed them could find our way to Travellers rest in their present Situation for the marked trees on which we had placed Considerable reliance are much fewer and more difficuelt to find than we had apprehended. those indians are most admireable pilots; we find the road wherever the Snow has disappeared tho it be only for a fiew paces. after haveing Smoked the pipe and Contemplating this Scene Sufficient to have dampened the Spirits of any except Such hardy travellers as we have become, we continued our march and at the dist. Of 3 m. decended a Steep mountain and passed two Small branches of the Chopunnish river just above their fok, and again assend the ridge on which we passed. at the distance of 7 m. arived at our Encampment of 16th Septr. last passed 3 Small branches passed on a dividing ridge rugid and we arived at a Situation very Similar to our Situation of last night tho the ridge was Somewhat higher and the Snow had not been So long disolved of course there was but little grass. here we Encamped for the night haveing traveled 28 Ms. over these mountains without releiveing the horses from their packs or their haveing any food. the Indians inform us that there is an abundance of the Mountain Sheep, or what they Call white Buffalow on those Mountains. we Saw 3 black tail or mule deer this evening but were unable to get a Shoot at them. we also Saw Several tracks of those animals in the snow. our Meat being exhosted we issued a point of Bears Oil to a mess which with their boiled roots made an agreeable dish. Jo. Potts leg which had been much Swelled and inflaimed for several days is much better this evening and givs him but little pain. we applied the poundd root & leaves of wild ginger from which he found great relief. Near our encampment we saw great numbers of the Yellow lilly with reflected petals in blume; this plant was just as foward here at this time as it was in the plains on the 10th of May. My head has not pained me so much to day as yesterday and last night.

[Lewis, June 28, 1806] Saturday June 28th 1806. This morning we collected our horses and set out as usual after an early breakfast. several of our horses had straggled to a considersble distance in surch of food but we were fortunate enough to find them in good time they look extreemly gant this morning, however the indians informed us that at noon we would arrive at a place where there was good food for them. we continued our rout along the dividing ridge passing one very deep hollow and at the distance of six miles passed our encampment of the 16 of September last, one and a half miles further we passed the road which leads by the fishery falling in on the wright immediately on the dividing ridge about eleven O'clock we arrived at an untimbered side of a mountain with a Southern aspect just above the fishery here we found an abundance of grass for our horses as the Indians had informed us. as our horses were very hungary and much fatiegued and from information no other place where we could obtain grass for them within the reach of this evening's travel we determined to remain at this place all night having come 13 miles only. the water was distant from our encampment we therefore melted snow and used the water principally. the whole of the rout of this day was over deep snows. we find the traveling on the snow not worse than without it, as the easy passage it gives us over rocks and fallen timber fully compensate for the inconvenience of sliping, certain it is that we travel considerably faster on the snow than without it. the snow sinks from 2 to 3 inches with a hors, is coarse and firm and seems to be formed of the larger and more dense particles of the snow; the surface of the snow is reather harder in the morning than after the sun shines on it a few hours, but it is not in that situation so dense as to prevent the horse from obtaining good foothold. we killed a small black pheasant; this bird is generally found in the snowey region of the mountains and feeds on the leaves of the pine and fir. there is a speceis of small whortleburry common to the hights of the mountains, and a speceis of grass with a broad succulent leaf which looks not unlike a flag; of the latter the horses are very fond, but as yet it is generally under the snow or mearly making it's appearance as it confined to the upper parts of the highest mountains.

[Clark, June 28, 1806] Saturday June 28th 1806 This morning we Colected our horses and Set out as usial after an early brackfast. we continued our rout along the dividig ridge over knobs & through deep hollows passed our encampmt of the 14 Sept. last near the forks of the road leaving the one on which we had Came one leading to the fishery to our right imediately on the dividing ridge. at 12 oClock we arived at an untimberd side of a mountain with a southern aspect just above the fishery here we found an abundance of grass for our horses as the guids had informed us. as our horses were hungary and much fatiegued and from information no other place where we could obtain grass for them within the reach of this evening's travel we deturmined to remain at this place all night haveing come 13 m. only. the water was distant from our Encampment we therefore melted Snow and used the water. the whole of the rout of this day was over deep Snow. we find the travelling on the Snow not worse than without it, as easy passage it givs us over rocks and fallen timber fully compensates for the inconvenience of sliping, certain it is that we travel considerably faster on the snow than without it. the Snow Sinks from 2 to 3 inches with a horse, is course and firm and seems to be formed of the larger particles the surface of the snow sees to be rather harder in the morning than after the Sun Shines on it a fiew hours, but it is not in that situation so dense as to prevent the horses from obtaining good foothold. I killed a Small black pheasant; this bird is generally found in the Snowey region of the mountains and feeds on the leaves of the pine & fir. there is a Species of Small huckleberry common to the hights of the mountains, and a Species of grass with a broad succulent leaf which looks not unlike a flag; of the latter the horses are very fond, but as yet it is generally under the Snow, or mearly makeing it's appearance as it confined to the upper part of the highest mountains.

[Lewis, June 29, 1806] Sunday June 29th 1806. We collected our horses early this morning and set out, having previously dispatched Drewyer and R. Fields to the warm springs to hunt. we pursued the hights of the ridge on which we have been passing for several days; it terminated at the distance of 5 ms. from our encampment and we decended to, and passed the main branch of the Kooskooske 11/2 ms. above the entrance of Quawmash creek wid falls in on the N. E. side. when we decended from this ridge we bid adieu to the snow. near the river we fund a deer which the hunters had killed and left us. this was a fortunate supply as all our oil was now exhausted and we were reduced to our roots alone without salt. the Kooskooske at this place is about 30 yds. wide and runs with great volocity. the bed as all the mountain streams is composed of smooth stones. beyond the river we ascended a very steep acclivity of a mountain about 2 Miles and arrived at it's summit where we found the old road which we had pased as we went out, coming in on our wright. the road was now much plainer and more beaten, which we were informed happened from the circumstance of the Ootslashshoots visiting the fishery frequently from the vally of Clark's river; tho there was no appearance of there having been here this spring. at noon we arrived at the quawmas flatts on the Creek of the same name and halted to graize our horses and dine having traveled 12 miles. we passed our encampment of the 13th of September at 10 ms. where we halted there is a pretty little plain of about 50 acres plentifully stocked with quawmash and from apperances this fromes one of the principal stages or encampments of the indians who pass the mountains on this road. we found after we had halted that one of our packhorses with his load and one of my riding horses were left behind. we dispatched J. Feilds and Colter in surch of the lost horses. after dinner we continued our march seven miles further to the warm springs where we arrived early in the evening and sent out several hunters, who as well as R Fields and Drewyer returned unsuccessful; late in the evening Colter and J. Fields joined us with the lost horses and brought with them a deer which they had killed, this furnished us with supper. these warm springs are situated at the base of a hill of no considerable hight on the N side and near the bank of travellers rest creek which at that place is about 10 yards wide. these springs issue from the bottoms and through the interstices of a grey freestone rock, the rock rises in iregular masy clifts in a circular range arround the springs on their lower side. immediately above the springs on the creek there is a handsome little quamas plain of about 10 acres. the prinsipal spring is about the temperature of the warmest baths used at the hot springs in Virginia. In this bath which had been prepared by the Indians by stoping the run with stone and gravel, I bathed and remained in 19 minutes, it was with dificulty I could remain thus long and it caused a profuse sweat two other bold springs adjacent to this are much warmer, their heat being so great as to make the hand of a person smart extreemly when immerced. I think the temperature of these springs about the same as the hotest of the hot springs in Virginia. both the men and indians amused themselves with the use of a bath this evening. I observed that the indians after remaining in the hot bath as long as they could bear it ran and plunged themselves into the creek the water of which is now as cold as ice can make it; after remaining here a few minutes they returned again to the warm bath, repeating this transision several times but always ending with the warm bath. I killed a small black pheasant near the quamash grounds this evening which is the first I have seen below the snowy region. I also saw some young pheasants which were about the size of Chickens of 3 days old. saw the track of two bearfoot indians who were supposed to be distressed rufugees who had fled from the Minnetares.

[Clark, June 29, 1806] Sunday June 29th 1806 We colected our horses and Set out haveing previously dispatched Drewyer & R. Field to the Warm Springs to hunt. we prosued the hights of the ridge on which we have been passing for several days; it termonated at the distance of 5 M. from our encampment, and we decended to & passed the main branch of Kooskooke 11/2 Ms. above the enterance of Glade Creek which falls in on the N. E. Side. we bid adew to the Snow. near the River we found a Deer which the hunters had killed and left us. this was a fortunate Supply as all our bears oil was now exhosted, and we were reduced to our roots alone without Salt. the river is 30 yds wide and runs with great velossity. the bead as all the Mountain streams is composed of Smooth Stone. beyond this river we assended a Steep Mountain about 2 Miles to it's Sumit where we found the old road which we had passed on as we went out. comeing in on our right, the road was now much plainer and much beaten. at noon we arived at the quawmash flatts on Vally Creek and halted to graize our horses and dined haveing traveled 12 Miles here is a pretty little plain of about 50 acres plentifully Stocked with quawmash and from appearance this forms one of the principal Stages of the indians who pass the mountains on this road. we found that one of our pack horss with his load and one of Capt. L.s. horses were missing we dispatched Jo. Field & Colter in serch of the lost horse's. after dinner we continued our march 7 ms further to the worm Springs where we arrived early in the evening, and Sent out Several hunters, who as well as R. Field & Drewyer returned unsuksessfull; late in the evening Jo. Field & Colter joined us with the lost horses and brought with them a Deer which J. F. had killed, this furnished us with a Supper.

Those Worm or Hot Springs are Situated at the base of a a hill of no considerable hight, on the N. Side and near the bank of travellers rest Creek which is at that place about 10 yds wide. these Springs issue from the bottom and through the interstices of a grey freestone rock, the rock rises in irregular masy clifts in a circular range, arround the Springs on their lower Side. imediately above the Springs on the Creek there is a handsom little quawmash plain of about 10 acres. the principal Spring is about the temperature of the Warmest baths used at the Hot Springs in Virginia. in this bath which had been prepared by the Indians by stopping the river with Stone and mud, I bathed and remained in 10 minits it was with dificulty I could remain this long and it causd a profuse swet. two other bold Springs adjacent to this are much warmer, their heat being so great as to make the hand of a person Smart extreemly when immerced. we think the temperature of those Springs about the Same as that of the hotest of the hot Springs of Virginia. both the Men and the indians amused themselves with the use of the bath this evening. I observe after the indians remaining in the hot bath as long as they could bear it run and plunge themselves into the Creek the water of which is now as Cold as ice Can make it; after remaining here a fiew minits they return again to the worm bath repeeting this transision Several times but always ending with the worm bath. Saw the tracks of 2 bearfooted indians-.

[Lewis, June 30, 1806] Monday June 30th 1806. We dispatched Drewyer and J. Fields early this morning to hunt on the road and indeavour to obtain some meat for us. just as we had prepared to set out at an early hour a deer came in to lick at these springs and one of our hunters killed it; this secured us our dinners, and we proceeded down the creek sometimes in the bottoms and at other times on the top or along the steep sides of the ridge to the N. of the Creek. at one mile from the springs we passed a stout branch of the creek on the north side and at noon having travelled 13 ms. we arrived at the entrance of a second Northen branch of the creek where we had nooned it on the 12 th of Septr. last. here we halted, dined and graized our horses. while here Sheilds took a small tern and killed a deer. at this place a road turns off to the wright which the indians informed us leads to Clarks river some distance below where there is a fine extensive vally in which the Shalees or Ootslashshoots sometimes reside. in descending the creek this morning on the steep side of a high hill my horse sliped with both his hinder feet out of the road and fell, I also fell off backwards and slid near 40 feet down the hill before I could stop myself such was the steepness of the declivity; the horse was near falling on me in the first instance but fortunately recovers and we both escaped unhirt. I saw a small grey squirrel today much like those of the Pacific coast only that the belly of this was white. I also met with the plant in blume which is sometimes called the lady's slipper or mockerson flower. it is in shape and appearance like ours only that the corolla is white, marked with small veigns of pale red longitudinally on the inner side. after dinner we resumed our march. soon after seting out Sheilds killed another deer and in the course of the evening we picked up three others which Drewyer had killed along the road making a total of 6 today. Deer are very abundant in the neighbourhood of travellers rest of both speceis, also some bighorns and Elk. a little before sunset we arrived at our old encampment on the south side of the creek a little above it's entrance into Clark's river. here we encamped with a view to remain two days in order to rest ourselves and horses & make our final arrangements for seperation. we came 19 ms. after dinner the road being much better than it has been since we entered the mountains we found no appearance of the Ootslashshoots having been here lately. the indians express much concern for them and apprehend that the Minnetares of fort de Prarie have distroyed them in the course of the last winter and spring, and mention the tracks of the bearfoot Indians which we saw yesterday as an evidence of their being much distressed.- our horses have stood the journey supprisingly well, most of them are yet in fine order, and only want a few days rest to restore them perfectly.-

[Clark, June 30, 1806] Monday June 30th 1806 We dispatched Drewyer & Jo. Field early this morning ahead to hunt. just as we had prepard. to set out at an early hour, a deer Came in to lick at the Springs and one of our hunters killed it; this Secired to us our dinner. and we proceeded down the Creek, Sometimes in the bottoms and at other times on the tops or along the Steep Sides of the ridge to the N of the Creek. at 11/2 m. we passd our encampment of the 12th of Septr. last. we noon'd it at the place we had on the 12 of Septr. last whiles here Shields killed a deer on the N. fork near the road. here a rode leads up the N. fork and passed over to an extensive vally on Clarks river at Some distance down that river as our guids inform us. after dinner we resumed our march. Soon after Setting out Shields killed another deer, and we picked up 3 others which G Drewyer had killed along the road. Deer are very abundant in the neighbourhood of travellers rest of boath Specis, also Some big horn and Elk. a little before Sunset we arrived at our old encampment on the S. Side of the Creek a little above its enterance into Clarks river. here we Encamped with a view to remain 2 days in order to rest ourselves and horses and make our final arrangements for Seperation. we found no signs of the Oatlashshots haveing been here lately. the Indians express much Concern for them and apprehend that the Menetarries of Fort d Prar have destroyed them in the course of the last Winter and Spring, and mention the tracts of the bearfooted indians which we Saw yesterday as an evidence of their being much distressed-. our horses have stood the journey Supirisinly well and only want a fiew days rest to restore them.

[Clark, June 30, 1806] Descended the mountain to Travellers rest leaveing those tremendious mountanes behind us-in passing of which we have experiensed Cold and hunger of which I shall ever remember. in passing over this part of the Rocky mountains from Clarks river, to the quawmash flats from the 14th to the 19th of Septr. 1805 we marched through Snow, which fell on us on the night of the 14th and nearly all the day of the 15 in addition to the cold rendered the air cool and the way difficuelt. our food was horses of which we eate three.- On our return we Set out from the quawmash flats on the 15th of June and commenes the assent of the rocky mountains; the air became cool and vigitation backward- on the 16th we met with banks of Snow and in the hollars and maney of the hill Sides the Snow was from 3 to 4 feet deep and Scercely any grass vegitation just commencing where the Snow had melted- on the 17th at meridian, the Snow became So deep in every derection from 6 to 8 feet deep we could not prosue the road there being no grass for our horses we were obliged to return to the quawmash flatts to precure meat to live on as well as grass for our horses- leaveing our baggage on the mountains We precured 5 Indians as pilots and on the 24th of June 1806 we again under took those Snowey regn. on the 26th we with our baggage arived at an open plain serounded with Snow where there was grass for horses on the 27th & 28th also passing over Snow 6 or 8 feet deep all the way on 29th passed over but little Snow- but saw great masses of it lying in different directions

[Lewis, July 1, 1806] Tuesday July 1st 1806. This morning early we sent out all our hunters. set Sheilds at work to repair some of our guns which were out of order Capt. Clark & my self consurted the following plan viz. from this place I determined to go with a small party by the most direct rout to the falls of the Missouri, there to leave Thompson McNeal and goodrich to prepare carriages and geer for the purpose of transporting the canoes and baggage over the portage, and myself and six volunteers to ascend Maria's river with a view to explore the country and ascertain whether any branch of that river lies as far north as Latd. 50 and again return and join the party who are to decend the Missouri, at the entrance of Maria's river. I now called for the volunteers to accompany me on this rout, many turned out, from whom I scelected Drewyer the two Feildses, Werner, Frazier and Sergt Gass accompanied me the other part of the men are to proceed with Capt Clark to the head of Jefferson's river where we deposited sundry articles and left our canoes. from hence Sergt Ordway with a party of 9 men are to decend the river with the canoes; Capt C. with the remaining ten including Charbono and York will proceed to the Yellowstone river at it's nearest approach to the three forks of the missouri, here he will build a canoe and decend the Yellowstone river with Charbono the indian woman, his servant York and five others to the missouri where should he arrive first he will wait my arrival. Sergt Pryor with two other men are to proceed with the horses by land to the Mandans and thence to the British posts on the Assinniboin with a letter to Mr. Heney whom we wish to engage to prevail on the Sioux Chefs to join us on the Missouri, and accompany them with us to the seat of the general government. these arrangements being made the party were informed of our design and prepared themselves accordingly. our hunters killed 13 deer in the course of this day of which 7 were fine bucks, deer are large and in fine order. the indians inform us that there are a great number of white buffaloe or mountain sheep of the snowey hights of the mountains West of this river; they state that they inhabit the most rocky and inaccessible parts, and run but badly, that they kill them with great ease with their arrows when they can find them. the indian warrior who overtook us on the 26th Ult. made me a present of an excellent horse which he said he gave for the good council we had given himself and nation and also to assure us of his attatchment to the white men and his desire to be at peace with the Minnetares of Fort de Prarie. we had our venison fleeced and exposed in the sun on pole to dry. the dove the black woodpecker, the lark woodpecker, the logcock, the prarie lark, sandhill crain, prarie hen with the short and pointed tail, the robin, a speceis of brown plover, a few curloos, small black birds, ravens hawks and a variety of sparrows as well as the bee martin and the several speceis of Corvus genus are found in this vally.

Windsor birst his gun near the muzzle a few days since; this Sheilds cut off and I then exchanged it with the Cheif for the one we had given him for conducting us over the mountains. he was much pleased with the exchange and shot his gun several times; he shoots very well for an inexperienced person.

The little animal found in the plains of the Missouri which I have called the barking squirrel weighs from 3 to 31/2 pounds. it's form is that of the squirrel. it's colour is an uniform light brick red grey, the red reather predominating. the under side of the neck and bely are lighter coloured than the other parts of the body. the legs are short, and it is wide across the breast and sholders in propotion to it's size, appears strongly formed in that part; the head is also bony muscular and stout, reather more blontly terminated wider and flatter than the common squirrel. the upper lip is split or divided to the nose. the ears are short and lie close to the head, having the appearance of being cut off, in this particular they resemble the guinea pig. the teeth are like those of the squrrel rat &c. they have a false jaw or pocket between the skin and the mustle of the jaw like that of the common ground squirrel but not so large in proportion to their size. they have large and full whiskers on each side of the nose, a few long hairs of the same kind on each jaw and over the eyes. the eye is small and black. they have five toes on each foot of which the two outer toes on each foot are much shoter than those in the center particularly the two inner toes of the fore feet, the toes of the fore feet are remarkably long and sharp and seem well adapted to cratching or burrowing those of the hind feet are neither as long or sharp as the former; the nails are black. the hair of this animal is about as long and equally as course as that of the common grey squrrel of our country, and the hair of the tail is not longer than that of the body except immediately at the extremity where it is somewhat longer and frequently of a dark brown colour. the part of generation in the female is placed on the lower region of the belly between the hinder legs so far forward that she must lie on her back to copolate. the whole length of this animal is one foot five inches from the extremity of the nose to that of the tail of which the tail occupyes 4 inches. it is nearly double the size of the whistleing squirrel of the Columbia. it is much more quick active and fleet than it's form would indicate. these squirrels burrow in the ground in the open plains usually at a considerable distance from the water yet are never seen at any distance from their burrows. six or eight usually reside in one burrow to which there is never more than one entrance. these burrows are of great debth. I once dug and pursued a burrow to the debth of ten feet and did not reach it's greatest debth. they generally associate in large societies placing their burrows near each other and frequently occupy in this manner several hundred acres of land. when at rest above ground their position is generally erect on their hinder feet and rump; thus they will generally set and bark at you as you approach them, their note being much that of the little toy dogs, their yelps are in quick succession and at each they a motion to their tails upwards. they feed on the grass and weeds within the limits of their village which they never appear to exceed on any occasion. as they are usually numerous they keep the grass and weeds within their district very closely graized and as clean as if it had been swept. the earth which they throw out of their burrows is usually formed into a conic mound around the entrance. this little animal is frequently very fat and it's flesh is not unpleasant. as soon as the hard frosts commence it shuts up it's burrow and continues within untill spring. it will eat grain or meat.

[Clark, July 1, 1806] Tuesday July 1st 1806 on Clark's river We Sent out all the hunters very early this morning by 12 OClock they all returned haveing killd. 12 Deer Six of them large fat Bucks, this is like once more returning to the land of liveing a plenty of meat and that very good. as Capt. Lewis and Myself part at this place we make a division of our party and such baggage and provisions as is Souteable. the party who will accompany Capt L. is G. Drewyer, Sergt. Gass, Jo. & R. Fields, Frazier & Werner, and Thompson Goodrich & McNear as far as the Falls of Missouri at which place the 3 latter will remain untill I Send down the Canoes from the head of Jeffersons river. they will then join that party and after passing the portage around the falls, proceed on down to the enterance of Maria where Capt. Lewis will join them after haveing assended that river as high up as Laid. 50° North. from the head of Jeffersons river I shall proceed on to the head of the Rockejhone with a party of 9 or 10 men and desend that river. from the R Rockejhone I Shall dispatch Sergt. Pryor with the horses to the Mandans and from thence to the Tradeing Establishments of the N. W. Co on the Assinniboin River with a letter which we have written for the purpose to engage Mr. H. Haney to endeaver to get Some of the principal Chiefs of the Scioux to accompany us to the Seat of our government &. we divide the Loading and apportion the horses. Capt L. only takes 17 horses with him, 8 only of which he intends to take up the Maria &c. One of the Indians who accompanied us Swam Clarks river and examined the Country around, on his return he informed us that he had discovered where a Band of the Tushepaws had encamped this Spring passed of 64 Lodges, & that they had passed Down Clarks river and that it was probable that they were near the quawmash flatts on a Easterly branch of that river. those guides expressed a desire to return to their nation and not accompany us further, we informed them that if they was deturmined to return we would kill some meat for them, but wished that they would accompy Capt. Lewis on the rout to the falls of Missouri only 2 nights and show him the right road to cross the Mountains. this they agreed to do. we gave a medal of the Small Size to the young man Son to the late Great Chief of the Chopunnish Nation who had been remarkably kind to us in every instance, to all the others we tied a bunch of blue ribon about the hair, which pleased them very much. the Indian man who overtook us in the Mountain, presented Capt. Lewis with a horse and said that he opened his ears to what we had said, and hoped that Cap Lewis would see the Crovanters of Fort De Prarie and make a good peace that it was their desire to be at peace. Shew them the horse as a token of their wishes &c.

[Lewis, July 2, 1806] Wednesday July 2ed 1806. We sent out the hunters early this morning, they returned not so succesfull as yesterday having killed 2 deer only. Sheilds continued repairing the gunns which he compleated by evening. all arrangements being now compleat we determined to set out in the morning. in the course of the day we had much conversation with the indians by signs, our only mode of communicating our ideas. they informed us that they wished to go in surch of the Ootslashshoots their friends and intended leaving us tomorrow morning, I prevailed on them to go with me as far as the East branch of Clark's River and put me on the road to the Missouri. I gave the Cheif a medal of the small size; he insisted on exchanging names with me according to their custom which was accordingly done and I was called Yo-me-kol-lick which interpreted is the white bearskin foalded. in the evening the indians run their horses, and we had several foot races betwen the natives and our party with various success. these are a race of hardy strong athletic active men. nothin worthy of notice transpired in the course of the day. Goodrich and McNeal are both very unwell with the pox which they contracted last winter with the Chinnook women this forms my inducement principally for taking them to the falls of the Missouri where during an intervail of rest they can use the murcury freely. I found two speceis of native clover here, the one with a very narrow small leaf and a pale red flower, the other nearly as luxouriant as our red clover with a white flower the leaf and blume of the latter are proportionably large. I found several other uncommon plants specemines of which I preserved. The leaf of the cottonwood on this river is like that common to the Columbia narrower than that common to the lower part of the Missouri and Mississippi and wider than that on the upper part of the Missouri. the wild rose, servise berry, white berryed honeysuckle, seven bark, elder, alder aspin, choke cherry and the broad and narrow leafed willow are natives of this valley. the long leafed pine forms the principal timber of the neighbourhood, and grows as well in the river bottoms as on the hills. the firs and larch are confined to the higher parts of the hills and mountains. the tops of the high mountains on either side of this river are covered with snow. the musquetoes have been excessively troublesome to us since our arrival at this place.

[Clark, July 2, 1806] Wednesday July 2nd 1806 Sent out 2 hunters this morning and they killed 2 Deer. the Musquetors has been So troublesom day and night Since our arrival in this Vally that we are tormented very much by them and Cant write except under our Bears. We gave the Second gun to our guides agreeable to our promis, and to each we gave Powder & ball I had the greater part of the meat dried for to Subsist my party in the Mountains between the head of Jeffersons & Clarks rivers where I do not expect to find any game to kill. had all of our arms put in the most prime order two of the rifles have unfortunately bursted near the muscle, Shields Cut them off and they Shute tolerable well one which is very Short we exchanged with the Indian whoe we had given a longer gun to induc them to pilot us across the Mountains. we caused every man to fill his horn with powder & have a sufficiency of Balls &c. the last day in passing down Travellers rest Creek Capt Lewis fell down the Side of a Steep Mountain near 40 feet but fortunately receved no dammage. his hors was near falling on him but fortunately recovered and they both escaped unhurt. I killed a Small grey squrrel and a Common pheasant. Capt L. Showed me a plant in blume which is Sometimes called the ladies Slipper or Mockerson flower. it is in shape and appearance like ours only that the corolla is white marked with Small veigns of pale red longitudinally on the inner Side, and much Smaller. The Indians and Some of our men amused themselves in running races on foot as well as with their horses.

[Lewis, July 3, 1806] Thursday July 3rd 1806. All arrangements being now completed for carrying into effect the several scheemes we had planed for execution on our return, we saddled our horses and set out I took leave of my worthy friend and companion Capt. Clark and the party that accompanyed him. I could not avoid feeling much concern on this occasion although I hoped this seperation was only momentary. I proceeded down Clark's river seven miles with my party of nine men and five indians. here the Indians recommended our passing the river which was rapid and 150 yds. wide. 2 miles above this place I passed the entrance of the East branch of Clark's River which discharges itself by two channels; the water of this river is more terbid than the main stream and is from 90 to 120 yds. wide. as we had no other means of passing the river we busied ourselves collecting dry timber for the purpose of constructing rafts; timber being scarce we found considerable difficulty in procuring as much as made three small rafts. we arrived at 11 A.M. and had our rafts completed by 3 P.M. when we dined and began to take over our baggage which we effected in the course of 3 hours the rafts being obliged to return several times. the Indians swam over their horses and drew over their baggage in little basons of deer skins which they constructed in a very few minutes for that purpose. we drove our horses in after them and they followed to the opposite shore. I remained myself with two men who could scarcely swim untill the last; by this time the raft by passing so frequently had fallen a considerable distance down the river to a rapid and difficult part of it crouded with several small Islands and willow bars which were now overflown; with these men I set out on the raft and was soon hurried down with the current a mile and a half before we made shore, on our approach to the shore the raft sunk and I was drawn off the raft by a bush and swam on shore the two men remained on the raft and fortunately effected a landing at some little distance below. I wet the chronometer by this accedent which I had placed in my fob as I conceived for greater security. I now joined the party and we proceeded with the indians about 3 Ms. to a small Creek and encamped at sunset. I sent out the hunters who soon returned with three very fine deer of which I gave the indians half These people now informed me that the road which they shewed me at no great distance from our Camp would lead us up the East branch of Clark's river and a river they called Cokahlarishkit or the river of the road to buffaloe and thence to medicine river and the falls of the Missouri where we wished to go. they alledged that as the road was a well beaten track we could not now miss our way and as they were affraid of meeting with their enimies the Minnetares they could not think of continuing with us any longer, that they wished now to proceed down Clark's river in surch of their friends the Shalees. they informed us that not far from the dividing ridge between the waters of this and the Missouri rivers the roads forked they recommended the left hand as the best rout but said they would both lead us to the falls of the Missouri. I directed the hunters to turn out early in the morning and indeavour to kill some more meat for these people whom I was unwilling to leave without giving them a good supply of provision after their having been so obliging as to conduct us through those tremendous mountains. the musquetoes were so excessively troublesome this evening that we were obliged to kindle large fires for our horses these insects tortured them in such manner untill they placed themselves in the smoke of the fires that I realy thought they would become frantic. about an hour after dark the air become so coald that the musquetoes disappeared.

We saw the fresh track of a horse this evening in the road near our camp which the indians supposed to be a Shale spye. we killed a prarie hen with the short and pointed tail she had a number of young which could just fly.

[Lewis, July 4, 1806] July 4th 1806. An Indian arrived alone from the West side of the mountains. he had pursued and overtook us here. sent out the hunters early to kill some meat to give the indians as they would not go with us further and I was unwilling after they service they had rendered to send them away without a good store of provision. they are going down Clark's River in surch of the Shalees their friends, and from thence intend returning by this rout home again, they fleesed their meat informed us that they should dry it and leave it for their homeward journey.- Set out at 12. had killed no deer.

[Lewis, July 4, 1806] Friday July 4th 1806. I arrose early this morning and sent out Drewyer and the Fieldses to hunt. at 6. A.M. a man of the Pallote pellows arrived from the West side of the Rocky mountains; he had pursued us a few days after our departure and overtook us at this place; he proved to be the same young man who had first attempted to pass the rocky mountains early in June last when we lay on the Kooskooske and was obliged to relinquish the enterprize in consequence of the debth and softness of the snow. I gave a shirt a handkercheif and a small quantity of ammunition to the indians. at half after eleven the hunters returned from the chase unsuccessfull. I now ordered the horses saddled smoked a pipe with these friendly people and at noon bid them adieu. they had cut the meat which I gave them last evening thin and exposed it in the sun to dry informing me that they should leave it in this neighbourhood untill they returned as a store for their homeward journey. it is worthy of remark that these people were about to return by the same pass by which they had conducted us through the difficult part of the Rocky Mountains, altho they were about to decend Clark's river several days journey in surch of the Shale's their relations, a circumstance which to my mind furnishes sufficient evidence that there is not so near or so good a rout to the plains of Columbia by land along that river as that which we came. the several war routs of the Minetarees which fall into this vally of Clark's river concenter at traveller's rest beyond which point they have never yet dared to venture in pursuit of the nations beyond the mountains. all the nations also on the west side of the mountain with whom we are acquainted inhabiting the waters of Lewis's river & who visit the plains of the Missouri pass by this rout. these affectionate people our guides betrayed every emmotion of unfeigned regret at seperating from us; they said that they were confidint that the Pahkees, (the appellation they give the Minnetares) would cut us off. the first 5 miles of our rout was through a part of the extensive plain in which we were encamped, we then entered the mountains with the East fork of Clark's river through a narrow confined pass on it's N. side continuing up that river five ms. further to the entrance of the Cokahlahishkit R which falls in on the N. E. side, is 60 yds. wide deep and rapid. the banks bold not very high but never overflow. the East fork below its junction with this stream is 100 yds. wide and above it about 90. the water of boath are terbid but the East branch much the most so; their beds are composed of sand and gravel; the East fork possesses a large portion of the former. neither of those streams are navigable in consequence of the rapids and shoals which obstruct their currents. thus far a plain or untimbered country bordered the river which near the junction of these streams spread into a handsome level plain of no great extent; the hills were covered with long leafed pine and fir. I now continued my rout up the N. side of the Cokahlahishkit river through a timbered country for 8 miles and encamped in a handsom bottom on the river where there was an abundance of excelence grass for our horses. the evening was fine, air pleasent and no musquetoes. a few miles before we encamped I killed a squirrel of the speceis common to the Rocky Mountains and a ground squirrel of a speceis which I had never before seen, I preserved the skins of both of these animals.

[Lewis, July 5, 1806] July 5th 1806. Set out at 6 A.M.- steered N. 75 E. 61/2 M. passed a stout C. N Side at 21/2 M. another just above saw an old indian encampment of 11 lodges of bark and leather on S. side at 31/2 M. killed a deer.

N. 25 E. 12 m. passing a small creek at one m. on S side on which there is a handsom and extensive Valley and plain for 10 or 12 ms. also another creek 12 yd. wide at 1/2 a mile further on N. sides and another 8 yds. wide on N. side at 5 ms further one & 1/2 m. short of the extremity of this course arrive at a high prarie on N. side from one to three miles in width extending up the river. halted and dined in the mouth of a little drane on the left of the plain where there was a considerable quantity of quawmash. saw a gang of antelopes here of which we killed one the does at this season herd with each other and have their young. the bucks are alone there are many wild horses on Clarkes river about the place we passed it we saw some of them at a distance. there are said to be many of them about the head of the yellowstone river.

East 6 m. to the entrance of Werner's Creek 35 yds. wide through a high extensive prairie on N. side. hills low and timbered with the long leafed pine, larch, and some fir. the road passes at some distance to the left of the river and this couses is with the river.

N. 22 W. 4 miles to a high insulated knob just above the entrance of a
Creek 8 yards wide which discharges itself into Werners Creek.

N. 75 E. 21/2 M. to the river passing through an extensive and handsom plain on Werner's Creek, crossing that creek at 1 m. and leaving a high prarie hill to the right seperating the plain from the river. saw two swan in this beautiful Creek.

East 3 m. to the entrance of a large creek 20 yds. wide Called

31 m. Seamans Creek passing a creek at 1 m. 8 yds. wide. this course with the river, the road passing through an extensive high prarie rendered very uneven by a vast number of little hillucks and sinkholes at the heads of these two creeks high broken mountains stand at the distance of 10 m. forming a kind of Cove generally of open untimbered country.- we encamped on the lower side of the last creek just above it's entrance. here a war party had encamped about 2 months since and conceald their fires.-

[Lewis, July 6, 1806]
July 6th 1806.
Set out a little after sunrise passed the creek a little above our
encampment.

East 14 M. to the point at which the river leaves the extensive plains and enters the mountains these plains I called the prarie of the knobs from a number of knobs being irregularly scattered through it. passed the N. fork 1 of the Cokahlarishkit Rivers at 7 M. it is 45 yds. wide deep and rapid. had some difficulty in passing it. passed a large crooked pond at 4 ms. further. great Number of the burrowing squirrls in this prarie of the speceis common to the plains of Columbia. saw some goats and deer. the hunters killed one of the latter. the trail which we take to be a returning war-party of the Minnetares of Fort de prarie becomes much fresher. they have a large pasel of horses. saw some Curloos, bee martains woodpeckers plover robins, doves, ravens, hawks and a variety of sparrows common to the plains also some ducks. the North fork is terbid as is also the main branch which is about 50 yds. wide the other streams are clear. these plains continue their course S 75 E. and are wide where the river leaves them. up this valley and creek a road passes to Dearbourn's river and thence to the Missouri.

N. 60 E 11/2 up the river. here we halted and dine and our hunters overtook us with a deer which they had killed. river bottoms narrow and country thickly timbered. Cottonwood and pine grow intermixed in the river bottoms musquitoes extreemely troublesome. we expect to meet with the Minnetares and are therefore much on our guard both day and night. the bois rague in blume.- saw the common small blue flag and peppergrass. the southern wood and two other speceis of shrub are common in the prarie of knobs. preserved specemines of them. passed several old indian encampments of brush lodges.-

S 80 E 2 m. to two nearly equal forks of the river here the road forks also one leading up each branch these are the forks of which I presume the indians made mention. passed a creek on N. side 12 yds. wide shallow and clear.

N 75 E. 8 m. to our encampment of this evening over a steep high

Ms. 25 balld toped hill for 2 m. thence through and to the left of a large low bottom 2 M. thence three miles through a thick wood along the hill side bottoms narrow. thence 1 m. to our encampment on a large creek some little distance above it's mouth through a beatifull plain on the border of which we passed the remains of

32 old lodges. they appear to be those of the Minnetares as are all those we have seen today. killed five deer and a beaver today. encamped on the creek much sign of beaver in this extensive bottom.

[Lewis, July 7, 1806] July 7 1806. Set out at 7 A.M. N. 75 E. 6 M. with the road through a level beatifull plain on the North side of the river much timber in the bottoms hills also timbered with pitch pine. no longleafed pine since we left the praries of the knobs. crossed a branch of the creek 8 yds. wid. on which we encamped at 1/4 m. also passed a creek 15 yd. wide at 1/4 further. North 6 ms.- passed the main creek at a mile 1/2 and kept up it on the wright hand side through handsom plain bottoms to the foot of a ridge which we ascended the main stream boar N W & W. as far as I could see it a wright hand fork falls into this creek at 1 M. above the commencement of this course.

N. 15 E. 8 m. over two ridges and again striking the wrighthand fork at 4 ms. then continued up it on the left hand side much appearance of beaver many dams. bottoms not wide and covered with low willow and grass. halted to dine at a large beaver dam the hunters killed 3 deer and a fawn. deer are remarkably plenty and in good order. Reubin Fields wounded a moos deer this morning near our camp. my dog much worried.

N. 10 E. 3 m. up the same creek on the east side through a handsome narrow plain.

N 45 E. 2 m. passing the dividing ridge betwen the waters of the Columbia and Missouri rivers at 1/4 of a mile from this gap which is low and an easy ascent on the W. side the fort mountain bears North Eaast, and appears to be distant about 20 Miles. the road for one and 3/4 miles desends the hill and continues down a branch.

N. 20 W. 7 ms. over several hills and hollows along the foot of the mountain hights passing five small rivulets running to the wright. saw some sighn of buffaloe early this morning in the valley where we encamped last evening from which it appears that the buffaloe do sometimes penetrate these mountains a few miles. we saw no buffaloe this evening. but much old appearance of dung, tracks &c. encamped on a small run under the foot of the mountain. after we encamped Drewyer killed two beaver and shot third which bit his knee very badly and escaped

[Lewis, July 8, 1806]
July 8th 1806.
Set out at 6 A.M.

N 25 W. 31/2 m. to the top of a hill from whence we saw the Shishequaw mountain about 8 M. distant, immediately before us. passed Dearborne's river at 3 m. this stream comes form the S. W. out of the mountains which are about 5 Ms. to our left. the bed of the river is about 100 yds. wide tho the water occupys only about 30 yds. it appears to spread over it's bottoms at certain seasons of the year and runs a mear torrant tearing up the trees by the roots which stand in it's bottom the Shishiquaw mountain is a high insulated conic mountain standing several miles in advance of the Eastern range of the rocky mountains. Country broken and mountanous to our wright.

North- 141/2 ms. through an open plain to Shishequaw Creek 20 yds. wide bottoms and considerable gantity of timber it leaves the mountain to the S E and enters the mountains. we struck it about 10 miles below the mountain which boar S. 32 W. from us. the road continued along the foot of the mountain to the West of north which not being anything like our course and the country becoming tolerably level at the commencement of this course we steered through the plains leaving the road with a view to strike Medicine river and hunt down it to it's mouth in order to procure the necessary skins to make geer, and meat for the three men whom we mean to leave at the falls as none of them are hunters. we halted and dined on Shishequaw Creek R. Fields killed a fine buck and a goat; Josh. Fields saw two buffaloe below us some distance which are the first that have been seen. we saw a great number of deer goats and wolves as we passed through the plains this morning but no Elk or buffaloe. saw some barking squirrils much rejoiced at finding ourselves in the plains of the Missouri which abound with game.

N. 50 E 2 m. to the discharge of Shishequaw Creek into the Medicine
Rivers through an extensive beautiful) and level bottom.

N. 85° E. 8 m. to our encampment of this evening on a large island the bottoms continue level low and extensive plains level and not very elivated partculary on the N. E. side of the river. the land of neither the plains nor bottoms is fertile. it is of a light colour intermixed with a considerable proportion of gravel the grass generally about 9 inghes high. the hunters were unsuccessful this evening. I killed a very large and the whitest woolf I have seen-

[Lewis, July 9, 1806] July 9th 1806. Set out early and had not proceeded far before it began to rain. the air extreemly cold. halted a few minutes in some old lodges until it cased to rain in some measure. we then proceeded and it rained without intermission wet us to the skin.

N. 80° E. 4 ms. through a handsome level wide bottom in which there is a considerable quanty of narrow leafed cottonwood timber. the river is generally about 80 yds. wide rapid yet I think it migt be navigated. it's bed is loose gravel and pebbles. the banks low but seldom overflow. water clear.

S 85 E 4 ms Still on the S W. side of the river through wide and level bottoms some timber. Joseph feilds killed a very fat buffaloe bull and we halted to dine. we took the best of the meat as much as we could possibly carry on our horses. the day continuing rainy and cold I concluded to remain all day. we feasted on the buffaloe. saw a number of deer wolves and Antelopes. killed two deer.

[Lewis, July 10, 1806] July 10th 1806. Set out early and continued down the S W bank of the river N 75 E 24 m. to our encampment in a grove of cottonwood timber. the latter part of this course for 7 miles there is no timber in the river bottom, the other parts of the river possesses bottoms of the wide leafed cottonwood. much the greater part of the bottom is untimbered. the bottoms are wide and level the high praries or plains are also beautiful level and smooth. great quantities of prickly pear of two kinds on the plains. the ground is renderd so miry by the rain which fell yesterday that it is excessively fatiegueing to the horses to travel. we came 10 miles and halted for dinner the wind blowing down the river in the fore part of the day was unfavourable to the hunters they saw several gangs of Elk but they having the wind of them ran off. in the evening the wind set from the West and we fell in with a few elk of which R. Fields and myself killed 3 one of which swam the river and fell on the opposite so we therefore lost it's skin I sent the packhorses on with Sergt. Gass directing them to halt and encamp at the first timber which proved to be about 7 ms. I retained frazier to assist in skining the Elk. we wer about this time joined by drewer. a large brown bear swam the river near where we were and drewyer shot and killed it. by the time we butchered thes 2 elk and bar it was nearly dark we loaded our horses with the best of the meat and pursud the party and found them encamped as they had been directed in the first timber. we did not reach them until 9 P.M. they informed us that they had seen a very large bear in the plains which had pursued Sergt. Gass and Thomson some distance but their horses enabled them to keep out of it's reach. they were affraid to fire on the bear least their horses should throw them as they were unaccustomed to the gun. we killed five deer 3 Elk and a bear today saw vast herds of buffaloe in the evening below us on the river. we hered them bellowing about us all night. vast assemblages of wolves. saw a large herd of Elk making down the river. passed a considerable rapid in medicine river after dark. the river about a hundred yards wide is deep and in many parts rappid and today has been much crouded with islands. from our encampment down we know the river and there is no rapids and scarcely any courant. goosberries are very abundant of the common red kind and are begining to ripen. no currants on this river. both species of the prickly pears just in blume.

[Lewis, July 11, 1806] July 11th 1806. the morning was fair and the plains looked beatifull the grass much improved by the late rain. the air was pleasant and a vast assemblage of little birds which croud to the groves on the river sung most enchantingly. we set out early. I sent the hunters down Medicine river to hunt Elk and proceeded with the party across the plain to the white bear Islands which I found to be 8 ms. distant my course S. 75 E.- through a level beautiful) and extensive high plain covered with immence birds of buffaloe.- it is now the season at which the buffaloe begin to coppelate and the bulls keep a tremendious roaring we could hear them for many miles and there are such numbers of them that there is one continual roar. our horses had not been acquainted with the buffaloe they appeared much allarmed at their appearance and bellowing. when I arrived in sight of the whitebear Islands the missouri bottoms on both sides of the river were crouded with buffaloe I sincerely belief that there were not less than 10 thousand buffaloe within a circle of 2 miles arround that place. I met with the hunters at a little grove of timber opposite to the island where they had killed a cowl and were waiting our arrival. they had met with no elk. I directed the hunters to kill some buffaloe as well for the benifit of their skins to enable us to pass the river as for their meat for the men I meant to leave at this place. we unloaded our horses and encamped opposite to the Islands. had the cow skined and some willows sticks collected to make canoes of the hides by 12 OCk. they killed eleven buffaloe most of them in fine order. the bulls are now generally much fatter than the cows and are fine beef. I sent out all hands with the horses to assist in buthering and bringing in the meat by 3 in the evening we had brought in a large quantity of fine beef and as many hides as we wanted for canoes shelters and geer. I then set all hands to prepare two canoes the one we made after the mandan fassion with a single skin in the form of a bason and the other we constructed of two skins on a plan of our own. we were unable to compleat our canoes this evening. the wind blew very hard. we continued our operations untill dark and then retired to rest. I intend giving my horses a couple of days rest at this place and deposit all my baggage which is not necessary to my voyage up medicine river.

[Lewis, July 12, 1806] July 12th 1806. we arrose early and resumed our operations in compleating our canoes which we completed by 10 A.M. about this time two of the men whom I had dispatched this morning in quest of the horses returned with seven of them only. the remaining ten of our best horses were absent and not to be found. I fear that they are stolen. I dispatch two men on horseback in surch of them. the wind blew so violently that I did not think it prudent to attempt passing the river.- at Noon Werner returned having found three others of the horses near Fort Mountain. Sergt. Gass did not return untill 3 P.M. not having found the horses. he had been about 8 ms. up medecine river. I now dispatched Joseph Fields and Drewyer in quest of them. the former returned at dark unsuccessfull and the latter continued absent all night. at 5 P.M. the wind abated and we transported our baggage and meat to the opposite shore in our canoes which we found answered even beyond our expectations. we swam our horses over also and encamped at sunset. quetoes extreemly troublesome. I think the river is somewhat higher than when we were here last summer. the present season has been much more moist than the preceeding one. the grass and weeds are much more luxouriant than they were when I left this place on the 13th of July 1805 saw the brown thrush, pigeons, doves &c.

the yellow Currants begining to ripen.

[Lewis, July 13, 1806] 13th July. removed above to my old station opposite the upper point of the white bear island. formed our camp and set Thompson &c at work to complete the geer for the horses. had the cash opened found my bearskins entirely destroyed by the water, the river having risen so high that the water had penitrated. all my specimens of plants also lost. the Chart of the Missouri fortunately escaped. opened my trunks and boxes and exposed the articles to dry. found my papers damp and several articles damp. the stoper had come out of a phial of laudinum and the contents had run into the drawer and distroyed a gret part of my medicine in such manner that it was past recovery. waited very impatiently for the return of Drewyer he did not arrive. Musquetoes excessively troublesome insomuch that without the protection of my musquetoe bier I should have found it impossible to wright a moment. the buffaloe are leaving us fast and passing on to the S. East. killed a buffaloe picker a beatifull bird.

[Lewis, July 14, 1806] 14th July Had the carriage wheels dug up found them in good order. the iron frame of the boat had not suffered materially. had the meat cut thiner and exposed to dry in the sun. and some roots of cows of which I have yet a small stock pounded into meal for my journey. I find the fat buffaloe meat a great improvement to the mush of these roots. the old cash being too damp to venture to deposit my trunks &c in I sent them over to the Large island and had them put on a high scaffold among some thick brush and covered with skins. I take this precaution lest some indians may visit the men I leave here before the arrival of the main party and rob them. the hunters killed a couple of wolves, the buffaloe have almost entirely disappeared. saw the bee martin. the wolves are in great numbers howling arround us and loling about in the plains in view at the distance of two or three hundred yards. I counted 27 about the carcase of a buffaloe which lies in the water at the upper point of the large island. these are generally of the large kind. Drewyer did not return this evening.-

[Lewis, July 15, 1806] 15 July 1806. Sent McNeal down this morning to the lower part of the portage to see whether the large perogue and cash were safe.- Drewyer returned without the horses and reported that he had tracked them to beyond our camp of the

[Lewis, July 15, 1806] Tuesday July 15th 1806. Dispatched McNeal early this morning to the lower part of portage in order to learn whether the Cash and white perogue remained untouched or in what state they were. the men employed in drying the meat, dressing deerskins and preparing for the reception of the canoes. at 1 P.M. Drewyer returned without the horses and reported that after a diligent surch of 2 days he had discovered where the horses had passed Dearborn's river at which place there were 15 lodges that had been abandoned about the time our horses were taken; he pursued the tracks of a number of horses from these lodges to the road which we had traveled over the mountains which they struck about 3 ms. South of our encampment of the 7th inst. and had pursued this road Westwardly; I have no doubt but they are a party of the Tushapahs who have been on a buffaloe hunt. Drewyer informed that there camp was in a small bottom on the river of about 5 acres inclosed by the steep and rocky and lofty clifts of the river and that so closely had they kept themselves and horses within this little spot that there was not a track to be seen of them within a quarter of a mile of that place. every spire of grass was eaten up by their horses near their camp which had the appearance of their having remained here some time. his horse being much fatiegued with the ride he had given him and finding that the indians had at least 2 days the start of him thought it best to return. his safe return has releived me from great anxiety. I had already settled it in my mind that a whitebear had killed him and should have set out tomorrow in surch of him, and if I could not find him to continue my rout to Maria's river. I knew that if he met with a bear in the plains even he would attack him. and that if any accedent should happen to seperate him from his horse in that situation the chances in favour of his being killed would be as 9 to 10. I felt so perfectly satisfyed that he had returned in safety that I thought but little of the horses although they were seven of the best I had. this loss great as it is, is not intirely irreparable, or at least dose not defeat my design of exploring Maria's river. I have yet 10 horses remaining, two of the best and two of the worst of which I leave to assist the party in taking the canoes and baggage over the portage and take the remaining 6 with me; these are but indifferent horses most of them but I hope they may answer our purposes. I shall leave three of my intended party, (viz) Gass, Frazier and Werner, and take the two Feildses and Drewyer. by having two spare horses we can releive those we ride. having made this arrangement I gave orders for an early departure in the morning, indeed I should have set out instantly but McNeal road one of the horses which I intend to take and has not yet returned. a little before dark McNeal returned with his musquet broken off at the breech, and informed me that on his arrival at willow run he had approached a white bear within ten feet without discover him the bear being in the thick brush, the horse took the allarm and turning short threw him immediately under the bear; this animal raised himself on his hinder feet for battle, and gave him time to recover from his fall which he did in an instant and with his clubbed musquet he struck the bear over the head and cut him with the guard of the guns and broke off the breech, the bear stunned with the stroke fell to the ground and began to scratch his head with his feet; this gave McNeal time to climb a willow tree which was near at hand and thus fortunately made his escape. the bear waited at the foot of the tree untill late in the evening before he left him, when McNeal ventured down and caught his horse which had by this time strayed off to the distance of 2 ms. and returned to camp. these bear are a most tremenduous animal; it seems that the hand of providence has been most wonderfully in our favor with rispect to them, or some of us would long since have fallen a sacrifice to their farosity. there seems to be a sertain fatality attatched to the neighbourhood of these falls, for there is always a chapter of accedents prepared for us during our residence at them. the musquetoes continue to infest us in such manner that we can scarcely exist; for my own part I am confined by them to my bier at least 3/4ths of my time. my dog even howls with the torture he experiences from them, they are almost insupportable, they are so numerous that we frequently get them in our thrats as we breath.

[Lewis, July 16, 1806] Wednesday July 16th 1806. I dispatched a man early this morning to drive up the horses as usual, he returned at 8 A.M. with one of them only. allarmed at this occurrence I dispatched one of my best hands on horseback in surch of them he returned at 10 A.M. with them and I immediately set out. sent Drewyer and R. Fields with the horses to the lower side of Medecine river, and proceeded myself with all our baggage and J. Fields down the missouri to the mouth of Medecine river in our canoe of buffaloe skins. we were compelled to swim the horses above the whitebear island and again across medicine river as the Missouri is of great width below the mouth of that river. having arrived safely below Medicine river we immediately sadled our horses and proceeded down the river to the handsom fall of 47 feet where I halted about 2 hours and took a haisty sketch of these falls; in the mean time we had some meat cooked and took dinner after which we proceeded to the grand falls where we arrived at sunset. on our way we saw two very large bear on the opposite side of the river. as we arrived in sight of the little wood below the falls we saw two other bear enter it; this being the only wood in the neighbourhood we were compelled of course to contend with the bear for possession, and therefore left our horses in a place of security and entered the wood which we surched in vain for the bear, they had fled. here we encamped and the evening having the appearance of rain made our beds and slept under a shelving rock. these falls have abated much of their grandure since I first arrived at them in June 1805, the water being much lower at preset than it was at that moment, however they are still a sublimely grand object. I determined to take a second drawing of it in the morning. we saw a few buffaloe as we passed today, the immence hirds which were about this place on our arrival have principally passed the river and directed their course downwards. we see a number of goats or antilopes always in passing through the plains of the Missouri above the Mandans. at this season they are thinly scattered over the plains but seem universally distributed in every part; they appear very inquisitive usually to learn what we are as we pass, and frequently accompany us at no great distance for miles, frequently halting and giving a loud whistle through their nostrils, they are a very pretty animal and astonishingly fleet and active. we spent this evening free from the torture of the Musquetoes. there are a great number of geese which usually raise their young above these falls about the entrance of Medicine river we saw them in large flocks of several hundred as we passed today. I saw both yesterday and today the Cookkoo or as it is sometimes called the rain craw. this bird is not met with west of the Rocky Mountains nor within them.

[Lewis, July 17, 1806] Thursday July 17th 1806. I arrose early this morning and made a drawing of the falls. after which we took breakfast and departed. it being my design to strike Maria's river about the place at which I left it on my return to it's mouth in the begining of June 1805. I steered my course through the wide and level plains which have somewhat the appearance of an ocean, not a tree nor a shrub to be seen. the land is not fertile, at least far less so, than the plains of the Columbia or those lower down this river, it is a light coloured soil intermixed with a considerable proportion of coarse gravel without sand, when dry it cracks and appears thursty and is very hard, in it's wet state, it is as soft and slipry as so much soft soap the grass is naturally but short and at present has been rendered much more so by the graizing of the buffaloe, the whole face of the country as far as the eye can reach looks like a well shaved bowlinggreen, in which immence and numerous herds of buffaloe were seen feeding attended by their scarcely less numerous sheepherds the wolves. we saw a number of goats as usual today, also the party coloured plover with the brick red head and neck; this bird remains about the little ponds which are distributed over the face of these plains and here raise their young. we killed a buffaloe cow as we passed throug the plains and took the hump and tonge which furnish ample rations for four men one day. at 5 P.M. we arrived at rose rivers where I purposed remaining all night as I could not reach maria's river this evening and unless I did there would be but little probability of our finding any wood and very probably no water either. on our arrival at the river we saw where a wounded and bleading buffaloe had just passed and concluded it was probable that the indians had been runing them and were near at hand. the Minnetares of Fort de prarie and the blackfoot indians rove through this quarter of the country and as they are a vicious lawless and reather an abandoned set of wretches I wish to avoid an interview with them if possible. I have no doubt but they would steel our horses if they have it in their power and finding us weak should they happen to be numerous wil most probably attempt to rob us of our arms and baggage; at all events I am determined to take every possible precaution to avoid them if possible. I hurried over the river to a thick wood and turned out the horses to graize; sent Drewyer to pursue and kill the wounded buffaloe in order to determine whether it had been wounded by the indians or not, and proceeded myself to reconnoitre the adjacent country having sent R. Fields for the same purpose a different rout. I ascended the river hills and by the help of my glass examined the plains but could make no discovery, in about an hour I returned to camp, where I met with the others who had been as unsuccessfull as myself. Drewyer could not find the wounded buffaloe. J. Fields whom I had left at camp had already roasted some of the buffaloe meat and we took dinner after which I sent Drewyer and R. Fields to resume their resurches for the indians; and set myself down to record the transactions of the day. rose river is at this place fifty yards wide, the water which is only about 3 feet deep occupys about 35 yds. and is very terbid of a white colour. the general course of this river is from East to west so far as I can discover it's track through the plains, it's bottoms are wide and well timbered with cottonwood both the broad and narrow leafed speceis. the bed of this stream is small gravel and mud; it's banks are low but never overflow, the hills are about 100 or 150 feet high; it possesses bluffs of earth like the lower part of the Missouri; except the debth and valocity of it's stream and it is the Missouri in miniture. from the size of rose river at this place and it's direction I have no doubt but it takes it's source within the first range of the Rocky mountains. the bush which bears the red berry is here in great plenty in the river bottoms The spies returned having killed 2 beaver and a deer. they reported that they saw no appearance of Indians.-

[Lewis, July 18, 1806] Friday July 18th 1806. We set out this morning a little before sunrise ascended the river hills and continued our rout as yesterday through the open plains at about 6 miles we reached the top of an elivated plain which divides the waters of the rose river from those of Maria's river. from hence the North mountains, the South mountains, the falls mountains and the Tower Mountain and those arround and to the East of the latter were visible. our course led us nearly parrallel with a creek of Maria's river which takes it's rise in these high plains at the place we passed them; at noon we struck this creek about 6 ms. from its junction with Maria's river where we found some cottonwood timber; here we halted to dine and graize our horses. the bed of this creek is about 25 yds. wide at this place but is nearly dry at present, the water being confined to little pools in the deeper parts of it's bed. from hence downwards there is a considerable quantity of timber in it's bottom. we passed immence herds of buffaloe on our way in short for about 12 miles it appeared as one herd only the whole plains and vally of this creek being covered with them; saw a number of wolves of both speceis, also Antelopes and some horses. after dinner we proceeded about 5 miles across the plain to Maria's river where we arrived at 6 P.M. we killed a couple of buffaloe in the bottom of this river and encamped on it's west side in a grove of cottonwood some miles above the entrance of the creek. being now convinced that we were above the point to which I had formerly ascended this river and faring that a fork of this stream might fall in on the Northside between this place and the point to which I had ascended it, I directed Drewyer who was with me on my former excurtion, and Joseph Fields to decend the river early in the morning to the place from whence I had returned, and examine whether any stream fell inn or not. I keep a strict lookout every night, I take my tour of watch with the men.

[Lewis, July 19, 1806] Saturday July 19th 1806. Drewyer and J. Fields set out early this morning in conformity to my instructions last evening. they returned at 1/2 after 12 OCk. and informed me that they had proceeded down the river to the place from which I had returned on the _____ of June last and that it was 6 miles distant. they passed the entrance of buffaloe Creek at 2 ms. the course of the river from hence downwards as far as they were is N. 80 E. they killed 8 deer and two Antelopes on their way; most of the deer were large fat mule bucks. having completed my observation of the sun's meridian Altitude we set out, ascended the river hills having passed the river and proceeded through the open plains up the N. side of the river 20 miles and encamped. at 15 miles we passed a large creek on N. side a little above it's entrance; there is but little running water in this creek at present, it's bed is about 30 yds. wide and appears to come from the broken Mountains so called from their raggid and irregular shape there are three of them extending from east to West almost unconnected, the center mountain terminates in a conic spire and is that which I have called the tower mountain they are destitute of timber. from the entrance of this creek they bore N. 10° W. the river bottoms are usually about 1/2 a mile wide and possess a considerable quantity of timber entirely cottonwood; the underbrush is honeysuckle rose bushes the narrow leafed willow and the bush which bears the acid red berry called by the french engages grease de buff. just as we halted to encamp R. Fields killed a mule doe. the plains are beautifull and level but the soil is but thin. in many parts of the plains there are great quantities of prickly pears. saw some herds of buffaloe today but not in such quantities as yesterday, also antelopes, wolves, gees, pigeons, doves, hawks, ravens crows larks sparrows &c. the Curlooe has disappeared.

[Lewis, July 20, 1806] Sunday July 20th 1806 We set at sunrise and proceed through the open plain as yesterday up the North side of the river. the plains are more broken than they were yesterday and have become more inferior in point of soil; a great quanty of small gravel is every where distributed over the surface of the earth which renders travling extreemly painfull to our bearfoot horses. the soil is generally a white or whiteish blue clay, this where it has been trodden by the buffaloe when wet has now become as firm as a brickbat and stands in an inumerable little points quite as formidable to our horses feet as the gravel. the mineral salts common to the plains of the missouri has been more abundant today than usual. the bluffs of the river are about 200 feet high, steep irregular and formed of earth which readily desolves with water, slips and precipitates itself into the river as before mentioned frequentlly of the bluffs of the Missouri below which they resemble in every particular, differing essencially from those of the Missouri above the entrance of this river, they being composed of firm red or yellow clay which dose not yeald readily to the rains and a large quantity of rock. the soil of the river bottom is fertile and well timbered, I saw some trees today which would make small canoes. the timber is generally low. the underbrush the same as before mentioned. we have seen fewer buffaloe today than usual, though more Elk and not less wolves and Antelopes also some mule deer; this speceis of deer seems most prevalent in this quarter. saw some gees ducks and other birds common to the country. there is much appearance of beaver on this river, but not any of otter. from the apparent decent of the country to the North and above the broken mountains I am induced to beleive that the South branch of the Suskashawan receives a part of it's waters from the plain even to the borders of this river and from the brakes visible in the plains in a nothern direction think that a branch of that river decending from the rocky mountains passes at no great distance from Maria's river and to the N. E. of the broken mountains. the day has proved excessively warm and we lay by four hours during the heat of it; we traveled 28 miles and encamped as usual in the river bottom on it's N. side. there is scarcely any water at present in the plains and what there is, lies in small pools and is so strongly impregnated with the mineral salts that it is unfit for any purpose except the uce of the buffaloe. these animals appear to prefer this water to that of the river. the wild liquorice and sunflower are very abundant in the plains and river bottoms, the latter is now in full blume; the silkgrass and sand rush are also common to the bottom lands. the musquetoes have not been troublesome to us since we left the whitebear islands.-

[Lewis, July 21, 1806] Monday July 21st 1806. We set out at sunrise and proceeded a short distance up the North side of the river; we found the ravines which made in on this side were so steep and numerous that we passed the river in doing which the pack horse which carried my instruments missed the ford and wet the instruments. this accident detained us about half an hor. I took the Instruments out wiped them and dryed their cases, they sustained no naterial injury. we continued on the S. side of the river about 3 miles when we again passed over to the N. side and took our course through the plains at some distance from the river. we saw a large herd of Elk this morning. the buffaloe still become more scarce. at 2 P.M. we struck a northern branch of Marias river about 30 yds. wide at the distance of about 8 miles from it's entrance. this stream is closely confined between clifts of freestone rocks the bottom narrow below us and above the rocks confine it on each side; some little timber below but not any above; the water of this stream is nearly clear. from the appearance of this rock and the apparent hight of the bed of the streem I am induced to beleive that there are falls in these rivers somewhere about their junction. being convinced that this stream came from the mountains I determined to pursue it as it will lead me to the most nothern point to which the waters of Maria's river extend which I now fear will not be as far north as I wished and expected. after dinner we set out up the North branch keeping on it's S. side; we pursued it untill dark and not finding any timber halted and made a fire of the dung of the buffaloe. we lay on the south side in a narrow bottom under a Clift. our provision is nearly out, we wounded a buffaloe this evening but could not get him.

[Lewis, July 22, 1806] Tuesday July 22ed 1806. We set out very early this morning as usual and proceeded up the river. for the first seven miles of our travel this morning the country was broken the land poor and intermixed with a greater quantity of gravel than usual; the ravines were steep and numerous and our horses feet have become extreemly soar in traveling over the gravel we therefore traveled but slow. we met with a doe Elk which we wounded but did not get her. the river is confined closely between clifts of perpendicular rocks in most parts. after the distance of seven miles the country became more level les gravly and some bottoms to the river but not a particle of timber nor underbrush of any discription is to be seen. we continued up the river on it's South side for 17 miles when we halted to glaize our horses and eat; there being no wood we were compelled to make our fire with the buffaloe dung which I found answered the purpose very well. we cooked and eat all the meat we had except a small peice of buffaloe meat which was a little tainted. after dinner we passed the river and took our course through a level and beautifull plain on the N. side. the country has now become level, the river bottoms wide and the adjoining plains but little elivated above them; the banks of the river are not usually more than from 3 to four feet yet it dose not appear ever to overflow them. we found no timber untill we had traveled 12 miles further when we arrived at a clump of large cottonwood trees in a beautifull and extensive bottom of the river about 10 miles below the foot of the rocky mountains where this river enters them; as I could see from hence very distinctly where the river entered the mountains and the bearing of this point being S of West I thought it unnecessary to proceed further and therefore encamped resolving to rest ourselves and horses a couple of days at this place and take the necessary observations. this plain on which we are is very high; the rocky mountains to the S. W. of us appear but low from their base up yet are partially covered with snow nearly to their bases. there is no timber on those mountains within our view;

they are very irregular and broken in their form and seem to be composed principally of clay with but little rock or stone. the river appears to possess at least double the vollume of water which it had where we first arrived on it below; this no doubt proceeds from the avapparation caused by the sun and air and the absorbing of the earth in it's passage through these open plains. The course of the mountains still continues from S. E. to N. W. the front rang appears to terminate abrubtly about 35 ms. to the N. W. Of us. I believe that the waters of the Suskashawan apporoach the borders of this river very nearly. I now have lost all hope of the waters of this river ever extending to N Latitude 50° though I still hope and think it more than probable that both white earth river and milk river extend as far north as latd. 50°- we have seen but few buffaloe today no deer and very few Antelopes; gam of every discription is extreemly wild which induces me to beleive that the indians are now, or have been lately in this neighbourhood. we wounded a buffaloe this evening but our horses were so much fatiegued that we were unable to pursue it with success.-

[Lewis, July 23, 1806] Wednesday July 23rd 1806 I dispatched Drewyer an Joseph fields this morning to hunt. I directed Drewyer who went up the river to observe it's bearings and the point at which it entered the mountains, this he did and on his return I observed the point at which the river entered to bear S 50° W. distant about ten miles the river making a considerable bend to the West just above us.

both these hunters returned unsuccessful and reported that there was no game nor the appearance of any in this quarter. we now rendered the grease from our tainted meat and made some mush of cows with a part of it, reserving as much meal of cows and grease as would afford us one more meal tomorrow. Drewyer informed us that there was an indian camp of eleven leather lodges which appeared to have been abandoned about 10 days, the poles only of the lodges remained. we are confident that these are the Minnetares of fort de prarie and suspect that they are probably at this time somewhere on the main branch of Maria's river on the borders of the buffaloe, under this impression I shall not strike that river on my return untill about the mouth of the North branch. near this place I observe a number of the whistleing squirrel of the specesi common to the plains and country watered by the Columbia river, this is the first instance in which I have found this squirrel in the plains of the Missouri. the Cottonwood of this place is also of the specesi common to the Columbia. we have a delightfull pasture for our horses where we are.

The clouds obscured the moon and put an end to further observation. the rok which makes its appearance on this part of the river is of a white colour fine grit and makes excellet whetstones; it lies in horizontal stratas and makes it's appearance in the bluffs of the river near their base. we indeavoured to take some fish but took only one small trout. Musquetoes uncommonly large and reather troublesome.

[Lewis, July 24, 1806] Thursday July 24th 1806. At 8 A.M. the sun made it's appearance for a few minutes and I took it's altitude but it shortly after clouded up again and continued to rain the ballance of the day I was therefore unable to complete the observations I wished to take at this place. I determined to remain another day in the hope of it's being fair. we have still a little bread of cows remaining of which we made a kettle of mush which together with a few pigeons that we were fortunate enough to kill served us with food for this day. I sent the hunters out but they shortly returned without having killed anything and declared that it was useless to hunt within 6 or 8 miles of this place that there was no appearance of game within that distance. the air has become extreemly cold which in addition to the wind and rain renders our situation extreemly unpleasant. several wolves visited our camp today, I fired on and wounded one of them very badly. the small specesi of wolf barks like a dog, they frequently salute us with this note as we pass through the plains.

[Lewis, July 25, 1806] Friday July 25th 1806. The weather still continues cold cloudy and rainy, the wind also has blown all day with more than usual violence from the N. W. this morning we eat the last of our birds and cows, I therefore directed Drewyer and J. Fields to take a couple of the horses and proceed to the S. E. as far as the main branch of Maria's river which I expected was at no great distance and indeavour to kill some meat; they set out immediately and I remained in camp with R. Fields to avail myself of every opportunity to make my observations should any offer, but it continued to rain and I did not see the sun through the whole course of the day R. Fields and myself killed nine pigeons which lit in the trees near our camp on these we dined. late in the evening Drewyer and J. Fields returned the former had killed a fine buck on which we now fared sumptuously. they informed me that it was about 10 miles to the main branch of Maria's River, that the vally formed by the river in that quarter was wide extensive and level with a considerable quantity timber; here they found some wintering camps of the natives and a great number of others of a more recent date or that had from appearance been evacuated about 6 weeks; we consider ourselves extreemly fortunate in not having met with these people. I determined that if tomorrow continued cloudy to set out as I now begin to be apprehensive that I shall not reach the United States within this season unless I make every exertion in my power which I shall certainly not omit when once I leave this place which I shall do with much reluctance without having obtained the necessary data to establish it's longitude-as if the fates were against me my chronometer from some unknown cause stoped today, when I set her to going she went as usual.

[Lewis, July 26, 1806] Saturday July 26th 1806. The moring was cloudy and continued to rain as usual, tho the cloud seemed somewhat thiner. I therefore posponed seting out untill 9 A.M. in the hope that it would clear off but finding the contrary result I had the horses caught and we set out biding a lasting adieu to this place which I now call camp disappointment. I took my rout through the open plains S. E. 5 ms. passing a small creek at 2 ms. from the mountains wher I changed my direction to S. 75 E. for 7 ms. further and struck a principal branch of Maria's river 65 yds. wide, not very deep, I passed this stream to it's south side and continued down it 2 ms. on the last mentioned course when another branch of nearly the same dignity formed a junction with it, coming from the S. W. this last is shallow and rappid; has the appearance of overflowing it's banks frequently and discharging vast torrants of water at certain seasons of the year. the beds of both these streams are pebbly particularly the S. branch. the water of the N. branch is very terbid while that of the S. branch is nearly clear not withstanding the late rains. I passed the S. branch just above it's junction and continued down the river which runs a little to the N of E 1 ms. and halted to dine and graize our horses here I found some indian lodges which appeared to have been inhabited last winter in a large and fertile bottom well stocked with cottonwood timber. the rose honeysuckle and redberry bushes constitute the undergrowth there being but little willow in this quarter both these rivers abov their junction appeared to be well stocked with timber or comparitively so with other parts of this country. here it is that we find the three species of cottonwood which I have remarked in my voyage assembled together that speceis common to the Columbia I have never before seen on the waters of the Missouri, also the narrow and broad leafed speceis. during our stay at this place R. Fields killed a buck a part of the flesh of which we took with us. we saw a few Antelopes some wolves and 2 of the smallest speceis of fox of a redish brown colour with the extremity of the tail black. it is about the size of the common domestic cat and burrows in the plains. after dinner I continued my rout down the river to the North of Eat about 3 ms. when the hills putting in close on the S side I determined to ascend them to the high plain which I did accordingly, keeping the Fields with me; Drewyer passed the river and kept down the vally of the river. I had intended to decend this river with it's course to it's junction with the fork which I had ascended and from thence have taken across the country obliquely to rose river and decend that stream to it's confluence with Maria's river. the country through which this portion of Maria's river passes to the fork which I ascended appears much more broken than that above and between this and the mountains. I had scarcely ascended the hills before I discovered to my left at the distance of a mile an assembleage of about 30 horses, I halted and used my spye glass by the help of which I discovered several indians on the top of an eminence just above them who appeared to be looking down towards the river I presumed at Drewyer. about half the horses were saddled. this was a very unpleasant sight, however I resolved to make the best of our situation and to approach them in a friendly manner. I directed J. Fields to display the flag which I had brought for that purpose and advanced slowly toward them, about this time they discovered us and appeared to run about in a very confused manner as if much allarmed, their attention had been previously so fixed on Drewyer that they did not discover us untill we had began to advance upon them, some of them decended the hill on which they were and drove their horses within shot of it's summit and again returned to the hight as if to wate our arrival or to defend themselves. I calculated on their number being nearly or quite equal to that of their horses, that our runing would invite pursuit as it would convince them that we were their enimies and our horses were so indifferent that we could not hope to make our escape by flight; added to this Drewyer was seperated from us and I feared that his not being apprized of the indians in the event of our attempting to escape he would most probably fall a sacrefice. under these considerations I still advanced towards them; when we had arrived within a quarter of a mile of them, one of them mounted his horse and rode full speed towards us, which when I discovered I halted and alighted from my horse; he came within a hundred paces halted looked at us and turned his horse about and returned as briskly to his party as he had advanced; while he halted near us I held out my hand and becconed to him to approach but he paid no attention to my overtures. on his return to his party they all decended the hill and mounted their horses and advanced towards us leaving their horses behind them, we also advanced to meet them. I counted eight of them but still supposed that there were others concealed as there were several other horses saddled. I told the two men with me that I apprehended that these were the Minnetares of Fort de Prarie and from their known character I expected that we were to have some difficulty with them; that if they thought themselves sufficiently strong I was convinced they would attempt to rob us in which case be their numbers what they would I should resist to the last extremity prefering death to that of being deprived of my papers instruments and gun and desired that they would form the same resolution and be allert and on their guard. when we arrived within a hundred yards of each other the indians except one halted I directed the two men with me to do the same and advanced singly to meet the indian with whom I shook hands and passed on to those in his rear, as he did also to the two men in my rear; we now all assembled and alighted from our horses; the Indians soon asked to smoke with us, but I told them that the man whom they had seen pass down the river had my pipe and we could not smoke untill he joined us. I requested as they had seen which way he went that they would one of them go with one of my men in surch of him, this they readily concented to and a young man set out with R. Fields in surch of Drewyer. I now asked them by sighns if they were the Minnetares of the North which they answered in the affermative; I asked if there was any cheif among them and they pointed out 3 I did not believe them however I thought it best to please them and gave to one a medal to a second a flag and to the third a handkercheif, with which they appeared well satisfyed. they appeared much agitated with our first interview from which they had scarcely yet recovered, in fact I beleive they were more allarmed at this accedental interview than we were. from no more of them appearing I now concluded they were only eight in number and became much better satisfyed with our situation as I was convinced that we could mannage that number should they attempt any hostile measures. as it was growing late in the evening I proposed that we should remove to the nearest part of the river and encamp together, I told them that I was glad to see them and had a great deel to say to them. we mounted our horses and rode towards the river which was at but a short distance, on our way we were joined by Drewyer Fields and the indian. we decended a very steep bluff about 250 feet high to the river where there was a small bottom of nearly 1/2 a mile in length and about 250 yards wide in the widest part, the river washed the bluffs both above and below us and through it's course in this part is very deep; the bluffs are so steep that there are but few places where they could ,be ascended, and are broken in several places by deep nitches which extend back from the river several hundred yards, their bluffs being so steep that it is impossible to ascend them; in this bottom there stand tree solitary trees near one of which the indians formed a large simicircular camp of dressed buffaloe skins and invited us to partake of their shelter which Drewyer and myself accepted and the Fieldses lay near the fire in front of the sheter. with the assistance of Drewyer I had much conversation with these people in the course of the evening. I learned from them that they were a part of a large band which lay encamped at present near the foot of the rocky mountains on the main branch of Maria's river one 1/2 days march from our present encampment; that there was a whiteman with their band; that there was another large band of their nation hunting buffaloe near the broken mountains and were on there way to the mouth of Maria's river where they would probably be in the course of a few days. they also informed us that from hence to the establishment where they trade on the Suskasawan river is only 6 days easy march or such as they usually travel with their women and childred which may be estimated at about 150 ms. that from these traders they obtain arm amunition sperituous liquor blankets &c in exchange for wolves and some beaver skins. I told these people that I had come a great way from the East up the large river which runs towards the rising sun, that I had been to the great waters where the sun sets and had seen a great many nations all of whom I had invited to come and trade with me on the rivers on this side of the mountains, that I had found most of them at war with their neighbours and had succeeded in restoring peace among them, that I was now on my way home and had left my party at the falls of the missouri with orders to decend that river to the entrance of Maria's river and there wait my arrival and that I had come in surch of them in order to prevail on them to be at peace with their neighbours particularly those on the West side of the mountains and to engage them to come and trade with me when the establishment is made at the entrance of this river to all which they readily gave their assent and declared it to be their wish to be at peace with the Tushepahs whom they said had killed a number of their relations lately and pointed to several of those present who had cut their hair as an evidince of the truth of what they had asserted. I found them extreemly fond of smoking and plyed them with the pipe untill late at night. I told them that if they intended to do as I wished them they would send some of their young men to their band with an invitation to their chiefs and warriors to bring the whiteman with them and come down and council with me at the entrance of Maria's river and that the ballance of them would accompany me to that place, where I was anxious now to meet my men as I had been absent from them some time and knew that they would be uneasy untill they saw me. that if they would go with me I would give them 10 horses and some tobacco. to this proposition they made no reply, I took the first watch tonight and set up untill half after eleven; the indians by this time were all asleep, I roused up R. Fields and laid down myself; I directed Fields to watch the movements of the indians and if any of them left the camp to awake us all as I apprehended they would attampt to seal steal our horses. this being done I fell into a profound sleep and did not wake untill the noise of the men and indians awoke me a little after light in the morning.-

[Lewis, July 27, 1806] July 27th 1806 Sunday. This morning at day light the indians got up and crouded around the fire, J. Fields who was on post had carelessly laid his gun down behind him near where his brother was sleeping, one of the indians the fellow to whom I had given the medal last evening sliped behind him and took his gun and that of his brothers unperceived by him, at the same instant two others advanced and seized the guns of Drewyer and myself, J. Fields seing this turned about to look for his gun and saw the fellow just runing off with her and his brothers he called to his brother who instantly jumped up and pursued the indian with him whom they overtook at the distance of 50 or 60 paces from the camp sized their guns and rested them from him and R Fields as he seized his gun stabed the indian to the heart with his knife the fellow ran about 15 steps and fell dead; of this I did not know untill afterwards, having recovered their guns they ran back instantly to the camp; Drewyer who was awake saw the indian take hold of his gun and instantly jumped up and sized her and rested her from him but the indian still retained his pouch, his jumping up and crying damn you let go my gun awakened me I jumped up and asked what was the matter which I quickly learned when I saw drewyer in a scuffle with the indian for his gun. I reached to seize my gun but found her gone, I then drew a pistol from my holster and terning myself about saw the indian making off with my gun I ran at him with my pistol and bid him lay down my gun which he was in the act of doing when the Fieldses returned and drew up their guns to shoot him which I forbid as he did not appear to be about to make any resistance or commit any offensive act, he droped the gun and walked slowly off, I picked her up instantly, Drewyer having about this time recovered his gun and pouch asked me if he might not kill the fellow which I also forbid as the indian did not appear to wish to kill us, as soon as they found us all in possession of our arms they ran and indeavored to drive off all the horses I now hollowed to the men and told them to fire on them if they attempted to drive off our horses, they accordingly pursued the main party who were drying the horses up the river and I pursued the man who had taken my gun who with another was driving off a part of the horses which were to the left of the camp, I pursued them so closely that they could not take twelve of their own horses but continued to drive one of mine with some others; at the distance of three hundred paces they entered one of those steep nitches in the bluff with the horses before them being nearly out of breath I could pursue no further, I called to them as I had done several times before that I would shoot them if they did not give me my horse and raised my gun, one of them jumped behind a rock and spoke to the other who turned arround and stoped at the distance of 30 steps from me and I shot him through the belly, he fell to his knees and on his wright elbow from which position he partly raised himself up and fired at me, and turning himself about crawled in behind a rock which was a few feet from him. he overshot me, being bearheaded I felt the wind of his bullet very distinctly. not having my shotpouch I could not reload my peice and as there were two of them behind good shelters from me I did not think it prudent to rush on them with my pistol which had I discharged I had not the means of reloading untill I reached camp; I therefore returned leasurely towards camp, on my way I met with Drewyer who having heared the report of the guns had returned in surch of me and left the Fieldes to pursue the indians, I desired him to haisten to the camp with me and assist in catching as many of the indian horses as were necessary and to call to the Fieldes if he could make them hear to come back that we still had a sufficient number of horses, this he did but they were too far to hear him. we reached the camp and began to catch the horses and saddle them and put on the packs. the reason I had not my pouch with me was that I had not time to return about 50 yards to camp after geting my gun before I was obliged to pursue the indians or suffer them to collect and drive off all the horses. we had caught and saddled the horses and began to arrange the packs when the Fieldses returned with four of our horses; we left one of our horses and took four of the best of those of the indian's; while the men were preparing the horses I put four sheilds and two bows and quivers of arrows which had been left on the fire, with sundry other articles; they left all their baggage at our mercy. they had but 2 guns and one of them they left the others were armed with bows and arrows and eyedaggs. the gun we took with us. I also retook the flagg but left the medal about the neck of the dead man that they might be informed who we were. we took some of their buffaloe meat and set out ascending the bluffs by the same rout we had decended last evening leaving the ballance of nine of their horses which we did not want. the Feildses told me that three of the indians whom they pursued swam the river one of them on my horse. and that two others ascended the hill and escaped from them with a part of their horses, two I had pursued into the nitch one lay dead near the camp and the eighth we could not account for but suppose that he ran off early in the contest. having ascended the hill we took our course through a beatiful level plain a little to the S of East. my design was to hasten to the entrance of Maria's river as quick as possible in the hope of meeting with the canoes and party at that place having no doubt but that they would pursue us with a large party and as there was a band near the broken mountains or probably between them and the mouth of that river we might expect them to receive inteligence from us and arrive at that place nearly as soon as we could, no time was therefore to be lost and we pushed our horses as hard as they would bear. at 8 miles we passed a large branch 40 yds. wide which I called battle river. at 3 P.M. we arrived at rose river about 5 miles above where we h ad passed it as we went out, having traveled by my estimate compared with our former distances and couses about 63 ms. here we halted an hour and a half took some refreshment and suffered our horses to graize; the day proved warm but the late rains had supplyed the little reservors in the plains with water and had put them in fine order for traveling, our whole rout so far was as level as a bowling green with but little stone and few prickly pears. after dinner we pursued the bottoms of rose river but finding inconvenient to pass the river so often we again ascended the hills on the S. W. side and took the open plains; by dark we had traveled about 17 miles further, we now halted to rest ourselves and horses about 2 hours, we killed a buffaloe cow and took a small quantity of the meat. after refreshing ourselves we again set out by moon light and traveled leasurely, heavy thunderclouds lowered arround us on every quarter but that from which the moon gave us light. we continued to pass immence herds of buffaloe all night as we had done in the latter part of the day. we traveled untill 2 OCk in the morning having come by my estimate after dark about 20 ms. we now turned out our horses and laid ourselves down to rest in the plain very much fatiegued as may be readily conceived. my indian horse carried me very well in short much better than my own would have done and leaves me with but little reason to complain of the robery.

[Lewis, July 28, 1806] July 28th 1806 Monday. The morning proved fair, I slept sound but fortunately awoke as day appeared, I awaked the men and directed the horses to be saddled, I was so soar from my ride yesterday that I could scarcely stand, and the men complained of being in a similar situation however I encourged them by telling them that our own lives as well as those of our friends and fellow travellers depended on our exertions at this moment; they were allert soon prepared the horses and we again resumed our march; the men proposed to pass the missouri at the grog spring where rose river approaches it so nearly and pass down on the S. W. side, to this I objected as it would delay us almost all day to reach the point by this circuetous rout and would give the enemy time to surprise and cut off the party at the point if they had arrived there, I told them that we owed much to the safety of our friends and that we must wrisk our lives on this occasion, that I should proceed immediately to the point and if the party had not arrived that I would raft the missouri a small distance above, hide our baggage and march on foot up the river through the timber untill I met the canoes or joined them at the falls; I now told them that it was my determination that if we were attacked in the plains on our way to the point that the bridles of the horses should be tied together and we would stand and defend them, or sell our lives as dear as we could. we had proceeded about 12 miles on an East course when we found ourselves near the missouri; we heared a report which we took to be that of a gun but were not certain; still continuing down the N. E. bank of the missouri about 8 miles further, being then within five miles of the grog spring we heared the report of several rifles very distinctly on the river to our right, we quickly repared to this joyfull sound and on arriving at the bank of the river had the unspeakable satisfaction to see our canoes coming down. we hurried down from the bluff on which we were and joined them striped our horses and gave them a final discharge imbrarking without loss of time with our baggage. I now learned that they had brought all things safe having sustaned no loss nor met with any accident of importance. Wiser had cut his leg badly with a knife and was unable in consequence to work. we decended the river opposite to our principal cash which we proceeded to open after reconnoitering the adjacent country. we found that the cash had caved in and most of the articles burried therin were injured; I sustained the loss of two very large bear skins which I much regret; most of the fur and baggage belonging to the men were injured. the gunpowder corn flour poark and salt had sustained but little injury the parched meal was spoiled or nearly so. having no time to air these things which they much wanted we droped down to the point to take in the several articles which had been buried at that place in several small cashes; these we found in good order, and recovered every article except 3 traps belonging to Drewyer which could not be found. here as good fortune would have it Sergt. Gass and Willard who brought the horses from the falls joined us at 1 P.M. I had ordered them to bring down the horses to this place in order to assist them in collecting meat which I had directed them to kill and dry here for our voyage, presuming that they would have arrived with the perogue and canoes at this place several days before my return. having now nothing to detain us we passed over immediately to the island in the entrance of Maria's river to launch the red perogue, but found her so much decayed that it was impossible with the means we had to repare her and therefore mearly took the nails and other ironwork's about her which might be of service to us and left her. we now reimbarked on board the white peroge and five small canoes and decended the river about 15 ms. and encamped on the S. W. side near a few cottonwood trees, one of them being of the narrow leafed speceis and was the first of that kind which we had remarked on our passage up the river. we encamped late but having little meat I sent out a couple of hunters who soon returned with a sufficient quantity of the flesh of a fat cow. there are immence quantities of buffaloe and Elk about the junction of the Missouri and Maria's rivers.- during the time we halted at the er.crance of Maria's river we experienced a very heavy shower of rain and hail attended with violent thunder and lightning.

[Lewis, July 29, 1806] Tuesday July 29th 1806. Shortly after dark last evening a violent storm came on from N. W. attended with rain hail Thunder and lightning which continued the greater part of the night. no having the means of making a shelter I lay in the water all night. the rain continued with but little intermission all day. I intend halting as soon as the weather proves fair in order to dry our baggage which much wants it. I placed the two Fieldses and Colter and Collins in the two smallest canoes with orderes to hunt, and kill meat for the party and obtain as many Elkskins as are necessary to cover our canoes and furnish us with shelters from the rain. we set out early and the currant being strong we proceeded with great rapidity. at 11 A.M. we passed that very interesting part of the Missouri where the natural walls appear, particularly discribed in my outward bound journey. we continued our rout untill late in the evening and encamped on the N. E. side of the river at the same place we had encamped on the 29th of May 1805. on our way today we killed 9 bighorns of which I preserved the skins and skeletons of 2 females and one male; the flesh of this aninmal is extreemly delicate tender and well flavored, they are now in fine order. their flesh both in colour and flavor much resembles mutton though it is not so strong as our mutton. the eye is large and prominant, the puple of a pale sea green and iris of a light yellowish brown colour. these animals abound in this quarter keeping themselves principally confined to the steep clifts and bluffs of the river. we saw immence hirds of buffaloe in the high plains today on either hand of the river. saw but few Elk. the brown Curloo has left the plains I presume it has raised it's young and retired to some other climate and country. as I have been very particular in my discription of the country as I ascended this river I presume it is unnecesssesary here to add any-thing further on that subject. the river is now nearly as high as it has been this season and is so thick with mud and sand that it is with difficulty I can drink it. every little rivulet now discharges a torrant of water bringing down immece boddies of mud sand and filth from the plains and broken bluffs.-

[Lewis, July 30, 1806] Wednesday July 30th 1806. The rain still continued this morning it was therefore unnecessary to remain as we could not dry our baggage I Consequently set out early as usual and pursued my rout downwards. the currant being strong and the men anxious to get on they plyed their oars faithfully and we went at the rate of about seven miles an hour. we halted several times in the course of the day to kill some bighorns being anxious to procure a few more skins and skeletons of this animal; I was fortunate enough to procure one other malle and female for this purpose which I had prepared accordingly. seven others were killed by the party also 2 buffaloe one Elk 2 beaver with & a female brown bear with tallons 6 1/4 inches in length. I preserved the skin of this bear also with the tallons; it was not large and in but low order. we arrived this evening at an island about 2 ms. above Goodriches Island and encamped on it's N. E. side. the rain continued with but little intermission all day; the air is cold and extreemly disagreeable. nothing extraordinary happened today

[Lewis, July 31, 1806] Thursday July 31st 1806. The rain still continuing I set out early and proceeded on as fast as possible. at 9 A.M. we fell in with a large herd of Elk of which we killed 15 and took their skins. the bottoms in the latter part of the day became wider better timbered and abound in game. the party killed 14 deer in the course of the day without attempting to hunt but little for them. we also killed 2 bighorns and 1 beaver; saw but few buffaloe. the river is still rising and excessively muddy more so I think than I ever saw it. we experienced some very heavy showers of rain today. we have been passing high pine hills all day. late in the evening we came too on the N. E. side of the river and took sheter in some indian lodges built of sticks, about 8 ms. below the entrance of North mountain creek. these lodges appeared to have been built in the course of the last winter. these lodges with the addition of some Elk skins afforded us a good shelter from the rain which continued to fall powerfully all night. I think it probable that the minnetares of Fort de Prarie visit this part of the river; we meet with their old lodges in every bottom.-

[Lewis, August 1, 1806] Friday August 1st 1806. The rain still continuing I set out early as usual and proceeded on at a good rate. at 9 A.M. we saw a large brown bear swiming from an island to the main shore we pursued him and as he landed Drewyer and myself shot and killed him; we took him on board the perogue and continued our rout. at 11 A.M. we passed the entrance of Mussel shell river. at 1 in the evening we arrived at a bottom on S. W. side where there were several spacious Indian lodges built of sticks and an excellent landing. as the rain still continued with but little intermission and appearances seemed unfavorable to it's becomeing fair shortly, I determined to halt at this place at least for this evening and indeavour to dry my skins of the bighorn which had every appearance of spoiling, an event which I would not should happen on any consideration as we have now passed the country in which they are found and I therefore could not supply the deficiency were I to loose these I have. I halted at this place being about 15 ms. below Missel shell river, had fires built in the lodges and my skins exposed to dry. shortly after we landed the rain ceased tho it still continued cloudy all this evening. a white bear came within 50 paces of our camp before we perceived it; it stood erect on it's hinder feet and looked at us with much apparent unconsern, we seized our guns which are always by us and several of us fired at it and killed it. it was a female in fine order, we fleesed it and extracted several gallons of oil. this speceis of bar are rearly as poor at this season of the year as the common black bear nor are they ever as fat as the black bear is found in winter; as they feed principally on flesh, like the wolf, they are most fatt when they can procure a sufficiency of food without rispect to the season of the year. the oil of this bear is much harder than that of the black bear being nearly as much so as the lard of a hog. the flesh is by no means as agreeable as that of the black bear, or Yahkah or partycoloured bear of the West side of the rocky mountains. on our way today we killed a buck Elk in fine order the skins and a part of the flesh of which we preserved. after encamping this evening the hunters killed 4 deer and a beaver. The Elk are now in fine order particularly the males. their horns have obtained their full growth but have not yet shed the velvet or skin which covers them. the does are found in large herds with their young and a few young bucks with them. the old bucks yet herd together in parties of two to 7 or 8.-

[Lewis, August 2, 1806] Saturday August 2cd 1806. The morning proved fair and I determined to remain all day and dry the baggage and give the men an opportunity to dry and air their skins and furr. had the powder parched meal and every article which wanted drying exposed to the sun. the day proved warm fair and favourable for our purpose. I permitted the Fieldses to go on a few miles to hunt. by evening we had dryed our baggage and repacked it in readiness to load and set out early in the morning. the river fell 18 inches since yesterday evening. the hunters killed several deer in the course of the day. nothing remarkable took place today. we are all extreemly anxious to reach the entrance of the Yellowstone river where we expect to join Capt. Clark and party.

[Lewis, August 3, 1806] Saturday August 3rd 1806. I arrose early this morning and had the perogue and canoes loaded and set out at half after 6 A.M. we soon passed the canoe of Colter and Collins who were on shore hunting, the men hailed them but received no answer we proceeded, and shortly after overtook J. and R. Fields who had killed 25 deer since they left us yesterday; deer are very abundant in the timbered bottoms of the river and extreemly gentle. we did not halt today to cook and dine as usual having directed that in future the party should cook as much meat in the evening after encamping as would be sufficient to serve them the next day; by this means we forward our journey at least 12 or 15 miles Pr. day. we saw but few buffaloe in the course of this day, tho a great number of Elk, deer, wolves, some bear, beaver, geese a few ducks, the party coloured covus, one Callamet Eagle, a number of bald Eagles, redheaded woodpeckers &c. we encamped this evening on N. E. side of the river 2 ms. above our encampment of the 12th of May 1805 soon after we encamp Drewyer killed a fat doe. the Fieldses arrived at dark with the flesh of two fine bucks, besides which they had killed two does since we passed them making in all 29 deer since yesterday morning. Collins and Colter did not overtake us this evening.

[Lewis, August 4, 1806] Monday August 4th 1806. Set out at 4 A.M. this morning. permited Willard and Sergt. Ordway to exchange with the Feildses and take their small canoe to hunt to-day. at 1/2 after eleven O'Ck. passed the entrance of big dry river; found the water in this river about 60 yds. wide tho shallow. it runs with a board even currant. at 3 P.M. we arrived at the entrance of Milk river where we halted a few minutes. this stream is full at present and it's water is much the colour of that of the Missouri; it affords as much water at present as Maria's river and I have no doubt extends itself to a considerable distance North. during our halt we killed a very large rattlesnake of the speceis common to our country. it had 176 scuta on the abdomen and 25 on the tail, it's length 5 feet. the scutae on the tail fully formed. after passing this river we saw several large herds of buffaloe and Elk we killed one of each of these animals and took as much of the flesh as we wished. we encamped this evening two miles below the gulph on the N. E. side of the river. Tonight for the first time this season I heard the small whippoorwill or goatsucker of the Missouri cry. Colter and Collins have not yet overtaken us. Ordway and Willard delayed so much time in hunting today that they did not overtake us untill about midnight. they killed one bear and 2 deer. in passing a bend just below the gulph it being dark they were drawn by the currant in among a parsel of sawyers, under one of which the canoe was driven and throwed Willard who was steering overboard; he caught the sawyer and held by it; Ordway with the canoe drifted down about half a mile among the sawyers under a falling bank, the canoe struck frequently but did not overset; he at length gained the shore and returned by land to learn the fate of Willard whom he found was yet on the sawyer; it was impossible for him to take the canoe to his relief Willard at length tied a couple of sticks together which had lodged against the sawyer on which he was and set himself a drift among the sawyers which he fortunately escaped and was taken up about a mile below by Ordway with the canoe; they sustained no loss on this occasion. it was fortunate for Willard that he could swim tolerably well.

[Lewis, August 5, 1806] Tuesday August 5th 1806. Colter and Collins not having arrived induced me to remain this morning for them. the hunters killed four deer this morning near our encampment. I remained untill noon when I again reimbarked and set out concluding that as Colter and Collins had not arrived by that time that they had passed us after dark the night of the 3rd inst. as Sergt Ordway informed me he should have done last evening had not the centinel hailed him. we continued our rout untill late in the evening when I came too and encamped on the South side about 10 miles below little dry river. on our way we killed a fat cow and took as much of the flesh as was necessary for us. The Feildses killed 2 large bear this evening one of them measured nine feet from the extremity of the nose to that of his tail, this is the largest bear except one that I have seen. we saw several bear today as we passed but did not kill any of them. we also saw on our way immence herds of buffaloe & Elk, many deer Antelopes, wolves, geese Eagles &c. but few ducks or prarie hens . the geese cannot fly at present; I saw a solitary Pillacon the other day in the same situation. this happens from their sheding or casting the fathers of the wings at this season.

[Lewis, August 6, 1806] Wednesday August 6th 1806. A little after dark last evening a violent storm arrose to the N. E. and shortly after came on attended with violent Thunder lightning and some hail; the rain fell in a mere torrant and the wind blew so violently that it was with difficulty I could have the small canoes unloaded before they filled with water; they sustained no injury. our situation was open and exposed to the storm. in attending to the canoes I got wet to the skin and having no shelter on land I betook myself to the orning of the perogue which I had, formed of Elkskin, here I obtained a few hours of broken rest; the wind and rain continued almost all night and the air became very cold. we set out early this morning and decended the river about 10 miles below Porcupine river when the wind became so violent that I laid by untill 4 P.M. the wind then abaiting in some measure we again resumed our voyage, and decended the river about 5 miles below our encampment of the 1st of May 1805 where we halted for the night on the S. W. side of the river. after halting we killed three fat cows and a buck. we had previously killed today 4 deer a buck Elk and a fat cow. in short game is so abundant and gentle that we kill it when we please. the Feildses went on ahead this evening and we did not overtake them. we saw several bear in the course of the day.

[Lewis, August 7, 1806] Thursday August 7th 1806. It began to rain about midnight and continued with but little intermission until 10 A.M. today. the air was cold and extreemly unpleasant. we set out early resolving if possible to reach the Yelowstone river today which was at the distance of 83 ms. from our encampment of the last evening; the currant favoured our progress being more rapid than yesterday, the men plyed their oars faithfully and we went at a good rate. at 8 A.M. we passed the entrance of Marthy's river which has changed it's entrance since we passed it last year, falling in at preasent about a quarter of a mile lower down. at or just below the entrance of this river we meet with the first appearance of Coal birnt hills and pumicestone, these appearances seem to be coextensive. here it is also that we find the first Elm and dwarf cedar on the bluffs, the ash first appears in the instance of one solletary tree at the Ash rapid, about the Elk rapid and from thence down we occasionly meet with it scattered through the bottoms but it is generally small. from Marthy's river to Milk river on the N. E. side there is a most beautifull level plain country; the soil is much more fertile here than above. we overtook the Feildses at noon. they had killed 2 bear and seen 6 others, we saw and fired on two from our perogue but killed neither of them. these bear resort the river where they lie in wate at the crossing places of the game for the Elk and weak cattle; when they procure a subject of either they lie by the carcase and keep the wolves off untill they devour it. the bear appear to be very abundant on this part of the river. we saw a number of buffaloe Elk &c as we passed but did not detain to kill any of them. we also saw an unusual flight of white gulls about the size of a pigeon with the top of their heads black. at 4 P.M. we arrived at the entrance of the Yellowstone river. I landed at the point and found that Capt. Clark had been encamped at this place and from appearances had left it about 7 or 8 days. I found a paper on a pole at the point which mearly contained my name in the hand wrighting of Capt. C. we also found the remnant of a note which had been attatched to a peace of Elk's horns in the camp; from this fragment I learned that game was scarce at the point and musquetoes troublesome which were the reasons given for his going on; I also learnt that he intended halting a few miles below where he intended waiting my arrival. I now wrote a note directed to Colter and Collins provided they were behind, ordering them to come on without loss of time; this note I wraped in leather and attatced onto the same pole which Capt. C. had planted at the point; this being done I instantly reimbarked and decended the river in the hope of reaching Capt. C's camp before night. about 7 miles below the point on the S. W. shore I saw some meat that had been lately fleased and hung on a pole; I directed Sergt. Ordway to go on shore examine the place; on his return he reported that he saw the tracks of two men which appeared so resent that he beleived they had been there today, the fire he found at the plce was blaizing and appeared to have been mended up afresh or within the course of an hour past. he found at this place a part of a Chinnook hat which my men recognized as the hat of Gibson; from these circumstances we included that Capt. C's camp could not be distant and pursued our rout untill dark with the hope of reaching his camp in this however we were disappointed and night coming on compelled us to encamp on the N. E. shore in the next bottom above our encampment of the 23rd and 24th of April 1805. as we came too a herd of buffaloe assembled on the shore of which we killed a fat cow.-

[Lewis, August 8, 1806] Friday August 8th 1806. Beleiving from the recent appearances about the fire which we past last evening that Capt Clark could be at no great distance below I set out early; the wind heard from the N. E. but by the force of the oars and currant we traveled at a good rate untill 10 A.M. by which time we reached the center of the beaver bends about 8 ms. by water and 3 by land above the entrance of White earth river. not finding Capt. Clark I knew not what calculation to make with rispect to his halting and therefore determined to proceed as tho he was not before me and leave the rest to the chapter of accedents. at this place I found a good beach for the purpose of drawing out the perogue and one of the canoes which wanted corking and reparing. the men with me have not had leasure since we left the West side of the Rocky mountains to dress any skins or make themselves cloaths and most of them are therefore extreemly bare. I therefore determined to halt at this place untill the perogue and canoe could be repared and the men dress skins and make themselves the necessary cloathing. we encamped on the N. E. side of the river; we found the Musquetoes extreemly troublesome but in this rispect there is but little choise of camps from hence down to St. Louis. from this place to the little Missouri there is an abundance of game I shall therefore when I leave this place travel at my leasure and avail myself of every opportunity to collect and dry meat untill I provide a sufficient quantity for our voyage not knowing what provision Capt C. has made in this rispect. I formed a camp unloaded the canoes and perogue, had the latter and one of the canoes drawn out to dry, fleased what meat we had collected and hung it on poles in the sun, after which the men busied themselves in dressing skins and making themselves cloaths. Drewyer killed 2 Elk and a deer this evening. the air is cold yet the Musquetoes continue to be troublesome.-

[Lewis, August 9, 1806] Saturday August 9th 1806. The day proved fair and favourable for our purposes. the men were all engaged dressing skins and making themselves cloathes except R & J. Fields whom I sent this morning over the river with orders to proceed to the entrance of the White earth river in surch of Capt. C. and to hunt and kill Elk or buffaloe should they find any convenient to the river. in the evening these men returned and informed me that they saw no appearance of Capt. Clark or party. they found no game nor was there a buffaloe.to be seen in the plains as far as the eye could reach. nothing remarkable took place in the course of the day. Colter and Collins have not yet overtaken us I fear some missfortune has happened them for their previous fidelity and orderly deportment induces me to beleive that they would not thus intentionally delay. the Perogue is not yet sufficiently dry for reparing. we have no pitch and will therefore be compelled to use coal and tallow.

[Lewis, August 10, 1806] Sunday August 10th 1806. The morning was somewhat cloudy I therefore apprehended rain however it shortly after became fair. I hastened the repairs which were necessary to the perogue and canoe which were compleated by 2 P.M. those not engaged about this business employed themselves as yester-day. at 4 in the evening it clouded up and began to rain which puting a stop to the opperation of skindressing we had nothing further to detain us, I therefore directed the vessels to be loaded and at 5 P.M. got under way the wind has blown very hard all day but did not prove so much so this evening as absolutely to detain us. we decended this evening as low nearly as the entrance of white Earth river and encamped on the S. W. side. the musquetoes more than usually troublesome this evening.

[Lewis, August 11, 1806] Monday August 11th 1806. We set out very early this morning. it being my wish to arrive at the birnt hills by noon in order to take the latitude of that place as it is the most northern point of the Missouri, enformed the party of my design and requested that they would exert themselves to reach the place in time as it would save us the delay of nearly one day; being as anxious to get forward as I was they plyed their oars faithfully and we proceeded rapidly. I had instructed the small canoes that if they saw any game on the river to halt and kill it and follow on; however we saw but little game untill about 9 A.M. when we came up with a buffaloe swiming the river which I shot and killed; leaving the small canoes to dress it and bring on the meat I proceeded. we had gone but little way before I saw a very large grizzly bear and put too in order to kill it, but it took wind of us and ran off. the small canoes overtook us and informed that the flesh of the buffaloe was unfit for uce and that they had therefore left it half after 11 A.M. we saw a large herd of Elk on the N. E. shore and I directed the men in the small canoes to halt and kill some of them and continued on in the perogue to the birnt hills; when I arrived here it was about 20 minutes after noon and of course the observation for the O's meridian Altitude was lost; jus opposite to the birnt hills there happened to be a herd of Elk on a thick willow bar and finding that my observation was lost for the present I determined to land and kill some of them accordingly we put too and I went out with Cruzatte only. we fired on the Elk I killed one and he wounded another, we reloaded our guns and took different routs through the thick willows in pursuit of the Elk; I was in the act of firing on the Elk a second time when a ball struck my left thye about an inch below my hip joint, missing the bone it passed through the left thye and cut the thickness of the bullet across the hinder part of the right thye; the stroke was very severe; I instantly supposed that Cruzatte had shot me in mistake for an Elk as I was dressed in brown leather and he cannot see very well; under this impression I called out to him damn you, you have shot me, and looked towards the place from whence the ball had come, seeing nothing I called Cruzatte several times as loud as I could but received no answer; I was now preswaded that it was an indian that had shot me as the report of the gun did not appear to be more than 40 paces from me and Cruzatte appeared to be out of hearing of me; in this situation not knowing how many indians there might be concealed in the bushes I thought best to make good my retreat to the perogue, calling out as I ran for the first hundred paces as loud as I could to Cruzatte to retreat that there were indians hoping to allarm him in time to make his escape also; I still retained the charge in my gun which I was about to discharge at the moment the ball struck me. when I arrived in sight of the perogue I called the men to their arms to which they flew in an instant, I told them that I was wounded but I hoped not mortally, by an indian I beleived and directed them to follow me that I would return & give them battle and releive Cruzatte if possible who I feared had fallen into their hands; the men followed me as they were bid and I returned about a hundred paces when my wounds became so painfull and my thye so stiff that I could scarcely get on; in short I was compelled to halt and ordered the men to proceed and if they found themselves overpowered by numbers to retreat in order keeping up a fire. I now got back to the perogue as well as I could and prepared my self with a pistol my rifle and air-gun being determined as a retreat was impracticable to sell my life as deerly as possible. in this state of anxiety and suspense remained about 20 minutes when the party returned with Cruzatte and reported that there were no indians nor the appearance of any; Cruzatte seemed much allarmed and declared if he had shot me it was not his intention, that he had shot an Elk in the willows after he left or seperated from me. I asked him whether he did not hear me when I called to him so frequently which he absolutely denied. I do not beleive that the fellow did it intentionally but after finding that he had shot me was anxious to conceal his knowledge of having done so. the ball had lodged in my breeches which I knew to be the ball of the short rifles such as that he had, and there being no person out with me but him and no indians that we could discover I have no doubt in my own mind of his having shot me. with the assistance of Sergt. Gass I took off my cloaths and dressed my wounds myself as well as I could, introducing tents of patent lint into the ball holes, the wounds blead considerably but I was hapy to find that it had touched neither bone nor artery. I sent the men to dress the two Elk which Cruzatte and myself had killed which they did in a few minutes and brought the meat to the river. the small canoes came up shortly after with the flesh of one Elk. my wounds being so situated that I could not without infinite pain make an observation I determined to relinquish it and proceeded on. we came within eight miles of our encampment of the 15th of April 1805 and encamped on N. E. side. as it was painfull to me to be removed I slept on board the perogue; the pain I experienced excited a high fever and I had a very uncomfortable night. at 4 P.M. we passed an encampment which had been evacuated this morning by Capt. Clark, here I found a note from Capt. C. informing me that he had left a letter for me at the entrance of the Yelow stone river, but that Sergt. Pryor who had passed that place since he left it had taken the letter; that Sergt. Pryor having been robed of all his horses had decended the Yelowstone river in skin canoes and had over taken him at this encampment. this I fear puts an end to our prospects of obtaining the Sioux Cheifs to accompany us as we have not now leasure to send and enjage Mr. Heney on this service, or at least he would not have time to engage them to go as early as it is absolutely necessary we should decend the river.

[Lewis, August 12, 1806] Thursday August 12th 1806. Being anxious to overtake Capt. Clark who from the appearance of his camps could be at no great distance before me, we set out early and proceeded with all possible expedition at 8 A.M. the bowsman informed me that there was a canoe and a camp he beleived of whitemen on the N. E. shore. I directed the perogue and canoes to come too at this place and found it to be the camp of two hunters from the Illinois by name Joseph Dickson and Forest Hancock. these men informed me that Capt. C. had passed them about noon the day before. they also informed me that they had left the Illinois in the summer 1804 since which time they had been ascended the Missouri, hunting and traping beaver; that they had been robed by the indians and the former wounded last winter by the Tetons of the birnt woods; that they had hitherto been unsuccessfull in their voyage having as yet caught but little beaver, but were still determined to proceed. I gave them a short discription of the Missouri, a list of distances to the most conspicuous streams and remarkable places on the river above and pointed out to them the places where the beaver most abounded. I also gave them a file and a couple of pounds of powder with some lead. these were articles which they assured me they were in great want of. I remained with these men an hour and a half when I took leave of them and proceeded. while I halted with these men Colter and Collins who seperated from us on the 3rd ist. rejoined us. they were well no accedent having happened. they informed me that after proceeding the first day and not overtaking us that they had concluded that we were behind and had delayed several days in waiting for us and had thus been unable to join us untill the present momet. my wounds felt very stiff and soar this morning but gave me no considerable pain. there was much less inflamation than I had reason to apprehend there would be. I had last evening applyed a poltice of peruvian barks at 1 P.M. I overtook Capt. Clark and party and had the pleasure of finding them all well. as wrighting in my present situation is extreemly painfull to me I shall desist untill I recover and leave to my frind Capt. C. the continuation of our journal. however I must notice a singular Cherry which is found on the Missouri in the bottom lands about the beaverbends and some little distance below the white earth river. this production is not very abundant even in the small tract of country to which it seems to be confined. the stem is compound erect and subdivided or branching without any regular order it rises to the hight of eight or ten feet seldom puting up more than one stem from the same root not growing in cops as the Choke Cherry dose. the bark is smooth and of a dark brown colour. the leaf is peteolate, oval accutely pointed at it's apex, from one and a 1/4 to 11/2 inches in length and from 1/2 to 3/4 of an inch in width, finely or minutely serrate, pale green and free from bubessence. the fruit is a globular berry about the size of a buck-shot of a fine scarlet red; like the cherries cultivated in the U States each is supported by a seperate celindric flexable branch peduncle which issue from the extremities of the boughs the peduncle of this cherry swells as it approahes the fruit being largest at the point of insertion. the pulp of this fruit is of an agreeable ascid flavour and is now ripe. the style and stigma are permanent. I have never seen it in blume.

[Clark, July 3, 1806] Thursday July 3rd 1806 we colected our horses and after brackfast I took My leave of Capt Lewis and the indians and at 8 A M Set out with _____ men interpreter Shabono & his wife & child (as an interpreter & interpretess for the Crow Inds and the latter for the Shoshoni) with 50 horses. we proceeded on through the Vally of Clarks river on the West Side of the river nearly South 18 Miles and halted on the upper Side of a large Creek, haveing Crossed 8 Streams 4 of which were Small. this vally is from 10 to 15 Ms. in width tolerably leavel and partially timberd with long leaf & pitch pine, Some cotton wood, Birch, and Sweet willow on the borders of the Streams. I observed 2 Species of Clover in this vally one the white Clover Common in the Western parts of the U. States, the other Species which is much Smaller than either the red or white both it's leaf & blossom the horses are excessively fond of this Species. after letting our horses graze a Sufficient length of time to fill themselves, and taking dinner of Venison we again resumed our journey up the Vally which we found more boutifully versified with Small open plains covered with a great variety of Sweet cented plants, flowers & grass. this evening we Crossed 10 Streams 8 of which were large Creeks which comes roleing their Currents with Velocity into the river. those Creeks take their rise in the mountains to the West which mountains is at this time Covered with Snow for about 1/5 of the way from their tops downwards. Some Snow is also to be Seen on the high points and hollows of the Mountains to the East of us. our Course this evening was nearly South 18 Ms. makeing a total of 36 miles today. we encamped on the N. Side of a large Creek where we found tolerable food for our horses. Labeish killed a Deer this evening. We Saw great numbers of deer and 1 bear today. I also observed the burring Squirel of the Species Common about the quawmarsh flatts West of the Rocky Mountains. Musquetors very troublesom.- one man Jo. Potts very unwell this evening owing to rideing a hard trotting horse; I give him a pill of Opiom which Soon releve him.

[Clark, July 4, 1806] Friday July 4th 1806 I order three hunters to Set out early this morning to hunt & kill Some meat and by 7 A.M. we Collected our horses took braekfast and Set out proceeded on up the Vally on the West Side of Clarks river crossing three large deep and rapid Creeks, and two of a Smaller Size to a Small branch in the Spurs of the mountain and dined. the last Creek or river which we pass'd was So deep and the water So rapid that Several of the horses were Sweped down Some distance and the Water run over Several others which wet Several articles. after Crossing this little river, I observed in the road the tracks of two men whome I prosume is of the Shoshone nation. our hunters joined us with 2 deer in tolerable order. on the Side of the Hill near the place we dined Saw a gange of Ibex or big horn Animals I Shot at them running and missed. This being the day of the decleration of Independence of the United States and a Day commonly Scelebrated by my Country I had every disposition to Selebrate this day and therefore halted early and partook of a Sumptious Dinner of a fat Saddle of Venison and Mush of Cows (roots) after Dinner we proceeded on about one mile to a very large Creek which we assended Some distance to find a foard to cross in crossing this creek Several articles got wet, the water was So Strong, alto the debth was not much above the horses belly, the water passed over the backs and loads of the horses. those Creeks are emensely rapid has great decnt the bottoms of the Creek as well as the low lands on each Side is thickly covered with large Stone after passing this Creek I inclined to the left and fell into the road on which we had passed down last fall near the place we had dined on the 7th of Sept. and continued on the road passing up on the W. Side of Clarks river 13 miles to the West fork of Sd. river and Encamped on an arm of the same I Sent out 2 men to hunt, and 3 in Serch of a foard to pass the river. at dark they all returned and reported that they had found a place that the river might be passed but with Some risque of the loads getting wet I order them to get up their horses and accompany me to those places &c. our hunters killed 4 deer to day. we made 30 ms. to day on a course nearly South Vally from 8 to 10 mes. wide. contains a good portion of Pitch pine. we passed three large deep rapid Creeks this after noon

[Clark, July 5, 1806] Saturday July 5th 1806 I rose at day light this morning despatched Labeash after a Buck which he killed late last evening; and I with the three men who I had Sent in Serch of a ford across the West fork of Clarks river, and examined each ford neither of them I thought would answer to pass the fork without wetting all the loads. near one of those places pointed out by Colter I found a practiable foard and returned to Camp, ordered everything packed up and after Brackfast we Set out passed 5 Chanels of the river which is divided by Small Islands in passing the 6th & last Chanel Colter horse Swam and with Some dificuelty he made the Opposite Shore, Shannon took a different derection from Colter rained his horse up the Stream and passed over very well I derected all to follow Shannon and pass quartering up the river which they done and passed over tolerably well the water running over the back of the 2 Smaller horses only. unfortunately my trunk & portmantue Containing Sea otter Skins flags Some curiosites & necessary articles in them got wet, also an esortment of Medicine, and my roots. about 1 mile we struk the East fork which had fallen and was not higher than when we passed it last fall we had not proceeded up this fork more than 1 mile eer we struck the road by which we passed down last fall and kept it at one mile we crossed the river at a very good foard and continued up on the East Side to the foot of the Mountain nearly opposite flour Crek & halted to let our horses graze and dry our wet articles. I saw fresh Sign of 2 horses and a fire burning on the side of the road. I prosume that those indians are spies from the Shoshones. Shannon & Crusat killed each a deer this morning and J. Shields killed a female Ibex or bighorn on the side of the Mountain, this Animal was very meager. Shannon left his tomahawk at the place he killed his deer. I derect him to return for it and join me in the Vally on the East Side of this mountain. gave Shields permission to proceed on over to the 1st Vally and there hunt untill my arival this evening at that place, after drying every article which detained us untill 1/2 past 4 P.M. we packed up and Crossed the Mountain into the vally where we first met with the flatheads here I overtook Shields he had not killed any thing. I crossed the river which heads in a high peecked mountain Covered with Snow N. E. of the Vally at about 20 Miles. Shields informed me that the Flat head indians passed up the Small Creek which we came down last fall about 2 miles above our Encampment of the 4th & 5th of, Septr. I proceeded up this South branch 2 Miles and encamped on the E. side of the Creek, and Sent out several men to examine the road. Shields returned at dark and informed me that the best road turned up the hill from the creek 3 Miles higher up, and appeared to be a plain beaten parth. as this rout of the Oat lash shoots can be followed it will evidently Shorten our rout at least 2 days and as the indians informed me last fall a much better rout than the one we came out. at all events I am deturmined to make the attempt and follow their trail if possible if I can prosue it my rout will be nearer and much better than the one we Came from the Shoshones, & if I should not be able to follow their road; our rout can't possibly be much wors. The hunters killed two deer this evening. The after part of the day we only come 8 miles makeing a total of 20 Miles-. Shannon Came up about Sunset haveing found his tomahawk.

[Clark, July 6, 1806] Sunday 6th July 1806 Some frost this morning the last night was so cold that I could not Sleep. we Collected our horses which were much scattered which detained us untill 9 A.M. at which time we Set out and proceeded up the Creek on which we camped 3 Miles and left the road which we came on last fall to our right and assended a ridge with a gentle Slope to the dividing mountain which Seperates the waters from the Middle fork of Clarks river from those and Lewis's river and passed over prosueing the rout of the Oat lash shute band which we met last fall to the head of a branch of Wisdom R and down the Said branch crossing it frequently on each Side of this handsom glades in which I observe great quantities of quawmash just beginning to blume on each side of those glades the timber is small and a great propotion of it Killed by the fires. I observe the appearance of old buffalow roads and some heads on this part of the mountain. The Snow appears to lying in considerable masses on the mountain from which we decended on the 4th of Septr. last. I observe great numbers of the whistleing Squirel which burrows their holes Scattered on each Side of the glades through which we passed. Shields killed a hare of the large mountain Species. the after part of the day we passed on the hill Side N of the Creek for 6 Ms. Creek and entered an extensive open Leavel plain in which the Indian trail Scattered in Such a manner that we Could not pursue it. the Indian woman wife to Shabono informed me that she had been in this plain frequently and knew it well that the Creek which we decended was a branch of Wisdom river and when we assended the higher part of the plain we would discover a gap in the mountains in our direction to the Canoes, and when we arived at that gap we would See a high point of a mountain covered with snow in our direction to the canoes. we proceeded on 1 mile and Crossd. a large Creek from the right which heads in a Snow Mountain and Fish Creek over which there was a road thro a gap. we assended a Small rise and beheld an open boutiful Leavel Vally or plain of about 20 Miles wide and near 60 long extending N & S. in every direction around which I could see high points of Mountains Covered with Snow. I discovered one at a distance very high covered with Snow which bore S. 80° E. The Squar pointed to the gap through which she said we must pass which was S. 56° E. She said we would pass the river before we reached the gap. we had not proceeded more than 2 Miles in the last Creek, before a violent Storm of wind accompand. with hard rain from the S W. imediately from off the Snow Mountains this rain was Cold and lasted 11/2 hours. I discovd. the rain wind as it approached and halted and formd. a solid column to protect our Selves from the Violency of the gust. after it was over I proceeded on about 5 Miles to Some Small dry timber on a Small Creek and encampd. made large fires and dryed our Selves. here I observed Some fresh Indian Signs where they had been gathering quawmash.

[Clark, July 7, 1806] Monday 7th July 1806 This morning our horses were very much Scattered; I Sent out men in every direction in Serch of them. they brought all except 9 by 6 oClock and informed me that they could not find those 9. I then ordered 6 men to take horses and go different directions and at a greater distance those men all returned by 10 A.M. and informed me that they had circles in every direction to 6 or 8 miles around Camp and could not See any Signs of them, that they had reasons to believe that the indians had Stolen them in the course of the night, and founded their reasons on the quallity of the horses, all being the most valuable horses we had, and Several of them so attached to horses of inferior quallity which we have they could not be Seperated from each other when driveing with their loads on in the course of the day. I thought it probable that they might be stolen by Some Skulking Shoshones, but as it was yet possible that they may have taken our back rout or rambled to a greater distance I deturmined to leave a Small party and hunt for them to day, and proceed on with the main party and all the baggage to the Canoes, raise them out of the water and expose them to the sun to dry by the time this party Should overtake me. I left Sergt. Ordway, Shannon, Gibson Collins & Labeech with directions to hunt this day for the horses without they Should discover that the Inds. had taken them into the Mountains, and prosue our trail &c. at 1/2 past 10 A M I set out and proceeded on through an open rich vally crossing four large Creeks with extensive low and mirey bottoms, and a Small river keeping the Course I had set out on S. 56° E after crossing the river I kept up on the N E. side, Sometimes following an old road which frequently disappeared, at the distance of 16 miles we arived at a Boiling Spring Situated about 100 paces from a large Easterly fork of the Small river in a leavel open vally plain and nearly oppost & E. of the 3 forks of this little river which heads in the Snowey Mountains to the S. E. & S W of the Springs. this Spring contains a very considerable quantity of water, and actually blubbers with heat for 20 paces below where it rises. it has every appearance of boiling, too hot for a man to endure his hand in it 3 seconds. I directt Sergt. Pryor and John Shields to put each a peice of meat in the water of different Sises. the one about the Size of my 3 fingers Cooked dun in 25 minits the other much thicker was 32 minits before it became Sufficiently dun. this water boils up through some loose hard gritty Stone. a little sulferish after takeing dininer and letting our horses graize 1 hour and a half we proceeded on Crossed this easterly branch and up on the N. Side of this middle fork 9 miles crossed it near the head of an Easterly branch and passed through a gap of a mountain on the Easterly Side of which we encamped near some butifull which fall into Willards Creek. I directed that the rambling horses should be hobbled, and the Sentinal to examine the horses after the moon rose. Emence beaver sign.

This extensive vally Surround with covered with snow is extreemly fertile covered esculent plants &c and the Creeks which pass through it contains emence numbers of beaver &c. I now take my leave of this butifull extensive vally which I call the hot spring Vally, and behold one less extensive and much more rugid on Willards Creek for near 12 miles in length. remarkable Cold night

[Clark, July 8, 1806] Tuesday July 8th 1806 Our horses being Scattered we were detained unill 8 A. M before we Set out. we proceeded on down Willards Creek on the S.W. Side about 11 miles near which the Creek passes through the mountain we then Steared S. 20° E. to the West branch of Jeffersons river in Snake Indian cove about 7 miles and halded two hours to let the horses graize. after dinner we proceeded on down the forke which is here but Small 9 Miles to our encampment of 17 Augt. at which place we Sunk our Canoes & buried Some articles, as before mentioned the most of the Party with me being Chewers of Tobacco become So impatient to be chewing it that they Scercely gave themselves time to take their Saddles off their horses before they were off to the deposit. I found every article Safe, except a little damp. I gave to each man who used tobacco about two feet off a part of a role took one third of the ballance myself and put up 2/3 in a box to Send down with the most of the articles which had been left at this place, by the Canoes to Capt. Lewis. as it was late nothing Could be done with the Canoes this evening. I examined them and found then all Safe except one of the largest which had a large hole in one Side & Split in bow. The Country through which we passed to day was diversified high dry and uneaven Stoney open plains and low bottoms very boggy with high mountains on the tops and North sides of which there was Snow, great quantities of the Species of hysoop & shrubs common to the Missouri plains are Scattered in those Vallys and hill Sides. The road which we have traveled from travellers rest Creek to this place an excellent road. and with only a few trees being cut out of the way would be an excellent waggon road one Mountain of about 4 miles over excepted which would require a little digging The distance is 164 Miles-. Shields killed an antelope

[Clark, July 9, 1806] Wednesday 9th July 1806 rose early had the horses brought up. after which I had the Canoes raised washed, brough down and drawn up on Shore to dry and repard. Set Several men to work digging for the Tobacco Capt. Lewis informed me he had buried in the place the lodge Stood when we lay here last Summer, they Serched diligently without finding anything. at 10 A M Sergt. Ordway and party arrived with the horses we had lost. he reported that he found those horses near the head of the Creek on which we encamped, makeing off as fast as they could and much Scattered. nothing material took place with his party in their absence. I had the Canoes repared men & lodes appotioned ready to embark tomorrow morning. I also formd. the party to accomp me to the river Rejhone from applicants and apportioned what little baggage I intended to carry as also the Spear horses. this day was windy and Cold. The Squar brought me a Plant the root of which the nativs eat. this root most resembles a Carrot in form and Size and Something of its colour, being of a pailer yellow than that of our Carrot, the Stem and leaf is much like the Common Carrot, and the taste not unlike. it is a native of moist land.- John Sheilds and Collins each killed a Deer this morning. the wind dried our Canoes very much they will be Sufficiently dry by tomorrow morning to Set out in them down the river.

[Clark, July 10, 1806] Thursday July 10th 1806 last night was very cold and this morning everything was white with frost and the grass Stiff frozend. I had Some water exposed in a bason in which the ice was 3/4 of an inch thick this morning. I had all the Canoes put into the water and every article which was intended to be Sent down put on board, and the horses collected and packed with what fiew articles I intend takeing with me to the River Rochejhone, and after brackfast we all Set out at the Same time & proceeded on Down Jeffersons river on the East Side through Sarviss Vally and rattle snake mountain and into that butifull and extensive Vally open and fertile which we Call the beaver head Vally which is the Indian name in their language Har na Hap pap Chah. from the No. of those animals in it & a pt. of land resembling the head of one this Vally extends from the rattle Snake Mountain down Jeffersons river as low as fraziers Creek above the big horn mountain and is from 12 to 30 miles in width and _____ miles on a direct line in length and Jeffersons river in passing through this Vally reives McNeals Creek, Track Creek, Phalanthrophy river, Wisdom river, Fields river and Fraziers Creek each throw in a considerable quantity of water and have innourmerable beaver and otter on them; the bushes in their low bottoms are the resort for great numbers of Deer, and in the higher parts of the Vally we see Antelopes scattered feeding. I saw also on the Sides of the rock in rattle snake mountain 15 big horn animals, those animals feed on the grass which grow on the Sides of the mountn. and in the narrow bottoms on the Water courses near the Steep Sides of the mountains on which they can make their escape from the pursute of wolves Bear &c. at Meridian I halted to let the horses Graze having Come 15 Miles I ordered the to land. Sergt. Ordway informed me that the party with him had Come on very well, and he thought the Canoes could go as farst as the horses &c. as the river now become wider and not So Sholl, I deturmined to put all the baggage &c. which I intend takeing with me to the river Rochejhone in the canoes and proceed on down with them myself to the 3 forks or Madisons & galletens rivers. leaveing the horses to be taken down by Sergt. Pryor and 6 of the men of the party to accompany me to the river Rochejhone and directed Sergt. Pryor to proceed on moderately and if possible encamp with us every night. after dinner had my baggage put on board and Set out, and proceeded on tolerable well to the head of the 3000 Mile Island on which we had encamped on the 11th of Augt last. the Canoes passed Six of my encampments assending, opposit this island I encamped on the East side. the Musquetors were troublesom all day and untill one hour after Sunset when it became Cool and they disappeared. in passing down in the Course of this day we saw great numbers of beaver lying on the Shores in the Sun. wild young Gees and ducks are common in this river. we killed two young gees this evening. I saw several large rattle Snakes in passing the rattle Snake Mountain they were fierce.

[Clark, July 11, 1806] Friday 11th July 1806 Sent on 4 of the best hunters in 2 Canoes to proceed on a fiew miles a head and hunt untill I came up with them, after an early brackfast I proceeded on down a very crooked Chanel, at 8 a. m I overtook one Canoe with a Deer which Collins had killed, at meridian passed Sergt. Pryors Camp near a high point of land on the left Side which the Shoshones call the beavers head. the wind rose and blew with great violence from the S W imediately off Some high mountains Covered with Snow. the violence of this wind retarded our progress very much and the river being emencly Crooked we had it imediately in our face nearly every bend. at 6 P M I passed Phalanthrophy river which I proceved was very low. the wind Shifted about to the N. E. and bley very hard tho much wormer than the forepart of the day. at 7 P M I arrived at the Enterance of Wisdom River and Encampd. in the Spot we had encamped the 6th of August last. here we found a Bayonet which had been left & the Canoe quite safe. I directed that all the nails be taken out of this Canoe and paddles to be made of her Sides & here I came up with Gibson & Colter whome I had Sent on a head for the purpose of hunting this morning, they had killed a fat Buck and 5 young gees nearly grown. Wisdom river is very high and falling. I have Seen great Nos. of Beaver on the banks and in the water as I passed down to day, also some Deer and great numbers young gees, Sand hill cranes &c. &c. Sgt. Pryor left a deer on the shore

[Clark, July 12, 1806] Saturday 12th, July 1806 Sergt. Pryor did not join me last night he has proceeded on down. the beaver was flacking in the river about us all the last night. this Morning I was detained untill 7 A M makeing Paddles and drawing the nails of the Canoe to be left at this place and the one we had before left here. after completing the paddles &c and takeing Some Brackfast I set out the Current I find much Stronger below the forks than above and the river tolerably streight as low as panther Creek when it became much more Crooked the Wind rose and blew hard off the Snowey mountains to the N. W. and renderd it very difficuelt to keep the canoes from running against the Shore at 2 P.M. the Canoe in which I was in was driven by a Suden puff of wind under a log which projected over the water from the bank, and the man in the Stern Howard was Caught in between the Canoe and the log and a little hurt after disingaging our selves from this log the canoe was driven imediately under a drift which projected over and a little abov the Water, here the Canoe was very near turning over we with much exertion after takeing out Some of the baggage hauled her out, and proceeded on without receiving any damage. the men in the other Canoes Seeing our Situation landed and come with as much Speed as possible through the briers and thick brush to our assistance. but from the thickness of the brush did not get up to our assistance untill we had got Clear. at 3 P M we halted at the enterance of Fields Creek and dined here Willard and Collins over took us with two deer which they had killd. this morning and by takeing a different Side of an Island from which we Came, we had passed them. after dinner I proceeded on and Encamped a little below our encampmt. of the 31st of July last. the Musquetoes very troublesome this evening Some old buffalow Signs. I killed 4 young gees and Collins killed 2 bever this evening.

[Clark, July 13, 1806] Sunday 13th July 1806 Set out early this morning and proceded on very well to the enterance of Madicines river at our old Encampment of the 27th July last at 12 where I found Sergt. Pryor and party with the horses, they had arived at this place one hour before us. his party had killed 6 deer & a white bear I had all the horses driven across Madicine & gallitines rivers and halted to dine and let the horses feed imediately below the enterance of Gallitine. had all the baggage of the land party taken out of the Canoes and after dinner the 6 Canoes and the party of 10 men under the direction of Sergt. Ordway Set out. previous to their departur I gave instructions how they were to proceed &c. I also wrote to Capt Lewis by Sergt. Ordway-. my party now Consists of the following persons Viz: Serjeant N. Pryor, Jo. Shields, G. Shannon William Bratton, Labiech, Windsor, H. Hall, Gibson, Interpreter Shabono his wife & Child and my man york; with 49 horses and a colt. the horses feet are very sore and Several of them can Scercely proceed on. at 5. P. M I Set out from the head of Missouri at the 3 forks, and proceeded on nearly East 4 miles and Encamped on the bank of Gallitines River which is a butifull navigable Stream. Saw a large Gange of Elk in the plains and Deer in the river bottoms. I also observe beaver and Several otter in galletines river as I passed along. Gibson killed an otter the fur of which was much longer and whiter than any which I had Seen. Willard killed 2 deer this morning. all the meat I had put into the Canoes except a Sufficiency for Supper. The Country in the forks between Gallitins & Madisens rivers is a butifull leavel plain Covered with low grass.- on the lower or N E. Side of Gallitins river the Country rises gradually to the foot of a mountain which runs nearly parrelal. those plains are indefferant or the Soil of which is not very rich they are Stoney & Contain Several Stratas of white rock. the Current of the river is rapid and near the mouth contains Several islands, it is navigable for Canoes. I saw Several Antelope Common Deer, wolves, beaver, Otter, Eagles, hawks, Crows, wild gees both old and young, does &c. &c. I observe Several leading roads which appear to pass to a gap of the mountain in a E. N E. direction about 18 or 20 miles distant. The indian woman who has been of great Service to me as a pilot through this Country recommends a gap in the mountain more South which I shall cross.-.

[Clark, July 14, 1806] Monday 14th July 1806 Sent Sheilds a head to kill a deer for our brackfast and at an early hour Set out with the party Crossed Gallitines river which makes a Considerable bend to the N. E. and proceeded on nearly S. 78° E through an open Leavel plain at 6 miles I Struck the river and crossed a part of it and attemptd to proceed on through the river bottoms which was Several Miles wide at this place, I crossed Several chanels of the river running through the bottom in defferent directions. I proceeded on about two miles crossing those defferent chanels all of which was damed with beaver in Such a manner as to render the passage impracticable and after Swamped as I may Say in this bottom of beaver I was compelled to turn Short about to the right and after Some difficuelty made my way good to an open low but firm plain which was an Island and extended nearly the Course I wished to proceed. here the Squar informed me that there was a large road passing through the upper part of this low plain from Madicins river through the gap which I was Stearing my Course to. I proceeded up this plain 4 miles and Crossed the main Chanel of the river, having passed through a Skirt of cotton timber to an open low plain on the N E. Side of the river and nooned it. the river is divided and on all the small Streams inoumerable quantities of beaver dams, tho the river is yet navagable for Canoes. I overtook Shields Soon after I set out; he had killed a large fat Buck. I saw Elk deer & Antelopes, and great deel of old Signs of buffalow. their roads is in every direction. The Indian woman informs me that a fiew years ago Buffalow was very plenty in those plains & Vallies quit as high as the head of Jeffersons river, but flew of them ever come into those Vallys of late years owing to the Shoshones who are fearfull of passing into the plains West of the mountains and Subsist on what game they Can Catch in the Mountains principally and the fish which they take in the E. fork of Lewis's river. Small parties of the Shoshones do pass over to the plains for a few days at a time and kill buffalow for their Skins and dried meat, and return imediately into the Mountains. after Dinner we proceeded on a little to the South of East through an open leavel plain to the three forks of the E branch of Gallitines River at about 12 miles, crossed the most Southerly of those forks and Struck an old buffalow road which I kept Continuing nearly the Same Course up the middle fork Crossed it and Camped on a small branch of the middle fork on the N E. Side at the commencement of the gap of the mountain- the road leading up this branch, Several other roads all old Come in from the right & left. emence quantities of beaver on this Fork quit down, and their dams very much impeed the navigation of it from the 3 forks down, tho I beleive it practicable for Small Canoes by unloading at a fiew of the worst of those dams. Deer are plenty. Shannon Shields and Sergt. Pryor each killed one which were very fat much more So than they are Commonly at this Season of the year. The Main fork of Galletins River turn South and enter them mountains which are yet Covered with Snow. Madisens river makes a Great bend to the East and enters the Same mountain. a leavel plain between the two rivers below the mountain.

[Clark, July 15, 1806] Tuesday 15th July 1806 we collected our horses and after an early brackft at 8 A M Set out and proceeded up the branch to the head thence over a low gap in the mountain thence across the heads of the N E. branch of the fork of Gallitins river which we Camped near last night passing over a low dividing ridge to the head of a water Course which runs into the Rochejhone, prosueing an old buffalow road which enlargenes by one which joins it from the most Easterly branch of the East fork of Galetins R. proceeding down the branch a little to the N. of East keeping on the North Side of the branch to the River rochejhone at which place I arrived at 2 P M. The Distance from the three forks of the Easterly fork of Galletines river (from whence it may be navigated down with Small Canoes) to the river Rochejhone is 18 miles on an excellent high dry firm road with very incoiderable hills. from this river to the nearest part of the main fork of Gallitine is 29 miles mostly through a leavel plain. from the head of the Missouri at the 3 forks 48 miles through a leavel plain the most of the way as may be seen by the remarks in the evening after the usial delay of 3 hours to give the horses time to feed and rest and allowing our Selves time also to Cook and eate Dinner, I proceeded on down the river on an old buffalow road at the distance of 9 miles below the mountains Shield River discharges itself into the Rochejhone on it's N W. side above a high rocky Clift, this river is 35 yards wide deep and affords a great quantity of water it heads in those Snowey Mountains to the N W with Howards Creek, it contains some Timber Such as Cotton & willow in it's bottoms, and Great numbers of beaver the river also abounds in those animals as far as I have Seen.

passed the creek and over a high rocky hill and encamped in the upper part of a large bottom. The horses feet are very sore many of them Can Scercely proceed on over the Stone and gravel in every other respect they are Sound and in good Sperits. I saw two black bear on the side of the mountains this morning. Several gangs of Elk from 100 to 200 in a gangue on the river, great numbers of Antelopes. one Elk only killed to day.

The Roche passes out of a high rugid mountain covered with Snow. the bottoms are narrow within the mountains but widen from 1/2 a m. to 2 ms. in the Vally below, those bottoms are Subject to over flow, they contain Some tall Cotton wood, and willow rose bushes & rushes Honey suckle &c. a Second bottom on the N E. Side which rises to about 20 feet higher the first & is 1 m. wide this bottom is coars gravel pebils & Sand with Some earth on which the grass grow very Short and at this time is quit dry this 2d bottom over flows in high floods on the opposit Side of the river the plain is much higher and extendes quite to the foot of the mountain. The mountains to the S. S. E on the East side of the river is rocky rugid and on them are great quantities of Snow. a bold Snow mountain which bears East & is imediately at & N W of the 3 forks of the East fork of Gallitins river may be Seen, there is also a high rugid Mtn. on which is Snow bearing North 15 or 20 miles . but fiew flowers to be Seen in those plains. low grass in the high plains, and the Common corse grass, rushes and a species of rye is the growth of the low bottoms. the mountains have Some scattering pine on them, and on the Spurs and hill Sides there is some scrubby pine. I can See no timber Sufficient large for a Canoe which will Carry more than 3 men and Such a one would be too Small to answer my purpose

[Clark, July 16, 1806] Wednesday 16th July 1806 I gave Labeech promission to proceed on early this morning a head and kill a fat Elk or Buffalow. our horses haveing rambled to a long distance down the river detained us much later than Common. we did not Set out untill 9 A M. we had not proceeded on far before I saw a buffalow & Sent Shannon to kill it this buffalow provd. to be a very fat Bull I had most of the flesh brought on an a part of the Skin to make mockersons for Some of our lame horses. proceeded on down the river without finding any trees Sufficently large for a Canoe about 10 miles and halted having passed over to an Island on which there was good food for our horses to let them graze & Dine. I have not Seen Labeech as yet. Saw a large gangue of about 200 Elk and nearly as many Antilope also two white or Grey Bear in the plains, one of them I Chased on horse back about 2 miles to the rugid part of the plain where I was compelled to give up the Chase two of the horses was So lame owing to their feet being worn quit Smooth and to the quick, the hind feet was much the worst I had Mockersons made of green Buffalow Skin and put on their feet which Seams to releve them very much in passing over the Stoney plains. after dinner I proceeded on Soon after I had set Out Labeech joined us with part of a fat Elk which he had killed. I passed over a Stoney point at which place the river runs Close to the high land on the N W. side crossed a small Creek and Encamped on the river a little below its Enterance. Saw emence heards of Elk feeding on the opposit side of the river. I saw a great number of young gees in the river. one of the men brought me a fish of a species I am unacquainted; it was 8 inches long formed like a trout. it's mouth was placed like that of the Sturgeon a red streak passed down each Side from the gills to the tail. The rocks which the high lands are faced with and which may also be seen in perpendicular Straters in the high plains, is a dark freestone. the greater part of this rock is of an excellent grit for Grindstones hard and sharp. observe the Silkgrass Sunflower & Wild indigo all in blume. but fiew other flowers are to be Seen in those plains. The river and Creek bottoms abound in Cotton wood trees, tho none of them Sufficiently large for Canoes. and the current of the Rochejhone is too rapid to depend on Skinn canoes. no other alternetive for me but to proceed on down untill I can find a tree Sufficently large &c. to make a Canoe.-

[Clark, July 17, 1806] Thursday 17th July 1806 The rain of last night wet us all. I had the horses all Collected early and Set out, proceeded ove the point of a ridge and through an open low bottom crossed a large Creek which heads in a high Snow toped Mountain to the N W. imediately opposit to the enterance of the Creek one Something larger falls in from the high Snow mountains to the S W. & South those Creeks I call Rivers across they contain Some timber in their Vallys at the distance of _____ Miles by water we arive at the enterance of two Small rivers or large Creeks which fall in nearly opposit to each other the one on the N E side is 30 yards wide. I call it Otter River the other Beaver R below the enterance of this Creek I halted as usial to let the Horses graze &c. I saw a Single Pelican which is the first which I have Seen on this river. after Dinner I proceeded on Down the Rochejhone passing over a low ridge through a Small bottom and on the Side of a Stoney hill for 2 miles and through a Small bottom and again on the Side of a high hill for 1 1/2 M. to a bottom in which we Incamped opposit a Small Island. The high lands approach the river on either side much nearer than it does above and their Sides are partially covered with low pine & Cedar, none of which are Suffecently large for Canoes, nor have I Seen a Cotton tree in the low bottoms Sufficently large for that purpose. Buffalow is getting much more plenty than they were above. not so many Elk & more deer Shannon killed one deer. I Saw in one of those Small bottoms which I passed this evening an Indian fort which appears to have been built last Summer. this fort was built of logs and bark. the logs was put up very Closely capping on each other about 5 feet and Closely chinked. around which bark was Set up on end so as to Cover the Logs. the enterance was also guarded by a work on each Side of it and faceing the river. this work is about 50 feet Diameter & nearly round. the Squaw informs me that when the war parties find themselves pursued they make those forts to defend themselves in from the pursuers whose Superior numbers might other wise over power them and cut them off without receiveing much injurey on hors back &c.

[Clark, July 18, 1806] Friday 18th July 1806 as we were about Setting out this morning two Buffalow Bulls came near our Camp Several of the men Shot at one of them. their being near the river plunged in and Swam across to the opposit Side and there died. Shabono was thrown from his horse to day in pursute of a Buffaloe, the hose unfortunately Steping into a Braroe hole fell and threw him over his head. he is a good deel brused on his hip Sholder & face. after brackfast I proceeded on as usial, passd. over points of ridges So as to cutoff bends of the river crossed a Small Muddy brook on which I found great quantities of the Purple, yellow & black currents ripe. they were of an excellent flavour. I think the purple Superior to any I have ever tasted. The river here is about 200 yards wide rapid as usial and the water gliding over corse gravel and round Stones of various sizes of an excellent grite for whetestones. the bottoms of the river are narrow. the hills are not exceeding 200 feet in hight the sides of them are generally rocky and composed of rocks of the same texture of a dark Colour of Grit well Calculated for grindstones &c. The high bottoms is composed of gravel and Stone like those in the Chanel of the river, with a mixture of earth of a dark brown colour The Country back from the river on each Side is generally open wavering plains. Some pine is to be Seen in every direction in those plains on the Sides of hills &c. at 11 A.M. I observed a Smoke rise to the S. S. E in the plains towards the termonation of the rocky mountains in that direction (which is Covered with Snow) this Smoke must be raisd. by the Crow Indians in that direction as a Signal for us, or other bands. I think it most probable that they have discovered our trail and takeing us to be Shoshone &c. in Serch of them the Crow Indians to trade as is their Custom, have made this Smoke to Shew where they are-or otherwise takeing us to be their Enemy made this Signal for other bands to be on their guard. I halted in a bottom of fine grass to let the horses graze.

Shields killed a fat Buck on which we all Dined. after dinner and a delay of 3 hours to allow the horses time to feed, we Set out at 4 P.M. I set out and proceeded down the river through a butifull bottom, passing a Indian fort on the head of a Small island near the Lard Shore and Encamped on a Small Island Seperated from the Lard Shore by a very narrow Chanel. Shields killed a Buffalow this evening which Caused me to halt sooner than Common to Save Some of the flesh which was So rank and Strong that we took but very little. Gibson in attempting to mount his horse after Shooting a deer this evening fell and on a Snag and sent it nearly two inches into the Muskeler part of his thy. he informs me this Snag was about 1 inch in diamuter burnt at the end. this is a very bad wound and pains him exceedingly. I dressed the wound.

[Clark, July 19, 1806] Saturday 19th July 1806. I rose early and dressed Gibsons wound. he Slept but very little last night and complains of great pain in his Knee and hip as well as his thy. there being no timber on this part of the Rochjhone sufficintly large for a Canoe and time is pracious as it is our wish to get to the U States this Season, conclude to take Gibson in a litter if he is not able to ride on down the river untill I can find a tree Sufficently large for my purpose. I had the Strongest and jentlesst Horse Saddled and placed Skins & blankets in Such a manner that when he was put on the horse he felt himself in as easy a position as when lying. this was a fortunate circunstance as he Could go much more at his ease than in a litter. passed Rose bud river on Sd Side I proceeded on about 9 miles, and halted to let the horses graze and let Gibson rest. his leg become So numed from remaining in one position, as to render extreemly painfull to him. I derected Shields to keep through the thick timber and examine for a tree sufficently large & Sound to make a Canoe, and also hunt for Some Wild Ginger for a Poltice for Gibsons wound. he joined me at dinner with 2 fat Bucks but found neither tree or Ginger. he informed me that 2 white bear Chased him on horsback, each of which he Shot from his horse &c. Currents are ripe and abundant, i, e, the Yellow, black & purple spcies. we passed over two high points of Land from which I had a View of the rocky Mounts. to the W. & S. S. E. all Covered with Snow. I also Saw a low mountain in an Easterly direction. the high lands is partially Covered with pine and form purpendcular Clifts on either side. afer dinner I proceeded on the high lands become lower on either Side and those of the Stard Side form Bluffs of a darkish yellow earth; the bottom widens to Several Ms. on the Stard Side. the timber which cotton wood principally Scattered on the borders of the river is larger than above. I have Seen Some trees which would make very Small Canoes. Gibsons thy became So painfull that he could not Set on the horse after rideing about 2 hours and a half I directed Sergt Pryor and one man to continue with him under the Shade of a tree for an hour and then proceed on to the place I Should encamp which would be in the first good timber for canoes for the below. It may be proper to observe that the emence Sworms of Grass hoppers have distroyed every Sprig of Grass for maney miles on this Side of the river, and appear to be progressing upwards. about 4 Miles below the place I left Sergt. Pryor with Gibson found some large timber near which the grass was tolerably good I Encamped under a thick grove of those trees which was not Sufficiently large for my purpose, tho two of them would mak small Canoes. I took Shields and proceeded on through a large timbered bottom imediately below in Serch of better trees for Canoes, found Several about the Same Size with those at my Camp. at dark I returned to Camp

Sergt. Pryor had arived with gibson. after my arival at this place the hunters killed Seven Elk, four Deer, and I wounded a Buffalow very badly near the Camp imediately after I arived. in the forepart of the day the hunters killed two deer an Antelope & Shot two Bear. Shabono informed me that he Saw an Indian on the high lands on the opposit Side of the river, in the time I was absent in the woods. I saw a Smoke in the Same direction with that which I had Seen on the 7th inst. it appeared to be in the Mountains.

[Clark, July 20, 1806] Sunday 20th July 1806 I directed Sergt. Pryor and Shields each of them good judges of timber to proceed on down the river Six or 8 miles and examine the bottoms if any larger trees than those near which we are encamped can be found and return before twelve oClock. they Set out at daylight. I also Sent Labech Shabono & hall to Skin & some of the flesh of the Elk Labeech had killed last evening they returned with one Skin the wolves haveing eaten the most of the other four Elk. I also Sent two men in Serch of wood Soutable for ax handles. they found some choke cherry which is the best wood which Can be precured in this Country. Saw a Bear on an Island opposit and Several Elk. Sergt. Pryor and Shields returned at half past 11 A M. and informed me that they had proceeded down the timbered bottoms of the river for about 12 miles without finding a tree better than those near my Camp. I deturmined to have two Canoes made out of the largest of those trees and lash them together which will Cause them to be Study and fully Sufficient to take my Small party & Self with what little baggage we have down this river. had handles put in the 3 Axes and after Sharpening them with a file fell the two trees which I intended for the two Canoes. those trees appeared tolerably Sound and will make Canoes of 28 feet in length and about 16 or 18 inches deep and from 16 to 24 inches wide. the men with the three axes Set in and worked untill dark. Sergt. Pryor dressed Some Skins to make him Clothes. Gibsons wound looks very well. I dressed it. The horses being fatigued and their feet very Sore, I Shall let them rest a fiew days. dureing which time the party intended for to take them by land to the Mandans will dress their Skins and make themselves Clothes to bare, as they are nearly naked. Shields killed a Deer & Buffalow & Shannon a faun and a Buffalow & York an Elk one of the buffalow was good meat. I had the best of him brought in and cut thin and Spread out to dry.

[Clark, July 21, 1806] Monday 21st July 1806 This morning I was informed that Half of our horses were absent. Sent out Shannon Bratten, and Shabono to hunt them. Shabono went up the river Shanon down and Bratten in the bottom near Camp, Shabono and Bratten returned at 10 A M and informed me that they Saw no Signs of the horses. Shannon proceeded on down the river about 14 miles and did not return untill late in the evening, he was equally unsuckcessfull. Shannon informed me that he Saw a remarkable large Lodge about 12 miles below, covered with bushes and the top Deckorated with Skins &c and had the appearance of haveing been built about 2 years. I Sent out two men on hors back to kill a fat Cow which they did and returned in 3 hours the men work very diligently on the Canoes one of them nearly finished ready to put in the water. Gibsons wound is beginning to heal. I am in great hope that it will get well in time for him to accompany Sgt.

Pryor with the horses to the Mandans. This evening late a very black Cloud from the S. E. accompanied with Thunder and lightning with hard winds which Shifted about and was worm and disagreeable. I am apprehensive that the indians have Stolen our horses, and probably those who had made the Smoke a fiew days passed towards the S. W. I deturmined to have the ballance of the horses guarded and for that purpose sent out 3 men, on their approach near the horses were So alarmed that they ran away and entered the woods and the men returned- a Great number of Geese which raise their young on this river passed down frequently Since my arival at this place. we appear to be in the beginning of the buffalow Country. the plains are butifull and leavel but the Soil is but thin Stoney and in maney parts of the plains & bottoms there are great quantity of prickly pears. Saw Several herds of buffalow Since I arived at this Camp also antilops, wolves, pigions, Dovs, Hawks, ravins, Crows, larks, Sparrows, Eagles & bank martins &c. &c. The wolves which are the constant attendants of the Buffalow are in great numbers on the Scerts of those large gangues which are to be Seen in every direction in those praries

[Clark, July 22, 1806] Tuesday 22nd of July 1806. The wind continued to blow very hard from the N. E. and a little before day light was moderately Cool. I Sent Sergt. Pryor and Shabono in Serch of the horses with directions to proceed up the river as far as the 1st narrows and examine particularly for their tracks, they returned at 3 P M and informed me that they had proceeded up the distance I derected them to go and could See neither horses nor tracks; the Plains imediately out from Camp is So dry and hard that the track of a horse Cannot be Seen without close examination. I therefore derected Sergt. Pryor Shannon Shabono & Bratten to incircle the Camp at Some distance around and find the tracks of the horses and prosue them, they Serched for tracks all the evening without finding which Course the horses had taken, the plains being so remarkably hard and dry as to render it impossible to See a track of a horse passing through the hard parts of them. begin to Suspect that they are taken by the Indians and taken over the hard plains to prevent our following them. my Suspicions is grounded on the improbibility of the horses leaveing the grass and rushes of the river bottoms of which they are very fond, and takeing imediately out into the open dry plains where the grass is but Short and dry. if they had Continued in the bottoms either up or down, their tracks Could be followed very well. I directed Labeech who understands traking very well to Set out early in the morning and find what rout the horses had taken if possible

[Clark, July 23, 1806] Wednesday 23rd July 1806. last night the wolves or dogs came into our Camp and eat the most of our dryed meat which was on a scaffold Labeech went out early agreeable to my directions of last evening. Sergt. Pryor and Windser also went out. Sgt. pryor found an Indian Mockerson and a Small piece of a roab, the mockerson worn out on the bottom & yet wet, and have every appearance of haveing been worn but a fiew hours before. those Indian Signs is Conclusive with me that they have taken the 24 horses which we lost on the night of the 10th instant, and that those who were about last night were in Serch of the ballance of our horses which they could not find as they had fortunately got into a Small Prarie Serounded with thick timber in the bottom. Labeech returned haveing taken a great Circle and informed me that he Saw the tracks of the horses makeing off into the open plains and were by the tracks going very fast. The Indians who took the horses bent their course reather down the river. the men finished both Canoes by 12 oClock to day, and I sent them to make Oars & get poles after which I sent Shields and Labeech to kill a fat Buffalow out of a gangue which has been in a fiew miles of us all day. I gave Sergt Pryor his instructions and a letter to Mr. Haney and directed that he G. Shannon & Windser take the remaining horses to the Mandans, where he is to enquire for Mr. H. Heney if at the establishments on the Assinniboin river to take 12 or 14 horses and proceed on to that place and deliver Mr. Heney the letter which is with a view to engage Mr. Heney to provale on some of the best informed and most influential Chiefs of the different bands of Sieoux to accompany us to the Seat of our Government with a view to let them See our population and resourses &c. which I believe is the Surest garentee of Savage fidelity to any nation that of a Governmt. possessing the power of punishing promptly every aggression. Sergt. Pryor is directed to leave the ballance of the horses with the grand Chief of the Mandans untill our arival at his village also to keep a journal of the of his rout courses distances water courss Soil production, & animals to be particularly noted. Shields and Labeech killed three buffalow two of them very fat I had as much of the meat Saved as we could Conveniently Carry. in the evening had the two Canoes put into the water and lashed together ores and everything fixed ready to Set out early in the morning, at which time I have derected Sergt. Pryor to Set out with the horses and proceed on to the enterance of the big horn river at which place the Canoes will meat him and Set him across the Rochejhone below the enterance of that river.

[Clark, July 23, 1806] Speech for Yellowstone Indians Children. The Great Spirit has given a fair and bright day for us to meet together in his View that he may inspect us in this all we say and do.

Children I take you all by the hand as the children of your Great father the President of the U. States of America who is the great chief of all the white people towards the riseing sun.

Children This Great Chief who is Benevolent, just, wise & bountifull has sent me and one other of his chiefs (who is at this time in the country of the Blackfoot Indians) to all his read children on the Missourei and its waters quite to the great lake of the West where the land ends and the sun sets on the face of the great water, to know their wants and inform him of them on our return.

Children We have been to the great lake of the west and are now on our return to my country. I have seen all my read children quite to that great lake and talked with them, and taken them by the hand in the name of their great father the Great Chief of all the white people.

Children We did not see the _____ or the nations to the North. I have come across over high mountains and bad road to this river to see the _____ Natn. I have come down the river from the foot of the great snowey mountain to see you, and have looked in every detection for you, without seeing you untill now

Children I heard from some of your people _____ nights past by my horses who complained to me of your people haveing taken 24 of their cummerads.

Children The object of my comeing to see you is not to do you injurey but to do you good the Great Chief of all the white people who has more goods at his command than could be piled up in the circle of your camp, wishing that all his read children should be happy has sent me here to know your wants that he may supply them.

Children Your great father the Chief of the white people intends to build a house and fill it with such things as you may want and exchange with you for your skins & furs at a very low price. & has derected me to enquire of you, at what place would be most convenient for to build this house. and what articles you are in want of that he might send them imediately on my return

Children The people in my country is like the grass in your plains noumerous they are also rich and bountifull. and love their read brethren who inhabit the waters of the Missoure

Children I have been out from my country two winters, I am pore necked and nothing to keep of the rain. when I set out from my country I had a plenty but have given it all to my read children whome I have seen on my way to the Great Lake of the West. and have now nothing.

Children Your Great father will be very sorry to here of the _____ stealing the horses of his Chiefs warrors whome he sent out to do good to his red children on the waters of Missoure.

_____ their ears to his good counsels he will shut them and not let any goods & guns be brought to the red people. but to those who open their Ears to his counsels he will send every thing they want into their country. and build a house where they may come to and be supplyed whenever they wish.

Children Your Great father the Chief of all the white people has derected me to inform his red children to be at peace with each other, and the white people who may come into your country under the protection of the Flag of your great father which you. those people who may visit you under the protection of that flag are good people and will do you no harm

Children Your great father has detected me to tell you not to suffer your young and thoughtless men to take the horses or property of your neighbours or the white people, but to trade with them fairly and honestly, as those of his red children below.

Children The red children of your great father who live near him and have opened their ears to his counsels are rich and hapy have plenty of horses cows & Hogs fowls bread &c.&c. live in good houses, and sleep sound. and all those of his red children who inhabit the waters of the Missouri who open their ears to what I say and follow the counsels of their great father the President of the United States, will in a fiew years be as hapy as those mentioned &c.

Children It is the wish of your Great father the Chief of all the white people that some 2 of the principal Chiefs of this _____ Nation should Visit him at his great city and receive from his own mouth. his good counsels, and from his own hands his abundant gifts, Those of his red children who visit him do not return with empty hands, he send them to their nation loaded with presents

Children If any one two or 3 of your great chiefs wishes to visit your great father and will go with me, he will send you back next Summer loaded with presents and some goods for the nation. You will then see with your own eyes and here with your own years what the white people can do for you. they do not speak with two tongues nor promis what they can't perform

Children Consult together and give me an answer as soon as possible your great father is anxious to here from (& see his red children who wish to visit him) I cannot stay but must proceed on & inform him &c.

[Clark, July 24, 1806] Thursday 24th July 1806. had all our baggage put on board of the two Small Canoes which when lashed together is very Study and I am Convinced will the party I intend takeing down with me. at 8 A M. we Set out and proceeded on very well to a riffle about 1 mile above the enterance of Clarks fork or big horn river at this riffle the Small Canoes took in a good deel of water which obliged us to land a little above the enterance of this river which the _____ has called Clarks fork to dry our articles and bail the Canoes. I also had Buffalow Skin tacked on So as to prevent the waters flacking in between the Two canoes. This last River is 150 yards wide at it's Mouth and 100 a Short destance up the water of a light Muddy Colour and much Colder than that of the Rochejhone a Small Island is Situated imediately in its mouth, the direction of this river is South and East of that part of the rocky mountains which Can be seen from its enterance and which Seem to termonate in that direction.- I thought it probable that this might be the big horn river, and as the Rochejhone appeared to make a great bend to the N. I deturmined to Set the horses across on S. Side. one Chanel of the river passes under a high black bluff from one mile below the place we built the Canoes to within 3 miles of the enterance of Clarks fork when the bottoms widen on each side those on the Stard Side from 1/2 to a mile in width. river much divided by Islands. at 6 ms. below the fork I halted on a large Island Seperated from the Stard. Shore by a narrow Channel, on this This being a good place to Cross the river I deturmined to wait for Sergt. pryor and put him across the river at this place. on this Island I observd a large lodge the Same which Shannon informed me of a fiew days past. this Lodge a council lodge, it is of a Conocil form 60 feet diamuter at its base built of 20 poles each pole 21/2 feet in Secumpheranc and 45 feet Long built in the form of a lodge & covered with bushes. in this Lodge I observed a Cedar bush Sticking up on the opposit side of the lodge fronting the dore, on one side was a Buffalow head, and on the other Several Sticks bent and Stuck in the ground. a Stuffed Buffalow skin was Suspended from the Center with the back down. the top of those poles were deckerated with feathers of the Eagle & Calumet Eagle also Several Curious pieces of wood bent in Circleler form with sticks across them in form of a Griddle hung on tops of the lodge poles others in form of a large Sturrip. This Lodge was errected last Summer. It is Situated in the Center of a butifull Island thinly Covered with Cotton wood under which the earth which is rich is Covered with wild rye and a Species of grass resembling the bluegrass, and a mixture of Sweet grass which the Indian plat and ware around their necks for its cent which is of a Strong sent like that of the Vinella after Dinner I proceeded on passed the enterance of a Small Creek and Some wood on the Stard. Side where I met with Sergt. Pryor, Shannon & Windser with the horses they had but just arived at that place. Sergt. Pryor informed me that it would be impossible for the two men with him to drive on the horses after him without tireing all the good ones in pursute of the more indifferent to keep them on the Course. that in passing every gangue of buffalow Several of which he had met with, the loos horses as Soon as they Saw the Buffalow would imediately pursue them and run around them. All those that Speed suffient would head the buffalow and those of less Speed would pursue on as fast as they Could. he at length found that the only practiacable method would be for one of them to proceed on and when ever they Saw a gang of Buffalow to Scear them off before the horses got up. This disposition in the horses is no doubt owing to their being frequently exercised in chasing different animals by their former owners the Indians as it is their Custom to chase every Speces of wild animal with horses, for which purpose they train all their horses. I had the horses drove across the river and Set Sergt. Pryor and his party across. H. Hall who cannot Swim expressed a Wiliness to proceed on with Sergt. Pryor by land, and as another man was necessary to assist in driveing on the horses, but observed he was necked, I gave him one of my two remaining Shirts a par of Leather Legins and 3 pr. of mockersons which equipt him Completely and Sent him on with the party by land to the Mandans. I proceeded on the river much better than above the enterance of the Clarks fork deep and the Current regularly rapid from 2 to 300 yards in width where it is all together, much divided by islands maney of which are large and well Supplyed with Cotton wood trees, Some of them large, Saw emenc number of Deer Elk and buffalow on the banks. Some beaver. I landed on the Lard Side walked out into the bottom and Killd the fatest Buck I every Saw, Shields killed a deer and my man York killed a Buffalow Bull, as he informed me for his tongue and marrow bones. for me to mention or give an estimate of the differant Spcies of wild animals on this river particularly Buffalow, Elk Antelopes & Wolves would be increditable. I shall therefore be silent on the Subject further. So it is we have a great abundance of the best of meat. we made 70 ms. to day Current rapid and much divided by islands. Campd a little below Pryers river of 35 yds. on S E.

[Clark, July 25, 1806] Friday 25th July 1806. We Set out at Sunrise and proceeded on very well for three hours. Saw a large gange of Buffalow on the Lard Bank. I concluded to halt and kill a fat one, dureing which time Some brackfast was ordered to be Cooked. we killed 2 Buffalow and took as much of their flesh as I wished. Shields killed two fat deer and after a delay of one hour and a half we again proceeded on. and had not proceeded far before a heavy shower of rain pored down upon us, and the wind blew hard from the S W. the wind increased and the rain continued to fall. I halted on the Stard. Side had Some logs set up on end close together and Covered with deerskins to keep off the rain, and a large fire made to dry ourselves.

the rain continued moderately untill near twelve oClock when it Cleared away and become fair. the wind Contined high untill 2 P M. I proceeded on after the rain lay a little and at 4 P M arived at a remarkable rock Situated in an extensive bottom on the Stard. Side of the river & 250 paces from it. this rock I ascended and from it's top had a most extensive view in every direction. This rock which I shall Call Pompy's Tower is 200 feet high and 400 paces in secumphrance and only axcessable on one Side which is from the N. E the other parts of it being a perpendicular Clift of lightish Coloured gritty rock on the top there is a tolerable Soil of about 5 or 6 feet thick Covered with Short grass. The Indians have made 2 piles of Stone on the top of this Tower. The nativs have ingraved on the face of this rock the figures of animals &c. near which I marked my name and the day of the month & year. From the top of this Tower I Could discover two low Mountains & the Rocky Mts. covered with Snow S W. one of them appeard to be extencive and bore S. 15° E. about 40 miles. the other I take to be what the indians Call the Little wolf Mtn. I can only see the Southern extremity of it which bears N 55° W about 35 Miles. The plains to the South rise from the distance of about 6 miles the width of the bottom gradually to the mountains in that derection. a large Creek with an extencive Vally the direction of which is S. 25° E. meanders boutifully through this plain. a range of high land Covered with pine appears to run in a N. & S. direction approaching the river below. on the Northerly Side of the river high romantic Clifts approach &jut over the water for Some distance both above and below. a large Brooks which at this time has Some running muddy water falls in to the Rochejhone imediately opposit Pompys Tower. back from the river for Some distance on that Side the hills are ruged & some pine back the plains are open and extensive. after Satisfying my Self Sufficiently in this delightfull prospect of the extensive Country around, and the emence herds of Buffalow, Elk and wolves in which it abounded, I decended and proceeded on a fiew miles, Saw a gang of about 40 Big horn animals fired at them and killed 2 on the Sides of the rocks which we did not get. I directed the Canoes to land, and I walked up through a crevis in the rocks almost inaxcessiable and killed 2 of those animals one a large doe and the other a yearlin Buck. I wished very much to kill a large buck, had there been one with the gang I Should have killd. him. dureing the time the men were getting the two big horns which I had killed to the river I employed my Self in getting pieces of the rib of a fish which was Semented within the face of the rock this rib is about 3 inchs in Secumpherance about the middle it is 3 feet in length tho a part of the end appears to have been broken off I have Several peces of this rib the bone is neither decayed nor petrified but very rotten. the part which I could not get out may be Seen, it is about 6 or 7 Miles below Pompys Tower in the face of the Lard. Clift about 20 feet above the water. after getting the big horn on board &c I proceeded on a Short distance and encamped, an earlyer than I intended on accout of a heavy cloud which was comeing up from the S. S W. and Some appearance of a Violent wind. I walked out and killed a Small Buck for his Skin which the party are in want of for Clothes. about Sunset the wind blew hard from the W. and Some little rain. I encamped on the Stard. Side imediately below the enteranc Shannons River about 22 Yards wide, and at this time discharges a great portion of water which is very Muddy. emence herds of Buffalow about our as it is now running time with those animals the bulls keep Such a grunting nois which is very loud and disagreeable Sound that we are compelled to Scear them away before we can Sleep. the men fire Several Shot at them and Scear them away.

[Clark, July 26, 1806] Saturday 26th July 1806. Set out this morning very early proceeded on Passed Creeks very well. the Current of the river reagulilarly Swift much divided by Stoney islands and bars also handsome Islands Covered with Cotton wood the bottoms extensive on the Stard. Side on the Lard. the Clifts of high land border the river, those clifts are composed of a whitish rock of an excellent grit for Grindstones. The Country back on each Side is wavering lands with Scattering pine. passed 2 Small Brooks on the Stard. Side and two large ones on the Lard. Side. I shot a Buck from the Canoe and killed one other on a Small Island. and late in the evening passed a part of the river which was rock under the Lard. Clifts fortunately for us we found an excellent Chanel to pass down on the right of a Stony Island half a mile below this bad place, we arived at the enterance of Big Horn River on the Stard. Side here I landed imediately in the point which is a Sof mud mixed with the Sand and Subject to overflow for Some distance back in between the two rivers. I walked up the big horn 1/2 a mile and crossed over to the lower Side, and formed a Camp on a high point. I with one of my men Labeech walked up the N E Side of Big horn river 7 miles to th enterance of a Creek which falls in on the N E. Side and is 28 yds wide Some running water which is very muddy this Creek I call Muddy Creek Some fiew miles above this Creek the river bent around to the East of South. The Courses as I assended it as follows Viz:

The bottoms of the Big Horn river are extencive and Covered with timber principally Cotton. it's Current is regularly Swift, like the Missouri, it washes away its banks on one Side while it forms extensive Sand bars on the other. Contains much less portion of large gravel than the R. Rochjhone and its water more mudy and of a brownish colour, while that of the rochejhone is of a lightish Colour. the width of those two rivers are very nearly the Same imediately at their enterances the river Rochejhone much the deepest and contain most water. I measured the debth of the bighorn quit across a 1/2 a mile above its junction and found it from 5 to 7 feet only while that of the River is in the deepest part 10 or 12 feet water on the lower Side of the bighorn is extencive boutifull and leavil bottom thinly covered with Cotton wood under which there grows great quantities of rose bushes. I am informed by the Menetarres Indians and others that this River takes its rise in the Rocky mountains with the heads of the river plate and at no great distance from the river Rochejhone and passes between the Coat Nor or Black Mountains and the most Easterly range of Rocky Mountains. it is very long and Contains a great perpotion of timber on which there is a variety of wild animals, perticularly the big horn which are to be found in great numbers on this river. Buffalow, Elk, Deer and Antelopes are plenty and the river is Said to abound in beaver. it is inhabited by a great number of roveing Indians of the Crow Nation, the paunch Nation and the Castahanas all of those nations who are Subdivided rove and prosue the Buffalow of which they make their principal food, their Skins together with those of the Big horn and Antilope Serve them for Clothes. This river is Said to be navagable a long way for perogus without falls and waters a fine rich open Country. it is 200 yds water & 1/4 of a Me. wd. I returned to Camp a little after dark, haveing killed one deer, finding my Self fatigued went to bead without my Supper. Shields killed 2 Bull & 3 Elk.

[Clark, July 27, 1806] Sunday 27th July 1806 I marked my name with red paint on a Cotton tree near my Camp, and Set out at an early hour and proceeded on very well the river is much wider from 4 to 600 yards much divided by Islands and Sand bars, passed a large dry Creek at 15 miles and halted at the enterance of River 50 yards wide on the Lard Side I call R. Labeech killed 4 Buffalow and Saved as much of their flesh as we could Carry took brackfast. The Buffalow and Elk is estonishingly noumerous on the banks of the river on each Side, particularly the Elk which lay on almost every point in large gang and are So jintle that we frequently pass within 20 or 30 paces of them without their being the least alarmd. the buffalow are Generally at a greater distance from the river, and keep a continueing bellowing in every direction, much more beaver Sign than above the bighorn. I Saw Several of those animals on the bank to day. the antilopes are Scerce as also the bighorns and the deer by no means So plenty as they were near the Rocky mountains. when we pass the Big horn I take my leave of the view of the tremendious chain of Rocky Mountains white with Snow in view of which I have been Since the 1st of May last.

about Sunset I Shot a very large fat buck elk from the Canoe near which I encamped, and was near being bit by a rattle Snake. Shields killed a Deer & a antilope to day for the Skins which the party is in want of for Clothes. this river below the big horn river resembles the Missouri in almost every perticular except that it's islands are more noumerous & Current more rapid, it's banks are generally low and falling in the bottoms on the Stard. Side low and exteneive and Covered with timber near the river such as Cotton wood willow of the different Species rose bushes and Grapevines together with the red berry or Buffalow Grees bushes & a species of shoemake with dark brown back of those bottoms the Country rises gradually to about 100 feet and has Some pine. back is leavel plains. on the Lard Side the river runs under the clifts and Bluffs of high which is from 70 to 150 feet in hight and near the river is Some Scattering low pine back the plains become leavel and extencive. the Clifts are Composed of a light gritty Stone which is not very hard. and the round stone which is mixed with the Sand and formes bars is much Smaller than they appeared from above the bighorn, and may here be termed Gravel. the Colour of the water is a yellowish white and less muddy than the Missouri below the mouth of this river.

[Clark, July 28, 1806] Monday 28th July 1806. Set out this morning at day light and proceeded on glideing down this Smooth Stream passing maney Isld. and Several Creeks and brooks at 6 miles passed a Creek or brook of 80 yards wide on the N W. Side Containing but little water. 6 miles lower passed a small Creek 20 yds wide on the Stard Side 18 Miles lower passed a large dry creek on the Lard Side 5 Miles lower passed a river 70 yards wide Containing but little water on the Lard Side which I call Table Creek from the tops of Several mounds in the Plains to the N W. resembling a table. four miles Still lower I arived at the enterance of a river 100 yards wide back of a Small island on the South Side. it contains Some Cotton wood timber and has a bold Current, it's water like those of all other Streams which I have passed in the Canoes are muddy. I take this river to be the one the Indians Call the Little Big Horn river. The Clifts on the South Side of the Rochejhone are Generally compd. of a yellowish Gritty Soft rock, whilest those of the N. is light Coloured and much harder in the evening I passd. Straters of Coal in the banks on either Side those on the Stard. Bluffs was about 30 feet above the water and in 2 vanes from 4 to 8 feet thick, in a horozontal position. the Coal Contained in the Lard Bluffs is in Several vaines of different hights and thickness. this Coal or Carbonated wood is like that of the Missouri of an inferior quallity. passed a large Creek on the Stard. Side between the 1st and 2nd Coal Bluffs passed Several Brooks the chanel of them were wide and contained but little running water, and encamped on the upper point of a Small island opposit the enterance of a Creek 25 Yards wide on the Stard. Side with water.

The Elk on the banks of the river were So abundant that we have not been out of Sight of them to day. J Shields killed 2 deer & Labeech killed an Antilope to day. the antilopes and deer are not Abundant. Beaver plenty

[Clark, July 29, 1806] Tuesday 29th July 1806 a Slight rain last night with hard thunder and Sharp lightening accompanied with a violent N. E. wind. I Set out early this morning wind So hard a head that w made but little way. in the fore part of the day, I saw great numbers of Buffalow on the banks. the country on either Side is like that of yesterday. passed three large dry Brooks on the Stard. Side and four on the Lard Side. great quantities of Coal in all the hills I passed this day. late in the evening I arived at the enterance of a River which I take to be the Lazeka or Tongue River it discharges itself on the Stard. Side and is 150 yards wide of water the banks are much wider. I intended to encamp on an eligable Spot imediately below this river, but finding that its water So muddy and worm as to render it very disagreeable to drink, I crossed the rochejhone and encamped on an island close to the Lard. Shore. The water of this river is nearly milk worm very muddy and of a lightish brown Colour. the Current rapid and the Chanel Contains great numbers of Snags. near its enterance there is great quantities of wood Such as is common in the low bottoms of the Rochejhone and Missouri. tho I believe that the Country back thro which this river passes is an open one where the water is exposed to the Sun which heats it in its passage. it is Shallow and throws out great quantities of mud and Some cors gravel. below this river and on the Stard Side at a fiew Miles from the Rochejhone the hills are high and ruged Containing Coal in great quantities. Beaver is very plenty on this part of the Rochejhone. The river widens I think it may be generally Calculated at from 500" yards to half a mile in width more Sand and gravelly Bars than above. cought 3 cat fish. they wer Small and fat. also a Soft Shell turtle.

[Clark, July 30, 1806] Friday 30th July 1806 Set out early this morning at 12 miles arived at the Commencement of Shoals the Chanel on the Stard Side near a high bluff. passed a Succession of those Shoals for 6 miles the lower of which was quit across the river and appeared to have a decent of about 3 feet. here we were Compeled to let the Canoes down by hand for fear of their Strikeing a rock under water and Splitting. This is by far the wost place which I have Seen on this river from the Rocky mountains to this place a distance of 694 miles by water. a Perogu or large Canoe would with Safty pass through the worst of those Shoals, which I call the Buffalow Sholes from the Circumstance of one of those animals being in them. the rock which passes the river at those Sholes appear hard and gritty of a dark brown Colour. the Clifts on the Stard. Side is about 100 feet in hight, on the Lard Side the Country is low and the bottom rises gradually back. here is the first appearance of Birnt hills which I have Seen on this river they are at a distance from the river on the Lard Side. I landed at the enterance of a dry Creek on the Lard side below the Shoals and took brackfast. Those Dry Rivers, Creeks &c are like those of the Missouri which take their rise in and are the Conveyance of the water from those plains. they have the appearanc of dischargeing emence torrents of water. the late rains which has fallen in the plains raised Sudenly those Brooks which receive the water of those plains on which those Suden & heavy Showers of rain must have fallen, Several of which I have Seen dischargeing those waters, whiles those below heading or takeing their rise in the Same neighbourhood, as I passed them appears to have latterly been high. those Broods discharge emencely of mud also, which Contributes much to the muddiness of the river. after Brackfast proceeded on the river much narrower than above from 3 to 400 yards wide only and only a fiew scattering trees to be Seen on the banks. at 20 miles below the Buffalow Shoals passed a rapid which is by no means dangerous, it has a number of large rocks in different parts of the river which Causes high waves a very good Chanel on the Lard. Side. this rapid I call Bear rapid from the Circumstance of a bears being on a rock in the Middle of this rapid when I arived at it. a violent Storm from the N. W. obliged us to land imediately below this rapid, draw up the Canoes and take Shelter in an old Indian Lodge above the enterance of a river which is nearly dry it has lately been very high and Spread over nearly 1/4 a mile in width. its Chanel is 88 yards and in this there is not more water than could pass through an inch auger hole. I call it Yorks dry R. after the rain and wind passed over I proceeded on at 7 Miles passed the enterance of a river the water of which is 100 yds wide, the bead of this river nearly 1/4 of a mile this river is Shallow and the water very muddy and of the Colour of the banks a darkish brown. I observe great quantities of red Stone thrown out of this river that from the appearance of the hills at a distance on its lower Side induced me to call this red Stone river. as the water was disagreeably muddy I could not Camp on that Side below its mouth. however I landed at its enteranc and Sent out and killed two fat Cows, and took as much of the flesh as the Canoes would conveniently Carry and Crossed the river and encamped at the enterance of a Brook on the Lard. Side under a large Spredding Cotton tree. The river on which we passed to day is not So wide as above containing but fiew islands with a Small quantity of Cotton timber. no timber of any kind to be Seen on the high lands on either Side.

In the evening below the enterance of redstone river I observed great numbers of Buffalow feeding on the plains, elk on the points and antilopes. I also Saw Some of the Bighorn animals at a distance on the hills. Gibson is now able to walk, he walked out this evening and killed an antilope.

[Clark, July 31, 1806] Saturday 31st of July 1806 I was much disturbed last night by the noise of the buffalow which were about me. one gang Swam the river near our Camp which alarmed me a little for fear of their Crossing our Canoes and Splitting them to pieces. Set out as usial about Sun rise passed a rapid which I call wolf rapid from the Circumstance of one of those animals being at the rapid. here the river approaches the high mountanious Country on the N W. Side those hills appear to be composed of various Coloured earth and Coal without much rock I observe Several Conical mounds which appear to have been burnt. this high Country is washed into Curious formed mounds & hills and is cut much with reveens. the Country again opens and at the distance of 23 miles below the Redston or War-har-sah River I landed in the enterance of a Small river on the Stard. Side 40 yards wid Shallow and muddy. it has lately been very high. haveing passed the Enterance of a River on the Lard Side 100 yards wide which has running water this river I take to be the one the Menetarries Call little wolf or Sa-a-shah River The high Country is entirely bar of timber. great quantities of Coal or carbonated wood is to be seen in every Bluff and in the high hills at a distance on each Side. Saw more

Buffalow and Elk and antilopes this evening than usial. 18 Miles below the last river on the Stard. Side, I passed one 60 yards wide which had running water. this Stream I call oak-tar-pon-er or Coal River has very steep banks on each side of it. passed Several large Brooks Some of them had a little running water, also Several Islands Some high black looking Bluffs and encamped on the Stard. Side on a low point. the country like that of yesterday is open extencive plains. as I was about landing this evening Saw a white bear and the largest I ever Saw eating a dead buffalow on a Sand bar. we fired two Shot into him, he Swam to the main Shore and walked down the bank. I landed and fired 2 more Shot into this tremendious animal without killing him. night comeing on we Could not pursue him he bled profusely. Showers all this day

[Clark, August 1, 1806] Sunday 1st of August 1806. We Set out early as usial the wind was high and ahead which caused the water to be a little rough and delayed us very much aded to this we had Showers of rain repeetedly all day at the intermition of only a fiew minits between them. My Situation a very disagreeable one. in an open Canoe wet and without a possibility of keeping my Self dry. the Country through which we passed is in every respect like that through which I passed yesterday. The brooks have all Some water in them from the rains which has fallen. this water is excessively muddy. Several of those brooks have Some trees on their borders as far as I can See up them. I observe Some low pine an cedar on the Sides of the rugid hills on the Stard. Side, and Some ash timber in the high bottoms. the river has more Sand bars today than usial, and more Soft mud. the current less rapid. at 2 P.M. I was obliged to land to let the Buffalow Cross over. not withstanding an island of half a mile in width over which this gangue of Buffalow had to pass and the Chanel of the river on each Side nearly 1/4 of a mile in width, this gangue of Buffalow was entirely across and as thick as they could Swim. the Chanel on the Side of the island the went into the river was crouded with those animals for 1/2 an hour. the other Side of the island for more than 3/4 of an hour. I took 4 of the men and killed 4 fat Cows for their fat and what portion of their flesh the Small Canoes Could Carry that which we had killed a few days ago being nearly Spoiled from the wet weather. encamped on an Island Close to the Lard Shore two gangues of Buffalow Crossed a little below us, as noumerous as the first.

[Clark, August 2, 1806] Monday August 2nd 1806. Musquetors very troublesom this morning I Set out early river wide and very much divided by islands and Sand and Mud bars. the bottoms more extencive and contain more timber Such as Cotton wood ash willow &c. The Country on the N W. Side rises to a low plain and extends leavel for great extent. Some high rugid hills in the forepart of this day on the S E. Side on which I saw the big horns but could not get near them. Saw emence numbers of Elk Buffalow and wolves to day. the wolves do catch the elk. I saw 2 wolves in pursute of doe Elk which I beleive they Cought they very near her when She entered a Small wood in which I expect they cought her as She did not pass out of the small wood during my remaining in view of it which was 15 or 20 minits &c. passed the enterance of Several brooks on each Side, a Small river 30 yds wide with Steep banks on the Stard. Side, which I call Ibex River the river in this days decent is less rapid crouded with Islds and muddy bars and is generally about one mile in wedth. as the islands and bars frequently hide the enterance of Brooks &c. from me as I pass'd maney of them I have not noticed. about 8 A. M this morning a Bear of the large vicious Species being on a Sand bar raised himself up on his hind feet and looked at us as we passed down near the middle of the river. he plunged into the water and Swam towards us, either from a disposition to attack't or from the Cent of the meat which was in the Canoes. we Shot him with three balls and he returned to Shore badly wounded. in the evening I saw a very large Bear take the water above us. I ordered the boat to land on the opposit Side with a view to attack't him when he Came within Shot of the Shore. when the bear was in a fiew paces of the Shore I Shot it in the head. the men hauled her on Shore and proved to be an old Shee which was so old that her tuskes had worn Smooth, and Much the largest feemale bear I ever Saw. after taking off her Skin, I proceeded on and encampd a little above the enterance of Jo. Feilds Creek on Stard. Side in a high bottom Covered with low Ash and elm. the Musquetors excessively troublesom.

I have noticed a great preportion Buck Elks on this lower part of the river, and but very few above. those above which are emencely noumerous are feemales Generally. Shields killed a Deer this morning dureing the time we were at Brackfast. we were very near being detained by the Buffalow today which were Crossing the river we got through the line between 2 gangues.

[Clark, August 3, 1806] Tuesday August 3rd,1806. last night the Musquetors was so troublesom that no one of the party Slept half the night. for my part I did not Sleep one hour. those tormenting insects found their way into My beare and tormented me the whole night. they are not less noumerous or troublesom this morn-ing. at 2 miles passed the enterance of Jo. Field's Creek 35 yds wide imediately above a high bluff which is falling into the river very fast. on the Side of this bluff I saw Some of the Mountain Bighorn animals. I assended the hill below the Bluff. the Musquetors were So noumerous that I could not Shute with any Certainty and therefore Soon returned to the Canoes. I had not proceeded far before I saw a large gangue of ewes & yearlins & fawns or lambs of the bighorn, and at a distance alone I saw a ram. landed and Sent Labeech to kill the ram, which he did kill and brought him on board. this ram is not near as large as maney I have Seen. however he is Sufficiently large for a Sample I directed Bratten to Skin him with his head horns & feet to the Skin and Save all the bone. I have now the Skin & bone of a Ram a Ewe & a yearlin ram of those big Horn animals. at 8. A.M. I arived at the junction of the Rochejhone with the Missouri, and formed my Camp imediately in the point between the two river at which place the party had all encamped the 26th of April-1805. at landing I observed Several Elk feeding on the young willows in the point among which was a large Buck Elk which I shot & had his flesh dryed in the Sun for a Store down the river. had the Canoes unloaded and every article exposed to dry & Sun. Maney of our things were wet, and nearly all the Store of meat which had been killed above Spoiled. I ordered it to be thrown into the river. Several Skins are also Spoiled which is a loss, as they are our principal dependance for Clothes to last us to our homes &c.

The distance from the Rocky Mountains at which place I struck the River Rochejhone to its enterance into the Missouri 837 Miles 636 Miles of this distance I decended in 2 Small Canoes lashed together in which I had the following Persons. John Shields, George Gibson, William Bratten, W. Labeech, Toust. Shabono his wife & child & my man York. The Rochejhone or Yellow Stone river is large and navagable with but fiew obstructions quite into the rocky mountains. and probably near it's source. The Country through which it passes from those Mounts. to its junction is Generaly fertile rich open plains the upper portion of which is roleing and the high hills and hill Sides are partially covered with pine and Stoney. The middle portion or from the enterance of Clarks Fork as low as the Buffalow Shoals the high lands Contain Some Scattering pine on the Lard. Side. on the Stard. or S. E. Side is Some hills thickly Supplied with pine. The lower portion of the river but fiew pines are to be Seen the Country opens into extencive plains river widens and Contains more islands and bars; of corse gravel sand and Mud. The Current of this river may be estimated at 4 Miles and 1/2 pr. hour from the Rocky Mts. as low as Clarks Fork, at 3 1/2 Miles pr. hour from thence as low as the Bighorn, at 3- Miles pr. hour from thence as low as the Tongue river, at 2 3/4 Miles pr. hour from thence as low as Wolf rapid and at 2 1/2 miles pr. hour from thence to its enterance into the Missouri

The Colour of the Water differs from that of the Missouri it being of a yellowish brown, whilst that of the Missouri is of a deep drab Colour containing a greater portion of mud than the Rochejhone. This delightfull river from indian information has it's extreem sources with the North river in the Rocky mountains on the confines of New Mexico. it also most probably has it's westerly sources connected with the Multnomah and those the main Southerly branch of Lewis's river while it's Easterly branches head with those of Clark's R. the bighorn and River Platte and may be said to water the middle portion of the Rocky Mountains from N W to S. E. for several hundred miles. the indians inform us, that a good road passes up this river to it's extreem source from whence it is buta short distance to the Spanish settlements. there is also a considerable fall on this river within the mountains but at what distance from it's source we never could learn like all other branches of the Missouri which penetrate the Rocky Mountains all that portion of it lying within those mountains abound in fine beaver and Otter, it's streams also which issuing from the rocky mountain and discharging themselves above Clark's fork inclusive also furnish an abundance of beaver and Otter and possess considerable portions of small timber in their values. to an establishment on this river at clarks Fork the Shoshones both within and West of the Rocky Mountains would willingly resort for the purposes of trade as they would in a great measure be relived from the fear of being attacked by their enimies the blackfoot Indians and Minnetares of fort de Prarie, which would most probably happen were they to visit any establishment which could be conveniently formed on the Missouri. I have no doubt but the same regard to personal safety would also induce many numerous nations inhabiting the Columbia and Lewis's river West of the mountains to visit this establishment in preference to that at the entrance of Maria's river, particularly during the first years of those Western establishments. the Crow Indians, Paunch Indians Castahanah's and others East of the mountains and south of this place would also visit this establishment; it may therefore be looked to as one of the most important establishments of the western fur trade. at the entrance of Clark's fork there is a sufficiency of timber to support an establishment, an advantage that no position possesses from thence to the Rocky Mountains. The banks of the yellowstone river a bold not very high yet are not subject to be overflown, except for a few miles immediately below where the river issues from the mountain. the bed of this river is almost entirely composed of loose pebble, nor is it's bed interrupted by chains of rock except in one place and that even furnishes no considerable obstruction to it's navigation. as you decend with the river from the mountain the pebble becomes smaller and the quantity of mud increased untill you reah Tongue river where the pebble ceases and the sand then increases and predominates near it's mouth. This river can be navigated to greater advantage in perogues than any other craft yet it possesses suficient debth of water for battauxs even to the mountains; nor is there any of those moving sand bars so formidable to the navigation of many parts of the Missouri. The Bighorn R and Clark's fork may be navigated a considerable distance in perogues and canoes. Tongue river is also navigable for canoes a considerable distance.

[Clark, August 4, 1806] Wednesday 4th August 1806 Musquetors excessively troublesom So much So that the men complained that they could not work at their Skins for those troublesom insects. and I find it entirely impossible to hunt in the bottoms, those insects being So noumerous and tormenting as to render it imposseable for a man to continue in the timbered lands and our best retreat from those insects is on the Sand bars in the river and even those Situations are only clear of them when the Wind Should happen to blow which it did to day for a fiew hours in the middle of the day. the evenings nights and mornings they are almost indureable perticelarly by the party with me who have no Bears to keep them off at night, and nothing to Screen them but their blankets which are worn and have maney holes. The torments of those Missquetors and the want of a Sufficety of Buffalow meat to dry, those animals not to be found in this neighbourhood induce me to deturmine to proceed on to a more eliagiable Spot on the Missouri below at which place the Musquetors will be less troublesom and Buffalow more plenty. (I will here obseve that Elk is Abundant but their flesh & fat is hard to dry in the Sun, and when dry is much easirSpoiled than either the Buffalow or Deer) I ordered the Canoes to be reloaded with our baggage & dryed meat which had been Saved on the Rochejhone together with the Elk killed at this place. wrote a note to Capt Lewis informing him of my intentions and tied it to a pole which I had Stuck up in the point. At 5 P. M Set out and proceeded on down to the 2d point which appeared to be an eligable Situation for my purpose killed a porcupine on this point the Musquetors were So abundant that we were tormented much worst than at the point. The Child of Shabono has been So much bitten by the Musquetor that his face is much puffed up & Swelled. I encamped on this extensive Sand bar which is on the N W. Side.

[Clark, August 5, 1806] Thursday 5th August 1806. The Musquetors was So troublesom to the men last night that they Slept but very little. indeed they were excessive troublesom to me. my Musquetor Bear has a number of Small holes worn through they pass in. I Set out at an early hour intending to proceed to Some other Situation. I had not proceded on far before I Saw a ram of the big horn Animal near the top of a Lard. Bluff I assended the hill with a view to kill the ram. the Misquetors was So noumerous that I could not keep them off my gun long enough to take Sight and by thair means missed. at 10 a.m. the wind rose with a gentle breeze from the N. W. which in Some measure thinned the Misquetors. I landed on a Sand bar from the South Point intending to form a Camp at this place and Continue untill Capt Lewis Should arive. and killed two Buck Elks and a Deer the best of their flesh & fat I had Saved. had all the dryed meat & fat put out to Sun and continued at this place untill late in the evening finding that there were no buffalow or fresh Sign I deturmined to proceed on accordingly Set out at 4 P. M and proceeded on but a fiew miles eeir I saw a Bear of the white Species walking on a Sand bear. I with one man went on the Sand bear and killed the Bear which proved to be a feemale very large and fat. much the fattest animale we have killed on the rout as this bear had got into the river before we killed her I had her toed across to the South Side under a high Bluff where formed a Camp, had the bear Skined and fleaced. our Situation was exposed to a light breeze of wind which continued all the forepart of the night from the S W. and blew away the misquetors.

[Clark, August 6, 1806] Friday 6th August 1806 I rose very wet. about 11 P M last night the wind become very hard for a fiew minits Suckceeded by Sharp lightning and hard Claps of Thunder and rained for about 2 hours very hard after which it continued Cloudy the balance of the night. as we were about Setting out a female Big horn animal came on the bluff imediately above us and looked down. I derected Labeech to Shoot it which he did, after Skinning this animal we Set out and proceeded on to a Sand bar on the S W. Side below the enterance of White earth river where I landed and had the meat Skins and bedding all put out to dry. wind hard from the N W. I halted on the N W. Side of this river in the bend above the white earth river, where I saw where the Indians had been digging a root which they eate and use in Seup, not more than 7 or 8 days past. This morning a very large Bear of white Specis, discovered us floating in the water and takeing us, as I prosume to be Buffalow imediately plunged into the river and prosued us. I directed the men to be Still. this animal Came within about 40 yards of us, and tacked about. we all fired into him without killing him, and the wind So high that we could not pursue him, by which means he made his escape to the Shore badly wounded. I have observed buffalow floating down which I suppose must have been drounded in Crossing above. more or less of those animals drown or mire in passing this river. I observed Several floating buffalow on the R. Rochejhone imediately below where large gangues had Crossed. The wind blew hard all the after part of the day. I derected the men to dress their Skins except one which I took with me and walkd. through the bottom to the foot of the hills I killed five deer and the man with me killed 2. four others were killed in the Course of the day by the party only 2 of those deer were fat owing as I suppose to the Musquetors which are So noumerous and troublesom to them that they Cannot feed except under the torments of millions of those Musquetors.

[Clark, August 7, 1806] Saturday 7th August 1806 Some hard rain this morning after daylight which wet us all. I formed a Sort of Camped and delayed untill 11 a.m. when it Stoped raining for a short time. I directed every thing put on board and proceeded on down. the rain Continued at intervales all day tho not hard in the evenig Saw a Bear on the bank but Could not get a Shoot at it. at 6 P M I landed on a Sand bar on the South Side and Campd. Soon after we landed the wind blew very hard for about 2 hours, when it lulled a little. the air was exceedingly Clear and Cold and not a misquetor to be Seen, which is a joyfull circumstance to the Party.

[Clark, August 8, 1806] Sunday 8th August 1806 A cool windey morning I derected Shields and Gibson to turn out and hunt this morning. at 8 A.M. Sergt. N. Pryor Shannon, hall & Windsor Came down the river in two Canoes made of Buffalow Skins. Sergt. Pryor informed me that the Second night after he parted with me on the river Rochejhone he arived about 4 P M on the banks of a large Creek which contained no running water. he halted to let the horses graze dureing which time a heavy Shower of rain raised the Creek so high that Several horses which had Stragled across the Chanel of this Creek was obliged to Swim back. here he deturmined to

Continue all night it being in good food for the horses. In the morning he could See no horses. in lookg about their Camp they discovered Several tracks within 100 paces of their Camp, which they pursued found where they had Caught and drove off all the horses. they prosued on five miles the Indians there divided into two parties. they Continued in pursute of the largest party five miles further finding that there was not the Smallest Chance of overtakeing them, they returned to their Camp and packed up their baggage on their backs and Steared a N. E. course to the River Rochejhone which they Struck at pompys Tower. there they killed a Buffalow Bull and made a Canoe in the form and shape of the mandans & Ricares (the form of a bason) and made in the following manner. Viz: 2 Sticks of 11/4 inch diameter is tied together So as to form a round hoop of the Size you wish the canoe, or as large as the Skin will allow to cover, two of those hoops are made one for the top or brim and the for the bottom the deabth you wish the Canoe, then Sticks of the Same Size are Crossed at right angles and fastened with a throng to each hoop and also where each Stick Crosses each other. then the Skin when green is drawn tight over this fraim and fastened with throngs to the brim or outer hoop So as to form a perfect bason. one of those Canoes will carry 6 or 8 Men and their loads. Those two Canoes are nearly the Same Size 7 feet 3 inches diamieter & 16 inchs deep 15 ribs or Cross Sticks in each. Sergt. Pryor informs me that the Cause of his building two Canoes was for fear of ones meating with Some accedent in passing down the rochejhone a river entirely unknown to either of them by which means they might loose their guns and amunition and be left entirely destitute of the means of precureing food. he informed me that they passed through the worst parts of the rapids & Shoals in the river without takeing a drop of water, and waves raised from the hardest winds dose not effect them. on the night of the 26th ulto. the night after the horses had been stolen a Wolf bit Sergt. Pryor through his hand when asleep, and this animal was So vicious as to make an attempt to Seize Windsor, when Shannon fortunately Shot him . Sergt. Pryers hand has nearly recovered. The Country through which St. Pryor Passed after he parted with me is a broken open Country. he passed one Small river which I have Called Pryors river which rises in a Mtn. to the South of Pompys tower. The note I left on a pole at the Mouth of the River Rochejhone Sergt. Pryor concluding that Capt. Lewis had passed took the note and brought it with him. Capt. Lewis I expect will be certain of my passing by the Sign which I have made and the encampment imediately in the point. Sergt. Pryor bing anxious to overtake me Set out Some time before day this morning and forgot his Saddlebags which contains his papers &c. I Sent Bratten back with him in Serch of them. I also Sent Shannon over to hunt the bottom on the opposit Side. Shields and Gibson returned at 10 A.M. with the Skins and part of the flesh of three deer which they had killed in this bottom. I derected them to take one of the Skin Canoes and proceed down to the next bottom and untill my arival which will be this evening if Sergt. Pryor returns in time. My object is to precure as many Skins as possible for the purpose of purchaseing Corn and Beans of the Mandans. as we have now no article of Merchindize nor horses to purchase with, our only resort is S kins which those people were very fond the winter we were Stationed near them. after dark Sergt. Pryor returned with his Saddlebeggs &c. they were much further up than he expected.

[Clark, August 9, 1806] Monday 9th August 1806 a heavy dew this morning. loaded the Canoes and proceeded on down about 6 miles and landed at the Camp of the 2 hunters Shields and Gibson whome I had Sent down to hunt last evening, they had killed five deer two of which were in good order which they brought in. here I took brackfast and proceeded on a fiew miles and I walked on Shore across a point of near 10 miles in extent in this bottom which was mostly open I saw Some fiew deer and Elk. I killed 3 of the deer which were Meagure the Elk appeared fat. I did not kill any of them as the distance to the river was too great for the men to Carry the meat at the lower part of this bottom a large Creek of runnig water 25 yds wide falls in which meanders through an open roleing plain of great extent. in the low bottoms of this Creek I observed Some timber Such as Cottonwood, ash & Elm. on my arival at the lower part of the bottom found that the canoes had been in waiting for me nearly two hours. The Squar brought me a large and well flavoured Goose berry of a rich Crimsin Colour, and deep purple berry of the large Cherry of the Current Speces which is common on this river as low as the Mandans, the engagees Call it the Indian Current. I landed opposit to a high plain on the S. E. Side late in the evening and walked in a Grove of timber where I met with an Elk which I killed. this Elk was the largest Buck I ever Saw and the fattest animal which have been killed on the rout. I had the flesh and fat of this Elk brought to Camp and cut thin ready to dry. the hunters killed nothing this evening.

[Clark, August 10, 1806] Tuesday 10th August 1806 had the flesh of the elk hung on poles to dry, and Sent out the the hunters. wind blew hard from the East all day. in the after part of the day it was cloudy & a fiew drops of rain. I finished a Copy of my Sketches of the River Rochejhone. Shields killed a black tail deer & an antilope. the other hunters killed nothing. deer are very Scerce on this part of the river. I found a Species of Cherry in the bottom the Srub or bush which are differant from any which I have ever Seen and not very abundant even in this Small tract of country to which it Seems to be confined. the Stem is compound erect and subdivided or branching without any regular order. it rises to the hight of 8 or 10 feet Seldom putting out more than one Stem from the Same root not growing in cops as the Choke Cherry does. the bark is Smooth and of a dark brown colour. the leaf is petialate, oval accutely pointed at it's apex, from 1 and a 1/4 to one and a 1/2 inch in length and from a half to 3/4 of an inch in wedth, finely or manutely Serrate, pale green and free from bubessance. The fruit is a globular berry about the Size of a buck Shot of a fine Scarlet red; like the cherries cultivated in the U. States each is supported by a Seperate Celindric flexable branch peduncle which issues from the extremities of the boughs. the peduncle of this cherry Swells as it approaches the fruit being largest at the point of insertion. the pulp of this fruit is of an agreeable ascid flavour and is now ripe. the Style and Stigma are permanent. I have never Seen it in blume. it is found on the high Stiff lands or hill Sides-. the men dug great parcel of the root which the Nativs call Hankee and the engagees the white apple which they boiled and made use of with their meat. This is a large insipid root and very tasteless. the nativs use this root after it is dry and pounded in their Seup.

[Clark, August 11, 1806] Wednesday 11th August 1806 I set out early this morning. at 10 A.M. landed on a Sand bar and brackfast dureing brackfast and my delay at this place which was 2 hours had the Elk meat exposed to the Sun. at Meridian I set out and had not proceeded more than 2 miles before I observed a Canoe near the Shore. I derected the Canoes to land here I found two men from the illinoies Jos. Dixon, and ____ Handcock those men are on a trapping expedition up the River Rochejhone. They inform me that they left the Illinois in the Summer 1804. the last winter they Spent with the Tetons in Company with a Mr. Coartong who brought up goods to trade The tetons robed him of the greater part of the goods and wounded this Dixon in the leg with a hard wad. The Tetons gave Mr. Coartong Some fiew robes for the articles they took from him. Those men further informed me that they met the Boat and party we Sent down from Fort Mandan near the Kanzas river on board of which was a Chief of the Ricaras, that he met the Yankton Chiefs with Mr. Deurion, McClellen & Several other traders on their way down. that the Mandans and Menitarrais wer at war with the Ricaras and had killed two of the latter. the Assinniboins were also at war with the Mandans &c and had prohibited the N W. traders from Comeing to the Missouri to trade. they have latterly killed one Trader near the Mous River and are now in wait for Mr. McKenzey one of the Clerks who have been for a long time with Menetarias. Those dificulties if true will I fear be a bar to our expectations of having the Mandan Minetarra & Ricara Chief to acompany us to the U. States. Tho we Shall endeavor to bring abot a peace between Mandans Menneteries & Ricaras and provail on Some of their Cheifs to accompany us to the U. States. proceeded on to a point on the S W Side nearly opposit the enterance of Goat pen creek and encamped found the Musquetors excessively troublesom.

[Clark, August 12, 1806] Thursday 12th August 1806 I set out early this morning and had not proceeded on far before Shannon discovered he had lost his Tomahk. I derected him to land his Skin Canoe and go back to our Camp of last night in Serch of it, and proceeded on my self with the two wood and one Skin Canoe to a large hottom on the N. E Side above the head of Jins island and landed to take brackfast as well as to delay untill Shannon & Gibson Should arive. Sent out Shields & Labiech to hunt deer in the bottom, at 2 P m. Shannon and gibson arived having found the tomahawk at our camp they killed 3 Elk &c. one of the Canoes of Buffalow Skin by accident got a hole peirced in her of about 6 inches diamuter. I derected two of the men to patch the Canoe with a piece of Elk skin over the hole, which they did and it proved all Sufficient, after which the Canoe did not leak one drop. The two hunters returned without haveing killed any thing. at meridian Capt Lewis hove in Sight with the party which went by way of the Missouri as well as that which accompanied him from Travellers rest on Clarks river; I was alarmed on the landing of the Canoes to be informed that Capt. Lewis was wounded by an accident-. I found him lying in the Perogue, he informed me that his wound was slight and would be well in 20 or 30 days this information relieved me very much. I examined the wound and found it a very bad flesh wound the ball had passed through the fleshey part of his left thy below the hip bone and cut the cheek of the right buttock for 3 inches in length and the debth of the ball. Capt L. informed me the accident happened the day before by one of the men Peter Crusat misstakeig him in the thick bushes to be an Elk. Capt Lewis with this Crusat and Several other men were out in the bottom Shooting of Elk, and had Scattered in a thick part of the woods in pursute of the Elk. Crusat Seeing Capt L. passing through the bushes and takeing him to be an Elk from the Colour of his Cloathes which were of leather and very nearly that of the Elk fired and unfortunately the ball passed through the thy as aforesaid. Capt Lewis thinking it indians who had Shot him hobbled to the canoes as fast as possible and was followered by Crusat, the mistake was then discovered. This Crusat is near Sighted and has the use of but one eye, he is an attentive industerous man and one whome we both have placed the greatest Confidence in dureing the whole rout.- After Capt. Lewis and my Self parted at Travellers rest, he with the Indians proceeded down the West Side of Clarks river Seven miles and crossed on rafts 2 miles below the East fork 120 yards wide, after Crossing the river he proceeded up the North Side of the east fork and encampd. here the Indians left him and proceeded down Clarks river in Serch of the Tushepaws. an Indian man Came up with Cap L. from the W. of the mountains and proceeded on with those who had accompanied us. Capt. L. proceeded up the E. fork of Clarks river 17 ms. to the enterance of Cokahlarishkit river or the river to buffalow, he proceeded up on the North Side of this river which is 60 yards wide crossing Several Small Streams and the N. fork, and passing over part of the dividing mountain onto the waters of Deabourns river in the plains and in a Derection to the N. extremity of Easte range of rocky mountains which pass the Missouri at the pine Island Rapid. from thence he bore his Course to the N E untill he Struck Meadcin river near where that river Enters the rocky Mts. and proceeded down Medicine river to the Missouri at the white bear Islands at the upper part of the portage. this rout is a very good one tho not the most derect rout, the most derect rout would be to proceed up the Missouri above Dearborns river and take a right hand road & fall on a South branch of the Cokatlarishkit R. and proceed down that river to the main road but the best rout would be from the falls of the Missouri by fort mountain and passing the N. extremity of that range of the Rocky Mountains which pass the Missouri at the pine Island rapid Course nearly S. W. and to the gap through which the great road passeds the dividing mountain the distance from the falls to this gap about 45 miles through a tolerable leavel plain on an old indian road. and the distance from thence to Clarks river is 105 miles. The total distance from the falls of the Missouri to Clarks river is only 150 miles of a tolerable road- Capt L. arived at the white Bear Islands and encampd. on the West Side of the Missouri and in the morning he discovered that the Indians had taken of Seven of his best horses, drewyer prosued the indians two day's on the rout towards Clarks river. he Saw their camp on Dearborns river near the road on which Capt. Lewis & party Come on a by place where they had left only one or two day at this encampment he Saw great appearanc of horses- on the return of Drewyer Capt L. took Drewyer & the 2 fieldses & proceeded on his intended rout up Marias river leaving Sergt. Gass, Thompson, Frazier, Werner, McNeal & Goodrich at the portage to prepare Geer and repar the wheels & Carrage against the arival of the Canoes and he also left 4 horses for the purpose of hauling the Canoes across. The Canoes arrived on the 16th, and on the 26th they had all except one across, the Plains becom So muddy from the emence rains which had fallen, that they Could not get her over the portage. on the 28th they joined Capt Lewis at the Grog Spring a fiew miles above the enterance of Marias river From the Falls of Missouri Capt. L. proceeded on with Drewyer & the 2 fieldses Courss

On the 26th of July Capt Lewis Set out on his return to the enterance of Marias river to meet with the party with, the Canoes from the falls. his course was through the plains

S. E. 5 Miles- passing a Small Creek from the mts

S. 70° E. 9 Miles to a principal branch of Marias River 65 yards wide not very deep at 7 mile. this last branch is Shallow and rapid about the Size of the former from the S W. both of those Streams Contain a great preportion of timber- here we find the 3 Specis of Cotton before mentioned

N 80° E. 4 miles down Marias river and met with 8 Indians of the Blackfoot nation with about 30 horses, those Indians professed friendship and Set out with him and encamped together the night of the 26th of July, thy informed him that there was two large bands of their nation in that quarter one of which would be at the enterance of Marias river in a fiew days. they also informed that a french Trader was with one of those bands, that they traded with the white people on the Suskashwen River at 6 easy days march or about 150 miles distant from whome they precured Guns Powder Lead blankets &c. in exchange for wolf and beaver Skins. Capt Lewis gave them a Flag Meadel & Handkerchief Capt. L. informed those Indians where he was from & where he had been and his objects & friendly views &c. of which they appeared to be well Satisfied.

"on the morning of the 27th at day light the indians got up and crouded around the fire, Jo. Field who was on post had carelessly laid his gun down behind him near where his brother was Sleeping. one of the Indians Slipd. behind him and took his gun and that of his brother unperceived by him, at the Same instant two others advanced and Seized the guns of Drewyer and Capt Lewis who were yet asleep. Jo. Fields Seeing this turned about to take his gun and Saw the fellow running off with his and his brothers, he called to his brother who instantly jumped up and prosued the indian with him whome they overtook at the distance of 50 or 60 paces Siezed their guns and rested them from him and R. Field as he Seized his gun Stabed the indian to the heart with his knif who fell dead; (this Cap L. did not know untill Some time after.) drewyer who awoke at the first alarm jumped up and Seized & rested his gun from the indian &c. Capt L. awoke and asked what was the matter Seeing Drewyer in a Scuffle for his gun he turned to get his gun and found her gorn, he drew a pistol from his holsters and prosued the Indian whom he Saw in possession of his gun making off he presented the pistol and the indian lay down the gun. the two Fields Came up and drew up to Shoot the Indian which Capt L. forbid the indians then attempted to drive off all the horses. Capt L. derected the men to fire on them if they attempted to drive off the horses, and prosued two fellows who Continued to drive of his horses he Shot the indian who had taken his gun and then in possession of his horse through the belly, he fell and raised on his elbow and fired at Capt L. the other made his escape into a nitch out of Sight with his bow and arrows and as Capt L. guns was empty and he without his Shot pouch he returnd. to the Camp where the 2 fields and Drewyer joind him having prosued the indians across the river the were now in possession of the most of their own as well as the indian horses and a gun Several bows & arrows and all the indians baggage the gun & Some feathers and flag they took and burnt all the other articles. and Saddled up a many of the best horses as they wished with Some Spear horses, and Set out for to intersept the party at Marias river and proceded on a little to the S. of East 112 Miles to the Missouri at the Grog Spring. here they met with Canoes and party decending joined them leaving their horses on the river bank, and proceeded on to the enterance of Marias river opened the deposits, found Several articles damaged. 3 Beaver traps could not be found, the red perogue unfit for Service, from thenc they proceeded without delay to the River Rochejhone See cources of Capt Lewis rout in next book."

at 2 P.M. Shannon & Gibson arived in the Skin Canoe with the Skins and the greater part of the flesh of 3 Elk which they had killed a fiew miles above. the two men Dixon & Handcock the two men we had met above came down intending to proceed on down with us to the Manclans. at 3 P M we proceded on all together having left the 2 leather Canoes on the bank. a little below the enterance of (Jos) Shabonos Creek we Came too on a large Sand point from the S. E. Side and Encamped. the wind blew very hard from the S W. and Some rain. I washed Capt L. wound which has become Sore and Somewhat painfull to him.

[Clark, August 13, 1806] Friday 13th August 1806 the last night was very Cold with a Stiff breeze from the N. W. all hands were on board and we Set out at Sunrize and proceeded on very well with a Stiff breeze astern the greater part of the day. passed the enterance of the Little Missouri river at 8 A.M. and arived at the Enterance of Myry river at Sun Set and encamped on the N E Side haveing came by the assistance of the wind, the Current and our oars 86 miles. below the little bason I with Drewyer walked through the N. E point. we Saw an Elk and Several deer. Drewyer wounded the Elk but could not get him. I joined the perogus & party again in the bend below and proceeded on. Some indians were Seen in a Skin Canoe below, they were decending from an old Camp of theirs on the S. W. Side, those I Suppose to be Some of the Minetaras who had been up on a hunting expedition, one Canoe was left at their Camp. we had not proceeded far before I discovered two indians on a high hill. nothing very remarkable took place. the Misquetors are not So troublesom this evening as they have been. the air is cool &c.

[Clark, August 14, 1806] Thursday 14th August 1806 Set out at Sunrise and proceeded on. when we were oppsit the Minetares Grand Village we Saw a number of the Nativs viewing of we derected the Blunderbuses fired Several times, Soon after we Came too at a Croud of the nativs on the bank oppsit the Village of the Shoe Indians or Mah-har-ha's at which place I saw the principal Chief of the Little Village of the Menitarre & the principal Chief of the Mah-har-has. those people were extreamly pleased to See us. the Chief of the little Village of the Menetarias cried most imoderately, I enquired the Cause and was informed it was for the loss of his Son who had been killed latterly by the Blackfoot Indians. after a delay of a fiew minits I proceeded on to the black Cats Village on the N. E. Side of the Missouri where I intended to Encamp but the Sand blew in Such a manner that we deturmined not to continu on that Side but return to the Side we had left. here we were visited by all the inhabitants of this village who appeared equally as well pleased to See us as those above. I walked up to the Black Cats village & eate some Simnins with him, and Smoked a pipe this Village I discovered had been rebuilt Since I left it and much Smaller than it was; on enquirey into the Cause was informed that a quarrel had taken place and Lodges had removed to the oppose Side. I had Soon as I landed despatched Shabono to the Minetarras inviting the Chiefs to visit us, & Drewyer down to the lower Village of the Mandans to ask Mr. Jessomme to Come and enterpret for us. Mr. Jessomme arived and I spoke to the chiefs of the Village informing them that we Spoke to them as we had done when we were with them last and we now repeeted our envitation to the principal Chiefs of all the Villages to accompany us and to the U States &c. &c. the Black Cat Chief of the Mandans, Spoke and informed me that he wished to Visit the United States and his Great Father but was afraid of the Scioux who were yet at war with them and had killed Several of their men Since we had left them, and were on the river below and would Certainly kill him if he attempted to go dow.i. I indeavored to do away with his objections by informig him that we would not Suffer those indians to hurt any of our red Children who Should think proper to accompany us, and on their return they would be equally protected, and their presents which would be very liberal, with themselves, Conveyed to their own Country at the expence of the U. States &c. &c. The chief promised us Some corn tomorrow. after the Council I directed the Canoes to cross the river to a brook opposit where we Should be under the wind and in a plain where we would be Clear of musquetors & after Crossing the Chief of the Mah har has told me if I would Send with him he would let me have some corn. I directed Sergt Gass & 2 men to accompany him to his Village, they Soon returned loaded with Corn. the Chief and his wife also came down. I gave his wife a fiew Needles &c.- The Great Chif of all the Menitarres the one eye Came to Camp also Several other Chiefs of the different Villages. I assembled all the Chiefs on a leavel Spot on the band and Spoke to them & see next book.

[Clark, August 15, 1806] Thursday August 15th 1806 Continued Mandans Vilg after assembling the Chiefs and Smokeing one pipe, I informed them that I Still Spoke the Same words which we had Spoken to them when we first arived in their Country in the fall of 1804. we then envited them to visit their great father the president of the U. States and to hear his own Councils and receive his Gifts from his own hands as also See the population of a government which Can at their pleasure protect and Secur you from all your enimies, and chastize all those who will Shut their years to his Councils. we now offer to take you at the expense of our Government and Send you back to your Country again with a considerable present in merchendize which you will recive of your great Father. I urged the necessity of their going on with us as it would be the means of hastening those Supples of Merchindize which would be Sent to their Country and exchanged as before mentioned for a moderate price in Pelteries and furs &c. the great Chief of the Menetaras Spoke, he Said he wished to go down and See his great father very much, but that the Scioux were in the road and would most certainly kill him or any others who Should go down they were bad people and would not listen to any thing which was told them. when he Saw us last we told him that we had made peace with all the nations below, Since that time the Seioux had killed 8 of their people and Stole a number of their horses. he Said that he had opened his ears and followed our Councils, he had made peace with the Chyennes and rocky mountains indians, and repieted the same objecctions as mentioned. that he went to war against none and was willing to receive all nations as friends. he Said that the Ricaras had Stolen from his people a number of horses at different times and his people had killed 2 Ricaras. if the Sieoux were at peace with them and Could be depended on he as also other Chiefs of the villages would be glad to go and See their great father, but as they were all afraid of the Sieoux they Should not go down &c.

The Black Cat Chief of the Mandans Village on the North Side of the Missouri Sent over and requested me to go over to his village which envertation I axceptd and crossed over to his village. he had a parcel of Corn about 12 bushuls in a pile in his lodge. he told me that his people had but little corn part of which they had given me. after takeing a Smoke he informed me that as the Sieoux were very troublesom and the road to his great father dangerous none of this village would go down with us. I told the Cheifs and wariers of the village who were there present that we were anxious that Some of the village Should go and See their great father and hear his good words & recve his bountiful gifts &c. and told them to pitch on Some Man on which they could rely on and Send him to See their Great father, they made the Same objections which the Chief had done before. a young man offered to go down, and they all agreeed for him to go down the charector of this young man I knew as a bad one and made an objection as to his age and Chareckter at this time Gibson who was with me informed me that this young man had Stole his knife and had it then in his possession, this I informed the Chief and directed him to give up the knife he delivered the knife with a very faint apology for his haveing it in his possession. I then reproached those people for wishing to Send Such a man to See and hear the words of So great a man as their great father; they hung their heads and Said nothing for Some time when the Cheif Spoke and Said that they were afraid to Send any one for fear of their being killed by the Sieux. after Smoking a pipe and relateing Some passages I recrossed to our Camp-. being informed by one of our enterpreters that the 2d Chief of the Mandans Comonly Called the little Crow intended to accompany us down, I took Charbono and walked to the Village to See this Chief and talk with him on the Subject. he told me he had deturmined to go down, but wished to have a council first with his people which would be in the after part of the day. I smoked a pipe with the little Crow and returned to the boat. Colter one of our men expressed a desire to join Some trappers who offered to become Shearers with and furnish traps &c. the offer a very advantagious one, to him, his Services Could be dispenced with from this down and as we were disposed to be of Service to any one of our party who had performed their duty as well as Colter had done, we agreed to allow him the prvilage provided no one of the party would ask or expect a Similar permission to which they all agreeed that they wished Colter every Suckcess and that as we did not wish any of them to Seperate untill we Should arive at St. Louis they would not apply or expect it &c. The Maharha Chief brought us Some Corn, as did also the Chief of the little village of the Menetarras on mules of which they have Several. The evening is Cool and windy. great number of the nativs of the different villages Came to view us and exchange robes with our men for their Skins- we gave Jo Colter Some Small articles which we did not want and Some powder & lead. the party also gave him Several articles which will be usefull to him on his expedittion.- This evening Charbono informed me that our back was scercely turned before a war party from the two menetarry villages followed on and attacked and killed the Snake Indians whome we had Seen and in the engagement between them and the Snake indians they had lost two men one of which was the Son of the principal Chief of the little village of the menitarras. that they had also went to war from the Menetarras and killed two Ricaras. he further informed me that a missunderstanding had taken place between the Mandans & minetarras and had verry nearly come to blows about a woman, the Menitarres at length presented a pipe and a reconsilliation took place between them

[Clark, August 16, 1806] Friday 16th August 1806 a cool morning. Sent up Sergt. Pryor to the mandan village, for Some Corn which they offered to give us. he informed that they had more Corn collected for us than our Canoes Could Carry Six load of which he brought down. I thanked the Chief for his kindness and informed him that our Canoes would not Carry any more Corn than we had already brought down. at 10 A. M the Chiefs of the different villages came to See us and Smoke a pipe &c. as our Swivel Could no longer be Serveceable to us as it could not be fireed on board the largest Perogue, we Concluded to make a present of it to the Great Chief of the Menetaras (the One Eye) with a view to ingratiate him more Strongly in our favour I had the Swivel Charged and Collected the Chiefs in a circle around it and adressed them with great ceremoney. told them I had listened with much attention to what the One Eye had Said yesterday and beleived that he was Sincere & Spoke from his heart. I reproached them very Severely for not attending to what had been Said to them by us in Council in the fall of 1804 and at different times in the winter of 1804 & 5, and told them our backs were Scercely turned befor a party followed and killed the pore defenceless snake indians whom we had taken by the hand & told them not to be afraid that you would never Strike them again &c. also mentioned the ricers &c. The little Cherry old Chief of the Menetarras Spoke as follows Viz: "Father we wish to go down with you to See our Great Father, but we know the nations below and are afraid of the Scioux who will be on the river and will kill us on our return home. The Scioux has Stolen our horses and killed 8 of our men Since you left us, and the Ricaras have also Struck us. we Staid at home and listened to what you had told us. we at length went to war against the Scioux and met with Ricaras and killed two of them, they were on their way to Strike us. We will attend to your word and not hurt any people all Shall be Welcom and we Shall do as you direct-." The One Eye Said his ears would always be open to the word of his great father and Shut against bad Council &c. I then a good deel of Ceremony made a preasent of the Swivel to the One Eye Chief and told him when he fired this gun to remember the words of his great father which we had given him. this gun had anounced the words of his great father to all the nations which we had Seen &c. &c. after the council was over the gun was fired & delivered, they Chief appeared to be much pleased and conveyed it immediately to his village &c. we Settled with and discharged Colter. in the evening I walked to the village to See the little Crow and know when he would be ready, took with me a flag intending to give him to leave at his lodge but to my astonishment he informed me he had declined going down the reason of which I found was through a jellousy between himself and the principal Chief he refused a flag & we Sent for Mr. Jessomme and told him to use his influn to provail on one of the Chiefs to acompany us and we would employ him. he informed us soon after that the big white Chief would go if we would take his wife & Son & Jessoms wife & 2 children we wer obliged to agree to do

[Clark, August 17, 1806] Saturday 17th of August 1806 a Cool morning gave some powder & Ball to Big White Chief Settled with Touisant Chabono for his Services as an enterpreter the pric of a horse and Lodge purchased of him for public Service in all amounting to 500$ 33 1/3 cents. derected two of the largest of the Canoes be fastened together with poles tied across them So as to make them Study for the purpose of Conveying the Indians and enterpreter and their families

we were visited by all the principal Chiefs of the Menetarras to take their leave of us at 2 oClock we left our encampment after takeing leave of Colter who also Set out up the river in Company with Messrs. Dickson & Handcock. we also took our leave of T. Chabono, his Snake Indian wife and their Son Child who had accompanied us on our rout to the pacific Ocean in the Capacity of interpreter and interpretes. T. Chabono wished much to accompany us in the Said Capacity if we could have provailed the Menetarre Chiefs to dcend the river with us to the U. States, but as none of those chiefs of whoes language he was Conversant would accompany us, his Services were no longer of use to the U States and he was therefore discharged and paid up. we offered to convey him down to the Illinois if he Chose to go, he declined proceeding on at present, observing that he had no acquaintance or prospects of makeing a liveing below, and must continue to live in the way that he had done. I offered to take his little Son a butifull promising Child who is 19 months old to which they both himself & wife wer willing provided the Child had been weened. they observed that in one year the boy would be Sufficiently old to leave his mother & he would then take him to me if I would be so freindly as to raise the Child for him in Such a manner as I thought proper, to which I agreeed &c.- we droped down to the Big white Cheifs Mandan Village 1/2 a mile below on the South Side, all the Indians proceeded on down by land. and I walked to the lodge of the Chief whome I found Sorounded by his friends the men were Setting in a circle Smokeing and the womin Crying. he Sent his bagage with his wife & Son, with the Interpreter Jessomme & his wife and 2 children to the Canoes provided for them. after Smoking one pipe, and distributing Some powder & lead which we had given him, he informed me that he was ready and we were accompd to the Canoes by all the Village Maney of them Cried out aloud. as I was about to Shake with the Grand Cheifs of all the Villages there assembled they requested me to Set one minit longer with them which I readily agreed to and directed a pipe to be lit. the Cheifs informed that when we first came to their Country they did not beleive all we Said we then told them. but they were now Convinced that every thing we had told them were true, that they Should keep in memory every thing which we had Said to them, and Strictly attend to our advice, that their young men Should Stay at home and Should no go again to war against any nation, that if any atacted them they Should defend themselves, that we might depend on what they Said, and requested us to inform their great father. the also requested me to tell the Ricaras to Come and See them, not to be afraid that no harm Should be done them, that they were anxious to be in peace with them.

The Seeoux they Said they had no dependance in and Should kill them whenever they Came into their Country to do them harm &c. I told them that we had always told them to defend themselves, but not to Strike those nations we had taken by the hand, the Sieoux with whome they were at war we had never Seen on our return we Should inform their great fathe of their conduct towards his faithfull red Children and he would take Such Steps as will bring about a lasting peace between them and his faithfull red children. I informed them that we should inform the ricaras what they had requested &c. The Grand Chief of the Mineterres Said that the Great Cheif who was going down with to see their great father was a well as if he went also, and on his return he would be fully informed of the words of his great father, and requested us to take care of this Gt. Chief. we then Saluted them with a gun and Set out and proceeded on to Fort Mandan where I landed and went to view the old works the houses except one in the rear bastion was burnt by accident, Some pickets were Standing in front next to the river. we proceeded on to the old Ricara village the S E wind was so hard and the waves So high that we were obliged to Come too, & Camp on the S W Side near the old Village. (18 mils)

[Clark, August 18, 1806] Monday 18th August 1806. moderate rain last night, the wind of this morning from the S. E. as to cause the water to be So rough that we Could not proceed on untill 8 a.m. at which time it fell a little & we proceeded on tho the waves were yet high and the wind Strong. Saw Several Indians on either Side of the river. at 9 A.M. I saw an Indian running down the beech and appd. to be anxious to Speak to us I derected the Canoes to land. this Indian proved to be the brother of the Chief we had on board and Came down from his Camp at no great distance to take his leave of his brother. the Chief gave him a par of Legins and took an effectunate leave of his brother and we procedeed on haveing previously Sent on 2 canoes with hunters to kill Some meat at 2 P. M we overtook the Canoe hunters, they had killed three deer which was divided and we halted and Cooked Some dinner on the Sandbar. wind Still high and from the Same point. The Chief pointed out Several places where he Said his nation formerly lived and related Some extroadinary Stories of their tredition. after Dinner we proceeded on, to a point on the N E. Side opposit the remains of an old Mandan village a little below the enterance of Chiss-che for River and the place we Encamped as we assended this river 20th of October 1804 haveing come 40 miles today. after landing which was a little before night the hunters run out into the bottom and Killed four deer. The winds blew hard from the S. E. all day which retarded our progress very much after the fires were made I set my self down with the big white man Chiefe and made a number of enquiries into the tredition of his nation as well as the time of their inhabiting the number of Villages the remains of which we see on different parts of the river, as also the cause of their evacuation. he told me his nation first Came out of the ground where they had a great village. a grape vine grew down through the Earth to their village and they Saw light Some of their people assended by the grape vine upon the earth, and Saw Buffalow and every kind of animal also Grapes plumbs &c. they gathered Some grapes & took down the vine to the village, and they tasted and found them good, and deturmined to go up and live upon the earth, and great numbers climbed the vine and got upon earth men womin and children. at length a large big bellied woman in climbing broke the vine and fell and all that were left in the Village below has remained there ever Since (The Mandans beleive when they die that they return to this village) Those who were left on earth made a village on the river below and were very noumerous &c. he Said that he was born in the Village Opposit to our Camp and at that time his nation inhabited 7 villages as large as that and were full of people, the Sieoux and Small pox killed the greater part of them and made them So weak that all that were left only made two Small villages when Collected, which were built near the old Ricaras village above. their troubles with the Scioux & Pawnees or Ricaras Compelled them to move and build a village where they now live.

he Said that the Menitarras Came out of the water to the East and Came to this Country and built a village near the mandans from whome they got Corn beens &c. they were very noumerous and resided in one village a little above this place on the opposit Side. they quarreled about a buffalow, and two bands left the village and went into the plains, (those two bands are now known bye the title Pounch, and Crow Indians.) the ballance of the Menetaras moved their village to where it now Stands where they have lived ever Since-

[Clark, August 19, 1806] Tuesday 19th of August 1806 Some rain last night and this morning the wind rose and blew with great Violence untill 4 P. M and as our camp was on a Sand bar we were very much distressd with the blows of Sand. I directed the hunters to proceed on down the bottom and kill and butcher Some meat and if the wind Should lie that I should proceed on down to their Camp &c. Capt. Lewis'es wounds are heeling very fast, I am much in hope of his being able to walk in 8 or 10 days-. at 4 P. M the wind Seased to blow with that violence which it had done all day we Set out and proceeded on down. the hunters which was Sent out this morning killed 4 Elk & 12 deer near the river we came too and brought in the most of the flesh and proceeded on to a Sand on the N E Side and Encamped. the wind rose and become very Strong from the S. E. and a great appearance of rain. Jessomme the Interpreter let me have a piece of a lodge and the Squars pitched or Stretched it over Some Sticks, under this piece of leather I Slept dry, it is the only covering which I have had Suffecient to keep off the rain Since I left the Columbia. it began to rain moderately Soon after night. The Indians appear well Satisfyed with the party and mode of proceedure. we decended only 10 miles to day Saw Some Elk and buffalow on the Shore near where we Encamped. the Elk beginning to run. the Buffalow are done running & the bulls are pore.

[Clark, August 20, 1806] Wednesday 20th of August 1806 a violent hard rain about day light this morning. all wet except myself and the indians. we embarked a little after Sun rise wind moderate and ahead. we proceeded on at meridn. passed the enterance of Cannonball river imediately above is the remains of a large Sieoux encampment which appears to have been made this Spring. at 3 P M passed the enterance of Wardepon River Saw great number of wolves on the bank Some Buffalow & Elk, tho not so abundant as near the River Rochejhone. passed the place where we left the last encampment of Ricaras in the fall 1804 and encamped on a Sandbar from the N. E. Side, having made 8 miles only, the wind blew hard all day which caused the waves to rise high and flack over into the Small Canoes in Such a manner as to employ one hand in throwing the water out. The plains begin to Change their appearance the grass is turning of a yellow colour. I observe a great alteration in the Corrent course and appearance of this pt. of the Missouri. in places where there was Sand bars in the fall 1804 at this time the main Current passes, and where the current then passed is now a Sand bar Sand bars which were then naked are now covered with willow Several feet high. the enteranc of Some of the Rivers & Creeks Changed owing to the mud thrown into them, and a layor of mud over Some of the bottoms of 8 inches thick.

[Clark, August 21, 1806] Thursday 21st August 1806 Musquetors very troublesom in the early part of last night and again this morning I directed Sergt. Ordway to proceed on to where there was Some ash and get enough for two ores which were wanting. Men all put their arms in perfect order and we Set out at 5 a.m. over took Sergt. ordway with wood for oars &c. at 8 A.M. Met three french men Comeing up, they proved to be three men from the Ricaras two of them Reevea & Greinyea wintered with us at the mandans in 1804 we Came too, those men informed us that they were on their way to the Mandans, and intended to go down to the Illinois this fall. one of them quit a young lad requested a passage down to the Illinois, we concented and he got into a Canoe to an Ore. Those men informd us that 700 Seeoux had passed the Ricaras on their way to war with the Mandans & Menitarras and that their encampment where the Squaws and Children wer, was Some place near the Big Bend of this river below. no ricaras had accompanied them but were all at home, they also informed us that no trader had arived at the Ricaras this Season, and that they were informed that the Pania or Ricara Chief who went to the United States last Spring was a year, died on his return at Smoe place near the Sieoux river &c. those men had nether powder nor lead we gave them a horn of powder and Some balls and after a delay of an hour we parted from the 2 men Reevey & Grienway and proceeded on. the wind rose and bley from the N. W. at half past 11 a.m. we arived in view of the upper Ricara villages, a Great number of womin Collecting wood on the banks, we Saluted the village with four guns and they returned the Salute by fireing Several guns in the village, I observed Several very white Lodges on the hill above the Town which the ricaras from the Shore informed me were Chyennes who had just arived-. we landed opposit to the 2d Villages and were met by the most of the men women and children of each village as also the Chyennes they all appeared anxious to take us by the hand and much rejoiced to See us return. I Steped on Shore and was Saluted by the two great Chiefs, whome we had made or given Medals to as we assend this river in 1804, and also Saluted by a great number both of Ricaras & Chyennes, as they appeared anxious to here what we had done &c. as well as to here Something about the Mandans & Minetarras. I Set my self down on the Side of the Bank and the Chiefs & brave men of the Ricaras & Chyennes formed a Cercle around me. after takeing a Smoke of Mandan tobacco which the Big white Chief who was Seated on my left hand furnished, I informed them as I had before informed the Mandans & Menitarras, where we had been what we had done and Said to the different nations in there favour and envited Some of their Chiefs to accompany us down and See their great father and receve from his own mouth his good Councils and from his own hands his bountifull gifts &c. telling pretty much the Same which I had told the mandans and menitarras. told them not to be afraid of any nation below that none would hurt them &c. a man of about 32 years of age was intreduced to me as 1st Chief of the nation this man they Call the grey eyes or _____ he was absent from the Nation at the time we passed up, the man whome we had acknowledged as the principal chief informed me that the Grey eyes was a greater Chief than himself and that he had given up all his pretentions with the Flag and Medal to the Grey eyes- The principal chief of the Chyenne's was then introduced he is a Stout jolley fellow of about 35 years of age whome the Ricaras Call the Grey Eyes I also told the ricaras that I was very Sorrey to here that they were not on friendly terms with their neighbours the Mandans & Menetarras, and had not listened to what we had Said to them but had Suffered their young men to join the Sieoux who had killed 8 Mandans &c. that their young men had Stolen the horses of the Minetarras, in retaliation for those enjories the Mandans & Menetarras had Sent out a war party and killed 2 ricaras. how could they expect other nations would be at peace with them when they themselves would not listen to what their great father had told them. I further informed them that the Mandans & Menetaras had opened their ears to what we had Said to them but had Staid at home untill they were Struk that they were Still disposed to be friendly and on good terms with the ricaras, they then Saw the great Chief of the Mandans by my Side who was on his way to see his great father, and was derected by his nation & the Menetaras & Maharhas, to Smoke in the pipe of peace with you and to tell you not to be afraid to go to their towns, or take the Birds in the plains that their ears were open to our Councils and no harm Should be done to a Ricara. The Chief will Speak presently The Grey eyes Chief of the ricaras made a very animated Speach in which he mentioned his williness of following the councels which we had given them that they had Some bad young men who would not listen to the Councels but would join the Seioux, those men they had discarded and drove out of their villages, that the Seioux were the Cause of their Missunderstanding &c. that they were a bad peoples. that they had killed Several of the Ricaras Since I Saw them. That Several of the chiefs wished to accompany us down to See their great father, but wished to see the Chief who went down last Sumer return first, he expressed Some apprehention as to the Safty of that Chiefs in passing the Sieoux. that the Ricaras had every wish to be friendly with the Mandans &c. that every mandan &c. who chose to visit the ricares should be Safe that he Should Continue with his nation and See that they followed the Council which we had given them &c.- The Sun being very hot the Chyenne Chief envited us to his Lodge which was pitched in the plain at no great distance from the River. I accepted the invitation and accompanied him to his lodge which was new and much larger than any which I have Seen it was made of 20 dressed Buffalow Skins in the Same form of the Sceoux and lodges of other nations of this quarter. about this lodges was 20 others Several of them of nearly the Same Size. I enquired for the ballance of the nation and was informed that they were near at hand and would arive on tomorrow and when all together amounted to 120 Lodges after Smokeing I gave a medal of the Small size to the Chyenne Chief &c. which appeared to alarm him, he had a robe and a fleece of fat Buffalow meat brought and gave me with the meadel back and informed me that he knew that the white people were all medecine and that he was afraid of the midal or any thing that white people gave to them. I had previously explained the cause of my gveing him the medal & flag, and again told him the use of the medal and the caus of my giveing it to him, and again put it about his neck delivering him up his preasent of a roab & meat, informing him that this was the medecene which his Great father directed me to deliver to all the great Chiefs who listened to his word and followed his councils, that he had done So and I should leave the medal with him as a token of his cincerity &c. he doubled the quantity of meat, and received the medal

The Big White chief of the Mandans Spoke at some length explainin the Cause of the misunderstanding between his nation and the ricaras, informing them of his wish to be on the most freindly termes &c. the Chyennes accused both nations of being in folt. I told to them all that if they eve wished to be hapy that they must Shake off all intimecy with the Seioux and unite themselves in a Strong allience and attend to what we had told them &c. which they promesed all to do and we Smoked and parted on the best terms, the Mandan Chief was Saluted by Several Chiefs and brave men on his way with me to the river- I had requested the ricaras & Chyennes to inform me as Soon as possible of their intentions of going down with us to See their great father or not. in the evening the Great Chief requested that I would walk to his house which I did, he gave me about 2 quarts of Tobacco, 2 beaver Skins and a trencher of boiled Corn & beans to eat (as it is the Custom of all the Nations on the Missouri to give Something to every white man who enters their lodge Something to eat) this Chief informed me that none of his Chiefs wished to go down with us they all wished to See the cheif who went down return first, that the Chyennes were a wild people and were afraid to go. that they Should all listen to what I had Said. I gave him Some ribon to Suspend his Medal to and a Shell which the Snake indians gave me for which he was very much pleased.

The interpreter informed me that the Cheifs of those villages had no intention of going down. one the Cheifs of the Village on the island talkd. of going down. I returned to the boat where I found the principal Chief of the lower vilege who had Cut part of his hair and disfigured himself in Such a manner that I did not know him, he informed me the Sieux had killed his nephew and that Was in tears for him &c. we deturmind to proceed down to the Island and accordingly took the chief on board and proceeded on down to the isd village at which place we arived a little before dark and were met as before by nearly every individual of the Village, we Saluted them and landed imediately oppost the town. The one arm 2d Cheif of this village whome we had expected to accompany us down Spoke to the mandan Cheif in a loud and thretening tone which Caused me to be Some what alarmed for the Safty of that Cheif, I inform the Ricaras of this village that the Mandans had opened their ears to and fold. our Councils, that this Cheif was on his way to see their Great Father the P. of U S. and was under our protection that if any enjorey was done to him by any nation that we Should all die to a man. I told the Ricaras that they had told us lies, they promised to be at peace with the mandans & Menetarras. that our back was Scrcely turned before they went to war & Killd. them and Stole their horses &c- The Cheif then envited me & the Mandan Chief to his house to talk there. I accompanied him, after takeing a very Serimonious Smoke the 2d Cheif informd. me that he had opened his ears to what we had Said to him at the time we gave him the medal that he had not been to war against any Natn. Since, that once been to See the mandans and they were going to kill him, they had not killed the Mandans, it was the Seeoux who killed them and not the ricaras, he Said that the Mandan Cheif was as Safe as if he was in his own Vilg that he had opened his ears and Could here as well as the mandans. I then informd them what I had told the upper villages and we all become perfectly reconsiled all to each other and Smoked in the most perfect harmony we had invatations to go into their lodges and eate. I at length went to the grand Chiefs Lodge by his particelar invitation, the Mandan Chief Stuck close to me the Chief had prepd. a Supper of boiled young Corn, beens & quashes of which he gave me in Wooden bowls. he also gave me near 2 quarts of the Tobacco Seed, & informed me he had always had his ears open to what we had Said, that he was well convinced that the Seeoux was the caus of all the trouble between the Mandans & them the Ricars had Stolen horses from the Mandan which had been returned all except one which could not be got, this mischief was done by Some young men who was bad. a long Conversation of explanations took place between the Ricara & mandan Chiefs which appeared to be Satisfactory on both Sides. the Chief gave a pipe with great form and every thing appeared to be made up. I returned to the river & went to bead. the Indians contd on board. made 22 miles today only.

[Clark, August 22, 1806] Friday 22nd August 1806. rained all the last night every person and all our bedding wet, the Morning cloudy, at 8 A M. I was requested to go to the Chiefs, I walkd up and he informed me that he Should not go down but would Stay and take Care of the village and prevent the young men from doing rong and Spoke much to the Same porpt of the Grey Eyes, the 2d Chief Spoke to the Same and all they Said was only a repitition of what they had Said before. the Chief gave me some Soft Corn and the 2d Chief Some Tobacco Seed- the Interpreter Garrow informed me that he had been Speeking to the Chiefs & warriers this morning and assured me that they had no intention of going down untill the return of the Cheif who went down last Spring was a year. I told the Cheifs to attend to what we had Said to them, that in a Short time they would find our words tru and Councils good. they promised to attend Strictly to what had been Said to them, and observed that they must trade with the Sieoux one more time to get guns and powder; that they had no guns or powder and had more horses than they had use for, after they got guns and powder that they would never again have any thing to do with them &c. &c. I returned the Canoes & derected the men to prepare to Set out. Some Chyennes from two Lodges on the Main S E. Shore Came and Smoked with me and at 11 A. M we Set out haveing parted with those people who appeared to be Sorry to part with us. at this nation we found a french man by the name of Rokey who was one of our Engagees as high as the Mandans this man had Spend all his wages, and requested to return with uswe agreed to give him a passage down. I directed 2 guns to be fired. we proceeded on passed the Marapa and the We ter hoo Rivers, and landed to dry our bedding and robes &c which were all wet. here we delayed untill 6 P M. and dryed our things which were much Spoiled.

I derected 5 of the hunters to proceed on to Grouse Island a fiew miles below and hunt on that island untill we arived, we proceded on to the main N E Shore below the Island and encamped, the hunters joined us without any thing. they Saw no game on the island. we made only 17 Miles to day. below the ricaras the river widens and the Sand bars are emencely noumerous much less timber in the bottoms than above

The Chyenne's are portly Indians much the complections of the Mandans & ricaras high Cheeks, Streight limbed & high noses the men are large, their dress in Sumner is Simpelly a roab of a light buffalow Skin with or without the hair and a Breach clout & mockerson Some ware leagins and mockersons, their ornaments are but fiew and those are composed principally of Such articles as they precure from other indians Such as blue beeds, Shell, red paint rings of brass broaches &c. they also ware Bears Claws about their necks, Strips of otter Skin (which they as well as the ricaras are excessively fond of) around their neck falling back behind. their ears are cut at the lower part, but fiew of them were ornements in them, their hair is generally Cut in the forehead above their eyes and Small orniminted plats in front of each Sholder the remainder of the hair is either twisted in with horse or buffalow hair divided into two plats over the Sholder or what is most common flow's back, Their women are homely, corse feetured wide mouthes they ware Simpially a leathe habit made in a plain form of two pieces of equal length and equal weadth, which is sewen together with Sinues from the tail to about half way from the hip to the arm, a String fastens the 2 pieces together over the Sholders leaveng a flap or lapells which fall over near half way ther body both before and behind. those dresses usially fall as low as mid leg, they are frequently ornemented with beeds and Shells & Elk tuskes of which all Indians are very fond of. those dresses are als frequently Printed in various regular figures with hot sticks which are rubed on the leather with Such velosity as to nearly burn it this is very handsom. they were their hair flowing and are excessively fond of ornamenting their ears with blue beeds- this nation peacbly disposed they may be estimated at from 350 to 400 men inhabetig from 130 to 150 Lodges, they are rich in horses & Dogs, the dogs Carry a great preportion of their light baggage. they Confess to be at war with no nation except the Sieoux with whome they have ever since their remembranc been on a difencive war, with the Bands of Sieoux. as I was about to leave the Cheifs of the Chyennes lodge he requested me to Send Some traders to them, that their country was full of beaver and they would then be encouraged to Kill beaver, but now they had no use for them as they could get nothing for their skins and did not know well, how to catch beaver. if the white people would come amongst them they would become acquainted and the white people would learn them how to take the beaver-. I promised the Nation that I would inform their Great father the President of the U States, and he would have them Supplied with goods, and mentioned in what manner they would be Supplied &c. &c.

I am happy to have it in my power to Say that my worthy friend Capt
Lewis is recovering fast, he walked a little to day for the first time.
I have discontinud the tent in the hole the ball came out

I have before mentioned that the Mandans Maharhas Menetarras &
Ricarras, keep their horses in the Lodge with themselves at night.

[Clark, August 23, 1806] Saturday 23rd August 1806 We Set out very early, the wind rose & became very hard, we passed the Sar-war-kar-na-har river at 10 A. M and at half past eleven the wind became So high and the water So rough that we were obliged to put to Shore and Continue untill 3 p. M. when we had a Small Shower of rain after which the wind lay, and we proceeded on. Soon after we landed I Sent Shields & Jo. & Reubin Fields down to the next bottom of timber to hunt untill our arival. we proceeded on Slowly and landed in the bottom. the hunters had killed three Elk and 3 Deer the deer were pore and Elk not fat had them fleece & brought in. the Musqueters large and very troublesom. at 4 P. M a Cloud from the N W with a violent rain for about half an hour after the rain we again proceeded on. I observe great quantities of Grapes and Choke Cheries, also a Speces of Currunt which I had never before observed the leas is larger than those above, the Currt. black and very inferior to either the yellow, red, or perple- at dark we landed on a Small Sand bar under a Bluff on the S W. Side and encamped, this Situation was one which I had Chosen to avoid the Musquetors, they were not very troublesom after we landed. we Came only 40 Miles to daye

My Frend Capt Lewis is recoverig fast the hole in his thy where the Ball passed out is Closed and appears to be nearly well. the one where the ball entered discharges very well-.

[Clark, August 24, 1806] Sunday 24th August 1806 a fair morning we Set out as usial about Sunrise and proceeded on untill 2 P M when the wind blew So hard from the N. W. that we could not proceed came too on the S W. Side where we continued untill 5 P.M. when the wind lay a little and we again proceeded on. at 8 a M. we passed La-hoo-catts Island, opposit the lower point of this Island on the S. W. Side near the top of the Bluff I observed a Stratea of White stone I landed and examined it found it to be a Soft White Stone containing very fine grit, when expd. to the Sun and become Dry this Stone will Crumble the Clay of this bluff to the above and below is remarkably Black. at half past 9 a.m. passed Good hope Island and at 11 a. m passed Caution Island a Short distance below this Island we came too. Sent out a hunter he Saw Several deer they were very wild and he returned without haveing killed any, the deer on this pt. of the Missouri is mostly the Mule or black tail Species. we Saw only 6 buffalow to day the Sieoux have been laterly encamped on the river and have Secured the most of the game opp. a large trail has passed on a derection to the enterance of the Chyenne this probably is the trail of a war party. at 5 P.M. we proceeded on a fiew miles and Encampd. on the gouge of the lookout bend of 20 miles around and 3/4 through, a little above an old tradeing house and 4 miles above of our outward bound encampment of the 1st of October 1804, haveing made 43 miles to day.

[Clark, August 25, 1806] Monday 25th August 1806 a cool clear morning a Stiff breeze ahead we Set out at the usial hour and proceeded on very well. I derected Shields Collins Shannon and the two fieldses to proceed on in the two small Canoes to the Ponia Island and hunt on that Island untill we came on, they Set out before day light The Skirt of timber in the bend above the Chyenne is not very Considerable the timber is Scattered from 4 to 16 miles on the S W Side of the river, and the thickest part is at the distance of 6 & 10 miles from the Chyenne, a narrow bottom of Small Cotton trees is also on the N E pt. at the distance of from 4 to 41/2 miles above the Chyenne imediately at the enterance of that river I observe but fiew large trees Some Small Growth and willows on the lower Side bottom on the Missouri about 1/2 a mile and extends up the Chyen 1 mile about a quarter of a mile above is a 2d bottom of Cotton timber, in the point above the Chyenne there is a considerable bottom of about 2 miles on that river and a large timbered bottom a Short distance above. at 8 A.M. we Came to at the mouth of the Chyenne to delay untill 12 to make a meridian observation and derected 3 hunters to proced up this river and hunt its bottoms untill twelve at which hou we Shall proceed on. the hunters returned with 2 deer the Chyenne discharges but little water which is much the colour of the missouri tho not So muddy I observe a very eligable Situation on the bank of the Chyenne on it's lower Side about 100 paces from it's enterance. this Situation is above the high floods and has a perfect Command of each river we obtained a Meridian altitude with the Sextt. and artificial Horizon 112° 50' 00"- after which we proceeded on passed the pania Island and came up with Shields and Collins they had killed two deer only at 3 P M we passed the place where we Saw the last encampement of Troubleson Tetons below the old ponia village on the S W Side. a very large timbered bottom on the N. E. Side imedialely below the Pania Island. Latd. of Chyenne is _____ North. at Sunset we landed about the Center of a large bottom on the N E Side a little below the enterance of No timber Creek and below our Encampment of 29th of Septr. 1804. dreyer killed a deer after we encamped. a little above our encampmt. the ricaras had formerly a large village on each Side which was destroyed by the Seioux. there is the remains of 5 other villages on the S W. Side below the Chyenne river and one on Le ho catts Isld. all those villages have been broken up by the Seioux. This day proved a fine Still day and the men played their oars and we made 48 miles to day. The 2 fields and Shannon did not join this evening which caused me to encamp earlier than usial for them. we Saw no game on the plains today. the Tetons have been on the river not long Since

[Clark, August 26, 1806] Tuesday 26th of August 1806 a heavy dew this morning the hunters or Shannon & the 2 fields came up at Sunrise and we Set out, they had killed only 2 Small deer one of which they had eat at 8 passed the place the Tetons were encamped at the time they attempted to Stop us in Septr. 1804, and at 9 A.M. passed the enterance of Teton River. Saw Several black tail or Mule deer and Sent out to kill them but they were wild and the hunters Could not get a Shot at either of them. a fiew miles below the Teton river I observed a buffalow Skin Canoe lying on the S Shore and a Short distance lower a raft which induces me to Suspect that the Tetons are not on the Missouri at the big bend as we were informed by the Ricaras, but up the Teton river. at Meridn. we halted on the N E. Side opposit a handsom leavel plain in which there is great quantities of plumbs which are not yet ripe. we passed the enteranc of Smoke Creek and landed and Continued two hours to Stop a leak in the perogue and fix the Stearing oare, Saw great quantities of Grapes, they are black tho not thurerly ripe. at 5 P.M. we landed a Louisells fort on Ceder Island, this fort is entire and every part appears to be in the Same state it was when we passed it in Septr. 1804. I observed the appearance of 3 fires in the houses which appeared to have been made 10 or 12 days past. we proceeded on about 10 miles lower and encamped on the S. W. Side opposit our outward bound encampment of the 21st of Septr. 1804, a fiew miles above Tylors River. we had a Stiff breeze from the S. E. which continued to blow the greater part of the night dry and pleasent. as we were now in the Country where we were informed the Sceoux were assembled we were much on our guard deturmined to put up with no insults from those bands of Seioux, all the arms &. in perfect order. Capt. L. is Still on the mending hand he walks a little. I have discontinued the tent in the hole where the ball entered, agreeable to his request. he tells me that he is fully Convinced that the wound is sufficiently heeled for the tents to be discontinued. we made 60 miles to day with the wind ahead greater part of the day-

[Clark, August 27, 1806] Wednesday 27th Augt. 1806 Set out before Sunrise a Stiff breeze a head from the East proceeded to the enterance of Tylors river on the S W Side and landed on a Sand bar and Sent out the hunters to kill Some meat, our Stock of meat being now exousted and this the most favourable place to precure a fresh Supply, the hunters returned in 3 hours without haveing killed any thing. they informed me that the bottoms were entirely beaten up and the grass laid flat by the emence number of Buffalow which had been here a Short time past. the deer had left the bottom. they Saw several Buffalow Bulls which they did not think proper to kill as they were unfit for use. here we discover the first Signs of the wild turkey. at 1 P M we halted in the big bend and killed a fat buck elk near the river, which was very timely as our meat was entirely exhosted. at 2 P. M we again proceeded on down saw Several Buffalow Bulls on each Side of the river also Some deer of the Common kind at 6 P.M. we herd the bellowing of the Buffalow Bulls in the lower Isld. of the Big bend below the Gouge which induced a belief that there was Some fat Cows, 5 men went out from the 2 Small Canoes which was a little a head, and killed two Cows one Bull and a Calf nether of them wer fat we droped the Perogue & Canoes to the lower part of the Island near to where the buffalow was killed and incamped haveing Come 45 Miles only to day. had the buffalow butched and brought in and divided. My friend Capt Lewis hurt himself very much by takeing a longer walk on the Sand bar in my absence at the buffalow than he had Strength to undergo, which Caused him to remain very unwell all night.

[Clark, August 28, 1806] Thursday 28th of August 1806 Capt Lewis had a bad nights rest and is not very well this morning. we Set out early and procded on very well, Saw a number of Buffalow bulls on the banks in different places. passd the 3 rivers of the Seioux pass at 9 A.M. a Short distance below on the S W Side Sent out Reubin & Joseph Feild to hunt for the Mule deer or the antilope neither of which we have either the Skins or Scellitens of, we detected those two men to proceed on down to the places we encamped the 16th & 17th of Septr. 1804 and which place the party had called pleasant Camp from the great abundance of Game Such as Buffalow Elk, antilopes, Blacktail or mule deer, fallow deer, common deer wolves barking Squirels, Turkies and a variety of other animals, aded to which there was a great abundance of the most delicious plumbs and grapes. this Situation which is a Short distance above the enterance of Corvus Creek we are deturmined to delay one day for the purpose of prcureing the sceletins of the Mule deer & antilope, and Some barking Squirels. a fiew miles below the place the 2 Fields were Set on Shore we Set Drewyer and Labeech on Shore with the Same directions which had been given to the 2 field's at 12 oClock we Landed on the S W. Side at the Same Spot which we had encamped on the 16th and 17th of September 1804, and formed a Camp, Sent out Serjt. Pryor, Shields, Go. Gibson, Willard and Collins to hunt in the plains up Corvus Creek for the Antilope and Mule deer Sent out Bratten and Frazier to kill the barking Squirel, and Gave directions to all of them to kill the Magpye if they Should See any of them Several of the men and the Squaws of the enterpreter Jessomme and the Mandan Chief went to Some plumb bushes in the bottom and geathered more plumbs than the party Could eate in 2 days, those blumbs are of 3 Speces, the most of them large and well flavored. our Situation is pleasent a high bottom thinly timbered and covered with low grass without misquitors. at 3 P. M Drewyer and Labeech arived, the latter haveing killd. a Deer of the Common Speceis only. in the evening late all the hunters returned without any Speces of animal we were in want of, they killed 4 Common deer and two buffalow a part of the best of the meat of those animals they brought in. we precured two of the barking Squirels only. as we Could not precere any Mule deer or antelope we concluded to Send the hunters on a head early in the morning and delay untill 10 A. M to give them time to hunt. I derected Shannon & Collins to go on the opposit Side, and Labeech and Willard to proceed down on this Side at Some distance from the river and join the party at the round Island &c. and R. Field to proceed on Slowly in the Small Canoe to that place and take in any thing which the hunters might kill. Made 32 miles to day

The hunters informed me that they Saw great numbers of Buffalow in the plains. I Saw Several herds of those animals on either Side to day at a distance.

[Clark, August 29, 1806] Friday 29th August 1806 a cloudy morning the hunters proceeded on agreeable to their orders of last night. I Sent out two men to the village of barking Squirels with direcitions to kill Some of them. they after 2 hours returned and informed me that not one of those Squirels were to be Seen out of their holes. the Skins of the party which they had been dressing Since yesterday being now completely dressed I derected all loose baggage to be put on board the Canoes and at 10 A.M. Set out and proceeded on passed the white river at 12 oClock and halted below the enterance of Shannons Creek where we were joined by Labeech Shannon and Willard, they had killed 2 common der but no Mule deer or antelopes. Willard informed me that he Saw 2 antelopes but Could not get near to them. Willard and Labiech waded white river a fiew miles above its enterance and inform me that they found it 2 feet water and 200 yards wide. the water of this river at this time nearly as white as milk. put Drewyer out to hunt on the S W. Side and proceeded on below the round Island and landed on the N. E. Side I with Several of the men went out in pursute of Buffalow. the men killed 2 Bulls near me they were very por I assended to the high Country and from an eminance, I had a view of the plains for a great distance. from this eminance I had a view of a greater number of buffalow than I had ever Seen before at one time. I must have Seen near 20,000 of those animals feeding on this plain. I have observed that in the country between the nations which are at war with each other the greatest numbers of wild animals are to be found- on my return to the river I killed 2 young deer. after Dinner we proceeded down the river about 3 mile to the Camp of Jo. & Rubin fields and Collins, and encamped on the S W. Side a little below our encampment of 13th Septr. 1804, haveing made 20 Miles only. neither of the hunters killed either a Black tail deer or an antilope. Jo. Fields & Shields each killed a porcupin and two others of the hunters Killed Deer, Drewyer did not join us untill 10 P.M. he informed that he Saw some antilopes and Mule deer but Could kill none of them. Jo. Field informed that he wounded female of the Mule deer a little below our Camp late in the evening and could not prosue her I directed him to Set out with 3 others and follow the Deer and get her if possible early in the morning.

[Clark, August 30, 1806] Saturday 30th of August 1806 Capt. Lewis is mending Slowly. we set out at the usial hour and proceeded on very well a fiew miles Jo Field who was on the Shore being behind I derected one of the Small Canoes with R. Fields & Shannon to continue on the point of a Sand bar untill he corns up. I took 3 hunters and walked on the N E Shore with a view to kill Some fat meet. we had not proceeded far before Saw a large plumb orchd of the most deelicious plumbs, out of this orchard 2 large Buck Elks ran the hunters killed them. I Stoped the Canoes and brought in the flesh which was fat and fine. here the party Collected as many plumbs as they could eate and Several pecks of which they put by &c. after a delay of nearly 2 hours we again proceeded on downwards passed 3 Small Islands and as we were about to land at the place appointed to wait for the 2 fields and Shannon, I saw Several men on horseback which with the help of a Spie glass I found to be Indians on the high hills to the N E we landed on the. S. W. Side and I sent out two men to a village of Barking Squirels to kill Some of those animals imedeatily after landing about 20 indians was discovered on an eminanc a little above us on the opposite Side. one of those men I took to be a freinch man from his a blanket Capoe & a handkerchief around his head. imediately after 80 or 90 Indian men all armed with fusees & Bows & arrows Came out of a wood on the opposite bank about 1/4 of a mile below us. they fired of their guns as a Salute we returned the Salute with 2 rounds. we were at a loss to deturmin of what nation those indians were. from their hostile appearance we were apprehensive they were Tetons. but from the Country through which they roved we were willing to believe them eithe the Yanktons, Ponars or Mahars either of which nations are well disposed towards the white people. I deturmined to find out who they were without running any resque of the party and indians, and therefore took three french men who could Speak the Mahar Pania and some Seioux and in a Small canoe I went over to a Sand bar which extended Sufficently near the opposite Shore to Converse. imedeately after I Set out 3 young men Set out from the opposite Side and Swam next me on the Sand bar. I derected the men to Speak to them in the Pania and mahar Languages first neither of which they could understand I then derected the man who could Speak a fiew words of Seioux to inquire what nation or tribe they belong to they informed me that they were Tetons and their Chief was Tar-tack-kah-sabbar or the black buffalow This Chief I knew very well to be the one we had seen with his band at Teton river which band had attempted to detain us in the fall of 1804 as we assended this river and with whome we wer near comeing to blows. I told those Indians that they had been deef to our councils and ill treated us as we assended this river two years past, that they had abused all the whites who had visited them since. I believed them to be bad people & Should not Suffer them to cross to the Side on which the party lay, and directed them to return with their band to their Camp, that if any of them come near our camp we Should kill them certainly. I lef them on the bear and returned to th party and examined the arms &c. those indians seeing Some Corn in the Canoe requested Some of it which I refused being deturmined to have nothing to do with those people. Several others Swam across one of which understood pania, and as our pania interpreter was a very good one we had it in our power to inform what we wished. I told this man to inform his nation that we had not forgot their treatment to us as we passed up this river &c. that they had treated all the white people who had visited them very badly; robed them of their goods, and had wounded one man whome I had Seen. we viewed them as bad people and no more traders would be Suffered to come to them, and whenever the white people wished to visit the nations above they would Come Sufficiently Strong to whip any vilenous party who dare to oppose them and words to the Same purpote. I also told them that I was informed that a part of all their bands were gorn to war against the Mandans &c, and that they would be well whiped as the Mandans & Menetarres & had a plenty of Guns Powder and ball, and we had given them a Cannon to defend themselves. and derected them to return from the Sand bar and inform their Chiefs what we had Said to them, and to keep away from the river or we Should kill every one of them &c. &c. those fellows requested to be allowed to Come across and make Cumerads which we positively refused and I directed them to return imediately which they did and after they had informed the Chiefs &c. as I Suppose what we had Said to them, they all Set out on their return to their Camps back of a high hill. 7 of them halted on the top of the hill and blackguarded us, told us to come across and they would kill us all &c. of which we took no notice. we all this time were extreamly anxious for the arival of the 2 fields & Shannon whome we had left behind, and were Some what consd. as to their Safty. to our great joy those men hove in Sight at 6 P.M. Jo. Fields had killed 3 black tail or mule deer. we then Set out, as I wished to See what those Indians on the hill would act. we Steared across near the opposit Shore, this notion put them Some agitation as to our intentions, some Set out on the direction towards their Camps others walked about on the top of the hill and one man walked down the hill to meet us and invited us to land to which invitation I paid no kind of attention. this man I knew to be the one who had in the fall 1804 accompaned us 2 days and is Said to be the friend to the white people. after we passd. him he returned on the top of the hill and gave 3 Strokes with the gun he had in his hand this I am informed is a great oath among the indians. we proceeded on down about 6 miles and encamped on a large Sand bar in the middle of the river about 2 miles above our encampment on Mud Island on the 10th Septr. 1804 haveing made 22 miles only to Day. Saw Several Indians on the hills at a distance this evening viewing us. our encampment of this evening was a very disagreable one, bleak exposed to the winds, and the Sand wet. I pitched on this Situation to prevent being disturbed by those Scioux in the Course of the night as well as to avoid the Musquetors-. Killed 9 whistleing squirels.

[Clark, August 31, 1806] Saturday 31st August 1806 all wet and disagreeable this morning. at half past 11 last night the wind Shifted about to the N. W. and it began to rain with hard Claps of thunder and lightning the Clouds passd over and the wind Shifted about to the S W. & blew with great violence So much So that all hands were obliged to hold the Canoes & Perogue to prevent their being blown off from the Sand bar, however a Suden Squal of wind broke the cables of the two Small Canoes and with Some dificuelty they were got to Shore Soon after the 2 Canoes in which Sergt. Pryor and the indians go in broke loose with wiser and Willard in them and were blown quite across the river to the N E. Shore where fortunately they arived Safe, I Sent Sergt. Jo Ordway with a Small perogue and 6 men to prosue the 2 Canoes and assist them in effecting a landing, those 2 Canoes being tied together 2 men could not manage them, the wind Slackened a little and by 2 A.M. Sergt Ordway with willard wiser and the 2 Canoes returned all Safe, the wind continud to blow and it rained untill day light all wet and disagreeable. all the party examind their arms and put them in order and we Set out and proceeded on down. Saw Several Indians on the hills untill we passed the Island of Cedar 9 A. M the morning Cloudy and wind down the the river at 4 P.M. passed the doome and lowest village of Barking Squirels. this is also the highest up the river where I observed the fox Squirel in the bottom above the doome on N. E Side I killed 2 fox Squirels. we Saw no game of any kind to day as the banks as usial. the Sun Shone with a number of flying Clouds. we encamped on the N. E. Side a little below our Encampment of the 5th of Septr. on no preserve Island haveing Come 70 Miles.

[Clark, September 1, 1806] Monday 1st of September 1806 Musquitors very troublesom last night, we set out at the usial hour and had not proceeded on far before the fog became So thick that we were oblige to come too and delay half an hour for the fog to pass off which it did in Some measure and we again proceded on R. Jo. Fields and Shannon landed on an Ponceras Island to try to kill Some deer which was Seen on the beech and the Canoes all passed them at 9 A. M we passed the enterance of River Quiequur which had the Same appearance it had when we passed up water rapid and of a milky white Colour about two miles below the Quicurre, 9 Indians ran down the bank and beckened to us to land, they appeared to be a war party, and I took them to be Tetons and paid no kind of attention to them further than an enquirey to what tribe they belonged, they did not give me any answer, I prosume they did not understand the man who Spoke to them as he Spoke but little of their language. as one Canoe was yet behind we landed in an open Commanding Situation out of Sight of the indians deturmined to delay untill they Came up. about 15 minits after we had landed Several guns were fired by the indians, which we expected was at the three men behind. I calld out 15 men and ran up with a fill determination to Cover them if possible let the number of the indians be what they might. Capt Lewis hobled up on the bank and formed the remainder of the party in a Situation well calculated to defend themselves and the Canoes &c. when I had proceeded to the point about 250 yards I discovered the Canoe about 1 mile above & the indians where we had left them. I then walked on the Sand beech and the indians came down to meet me I gave them my hand and enquired of them what they were Shooting at, they informed me that they were Shooting off their guns at an old Keg which we had thrown out of one of the Canoes and was floating down. those Indians informed me they were Yanktons, one of the men with me knew one of the Indians to be the brother of young Durion's wife. finding those indians to be Yanktons I invited them down to the boats to Smoke. when we arived at the Canoes they all eagerly Saluted the Mandan Chief, and we all Set and Smoked Several pipes. I told them that we took them to be a party of Tetons and the fireing I expected was at the three men in the rear Canoe and I had went up with a full intention to kill them all if they had been tetons & fired on the Canoe as we first expected, but finding them Yanktons and good men we were glad to See them and take them by the hand as faithfull Children who had opened their ears to our Councils. one of them Spoke and Said that their nation had opened their years, & done as we had directed them ever Since we gave the Meadel to their great Chief, and Should Continue to do as we had told them we enquired if any of their Chiefs had gone down with Mr. Durion, the answered that their great Chief and many of their brave men had gone down, that the white people had built a house near the Mahar village where they traded. we tied a piec of ribon to each mans hair and gave them Some Corn of which they appeared much pleased. The Mandan Cheif gave a par of elegant Legins to the principal man of the indian party, which is an indian fashion. the Canoe & 3 men haveing joined us we took our leave of this party telling them to return to their band and listen to our councils which we had before given to them. Their band of 80 Lodges were on plum Creek a fiew miles to north. those nine men had five fusees and 4 bows & quivers of arrows. at 2 P.M. we came too on the upper point of bon homme opposit the antient fortification and Sent out men to hunt on each Side and on the island. and the canoes on each Side of the island to receive any meat might be killed I walked on the N. E. main Shore found the bottom rich and thickly covered with Peavine rich weed grass interwoven in Such a manner with grape vines that I could not get through and was obliged to assend a high plains the passing through which I also found tiresom. the grass was nearly as high as my head and the musquitors excessively bad. at the lower point of the Island all the Canoes & hunters Came together. Labeech killed an Elk only the flesh of which was brought on in the perogue. at this island we brought 2 years together or on the 1st of Septr. 1804 we Encamped at the lower point of this Island. after we all Came together we again proceeded on down to a large Sand bar imediately opposit to the place were we met the Yanktons in Council at the Calumet Bluffs and which place we left on the it of Septr. 1804. I observed our old flag Staff or pole Standing as we left it. the musquitors excessively troublesom untill about 10 P.M. when the S W wind became Strong and blew the most of them off. we came 52 miles to day only with a head wind. the Country on either Side are butifull and the plains much richer below the Queiquer river than above that river.

[Clark, September 2, 1806] Tuesday 2nd of September 1806 Set out at the usial hour passed the River Jacque at 8 A.M. in the first bottom below on the N. E. Side I observed the remains of a house which had been built since we passed up, this most probably was McClellins tradeing house with the Yanktons in the Winter of 1804 & 5 the wind was hard a head & continued to increas which obliged us to lay by nearly all day. as our Store of meat, I took with me 8 men and prosued a Small Gang of Cows in the plains 3 miles and killed two which was in very good order, had them butchered and each man took a load as much as he Could Carry and returned to the Canoes, the wind Still high and water rough we did not Set out untill near Sun Set we proceded to a Sand bar a Short distance below the place we had Come too on account of the wind and Encamped on a Sand bar, the woods being the harbor of the Musquetors and the party without the means of Screaning themselves from those tormenting insects. on the Sand bars the wind which generaly blows moderately at night blows off those pests and we Sleep Soundly. The wind Continued to blow hard from the Same point S. E untill 3 P. M I saw in my walk to day Lynn and Slipery Elm. the plains are tolerably leavel on each Side and very fertile. I saw 4 prarie fowls Common to the Illinois, those are the highest up which have been Seen, white Oak is very Common also white ash on the riveens and high bottoms. two turkys killed to day of which the Indians very much admired being the first which they ever Saw. Capt L. is mending fast- we made only 22 Miles to day.

[Clark, September 3, 1806] Wednesday 3rd of September 1806 Wind Continued to blow very hard this morning. it Shifted last night to the S. W. and blew the Sand over us in Such a manner as to render the after part of the night very disagreeable. the wind luled a little and we Set out and proceeded on with the wind a head passed the enterance of redstone River on the N E. Side at 11 A M. and at half past 4 P. M we Spied two boats & Several men, our party peyed their Ores and we Soon landed on the Side of the Boats the men of these boats Saluted us with their Small arms I landed & was met by a Mr. James Airs from Mackanaw by way of Prarie Dechien and St. Louis. this Gentleman is of the house of Dickson & Co. of Prarie de Chian who has a Licence to trade for one year with the Sieoux he has 2 Batteaux loaded with Merchendize for that purpose. This Gentleman receved both Capt. Lewis and my Self with every mark of friendship he was himself at the time with a chill of the agu on him which he has had for Several days. our first enquirey was after the President of our country and then our friends and the State of the politicks of our country &c. and the State Indian affairs to all of which enquireys Mr. Aires gave us as Satisfactory information as he had it in his power to have Collected in the Illinois which was not a great deel. soon after we Landed a violent Storm of Thunder Lightning and rain from the N W. which was violent with hard Claps of thunder and Sharp Lightning which continued untill 10 P M after which the wind blew hard. I set up late and partook of the tent of Mr. Aires which was dry. Mr. Aires unfortunately had his boat Sunk on the 25 of July last by a violent Storm of Wind and hail by which accident he lost the most of his usefull articles as he informd. us. this Gentleman informed us of maney Changes & misfortunes which had taken place in the Illinois amongst others the loss of Mr. Cady Choteaus house and furniture by fire. for this misfortune of our friend Choteaus I feel my Self very much Concernd &c. he also informed us that Genl. Wilkinson was the governor of the Louisiana and at St. Louis. 300 of the american Troops had been Contuned on the Missouri a fiew miles above it's mouth, Some disturbance with the Spaniards in the Nackatosh Country is the Cause of their being Called down to that Country, the Spaniards had taken one of the U, States frigates in the Mediteranean, Two British Ships of the line had fired on an American Ship in the port of New York, and killed the Capts. brother. 2 Indians had been hung in St. Louis for murder and several others in jale. and that Mr. Burr & Genl. Hambleton fought a Duel, the latter was killed &c. &c. I am happy to find that my worthy friend Capt L's is so well as to walk about with ease to himself &c., we made 60 Miles to day the river much crowded with Sand bars, which are very differently Situated from what they were when we went up.

[Clark, September 4, 1806] Thursday 4th September 1806 The Musquitors became troublesom early this morning I rose at the usial hour found all the party as wet as rain could make them. as we were in want of Some tobacco I purposed to Mr. Airs to furnish us with 4 Carrots for which we would Pay the amount to any Merchant of St. Louis he very readily agreed to furnish us with tobacco and gave to each man as much as it is necessary for them to use between this and St. Louis, an instance of Generossity for which every man of the party appears to acknowledge. Mr. Airs also insisted on our accepting a barrel of flourwe gave to this gentleman what Corn we Could Spear amounting to about 6 bushels, this Corn was well Calculated for his purpose as he was about to make his establishment and would have it in his power to hull the Corn & The flower was very acceptable to us. we have yet a little flour part of what we carried up from the Illinois as high as Maria's river and buried it there untill our return &c. at 8 A. M we took our leave and Set out, and proceeded on very well, at 11 A.M. passed the Enterance of the big Sieoux River which is low, and at meridian we came too at Floyds Bluff below the Enterance of Floyds river and assended the hill, with Capt Lewis and Several men, found the grave had been opened by the nativs and left half Covered. we had this grave Completely filled up, and returned to the Canoes and proceeded on to the Sand bar on which we encamped from the 12th to the 20th of August 1804 near the Mahar Village, here we came to and derected every wet article put out to dry, all the bedding of the party and Skins being wet. as it was late in the evening we deturmined to continue all night. had issued to each man of the party a cup of flour. we See no Species of Game on the river as usial except wild geese and pelicans. I observed near Sergt Floyds Grave a number of flurishing black walnut trees, these are the first which I have seen decending the river. a little before night Several Guns were heard below and in a direction towards the Mahar village which induced us to suspect that Mr. McClellin who we was informed was on his way up to trade with the Mahars had arived at the Creek below and that those reports of Guns was Some of his party out hunting. every thing being dry we derected the Perogue & Canoes to be loaded and in readiness to Set out in the morning early. at dark the Musquetors became troublesom and continued So all night the party obtained but little Sleep- we made 36 miles only to daye.

[Clark, September 5, 1806] Friday 5th September 1806 The Musquetors being So excessively tormenting that the party was all on board and we Set out at day light and proceeded on very well. here the river is bordered on both sides with timber &c becoms much narrower more Crooked and the Current more rapid and Crouded with Snags or Sawyers than it is above, and continus So all day. We did not meet with McClellen as we expected at the Creek. the report of the guns which was heard must have been the Mahars who most probably have just arrived at their village from hunting the buffalow. this is a Season they usialy return to their village to Secure their Crops of Corn Beens punkins &c &c. proceeded on very well passd. the blue Stone bluff at 3 P. M here the river leaves the high lands and meanders through a low rich bottom. Encamped on the S W Side on a Sand bar at a cut off a little below our Encampment of the 9th of August 1804. haveing made 73 Miles to day- Capt. Lewis still in a Convelesent State. We Saw no game on the Shores to day worth killig only Such as pelicans Geese ducks, Eagles and Hawks &c.-

[Clark, September 6, 1806] Saturday 6th of September 1806 The Musquetors excessively troublesom we Set out early at the great Cut off Saw a herd of Elk, we landed and Sent out Several hunters to kill Some of the Elk, they returnd. without killing any as the Elk was wild and ran off much fritened. I Sent the two Small Canoes on a head with derections to hunt in two bottoms below, and after a delay of half an hour proceeded on wind-hard a head at the lower point 7 of Pelecan Island a little above the Petite River de Seeoux we met a tradeing boat of Mr. Ag. Choteaux of St Louis bound to the River Jacque to trade with the Yanktons, this boat was in Care of a Mr. Henry Delorn, he had exposed all his loading and Sent out five of his hands to hunt they Soon arived with an Elk. we purchased a gallon of whiskey of this man and gave to each man of the party a dram which is the first Spiritious licquor which had been tasted by any of them Since the 4 of July 1805. Several of the party exchanged leather for linen Shirts and beaver for Corse hats. Those men Could inform us nothing more than that all the troops had movd. from the Illinois and that Genl. Wilkinson was prepareing to leave St. Louis. We advised this trader to treat the Tetons with as much Contempt as possible and Stated to him where he would be benefited by such treatment &c &c. and at 1 P. M Set out those men gave us 2 Shots from a Swivell they had on the bow of their boat which we returned in our turn. proceeded on about 3 miles and Came up with two of the hunters, they had not killd. any thing. at 5 miles we over took the Canoe of the other hunters with Shannon in it floating down, the two fields being in the woods behind we Came too on a Sand bar on the N. E. Side and delayed all the after part of the day for the two Fields, Sent out 3 men to hunt in the bottom up the river and observe if they Saw any Sign of the hunters. the evening proved Cloudy and the wind blew hard two pelicans were killed to day. we came 30 Miles only to day the 2 fieldses did not join us I think they are below. The Chief & the Squaws & children are awarey of their journey. Children cry &c.

[Clark, September 7, 1806] Sunday 7th September 1806 as we were doubtfull that the two fieldses were behind I derected Sergt. Ordway with 4 men to Continue untill Meridian and if those men did not arive by that hour to proceed on. if we met with them at any Short distance a gun Should be fired which would be a Signal for him to proceed on. we had proceeded on about 8 miles by water and the distance through not more than 1 mile when we Saw the fire of those 2 men, I derected a gun fired as a Signal for Sergt. ordway to proceed on, and took the boys on board. they had killed nothing & informed me they had been Somewhat almd. at our delay, that the distance across from the little Sieoux river was about 1 1/2 miles only, the bottoms thick and Grass very high. we proceded on with a Stiff Breeze ahead (note the evaperation on this portion of the Missouri has been noticed as we assended this river, and it now appears to be greater than it was at that time. I am obliged to replenish my ink Stand every day with fresh ink at least 9/10 of which must evaperate.) we proceeded on to a bottom on the S W Side a little above the Soldiers river and Came too and Sent out all the hunters. they killed 3 Elk which was at no great distance we Sent out the men and had the flesh brought in Cooked and Dined. Sergt. Ordway Came up & after takeing a Sumptious Dinner we all Set out at 4 P M wind ahead as usial. at Dusk we came too on the lower part of a Sand bar on the S W side found the Musquetors excessively tormenting not withstanding a Stiff breeze from the S. E. a little after dark the wind increased the Musquetors dispersed our Camp of this night is about 2 miles below our Encampment of the 4th of august 1804 ascending we came 44 miles to day only

[Clark, September 8, 1806] Munday 8th September 1806 Set out very early this morning, passed an old tradeing house on the S W Side a few miles above the Council bluffs, at 11 A M we Came too at the bluffs and Capt Lewis and myself walked up on the bluffs and around to examine the Country and Situation more particularly, the Situation appeared to us eaqually as eligable as when we passed up for an establishment, the hill high and Commanding with a high rich bottom of great extent below. we proceeded on very well all being anxious to get to the River Platt to day they ply'd their orers very well, and we arived at our old encampment at White Catfish Camp 12 miles above the river platt at which place we lay from the 22th to the 26th of July 1804 here we encamped haveing made 78 Miles to day. The Missouri at this place does not appear to Contain more water than it did 1000 Miles above this, the evaperation must be emence; in the last 1000 miles this river receives the water 20 rivers and maney Creeks Several of the Rivers large and the Size of this river or the quantity of water does not appear to increas any-

[Clark, September 9, 1806] Tuesday 9th September 1806 Set out early at 8 A. M passed the enterance of the great river Platt which is at this time low the water nearly clear the Current turbelant as usial; the Sand bars which Choked up the Missouri and Confined the river to a narrow Snagey Chanel are wastd a way and nothing remains but a fiew Small remains of the bear which is covered with drift wood, below the R. Platt the Current of the Missouri becomes evidently more rapid than above and the Snags much more noumerous and bad to pass late in the evening we arived at the Bald pated prarie and encamped imediately opposit our encampment of the 16th and 17th of July 1804. haveing made 73 miles only to day. The river bottoms are extencive rich and Covered with tall large timber, and the hollows of the reveins may be Said to be covered with timber Such as Oake ash Elm and Some walnut & hickory. our party appears extreamly anxious to get on, and every day appears produce new anxieties in them to get to their Country and friends. My worthy friend Cap Lewis has entirely recovered his wounds are heeled up and he Can walk and even run nearly as well as ever he Could. the parts are yet tender &c. &.

The Musquetors are yet troublesom, tho not So much So as they were above the River platt. the Climate is every day preceptably wormer and air more Sultery than I have experienced for a long time. the nights are now So worm that I sleep Comfortable under a thin blanket, a fiew days past 2 was not more than Sufficient

[Clark, September 10, 1806] Wednesday 10th of September 1806 we Set out very early this morning and proceeded on very well with wind moderately a head at _____ P M we met a Mr. Alexander La fass and three french men from St. Louis in a Small perogue on his way to the River Platt to trade with the Pania Luup or Wolf Indians. this man was extreemly friendly to us he offered us any thing he had, we axcepted of a bottle of whisky only which we gave to our party, Mr. la frost informed us that Genl. Wilkinson and all the troops had decended the Mississippi and Mr. Pike and young Mr. Wilkinson had Set out on an expedition up the Arkansaw river or in that direction after a delay of half an hour we proceedd on about 3 miles and met a large perogue and 7 Men from St. Louis bound to the Mahars for the purpose of trade, this perogue was in Charge of a Mt. La Craw, we made Some fiew enquiries of this man and again proceeded on through a very bad part of the river Crouded with Snags & Sawyers and incamped on a Sand bar about 4 miles above the Grand Nemahar. we find the river in this timbered Country narrow and more moveing Sands and a much greater quantity of Sawyers or Snags than above. Great caution and much attention is required to Stear Clear of all those dificuelties in this low State of the water. we made 65 Miles to day. we Saw Deer rackoons and turkies on the Shores to day one of the men killed a racoon which the indians very much admired.

[Clark, September 11, 1806] Thursday 11th Septr. 1806 a heavy Cloud and wind from the N W. detained us untill after Sunrise at which time we Set out and proceeded on very well, passed the nemahar which was low and did not appear as wide as when we passed up. Wolf river Scercely runs at all, at 3 P. M we halted a little above the Nadawa river on the S. Side of the Missouri to kill Some meat that which we killed a fiew days past being all Spoiled. Sent out 6 hunters they killed and brought in two Deer only, we proceeded on a fiew miles below the Nadawa Island and encamped on a Small Isld. near the N. E. Side, haveing Came 40 Miles only to day, river rapid and in maney places Crouded with Snag's. I observe on the Shores much deer Sign- the mosquitoes are no longer troublesome on the river, from what cause they are noumerous above and not So on this part of the river I cannot account. Wolves were howling in different directions this evening after we had encamped, and the barking of the little prarie wolves resembled those of our Common Small Dogs that 3/4 of the party believed them to be the dogs of Some boat assending which was yet below us. the barking of those little wolves I have frequently taken notice of on this as also the other Side of the Rocky mountains, and their Bark so much resembles or Sounds to me like our Common Small Cur dogs that I have frequently mistaken them for that Speces of dog- The papaws nearly ripe

[Clark, September 12, 1806] Friday 12th of September 1806 a thick fog a litile before day which blew off at day light. a heavy Dew this morning. we Set out at Sunrise the usial hour and proceeded on very well about 7 miles met 2 perogues from St. Louis one contained the property of Mr. Choteau bound to the panias on River Platt, the other going up trapping as high as the Mahars. here we met one of the french men who had accompanied us as high as the Mandans he informed us that Mr. McClellan was a fiew miles below the wind blew a head Soon after we pased those perogues, we Saw a man on Shore who informed us that he was one of Mr. McClellens party and that he was a Short distance below, we took this man on board and proceeded on and Met Mr. McClellin at the St. Michl. Prarie we came too here we found Mr. Jo. Gravelin the Ricaras enterpreter whome we had Sent down with a Ricaras Chief in the Spring of 1805 and old Mr. Durion the Sieux enterpreter, we examined the instructions of those interpreters and found that Gravelin was ordered to the Ricaras with a Speach from the president of the U. States to that nation and some presents which had been given the Ricara Cheif who had visited the U. States and unfortunately died at the City of Washington, he was instructed to teach the Ricaras agriculture & make every enquirey after Capt Lewis my self and the party Mr. Durion was enstructed to accompany Gravelin and through his influence pass him with his presents & by the tetons bands of Sieux, and to provale on Some of the Principal chiefs of those bands not exceeding six to Visit the Seat of the Government next Spring he was also enstructed to make every enquirey after us. we made Some Small addition to his instructions by extending the number of Chiefs to 10 or 12 or 3 from each band including the Yanktons &c. Mr. McClellin receved us very politely, and gave us all the news and occurrences which had taken place in the Illinois within his knowledge the evening proveing to be wet and Cloudy we Concluded to continue all night, we despatched the two Canoes a head to hunt with 5 hunters in them

[Clark, September 13, 1806] Saturday 13th September 1806 rose early Mr. McClellen gave each man a Dram and a little after Sunrise we Set out the wind hard a head from the S E at 8 A M we landed at the Camp of the 5 hunters whome we had Sent a head, they had killed nothing, the wind being too high for us to proceed in Safty through the emecity of Snags which was imediately below we concluded to lye by and Sent on the Small Canoes a Short distance to hunt and kill Some meat, we Sent out 2 men in the bottom they Soon returned with one turky and informed that the rushes was so high and thick that it was impossible to kill any deer. I felt my Self very unwell and derected a little Chocolate which Mr. McClellen gave us, prepared of which I drank about a pint and found great relief at 11 A.M. we proceeded on about 1 mile and come up with the hunters who had killed 4 deer, here we delayed untill 5 P. M when the hunters all joined us and we again proceded on down a fiew miles and encamped on the N E Side of the Missouri haveing decended 18 Miles only to day. the day disagreeably worm. one man George Shannon left his horn and pouch with his powder ball and knife and did not think of it untill night. I walked in the bottom in the thick rushes and the Growth of timber Common to the Illinois Such as cotton wood, Sycamore, ash mulberry, Elm of different Species, walnut, hickory, horn beem, pappaw arrow wood willow, prickly ash, &c and Grape vines, pees of 3 species &c &c. Birds most Common the buzzard Crow the hooting owl and hawks, &c. &c.-

[Clark, September 14, 1806] Sunday 14th Sept. 1806 Set out early and proceeded on very well. this being the part of the Missouri the Kanzas nation resort to at this Season of the year for the purpose of robbing the perogues passing up to other nations above, we have every reason to expect to meet with them, and agreeably to their Common Custom of examining every thing in the perogues and takeing what they want out of them, it is probable they may wish to take those liberties with us, which we are deturmined not to allow of and for the Smallest insult we Shall fire on them. at 2 P.M. a little below the lower of the old Kanzas Village we met three large boats bound to the Yanktons and Mahars the property of Mr. Lacroy, Mr. Aiten & Mr. Coutau all from St. Louis, those young men received us with great friendship and pressed on us Some whisky for our men, Bisquet, Pork and Onions, & part of their Stores, we continued near 2 hours with those boats, makeing every enquirey into the state of our friends and Country &c. those men were much affraid of meeting with the Kanzas. we Saw 37 Deer on the banks and in the river to Day 5 of which we killed those deer were Meager. we proceeded on to an Island near the middle of the river below our encampment of the 1st of July 1804 and encamped haveing decended only 53 miles to day. our party received a dram and Sung Songs untill 11 oClock at night in the greatest harmoney.

[Clark, September 15, 1806] Monday 15th of September 1806 we set out early with a Stiff Breeze a head saw Several deer Swiming the river soon after we Set out. at 11 A.M. passed the enterance of the Kanzas river which was very low, about a mile below we landed and Capt Lewis and my Self assended a hill which appeared to have a Commanding Situation for a fort, the Shore is bold and rocky imediately at the foot of the hill, from the top of the hill you have a perfect Command of the river, this hill fronts the Kanzas and has a view of the Missouri a Short distance above that river. we landed one time only to let the men geather Pappaws or the Custard apple of which this Country abounds, and the men are very fond of. we discovered a Buck Elk on a Small Island, and sent the 2 fields and Shannon in pursute of it they Soon Came up with and killed the Elk, he was large and in fine order we had his flesh Secured and divided. as the winds were unfabourable the greater part of the day we only decended 49 Miles and encamped a Short distance Above Hay Cabin Creek we are not tormented by the Musquetors in this lower portion of the river, as we were above the river plat and as high up as the Rochejhone and for a fiew miles up that river, and above its enterance into the Missouri. we passd Some of the most Charming bottom lands to day and the uplands by no means bad, all well timberd. the weather disagreeably worm and if it was not for the constant winds which blow from the S. and S E. we Should be almost Suficated Comeing out of a northern Country open and Cool between the Latd. Of 46° and 49° North in which we had been for nearly two years, rapidly decending into a woody Country in a wormer Climate between the Latds. 38°& 39° North is probably the Cause of our experiencing the heat much more Senceable than those who have Continued within the parralel of Latitude.

[Clark, September 16, 1806] Tuesday 16th September 1806 we Set out early this morning and proceded on tolerably well the Day proved excessively worm and disagreeable, So much So that the men rowed but little, at 10 A M we met a large tradeing perogue bound for the Panias we continued but a Short time with them. at 11 A. M we met young Mr. Bobidoux with a large boat of six ores and 2 Canoes, the licenes of this young man was to trade with the Panias Mahars and ottoes reather an extroadanary a license for young a man and without the Seal of the teritory anexed, as Genl. Wilkensons Signeture was not to this instrement we were Somewhat doubtfull of it. Mr. Browns Signeture we were not acquainted with without the Teritorial Seal. we made Some enquireys of this young man and Cautioned him against prosueing the Steps of his brother in attempting to degrade the American Charector in the eyes of the Indians. we proceeded on to an Island a little above our encampment of the 16th & 17th of June 1804 haveing Came 52 miles only to day.

[Clark, September 17, 1806] Wednesday 17th September 1806 We Set out as usial early pass the Island of the little Osage Village which is considered by the navigater of this river to be the worst place in it. at this place water of the Missouri is confined between an Island and the S E main Shore and passes through a narrow chanel for more than 2 miles which is crouded with Snags in maney places quite across obligeing the navigater to pica, his passage between those Snags as he can, in maney places the current passing with great velocity against the banks which cause them to fall &c. at 11 A.M. we met a Captain McClellin late a Capt. of Artily of the U States Army assending in a large boat. this gentleman an acquaintance of my friend Capt. Lewis was Somewhat astonished to See us return and appeared rejoiced to meet us. we found him a man of information and from whome we received a partial account of the political State of our Country, we were makeing enquires and exchangeing answers &c. untill near mid night. this Gentleman informed us that we had been long Since given out by the people of the U S Generaly and almost forgotton, the President of the U. States had yet hopes of us; we received some civilities of Capt. McClellin, he gave us Some Buisquit, Chocolate Sugar & whiskey, for which our party were in want and for which we made a return of a barrel of corn & much obliges to him. Capt. McClellin informed us that he was on reather a speculative expedition to the confines of New Spain, with the view to entroduce a trade with those people. his plan is to proceede up this river to the Entcrance of the river platt there to form an establishment from which to trade partially with the Panas & Ottoes, to form an acquaintance with the Panias and provail Some of their principal Chiefs to accompany him to Santa Fee where he will appear in a stile calculated to atract the Spanish government in that quarter and through the influence of a handsome present he expects to be promited to exchange his merchindize for Silver & gold of which those people abound. he has a kind of introductory Speach from Govr. Wilkinson to the Panias and Ottoes and a quantity of presents of his own which he purposes distributing to the Panias and ELeatans with a view to gain their protection in the execution of his plans, if the Spanish Governmt. favour his plans, he purposes takeing his merchendize on mules & horses which Can easily be procured of the panias, to Some point convenient to the Spanish Settlements within the Louisiana Teritory to which place the inhabitants of New mexico may meet him for the purpose of trade &c. Capt McClellins plan I think a very good one if strictly prosued &c.

we Sent 5 hunters a head with directions to halt below Grand river and hunt untill we arived which would be in the morning. This day proved worme. we decended only 30 miles to day and encamped 4 miles above Grand river on S E. Side.

[Clark, September 18, 1806] Thursday 18th of September 1806 we rose early Capt McClellin wrote a letter and we took our leave, and proceeded on passed the Grand river at 7 A M. a Short distance below we came up with our hunters, they had killed nothing. at 10 oClock we Came too and gathered pottows to eate we have nothing but a fiew Buisquit to eate and are partly compelled to eate poppows which we find in great quantities on the Shores, the weather we found excessively hot as usial. the lands fine particularly the bottoms. a charming Oake bottom on the S E Side of the Missouri above the 2 Charletons rivers we find the Current of this part of the Missouri much more jentle than it was as we assended, the water is now low and where it is much confin'd it is rapid. we saw very little appearance of deer, Saw one bear at a distance and 3 turkeys only to day. our party entirely out of provisions Subsisting on poppaws. we divide the buiskit which amounted to nearly one buisket per man, this in addition to the poppaws is to last is down to the Settlement's which is 150 miles the party appear perfectly contented and tell us that they can live very well on the pappaws. we made 52 miles to day only. one of our party J. Potts complains very much of one of his eyes which is burnt by the Sun from exposeing his face without a cover from the Sun. Shannon also complains of his face & eyes &c. Encamped on an Island nearly opposit to the enterance of Mine river.

[Clark, September 19, 1806] Friday 19th of Sept. 1806 Set out this morning a little after day & proceeded on very well the men ply their oares & we decended with great velocity, only Came too once for the purpose of gathering pappows, our anxiety as also the wish of the party to proceed on as expeditiously as possible to the Illinois enduce us to continue on without halting to hunt. we Calculate on ariveing at the first Settlements on tomorrow evening which is 140 miles, and objecet of our party is to divide the distance into two days, this day to the Osarge River, and tomorrow to the Charriton a Small french Village- we arived at the Enterance of Osage River at dark and encamped on the Spot we had encamped on the 1st & 2d of June 1804 haveing Came 72 miles. a very singular disorder is takeing place amongst our party that of the Sore eyes. three of the party have their eyes inflamed and Sweled in Such a manner as to render them extreamly painfull, particularly when exposed to the light, the eye ball is much inflaimed and the lid appears burnt with the Sun, the cause of this complaint of the eye I can't account for. from it's Sudden appearance I am willing to believe it may be owing to the reflection of the Sun on the water

[Clark, September 20, 1806] Saturday 20th Septr. 1806 as three of the party was unabled to row from the State of their eyes we found it necessary to leave one of our Crafts and divide the men into the other Canoes, we left the two Canoes lashed together which I had made high up the River Rochejhone, those Canoes we Set a drift and a little after day light we Set out and proceeded on very well. The Osage river very low and discharges but a Small quantity of water at this time for so large a river. at meridian we passed the enterance of the Gasconnade river below which we met a perogue with 5 french men bound to the Osarge Gd. village. the party being extreemly anxious to get down ply their ores very well, we Saw Some cows on the bank which was a joyfull Sight to the party and Caused a Shout to be raised for joy at _____ P M we Came in Sight of the little french Village called Charriton the men raised a Shout and Sprung upon their ores and we soon landed opposit to the Village. our party requested to be permited to fire off their Guns which was alowed & they discharged 3 rounds with a harty Cheer, which was returned from five tradeing boats which lay opposit the village. we landed and were very politely received by two young Scotch men from Canada one in the employ of Mr. Aird a Mr. _____ and the other Mr. Reed, two other boats the property of Mr. Lacomb & Mr. _____ all of those boats were bound to the Osage and Ottoes. those two young Scotch gentlemen furnished us with Beef flower and Some pork for our men, and gave us a very agreeable supper. as it was like to rain we accepted of a bed in one of their tents. we purchased of a Citizen two gallons of Whiskey for our party for which we were obliged to give Eight dollars in Cash, an imposition on the part of the Citizen. every person, both French and americans Seem to express great pleasure at our return, and acknowledged them selves much astonished in Seeing us return. they informed us that we were Supposed to have been lost long Since, and were entirely given out by every person &c.

Those boats are from Canada in the batteaux form and wide in perpotion to their length. their length about 30 feet and the width 8 feet & pointed bow & Stern, flat bottom and rowing Six ores only the Skeneckeity form. those Bottoms are prepared for the navigation of this river, I beleive them to be the best Calculated for the navigation of this river of any which I have Seen. they are wide and flat not Subject to the dangers of the roleing Sands, which larger boats are on this river. the American inhabitants express great disgust for the govermt of this Teritory. from what I can lern it arises from a disapmt. of getting all the Spanish Grants Confirmed-. Came 68 ms. to day.

[Clark, September 21, 1806] Sunday 21st Septr. 1806 rose early this morning Colected our men Several of them had axcepted of the invitation of the Citizens and visited their families. at half after 7 A. M we Set out. passed 12 canoes of Kickapoos assending on a hunting expedition. Saw Several persons also Stock of different kind on the bank which reviv'd the party very much. at 3 P M we met two large boats assending. at 4 P M we arived in Sight of St. Charles, the party rejoiced at the Sight of this hospital village plyed thear ores with great dexterity and we Soon arived opposit the Town, this day being Sunday we observed a number of Gentlemen and ladies walking on the bank, we Saluted the Village by three rounds from our blunderbuts and the Small arms of the party, and landed near the lower part of the town. we were met by great numbers of the inhabitants, we found them excessively polite. we received invitations from Several of those Gentlemen a Mr. Proulx, Taboe, Decett, Tice Dejonah & Quarie and several who were pressing on us to go to their houses, we could only visit Mr. Proulx and Mr. Deucett in the course of the evening. Mr. Querie under took to Supply our party with provisions &c. the inhabitants of this village appear much delighted at our return and seem to vie with each other in their politeness to us all. we Came only 48 miles today. the banks of the river thinly Settled &c.

[Clark, September 22, 1806] Monday 22nd of Sept. 1806 This morning being very wet and the rain Still Continueing hard, and our party being all Sheltered in the houses of those hospitable people, we did not think proper to proceed on untill after the rain was over, and continued at the house of Mr. Proulx. I took this oppertunity of writeing to my friends in Kentucky &c. at 10 A M. it seased raining and we Colected our party and Set out and proceeded on down to the Contonemt. at Coldwater Creek about 3 miles up the Missouri on it's Southern banks, at this place we found Colo. Hunt & a Lieut Peters & one Company of Artillerists we were kindly received by the Gentlemen of this place. Mrs. Wilkinson the Lady of the Govr. & Genl. we wer Sorry to find in delicate health.

we were honored with a Salute of _____ Guns and a harty welcom at this place there is a publick Store kept in which I am informed the U. S have 60000$ worth of indian Goods

[Clark, September 23, 1806] Thursday 23rd of Septr. 1806 we rose early took the Chief to the publick store & furnished him with Some clothes &c. took an early breckfast with Colo. Hunt and Set out decended to the Mississippi and down that river to St. Louis at which place we arived about 12 oClock. we Suffered the party to fire off their pieces as a Salute to the Town. we were met by all the village and received a harty welcom from it's inhabitants &. here I found my old acquaintance Majr. W. Christy who had Settled in this town in a public line as a Tavern Keeper. he furnished us with Store rooms for our baggage and we accepted of the invitation of Mr. Peter Choteau and took a room in his house we payed a friendly visit to Mr August Chotau and Some of our old friends this evening. as the post had departed from St. Louis Capt Lewis wrote a note to Mr. Hay in Kahoka to detain the post at that place untill 12 tomorrow which was reather later than his usial time of leaveing it

[Clark, September 24, 1806] Wednesday 24th of September 1806 I sleped but little last night however we rose early and Commencd wrighting our letters Capt. Lewis wrote one to the presidend and I wrote Govr. Harrison & my friends in Kentucky and Sent of George Drewyer with those letters to Kohoka & delivered them to Mr. Hays &. we dined with Mr. Chotoux to day, and after dinner went to a Store and purchased Some Clothes, which we gave to a Tayler and derected to be made. Capt Lewis in opening his trunk found all his papers wet, and Some Seeds spoiled

[Clark, September 25, 1806]
Thursday 25th of Septr. 1806
had all of our Skins &c. Suned and Stored away in a Storeroom of Mr. Caddy Choteau. payed Some visits of form, to the gentlemen of St. Louis. in the evening a dinner & Ball

[Clark, September 26, 1806] Friday 26th of September 1806 a fine morning we commenced wrighting &c.

PROUDLY PRINTED IN THE UNITED STATES OF AMERICA.

OFFICE OF
HISTORICAL DOCUMENTS
AND ARCHIVES,

a division comprised of volunteers and students of Northwest history

hosted in part by the Northwest's very own

RIVER CANYON PRESS

UMPQUA, OREGON

"Preserving America's Story, One Story At A Time"

Our growing list of preserved heritage books include:

Shea's Library of American Linguistics, XII. Dictionary of The Chinook Jargon, or, Trade Language of Oregon. *George Gibbs.* 1863

Lay Morals and Other Papers. *Robert Louis Stevenson.* 1911

Northern California, Oregon, and The Sandwich Islands. *Charles Nordhoff.* 1875

The Sketch Book of Geoffrey Crayon, Gent. *Washington Irving.* 1820

The Log School-House on The Columbia. A Tale of The Pioneers of The Great Northwest. *Hezekiah Butterworth.* 1890

Confidence. *Henry O. M. James.* 1820

Tractatus Logico-Philosophicus. *Ludwig Wittgenstein.* 1918

Marley's Chain. *Alan E. Nourse.* 1952

Legends of The Northwest. *H. L. Gordon.* 1881

Become A Member Of The

Pacific Northwest Literacy Alliance

www.PacificNorthwestLiteracy.org

Made in the USA
Las Vegas, NV
15 December 2022

61810054R00324